TRADE MARK LAW
A Practical Anatomy

TRADE MARK LAW

A PRACTICAL ANATOMY

JEREMY PHILLIPS
Intellectual Property Consultant
Slaughter and May

Professorial Fellow
Queen Mary Intellectual Property Research Institute

Professor, Magister Lucentinus
University of Alicante

Visiting Professor at the Faculty of Laws
University College London

Visiting Professor
School of Finance and Law, Bournemouth University

Editor
European Trade Mark Reports

OXFORD
UNIVERSITY PRESS

Great Clarendon Street, Oxford OX2 6DP

Oxford University Press is a department of the University of Oxford.
It furthers the University's objective of excellence in research, scholarship,
and education by publishing worldwide in

Oxford New York

Auckland Bangkok Buenos Aires Cape Town Chennai
Dar es Salaam Delhi Hong Kong Istanbul Karachi Kolkata
Kuala Lumpur Madrid Melbourne Mexico City Mumbai Nairobi
São Paulo Shanghai Taipei Tokyo Toronto

Oxford is a registered trade mark of Oxford University Press
in the UK and in certain other countries

Published in the United States
by Oxford University Press Inc., New York

© Jeremy Phillips December 2003

The author hereby asserts his moral rights under the Copyright, Designs and
Patents Act 1988.
Neither the author nor the publisher accept any liability in respect of any loss or damage arising
from the preparation or consumption of all or any of the recipes reproduced in Chapter 18.
No express or implied warranty is given in particular as to the suitability of any such recipe for
consumption by trade mark lawyers.

Database right Oxford University Press (maker)

First published December 2003

All rights reserved. No part of this publication may be reproduced,
stored in a retrieval system, or transmitted, in any form or by any means,
without the prior permission in writing of Oxford University Press,
or as expressly permitted by law, or under terms agreed with the appropriate
reprographics rights organization. Enquiries concerning reproduction
outside the scope of the above should be sent to the Rights Department,
Oxford University Press, at the address above

You must not circulate this book in any other binding or cover
and you must impose this same condition on any acquirer

British Library Cataloguing in Publication Data
Data available

Library of Congress Cataloging in Publication Data
Data available

ISBN 0–19–926796–0
ISBN 0–19–926826–6 (pbk)

1 3 5 7 9 10 8 6 4 2

Typeset in Garamond by
Cambrian Typesetters, Frimley, Surrey

Printed in Great Britain
on acid-free paper by
Antony Rowe Ltd, Chippenham

To Sara

CONTENTS—SUMMARY

Foreword by The Rt. Hon. Sir Robin Jacob   xvii
Preface and Acknowledgements   xix
Tables of Cases   xxv
Table of Treaties and Legislation   lxxxi
Abbreviations   lxxxvii

A INTRODUCING TRADE MARK LAW

1. Petty Matters: About this Book   3
2. Why Trade Marks?   15
3. Trade Mark Law and Trade Mark Registration Systems   35

B REGISTRABLE TRADE MARKS

4. Registrability: The Basic Principles   55
5. Registrability of Specific Types of Trade Mark   117
6. Trade Marks and Generic Terms   169

C LAWFUL AND UNLAWFUL USE OF TRADE MARKS

7. Infringing Acts   191
8. Non-infringing Acts   215
9. Exhaustion of Trade Mark Rights   269
10. Identical and Similar Marks, Goods and Services   307
11. Reputation, Unfair Advantage and Detriment   361
12. Well-known Marks, Famous Marks and Dilution   393
13. The Killing Fields: Opposition, Cancellation and Revocation   421
14. Trade Marks in Court   469

D TRADE MARKS IN INDUSTRY AND COMMERCE

15. Transactions Involving Trade Marks   511
16. Trade Marks in Specific Sectors   543
17. Trade Marks on the Internet   569
18. Geographical Indications and other Forms of Protection   599

E ISSUES FOR TRADE MARK OWNERS

19	Choosing a Trade Mark	627
20	The Psychology of Trade Marks	637
21	Trade Marks, Images, Icons and Social Responsibility	651

Bibliography 669
Glossary 681
Index of Word Marks 689
Index 701

CONTENTS

Foreword by The Rt. Hon. Sir Robin Jacob — xvii
Preface and Acknowledgements — xix
Tables of Cases — xxv
Table of Treaties and Legislation — lxxxi
Abbreviations — lxxxvii

A INTRODUCING TRADE MARK LAW

1 Petty Matters: About this Book

A. Pedantry and conceptual preoccupation: the true signs of the trade mark expert	1.01
B. Conventions employed in writing this book	1.06
C. Important definitions and distinctions	1.09
D. A word about jurisdictions	1.25
E. Case law	1.28
F. Trade marks and history	1.38

2 Why Trade Marks?

A. Introduction	2.01
B. The interested parties	2.05
C. The function of the trade mark system	2.16
D. Conclusion	2.59

3 Trade Mark Law and Trade Mark Registration Systems

A. Introduction	3.01
B. Sources of trade mark law	3.05
C. Trade mark registration systems	3.19
D. Community trade marks and the trade marks of EU Member States	3.47
E. Conclusion	3.52

B REGISTRABLE TRADE MARKS

4 Registrability: The Basic Principles

A. Introduction	4.01
B. Absolute bars to registration	4.16
C. Graphic representation and the function of the register	4.24
D. Signs may not be registrable if consumers do not regard them as being trade marks	4.31
E. Signs which are not registrable on policy grounds	4.32
F. Signs which other traders may wish to use	4.50
G. Distinctiveness	4.88
H. Descriptive marks	4.128
I. Distinctiveness acquired through use	4.163
J. Relative grounds of unregistrability: a reminder	4.179
K. Conclusion	4.180

5 Registrability of Specific Types of Trade Mark

A. Introduction	5.01
B. Are there minimum and maximum criteria for registrability?	5.04
C. Identifiers which may not serve as trade marks	5.12
D. Cultural emblems	5.17
E. Locators	5.25
F. Issues relating to letters and numbers	5.30
G. Geographical marks	5.44
H. Trade dress and business formats	5.56
I. Names, titles and cultural icons	5.57
J. Slogans	5.73
K. Technology standards	5.78
L. Product surfaces and shapes	5.79
M. Non-traditional trade marks	5.117
N. Registration and the conduct of the applicant	5.145
O. Building up a portfolio of registrations in order to cover unprotectable classes	5.146
P. Conclusion	5.151

6 Trade Marks and Generic Terms

A.	Introduction	6.01
B.	'Fencing in the commons': competing public and private claims upon words	6.07
C.	Legal issues relating to generic terms	6.22
D.	Conclusion	6.45

C LAWFUL AND UNLAWFUL USE OF TRADE MARKS

7 Infringing Acts

A.	Introduction	7.01
B.	The scope of trade mark infringement	7.03
C.	Specific instances of infringing use	7.16
D.	Further observations concerning infringing use	7.26
E.	The 'course of trade' requirement	7.38
F.	Infringement by the trade mark owner	7.52
G.	Secondary infringements and infringers	7.55
H.	The United States perspective	7.63
I.	Conclusion	7.65

8 Non-infringing Acts

A.	Introduction	8.01
B.	Taxonomy of non-infringing acts	8.02
C.	Acts for which specific defences are provided	8.13
D.	Acts which are permitted in principle, even without a statutory defence	8.52
E.	Limitation of actions	8.90
F.	Comparative advertising	8.93
G.	The effect of consent	8.177
H.	Conclusion	8.179

9 Exhaustion of Trade Mark Rights

A.	Introduction	9.01
B.	The legal basis of modern exhaustion law	9.22
C.	The requirement of consent	9.36
D.	Legitimate reasons for prohibiting further use of a trade mark	9.53

	E. Exhaustion and its relationship with other legal rights	9.65
	F. Some interesting problems relating to exhaustion	9.75
	G. Conclusion	9.95
10	**Identical and Similar Marks, Goods and Services**	
	A. Introduction	10.01
	B. Identical and similar marks	10.10
	C. Identical and similar goods and services	10.76
	D. Likelihood of confusion	10.103
	E. Likelihood of association	10.143
	F. Conclusion	10.156
11	**Reputation, Unfair Advantage and Detriment**	
	A. Introduction	11.01
	B. Reputation	11.30
	C. Unfair advantage and detriment	11.52
	D. Conclusion	11.95
12	**Well-known Marks, Famous Marks and Dilution**	
	A. Introduction	12.01
	B. Europe	12.25
	C. Famous mark protection in the United States	12.49
	D. Conclusion	12.69
13	**The Killing Fields: Opposition, Cancellation and Revocation**	
	A. Introduction	13.01
	B. Opposition	13.16
	C. Cancellation	13.35
	D. Revocation	13.46
	E. Suspension of trade mark applications and of hostilities in general	13.70
	F. Trade mark systems and 'bad faith'	13.72
	G. Conclusion	13.149

14 Trade Marks in Court

A.	Introduction	14.01
B.	Preliminary issues in trade mark litigation	14.06
C.	Injunctive relief	14.29
D.	Pecuniary relief	14.76
E.	Dealing with infringing goods	14.95
F.	Liability for making groundless threats	14.101
G.	Declaration of non-infringement	14.116
H.	Competition law	14.118
I.	Conclusion	14.123

D TRADE MARKS IN INDUSTRY AND COMMERCE

15 Transactions Involving Trade Marks

A.	Introduction	15.01
B.	The nature of trade mark transactions	15.02
C.	Basic legal provisions governing transactions	15.14
D.	Classification of trade mark licences	15.26
E.	The consequences of being a licensee	15.35
F.	Internal transactions and external transactions	15.42
G.	Some examples of trade mark transactions	15.47
H.	Important issues in trade mark licences	15.71
I.	Litigation of trade mark transactions	15.88
J.	The valuation of trade marks	15.93
K.	Conclusion	15.98

16 Trade Marks in Specific Sectors

A.	Introduction	
B.	Pharmaceutical marks	16.01
C.	Retail sales service marks	16.37
D.	Celebrity trade marks	16.50
E.	Conclusion	16.73

17 Trade Marks on the Internet

A.	Introduction	17.01
B.	Use of another's trade mark as a domain name	17.02
C.	Use of another's trade mark on a web page	17.51
D.	Use of another's trade mark as a metatag	17.64
E.	Use of another's trade mark as the name of an Internet service provider	17.73
F.	Conclusion	17.74

18 Geographical Indications and other Forms of Protection

A.	Introduction	18.01
B.	The protection of geographical indications	18.04
C.	GIs in the European Union	18.21
D.	GIs under national law in Europe	18.38
E.	The interface between GI protection and trade mark protection	18.41
F.	Case law of the European Court of Justice	18.47
G.	Future plans for GIs	18.52
H.	Company name registrations	18.54
I.	Protection of titles	18.55
J.	Certification marks, guarantee marks and collective marks	18.56
K.	Conclusion	18.60

E ISSUES FOR TRADE MARK OWNERS

19 Choosing a Trade Mark

A.	Introduction	19.01
B.	Legal considerations	19.03
C.	Cultural considerations	19.10
D.	Business considerations	19.19
E.	Psychological considerations	19.24
F.	Conclusion	19.25

20 The Psychology of Trade Marks

A.	Introduction	20.01
B.	The trade mark as an icon of brand loyalty	20.03

C. Branding strategy in action		20.13
D. Some aspects of brand psychology		20.26
E. Conclusion		20.32

21 Trade Marks, Images, Icons and Social Responsibility

A. Introduction		21.01
B. *No Logo*: the thesis		21.03
C. No excuse: formulating a response		21.15
D. No chance: brand power and goodwill		21.24
E. No change: why the public's best weapons may never be adequately utilized		21.29
F. No fear: why the consumer apocalypse may never happen		21.38
G. No Armageddon: the threat of trade mark litigation		21.40
H. Conclusion		21.44

Bibliography	669
Glossary	681
Index of Word Marks	689
Index	701

FOREWORD

I am honoured to be asked to write this Foreword. And it is a great pleasure. I will tell you why. Many years ago a Chancery Judge (Eve, Clauson, Romer?) heard a wholly unmemorable appeal about the registrability of a mark—was it the sort of thing that was too descriptive was the kind of question. He began with words to the effect that he had to decide a matter 'in this not very interesting branch of the law.' I can't actually re-find the case—an interesting task for a diligent pupil or trainee. Whoever the Judge was, he was completely wrong. For trade mark law is astonishingly deceptive. Curiously, the less you know about it the more you think it must be simple—we all know what a trade mark is, obviously you cannot register descriptive words and people mustn't use someone else's mark or something confusingly similar. That's about all there is to it, isn't it? Well that view could hardly be more wrong. Anyone who has had to delve into the subject discovers, astonishingly, that it is fraught with genuine intellectual difficulties. That was true under the old law, as my late pupil master, Anthony Walton QC, so comically indicated in his address of welcome to me when I was appointed [1993] FSR 764. One of the points he described as Gödel Undecidable is 'what is a trade mark actually for?' And there were several other such trade mark points, all of which have re-surfaced under the new law. He begged me not to decide such points because they gave much work to lawyers.

Anthony would have been glad to know that none of these points, in their new form, has been decided. On the contrary I think it is fair to say that notwithstanding a mass of decisions from the ECJ since the Directive came into effect (was it really only 9 years ago?) trade mark law is more confusing, more uncertain, than it has been for years—indeed more so than when there were not so many 'helpful' interpretations from the Court. New concepts or at least forms of words have appeared—'global appreciation', 'lexical invention', 'guarantee of origin' and so on, but we are no closer to having clearly defined rules of law.

What has Jeremy Phillips done about this? Has he provided clear answers to the problems of trade mark law? By reading this book can we know what a trade mark is or is for? Most decidedly not. What we can and do get is something much more exciting. We get deep insight into the intellectual problems involved. This book makes you think. And it makes you understand at a profound level why some basic questions of trade mark law remain uncertain and probably always will be. He makes you understand that trade mark law has a lot in common with quantum mechanics. Each have at their heart an uncertainty principle.

Foreword

Not only has Jeremy done this, but he has done it with a deceptively light touch. Unlike most law books, if you open this book at almost any page you are likely positively to enjoy what you read and often you will have a silent chuckle. And because Jeremy is essentially dealing with principles, this book should be of interest to trade mark lawyers everywhere—it does not matter what the details of your legal system are, the underlying intellectual problems find their way to the surface. I do not say the reader will necessarily agree with what he says. They may well not—but they will be provoked to think and to work out their own answers. This is not the sort of law book which sends you to sleep. Read it and enjoy.

The Rt. Hon. Sir Robin Jacob, a Lord Justice of Appeal
Royal Courts of Justice,
October 2003

PREFACE AND ACKNOWLEDGEMENTS

Why have I written this book?

Where do I start?

My sole aim in writing this book is to explain, to any reader willing to read it, how the trade mark system works. This book has no hidden agenda. It is not an apology for trade marks, nor is it an onslaught on them. I have not written it specifically for the education of students, nor for the edification of practitioners. I have not sought to pump it full of supercharged footnotes, nor have I padded it out with useless and voluminous appendices of familiar and accessible materials. My purpose is to celebrate the joys of trade mark law, to point out its iniquities, laugh at its anomalies, gasp with admiration at its lean and muscled functionality and growl with indignation at its abuse.

I cannot claim that I am better qualified than anyone else to write this book. Trade mark law has however been a major a part of my life for so long that I can bring many different perspectives to bear when writing it. As an academic I have taught and researched the subject. As a writer, editor and publisher I have explored its furthest ramifications. As a consumer and then in business I have made brand-based decisions. As an actual or potential litigant I have made fine judgments in the knowledge that I should have to pay from my own pocket if I were wrong. As an administrator I have carried some of the responsibility for a mark's protection. As intellectual property consultant to a Magic Circle law firm I have advised on many issues, both practical and theoretical, involving some of the world's most powerful brand portfolios. Since 1973 trade marks have been my bread, my butter and my jam.

This book is my trade mark manifesto. Being self-employed I am grateful that no angry employer can dismiss me for my words, nor can any academic faculty stifle or misdirect my endeavours or take away my tenure. My old teacher Harry Bloom taught me many valuable things. One was that the best way to enjoy academic freedom is to avoid being an employee of a university. Another was that there is no value in writing anything that is intended to be taken seriously if it is not firmly based on truth. A third is that, if you have nothing to say, say nothing. But for me there is a lot to say. Being able to write what I want is a delicious indulgence and the insecurity of self-employment is a small price to pay for it.

Other people's books

I should like to say a few words about trade mark books that I have not written as well as this one which I have. Colleagues and students will recall some harsh judgments which I have issued concerning other people's books. For the record, they are too long on detail or contain too little of it; they are too full of their authors' opinions or devoid of any meaningful comments; they tediously parrot the law or they dangerously paraphrase it. Having spent much of the past nine months revisiting these works, I should like to retract my strident criticisms of them—well, most of my criticisms at any rate—and pay tribute to the use I have made of them.

Methodology

I wrote this book from scratch in forty-two weeks between September 2002 and June 2003, knowing that I would have to stop writing at the moment my allotted time expired. To do so, I gave up teaching for the year and plunged into a frantic schedule of reading, writing and revision. I started from the bottom upwards, with sources and footnotes which I later sought to stitch into paragraphs and chapters. For this reason this book may feel rather strange to those who are used to reading more conventional texts on the subject. Perceptive readers may sense that some of the paragraphs in my text have been subject to a good deal of cutting and pasting before they found their final home, though I have done may best to minimize this effect.

I tried to read primary sources first, such as cases, statutes, Directives, Regulations and treaties. Only then did I look at what my colleagues wrote in their books and articles, partly to see whether I had independently reached consensus with them and partly as a sort of sanity check when, having written on a particular topic, my opinions seemed at odds with conventional wisdom and led me to suspect that I had missed something obvious. From this exercise I came to conclude that there are many issues within trade mark law which are far from cut and dried and that there is still plenty of space for competing, or complementary, opinions.

Who is to blame? Who is to be thanked?

All responsibility for the content of this book is mine and mine alone. Many of those whom I have thanked in the following paragraphs hold views which are very different to my own and some of them were anxious that nothing I have written should be taken as an expression of their own views. I have solicited comments on draft chapters from people whose views diverge from my own for two reasons: (i) to learn from their criticisms and (ii) to see if my own theories can withstand their criticisms. The comments I have received, whether I have agreed with them or not, have improved both the general quality of the text and my own depth of understanding of the subject.

Preface and Acknowledgements

It is impossible to describe the zeal with which many of my critics fell to their task of appraising and criticizing my draft chapters. Some, not content with firing broadsides at my own text and picking holes in my reasoning, were even determined to rewrite text for which I assumed no responsibility: their targets included *verbatim* quotes from the Agreement on Trade-Related Aspects of Intellectual Property Law (TRIPs) and the Paris Convention, not to mention the subtle barbs of Saki and the pungent prose of Naomi Klein, all of which were garnished with helpful suggestions for improvement. My introductory stories were subject to the most demanding of literary criticism, the character of Maude in Chapter 14 was psychoanalysed and even my poems were tested to destruction against the rigorous demands of style and metre. A word of recommendation for readers who may yet also be writers: no one will perform a better hatchet job on your draft than former students whose essays you once covered with red ink and sharp comments.

Before addressing the debts of gratitude that fall to be paid to individuals who have helped me, it would be improper to acknowledge the collective support which I have enjoyed from the Intellectual Property Group of Slaughter and May. This hugely talented team of colleagues both past and present has provided a friendly and hospitable culture in which the seeds of my thoughts have germinated. Partners **Nigel Swycher**, **Susie Middlemiss**, **Cathy Connolly** and **Rob Sumroy**, aided and abetted in particular by (in alphabetical order) **Carina Badger**, **Martin Cook**, **Dominic Dryden**, **David Morris**, **Mark Parsons**, **Rhys Steigerwald** and **Richard Watts**, have all contributed to this volume in more ways than they may realize.

In paying debts of gratitude to individuals, first and foremost of my creditors is my stalwart Research Assistant, **Ilanah Simon** (Queen Mary Intellectual Property Research Institute), my partner on the www.ipkat.com weblog. Ilanah deserves particular praise for the astonishingly high level of critical comment to which she has exposed my text and thanks for the many long hours during which she has identified and challenged inconsistencies in my approach. So detailed and cogent were her many criticisms that I almost feel tempted to say that any errors which remain in this book are her responsibility, not mine. In the world of trade mark scholarship she is a true Miss Whiplash, before whom the pale white pages of A4 quail in anticipation of her stern correction. I must confess that, on a couple of rare occasions, it was with a sense of glee that I chanced upon some of my own mistakes which Ilanah had missed. Thank you, Ilanah.

Another person who has greatly contributed to my understanding of the subject is trade mark attorney **Claire Lazenby**. Her critical eye and trenchant comments—some of which were at least as provocative as anything in this book—kept me on my toes.

Preface and Acknowledgements

Mention should also be made of the following:

(i)   My students (past and present) for posing so many questions concerning trade mark law which have remained with me, in particular **Suzanna Hawkes, Eva Lehnert, Noam Shemtov** and **Tom O'Shea**.

(ii) Academics, in alphabetical order: **Subathira Amarasingham, Catherine Colston** (University of Strathclyde), **Jennifer Davis** (Woolfson College, Cambridge), **Professor Gerald Dworkin** (Intellectual Property Academy, Singapore), **Catherine Ng** (St Peter's College, Oxford), **Spyros Maniatis** (Queen Mary), **Professor Ruth Soetendorp** (Bournemouth), **Professor Paul Torremans** (University of Nottingham), **Uma Suthersanen** (Queen Mary) and **Professor David Vaver** (St Peter's College, Oxford).

(iii) Solicitors and trainees, barristers and trade mark attorneys in private practice in the United Kingdom who have encouraged me, provided me with information or who have given me helpful comments include the following, in alphabetical order: **Richard Abnett** (Reddie & Grose), **Lucy Adler** (Harbottle & Lewis), **Ray Black** (S. J. Berwin, London), **Hugh Brett** (White & Case), **Nina Burden** (Charles Russell), **Anna Carboni** (Wilberforce Chambers), **Larry Cohen** (McDermott Will & Emery), **Michael Edenborough** (Hogarth Chambers), **John Groom** (Hallmark IP), **Carolyn Jones** (Richards Butler), **Ian Karet** (Linklaters), **Louise Gellman** (Nabarro Nathanson), **Tibor Gold** (Kilburn & Strode), **Gill Grassie** (Maclay Murray & Spens), **Naomi Gross** (Herbert Smith), **Gurminder Panesar** (Taylor Wessing), **Tim Pinto** (Taylor Wessing) and **Michael Skrein** (Richards Butler).

(iv) Private practitioners from outside the United Kingdom who have encouraged me, provided me with information or who have given me helpful comments include the following, in alphabetical order: **Juliette Biardeaud** (Gilbey de Haas, Paris), **Sheldon Burshtein** (Blake Cassels & Graydon, Toronto), **Fabrizio Jacobacci** (Jacobacci e Associati, Turin), **Bas Kist** (Shieldmark, Amsterdam), **Sheldon H Klein** (Arent Fox Plotkin & Kahn, Washington DC), **Roland Kunze** (Wuesthoff & Wuesthoff, Munich), **Willem Leppink** (NautaDutilh, Rotterdam), **Patricia McGovern** (L K Shields, Dublin), **Neil Wilkof** (Herzog Fox & Neeman, Tel-Aviv), **Steven Nemetz** (Blaney McMurtry, Toronto) and **Gert Würtenburger** (Wuesthoff & Wuesthoff, Munich).

(v)   On the side of those who work with or for trade mark-owning businesses, the following have given me the benefit of their thoughts or comments: **Jeffrey Belson** (Hewlett Packard), **Bob Boad** (BP), **Dawn Franklin** (Brandright), **Kelvin King** (Valuation Consulting), **Daniele Le Carval** (Procter & Gamble), **Tove Graulund** (Arla Foods), **John Noble**

Preface and Acknowledgements

(British Brands Group), **Lyndon Miles** (Investec), **Frederick Mostert** (Richemont) and **Naomi Runquist** (GlaxoSmithKline).

(vi) **Sir Robin Jacob** (Patents Court and now Court of Appeal, London), **David Keeling**, **Stefano Sandri** and **Kerstin Sundström** (OHIM Board of Appeal members), **Bojan Pretnar** (WIPO).

(vii) Many members of the Editorial Board of the *European Trade Mark Reports* have provided me with information concerning their respective jurisdictions.

(viii) To the organization of European trade mark proprietors, MARQUES, I am indebted for numerous insights, gleaned from their excellent conferences, as to the gap which sometimes exists between what trade mark owners want and what their legal representatives think they want.

(ix) My thanks are also owed to certain individuals who do not fit conveniently within any of the previous categories: **Chavi Phillips** (Brent Cross) gave me valuable information on brand and market-related issues, **Barney Phillips** (Barnstormers Publicity) advised me on several marketing issues and **Rachel Simon** provided the delicious 'geographical indications' recipes for Chapter 18.

This book was conceived out of wedlock, being two-fifths completed before I had even identified a possible publisher. My association with Oxford University Press has therefore been rather short, but entirely congenial. That this is so is entirely due to the efforts of **Chris Rycroft**, who has done an admirable job of endeavouring to steer me wide of all obstacles while surfing the crest of my various enthusiasms.

Further contributions to this book were made by others who inspired, encouraged or provoked me, challenged my thought-processes and generally enabled me to cultivate a far wider perception of trade marks than I would have achieved on my own. This category includes my old PhD supervisor **Harry Bloom** (lawyer, novelist, script-writer, journalist and dreamer), the imposing and demanding figure of **John Murphy** (founder of Interbrand and now the power behind the St Peter's Ale and Plymouth Gin brands), the occasionally outrageous former PTMG President **Derek Rossitter** and two other very different personalities whose opinions I have always valued and respected, **Florent Gevers** (Gevers) and **Charles Gielen** (NautaDutilh). Also in this category but known to me only by her writing is **Naomi Klein**, whose *No Logo* helped spark off the chain reaction which led to this book being written.

A final prefatory word: my late father **Louis Phillips** was a solicitor who did not believe in law books. Apart from the fact that they cost too much, they lacked utility: if you were a good lawyer you didn't need them and if you weren't a good lawyer they wouldn't help you. He did however believe in giving his unconditional support and devoted love to all his family and friends. He would never have read the book but he would been so proud to see my name on its cover.

Jeremy Phillips

jjip@btinternet.com

Temple Fortune, August 2003

TABLES OF CASES

A. Cases in alphabetical order	xxv
B. Cases by jurisdiction	li

A. Cases in alphabetical order

1-800 Flowers Inc. v Phonenames Ltd [2000] ETMR 369, [2000] IP&T 325 (HC); [2001]
  EWCA Civ 721, [2002] FSR 191, [2001] IP&T 810 ....5.28, 7.31, 17.52
A. Menarini—Industrie Farmaceutiche Riunite SRL (European Federation of Pharmaceutical
  Industries and Associations, intervening) v Commission Case T-179/00 [2002]
  ETMR 1131 ....16.28
AAH Pharmaceuticals Ltd v Vantagemax Plc [2002] EWHC 990 (Ch), [2003]
  ETMR 205 ....10.13, 10.18
Aaro Forsman OY's application; opposition of Gilvaria OY [2000] ETMR 142 ....5.24
ABB Sadelmi SpA's application; opposition of the European Patents Organisation, Case 3552/2002,
  28 November 2002 (unreported) 10.54
ABN Amro Holding N.V.'s application Case R 190/1999-3 [2001] ETMR 90 ....4.57, 5.17
ABSOLUT trade mark [2001] ETMR 21 ....4.59
Absperrpoller trade mark application [1997] ETMR 176 ....5.108
ACUPREL V AQUAPRED, noted in [2003] ETMR 653 ....10.123
Adidas A.G. v N.V. Famco [1998] ETMR 616 ....14.27
Adidas AG's application [1996] ETMR 66 ....10.118
Adidas AG's reference Case C-223/98 [1999] ETMR 960 ....14.25
Adidas-Saloman AG v Microhaven Ltd and others, 24 March 2003 (unreported) 9.93
Adidas-Salomon AG's application, Case 2000:119, Finnish Supreme Court 14.98
Adidas-Salomon AG and Adidas Benelux BV v Fitnessworld Trading Ltd, Case C-408/01,
  Opinion of 10 July 2003 (unreported) (ECJ) 7.51, 7.51A, 10.23, 11.22A, 11.58, 11.61,
    11.93, 11.95
Adolf Ahler AG's application Case R 91/1998-2, 28 May 1999 (unreported) 5.33
Advernet S.L. v Ozucom S.L. [1999] ETMR 1037 ....17.15
Aimo-Boot v Fabre [1999] ETMR 55 (Tribunal de Grande Instance de Paris) 4.99
Ajlan bin Abdullaziz Al-Ajlan Brothers Co's application; opposition by Al-Masaraat International
  Trading & Contracting Co. Ltd [2000] ETMR 710 ....4.107
Aktiebolaget Volvo and another v Heritage (Leicester) Ltd [2000] ETMR 940 ....7.26, 8.30
Aktsionernoe Obchtchestvo Zakritogo Tipa Torgovy Dom Potomkov Postavchtchika Dvora Ego
  Imperatorskago Velitschestva PA Smirnova v UDV North America Inc, Chancery
  Division, [2002] EWHC 2911 (Ch), 18 October 2002 ....4.47
Al Gatto Nero Srl v Le Chat Noir [1997] ETMR 371 ....10.51
Alcar Group v Corporate Performance Systems Ltd 109 FSupp 2d 948 (ND Ill 2000) 14.17
Alcon Inc v OHIM, Dr Robert Winzer Pharma GmbH intervening, Case T-237/01,
  Court of First Instance, 5 March 2003 (unreported) 4.174, 5.38, 6.22, 6.41
Alfa-Tel's application; opposition of Alcatel Altshom Compagnie Générale d'Electricité noted in
  [2001] ETMR 621 ....10.61

Tables of Cases

Alfred Ritter GmbH & Co. KG and CK Chocolade A/S v Ion SA Cocoa & Chocolate
   Manufacturers [1997] ETMR 103 ....8.56
Alghussein Establishment v Eton College [1991] 1 All ER 267 (HL) 15.78
'Alles Wird Teurer' [1999] ETMR 49 ....8.67
Allied Domecq plc's application [1997] ETMR 253 ....4.31, 5.19
Allied Domecq Spirits & Wine Ltd v Murray McDavid Ltd [1998] ETMR 61 ....8.21, 14.65
Altecnic Ltd v Reliance Water Controls Ltd [2001] RPC 13 ....13.107
ALVORADA trade mark [2003] ETMR 623 ....7.28, 13.99
AM General Corp v DaimlerChrysler Corp, No. 02-1816 (7th Cir 18 November 2002) 12.40
America Online Inc's application Case R 209/2000-3 [2002] ETMR 59 ....4.31, 4.165
American Cyanamid v Ethicon [1975] AC 396 ....1.37, 14.63, 14.69
American Home Products Corp's application [2001] ETMR 536 ....4.138
Amp Inc. v Utilux Pty Ltd [1972] RPC 103 ....5.91
Anheuser-Busch Inc v Budejovicky Budvar Narodni Podnik [2002] ETMR 1182
   (Portugal) 18.40
Anheuser-Busch Inc v Budejovicky Budvar Narodni Podnik [2001] ETMR 74
   (Switzerland) 3.08, 18.40
Anheuser-Busch Inc v Budejovicky Budvar Narodni Podnik [2000] RPC 906, [2000]
   IP&T 617 (CA) 8.51
Anne Frank Stichting's trade marks [1998] ETMR 687 ....16.63
Anne of Green Gables Licensing Authority and Heirs of L.M. Montgomery v. Avonlea Traditions, 10
   March 2000, OSCJ 15.13
Ansul BV v Ajax Brandbeveiliging BV, Case C-40/01, 2 July 2002 (Advocate General's Opinion),
   11 March 2003 (ECJ) 13.54, 13.57
Antoni and Alison's application Case R 4/97-2 [1998] ETMR 460 ....5.101, 5.105
AOM Minerve SA v INPI and another noted in [2001] ETMR 1209 ....7.12, 10.14
APHRODISIA trade mark [1977] FSR 133 ....4.36
Aquatherm GmbH v Wavin SpA [2002] EIPR N-33 ....5.123
A/S Arovit Petfood's application; opposition of Chivas Brothers Ltd, Case R 165/2002-1,
   26 March 2003 ....11.80
Arsenal Football Club plc v Matthew Reed, Case C-206/01 [2002] ETMR 975, [2003] RPC 144
   (Advocate General); [2003] ETMR 227 (ECJ); [2003] IP&T 43 (ECJ) 2.30, 2.33,
                              2.38, 7.40, 7.42, 7.43, 7.49–7.51A, 17.67
Arsenal Football Club plc v Matthew Reed [2001] ETMR 860, [2001] IP&T 810 (HC) ...2.38, 7.19,
                              8.85–8.88
Arsenal Football Club plc v Matthew Reed [2002] EWCA 2695 (Ch); [2003] IP&T 75,
   [2003] ETMR 453 (HC); [2002] EWCA Civ 96, 21 May 2003 ....7.50, 8.88
Artistic Upholstery Ltd v Art Forma (Furniture Ltd) [2000] FSR 311, [2000] IP&T 147 ......13.101
A/S: look up next word of name
Askey Computer Corp's application; opposition of Nokia Telecommunications OY [2000]
   ETMR 214 ....10.73, 10.118
Asprey & Garrard Ltd v WRA (Guns) Ltd and Asprey [2001] EWCA Civ 1499, [2002]
   ETMR 933 ....10.12
Associated Newspapers Ltd and another v Express Newspapers [2003] EWHC 1322 (Ch),
   11 June 2003, (unreported) (HC) 4.124, 10.79
Association Greenpeace France v SA Société Esso [2003] ETMR 441, reversed 26 February 2003
   [2003] ETMR 867(Cour d'appel de Paris) 8.61, 21.39
AstraZeneca AB v Orifarm A/S, noted in [2002] EIPR N-92 ....14.85
SA Ateliers Réunis Caddie v Sarl Société Nouvelle de Presse et de Communication (SNPC) [1999]
   ETMR 45 ....6.25, 8.78
Atlan v INPI and SA Promodès [2001] ETMR 88 ....10.15
Audio Medical Devices Ltd's application; opposition of Audi AG [1999] ETMR 1010 ....11.74
Aunt Jemima Mills Co. v Rigney & Co., 247 F. 407 (2d Cir 1917), cert. denied, 245 U.S. 672
   (1918) 10.102

A. Cases in alphabetical order

AUVI trade mark [1995] FSR 288 High Court (Singapore) 19.05
AV by Versace Inc v Gianni Versace SpA 126 FSupp 2d 328 (SDNY 2001) 14.17
Aventis Pharma Aktiebolag v Paranova Läkemedel Aktiebolag [2001] ETMR 652 ....16.24
Aventis Pharma Deutschland GmbH v Kohlpharma GmbH and another Case C-433/00 [2003]
    ETMR 143, [2003] IP&T 183 ....16.12
Avery Dennison Corp. v Sumpton 189 F3d 368, 51 USPQ 2d 1801 (9th Cir 1999) 12.69
Avnet Incorporated v Isoact Ltd [1997] ETMR 562 ....10.98, 17.73
Axion SA and Christian Belce v Office for Harmonisation in the Internal Market, Joined Cases T-
    324/01 and T-110/02, 30 April 2003 (unreported) 5.144A
Azienda Agragia Perda Rubia v Cantina Sociale Ogliastria noted in [2001] ETMR 1114 ....14.38

BABY-DRY: see Procter & Gamble
Bacardi y Compañía SA España v Dimexco SL and Destilerias de l'Urgell SA [2003]
    ETMR 326 ....9.52
Bach Flower Remedies Ltd v Healing Herbs Ltd [1999] IP&T 146 ....4.91
Ball v The Eden Project Ltd and another [2001] ETMR 966 (HC) 13.89
Bandera, re [1999] ETMR 337 ....13.61
Bank für Arbeit und Wirtschaft v OHIM (EASYBANK) Case T-87/00 [2001] ECR II-1259,
    [2001] ETMR 761, [2001] IP&T 1142 ....4.117, 4.138
Barclays Bank plc v RBS Advanta [1996] RPC 307; [1997] ETMR 199 ....8.115, 8.142,
    8.145, 8.149, 8.150, 8.151
SA Bardinet v S.C.P. Ego-Fruits (S.C.P. Belat-Desprat intervening) [2002] ETMR 1043 ....4.174,
    6.27, 6.29, 8.79
Barilla Alimentares SpA v Danis Srl and others [1996] ETMR 43 ....10.65
Barilla Alimentares SpA v Danis Srl and others [2003] ETMR N-4 ....14.22
BASF plc v C.E.P. (UK) plc [1996] ETMR 51 ....7.14, 11.83
Bata Ltd v Face Fashions CC [2002] EIPR N-9 ....10.40
Bayerische Motorenwerke AG (BMW) and BMW Nederland BV v Deenik Case C-63/97 [1999]
    ETMR 339 ....8.30, 9.32, 17.08
Baywatch Production Co. Inc. v The Home Video Channel [1997] FSR 22 ....7.14, 11.83
Beautimatic International Ltd v Mitchell International Pharmaceuticals Ltd and another [1999]
    ETMR 912, [1999] IP&T 59 ....7.18, 7.23, 7.30, 14.34
BECOME WHAT YOU ARE trade mark, Republic of Turkey Appellate Court, Eleventh Tribunal,
    [2003] ETMR 879 ....5.74
Beecham Group plc v Munro Wholesale Medical Supplies Ltd [2001] ETMR 318 ....14.51,
    14.63, 16.25
Beiersdorf A.G.'s trade mark; application for cancellation by L'Oréal Case C000835728/1
    [2001] ETMR 187 ....8.82, 13.35, 13.68
Belgacom v Benelux Trade Mark Office [2000] ETMR 286 ....5.127
Belgium (Kingdom of) v Spain (Kingdom of) Case C-388/95 [2000] ETMR 999 ....18.50
Belmont Olympic SA's application; opposition of the Comité International Olympique [2000]
    ETMR 919 ....12.32
Benckiser N.V. and Benckiser Italia SpA v Henkel SpA and others [1999] EMR 614 ......14.61, 14.95
Benincasa v Dentalkit Srl Case C-296/95 [1997] ETMR 447 ....15.54
Bertucci v McDonald's Corp and others [1999] ETMR 742 ....10.139
Bette Midler v Ford Motor Co 849 F2d 460 (9th Cir 1988) 16.52
Betts v Wilmott (1871) LR 6 Ch App 239 ....9.02
BETTY'S KITCHEN CORONATION STREET trade mark [2001] RPC 825 ....13.95
BEVETE COCA COLA Court of Milan, 10 March 1980, Giur. Ann. Dir Ind. 80, 271 ....13.126
Biba Group Ltd v Biba Boutique [1980] RPC 413 ....8.34
Bio-Claire International Ltd v Benelux Trade Marks Office [1998] ETMR 251 ....4.156
BioID v OHIM, Case T-91/01, [2003] ETMR 766 ....4.62, 5.30, 5.41
Björnekulla Fruktindustrier Aktiebolag v Procordia Food Aktiebolag [2002] ETMR 464 ....4.95,
    6.32, 12.43

Björnekulla Fruktindustrier Aktiebolag v Procordia Food Aktiebolag, Svea Hovrätt, 14 October 2002
 (unreported, reference to ECJ as Case C-367/02) 6.32
Black & Decker Corp's application Case R 99/1999-1 [1999] ETMR 845 (MULTI 2 'N 1) 4.111
BMW: see also Bayerische Motorenwerke AG
BMW GRUR 1986, 759 ....8.67
Board of Appeal for Patents and Trade Marks v Danish Association of Pharmacists WTLR,
 1 April 2003 ....4.54
BOCM Pauls Ltd and Scottish Agricultural College's application [1997] ETMR 420 ....4.49, 5.53
Boehringer Ingelheim Danmark A/S and others v Orifarm A/S [2002] ETMR 223 ....16.24
Boehringer Ingelheim KG and Boehringer Ingelheim Pharma KG v Swingward Ltd, Case C-143/00
 [2002] ETMR 898 ....9.83, 16.13, 16.18
Boehringer Ingelheim Pharma KG v Eurim-Pharm Arzneimittel GmbH [2003] ETMR 491 ....14.16,
 14.99
Boehringer Ingelheim Pharma KG v GTO Expeditie BV and others, Court of The Hague,
 19 February 2003 ....14.24
Bongrain SA's trade mark application, EWHC 531 (Ch) 5.82
Bonnier Media Ltd v Greg Lloyd Smith and Kestrel Trading Corp, [2002] ETMR 1050, Court of
 Session (Scotland) 9.09, 14.13
BONUS trade mark application [1997] ETMR 413 ....4.81
Bord Telecom Eireann plc's application [2001] ETMR 790 ....4.115
Borden Inc v Federal Trade Commission, 674 F2d 498 (6th Cir 1982) 15.32
Borie Manoux Sarl v Directeur de l'Institut de la Propriété Industrielle Case C-81/01 [2003]
 ETMR 367 ....18.45
Boston Pizza International Inc v Boston Chicken Inc, (2003) WTLR 11 April 2003 ....4.172
Boston Professional Hockey Assoc., Inc. v. Dallas Cap & Emblem Mfg., Inc., 510 F2d 1004 (5th Cir.
 1975) 7.64
Bouchard Pere & Fils v Pascal Bouchard, Cour de Cassation, 2 July 2002 ....7.12
BP Amoco plc v John Kelly Ltd, [2001] IP&T 787; noted in [2001] ETMR 1021 ....5.128
Brackenbrough's application; opposition of Säntis Management AG Case 1517/2000 [2001]
 ETMR 412 ....10.48
Brain v Ingledew Brown Bennington & Garret [1996] FSR 341 ....14.113
Braun Aktiengesellschaft v Elbeka Electro BV [1998] ETMR 259 ....14.23, 14.100
Bravado Merchandising Services Ltd v Mainstream Publishing (Edinburgh) Ltd [1996]
 FSR 205 ....7.48, 8.43, 8.86, 16.68
Bravilor Bonamat BV v Boumann Hotelbenodigdheden BV (District Court, Amsterdam), 10 August
 2000; (2002) 92 TMR 273 ....17.08
Bravo Industry of Coffees SA (also Trading as Bravo SA) v Fiat Auto SpA [1997] ETMR 167 ....11.47
Bristol-Myers Squibb v Paranova A/S; C.H. Boehringer Sohn and others v Paranova A/S; Bayer
 Aktiengesellschaft and another v Paranova A/S Joined cases C-427/93, C-429/93 & C-436/93
 [1996] ETMR 1 ....16.11, 16.13, 16.17, 16.26
British Airways plc v Ryanair Ltd [2001] ETMR 235, [2001] IP&T 373 ....2.48, 4.160, 8.111,
 8.134–8.135, 8.143, 8.145, 8.153, 8.154
British American Tobacco Cigaretten-Fabriken GmbH v Commission Case C-35/83 [1985]
 ECR 363 ....15.41
British-American Tobacco (Holdings) Ltd's application; opposition of Fabriques de Tabac Réunis
 SA Case B598 [1999] ETMR 32 ....10.139
British Petroleum Company plc's application Cases R 55/1998-2 and R 60/1998-2 [1999]
 ETMR 282 ....5.104
British Sugar plc v James Robertson & Sons Ltd [1997] ETMR 118; [1996] RPC 281 ....4.127,
 5.49, 7.49, 8.59
British Telecommunications plc v Nextcall Telecom plc [2000] ETMR 943, [2000]
 IP&T 478 ....14.40
British Telecommunications plc and others v One in a Million Ltd and others [1999]
 ETMR 61 ....17.07, 17.16, 17.17

A. Cases in alphabetical order

Bromberg v Carmel Self Service Inc, 198 USPQ 176 (TTAB 1978) 19.14
Brookfield Communications Inc v West Coast Entertainment Corp, 174 F3d 1056 (9th Cir, 22 April
    1999) 10.126
Brother Records Inc. v Jardine 318 F3d 900 (9th Cir. 2003) 8.36, 16.64
Brunswick Corp v British Seagull Ltd, 35 F. 3d 1527, 1532 (CA Fed. 1994) 5.93
Budejovicky Budvar NP v Rudolf Ammersin GmbH, Case C-216/01, Advocate General Opinion
    22 May 2003 ....18.40
Budejovicky Budvar Narodni Podnik v Anheuser-Busch Inc [2002] ETMR 1182
    (SC Portugal) 3.08, 18.40
Budejovicky Budvar Narodni Podnik v Anheuser-Busch Inc WTLR, 3 July 2003 (Examination
    Committee of the Romanian State Office for Inventions and Trade Marks) 10.33
BUDGET BILUTHYRNING AB (Svea CA, 27 Nov 1981) 13.96
Bulmer (HP) Ltd v J Bollinger SA (No. 3) [1978] RPC 79 ....18.38
Burberrys Ltd v EMEC Co Ltd and Textjournal Co Ltd [1998] IP Asia LR 129 ....9.66
Burroughs Inc. and another v Picha, Valiza Films and others [1978] EIPR European Digest,
    December, p. iv 8.68
Buy.Com Inc's application R 638/2000-4 [2002] ETMR 540 ....4.166, 5.26, 17.05
BVBA: see Kruidvat

C. A. Sheimer (M.) Sdn. Bhd's application; opposition by Visa International Service Association [1999]
    ETMR 519 (Registry); [2000] RPC 484 (LCAP) 11.81, 13.102, 13.108
Cabot Safety Intermediate Corp's application Case R 381/2000-1 [2001] ETMR 949 ....5.115
Caesar's World Inc v Caesar's Palace.com and others 112 FSupp2d 502 (EDVa 2000) 17.30
CAFFREY's application; opposition of CAFRE [2002] EntLR N-87 (Hungarian Supreme Court) Pfk. IV
    25.022/1999 ....10.139
Cahill May Roberts Ltd's application for a declaration of invalidity; Medicine Shoppe International's
    trade mark Case C000172734/1 [2000] ETMR 794 ....13.38
Caixa d'Estalvis y Pensions de Barcelona v Namezero.com Decision 2001-0360 [2001]
    ETMR 1239 ....17.41
Callaway Golf Company v Big Bertha Srl WTLR, 20 June 2003 (Bundesgerichtshof,
    Germany) 10.88
Calvin Klein Trademark Trust v Cowboyland A/S, Dansk Supermarked Administration A/S,
    HBN Marketing ApS, Progress (in the name of Peter Jensen) and Bilka Lavprisvarehus A/S,
    Case C-4/98 (removed from the Register on 27 March 1999) 9.85
Camel Tours (1988) 19 IIC 695 ....11.64
Campina Melkunie BV v Benelux Merkenbureau Case C-265/00 31 Jan 2002(AG) 4.154
Campina Melkunie BV v Bureau Benelux des Marques [2001] ETMR 392 ....4.171
Campomar S.L's application; opposition of Nike International Ltd Case 102/1999 [2000]
    ETMR 50 ....11.71
Campomar Sociedad, Limitada v Nike International Ltd [2000] HCA 12 ....10.116
Canal+ Image UK Ltd v VanityMail Services Inc. Decision FA0006000094946 [2001]
    ETMR 418 ....17.46
CANNON trade mark application [1998] ETMR 77 ....10.80
Canon Kabushiki Kaisha v Metro-Goldwyn-Mayer Inc Case C-39/97 [1999] ETMR 1 ....
    2.30, 10.81, 10.102, 10.111, 12.69, 21.04
Canon Kabushiki Kaisha's application Case R 182/1999-1 [1999] ETMR 845 (WebRecord) 4.115
Car Wheel Rim trade mark application [1998] ETMR 584 ....5.108
Sarl Cargo Communication v La Cité des Sciences et de l'Industrie [1999] ETMR 545 ....4.111
Carl Kühne GmbH and Co. KG Rich. Hengstenberg GmbH and another v Jütro Konservenfabrik
    GmbH & Co. KG Case C-269/99 [2003] ETMR 36 ....18.35
Carlill v Carbolic Smoke Ball Company [1893] 1 QB 256 ....2.48
Carpoint SpA v Microsoft Corp [2000] ETMR 802 ....14.13
Cartier International BV v Hammer Diamonds A/S noted in [2002] ETMR] 1041 ....10.60
Casaubon and Vingt et Unième Siècle v 21st Century Film France [1999] ETMR 787 .....5.21, 10.52

Caterham Car Sales & Coachworks Ltd's application Case R 63/1999-3 [2000] ETMR 14 ....5.40
SA Caviar Anzali v L'Institut National de La Propriété Industrielle, Sté Brugis (third party) [2000]
    ETMR 513 ....10.90
Centrafarm v American Home Products Corp [1978] ECR 1823 ....16.11
Centro Botanico Srl, Angelo Naj Oleari and Gruppo Cartorama SpA v Modafil di A. Toniolo &
    C. Sas [2003] ETMR 500 ....5.64, 14.80
Century 21 Real Estate Corp's application Case R 135/1998-2 [1999] ETMR 781 ....5.21
Chambre Syndicale Nationale de la Confiserie v Optos-Opus Sarl, (2003) 762 PIBD III-216 .....4.39
'Champagner Bekommen, Sekt Bezahlen' [2002] ETMR 1091 ....8.104, 18.38
Sté Chanel v SA Citycom [2000] ETMR 1068 ....17.53
Chanel SA Genève of Geneva and Chanel SA of Glaris v EPA AG [1997] ETMR 352 ....9.57
Chanelle Pharmaceuticals Mfg. Ltd v Chanel Ltd [2003] ETMR 64 ....10.68
Checkpoint Systems Inc. v Check Point Software Technologies Inc, 104 FSupp 2d 427 (DNJ, 12 July
    2000) 10.126
Chemfinder Cambridgesoft Corp's application Case R 211/1998-2 [2000] ETMR 250 ....4.118
Chiciak, Fromagèrie Chiciak and Fol Joined Cases C-129 and 130/97 [1998] ETMR 550 ......18.47
Chloé Société Anonyme v Føtex A/S [1997] ETMR 131 ....14.22
Choay SA v Boehringer Ingelheim International GmbH Case R 273/1999-1 [2001] ETMR
    693 ....10.56, 16.32
Chocosuisse, Kraft Jacobs Suchard (Schweiz) AG and Chocoladefabriken Lindt & Sprüngli
    (Schweiz) AB v Cadbury Ltd [1998] ETMR 205 (High Court); [1999] ETMR 1020
    (Court of Appeal) 18.38
Christian Dior: see Parfums Christian Dior
Christian Dior Couture SA v Fashion TV Paris and others [2001] ETMR 126 ....8.65
Christian Dior Couture SA v Liage International Inc. Decision 2000-0098 [2000] ETMR
    773 ....17.43
Christien t/a Rose's Lace Boutique and another v BVBA Parcles [2000] ETMR 1 ....14.50
Citicorp v Link Interchange Network Ltd [2002] ETMR 1146 ....10.118
Claerin/Klarein: see Lucas Bols v Colgate-Palmolive
Claritas (UK) Ltd v Post Office and Postal Preference Service Ltd [2001] ETMR 679 ....14.122
CLASSE E, BGH, GRUR 2001, 242, 244 ....13.90
Cline v I-888-Plumbing Group 146 F Supp 2d 351, 362 (SDNY 2001) 5.29
Clinique Laboratories Inc's application Case R 73/1998-2 [1999] ETMR 750 ....4.111, 5.74
CLT-UFA Société Anonyme v This Domain is for Sale and Sean Gajadhar Decision 2000-0801
    [2001] ETMR 446 ....17.47
CNL-Sucal NV v Hag GF AG [1990] 3 CMLR 571 ('HAG II') 2.30, 3.13, 9.92
Cobra Beer Ltd's application; opposition of Alpabob AG Case 811/1999 [2000]
    ETMR 638 ....10.84
Coflexip SA v Stolt Comex Seaway MS Ltd [1999] FSR 473 (Patents Court), [2001] RPC 182
    (Court of Appeal) 14.34
Cola Test (1987) GRUR 49 ....8.95
Colgate-Palmolive Ltd and another v Markwell Finance Ltd and another [1988] RPC 283 ....2.25,
                                                                                    9.13, 9.16
Comercial Iberica de Exclusivas Deportivas SA (Cidesport) v Nike International Ltd and American
    Nike SA [2000] ETMR 189 ....10.36, 10.61
Comité Interprofessionel du Vin de Champagne v SA Parfums Caron (1999) 685 PIBD,
    III-442 ....18.34
Commission of the European Communities v Federal Republic of Germany Case C-325/00
    [2003] ETMR 417 ....20.11
Commission of the European Communities v French Republic, Case C-6/02, 6 March 2003
    (ECJ) 18.21, 20.11
Community Concepts AG v OHIM Case T-360/99 [2001] ETMR 176 ....4.117
CompAir Ltd v Naber + Co KG, Case R 590/1999-2, OHIM OJ 2/2003, 341 ....13.34
Compare! (1999) GRUR Int 453 ....8.136

A. Cases in alphabetical order

ConAgra Foods Inc v Fetherstonhaugh & Co., (Federal Court of Canada), WTLR
    2 April 2003 ....13.57
Consejo Regulador de las Denominaciones Jerez-Xeres-Sherry y Manzanilla de Sanlucar de
    Barrameda v Mathew Clark & Sons Ltd [1992] FSR 525 (HC) 18.38
Consorzio del Prosciutto di Parma v Marks & Spencer Plc [1991] RPC 351 ....18.32
Consorzio del Prosciutto di Parma and Salumificio S. Rita Case C-108/01, 20 May
    2003 ....18.32, 18.51
Consorzio per la Promozione dello Speck v Christanell, Handle Tyrol and Lidl Italia Srl, noted in
    [1998] ETMR 537 ....14.17, 18.10
Consorzio per la Tutela del Formaggio Gorgonzola v Käserei Champignon Hofmeister GmbH & Co.
    KG and Eduard Bracharz GmbH [1999] ETMR 454 (ECJ) 3.08, 18.33
Continental Graphics Corp, re 52 USPQ 2d 1374 (TTAB 1999) 1.26
Corning InCorp's application Case R 449/1999-2 [2001] ETMR 933 ....5.05
Corsair Toiletries Ltd's application; opposition by Jane Austen Memorial Trust [1999] ETMR
    1038 ....16.57
Société Corsetel v INPI and France Telecom [2001] ETMR 930 ....10.64
CORVINA trade mark, Polish Patent Office, 18 December 2001 (unreported) 13.99
Cosmedent Inc's application Case R 29/1998-3 [1998] ETMR 658 ....4.157
Cowbell AG v ICS Holdings Ltd 2001 (3) SA 941 ....1.26
Cuisine de la Mer Cuisimer SA v Maumenee, SA Meralim and Rambour [2000] ETMR 880 ....10.27,
    10.45, 10.73

D'Ieteren v Benelux Trade Marks Office [2003] ETMR 842, CA Brussels 4.22, 4.99
D. Green & Co. (Stoke Newington) Ltd and Plastico Ltd v Regalzone Ltd [2001] EWCA Civ 639,
    [2002] ETMR 241, [2001] IP&T 1071 ....4.95, 6.33
DAAWAT trade mark [2003] RPC 187 ....13.101
DaimlerChrysler A.G. v Alavi [2001] ETMR 1069, [2001] IP&T 496 ....11.36, 11.46,
    11.67, 11.69, 11.76
DaimlerChrysler AG v OHIM Case T-356/00 [2002] IP&T 815, [2003] ETMR 778
    (CARCARD) 5.149
DaimlerChrysler Aktiengesellschaft's application; opposition of Succession Picasso 22/2001
    [2002] ETMR 346 ....16.60
DaimlerChrysler Corp v OHIM, Case T-128/01, 6 March 2003 (unreported) 4.109
Dairygold Co-operative Society Ltd's application [2001] ETMR 1279 (the 'white meat'
    applications), Ireland 3.50
Dairygold Co-operative Society Ltd's application; opposition of Austin Nichols & Co. Inc [2002]
    ETMR 1084 (ORANGO/ORANGINA) 10.118
Daishowa Seiki Co. Ltd's application R 991/2000-3 [2002] ETMR 403 ....4.85
Dann and Backer v Société Provençale d'Achat et de Gestion (SPAG), Case R 1072/2000-2,
    [2003] ETMR 888, OHIM Second Board of Appeal 10.71
Danone: see Gervais Danone
Dansk Supermarked Case 58/80 [1981] ECR 181 ....6.36
Dante Bigi Case C-66/00 [2003] ETMR 707 ....18.31
Dart Industries Inc. v OHIM, Case T-360/00 [2003] ETMR 406, [2003] IP&T 203 ....4.78,
    4.87, 4.100, 4.110
Data Professionals Srl v Mercantile Sistemi Srl [1998] ETMR 670 ....10.93
Davide Campari Milano SpA v Özal/Finkol Giyim Sanayi ve Ticaret Ltd Şti [2002]
    ETMR 856 ....13.98
Davidoff: see Zino Davidoff
Davidoff & Cie SA and another v PLD International Corp 263 F3d 1297 (11 Cir 2001) 9.57
Davidoff & Cie. and Zino Davidoff SA v Gofkid Ltd Case C-292/00 [2002] ETMR 1219,
    [2003] FSR 50 (Advocate-General's Opinion); [2003] ETMR 534 (ECJ) 7.11, 10.18,
    11.84, 11.87, 11.91, 11.92, 11.93, 11.95, 12.27
Davidoff & Cie SA v Muriel Case FA 0211000129124, (2003) WTLR 4 April 2003 ....17.18

Dax Cosmetics Zaklady Kosmetyczno-Chemiczne Jacek Majdax I Wojciech Szulc SC's appeal
   [2001] ETMR 506 ....4.131
De Boer Stalinrichtingen BV's application Case R 175/2000-4 [2001] ETMR 899 ....5.06
Decon Laboratories Ltd v Fred Baker Scientific Ltd and another [2001] ETMR 486 ....13.80, 13.101,
   13.125, 13.128, 13.130, 13.131, 13.132, 13.142
Deere & Company v MTD Products Inc, 41 F3d 39 (2d Cir 1994) 8.175
Demon Ale trade mark [2000] RPC 345 ....13.91, 13.110
Denmark, Germany and France v The Commission Joined cases C-289, 293 and 299/96 [1999]
   ETMR 478 ....18.16
Denner A.G. v Rivella A.G. noted in [2001] ETMR 826 ....10.131
Deutsche Renault AG v Audi AG Case C-317/91 [1995] FSR 738 ....6.36
Deutsche Telekom A.G.'s trade mark; Veiga's application for cancellation Case 000267724/1,
   noted in [2000] ETMR 939 ....10.120
Deutsche Telekom AG, B***** v R***** AG, C***** Gelleschaft *** mbH [2003] ETMR 170 ....4.69,
   10.120
Deutsche Telekom v Deutsche Krankenversicherung, Case C-367/02, reference to ECJ 10.151
Deutscher Teeverband E.V.'s application for cancellation (TEEKAMPAGNE) [2000]
   ETMR 546 ....13.35
Diageo plc v John Zuccarini and Cupcake Patrol Decision 2000-0996 [2001] ETMR 466 ......17.38
Dial-A-Mattress Operating Corp, re 240 F3d 1341 (Fed Cir 2001) 5.29
Diana, Princess of Wales: see Executrices
Din Bank A/S's trade mark; application for declaration of invalidity by Deutsche Bank
   Aktiengesellschaft Case 144C 001027374/1, OHIM Cancellation Division,
   1 October 2001 (unreported) 10.120
DIMPLE (1985) 17 GRUR 529 ....11.29, 11.60–11.64, 11.94
Discovery Communications Inc. v Discovery FM Ltd [2000] ETMR 516 ....14.67
Disparagement of Trade Marks 1, GRUR 1994, 808 (MARS) 8.67
Disparagement of Trade Marks 2, GRUR 1995, 57 (NIVEA) 8.67
Diversified Marketing Inc. v Estée Lauder Inc. 705 F Supp 128 (SDNY 1988) 8.95
DKV Deutsche Krankenversicherung AG v OHIM (COMPANYLINE) Case C-104/00 P
   [2003] ETMR 241 ....4.63, 4.102, 6.34
DKV Deutsche Krankenversicherung AG v OHIM (EuroHealth) Case T-359/99 [2001]
   ECR II-1645, [2001] ETMR 919, [2001] IP&T 149 ....5.53
Dolby Laboratories Licensing Corp's application, 11 February 1999 (Paraguayan Trade Mark
   Office) 5.139
Douglas and others v Hello! Ltd [2001] QB 967 (CA) 16.54
Douglas, Zeta-Jones and another v Hello! Ltd and others, High Court, 11 April 2003 ....7.59
Dr Karl Thomae GmbH, supported by the European Federation of Pharmaceutical Industries and
   Associations (EFPIA) v Commission of the European Communities, supported by the
   Council of the European Union, Case T-123/00, Court of First Instance
   (Fifth Chamber), 10 December 2002 (unreported) 16.06
Dr Martens International Trading GmbH's application; opposition of Lloyd Schuhfabrik Meyer & Co.
   GmbH Case 165/2000 [2000] ETMR 1151 ....10.58, 10.69
Dr Robert Winzer Pharma GmbH's application to cancel a trade mark of Alcon Pharmaceuticals Ltd,
   Case C000090134/1, [2000] ETMR 217 ....5.38, 8.82
DSG Retail Ltd (t/a Currys) v Comet Group plc, [2002] EWHC 116 (QB), [2002] FSR 899 ....8.154
Du Pont de Nemours (E.I.) and Company v AMA VOF Antoon Michielsen Automobiles (trading as
   Protech Nederland Teflon Lakbescherming) and others [2001] ETMR 777 ....6.41, 8.82
Du Pont du Nemours: see also E.I. du Pont
Ducks UnLtd's application; opposition of Dr Rehfeld Handelsgesellschaft mbH Case 849/1999
   [2000] ETMR 820 ....10.85
DUPLO/DUPLO Case R 802/1999-1, 5 June 2000 (unreported) 11.47
DURACELL trade mark [1999] ETMR 583 ....12.33
Durferrit GmbH v OHIM, Kolene Corp Intervening, Case T-224/01, 9 April 2003 ....4.35, 13.03

A. Cases in alphabetical order

'Dyed Jeans' [1997] ETMR 530 .... 9.56
Dyson Appliances Ltd v Hoover Ltd (No.2) [2001] RPC 544 .... 14.47
Dyson Ltd v Registrar of Trade Marks [2003] EWHC 1062 (Ch) 15 May 2003 .... 5.82

E.I. du Pont de Nemours & Co., In re 476 F2d 1357, 177 USPQ 563 (CCPA 1973) 10.125
Eastman Kodak Company Corp v Grundul and the Russian Scientific and Research Institute for the
    Development of Public Networks [2002] ETMR 776 .... 9.35, 17.08
Ecco Sko A/S v Nike Denmark ApS [2001] ETMR 371 .... 8.58
Echodent AB's application Case R 773/2001-2 [2002] ETMR 1240 .... 4.115
Edgar Rice Burroughs Inc v Beukenoord BV and others [2001] ETMR 1300 (CA, Amsterdam) .. 6.38,
    16.68
Einstein, re, Trade Mark [2001] EIPR N-136 .... 16.62
Einstein Stadtcafé Verwaltungs- und Betriebsgesellschaft mbH's application; opposition of the Hebrew
    University of Jerusalem Case 506/2000 [2000] ETMR 952 .... 16.62
Eiretel Ltd's application; opposition by Airtel Movil SA and another [2003] EIPR N-7 .... 10.68
Eli Lilly & Co. v Salenab Nigeria Ltd (FHC/LCS/534/99), Federal High Court, noted in WTLR,
    1 April 2003 .... 13.72
Elite Industries Ltd v Graziella Import Export Srl, Case 1409/2002, (2003) WTLR
    17 June 2003 .... 9.56
Ellos AB v OHIM Case T-219/00 [2003] IP&T 384 .... 4.134
Elvis Presley Trade Marks [1997] RPC 543 (ChD), 567 (CA) 8.89, 16.53
Emaco Ltd and Aktienbolaget Electrolux v Dyson Appliances Ltd [1999] ETMR 903 ... 8.128–8.129,
    8.133, 8.156, 14.89
Emergency One v American Fire Eagle Engine Company 332 F3d 264, 67 USPQ 2d 1124
    (4th Cir NC 2003) 14.35A
Empresa Licorera de Santander's trade mark application, 8 March 2002 (Colombia Trade Mark
    Office) 4.173
Enterprise Rent-a-Car Co v Advantage Rent-a-Car Inc WTLR 18 July 2003 (CAFC) 12.42
EQUI 2000, BGH, GRUR 2000, 1032, 1034 .... 13.90
Erich Perner Kunststoffwerke v Pressman Toy Corp [1997] ETMR 159 .... 13.65
ERGOPANEL trade mark application [1997] ETMR 495 .... 4.71
Erpo Möbelwerk GmbH v OHIM Case T-138/00 [2002] ETMR 430 .... 4.113, 4.132
ESA (European Space Agency) v ETOS BV, Haarlem District Court, [2003]
    ETMR 655 .... 5.23
Esprit International v Commissioner of the Japanese Patent Office Heisei (gyo-ke) 105,
    31 January 2001 .... 16.42
Esquire Electronics v Executive Video 1986 (2) 576 AD 7.34
Esso Société Anonyme Française SA v Association Greenpeace France and Société Internet.Fr,
    [2003] ETMR 441 .... 8.61, 8.68, 14.39, 17.68
Estée Lauder Cosmetics and others v Fragrance Counter Inc. and Excite Inc. [2000]
    ETMR 843 .... 17.29, 17.70
Estée Lauder Inc. v Fragrance Counter 1999 US Dist. LEXIS 14825 (SDNY 1999) 17.29
Etat Française v Bernard Matthews plc [2002] EWHC 190, [2002] ETMR 1098, [2003]
    ETMR 13 .... 13.97
Eurocool Logistik GmbH v OHIM Case T-34/00 [2003] ETMR 51 .... 5.53
Euromarket Designs Incorporated v Peters and another [2000] ETMR 1025, [2001] IP&T
    1308 .... 7.31, 17.09
Europabank N.V. v Banque pour l'Europe SA [1997] ETMR 143 .... 4.42
European Ltd v The Economist Newspaper Ltd [1998] ETMR 307 .... 5.47, 8.17
Executrices of the Estate of Diana Princess of Wales' application [2001] ETMR 254 .... 16.57

Sté Fabrication et d'Outillage de la Brie (SFOB) v Sté Notter GmbH, Cour d'appel de Paris,
    13 March 2002 (unreported) 17.69
Fada Pty Ltd (t/a Pacific Coast Eco-Bananas)'s application (2003) WTLR 19 May 2003 .... 5.130

Farley's application; opposition by the joint ownership on the monopoly of the intellectual property attached to the work of Pablo Picasso [2002] ETMR 336 ......16.60
Farmaceutici Dott. Ciccarelli v Aboca di Mercati Valentino SaS [2003] EIPR N-72 ......14.117
Farside Clothing Ltd et al. v Caricline Ventures Ltd, 2002 FCA 466, 12 November 2002 ......13.36
Fédération Nationale d'Agriculture Biologique des Régions de France (FNAB), Syndicat Européen des Transformateurs et Distributeurs de Produits de l'Agriculture Biologique (SETRAB) and Est Distribution Biogram Sarl v Council of the European Union, Case T-268/99, 11 July 2000 ......4.45
Feta: see Denmark, Germany and France v The Commission
Sté Felix the Cat Productions Inc. v Sté Polygram [1999] ETMR 370 ......10.43, 10.55
Ferrari SpA v Power Horse and others [1997] ETMR 84 ......14.32, 14.39
Ferrero oHG mbH v Annie Cornelia Beekenkamp, Case R 214/2000-4, 4 December 2002 (unreported) 11.41, 11.47, 12.58
Ferrero oHG mbH v Jordi Tarrida Llopart, Case R 186/2001-1 [2003] ETMR 188 ......11.44, 12.58
Ferring Arzneimittel GmbH v Eurim-Pharm Arzneimittel GmbH Case C-172/00 [2003] ETMR 115 ......9.60, 16.30
Fertin A/S's application Case R 382/1999-1 [2000] ETMR 652 ......4.114
Fieldturf Inc's application Case R 462/2001-1, 15 May 2002 (unreported) 5.73
Figueroa v United States (argued before the US Court of Federal Claims, 14 November 2002) 2.08
First National Bank of Southern Africa Ltd v Barclays Bank plc (2003) WTLR 1 May 2003 ......4.178
Football Association Ltd, G.B. v Distributors of Football Strips [1997] ETMR 229 ......14.45
FOR YOU trade mark application [2001] ETMR 28 ......4.137
Ford Motor Company v Association of Former Ford Distributors (2003) WTLR 5 June 2003 ......8.12
Ford Motor Company v OHIM Case T-91/99 [2000] ETMR 554, [2000] IP&T 597 (OPTIONS) 4.95, 4.177
Ford Motor Company's application Case R 433/1999-1 [2000] ETMR 679 (TDdi) 5.39
Format Gesellschaft M.B.H. and another v Wirtschafts-Trend Zeitschriftenverlags Ges m.b.H. [2002] ETMR 472 ......14.62, 17.15, 17.16, 17.19
FPOE v Nic.at [2003] ETMR 25 ......17.25
Société France Cartes v Naipes Heraclio Fournier SA [2002] ETMR 1119 ......5.89
Frank Reddaway & Co. Ltd v George Banham & Co. Ltd [1896] AC 199 ......4.161, 6.18
Fratelli Graffione SNC v Ditta Fransa Case C-313/94 [1997] ETMR 71 ......4.55
French Connection Ltd v Sutton [2000] ETMR 341 ......4.37, 14.26, 14.44
Fresh Breath Co. Ltd's application [2000] ETMR 644 ......4.104
Fritidsresor AB v Atlas Mediterraneo Svergie AB, Brandnews 1/2003, p. 1 ......10.100
Frits Loendersloot trading as F. Loendersloot Internationale Expeditie v George Ballantine & Son Ltd and others Case C-349/95 [1998] ETMR 10 ......9.57
Fromex SA's application; opposition of K. H. de Jong's Exporthandel BV Case B 43457 [1999] ETMR 989 ......10.45
FROOT LOOPS trade mark [1998] RPC 240 ......19.06
FSS Trade Mark [2001] RPC 40 ......13.147
FTOS [1999] ETMR 338 ......18.55
Fuji Film Co Ltd v Noh WLTR, 21 July 2003 ......9.56
Fuji Photo Film Co. Ltd's application Case R 4/1998-2 [1998] ETMR 343 (IX) 5.34
Fuji Photo Film Co. Ltd's application Case R 44/1998-3 [1999] ETMR 505 (SUPREME) 4.84
Füllkörper trade mark application [1997] ETMR 431 ......4.12, 5.88

Gaweda v Poland [2002] ETMR 691 ......4.56
GE trade mark [1972] FSR 225 ......4.182
General Motors Corp v Yplon SA Case C-375/97 [1999] All ER 865; [1999] ETMR 950 (ECJ); [1999] ETMR 120 (Advocate General's Opinion) 11.33, 11.38, 11.44, 11.92, 12.27, 12.38, 12.53, 12.67, 12.69
GENESCAN trade mark [2002] ETMR 329 ......4.69, 4.149

A. Cases in alphabetical order

Gerber Products Co. v Gerber Foods International Ltd [2002] EWHC 428, [2002] ETMR 882;
 [2002] EWCA Civ 1888, 12 December 2002 ....13.57
Gerber Garment Technology Ltd v Lectra Systems Ltd [1997] RPC 443 (CA) 14.83
Gerolsteiner Brunnen GmbH & Co. v Putsch GmbH, Case C-100/02, 10 July 2003 (unreported)
 (ECJ Opinion of AG Stix-Hackl) 8.19
Sté Gervais Danone v Société Le Riseau Voltaire, Société Gandhi, Valentin Lacambre [2003]
 ETMR 321 ....8.61, 14.39, 17.24, 21.39
Ghazilian's application [2002] ETMR 631 ....4.37
Giacomelli Sport SpA's application Case R 46/1998-2 [2000] ETMR 277 ....16.44
Gillette Company's trade mark; application for a declaration of invalidity by Warner-Lambert &
 Company Case 000703579 [2002] ETMR 733 ....5.36, 6.22
Glaverbel v OHIM Case T-36/01 [2003] ETMR 425 ....5.79
Glaxo Group and others v Dowelhurst Ltd and others [2000] ETMR 118 ....14.119
Glaxo Group and others v Dowelhurst Ltd and others (No. 2) [2000] ETMR 415 ....14.119
Glaxo Group and others v Dowelhurst Ltd and others [2003] EWHC 110 (Ch), [2003] 2 CMLR 248
 6 February 2003 ....16.14, 16.26, 16.29
Glaxo Group Ltd v Knoll Aktiengesellschaft [1999] ETMR 358 ....16.31
Glaxo Group Ltd's trade mark; Riker Laboratories Inc's application for a declaration of invalidity [2001]
 ETMR 96 ....5.132
Glen Catrine Bonded Warehouse Ltd's application for revocation [1996] ETMR 56...........13.59
Gleneagles Hotels Ltd v Quillco 100 Ltd and Toni Antioniou, 1 April 2003, Court of Session, Scotland
 (unreported) 14.71
Glenn Miller Productions Inc. and another v Stichting Bill Bakers Big Band Corp [1999]
 ETMR 247 ....8.44
Global Asset Management Ltd's application Case R 426/1999-2 noted in [2001] ETMR 131 ....4.171
GlobalSantaFe Group v Globalsantafe.com (2003) WTLR 15 April 2003 ....17.30
Glow Industries Inc v Jennifer Lopez, Coty Inc & Does 1-20, 252 FSupp2d 962 (CD Cal 2002) 10.130
Gödecke AG v Teva Pharmaceutical Industries Ltd 15 May 2000 (2001) 32 IC 326 (OHIM Board of
 Appeal) 16.34
GOLDEN LIGHTS (RÅ 1984 Ab 122) 13.120
Gorgonzola: see Consorzio per la Tutela del Formaggio Gorgonzola
Gorgonzola/Cambozola [1999] ETMR 135 ....18.33
Goulbourn v OHIM, Redcats SA intervening, Case T-174/01, 12 March 2003 ....13.51
SA GPT v Sté Cartier France [1998] ETMR 382 ....4.47
Gromax Plasticulture Ltd v Don & Low Nonwovens Ltd [1999] RPC 367 ....13.100, 13.136
Grosz Sp. Z.o.o.'s application, Polish Patent Office, Board of Appeals 29 April 1998
 (unreported) 4.57, 5.17
Groupement d'Achat des Centres Leclerc v Comité National Olympique et Sportif Français
 and others [2001] ETMR 367 ....12.35
GTR Group's application; opposition of Jean Patou [1999] ETMR 164 ....10.106
Gua Giù SNC v FC Internazionale Milano SpA, noted at [2003] EIPR N-73 ....7.50
Guaber Srl v Greece [1999] ETMR 879 ....16.56
Guimont, Jean-Pierre Case C-448/989 [2001] ETMR 145 ....18.38, 18.48
Gulf International Lubricants Ltd v Gulf Oil Estonia AS WTLR, 4 July 2003 (Patent and Trade
 Mark Office, Board of Appeal, Estonia) 13.96
Gut Springenheide GmbH, Tusky v Oberkreisdirektor des Kreises Steinfurt etc. Case C-210/96
 noted in [1999] ETMR 425 ....4.90, 10.134

Haci Keles v Sté Megafonte and Evelyne Sitbon [1997] ETMR 515 ....10.101
HAG I: see Van Zuylen Freres v HAG AG [1974] ECR 731
HAG II: see CNL-Sucal NV v Hag GF AG [1990] 3 CMLR 571
HAMMARBY MARINCENTER trade mark (RÅ 1988 not 296) 13.97
Harbinger Corp v OHIM Case T-345/99 [2001] ETMR 11, [2001] IP&T 1496 ....4.20
Harcourt Brace & Co's application Case R 130/1999-1 [2000] ETMR 382 (IDEAL) 4.82

Harding v Smilecare Ltd [2002] FSR 37 ....10.100
Harjo v Pro Football Inc, 50 USPQ 2d 1705 (TTAB 1999) 19.14
Harvest Technologies LLC's application Case R 33/1998-2 [1999] ETMR 503 ....4.133
Henkel KGaA v OHIM Case T-30/00 [2002] ETMR 278 (bicoloured rectangular detergent
    tablet) 4.166, 5.126
Henkel KgaA's application WTLR, 11 July 2003 ....4.84
HENNAFLOR trade mark noted in [2001] ETMR 132 ....13.59
Herbalife International Inc's application; opposition of Haka Kunz GmbH Case B 52037 [1999]
    ETMR 882 ....10.69
Hermans Groep BV v Gillette Nederland BV and The Gillette Company Inc. [2002]
    ETMR 150 ....8.25
Hermès International v FHT Marketing Choice BV Case C-53/96 [1998] ETMR 425 ...14.56, 14.74
Hershey Foods Corp v OHIM, Case T-198/00, [2003] ETMR 795 ....10.53
High Lights (newsletter of Law Offices of Dr Ali Laghaee & Associates Inc), vol. 3, January 2003,
    p. 1 ....5.115
Hij Mannenmode BV v Nienhaus & Lotz GmbH [1999] ETMR 730 ....4.137, 10.153, 13.13
Hilton International Co. and another v Raclet SA noted in [2001] ETMR 1113 ....11.81
Hodgkinson Corby Ltd and another v Wards Mobility Services Ltd [1995] FSR 169 ....2.46,
                                                                                8.02, 8.159
Hoffmann-La Roche v Centrafarm Case 102/77 [1978] ECR 1139 ....16.11
Hoffmann-La Roche v Commission Case 88/76 [1979] ECR 461 ....9.73
Hola SA's trade mark; application for cancellation by G + J Gruner + Jahr Polska Sp. Z.o.o. & Co.
    Spolka Komandytowa [2002] ETMR 257 ....10.115
HOLLY HOBBIE trade mark [1984] FSR 199; [1984] RPC 329 ....15.58
Hollywood SAS. v Souza Cruz SA Case R 283/1999-3 [2002] ETMR 705 ....11.10, 11.14,
                        11.26, 11.50, 11.53, 11.55, 11.58, 11.77, 12.51, 12.69
Hölterhoff v Freiesleben Case C-2/00 [2002] ETMR 917, [2003] IP&T 163 ....6.33, 7.29,
                                                                                8.26, 8.46
Home A/S v Home From Home Relocation Services by Annemette Krogh Pedersen [2003]
    ETMR 605 ....10.100
Homer v Homer's Bar Maunlua OY and Homer's Bar Pihlajanmäki OY [1998] ETMR 591 ......5.68
Honda Giken KKK and another v H-D Michigan Inc 43 USPQ 2d 1526 (TTAB 1997) 5.136
Honda Italia Industriale SpA v Kama Italia Import and Export Srl WTLR, 12 May 2003 ....5.82
Horphag Research Ltd v Pellegrini (t/a Healthdiscovery.com), 328 F3d 1108
    (9th Cir. 2003) 17.72
House of Stitches Pty Ltd's application; opposition of Bellini Warenvertriebsgesellschaft mbH Case B
    16560 [1999] ETMR 994 ....10.17
Hugo Boss (4 Ob 174/02w), (2003) WTLR 6 May 2003 ....14.27
Sté Hugo Boss v Dernières Nouvelles d'Alsace and others [1998] ETMR 197 ......8.74, 11.94, 14.39
Humic SA's application; opposition of Sapec-Agro SA Case B911 [1999] ETMR 26............10.84
Hutchison Personal Communications Ltd v Hook Advertising Ltd and Others [1996]
    FSR 549 ....19.05

IBP Industrial Products Ltd's application, Case R 736/1999-2, 27 July 2001, OHIM Journal
    12/2002, p. 2299 ....5.53
Icart SA's application; opposition of Beiersdorf A.G. Case B 1794 [2000] ETMR 180 ....10.121
ICC (Development) International v Philips, 31 January 2003 (High Court, Delhi) 8.64, 16.72
Idaho Potato Commission v M&M Produce Farm and Sales 335 F3d 130, 67 USPQ 2d 1348
    (2d Cir NY 2003) 15.41
Ide Line Aktiebolag v Philips Electronics NV [1997] ETMR 377 ....5.91
IHT Internationale Heiztechnik GmbH v Ideal Standard GmbH Case C-9/93 [1994] ECR I-2789,
    [1994] 3 CMLR 857, [1995] FSR 59 ....9.92
Iliad SA v Cédric A. Trbunal de Grande Instance de Paris, 7 January 2003 ....14.46
In Over Our Heads Inc, in re, 16 USPQ 2d 1653 (TTAB 1990) 19.15

A. Cases in alphabetical order

Inditex SA v Compagna Mercantile SRL [2002] ETMR 9 ....17.05
Indústria e Comércio de Cosméticos Natura A.S's application [2001] ETMR 783 ....12.34, 12.45
Infamous Nut Co. Ltd's trade marks [2003] RPC 126 ....13.24
Inland Revenue Commissioners v Muller & Co's Margarine Ltd [1901] AC 217 ....21.25
Inlima S.L's application; opposition of Adidas A.G. [2000] ETMR 325 ....11.81
Institut Für Lernsysteme GmbH v OHIM, Case T-388/00, 23 October 2002 (Court of First
    Instance, unreported) 10.74, 10.140
Institut National des Appellations d'Origine v Handelshuset OPEX AB (Case 99-004),
    WTLR 7 April 2003 ....18.59
Intel Corp v Distilleerijen Erven Lucas Bols BV noted in [2001] ETMR 1300 ....8.58
Intel Corp v Sihra [2003] EWHC 17 (Ch), 24 January 2003 ....11.57, 11.72
Inter Lotto (UK) Ltd v Camelot Group plc, [2003] EWHC 1256 (Ch), [2003] 3 All ER 191 ....14.08
Inter Service Srl's application; opposition of Sephora SA, Case B 95804, OHIM Opposition Division,
    23 February 2003 (unreported) 11.36
Interactive Products Corp v a2z Mobile Office Solutions Inc, 326 F3d 687 (6th Circ.
    2003) 17.22
Interdigital Communications Corp's application Case R 50/98-3 [1999] ETMR 758 ....5.78
Intergro v Interbuy [2003] ETMR 152 ....13.93
Interkrenn Maschinen Vertriebs GmbH's Trade Mark; Application for Declaration of Invalidity by
    Horst Detmers [2002] ETMR 312 ....13.119
International Bancorp LLC and others v Société des Bains et Mer du Cercle des Etrangers à Monaco,
    No. 02-1364, 3 December 2002 (EDVa 2002) 14.11
International Business Machine Corp's application R 10/1998-2 [1998] ETMR 643 ....10.11
International Flavors & Fragrances Inc, Re 51 USPQ 2d 1513 (Fed Cir 1999) 3.27
International Order of Job's Daughters v. Lindeburg and Co., 633 F2d 912; 208 USPQ 718
    (9th Cir. 1980) 7.64
International Paper Company's application Case R 868/200-2 [2003] ETMR 92 ....5.54
Interpol: see Organisation Internationale de Police Criminelle Interpol
Iris v Urus GRUR Int 1966, 457 ....14.86
Italian Leather SpA v WECO Polstermöbel GmbH & Co. Case C-80/00 [2003] ETMR 130 ....14.09

J B Cosmetics SP. ZO. O. Kamienczyk N/Bugiem's trade mark noted in [2000] ETMR 722 ....12.40,
    13.98
JAN III SOBIESKI trade mark [1999] ETMR 874...16.58
Jansen Pharmaceutica N.V. v Patent and trade Marks Office [2001] ETMR 663 ....5.104
JANE AUSTEN application, Trade Marks Registry, 12 July 1999 ....13.104
SA Jean Lempereur v SA Jifi-Madison [1999] ETMR 1005 ....13.13
Jean Patou SA v Sté Zag Zeitschriftn Verlag A.G. and another [1999] ETMR 157 ....13.64, 13.38
Jellinek's application (1946) 63 RPC 59 ....10.86
Jimmy Nicks Property Company Ltd's application [1999] ETMR 445 ....5.08, 5.56
Jo-Bolaget Fruktprodukter HB v State Ministry of Industry and Commerce [2002]
    ETMR 161 ....4.106
John Lewis of Hungerford Ltd's Trade Mark Application [2001] ETMR 1193 ....4.27
John Walker & Sons Ltd and another v Henry Ost and Company Ltd and another [1970]
    FSR 63 ....14.17
Johnson & Johnson v Bandhaye Pezeshki Co., (Iran, noted in Raysan email circular,
    3 March 2003) 10.72
Johnson (S.C.) & Son Inc v The Clorox Company, 241 F3d 232 (2d Cir, 2001) 8.174
Jordan Grand Prix Ltd v Vodafone Group Plc, [2003] EWHC 1965 (Comm), 4 August 2003
    (unreported) (Commercial Court) 15.62A
Josef Rupp Gesellschaft mbH's trade mark; application for a declaration of invalidity by the
    Danish Dairy Board Case C000576066/1 [2002] ETMR 395 ....5.99
Joseph Crosfield & Son's application ('PERFECTION') (1909) 26 RPC 837 ....6(Intro)
Jullien v Verschuere Case A 82/5, 20 May 1983, Jur. 1983 vol. 4 p. 36 ....10.144

Jupiter Unit Trust Managers Ltd v Johnson Fry Asset Managers plc, 19 Apr 2000 (HC) 8.155
Jusline GmbH v O***** [1999] ETMR 173 ....17.20

K trade mark [2001] ETMR 1181 ....4.67, 5.32
SA Kaasmakerij Passendale v Coopératives Réunies de l'Industrie du Lait Coberco noted in
  [2000] ETMR 840 ....5.06
Kabushiki Kaisha Fernandes v OHIM, Case T-39/01, 12 December 2002 ....13.30
Kabushiki Kaisha Yakult Honsha and others v Danone Nederland BV and others [1998]
  ETMR 465 ....5.103
Kaysersberg SA and another v Scott Paper and others [1997] ETMR 188 ....13.35
Kellogg Company v Pehuamar SA (2003) WTLR 22 May 2003 ....6.04
Kenman Kandy Australia Pty Ltd v Registrar of Trade Marks [2002] FCAFC 273 ....5.84
Khris, Taïg v INPI, ex parte Loius Vuitton Malletier [2001] ETMR 194 ....16.55
KIKU trade mark [1978] FSR 246 ....4.144
Kimberley-Clark Ltd v Fort Sterling Ltd [1997] FSR 877 ....8.95, 10.138
Kimpton Hotel & Restaurant Group Inc., re 55 USPQ 2d 1154 (TTAB 2000) 5.49
Kodak: see Eastman Kodak
Koninklijke KPN Nederland NV v Benelux Trade Marks Office Case C-363/99, 31 January 2002
  (AG) 4.140
Koninklijke Philips Electronics NV v Remington Consumer Products Ltd, Case C-299/99 [2002]
  ETMR 955 ....4.113, 5.90, 5.91
Korea Telecom Co. Ltd's application, Korean Patent Court, 29 August 2002 (INTA Bulletin 57
  (2003) no. 21, p. 4) 4.135
Korean Florist Association v Kordes (2003) WTLR 14 March 2003 ....6.29
KP Permanent Make-Up Inc v Lasting Impression I, Inc, No. 01-56055 (9th Cir 30 Apr. 2003) ...3.45
Kraft Jacobs Suchard Ltd's application; opposition by Nestlé UK Ltd [2001] ETMR 54 ....19.08
Kruidvat v Commission of the European Communities Case T-87/92 [1997] ETMR 395 ...9.61, 9.69
Kundry SA's application; opposition by the President and Fellows of Harvard College [1998]
  ETMR 178 ....10.48
KWS Saat AG v OHIM, Case T-173/00 [2003] ETMR 288, [2003] IP&T 14 ....4.108, 5.126

L'Oréal (UK) Ltd and another v Johnson & Johnson and another [2000] ETMR 691, [2000]
  IP&T 789 ....14.114
L'Oréal's application [2000] ETMR 10 ....5.68
La Chemise Lacoste SA and SIDAS SpA v Centro Tessile Srl [1997] ETMR 520, Milan CA 2.25
Labatt Brewing Co. Ltd v Molson Canada, Federal Court Trial Division, Canada, noted in
  (2003) WTLR 16 May 2003 ....4.171
Laboratoire Garnier & Cie v Sté Copar [1998] ETMR 114; [2000] ETMR 1124 ....8.29
Laboratories Goemar SA's trade marks; application for revocation by La Mer Technology Inc
  [2002] ETMR 382 ....13.57
Laboratories Goemar SA, Re [2003] EWHC 1382 (Ch), 20 June 2003 (unreported) (HC) 13.57
Laboratorios Menarini SA v Takeda Chemical Industries Ltd Case R 222/1999-2 [2001]
  ETMR 703 ....10.91
Lancaster Group GmbH v Parfume Discount Sjaelland SpA, noted in [2002] EIP
  N-47 ....9.57
Lancôme Parfums et Beauté & Cie Snc v Jacques Bogart SA (2003) 761 PIBD III-187 ....10.70
Lancôme Parfums et Beauté & Cie's trade mark; application for revocation by Laboratoires Décléor
  [2001] ETMR 981 ....13.109, 13.116
Landré GmbH v International Paper Company Case R 39/2000-1 [2001] ETMR 794 ....10.111
Last Minute Network Ltd's application R 1068/2000-2 [2002] ETMR 534 ....4.170
Sarl Le Book Editions v Sté EPC Edition Presse Communication and another [1999]
  ETMR 554 ....7.36, 10.144
Le Lido SA v Nationale Stichting tot Exploitatie van Casinospelen in Nederland and another
  [1997] ETMR 537 ....13.40

A. Cases in alphabetical order

Legal & General Group plc v Image Plus (2003) 157 Trademark World 17 ....17.37
Lego and another v Distributor of B***** Building Blocks [2001] ETMR 907 ....10.138
Leonard Cheshire Foundation v Darke Decision 2000-0131 [2001] ETMR 991 ....17.37, 17.50,
 21.39
Leroy Merlin Participations (S.A) v K-2 Corp Case R 66/2001-4 [2003] ETMR 113 ....5.67
Les Editions Albert René v Hauser (2003) WTLR 17 April 2003 ....10.68
Les Editions Albert René Sarl v Madaleno WTLR, 23 July 2003 (Court of Golegā) 14.87A
Levi Spa v Iniziative Srl [2003] ETMR N-3 ....14.56
Levi Strauss & Co. and Levi Strauss Continental v Parkway Ltd [2000] ETMR 977 ....9.72
Levi Strauss & Co and Levi Strauss (UK) Ltd v Tesco Stores: see Zino Davidoff SA v A & G
 Imports Ltd (ECJ)
Levi Strauss & Co and Levi Strauss (UK) Ltd v Tesco Stores Ltd and others [2002] EWHC 1556
 (Ch), [2002] ETMR 1153, [2003] IP&T 117, [2003] RPC 319 ....2.12, 9.74, 9.82
LG Electronics Inc v NCR Financial Solutions Group Ltd [2003] FSR 428 ....15.25
Libertel Groep BV v Benelux-Merkenbureau, Case C-104/01 [2003] ETMR 508 (AG), [2003]
 ETMR 807 (ECJ) 5.102, 5.125, 5.127, 5.128
Lidl Stiftung & Co. KG v Heinz Iberica, S.A, Case R 232/200-4 [2003] ETMR 312 ....10.137
Lidl Stiftung & Co. K.G. v The Savoy Hotel Case R 729/1999-2 [2001] ETMR 1284 ....10.139
Lifesource International Inc.'s application; opposition of Novartis Nutrition A.G. Case 2844/2000
 [2001] ETMR 1227 ....13.23
Likoerflasche trade mark [2002] ETMR 456 ....5.103, 5.115
Linda Jackson Pty Ltd's application; opposition of Jackson International Trading Company Kurt D.
 Brühl Gesellschaft mbH & Co. K.G. Case 520/2000 [2001 ETMR 376 ....5.70
Linde AG, Winward Industries Inc. and Rado Uhren AG, 24 October 2002, ECJ Joined Cases
 C-53/01 to C-55/01 [2003] ETMR 354 (AG), [2003] ETMR 963 (ECJ) 4.67, 4.125,
 5.82, 5.83
SA Lindt & Sprüngli v Sté Chocometz [1999] ETMR 315 ....8.72, 8.75
Lipton Ltd, Van Den Berg & Jurgens BV, Unilever Belgium and Unilever NV v Sara Lee/De NV
 and Douwe Egberts [2002] ETMR 1073 ....5.110, 6.35
Liqueur Bottle: see Likoerflasche
Lloyd Schuhfabrik Meyer & Co. GmbH v Klijsen Handel BV Case C-342/97 [1999]
 ETMR 690 ....4.90, 4.92, 10.62, 10.132, 10.134, 11.35, 12.14
Loendersloot: see Frits Loendersloot
Loewe SA's application; opposition by Logoathletic Inc. Case B 37889 [2000]
 ETMR 40 ....10.73
Lombard Risk Systems Ltd's application Case R 4/1999-2 [2000] ETMR 1055 ....4.65
London Borough of Hackney v Cedar Trading Ltd [1999] ETMR 801 ....2.04, 9.54
Long John Silver's Inc's application; opposition of Swedish Match Sverige A.B. Case 458/2000
 [2001] ETMR 120 ....10.101, 16.67
Louis Vuitton Distribuição v Caliente Comércio de Modas (2003) WTLR 30 May 2003 ....14.91
Løvens Kemiske Fabrik Produktionsaktielskab v Orifarm A/S, WTLR 20 March 2003,
 [2003] EIPR N-68 ....16.17, 16.26, 16.29
Løvens Kemiske Fabrik Produktionsaktielskab v Paranova A/S [2001] ETMR 302 ....16.17
Lube A/S v Dansk Droge A/S [2001] ETMR 343 ....10.119, 14.69
Lucas Bols v Colgate-Palmolive (1976)7 IIC 420 (CLAERYN/KLAREIN) 11.53, 11.55
Luijckx BV v ECC [2000] ETMR 530 ....5.98
Lyon v SA Rhums Martiniquais Saint-James [1999] ETMR 188 ....10.55, 10.61

M&R Marketing Systems Inc's application Case R 1167/2000-1 [2002] ETMR 317 ....4.82
McCain Foods (Australia) Pty Ltd v ConAgra Inc, New Zealand Court of Appeal, 6 June 2002
 (unreported) 4.175
McCain International Ltd v Country Fair Foods Ltd and another [1981] RPC 69 ....6.18
McCann-Erickson Advertising Ltd's application; opposition of Momentum Integrated
 Communications Ltd Case 2149/2000 [2001] ETMR 540 ....13.29

McDonalds Corp v Joburgers Drive-Inn Restaurant (Pty) Ltd and Anor & McDonalds Corp v
    Dax Prop CC and Anor [1996] (4) All SA 4 ....12.65
McDonald's Corp v McDonald's Corp Ltd & Vincent Chang [1997] FSR 760 ....12.41, 14.64
McDonald's Corp and McDonald's Deutschland Inc v Rahmer [2000] ETMR 91 ....12.40
McDonald's Corp USA and McDonald's Restaurants Denmark A/S v Pedersen [1997]
    ETMR 151 ....1.21
Madgecourt Ltd's application; opposition of Fédération des Industries de la Parfumerie [2000]
    ETMR 825 ....4.46
Mag Instrument Inc. v California Trading Company Norway, Ulsteen [1998] ETMR 85 ....3.14
Mag Instrument Inc. v OHIM Case T-88/00 [2002] ETMR 665 ....5.95
Magazijn 'De Bijenkorf' BV v Accelerated Information BV [2002] ETMR 676 ....17.08
Magna Ltd v Abdullah Ismail [1998] IP Asia LR 176 ....6.41
Magnetics v Diskcopy, Tel Aviv District Court 2001, CF 751/00 ....17.19
Maizoro SA de CV v Kellogg Company (2003) WTLR 6 May 2003 ....13.48
Majestic Distilling Co., In re, 315 F3d 1311 (Fed. Cir. 2003) 10.106
Mainland Products Ltd v Bonlac Foods [1998] IP Asia LR 289 ....4.82
Manpower ***** v Manpower Austria P***** GmbH, ***** [2002] ETMR 845 ....4.176
Manpower Inc v Manpower Temporar Personal GmbH (2003) 16 April 2003 ....13.63
Manton and others v Van Day and others noted in [2001] ETMR 1114 ....16.64
Marc Brown's trade mark application; opposition of LTJ Diffusion [2002] ETMR 653 ....10.29,
    10.31, 10.39
Marca Mode C.V., Adidas A.G. and Adidas Benelux BV Case C-425/98 [2000] ETMR 723,
    [2000] IP&T 968 ....10.154
Marco-Chemie Eugen Martin KG Chemische Fabrik v Aldemar AG, Case R 644/2000-4, OHIM OJ
    2/2003, 375 ....13.28
Marie Claire Album SA v Ipko-Amcor BV (Case 00/2268), District Court, The Hague 12.44
Marks & Spencer plc's application Case R 95/1998-3 [2000] ETMR 168 ....4.136
MARLBORO–SCOTCH WHISKY Industrial Property Bulletin 10/1981, p. 1980 (Civil Court 3,
    Lisbon) 12.34
Marleasing Case 106/89 [1990] ECR I-4135 ....8.111
MARS (1995) 26 IIC 282, I ZR 79/92 ....11.76
Mars v Miski, Supreme Court (Peru), 13 February 2003 ....12.42
Mars BV v Société des Produits Nestlé SA [1999] ETMR 862 ....10.43
Marshak v Green 746 F2d 927, 929 (2d Cir 1984) 15.19
Master Foods Ltd's application [2001] ETMR 667 ....5.73
Matratzen v OHIM Case T-6/01 [2003] ETMR 392 ....4.95, 4.144, 6.35, 6.36, 10.62
Matsushita Electric Works' application Case R 332/1999-1 [2000] ETMR 962 ....4.111, 4.123,
    4.144
Mattel Inc. v MCA Records Inc., 296 F3d 894 (9th Cir. 2000); cert. denied 123
    SupCt 993 ....8.66, 8.71, 21.01
Maxim's Ltd v Dye [1977] 1 WLR 1155 ....8.49
Mecklermedia Corp v Benelux Trade Mark Office [2001] ETMR 523 ....5.26
Mecklermedia Corp and another v D.C. Congress GmbH [1997] ETMR 265 ....5.26, 14.12
Medical Research Industries Inc.'s application Case R 639/1999-2, 23 May 2001
    (unreported) 4.36
Medinol Ltd v NeuroVasx Inc., (2003) WTLR 12 June 2003 (TTAB) 13.99
Medtronic Inc's application Case R 51/1998-1 [1999] ETMR 504 ....4.85
Mega Bloks Inc v Lego System A/S (Case HG000095/ZO7, Zurich Commercial Court) 5.82
Mega Press and Sumo Editions v Pressimage and Guidicelli [2000] ETMR 403 ....8.83
Melitta SystemService and another v Coffilter International (2003) 17 WIPR 6 ....8.26
Memory (Ireland) Ltd v Telex Computers (Ireland) Ltd, High Court, [1978] EIPR European Digest,
    December, p. v 10.135
Menarini: see A. Menarini
Merck & Co. Inc v Primecrown Ltd, Joined Cases C-267/95 and 268/95 [1997] FSR 237 ......16.08

A. Cases in alphabetical order

Merck and Company's trade mark; SmithKline Beecham plc's application for a declaration of invalidity [2000] ETMR 75 .... 6.39
Merck, Sharp & Dohme GmbH v Paranova Pharmazeutika Handels GmbH, Case C-443/99 [2002] ETMR 923 .... 9.83
Mercury Communications Ltd v Mercury Interactive (UK) Ltd [1995] FSR 850 .... 10.94
Merri Mayers-Head's application; opposition of Jean Patou [1997] ETMR 577 .... 10.12
Merz & Krell GmbH Case C-517/99 [2002] ETMR 231 .... 4.59, 4.60, 4.81, 4.83, 4.176, 6.37
Messe München GmbH v OHIM Case T-32/00 [2001] ETMR 135, [2001] IP&T 298 .... 5.41
Mickey Dees (Nightclub) Trade Mark [1998] RPC 359 .... 13.97
Microsoft Corp v Computer Future Distribution Ltd [1998] ETMR 597 .... 9.58
Microsoft Corp's application Case R 26/1998-3 [1999] ETMR 386 (NETMEETING) 4.117, 4.133
Midland Wheel Supplies Ltd's application for revocation [2000] ETMR 256 .... 6.23
Midler v. Ford Motor Co., 849 F.2d 460 (9th Cir 1988) 16.52
Milan AC SpA and Juventus FC SpA v Topps Italia Srl [1999] ETMR 182 .... 7.44
Milliken & Company's application R 66/1998-1 [1999] ETMR 575 (COMFORT PLUS) 4.139
Mitsubishi HiTec Paper Bielefeld v OHIM Case T-331/99 [2001] ETMR 614, [2001] IP&T 459 .... 4.63
Mitutoyo Corp's application [1999] ETMR 39 .... 11.48
Molkerei Groddbraunshain GmbH and Bene Nahrungsmittel GmbH v Commission Case C-447/98 P [2002] ETMR 605 .... 18.35, 18.39
Monster Board BV, The v VNU Business Publications BV [2002] ETMR 1 .... 17.08, 17.67
MONTAZS trade mark noted at [2001] ETMR 275 .... 8.42
Montblanc-Simplo GmbH v Staples Inc (unreported, D. Mass. 3 May 2001) 9.57
Montex Holdings Ltd v Controller [2000] ETMR 658 .... 13.18
Montres Rolex SA v Fogtmann [2001] ETMR 424 .... 17.08
Montres Rolex SA v PT Permona (Case 951/80), Court of Appeal, Iran 10.112
Morgan Crucible Company plc v AB Svejseteknik ApS [2001] EIPR N-78 .... 14.22
Moseley et al., dba Victor's Little Secret v V Secret Catalogue Inc 537 US 418, 123 Sup Ct 1115 (2003) 11.21, 11.22, 11.46, 12.53, 21.01
Mothercare Ltd's application [1968] IR 359 .... 4.139
Multiple Marketing Ltd's trade mark; Surene Pty's application for cancellation Case C000479899/1 noted in [2001] ETMR 131 .... 13.94
Musidor BV v Tansing (t/a Apple Music House) (1994) ALR 593 .... 7.48
Myles Ltd's application Case R 711/1999-3, [2003] ETMR 718 .... 3.27, 5.117, 5.119
Mystery Drinks GmbH v OHIM, Karlsberg Brauerei KG Weber Intervening, Case T-99/01, Court of First Instance, 15 January 2003 (unreported) 10.29, 10.114

Nabisco v P. F. Brands Inc, 191 F3d 208 (2d Cir 1999) 7.12, 12.52
NAD Electronics Inc. and another v NAD Computer Systems Ltd [1997] FSR 380 .... 8.34
Narada Productions Inc., re 57 USPQ 2d 1801 (TTAB 2001) 5.49
National Academy of Recording Arts & Sciences Inc. v International Federation of Phonographic Industry Denmark [2001] ETMR 219 .... 14.42
National Canine Defence League's application; opposition of Geoffrey Inc., Case O-213-03, 29 July 2003 (unreported) (Trade Mark Registry) 11.73
National Car Rental Systems, Inc's application, Case R194/2000-3, OHIM OJ 1/2003, 67 ...... 5.125
Nationsbanc Montgomery Securities LLC's application Case R 77/1999-2 [2000] ETMR 245 .... 5.25
Natural Resources Inc v Origin Clothing Ltd [1995] FSR 280 .... 10.105, 10.109, 13.66
Neil King's application; opposition of Hard Rock International plc and another [2000] ETMR 22 .... 10.63
Nestlé UK Ltd v Zeta Espacial SA [2000] ETMR 226 .... 13.59
Netherlands v Goldnames Inc. Decision 2001-0520 [2001] ETMR 1062 .... 17.36
Netherlands v Humlum Decision 2002-0248 [2001] ETMR 1213 .... 17.49
Neurone Tech v Neurones and de Chammard [1999] ETMR 611 .... 4.70
NeutralRed trade mark [1998] ETMR 277 .... 13.90

New Kids on the Block v New America Pub. Inc, 971 F2d 302 (9th Cir 1992) 8.13
NGK Spark Plug Co. Ltd v Biltema Sweden Aktiebolag [2000] ETMR 507 ....3.14
Nichols (N. N.) plc v Mehran Bottles (Private) Ltd, noted in (2001) 91 TMR 477 ....14.50
Nichols plc, Re [2002] EWHC 1424 (Ch), [2003] ETMR 180, [2003] RPC 301 ....5.67
Nijs et al. v Ciba-Geigy IngCons 1984, 317 ....7.56
Nissan Motor Iberica's application [1999] ETMR 338 ....10.66
No Ordinary Designer Label Ltd v Comercial Fenicia de Exportación, S.L. [2002]
  ETMR 527 ....10.152
Nogueras v City of Barcelona (2003) WTLR 9 June 2003 (US Court of Appeals, 4th Cir.) 14.09
Nordic Saunas Ltd's trade mark; application for revocation by Nordic Timber Council AB [2002]
  ETMR 210 ....5.47
Northern & Shell Plc v Conde Nast and National Magazines Distributors Ltd and another
  [1995] RPC 117 ....8.177
Northern Foods Grocery Group Ltd's application; opposition by Horace M. Ostwald [2002]
  ETMR 516 ....10.44, 10.46, 10.140
Norton Co. v Newage Industries 204 USPQ 382 (EDPA 1979) 8.176
Norwegian Government v Astra Norge AS [2000] ECDR 20 ....9.66
Norwich Pharmacal Co. v Commissioners for Customs and Excise [1974] AC 133 (HL) 14.24
Notetry Ltd's application Case R 78/1998-1 [1999] ETMR 435 ....5.105
Notetry Ltd's application (unreported), trade mark Registry transcript O/258/97,
  29 December 1997 ....5.131

Oasis Stores Ltd's application; opposition of Ever Ready plc [1999] ETMR 531 ....11.81
Oberhauser v OHIM, Case T-104/01, [2003] IP&T 279, [2003] ETMR 739 ....10.32
Objective loss calculation, Bundesgerichtshof, I ZR 16/93, 2 February 1995 ....14.93
Odol, 25 Juristiche Wochenschrift 502, XXV Markenschutz und Wettbewerb 265 (1925)
Odyssée Interactive v L'Ile des Médias, Tribunal de Grande Instance de Grenoble, 2 December
  2002 ....14.09
OHIM v Wm Wrigley Jr Company, Case C-191/01 P, 10 April 2003, Opinion of Advocate General
  Jacob 4.75, 4.77, 4.129, 4.139, 4.141
Ohio Art Company and Bandai GmbH Toys and Entertainment v CreCon Spiel U. Hobbyartikel
  GmbH [2000] ETMR 756 ....3.51, 10.137
Omega SA v Omega Engineering Ltd [2003] EWHC, 3 June 2003 ....13.64
OMEPRAZOK Trade Mark [2003] ETMR 662 ....13.111, 16.05
Optimum Healthcare Ltd's application [2003] ETMR 628 ....4.117
Optos-Opus Sarl v SA Haribo Ricqlès Zan SA and others [1999] ETMR 362 ....4.39, 5.22
Orange Personal Communications Services Ltd's application Case R 7/97-3 [1998]
  ETMR 337 ....5.123
Orangex C.A. v Juan José Llombart Gavalda Case R 662/2001-1 [2003] ETMR 302 ....10.57
Orient Watch Co. Ltd v Rita HB, noted in [2002] EIPR N-94 ....13.86
Organic Essential Inc's application Case R 146/2001-4, 22 May 2002 (unreported) 4.143
Organisation Internationale de Police Criminelle Interpol v Sté Alexandre William Setruck [1998]
  ETMR 664
OXYFRESH Trade Mark, Trade Mark Registry, 25 March 1999 ....13.90

PACCAR Inc v TeleScan Technologies LLC, 319 F3d 243 (6th Cir. 2003) 7.35
Pacific Supply Co-op v. Farmers Union Cent. Exch., Inc., 318 F.2d 894, 908-09
  (9th Cir 1963) 15.13
PAG Ltd v Hawke-Woods Ltd [2002] ETMR 811 ....8.27
Paniberica [2002] EIPR N-8 ....4.98
SA Papeterie Hamelin v Wiggins Teape Ltd [2000] ETMR 1047 ....14.30
Paranova AS v Merck & Co Inc, Case C-3/02, request for advisory opinion, 17 December
  2002 ....16.27
Paranova Oy, Case C-113/01, 8 May 2003 ....16.30

A. Cases in alphabetical order

Parfums Christian Dior SA v Etos BV [2000] ETMR 1057 ....9.72
Parfums Christian Dior SA v Evora BV Case C-337/95 [1998] ETMR 26 ....9.62
Parfums Christian Dior SA v Tuk Consultancy BV Case C-300/98 [2001] ETMR 277 ....14.73
Parke, Davis & Co. v Probel Case 24/67[1968] ECR 55 ....9.66
Parks v LaFace Records No. 99-2495, 12 May 2003 (6th Cir. 2003) 21.01
'Partner With The Best' trade mark application [1998] ETMR 679 ....4.53, 5.73
Payless Car Rental System Inc's application; opposition of Canary Islands Car SA Case 198/2000
    [2000] ETMR 1136 ....13.28
Pebble Beach Company v Lombard Brands Ltd [2003] ETMR 252 ....11.56, 11.63, 14.68
Penny Makinson's application Case R 68/1998-3 [1999] ETMR 234 ....4.158
People for the Ethical Treatment of Animals v Doughney 263 F 3d 359, 60 USPQ 2d 1209
    (4th Cir 2001) 17.06
PepsiCo Inc v Productos Industriales, Comerciales y Agrícolas, Sociedad Anonima, Case 128-97, 19
    May 1998 (noted in (2001) 91 TMR 407 ....10.37
Perfetti SpA, Van Melle NV and Van Nelle Nederland BV v MIC [2002] ETMR 52 (WIPO) 17.16
Pfeiffer Grosshandel GmbH v Löwa Warenhandel GmbH Case C-255/97 [1999] ETMR 603 ....3.47
Pfizer Inc. v Monaco Télématique en Abrégé MC TEL [2001] ETMR 169 ....12.46
Pfizer Inc. and Pfizer A/S v Durascan Medical Products A/S [1997] ETMR 86 ....7.14, 16.31
Pfizer Inc. and Pfizer BV v Lestre Nederlandse Reformadviefbureau E.N.R.A. [2001]
    ETMR 155 ....6.40, 10.88
Pfizer Ltd and Pfizer Incorporated v Eurofood Link (United Kingdom) Ltd [2000] ETMR 896,
    [2000] IP&T 280 ....3.49, 11.83, 12.15, 12.35, 12.42, 12.51
Pharmacia & Upjohn SA v Paranova A/S Case C-379/97 [1999] ETMR 937, [1999] IP&T 88 ...9.86,
    16.07, 16.24
Philip Morris Inc v Tsypkin (2003) WTLR 7 May 2003 ....17.18
Philip Morris Products Inc and another v Rothmans International Enterprises Ltd and another
    [2001] EWCA Civ 1043, [2001] ETMR 1250 ....15.85
Philip Morris Products Inc's application; opposition of R. J. Reynolds Tobacco Company [1997]
    ETMR 511 ....4.48
Philip Morris Products SA's application Case R 687/2000-2 [2002] ETMR 403 ....4.149
Philips: see Koninklijke
Philips Electronics NV v Remington Consumer Products [1998] ETMR 124 (High Court);
    [1999] ETMR 816 (Court of Appeal) 4.166, 4.168, 5.82, 5.109, 5.110, 7.49
Philips Electronics N.V. v Remington Consumer Products Ltd (No. 2) [1999] ETMR
    835 ....13.33, 13.71
Philosophy Inc. v Ferretti Studio Srl [2002] EWCA Civ 921, [2003] ETMR 97, [2003]
    RPC 287 ....13.46, 13.60
Philmac Pty Ltd v Registrar of Trade Marks [2002] FCA 155 ....5.129
Phytheron International SA v Jean Bourdon SA Case C-352/95 [1997] ETMR 211 ....9.94
Pilkington plc's application Case R 81/1999-3 [2000] ETMR 1130 (K GLASS) 6.37
Pilkington plc's application [2002] ETMR 206 (GL@ss) 5.42
Pilsen Urquell v Industrie Poretti SpA [1998] ETMR 168 ....18.46
Pink Fibreglass, re [2002] EIPR N-39 ....5.125
Pippig Augenoptik GmbH & Co. KG v Hartlauer Handelsgesellschaft mbH, Verlassenschaft
    Nach Dem Verstorbenen Franz Josef Hartlauer, Case C-44/01, 8 April 2003
    (unreported) 8.116, 8.118, 8.119, 8.146, 8.147
Piromalli's trade mark; application for cancellation by Greci Industria Alimentare SpA, Case 133C
    000372920/1, 13 February 2002 (unreported) 4.59
Pistre and others v France Joined cases C-321 to 324/94 [1997] ETMR 457 ....4.55
Pitman Training Ltd and Another v Nominet UK and another [1997] FSR 797 ....15.92
Pizza Hut Inc v Papa John's International Inc, 27 F3d 489 (5th Cir 2000) 8.174
Pizza Pizza Ltd v Registrar of Trade-marks (1989) 26 CPR (3d) 355 ....5.28
Playboy Enterprises Inc v Giannattasio (2003) WTLR 30 May 2003 ....10.129, 17.10
Playboy Enterprises, Inc v Terri Welles 279 F3d 796 (9th Cir. 2002) 8.36

Pliva D.D. Zagreb's application noted in [2000] ETMR 594 ....16.31
Polo/Lauren Company L.P. v PT Dwidua Langgeng Pratama International Freight Forwarders
    Case C-383/98 [2000] ETMR 535, [2000] IP&T 1128 ....7.21
Polaroid Corp v Polarad Electronics Corp 287 F2d 492 (2d Cir 1961) 10.125
Polyglycoat Corp v Environmental Chemicals Inc. 509 F Supp 36 (SDNY 1980) 8.176
Pomaco Ltd's trade mark; application for revocation by Reed Consumer Books Ltd [2001]
    ETMR 1013 ....13.67
Porczynska Marzena Gappol Przedsiebiorstwo Prywatne's trade mark; The Gap Inc's application
    for cancellation [2001] ETMR 1056 ....13.115
Porous Media Corp v. Pall Corp, 173 F.3d 1109, 1120-21 (8th Cir 1999) 8.173
Poulsen Roser ApS' application Case R 746/2001-1 [2003] ETMR 112 ....4.95
Praktiker Bau- und HeimwerkemÄrkte AG, reference by the Bundespatentgericht to the European
    Court of Justice, 15 October 2002 ....16.45
Precision Dynamics Corp's application; opposition of Visa International Service Association Case
    3479/2002, 29 November 2002 (unreported) 10.92
Premier Brands UK Ltd v Typhoon Europe Ltd [2000] ETMR 1071, [2002] EWCA Civ 1043, [2002]
    ETMR 787, [2003] FSR 69 ....11.13, 11.14, 11.42, 11.44, 11.54, 11.61,
                                                                11.66, 11.83, 11.94
Premier Luggage and Bags Ltd v Premier Co (UK) Ltd and another [2002] ETMR 787
    (CA) 7.29, 10.147
Primark Stores Ltd and Primark Holdings v Lollypop Clothing Ltd [2001] ETMR 334 ....9.39
Société Prime TV v Top Tele, Cour de Cassation (Chambre Commerciale),
    26 March 2002 ....4.104
Prince plc v Prince Sports Group Ltd [1998] FSR 21 ....14.111
Principles Retail Ltd's application' opposition of Manifattura Lane Gaetano Marzotto & Figli
    SpA Case 355/1999 [2000] ETMR 240 ....10.59
SNC Prisma Presse v SA Europe 1 Telecompagnie [1998] ETMR 515 ....10.101
Sté Prisma Presse and Sté Gruner und Jahr Communication GmbH v SA Editions Economica [1999]
    ETMR 549 ....4.105
Procter & Gamble Company v OHIM Case C-383/99 P [2002] ETMR 22 (BABY-DRY)1.36, 4.63, 4.71,
                        4.76, 4.78, 4.96, 4.98, 4.99, 4.100, 4.104, 4.111, 4.133, 4.147,
                                                4.148, 4.149, 4.181, 6.15, 10.117
Procter & Gamble Company v OHIM Case T-117/00 [2002] ETMR 174 (bicoloured tablet) 4.79,
                                                                5.126, 5.133
Procter & Gamble Company v OHIM Case T-122/99 [2000] ETMR 580 (shaped soap) 5.96
Procter & Gamble Company v OHIM Case T-63/01, [2003] ETMR 549 (shaped soap) 5.96
Procter & Gamble Company and another v Randy L. Haugen and others, US Court of Appeals
    10th Cir, 23 August 2000 ....8.173
Procter & Gamble Company's application Case R 116/1998-3 [1999] ETMR 664 (OHIM)
    (COMPLETE) 4.13, 4.84
Procter & Gamble Company's application Case R 110/1998-3 [2000] ETMR 174
    (PERFECT BROW) 5.148
Procter & Gamble Company's application Case R 74/1998-3 [1999] ETMR 776 ....5.87, 5.96
Procter & Gamble Company's application [2000] ETMR 703 (shaped soap: Ireland) 5.95, 5.97
Procter & Gamble Company's application Case R 85/1998-2 [1999] ETMR 559
    (SWEDISH FORMULA) 4.158
Procter & Gamble's trade mark application, re [1999] ETMR 375 (bottles with 'ghosted'
    labels) 4.31
Professional Golfers Association v Bankers L & C Co., 514 F2d 665, 671 (5th Cir 1975) 15.38
Pronuptia de Paris GmbH v Pronuptia de Paris Irmgard Schillgalis, Case C-161/84 [1986]
    ECR 353 ....15.55
Prudential Assurance Co. Ltd v Prudential Insurance Company of America [2002]
    EEWHC 534 (Ch), [2002] ETMR 1013, [2003] FSR 97; [2003] EWCA Civ 327,
    [2003] ETMR 873 ....14.05, 14.14, 15.91

A. Cases in alphabetical order

Qlicksmart Pty Ltd's application Case R 1/1998-2 [1999] ETMR 190 ....5.138
Qualitex Co. v Jacobson Products Co. 514 US 159 (1995) 1.36, 5.125
Quality Bakers The Hague Court of Appeal, 27 April 2000 ....12.43
Queen v Virtual Countries Inc., WIPO D 2002-0754, 27 November 2002 ....5.52
Queen's Club trade mark application [1997] ETMR 345 ....10.84
QUICK (1959) GRUR 182 ....11.65

R Cable y Telecommunicationes Galicia SA's application; opposition of Ricoh Company Ltd, Case
    3475/2002, 28 November 2002 (unreported) 10.141
R v Johnstone [2003] ETMR 1, affirmed on appeal at [2003] 3 UKHL 28 ....7.51, 7.51A, 9.49
R v Secretary of State for Health, ex. P. British American Tobacco (Investments) Ltd and Imperial
    Tobacco Ltd, supported by Japan Tobacco Inc. and JT International SA, Case C-491/01
    noted in [2002] ETMR 1244 ....15.02
Ravil Sarl v Bellon Import Sarl and Biraghi SpA, Case C-469/00, 20 May 2003 ....18.32, 18.40,
                                                                                        18.51
Reality Group Ltd v Chance [2002] FSR 13 ....7.28
Sté Recife v Sté Recife [2001] ETMR 182 ....13.37
Reckitt & Colman v Borden [1990] RPC 340 ....10.123
Recot Inc v M. C. Becton 56 USPQ 2d 1859 (TTAB 2000) 10.137
Red Bull Sweden AB v Energi Trading I Skara Handelsbolag and Energi Trading I Skara AB
    (in bankruptcy) [2002] ETMR 758 ....14.104
Reddaway: see Frank Reddaway
Reebok International Ltd v SA Cora and others [1999] ETMR 649 ....9.57
Reed Elsevier (UK) Limited and Totaljobs.Com Limited (No 2) [2003] InfoTLR 60 .....14.84, 14.88
Reed Executive Plc and Reed Solutions Plc v Reed Business Information Ltd, Reed Elsevier (UK)
    Ltd and Totaljobs.Com Ltd, [2003] RPC 207, [2003] IP&T 220 ....8.35, 17.63, 17.71
Reed Executive Plc and Reed Solutions Plc v Reed Business Information Ltd, Reed Elsevier (UK)
    Ltd and Totaljobs.Com Ltd (No. 2), [2002] EWHC 2722 (Ch), [2003] Info TLR 60 ...14.22
Société Reed Expositions France (Formerly Groupe Miller Freeman) v Société Tigest Sarl [2003]
    ECDR 206 ....8.31
Société Reed Expositions France (Formerly Groupe Miller Freeman) v Société Tigest Sarl,
    Cour D'appel de Paris, 12 September 2001 (unreported) 8.62, 14.87
Reemtsma Cigaretten Fabriken Gesellschaft Mit Beschrankter Haftung v Turkish Patent Institute,
    5th Commercial Court of Ankara, Decision 1998/777-1999/225, 22 April 1999 ....4.12
Reemtsma Cigarettenfabriken GmbH v NV Sumatra Tobacco Trading Company (2003)
    WTLR 22 April 2003 ....13.58
REETRUCK trade mark application noted in [2002] EIPR N-115 ....10.27
Retail Services Inc v Freebies Publishing 247 FSupp2d 822 (EDVa 2003) 17.21
Revenue Technologies Corporation, re (2003) WTLR 5 June 2003 (TTAB) 4.102
Rewe Zentral AG v OHIM Case T-79/00 [2002] ETMR 1109 ....4.61, 4.131, 13.31
Rhône Poulenc v Reckitt Benckiser WTLR, 18 July 2003 (Colombian Trade Mark Office) 10.79
Ringling Bros.-Barnum & Bailey Combined Shows, Inc. v Utah Division of Travel Development
    170 F3d 449 (4th Cir 1999) 11.70
Roadtech Computer Systems Ltd v Mandata (Management and Data Services) Ltd [2000]
    ETMR 970 ....17.69
Robelco NV v Robeco Groep NV, Case C-23/01, [2003] ETMR 671 ....6.24
Robert Bosch GmbH v OHIM, Joined Cases T-79/01 And T-86/01, 20 November 2002
    (unreported) 4.100
Rosenbluth International Inc's application Case R 190/1998-2 [2000] ETMR 934 ....4.121
Société Roullet Fransac Sarl v v Secret Catalogue Inc. [2001] ETMR 1187 ....4.39
Roux Laboratories Inc. v Clairol Inc. 427 F.2d 823 ....5.73
Rowling v Uitgeverji Byblos, District Court of Amsterdam, 3 April 2003 (unreported) 4.31, 14.66,
                                                                                        16.66
Royal Berkshire Polo Club's application, noted in [2001] ETMR 826 ....8.59

Rugby Football Union and Nike European Operations Netherlands BV v Cotton Traders Ltd [2002]
    EWHC 467 (Ch), [2002] ETMR 861 ....13.35
Sarl RWS Translations Ltd v Getten and Sté Translations [1999] ETMR 258 ....4.70
Rynkeby Foods A/S v Ministry of Foods, Agriculture and Fisheries [2002] ETMR 136 ....4.176
Rytz Cie SA v Rytz Industriebau A.G. [2001] ETMR 363 ....8.50

SA: look up next word of name
S-P's trade mark application; application by K.S. to suspend the trade mark registration proceedings
    noted in [1999] ETMR 335 ....13.70
Sabèl BV v Puma AG, Rudolf Dassler Sport, Case C-251/95 [1998] ETMR 1 ....10.23, 10.26, 10.28,
                    10.38, 10.43, 10.51, 10.60, 10.61, 10.62, 10.73, 10.104, 10.132, 10.146,
                                          10.154, 11.10, 11.83, 11.86, 13.24
Sabena v Ryanair, Brussels Commercial Court, 10 July 2001 ....8.140, 8.148
Sacher, re noted in [2000] ETMR 185 ....14.17
Safeway Stores plc v Hachette Filipacchi Presse [1997] ETMR 552 ....13.61
Saint-Tropez v Valais and another [1999] ETMR 310 ....4.38
Salamander AG v Industria de Calcados Kissol Ltda, Too Vitl and Centra Anstalt [1998]
    ETMR 94 ....7.21
Samara Brothers Inc v Wal-Mart Stores Inc, 165 F3d 120, (2d Cir 1998), 120 SCt 1339 (2000) ...5.11
Sanofi-Synthélabo SpA v 3M Healthcare Ltd and another [2002] EWHC 707 (Ch), [2003]
    ETMR 586 ....15.85
Sanrio Co. Ltd v Dong-A Pencil Co. Ltd, Seoul High Court, Case 2002Na32648, 27 November
    2002 ....8.41
Sari (P.T.) Incofood Corporation v Department of Intellectual Property and others (2003)
    17 WIPR 9..4.130
Sarl: look up next word of name
SAT.1 SattellitenFernsehen GmbH v OHIM Case T-323/00 [2002] IP&T 928, [2003]
    ETMR 635 ....4.101
Scandecor Development AB v Scandecor Marketing AB and others [1999] FSR 26
    (CA) 13.41, 15.84
Scandecor Development AB v Scandecor Marketing AB and others [2001] UKHL 21, [2001]
    ETMR 800, [2001] IP&T 676 ....8.34, 15.18, 15.87
Scania C.V. A.B. v Leif Westlye Decision 2000-0169 [2000] ETMR 767 ....17.42
Scapino BV and Ron Suwandi Sports BV v Basic Trademark SA [2001] ETMR 294 ....9.44
Schieving-Nijstad V.O.F. and others v Groeneweld Case C-89/99 [2002] ETMR 34 ....14.74
Schutzverband Gegen Unwesen in der Wirtschaft eV v Warsteiner Brauerei Haus Bramer GmbH
    & Co. KG Case C-312/98 [2003] ETMR 76 ....18.39
Schutzverband Gegen Unwesen in der Wirtschaft eV v Warsteiner Brauerei Haus Bramer GmbH
    & Co. KG, [2002] EIPR N-110 ....18.39
Scotch Whisky Association v Glen Kella [1997] ETMR 470, HC 14.36
Scottish & Newcastle plc's application; opposition of Red Bull GmbH Case 863/2000
    [2000] ETMR 1143 ....10.150
Sebago Inc. and Ancienne Maison Dubois et Fils SA v GB-UNIC SA, Case C-173/98,
    [1999] ETMR 467 (Advocate General), 681 (ECJ) 9.51, 9.52
Sebago Inc. and Ancienne Maison Dubois et Fils SA v GB-UNIC SA, Case C-173/98,
    [1998] ETMR 187 (Brussels Tribunal of Commerce) 9.72
SECOND SKIN trade mark [2002] ETMR 326 ....13.61
Seder's application; opposition of Funk Case 151/1999 [2000] ETMR 685 ....10.64
Senso di Donna's trade mark; Kim Carl Meller's application for a declaration of invalidity Case
    C000616979/1 [2001] ETMR 38 ....10.42, 13.125
Series 5 Software Ltd v Clarke [1996] FSR 273 ....1.37
Seven-Up Bottling Co. v. Seven-Up Co., 561 F.2d 1275, 1279 (8th Cir 1977) 15.13
Shield Mark BV v Kist, trading as Memex [2000] ETMR 147 (Hague Court of Appeal);
    [2002] ETMR 2002 (Hoge Raad) 5.134, 5.136

A. Cases in alphabetical order

Shield Mark BV v Kist, trading as Memex, Case C-283/01 [2003] ETMR 822 ....5.134, 5.136
Sieckmann v Deutsches Patent- und Markenamt, Case C-273/00 [2003] ETMR 466 ....5.10, 5.117, 5.118
Silhouette International Schmiedt GmbH & Co. KG v Hartlauer Handelsgesellschaft mbH Case C-355/96 [1998] ETMR 539 ....1.36, 3.14, 9.64
Sirena Srl v Eda Srl Case 40/70 [1971] ECR 69 ....14.118, 14.120
Skis Rossignol SA and another v SA Head Tyroli\ Sports & HTM Sport SpA [1999] ETMR 450 ....14.60
SKYLIFT trade mark, Trade Mark Registry (C. J. Bowen), 19 July 2000 ....13.113
Slim International and Antineas Graikou v Delta Protypos Milk Industry [2000] ETMR 409 ...10.12, 10.33, 14.66
SMARTWEB trade mark application [2003] ETMR 272 ....4.144, 16.49
SmithKline Beecham plc and others v Antigen Pharmaceuticals Ltd [1999] ETMR 512 ....14.51
SNC: look up next word of name
Société: look up next word of name
SA Société des Participations du Commissariat à l'Energie Atomique (CEA) v Greenpeace France et al, Tribunal de Grande Instance de Paris, 2 August 2002, affirmed by the Cour d'appel de Paris [2003] ETMR 870 ....8.61, 8.68
SA Société LTJ Diffusion v SA Sadas Case C-291/00 [2002] ETMR 441, [2003] FSR 1 (Advocate General), unreported judgment of 20 March 2003 (ECJ) 1.03, 10.10, 10.18
SA Société LTJ Diffusion v Société SA Sadas Vertbaudet [2001] ETMR 76 ....10.10
Société des Produits Nestlé SA v Mars UK Ltd, [2002] EWHC 2533 (Ch), 2 December 2002, [2003] FSR 684 (HC) 4.169, 5.77
Société des Produits Nestlé SA v Pro Fiducia Treuhand AG [2002] ETMR 351 ....12.41, 17.22, 17.48
Société des Produits Nestlé SA v Turkish Patent Institute, 9th Commercial Court of Ankara, Case no. 2000/783, Decision 2001/382, 9 May 2001 ....4.12
Société des Produits Nestlé SA v Unilever plc, [2002] EWHC 2709 (Ch), [2003] ETMR 681 ....5.87, 13.104
Software Products International Inc's trade marks; applications by Microsoft Corp for declarations of invalidity, unreported UK Trade Mark Registry transcript O/256/97 of 30 December 1997 ....13.98
Sony Computer Entertainment Inc v Lee, WTLR 8 April 2003 ....14.46
Sony Computer Entertainments Inc. v Tesco Stores Ltd [2000] ETMR 102 ....9.57
Sony Europe v Time Tron Corp, Austrian Supreme Court, June 2002 ....1.02
Sony Walkman trade mark [2000] ETMR 890; [2003] EIPR N-87 ....8.79
South African Breweries International (Finance) BV v Laugh It Off Promotions (2003) WTLR 28 May 2003 ....8.66, 12.26
South Cone Incorporated v Bessant and others (trading as Reef) [2002] EWCA Civ 763, [2003] RPC 5 ....13.127
SpeechWorks Ltd v SpeechWorks International Incorporated [2000] ETMR 982 ....14.17, 14.69
Spolka Akcyjna PPCH's trade mark [2001] ETMR 770 ....13.41
Sporty's Farm LLC v Sportsman's Market, Inc 202 F3d 489 (2d Cir. 2000); cert. denied 147 LEd2d 984 (Sup Ct 2000) 17.31
Sprints Ltd v Comptroller of Customs (Mauritius) and another [2000] IP&T 735 ....15.02
Sté: look up next word of name
Stephanskreuz trade mark application [1997] ETMR 182 ....10.124
Stillwater Designs and Audio Inc's application; opposition of Josefina Fernandez de la Fuenta Abellan Case B 7049 [2000] ETMR 35 ....10.73
Stokke Fabrikker and another v Playmaster of Sweden AB (Ltd) and another [1998] ETMR 395 ....5.92
Streamserve Inc v OHIM, Case T-106/00 [2003] ETMR 751, [2003] IP&T 439 ....4.04
Sarl Succès de Paris v SA Parfums Van Cleef et Arpels [1999] ETMR 869 ....10.15
Succession Picasso v DaimlerChrysler Aktiengesellschaft R 0247/2001-3 [2002] ETMR 953 ....16.60
SunAmerica Corp v Sun Life Assurance Co. of Canada, 77 F.3d 1325, 1345 (11th Cir 1996) 12.56

Sunrider v OHIM (VITALITE) Case T-24/00 [2001] ECR II-449, [2001] ETMR 605,
    [2001] IP&T 452 ....4.115
Swatch Group (US) Inc v Movado Corp (2003) WTLR 27 May 2003 ....10.129
Sweetmasters Ltd's application; opposition of Société des Produits Nestlé, 25 February 2002
    (UK Trade Mark Registry) 10.103
Swizzels Matlow Ltd's application [2000] ETMR 58 ....5.106
Sarl Sygroup and SA DCM v Société Sylab Ypsis and Jean Lagadec [2001] ETMR 1275 ....7.24
Sykes Enterprises Inc v OHIM, Case T-130/01 [2003] IP&T 213, [2003] ETMR 731 ....5.75
Symonds Cider & English Wine Co. Ltd v Showerings (Ireland) Ltd [1997] ETMR 238 ....14.63
Syndicate Sales Inc v Hampshire Paper Corp 192 F3d 633, 52 USPQ 2d 1035
    (7th Cir 1999) 12.69
System 3R International AB v Erowa AG and Erowa Nordic AB, Stockholm District Court
    [2003] ETMR 916 ....8.22, 10.13

Taam Teva (1988) Tivoli Ltd v Ambrosia Superb Ltd (2003) WTLR 15 May 2003 ....10.71
Tabasco Restaurant v Proprietor of the Tabasco Registered trade mark [1998] ETMR 100 ....8.79
Taittinger SA v Allbev Ltd [1994] 4 All ER 75 ....18.38
Tajer Firma Handlowa Sciwiarski Tadeusz's trade mark; Multibond Inc.'s application for
    Cancellation [2002] ETMR 491 ....13.86
Tastee Freez International Ltd's application [1960] RPC 255 ....8.16
Taubman Company v Mishkoff 319 F3d 770 (6th Cir. 2003) 8.63
Taurus-Film v OHIM (Cine Action) Case T-135/99 [2001] ECR II-379, [2001] ETMR 594,
    [2001] IP&T 436 ....4.111
Tax Free trade mark application [1998] ETMR 193 ....4.69, 8.16
TDC Forlag A/S v Medieforlaget Danmark A/S [2003] ETMR 158 ....6.40
Team Lotus Ventures Ltd's application; opposition of Group Lotus Ltd [1999] ETMR 669 ....4.50
Teknek Electronics Ltd v KSM International Ltd [1998] ETMR 522 ......8.137-8.139, 8.157, 14.59
Telecom Plus plc's application, 26 November 2002 (UK Trade Marks Registry) 4.28
Telefon & Buch Verlags GmbH v OHIM joined cases T-357 and 358/99 [2001] ETMR 1004,
    [2001] IP&T 1158 ....5.07
Tele-Mægleren ApS v Netsource Danmark A/S [2000] ETMR 523 ....8.28
Terrapin v Terranova Case 119/75 [1976] ECR 1039 ....6.36
Thank You Candy Co. Ltd's application, UK Trade Mark Registry 19 October 1995 ....4.106
Thomson Holidays v Norwegian Cruise [2002] EWCA Civ 1828, [2003] IP&T 299 ....13.69
Three Stripes trade mark [2002] ETMR 553 ....10.154
Tilia International's application Case R 57/1998-1 [1999] ETMR 191 ....4.155
Times Mirror Magazine Inc v Las Vegas Sports News LLC, 212 F3d 157, 167 (3d Cir 2000) 12.52,
                                                                                     12.69
Tong Hwei Enterprise Co. Ltd's application Case R 374/2000-1 [2001] ETMR 961 ....4.86
Tong Yang Confectionery Corp's trade mark; application for cancellation by Lotte Confectionery
    Co. Ltd [2002] ETMR 219 ....6.35
TORREMAR trade mark [2003] RPC 89 ....13.25
Torres Valls, re Spanish Supreme Court, 6 July 2001, noted in [2002] ETMR N-53 ....5.62
Toshiba Europe GmbH v Katun Germany GmbH Case C-112/99 [2002] ETMR 295 ....8.95, 8.116,
                                                                              8.117, 8.118
Toys 'R' Us (Canada) Ltd v Manjel Inc, Federal Court of Canada, noted in (2003) WTLR
    19 May 2003 ....1.20
Travelex Global and Financial Services Ltd (formerly Thomas Cook Group Ltd) and
    Interpayment Services Ltd v Commission, Case T-195/00, Court of First Instance,
    10 April 2003 ....8.11, 10.105
Trebor Bassett Ltd v The Football Association [1997] FSR 211 ....7.45
Treatment of overheads in profit calculations [2002] ECDR 289 ....14.93
Tria Robit Agency v Jason (2003) WTLR 23 April 2003 ....4.172
            Trillium Digital Systems Inc.'s trade mark; Harte-Hanks Data Technologies' application

A. Cases in alphabetical order

for a declaration of invalidity Case C000053447/1 noted in [2000] ETMR 1054 . . . . . .13.80,
13.125, 13.130, 13.132, 13.135
TV4 and TV Spartacus KB v Bröderna Lindströms Forlags AB, noted in Brandnews 2/2003 . . . . . .8.65
Twelve Islands Shipping Company Ltd v Turkish Patent Institute, 11th Civil Chamber of the
Supreme Court, Decision 2000/3866–2000/4995, 1 June 2000 . . . . .4.12
Two Pesos Inc v Taco Cabana 932 F2d 1113 (CA5 1991), 505 US 763 (1992) 4.114, 5.09
Ty Inc v Perryman 306 F3d 509 (7th Cir. 2002); cert. denied 123 SupCt 1750 (Sup Ct 2003) 8.32,
17.18
Ty Nant Spring Water Ltd v Lemon & Co. Srl [1999] ETMR 969 . . . . .14.26
Ty Nant Spring Water Ltd's application Case R 5/1999-3 [1999] ETMR 974 . . . . .4.177

UNIC Centre Sarl v Harrow Crown Court and others [2000] ETMR 595, [2000] IP&T 205 . . .14.05
Unilever NV. v Arctic HR 24 January 2003, Case C01/036 . . . . .13.117
Unilever N.V. v Raisio Yhtyma OY and others [1999] ETMR 847 . . . . .10.75, 10.148
Unilever plc v OHIM Case T-194/01, 5 March 2003 (unreported) 2.29, 5.80
Unilever plc and another v Cussons (New Zealand) Pty. Ltd [1998] RPC 369 . . . . .13.66
Unilever plc's application [1999] ETMR 406 (MISTER LONG) 5.69
Unione Calcio Sampdoria SpA v Titan Hancocks Decision 2000-0523 [2000] ETMR 1017 . . . . .17.44
United Biscuits (UK) Ltd v Asda Stores Ltd [1997] RPC 513 . . . . .7.54, 14.46
United Biscuits Ltd v Irish Biscuits Ltd [1971] IR 16 . . . . .10.123
United Brands v Commission Case 27/76 [1978] ECR 207 . . . . .10.78
Upjohn v Paranova: see Pharmacia & Upjohn SA v Paranova A/S
USA Detergents Inc's application Case R 20/97-1 [1998] ETMR 562 . . . . .4.84

Valigeria Roncato SpA's application Case R 164/1998-1 [2000] ETMR 46 . . . . .5.98
Valliant-Saunders' application; opposition of Cadbury Trebor Allan (noted in Marketing Law,
26 May 2003 . . . . .10.127
Van Doren + Q GmbH v Lifestyle + Sportswear Handelsgesellschaft mbG, Case C-244/00
[2003] ETMR 561 (AG), [2003] ETMR 922 (ECJ) 9.45, 9.46
Van Zuylen Freres v HAG AG 1974] ECR 731 ('HAG I') 3.13, 9.92
Vekaria v Kalatizadeh Case R 410/2001-1, noted in [2003] ETMR 111 .10.15
Vennootschap onder Firma Senta Aromatic Marketing's application, Case R 156/1998-2
[1999] ETMR 429 (OHIM) 4.26, 5.117
Verbraucherschutzverein EV v Sektkellerei G. C. Kessler GmbH und Co. Case C-303/97 [1999]
ETMR 269 . . . . .18.37, 18.42
Verify International N.V.'s application; opposition of Jörg Pohlmann Case 110/2000 [2000]
ETMR 716 . . . . .10.64
Viasat Inc v Sociedad Telefónica SA, WTLR 3 April 2003 . . . . .13.17
Videogruppo SpA v Agenzia GP Srl [2002] ETMR 1003 . . . . .13.88
Viking-Umwelttechnik GmbH v OHIM, Case T-316/00 [2003] ETMR 196,
[2003] IP&T 25 . . . . .4.102, 5.111, 5.124, 5.131
Vine Products Ltd v Mackenzie & Co. Ltd (No. 3) [1967] FSR 402 . . . . .18.38
Visa International (U.S.) v Editions Jibena [1998] ETMR 580 . . . . .13.50
Visa International Service Association's application Case R 46/1999-1 [2000]
ETMR 263 . . . . .4.111, 5.73
Vita Sulfal GRUR Int 1961, 354 . . . . .14.86
VN Legetøj A/S v Patentankenævnet [2001] ETMR 529 . . . . .4.51, 18.55
Vodafone Group Plc and another v Orange Personal Communications Services Ltd [1997]
FSR 34 . . . . .8.130-8.133, 8.152
Volkswagen AG and Audi AG v Garage X noted in [2003] ETMR 225 . . . . .8.30
Volkswagen A.G's application; opposition of FIAT Veicoli Industriali SpA (Iveco SpA) Case 1269/1999
[2000] ETMR 320 . . . . .13.27
Volkswagen AG SA v Société Renault SA, Tribunal de Grande Instance de Paris, 23 September 1991,
PIBD 22 October 1991 . . . . .8.120

Volkswagen Leasing GmbH's trade mark; International Fleet Management N.V.'s application for cancellation Case C000525824/1 [2001] ETMR 1170 ....13.39
Volvo Ltd v D.S. Larm Ltd and Dick Edvinsson [2000] ETMR 299 ....7.29, 8.30, 14.31
Vranken SA v Champagne H. Germain et Fils SA [1998] ETMR 390 ....8.45
Vzao Sojuzplodimport's application; opposition of Latvijas Balzams Case 62/1999 [2000] ETMR 618 ....13.32

Wackers application, Trade Mark Registry (G. W. Salthouse), 27 November 1998 ....13.114
Wagamama Ltd v City Centre Restaurants plc [1996] ETMR 307 ....10.145
Warman International Ltd's application Case R 82 /1999 [2000] ETMR 1159 ....5.98
Warnaco Inc's application [1997] ETMR 505 ....4.83
Warsteiner Brauerei Gaus GmbH & Co. KG's application; opposition of Brauerei Beck GmbH & Co. Case 57/1998 [1999] ETMR 225 ....10.49, 13.22
Waterford Wedgwood Plc v David Nagli Ltd [1998] FSR 92 ....7.22
Wellcome Foundation Co. Ltd v Dairy Farm Management Co. Ltd [1998] IP Asia LR 40 ....13.06
West v Nicolas Feuillatte SA and Yvon Mau SA, Cour d'appel de Reims 13 November 2002 ....6.28
West (t/a Eastenders) v Fuller Smith and Turner plc [2002] FSR 822, [2003] ETMR 376; [2003] EWCA Civ 48, 31 January 2003 ....4.64, 4.96, 13.69
?What If! Holdings Ltd v The What If Group BV [2003] ETMR 481 ....8.49, 14.43
Windsurfing Chiemsee Produktions- und Vertriebs GmbH v Boots- und Segelzubehör Walter Huber and Franz Attenberger Joined Cases C-108 and 109/97 [1999] ETMR 585 ....4.67, 4.74, 4.75, 4.78, 4.163, 5.50, 6.19, 8.19, 11.35, 12.14, 20.11
Wilhelm Kaimann's application, Trade Mark Registry, 19 May 1999 ....13.106
Winterson v Hogarth Decision 200-0235 [2000] ETMR 783 ....17.36
Wm. Wrigley Jr. Company's application [1999] ETMR 214 (colour green) 4.67, 5.126
Wm. Wrigley Jr. Company's application Case T-193/99 [2001] ETMR 623 (DOUBLEMINT) 4.96, 4.117
Sarl Wolke Inks & Printers GmbH v SA Imaje [2003] ETMR 849 ....6.44, 8.27
Woolworths' Trade Mark Application [1999] FCA 1020 (Australian Federal CA) 16.48
World Wide Fund for Nature and World Wildlife Fund Inc. v World Wrestling Federation Entertainment Inc. [2002] EWCA Civ 196, [2002] ETMR 564, [2003] IP&T 98 ....5.35, 15.90
World Wide Fund for Nature and World Wildlife Fund Inc. v World Wrestling Federation Entertainment Inc. and another, [2003] EWCA Civ 401, 27 March 2003 ....14.41
Wrigley: see Wm. Wrigley
WWF Danmark and WWF-World Wide Fund for Nature v Den Blå Avis A/S [1999] 300 ......14.82
Wyeth (formerly American Home Products Corp) v Knoll Aktiengesellschaft, reported as Knoll AG's trade mark [2003] RPC 175 ....13.130, 13.136, 13.137, 13.142

XTC trade mark [1998] ETMR 268 ....8.40

Yakult: see Kabushiki Kaisha Yakult
Yellow/Black trade mark application [1999] noted in ETMR 677 ....5.131
Yellow/Green trade mark application [2002] WRP 450 ....5.131
YES trade mark [1998] ETMR 386; [2000] ETMR 883 ....4.83
York trade mark [1981] FSR 33 ....4.177
Yuen v McDonald's Corp and another (unreported, Chancery Division, 27 November 2001) 1.21
Yves Saint Laurent Parfums SA v Institut National des Appellations d'Origine [1994] ECC 385 ..11.29
Yves Saint Laurent Parfums SA v Javico International Case C-306/96 [1998] ECR I-1983 ....9.19

Zakritoe Aktsionernoe Obchtechestevo 'Torgovy Dom Potomkov Postavechtchika Dvora Ego Imperatorskago Velitschestva Pa Smirnova' v Diageo North America Inc, [2003] EWHC 970 (Ch), 7 April 2003 ....4.41

Zanella SNC's application; opposition by Zanella Confezioni SpA Case B 42053 [2000] ETMR 69 ....10.97
Zapf Creation AG v OHIM Case T-140/00 [2002] ETMR 128 ....4.113, 4.122, 4.133
Zaras, re [2003] ECC 34 ....17.23
ZDF v Karl-May-Verlag, 5 December 2002, Bundesgerichtshof 5.72, 16.69
Zewillis v Baan Nordic A/S, Østre Landsret, Case B-3553-97, 26 November 1999 ....17.07
Zino Davidoff SA v A & G Imports Ltd [1999] ETMR 700, [2000] IP&T 101 ....9.37, 9.41
Zino Davidoff SA v A & G Imports Ltd; Levi Strauss & Co and Levi Strauss (UK) Ltd v Tesco Stores, Tesco plc and Costco Wholesale Ltd Joined Cases C-414/99, C-415/99 and C-416/00 [2002] ETMR 109 (ECJ) 1.36, 9.37, 9.41
Zino Davidoff SA v M & S Toiletries Ltd [2000] ETMR 622, [2000] IP&T 955 ....14.52
Zino Davidoff SA v M & S Toiletries Ltd (No. 2) [2001] ETMR 112 ....9.45

B. Cases by jurisdiction

Argentina
Kellogg Company v Pehuamar SA (2003) WTLR 22 May 2003 ....6.03

Australia
Campomar Sociedad, Limitada v Nike International Ltd [2000] HCA 12 ....10.116
Fada Pty Ltd (t/a Pacific Coast Eco-Bananas)'s application (2003) WTLR 19 May 2003 ....5.130
Kenman Kandy Australia Pty Ltd v Registrar of Trade Marks [2002] FCAFC 273 ....5.84
Musidor BV v Tansing (t/a Apple Music House) (1994) ALR 593 ....7.48
Philmac Pty Ltd v Registrar of Trade Marks [2002] FCA 155 ....5.129
Woolworths' Trade Mark Application [1999] FCA 1020 ....16.48

Austria
Deutsche Telekom AG, B***** v R***** AG, C***** Gelleschaft *** mbH [2003] ETMR 170 ....4.69, 10.120
Football Association Ltd, G.B. v Distributors of Football Strips [1997] ETMR 229 ....14.45
Format Gesellschaft M.B.H. and another v/ Wirtschafts-Trend Zeitschriftenverlags Ges m.b.H. [2002] ETMR 472 ....14.62, 17.15, 17.16, 17.19
FPOE v Nic.at [2003] ETMR 25 ....17.25
Hugo Boss (4 Ob 174/02w), (2003) WTLR 6 May 2003 ....14.27
Jusline GmbH v O***** [1999] ETMR 173 ....17.20
Lego and another v Distributor of B***** Building Blocks [2001] ETMR 907 ....10.138
Manpower ***** v Manpower Austria P***** GmbH, ***** [2002] ETMR 845 ....4.176
Sacher, re noted in [2000] ETMR 185 ....14.17
Sony Europe v Time Tron Corp, Austrian Supreme Court, June 2002 ....1.02
Sony Walkman trade mark [2000] ETMR 890; [2003] EIPR N-87 ....8.79
Tabasco Restaurant v Proprietor of the Tabasco Registered trade mark [1998] ETMR 100 ....8.79
XTC trade mark [1998] ETMR 268 ....8.40

Belgium
Adidas A.G. v N.V. Famco [1998] ETMR 616 ....14.27
Belgacom v Benelux Trade Mark Office [2000] ETMR 286 ....5.127
Christien t/a Rose's Lace Boutique and another v BVBA Parcles [2000] ETMR 1 ....14.50
D'Ieteren v Benelux Trade Marks Office [2003] ETMR 842, CA Brussels 4.22, 4.99
SA Kaasmakerij Passendale v Coopératives Réunies de l'Industrie du Lait Coberco noted in [2000] ETMR 840 ....5.06
Lipton Ltd, Van Den Berg & Jurgens BV, Unilever Belgium and Unilever NV v Sara Lee/De NV and Douwe Egberts [2002] ETMR 1073 ....5.110, 6.35

Nijs et al. v Ciba-Geigy IngCons 1984, 317 . . . . .7.56
Reebok International Ltd v SA Cora and others [1999] 649 . . . . .9.57
Sabena v Ryanair, Brussels Commercial Court, 10 July 2001 . . . . .8.140, 8.148
Sebago Inc. and Ancienne Maison Dubois et Fils SA v GB-UNIC SA, Case C-173/98 [1998]
    ETMR 187 . . . . .9.72

Benelux Court of Justice
Campina Melkunie BV v Bureau Benelux des Marques [2001] ETMR 392 . . . . .4.171
Campina Melkunie BV v Benelux Merkenbureau Case C-265/00, 31 Jan 2002 (AG) 4.154
Claerin/Klarein: see Lucas Bols v Colgate-Palmolive
Erich Perner Kunststoffwerke v Pressman Toy Corp [1997] ETMR 159 . . . . .13.65
Europabank N.V. v Banque pour l'Europe SA [1997] ETMR 143 . . . . .4.42
Intergro v Interbuy [2003] ETMR 152 . . . . .13.93
Jullien v Verschuere Case A 82/5, 20 May 1983, Jur. 1983 vol. 4 p. 36 . . . . .10.144
Lucas Bols v Colgate-Palmolive (1976)7 IIC 420 (CLAERYN/KLAREIN) 11.53

Brazil
Ford Motor Company v Association of Former Ford Distributors (2003) WTLR
    5 June 2003 . . . . .8.12
Louis Vuitton Distribuição v Caliente Comércio de Modas (2003) WTLR 30 May 2003 . . . . .14.91

Canada
Anne of Green Gables Licensing Authority and Heirs of L.M. Montgomery v. Avonlea Traditions,
    10 March 2000, (OSCJ) 15.13
Boston Pizza International Inc v Boston Chicken Inc, (2003) WTLR 11 April 2003 . . . . .4.172
ConAgra Foods Inc v Fetherstonhaugh & Co., WTLR 2 April 2003 . . . . .13.57
Farside Clothing Ltd et al. v Cariclime Ventures Ltd, 2002 FCA 466, 12 November 2002 . . . . . . .13.36
Labatt Brewing Co. Ltd v Molson Canada, Federal Court Trial Division, Canada, noted in (2003)
    WTLR 16 May 2003 . . . . .4.171
Pizza Pizza Ltd v Registrar of Trade-marks (1989) 26 CPR (3d) 355 . . . . .5.28
Toys 'R' Us (Canada) Ltd v Manjel Inc, Federal Court of Canada, noted in (2003) WTLR 19 May
    2003 . . . . .1.20
Valliant-Saunders' application; opposition of Cadbury Trebor Allan (noted in Marketing Law,
    26 May 2003 . . . . .10.127

Colombia
Empresa Licorera de Santander's trade mark application, 8 March 2002 . . . . .4.173
Rhône Poulenc v Reckitt Benckiser WTLR, 18 July 2003 (Colombian Trade Mark
    Office) 10.79
Viasat Inc v Sociedad Telefónica SA, WTLR 3 April 2003 . . . . .13.17

Czech Republic
Alfa-Tel's application; opposition of Alcatel Altshom Compagnie Générale d'Electricité noted in
    [2001] ETMR 621 . . . . .10.61
DURACELL trade mark noted in [1999] ETMR 583 . . . . .12.33
HENNAFLOR trade mark noted in [2001] ETMR 132 . . . . .13.59

Denmark
Alfred Ritter GmbH & Co. KG and CK Chocolade A/S v Ion SA Cocoa & Chocolate Manufacturers
    [1997] ETMR 103 . . . . .8.56
AstraZeneca AB v Orifarm A/S, noted in [2002] EIPR N-92 . . . . .14.85
Board of Appeal for Patents and Trade Marks v Danish Association of Pharmacists WTLR,
    1 April 2003 . . . . .4.54
Boehringer Ingelheim Danmark A/S and others v Orifarm A/S [2002] ETMR 223 . . . . .16.24

B. Cases by jurisdiction

Chloé Société Anonyme v Føtex A/S [19979] ETMR 131 ....14.22
Ecco Sko A/S v Nike Denmark ApS [2001 ETMR 371 ....8.58
Glaxo Group Ltd v Knoll Aktiengesellschaft [1999] ETMR 358 ....16.31
Home A/S v Home From Home Relocation Services by Annemette Krogh Pedersen [2003]
    ETMR 605 ....10.100
Lancaster Group GmbH v Parfume Discount Sjaelland SpA, noted in [2002]
    ETMR N-47 ....9.57
Løvens Kemiske Fabrik Produktionsaktielskab v Orifarm A/S, WTLR 20 March 2003, [2003]
    EIPR N-68 ....16.17, 16.26, 16.29
Løvens Kemiske Fabrik Produktionsaktielskab v Paranova A/S [2001] ETMR 302 ....16.17
Lube A/S v Dansk Droge A/S [2001] ETMR 343 ....10.119, 14.69
McDonald's Corp USA and McDonald's Restaurants Denmark A/S v Pedersen [1997]
    ETMR 151 ....1.21
Melitta SystemService and another v Coffilter International (2003) 17 WIPR 6 ....8.26
Montres Rolex SA v Fogtmann [2001] ETMR 424 ....17.08
Morgan Crucible Company plc v AB Svejseteknik ApS [2001] EIPR N-78 ....14.22
National Academy of Recording Arts & Sciences Inc. v International Federation of Phonographic
    Industry Danmark [2001] ETMR 219 ....14.42
Pfizer Inc. and Pfizer A/S v Durascan Medical Products A/S [1997] ETMR 86 ....16.31
Rynkeby Foods A/S v Ministry of Foods, Agriculture and Fisheries [2002] ETMR 136 ....4.176
TDC Forlag A/S v Medieforlaget Danmark A/S [2003] ETMR 158 ....6.40
Tele- Mægleren ApS v Netsource Danmark A/S [2000] ETMR 523 ....8.28
VN Legetøj A/S v Patentankenævnet [2001] ETMR 529 ....4.51, 18.55
WWF Danmark and WWF-World Wide Fund for Nature v Den Blå Avis A/S [1999] 300 ......14.82
Zewillis v Baan Nordic A/S, Østre Landsret, Case B-3553-97, 26 November 1999 ....17.07

England and Wales
1-800 Flowers Inc. v Phonenames Ltd [2000] ETMR 369, [2000] IP&T 325 (HC);
    [2001] EWCA Civ 721 [2002] FSR 191, [2001] IP&T 810 ....5.28, 7.31, 17.52
AAH Pharmaceuticals Ltd v Vantagemax Plc [2002] EWHC 990 (Ch), [2003]
    ETMR 205 ....10.13, 10.18
Adidas-Saloman AG v Microhaven Ltd and others, 24 March 2003 (unreported) 9.93
Ajlan bin Abdullaziz Al-Ajlan Brothers Co's application; opposition by Al-Masaraat International
    Trading & Contracting Co. Ltd [2000] ETMR 710 ....4.107
Aktiebolaget Volvo and another v Heritage (Leicester) Ltd [2000] ETMR 940 ....7.26, 8.30
Aktsionernoe Obchtchestvo Zakritogo Tipa Torgovy Dom Potomkov Postavchtchika Dvora Ego
    Imperatorskago Velitschestva PA Smirnova v UDV North America Inc, Chancery
    Division, [2002] EWHC 2911 (Ch), 18 October 2002 ....4.47
Alghussein Establishment v Eton College [1991] 1 All ER 267 (HL) 15.78
Allied Domecq plc's application [1997] ETMR 253 ....4.31, 5.19
Altecnic Ltd v Reliance Water Controls Ltd [2001] RPC 13 ....13.107
American Cyanamid v Ethicon [1975] AC 396................................1.37, 14.63, 14.69
Amp Inc. v Utilux Pty Ltd [1972] RPC 103 ....5.91
Anheuser-Busch Inc v Budejovicky Budvar Narodni Podnik [2000] RPC 906, [2000]
    IP&T 617 (CA) 8.51
Anne Frank Stichting's trade marks [1998] ETMR 687 ....16.63
Artistic Upholstery Ltd v Art Forma (Furniture Ltd) [2000] FSR 311, [2000] IP&T 147 ......13.101
Arsenal Football Club plc v Matthew Reed, Case C-206/01 [2002] ETMR 975, [2003]
    RPC 144 (Advocate General); [2003] ETMR 227 (ECJ); [2003] IP&T 43
    (ECJ) 2.30, 2.33, 2.38, 7.40, 7.42, 7.43, 7.49-7.51
Arsenal Football Club plc v Matthew Reed [2001] ETMR 860, [2001] IP&T 810 (HC) ...2.38, 7.19,
    8.85-8.88
Arsenal Football Club plc v Matthew Reed [2002] EWCA 2695 (Ch) [2003] IP&T 75, [2003]
    ETMR 453 (HC); [2002] EWCA Civ 96, 21 May 2003 ....7.50, 7.51A, 8.88

Tables of Cases

Asprey & Garrard Ltd v WRA (Guns) Ltd and Asprey [2001] EWCA Civ 1499, [2002]
  ETMR 933 ....10.12
Associated Newspapers Ltd and another v Express Newspapers [2003] EWHC 1322 (Ch),
  June 2003 (unreported) (HC) 4.124, 10.79
Audio Medical Devices Ltd's application; opposition of Audi AG [1999] ETMR 1010 ....11.74
Avnet Incorporated v Isoact Ltd [1997] ETMR 562 ....10.98, 17.73

Bach Flower Remedies Ltd v Healing Herbs Ltd [1999] IP&T 146 ....4.91
Ball v The Eden Project Ltd and another [2001] ETMR 966 (HC) 13.89
Barclays Bank plc v RBS Advanta [1996] RPC 307; [1997] ETMR 199 ....8.115, 8.125-8.127,
  8.142, 8.145, 8.149, 8.150, 8.151
BASF plc v C.E.P. (UK) plc [1996] ETMR 51 ....7.14, 11.83
Baywatch Production Co. Inc. v The Home Video Channel [1997] FSR 22 ....7.14, 11.83
Beautimatic International Ltd v Mitchell International Pharmaceuticals Ltd and another
  [1999] ETMR 912, [1999] IP&T 59 ....7.18, 7.23, 7.30, 14.34
Betts v Wilmott (1871) LR 6 Ch App 239 ....9.02
BETTY'S KITCHEN CORONATION STREET trade mark [2001] RPC 825 ....13.95
Biba Group Ltd v Biba Boutique [1980] RPC 413 ....8.34
BOCM Pauls Ltd and Scottish Agricultural College's application [1997] ETMR 420 ....4.49, 5.53
Bongrain SA's trade mark application, EWHC 531 (Ch) 5.82
Brain v Ingledew Brown Bennington & Garret [1996] FSR 341 ....14.113
British Airways plc v Ryanair Ltd [2001] ETMR 235, [2001] IP&T 373 ....2.48, 4.160,
  8.111, 8.134-8.135, 8.143, 8.145, 8.153, 8.154
British Sugar plc v James Robertson & Sons Ltd [1997] ETMR 118; [1996] RPC 281 ....4.127,
  5.49, 7.49, 8.59
British Telecommunications plc and others v One in a Million Ltd and others [1999]
  ETMR 61 ....17.07, 17.16, 17.17
British Telecommunications plc v Nextcall Telecom plc [2000] ETMR 943, [2000] IP&T 478 ...14.40
Bulmer (HP) Ltd v J Bollinger SA (No.3) [1978] RPC 79 ....18.38

C. A. Sheimer (M.) Sdn. Bhd's application; opposition by Visa International Service Association
  [1999] ETMR 519 (Registry); [2000] RPC 484 (LCAP) 11.81, 13.102, 13.108
Carlill v Carbolic Smoke Ball Company [1893] 1 QB 256 ....2.48
Chocosuisse, Kraft Jacobs Suchard (Schweiz) AG and Chocoladefabriken Lindt & Sprüngli
  (Schweiz) AB v Cadbury Ltd [1998] ETMR 205 (HC); [1999] ETMR 1020 (CA) 18.38
Citicorp v Link Interchange Network Ltd [2002] ETMR 1146 ....10.118
Claritas (UK) Ltd v Post Office and Postal Preference Service Ltd [2001] ETMR 679 ....14.122
Coflexip SA v Stolt Comex Seaway MS Ltd [1999] FSR 473 (Patents Court), [2001] RPC 182
  (Court of Appeal) 14.34
Colgate-Palmolive Ltd and another v Markwell Finance Ltd and another [1988] RPC 283 ....2.25,
  9.13, 9.16
Consejo Regulador de las Denominaciones Jerez-Xeres-Sherry y Manzanilla de Sanlucar de Barrameda v
  Mathew Clark & Sons Ltd [1992] FSR 525 (HC) 18.38
Consorzio del Prosciutto di Parma v Marks & Spencer Plc [1991] RPC 351 ....18.32
Corsair Toiletries Ltd's application; opposition by Jane Austen Memorial Trust [1999]
  ETMR 1038 ....16.57

D. Green & Co. (Stoke Newington) Ltd and Plastico Ltd v Regalzone Ltd [2001] EWCA Civ 639,
  [2002] ETMR 241, [2001] IP&T 1071 ....4.95, 6.33
DAAWAT trade mark [2003] RPC 187 ....13.101
DaimlerChrysler A.G. v Alavi [2001] ETMR 1069, [2001] IP&T 496 ....11.36, 11.46, 11.66,
  11.69, 11.76
Davidoff: see Zino Davidoff
Decon Laboratories Ltd v Fred Baker Scientific Ltd and another [2001] ETMR 486 ....13.80,
  13.101, 13.125, 13.128, 13.130, 13.131, 13.132, 13.142

B. Cases by jurisdiction

Demon Ale trade mark [2000] RPC 345 ....13.91, 13.110
Diana, Princess of Wales: see Executrices
Douglas and others v Hello! Ltd [2001] QB 967 (CA) 16.54
Douglas, Zeta-Jones and another v Hello! Ltd and others, 11 April 2003 (HC) 7.59
DSG Retail Ltd (t/a Currys) v Comet Group plc, [2002] EWHC 116 (QB), [2002] FSR 899 ....8.154
Dyson Appliances Ltd v Hoover Ltd (No.2) [2001] RPC 544 ....14.47
Dyson Ltd v Registrar of Trade Marks [2003] EWHC 1062 (Ch) 15 May 2003 ....5.82

Eiretel Ltd's application; opposition by Airtel Movil SA and another [2003] EIPR N-7 ....10.68
Elvis Presley Trade Marks [1997] RPC 543 (ChD), 567 (CA) 8.89, 16.53
Emaco Ltd and Aktienbolaget Electrolux v Dyson Appliances Ltd [1999] ETMR 903 ....8.128-8.129,
    8.131, 8.156, 14.89
Etat Française v Bernard Matthews plc [2002] EWHC 190, [2002] ETMR 1098, [2003]
    ETMR 13 ....13.97
Euromarket Designs Incorporated v Peters and another [2000] ETMR 1025, [2001] IP&T
    1308 ....7.31, 17.09
European Ltd, The v The Economist Newspaper Ltd [1998] ETMR 307 ....5.47, 8.17
Executrices of the Estate of Diana Princess of Wales' application [2001] ETMR 254 ....16.57
Farley's application; opposition by the joint ownership on the monopoly of the intellectual property
    attached to the work of Pablo Picasso [2002] ETMR 336 ....16.60
Frank Reddaway & Co. Ltd v George Banham & Co. Ltd [1896] AC 199 ....4.161, 6.18
French Connection Ltd v Sutton [2000] ETMR 341 ....4.37, 14.26, 14.44
Fresh Breath Co. Ltd's application [2000] ETMR 644 ....5.104
FROOT LOOPS trade mark [1998] RPC 240 ....19.06
FSS Trade Mark [2001] RPC 40

GE trade mark [1972] FSR 225 ....4.182
Gerber Products Co. v Gerber Foods International Ltd [2002] EWHC 428, [2002] ETMR 882;
    [2002] EWCA Civ 1888 12 December 2002 ....13.57
Gerber Garment Technology Ltd v Lectra Systems Ltd [1997] RPC 443 (CA) 14.83
Ghazilian's application [2002] ETMR 631 ....4.37
Glaxo Group and others v Dowelhurst Ltd and others [2000] ETMR 118 ....14.119
Glaxo Group and others v Dowelhurst Ltd and others (No. 2) [2000] ETMR 415 ....14.119
Glaxo Group and others v Dowelhurst Ltd and others, [2003] EWHC 110 (Ch), [2003] 2 CMLR
    248, 6 February 2003 ....16.14, 16.26, 16.29
Glaxo Group Ltd's trade mark; Riker Laboratories Inc's application for a declaration of invalidity
    [2001] ETMR 96 ....5.132
Glen Catrine Bonded Warehouse Ltd's application for revocation [1996] ETMR 56 ....13.59
Green: see D. Green
Gromax Plasticulture Ltd v Don & Low Nonwovens Ltd [1999] RPC 367 ....13.100, 13.136
GTR Group's application; opposition of Jean Patou [1999] ETMR 164 ....10.106

Harding v Smilecare Ltd [2002] FSR 37 ....10.100
Hodgkinson Corby Ltd and another v Wards Mobility Services Ltd [1995] FSR 169 ....2.46, 8.02,
    8.159
HOLLY HOBBIE trade mark [1984] FSR 199; [1984] RPC 329 ....15.58
Hutchison Personal Communications Ltd v Hook Advertising Ltd and Others [1996]
    FSR 549 ....19.05

Infamous Nut Co. Ltd's trade marks [2003] RPC 126 ....13.24
Inland Revenue Commissioners v Muller & Co's Margarine Ltd [1901] AC 217 ....21.25
Inlima S.L's application; opposition of Adidas A.G. [2000] ETMR 325 ....11.81
Intel Corp v Sihra [2003] EWHC 17 (Ch), 24 January 2003 ....11.57, 11.72
Inter Lotto (UK) Ltd v Camelot Group plc, [2003] EWHC 1256 (Ch), [2003]
    3 All ER 191 ....14.08

JANE AUSTEN application, Trade Marks Registry, 12 July 1999 ....13.105
Jellinek's application (1946) 63 RPC 59 ....10.86
John Lewis of Hungerford Ltd's Trade Mark Application [2001] ETMR 1193 ....4.27
John Walker & Sons Ltd and another v Henry Ost and Company Ltd and another
    [1970] FSR 63..14.17
Jordan Grand Prix Ltd v Vodafone Group Plc, [2003] EWHC 1965 (Comm), 4 August 2003
    (unreported) (Commercial Court)...15.62A
Joseph Crosfield & Son's application ('PERFECTION') (1909) 26 RPC 837 ....6Intro
Jupiter Unit Trust Managers Ltd v Johnson Fry Asset Managers plc, 19 Apr 2000 (HC) 8.155

Kimberley-Clark Ltd v Fort Sterling Ltd [1997] FSR 877 ....8.95, 10.138
Kraft Jacobs Suchard Ltd's application; opposition by Nestlé UK Ltd [2001] ETMR 54 ....19.08
Kundry SA's application; opposition by the President and Fellows of Harvard College [1998]
    ETMR 178 ....10.48

Laboratories Goemar SA's trade marks; application for revocation by La Mer Technology Inc
    [2002] ETMR 382 ....13.57
Laboratories Goemar SA, Re [2003] EWHC 1382 (Ch), 20 June 2003 (unreported) (HC) 13.57
LG Electronics Inc v NCR Financial Solutions Group Ltd [2003] FSR 428 ....15.25
L'Oréal (UK) Ltd and another v Johnson & Johnson and another [2000] ETMR 691, [2000]
    IP&T 789 ....14.114
Levi Strauss & Co and Levi Strauss (UK) Ltd v Tesco Stores Ltd and others [2002] EWHC 1556
    (Ch), [2002] ETMR 1153, [2003] IP&T 117, [2003] RPC 319 ....2.12, 9.74, 9.82
London Borough of Hackney v Cedar Trading Ltd [1999] ETMR 801 ....2.04, 9.54

Madgecourt Ltd's application; opposition of Fédération des Industries de la Parfumerie [2000]
    ETMR 825 ....4.46
Manton and others v Van Day and others noted in [2001] ETMR 1114 ....16.64
Maxim's Ltd v Dye [1977] 1 WLR 1155 ....8.49
McCain International Ltd v Country Fair Foods Ltd and another [1981] RPC 69 ....6.18
Mecklermedia Corp and another v D.C. Congress GmbH [1997] ETMR 265 ....14.12
Merck and Company's trade mark; SmithKline Beecham plc's application for a declaration of
    invalidity [2000] ETMR 75..6.39
Mercury Communications Ltd v Mercury Interactive (UK) Ltd [1995] FSR 850 ....10.94
Merri Mayers-Head's application; opposition of Jean Patou [1997] ETMR 577 ....10.12
Mickey Dees (Nightclub) Trade Mark [1998] RPC 359 ....13.97
Microsoft Corp v Computer Future Distribution Ltd [1998] ETMR 597 ....9.58
Midland Wheel Supplies Ltd's application for revocation [2000] ETMR 256 ....6.23

NAD Electronics Inc. and another v NAD Computer Systems Ltd [1997] FSR 380 ....8.34
National Canine Defence League's application; opposition of Geoffrey Inc., Case O-213-03,
    29 July 2003 (unreported) (Trade Mark Registry) 11.73
Natural Resources Inc v Origin Clothing Ltd [1995] FSR 280 ....10.105, 10.109, 13.66
Neil King's application; opposition of Hard rock International plc and another [2000]
    ETMR 22 ....10.63
Nestlé UK Ltd v Zeta Espacial SA [2000] ETMR 226 ....13.59
Nichols plc, Re [2002] EWHC 1424 (Ch), [2003] ETMR 180, [2003] RPC 301 ....5.67
Nordic Saunas Ltd's trade mark; application for revocation by Nordic Timber Council AB [2002]
    ETMR 210 ....5.47
Northern & Shell Plc v Conde Nast and National Magazines Distributors Ltd and another
    [1995] RPC 117 ....8.177
Norwich Pharmacal Co. v Commissioners for Customs and Excise [1974] AC 133 (HL) 14.24
Notetry Ltd's application (unreported), trade mark Registry transcript O/258/97,
    29 December 1997 ....5.131

B. Cases by jurisdiction

Oasis Stores Ltd's application; opposition of Ever Ready plc [1999] ETMR 531 ....11.81
Omega SA v Omega Engineering Ltd [2003] EWHC, 3 June 2003 ....13.64
OXYFRESH Trade Mark, Trade Mark Registry, 25 March 1999 ....13.90

PAG Ltd v Hawke-Woods Ltd [2002] ETMR 811 ....8.27
Pfizer Ltd and Pfizer Incorporated v Eurofood Link (United Kingdom) Ltd [2000] ETMR 896,
　　[2000] IP&T 280 ....3.49, 7.14, 11.83, 12.15, 12.35, 12.42, 12.51
Philip Morris Products Inc and another v Rothmans International Enterprises Ltd and another
　　[2001] EWCA Civ 1043, [2001] ETMR 1250 ....15.85
Philips Electronics N.V. v Remington Consumer Products Ltd (No. 2) [1999]
　　ETMR 835 ....13.33, 13.71
Philips Electronics NV v Remington Consumer Products [1998] ETMR 124 (High Court);
　　[1999] ETMR 816 (Court of Appeal) 4.166, 4.168, 5.82, 5.109, 5.111, 7.49
Philosophy Inc. v Ferretti Studio Srl [2002] EWCA Civ 921, [2003] ETMR 97, [2003]
　　RPC 287 ....13.46, 13.60
Pilkington plc's application [2002] ETMR 206 ....5.42
Pitman Training Ltd and another v Nominet UK and another [1997] FSR 797 ....15.92
Pomaco Ltd's trade mark; application for revocation by Reed Consumer Books Ltd [2001]
　　ETMR 1013 ....13.67
Premier Brands UK Ltd v Typhoon Europe Ltd [2000] ETMR 1071, [2002] EWCA Civ 1043,
　　[2002] ETMR 787, [2003] FSR 69 ....11.13, 11.14, 11.42. 11.44, 11.54, 11.61,
　　　　　　　　　　　　　　　　　　　　　　　　　　　　　　　　　　11.66, 11.83, 11.94
Premier Luggage and Bags Ltd v Premier Co (UK) Ltd and another [2002] ETMR 787 (CA) 7.29,
　　　　　　　　　　　　　　　　　　　　　　　　　　　　　　　　　　　　　10.147
Primark Stores Ltd and Primark Holdings v Lollypop Clothing Ltd [2001] ETMR
　　334 ....9.39
Prince plc v Prince Sports Group Ltd [1998] FSR 21 ....14.111
Procter & Gamble's trade mark application, re [1999] ETMR 375 (bottles with 'ghosted'
　　labels) 4.31
Prudential Assurance Co. Ltd v Prudential Insurance Company of America [2002] EEWHC 534
　　(Ch), [2002] ETMR 1013, [2003] FSR 97; [2003] EWCA Civ 327, [2003]
　　ETMR 873 ....14.05, 14.14, 15.91

R v Johnstone [2003] ETMR 1, affirmed on appeal at [2003] 3 UKHL 28 ....7.51, 7.51A, 9.49
Reality Group Ltd v Chance [2002] FSR 13 ....7.28
Reckitt & Colman v Borden [1990] RPC 340 ....10.123
Reddaway: see Frank Reddaway
Reed Elsevier (UK) Limited and Totaljobs.Com Limited (No 2) [2003] InfoTLR 60 .....14.84, 14.88
Reed Executive Plc and Reed Solutions Plc v Reed Business Information Ltd, Reed Elsevier (UK)
　　Ltd and Totaljobs.Com Ltd, [2003] RPC 207, [2003] IP&T 220 ....8.35, 17.63, 17.71
Reed Executive Plc and Reed Solutions Plc v Reed Business Information Ltd, Reed Elsevier (UK) Ltd
　　and Totaljobs.Com Ltd (No. 2), [2002] EWHC 2722 (Ch), [2003] Info TLR 60 ......14.22
REETRUCK trade mark application noted in [2002] EIPR N-115 ....10.27
Roadtech Computer Systems Ltd v Mandata (Management and Data Services) Ltd [2000]
　　ETMR 970 ....17.69
Royal Berkshire Polo Club's application. noted in [2001] ETMR 826 ....8.59
Rugby Football Union and Nike European Operations Netherlands BV v Cotton Traders Ltd
　　[2002] EWHC 467 (Ch), [2002] ETMR 861 ....13.35

Safeway Stores plc v Hachette Filipacchi Presse [1997] ETMR 552 ....13.61
Sanofi-Synthélabo SpA v 3M Healthcare Ltd and another [2002] EWHC 707 (Ch), [2003]
　　ETMR 586 ....15.85
Scandecor Development AB v Scandecor Marketing AB and others [1999] FSR 26
　　(Court of Appeal) 13.41, 15.84

Scandecor Development AB v Scandecor Marketing AB and others [2001] UKHL 21,
    [2001] ETMR 800, [2001] IP&T 676 ....8.34, 15.18, 15.87
Scotch Whisky Association v Glen Kella [1997] ETMR 470, HC 14.36
SECOND SKIN trade mark [2002] ETMR 326 ....13.61
Series 5 Software Ltd v Clarke [1996] FSR 273 ....1.37
SKYLIFT trade mark, Trade Mark Registry, 19 July 2000 ....13.113
Société des Produits Nestlé SA v Mars UK Ltd, [2002] EWHC 2533 (Ch), 2 December 2002,
    [2003] FSR 684 (HC) 4.169, 5.77
Société des Produits Nestlé SA v Unilever plc, [2002] EWHC 2709 (Ch), [2003] ETMR 681 ....5.87,
    13.104
Software Products International Inc's trade marks; applications by Microsoft Corp for declarations
    of invalidity, unreported UK Trade Mark Registry transcript O/256/97 of 30 December
    1997 ....13.98
Sony Computer Entertainments Inc. v Tesco Stores Ltd [2000] ETMR 102 ....9.57
South Cone Incorporated v Bessant and others (trading as Reef) [2002] EWCA Civ 763,
    [2003] RPC 5 ....13.127
Sweetmasters Ltd's application; opposition of Société des Produits Nestlé, 25 February 2002
    (UK Trade Mark Registry) 10.103
Swizzels Matlow Ltd's application [2000] ETMR 58 ....5.106

Taittinger SA v Allbev Ltd [1994] 4 All ER 75 ....18.38
Tastee Freez International Ltd's application [1960] RPC 255 ....8.16
Team Lotus Ventures Ltd's application; opposition of Group Lotus Ltd [1999] ETMR 669 ....4.50
Telecom Plus plc's application, 26 November 2002 (UK Trade Marks Registry) 4.28
Thank You Candy Co. Ltd's application, UK Trade Mark Registry 19 October 1994 ....4.106
Thomson Holidays v Norwegian Cruise [2002] EWCA Civ 1828, [2003] IP&T 299 ....13.69
TORREMAR trade mark [2003] RPC 89 ....13.25
Trebor Bassett Ltd v The Football Association [1997] FSR 211 ....7.45

UNIC Centre Sarl v Harrow Crown Court and others [2000] ETMR 595, [2000] IP&T 205 ...14.05
Unilever plc's application [1999] ETMR 406 (MISTER LONG) 5.69
United Biscuits (UK) Ltd v Asda Stores Ltd [1997] RPC 513 ....7.54, 14.46

Vine Products Ltd v Mackenzie & Co. Ltd (No. 3) [1967] FSR 402 ....18.38
Vodafone Group Plc and another v Orange Personal Communications Services Ltd [1997]
    FSR 34 ....8.130-8.133, 8.152

Wackers application, Trade Mark Registry, 27 November 1998 ....13.114
Wagamama Ltd v City Centre Restaurants plc [1996] ETMR 307 ....10.145
Warnaco Inc's application [1997] ETMR 505 ....4.83
Waterford Wedgwood Plc v David Nagli Ltd [1998] FSR 92 ....7.22
West (t/a Eastenders) v Fuller Smith and Turner plc [2002] FSR 822, [2003] ETMR 376;
    [2003] EWCA Civ 48, 31 January 2003 (unreported) 4.64, 4.96, 13.69
Wilhelm Kaimann's application, Trade Mark Registry, 19 May 1999 ....13.106
World Wide Fund for Nature and World Wildlife Fund Inc. v World Wrestling Federation
    Entertainment Inc. [2002] EWCA Civ 196, [2002] ETMR 564,
    [2003] IP&T 98 ....5.35, 15.90
World Wide Fund for Nature and World Wildlife Fund Inc. v World Wrestling Federation
    Entertainment Inc. and another, [2003] EWCA Civ 401, 27 March 2003 ....14.41
Wyeth (formerly American Home Products Corp) v Knoll Aktiengesellschaft, reported as Knoll AG's
    trade mark [2003] RPC 175 ....13.130, 13.136, 13.137, 13.142

York trade mark [1981] FSR 33 ....4.177
Yuen v McDonald's Corp and another (unreported, Chancery Division, 27 November 2001) 1.21

B. Cases by jurisdiction

Zakritoe Aktsionernoe Obchtechestevo 'Torgovy Dom Potomkov Postavechtchika Dvora Ego
    Imperatorskago Velitschestva Pa Smirnova' v Diageo North America Inc, [2003] EWHC
    970 (Ch), 7 April 2003 ....4.41
Zino Davidoff SA v A & G Imports Ltd [1999] ETMR 700, [2000] IP&T 101 ....9.37, 9.41

Estonia
Gulf International Lubricants Ltd v Gulf Oil Estonia AS WTLR, 4 July 2003 (Patent and Trade Mark
    Office, Board of Appeal, Estonia) 13.96
Henkel KgaA's application WTLR, 11 July 2003 ....4.84

European Court of Human Rights
Gaweda v Poland [2002] ETMR 691 ....4.56

European Free Trade Area Court
Mag Instrument Inc. v California Trading Company Norway, Ulsteen [1998] ETMR 85 ....3.14
Norwegian Government v Astra Norge AS [2000] ECDR 20 ....9.66
Paranova AS v Merck & Co Inc, Case C-3/02, request for advisory opinion, 17
    December 2002 ....16.27

European Union: Court of Justice of the European Communities
Adidas AG's reference Case C-223/98 [1999] ETMR 960 ....14.25
Ansul BV v Ajax Brandbeveiliging BV, Case C-40/01, 11 March 2003 (unreported) 13.54, 13.57
Arsenal Football Club plc v Matthew Reed, Case C-206/01 [2003] ETMR 227,
    [2003] IP&T 43 ....2.30, 2.33, 2.38, 7.40, 7.42, 7.43, 7.49-7.51, 17.67
BABY-DRY: see Procter & Gamble
Bayerische Motorenwerke AG (BMW) and BMW Nederland BV v Deenik [1999] ETMR 339 ...8.30,
    9.32, 17.08
Belgium (Kingdom of) v Spain (Kingdom of) Case C-388/95 [2000] ETMR 999 ....18.50
Benincasa v Dentalkit Srl Case C-296/95 [1997] ETMR 447 ....15.54
Björnekulla Fruktindustrier Aktiebolag v Procordia Food Aktiebolag, Case C-367/02
Boehringer Ingelheim KG and Boehringer Ingelheim Pharma KG v Swingward Ltd, Case C-143/00
    [2002] ETMR 898 ....9.83, 16.13, 16.18
Borie Manoux Sarl v Directeur de l'Institut de la Propriété Industrielle Case C-81/01 [2003] ETMR
    367 ....18.45
Bristol-Myers Squibb v Paranova A/S; C.H. Boehringer Sohn and others v Paranova A/S;
    Bayer Aktiengesellschaft and another v Paranova A/S Joined cases C-427/93,
    C-429/93 & C-436/93 [1996] ETMR 1 ....16.11, 16.17, 16.26
British American Tobacco Cigaretten-Fabriken GmbH v Commission Case C-35/83
    [1985] ECR 363 ....15.41
Calvin Klein Trademark Trust v Cowboyland A/S, Dansk Supermarked Administration A/S, HBN
    Marketing ApS, Progress (in the name of Peter Jensen) and Bilka Lavprisvarehus A/S,
    Case C-4/98 (removed from the Register on 27 March 1999) 9.85
Canon Kabushiki Kaisha v Metro-Goldwyn-Mayer Inc Case C-39/97 [1999] ETMR 1 ....2.30,
    10.81, 10.102, 10.111, 12.69, 21.04
Carl Kühne GmbH and Co. KG Rich. Hengstenberg GmbH and another v Jütro Konservenfabrik
    GmbH & Co. KG Case C-269/99 [2003] ETMR 36 ....18.35
Centrafarm v American Home Products Corp [1978] ECR 1823 ....16.11
Chiciak, Fromagèrie Chiciak and Fol Joined Cases C-129 and 130/97 [1998] ETMR 550 ......18.47
Christian Dior: see Parfums Christian Dior
CNL-Sucal NV v Hag GF AG [1990] 3 CMLR 571 ('HAG II') 2.30, 3.13, 9.92
Commission of the European Communities v Federal Republic of Germany Case C-325/00
    [2003] ETMR 417 ....20.11
Commission of the European Communities v French Republic, Case C-6/02, 6 March 2003 ...18.21,
    20.11

Consorzio del Prosciutto di Parma and Salumificio S. Rita Case C-108/01,
    20 May 2003 . . . . .18.32, 18.51
Consorzio per la Tutela del Formaggio Gorgonzola v Käserei Champignon Hofmeister GmbH & Co.
    KG and, Eduard Bracharz GmbH [1999] ETMR 454 . . . . .3.08, 18.33
Dansk Supermarked Case 58/80 [1981] ECR 181 . . . . .6.36
Dante Bigi Case C-66/00 [2003] ETMR 707 . . . . .18.31
Davidoff: see also Zino Davidoff
Davidoff & Cie. and Zino Davidoff SA v Gofkid Ltd Case C-292/00 [2003] ETMR 534 . . . . .7.11,
    10.18, 11.84, 11.87, 11.91, 11.92, 11.93, 11.95
Denmark, Germany and France v The Commission Joined cases C-289, 293 and 299/96 [1999]
    ETMR 478 . . . . .18.16
Deutsche Renault AG v Audi AG Case C-317/91 [1995] FSR 738 . . . . .6.36
Deutsche Telekom v Deutsche Krankenversicherung, Case C-367/02 . . . . .10.151
DKV Deutsche Krankenversicherung AG v OHIM (COMPANYLINE) Case C-104/00 P [2003] ETMR
    241 . . . . .4.63, 4.102, 6.34
Ferring Arzneimittel GmbH v Eurim-Pharm Arzneimittel GmbH Case C-172/00 [2003]
    ETMR 115 . . . . .9.60, 16.30
Feta: see Denmark, Germany and France v The Commission
Fratelli Graffione SNC v Ditta Fransa Case C-313/94 [1997] ETMR 71 . . . . .4.55
Frits Loendersloot trading as F. Loendersloot Internationale Expeditie v George Ballantine & Son Ltd
    and others Case C-349/95 [1998] ETMR 10 . . . . .9.57
General Motors Corp v Yplon SA Case C-375/97 [1999] All ER 865; [1999] ETMR 950 (ECJ);
    [1999] ETMR 120 (Advocate General's Opinion) 11.33, 11.38, 11.44, 11.92,
    12.27, 12.38, 12.53, 12.67, 12.69
Gorgonzola: see Consorzio per la Tutela Formaggio Gorgonzola
Green: see D. Green
Guimont, Jean-Pierre Case C-448/989 [2001] ETMR 145 . . . . .18.38, 18.48
Gut Springenheide GmbH, Tusky v Oberkreisdirektor des Kreises Steinfurt etc. Case C-210/96
    noted in [1999] ETMR 425 . . . . .4.90, 10.134
HAG I: see Van Zuylen Freres v HAG AG 1974] ECR 731
HAG II: see CNL-Sucal NV v Hag GF AG [1990] 3 CMLR 571
Hermès International v FHT Marketing Choice BV Case C-53/96 [1998] ETMR 425 . . .14.56, 14.74
Hoffmann-La Roche v Commission Case 88/76 [1979] ECR 461 . . . . .9.73
Hoffmann-La Roche v Centrafarm Case 102/77 [1978] ECR 1139 .16.11
Hölterhoff v Freiesleben Case C-2/00 [2002] ETMR 917, [2003] IP&T
    163 . . . . .6.33, 7.29, 8.26, 8.46
IHT Internationale Heiztechnik GmbH v Ideal Standard GmbH Case C-9/93 [1994] ECR I-2789,
    [1994] 3 CMLR 857, [1995] FSR 59 . . . . .9.92
Italian Leather SpA v WECO Polstermöbel GmbH & Co. Case C-80/00 [2003] ETMR 130 . . . .14.09
Karl Thomae: see Dr Karl Thomae
Koninklijke Philips Electronics NV v Remington Consumer Products Ltd, Case C-299/99 [2002]
    ETMR 955 . . . . .4.113, 5.90, 5.91
Levi Strauss & Co and Levi Strauss (UK) Ltd v Tesco Stores: see Zino Davidoff SA v A & G
    Imports (ECJ)
Libertel Groep BV v Benelux-Merkenbureau, Case C-104/01 [2003] ETMR 508;
    [2003] ETMR 807 (ECJ) 5.102, 5.125, 5.127, 5.128
Linde AG, Winward Industries Inc. and Rado Uhren AG, 24 October 2002, Joined Cases C-53/01
    to C-55/01[2003] ETMR 354 (AG); [2003] ETMR 963 (ECJ) 4.67, 4.125, 5.82, 5.83
Lloyd Schuhfabrik Meyer & Co. GmbH v Klijsen Handel BV Case C-342/97 [1999]
    ETMR 690 . . . . .4.90, 4.92, 10.62, 10.132, 10.134, 11.35, 12.14
Loendersloot: see Frits Loendersloot
Marca Mode C.V., Adidas A.G. and Adidas Benelux BV Case C-425/98 [2000] ETMR 723,
    [2000] IP&T 968 . . . . .10.154
Marleasing Case 106/89 [1990] ECR I-4135 . . . . .8.111

B. Cases by jurisdiction

Merck & Co. Inc v Primecrown Ltd, Joined Cases C-267/95 and 268/95 [1997]
FSR 237 ....16.08
Merck, Sharp & Dohme GmbH v Paranova Pharmazeutika Handels GmbH, Case C-443/99
[2002] ETMR 923 ....9.83
Merz & Krell GmbH Case C-517/99 [2002] ETMR 231 ....4.59, 4.61, 4.81, 4.83, 4.176, 6.37
Molkerei Groddbraunshain GmbH and Bene Nahrungsmittel GmbH v Commission Case
C-447/98 P [2002] ETMR 605 ....18.35, 18.39
Paranova Oy, Case C-113/01, 8 May 2003 ....16.30
Parfums Christian Dior SA v Evora BV Case C-337/95 [1998] ETMR 26 ....9.62
Parfums Christian Dior SA v Tuk Consultancy BV Case C-300/98 [2001] ETMR 277 ....14.73
Parke, Davis & Co. v Probel Case 24/67 [1968] ECR 55 ....9.66
Pharmacia & Upjohn SA v Paranova A/S Case C-379/97 [1999] ETMR 937, [1999] IP&T 88 ...9.86,
16.07, 16.24
Philips: see Koninklijke
Phytheron International SA v Jean Bourdon SA Case C-352/95 [1997] ETMR 211 ....9.94
Pippig Augenoptik GmbH & Co. KG v Hartlauer Handelsgesellschaft mbH, Verlassenschaft
Nach Dem Verstorbenen Franz Josef Hartlauer, Case C-44/01, 8 April 2003
(unreported) 8.116, 8.118, 8.119, 8.146, 8.147
Pistre and others v France Joined cases C-321 to 324/94 [1997] ETMR 457 ....4.55
Polo/Lauren Company L.P. v PT Dwidua Langgeng Pratama International Freight Forwarders
Case C-383/98 [2000] ETMR 535, [2000] IP&T 1128 ....7.21
Pfeiffer Grosshandel GmbH v Löwa Warenhandel GmbH Case C-255/97 [1999] ETMR 603 ....3.47
Procter & Gamble Company v OHIM Case C-383/99 P [2002] ETMR 22 (BABY-DRY) 1.36,
4.63, 4.71, 4.76, 4.78, 4.96, 4.98, 4.99, 4.100, 4.104, 4.111, 4.133,
4.147, 4.148, 4.149, 4.181, 6.15, 10.117
Pronuptia de Paris GmbH v Pronuptia de Paris Irmgard Schillgalis, Case C-161/84 [1986]
ECR 353 ....15.55
Ravil Sarl v Bellon Import Sarl and Biraghi SpA, Case C-469/00, 20 May 2003 ....18.32, 18.40, 18.51
Robelco NV v Robeco Groep NV, Case C-23/01, [2003] ETMR 671 ....6.24
Sabèl BV v Puma AG, Rudolf Dassler Sport, Case C-251/95 [1998] ETMR 1 ....10.23, 10.26,
10.28, 10.38, 10.43, 10.51, 10.60, 10.61, 10.62, 10.73, 10.104, 10.132, 10.146,
10.154, 11.10, 11.83, 11.86, 13.24
Schieving-Nijstad V.O.F. and others v Groeneweld Case C-89/99 [2002] ETMR 34 ....14.74
Schutzverband Gegen Unwesen in der Wirtschaft eV v Warsteiner Brauerei Haus Bramer
GmbH & Co. KG Case C-312/98 [2003] ETMR 76 ....18.39
Sebago Inc. and Ancienne Maison Dubois et Fils SA v GB-UNIC SA, Case C-173/98, [1999]
ETMR 681 ....9.51, 9.52
Sieckmann v Deutsches Patent- und Markenamt, Case C-273/00 [2003] ETMR 466 ....5.10,
5.117, 5.118
Silhouette International Schmiedt GmbH & Co. KG v Hartlauer Handelsgesellschaft mbH
Case C-355/96 [1998] ETMR 539 ....1.36, 3.14, 9.64
Sirena Srl v Eda Srl Case 40/70 [1971] ECR 69 ....14.118, 14.120
SA Société LTJ Diffusion v SA Sadas Case C-291/00, unreported judgment of 20 March 2003 ...1.03,
10.10
Terrapin v Terranova Case 119/75 [1976] ECR 1039 ....6.36
Toshiba Europe GmbH v Katun Germany GmbH Case C-112/99 [2002] ETMR 295 ....8.95,
8.116, 8.117, 8.118
United Brands v Commission Case 27/76 [1978] ECR 207 ....10.78
Upjohn v Paranova: see Pharmacia & Upjohn SA v Paranova A/S
Van Doren + Q GmbH v Lifestyle + Sportswear Handelsgesellschaft mbG, Case C-244/00, 8 April
2003 (unreported) 9.45, 9.46
Van Zuylen Freres v HAG AG 1974] ECR 731 ('HAG I') 3.13, 9.92
Verbraucherschutzverein EV v Sektkellerei G. C. Kessler GmbH und Co. Case C-303/97
[1999] ETMR 269 ....18.37, 18.42

Tables of Cases

Windsurfing Chiemsee Produktions- und Vertriebs GmbH v Boots- und Segelzubehör Walter
    Huber and Franz Attenberger Joined Cases C-108 and 109/97 [1999]
    ETMR 585 ....4.67, 4.74, 4.75, 4.78, 4.163, 5.50, 6.19, 8.19, 11.35, 12.14, 20.11
Yves Saint Laurent Parfums SA v Javico International Case C-306/96 [1998] ECR I-1983 ....9.19
Zino Davidoff SA v A & G Imports Ltd; Levi Strauss & Co and Levi Strauss (UK) Ltd v Tesco Stores,
    Tesco plc and Costco Wholesale Ltd Joined Cases C-414/99, C-415/99 and C-416/00
    [2002] ETMR 109 ....1.36, 9.37, 9.41, 9.74

European Union: Court of Justice of the European Communities: Advocate Generals' Opinions
Adidas-Salomon AG and Adidas Benelux BV v Fitnessworld Trading Ltd, Case C-408/01, Opinion of
    10 July 2003 (unreported) (ECJ) 7.51, 7.51A, 10.23, 11.22A, 11.58, 11.61,
                                                                      11.93, 11.95
Ansul BV v Ajax Brandbeveiliging BV: C-40/01, 2 July 2002
Arsenal Football Club plc v Matthew Reed, Case C-206/01 [2002] ETMR 975,
    [2003] RPC 144 ....2.38
Aventis Pharma Deutschland GmbH v Kohlpharma GmbH and another Case C-433/00 [2003]
    ETMR 143, [2003] IP&T 183 ....16.12
Budejovicky Budvar NP v Rudolf Ammersin GmbH, Case C-216/01, 22 May 2003 ....18.40
Campina Melkunie BV v Benelux Merkenbureau Case C-265/00, 31 January 2002 ....4.154
Davidoff & Cie. and Zino Davidoff SA v Gofkid Ltd Case C-292/00 [2002] ETMR 1219,
    [2003] FSR 50 ....12.27
General Motors Corp v Yplon SA Case C-375/97 [1999] All ER 865; [1999] ETMR 950 (ECJ);
    [1999] ETMR 120 (Advocate General's Opinion) 11.33, 11.38, 11.44, 11.92,
                                                         12.27, 12.38, 12.53, 12.67, 12.69
Gerolsteiner Brunnen GmbH & Co. v Putsch GmbH, Case C-100/02, 10 July 2003
    (unreported) (ECJ Opinion of AG Stix-Hackl) 8.19
Koninklijke KPN Nederland NV v Benelux Trade Marks Office Case C-363/99, 31 January 2002
    (POSTKANTOOR) 4.140
Libertel Groep BV v Benelux-Merkenbureau, Case C-104/01 [2003] ETMR 508
Linde AG, Winward Industries Inc. and Rado Uhren AG, 24 October 2002, Joined Cases C-53/01
    to C-55/01 [2003] ETMR 354 ....5.82
OHIM v Wm Wrigley Jr Company, Case C-191/01 P, 10 April 2003 ....4.75, 4.77, 4.129,
                                                                               4.139, 4.141
R. v Secretary of State for Health, ex. P. British American Tobacco (Investments) Ltd and Imperial
    Tobacco Ltd, supported by Japan Tobacco Inc. and JT International SA, Case C-491/01
    noted in [2002] ETMR 1244 ....15.02
Sebago Inc. and Ancienne Maison Dubois et Fils SA v GB-UNIC SA, Case C-173/98,
    [1999] ETMR 467
Shield Mark BV v Kist, trading as Memex, Case C-283/01 [2003] ETMR 822 ....5.134, 5.136
SA Société LTJ Diffusion v SA Sadas Case C-291/00 [2002] ETMR 441, [2003] FSR 1 ....10.18
Van Doren + Q GmbH v Lifestyle + Sportswear Handelsgesellschaft mbG, Case C-244/00 [2003]
    ETMR 561 (AG), [2003] ETMR 922 (ECJ) 9.45, 9.46

European Union: Court of First Instance of the European Communities
A. Menarini—Industrie Farmaceutiche Riunite SRL (European Federation of Pharmaceutical
    Industries and Associations, intervening) v Commission Case T-179/00 [2002]
    ETMR 1131 ....16.28
Alcon Inc v OHIM, Dr Robert Winzer Pharma GmbH intervening, Case T-237/01, 5 March 2003
    (unreported) 4.174, 5.38, 6.22, 6.41
Axion SA and Christian Belce v Office for Harmonisation in the Internal Market, Joined Cases
    T-324/01 and T-110/02, 30 April 2003 (unreported) 5.144A
Bank für Arbeit und Wirtschaft v OHIM (EASYBANK) Case T-87/00 [2001] ECR II-1259,
    [2001] ETMR 761, [2001] IP&T 1142 ....4.117, 4.138
BioID v OHIM, Case T-91/01, [2003] ETMR 766 ....4.62, 5.30, 5.41

B. Cases by jurisdiction

BVBA: see Kruidvat
Community Concepts AG v OHIM Case T-360/99 [2001] ETMR 176 ....4.117
DaimlerChrysler AG v OHIM Case T-356/00 [2002] IP&T 815, [2003] ETMR 778
    (CARCARD) 5.149
DaimlerChrysler Corp v OHIM, Case T-128/01, 6 March 2003 (unreported) 4.109
Dart Industries Inc. v OHIM, Case T-360/00 [2003] ETMR 406, [2003] IP&T 203 ....4.78,
    4.87, 4.100, 4.110
DKV Deutsche Krankenversicherung AG v OHIM (EuroHealth) Case T-359/99 [2001]
    ECR II-1645, [2001] ETMR 919, [2001] IP&T 1149 ....5.53
Dr Karl Thomae GmbH, supported by the European Federation of Pharmaceutical Industries and
    Associations (EFPIA) v Commission of the European Communities, supported by the
    Council of the European Union, Case T-123/00, Court Of First Instance (Fifth Chamber),
    10 December 2002 (unreported) 16.06
Durferrit GmbH v OHIM, Kolene Corp Intervening, Case T-224/01, 9 April 2003 ....4.34,
    10.89, 13.03
Ellos AB v OHIM Case T-219/00 [2003] IP&T 384 ....4.134
Erpo Möbelwerk GmbH v OHIM Case T-138/00 [2002] ETMR 430 ....4.113, 4.132
Eurocool Logistik GmbH v OHIM Case T-34/00 [2003] ETMR 51 ....5.53
Fédération Nationale d'Agriculture Biologique des Régions de France (FNAB), Syndicat Européen
    des Transformateurs et Distributeurs de Produits de l'Agriculture Biologique (SETRAB)
    and Est Distribution Biogram Sarl v Council of the European Union, Case T-268/99,
    11 July 2000 ....4.45
Ford Motor Company v OHIM Case T-91/99 [2000] ETMR 554, [2000]
    IP&T 502 ....4.95, 4.177
Glaverbel v OHIM Case T-36/01 [2003] ETMR 425 ....5.79
Goulbourn v OHIM, Redcats SA intervening, Case T-174/01, 12 March 2003 ....13.51
Harbinger Corp v OHIM Case T-345/99 [2001] ETMR 11, [2001] IP&T 1496 ....4.20
Henkel KGaA v OHIM Case T-30/00 [2002] ETMR 278 (bicoloured rectangular detergent
    tablet) 4.166, 5.126
Hershey Foods Corp v OHIM, Case T-198/00, [2003] ETMR 795 ....10.53
Institut Für Lernsysteme GmbH v OHIM, Case T-388/00, 23 October 2002 ....10.74, 10.140
Kabushiki Kaisha Fernandes v OHIM, Case T-39/01, 12 December 2002 ....13.30
Kruidvat v Commission of the European Communities Case T-87/92 [1997] ETMR 395 ...9.61, 9.69
KWS Saat AG v OHIM, Case T-173/00 [2003] ETMR 288, [2003] IP&T 14 ....4.108, 5.126
Mag Instrument Inc. v OHIM Case T-88/00 [2002] ETMR 665 ....5.95
Matratzen v OHIM Case T-6/01 [2003] ETMR 392 ....4.95, 4.144, 6.35, 6.36, 10.62
Menarini: see A. Menarini
Messe München GmbH v OHIM Case T-32/00 [2001] ETMR 135, [2001] IP&T 298 ....5.41
Mitsubishi HiTec Paper Bielefeld v OHIM Case T-331/99 [2001] ETMR 614, [2001]
    IP&T 459 ....4.63
Mystery Drinks GmbH v OHIM, Karlsberg Brauerei KG Weber Intervening, Case T-99/01,
    Court of First Instance, 15 January 2003 (unreported) 10.29, 10.114
Oberhauser v OHIM, Case T-104/01, [2003] IP&T 279, [2003] ETMR 739 ....10.32
Procter & Gamble Company v OHIM Case T-117/00 [2002] ETMR 174 (bicoloured tablet) 4.79,
    5.126, 5.133
Procter & Gamble Company v OHIM Case T-122/99 [2000] ETMR 580 (shaped soap) 5.87, 5.96
Procter & Gamble Company v OHIM Case T-63/01, [2003] ETMR 549 (shaped soap) 5.96
Procter & Gamble Company's application Case T-122/99 [2000] ETMR 580 (shaped soap)
Rewe Zentral AG v OHIM Case T-79/00 [2002] ETMR 1109 ....4.61, 4.131, 13.31
Robert Bosch GmbH v OHIM, Joined Cases T-79/01 And T-86/01, 20 November 2002
    (unreported) 4.100
SAT.1 SattellitenFernsehen GmbH v OHIM Case T-323/00 [2002] IP&T 928, [2003] ETMR
    635 ....4.101
Streamserve Inc v OHIM, Case T-106/00 [2003] ETMR 751 ....4.04

Sunrider v OHIM (VITALITE) Case T-24/00 [2001] E.C.R. II-449, [2001] ETMR 605,
 [2001] IP&T 452 .... 4.115
Sykes Enterprises Inc v OHIM, Case T-130/01 [2003] IP&T 213, [2003] ETMR 731 .... 5.75
Taurus-Film v OHIM (Cine Action) Case T-135/99 [2001] ECR II-379, [2001] ETMR 594,
 [2001] IP&T 436 .... 4.111
Travelex Global and Financial Services Ltd (formerly Thomas Cook Group Ltd) and
 Interpayment Services Ltd v Commission, Case T-195/00, Court of First Instance,
 10 April 2003 .... 8.11, 10.105
Unilever plc v OHIM Case T-194/01, 5 March 2003 (unreported) 2.29, 5.80
Viking-Umwelttechnik GmbH v OHIM, Case T-316/00 [2003] ETMR 196, [2003]
 IP&T 25 .... 4.102, 5.111, 5.124, 5.131
Wm. Wrigley Jr. Company's application Case T-193/99 [2001] ETMR 623
 (DOUBLEMINT) 4.96, 4.117
Zapf Creation AG v OHIM Case T-140/00 [2002] ETMR 128 .... 4.113, 4.122, 4.133

Finland
Aaro Forsman OY's application; opposition of Gilvaria OY [2000] ETMR 142 .... 5.24
Adidas-Salomon AG's application, Case 2000:119, Finnish Supreme Court 14.98
Askey Computer Corp's application; opposition of Nokia Telecommunications OY [2000]
 ETMR 214 .... 10.73, 10.118
Homer v Homer's Bar Maunlua OY and Homer's Bar Pihlajanmäki OY
 [1998] ETMR 591 .... 5.68
L'Oréal's application [2000] ETMR 10 .... 5.68
Philip Morris Products Inc's application; opposition of R. J. Reynolds Tobacco Company [1997]
 ETMR 511 .... 4.48
Salamander AG v Industria de Calcados Kissol Ltda, Too Vitl and Centra Anstalt [1998]
 ETMR 94 .... 7.21
Salmi-Leather Oy v Oy Fidan Ltd [1997] EIPR D174-175

France
Aimo-Boot v Fabre [1999] ETMR 55 (Tribunal de Grande Instance de Paris) 4.99
AOM Minerve SA v INPI and another noted in [2001] ETMR 1209 .... 7.12, 10.14
Association Greenpeace France v SA Société Esso [2003] ETMR 441, reversed 26 February 2003
 [2003] ETMR 867(Cour d'appel de Paris) 8.61, 21.39
SA Ateliers Réunis Caddie v Sarl Société Nouvelle de Presse et de Communication (SNPC) [1999]
 ETMR 45 .... 6.25, 8.78
Atlan v INPI and SA Promodès [2001] ETMR 88 .... 10.15
SA Bardinet v S.C.P. Ego-Fruits (S.C.P. Belat-Desprat intervening) [2002] ETMR 1043 .... 4.174,
 6.27, 6.29, 8.79
Bertucci v McDonald's Corp and others [1999] ETMR 742 .... 10.139
Bouchard Pere & Fils v Pascal Bouchard, Cour de Cassation, 2 July 2002 .... 7.12
Burroughs Inc. and another v Picha, Valiza Films and others [1978] EIPR European Digest,
 December, p. iv 8.68
Sarl Cargo Communication v La Cité des Sciences et de l'Industrie [1999] ETMR 545 .... 4.111
Casaubon and Vingt et Unième Siècle v 21st Century Film France [1999]
 ETMR 787 .... 5.21, 10.52
SA Caviar Anzali v L'Institut National de La Propriété Industrielle, Sté Brugis (third party) [2000]
 ETMR 513 .... 10.90
Sté Chanel v SA Citycom [2000] ETMR 1068 .... 17.53
Chambre Syndicale Nationale de la Confiserie v Optos-Opus Sarl, (2003) 762 PIBD III-216 ..... 4.39
Christian Dior Couture v Fashion TV Paris and others [2001] ETMR 126 .... 8.65
Société Corsetel v INPI and France Telecom [2001] ETMR 930 .... 10.64
Comité Interprofessionel du Vin de Champagne v SA Parfums Caron, (1999) 685 PIBD,
 III-442 .... 18.34

B. Cases by jurisdiction

Cuisine de la Mer Cuisimer SA v Maumenee, SA Meralim and Rambour [2000] ETMR 880 . . . .10.27, 10.45, 10.73
Danone: see Gervais Danone
Esso Société Anonyme Française SA v Association Greenpeace France and Société Internet.Fr [2003] ETMR 441 . . . . .8.61, 8.68, 14.39, 17.68
Sté Fabrication et d'Outillage de la Brie (SFOB) v Sté Notter GmbH, Cour d'appel de Paris, 13 March 2002 (unreported) 17.69
Sté Felix the Cat Productions Inc. v Sté Polygram [1999] ETMR 370 . . . . .10.43, 10.55
Sté Gervais Danone v Société Le Riseau Voltaire, Société Gandhi, Valentin Lacambre [2003] ETMR 321 . . . . .8.61, 14.39, 17.24, 21.39
Groupement d'Achat des Centres Leclerc v Comité National Olympique et Sportif Français and others [2001] ETMR 367 . . . . .12.35
SA GPT v Sté Cartier France [1998] ETMR 382 . . . . .4.47
Haci Keles v Sté Megafonte and Evelyne Sitbon [1997] ETMR 515 . . . . .10.101
Hilton International Co. and another v Raclet SA noted in [2001] ETMR 1113 . . . . .11.81
Sté Hugo Boss v Dernières Nouvelles d'Alsace and others [1998] ETMR 197 . . . . . .8.74, 11.94, 14.39
Iliad SA v Cédric A. Trbunal de Grande Instance de Paris, 7 January 2003 . . . . .14.46
Interpol: see Organisation Internationale de Police Criminelle Interpol
SA Jean Lempereur v SA Jifi-Madison [1999] ETMR 1005 . . . . .13.13
Jean Patou SA v Sté Zag Zeitschriftn Verlag A.G. and another [1999] ETMR 157 . . . . .13.64, 14.38
Khris, Taïg v INPI, ex parte Loius Vuitton Malletier [2001] ETMR 194 . . . . .16.55
Laboratoire Garnier & Cie v Sté Copar [1998] ETMR 114; [2000] ETMR 1124 . . . . .8.29
Lancôme Parfums Beauté & Cie Snc v Jacques Bogart SA (2003) 761 PIBD III-187 . . . . .10.70
Sarl Le Book Editions v Sté EPC Edition Presse Communication and another [1999] ETMR 554 . . . . .7.36, 10.142
Levi Strauss & Co. and Levi Strauss Continental v Parkway Ltd [2000] ETMR 977 . . . . .9.72
SA Lindt & Sprüngli v Sté Chocometz [1999] ETMR 315 . . . . .8.72, 8.75
Lyon v SA Rhums Martiniquais Saint-James [1999] ETMR 188 . . . . .10.55, 10.61
Mega Press and Sumo Editions v Pressimage and Guidicelli [2000] ETMR 403 . . . . .8.83
Neurone Tech v Neurones and de Chammard [1999] ETMR 611 . . . . .4.70
Odyssée Interactive v L'Ile des Médias, Tribunal de Grande Instance de Grenoble, 2 December 2002 . . . . .14.09
Optos-Opus Sarl v SA Haribo Ricqlès Zan SA and others [1999] ETMR 362 . . . . .4.39, 5.22
Organisation Internationale de Police Criminelle Interpol v Sté Alexandre William Setruck [1998] ETMR 664
SA: look up next word of name
SA Papeterie Hamelin v Wiggins Teape Ltd [2000] ETMR 1047 . . . . .14.30
SA Société LTJ Diffusion v Société SA Sadas Vertbaudet [2001] ETMR 76 . . . . .10.10
SA Société des Participations du Commissariat à l'Energie Atomique (CEA) v Greenpeace France et al, Tribunal de Grande Instance de Paris, 2 August 2002, affirmed by the Cour d'appel de Paris [2003] ETMR 870 . . . . .8.61, 8.68
Sarl: look up next word of name
Société Prime TV v Top Tele, Cour de Cassation (Chambre Commerciale), 26 March 2002 . . . . .4.104
SNC Prisma Presse v SA Europe 1 Telecompagnie [1998] ETMR 515 .10.101
Sté Prisma Presse and Sté Gruner und Jahr Communication GmbH v SA Editions Economica [1999] ETMR 549 . . . . .4.105
Sté Recife v Sté Recife [2001] ETMR 182 . . . . .13.37
Société Reed Expositions France (Formerly Groupe Miller Freeman) v Société Tigest Sarl [2003] ECDR 206 . . . . .8.31, 8.62, 14.87
Société Roullet Fransac Sarl v v Secret Catalogue Inc. [2001] ETMR 1187 . . . . .4.39
Sarl RWS Translations Ltd v Getten and Sté Translations [1999] ETMR 258 . . . . .4.70
Saint-Tropez v Valais and another [1999] ETMR 310 . . . . .4.38

Skis Rossignol SA and another v SA Head Tyroli Sports & HTM Sport SpA [1999] ETMR 450 . . 14.60
Société: look up next word of name
Sté: look up next word of name
Sarl Succès de Paris v SA Parfums Van Cleef et Arpels [1999] ETMR 869 . . . . .10.15
Sarl Sygroup and SA DCM v Société Sylab Ypsis and Jean Lagadec [2001] ETMR 1275 . . . . .7.24
Visa International (U.S.) v Editions Jibena [1998] ETMR 580 . . . . .13.50
Volkswagen AG SA v Société Renault SA, Tribunal de Grande Instance de Paris, 23 September 1991,
    PIBD 22 October 1991 . . . . .8.120
Vranken SA v Champagne H. Germain et Fils SA [1998] ETMR 390 . . . . .8.45
West v Nicolas Feuillatte SA and Yvon Mau SA, Cour d'appel de Reims 13 November 2002 . . . . . .6.28
Sarl Wolke Inks & Printers GmbH v SA Imaje, Cour d'appel de Paris, 19 October 2001
    (unreported) 6.44, 8.27
Yves Saint Laurent Parfums SA v Institut National des Appellations d'Origine [1994]
    ECC 385 . . . . .11.29

Germany
ABSOLUT trade mark [2001] ETMR 21 . . . . .4.59
Absperrpoller trade mark application [1997] ETMR 176 . . . . .5.108
'Alles Wird Teurer' [1999] ETMR 49 . . . . .8.67
Boehringer Ingelheim Pharma KG v Eurim-Pharm Arzneimittel GmbH [2003] ETMR 491 . . . .14.16,
    14.99
BONUS trade mark application [1997] ETMR 413 . . . . .4.81
BMW GRUR 1986, 759 . . . . .8.67
Callaway Golf Company v Big Bertha Srl WTLR, 20 June 2003 (Bundesgerichtshof,
    Germany) 10.88
Camel Tours (1988) 19 IIC 695 . . . . .11.64
CANNON trade mark application [1998] ETMR 77 . . . . .10.80
Car Wheel Rim trade mark application [1998] ETMR 584 . . . . .5.108
'Champagner Bekommen, Sekt Bezahlen' [2002] ETMR 1091 . . . . .8.104, 18.38
CLASSE E , BGH, GRUR 2001, 242, 244 . . . . .13.90
Cola Test (1987) GRUR 49 . . . . .8.95
Compare! (1999) GRUR Int 453 . . . . .8.136
DIMPLE (1985) 17 GRUR 529 . . . . .11.29, 11.60-11.64, 11.94
Disparagement of Trade Marks 1, GRUR 1994, 808 (MARS) 8.67
Disparagement of Trade Marks 2, GRUR 1995, 57 (NIVEA) 8.67
'Dyed Jeans' [1997] ETMR 530 . . . . .9.56
EQUI 2000, BGH, GRUR 2000, 1032, 1034 . . . . .13.90
ERGOPANEL trade mark application [1997] ETMR 495 . . . . .4.71
Estée Lauder Cosmetics and others v Fragrance Counter Inc. and Excite Inc. [2000] ETMR
    843 . . . . .17.29, 17.70
FOR YOU trade mark application [2001] ETMR 28 . . . . .4.137
FTOS [1999] ETMR 338 . . . . .18.55
Füllkörper trade mark application [1997] ETMR 431 . . . . .4.12, 5.88
GENESCAN trade mark [2002] 329 . . . . .4.69, 4.149
Gorgonzola/Cambozola [1999] ETMR 135 . . . . .18.33
Iris v Urus GRUR Int 1966, 457 . . . . .14.86
K trade mark [2001] ETMR 1181 . . . . .4.67, 5.32
Les Editions Albert René v Hauser (2003) WTLR 17 April 2003 . . . . .10.68
Likoerflasche trade mark [2002] ETMR 456 . . . . .5.103, 5.115
Liqueur Bottle: see Likoerflasche
MARS (1995) 26 IIC 282, I ZR 79/92 . . . . .11.76
McDonald's Corp and McDonald's Deutschland Inc v Rahmer [2000] ETMR 91 . . . . .12.40
NeutralRed trade mark [1998] ETMR 277 . . . . .13.90
Objective loss calculation, Bundesgerichtshof, I ZR 16/93, 2 February 1995 . . . . .14.93

B. Cases by jurisdiction

Odol, 25 Juristiche Wochenschrift 502, XXV Markenschutz und Wettbewerb 265 (1925)
Ohio Art Company and Bandai GmbH Toys and Entertainment v CreCon Spiel U.
    Hobbyartikel GmbH [2000] ETMR 756 ....3.51, 10.137
OMEPRAZOK Trade Mark [2003] ETMR 662 ....13.111, 16.05
'Partner With The Best' trade mark application [1998] ETMR 679 ....4.53, 5.73
Praktiker Bau- und HeimwerkemÄrkte AG, reference by the Bundespatentgericht to the European
    Court of Justice, 15 October 2002 ....16.45
Queen's Club trade mark application [1997] ETMR 345 ....10.84
QUICK (1959) GRUR 182 ....11.65
Schutzverband Gegen Unwesen in der Wirtschaft eV v Warsteiner Brauerei Haus Bramer GmbH
    & Co. KG, [2002] EIPR N-110 ....18.39
SMARTWEB trade mark application [2003] ETMR 272 ....4.144, 16.49
Stephanskreuz trade mark application [1997] ETMR 182 ....10.124
Tax Free trade mark application [1998] ETMR 193 ....4.69, 8.16
Three Stripes trade mark [2002] ETMR 553 ....10.154
Treatment of overheads in profit calculations [2002] ECDR 289 ....14.93
Vita Sulfal GRUR Int 1961, 354 ....14.86
Sarl Wolke Inks & Printers GmbH v SA Imaje [2003] ETMR 849
Yellow/Black trade mark application [1999] noted in ETMR 677 ....5.131
Yellow/Green trade mark application [2002] WRP 450
YES trade mark [1998] ETMR 386; [2000] ETMR 883 ....4.83
ZDF v Karl-May-Verlag, 5 December 2002, Bundesgerichtshof 5.72, 16.69

Greece
Bravo Industry of Coffees SA (also Trading AS Bravo SA) v Fiat Auto SpA [1997] ETMR 167 ....11.47
Guaber Srl v Greece [1999] ETMR 879 ....16.56
Slim International and Antineas Graikou v Delta Protypos Milk Industry [2000] ETMR 409 ...10.12,
    10.33, 14.66
Zaras, re [2003] ECC 34 ....17.23

Guatemala
PepsiCo Inc v Productos Industriales, Comerciales y Agrícolas, Sociedad Anonima, Case 128-97,
    19 May 1998 (noted in (2001) 91 TMR 407) 10.37

Hungary
CAFFREY's application; opposition of CAFRE [2002] EntLR N-87 (Hungarian Supreme Court) Pfk. IV
    25.022/1999 ....10.139
Manpower Inc v Manpower Temporar Personal GmbH (2003) 16 April 2003 ....13.63
MONTAZS trade mark noted at [2001] ETMR 275 ....8.42

India
ICC (Development) International v Philips, 31 January 2003 (High Court, Delhi) 8.64, 16.72

Indonesia
Reemtsma Cigarettenfabriken GmbH v NV Sumatra Tobacco Trading Company (2003) WTLR 22
    April 2003 ....13.58

Iran
High Lights (newsletter of Law Offices of Dr Ali Laghaee & Associates Inc), vol. 3, January 2003,
    p. 1 ....5.115
Johnson & Johnson v Bandhaye Pezeshki Co., (noted in Raysan email circular, 3 March 2003) ...10.72
Montres Rolex SA v PT Permona (Case 951/80), Court of Appeal 10.115

Ireland
American Home Products Corp's application [2001] ETMR 536 ....4.138

APHRODISIA trade mark [1977] FSR 133 ....4.36
Bord Telecom Eireann plc's application [2001] ETMR 790 ....4.115
Chanelle Pharmaceuticals Mfg. Ltd v Chanel Ltd [2003] ETMR 64 ....10.68
Dairygold Co-operative Society Ltd's application [2001] ETMR 1279 (the 'white meat'
   applications) 3.50
Dairygold Co-operative Society Ltd's application; opposition of Austin Nichols & Co. Inc [2002]
   ETMR 1084 (ORANGO/ORANGINA) 10.118
KIKU trade mark [1978] FSR 246 ....4.144
Master Foods Ltd's application [2001] ETMR 667 ....5.73
Memory (Ireland) Ltd v Telex Computers (Ireland) Ltd, High Court, [1978] EIPR European
   Digest, December, p. v 10.135
Montex Holdings Ltd v Controller [2000] ETMR 658 ....13.18
Mothercare Ltd's application [1968] IR 359 ....4.139
Procter & Gamble Company's application [2000] ETMR 703 (shaped soap: Ireland) 5.95, 5.97
SmithKline Beecham plc and others v Antigen Pharmaceuticals Ltd [1999] ETMR 512 ....14.51
Symonds Cider & English Wine Co. Ltd v Showerings (Ireland) Ltd [1997] ETMR 238 ....14.63
United Biscuits Ltd v Irish Biscuits Ltd [1971] IR 16 ....10.123

Israel
Magnetics v Diskcopy, Tel Aviv District Court 2001, CF 751/00 ....17.19
Taam Teva (1988) Tivoli Ltd v Ambrosia Superb Ltd (2003) WTLR 15 May 2003 ....10.71

Italy
Al Gatto Nero Srl v Le Chat Noir [1997] ETMR 371 ....10.51
Aquatherm GmbH v Wavin SpA [2002] EIPR N-33 ....5.123
Azienda Agragia Perda Rubia v Cantina Sociale Ogliastria noted in [2001] ETMR 1114 ....14.38
Barilla Alimentares SpA v Danis Srl and others [1996] ETMR 43 ....10.65
Barilla Alimentares SpA v Danis Srl and others, noted at [2003] ETMR N-4 ....14.22
Benckiser N.V. and Benckiser Italia SpA v Henkel SpA and others [1999] ETMR 614 ....14.61, 14.95
BEVETE COCA COLA Court of Milan, 10 March 1980, Giur. Ann. Dir Ind. 80, 271 ....13.126
Carpoint SpA v Microsoft Corp [2000] ETMR 802 ....14.13
Centro Botanico Srl, Angelo Naj Oleari and Gruppo Cartorama SpA v Modafil di A. Toniolo &
   C. Sas [2003] ETMR 500 ....5.64, 14.80
Consorzio per la Promozione dello Speck v Christanell, Handle Tyrol and Lidl Italia Srl, noted in
   [1998] ETMR 537 ....14.17, 18.10
Data Professionals Srl v Mercantile Sistemi Srl [1998] ETMR 670 ....10.93
Farmaceutici Dott. Ciccarelli v Aboca di Mercati Valentino SaS, noted at [2003] EIPR N-72 ...14.117
Ferrari SpA v Power Horse and others [1997] ETMR 84 ....14.32, 14.39
Gua Giù SNC v FC Internazionale Milano SpA, noted at [2003] EIPR N-73 ....7.50
Honda Italia Industriale SpA v Kama Italia Import and Export Srl WTLR, 12 May 2003 ....5.82
Inditex SA v Compagna Mercantile SRL [2002] ETMR 9 ....17.05
Kaysersberg SA and another v Scott Paper and others [1997] ETMR 188 ....13.35
La Chemise Lacoste SA and SIDAS SpA v Centro Tessile Srl [1997] ETMR 520, Milan CA 2.28
Levi Spa v Iniziative Srl [2003] ETMR N-3 ....14.56
Milan AC SpA and Juventus FC SpA v Topps Italia Srl [1999] ETMR 182 ....7.44
Pilsen Urquell v Industrie Poretti SpA [1998] ETMR 168 ....18.46
Playboy Enterprises Inc v Giannattasio (2003) WTLR 30 May 2003 ....10.129, 17.10
Ty Nant Spring Water Ltd v Lemon & Co. Srl [1999] ETMR 969 ....14.26
Videogruppo SpA v Agenzia GP Srl [2002] ETMR 1003 ....13.88

Jamaica
McDonald's Corp v McDonald's Corp Ltd & Vincent Chang [1997] FSR 760 ....12.41, 14.64

Japan
Einstein, re, Trade Mark [2001] EIPR N-136 ....16.62

B. Cases by jurisdiction

Esprit International v Commissioner of the Japanese Patent Office Heisei (gyo-ke) 105, 31 January
2001 .... 16.42

Latvia
Cartier International BV v Hammer Diamonds A/S noted in [2002] ETMR] 1041 .... 10.60
Intel Corp v Distilleerijen Erven Lucas Bols BV noted in [2001] ETMR 1300 .... 8.58
Tria Robit Agency v Jason (2003) WTLR 23 April 2003 .... 4.172

Malaysia
Sony Computer Entertainment Inc v Lee, WTLR 8 April 2003 .... 14.46

Mauritius
Sprints Ltd v Comptroller of Customs (Mauritius) and another [2000] IP&T 735 .... 15.02

Monaco
Pfizer Inc. v Monaco Télématique en Abrégé MC TEL [2001] ETMR 169 .... 12.46

National Arbitration Forum
Davidoff & Cie SA v Muriel Case FA 0211000129124 (2003) WTLR 4 April 2003 .... 17.18

Netherlands
Bio-Claire International Ltd v Benelux trade marks Office [1998] ETMR 251 .... 4.156
Boehringer Ingelheim Pharma KG v GTO Expeditie BV and others, Court of The Hague,
19 February 2003 .... 14.24
Braun Aktiengesellschaft v Elbeka Electro BV [1998] ETMR 259 .... 14.23, 14.100
Bravilor Bonamat BV v Boumann Hotelbenodigdhenden BV (District Court, Amsterdam),
10 August 2000; (2002) 92 TMR 273
Campina Melkunie BV v Unilever NV and Iglo-Ola BV IER 32 (1998); (2000) 90 TMR 252
Du Pont de Nemours (E.I.) and Company v AMA VOF Antoon Michielsen Automobiles
(trading as Protech Nederland Teflon Lakbescherming) and others [2001]
ETMR 777 .... 6.41, 8.82
Edgar Rice Burroughs Inc v Beukenoord BV and others [2001] ETMR 1300 (CA, Amsterdam) ..6.38,
16.68
ESA (European Space Agency) v ETOS BV, Haarlem District Court, [2003] ETMR 655 .... 5.23
Glenn Miller Productions Inc. and another v Stichting Bill Bakers Big Band Corp [1999]
ETMR 247 .... 8.44
Hermans Groep BV v Gillette Nederland BV and The Gillette Company Inc. [2002]
ETMR 150 .... 8.25
Hij Mannenmode BV v Nienhaus & Lotz GmbH [1999] ETMR 730 .... 4.137, 10.153, 13.13
Kabushiki Kaisha Yakult Honsha and others v Danone Nederland BV and others [1998]
ETMR 465 .... 5.103
Le Lido SA v Nationale Stichting tot Exploitatie van Casinospelen in Nederland and another
[1997] ETMR 537 .... 13.40
Lego v Oku Hobby Speelgoed BV [1999] EIPR N83
Luijckx BV v ECC [2000] ETMR 530 .... 5.98
Marie Claire Album SA v Ipko-Amcor BV (Case 00/2268), District Court, The Hague
(unreported) 12.44
Mars BV v Société des Produits Nestlé SA [1999] ETMR 862 .... 10.43
Mecklermedia Corp v Benelux Trade Mark Office [2001] ETMR 523 .... 5.26
Monster Board BV, The v VNU Business Publications BV [2002] ETMR 1 .... 17.08, 17.67
Parfums Christian Dior SA v Etos BV [2000] ETMR 1057 .... 9.72
Pfizer Inc. and Pfizer BV v Lestre Nederlandse Reformadviefbureau E.N.R.A. [2001]
ETMR 155 .... 6.40, 10.88
Quality Bakers The Hague Court of Appeal, 27 April 2000 .... 12.43

Rowling v Uitgeverji Byblos, District Court of Amsterdam, 3 April 2003 (unreported) 4.31,
                                                                                                           14.66, 16.66
Scapino BV and Ron Suwandi Sports BV v Basic Trademark SA [2001] ETMR 294 .... 9.44
Shield Mark BV v Kist, trading as Memex [2000] ETMR 147 (Hague Court of Appeal);
        [2002] ETMR 2002 (Hoge Raad) 5.134, 5.136
Unilever N.V. v Arctic HR 24 January 2003, Case C01/036 .... 13.117
Unilever N.V. v Raisio Yhtyma OY and others [1999] ETMR 847 .... 10.75, 10.148
?What If! Holdings Ltd v The What If Group BV [2003] ETMR 481 .... 8.49, 14.43
Yakult: see Kabushiki Kaisha Yakult

New Zealand
Mainland Products Ltd v Bonlac Foods [1998] IP Asia LR 289 .... 4.82
McCain Foods (Australia) Pty Ltd v ConAgra Inc, New Zealand Court of Appeal, 6 June 2002
        (unreported) 4.175
Unilever Plc and another v Cussons (New Zealand) Pty. Ltd [1998] RPC 369 .... 13.66

Nigeria
Eli Lilly & Co. v Salenab Nigeria Ltd, (FHC/LCS/534/99), Federal High Court, noted in WTLR,
        1 April 2003 .... 13.72

Northern Ireland
BP Amoco plc v John Kelly Ltd, [2001] IP&T 787; noted in [2001] ETMR 1021 .... 5.127

Norway
Jo-Bolaget Fruktprodukter HB v State Ministry of Industry and Commerce [2002]
        ETMR 161 .... 4.106

Office for Harmonisation in the Internal Market: Boards of Appeal
ABN Amro Holding N.V.'s application Case R 190/1999-3 [2001] ETMR 90 .... 4.57, 5.17
Adolf Ahler AG's application Case R 91/1998-2, 28 May 1999 (unreported) 5.33
America Online Inc's application Case R 209/2000-3 [2002] ETMR 59 .... 4.31, 4.165
Antoni and Alison's application Case R 4/97-2 [1998] ETMR 460 .... 5.101, 5.105
A/S Arovit Petfood's application; opposition of Chivas Brothers Ltd, Case R 165/2002-1,
        26 March 2003 .... 11.80
Black & Decker Corp's application Case R 99/1999-1 [1999] ETMR 845 (MULTI 2 'N 1) 4.111
British Petroleum Company plc's application Cases R 55/1998-2 and R 60/1998-2 [1999]
        ETMR 282 .... 5.104
Buy.Com Inc's application Case R 638/2000-4 [2002] ETMR 540 .... 4.166, 5.26, 17.05
Cabot Safety Intermediate Corp's application Case R 381/2000-1 [2001] ETMR 949 .... 5.115
Canon Kabushiki Kaisha's application Case R 182/1999-1 [1999] ETMR 845 (WebRecord) 4.115
Caterham Car Sales & Coachworks Ltd's application Case R 63/1999-3 [2000] ETMR 14 .... 5.40
Century 21 Real Estate Corp's application Case R 135/1998-2 [1999] ETMR 781 .... 5.21
Chemfinder Cambridgesoft Corp's application Case R 211/1998-2 [2000] ETMR 250 .... 4.118
Choay SA v Boehringer Ingelheim International GmbH Case R 273/1999-1 [2001]
        ETMR 693 .... 10.56, 16.32
Christian Science Board of Directors of the First Church of Christ, Scientist, Case R 801/1999-1,
        21 May 2002 (unreported)
Clinique Laboratories Inc's application Case R 73/1998-2 [1999] ETMR 750 .... 4.111, 5.74
CompAir Ltd v Naber + Co KG, Case R 590/1999-2, OHIM OJ 2/2003, 341 .... 13.34
Corning InCorp's application Case R 449/1999-2 [2001] ETMR 933 .... 5.05
Cosmedent Inc's application Case R 29/1998-3 [1998] ETMR 658 .... 4.157
Dann and Backer v Société Provençale d'Achat et de Gestion (SPAG), Case R 1072/2000-2,
        [2003] ETMR 888 OHIM Second Board of Appeal 10.71
Daishowa Seiki Co. Ltd's application Case R 991/2000-3 [2002] ETMR 403 .... 4.85

B. Cases by jurisdiction

De Boer Stalinrichtingen BV's application. Case R 175/2000-4 [2001] ETMR 899 ....5.06
DUPLO/DUPLO Case R 802/1999-1, 5 June 2000 (unreported) 11.47
Echodent AB's application Case R 773/2001-2 [2002] ETMR 1240 ....4.115
Ferrero oHG mbH v Annie Cornelia Beekenkamp, Case R 214/2000-4, 4 December 2002
  (unreported) 11.41, 11.47, 12.58
Ferrero oHG mbH v Jordi Tarrida Llopart, Case R 186/2001-1 [2003] ETMR 188 ......11.44, 12.58
Fertin A/S's application Case R 382/1999-1 [2000] ETMR 652 ....4.114
Fieldturf Inc's application Case R 462/2001-1, 15 May 2002 (unreported) 5.73
Ford Motor Company's application Case R 433/1999-1 [2000] ETMR 679 (TDdi) 5.39
Société France Cartes v Naipes Heraclio Fournier SA Case R 766/2000-2 [2002]
  ETMR 1119 ....5.89
Fuji Photo Film Co. Ltd's application Case R 4/1998-2 [1998] ETMR 343 (IX) 5.34
Fuji Photo Film Co. Ltd's application Case R 44/1998-3 [1999] ETMR 505 (SUPREME) 4.84
Giacomelli Sport SpA's application Case R 46/1998-2[2000] ETMR 277 ....16.44
Global Asset Management Ltd's application Case R 426/1999-2 noted in [2001] ETMR 131 ....4.171
Gödecke AG v Teva Pharmaceutical Industries Ltd 15 May 2000 (2001) 32 IC 326 (OHIM Board
  of Appeal) 16.34
Harcourt Brace & Co's application Case R 130/1999-1 [2000] ETMR 382 (IDEAL) 4.82
Harvest Technologies LLC's application Case R 33/1998-2 [1999] ETMR 503 ....4.133
Herbalife International Inc's application; opposition of Haka Kunz GmbH Case B 52037
  [1999] ETMR 882 ....10.69
Hollywood SAS. v Souza Cruz SA Case R 283/1999-3 [2002] ETMR 705 ....11.10, 11.14,
  11.26, 11.50, 11.53, 11.55, 11.58, 11.77, 12.51, 12.69
IBP Industrial Products Ltd's application, Case R 736/1999-2, 27 July 2001, OHIM Journal
  12/2002, p. 2299 ....5.53
Icart SA's application; opposition of Beiersdorf A.G. Case B 1794 [2000] ETMR 180 ....10.121
Interdigital Communications Corp's application Case R 50/98-3 [1999] ETMR 758 ....5.78
International Business Machine Corp's application R 10/1998-2 [1998] ETMR 643 ....10.11
International Paper Company's application Case R 868/200-2 [2003] ETMR 92 ....5.54
Laboratorios Menarini SA v Takeda Chemical Industries Ltd Case R 222/1999-2 [2001]
  ETMR 703 ....10.91
Landré GmbH v International Paper Company Case R 39/2000-1 [2001] ETMR 794 ....10.111
Last Minute Network Ltd's application Case R 1068/2000-2 [2002] ETMR 534 ....4.170
Leroy Merlin Participations (S.A) v K-2 Corp Case R 66/2001-4 [2003] ETMR 113 ....5.67
Lidl Stiftung & Co. KG v Heinz Iberica, S,A, Case R 232/200-4 [2003] ETMR 312 ....10.137
Lidl Stiftung & Co. K.G. v The Savoy Hotel Case R 729/1999-2 [2001] ETMR 1284 ....10.139
Lombard Risk Systems Ltd's application Case R 4/1999-2 [2000] ETMR 1055 ....4.65
Long John Silver's Inc's application; opposition of Swedish Match Sverige A.B. Case 458/2000
  [2001] ETMR 120 ....10.101, 16.67
M&R Marketing Systems Inc's application Case R 1167/2000-1 [2002] ETMR 317 ....4.82
Marco-Chemie Eugen Martin KG Chemische Fabrik v Aldemar AG, Case R 644/2000-4, OHIM
  OJ 2/2003, 375 ....13.28
Marks & Spencer plc's application Case R 95/1998-3 [2000] ETMR 168 ....4.136
Matsushita Electric Works' application Case R 332/1999-1 [2000] ETMR 962 ....4.111, 4.123,
  4.144
Medical Research Industries Inc.'s application Case R 639/1999-2, 23 May 2001 (unreported) 4.36
Medtronic Inc's application Case R 51/1998-1 [1999] ETMR 504 ....4.85
Microsoft Corp's application Case R 26/1998-3 [1999] ETMR 386 (NETMEETING) ....
  4.117, 4.133
Milliken & Company's application R 66/1998-1 [1999] ETMR 575 (COMFORT PLUS) 4.139
Myles Ltd's application Case R 711/1999-3, [2003] ETMR 718 ....3.27, 5.117, 5.119
National Car Rental Systems, Inc's application, Case R194/2000-3, OHIM OJ 1/2003, 67 .....5.125
Nationsbanc Montgomery Securities LLC's application Case R 77/1999-2 [2000]
  ETMR 245 ....5.25

No Ordinary Designer Label Ltd v Comercial Fenicia de Exportación, S.L. [2002] ETMR
   527 ....10.152
Northern Foods Grocery Group Ltd's application; opposition by Horace M. Ostwald [2002] ETMR
   516 ....10.44, 10.46, 10.140
Notetry Ltd's application Case R 78/1998-1 [1999] ETMR 435 ....5.105
Optimum Healthcare Ltd's application [2003] ETMR 628 ....4.117
Orange Personal Communications Services Ltd's application Case R 7/97-3 [1998]
   ETMR 337 ....5.123
Orangex C.A. v Juan José Llombart Gavalda Case R 662/2001-1 [2003] ETMR 302 ....10.57
Organic Essential Inc's application Case R 146/2001-4, 22 May 2002 (unreported) 4.143
Penny Makinson's application Case R 68/1998-3 [1999] ETMR 234 ....4.158
Philip Morris Products SA's application Case R 687/2000-2 [2002] ETMR 403 ....4.149
Pilkington plc's application Case R 81/1999-3 [2000] ETMR 1130 (K GLASS) 6.37
Poulsen Roser ApS' application Case R 746/2001-1 [2003] ETMR 112 ....4.95
Procter & Gamble Company's application Case R 116/1998-3 [1999] ETMR 664
   (COMPLETE) 4.13, 4.84
Procter & Gamble Company's application Case R 110/1998-3 [2000] ETMR 174
   (PERFECT BROW) 5.148
Procter & Gamble Company's application Case R 74/1998-3 [1999] ETMR 776
   (shaped soap) 5.96
Procter & Gamble Company's application Case R 85/1998-2 [1999] ETMR 559
   (SWEDISH FORMULA) 4.158
Qlicksmart Pty Ltd's application Case R 1/1998-2 [1999] ETMR 190 ....5.138
Rosenbluth International Inc's application Case R 190/1998-2 [2000] ETMR 934 ....4.121
Succession Picasso v DaimlerChrysler Aktiengesellschaft Case R 0247/2001-3 [2002]
   ETMR 953 ....16.60
Telefon & Buch Verlags GmbH v OHIM joined cases T-357 and 358/99 [2001] ETMR 1004,
   [2001] IP&T 1158 ....5.07
Tilia International's application Case R 57/1998-1 [1999] ETMR 191 ....4.155
Tong Hwei Enterprise Co. Ltd's application Case R 374/2000-1 [2001] ETMR 961 ....4.86
Ty Nant Spring Water Ltd's application Case R 5/1999-3 [1999] ETMR 974 ....4.177
USA Detergents Inc's application Case R 20/97-1 [1998] ETMR 562 ....4.84
Valigeria Roncato SpA's application Case R 164/1998-1 [2000] ETMR 46 ....5.98
Vekaria v Kalatizadeh Case R 410/2001-1, noted in [2003] ETMR 111 ....10.15
Vennootschap onder Firma Senta Aromatic Marketing's application, Case R 156/1998-2
   [1999] ETMR 429 ....4.26, 5.117
Visa International Service Association's application Case R 46/1999-1 [2000]
   ETMR 263 ....4.111, 7.73
Warman International Ltd's application Case R 82 /1999 [2000] ETMR 1159 ....5.98
Wm. Wrigley Jr. Company's application [1999] ETMR 214 ....4.67, 5.126
Wrigley: see Wm. Wrigley

Office for Harmonisation in the Internal Market: Cancellation Divisions
Beiersdorf AG's trade mark; application for cancellation by L'Oreal Case C000835728/1
   [2001] ETMR 187 ....8.82, 13.35, 13.68
Cahill May Roberts Ltd's application for a declaration of invalidity; Medicine Shoppe International's
   trade mark Case C000172734/1 [2000] ETMR 794 ....13.38
Deutsche Telekom A.G.'s trade mark; Veiga's application for cancellation Case 000267724/1,
   noted in [2000] ETMR 939 ....10.120
Deutscher Teeverband E.V.'s application for cancellation (TEEKAMPAGNE) [2000] ETMR
   546 ....13.35
Din Bank A/S's trade mark; application for declaration of invalidity by Deutche Bank
   Aktiengesellschaft Case 144C 001027374/1, OHIM Cancellation Division,
   1 October 2001 (unreported) 10.120

B. Cases by jurisdiction

Dr Robert Winzer Pharma GmbH's application to cancel a trade mark of Alcon Pharmaceuticals
 Ltd, Case C000090134/1, [2000] ETMR 217 ....5.38, 8.82
Gillette Company's trade mark; application for a declaration of invalidity by Warner-Lambert &
 Company Case 000703579 [2002] ETMR 733 ....5.36, 6.22
Interkrenn Maschinen Vertriebs GmbH's Trade Mark; Application for Declaration of Invalidity by
 Horst Detmers [2002] ETMR 312...13.119
Josef Rupp Gesellschaft mbH's trade mark; application for a declaration of invalidity by the Danish
 Dairy Board Case C000576066/1 [2002] ETMR 395..............................5.99
Lancôme Parfums et Beauté & Cie's trade mark; application for revocation by Laboratoires Décléor
 [2001] ETMR 981 ....13.109, 13.116
Multiple Marketing Ltd's trade mark; Surene Pty's application for cancellation Case C000479899/1
 noted in [2001] ETMR 131 ....13.94
Piromalli's trade mark; application for cancellation by Greci Industria Alimentare SpA, Case 133C
 000372920/1, 13 February 2002 (unreported) 4.59
Senso di Donna's trade mark; Kim Carl Meller's application for a declaration of invalidity Case
 C000616979/1 [2001] ETMR 38 ....10.42, 13.125
Trillium Digital Systems Inc.'s trade mark; Harte-Hanks Data Technologies' application for a
 declaration of invalidity Case C000053447/1 noted in [2000] ETMR 1054 ....13.80,
 13.125, 13.130, 13.132, 13.135
Volkswagen Leasing GmbH's trade mark; International Fleet Management N.V.'s application for
 cancellation Case C000525824/1 [2001] ETMR 1170 ....13.39

Office for Harmonisation in the Internal Market: Opposition Divisions
ABB Sadelmi SpA's application; opposition of the European Patents Organisation, Case 3552/2002
 of 28 November 2002 (unreported) 10.54
Belmont Olympic SA's application; opposition of the Comité International Olympique [2000]
 ETMR 919 ....12.32
Brackenbrough's application; opposition of Säntis Management AG Case 1517/2000 [2001]
 ETMR 412 ....10.48
British-American Tobacco (Holdings) Ltd's application; opposition of Fabriques de Tabac Réunis
 SA Case B598 [1999] ETMR 32 ....10.139
Campomar S.L's application; opposition of Nike International Ltd Case 102/1999 [2000] ETMR
 50 ....11.71
Cobra Beer Ltd's application; opposition of Alpabob AG Case 811/1999 [2000] ETMR 638 ....10.84
DaimlerChrysler Aktiengesellschaft's application; opposition of Succession Picasso 22/2001 [2002]
 ETMR 346 ....16.60
Dr Martens International Trading GmbH's application; opposition of Lloyd Schuhfabrik Meyer & Co.
 GmbH Case 165/2000 [2000] ETMR 1151 ....10.58, 10.69
Ducks UnLtd's application; opposition of Dr Rehfeld Handelsgesellschaft mbH Case 849/1999
 [2000] ETMR 820 ....10.85
Einstein Stadtcafé Verwaltungs- und Betriebsgesellschaft mbH's application; opposition of the
 Hebrew University of Jerusalem Case 506/2000 [2000] ETMR 952 ....16.62
Fromex SA's application; opposition of K. H. de Jong's Exporthandel BV Case B 43457 [1999]
 ETMR 989 ....10.45
House of Stitches Pty Ltd's application; opposition of Bellini Warenvertriebsgesellschaft mbH
 Case B 16560 [1999] ETMR 994 ....10.17
Humic SA's application; opposition of Sapec-Agro SA Case B911 [1999] ETMR 26............10.84
Inter Service Srl's application; opposition of Sephora SA, Case B 95804, OHIM Opposition
 Division, 23 February 2003 (unreported) 11.36
Lifesource International Inc.'s application; opposition of Novartis Nutrition A.G. Case 2844/2000
 [2001] ETMR 1227 ....13.23
Linda Jackson Pty Ltd's application; opposition of Jackson International Trading Company Kurt D.
 Brühl Gesellschaft mbH & Co. K.G. Case 520/2000 [2001 ETMR 376 ....5.70
Loewe SA's application; opposition by Logoathletic Inc. Case B 37889 [2000] ETMR 40 ....10.73

Marc Brown's trade mark application; opposition of LTJ Diffusion [2002] ETMR 653 ....10.29, 10.31, 10.39
McCann-Erickson Advertising Ltd's application; opposition of Momentum Integrated Communications Ltd Case 2149/2000 [2001] ETMR 540 ....13.29
Payless Car Rental System Inc's application; opposition of Canary Islands Car SA Case 198/2000 [2000] ETMR 1136 ....13.28
Precision Dynamics Corp's application; opposition of Visa International Service Association Case 3479/2002, 29 November 2002 (unreported) 10.92
Principles Retail Ltd's application' opposition of Manifattura Lane Gaetano Marzotto & Figli SpA Case 355/1999 [2000] ETMR 240 ....10.59
R Cable y Telecommunicationes Galicia SA's application; opposition of Ricoh Company Ltd, Case 3475/2002, 28 November 2002 (unreported) 10.141
Scottish & Newcastle plc's application; opposition of Red Bull GmbH Case 863/2000 [2000] ETMR 1143 ....10.150
Seder's application; opposition of Funk Case 151/1999 [2000] ETMR 685 ....10.64
Stillwater Designs and Audio Inc's application; opposition of Josefina Fernandez de la Fuenta Abellan Case B 7049 [2000] ETMR 35 ....10.73
Verify International N.V.'s application; opposition of Jörg Pohlmann Case 110/2000 [2000] ETMR 716 ....10.64
Volkswagen A.G's application; opposition of FIAT Veicoli Industriali SpA (Iveco SpA) Case 1269/1999 [2000] ETMR 320 ....13.27
Vzao Sojuzplodimport's application; opposition of Latvijas Balzams Case 62/1999 [2000] ETMR 618 ....13.32
Warsteiner Brauerei Gaus GmbH & Co. KG's application; opposition of Brauerei Beck GmbH & Co. Case 57/1998 [1999] ETMR 225 ....10.49, 13.22
Zanella SNC's application; opposition by Zanella Confezioni SpA Case B 42053 [2000] ETMR 69 ....10.97

Pakistan
Magna Ltd v Abdullah Ismail [1998] IP Asia LR 176 ....6.41
Nichols (N. N.) plc v Mehran Bottles (Private) Ltd, noted in (2001) 91 TMR 477 ....14.50

Paraguay
Dolby Laboratories Licensing Corp's application, 11 February 1999 (Paraguayan Trade Mark Office) 5.139

Peru
Mars v Miski, Supreme Court, 13 February 2003, noted in (2003) 4 WIPR 13 ....12.42

Poland
CORVINA trade mark, Polish Patent Office, 18 December 2001 (unreported) 13.99
Dax Cosmetics Zaklady Kosmetyczno-Chemiczne Jacek Majdax I Wojciech Szulc SC's appeal [2001] ETMR 506 ....4.131
Grosz Sp. Z.o.o.'s application, Polish Patent Office, Board of Appeals 29 April 1998 (unreported) 4.57, 5.17
Hola SA's trade mark; application for cancellation by G + J Gruner + Jahr Polska Sp. Z.o.o. & Co. Spolka Komandytowa [2002] ETMR 257 ....10.115
J B Cosmetics SP. ZO. O. Kamienczyk N/Bugiem's trade mark noted in [2000] ETMR 722 ....12.40, 13.98
JAN III SOBIESKI trade mark [1999] ETMR 874 ....16.58
Krzysztof Wozniak 'Rolex' Przedsiebiorstwo Produkcyjno-Handlowo-Uslugowe's application, [2003] ETMR 699
Pliva D.D. Zagreb's application noted in [2000] ETMR 594 ....16.31
Porczynska Marzena Gappol Przedsiebiorstwo Prywatne's trade mark; The Gap Inc's application for cancellation [2001] ETMR 1056 ....13.115

B. Cases by jurisdiction

S-P's trade mark application; application by K.S. to suspend the trade mark registration
    proceedings noted in [1999] ETMR 335 ....13.70
Spolka Akcyjna PPCH's trade mark[2001] ETMR 770 ....13.40
Tajer Firma Handlowa Sciwiarski Tadeusz's trade mark; Multibond Inc.'s application for
    Cancellation [2002] ETMR 491 ....13.86
Tong Yang Confectionery Corp's trade mark; application for cancellation by Lotte Confectionery
    Co. Ltd [2002] ETMR 219 ....6.35

Portugal
Adidas AG's application [1996] ETMR 66 ....10.118
Budejovicky Budvar Narodni Podnik v Anheuser-Busch Inc [2002] ETMR 1182 ....3.08, 18.40
COKE, Colectânea de Jurisprudência, ano XV, tom. IV, p. 119
Indústria e Comércio de Cosméticos Natura A.S's application [2001] ETMR 783 ....12.34, 12.45
Jansen Pharmaceutica N.V. v Patent and trade marks Office [2001] ETMR 663 ....5.104
Les Editions Albert René Sarl v Madaleno WTLR, 23 July 2003 (Court of Golegã) 14.87A
MARLBORO—SCOTCH WHISKY Industrial Property Bulletin 10/1981, p. 1980 (Civil Court 3,
    Lisbon) 12.34

Privy Council
Sprints Ltd v Comptroller of Customs (Mauritius) and another [2000] IP&T 735
Unilever Plc and another v Cussons (New Zealand) Pty. Ltd [1998] RPC 369 ....13.66

Romania
Budejovicky Budvar Narodni Podnik v Anheuser-Busch Inc WTLR, 3 July 2003 (Examination
    Committee of the Romanian State Office for Inventions and Trade Marks) 10.33
Elite Industries Ltd v Graziella Import Export Srl, Case 1409/2002, (2003) WTLR
    17 June 2003 ....9.56

Russian Federation
Eastman Kodak Company Corp v Grundul and the Russian Scientific and Research Institute for the
    Development of Public Networks [2002] ETMR 776 ....9.35, 17.08

Scotland (see also England and Wales)
Allied Domecq Spirits & Wine Ltd v Murray McDavid Ltd [1998] ETMR 61 ....8.21, 14.65
Beecham Group plc v Munro Wholesale Medical Supplies Ltd [2001] ETMR 318 ....14.51,
    14.63, 16.25
Bonnier Media Ltd v Greg Lloyd Smith and Kestrel Trading Corp [2002] ETMR 1050
    Court of Session 9.09, 14.13
Bravado Merchandising Services Ltd v Mainstream Publishing (Edinburgh) Ltd [1996]
    FSR 205 ....7.48, 8.43, 8.86, 16.68
Discovery Communications Inc. v Discovery FM Ltd [2000] ETMR 516 ....14.67
Gleneagles Hotels Ltd v Quillco 100 Ltd and Toni Antioniou, 1 April 2003, Court of Session
    (unreported) 14.71
Jimmy Nicks Property Company Ltd's application [1999] ETMR 445 ....5.08, 5.56
Pebble Beach Company v Lombard Brands Ltd [2003] ETMR 252 ....11.56, 11.63, 14.68
SpeechWorks Ltd v SpeechWorks International Incorporated. [2000] ETMR
    982 ....14.17, 14.69
Teknek Electronics Ltd v KSM International Ltd [1998] ETMR 522 ....8.137-8.139,
    8.157, 14.59
Zino Davidoff SA v M & S Toiletries Ltd [2000] ETMR 622, [2000] IP&T 955 ....14.52
Zino Davidoff SA v M & S Toiletries Ltd (No. 2) [2001] ETMR 112 ....9.45

Singapore
AUVI trade mark [1995] FSR 288 High Court (Singapore) 19.05

South Africa

Bata Ltd v Face Fashions CC [2002] EIPR N-9 .... 10.40
Cowbell AG v ICS Holdings Ltd 2001 (3) SA 941 .... 1.26
Esquire Electronics v Executive Video 1986 (2) 576 AD 7.34
First National Bank of Southern Africa Ltd v Barclays Bank plc (2003) WTLR 1 May 2003 ..... 4.178
McDonalds Corp v Joburgers Drive-Inn Restaurant (Pty) Ltd and Anor & McDonalds Corp v
    Dax Prop CC and Anor [1996] (4) All SA 4 .... 12.65
South African Breweries International (Finance) BV v Laugh It Off Promotions (2003) WTLR
    28 May 2003 .... 8.66, 12.26

South Korea

Burberrys Ltd v EMEC Co Ltd and Textjournal Co Ltd [1998] IP Asia LR 129 .... 9.66
Fuji Film Co Ltd v Noh WLTR, 21 July 2003 .... 9.56
Korea Telecom Co. Ltd's application, Korean Patent Court, 29 August 2002 (INTA Bulletin 57
    (2003) no. 21, p. 4) 4.135, 6.29
Korean Florist Association v Kordes (2003) WTLR 14 March 2003
Sanrio Co. Ltd v Dong-A Pencil Co. Ltd, Seoul High Court, Case 2002Na32648, 27
    November 2002 .... 8.41

Spain

ACUPREL V AQUAPRED, noted in [2003] ETMR 653 .... 10.123
Advernet S.L. v Ozucom S.L. [1999] ETMR 1037 .... 17.15
Bacardi y Compañía SA España v Dimexco SL and Destilerias de l'Urgell SA [2003] ETMR 326 ..9.52
Bandera, re [1999] ETMR 337 .... 13.61
Comercial Iberica de Exclusivas Deportivas SA (Cidesport) v Nike International Ltd and American
    Nike SA [2000] ETMR 189 .... 10.36, 10.61
Nissan Motor Iberica's application [1999] ETMR 338 .... 10.66
Orient Watch Co. Ltd v Rita HB, noted in [2002] EIPR N-94 .... 13.86
Paniberica [2002] EIPR N-8 .... 4.98
REETRUCK trade mark application, noted in [2002] EIPR N-115 .... 10.27
Torres Valls, re, noted in [2002] EIPR N-53 .... 5.62

Sweden

Aventis Pharma Aktiebolag v Paranova Läkemedel Aktiebolag [2001] ETMR 652 .... 16.24
Björnekulla Fruktindustrier Aktiebolag v Procordia Food Aktiebolag [2002] ETMR 464 ...4.95, 6.32,
    12.43
Björnekulla Fruktindustrier Aktiebolag v Procordia Food Aktiebolag, Svea Hovrätt, 14 October
    2002 (unreported, reference to ECJ as Case C-367/02 .... 6.32
BUDGET BILUTHYRNING AB (Svea CA, 27 Nov 1981) 13.96
Fritidsresor AB v Atlas Mediterraneo Svergie AB, Brandnews 1/2003, p. 1 .... 10.100
GOLDEN LIGHTS (RÅ 1984 Ab 122) 13.120
HAMMARBY MARINCENTER trade mark (RÅ 1988 not 296) 13.97
Ide Line Aktiebolag v Philips Electronics NV [1997] ETMR 377 .... 5.91
Institut National des Appellations d'Origine v Handelshuset OPEX AB (Case 99-004),
    WTLR 7 April 2003 .... 18.59
Mitutoyo Corp's application [1999] ETMR 39 .... 11.48
NGK Spark Plug Co. Ltd v Biltema Sweden Aktiebolag [2000] ETMR 507 .... 3.14
Pink Fibreglass, re [2002] EIPR N-39
Red Bull Sweden AB v Energi Trading I Skara Handelsbolag and Energi Trading I Skara AB
    (in bankruptcy) [2002] ETMR 758 .... 14.104
Stokke Fabrikker and another v Playmaster of Sweden AB (Ltd) and another [1998]
    ETMR 395 .... 5.92
System 3R International AB v Erowa AG and Erowa Nordic AB, Stockholm District Court,
    [2003] ETMR 916 .... 8.22, 10.13

B. Cases by jurisdiction

TV4 and TV Spartacus KB v Bröderna Lindströms Forlags AB, noted in Brandnews 2/2003 ......8.65
Volvo Ltd v D.S. Larm Ltd and Dick Edvinsson [2000] ETMR 299 ....7.29, 8.30, 14.31

Switzerland
Anheuser-Busch Inc v Budejovicky Budvar Narodni Podnik [2001] ETMR 74 ....3.08, 18.40
Chanel SA Genève of Geneva and Chanel SA of Glaris v EPA AG [1997] ETMR 352 ....9.57
Denner A.G. v Rivella A.G. noted in [2001] ETMR 826 ....10.131
Mega Bloks Inc v Lego System A/S (Case HG000095/ZO7, Zurich Commercial Court) 5.82
Rytz Cie SA v Rytz Industriebau A.G. [2001] ETMR 363 ....8.50
Volkswagen AG and Audi AG v Garage X noted in [2003] ETMR 225 ....8.30

Thailand
Sari (P.T.) Incofood Corporation v Department of Intellectual Property and others (2003)
    17 WIPR 9 ....4.130
Wellcome Foundation Co. Ltd v Dairy Farm Management Co. Ltd [1998] IP Asia LR 40 ....13.06

Turkey
ALVORADA trade mark [2003] ETMR 623 ....7.28, 13.99
BECOME WHAT YOU ARE trade mark, Republic of Turkey Appellate Court, Eleventh Tribunal,
    [2003] ETMR 879 ....5.74
Davide Campari Milano SpA v Özal/Finkol Giyim Sanayi ve Ticaret Ltd Şti [2002]
    ETMR 856 ....13.98
Reemtsma Cigaretten Fabriken Gesellschaft Mit Beschrankter Haftung v Turkish Patent Institute,
    5th Commercial Court of Ankara, Decision 1998/777-1999/225, 22 April 1999 ....4.12
Société Des Produits Nestlé SA v Turkish Patent Institute, 9th Commercial Court of Ankara,
    Case no. 2000/783, Decision 2001/382, 9 May 2001 ....4.12
Twelve Islands Shipping Company Ltd v Turkish Patent Institute, 11th Civil Chamber of the Supreme
    Court, Decision 2000/3866–2000/4995, 1 June 2000 ....4.12

United States
Alcar Group v Corporate Performance Systems Ltd 109 FSupp 2d 948 (ND Ill 2000) 14.17
AM General Corp v DaimlerChrysler Corp, No. 02-1816 (7th Cir 18 November 2002) 12.40
Aunt Jemima Mills Co. v Rigney & Co., 247 F. 407 (2d Cir 1917), cert. denied, 245 U.S. 672
    (1918) 10.102
AV by Versace Inc v Gianni Versace SpA 126 FSupp 2d 328 (SDNY 2001) 14.17
Avery Dennison Corp. v Sumpton 189 F3d 368, 51 USPQ 2d 1801 (9th Cir 1999) 12.69
Bette Midler v Ford Motor Co 849 F2d 460 (9th Cir 1988) 16.52
Borden Inc v Federal Trade Commission, 674 F2d 498 (6th Cir 1982) 15.32
Boston Professional Hockey Assoc., Inc. v. Dallas Cap & Emblem Mfg., Inc., 510 F2d 1004
    (5th Cir. 1975) 7.64
Bromberg v Carmel Self Service Inc, 198 USPQ 176 (TTAB 1978) 19.14
Brookfield Communications Inc v West Coast Entertainment Corp, 174 F3d 1056 (9th Cir,
    22 April 1999) 10.126
Brother Records Inc. v Jardine 318 F3d 900 (9th Cir. 2003) 8.36, 16.64
Brunswick Corp v British Seagull Ltd, 35 F. 3d 1527, 1532 (CA Fed. 1994) 5.93
Caesar's World Inc v Caesar's Palace.com and others 112 FSupp2d 502 (EDVa 2000) 17.30
Checkpoint Systems Inc. v Check Point Software Technologies Inc, 104 FSupp 2d 427 (DNJ,
    12 July 2000) 10.126
Cline v 1-888-Plumbing Group 146 F Supp 2d 351, 362 (SDNY 2001) 5.29
Continental Graphics Corp, re 52 USPQ 2d 1374 (TTAB 1999) 1.26
Davidoff & Cie SA and another v PLD Interntional Corp 263 F3d 1297 (11 Cir 2001) 9.57
Deere & Company v MTD Products Inc, 41 F3d 39 (2d Cir 1994) 8.175
Dial-A-Mattress Operating Corp, re 240 F3d 1341 (Fed Cir 2001) 5.29
Diversified Marketing Inc. v Estée Lauder Inc. 705 F Supp 128 (SDNY 1988) 8.95

lxxvii

E.I. du Pont de Nemours & Co., In re 476 F2d 1357, 177 USPQ 563 (CCPA 1973) 10.125
Emergency One v American Fire Eagle Engine Company 332 F3d 264, 67 USPQ 2d 1124
 (4th Cir NC 2003) 14.35A
Enterprise Rent-a-Car Co v Advantage Rent-a-Car Inc 330 F3d 1333, 66 USPQ 2d 1811
 (Fed Cir 2003)
Enterprise Rent-a-Car Co v Advantage Rent-a-Car Inc WTLR 18 July 2003 (CAFC) 12.42
Estée Lauder Inc. v Fragrance Counter 1999 US Dist. LEXIS 14825 (SDNY 1999) 17.29
Figueroa v United States (argued before the US Court of Federal Claims, 14 November 2002) 2.08
GlobalSantaFe Group v Globalsantafe.com (2003) WTLR 15 April 2003 .17.30
Glow Industries Inc v Jennifer Lopez, Coty Inc & Does 1-20, 252 FSupp2d 962
 (CD Cal 2002) 10.130
Harjo v Pro Football Inc, 50 USPQ 2d 1705 (TTAB 1999) 19.14
Honda Giken KKK and another v H-D Michigan Inc 43 USPQ 2d 1526 (TTAB 1997) 5.136
Horphag Research Ltd v Pellegrini (t/a Healthdiscovery.com), 328 F3d 1108 (9th Cir. 2003) 17.72
Horphag Research Ltd. v Pellegrini, 337 F3d 1036 (9th Cir Cal 2003)
Idaho Potato Commission v M&M Produce Farm and Sales 335 F3d 130, 67 USPQ 2d 1348
 (2d Cir NY 2003) 15.41
In Over Our Heads Inc, in re, 16 USPQ 2d 1653 (TTAB 1990) 19.15
Interactive Products Corp v a2z Mobile Office Solutions Inc, 326 F3d 687 (6th Circ. 2003) 17.12
International Bancorp LLC and others v Société des Bains et Mer du Cercle des Etrangers à Monaco,
 No. 02-1364, 3 December 2002 (EDVa 2002) 14.11
International Flavors & Fragrances Inc, Re 51 USPQ 2d 1513 (Fed Cir 1999) 3.27
International Order of Job's Daughters v. Lindeburg and Co., 633 F2d 912; 208 USPQ 718
 (9th Cir. 1980) 7.64
Johnson (S.C.) & Son Inc v The Clorox Company, 241 F3d 232 (2d Cir, 2001) 8.174
Kimpton Hotel & Restaurant Group Inc., re 55 USPQ 2d 1154 (TTAB 2000) 5.49
KP Permanent Make-Up Inc v Lasting Impression I, Inc, No. 01-56055 (9th Cir 30 Apr. 2003) . . .3.45
Majestic Distilling Co., In re, 315 F3d 1311 (Fed. Cir. 2003) 10.106
Marshak v Green 746 F2d 927, 929 (2d Cir 1984) 15.19
Mattel Inc. v MCA Records Inc., 296 F3d 894 (9th Cir. 2000); cert. denied 123
 SupCt 993 . . . . .8.66, 8.71, 21.01
Medinol Ltd v NeuroVasx Inc., (2003) WTLR 12 June 2003 (TTAB) 13.99
Midler v. Ford Motor Co., 849 F.2d 460 (9th Cir 1988)
Montblanc-Simplo GmbH v Staples Inc (unreported, D. Mass. 3 May 2001) 9.57
Moseley et al., dba Victor's Little Secret v V Secret Catalogue Inc 537 US 418, 123 SupCt 1115
 (2003) 11.21, 11.22, 11.46, 12.53, 21.01
Nabisco v P. F. Brands Inc, 191 F3d 208 (2d Cir 1999) 7.12, 12.52
Narada Productions Inc., re 57 USPQ 2d 1801 (TTAB 2001) 5.49
New Kids on the Block v New America Pub. Inc, 971 F2d 302 (9th Cir 1992) 8.13
Nogueras v City of Barcelona (2003) WTLR 9 June 2003 (US Court of Appeals, 4th Cir.) 14.09
Norton Co. v Newage Industries 204 USPQ 382 (EDPA 1979) 8.176
PACCAR Inc v TeleScan Technologies LLC, 319 F3d 243 (6th Cir. 2003) 7.35
Pacific Supply Co-op v. Farmers Union Cent. Exch., Inc., 318 F.2d 894, 908-09 (9th Cir
 1963) 15.13
Parks v LaFace Records No. 99-2495, 12 May 2003 (6th Cir. 2003) 21.01
People for the Ethical Treatment of Animals v Doughney 263 F 3d 359, 60 USPQ 2d 1209
 (4th Cir 2001) 17.06
Pizza Hut Inc v Papa John's International Inc, 27 F3d 489 (5th Cir 2000) 8.174
Playboy Enterprises, Inc v Terri Welles 279 F3d 796 (9th Cir. 2002) 8.36
Polaroid Corp v Polarad Electronics Corp 287 F2d 492 (2d Cir 1961) 10.125
Polyglycoat Corp v Environmental Chemicals Inc. 509 F Supp 36 (SDNY 1980) 8.176
Porous Media Corp. v. Pall Corp., 173 F.3d 1109, 1120-21 (8th Cir 1999) 8.173
Procter & Gamble Company and another v Randy L. Haugen and others, US Court of Appeals 10th
 Cir, 23 August 2000 . . . . .8.173

B. Cases by jurisdiction

Professional Golfers Association v Bankers L & C Co., 514 F2d 665, 671 (5th Cir 1975) 15.38
Qualitex Co. v Jacobson Products Co. 514 US 159 (1995) 1.36, 5.125
Recot Inc v M. C. Becton 56 USPQ 2d 1859 (TTAB 2000) 10.137
Revenue Technologies Corporation, re (2003) WTLR 5 June 2003 (TTAB) 4.102
Retail Services Inc v Freebies Publishing 247 FSupp2d 822 (EDVa 2003) 17.21
Ringling Bros.-Barnum & Bailey Combined Shows, Inc. v Utah Division of Travel Development
    170 F3d 449 (4th Cir 1999) 11.70
Roux Laboratories Inc. v Clairol Inc. 427 F.2d 823 ....5.73
Samara Brothers Inc v Wal-Mart Stores Inc, 165 F3d 120 (2d Cir 1998), 120 SCt 1339 (2000) ...5.11
Seven-Up Bottling Co. v. Seven-Up Co., 561 F.2d 1275, 1279 (8th Cir 1977) 15.13
Sporty's Farm LLC v Sportsman's Market, Inc 202 F3d 489 (2d Cir. 2000); cert. denied 147
    LEd2d 984 (Sup Ct 2000) 17.31
SunAmerica Corp v Sun Life Assurance Co. of Canada, 77 F.3d 1325, 1345 (11th Cir 1996) 12.56
Swatch Group (US) Inc v Movado Corp (2003) WTLR 27 May 2003 ....10.129
Syndicate Sales Inc v Hampshire Paper Corp 192 F3d 633, 52 USPQ 2d 1035 (7th Cir 1999) ...12.69
Taubman Company v Mishkoff 319 F3d 770 (6th Cir. 2003) 8.63
Times Mirror Magazine Inc v Las Vegas Sports News LLC, 212 F3d 157, 167 (3d Cir 2000) 12.52,
    12.69
Two Pesos Inc v Taco Cabana 932 F2d 1113 (CA5 1991), 505 US 76 (1992) 4.114, 5.09
Ty Inc v Perryman 306 F3d 509 (7th Cir. 2002); cert. denied 123 SupCt 1750 (Sup Ct 2003) 8.32,
    17.18

Venezuela
Maizoro SA de CV v Kellogg Company (2003) WTLR 6 May 2003 ....13.48

World Intellectual Property Organization Arbitration and Mediation Center
Caixa d'Estalvis y Pensions de Barcelona v Namezero.com Decision 2001-0360 [2001] ETMR
    1239 ....17.41
Canal+ Image UK Ltd v VanityMail Services Inc. Decision FA0006000094946 [2001] ETMR
    418 ....17.46
Christian Dior Couture SA v Liage International Inc. Decision 2000-0098 [2000] ETMR
    773 ....17.43
CLT-UFA Société Anonyme v This Domain is for Sale and Sean Gajadhar Decision 2000-0801
    [2001] ETMR 446 ....17.47
Diageo plc v John Zuccarini and Cupcake Patrol Decision 2000-0996 [2001] ETMR 466 ......17.38
Legal & General Group plc v Image Plus (2003) 157 Trademark World 17 ....17.37
Leonard Cheshire Foundation v Darke Decision 2000-0131 [2001] ETMR 991 ....17.37, 17.50
Magazijn 'De Bijenkorf' BV v Accelerated Information BV [2002] ETMR 676 ....17.08
Netherlands v Goldnames Inc. Decision 2001-0520 [2001] ETMR 1062 ....17.36
Netherlands v Humlum Decision 2002-0248 [2001] ETMR 1213 ....17.49
Perfetti SpA, Van Melle NV and Van Nelle Nederland BV v MIC [2002] ETMR 52 ....17.16
Philip Morris Inc v Tsypkin (2003) WTLR 7 May 2003 ....17.18
Queen v Virtual Countries Inc., WIPO D 2002-0754, 27 November 2002 ....5.52
Scania C.V. A.B. v Leif Westlye Decision D2000-0169 [2000] ETMR 767 ....17.42
Société des Produits Nestlé SA v Pro Fiducia Treuhand AG [2002] 351 ....12.41, 17.22, 17.48
Unione Calcio Sampdoria SpA v Titan Hancocks Decision 2000-0523 [2000] ETMR 1017 .....17.44
Winterson v Hogarth Decision 200-0235 [2000] ETMR 783 ....17.36

TABLE OF TREATIES AND LEGISLATION

Austria
General Civil Code 17.25
    Art 1302 ....7.58
Trade Mark Law
    Art 54 ....7.60

Benelux
Old Uniform Benelux Trade Mark Law
    Art 13A 10.144
Uniform Benelux Trade Mark Law
    Art 4(6) 13.92
    Art 6(4)(a) 13.117

Denmark
Trade Mark Act
    s 14(5) 4.51

European Union
EC Treaty
    Art 28 ....4.55, 20.11
    Art 50 ....16.45
    Art 81 (ex Art 85) 9.19, 14.118, 14.119,
              15.55
    Art 81(3) 15.56
    Art 82 (ex Art 86) 9.73, 9.88, 14.120
    Art 85(3) 15.55

Regulations
Certificates of Specific Character for agricultural
    products and foodstuffs, Reg 2082/
    92 ....18.23
    Art 16 ....18.29
Community Trade Mark (CTM) Regulation, Reg
    40/94 ....3.09, 4.52, 4.59, 4.75,
    5.88, 6.24, 7.26, 7.38, 8.50, 8.108, 8.109,
    8.123, 9.29, 9.37, 9.56, 9.85,10.144,
    10.145, 11.23, 11.24, 12.09,13.24,
    13.51, 13.83, 13.128, 14.105, 15.34,
    16.11, 16.15, 16.18, 16.42,16.50, 8.09
    Reg 4 ....14.111
    Art 4 ....4.05, 4.24, 4.28, 5.57
    Art 4(2)(d) 12.25
    Art 5 ....7.10
    Art 5(2) 12.25
    Art 7(1)(c) ...4.73, 4.78, 4.128, 4.129, 5.14,
              5.83

    Art 7(1)(d) 4.58, 4.72
    Art 7(1)(e) 5.83
    Art 7(1)(e)(i) 5.86
    Art 7(1)(e)(ii) 5.90
    Art 7(1)(f) 4.32
    Art 7(3) 8.167
    Art 8(1) 10.07, 10.143
    Art 8(1)(b) 8.108, 11.82, 16.47
    Art 8(2)(c) 12.26
    Art 8(3) 13.79
    Art 8(4) 8.47, 13.29
    Art 8(5) 11.09, 11.50, 11.82
    Art 9(1) 7.09, 7.20, 7.55, 8.74, 10.143, 17.09
    Art 9(1)(a) 10.07
    Art 9(1)(b) 8.108, 10.07, 11.82, 16.47
    Art 9(1)(c) 11.09, 11.25, 11.50, 11.82, 12.26,
       12.53
    Art 9(2) 7.16
    Art 10 ....8.80
    Art 12 ....4.149, 4.46, 8.09, 8.13, 8.38, 9.31
    Art 12(1) 4.69
    Art 12(2)d) 15.24
    Art 13 ....9.27, 9.28, 16.26
    Art 14(2) 8.81
    Art 15(1) 13.12, 15.48
    Art 15(2) 13.61
    Art 16(1) 15.17
    Art 17(1) 15.23
    Art 17(2) 15.08, 15.17
    Art 17(3) 15.17
    Art 17(4) 15.24
    Art 18 ....15.17
    Art 22 ....15.17, 15.17
    Art 22(3) 15.30
    Art 34 ....3.48
    Art 41 ....13.03
    Art 42 ....13.03
    Art 42(1) 13.09, 13.14
    Art 50 ....12.14
    Art 50(1)(a) 13.46
    Arts 50(1)(b), (c) 13.47
    Art 51 ....3.51, 13.14
    Art 51(a) 13.132
    Art 51(1)(b) 13.78, 13.133
    Art 51(3) 13.132
    Art 52 ....12.26

Table of Treaties and Legislation

Community Trade Mark (CTM) Regulation, Reg 40/94 (*cont.*):
- Art 52(1) 13.14
- Art 52(2) 4.50, 13.14
- Art 53(1) 8.91, 13.78
- Art 53(2) 8.91, 13.78
- Art 55(1)(a), (b) 13.14
- Art 91 ....3.48
- Art 92 ....14.19
- Art 95 ....14.20
- Art 96 ....3.51
- Art 96(6) 3.51
- Art 97(1) 3.48
- Art 97(2) 3.48, 8.47, 14.19
- Art 97(3) 3.48
- Art 98 ....14.19
- Art 99 ....14.19, 14.50, 14.66
- Art 105(1) 14.13
- Art 105(2) 14.13
- Art 105(3) 14.13
- Art 105(4) 14.13
- Art 107(2) 13.78
- Art 108 ....3.48

Counterfeit or pirated goods (Intellectual Property Rights), Council Reg 3295/94 ....14.25
- Art 8(1) 14.98

Franchise Agreements, Reg 4087/88 ....15.55

Jurisdiction and the Recognition and Enforcement of Judgments in civil and commercial matters (Brussels Regulation), Council Reg 44/2001 ....14.10
- Art 22(4) 14.10

Medicinal Products: authorization and supervision (European Agency for the Evaluation of Medicinal Products), Council Reg 2309/93 ....16.12

Organic Production of agricultural production, Council Reg 1804//1999 ....4.45
- Art 2 ....4.45

Organic Production of agricultural production, Council Reg 2092/91 ....4.45

Protection of Geographical Indications, Council Reg 2081/92 .....18.22, 18.23, 18.32, 18.36, 18.38, 18.39, 18.53, 18.59
- Art 2 ....18.09
- Art 2(2) 18.22
- Art 2(3) 18.22
- Art 3 ....18.28
- Art 3(1) 18.09
- Art 4 ....18.09
- Art 5 ....18.09
- Art 7 ....18.09
- Art 12 ....18.29
- Art 13 ....18.09
- Art 13(1) 18.30
- Art 13(1)(d) 18.09
- Art 13(3) 18.09
- Art 14(1) 18.34
- Art 14(2) 18.34

Protection of Geographical Indications, Implementing Regulations, Commission Reg 2037/93 ....18.22

Protection of Names of Wines and Grape Musts, Reg 2392/89 as amended by Reg 2603/95 ....18.36, 18.37, 18.45

Protection of names of sparkling and aerated wines, Reg 2333/92 [1992] OJ L231/9 ..18.36, 18.37, 18.42, 18.43
- Art 13(2) 18.41

Vertical Agreements and concerted practices, Reg 2790/99 ....15.56

Directives

E-Commerce Directive, Dir 2000/31
- Art 12 ....14.39, 17.60

Liability for Defective Products Council Dir 1985/374
- Art 3 ....2.37

Misleading and Comparative Advertising, Dir 84/450, as amended by Dir 97/55 ....8.102, 8.111, 8.118, 8.120, 8.136
- Recitals 13-15 ....8.110
- Recital 13 ....8.110
- Recital 14 ....8.110
- Recital 15 ....8.110, 8.113
- Art 2 ....8.103
- Art 2(2a) 8.117
- Art 3a 8.105, 8.119
- Art 3a(1)(c) 8.117
- Art 3a(b) 8.106
- Art 3a(c) 8.107
- Art 3a(d) 8.108
- Art 3a(e) 8.109
- Art 3a(g) 8.109
- Art 4 ....8.112
- Art 5 ....8.114
- Art 7 ....8.119

Trade Mark Harmonization, Council Dir 89/104 ....3.10, 4.19, 4.52, 4.59, 4.75, 5.88, 7.18, 7.26, 7.38, 8.50, 8.106, 8.108, 8.109, 8.110, 8.111, 8.123, 9.25, 9.28, 9.29, 9.37, 9.56, 9.85, 10.144, 10.145, 11.23, 11.24, 11.30, 12.09, 12.26, 12.29, 13.51, 13.73, 13.79, 13.83, 13.87, 13.90, 13.128, 14.08,

Trade Mark Harmonization, Council Dir
  89/104 (cont.):
    14.105, 15.15, 15.34, 16.11, 16.15,
    16.18, 16.42, 16.50
  Preamble 12.25
  Recital 10 ....7.42
  Recital 11 ....13.77
  Art 2 ....4.05, 4.24, 4.31, 5.57, 16.45
  Art 3 ....13.144, 18.58
  Art 3(1)(c) 4.73, 4.128, 5.14, 5.45,
                                5.83, 18.58
  Art 3(1)(d) 4.58, 4.72
  Art 3(1)(e) 5.83, 5.86, 5.90
  Art 3(1)(f) 4.32
  Art 3(1)(g) 4.41
  Art 3(2)(d) 13.75
  Art 3(3) 4.171, 8.167
  Art 4 ....10.08, 13.144, 18.58
  Art 4(1) 10.07, 10.143
  Art 4(1)(a) 10.19
  Art 4(1)(b) 8.108, 11.82, 11.86, 16.47
  Art 4(2)(d) 12.28
  Art 4(3) 11.82
  Art 4(4)(a) 11.09, 11.50, 12.27
  Art 4(4)(g) 13.76, 13.93, 13.120
  Art 5 ....7.25, 8.160
  Art 5(1) 7.07, 7.20, 7.55, 8.74, 8.125,
                          10.07, 10.143, 17.09
  Art 5(1)(a) 7.51A, 10.18, 18.30
  Art 5(1)(b) 8.108, 11.82, 11.86, 12.69,
                                16.47, 18.30
  Art 5(2) 7.07, 7.51, 7.51A, 8.55, 11.08,
          11.25, 11.37, 11.50, 11.82, 11.85,
          11.89, 11.90, 11.93, 12.27, 12.53,
                                12.69, 18.09
  Art 5(3) 7.16, 7.45
  Art 5(5) 6.24, 8.162
  Art 6 ....8.38
  Art 6(1) 4.69, 4.149, 5.46, 8.09, 8.13,
                          8.38, 8.123, 8.161, 9.34
  Art 6(2) 8.47
  Art 7 .....9.02, 9.26, 9.28, 9.31, 9.32, 9.33,
                                9.34, 16.26
  Art 7(1) 9.28
  Art 8 ....15.15
  Art 8(2) 15.37
  Art 9 ....8.91
  Art 9(1) 13.77
  Art 10(2) 13.61
  Art 12 ....18.58
  Art 12(1) 8.166, 13.12, 13.46
  Art 12(2)(a) 6.32, 13.47
  Art 12(2)(b) 13.47
  Art 15 ....18.58
  Art 15(1) 8.166

Processing of Personal Data/Privacy Protection,
  Dir 2002/58
  Art 13(2) 10.78
Dir 76/768 (deleted) 9.57

Finland
Law against Transactions Contrary to Good
  Business Practice 8.111

France
Civil Procedural Code
  Art 552 ....14.103
  Art 700 ....14.77
  Art 1382 ....14.103
Intellectual Property Code
  Art L713-5 ....12.35
  Art 716-5 ....15.28
  Art L716-7 ....14.55
Loi No 2001-741, 23 Aug 2001 ....8.120
Decree 88-1206 Emmenthal cheese 18.48

Germany
Civil Procedural Code 14.54
Markengesetz
  s 50(1)(4) 13.78
  s 55(2)(2) 4.51
Partnership Law 25 July 194 (BGBl I 1994,
  1774) 4.53
Trade Marks Act
  s 5 ....18.55
  s 15 ....18.55

International Treaties and Agreements
Andean Pact
  Decision 344, Art 83(d) 12.38
Bangui Agreement (OAPI) 3.09
Banjul Protocol on Marks (ARIPO) 3.09
Benelux Treaty on Uniform Trade Mark Law
  1962 (Additional Protocols 1983,
  1992) 3.09
Berne Convention for the Protection of Literary
  and Artistic Works
  Art 6bis 14.90
Brussels Convention 1968 ....14.1015.54
Cartagena Agreement (Andean Pact states) ..3.09
Convention on International Exhibitions, Paris,
  22 Nov 1928 ....12.63
EFTA Agreement on the establishment of a
  surveillance authority and a Court of
  Justice
  Art 34 ....3.14
European Convention on Human Rights
  Art 6 ....9.48, 9.49, 9.74
  Art 8 ....4.56, 16.54

Table of Treaties and Legislation

European Convention on Human Rights (*cont.*):
    Art 10 . . . . .8.60, 8.62, 9.74, 9.82
    First Protocol, Art 1 . . . . .9.74, 9.82
European Patent Convention
    Art 53 . . . . .4.40
Lisbon Agreement for the protection of
    Appelations of Origin and their
    International Registration 1958, as
    amended 1979 . . . . .18.09, 18.11
Madrid Agreement on the International
    Registration of Marks, 1891
    (WIPO) 3.06, 3.25, 9.22,
                        13.42-13.45, 15.03
    Art 6(2) 13.44
    Art 6(3) 13.44
Madrid Protocol, 1989 (WIPO) 1.38, 3.06,
          3.25, 9.22, 13.42, 13.45, 15.03
Nice Agreement concerning the International
    Classification of Goods and Services for
    the Purposes of Registration of marks
    1952, as amended . .3.30, 13.138, 18.09
Paris Convention on the Protection of Industrial
    Property (1883), as amended to
    1979 . . . . . .3.06, 3.19, 4.13, 4.15, 8.50,
         11.30, 12.08, 12.09, 12.11, 12.25,
                14.105, 14.107, 15.34
    Art 1(2) .16.39, 18.09
    Art 2 . . . . .9.23
    Art 5A(2) 15.31
    Art 5A(5) 15.31
    Art 5B 15.31
    Art 6(1) 4.09
    Art 6*bis* 4.39, 7.06, 9.20, 12.05, 12.07,
        12.11, 12.25, 12.28, 12.30, 12.35, 12.44,
                           13.77, 17.43
    Art 6*bis*(1) 12.25
    Art 6*bis*(3) 7.06, 11.07
    Art 6*ter* 5.23
    Arts 6*ter*(1)(a), (b) 4.08
    Art 6*ter*(1)(c) 5.23
    Art 6*quater* 15.21
    Art 6(2) 4.09
    Art 6*quinquies* .4.10
    Art 6*quinquies*B 4.11
    Art 6*sexies* 16.39
    Art 7 1 . . . . .6.39
    Art 7*bis* 18.56
    Art 8 . . . . .4.14
    Art 10*bis* 18.19
    Art 10*bis*(2) 8.123
    Art 10*bis*(3) .14.105
    Art 10*ter* 18.09
    Art 28 . . . . .4.12
Stresa Convention .3.08

Trademark Law Treaty 1994 . . . . .3.06, 9.22
TRIPS Agreement: Agreement on Trade Related
    Aspects of Intellectual Property Law,
    1994 . . . . . .1.31, 1.38, 3.06, 3.07, 3.19,
        3.38, 4.06, 4.25, 4.26, 4.50, 5.88, 7.10,
          7.38, 7.55, 8.50, 8.179, 9.97, 11.08,
          11.30, 12.08, 12.09, 14.105, 14.106,
         14.107, 15.03, 15.34, 16.50, 18.38
    Art 2(1) 7.06
    Art 3 . . . . .18.07
    Art 6 . . . . .9.23, 9.24
    Arts 15-21 . . . . .9.23
    Art 15 . . . . .4.04, 4.24, 4.31, 5.57
    Art 15(1) 4.88
    Art 15(3) 13.124, 13.132
    Art 15(4) 16.39
    Art 16 . . . . .7.05, 10.07, 10.143, 12.07
    Art 16(1) 7.14, 7.20, 10.06, 10.19
    Art 16(2) 7.06
    Art 16(3) 11.07, 12.11
    Art 17 . . . . .8.08, 8.15
    Art 19(1) 13.11, 13.59
    Art 21 . . . . .15.14, 15.22, 15.31
    Art 22 . . . . .18.12
    Art 22(1) 18.12
    Art 22(2)(a) 18.15
    Art 22(2)(b) 18.15, 18.19
    Art 23(4) 18.20
    Art 24 . . . . .18.20
    Art 31 . . . . .15.31
    Art 41(1) 14.03
    Art 41(2) 14.03
    Art 41(4) 14.03
    Art 44 . . . . .14.03
    Art 45 . . . . .14.03
    Art 46 .14.03, 14.96
    Art 47 . . . . .14.03
    Art 48(1) 14.106
    Art 50 .14.03, 14.50
    Art 50(6) 14.73, 14.74
    Arts 51-60 . . . . .9.23
Universal Declaration of Human Rights
    Art 12 . . . . .16.54
WIPO Recommendations for the Protection of
    Well-known Marks 12.60-12.66
    Art 1 . . . . .12.66
    Art 2 12.62, 12.63, 12.69
    Arts 2(1)(b)(1), (2), (3), (4), (5),
        (6) 12.69
    Art 2(2)(a) 12.69
    Art 2(2)(b) 12.69
    Art 2(2)(c) 12.69
    Art 2(2)(d) 12.69
    Art 2(3) 12.64

Table of Treaties and Legislation

WIPO Recommendations for the Protection
of Well-known Marks (*cont.*):
    Art 3 .... 12.66
    Art 4 .... 12.66
    Art 5 .... 12.66

Ireland
Civil Liability Act 1961
    s 11(1) 7.59
    s 12(2) 7.59
Trade Marks Act 1996
    s 13(3) 14.08
    s 14(5) 7.18
    s 24 .... 14.103
    s 29(4) 15.09
    s 34(2) 15.30
    s 35(2) 15.28
    s 45(3) 14.08
    s 54(1) 18.56
    s 55(1) 18.56
    s 57(4) 14.111

Italy
Trade Marks Law
    Art 22(2) 13.87, 13.120
    Art 61 .... 14.66

Monaco
Sovereign Decree No 5687 of 29 Oct
    1975 .... 12.30

Portugal
Industrial Property Code
    Art 214(6) 13.78

Spain
Law 32/1988
    Art 11 .... 4.98

Sweden
Trade Mark Law, SOU 1958:10 .... 13.96,
                             13.119, 13.122
SOU 2001: 26 .... 13.123

Turkey
Commercial Code
    Art 21(2) 13.99
Decree-Law on Trade Marks 556
    Ar 61(a)(c) 7.57
    Art 61(e) 7.57

United Kingdom
Anzac (Restriction on Trade Use of Word) Act
    1916 .... 4.17

Competition Act 1998
    s 2 .... 14.118
    s 18 .... 14.120
Contracts (Rights of Third Parties) Act
    1999 .... 9.04
Copyright, Designs and Patents Act 1988
    s 240 .... 15.31
Food Safety Act 1990 .... 2.04
Patents Act 1977
    s 57 .... 15.33
    s 57A 15.33
Registered Designs Act 1949
    s 10 .... 15.31
Trade Marks Act 1938 .... 13.57, 13.128
    s 63(1) 1.14
Trade Marks Act 1963 .... 13.18
Trade Marks Act 1994 .... 16.15
    s 3(6) 13.127, 13.141
    s 5(4)(b) 4.50
    s 9 .... 2.11
    s 9(3) 8.50, 14.08
    ss 10(1)-(3) 8.160
    s 10(4) 7.45
    s 10(5) 7.18
    s 10(6) 8.121, 8.122, 8.123, 8.124,
                      8.125, 8.127, 8.130, 8.139, 8.161,
                      8.162, 8.163
    s 11 .... 8.38
    s 11(2) 8.161
    s 21 .... 14.103
    s 21(1) 14.108, 14.110
    s 21(2) 14.109
    s 25(4) 14.25
    s 25(3) 15.07, 15.25
    s 25(4) 14.07, 15.09
    s 28(4) 15.34
    s 30(2) 15.30
    s 31(1) 15.28
    s 32(3) 13.83, 13.125,
                      13.127
    s 40(3) 2.11, 14.08
    s 43(3) 8.50
    s 47(1) 4.171
    s 49(1) 18.56
    s 50(1) 18.56
    s 52 .... 14.111
    s 56 .... 12.25
    s 72 .... 14.20
    s 92(5) 9.49
Civil Procedure Rules (CPR)
    r 25(1)(f), (g) 14.54
Trade Mark Rules 2000, SI 2000/136
    r 2 .... 3.22

Table of Treaties and Legislation

United States of America
Constitution
    Art 1, s 8 ....3.12
Anticybersquatting Consumer Protection Act
    1999.........................17.27
Federal Trademark Dilution Act 1995, 15 USc,
    s 1127 ....11.17
Lanham Act (15 USC) 12.55, 12.68, 14.17,
                                16.41, 17.21
    s 2(a) 4.32
    s 2(e)(3) 4.44, 5.49
    s 32 ....7.63
    s 43 (s 1125) 6.26, 12.13. 12.49, 12.67, 12.69
    s 43(a) 8.172
    s 43(a)(1) 17.60
    s 43(c)(1) 12.52, 17.60
    ss 43(c)(1)(A), (B), (C), (D), (E), (F), (G),
        (H) 12.69
    s 43(c)(4) 8.13
    s 43(d) 17.27
    s 45 ....12.50
    s 106(3) 6.03
    s 1051(b)(1) 13.125
    s 1125(1)(1)(A) 21.04
    s 1125(a)(1)(B) 8.172
    s 1126(e) 13.125
    s 1127 ....12.11
Patent and Trademark Fee Modernization Act
    2003........................2.08

ABBREVIATIONS

AC	*Appeal Cases* (House of Lords)
AIPLA	American Intellectual Property Law Association
All ER	*All England Reports*
ARIPO	African Regional Industrial Property Organisation
CA	Court of Appeal, England and Wales
CAFC	Court of Appeal for the Federal Circuit
CCPA	Court of Customs and Patent Appeals (United States)
CFI	Court of First Instance [of the European Communities]
CIPA	Chartered Institute of Patent Agents
CL&SR	*Computer Law and Security Report*
CLR	*Commonwealth Law Reports*
CMLR	*Common Market Law Reports*
Colum L Rev	*Columbia Law Review*
CPR	Civil Procedure Rules (England and Wales)
CTM	Community Trade Mark
ECC	*European Commercial Cases*
ECDR	*European Copyright and Design Reports*
ECJ	European Court of Justice (Court of Justice of the European Communities)
ECLR	Electronic Commerce and Law Report (BNA)
ECR	*European Court Reports*
ECR I	European Court Reports (European Court of Justice)
ECR II	European Court Reports (Court of First Instance)
ECTA	European Communities Trade Mark Association
EEA	European Economic Area
EFTA	European Free Trade Association
EIPR	*European Intellectual Property Review*
Ent LR	*Entertainment Law Review*
ETMR	*European Trade Mark Reports*
EWCA	England and Wales Court of Appeal
EWHC	England and Wales High Court
FCAFC	Federal Court of Australia Full Court
Fordham Int Prop, Media and Ent Law Jl	*Fordham Intellectual Property, Media and Entertainment Law Journal*

FSR	*Fleet Street Reports*
GRUR	*Deutsche Vereinigung für gewerblichen Rechtsschutz und Urheberrecht*
GRUR Int	*Deutsche Vereinigung für gewerblichen Rechtsschutz und Urheberrecht* (International Edition)
Harv Law Rev	*Harvard Law Review*
HC	High Court, England and Wales
HL	House of Lords (United Kingdom)
IIC	*International Review of Industrial Property and Copyright Law*
Info TLR	*Information Technology Law Reports*
Ing Cons	*L'Ingénieur-Conseil*
INTA	International Trademark Association
INTA Bull	*INTA Bulletin*
IP&T	*Intellectual Property and Technology Cases*
IPQ	*Intellectual Property Quarterly*
IR	*Irish Reports*
ISP	Internet service provider
ITMA	Institute of Trade Mark Attorneys
JBL	*Journal of Business Law*
JWIP	*Journal of World Intellectual Property*
LCAP	Lord Chancellor's Appointed Person
LES	Licensing Executives Society
MARQUES	Association of European Trade Mark Owners
MIP	*Managing Intellectual Property*
MLR	*Modern Law Review*
OAMI	Spanish acronym for OHIM
OAPI	Organisation Africaine de la Propriété Industrielle (African Industrial Property Organization)
OHIM	Office for Harmonisation in the Internal Market
OHIM OJ	OHIM Official Journal
OSCJ	Ontario Supreme Court of Justice
Paris Convention	Paris Convention for the Protection of Industrial Property
PC	Privy Council
PDO	Protected Designation of Origin
PGI	Protected Geographical Indication
PTMG	Pharmaceutical Trade Marks Group
QBD	Queen's Bench Division (United Kingdom)
RPC	*Reports of Patent Cases*
Texas L Rev	*Texas Law Review*
TGI	Tribunal de Grande Instance (France)
TLD	Top-level domain

Abbreviations

TLR	*Tulane Law Review*
TMR	*Trademark Reporter*
TRIPs	Agreement on Trade-Related Aspects of Intellectual Property Law
TTAB	Trademark Trial Appeal Board (US)
US	*United States Supreme Court Reports*
USPQ	*United States Patent Quarterly*
USPTO	United States Patents and Trademarks Office
WIPO	World Intellectual Property Organization
WIPR	*World Intellectual Property Reporter*
WLR	*Weekly Law Reports* (UK)
WTLR	*World Trademark Law Report*
WTO	World Trade Organization

PART A

INTRODUCING TRADE MARK LAW

1

PETTY MATTERS: ABOUT THIS BOOK

A.	Pedantry and conceptual preoccupation: the true signs of the trade mark expert	1.01
B.	Conventions employed in writing this book	1.06
C.	Important definitions and distinctions	
	(1) Trade marks and service marks	1.09
	(2) Registered and unregistered trade marks	1.10
	(3) Trade marks and 'signs'	1.12
	(4) Trade marks, trade names, business names and company names	1.13
	(5) Trade marks and brands	1.14
	(6) Trade marks and 'house marks'	1.22
D.	A word about jurisdictions	1.25
E.	Case law	
	(1) The hierarchy of nations	1.28
	(2) Cases as precedents	1.32
	(3) Cases as examples	1.33
	(4) Cases as working hypotheses	1.35
	(5) Cases as landmarks	1.36
F.	Trade marks and history	1.38

A. Pedantry and conceptual preoccupation: the true signs of the trade mark expert

Nearly all trade mark enthusiasts are pedants. They are the sort of people who correct you in the course of conversation and remind you that, when you say 'Hoover', you really mean 'vacuum cleaner'. When you ask for a Coke, you surely mean 'a carbonated cola beverage flavoured with vegetable extract'. Your Frisbee is, to them, a 'moulded plastic flying disc' and your coat is kept done up not with Velcro but with 'hook and loop fasteners'. **1.01**

This pedantry highlights the constant tension between legal rules and living language. If the entire Austrian nation calls a personal stereo system a 'walkman', regardless of that word's contrivance as a freshly coined term, then it is indeed a **1.02** common noun, a walkman, and has ceased in Austria to be a trade mark.[1] Other words start their lives as perfectly ordinary words but are captured by traders and elevated to the status of a trade mark, such as APPLE, ORANGE and PENGUIN. Some words start off as trade marks, are mutated by the public and then reclaimed by the trade mark owner: hence MERC, CHEVY and COKE. The constant flow of words from common use to trade mark use and back again enriches both common speech and private pockets.

1.03 True trade mark aficionados also tirelessly patrol a number of fault lines other than that which divides legal property from living language. In our calling we are drawn repeatedly to contemplate issues of verbal and conceptual preoccupation which many of our fellow lawyers, and certainly most of our fellow humans, find inexplicable. One of these issues is our constant need to know what is 'identical' and what is 'similar'. There are many fine disciplines and specializations within the legal world, but only a trade mark lawyer can argue with logic and conviction that the trade mark ARTHUR ET FELICIE is identical to the trade mark ARTHUR.[2] But that is not all. We devise rules to establish whether soft drinks are 'similar' to beer and whether fish-hooks are similar to fishing rods. We rule whether services provided *for* dentists are similar to services provided *by* dentists. In terms of marks and signs themselves we alone hold the key to whether ORANGE XPRESS is similar to ORANGEX or whether the word APPLE is similar to a picture of an apple.

1.04 The reader of any typical book on trade mark law may be perplexed both by the provisions of trade mark law itself and by the way they translate into commercial practices. In terms of commercial competition between businesses, trade mark law is the law of the jungle. It may be obtuse or convoluted. It may be momentarily inconvenient for those whose daily lives are subject to it. But above all it must be obeyed.

1.05 The reader's perplexities as to the nature and effects of trade mark law will not be cured even by clear and unambiguous writing. Lack of clarity of expression should not however exacerbate them. Accordingly I have taken great care to write in terms of simplicity, even at the risk of promoting generalities over precise factual accuracy. For those for whom more legal information is sought, particularly in terms of the law in any specific country and not in the world painted between the covers of this book, refuge will be found in countless other volumes with which this book is not in competition.

---

[1] See *Sony Europe v Time Tron Corp*, June 2002 (unreported) (Austrian Supreme Court).
[2] *SA Société LTJ Diffusion v SA Sadas*, Case C-291/00, judgment of 20 March 2003 (unreported) (ECJ).

B. Conventions employed in writing this book

1.06 In this book I have generally written trade marks in capitals to distinguish them from corporations (initial capitals) and common parts of speech (lower case). Thus APPLE is a trade mark owned by Apple Corp, while an apple a day keeps the doctor away. I have not peppered my prose with clones of the ® symbol since to have done so would have made the text clumsy and vulgar (imagine, for example, a sentence such as 'Come to McDonalds® and enjoy a Big Mac® with Mickey Mouse®, Donald Duck® and all their friends from DisneyWorld®'). Geographical indications have been written with an initial capital (for example, Champagne, Gorgonzola).

1.07 I have used the spelling 'trade mark' in general rather than 'trademark'. 'Trade mark' is normally used in the European Union and in much of the old Commonwealth; 'trademark' is normally used by the World Intellectual Property Organization (WIPO), the World Trade Organization (WTO) and in the United States. Canada, that haven of rugged individuality, uses 'trade-mark'. On the subject of spelling, I have preferred the English spelling of the noun 'licence' to the American 'license', thus enabling it to be readily distinguished from the verb 'to license'.

1.08 Almost throughout the English-speaking world, with the exception of England, the person who sues another in court is called a 'plaintiff'.[3] But in 1999 England was smitten by a wave of law reforms which resulted in the banishing from that jurisdiction of most Latin phrases (thus severing English usage from that of those many continental jurisdictions which persist in using them) as well as the replacement of 'plaintiff' with 'claimant'. Apparently someone thought that people in England might not understand what 'plaintiff' meant, notwithstanding the long-standing popularity of televised American courtroom dramas in which the p-word is ubiquitous. Out of a profound respect for the reforming zeal of those in power who know so much better than we do and who so kindly make these decisions for us, this book will describe plaintiffs as claimants unless the word appears in a quote.

C. Important definitions and distinctions

(1) Trade marks and service marks

1.09 A trade mark is a mark which is used in relation to goods (for example, CROSS for pens, ROLEX for watches), while a service mark is a mark which is used in relation

---

[3] Scotland is an exception, the claimant being termed 'pursuer'.

to services (for example, FINNAIR for air-travel services or AMERICAN EXPRESS for the provision of financial services). Unless the context provides otherwise, use of the term 'trade mark' in this book includes both trade marks and service marks.

(2) Registered and unregistered trade marks

1.10 Many people use the term 'trade mark' to indicate either a legal status (where, following an initial application, a trade mark has been issued by a granting authority such as a government trade mark registry or patent office) or a purely factual one (where a business entity does not seek to fulfil the legal formalities of registration but goes ahead and calls its garden fertilizer SUPA-GRO anyway). Many *de facto* trade marks can be turned into registered trade marks by complying with the formalities of registration, though some trade marks can never be registered, however distinctive they may appear to be. The distinction is a little bit like marriage: some people get married and then move in together; others live together first and get married subsequently; others again live together and dispense with all the formalities of marriage; some, finally, may lack the capacity to contract marriage at all.[4]

1.11 In some circles, particularly within Europe, it is common to find the words 'trade mark' reserved for registered trade marks, leaving the word 'sign' for any trade mark which, though it may be used, has not been registered. This usage is often employed in countries which do not recognize the terminology of the 'unregistered trade mark'[5] which, to them, sounds like a contradiction in terms. In other circles, particularly the United States, the word 'trademark' is widely and indiscriminately used for every species of mark whether registered or not.

(3) Trade marks and 'signs'

1.12 In this book the words 'trade mark' generally refer to a registered trade mark, unless the contrary is clearly expressed. The words 'unregistered trade mark' and 'sign' will be used to describe, respectively, a trade mark which has not been registered but which has been used and a putative trade mark which may or may not be registrable, irrespective of whether it has been (or will be) used.

(4) Trade marks, trade names, business names and company names

1.13 A trade name (or trading name) is a name under which a business trades. This may or may not be a registered trade mark. I have accordingly avoided using the term 'trade name' as a synonym for 'trade mark'. I have also sought to avoid making such

---

[4] The analogy may be carried further: just as a marriage may be annulled for non-consummation, so too may a trade mark be revoked for non-use.
[5] In *The Law of Passing Off* (1994), ch 6, Christopher Wadlow prefers to call such entities 'indicia'.

C. Important definitions and distinctions

use of the terms 'business name' and 'company name', which in most jurisdictions are legal terms of art in their own right.

(5) Trade marks and brands

1.14 The words 'trade mark' and 'brand' are often used synonymously. For example, a beer drinker might announce to his friends: 'My favourite beer is HEINEKEN'. This statement would be interpreted by a trade mark lawyer as meaning 'The trade mark which identifies my favourite brand of beer is HEINEKEN'. But this same statement may convey to someone in the beer trade the same information as 'My favourite beer is manufactured under licence from Heineken and sold under the HEINEKEN trade mark'. The use of 'trade mark' and 'brand' as synonyms stems from the fact that the notion of 'brand' was once integral to trade mark law: the word 'brand' quite literally meant a sign which was seared into the hide of a farmer's cattle so as to distinguish his herds from those of his neighbours.[6] Indeed, until as late as 1994, the definition of 'trade mark' in the UK included the word 'brand' when used in that sense.[7]

1.15 The historical consanguinity of brands and trade marks does not mean that, in modern parlance, the terms 'trade mark' and 'brand' still share a common meaning. Nowadays a *trade mark* is a sign which is controlled by its legal proprietor. He alone can use, permit or prohibit its use on the products or services for which he holds a registration certificate, or on products or services which the consuming public would think were connected to him if that sign were used on or in connection with them. A *brand* however is a form of shorthand, a signal by which the consuming public can identify and relate to actual goods or services.

1.16 To give an example, COCA COLA is many people's preferred choice of soft drink. The words COCA COLA are a registered trade mark which its proprietor, the Coca-Cola Company, may apply to soft drinks and also to associated marketing tools such as sweatshirts, coasters, pens and badges. Control of the COCA COLA trade mark does not only enable the Coca-Cola Company to stop fraudsters manufacturing their own concoctions and selling them as COCA COLA but it also prevents legitimate competitors from selling soft drinks with confusingly similar names. Finally, the ability to license the use of the trade mark COCA COLA permits the carefully controlled manufacture of the genuine Coca-Cola Company's product under the COCA COLA trade mark in situations in which direct manufacture by the Coca-Cola Company would not be feasible.

1.17 Trade marks may serve the primary function of distinguishing the goods of one manufacturer from those of another (for example, the COCA COLA and PEPSI COLA

---

[6] On the dual meaning of 'brand', see *Riding for the Brand* (American Express, 1985).
[7] Trade Marks Act 1938, s 63(1).

trade marks enable consumers to discern between the products made respectively by Coca-Cola and Pepsico), but they also have a secondary function of distinguishing different goods made by the same manufacturer (for example, COCA COLA and DIET COKE). The secondary trade mark is usually used together with the primary trade mark (for example, 'I'll have a BACARDI BREEZER, please', which is almost a tautology if one considers that no drinks company other than Bacardi makes and sells the BREEZER product), but it is sometimes used even in the absence of the primary trade mark.

1.18 COCA COLA is also a brand of soft drink; it is the name by which the drink is known and by which it is requested in restaurants and bars. Drinks sold under the COCA COLA brand are marketed with a bundle of intellectual property rights such as the distinctive Coca-Cola typeface and logo, the 'curved bottle' emblem and highly recognizable container design. The brand carries with it an ethos which is either derived from provable fact (for example, the fact that 80 per cent of Fortune 500 companies use a particular brand of software) or from manipulative marketing (for example, encouraging preferably young and attractive people to buy a fashion product by showing advertisements populated by young and attractive people who wear it). It is the brand which announces to the public a set of values: this product is expensive (or economical), fashionable (or utilitarian), durable (or disposable), and so on.

1.19 The COCA COLA drink may be additionally graced by a *sub-brand*, which conveys the same fundamental values as the brand and seeks to transfer them, with appropriate modification, to a different product. For example, DIET COKE and PEPSI MAX are sub-brands. They send out the message that products bearing the sub-brand represent the same values as ordinary COCA COLA or PEPSI COLA, but tailor that message for specific sub-audiences. For example, FORD FOCUS conveys the values of FORD (solid performance criteria, pleasing design, easy availability of cheap spare parts, power without ostentation, etc) to the sub-brand FOCUS. Although the Ford Motor Corporation also owns the JAGUAR trade mark, it has not employed JAGUAR as a sub-brand: a new FORD JAGUAR brand would send out mixed and inherently confusing messages to the car-buying public.

1.20 This book is primarily concerned with trade marks, but it must of necessity also address a number of issues relating to brands. Not the least of these is the fact that the legal monopoly in the use of the registered trade mark is the prime means of establishing and preserving the brand against the external erosion of its ethos and values by competitors and third parties.[8] Where the trade mark protection is cogent, the brand value remains unassailed. Consider the fate of TOYS "я" US—a

---

[8] I am indebted to my colleague Spyros Maniatis for reminding me that the trade mark monopoly provides no protection against the erosion of a company's ethos and values from within itself.

remarkable brand innovation in its time but the innovator could not retain legal control of the '"я" us' suffix.[9] Now every locality in the English-speaking world seems to have an '"я" us' store (DRAINS "я" US, KITCHENS "я" US) and an Internet search has yielded such horrors as RATZ "я" US (for keepers of pet rats) and VAC "я" US (suppliers of vacuum cleaner dust bags). Uses of the ' "я" US' suffix may even be socially undesirable where the object of the exploitation is to target children and lead them from a friendly toy shop to more sinister products or unsuitable social environments. In any event the inability of the trade mark to protect the suffix has greatly limited its brand value and the opportunity to extend the message conveyed by TOYS "я" US into appropriately related areas.

1.21 This book must also concern itself with the other side of the coin, addressing the attempts made by brand owners to extend their brand into areas felt by many to belong to the public at large. For example, the McDonald's hamburger empire has clearly established its entitlement to protection of the word MCDONALD'S, but it has fought to extend its control to cover the prefixes MC and MAC. This move was initially prompted by unworthy attempts of other traders to cash in on the 'MC ethos', but has been taken to limits which objective observers who exist outside that corporation find unacceptable and indeed risible.[10] Nonetheless, McDonald's has had far greater success in gaining control of the 'MC' prefix—which it did not invent and which it shares with many other well-known brands[11]—than TOYS "я " US has had in controlling its own invented and original suffix.

(6) Trade marks and 'house marks'

1.22 Some trade marks are called 'house marks' because they serve to link products, in the mind of the consumers, with the retail outlet or 'house' in which they are sold rather than with their manufacturer.

1.23 House marks are no different in legal terms to any other type of trade mark and the words 'house mark' are not a legal term of art. Nonetheless, their commercial behaviour is different, in that they seek to unify in the retailer, in the mind of consumers, the usually distinct goodwill which they experience in buying the products of one company from the premises or website of another. For example, where I go to HARRODS to purchase my CHIVAS REGAL whisky my shopping decision is linked

---

[9] See eg *Toys 'R' Us (Canada) Ltd v Manjel Inc* (Federal Court of Canada) noted in WTLR 19 May 2003.
[10] For good examples, see *Yuen v McDonald's Corp and another*, 27 November 2001 (unreported) (Chancery Division) where the proprietor of an oriental restaurant was able to register McCHINA as a trade mark in the face of vigorous opposition, and *McDonald's Corporation USA and McDonald's Restaurants Denmark A/S v Pedersen* [1997] ETMR 151 where the Danish Supreme Court allowed a hot-dog salesman to trade under the somewhat spurious nickname of 'McAllan'.
[11] eg McDONNELL DOUGLAS, McDOUGALLS, McINTOSH.

to my attitudes towards both the HARRODS brand of retail service and the CHIVAS REGAL brand of whisky. But if I went to a TESCO supermarket to purchase a TESCO's own-brand whisky, I would have consolidated in Tesco stores the two strains of goodwill which would otherwise have been dissipated between producer and retailer.

1.24 In modern usage the notion of the house mark has been extended by analogy so as to cover the use of a trade mark as a primary brand (sometimes called an 'umbrella brand') beneath which goods are supplied as sub-brands. For example, FORD could be termed a house brand within which a stable of products such as the FOCUS, TAURUS, MUSTANG and THUNDERBIRD are sold to the public.

D. A word about jurisdictions

1.25 This book portrays a generalized picture of trade mark law, drawing on international treaties as well as statutes and case law from a wide range of countries. Inevitably, given the central prominence of European trade mark law in current international legal developments, as well as the easy availability of European source materials to this writer, the book has a strong European flavour to it and it is aimed principally—but by no means exclusively—at readers who are involved with trade marks in Europe. Where propositions or comments are intended to apply in respect of a single country or a specific group of countries, the text indicates this accordingly. In all other situations the law is as one might expect to find it in any European Union Member State, allowing for national variations in matters of relative detail. Nothing in this book should be taken as legal advice, or as a substitute for it, on the substantive legal provisions of any jurisdiction as they apply to any specific factual situation.

1.26 The fact that the case law of a large number of jurisdictions is discussed should not lead the reader to assume that this work has a *comparative* element to it in the sense that it actively seeks to draw comparisons based on differences between the laws of different countries. Following more than 120 years of co-operation and ultimately harmonization among national trade mark systems, it is tempting to suggest that there is practically nothing that can be gained from adopting a comparative approach of that nature. Instead, the approach taken in this book is *synthetic* rather than comparative: it assumes that all trade mark systems have the same objectives and that, in the preponderant majority of factual situations, a given set of trade mark-related facts produces the same outcome in each country. In any event, this book assumes that the operation of most trade mark systems for the most part displays an attraction towards the same normative behaviour.[12]

---

[12] This normative behaviour can be displayed in the now frequent citation in European courts of

E. Case law

Since trade mark cases frequently depend on how a judge or registry official perceives the similarities and differences between two marks, the same result cannot be guaranteed even when different tribunals in different countries are looking at exactly the same set of facts; the same is true for different individuals in the same country. This 'natural variation' factor demonstrates the degree to which human intervention comes into play in the field of trade mark law and is indeed one of the features which makes the subject so compellingly interesting.

There is more to be learned about trade mark law, at least in the introductory phase of one's learning, if one looks at the way trade mark systems actually behave. It is also more fun to treat trade mark systems as living organisms than to expend one's energy in isolating and theorizing to death the often trivial differences that still exist between many of them. **1.27**

E. Case law

(1) The hierarchy of nations

Many of the cases woven into the tapestry of this text are from countries which have little clout in terms of the development of trade mark law. Their inclusion has been criticized by some of my friends who have read the book in draft on the basis that 'no one really cares what happens in Paraguay'. I have been asked: 'A case from *Iran*? You must be joking!' I am not. **1.28**

Everyone in trade marks knows that there is a great hierarchy of nations. At the pinnacle sits the United States. In recognition of this, even those of us whose trade mark law has no formal dilution doctrine[13] feel struck by an urgent need to read the US Supreme Court decision in the VICTORIA'S SECRET case the day it is handed down. At the next level down we find the past, present and future of serious competition with the Americans: Japan, the European Union and China respectively, together with their economic satellites. Then come a number of earnest and worthy jurisdictions (such as Australia and Canada) whose undoubted expertise in trade mark law struggles to radiate light in the presence of the many powerful legal luminaries above it. Beneath them are countries in the holiday zone and, at the very bottom, the lands so tragically beset by war, disease, poverty and producers of documentary television programmes. **1.29**

This perception of a hierarchy of nations—a perception which many experienced **1.30**

US concepts such as 'dilution and tarnishment' and by the application of the European test of confusing similarity by the US Trademark Trial Appeal Board in *Re Continental Graphics Corp* 52 USPQ 2d 1374 (TTAB 1999) and South Africa's Supreme Court of Appeal in *Cowbell AG v ICS Holdings Ltd* 2001 (3) SA 941.

[13] On dilution and the VICTORIA'S SECRET case, see Chapter 12.

readers may share—stands as a pernicious barrier to our understanding of how trade marks work in law and practice. Major and respected corporations cannot simply choose to litigate their trade marks in the United States or Europe. They must sue where their rights are jeopardized or infringed, which may turn out to be countries at the lower end of the hierarchy.

1.31 Many of these countries have, in the years following the Agreement on Trade-Related Aspects of Intellectual Property Law (TRIPs) in 1994, passed trade mark legislation which is remarkably close to our own. Owners of well-known marks are frequent visitors to their courts and trade mark registries. Their lawyers—if you only take the trouble to listen to them—have developed their own methods for dealing with difficult issues both in court and out of it. I fervently believe that, just as we expect them to learn from our ways, we too can learn from theirs. I also believe that, before criticizing the legal institutions which we have introduced, we should at least consider whether they work better or worse than the legal techniques adopted elsewhere. It is thus without apology that decisions from some of the less prominent jurisdictions are included in this book.

(2) Cases as precedents

1.32 This book refers to a very large number of court cases and administrative decisions. Some of these are very important. Decisions of the European Court of Justice are binding on all European Union Member States and, in countries which operate a precedent-based legal system, decisions of superior courts bind lower courts, and so on. At the other end of the spectrum are decisions by trade mark examiners in registry hearings and decisions of administrative bodies such as the Boards and Divisions of the Office of Harmonisation in the Internal Market (OHIM). These may have little or no value as precedents at all, although they may have persuasive value in suggesting to a court or registry a position or course of action which it may adopt when no other guidance presents itself.

(3) Cases as examples

1.33 Most of the cases and administrative decisions referred to in this book are not cited for the solid statements of binding law which they contain. They are cited as being illustrative of the way in which trade mark examiners and tribunals behave when faced with a particular type of problem. Regular 'file-'em high' trade mark attorneys place great importance in knowing what examiners and appeal boards do, since it is what they do that lies at the heart of every trade mark system. To give an analogy: the professor of zoology knows more about the anatomy, the physiognomy and the digestive system of the lion than does the humble zoo-keeper, but it's the zoo-keeper who goes into the cage with the lions every day and it's the zoo-keeper who knows what keeps his lions happy and what they like to eat. In similar manner, lofty academics and distinguished judges may know far more about

the economics of the judicial system.

trade mark law than the humble trade mark attorney, but he too faces daily lions in the registry.

Most contested trade mark applications and oppositions never get to court: it is the exceptional cases that find themselves litigated and then scrutinized under the jurisprudential microscope. This book seeks to bridge some of the gap that exists between theory and practice, between scholarship and professional intuition, by explaining issues in a manner which is, as far as possible, sympathetic to each. That is why it is as much concerned with how trade mark systems work as with what the law is and why it cites so many low-level examples of the law's application before trade mark examiners as well as *ex cathedra* pronouncements from appellate courts and scholars.[14]

1.34

(4) Cases as working hypotheses

Many readers will feel tempted to skip the parts of this book which discuss cases decided in jurisdictions other than their own, since they may not always appear to be either relevant or useful in the explanation of their own law. Such readers should be reminded that it is not only from the result of a case that one can draw lessons: the reasoning which led to that result may be a far more valuable resource for the lawyer or trade mark attorney. Accordingly they should remember that the arguments offered in these cases frequently offer hypotheses which readers can try out before the judges or trade mark examiners in their own jurisdictions.

1.35

(5) Cases as landmarks

A small number of cases are landmark decisions which can, where appropriate, change the behaviour of courts, trade mark registries, legal practitioners, trade mark owners or brand managers. These cases are few and far between. Examples from the European Court of Justice include the BABY-DRY case[15] (which set a new, low standard of registrability for trade marks), *Silhouette*[16] (which gave countries no choice between 'global' and regional exhaustion of rights) and *Davidoff v A & G Imports*[17] (a nail in the coffin for non-EEA parallel traders in cheap but genuine branded products). Landmark cases from the United States include *Qualitex*[18] (on the registration of colours as trade marks), and so on.

1.36

---

[14] In civil-law jurisdictions such as Germany, the contribution played by scholarly comment is highly respected. In common-law countries such as the UK, scholarly comment plays a far smaller role in developing and applying the law.
[15] *Procter & Gamble Company v OHIM*, Case C-383/99 P [2002] ETMR 22.
[16] *Silhouette International Schmiedt GmbH & Co KG v Hartlauer Handelsgesellschaft mbH*, Case C-355/96 [1998] ETMR 539.
[17] *Zino Davidoff SA v A & G Imports Ltd; Levi Strauss & Co and Levi Strauss (UK) Ltd v Tesco Stores, Tesco plc and Costco Wholesale Ltd*, Joined Cases C-414/99, C-415/99 and C-416/00 [2002] ETMR 109.
[18] *Qualitex Co v Jacobson Products Co* 514 US 159 (Supreme Court, 1995).

1.37 What makes a case a landmark decision? It is not the court, it is not the identity or scale of the litigants and it is not the facts. It is what lawyers, trade mark attorneys and their clients do with the case *after* it has been decided. Do they cite it in other cases in which they are involved or do they ignore or downplay it?[19] Do they disinvest from proprietary drugs companies and plough their money into generic drugs? Do they brush the dust off a pile of formerly unsuccessful trade mark applications and file them again? A case is a landmark when it serves as a landmark, to guide the conduct of others. In some respects, therefore, it is for us as trade mark lawyers, as scholars and as writers to determine what those landmarks are. We have it in our power. Readers may find, among the many cases discussed, some sunken treasures which might, when ebbs the tide of unfamiliarity, achieve great value as landmarks in the future.

F. Trade marks and history

1.38 There are many excellent publications on the history of trade marks and trade mark law. This book is not one of them, because its subject matter is the laying bare of the aspirations and functional reality of trade mark law as it stands today. Trade mark law and practice as we know it today more or less started afresh in the mid-1990s, with the establishment of the internationally accepted TRIPs[20] norms, the implementation of the Community trade mark and Madrid Protocol systems and the introduction of Federal anti-dilution laws in the United States.[21] This book only looks before that year when (i) post-1994 trade mark law cannot be satisfactorily explained or understood without doing so or when (ii) the pre-1994 period provides good examples of some commercial or legal phenomenon which is under discussion.

1.39 Trade marks did not always exist; nor did trade mark law. Something must have triggered their creation and, once they came to be, other factors must have shaped their features and ensured their continued existence. We accordingly commence our review of trade marks by asking, and attempting to answer, the question 'why trade marks?'

---

[19] British readers may ask whatever happened to *Series 5 Software Ltd v Clarke* [1996] FSR 273 and the line of cases which briefly followed it; see Jeremy Phillips, 'Interlocutory Injunctions and Intellectual Property: A Review of *American Cyanamid v Ethicon* in the Light of *Series 5 Software*' [1997] JBL 486.
[20] TRIPs is discussed in the following chapter.
[21] On which, see Chapter 12.

2

WHY TRADE MARKS?

A. **Introduction**
    'It's the trade mark that makes the difference'
    The moral of the story   2.01
  (1) What do trade marks do?   2.02
  (2) Can anything else do what a trade mark does?   2.03
  (3) Is there anything that trade marks cannot do?   2.04

B. **The interested parties**
  (1) Who benefits from trade marks?
    (a) The trade mark owner   2.05
    (b) Other honest traders   2.06
    (c) Other dishonest traders   2.07
    (d) The state   2.08
    (e) The legal profession   2.09
    (f) Purchasers and ultimate consumers of trade marked goods and services   2.10
  (2) Who are the victims of trade mark law?
    (a) Infringers   2.11
    (b) Purchasers and ultimate consumers of trade marked goods and services   2.12
  (3) What exactly is the position of the consumer under trade mark law?   2.13

C. **The function of the trade mark system**
  (1) What function is the trade mark system intended to serve?   2.16
    (a) To identify the actual physical origin of goods and services   2.24
    (b) To guarantee the identity of the origin of goods and services   2.30
    (c) To guarantee the quality of goods and services   2.34
    (d) To serve as a badge of support or affiliation   2.38
    (e) To enable the consumer to make a lifestyle statement   2.39
  (2) The pathology of trade marks   2.42
  (3) The morality of trade mark law   2.44
    (a) Not all copying is regarded as wrong   2.46
    (b) Not all lying is regarded as wrong   2.48
    (c) Not all copying of trade marks is made unlawful by trade mark law   2.49
    (d) Trade mark law makes unlawful apparently morally neutral acts which have nothing to do with copying or lying   2.50
    (e) Trade mark law penalizes conduct which is not intended to be unlawful   2.51
  (4) The real function of the trade mark system?   2.53

D. **Conclusion**   2.59

Chapter 2: Why Trade Marks?

A. Introduction

'It's the trade mark that makes the difference'

It was a beautiful afternoon for a little time off. Some 6,000 delegates attending the International Trademark Association's 1997 meeting in San Diego surged out of the conference centre to enjoy some leisure time before the Grand Finale at the city's famous zoo. Some went shopping downtown; others cruised the limpid bay; others again braved the city tram to the national border with Mexico and a short taxi ride to Tijuana. My wife and I were among them.

The taxi ride took us to a dusty main street where barefoot children played and pedlars touted their wares from all corners. A mule twitched its tail at the roadside while its owner stopped off for a refreshing tequila. Nearby a couple of native dogs scratched idly at their fleas.

Fortified by a couple of margaritas, our party decided to tour the main street's main attraction: the stores full of counterfeit goods. Handbags seemed to be the flavour of the month. From fairly primitive jobs to expertly stitched and highly finished articles, they all bore illustrious trade marks—particularly LOUIS VUITTON.

We ventured into one of the shops and my wife began to give the bags some serious scrutiny. No more than a fraction of a second could have elapsed after she gave the impression of being a serious customer when suddenly the shopkeeper appeared, earnestly pressing all manner of merchandise before her and urging her to purchase. We persuaded the shopkeeper to lay off for a while so that we could check out the handbags undisturbed.

It soon became apparent that the store stocked two classes of handbag: counterfeit bags, the most expensive of which cost as much as US$20 (all prices were marked in dollars), and non-branded handbags, which cost in the range of US$5. Some of the bags were identical, except that a trade mark had been appended to the $20 bags but not to the $5 bags. My wife's curiosity was aroused. She picked up two identical bags, one counterfeit brand and one 'generic', and asked why one cost four times as much as the other.

'It's like this,' the shopkeeper explained. 'This one has to cost more because it's got the trade mark on it. It's the brand that makes it more valuable'.

The moral of the story

2.01 Even overt and unashamed trade mark infringers such as the Mexican shopkeeper are willing to concede that the addition of a trade mark to goods adds to their value. In this case it was a matter of cynical exploitation of the gullibility or greed of luxury-goods shoppers from across the border. In many other cases there is no cynicism: there is a genuine desire to enhance the purchaser's well-being or happiness by conveying, through the medium of the trade mark, the fact that there is something right about a product: it relieves pain; it is manufactured to reliably high standards; it is fashionable, and so on. This chapter will investigate a little further some of the things that justify the existence of trade marks.

B. The interested parties

(1) What do trade marks do?

2.02 Some trade marks tell purchasers of goods and services that those goods or services are connected with a particular manufacturer or seller. Other trade marks promise purchasers that those goods or services will help them cultivate a particular image. Other trade marks give purchasers information about the goods or services they are buying. Other trade marks probably do nothing at all. The same trade mark may do all or any of these things, depending on (i) how the trade mark owner uses it and (ii) how the purchaser views it.

(2) Can anything else do what a trade mark does?

2.03 No. Not in the same way, at any rate. The trade mark forges a powerful yet intimate link between three discrete entities: the trade mark proprietor, his market and the goods or services for which it is registered. Other similar legal devices such as certification marks, collective marks, protected geographical indications and protected designations of origin, which function in many ways in a manner similar to trade marks, are described in Chapter 18.

(3) Is there anything that trade marks cannot do?

2.04 Yes. Trade marks are not regarded as an adequate means of conveying to the consuming public the ingredients of trade mark-protected foods and drinks. Thus, where cans of drink bearing the COCA-COLA trade mark and a list of ingredients in Dutch were imported from the Netherlands into the UK and the importer was prosecuted under the Food Safety Act 1990, the argument that, since consumers would recognize the famous trade mark on the cans, they would know that the ingredients were the same, was rejected.[1]

B. The interested parties

(1) Who benefits from trade marks?

(a) The trade mark owner

2.05 Armed with a trade mark registration, the trade mark owner has the law's backing in his efforts to stop competitors making exact copies of his products or using that same trade mark on his own products, thus deceiving or confusing the trade mark owner's customers into making a purchase on the basis of their misplaced trust in the legitimacy of that product. With a trade mark a trader can protect the reputation in his goods or services and the goodwill which attracts customers to choose to give him their business. The law benefits the trade mark owner by enabling

---

[1] *London Borough of Hackney v Cedar Trading Ltd* [1999] ETMR 801 (Divisional Court).

him, where appropriate: (i) to stop any trade which makes unlawful use of his trade mark; (ii) to collect damages for his loss or gather up the wrongdoer's profits; and (iii) to secure the destruction of any infringing goods.

(b) Other honest traders

2.06 Even if you do not have a trade mark of your own, you can benefit from the use of trade marks belonging to others, so long as that use is not abusive. You can use their trade marks in advertisements and other promotional ways in order to advertise the sale or repair of their products or to indicate that your goods are technically compatible with theirs. This information enables a trader who is not the trade mark owner legitimately to harvest the benefit of the goodwill which exists in another's trade mark. Other trade mark owners can also benefit from the honest use of a competitor's trade mark in the course of their own comparative advertising.[2]

(c) Other dishonest traders

2.07 The existence of another's valuable and attractive branded products is always an incentive to dealers in infringing and counterfeit goods. This is because, as indicated in the story with which this chapter commenced, even the unlawful use of another's trade mark becomes an easy and convenient way to introduce one's products to prospective customers. In this sense even an infringing use of a trade mark—if that mark is well enough known—helps to protect the illicit trader's investment in his stock, his distribution system and his other overheads.

(d) The state

2.08 Each trade mark granting authority charges applicants for their trade mark applications and extracts further fees for subsequent significant events in a trade mark's life such as its occasional renewal or the recordal of details of its assignment to another person. The sums derived from administering the trade mark system can be considerable. In year ending 31 March 2001, the turnover of trade mark procedures in the UK Trade Mark Registry touched £18.54 million, against expenditure of £13.284 million, netting a surplus of £5.256 million.[3] Assertions that the income derived from patent and trade mark filing fees has been diverted so as to subsidize other government activities has led to litigation[4] and even the possibility of legislation[5] in the United States.

---

[2] Many examples of both honest and dishonest uses of another's trade mark are given in Chapter 8.
[3] UK Patents Office's *Annual Report* (2001), p 45.
[4] See *Figueroa v United States* (argued before the US Court of Federal Claims, 14 November 2002).
[5] The US Patent and Trademark Fee Modernization Act 2003, approved by the Subcommittee on Court, the Internet and Intellectual Property; see Sam Mamudi, 'Lawmakers Vote to End Diversion', *MIP Week*, 1 June 2003, who states that the US budget for 2004 proposes to divert $99.7m of the United States Patent and Trademark Office (USPTO) fees for the funding of other areas of Federal government.

B. The interested parties

(e) The legal profession

2.09 The trade mark system is driven by professional legal and paralegal advisers who act on behalf of their clients in: (i) applying for trade marks; (ii) opposing the grant and seeking the cancellation of other people's trade mark applications; (iii) suing infringers; and (iv) engaging in transactions for the commercialization of the trade mark. It is not possible to estimate the total number of lawyers and paralegals who depend on the trade mark system for their sustenance, since many trade mark specialists also deal in related areas of law. However, they are considerable in number,[6] as presumably is their aggregated earning power.

(f) Purchasers and ultimate consumers of trade marked goods and services

2.10 If the trade mark on the package says ZANTAC, its purchaser is looking for assurance that he is buying GlaxoSmithKline's treatment for his gastrointestinal ailments and not a concoction of herbs, sugar and colourings conjured up by some charlatan. In the developing world, where trade mark protection is weak and difficult for trade mark owners to police, not only fake pharmaceutical products but also home-made spirits, soft drinks, low-quality brake pads, ineffectual contraceptives and a host of other products are sold under the well-respected trade marks of legitimate traders, with potentially fatal results. In the service sector too, it is well known that travellers have been misled into making Internet or telephone reservations with unpleasant hotels in unsavoury locations on the strength of the misappropriation by the latter of an internationally known and respected trade name.

(2) Who are the victims of trade mark law?

(a) Infringers

2.11 While no sympathy should be felt for those dishonest traders who package worthless treatments in boxes bearing the trade marks of what are often life-saving products, it should be conceded that by no means all trade mark infringers are the perpetrators of actions of moral obloquy. Trade mark infringement in most instances does not depend on the subjective intention, the attitude or even the knowledge of the infringer but upon the objectively verifiable answer to the question: 'did the alleged infringer perform an infringing act?' Accordingly, a trader who does not even know that his competitor exists and who is quite unaware of

---

[6] The International Trademark Association lists more than 4,200 in-house and private practitioners among its full and associate members. The American Intellectual Property Law Association claimed more than 10,000 members in 2002. In the same year the Office for Harmonisation in the Internal Market (OHIM) (the EU's own trade mark office) announced that it had registered 5,881 individuals as being qualified to represent clients in proceedings before it, in addition to those EU practitioners who, being authorized to represent clients before national offices, do not need to register with OHIM.

the latter's trade mark application is still liable for infringing it—and this is the case in the UK even if the trade mark application was filed only one day before the alleged infringing use and no record of its existence would have been found even if the alleged infringer had checked the trade mark register first.[7] The trade mark laws of most countries provide for various innocent uses of another's trade mark to be protected from liability, thus enabling any biological Helena Rubinsteins or Harry Potters to make honest use of their own names without incurring liability.

(b) Purchasers and ultimate consumers of trade marked goods and services

2.12 To date, the trade mark laws of most countries have not adopted the principle of global exhaustion of rights.[8] This means that a trade mark owner can prevent the importation and resale of products bearing the trade mark which were first marketed in another jurisdiction, even though the trade mark owner has already had the benefit of being able to sell (or license the sale of) that product for profit in the country where it was first marketed. The result of the exhaustion doctrine being applied on a regional basis in Europe is that Levi Strauss can force European purchasers of its jeans to pay higher prices than would be paid by consumers in the United States[9] for exactly the same items of clothing.

(3) What exactly is the position of the consumer under trade mark law?

2.13 The position of the consumer in trade mark law is a matter of debate.[10] The astute reader will have spotted that consumers are listed both among the beneficiaries of trade mark law and among its victims. Both these statements are true and there is no contradiction between them. When, as will eventually be the case, the doctrine of global exhaustion of rights prevails, consumers will greatly benefit from the protection that trade mark law gives to producers and suppliers of goods without their having to pay the price of living in partitioned markets. However, to say that purchasers and ultimate consumers of trade marked goods and services benefit from the existence of the trade mark system is not the same as saying that they benefit from rights granted under trade mark law. It is not normal for the trade mark

---

[7] Trade Marks Act 1994, ss 9, 40(3).
[8] Exhaustion of rights is discussed in detail in Chapter 9.
[9] See *Levi Strauss & Co and Levi Strauss (UK) Ltd v Tesco Stores Ltd and others* [2002] ETMR 1153 (HC).
[10] Jennifer Davis, 'To Protect or Serve? European Trade Mark Law and the Decline of the Public Interest' [2003] EIPR 180–7 weaves an elegant case, based on what judges and Advocates General say rather than on what the law actually does, for the proposition that consumers are, or at least have been, more than the mere canaries which the account in this book suggests. See also Felix Cohen's classic work, 'Transcendental Nonsense and the Functional Approach' (1935) 35 Colum L Rev 809, 814–17, where he was the first to question the justification of protection of trade marks against dilution on the basis that it did not appear to serve any legitimate function in terms of consumer protection.

C. The function of the trade mark system

law of any country to grant enforceable rights or interests to consumers; nor are such rights required under international law.

2.14 What does this mean in practice? If I go to my local Asda store to buy a well-known brand of breakfast cereal but purchase instead an own-brand lookalike product of similar shape, size and colour, I have been confused and possibly deceived by the similarity of the two products. If it transpires that the Asda product infringes a trade mark, the trade mark owner can sue Asda for damages for infringement of rights protected by domestic trade mark legislation. All I can do is complain to the store manager and hope that he will take pity on me. He might point out, with some justification, that it was my own fault that I bought the wrong breakfast cereal. As a highly literate lawyer with two degrees I might have been expected to read the legend on the cereal box carefully, either at the point at which I picked it up and dropped it into my shopping trolley or later when I removed it from the trolley and handed it to the assistant at the checkout. I might remonstrate that the whole point of trade mark law is to prevent the sale of products that confuse the public through the similarity of consumer identifiers, but his rejoinder would be that I am not the trade mark owner.

2.15 The choice of the consumer as the yardstick to measure confusion is found throughout the world and the consumer's personal characteristics may vary, depending on the country and the nature of the goods or services consumed. Sometimes he or she is the 'average consumer', sometimes the 'relevant consumer' of the goods or services in question. The number or proportion of consumers who need to be confused may also vary from country to country. In all cases, however, the position of the consumer is not the position of a person whom the law protects. The consumer is a piece of human litmus paper, dipped into the marketplace and employed as the acid test of whether the trade mark owner can successfully sue the maker or seller of the allegedly similar product, or a canary in a cage, taken down the coal mine to see if the air is wholesome. If the canary dies, the miners know they must leave the mine; in the same way, if the consumer is confused, the copyists know they must cease their acts of imitation. Neither the consumer nor the canary derives any great personal benefit from its experience.

C. The function of the trade mark system

(1) What function is the trade mark system intended to serve?

2.16 Before considering the explanations which may been offered in justification of the trade mark system, it is necessary to say a few words about theories in general.

2.17 Many theories as to the actual or intended function of the trade mark system are built upon models. The exercise of model-building is a frequently employed approach to the understanding of the operation of any self-enclosed system as well as to conducting systems analysis of subject matter which has an impact on the world outside it. The system for processing trade mark applications is not actually self-enclosed since it involves the interaction of a body of often self-selected parties such as trade mark applicants and opponents. It is however a relatively tightly focused system. The system for enforcing trade mark rights is not self-enclosed: it involves entire markets, nationally and beyond, not to mention (among others) businesses, lawyers, importers, designers, hauliers, consumers and bailiffs.

2.18 Model-building involves starting with the totality of the real world and then seeking to identify within it those features which are deemed to be relevant to the subject under study—in this case the trade mark system—and omitting the rest. Some things are clearly relevant to all trade mark systems (for example, the rule of law, consumer choice, credit and the existence of a marketplace for commodities), while other things equally clearly are of little or no direct relevance (the number of hours domestic cats spend asleep, number of decimal places to which π can be calculated or the gestation period of the latest *Harry Potter* novel). Other factors fall somewhere in between these two extremes (for example, peer-group pressure, the availability of disposable income generated by pension schemes and social attitudes towards leisure activities) and may or may not be relevant to a given model. So far, so good.

2.19 This process of identification is followed by the extraction of those features and their subsequent reincorporation into a simplified working model which the analyst then employs in order to demonstrate and explain the system. The more closed the system, the easier it is to identify and extract its arguably salient features and to constitute them into a model; the more open the system, the more controversy exists at its periphery as to what should be included in the model and what should be omitted.

2.20 Some models are essentially static in character, since they seek to describe the various functions of an apparently unchanging system. Others are dynamic, incorporating self-correcting or evolutionary features which project the functions of a system through linear time or through patterns of economic, social or political change. Indeed, the incorporation of the concept of proactive and reactive consumers into the model can be said to add a certain degree of democratization to a dynamic model of trade mark protection.

2.21 Although the building of models is a highly respected academic method, particularly for economists, it is also an approach which those who adopt more existentialist or phenomenological approaches regard as being misleading almost to the point of dishonesty. The making of models has no justification for anyone whose aim is to understand or experience a system *as a whole* rather than to create a working model to aid its explanation. Indeed the model-building exercise may be seen

C. The function of the trade mark system

as a deliberate refusal to absorb the very detail which characterizes the vital fibre of a trade mark system in daily operation.

2.22 In truth, neither approach is ideal. The model-builders produce models which imperfectly and inaccurately describe the function and operation of the trade mark system because they produce generalizations which work well in principle but stubbornly refuse to snuggle down with many individual cases. The existentialists and phenomenologists may experience the ultimate truth of the trade mark system; they may indeed intuit the phenomenon of the trade mark system at a level which enables them to exploit their perspectives commercially—but one's own experiences and realizations are both difficult to quantify and to share with others.

2.23 This foregoing discussion is intended to explain that the reader should not expect too much from any purported justifications of the trade mark system and evaluations of its operation. No profound truth will be found in them, but a good deal of useful guidance may nonetheless be derived from them.[11]

(a) To identify the actual physical origin of goods and services

2.24 The theory that the trade mark is designed to serve as a badge of origin of goods and services is of ancient provenance and has been long respected.[12] The idea is simple: if you see the name PORSCHE on a car, you know that it has been made and designed by a particular car maker and by no one else. You can depend on your PORSCHE not being made by FIAT or HYUNDAI. Your PORSCHE is made in Germany, by a skilled and highly trained workforce, and that is that. As one commentator has put it:

> A brand itself is a seal of authenticity, a practical method for consumers to appreciate the quality of goods by viewing the mark rather than inspecting each product.[13]

2.25 This justification of trade marks supports the principle of international exhaustion of trade mark rights.[14] For example, let us say that a batch of ZANTAC indigestion tablets is manufactured in a factory and that half the pills are first marketed in Switzerland, half in Germany. It cannot be said that the need to guarantee the physical origin of ZANTAC pills justifies the exercise of a trade mark right so as to prevent the Swiss-marketed pills, but not the German ones, being imported into the UK. The protection of the public against the effects of international exhaustion is better served by the need to guarantee the quality of goods rather than their

---

[11] For further reading on this subject, see Anselm Kamperman Sanders and Spyros Maniatis, 'A Consumer Trade Mark: Protection Based on Origin and Quality' [1993] EIPR 406.
[12] This notion was accepted in the context of the hallmarking of precious metals and in early trade mark systems but its obsolescence was pointed out as early as 1925 by Frank Schechter in his treatise *The Historical Foundation of Trade-mark Law*.
[13] Frederick Mostert, 'Authenticity: The Timeless Quest' (2003) 156 *Trademark World* 22, 24.
[14] See Chapter 9, paras 9.09–9.14.

source or authenticity. For example, where high grade COLGATE toothpaste is marketed in Europe and a lower grade COLGATE toothpaste is marketed in Brazil, the European public wants assurance that the toothpaste it buys under the COLGATE trade mark is the product it prefers—even though both may be legitimately described as COLGATE products.[15]

2.26 This same justification requires some qualification if it is to apply to the trading conditions found in the modern world. It happens with increasing frequency that trade mark owners license the making of products bearing their trade mark because it is too expensive to make and send them round the world from just one factory; or they outsource all their manufacture to factories in parts of the world where labour or materials are cheap. Beer and soft drinks are typically made under licence by companies other than the trade mark owner since they are not much more than flavoured water and the cost of transporting quantities of water to ultimate consumers in other countries can substantially exceed the cost of initial manufacture. The use of outsourcing is a widespread and well-catalogued phenomenon: the same company's running shoes may come from China, the Philippines, Indonesia or any of a large number of countries vying with each other for manufacturing contracts.

2.27 In cases such as these, the trade mark is not a badge of the physical origin of the mark, but it might be seen as a badge of the metaphysical origin of the goods—the design, styling, ethos and other intangible factors which are chosen by the same arbiters of taste: Nike, Adidas, Tommy Hilfiger, Heineken or whoever. No one honestly believes that the Disney Corporation actually makes MICKEY MOUSE watches or toothbrush-holders, but most people assume that Disney gets some money from their sale and have no hesitation in suing them rather than the manufacturer if any MICKEY MOUSE goods proved defective.[16]

2.28 The identification of a product as originating from the trade mark owner can however be viewed either objectively or subjectively. Objectively, the consumer views the trade mark and makes the assumption that the goods to which it is attached are connected to the trade mark owner, or at least to someone connected with him. Subjectively, it is the trade mark owner who 'identifies' goods, literally giving them an identity, by putting his trade mark on them before they reach the market governed by the trade mark right. It is in this latter sense that 'identification' has been treated in at least one major piece of litigation.[17] The trade mark monopoly, which protects the owner's right to impose an identity on goods enter-

---

[15] See eg *Colgate-Palmolive Ltd and another v Markwell Finance Ltd and another* [1988] RPC 283 (HC).
[16] See the comments on Product Liability at para 2.37 below.
[17] *La Chemise Lacoste SA and SIDAS SpA v Centro Tessile Srl* [1997] ETMR 520 (Milan Court of Appeal).

C. The function of the trade mark system

ing the market, thus covers even goods lawfully made by or with the trade mark owner's blessing in a third country but which have been imported without the trade mark owner having had the chance to 'identify' them within the market of importation.

2.29 The use of a trade mark as a means of indicating the actual source of goods has not been accepted by the European Court of Justice (ECJ) as being either a sufficient or a necessary justification for the trade mark system. As the Court of First Instance has recently said:

> ... *it is not necessary for a mark to convey exact information about the identity of the manufacturer of the product or the supplier of the services.* It is sufficient that the mark enables members of the public concerned to distinguish the product or service that it designates from those which have a different trade origin and to conclude that all the products or services that it designates have been manufactured, marketed or supplied under the control of the owner of the mark and that the owner is responsible for their quality [emphasis added].[18]

(b) To guarantee the identity of the origin of goods and services

2.30 This is the ECJ's preferred and apparently sole justification for trade mark protection. In the now celebrated case of *Arsenal v Reed*[19] the Court said:

> ... according to the settled case-law of the Court, the essential function of the trade mark is to *guarantee the identity of the origin of the marked product* to the consumer or end user by enabling him, without any possibility of confusion, to distinguish the product or service from others which have another origin. For the trade mark to be able to fulfil its essential role in the system of undistorted competition ..., it must offer *a guarantee that all the goods or services bearing it have originated under the control of a single undertaking* which is responsible for their quality [emphasis added].[20]

2.31 This definition addresses the relationship of the trade mark owner to his competitors by enabling him to keep his channel of communication to the consumer free from interference by other, unauthorized uses of the same or similar trade marks. The relationship that the law seeks to protect is one of 'undistorted competition' between two or more competitors.

2.32 Precisely what constitutes the difference is between guaranteeing 'the identity of the origin' and guaranteeing the origin itself is a matter of speculation. I do not believe that the court intended the two terms to convey any different nuance of meaning. Rather, it is submitted that the word 'identity' is used to convey the notion of 'one-ness', that the origin be identical in respect of all goods bearing the same mark.

---

[18] *Unilever plc v OHIM*, Case T-194/01, 5 March 2003 (unreported), para 43.
[19] See further para 2.38 below.
[20] *Canon Kabushiki Kaisha v Metro-Goldwyn-Mayer Inc*, Case C-39/97 [1999] ETMR 1, para 28, citing *CNL-Sucal NV v Hag GF AG* [1990] 3 CMLR 571 ('HAG II'), paras 13, 14.

2.33 It was on the basis that the guarantee of identity of the origin of goods and services was under threat that the ECJ gave its ruling in *Arsenal v Reed*[21] that the unauthorized use of a trade mark as a 'badge of loyalty' towards a football team constituted an infringement of the ARSENAL trade mark.

(c) To guarantee the quality of goods and services

2.34 When consumers are no longer concerned with the physical origin of goods or services, what is it that does concern them? In the previous chapter we saw how the ECJ believed that consumers sought instead a guarantee of the 'identity of the origin' of goods or services, but American trade mark theory has been influenced by a quite different notion—that the consumer seeks an assurance that relates to the quality of the goods or services to which the trade mark testifies:

> the true functions of a trademark are, then, *to identify a product as satisfactory* and thereby *to stimulate further purchases* by the consuming public [emphasis added].[22]

2.35 In other words, the trade mark promises the consumer satisfaction and the chance of repeating satisfaction. It will be immediately noticed that these functions exist only as between the trade mark owner and the actual or potential consumer. This theory is in harmony with the 'actual physical origin' justification (see further paras 2.24–2.29 above), although that theory is neutral to the question of consumer satisfaction. This theory is also in complete contrast with the 'guarantee of identity of origin' theory (see further paras 2.30–2.33 above). By the 'guarantee of quality' view, trade marks bind the trade mark owner, as brand exploiter, to his customers, while the 'guarantee of identity of origin' theory sees trade marks as a sort of buffer which stops competing businesses getting too close together.

2.36 As early as 1970 it was apparent that this justification of the trade mark system was not favoured in Europe. It is difficult to find a more outspoken dismissal of it than this:

> ...[T]he quality or guarantee function has in my view no independent legal significance. It is derived from the basic function of identifying the origin of goods and simply means that the public, from its knowledge that trademarked artefacts have the same origin, often believes these to be of the same quality. But this expectation to the extent that it really exists is not protected by trademark law. Protection against deception of quality is rather a matter for criminal law or the law against unfair competition.[23]

2.37 The law in Europe has gone even further than this by demonstrating that a guarantee or at least an expectation that goods bearing a trade mark will be of good quality is not a justification for the protection of the trade mark but a burdensome

---

[21] See further para 2.38 below.
[22] Frank Schechter, 'The Rational Basis of Trademark Protection' (1927) 40 Harv LR 813.
[23] Friedrich-Karl Beier, 'Territoriality of Trade Mark Law and International Trade' (1970) 1 IIC 48–72, 64.

C. The function of the trade mark system

responsibility which flows from it. Accordingly a European consumer who purchases a defective product may seek compensation from the product's producer. For this purpose 'producer' is defined as

> the manufacturer of a finished product, the producer of any raw material or the manufacturer of a component part and any person who, by putting his name, trade mark or other distinguishing feature on the product presents himself as its producer.[24]

(d) To serve as a badge of support or affiliation

2.38 The argument that the use of a sign as a badge of support or affiliation was in some way removed from the normal scope of a trade mark's functions was reviewed in some depth by the ECJ in *Arsenal v Reed*. This case arose from an attempt by Arsenal to prevent the unauthorized sale of clearly unofficial football memorabilia such as hats and scarves bearing Arsenal's trade marks. The referring court[25] found some merit in the argument that the trade mark was being used by the defendant as a badge of allegiance for support of Arsenal the football team, rather than as an indication of any connection with Arsenal the public limited company. Before the ECJ Advocate General Ruiz-Jarabo denied that there was a dichotomy between the use made of a football team's name by its trade mark owner (as a way of making money) and the use made of the team's name by its supporters (as a badge of loyalty or support); his view was adopted by the ECJ.[26] If this view is right, then the ability to exploit a trade mark as a badge of loyalty or affiliation by the trade mark owner himself falls within the scope of the justifications for the trade mark system.

(e) To enable the consumer to make a lifestyle statement

2.39 Once a trade mark is created and used, it remains not only the private property of the trade mark owner but also the toy of the consumer, to do with as he chooses. It is therefore necessary to examine the justification of the trade mark system from the consumer's point of view—and from that view the use of a trade mark as a lifestyle statement is a phenomenon which has enriched both trade mark owners and dealers in counterfeit products ever since trade marks became fashion statements.

2.40 Fashion trade marks do much more than simply indicate the origin or quality of manufactured products. They enable consumers to buy goods which speak to the world and declare: 'this is the sort of person I am'. Thus by wearing clothes bearing the BENETTON label a person declares: 'I am a BENETTON person, with

---

[24] Council Directive 1985/374 on the approximation of the laws, regulations and administrative provisions of the Member States concerning liability for defective products, art 3.
[25] *Arsenal Football Club plc v Matthew Reed* [2001] ETMR 860 (HC).
[26] *Arsenal Football Club plc v Matthew Reed*, Case C-206/01 [2002] ETMR 975, [2003] RPC 144 (Advocate General's Opinion); [2003] ETMR 227 (ECJ). On the subsequent history of this ECJ reference, see further Chapter 7, paras 7.52–7.54.

BENETTON values', meaning: 'I am (or think I am) young, beautiful, affluent, stylish, not carrying any hang-ups about race, gender or politics and dedicated to the pursuit of my personal relationships with like-minded people'. A person who wears NIKE sportswear announces: 'I am young, oriented towards physically stimulating challenges and achievements and have a cool, couldn't-careless, attitude'. The wearer of the BURBERRY check or HERMES silk indicates: 'I am wealthy enough to appreciate good style that is not found on every street corner; I am discreet in my thoughts and actions, selective in my personal alliances and cultivate a touch of personal class'. Of course, the message purchased by the consumer is not necessarily the message perceived by others. The BENETTON message may be received unsympathetically as: 'You are a spoilt, selfish, fashion-conscious poseur whose transient values will pass upon the onset of personal maturity'. The same mixed messages can be conveyed by many trade marks which have become 'in-your-face' brands, for example, ROLLS ROYCE, HÄAGEN-DAZS and ROLEX.

2.41 Most trade marks however either (i) have no lifestyle-proclaiming function at all or (ii) have a lifestyle-proclaiming function which speaks to the consumer at the point of sale but which does not thereafter enable the consumer to proclaim that lifestyle to others. In the first category are trade marks such as BOEING, HEWLETT PACKARD or NESTLÉ. These trade marks represent brands which are so universal in their market application that they convey no lifestyle at all. Rich and poor, young and old, beautiful and ugly—all fly on BOEING aeroplanes, use HEWLETT PACKARD computer hardware and imbibe NESTLÉ products. The second category includes trade marks such as ANDREX, DINERS CLUB CARD and JOY. The brand affiliation of commodities such as toilet rolls, charge cards and perfumes will generally be unknown to those whom the lifestyle aspirant most wishes to impress.

(2) The pathology of trade marks

2.42 A large number of trade marks lead unexceptionable lives. They are not challenged in the course of application by the granting authorities; they are not opposed by competitors; they are not infringed; they just sit quietly on the trade marks register, a mute testimony to their owners' rights. This book is not the story of their lives. It deals for the most part with things that go wrong with trade marks: the ailments of unregistrability, invalidity, revocability, dilution, tarnishment and infringement. But do not forget that the trade mark system was developed for the sake of the good order of trade and commerce, not as an adversarial game between owner and infringer, applicant and granting authority.

2.43 A surprising number of trade mark disputes reach the courts or inferior tribunals within trade mark registries. Examine the list of legal cases cited in this book and

C. *The function of the trade mark system*

collected in the tables of cases and you will see not only how much litigation there is but how much of it is brought by trade mark owners (or aspiring owners) against trade mark registries. The strategic commercial value of a trade mark can be immense; the cost of acquiring it is usually trivial and its benefits are potentially eternal. Moreover, unlike most other assets, a trade mark becomes more valuable the more you use it. Is it any wonder, then, that so many trade mark disputes are fought to the bitter end rather than discreetly settled by mediation or other means? It is for this reason that trade mark law appears so dispute-oriented and so much of what we learn about the system is gleaned from watching the bits that go wrong rather than the bits that work smoothly.

(3) The morality of trade mark law

Trade mark law is like an iceberg, the vast bulk of which generally remains submerged beneath the line of vision of legal practitioners and the courts. The bits of law which most businesses and the public see are the bits that address the issues that most keenly affect them: Can I copy this mark? How much do I have to change that mark before I can't be sued for copying it? Can I use my competitor's mark in my own advertisements? Does the fact it doesn't say KELLOGG'S on the box mean it isn't made by Kellogg's? Why can't I register BRITE-KLEEN for toothpaste if I can register it for corn plasters? Do I really need permission before stitching my favourite football team's name on to my scarf? The rules that address these issues are however the exception. Most trade mark law deals with procedures and mechanisms that govern filing of applications, oppositions, revocations and cancellations, with renewals and with establishing, maintaining and amending records. This book focuses more on the high-profile issues which drive trade mark law rather than on the interstitial rules that hold every national and supranational system together. **2.44**

All trade mark law is man-made law: it is an arbitrary set of rules the majority of which, being procedural, possess a content that cannot be said to reflect any clearly recognizable principle of morality. In that sense much trade mark law addresses conduct which we would view as *malum prohibitum*, not *malum per se* (conduct which is wrong because it is prohibited, not inherently wrong in itself). At the heart of the trade mark system, however, lie rules with high moral content—the assumptions that copying and lying are wrong. Copying is what happens when I take your trade mark and put it on my goods, while lying is what I do when I represent that my products are in some way connected to yours when in fact they are not. These assumptions are however subject to several qualifications which are outlined below. **2.45**

(a) *Not all copying is regarded as wrong*

Even dismissing the trite dictum that imitation is the sincerest form of flattery, we **2.46** both teach and learn by copying. Such social phenomena as peer-group pressure and such psychological concepts as the fear of being thought different or an 'outsider' give copying an unchallengeable badge of legitimacy as a norm of human conduct. Success in the fashion industry depends on the urge of consumers to emulate their heroes or friends. Indeed, even in legal terms it cannot be said that copying is wrong. This view has been expressed in typically succinct form by one English judge in the following words:

> Some think that copying is unethical; others do not. Often the copyist of today becomes the innovator of tomorrow. Copying is said by some to be part of the lifeblood of competition, the means of breaking *de facto* market monopolies and keeping down the price of articles not protected by special monopolies such as patents or registered designs. Others say that copyists are parasites on innovators. None of this matters. Certainly it is not the law that copying as such is unlawful: the common law (and I am concerned with the common law) leans against monopolies.[27]

2.47 While this observation specifically addresses patents and registered design protection, it appears to be equally applicable to trade marks, particularly those trade marks which give a snappy and convenient name to a previously unknown product. And while the words are spoken by a common-law judge, their sentiment appears to be shared even by those civil-law jurisdictions in which 'slavish imitation' is treated as a legal wrong.[28]

(b) Not all lying is regarded as wrong

2.48 Small and relatively harmless lies are all part and parcel of advertising and marketing in a free-market economy, where consumers must learn at an early age not to believe everything they read or hear. Indeed, all generalizations—to the extent that they do not apply to specific cases—are almost by definition lies. We learn to call boastful advertising a mere 'puff'[29] and to remember that airlines are allowed to be quite economical with the truth when they compare their prices with those of their competitors.[30] We also latch on to the kernel of hidden truth contained in an advertising metaphor and discard the outer husk of falsity in which it is wrapped (no one expects 'man-sized' paper tissues to be the size of a man, nor holds exaggerated expectations as to the friendship offered by 'forest friendly' toilet rolls). The extent to which we not only tolerate these untruths but refuse even to call them lies demonstrates the extent to which we do not regard them as being wrong.

---

[27] Jacob J in *Hodgkinson Corby Limited and another v Wards Mobility Services Limited* [1995] FSR 169, 172.
[28] eg France and Italy.
[29] eg *Carlill v Carbolic Smoke Ball Company* [1893] 1 QB 256 (CA).
[30] See *British Airways plc v Ryanair Ltd* [2001] ETMR 235 (HC).

C. The function of the trade mark system

(c) Not all copying of trade marks is made unlawful by trade mark law

The trade mark laws of all countries include a range of defences to commercial activities which incense trade mark owners. These defences, which are discussed below,[31] only come into play once there is an act of copying which otherwise constitutes an infringement.

2.49

(d) Trade mark law makes unlawful apparently morally neutral acts which have nothing to do with copying or lying

Thus a trader who buys genuine MAG torches in the United States and imports them into the European Economic Area where he sells them at a profit has violated trade mark law, even though he has neither copied nor lied. The same can be said of the trader who innocently selects a fancy name under which to sell his product, with neither actual knowledge nor the opportunity to discover that a competitor has already filed an application to register the same trade mark for the same product.

2.50

(e) Trade mark law penalizes conduct which is not intended to be unlawful

Where a trader opts to use a sign which is actually different from a competitor's registered trade mark, he may have no idea whether his sign will be found to be confusingly similar to that mark. Similarity of marks is a matter of personal judgment and one man's confusion is another man's certainty. Any reader who does not believe this should match his own judgment as to confusing similarity against the decisions of the OHIM Opposition Division in respect of Community trade mark applications[32] and see how often he agrees with them.

2.51

Further issues involving the morality of trade mark law are addressed in Chapters 9 and 21.

2.52

(4) The real function of the trade mark system?

The real function of the trade mark system is not stated in trade mark legislation or in the *travaux préparatoires* to international treaties, nor even in trade mark books. The function of a key, a spade or a cup is as much defined by the uses to which it is in fact put as to the use it is designed to possess in theory. So too with the trade mark system, we must examine its function in the real world as well as its intended purpose on the legal draftsman's desk.

2.53

I believe that the function of the trade mark system in every developed economy is to establish an equilibrium of creative tension between the sometimes conflicting and sometimes coterminous interests of

2.54

---

[31] See Chapter 8.
[32] These decisions may be found at http://oami.eu.int/search/legaldocs/la/EN_Opposition_index.cfm.

(i) those who own trade marks;
(ii) those who compete directly or indirectly with them;
(iii) those who do not compete with them at all;
(iv) those consumers who choose to use their products and services; and
(v) those consumers who choose not to use their products and services.

2.55 In this state of equilibrium one should seek to maximize the benefits of the system for each group, save to the extent that each group's benefit inflicts detriment upon members of the other groups.

2.56 This definition is complex because trade mark law does not just exist for trade mark owners: it exists for everyone. It must accordingly apply to at least the following sets of relationships:

(i) the trade mark owner *vis-à-vis* the competing businesses (for example, PENGUIN chocolate-covered biscuits versus similar PUFFIN biscuits);
(ii) the trade mark owner *vis-à-vis* the non-competing business (for example, VISA for financial services versus VISA for condoms);
(iii) the trade mark owner *vis-à-vis* the consumer (for example, the registrability and use of deceptive trade marks);
(iv) the competing business *vis-à-vis* the consumer (for example, the ability of a parallel importer of pharmaceutical products to persuade foreign consumers that a medicine covered in sticky labels is safe to take); and
(v) the consumer *vis-à-vis* the non-competing business (for example, where a prospective purchaser of a Volkswagen wishes to obtain information on the Internet from one of three major companies which own POLO trade marks without becoming enmeshed in websites or pop-up banners relating to the other two).

2.57 A still more complex version of this definition factors in the special interests of: (vi) the owners of famous trade marks; (vii) licensees and assignees of trade marks; (viii) government departments and administrative agencies; and (ix) litigants. But for the purposes of this book, the simple definition will suffice.

2.58 If any existing known trade mark system is measured against this regrettably complex functional definition, it can be seen that the definition works fairly well. All trade mark systems are forced to make a series of compromises between the various sets of competing or complementary interests: it is how a trade mark system works at the points of intersection between those conflicting interests, when they are litigated, that the strengths and weaknesses of that system can be assessed. A country whose trade mark laws fail to protect even blatant infringements, or where the green shoots of innovative enterprise are trampled underfoot by the broad enforcement of existing entrenched trade marks, or whose consumers are laid open to cynical exploitation by amoral parasitic traders, will have demonstrated the extent to which it will have fallen short of the definition's ideal state of equilibrium.

D. Conclusion

2.59 This chapter has sought to explain the book's main aims and objectives and to set the scene, in outline, for the development of further themes in the theory and daily practice of trade mark law. It considers the moral bases of trade mark law as well as the legal framework within which the law is enacted, interpreted and applied.

3

TRADE MARK LAW AND TRADE MARK REGISTRATION SYSTEMS

A. **Introduction**
   A tale from Dickens
   The moral of the story 3.01
B. **Sources of trade mark law**
   (1) Where does trade mark law come from? 3.05
   (2) Treaties and regional agreements
       (a) International multilateral conventions and treaties 3.06
       (b) International bilateral treaties 3.08
       (c) Regional treaties 3.09
   (3) National statutes and subordinate legislation 3.11
   (4) Case law
       (a) Decisions of the European Court of Justice, the Court of First Instance of the European Communities and the European Free Trade Association Court 3.13
       (b) Decisions of national courts 3.15
   (5) Practice statements and rulings of regional and national trade mark registries 3.16
   (6) The learned writings of academic and professional experts 3.18
C. **Trade mark registration systems**
   (1) Do countries have to operate a trade mark registration system? 3.19
   (2) Modern registration systems: the theory 3.20
   (3) National registration 3.21
   (4) Regional registration 3.23
   (5) International registration 3.25
   (6) The main features of trade mark registration systems
       (a) Registration means that there is a register 3.26
       (b) What functions does the register perform? 3.27
       (c) Dividing the register into classes: the Nice Treaty 3.29
       (d) Examination of applications: what gets examined? 3.33
       (e) Examination of applications: the only way? 3.35
       (f) Interaction between trade mark applicant and examiner 3.39
       (g) Publication of the application 3.40
       (h) An opportunity for applications to be opposed 3.41
       (i) An opportunity for an applicant to amend his application and/or make a disclaimer 3.42
       (j) Grant and certification of a trade mark 3.44
       (k) Post-grant challenge 3.46
D. **Community trade marks and the trade marks of EU Member States** 3.47
   (1) The same mark can be registered under both CTM and national law 3.49
   (2) National courts can annul Community registrations 3.51
E. **Conclusion** 3.52

A. Introduction

A tale from Dickens[1]

The Circumlocution Office was (as everybody knows without being told) the most important Department under Government. No public business of any kind could possibly be done at any time without the acquiescence of the Circumlocution Office. Its finger was in the largest public pie, and in the smallest public tart. It was equally impossible to do the plainest right and to undo the plainest wrong without the express authority of the Circumlocution Office. If another Gunpowder Plot had been discovered half an hour before the lighting of the match, nobody would have been justified in saving the parliament until there had been half a score of boards, half a bushel of minutes, several sacks of official memoranda, and a family-vault full of ungrammatical correspondence, on the part of the Circumlocution Office.

This glorious establishment had been early in the field, when the one sublime principle involving the difficult art of governing a country was first distinctly revealed to statesmen. It had been foremost to study that bright revelation and to carry its shining influence through the whole of the official proceedings. Whatever was required to be done, the Circumlocution Office was beforehand with all the public departments in the art of perceiving—how not to do it.

Through this delicate perception, through the tact with which it invariably seized it, and through the genius with which it always acted on it, the Circumlocution Office had risen to overtop all the public departments; and the public condition had risen to be—what it was.

It is true that How not to do it was the great study and object of all public departments and professional politicians all round the Circumlocution Office. It is true that every new premier and every new government, coming in because they had upheld a certain thing as necessary to be done, were no sooner come in than they applied their utmost faculties to discovering How not to do it. It is true that from the moment when a general election was over, every returned man who had been raving on hustings because it hadn't been done, and who had been asking the friends of the honourable gentleman in the opposite interest on pain of impeachment to tell him why it hadn't been done, and who had been asserting that it must be done, and who had been pledging himself that it should be done, began to devise, How it was not to be done.

It is true that the debates of both Houses of Parliament the whole session through, uniformly tended to the protracted deliberation, How not to do it. It is true that the royal speech at the opening of such session virtually said, My lords and gentlemen, you have a considerable stroke of work to do, and you will please to retire to your respective chambers, and discuss, How not to do it. It is true that the royal speech, at the close of such session, virtually said, My lords and gentlemen, you have through several laborious months been considering with great loyalty and patriotism, How not to do it, and you have found out; and with the blessing of Providence upon the harvest (natural, not political), I now dismiss you. All this is true, but the Circumlocution Office went beyond it.

Because the Circumlocution Office went on mechanically, every day, keeping this wonderful, all-sufficient wheel of statesmanship, How not to do it, in motion.

---

[1] From Charles Dickens, *Little Dorrit*, ch 10 ('Containing the Whole Science of Government').

A. Introduction

Because the Circumlocution Office was down upon any ill-advised public servant who was going to do it, or who appeared to be by any surprising accident in remote danger of doing it, with a minute, and a memorandum, and a letter of instructions that extinguished him. It was this spirit of national efficiency in the Circumlocution Office that had gradually led to its having something to do with everything. Mechanicians, natural philosophers, soldiers, sailors, petitioners, memorialists, people with grievances, people who wanted to prevent grievances, people who wanted to redress grievances, jobbing people, jobbed people, people who couldn't get rewarded for merit, and people who couldn't get punished for demerit, were all indiscriminately tucked up under the foolscap paper of the Circumlocution Office.

Numbers of people were lost in the Circumlocution Office. Unfortunates with wrongs, or with projects for the general welfare (and they had better have had wrongs at first, than have taken that bitter English recipe for certainly getting them), who in slow lapse of time and agony had passed safely through other public departments; who, according to rule, had been bullied in this, over-reached by that, and evaded by the other; got referred at last to the Circumlocution Office, and never reappeared in the light of day. Boards sat upon them, secretaries minuted upon them, commissioners gabbled about them, clerks registered, entered, checked, and ticked them off, and they melted away. In short, all the business of the country went through the Circumlocution Office, except the business that never came out of it; and its name was Legion.

The moral of the story

3.01 Trade marks are granted by bureaucratic institutions and it is the case that, however good a set of trade mark laws may be, the excellence of a trade mark system is judged by the quality of its administration and not merely by the quality of its laws.

3.02 Legal practitioners, trade mark attorneys, trade mark registry administrators and traders generally take it for granted that a great deal of time should elapse between the date of application to register a trade mark and the date upon which the application is granted or refused. But why should this be the case? If you ask for a bank loan, the bank expresses its intention of imposing a number of conditions upon the loan and seeks security for it, the necessary security and the means and frequency of repayment are evidenced and agreed, the entire transaction can take days. But if you apply to register FROOTIE TOOT as a trade mark for an ice lolly you can expect to wait many months or even years before getting an answer.

3.03 Charles Dickens was no admirer of bureaucracy. The Circumlocution Office, described above, may have been modelled on the bureaucratic and improbable means of granting patents which he mercilessly pilloried in his short story *The Poor Man's Tale of a Patent*.[2] But the patent system which he attacked for its cumbersome and meaningless rituals could deliver a granted patent in all of six weeks; nowadays between thirty and forty-two months can be expected to elapse between filing a patent and getting it.

---

[2] See Jeremy Phillips, *Charles Dickens and 'The Poor Man's Tale of a Patent'* (1984).

3.04 Trade mark systems, then, depend on the quality of their law and on their administrative capabilities. This chapter will examine each of these phenomena. As a result of this, the reader should be in a better position to understand why, even if a trade mark application takes a lot more time to process than it should, it needs to take more time than many people imagine.

B. Sources of trade mark law

(1) Where does trade mark law come from?

3.05 There are many sources of trade mark law, bringing their influence to bear at many different levels of the trade mark system. These sources are as follows: (i) international multilateral conventions; (ii) international bilateral treaties; (iii) regional treaties; (iv) national statutes and subordinate legislation; (v) decisions of courts in trade mark disputes (case law); (vi) practice statements and rulings of regional and national trade mark registries; and (vii) the learned writings of academic and professional experts. These are described briefly below.

(2) Treaties and regional agreements

(a) International multilateral conventions and treaties

3.06 One of the reasons why the trade mark laws of so many countries are so similar to each other and why there is such a high degree of compatibility between the national trade mark systems of different jurisdictions is that both these issues have been shaped for nearly 120 years by a range of international conventions to which very many countries are signatory. The main conventions are

   (i) the Paris Convention on the Protection of Industrial Property, which requires countries to protect trade marks, to provide 'grace periods' within which an applicant from one country can file his mark in other countries ahead of local competitors, and to treat applicants from other Member States no worse than one would treat one's own national applicants;
   (ii) the Madrid Agreement on the International Registration of Marks, which enables a trade mark owner to apply, through one application, for registration in other countries;
   (iii) the Madrid Protocol, which extends and amends some aspects of the Madrid Agreement;
   (iv) the Agreement on Trade-Related Aspects of Intellectual Property Law (TRIPs), which spells out the minimum acceptable levels of legal protection to which trade mark owners should be entitled; and
   (v) the Trademark Law Treaty, which seeks to reduce the degree of unnecessary red tape associated with so eminently bureaucratic a task as filing trade marks.

B. Sources of trade mark law

Most international treaties are unenforceable if the countries that sign them subsequently choose to ignore their obligations and, since no country has yet gone to war with another over a trade mark, many treaty obligations are more honoured in the breach than in their observation. However, TRIPs has quite a sophisticated dispute-resolution mechanism which can result in trading sanctions being imposed on recalcitrant Member States.[3] **3.07**

(b) International bilateral treaties

Since the major international conventions are so well known in legal circles, little attention has been paid to bilateral treaties. They are the varicose veins of trade mark law, a web of often unsightly provisions which, if ignored, can hinder and ultimately block the flow of commerce between nations. There is no convenient source to which one can turn for information concerning them, which is why they are often overlooked. Bilateral treaties which may have recently surprised trade mark litigants include the Stresa Convention,[4] agreements struck by the former Czechoslovakia with both Portugal[5] and Switzerland[6] for the protection of indications of provenance, designations of origin and other geographical designations. **3.08**

(c) Regional treaties

Here we mention treaties made between regional blocs of countries for the purpose of regulating aspects of trade mark law. In this category fall such legal arrangements as: the Benelux Treaty on the Uniform Trade Mark Law,[7] which provides for three countries—Belgium, Luxembourg and the Netherlands—to share a single trade mark system; the Community Trade Mark (CTM) Regulation; the Cartagena Agreement which provides for co-operation in trade mark matters between the Member States of the Andean Pact;[8] the Banjul Protocol on Marks;[9] and the 1999 revised Bangui Agreement on an African **3.09**

---

[3] Member States in breach of TRIPs may become the victims of trade sanctions and tariff reprisals. Up-to-date news, background materials and legal sources can be found on the World Trade Organization's website www.wto.org.

[4] Despite its grand name ('International Convention of Stresa, 1 June 1951, on the use of designations of origin and names of cheeses'), this convention appears to bind just France and Italy; see *Consorzio per la Tutela del Formaggio Gorgonzola v Käserei Champignon Hofmeister GmbH & Co KG and Eduard Bracharz GmbH* [1999] ETMR 454 (ECJ).

[5] *Budejovicky Budvar Narodni Podnik v Anheuser-Busch Inc* [2002] ETMR 1182 (Supreme Court, Portugal).

[6] See *Anheuser-Busch Inc v Budejovicky Budvar Narodni Podnik* [2001] ETMR 74 (Schweizerisches Bundesgericht).

[7] Convention concerning Trade Marks of 19 March 1962 with an Annex, Uniform Benelux Law on Marks (amended by Protocol of 10 November 1983, amending the Uniform Benelux Law on Trade Marks and by the Protocol of 2 December 1992, amending the Uniform Benelux Law on Marks).

[8] Bolivia, Colombia, Ecuador, Peru, Venezuela.

[9] This protocol operates under the auspices of the African Regional Industrial Property Organization (ARIPO). The five nations currently operating within the Protocol are Malawi, Lesotho, Swaziland, Tanzania and Zimbabwe. For details of ARIPO, see aripo.wipo.net.

Industrial Property Organization (OAPI).[10] These treaties reflect a recognition by smaller jurisdictions that efficiencies and economies of scale can be gained by combining their resources and perhaps also a somewhat begrudging concession that national trade mark law is an ultimately parochial pastime and that global trade mark protection will eventually evolve as an alternative to national registration if not as a complete replacement for it.

3.10 A different sort of regional agreement is the European Union's trade mark harmonization Directive.[11] This Directive does not so much regulate relations between states or require co-operation between them. Instead, it demands that its signatories adopt a common standard for their respective national laws, this standard consisting both of compulsory and optional legal norms. These norms have been given scope for interpretation and subsequent development through the jurisprudence of the Court of Justice of the European Communities (usually referred to as the European Court of Justice and abbreviated to ECJ).

(3) National statutes and subordinate legislation

3.11 Most countries have their own national trade mark legislation, passed by their national legislature and supplemented by subordinate legislation on its implementation and day-to-day operation. There are however some exceptions, as has been mentioned in the previous paragraph.

3.12 Some jurisdictions have unusual arrangements for domestic trade mark legislation. For example, the United States of America is both a single entity and an alliance of fifty-one separate jurisdictions.[12] The US accordingly simultaneously operates a Federal trade mark system in respect of trade marks for use in 'interstate commerce'[13] and a large number of separate State trade mark systems. Although many people outside the US are unaware of the existence of State registration, it is a significant form of legal protection which non-US businesses ignore at their peril.[14]

---

[10] This agreement provides for a single patent and trade mark office to process the industrial property rights of no fewer than fifteen countries: Benin, Burkina Faso, Cameroon, Central African Republic, Chad, Congo, Gabon, Guinea, Guinea Bissau, Ivory Coast, Mali, Mauretania, Niger, Senegal and Togo. For details of OAPI, see oapi.wipo.net.

[11] Council Directive 89/104.

[12] The fifty states of the Union together with Puerto Rico.

[13] United States Constitution, art 1, s 8, gives power to the Congress 'to regulate commerce with foreign nations, and among the several states, and with the Indian tribes'. It is to this provision, remarkably, that the big brand-owning corporations owe the powerful protection conferred upon their trade marks under United States law.

[14] On State registration and protection, see the impressive loose-leaf publication of the International Trademark Association, *State Trademark and Unfair Competition Law*, which extends to some 1,600 pages.

B. Sources of trade mark law

(4) Case law

(a) Decisions of the European Court of Justice, the Court of First Instance of the European Communities and the European Free Trade Association Court

3.13 As a matter of European Union law,[15] all Member States of that Union are bound by EU law even where it is inconsistent with national law. EU legal doctrine, which embraces many points of national and EU trade mark law, is frequently developed by the ECJ, to which national courts refer difficult issues for a preliminary ruling. EU legal doctrine is also developed by the Court of First Instance of the European Communities (usually shortened to the Court of First Instance or CFI) when an appeal is made from a decision of the Office for Harmonisation in the Internal Market (often referred to as OHIM or OAMI), the body which administers the CTM system. The ECJ also hears appeals against decisions of the CFI. Once the ECJ or CFI makes a pronouncement on the meaning of a provision of European trade mark law, it is not open to a national court in the European Union to challenge that decision directly. It is however open to a national court to make a reference to the ECJ even on an issue upon which it has already ruled, in the hope that the ECJ will see the error of its ways and issue a different ruling.[16] Courts in countries belonging to the European Economic Area but not the European Union[17] treat decisions of the ECJ as being advisory only, although they are likely to be influential.

3.14 The Court of the European Free Trade Association (EFTA) has jurisdiction to rule on trade mark issues involving those countries which are part of the EEA but which are not part of the EU.[18] The EFTA Court's rulings are only advisory, not binding, and the ECJ will simply ignore that court's approach in favour of its own.[19]

(b) Decisions of national courts

3.15 Courts in common-law jurisdictions have traditionally regarded themselves as being bound by decisions of higher courts within their own countries; they will

---

[15] On the supremacy of European law over domestic law, see Craig and De Búrca, *EU Law: Text, Cases and Materials* (2002), ch 6.

[16] This has in fact happened in the field of trade mark law when the ECJ's decision in *Van Zuylen Freres v HAG AG* [1974] ECR 731 ('HAG I') was subsequently reversed in *CNL-Sucal NV v Hag GF AG* [1990] 3 CMLR 571 ('HAG II').

[17] At the time of writing, Iceland, Liechtenstein and Norway.

[18] Agreement Between the EFTA States on the establishment of a surveillance authority and a Court of Justice, art 34.

[19] See the EFTA Court's decision in *Mag Instrument Inc v California Trading Company Norway, Ulsteen* [1998] ETMR 85, which was not even mentioned by the ECJ in *Silhouette International Schmiedt GmbH & Co KG v Hartlauer Handelsgesellschaft mbH*, Case C-355/96 [1998] ETMR 539. Both of these decisions were first considered by the Swedish Court of Appeal in *NGK Spark Plug Co Ltd v Biltema Sweden Aktiebolag* [2000] ETMR 507, which held that Swedish law did not explicitly reject the principle of global exhaustion but nonetheless followed *Silhouette* in preference to *Mag*.

also generally, as a matter of judicial comity, refuse to dissent from the view of a court of equivalent status without giving at least a reasoned statement as to why they have done so. This practice is nowadays increasingly found outside the common-law world and readers of judgments delivered in jurisdictions within not only the United States and the British Isles but also Germany, Austria, Poland and Italy, among others, will find references to legal doctrine as discussed and explained by earlier decisions within those jurisdictions. In other countries the citation of earlier cases is still a relatively infrequent event, for example, in France, Finland, Portugal and Switzerland.

(5) Practice statements and rulings of regional and national trade mark registries

3.16 The decisions made by hearing officers in applications and opposition proceedings before national trade mark registries are relatively low-level events; in many countries the decisions of hearing officers are not made publicly available at all while, in others, they are made available but are rarely accorded any serious attention by trade mark lawyers. Yet in one respect they are vital: they provide the most important form of guidance as to what a trade mark registry actually does when confronted with a specific situation. Indeed, when the law changes (as most European trade mark laws did in the mid-1990s), office practice and the decisions of hearing officers may form the level to which reference is made in default of any more current or appropriate guidance. Some countries, as well as OHIM, helpfully publish the instruction manuals that guide trade mark examiners as to how to deal with certain issues, on the basis that it is important for hearing officers to behave consistently when facing those issues. These manuals, and the decisions of individual hearing officers, may not have the force of law but, on a behavioural view, how a trade mark registry deals with its case load *is* the law unless any higher authority interferes with it. In the absence of any other guidance, the manuals act as a common focus for predicting how higher authorities will act, rather than relying on the subjective guesses of individual trade mark practitioners.

3.17 Registries also promulgate their own orders, which one ignores at one's peril. They may deal with purely procedural issues (such as the dates when a registry is closed over a holiday period) or serious substantive issues (such as indicating how the registry proposes to treat a particular type of application in the future).

(6) The learned writings of academic and professional experts

3.18 In civil-law jurisdictions the writings of scholars and experts have long been valued as a source of law. Even today, anyone reading the transcripts of trade mark cases from countries such as Austria, Germany and Greece will often be struck by the large number of scholarly citations considered by the judges. Although common-law jurisdictions such as the United States and the UK formerly paid relatively little attention to scholarly doctrine, the practice of citing scholarly opinions—particularly in fields of legal application in which there is no more directly relevant source of law—appears to have increased in recent years, particularly in the United States. In truth scholarly writings have made their influence felt even when their use has not been acknowledged, since many trade mark practitioners will read and imbibe the writings of learned commentators which are then presented as their own submissions in court.

C. Trade mark registration systems

(1) Do countries have to operate a trade mark registration system?

3.19 In theory, no. Neither the Paris Convention nor TRIPs explicitly imposes an obligation on any country to operate a system for the registration of trade marks: they merely stipulate the parameters within which a country's trade mark registration system must operate. In practice, however, the great majority of countries do operate registration systems. Only a few still accord protection on the basis that the trade mark owner has advertised his interest through placing a 'cautionary notice' in a local newspaper.[20]

(2) Modern registration systems: the theory

3.20 Most trade mark registrations today are striving to achieve the same aims: (i) to grant trade mark applications unless there is a clear reason for not doing so; (ii) to keep staff costs to a minimum through the most efficient use of information technology; and (iii) to ensure that registry practice meets the needs of its users and their professional representatives.

(3) National registration

3.21 Most countries operate a national system for the registration of trade marks. The operation of the national trade mark registry (which is usually a branch of that country's patent office) is governed by national law. Although there have been suggestions from time to time that patent offices should be privatized, all national trade mark registries remain part of their country's civil service.

3.22 When a trade mark is granted by a national trade mark registry, the resulting monopoly is normally coterminous with the borders of the granting jurisdiction. This is not always the case. For example, French trade marks extend to a number

---

[20] Eritrea still operates a 'cautionary notice' system. Even in some jurisdictions in which registration has replaced cautionary notices, local practitioners sometimes advise placing newspaper advertisements anyway, to be on the safe side.

(4) Regional registration

3.23 Where a group of countries join together to form a single system for the grant of trade marks, they do so by means of a regional trade mark registry such as OHIM (for EU countries) or the Benelux Trade Mark Office (for Belgium, the Netherlands and Luxembourg). The legal basis for the operation of such systems is not national law but the treaty or international regulation establishing the office and any subordinate legislation issued under the treaty for the operation of that office.

3.24 The trade mark, once issued, will cover the territory provided for under the treaty. Where the number of countries within a regional system increases, careful provision must be made for the extent of protection conferred in the enlarged region upon trade marks registered prior to enlargement.[23]

(5) International registration

3.25 Although the term 'international trademark' is frequently heard in trade mark circles, its use should not encourage listeners to think that it is possible to obtain a form of trade mark registration which confers global protection upon a trade mark proprietor. The Madrid Agreement and Madrid Protocol provide a mechanism whereby, starting with a single national trade mark registration or application, an applicant can obtain protection in a multiplicity of countries (currently around seventy between the two treaties). The two Madrid schemes are administered by the International Bureau of the World Intellectual Property Organization (WIPO) in Geneva.

(6) The main features of trade mark registration systems

(a) Registration means that there is a register

3.26 The very term 'registration' presupposes the existence of a register. This is a list of trade marks, together with:

(i) a record of the goods and services for which they are registered;
(ii) the date of registration;

---

[21] French Antarctica, Guadeloupe, French Guiana, Martinique, Mayotte, New Caledonia, French Polynesia, Réunion, St Pierre and Miquelon, French Southern Territories, Wallis and Futuna Islands.
[22] Trade Mark Rules 2000, SI 2000/136, r 2.
[23] On the problems of enlargement of a regional trade mark system, see eg Tibor Gold, 'Community Trade Marks in Transition' (2003) 126 MIP 55–9.

C. Trade mark registration systems

(iii) the details of their proprietors; and

(iv) in some cases the details of the professional representatives who acted for the proprietors in the application process. The register will also record various things that are done with, or to, trade marks after the application is granted.

(b) What functions does the register perform?

3.27 The register is in principle a publicly accessible document to which all may turn for information. It performs, among others, the following useful functions:[24]

(i) enables prospective trade mark applicants to see whether the mark they propose to register has already been taken,[25] whether for the goods or services for which they wish to use that mark or for other related goods or services;

(ii) enables the competitors of trade mark owners to see which words, logos and other marks cannot be used as trade marks or in the commercial promotion of their businesses because they have already been appropriated as registered trade marks;

(iii) it enables competitors, when confronted by a trade mark registration symbol (®), to ascertain precisely what the registered trade mark consists of;

(iv) it provides would-be licensees of registered trade marks with details as to those to whom they should address requests for the grant of a licence; and

(v) it provides ideas and often inspiration for those who are seeking to create an effective trade mark and who wish to study the manner in which others achieve that end.

3.28 It is often advisable to re-check the contents of the register, since there is always a lapse of time between the receipt of information by the trade marks registry and its entry on to the register.

(c) Dividing the register into classes: the Nice Treaty

3.29 Among the lay public it is often believed that, once a trade mark has been registered, it confers protection against unauthorized use in all areas of commerce.

---

[24] An 'official' view of the function of the register in relation to representations of trade marks may be found in *Myles Ltd's application*, Case R 711/199-3, 5 December 2001 (OHIM): 'the representation must be complete and encompass the trade mark as a whole. In addition, it must be so clear and precise that the Office is able to undertake the examination for absolute and relative grounds for refusal, publish the trade mark in the Community Trade Marks Bulletin and register it in the Register of Community Trade Marks. Such a representation must also be so unequivocal that competitors can undertake investments in reliance on the precisely-outlined scope of the trade mark and the courts and parties are in a position to establish and assess properly any trade mark infringements' (para 11).

[25] For this reason each registration should be for a single trade mark and not for an infinitely variable group or combination of marks. Thus in *Re International Flavors & Fragrances Inc* 51 USPQ 2d 1513 (Fed Cir 1999) three applications to register the designations LIVING xxxx, LIVING xxxx FLAVOUR and LIVING xxxx FLAVOURS, where the 'xxxx' was intended to be substituted by any of a number of words which would not appear on the register, were rejected.

This is only true in the improbable situation in which (i) a trade mark has been registered for all possible goods and services for which registration is possible, or the rather less improbable but still none-too-common situation in which (ii) a trade mark is so famous that it is inconceivable that anyone other than the trade mark owner or his licensees could use it without confusing the public or damaging the mark's reputation. In all other situations the protection conferred by registration is limited by the applicant's designation of the goods or services for which he requires protection.

3.30 For the benefit of trade mark applicants, trade mark registries and (according to some opinions) the public at large, the scheme of designation of goods and services in most countries is determined by the classification system set out by the Nice Agreement.[26] This Agreement, which was concluded in 1952, initially divided up into forty-two classes all goods and services in which trade took place. As commerce becomes more sophisticated and the range of goods and services increases, the Nice Classification is from time to time amended.[27]

3.31 The operation of this system by national and regional trade mark systems makes it easier for trade mark applicants to check whether a mark is free for use. For example, pharmaceutical products are registered in Class 5. If a drugs company wishes to register the trade mark POXYCILLIN for a new antibiotic, it will be known which part of the trade mark register to search for earlier identical or similar registrations even in countries with whose laws it has little familiarity, so long as those countries employ the Nice categorization.

3.32 Not all countries are signatory to the Nice classification scheme[28] but the trend towards greater homogenization of national and regional trade mark systems is likely to result in its eventual adoption worldwide.

(d) Examination of applications: what gets examined?

3.33 The examination process is multifaceted. First, the trade mark registry needs to examine the application in order to ascertain that it is indeed a trade mark application. Secondly the examiner will need to be sure that the examination is for something which fits the formal criteria for a 'trade mark'. Thirdly the examiner will consider whether any inherent defect in the trade mark precludes it from being registered. In many countries the examiner will also check to see whether the applicant's trade mark has already been registered by another applicant in respect of the same goods or services.

---

[26] Nice Agreement Concerning the International Classification of Goods and Services for the Purposes of the Registration of Marks of 15 June 1957, most recently amended on 28 September 1979.
[27] The Nice Classification is now in its seventh edition, containing forty-five classes (classes 1–34 for goods, 35–45 for services).
[28] Only seventy countries were Nice signatories at the beginning of 2003. Significant omissions include (in alphabetical order) Argentina, Brazil, Canada, Chile, India, Malaysia and Pakistan.

C. Trade mark registration systems

3.34 Trade mark registries have adopted different approaches towards the examination of a trade mark. Some, for example, the British registry prior to 1994, operated a principle sometimes called 'purity of the register': no trade mark should be registered unless it was truly meritorious of registration. Others, including the great majority of continental European trade mark systems, preferred to operate a presumption of registrability, allowing an application to proceed to grant unless there was a good reason why it should not be granted. In some registries, examiners were accorded a wide degree of discretion in determining whether a mark should be registered, in order to 'achieve justice in the individual case'. Other registries operated on the basis that examiners should be accorded as little discretion as possible, in order that 'distributive justice' in the Aristotelian sense should be achieved by the greatest degree of consistency in the application of the same legal rules to comparable trade marks. The current norm is for registration to be the natural consequence of a trade mark application which is not beset by any raging problem and for examiners to be administrators rather than judges, applying legal rules rather their own judgment.

(e) Examination of applications: the only way?

3.35 It is nowadays the norm for a trade mark right to be based upon an application for registration which is examined. There are however systems even today which are based upon deposit or notice.

3.36 A *depository* system is one under which an applicant can deposit any trade mark he wishes; the deposit, which is not examined for validity or anything other than compliance with formalities, is not accorded any high degree of presumed validity.[29] Once a mark is deposited, it will however give its owner an earlier and therefore superior right to anyone else who subsequently deposits the same mark for the same goods or services. Accordingly if I deposited the word mark FIZZPOP for confectionery on 10 February 1999, I will have a superior right to that mark to Mongoose, who deposited the same mark on 15 March 2001 but an inferior right as against Bandicoot, who deposited it on 19 August 1997. If I use the mark, Bandicoot may sue me for infringing his deposited mark; if Mongoose uses the mark and Bandicoot is indifferent to it or has ceased trading, then I can sue for infringement. Depository systems are cheap to maintain, but they create a proliferation of weak and unexamined deposited marks, many of which are of little or no legal force or commercial significance.

3.37 A *notice-based* system does not even require the deposit of a trade mark, far less a formal application. All that is needed is that the person asserting his entitlement to a trade mark should advertise that fact by publishing a formal cautionary notice

---

[29] Countries which examine for formalities only include Algeria, Angola, Burundi, Morocco, Rwanda, Somalia, St Helena, Cambodia, Lebanon and Myanmar.

of its claim to the trade mark in a national or official newspaper. Such a system works in jurisdictions in which there are very few trade marks (such as Eritrea) and should work even better if everyone reads the newspapers and keeps their own record of their competitors' advertisements.

3.38 Depository and notice-based systems have become increasingly rare in recent years, for a number of reasons. These include: (i) the perception that any trade mark system which fails to provide for the examination of trade marks is unlikely to be seen as an encouragement to make investment in the development of new brands; (ii) the increasing trend towards compatibility of domestic trade mark law with TRIPs norms; and (iii) the degree of advice and assistance which has been made available to developing countries by WIPO for the establishment of trade mark examination systems and for the training of trade mark examiners.

(f) Interaction between trade mark applicant and examiner

3.39 Once an application for trade mark registration is lodged, it may proceed smoothly until the trade mark is registered. Quite often, however, the application becomes an interactive process in which the examiner raises objections concerning the trade mark or seeks clarification from the applicant as to various issues arising from the application. If the issues raised are not dealt with to the examiner's satisfaction, the application may not be able to proceed further.

(g) Publication of the application

3.40 It is normal for trade mark applications to be published so that interested parties—normally competitors—can respond to the consequences which arise from the fact that those marks will become the basis for the private monopolies enjoyed by their proprietors and for the assertion of their earlier rights against later users. It is the trade mark as published which determines the nature of the proprietor's rights. Where (as with CTMs) the applicant may file his application by fax, it is the version of the sign which comes out of the receiving office's fax, not the version which the applicant feeds in, which is published.

(h) An opportunity for applications to be opposed

3.41 Where a competitor or other interested third party objects to the grant of an application for a trade mark which has been published, it is normal for trade mark systems to operate a mechanism whereby that application can be opposed. (The grounds upon which a trade mark can be opposed are discussed in Chapter 13.)

(i) An opportunity for an applicant to amend his application and/or make a disclaimer

3.42 Before a trade mark application is finally disposed of by the registry, an applicant is generally given the opportunity to amend the application. This amendment

C. Trade mark registration systems

may relate to his own personal details, such as a change of name or address, or to matters which affect the scope of the granted monopoly such as the making of changes in the classes of goods or services for which registration of the mark is sought or the amendment of the specification of goods or services listed in each class.

3.43 In some jurisdictions, including that of the CTM, applicants may inform the registry that they disclaim a monopoly entitlement in respect of specific features of a trade mark which could not be lawfully monopolized. The making of disclaimers may help avoid the risk of registry objections that an applicant has sought to appropriate for himself any words or signs which others should be entitled to use; disclaimers may also serve the role of heading off unwanted oppositions lodged by competitors who are concerned that words or signs the use of which they have an interest in may be drawn within the scope of the applicant's granted trade mark right.

(j) Grant and certification of a trade mark

3.44 When the trade mark registry is satisfied that there are no bars to registration, the application will be completed by the grant of a valid trade mark registration. The granting office will issue a certificate to the effect that the trade mark has been granted. The certificate will identify the trade mark's owner and will provide sufficient salient details to satisfy a court of law as to the nature of the granted trade mark, the date from which protection was granted and its initial ownership.

3.45 Once a trade mark application is granted, the registered trade mark is presumed to be valid. This means both that, in infringement proceedings in which the defendant does not contest the trade mark's validity, the trade mark proprietor does not have to establish afresh that his trade mark is valid: all he has to do is to produce his registration certificate. It also means that, where the trade mark's validity is granted, it is for the party alleging invalidity to prove invalidity. The presumption of validity has been held in the United States to extend to a trade mark's 'most salient features', even if those features are allegedly descriptive or generic.[30]

(k) Post-grant challenge

3.46 It is a feature of most national trade mark systems that, once the administrative procedure leading to the grant of a trade mark has been completed by the grant of a registered trade mark, it is open to any third party to challenge the validity of the granted mark on absolute grounds. Additionally, where a mark is validly granted but another trade mark owner or trader believes that the grant was made in violation of its rights, that interested party can seek cancellation of the registration on

---

[30] *KP Permanent Make-Up Inc v Lasting Impression I, Inc*, No 01-56055 (9th Cir 30 April 2003): word-and-device mark including the allegedly generic term MICRO COLORS held presumptively valid.

relative grounds. Sometimes this challenge is designed to be effected through the granting office (as is the case for CTMs, which may be challenged through an application made to OHIM's Cancellation Division); sometimes the challenge is launched through the courts. (Challenges to the validity of a granted trade mark through cancellation and revocation proceedings are discussed in greater detail in Chapter 13.)

D. Community trade marks and the trade marks of EU Member States

3.47 The CTM system and the national trade mark systems of EU Member States[31] are designed to coexist, since neither is capable of replicating the benefits conferred by the other. Since national laws may prevent a trade name or trade mark which is lawfully used in one Member State from being used in others,[32] protection under national law will remain necessary notwithstanding the increasing extent to which CTMs are sought and granted.

3.48 The CTM courts[33] of the Member States are also their national trade mark courts; when CTMs are litigated,[34] these courts apply the CTM Regulation as far as possible[35] but, where it is silent, the courts apply national rules on procedure and evidence, as well as national rules on remedies and enforcement.[36] A CTM application can, in appropriate circumstances, be converted into separate national applications.[37] A national registration can grant seniority to a subsequent CTM application.[38] Rulings of the ECJ will bind, and decisions of the CFI will influence, the interpretation of both Community and national trade mark law, and so on. In the following subheadings we consider some of the more interesting facets of this coexistence.

(1) The same mark can be registered under both CTM and national law

3.49 There is no reason why the same trade mark may not be separately registered by the same proprietor as a CTM and under national law, as is the case with

---

[31] Henceforward, 'national' also includes the regional Benelux system.
[32] *Pfeiffer Grosshandel GmbH v Löwa Warenhandel GmbH*, Case C-255/97 [1999] ETMR 603 (ECJ).
[33] Council Regulation 40/94, art 91. For a current list of CTM courts, see the OHIM website at http://oami.eu.int/pdf/aspects/Co026-ann.pdf.
[34] For a helpful and straightforward account of CTM enforcement, see Gert Würtenburger, 'Enforcement of Community Trade Mark Rights' [2002] IPQ 402–17.
[35] Council Regulation 40/94, art 97(1).
[36] ibid, art 97(2) and (3).
[37] ibid, arts 108 et seq.
[38] ibid, art 34.

D. Community and EU trade marks

VIAGRA.[39] It may happen that the two registrations are not coextensive, since the existence of other marks on the national and CTM register will determine the spread of goods or services within any given class[40] for which registration is available.

3.50 The fact that the same trade mark can be registered in one or both of two overlapping systems has an interesting twist to it where two applicants are competing for control of the same mark. Thus in an Irish application[41] Dairygold sought to register the words PORK—THE OTHER WHITE MEAT as a trade mark for pork and pork products. The examiner objected that this application was both descriptive and devoid of distinctive character. At the hearing Dairygold explained that an application had been made by a third party to register a virtually identical mark as a CTM and that Dairygold was basing its opposition to CTM registration on this very application. Effectively, therefore, the Hearing Officer was faced with the following choice: (i) allow Dairygold's application, with the result that PORK—THE OTHER WHITE MEAT is registered in Ireland but can then be used to oppose the CTM application; or (ii) refuse the application, in which case the CTM application would proceed unopposed. In either case the words PORK—THE OTHER WHITE MEAT would be the subject of an Irish trade mark monopoly. In the event, the Hearing Officer's decision to reject the application appears to have been justified since the CTM application seems to have sunk without trace.[42]

(2) National courts can annul Community registrations

3.51 Although proceedings to cancel a CTM registration must be brought before OHIM's Cancellation Division,[43] the invalidity of a CTM may be pleaded as a counterclaim in infringement proceedings,[44] with the result that a national court, in its capacity as a CTM court, declares the CTM invalid.[45] Once this happens the court's decision is sent to OHIM, which is obliged to accept it.[46]

---

[39] *Pfizer Ltd and Pfizer Incorporated v Eurofood Link (United Kingdom) Ltd* [2000] ETMR 896 (HC).
[40] On the class system, see paras 3.29–3.32 below.
[41] *Dairygold Co-operative Society Ltd's application* [2001] ETMR 1279 (Irish Patent Office).
[42] A search of the OHIM database on 6 March 2003 revealed only three trade marks containing the word 'pork', none of which made any reference to white meat.
[43] Council Regulation 40/94, art 51.
[44] But not proceedings for a declaration that the defendant was not entitled to seek discontinuance of use of the claimant's mark; see *Ohio Art Company and Bandai GmbH Toys and Entertainment v CreCon Spiel U Hobbyartikel GmbH* [2000] ETMR 756 (Landgericht, Munich).
[45] See Council Regulation 40/94, art 96.
[46] ibid, art 96(6).

E. Conclusion

3.52 In this chapter we have surveyed the institutional structure of trade mark systems: where the law comes from, how trade marks are administered and where they are enforced. The institutional structure is not complex and it has responded, on the whole, fairly well to the competing demands of applicants, competitors, consumers and administrators.

3.53 Now we move on to the next stage, and the following three chapters review the parameters of protection within which trade mark-granting authorities discharge their various duties.

PART B

REGISTRABLE TRADE MARKS

4

REGISTRABILITY: THE BASIC PRINCIPLES

A. Introduction
    'But I tell you, I want it registered'
    The moral of the story   4.01
    (1) What makes a trade mark registrable?   4.04
    (2) A short note on the terminology of registrability   4.07
    (3) Registration under international law   4.08

B. Absolute bars to registration
    (1) How absolute bars to registration function   4.16
    (2) Grounds of unregistrability are independent of each other   4.20

C. Graphic representation and the function of the register   4.24

D. Signs may not be registrable if consumers do not regard them as being trade marks   4.31

E. Signs which are not registrable on policy grounds
    (1) Immoral and illegal marks   4.32
    (2) Deceptive marks   4.41

F. Signs which other traders may wish to use
    (1) Marks which infringe copyright, design and other intellectual property rights   4.50
    (2) Publicly reserved terms are not registrable   4.53
    (3) Generic terms and customary trade terms are not registrable   4.58
    (4) The need to keep a word or other sign available for all to use   4.67
        (a) *Freihaltebedürfnis* and the scope of protection of granted applications   4.69
        (b) *Freihaltebedürfnis* in ECJ and CFI case law   4.72
        (c) Is *Freihaltebedürfnis* relevant only to word marks?   4.79
    (5) When are laudatory terms registrable?   4.81

G. Distinctiveness   4.88
    (1) Distinctiveness is in the eyes of the relevant average consumer   4.90
    (2) Distinctiveness cannot be arithmetically quantified   4.92
    (3) Distinctiveness is presumed unless it is disproved   4.94
    (4) Distinctiveness must exist throughout the territory in which the trade mark is to be registered   4.95
    (5) Distinctiveness is not to be considered in abstract but must be considered in relation to the goods or services for which the mark is to be used   4.97
    (6) Distinctiveness is to be considered in relation to the trade mark as a whole, not in relation to its component parts   4.98
    (7) Descriptiveness and other negative traits of a trade mark must also relate to the mark as a whole, not merely to its individual components   4.104
    (8) The weak distinctive character of a word mark can be strengthened by the addition of figurative elements   4.105

(9) Signs in common use are not disqualified from being monopolized	4.106
(10) Distinctiveness is enhanced by a mark's memorable nature	4.110
(11) Banality and the lack of originality, imagination or arbitrary embellishments do not prove a lack of distinctiveness	4.111
(12) Allusiveness does not prove a lack of distinctiveness	4.114
(13) Lexical invention, grammatical error and perversity do not prove the existence of distinctiveness	4.116
(14) An inability to guess a product's nature from its trade mark does not make the trade mark distinctive	4.118
(15) The fact that competitors do not use a term does not prevent it being descriptive rather than distinctive	4.123
(16) The fact that competitors also use a term does not prevent it being distinctive	4.124
(17) The same level of distinctiveness is required of all types of mark	4.125
H. Descriptive marks	
(1) Exclusively descriptive marks cannot be registered	4.128
(a) Allusiveness does not constitute exclusive descriptiveness	4.133
(b) Descriptiveness of the market or of the ultimate user	4.136
(c) Descriptiveness of the function	4.138
(d) Ambiguous terms	4.139
(e) Descriptiveness in multilingual jurisdictions	4.140
(f) A new approach?	4.141
(2) Immaterial descriptiveness	4.143
(3) Is a low threshold of inherent distinctiveness desirable?	4.146
(4) Is there such a thing as an invented descriptive mark?	4.150
(a) Fusion of existing words	4.154
(b) Existing words in unused and unnatural formations	4.157
(c) Words that describe something that does not exist	4.158
(5) Why not register descriptive trade marks?	4.159
I. Distinctiveness acquired through use	4.163
(1) Not all use is evidence of 'distinctiveness acquired through use'	4.167
(2) How much proof will establish that distinctiveness has been acquired?	4.171
(3) Whose use will count as evidence of distinctiveness acquired through use?	4.175
(4) Acquired distinctiveness can overcome even absolute bars to registrability	4.176
J. Relative grounds of unregistrability: a reminder	4.179
K. Conclusion	4.180

A. Introduction

'But I tell you, I want it registered'

The five of them stood in a neat little row. Handsome, well groomed and articulate, these Scandinavian businessmen were latter-day Vikings. Their business—the international transportation of fresh smorgasbords—had conquered much of the world. Their company, International Smorgasbord Transportation Inc, sent chills down the spines of their business rivals. Mighty Volvo trucks with throbbing engines towed vast white containers bearing their name as they power-surged along the world's motorways. Their success was a tribute to their skill, their patience and, above all, their determination. They did not shirk from doing what was necessary.

A. Introduction

Nor did Mark Fast, Toby Throttle's principal at FastMark Trade Mark Attorneys. The development of his thriving trade mark filing practice was not a matter of mere chance: it took skill, patience and, above all, diplomacy with clients. Diplomacy today took him to a sports event, where he and one of his long-term clients were sharing a coveted session in a well-stocked hospitality suite. Throttle would mind the shop till Mark returned, flushed and happy, at the end of a productive afternoon's diplomacy.

But Throttle was beginning to rue the day he passed the Institute's examinations and became a fully fledged trade mark attorney. For one thing, he was outnumbered five to one by the Scandinavian contingent. For another thing, he had run out of ways to say 'no'.

'You just can't register INTERNATIONAL SMORGASBORD TRANSPORTATION as a trade mark'. Throttle repeated the mantra but was fast losing faith in it. 'For one thing, it totally describes your business. For another, it's the only convenient way anyone can refer to what your company does. It doesn't distinguish your business from your competitors'.

'No. We must register it. It is the name of our company and the name of our business. We are famous for it. And our business is already distinguished. It is the most distinguished smorgasbord haulage company in the world'. With a generous gesture of his hand the pale-faced speaker stroked the bristles on his scalp and nodded courteously, adding 'That is why we have come here. To have our trade mark registered'.

'Let me explain again,' began Throttle. 'You transport smorgasbords, internationally. That means that INTERNATIONAL SMORGASBORD TRANSPORTATION literally and exactly describes everything you do. You can't register it because your competitors need to use it too'.

'But that's why we want to register it. We don't want our competitors to use it'.

Throttle had a sudden idea. 'Look, I'll give you an example. You can't register the word SMORGASBORD for a smorgasbord. If someone else was allowed to register smorgasbord, you wouldn't be able to use it in your name. You'd be an infringer'.

A Nordic frown passed imperceptibly across five momentarily perplexed faces. Then the lead Viking spoke. 'Does this mean that no one has registered SMORGASBORD for smorgasbords?'

'Yes,' asserted Throttle, hoping he was right.

'In that case, *we'll* register it,' exclaimed the triumphant client. 'After we've registered INTERNATIONAL SMORGASBORD TRANSPORTATION, that is. Thank you'. He turned to his colleagues and added in English, for Throttle's benefit: 'I tell you, these English trade mark attorneys are so very clever'.

'But you *can't* register them,' Throttle spluttered, the compliment weighing heavily on his undeserving shoulders. 'Look, unless you either change your business or the name you want to register, I don't think I can help you'.

'Ah,' beamed the Viking in chief. His countenance was a picture of revelation. The penny had dropped. 'We have to make a change. Yes, we can make a change. It is not our policy to change but, yes, on this occasion we will change'. He beckoned to his colleagues, who huddled closely round the table, whispering earnestly in a tongue unfamiliar to Throttle. The young man fingered his mobile, wondering whether to bring Mr Fast up to speed or whether his promotion might be better advanced by leaving the man to his earthly pleasures for a little longer.

'Mr Throttle,' said the Viking. 'I think we have solved your problem. We have decided to change our trade mark. From now on we will no longer be known as IN-TERNATIONAL SMORGASBORD TRANSPORTATION. We will be known as this'. He handed Throttle a piece of paper which bore the neat inscription INTERNATIØNAL SMØRGASBØRD TRANSPØRTATIØN. 'And when you have finished this, we start on SMORGASBORD . . .'

The moral of the story

4.01 Some trade marks are automatically and inherently registrable. The best examples of such trade marks are invented words which have neither an inherent meaning nor an allusive quality in relation to the products or services for which they are to be registered. KODAK, XEROX, VIAGRA, ROLEX, HÄAGEN-DAZS and EXXON all fall into this category. For many trade marks, however, the application process represents a journey pitted with obstacles, delays, frustration and often ultimately disappointment. The registration process is a refining process in which many weak or unworthy marks (such as the lamentable INTERNATIONAL SMORGASBORD TRANSPORTATION in our story) are sifted out and eliminated by the granting authorities, whittled down by competitors and finally abandoned by their erstwhile champions. Much of this chapter and the chapter which follows it deal with the reasons for this sifting and refining process, as well as their practical consequences for trade mark applicants.

4.02 This chapter discusses signs which are capable of serving as trade marks. It does not consider problems which arise where a sign is capable of serving as a trade mark but cannot be registered because it is similar to an existing trade mark or because it interferes in any way with some other legal right. Those problems are discussed in Chapter 10.

4.03 The basic requirements of registrability are reviewed in this chapter. The application of these basic principles in specific instances—for example, in respect of trade marks for colours, sounds or scents—is covered in Chapter 5.

(1) What makes a trade mark registrable?

4.04 The fact that other apparently comparable marks have already been registered is not a ground of registration:[1] a trade mark is registrable only if it satisfies the criteria of registrability which the law lays down. What then are these criteria? Article 15 of the Agreement on Trade-Related Aspects of Intellectual Property Law (TRIPs) gives some guidance on this question, by indicating the minimum level of registrability which is expected of the trade mark laws of those very many countries which are members of the World Trade Organization (WTO):

---

[1] *Streamserve Inc v OHIM*, Case T-106/00 [2003] ETMR 751 (CFI).

A. Introduction

Protectable subject matter
Any sign, or any combination of signs, capable of distinguishing the goods or services of one undertaking from those of other undertakings, shall be capable of constituting a trademark. Such signs, in particular, including personal names, letters, numerals, figurative elements and combinations of colours as well as any combinations of such signs, shall be eligible for registration as trademarks. Where signs are not inherently capable of distinguishing the relevant goods or services, Members may make registrability depend on distinctiveness acquired through use. Members may require, as a condition of registration, that signs be visually perceptible.

The EU's Directive 89/104 adopts a simplified version of the same formula: **4.05**

Signs of which a trade mark may consist
A trade mark may consist of any sign capable of being represented graphically, particularly words, including personal names, designs, letters, numerals, the shape of goods or of their packaging, provided that such signs are capable of distinguishing the goods or services of one undertaking from those of other undertakings.[2]

From this it can be seen that the fundamental requirements for the protection of a registered trade mark are that it be (i) a 'sign' and (ii) inherently capable of distinguishing the goods or services of competing businesses and, at the option of the country providing protection, (iii) capable of distinguishing goods or services on account of the use to which it has been put. In addition a TRIPs Member State *may* require that signs 'be visually perceptible', while EU Member States *must* require that they be 'capable of being represented graphically', a concept discussed below (see paras 4.24–4.30). **4.06**

(2) A short note on the terminology of registrability

Terms relating to the concept of distinctiveness such as 'distinctiveness' itself, 'distinctive', 'capacity to distinguish' and 'distinctive character' are frequently found in trade mark law, at international, regional and domestic level. In Europe the term is employed within the context of: (i) what constitutes a sign of which a mark may consist; (ii) grounds for refusing registration; (iii) the acquisition by an initially unregistrable sign of subsequently registrable status; and (iv) the invalidation of a registered trade mark. In the absence of irrefragable evidence to the contrary, this book assumes that the word 'distinctive' and its cognate terms bear, and will continue to bear, the same meaning in every context, even if it is used for different legal ends. **4.07**

---

[2] First Council Directive 89/104, art 2 (see also Council Regulation 40/94, art 4).

(3) Registration under international law

4.08 International conventions tend to concentrate on the positive aspects of trade mark registration rather than the negative. Even so, the Paris Convention takes the trouble to stipulate the sort of signs to which countries must refuse registration, not on the basis that they do not constitute trade marks at all but because there is something inherently wrong with them. Thus the Convention requires Member States to refuse registration to the emblems, flags and armorial bearings of Member States and international intergovernmental organizations.[3]

4.09 The Convention does however leave it to each country to determine its own conditions for filing and registration,[4] while also stating two grounds upon which trade mark applications *cannot* be refused. First

> ... [a]n application for the registration of a mark filed by a national of a country of the Union may not be refused ... on the ground that the filing, registration or renewal has not been effected in its country of origin.[5]

4.10 This provision is complemented by what is sometimes referred to as the *telle-quelle* principle:[6] the rule that a trade mark which has been registered in its country of origin should also be accepted for filing and registration in other Paris Union Member States.[7] Putting the two together:

(i) Paris Union country A may not refuse to register a mark on the basis that its home country B rejected the same application; but
(ii) Paris Union country A must accept an application to register a mark on the basis that its home country B accepted the same application.

4.11 This looks a lot worse than it is, since the Convention subsequently lists situations in which the *telle-quelle* principle does not apply: where the applicant's mark clashes with third-party rights, is devoid of distinctive character, is contrary to morality or is contrary to public order[8] in the country in which *telle-quelle* registration is sought.

4.12 The operation of the *telle-quelle* principle appears to vary from country to country. In Turkey, for example, it appears to have resulted in the registration as trade marks of subject matter which had not hitherto been regarded as registrable under

---

[3] Paris Convention, art 6*ter*(1)(a) and (b).
[4] ibid, art 6(1).
[5] ibid, art 6(2).
[6] Since '*telle-quelle*' is a French term which has no obvious English translation, it has been to a large extent ignored by English-speaking countries. There is however a sizeable volume of jurisprudence on it from civil-law jurisdictions.
[7] Paris Convention, art 6*quinquies*.
[8] ibid, art 6*quinquies* B.

B. Absolute bars to registration

national law: a cigarette packet,[9] the packaging of a chocolate bar[10] and a bottle shape.[11] The German courts have however concluded that *telle-quelle* registration is unavailable in Germany where the subject matter of the trade mark registration in the applicant's home country is not recognized as registrable subject matter in the country of the subsequent application.[12] There is no convenient means by which a consistent interpretation of the Paris Convention's provisions can be imposed.[13]

The *telle-quelle* doctrine is inapplicable to Community Trade Marks (CTMs) because the EU is not a party to the Paris Convention.[14]   **4.13**

The second ground upon which a trade mark may not be refused registration is that   **4.14**

> The nature of the goods to which a trademark is to be applied shall in no case form an obstacle to the registration of the mark.[15]

This provision means that, for example, it should be possible to register trade marks in Paris Convention Member States for alcoholic drinks, contraceptives and chewing gum even in countries in which those commodities are either illegal or their use is closely circumscribed by religious sensitivities or law.   **4.15**

B. Absolute bars to registration

(1) How absolute bars to registration function

As mentioned in the Moral of the Story above, this chapter deals with the question of whether a trade mark is inherently registrable, that is to say, whether a sign which is intended for registration can slip between the 'absolute' legal bars to registration. 'Absolute' bars to registration may be contrasted with 'relative' bars, where there is nothing inherently wrong with an applicant's sign but he still cannot register it because it is too close to a trade mark or other legally protected right of another person. ('Relative' bars to registration are dealt with in detail in Chapter 10.)   **4.16**

---

[9] *Reemtsma Cigaretten Fabriken Gesellschaft mit Beschrankter Haftung v Turkish Patent Institute*, Decision 1998/777-1995/225, 22 April 1999 (5th Commercial Court of Ankara).
[10] *Société des Produits Nestlé SA v Turkish Patent Institute*, Case no 2000/783, Decision 2001/382, 9 May 2001 (9th Commercial Court of Ankara).
[11] *Twelve Islands Shipping Company Ltd v Turkish Patent Institute*, Decision 2000/3866-2000/4995, 1 June 2000 (Turkish Supreme Court).
[12] *Füllkörper trade mark application* [1997] ETMR 431 (Bundespatentgericht).
[13] Both the Paris Convention, art 28, and the WTO (in respect of TRIPs-related disputes) have dispute-resolution mechanisms, but these apply only as between signatory states and cannot be invoked by trade mark applicants.
[14] *Procter & Gamble Company's application*, Case R 116/1998-3 [1999] ETMR 664 (OHIM): the applicant's sign was COMPLETE.
[15] Paris Convention, art 8.

4.17 Most countries have rules which prohibit the registration of certain types of trade mark under any circumstances. Why should this be so? Surely, it may be argued, if a business uses a particular word or sign to designate its goods or services, then the law should protect it against damage done through unauthorized use by competitors? There is however a public interest in ensuring that certain words and terms are kept free for everyone to use (for example, the word 'apple' for apples) and that other words are reserved so that no one can use them at all (for example, INTERPOL). How does this work in practice? In the UK, for example, a frequently used public-interest word like POLICE has been the subject of trade mark registrations for goods and services in a large number of classes. This seems perfectly reasonable: no one is either harmed or confused, by the manufacture and sale of CDs recorded by a group calling itself The Police, into believing that the nation's law enforcement agency has expanded its activities so far beyond the execution of its public duties. In contrast the word ANZAC, the significance of which is lost on most people today, is barred from registration as a trade mark without regard to the goods or services for which registration may have been sought.[16]

4.18 Some of the bars to registration discussed in this chapter relate to the form which the trade mark takes, while others relate to its meaning. Bars relating to the form of a trade mark may relate to whether it constitutes a sign, whether it can distinguish goods or services and whether it is capable of being graphically represented. Bars relating to the meaning of a trade mark may relate to whether its meaning is descriptive or generic, whether it is deceptive, whether it is the same as or similar to a word which has been reserved exclusively for non-trade mark use, as well as whether a trade mark is contrary to public policy or morality. (Further bars to registration which are not inherent in the nature of the mark itself, such the absence of good faith on the part of the applicant and the similarity of the applicant's trade mark to an earlier mark or other protected piece of intellectual property, are discussed respectively in Chapters 5 and 10 below.)

4.19 Figure 4.1 illustrates the structure of absolute bars to registration in EEA Member States under Council Directive 89/104.

(2) Grounds of unregistrability are independent of each other

4.20 Some of the grounds of rejection of a trade mark application overlap with one another. Notwithstanding the existence of conceptual overlap, the grounds of

---

[16] 'Anzac' (Restriction on Trade Use of Word) Act 1916. ANZAC is the acronym of the Australia and New Zealand Army Corps.

B. Absolute bars to registration

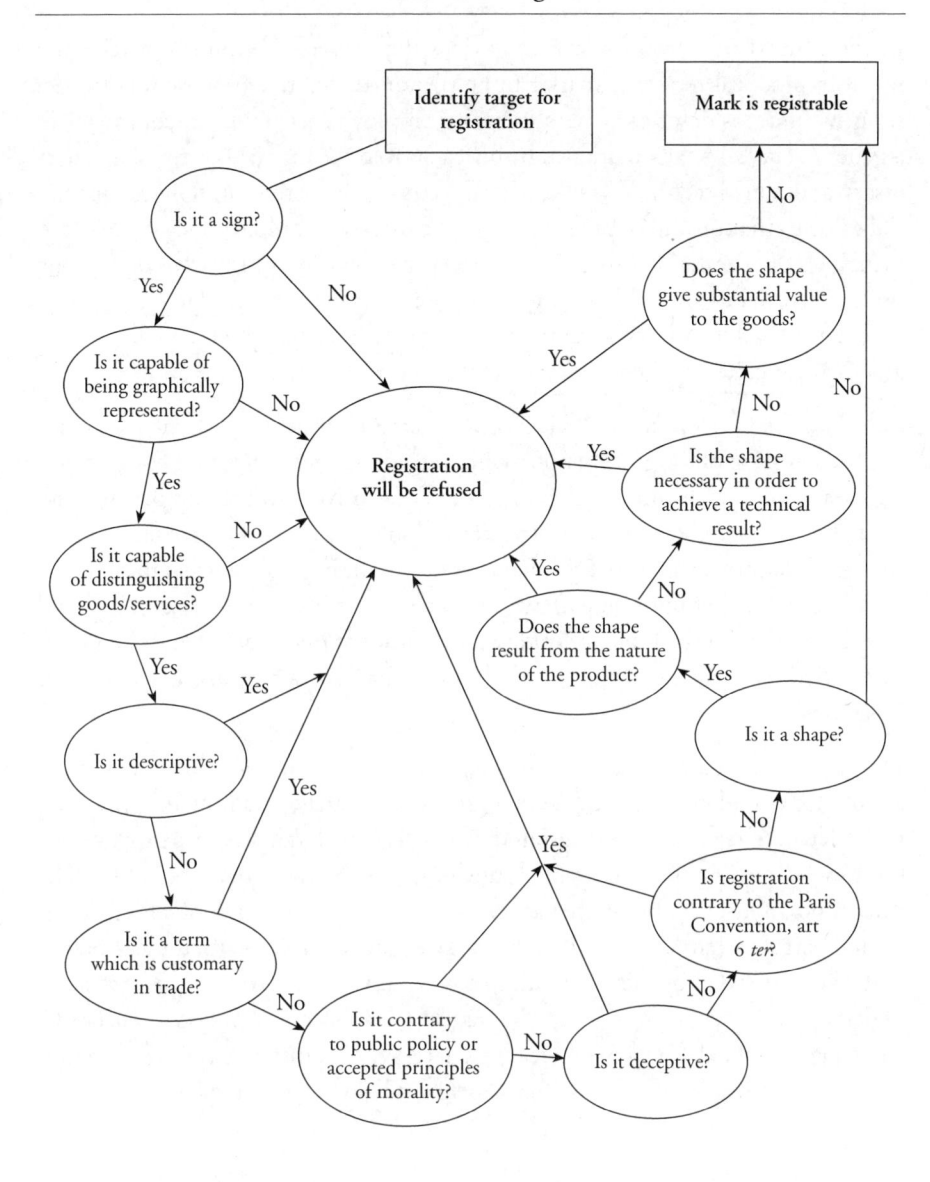

Figure 4.1 Refusal of registration on absolute grounds (Council Directive 89/104, art 3).

rejection are 'neither interdependent nor mutually exclusive'.[17] Each stands alone and they do not need to be applied cumulatively: a trade mark need fall foul of only one of the criteria which bar it from registration and it will not be registrable.

---

[17] *Harbinger Corp v OHIM*, Case T-345/99 [2001] ETMR 11 (TRUSTEDLINK) (CFI), para 31.

4.21 In the context of European law, what does the overlap of grounds of rejection mean in practical terms? A mark can be (i) non-distinctive because it is (ii) descriptive and it is descriptive because (iii) it employs a term used in commerce in a generic sense. A shape mark can be unregistrable because (i) it is the shape necessary to obtain a technical result, with the consequence that (ii) it gives substantial value to that product. A mark can be (i) contrary to public policy or accepted principles of morality because (ii) it is deceptive, and so on. In terms of drafting policy, it is safer to ensure that the grounds of rejection are phrased in terms which do overlap than to risk the acceptance for registration of signs which fall between any gaps which legal ingenuity may identify.

4.22 Since the absolute grounds of rejection overlap, one must be particularly careful in the expression of the ground upon which an application is rejected. A mark may be both devoid of distinctive character and descriptive, but the fact that it is devoid of distinctive character cannot be derived solely from a finding of fact that the mark is descriptive. Thus in a Belgian case in which the applicant sought to register WECOVER (the conjunction of 'we' and 'cover') for insurance services, it would have been open for the Benelux Trade Marks Office to find that the mark was non-distinctive and that it was descriptive, but not that it was non-distinctive *because* it was descriptive.[18]

4.23 Does it really matter that the grounds of rejection of an application do not have to be established cumulatively and that each stands alone? Surely, a trade mark application which has been rejected on three grounds is a bit like a wolf that has been shot by three hunters—it can't be three times more unregistrable any more than the wolf can be three times more dead. But in the case of trade marks some grounds of refusal of registration are only temporary and can be removed by extensive use (in the case of lack of distinctiveness) or by shifts in terminology within a field of commerce (in the case of descriptive or generic terms). Since a trade mark application, once refused, can be subsequently refiled, the causes of death of an earlier application may provide the applicant with valuable information for the reformulation of a later one.

C. Graphic representation and the function of the register

4.24 Article 15 of TRIPs provides that 'Members may require, as a condition of registration, that signs be visually perceptible'. In contrast, Directive 89/104 and the CTM Regulation provide that a trade mark may consist of 'any sign . . . provided that such signs are capable of distinguishing the goods or services of one undertaking from those of other undertakings'.[19]

---

[18] *D'Ieteren v Benelux Trade Marks Office* [2003] ETMR 842 (CA, Brussels), para 7.
[19] Council Directive 89/104, art 2; Council Regulation 40/94, art 4.

C. Graphic representation and the function of the register

4.25 The qualification that a mark be graphically represented or visually perceptible reveals a clear difference between the approaches taken by TRIPs and the EU, particularly since the EU demands as an absolute precondition for registration that a sign be 'represented graphically', while TRIPs leads with the requirement that a sign be distinctive and only mentions 'visual perceptibility' as an optional extra. This divergence is quite deliberate. The 'graphic representation' formula can be found in the two drafts[20] which preceded the final version of TRIPs but it was jettisoned in the final draft. The fact that a trade mark is visually perceptible may mean that, of necessity, it must be graphically represented on the principle that anything which can be seen can be visually recorded and that anything which can be visually recorded must be graphically represented. On the other hand, a literal interpretation of the TRIPs approach allows Members to exclude invisible marks such as sounds and smells from registrability and such marks are not listed as being 'in particular' eligible for registrability.[21]

4.26 The TRIPs requirement of visual perceptibility is in fact ambiguous. It can mean that a sign may not be registered unless it is a sign that can be seen, such as the word PEPSI or the BMW roundel. It can also mean that a sign may be registered whether it can be seen or not, so long as a visually perceptible description of it can be entered in the trade mark register so that people can read the register and understand the nature of the mark even if it is invisible. On the first interpretation, trade marks for sounds (such as advertising jingles) and scents (such as the smell of grass in respect of tennis balls[22]) may be excluded from registration. On the second interpretation, trade marks for sounds may be registered because those sounds can be represented by musical notation and trade marks for scents may be registered if an acceptable means can be found for enabling them to be recorded visually on the register in an appropriately intelligible form.

4.27 This is not an academic point: it is a matter of acute importance. The trade mark register is not supposed to be the result of an academic exercise in turning intangible concepts such as sounds and scents into words and pictures: it is a practical tool for any businessman who wants to go into business and who wants to know if he will get into legal trouble if he gives his goods a particular name, appearance, colour or smell. If the register cannot give him that information, it has failed in its primary objective. A person who is capable of recognizing words and pictures can scan the pages of the register and readily appreciate which words and pictures have

---

[20] The W/76 draft of 23 July 1990 and the Brussels draft of later that year; see Daniel Gervais, *The TRIPs Agreement: Drafting History and Analysis* (1998), pp 102–4.

[21] See also Michael Blakeney, 'The Impact of the TRIPs Agreement in the Asia Pacific Region' [1996] EIPR 544–54, 548.

[22] Which was in fact registered as a CTM; see *Vennootschap onder Firma Senta Aromatic Marketing's Application*, Case R 156/1998-2 [1999] ETMR 429 (OHIM) and the discussion of olfactory marks in Chapter 5.

been appropriated by other businesses, but can he so easily recognize a sound or smell? Olfactory marks cause particular problems, both because our perception of smells is acutely subjective and because objectivized means of recording smells such as the use of 'electronic noses' do not describe an odour in such a manner as to enable a competitor, consulting the trade mark register, readily to understand what has in fact been registered. As Geoffrey Hobbs QC put it:

> In the case of a person without the necessary experience of the article the sign cannot be identified [by looking at the register] no matter what technical skills they possess or bring to bear.[23]

4.28 To give some idea of the problems faced by trade mark examiners, readers may wish to conjure up a clear image of the following trade mark:

> A pictorial representation of a pig, not being a photographic representation, with a slot in its back, presented generally in profile with a curly tail in the form of a telephone wire, portrayed generally in the colour pink.[24]

4.29 The range of porcine depictions falling within this description is vast. Apart from the fact that every pig presumably favours either its left or its right profile, pigs vary greatly in appearance and slots may run either along the spine or across it. An all-encompassing claim of this nature would appear more natural to patent law than to trade marks.

4.30 Our current perception of the register may be in need of an upgrade. For example, with modern technology there is no reason why one should not be able to access the register by computer and, on clicking the relevant icon, be treated to the sound of a musical or noise mark, the colours and configuration of multicoloured product marks, the visual perspective of three-dimensional shape marks or the sequential element of motion trade marks. If the register can respond to the challenge of communicating the aesthetic or sensual impact of a trade mark other than through graphic representation alone, it would be able to overcome the difficulties we have mentioned above.

D. Signs may not be registrable if consumers do not regard them as being trade marks

4.31 If a sign is 'capable of distinguishing . . . goods or services', it is 'capable of constituting a trademark'.[25] If consumers of an alcoholic beverage can be expected to

---

[23] *John Lewis of Hungerford Ltd's Trade Mark Application* [2001] ETMR 1193 (LCAP).
[24] *Telecom Plus plc's application*, 26 November 2002 (UK Trade Marks Registry).
[25] TRIPs, art 15; see also the equivalent provisions in Council Directive 89/104, art 2, and Council Regulation 40/94, art 4.

regard the word mark AD2000 on a bottle as an indication of a date,[26] or if computer users view the phrase YOU'VE GOT MAIL on their computer screens as a message that they have received e-mail,[27] those signs will not be registrable as trade marks. This is because, if they are not regarded by the relevant public as even being trade marks, they cannot fulfil the role of trade marks in distinguishing goods or services.[28] Shoppers may view bottles containing the household cleaning products of various manufacturers on the supermarket shelves in the same manner. Even if those bottles are different in their shape and colour, if those differences are not used by shoppers as a means of identifying the brand of their choice but are merely regarded as 'typical' for those products, their differences—whether separately or in aggregate—will not be regarded as trade marks.[29]

E. Signs which are not registrable on policy grounds

(1) Immoral and illegal marks

4.32 Directive 89/104 provides that 'trade marks which are contrary to public policy or to accepted principles of morality' may not be granted. A deficiency of this nature is an absolute bar to registration.[30] Provisions of this nature can be found in the law or practice of most countries, though sometimes the terminology is different. For example, in Poland marks may not be registered if they are 'contrary to principles of social coexistence'. This verbal formula, implanted in Polish trade mark law during the era of Communism, has survived that country's transition to a market economy and now appears to mean much the same as 'contrary to public policy'.

4.33 Deceptive marks are also contrary to 'public policy or to accepted principles of morality', but they are dealt with separately both under the trade mark law of most countries and in this chapter (see paras 4.41–4.49).

4.34 Public policy and morality are concepts which we can all understand, but the standards of which we find it exceedingly difficult to identify and apply to specific sets of facts. In many parts of Europe those terms are most closely associated with sexual mores, but there is no reason why they should be so limited in their application.[31] Thus it has been argued that an attempt by a trade mark applicant to

---

[26] *Allied Domecq plc's application* [1997] ETMR 253 (LCAP).
[27] *America Online Inc's application*, Case R 209/2000-3 [2002] ETMR 59 (OHIM).
[28] It has been questioned whether a book title may serve as a trade mark; see *Rowling v Uitgeverij Byblos*, 3 April 2003 (unreported) (District Court of Amsterdam) where 'an application has been filed for the HARRY POTTER trade mark for various classes of goods and the book class is only one of these'. (But *Harry Potter* was the title of a series of books, rather than an individual book.)
[29] *Re Procter & Gamble's trade mark application* [1999] ETMR 375 (CA).
[30] Council Directive 89/104, art 3(1)(f). See also Council Regulation 40/94, art 7(1)(f).
[31] In the United States, in contrast, many types of trade mark which would be regarded by most Europeans as quite unobjectionable may be challenged under section 2(a) of the Lanham Act as

register a mark for an overwide specification for goods or services could in theory fall, at least in the UK, within this ground of absolute refusal of protection.[32] The Court of First Instance (CFI) has however ruled that the fact that an application to register a trade mark is made in bad faith does not make that mark 'contrary to public policy or accepted principles of morality'.[33]

4.35 Who is the custodian of public policy and morality? At the conference of the European Communities Trade Mark Association in 1996 the OHIM Head of Examination Division Vincent O'Reilly, in response to a question from the floor, informed a generally amused audience that the standard of 'accepted principles of morality' to be applied at OHIM when considering trade mark applications was that of the local man in the street in Alicante, Spain. Whether this has been the case remains to be seen, but the Office's efforts to protect these principles of morality have so far not been challenged in court. At the time of writing, only six applications to register CTMs had been rejected as being contrary to the acceptable standards of public policy and morality. They consisted of three obscene word marks[34] together with BILLCLINTON,[35] FIDEL CASTRO[36] and JOHANNES PAUL II.[37]

4.36 Even from this small number of failed applications, which may be contrasted with some applications which have succeeded, we can discern that OHIM's attitude towards trade marks with sexual content is rather more relaxed than that of some national offices within the EU. For example, an application to register the word SEX PATCH in respect of 'transdermal patches for inducing libido' was rejected on the grounds that the mark was descriptive and non-distinctive,[38] without any reference to immorality. Even in the predominantly Catholic Republic of Ireland of the 1970s, when sex was something that took place either behind closed doors or in the imagination, the Irish High Court ruled that sexual content would not of itself prevent the grant of a trade mark.[39]

---

being scandalous or immoral; see eg Stephen R Baird, 'Moral Intervention in the Trademark Arena: Banning the Registration of Scandalous and Immoral Trademarks' (1993) 83 TMR 661–800 and Theodore H Davis Jr, 'Registration of Scandalous, Immoral and Disparaging Matter Under Section 2(a) of the Lanham Act: Can One Man's Vulgarity be Another's Registered Trademark?' (1993) 83 TMR 801.

[32] David Wilkinson, 'Broad Trade Mark Specifications' [2002] ETMR 227–31, 230–1.
[33] *Durferrit GmbH v OHIM, Kolene Corporation Intervening*, Case T-224/01, 9 April 2003, para 76.
[34] Applications numbered 65839 (BALLE) for wines, spirits etc; 99103 (BOLLOX) for adult board games; and 06399 (F*** OF THE YEAR [asterisks supplied by the author]) for films, magazines and television broadcasts.
[35] Application no 956540 (perfumery; alcoholic beverages; tobacco goods).
[36] Application no 921155 (tea, coffee; beer; tobacco and smokers' products).
[37] Application no 958280 (non-alcoholic and alcoholic beverages; smokers' articles).
[38] *Medical Research Industries Inc's application*, Case R 639/1999-2, 23 May 2001 (unreported). A similar fate befell SEXCAM (Case R 0212/2001-4).
[39] APHRODISIA *Trade Mark* [1977] FSR 133 (Irish High Court).

E. Signs which are not registrable on policy grounds

4.37 In contrast with the approach taken by OHIM, a good example of 'how not to do it' may be found in the attempt of the UK Registry and Lord Chancellor's Appointed Person to suppress an application to register the word mark TINY PENIS for clothing.[40] Once it was conceded that neither the words 'tiny' nor 'penis' were inherently obscene or immoral, it became necessary to base the decision to refuse the mark upon the sense of outrage which consumers might experience when viewing that mark, a sense of outrage which has probably been dulled in recent years by the sight of so many people in that jurisdiction wearing FCUK T-shirts and carrying FCUK shopping bags.[41]

4.38 For the French, public policy and morality have nothing to do with sex but are indissolubly linked with two passions which are deeply engrained in the Gallic psyche: civic pride[42] and good food. On that basis the municipality of Saint-Tropez[43] applied for cancellation of the trade mark LA PIZZA DE ST-TROPEZ on the ground that that mark represented an attempt to 'take over a unique and inalienable name' and 'seize the patrimony belonging to businesses established in the district'; not only that, but 'the district finds that a second-rate image had been imposed upon itself by the association of its name with a product of mass consumption'. The court rejected this claim, not on the basis that it was unfounded in law but on the ground that no evidence of damage through this trivialization had been brought; the mark was however cancelled as being likely to mislead the public as to the origin of products which had no association with Saint-Tropez.

4.39 Two other French decisions are worthy of note, in that they demonstrate the potential breadth of scope which public policy and morality issues can be given within the trade mark system. In the first of these, a trade mark owner had registered the word HALLOWEEN in respect of confectionery. Haribo, having used the word HALLOWEEN in conjunction with its own name in respect of confectionery, was faced with an action for infringement in which it argued that the trade mark owner was unlawfully seeking to take over the name of a well-known public celebratory event in order to prevent others making reference to Halloween when selling their own seasonal products. The court rejected this argument, which might have fared better if it had been made as part of the claim that the trade mark was wrongly registered rather than as a defence to the allegations of infringement.[44] In the second

---

[40] *Ghazilian's application* [2002] ETMR 631.
[41] Rattee J cast aspersions, *obiter*, upon the validity of the FCUK trade mark in *French Connection Ltd v Sutton* [2000] ETMR 341, 361. At the time of writing it has been registered in fifteen classes.
[42] See eg Gabriel Chevallier, *Clochemerle*; Marcel Pagnol, *Jean de Florette*; *Manon de Source*.
[43] *Saint-Tropez v Valais and another* [1999] ETMR 310 (Tribunal de Grande Instance de Paris).
[44] *Optos-Opus Sarl v SA Haribo Ricqlès Zan SA and others* [1999] ETMR 362 (Tribunal de Grande Instance de Paris). In a subsequent case the Cour d'appel de Paris cancelled the HALLOWEEN trade mark's registration for confectionery products not on the basis that Halloween was a festival but on the ground that, this being an event associated with confectionery, the mark should be available for other traders to use; see *Chambre Syndicale Nationale de la Confiserie v Optos-Opus Sarl* (2003) PIBD III-216.

case[45] the owner of the VICTORIA'S SECRET trade mark for women's clothes sought to invalidate the VICTORIA'S SECRET trade mark for alcoholic beverages. At the time of the second registration VICTORIA'S SECRET had not yet become a famous mark under Article 6*bis* of the Paris Convention, but the drinks mark was still annulled: if it had been allowed to remain on the register for drinks, the claimant could not have continued advertising his own lingerie under the VICTORIA'S SECRET trade mark without making it look as though he was sponsoring the defendant's drinks, thus infringing a little-known provision of the Drinking Establishment Code.

4.40 In closing this discussion, it may be asked whether a prohibition of trade mark registration provides the most appropriate legal basis for addressing the issue of social responses to trade marks which are contrary to accepted principles or contrary to public policy. The national laws of all civilized countries—even those which make constitutional provision for the protection of freedom of speech—generally have countervailing laws which address issues of public obscenity and offence. For example, irrespective of the provisions of trade mark law, any overt commercial exploitation of terms such as 'wog', 'wap', 'chink', 'kraut', 'yid', 'nigger', 'poof', 'queer' or 'coon' (and their non-English equivalents) is likely to be proscribed by laws against intolerance of racial origin or sexual preferences, while similar provisions are generally available to restrict similar use of obscene materials. In these circumstances what value is served by the duplication of these laws at administrative level by requiring trade mark examiners to weed out applications which may never be commercially useful? By way of comparison, the equivalent provisions of patent law have proved an unwieldy and ultimately unsuccessful mechanism for the suppression of undesirable inventions.[46]

(2) Deceptive marks

4.41 Directive 89/104 also provides that trade marks shall not be registered if they are of 'such a nature as to deceive the public, for instance as to the nature, quality or geographical origin of the goods or service'.[47] As in the case of marks which are immoral or contrary to public policy, deceptive marks are also universally barred from registrability. This provision is designed to protect the public, by which is meant those people who are consumers of the goods or services for which registration is sought. Accordingly, where a trade mark for vodka is registered in the UK in Cyrillic script, our concern is that vodka drinkers, rather than the public at large, should not be deceived by it.[48]

---

[45] *Société Roullet Fransac Sarl v V Secret Catalogue Inc* [2001] ETMR 1187 (Cour d'appel de Paris).
[46] See European Patent Convention, art 53 and the cases decided under that provision.
[47] Council Directive 89/104, art 3(1)(g).
[48] *Zakritoe Aktsionernoe Obchtechestevo 'Torgovy Dom Potomkov Postavechtchika Dvora Ego*

E. Signs which are not registrable on policy grounds

4.42 The policy behind preventing the registration of deceptive marks has never been questioned, but there is a sense in which many perfectly legitimate trade marks are also deceptive. The raisins sold under the SUN MAID trade mark are not gathered by sun maids; no birds' eyes roll out of the BIRDS EYE frozen pea packets; the contents of the AMBROSIA tin are only creamed rice, not the food of the gods, and KIWI shoe polish has never yet been extracted from flightless birds from the Antipodes. Why are these marks not deceptive? If we allow these marks to be registered because they contain deceptions so fanciful that they would never muster credibility, we are rewarding the biggest lies over their smaller companions. Or do we tolerate such lies because, in at least some of these instances, the brand owner educates his consuming public to associate the word with him and not with the contents of his products? Or could it be that the public isn't bothered about the deceit. The last of these suggestions may well be the right answer. When the validity of the trade mark EUROPABANK, owned by a small regional bank that did not trade throughout Europe, was challenged for deceptiveness, the Benelux Court of Justice rejected that challenge and stated:

> The use of a geographical indicator in respect of services will only be deceptive if the fact that the public's belief that the service is offered throughout that territory has a determining effect upon the belief held by the public concerning the nature, origin, quality or equivalent characteristics of the services offered under the trade mark.[49]

4.43 In other words, if I am particular only to clean my shoes with the extract of a kiwi, but would not use any other product, the image of that bird together with the word KIWI would induce me to purchase a product that was made from something quite different and, from my point of view, undesirable. If however I am neutral to the gender or the marital status of those persons who are portrayed as having harvested baskets of grapes, the trade mark SUN MAID cannot be said to have deceived me into the mistaken exercise of my consumer choice.

4.44 In the United States a mark may not be registered if it is 'deceptively misdescriptive'.[50] This formula is more succinct than its European counterpart and at first blush appears to deal more effectively with the problem of whether KIWI is a deceptive mark. But does it? We know that KIWI, to the extent that it is misdescriptive, is not *deceptively* misdescriptive because no one expects the contents of the shoe-polish tin to have anything to do with kiwis. This expectation is not however something which is natural and inherent: it is based on our knowledge of shoe polish and our expectation that it is derived from non-ornithological matter. If a

---

Imperatorskago Velitschestva Pa Smornova' v Diageo North America Inc, 7 April 2003 (unreported) (Chancery Division): hearing officer wrong to hold that trade marks in Cyrillic script were not deceptive.

[49] *Europabank NV v Banque pour l'Europe SA* [1997] ETMR 143, 144.
[50] Lanham Act, s 2(e)(3); 15 USC, s 1052(e)(3). This provision is discussed in Chapter 5, paras 5.44–5.55.

product with which we are unfamiliar is given a trade mark consisting of a word with which we are familiar, it may be a matter of chance as to whether (i) we believe in the misdescriptive character of the term and are deceived or (ii) we do not believe in its misdescriptive character and are not deceived.

4.45 In Europe terms such as BIO- and ECO-, when used in marketing and branding, convey such strong meanings that it is clear that trade marks incorporating them will suggest some organic or ecologically acceptable content, or means of processing, on the part of any goods bearing them. However, Europe is an ancient continent and trade marks containing words such as BIO have been in use before those words obtained their current nuances. Accordingly Community legislation has stepped in to provide that, while trade marks including the word BIO should ultimately be reserved for appropriately organic products, a twilight period has been established during which those marks may continue to be used on non-organic products, so long as they are clearly marked as being so.[51] Once that twilight period expires on 1 July 2006, those trade marks may continue to be used only in respect of organic produce,[52] and if they are not, then they will have become automatically deceptive.

4.46 Many of the deceptions to which trade mark registries take offence relate to geographical indications. If, as is generally the case, a false representation by a trader that his goods come from a particular region may render him criminally liable, it would be anomalous for the law to accord him a protectable monopoly in a trade mark which makes that representation. A perfect example of a deceptive mark being rejected is that of the trade mark MCL PARFUMS DE PARIS, which the applicant sought to register for perfumes which had no connection with Paris, or indeed anywhere else in France. The applicant offered to establish a 'French connection' by buying ingredients from France for products which were however to be assembled in a region of Europe that was not in the slightest associated with the perfume industry, but the UK Registry would have none of it.[53] If Paris had not been associated with perfume, there would have been no problem (so, for example, PARFUMS DE CALAIS would be registrable).

---

[51] See Council Regulation 1804/1999 supplementing Regulation 2092/91 on organic production of agricultural products and indications referring thereto on agricultural products and foodstuffs so as to include livestock production, especially art 2. The operation of this provision has been scrutinized by the CFI in *Fédération Nationale d'Agriculture Biologique des Régions de France (FNAB), Syndicat Européen des Transformateurs et Distributeurs de Produits de l'Agriculture Biologique (SE-TRAB) and Est Distribution Biogram Sarl v Council of the European Union*, Case T-268/99, 11 July 2000 (unreported) (ECJ).

[52] Use of the word 'organic' is also carefully controlled by EU legislation; see Council Regulation 2092/91 itself.

[53] *Madgecourt Ltd's application; opposition of Fédération des Industries de la Parfumerie* [2000] ETMR 825 (UK Trade Marks Registry).

E. Signs which are not registrable on policy grounds

4.47 In the MCL PARFUMS DE PARIS case, the opponents (an association of French *parfumiers*) had a connection with Paris but the trade mark applicant did not. But sometimes the boot is on the other foot. In the French case of *GPT v Cartier France*[54] GPT sued Cartier for infringement of its SAINT-PETERSBOURG trade mark, which was registered for jewellery. Cartier challenged the validity of the registration, pointing out that St Petersburg was the seat of the Imperial Court prior to the Russian Revolution and that, in the pre-revolutionary era, Cartier had supplied jewellery to the Russian elite. GPT, however, had no connection with the city at all and was merely seeking to cash in on its luxury reputation for its own ends. The court rejected this plea. Whatever reputation St Petersburg had as a centre for jewellery and luxury goods was lost some eighty years earlier and would therefore be lost on the French public. Once that reputation had been lost, anyone was free to register the name of the city. Cartier didn't but GPT did. This is not the only deceptive case arising out of the hijacking of Imperial Russian heritage: a Russian company has sought, so far unsuccessfully, the cancellation of a number of SMIRNOFF vodka trade mark registrations in the UK on the ground that their use, in conjunction with the word 'Moscow' and the Russian Imperial Court regalia on the bottles' labels, misled the public as to the origin of the vodka.[55] The trade mark owner had argued that the material in question was purely decorative and would not be regarded by vodka drinkers as constituting a misrepresentation as to the vodka's origin.

4.48 Some denials of deception are frankly difficult to accept. Thus in Finland an application to register DE-NIC for cigarettes which were not nicotine-free was refused. The applicant maintained that the word DE-NIC was an invented word and that it was not an abbreviation of 'de-nicotinized' in any language. That may well have been so, but so strong was the conceptual force of the word DE-NIC that the Finnish Supreme Administrative Court had no difficulty in refusing the application.[56]

4.49 An aesthetically elegant application of law and logic combined to scupper an application to register the word EUROLAMB in respect of meat. If the mark was for use in relation to meat originating outside Europe, then the front end of the trade mark, the term EURO-, was deceptive; if however the meat came from Europe, EURO- was descriptive. At the tail of the trade mark was -LAMB. If the meat was not lamb, then -LAMB was deceptive; if however the meat was lamb, then -LAMB was descriptive.[57]

---

[54] *SA GPT v Sté Cartier France* [1998] ETMR 382 (Tribunal de Grande Instance de Paris).
[55] *Aktsionernoe Obchtchestvo Zakritogo Tipa Torgovy Dom Potomkov Postavchtchika Dvora Ego Imperatorskago Velitschestva PA Smirnova v UDV North America Inc*, 18 October 2002 (Chancery Division, Pumfrey J).
[56] *Philip Morris Products Inc's application; opposition of R J Reynolds Tobacco Company* [1997] ETMR 511.
[57] *BOCM Pauls Ltd and Scottish Agricultural College's application* [1997] ETMR 420 (UK Trade Marks Registry).

F. Signs which other traders may wish to use

(1) Marks which infringe copyright, design and other intellectual property rights

4.50 Although this bar to registrability is not addressed by TRIPs or by either of the major pieces of European legislation,[58] it has found its way into UK legislation which provides that a sign may not be registered if its use is liable to be prevented

> by virtue of an earlier right . . ., in particular by virtue of the law of copyright, design right or registered design.[59]

4.51 It has also found its way into the German law through a bar on the registration of others' company names and titles[60] and into the Danish law with a provision that a mark may not, without authorization,

> consist of or contain any part that can be understood as a distinctive title of another's work, which is protected by copyright.[61]

4.52 The fact that a sign infringes copyright or design right does not act as a bar to its registration under either the CTM Regulation or the Directive. Accordingly, in the absence of a provision such as that which operates in the UK, once registration is secured the trade mark proprietor has five years in which to secure a licence to use the copyright work as a trade mark, failing which his registration is open to revocation proceedings. Another approach would be to conclude that an application to register someone else's copyright or design-protected work as a trade mark would be regarded as having been made in bad faith.[62]

(2) Publicly reserved terms are not registrable

4.53 Recent German case law has reminded us that some words may not be used as trade marks at all, not because they are inherently deceptive or immoral (which they may not be) but because their use is regulated or limited by statute. This was the fate of the trade mark PARTNER WITH THE BEST[63] where the word 'partner', together with corporate designations such as AG, GmbH, KG and oHG, is barred

---

[58] Council Regulation 40/94, art 52(2) does however provide that a granted CTM may be invalidated where its use is prohibited by any national copyright, industrial design right, right of personal portrayal or right to a name.

[59] Trade Marks Act 1994, s 5(4)(b); see *Team Lotus Ventures Ltd's application; opposition of Group Lotus Ltd* [1999] ETMR 669, where the UK Trade Marks Registry refused an application which infringed copyright in the opponent's logo.

[60] Markengesetz, s 55(2)(2) (Germany).

[61] Trade Mark Act, s 14(5) (Denmark). On the operation of this provision, see *VN Legetøj A/S v Patentankenævnet* [2001] ETMR 529 in which the Maritime and Commercial Court ruled FLIPPER unregistrable: the title of the film of the same name was an obstacle to registration.

[62] On the doctrine of bad faith, see Chapter 13.

[63] *'Partner With The Best' trade mark application* [1998] ETMR 679 (Bundespatentgericht).

F. Signs which other traders may wish to use

from being part of a trade mark by the Partnership Law.[64] In similar fashion many countries prohibit the registration of terms such as 'incorporated' or 'limited' to the extent that they imply a degree of personal legal status on the part of the trade mark owner or user. The reason for this is to protect members of the public against the impression that they are dealing with goods or services provided by a more commercially substantial enterprise than is in fact the case.

4.54 'Partner' is a word which may be found in any area of commercial activity, but some reserved terms are narrower in their area of application, for example, *apoteket* (the Danish word for pharmacy). The Danish Supreme Court has ruled that, while *apoteket* is a reserved term which cannot be registered as part of a trade mark for healthcare products and services, that reservation does not prevent its incorporation into terms which have no healthcare significance. Accordingly the trade mark BETON-APOTEKET ('concrete pharmacy') was registrable: its use would not erroneously lead consumers to conclude that, in relation to products for the repair and protection of concrete, the trade mark applicant had any medical skills.[65]

4.55 The extent to which national law may reserve the use of terms as trade marks is limited in the EU by the EC Treaty itself. EU Member States may prohibit the use in their own territory of trade marks which are lawfully registered and used in other Member States, so long as the risk of misleading consumers outweighs the requirement of the free movement of goods.[66] The Treaty will not however allow Member States to impose qualitative restrictions on imports[67] by even subtle means like reserving the use of words such as 'montagne' (French for 'mountain') to traders who produce, prepare, make and package their goods in mountain areas on French territory. The European Court of Justice (ECJ) had no difficulty in declaring such a reservation contrary to Community trading principles.[68]

4.56 The European Court of Human Rights[69] has ruled that a provision of the Polish Press Law which prevented the registration of periodical titles (for publication purposes, not for trade mark purposes) which were deceptive or contrary to public policy was itself contrary to principles of freedom of speech. This being so, it may be asked whether the titles in question (*Germany: A Thousand-Year-Old Enemy of Poland* and *The Social and Political Monthly: A European Moral Tribunal*)

---

[64] Partnership Law of 25 July 1994 (BGBl I 1994, 1744).
[65] *Board of Appeal for Patents and Trade Marks v Danish Association of Pharmacists* WTLR, 1 April 2003.
[66] *Fratelli Graffione SNC v Ditta Fransa*, Case C-313/94 [1997] ETMR 71 (ECJ): COTONELLE products, imported from France to Italy, were banned there because they falsely suggested that the goods sold under that mark contained cotton.
[67] EC Treaty, art 28.
[68] *Pistre and others v France*, Joined Cases C-321 to 324/94 [1997] ETMR 457.
[69] *Gaweda v Poland* [2002] ETMR 691.

would be acceptable as titles of periodicals for freedom of speech purposes but nonetheless remain contrary to public policy under trade mark law. It is quite possible that this would be the case, since the aims, and therefore the criteria of public policy, under human rights law[70] are not coterminous with those of trade mark law.

4.57 Curiously an application to register as a CTM a sign including the word 'euro' and a representation of the euro symbol for business and financial services was rejected not on the ground that it was reserved for use as a currency sign but because it could never be distinctive of those services in the eyes of European consumers. The use of the word 'never' is unusual since persistent long-term use of a sign as a trade mark is generally understood to be capable of earning its user the right of registration. The OHIM Board of Appeal[71] however felt that no specific shaping of the word 'euro' or the euro sign could convey any meaning in the eyes of consumers other than that of a unit of currency. In the light of its position one may speculate as to how the Board would have responded to evidence of distinctiveness acquired through use.

(3) Generic terms and customary trade terms are not registrable

4.58 In Europe both the Directive 89/104[72] and the CTM Regulation[73] prohibit the registration of

> trade marks which consist exclusively of signs or indications which have become customary in the current language or in the bona fide and established practices of the trade.

4.59 This exclusion, which is found in all fully functional trade mark systems, prevents the registration of terms which traders or the public—or any specific segment of it—have invested with a particular meaning. Such terms may be generic, in the sense that they describe or refer to a particular class of goods or services (for example, BRUSCHETTA, for a category of food which included bruschetta[74]), or they may simply be specialist jargon of the sort employed by lawyers, accountants, pigeon-fanciers, scientists or bridge players. Although the language of the Directive

---

[70] See European Convention on Human Rights, art 8.
[71] *ABN Amro Holding NV's application*, Case R 190/1999-3 [2001] ETMR 90. A similar view was taken in *Grosz Sp Zoo's application*, 29 April 1998 (unreported) (Polish Patent Office, Board of Appeals) where an application to register the Polish unit of currency GROSZ failed for want of distinctiveness, not on the ground of public policy.
[72] Council Directive 89/104, art 3(1)(d).
[73] Council Regulation 40/94, art 7(1)(d).
[74] 'Bruschetta' is an Italian dish comprising 'a slice of toasted bread served with garlic, oil, tomato or other salted or sweet sauces' for which the CTM registration was cancelled; see *Piromalli's trade mark; application for cancellation by Greci Industria Alimentare SpA*, Case 133C 000372920/1, 13 February 2002 (unreported) (OHIM).

F. Signs which other traders may wish to use

and the CTM Regulation do not state this explicitly,[75] this exclusion only applies where the putative trade mark/generic term is used in the context of the goods or services for which it is generic. Thus the fact that the word 'absolute' was used as a trade term in areas of activity other than the manufacture and sale of vodka did not prevent the registration of the word mark ABSOLUT for that commodity.[76]

4.60 Is it necessary that a term be descriptive before it can be regarded as 'customary in the current language'? The ECJ considered that it did not.[77] This conclusion can be deduced from the fact that exclusively descriptive terms are already excluded from registrability: a separate provision for the exclusion of signs consisting exclusively of terms which are 'customary in the current language' would only succeed in excluding that which has already been excluded.

4.61 The judicial explanation which the CFI has given for the non-registrability of generic and trade terms is that such signs

> do not enable the relevant public to repeat the experience of a purchase, if it proves to be positive, or to avoid it, if it proves to be negative, on the occasion of a subsequent acquisition of the goods or services concerned.[78]

4.62 If that rationale were rigidly applied, marks such as LITE would correctly be excluded from registrability while those which *do* enable a consumer to make a repeat purchase would be registrable. However, the exclusion has been understood as including not only these marks but also those where there is evidence that, if they *could* have been used in such a way, they would not have enabled consumers to make or avoid that crucial repeat purchase. This takes the exclusion from the realm of market reality to the realm of surmise and thus enabled the CFI to refuse registration to the mark BIOID in respect of (among other things) computer programs and services used for 'the identification and/or verification of live organisms based on one or more specific biometric characteristics'.[79]

4.63 Courts and trade mark registries have taken pains to protect the public against the misappropriation of everyday words and to protect trading interests against the ring-fencing by private monopolies of words which they would normally expect to be able to use. Thus, since the words 'giro' and 'form' were used on a daily basis in relation to giros and forms, the word mark GIROFORM was held by the CFI[80] to

---

[75] *Merz & Krell GmbH*, Case C-517/99 [2002] ETMR 231, para 27.
[76] *ABSOLUT trade mark* [2001] ETMR 21 (Bundesgerichtshof).
[77] *Merz & Krell GmbH*, Case C-517/99 [2002] ETMR 231, para 35.
[78] *Rewe Zentral AG v OHIM*, Case T-79/00 [2002] ETMR 1109 (LITE for foods and drinks), para 26.
[79] *BioID v OHIM*, Case T-91/01, 5 December 2002 (unreported) (CFI).
[80] *Mitsubishi HiTec Paper Bielefeld v OHIM*, Case T-331/99 [2001] ETMR 614 (a pre-*BABY-DRY* case but one which would probably be decided the same today, following the approach of the ECJ in *COMPANYLINE*).

be unregistrable for paper products and printed forms. This was so even though the fusion of the two words was not itself a customary usage.

4.64 European trade mark law only objects to the appropriation of terms which are in fact customary: it does not however bar the registration of terms which, though not customary themselves, allude to a term which is customary. Accordingly the fact that brewers had used the terms 'Extra Special Bitter' or 'Extra Strong Bitter' in the course of their trade did not prevent the registration of the three letter mark E.S.B.[81]

4.65 Anyone reading authors even as recent as Damon Runyan[82] will soon be aware of the speed at which language changes. Not only do words change their meanings but the physical objects to which they are attached may disappear from our lives. Stories like *Black Beauty*[83] may still tantalize children, but the vocabulary related to horses, the vehicles they pull and the means by which they are attached to them are now quite unfamiliar to most of us who live in modern urban areas. The generic commonplaces of the era of the horse (ostler, blinker, halter, cob, crupper) are now known mainly to those whose pastime is keeping horses or doing crossword puzzles. This phenomenon causes us as lawyers to ask: do generic terms have a 'half-life' in which they are no longer used as generic terms but may still be associated with a class of products which has become obsolete? The answer to this is apparently yes: an OHIM Board of Appeal[84] refused to allow the registration of OBERON as a trade mark for computer software, that word having formerly served as a little-known programming language. The word OBERON would not therefore appear to consumers as a trade mark: it would appear to them to communicate information about the product itself. This decision, which seems unduly broad in its view of terms customary in the trade, may not be a good indicator of the sort of words which fall short of registrability.

4.66 Issues involving genericity are discussed further in Chapter 6.

(4) The need to keep a word or other sign available for all to use

4.67 In German law the doctrine of *Freihaltebedürfnis* (the need to keep a word or other

---

[81] *West (t/a Eastenders) v Fuller Smith and Turner plc* [2002] FSR 822, affirmed by the Court of Appeal on 31 January 2003.
[82] Damon Runyan, who died in 1946, wrote a series of delightful short stories based on the adventures of disreputable Broadway characters whose rich and colourful argot has fast become unintelligible to all but the patient and advanced reader.
[83] Anna Sewell's *Black Beauty* was first published in 1877 when the horse was the principal means of transport in Europe.
[84] *Lombard Risk Systems Ltd's application*, Case R 4/1999-2 [2000] ETMR 1055.

F. Signs which other traders may wish to use

mark[85] free for general use), as its name suggests, may prevent the registration of a trade mark if it can be shown[86] that it should be kept available for all traders and not monopolized by just one of them. This doctrine is specifically German and it cannot apply in the face of evidence that a word—however desirable its free use may be—has actually acquired distinctive character in respect to goods or services for which registration is sought.[87] Nonetheless its influence can be detected in other jurisdictions, particularly within Europe. Accordingly it will be discussed at some length here.

An extreme case of *Freihaltebedürfnis* would be the word BANANA, which should be kept available for use by all traders in bananas. Unfortunately many of the cases in which *Freihaltebedürfnis* is raised as an objection to a mark's registration are not extreme cases. They are cases in which the arguments are finely balanced and where other traders could manage to run their businesses without using the applicant's mark but might prefer not to be put to that inconvenience. More to the point, other traders should not be forced to be more inventive in their circumvention of a registered trade mark which inconveniences trade than the applicant was in selecting it in the first place.   4.68

(a) Freihaltebedürfnis *and the scope of protection of granted applications*

The concept of *Freihaltebedürfnis* must be understood in conjunction with the concept of the scope of protection given to a granted trade mark. If the scope of protection is wide, then *Freihaltebedürfnis* comes into play more; if the scope is narrow, then *Freihaltebedürfnis* may not even be needed.[88] Also, where a trade mark consists of words and images, for example, in relation to the words 'TAX FREE for tourists Europe Tax-Free Shopping' with a strikingly coloured device, use of the term 'tax free' by itself would not constitute an infringement of that mark since the protection conferred by registration would be confined to that particular colour combination and device, with the result that *Freihaltebedürfnis* need not be applied.[89] Finally, there is a point of remoteness beyond which there is no realistic need to keep a mark free. BANANA should be kept free for all who sell or grow   4.69

---

[85] The vast majority of problems have been caused by words, but the concept is relevant to other types of mark such as colours (see eg *Wm Wrigley Jr Company's application* [1999] ETMR 214) and product shapes (*Linde AG, Winward Industries Inc and Rado Uhren AG*, 24 October 2002, Joined Cases C-53/01 to C-55/01 [2003] ETMR 354 (Opinion of Advocate General Ruiz Jarabo)).

[86] This is important. The need to keep free must be *proved* and cannot be assumed; *K trade mark* [2001] ETMR 1181 (Bundesgerichtshof).

[87] *Windsurfing Chiemsee Produktions- und Vertriebs GmbH v Boots- und Segelzubehör Walter Huber und Franz Attenberger*, Joined Cases C-108 and 109/97 [1999] ETMR 585 (ECJ), paras 44–5.

[88] See the *Deutsche Telekom* case [2003] ETMR 170 where the Austrian appellate court considered that the scope of protection of a particularly weak trade mark was so narrow that competitors were not unduly inconvenienced by it.

[89] *Tax Free trade mark application* [1998] ETMR 193 (Bundespatentgericht).

bananas, but what of people who trans-ship fruit or who make fruit-flavoured ice-cream? The answer to this question too will depend on the scope of protection of the BANANA and on the defences available to others. Descriptive use should always be kept free, even for more remote products, but the big issue is which of three ways may be employed to achieve this: (i) by refusing registration from the outset; (ii) by allowing registration but not considering such descriptive use as an infringement (for example, by requiring 'trade mark use' as a precondition of infringement)[90] or (iii) by allowing a special defence of descriptive use (as we do in Europe).[91] This issue was addressed by the Bundesgerichtshof in GENESCAN, where the need to keep the word 'genescan' available for the operation of genetic analysis and sequencing did not extend to the provision of a computer program which would facilitate such analysis and sequencing.[92]

4.70 Given the potential conceptual overlap between *Freihaltebedürfnis* and the two mandatory legal barriers of absence of distinctive quality and descriptiveness, it is highly likely that the employment of the doctrine of *Freihaltebedürfnis* will not lead to the unregistrability or cancellation of any trade marks which might not anyway fall foul of the twin requirements of non-distinctiveness and descriptiveness. Thus in France an argument that the word mark TRANSLATIONS should be kept available for translation companies was rejected on the basis of the mark's distinctiveness alone,[93] while the registrability of NEURONE in the face of 'neural networks' was held valid for computer products on the basis that it was neither commonplace nor descriptive.[94]

4.71 It is possible to regard it as necessary to keep even an invented word or 'syntactically unusual juxtaposition'[95] free for general use if that word contains a meaning which is derived from those goods. Thus the word mark ERGOPANEL could not be registered for goods which had control consoles:[96] those consoles were 'ergonomic panels' and ERGOPANEL was too good a word, once coined, to leave in private hands.

---

[90] 'Trade mark use' is discussed in detail in Chapters 7 and 8.
[91] Council Directive 89/104, art 6(1); Council Regulation 40/94, art 12(1).
[92] *GENESCAN trade mark* [2002] ETMR 329, 332.
[93] *Sarl RWS Translations Ltd v Getten and Sté Translations* [1999] ETMR 258 (Cour d'appel de Paris). In this remarkable case an English translation company infringed the TRANSLATIONS trade mark for translation. The French term for translation is *traduction* and there would have been no reason why the word TRANSLATION should have been left open for use by foreigners alone.
[94] *Neurone Tech v Neurones and de Chammard* [1999] ETMR 611 (Cour de Cassation, Chambre Commerciale, Paris).
[95] This term, coined in *Procter & Gamble Company v OHIM*, Case C-383/99 P [2002] ETMR 22, paras 43–8, is sometimes referred to in OHIM circles as a 'suj'.
[96] *ERGOPANEL trade mark application* [1997] ETMR 495 (Bundespatentgericht).

F. Signs which other traders may wish to use

(b) Freihaltebedürfnis in ECJ and CFI case law

The two central planks of European trade mark legislation, Directive 89/104 and the CTM Regulation, both bar the registration of   **4.72**

> trade marks which consist exclusively of signs or indications which have become customary in the current language or in the bona fide and established practices of the trade.[97]

They also bar the registration of signs which consist exclusively of   **4.73**

> signs or indications which may serve, in trade, to designate the kind, quality, quantity, intended purpose, value, geographical origin, time of production of the goods or of rendering of the service, or other characteristics of the goods or service.[98]

The first of these bars might be regarded as a pure form of *Freihaltebedürfnis,* while the second, discussed in greater depth below,[99] is a bar on the registration of any mark comprised of purely descriptive terms. The ECJ has made it plain that this second bar   **4.74**

> pursues an aim which is in the public interest, namely that descriptive signs or indications relating to the categories of goods or services in respect of which registration is applied for may be freely used by all, including as collective marks or as part of complex or graphic marks,[100]

from which we can see that it is intended to fulfil the same function as *Freihaltebedürfnis.*

In one sense *Freihaltebedürfnis* goes further than the new European position, barring registration of those signs or indications which may not have become customary but which are nonetheless to be kept available to those who work within a particular trade or profession. In another sense it is the phraseology of Directive 89/104 and the CTM Regulation which runs wider, in that it does not limit the bar to registration to just those cases where there is a 'real, serious or current need' to keep the mark available for use by others.[101] *Freihaltebedürfnis* really lies in a limbo between lack of distinctiveness (since a word which competitors may readily seek to use may have little or no inherently distinctive quality) and descriptiveness (to the extent that such a word may have descriptive qualities), but it is neither of them.   **4.75**

---

[97] Council Directive 89/104, art 3(1)(d); Council Regulation 40/94, art 7(1)(d).
[98] Council Directive 89/104, art 3(1)(c); Council Regulation 40/94, art 7(1)(c).
[99] See paras 4.128–4.142 below.
[100] *Windsurfing Chiemsee Produktions- und Vertriebs GmbH v Boots- und Segelzubehör Walter Huber and Franz Attenberger,* Joined Cases C-108 and 109/97 [1999] ETMR 585, para 25.
[101] *OHIM v Wm Wrigley Jr Company,* Case C-191/01 P, 10 April 2003 (Opinion of Advocate General Jacobs), para 17, citing *Windsurfing Chiemsee,* paras 29–35.

4.76 The ECJ has itself pointed out in the BABY-DRY case[102] that the juxtaposition of current European law on registration and defences to infringement will protect the interests of other traders in making *bona fide* use of the sort of marks that would have been unregistrable under the *Freihaltebedürfnis* principle:

> ... trade marks are not to be registered if they are devoid of distinctive character ... or if they consist exclusively of signs or indications which may serve, in trade, to designate the kind, quality, quantity, intended purpose, value, geographical origin, time of production of the goods or of rendering of the service, or other characteristics of the goods or service ...
>
> ... the rights conferred by the trade mark do not entitle the proprietor to prohibit a third party from using, in the course of trade, indications concerning the kind, quality, quantity, intended purpose, value, geographical origin, the time of production of the goods or the time of rendering the service, or other characteristics of the goods or service, provided he uses them in accordance with honest practices in industrial or commercial matters.
>
> It is clear from those two provisions taken together that the purpose of the prohibition of registration of purely descriptive signs or indications as trade marks is ... to prevent registration ... of signs or indications which, because they are no different from the usual way of designating the relevant goods or services or their characteristics, could not fulfil the function of identifying the undertaking that markets them and are thus devoid of the distinctive character needed for that function.

4.77 This statement, particularly its second paragraph, demonstrates that the need to keep certain signs free for others to use is an issue which cannot be disposed of without also addressing the limits of the trade mark monopoly in the first place. However, the ECJ may not be eager to force competitors to rely on the defence of using a word in a descriptive manner. As Advocate General Jacobs said:

> It may be feared that the approach in question is liable to shift the balance of power in favour of a trade mark owner with monopolistic ambitions who may assert, or threaten to assert, his rights against an alleged 'infringer' who merely seeks to use descriptive terms descriptively and honestly. In the real world, a defence under Article 12(b) might be worth rather less than its ostensible value in law.
>
> That danger cannot be ignored. A trade mark owner wishing to monopolise not only his trade mark but the area around it may threaten unmeritorious proceedings against a competitor, who may capitulate rather than incur the costs of litigation as well as risk an adverse outcome.[103]

4.78 In the wake of BABY-DRY and *Windsurfing Chiemsee*,[104] which analyses the need to keep a sign free within the context of its possible function as an indicator of

---

[102] *Procter & Gamble Company v OHIM*, Case C-383/99 P [2002] ETMR 22, paras 35–7.
[103] *OHIM v Wm Wrigley Jr Company*, Case C-191/01 P, 10 April 2003, paras 94–5.
[104] *Windsurfing Chiemsee Produktions- und Vertriebs GmbH v Boots- und Segelzubehör Walter Huber and Franz Attenberger*, Joined Cases C-108 and 109/97 [1999] ETMR 585 (ECJ).

F. Signs which other traders may wish to use

geographical origin, the CFI,[105] allowing an application to register the word mark ULTRAPLUS for plastic microwave ovenware to proceed, struck a good balance between *Freihaltebedürfnis,* descriptiveness, distinctiveness and the ability of a sign to function as a trade mark. This is how it approached these issues:

> 21. Article 7(1)(c) of Regulation 40/94 . . . pursues an aim which is in the public interest, namely that descriptive signs or indications may be freely used by all. . . .
>
> 22. From that point of view, the signs and indications referred to in Article 7(1)(c) . . . are those which may serve in normal usage from the point of view of the relevant public to designate, either directly or by reference to one of their essential characteristics, the goods or services in respect of which registration is sought . . . Accordingly, a sign's descriptiveness can only be assessed by reference to the goods or services concerned and to the way in which it is understood by a specific intended public . . .
>
> 23. In the present case, the Board of Appeal found . . . that the sign consists of, first, the prefix 'ultra', which means 'going beyond, surpassing, transcending the limits of . . .' or 'exceeding in quantity, number, scale, minuteness, . . .' and, second, the suffix 'plus', which means that the product is 'of superior quality; excellent of its kind'. It considered that those two words are laudatory terms used to claim the excellence of the products in question. Thus it found that UltraPlus is descriptive for any type of goods or services.
>
> 24. [I]f the term consisted of, for example, the prefix 'ultra' and an adjective, it could indeed be held that the adjective directly and immediately informs the consumer about a characteristic of the product and that, since the prefix merely reinforces the characterisation thus given to the product, a sign composed in this way is descriptive.
>
> 25. However . . . 'ultra' does not designate a quality, quantity or characteristic of the ovenware which the consumer is able to understand directly. That word . . . is only capable of reinforcing the designation of a quality or characteristic by another word. . . . 'plus' does not in itself designate a quality or characteristic of the plastic ovenware concerned which the consumer is able to understand directly and which could be reinforced by the word 'ultra'.
>
> 26. . . . it is not apparent . . . that the relevant public would immediately and without further reflection make a definite and direct association between plastic ovenware and UltraPlus . . .
>
> 27. When an undertaking extols, indirectly and in an abstract manner, the excellence of its products by way of a sign such as UltraPlus, yet without directly and immediately informing the consumer of one of the qualities or specific characteristics of the ovenware, it is a case of evocation and not designation for the purposes of Article 7(1)(c) . . .
>
> 28. . . . the Office's arguments that UltraPlus designates the very good quality of the goods, and in particular—as was alleged at the hearing—the excellence of the plastic which makes the products light and resistant to changes in temperature, do not make it possible to characterise the sign as descriptive. Such characteristics are neither indicated nor singled out by the sign at issue and remain, where the public

---

[105] *Dart Industries Inc v OHIM,* Case T-360/00 [2003] ETMR 406, discussed in Ilanah Simon, 'What's Cooking at the CFI? More Guidance on Descriptive and Non-distinctive Trade Marks' [2003] EIPR 322.

might imagine that they are alluded to, too vague and indeterminate to render that sign descriptive of the goods in question . . .

29. It follows . . . that, in failing to relate its analysis to the goods in question and in failing to show that UltraPlus may serve to designate those goods directly, the Board of Appeal infringed Article 7(1)(c) . . .

30. Finally . . . the fact that a sign is not descriptive does not automatically mean that it is distinctive. That character may also be lacking if the relevant public cannot perceive in that sign an indication of the commercial origin of the goods . . .

(c) Is Freihaltebedürfnis *relevant only to word marks?*

4.79 Most *Freihaltebedürfnis* cases involve word marks, but the concept of keeping elements of a trade mark open for all to use is capable of applying equally to logos, shapes, colours and any other feature of a trade mark. This principle should however be applied sparingly. After all, every case in which a trade mark application is granted is a case in which the freedom of choice of the applicant's competitors has diminished. The CFI has itself noted:

> [T]he interest that competitors of an applicant for a three-dimensional mark consisting of the product's design may have in being able freely to choose shapes and colours for their own products is not in itself a ground for refusing registration of such a mark . . .[106]

4.80 One further point to consider is the applicability of *Freihaltebedürfnis* to trade marks for signs which have acquired distinctiveness through use. Once a sufficiently large proportion of the public has been schooled to understand that a sign, formerly free for use by all, has been vested with a new meaning which identifies the products or services of the person who uses that sign, the reason for keeping it free for use by competitors disappears.

(5) When are laudatory terms registrable?

4.81 Terms which praise a product or service in a direct manner are generally not inherently registrable as trade marks. This may be because: (i) they are terms customarily used in trade or by the public with regard to those goods or services—irrespective of whether those terms are descriptive of the goods for which registration is sought;[107] (ii) they are regarded as terms which should be kept available for all traders to use;[108] or (iii) the registration of laudatory terms is explicitly or by implication prohibited by national legislation.

4.82 Once a term has been so heavily and extensively used that it has acquired secondary meaning as a trade mark, the fact that it is laudatory will no longer be a bar

---

[106] *Procter & Gamble Company v OHIM*, Case T-117/00 [2002] ETMR 174, para 72.
[107] *Merz & Krell GmbH*, Case C-517/99 [2002] ETMR 231 (ECJ): BRAVO for typewriters.
[108] eg BONUS in the German Bundespatentgericht's *BONUS trade mark application* [1997] ETMR 413.

F. Signs which other traders may wish to use

to registration, even if its trade mark meaning does not fully eradicate the original laudatory meaning.[109] Thus the word IDEAL is not in general registrable for any goods or services;[110] but where evidence was adduced to show that the word IDEAL was clearly used and recognized as a trade mark for rubber stamps and ink pads, its registration in that somewhat specialized market was no longer objectionable.[111]

4.83 What constitutes a laudatory term is a matter of cultural relativism. For example, the Germans have regarded the word BRAVO as a laudatory term for typewriters[112] even though many people may wonder whether other manufacturers of such products would be seriously inconvenienced by the appropriation of that term for a machine which rarely if ever elicits such a response. After some uncertainty that same nation concluded that the word YES was not a term of approbation for cigarettes.[113] The British have considered the words THE PERFECTIONISTS unregistrable in respect of bras and panties[114] on the basis that the approbation related to the makers of such underwear, even though the Danes and Australians had no such hang-ups about that mark's registration.

4.84 Practice before the OHIM Boards of Appeal has been somewhat unsettled. The word SUPREME has been held to be unregistrable for all goods and services on the basis that it is 'without any originality or distinctiveness' rather than on account of its laudatory character,[115] while COMPLETE was rejected for being descriptive of goods having 'every necessary part or element' and for describing 'the intended purpose of those goods (ie to complete or perfect)'.[116] The word XTRA could not be registered because, being 'descriptive of better than expected quality' it was thus devoid of distinctive quality.[117]

4.85 Not all laudatory terms have had such a rough time before OHIM, though. Although the word MAXIMA was refused registration for surgical and medical goods, on the ground that the word bore a connotation of 'biggest and best' and 'suggested that a product represented the highest technical achievement in a particular field', the Board of Appeal noted realistically that

---

[109] *Mainland Products Ltd v Bonlac Foods* [1998] IP Asia LR 289 (New Zealand High Court): VINTAGE was validly registered for cheese, even though the word's original meaning had not been extinguished.
[110] *Harcourt Brace & Co's application*, Case R 130/1999-1 [2000] ETMR 382 (OHIM).
[111] *M&R Marketing Systems Inc's application*, Case R 1167/2000-1 [2002] ETMR 317 (OHIM).
[112] See facts relating to *Merz & Krell GmbH*, Case C-517/99 [2002] ETMR 231 (ECJ).
[113] *YES trade mark* [1998] ETMR 386; [2000] ETMR 883 (Bundesgerichtshof).
[114] *Warnaco Inc's application* [1997] ETMR 505 (UK Trade Mark Registry).
[115] *Fuji Photo Film Co Ltd's application*, Case R 44/1998-3 [1999] ETMR 505.
[116] *Procter & Gamble Company's application*, Case R 116/1998-3 [1999] ETMR 664, 665. Cf *Henkel KgaA's application* WTLR, 11 July 2003, in which the Estonian Board of Appeal allowed the registration of X-TRA on the ground that the word 'extra' was meaningless to at least 80 per cent of Estonians.
[117] *USA Detergents Inc's application*, Case R 20/97-1 [1998] ETMR 562.

the products in question would normally be purchased by highly trained individuals who were unlikely to be influenced by any subliminal message, contained in a trade mark, that the products were in some way superior to competing products.[118]

4.86 Recent OHIM practice has been even kinder to applicants. Apart from allowing the registration of IDEAL for rubber stamps and ink pads (mentioned above), OHIM dealt a mighty blow in favour of the registration of apparently no-hope trade marks when a Board of Appeal allowed the registration of the word THE for screws, nuts, bolts and threaded rods.[119] The examiner had rejected the application, arguing that the mark meant 'the best', 'only' or 'most remarkable' but the Board disagreed: THE only had such a connotation when followed by another word (for example, THE BEST, THE TOP). But by itself, stripped of a qualifying word, the word THE was quite devoid of connotations. Indeed, it was even fanciful because it needed something further to complete it.

4.87 The CFI allowed the application to register ULTRAPLUS for plastic ovenware. While 'ultra' and 'plus' might each be individually unregistrable on account of their laudatory nature, their combination was both meaningless and 'easily and instantly memorised by the relevant public'.[120]

G. Distinctiveness

4.88 Of all the criteria relating to registrability, distinctiveness is the most important. The TRIPs provisions relating to trade mark registration[121] make the fact that a sign is 'capable of distinguishing' goods or services the sole essential determinant of its suitability for registration.

4.89 How do we know if a trade mark is distinctive in the sense of being inherently capable of distinguishing the goods or services of one undertaking from those of other undertakings? The courts and trade mark registries have laid down various criteria of distinctiveness, some of which have been canonized into significant rules while others have been discarded as being of little assistance in the quest for distinctive character. In the following paragraphs we consider the meaning of this concept, both in legal and practical terms.

---

[118] *Medtronic Inc's application*, Case R 51/1998-1 [1999] ETMR 504. The same approach was taken in *Daishowa Seiki Co Ltd's application*, Case R 991/2000-3 [2002] ETMR 403, where an OHIM Board of Appeal considered that purchasers of metal machine tool parts would not be influenced by the laudatory connotations of the word mark BIG PLUS.
[119] *Tong Hwei Enterprise Co Ltd's application*, Case R 374/2000-1 [2001] ETMR 961. The word mark THE was chosen because it was an acronym of the applicant's name.
[120] *Dart Industries Inc v OHIM*, Case T-360/00 [2003] ETMR 406, 415.
[121] TRIPs, art 15(1).

G. Distinctiveness

(1) Distinctiveness is in the eyes of the relevant average consumer

In seeking to establish a test of inherent distinctive character the courts have been motivated by the need to identify as being objectively registrable only those marks which are indeed capable of distinguishing the applicant's goods or services. They have however been required to focus their attention *not* on what they as judges regard as distinctive but on what the average consumer of the relevant goods or services in question would regard as distinctive.[122] This consumer 'normally perceives a mark as a whole and does not proceed to analyse its various details'; he or she is 'reasonably well-informed and reasonably observant and circumspect' and possesses a level of attention which is 'likely to vary according to the category of goods or services in question'.[123]

4.90

When considering the registrability of a sign, judges are reluctant to allow the test of what the relevant consumer would regard as distinctive to degenerate into a process of allowing litigants to parade cohorts of allegedly typical relevant consumers before the courts as 'evidence' of how a relevant consumer would regard a particular sign.[124]

4.91

(2) Distinctiveness cannot be arithmetically quantified

In *Lloyd Schuhfabrik Meyer v Klijsen*, admittedly a case dealing with infringement of trade marks and not their registrability, the ECJ observed:

4.92

> It is not possible to state in general terms, for example, by referring to given percentages relating to the degree of recognition attained by the mark within the relevant section of the public, when a mark has a strong distinctive character.[125]

This is an important statement. Obviously if a trade mark is recognized by 100 per cent of consumers as designating the goods or services of its owner it is a strongly distinctive mark while, if no one recognizes it as having that function, it is entirely non-distinctive. But there is no one 'cut-off point', in absolute or percentage terms, beneath which a distinctive mark ceases to be a distinctive mark. In respect of goods and services which are rarely purchased and which are of long duration, a consumer may only occasionally make a foray into the market for such goods or services and will be unlikely to make a keen study of them before he needs to do so. Other branded products and services maintain a high profile within society at large, even among those who do not purchase them at all and

4.93

---

[122] *Lloyd Schuhfabrik Meyer & Co GmbH v Klijsen Handel BV*, Case V-342/97 [1999] ETMR 690 (ECJ), paras 25–6.
[123] *Gut Springenheide GmbH, Tusky v Oberkreisdirektor des Kreises Steinfurt etc*, Case C-210/96 [1999] ETMR 425 (ECJ), para 31.
[124] *Bach Flower Remedies Ltd v Healing Herbs Ltd* [1999] IP&T 146 (CA), 160, 169.
[125] *Lloyd Schuhfabrik Meyer & Co GmbH v Klijsen Handel BV*, Case V-342/97 [1999] ETMR 690, 699.

will therefore possess a high degree of recognition. But the quantification of distinctiveness confuses two concepts: there is the degree of recognition among members of the public that there exists a particular trade mark and there is the ability of the trade mark to serve as such in identifying goods and services before the market of relevant consumers for them. The degree of recognition can be readily quantified, and frequently is, in market surveys. The ability of the trade mark cannot so readily be quantified because it comprehends both that mark's *actual ability* to distinguish and its *potential* to do so. The degree of actual recognition is not a measure of capacity to distinguish.

(3) Distinctiveness is presumed unless it is disproved

4.94 The modern trade mark registry operates more efficiently if decision-making and the exercise of discretion are limited to only those situations in which they are absolutely necessary and it should not therefore be necessary for trade mark applicants to vouch for the distinctive nature of their trade marks if that distinctive nature has not first been challenged. Ideally, an application to register a mark should be the first leg of a journey on an administrative conveyor belt which leads automatically from filing to grant unless some fault is detected in the application.

(4) Distinctiveness must exist throughout the territory in which the trade mark is to be registered

4.95 This is a matter of great importance to multicultural Europe, where a word or figurative mark[126] may be entirely distinctive in part of the EU but descriptive[127] or non-distinctive[128] in others. In theory a trade mark cannot be partially valid within its territory: either it is distinctive of goods or it is not. Cases which suggest that there is such a thing as a partially distinctive mark[129] reach this conclusion by finding that some consumers find the mark distinctive while others do not, but (i) they have not drawn this conclusion on a geographical basis and (ii) they have done so in respect of a mark which was formerly entirely distinctive and which has begun to lose its distinctive character.

---

[126] *Poulsen Roser ApS' application*, Case R 746/2001-1 [2003] ETMR 112 (OHIM): accurate depiction of a rose may be distinctive in Denmark, but would need to be shown to be distinctive throughout the territory of EU before a CTM could be granted.

[127] eg *Matratzen v OHIM*, Case T-6/01 [2003] ETMR 392 (CFI), where the word mark MATRATZEN was entirely distinctive in Spain but generic (meaning 'mattresses') in Germany.

[128] In *Ford Motor Company v OHIM*, Case T-91/99 [2000] ETMR 554 (CFI) the word mark OPTIONS was refused for insurance services: it was distinctive in all EU countries save France and the UK.

[129] See eg *D Green & Co (Stoke Newington) Ltd and Plastico Ltd v Regalzone Ltd* [2002] ETMR 241 (HC): SPORK for a combination spoon and fork; *Björnekulla Fruktindustrier Aktiebolag v Procordia Food Aktiebolag* [2002] ETMR 464 (Stockholm District Court): BOSTONGURKA for cucumbers.

G. Distinctiveness

It might be thought that, even if the diminishing distinctiveness of a trade mark over time does not automatically render it invalid, it should nevertheless be impossible to register a partially distinctive mark from scratch. This is not however the case. So long as the applicant's sign has a distinctive character, the fact that for some consumers it has a descriptive connotation will not disqualify it from registration.[130] **4.96**

(5) Distinctiveness is not to be considered in abstract but must be considered in relation to the goods or services for which the mark is to be used

A trade mark such as PC would never be considered distinctive of personal computers, but it might serve as a perfectly good trade mark for quails' eggs. **4.97**

(6) Distinctiveness is to be considered in relation to the trade mark as a whole, not in relation to its component parts

It is no longer regarded as acceptable practice to divide an applicant's trade mark into salami slices and to consider the fitness of each slice for registration.[131] As the ECJ stated in BABY-DRY: **4.98**

> As regards trade marks composed of words . . . descriptiveness must be determined not only in relation to each word taken separately but also in relation to the whole which they form. Any perceptible difference between the combination of words submitted for registration and the terms used in the common parlance of the relevant class of consumers to designate the goods or services or their essential characteristics is apt to confer distinctive character on the word combination enabling it to be registered as a trade mark.[132]

In that case, a salami-slicer would seek to reason as follows: (i) BABY is a non-distinctive term in respect of babies' nappies since it indicates the use or destination of individual nappies; (ii) DRY is a non-distinctive term in respect of babies' nappies since it indicates the urine-retaining function played by nappies; (iii) based on the previous premisses, and assuming that a trade mark cannot be more distinctive than the sum of its parts, the trade mark BABY-DRY is also non-distinctive. This reasoning, which has been held to be unacceptable for CTMs, has also been rejected by some national courts.[133] **4.99**

---

[130] *West (t/a Eastenders) v Fuller Smith & Turner plc*, 31 January 2003 (unreported) (CA), citing BABY-DRY [2002] ETMR 22 and *Wm Wrigley Jr Co v OHIM* [2001] ETMR 623.

[131] In *Paniberica* [2002] EIPR N-8 (Supreme Court, Spain) the court considered that Law 32/1988, art 11 actually prohibited it from breaking PANIBERICA down into its components PAN- and IBERICA, since only a global appreciation of the mark was admissible.

[132] *Procter & Gamble Company v OHIM* Case C-383/99 P [2002] ETMR 22, para 40.

[133] See eg *Aimo-Boot v Fabre* [1999] ETMR 55 (Tribunal de Grande Instance de Paris): AUDIO FEELING distinctive for hi-fi audio equipment; *D'Ieteren v Benelux Trade Marks Office* [2003] ETMR 842 (CA, Brussels): WECOVER distinctive for insurance services.

Chapter 4: Registrability: The Basic Principles

4.100   The ECJ may have pronounced on high that trade marks must be considered in their entirety but the salami-slicers are still alive and well in the same building, in the CFI. In an application to register as CTMs the word marks KIT PRO and KIT SUPER PRO for goods in Class 12 (parts for repairing drum brakes in land vehicles), the CFI upheld OHIM's refusal of these applications on the ground that, since the words 'kit' 'pro' and 'super' were commonly used in marketing for all kinds of products and services, they were devoid of distinctive character and could not be registered.[134] Can KIT SUPER PRO really be less distinctive for drum brake parts than BABY-DRY for nappies or ULTRAPLUS[135] for plastic ovenware? In the case of KIT PRO and SUPER KIT PRO the CFI justified the salami-slicing in a much-cited passage from *BABY-DRY*:

> Since this is a trade mark made up of several components (a compound mark), for the purposes of assessing its distinctive character it must be considered as a whole. However, that is not incompatible with an examination of each of the mark's individual components in turn.[136]

4.101   This process was taken to an extreme length when the fairly short and succinct trade mark SAT.2 was taken to be a compound trade mark and analysed in terms of the capacity to distinguish the elements 'SAT', '.' and '2'.[137]

4.102   The consequence of these doctrinal developments is that the court has two options. If it wants to find a compound trade mark valid, then its whole is greater than the sum of its parts while, if the court wants to find it invalid, it is the individual parts which condemn it to unregistrability.[138] The court may as well have said:

> Since this is an entire salami, its registrability must be considered as a whole. However, that is not incompatible with cutting it up and examining each slice of it separately.

4.103   In defence of salami-slicing, a small role may remain for it in respect of applications to register a combination of colours where the applicant specifies neither the proportion of each colour to the other nor the appearance of products to which the colour combination has been applied.[139] In such cases global appreciation is

---

[134] *Robert Bosch GmbH v OHIM*, 20 November 2002, Joined Cases T-79/01 and T-86/01 (CFI (Fourth Chamber)).
[135] *Dart Industries Inc v OHIM*, Case T-360/00 [2003] ETMR 406.
[136] *Procter & Gamble Company v OHIM*, Case C-383/99 P [2002] ETMR 22, para 40.
[137] *SAT 1 SattellitenFernsehen GmbH v OHIM*, Case T-323/00 [2002] IP&T 928 (CFI). The mark was in fact held registrable for some services but not others.
[138] This is effectively what the ECJ did in *DKV Deutsche Krankenversicherung AG v OHIM (COMPANYLINE)*, Case C-104/00 P [2003] ETMR 241, when it ruled that COMPANYLINE lacked distinctive character for insurance and financial services in Class 36. Cf the approach taken by the majority in the TTAB decision in *Re Revenue Technologies Corporation* WTLR, 5 June 2003, allowing MARKETPRICE for 'business consulting services in the fields of product and service pricing'.
[139] eg the colours green and grey for garden equipment: *Viking-Umwelttechnik GmbH v OHIM*, Case T-316/00 [2003] ETMR 196 (CFI).

G. Distinctiveness

impossible and an application can only be judged on the distinctiveness of its constituent parts. Salami-slicers may also be useful where the scope of protection given to distinctive combinations of individually non-distinctive terms is wide. For example, registration of the word mark ULTRAPLUS would be harmful if it conferred a monopoly which enabled the trade mark proprietor to suppress the use by competitors of the separate words 'ultra' and 'plus'.

(7) Descriptiveness and other negative traits of a trade mark must also relate to the mark as a whole, not merely to its individual components

It follows that, if distinctiveness is assessed by reference to the mark as a whole, when taken in the context of the goods or services for which its registration is sought, the same should be true for an assessment of those qualities of a trade mark which prevent it attaining the status of registrability: descriptiveness, deceptiveness, genericity and so on. This position is however inconsistent with the French concept of 'negative distinctiveness': that the distinctiveness of a trade mark is defined as the non-necessary, non-generic, unusual or non-descriptive characteristics of a sign. By that test, which has been recently consecrated by the Cour de Cassation,[140] it is difficult to conceive how BABY-DRY could ever be registered for babies' nappies. **4.104**

(8) The weak distinctive character of a word mark can be strengthened by the addition of figurative elements

In principle, inherent distinctiveness can be created by a trade mark's overall appearance even if it contains a verbal element which is by itself non-distinctive. However, the weaker a word mark is, the stronger will need to be the figurative element which surrounds it. Taking one French case, the word mark GEO (see Figure 4.2) is not a strong mark for books and printed matter, since it is very short and highly reminiscent of many words beginning with the prefix GEO- and which are either the title or the subject matter of publications. But once the word GEO is cast in a striking visual format, its overall distinctiveness can be greatly enhanced[141] and registration will be secured—even though the scope of protection conferred by its registration may be very narrow. **4.105**

Figure 4.2 The word mark GEO.

---

[140] *Société Prime TV v Top Tele*, 26 March 2002 (Cour de Cassation (Chambre Commerciale)).
[141] *Sté Prisma Presse and Sté Gruner und Jahr Communication GmbH v SA Editions Economica* [1999] ETMR 549 (TGI de Paris).

(9) Signs in common use are not disqualified from being monopolized

4.106 Registration of the word mark GOD MORGON APELSINJUICE MED FRUKTKÖTT (Swedish for 'Good morning orange juice with pulp') in Norway was not held to be contingent upon the applicant disclaiming exclusive use of the words GOD MORGON. Although these words are spoken daily by millions of people who drink orange juice, they could nonetheless be appropriated by a trade mark monopoly. The words were not devoid of distinctive character and there was nothing in their meaning which dictated that they should be kept free for other orange juice makers to use.[142] The word mark THANK YOU was however ruled to be lacking in distinctive character for chocolates: a recipient, when presented by a donor with a box of chocolates, will normally articulate the polite and formal response 'thank you'.[143]

4.107 Not just verbal but visual clichés can be registered. The fact that signs such as globes[144] are so frequently used as to become hackneyed commonplaces does not deprive them of registrability, so long as they fulfil the regular criteria of registrability.

4.108 Can a colour be commonplace? The CFI appears to suggest that it can. In one case that court found that, since it was 'not rare' to come across orange-coloured agricultural machines, that use was 'commonplace'.[145] This reasoning would seem to have forgotten the law of the excluded middle: there are surely some degrees of frequency of occurrence which lie between the opposing poles of the rare and the commonplace: we even have at least three convenient terms by which to describe them (occasional; not infrequent; frequent). This excluded middle would also appear to be the natural habitat of the partially distinctive mark.[146]

4.109 Once a sign is above the level of the commonplace, even if the kindest thing said about it is that it is 'not exactly commonplace', the CFI has held that it possesses sufficient distinctiveness to qualify it for registration.[147]

(10) Distinctiveness is enhanced by a mark's memorable nature

4.110 The fact that a trade mark is easily memorable leans towards its being more likely to be found distinctive. This is because a mark's memorability facilitates the making of repeat purchases by contented customers.[148]

---

[142] *Jo-Bolaget Fruktprodukter HB v State Ministry of Industry and Commerce* [2002] ETMR 161 (Borgarting Lagmansrett).
[143] *Thank You Candy Co Ltd's application*, 19 October 1995 (unreported) (UK Trade Mark Registry).
[144] *Ajlan bin Abdullaziz Al-Ajlan Brothers Co's application; opposition by Al-Masaraat International Trading & Contracting Co Ltd* [2000] ETMR 710 (LCAP, Geoffrey Hobbs QC).
[145] *KWS Saat AG v OHIM*, Case T-173/00 [2003] ETMR 288 (CFI), para 40.
[146] Discussed further at paras 4.95–4.96 below.
[147] *DaimlerChrysler Corp v OHIM*, Case T-128/01, 6 March 2003 (unreported).
[148] *Dart Industries Inc v OHIM*, Case T-360/00 [2003] ETMR 406, para 48.

G. Distinctiveness

(11) Banality and the lack of originality, imagination or arbitrary embellishments do not prove a lack of distinctiveness

Before the watershed of the BABY-DRY case, some trade mark applications were rejected on the grounds of banality or lack of originality, but others were not. Thus the OHIM Board of Appeal rejected an application to register the trade mark MULTI 2'N I for an entire range of tools and tool-parts on the basis that there was 'nothing fanciful or capricious' in the combination of commonplace elements into a mark which was 'banal'.[149] Likewise the CFI, even after conceding that signs need not be original or fanciful, nonetheless ruled the words CINE ACTION to be devoid of distinctive character for a large number of film-related services including the 'showing and rental of films' on the basis that they lacked a 'minimum of imagination'.[150] In contrast, after the slogan BEAUTY ISN'T ABOUT LOOKING YOUNG BUT LOOKING GOOD was rejected by an OHIM examiner for being both banal and unoriginal, the Board of Appeal remitted the application for further consideration: the slogan was not banal but was an expression which fell within 'cosmetic philosophy'.[151] Nor was its lack of originality fatal. A similar position was adopted by the Tribunal de Grand Instance de Paris when it affirmed the validity of the trade mark TECHNOCITE for a techno(logy) city, observing that trade mark rights are not accorded on the basis of creativity.[152]

4.111

The law does not actually require there to be any exercise of imagination; that is left to other fields of intellectual property law. If trade marks such as personal names are not subjected to the 'minimum of imagination' standard, it seems unfair to require it of other types of trade mark.

4.112

The CFI has now ruled on several occasions that the mere fact that a mark is unimaginative does not mean that it is devoid of distinctive character. Thus NEW BORN BABY is not the most scintillatingly imaginative of terms for a child's doll but may still be registered.[153] Also DAS PRINZIP DER BEQUEMLICHKEIT (German for 'the principle of comfort') could be registered for household and office furniture, notwithstanding the OHIM Board of Appeal's conclusion that the mark lacked

4.113

---

[149] *Black & Decker Corp's application*, Case R 99/1999-1 [1999] ETMR 846.
[150] *Taurus-Film v OHIM (Cine Action)*, Case T-135/99 [2001] ETMR 594, 602. See also *Matsushita Electric Works' application*, Case R 332/1999-1 [2000] ETMR 962 (BLOOD PRESSURE WATCH demonstrated no 'imaginative surplus' in respect of sphygmomanometers, discussed further at para 4.123).
[151] *Clinique Laboratories Inc's application*, Case R 73/1998-2 [1999] ETMR 750. This decision is in stark contrast with *Visa International Service Association's application*, Case R 46/1999-1 [2000] ETMR 263 ('THE WORLD'S BEST WAY TO PAY AND BE PAID'), where even the rhyme of 'way', 'pay' and 'paid' failed to save the slogan mark from the stigma of banality.
[152] *Sarl Cargo Communication v La Cité des Sciences et de l'Industrie* [1999] ETMR 545.
[153] *Zapf Creation AG v OHIM*, Case T-140/00 [2002] ETMR 128. The mark NEW BORN BABY would not apparently be registrable for newborn babies.

originality.¹⁵⁴ Finally, the ECJ has also stated that the addition of capricious elements and embellishments is not a precondition for registration of a product shape as a trade mark.¹⁵⁵

(12) Allusiveness does not prove a lack of distinctiveness

4.114 A trade mark may allude to the nature or function of the goods or services for which registration is sought, since allusion is a suggestive rather than a descriptive attribute which does not negate the distinctive role which a trade mark is to play, so long as the monopolization of the allusion does not exclude other traders from being able to use the images or words which are part of their ordinary stock in trade. Thus a toothlike image (see Figure 4.3) was not precluded from registration in respect of dental products, there being many other ways in which a tooth could be portrayed by the applicant's competitors.¹⁵⁶ Indeed, many well-known marks today have allusive qualities: for example, LINGUAPHONE for recorded foreign language course materials, AQUASCUTUM and DRIZABONE for waterproof clothing, GARDOL for toothpaste which guards against tooth decay. In the United States too it is established that a trade mark's suggestive nature does not impair its inherently distinctive nature and it is not therefore necessary to furnish evidence of use which has conveyed it from the suggestive to the distinctive.¹⁵⁷

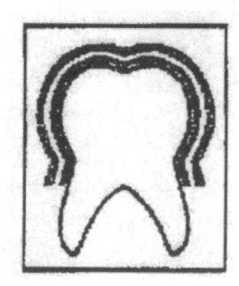

Figure 4.3 A toothlike image which was not precluded from registration in respect of dental products.

4.115 One test suggested by the CFI¹⁵⁸ is whether the applicant's trade mark conveys a 'clear and unambiguous message' as to the function of the goods for which registration is sought. On this basis VITALITE—despite its evocative French form 'vitalité'—did not transmit a clear and unambiguous message that it was connected with baby foods. Likewise the word FORMATIL was registrable for dental products even though it was comprised of the Swedish words 'forma' and 'till', meaning 'shape a filling',¹⁵⁹ since not all dental products are used for shaping fillings. Less fortunate was an Irish application to register the word KEYMAIL for telecommuni-

---

¹⁵⁴ *Erpo Möbelwerk GmbH v OHIM*, Case T-138/00 [2002] ETMR 430.
¹⁵⁵ *Koninklijke Philips Electronics NV v Remington Consumer Products Ltd*, Case C-299/99 [2002] ETMR 955.
¹⁵⁶ *Fertin A/S's application*, Case R 382/1999-1 [2000] ETMR 652 (OHIM).
¹⁵⁷ *Two Pesos Inc v Taco Cabana Inc* 23 USPQ 2d 1081 (US Supreme Court).
¹⁵⁸ *Sunrider v OHIM* (VITALITE), Case T-24/00 [2001] ECR II-449; [2001] ETMR 605; [2001] IP&T 452 (CFI).
¹⁵⁹ *Echodent AB's application*, Case R 773/2001-2 [2002] ETMR 1240 (OHIM).

G. Distinctiveness

cation services, specifically those relating to secure e-mail. The applicant argued that the word was at most allusive, but the hearing officer thought otherwise: although 'key' had several possible meanings, its combination with the word 'mail' in the context of electronic mail meant that it exclusively designated e-mail security.[160] The same result has been achieved by OHIM in respect of WEBRECORD: as a free-floating word it could be connected to the recording of the activities of spiders but, once an application is made to register it for computer software, the ambiguity drops away.[161]

(13) Lexical invention, grammatical error and perversity do not prove the existence of distinctiveness

4.116 The highest form of inherent distinctiveness is that achieved by invented words. The history of trade marks has repeatedly testified to this truism in the form of marks such as KODAK, XEROX, BOVRIL, ROLEX, ZANTAC and COLIBRI. Some invented words are formed from the contraction of existing words (for example, ADIDAS from the name of the business's founder Adi Dassler and LEGO from the Danish words 'leg godt', meaning 'play well'[162]) or from the metamorphosis of existing words (for example, TAMPAX from 'tampon'). Nonetheless in the eye of the consumer they are not words drawn from everyday parts of speech: they are inventions which serve admirably to set one manufacturer's goods or services apart from those of other undertakings.

4.117 Many trade mark applicants have cloaked the paucity of their own poor offerings with the rich dignity of the term 'invention'. Thus word marks such as IN-VESTORWORLD[163] have been refused registration on the basis that their descriptive or otherwise non-distinctive quality has not been disguised by a *de minimis* level of invention. Other words, not necessarily more inventive, have been accorded registration on the basis that their 'meaning' was meaningless (NETMEETING),[164] ambiguous (DOUBLEMINT)[165] or at least not easy to guess (EASYBANK),[166] rather than on the basis of invention alone. This demonstrates that the presence or absence of lexical invention is no longer a determinative criterion of distinctiveness.

---

[160] *Bord Telecom Eireann plc's application* [2001] ETMR 790 (Irish Patents Office).
[161] *Canon Kabushiki Kaisha's application*, Case R 182/1999-1 [1999] ETMR 845.
[162] Jeremy Phillips, 'An Empire Made of Bricks: A Brief Appraisal of LEGO' [1987] EIPR 363–6.
[163] *Community Concepts AG v OHIM*, Case T-360/99 [2001] ETMR 176 (CFI).
[164] *Microsoft Corp's application*, Case R 26/1998-3 [1999] ETMR 386 (OHIM).
[165] *Wm Wrigley Jr Company's Application*, Case T-193/99 [2001] ETMR 623 (CFI), currently under appeal. Cf *Optimum Healthcare Ltd's application* [2003] ETMR 628 in which an OHIM Board of Appeal refused ALOESORB notwithstanding the fact that 'sorb' could mean 'absorb' or 'adsorb'.
[166] *Bank für Arbeit und Wirtschaft AG v OHIM*, Case T-87/00 [2001] ETMR 761 (CFI).

(14) An inability to guess a product's nature from its trade mark does not make the trade mark distinctive

4.118 Is the word CHEMFINDER distinctive in respect of 'computer programs for use in chemical searching and information integration'? No, said the OHIM examiner: 'chem' is short for 'chemical' and 'finder' is 'a thing that finds' so those words are both descriptive. Put the two together and you have added nothing to make CHEMFINDER less so. On appeal the applicant argued:

> Imagine that one person overhears a conversation in which someone says: 'I have just bought a CHEMFINDER computer program' or 'I have just been looking at a CHEMFINDER instruction manual'.... [T]hese references to CHEMFINDER would be virtually meaningless to the listener.[167]

4.119 Accordingly, if those references are meaningless, they cannot also be descriptive. If they are not descriptive and their meaning cannot be divined by guesswork on the part of the listening consumer, it follows that the word mark CHEMFINDER must therefore be distinctive.

4.120 The Board of Appeal pinpointed the fallacy of this otherwise attractive argument, which is that it presupposes that the person overhearing the conversation does not know what the product is. The word 'chemfinder' may mean nothing to the man in the street, but it will mean a great deal to a person who is involved in the use of computer software in the retrieval of chemical information. The crux of distinctiveness is therefore that it only makes sense to guess a mark's meaning in relation to the specific goods or services to which that mark applies.

4.121 Building on this argument we can state with confidence that, where the person who overhears a conversation actually knows what the product is but still can't pinpoint the trade mark's descriptive element, that mark will be distinctive. This point was made in an application to register the words VISION DIRECT for 'computer software used in connection with the management of travel expenses'.[168] The OHIM examiner considered that the mark merely suggested a device or tool which visualizes or displays data immediately on-screen. The Board of Appeal disagreed and allowed the application. The examiner's conclusion required more of a leap of imagination than went into the creation of the trade mark in the first place, because it regarded a mere allusion to a characteristic of the computer program to be regarded as an actual description of it.

4.122 In a variant on the approach taken in *VISION DIRECT* the CFI criticized the OHIM Board of Appeal for refusing an application while failing to show that 'persons targeted' by the applicant's trade mark—presumably adults who buy toys rather than

---

[167] *Chemfinder Cambridgesoft Corp's application*, Case R 211/1998-2 [2000] ETMR 250, 253.
[168] *Rosenbluth International Inc's application*, Case R 190/1998-2 [2000] ETMR 934.

G. Distinctiveness

impecunious tiny tots—would, 'without further reflection, instantly take the sign NEW BORN BABY to designate a quality or other characteristics of dolls'.[169] This decision would appear to endorse the broad approach of *CHEMFINDER*, only substituting 'reflection' for 'guesswork'.

(15) The fact that competitors do not use a term does not prevent it being descriptive rather than distinctive

A sphygmomanometer is a device which, worn in the manner of a wristwatch, enables a reading to be taken of the wearer's blood pressure. When Matsushita sought to register the words BLOOD PRESSURE WATCH for sphygmomanometers, it pointed out that none of its competitors had used the term 'blood pressure watch'; accordingly the term should be regarded as distinctive. The OHIM examiner and Board of Appeal disagreed.[170] Lack of use by competitors may be relevant to issues such as whether a term is generic, but it does not address the issue of inherent distinctiveness.

4.123

(16) The fact that competitors also use a term does not prevent it being distinctive

It was argued that, since the word 'mail' was commonly used in the titles of many newspapers, it was not unique to the trade mark proprietor and that, therefore, the trade mark THE MAIL could not distinguish its owner's newspapers from those of other publishers. This argument was rejected on the basis that uniqueness is not of itself a prerequisite of distinctiveness.[171]

4.124

(17) The same level of distinctiveness is required of all types of mark

The ECJ ruled in the *Linde* case that

4.125

> neither the scheme of the Directive nor the wording of that provision indicate that stricter criteria than those used for other categories of trade mark ought to be applied when assessing the distinctiveness of a three-dimensional shape of goods mark.[172]

The law does not impose different standards, but the exigencies of practical reality will impose demands from which the law shrinks. Generations of members of the consuming public, practically throughout the world, have been schooled to identify the source of goods by looking at a word, label or other badge of origin

4.126

---

[169] *Zapf Creation AG v OHIM*, Case T-140/00 [2002] ETMR 128, 133 (CFI).
[170] *Matsushita Electric Works' application*, Case R 332/1999-1 [2000] ETMR 962.
[171] *Associated Newspapers Ltd and another v Express Newspapers* [2003] EWHC 1322 (Ch), paras 52–5.
[172] *Linde AG, Winward Industries Inc and Rado Uhren AG*, Joined Cases C-53/01 to C-55/01 [2003] ETMR 963.

that has been attached to them, not by looking at the shape of the goods themselves. There are some notable exceptions though, for example, the curvy Coca Cola bottle which was first perceived as an indicator of the source of its contents at a time when plain bottle shapes constituted the norm for soft drinks.

4.127 Although it is quite possible that consumers may come to identify a product shape as a trade mark quite of their own accord, there is no certainty that they will do so unless prompted to do so by advertising or marketing techniques. Accordingly we as consumers need to be positively educated to view as a trade mark anything which does not fit our own 'default' view of what a trade mark is. When it comes to weak or non-distinctive word marks, for example, we may pick up from the supermarket shelf a product called TREAT and regard that word as: (i) a trade mark, albeit a weak one because of its laudatory connotations;[173] (ii) a descriptive or deceptive indication of its contents; or possibly even (iii) a piece of literary decoration with no significance whatsoever. If the word TREAT is displayed where we would expect a trade mark to be, we would probably treat it as a trade mark. But product shapes (and colours) are different since, without consumer education, we would probably pick an apparently unmarked product up, rotate it and then turn it upside down to look for a label or word that gives us the clue as to its provenance. For this reason, establishment of the same level of acquired distinctiveness by an applicant to register a shape as a trade mark will almost inevitably involve a lot more work on his part.

H. Descriptive marks

(1) Exclusively descriptive marks cannot be registered

4.128 The bar to the registration of exclusively descriptive marks is one of the characteristics of a mature trade mark system. In the EU the non-registrability of a sign is couched in terms which have already been discussed above within the context of *Freihaltebedürfnis*:[174] a sign may not be registered if it

> consists exclusively of signs or indications which may serve, in trade, to designate the kind, quality, quantity, intended purpose, value, geographical origin, or the time of production of the goods or of the rendering of the service, or other characteristics of the goods or service.[175]

4.129 The role of the word 'exclusively' should be noted carefully. As has been observed:

> The word 'exclusively' in that provision qualifies the verb 'consist'; it refers to the elements of which the mark is composed and not to their capacity to designate

---

[173] *British Sugar plc v James Robertson & Sons Ltd* [1997] ETMR 118; [1996] RPC 281 (HC).
[174] See, in particular, Chapter 14, paras 4.67–4.80.
[175] Council Directive 89/104, art 3(1)(c); Council Regulation 40/94, art 7(1)(c).

H. Descriptive marks

characteristics. In order for registration to be precluded . . ., all the elements must have such a descriptive capacity; it is not necessary . . . that they can have no other, non-descriptive, meaning. A decision on registrability which is based on the latter criterion in the context of Article 7(1)(c) is prima facie wrong in law.[176]

4.130 In this context it was argued that the word DOUBLEMINT should not be registrable for mint-flavoured chewing gum. Although it does not exclusively describe mint-flavoured chewing gum, it consists exclusively of terms which consumers of chewing gum would perceive as being descriptive of its flavour.[177]

4.131 Applications to register completely descriptive marks cause little difficulty because they are easy to detect and to reject. A simple misspelling does not disguise the meaning of LITE ('light') in respect of food and drink and the application to register it as a CTM was so devoid of distinctive character that not even a finding that the applicant's procedural rights had been violated could save it.[178] Adopting similar reasoning, the adjectival form of the Polish word for 'marigold' was no less descriptive than the word 'marigold' itself, for marigold-based cosmetics.[179]

4.132 If a trade mark is genuinely not *exclusively* descriptive, an application to register it cannot be refused on that ground. Thus BEQUEMLICHKEIT (German for 'comfort') would not be registrable for comfortable furniture, but DAS PRINZIP DER BEQUEMLICHKEIT ('the principle of comfort') could be.[180]

(a) Allusiveness does not constitute exclusive descriptiveness

4.133 An application to register as a CTM the word BLOODSTREAM in respect of equipment for treating and recovering blood products was allowed to proceed. The examiner considered the word descriptive; the Board of Appeal thought otherwise. 'Bloodstream' described the flow of blood through a circulatory system; it hinted at the nature of the equipment but could not be said to describe it.[181] Similar conclusions have been reached in respect of NETMEETING for conferencing software,[182] NEW BORN BABY for children's dolls[183] and BABY-DRY for disposable nappies.[184]

---

[176] *OHIM v Wm Wrigley Jr Company*, Case C-191/01 P, 10 April 2003 (Opinion of Advocate General Jacobs), para 39.
[177] ibid, paras 37–48. A similar result was reached by the Thai Supreme Court in *Sari (PT) Incofood Corporation v Department of Intellectual Property and others* (2003) 17 WIPR 9, where the combination of the geographical term 'Java' and the generic term 'café' into the word JAVACAFE did not render that combination of exclusively descriptive terms registrable.
[178] *Rewe Zentral AG v OHIM*, Case T-79/00 [2002] ETMR 1109 (CFI).
[179] *Dax Cosmetics Zaklady Kosmetyczno-Chemiczne Jacek Majdax I Wojciech Szulc SC's appeal* [2001] ETMR 506 (Polish Patent Office): NAGIETKOWY.
[180] *Erpo Möbelwerk GmbH v OHIM*, Case T-138/00 [2002] ETMR 430 (CFI).
[181] *Harvest Technologies LLC's application*, Case R 33/1998-2 [1999] ETMR 503.
[182] *Microsoft Corp's application*, Case R 26/1998-3 [1999] ETMR 386 (OHIM).
[183] *Zapf Creation AG v OHIM*, Case T-140/00 [2002] ETMR 128 (CFI).
[184] *Procter & Gamble Company v OHIM*, Case C-383/99 P [2002] ETMR 22 (ECJ).

4.134 Sometimes a court may run into difficulty in dealing with a trade mark that has ended up in a no-man's land between descriptiveness and allusiveness. European law suggests that, unless the mark is *exclusively* descriptive, it should be registered. If this is the case, the courts should give a broad degree of scope to the notion of what constitutes exclusive descriptiveness in order for them to be able to refuse applications for marks which they feel are essentially unmeritorious. Unfortunately this does not always happen. Thus, somewhat anomalously, the CFI held the word ELLOS (the Spanish third-person plural masculine pronoun) unregistrable for clothes, since the masculine form of the word 'they' indicated clothes for men, while nonetheless registrable for mail-order sales of the same articles.[185] It is difficult to be convinced that a Spanish word meaning 'they' was 'an essential characteristic of the goods in question and would be taken into account by the relevant public'.[186]

4.135 Outside Europe different concepts may apply. For example, in Korea it is recognized that an applicant's mark may fall into the gap between descriptiveness and suggestiveness; where it does, the application will be refused.[187]

(b) Descriptiveness of the market or of the ultimate user

4.136 Sometimes it is not the goods or services that the mark allegedly describes, but rather the intended market or ultimate user. The OHIM Board of Appeal refused the word mark PETIT BEBE (French for 'little baby') for children's clothes on the ground that they described the intended purpose of the goods as clothes for *petits bébés*, despite keen argument from the applicant that the words were too vague to be regarded as descriptive of anything.[188] On the face of it, it seems anomalous that NEW BORN BABY should not be descriptive for children's dolls while PETIT BEBE is descriptive for children's clothes, the one being allegedly descriptive of the product itself and the other being descriptive of the bodies upon which the trade marked goods were to be worn. But which approach should be preferred? The approach taken in *NEW BORN BABY* has been criticized and at least the English version of the judgment is difficult to understand, but it is in the spirit of the ECJ decision in *BABY-DRY* and should be seen as supporting the principle that obstacles to registration should be restrictively interpreted and sparingly applied to the facts of individual cases.

4.137 In the Netherlands the trade marks YOU, YOURS and FOR YOU have been found not to be exclusively descriptive of clothing; the argument that those trade marks re-

---

[185] *Ellos AB v OHIM*, Case T-219/00 [2003] IP&T 384.
[186] ibid, para 34.
[187] *Korea Telecom Co Ltd's application* (2003) 57(21) INTA Bull 4 (Korean Patent Court). It is difficult to reconcile this ruling with the facts of the case, in which the mark MEGA-PASS was refused for 'telecommunication and broadcasting business services'.
[188] *Marks & Spencer plc's application*, Case R 95/1998-3 [2000] ETMR 168.

H. Descriptive marks

ferred to the trade mark owner's customers was not surprisingly rejected.[189] A similar conclusion was reached by the German Bundesgerichtshof with regard to the words FOR YOU for cigarettes.[190]

(c) Descriptiveness of the function

4.138 Description of a product's function can be a sufficient ground upon which a trade mark fails. Thus in Ireland the word FLU-SHIELD could not be registered as a vaccine against influenza even though the precise mechanism by which a person is shielded from flu is not itself described and the notion of a 'flu-shield' may be regarded as nothing other than a pale metaphor.[191] In contrast, where all that is described is an ideal end to be achieved rather than the function itself, the applicant may be more fortunate. Thus the words FLU-SHIELD may conjure up the notion in the minds of the public that the vaccine shields the patient from the flu by being injected into him and setting up a specific defence. In contrast, while EASYBANK suggests the idea of easy banking, that suggestion is weak and allusive; it does not explain how this end is to be achieved.[192]

(d) Ambiguous terms

4.139 The fact that words employed as a trade mark or any other trade description may be literally ambiguous has long been recognized. Thus in Ireland the trade mark MOTHERCARE was described as encompassing both the care which a mother lavished on her child and the care which a child bestowed upon his mother.[193] But the modern approach is not to take the trade mark in abstract but to consider it in the light of the goods or services specified in the application. Thus the concept of 'comfort' may refer to physical comfort ('His lordship retired to the comfort of his favourite armchair'), to psychological comfort (as in the expressions 'comfort blanket' and 'Job's comforters'), to ease ('Bayern Munich comfortably held their two-goal lead') and to financial security ('Is he very rich?'; 'No, but he's quite comfortably off'). If you put the words COMFORT PLUS on a carpet, the ambiguities begin to evaporate and the words become descriptive and unregistrable.[194] In essence, if the words are sufficiently ambiguous that consumers of the goods or services in question would not be immediately able to identify a specific meaning when seeing them, then they will be registrable. Consumers of chewing gum, however, when seeing the word DOUBLEMINT, might be expected to draw immediate assumptions as to which of

---

[189] *Hij Mannenmode BV v Nienhaus & Lotz GmbH* [1999] ETMR 730 (Utrecht District Court).
[190] *FOR YOU trade mark application* [2001] ETMR 28.
[191] *American Home Products Corp's application* [2001] ETMR 536 (Irish Patents Office). The mark was however registered in the UK (no 2181057, registered on 22 October 1999).
[192] *Bank für Arbeit und Wirtschaft AG v OHIM*, Case T-87/00 [2001] ETMR 761 (CFI).
[193] *Mothercare Ltd's application* [1968] IR 359 (High Court, Dublin).
[194] *Milliken & Company's application*, R 66/1998-1 [1999] ETMR 575 (OHIM).

the meanings of 'double' and 'mint' are intended, with the result that DOUBLEMINT would not be registrable.[195]

(e) Descriptiveness in multilingual jurisdictions

4.140 The Advocate General has advised the ECJ that, in determining whether a sign is of an exclusively descriptive character, it is necessary for the examining authority in a multilingual jurisdiction to consider the meaning of that sign in each of the operative languages.[196]

(f) A new approach?

4.141 In *OHIM v Wm Wrigley*[197] the Advocate General suggested that there is no clear-cut distinction between those indications which designate a characteristic of goods or services and those which merely allude suggestively to it. Accordingly he proposed a sliding scale between the two extremes of 'characteristic designations' and 'suggestive allusions'. In the light of existing practice and case law, and with a view to establishing a slightly greater degree of objectivity, the assessment of the trade mark should be conducted from three points of view:

(i) How does a term relate to a product or one of its characteristics? The more factual and objective that relationship, the more likely it is that the term may be used as a designation in trade (for example, the word SUNNY in the trade mark SUNNY DELIGHT orange drink relates less factually to the product than the word ORANGE in the phrase ORANGE MAID for orange-flavoured ice lollies).

(ii) How is a term is perceived? The more ordinary, definite and down-to-earth a term is, the more readily a consumer will apprehend any designation of a characteristic and thus the more likely the term is not to qualify for registration as a trade mark (for example, TASTY is more obviously a quality of a food product than the word PALATABLE).

(iii) How significant is the characteristic in relation to the product, in particular in the consumer's mind? Where the characteristic designated is essential or central to the product, the case for refusing registration is compelling (for example, prefixes like TURBO- will spark off a strong significance in the minds of purchasers of cars, but not for purchasers of potatoes).

4.142 Once a proposed trade mark has been assessed separately from each of these three proposed points of view, a mark should be refused registration (i) if, overall, it appears to be nearer the 'non-registrable' end of the scale when taking the three

---

[195] *OHIM v Wm Wrigley Jr Company*, Case C-191/01 P, 10 April 2003 (Opinion of Advocate General Jacobs), para 27.
[196] *Koninklijke KPN Nederland NV v Benelux Trade Marks Office*, Case C-363/99, 31 January 2002 (POSTKANTOOR).
[197] *OHIM v Wm Wrigley Jr Company*, Case C-191/01 P, 10 April 2003, paras 60–7.

H. Descriptive marks

points of view into account or (ii) if, from even one point of view, it is particularly near that end of the scale. At the time of writing, it is not known how, or indeed whether, the ECJ will respond to this suggestion which, on an objective consideration, appears rather more complex for a test which ultimately depends upon the subjective impressions of the person applying it.

(2) Immaterial descriptiveness

It may be safely assumed that the descriptiveness, or indeed the genericity, of a trade mark will only hinder its registrability where it is material to the consumer's decision to purchase the goods or services to which it is attached. The OHIM Board of Appeal accordingly ruled that the trade mark ORGANIC ESSENTIALS was registrable for cotton balls and tampons: while those goods were both 'organic', being made of cotton, and 'essential', being essential for feminine hygiene, there was no evidence that anyone ever referred to them as 'organic essentials'.[198] The term was therefore descriptive, but irrelevantly so. On the same basis the generic term POISON is registrable in respect of the perfume of that name even though the product, if consumed orally and in sufficient quantity, is poisonous. Likewise there was no bar to registration of the word-and-device mark DEATH in respect of cigarettes even though those products, if consumed in the normal manner, will be likely to accelerate the consumer's death (see Figure 4.4).[199] Nor was the highly successful trade mark TRIVIAL PURSUIT unregistrable in respect of the board game which was, to all intents and purposes, a trivial pursuit.

4.143

Figure 4.4 There was no bar to registration of this word-and-device mark in respect of cigarettes.

A further species of immaterial descriptiveness was recognized by the CFI when it concluded that a national trade mark is not descriptive if the element of description is couched in a language which the nationals of that country do not understand. Thus the fact that MATRATZEN is the German word for 'mattresses' will make it unregistrable as a trade mark in Germany but should not affect its validity in Spain.[200] In similar vein, the registration of KIKU was permitted for perfume in Ireland, whose inhabitants were deemed to be unaware of the fact that 'kiku' was the Japanese word for a chrysanthemum,[201] while the words BLOOD PRESSURE

4.144

---

[198] *Organic Essential Inc's application*, Case R 146/2001-4, 22 May 2002 (unreported).
[199] See eg UK trade marks 1481627, 1569155.
[200] *Matratzen v OHIM*, Case T-6/01 [2003] ETMR 392.
[201] *KIKU Trade Mark* [1978] FSR 246 (Supreme Court).

WATCH have been registered in Germany for sphygmomanometers, where they conveyed no descriptive meaning to non-English speaking Germans.[202] The English words 'smart' and 'web' have, however, been assumed to be descriptive in Germany when combined to form SMARTWEB for Internet-related services.[203] The effect of the imbalance of linguistic abilities within Europe means that countries whose inhabitants are relatively poor linguists (for example, those who live in the UK, Ireland and Spain) will register more trade marks than those whose inhabitants are excellent linguists (for example, the inhabitants of Germany, the Netherlands and Scandinavia).

4.145 In terms of European trade mark practice, the linguistic dimension which the law accords to descriptiveness may thus seem in theory to be somewhat ambivalent. While an application for a CTM will fail on absolute grounds if it is descriptive in *any* of the eleven languages of the EU (twenty-one after the next round of accessions), it can also fail on relative grounds if a prior national mark has been registered before it. This is so even if that prior national mark is descriptive in every language of the EU except that of the one country in which it is registered. Though this approach displays apparent inconsistency, it is manifestly correct. The reason why a CTM may not be registered if it is descriptive in any EU country is that it will deprive the inhabitants of that country of a normal means of describing or otherwise alluding to the goods or services which the registration of that CTM would cover; but the facility of the owner of even a marginally distinctive mark—registered in just one country but descriptive everywhere else—to launch successful opposition proceedings is based on the premiss that consumers in the country are entitled to be protected against the confusion which would result if two or more traders were allowed to use the same or confusingly similar marks for their goods or services. This theoretical ambivalence does not however result in any great injustice: even if the holder of an earlier national trade mark does not oppose the CTM application, that application would still fail once it was shown to be descriptive in any EU Member State.

(3) Is a low threshold of inherent distinctiveness desirable?

4.146 If there is a low threshold of inherent distinctiveness, any mark which possesses any degree of distinctiveness at all is theoretically registrable. We have moved a long way from the old British notion of 'purity of the trade mark register', the idea that only really deserving trade marks should be registered at all. It is now widely accepted that, so long as a trade mark can serve the function of assisting consumer choice between competing products or services, it can be registered. But is this a good thing or a bad thing?

---

[202] *Matsushita Electric Works' application*, Case R 332/1999-1 [2000] ETMR 962 (OHIM).
[203] SMARTWEB *trade mark application* [2003] ETMR 272 (Bundespatentgericht).

H. Descriptive marks

Within the context of multicultural regions such as the EU, the lowest level of distinctiveness is as good a place as any to place the Plimsoll line of registrability. This is because a minimalist level of 'distinctiveness' is easier for trade mark examiners to identify throughout the Union. Anything which is not actually descriptive, which is used as a common term in trade and which is neither deceptive nor immoral—and which possesses the formal characteristics of a trade mark—can thus be assured of registration anywhere in Europe. That is why the BABY-DRY rule, whatever its undesirable side-effects are or may be, is an ideal common denominator for national and regional trade mark registries. **4.147**

But 'low-level' distinctiveness has its critics. First, the lower the level of inherent descriptiveness, the more words and images are capable of being clawed away from the public and from other traders, to be locked away as private fiefdoms by those fortunate enough to register them. This criticism is met by the counter-argument that, if anyone is perspicacious enough to register a marginally distinctive mark and consumers actually rely on it in order to distinguish his goods from those of other traders, what justification is there for other traders to be allowed to take unfair advantage of his efforts and cream off those customers who are confused into thinking that they are getting that perspicacious proprietor's products? A second criticism is that the registration of scarcely distinctive marks enables a build-up of highly similar trade marks and non-trade mark advertising and marketing usages by competing concerns, each of whose trade marks differ from the others in very small details. So if BABY-DRY is registrable, but the words 'baby' and 'dry' remain free for use, we can imagine the market being invaded by DRY-BABY products as well as BABY-DRY ones, not to mention slogans such as 'helps keep your baby dry', thus potentially puzzling first-time consumers who seek to distinguish them. **4.148**

After *BABY-DRY* we have seen a series of cases in which very weak trade marks have been granted both on a pan-European basis and under national law. Thus the word mark LABEL has been accepted for cigarettes,[204] being a less well-used alternative to the word 'brand', while GENESCAN has been accepted both in Germany and in the UK for computer software for gene sequencing.[205] There are many other examples. So far we have no concrete examples of litigation arising from the anguish caused by competitors who have been unable to describe their products or services on account of these weak registrations, so we can infer that: (i) these marks are not as troublesome in practice as they are in theory; or (ii) that competitors are more resourceful than the law supposes; or that (iii) consumers buy PAMPERS which are sub-branded BABY-DRY without even considering that the words BABY-DRY are a registered trade mark and not a cute catchphrase or generic **4.149**

---

[204] *Philip Morris Products SA's application*, Case R 687/2000-2 [2002] ETMR 403 (OHIM).
[205] *GENESCAN Trade Mark* [2002] ETMR 329 (Bundesgerichtshof).

descriptor; that (iv) defences to infringement actions[206] which permit the honest descriptive use of matter contained in another's trade mark adequately balance the interests of the trade mark proprietor and his competitors; or finally that (v) that trade mark owners are not willing to strain their trade mark monopolies to the limits by suing users of closely similar marks for fear of attracting a counterclaim for cancellation of their own registered trade marks.

(4) Is there such a thing as an invented descriptive mark?

4.150 There is an interface between distinctive and descriptive marks which lies at the focal point for some of the most vigorously contested litigation in trade marks: the point at which invented words become descriptive. Consider this: some words are (i) inherently descriptive and therefore unregistrable for goods which they describe (SWEET for honey, FRESH for eggs, ECONOMICAL for fuel-burning goods), while other words are inherently distinctive either because (ii) they are non-inventive but not descriptive (APPLE for computers, CROSS for pens) or because (iii) they are truly inventive (VELCRO, POLAROID, PEPSI), in which case they are registrable.

4.151 This taxonomy is an unhelpful truism for lawyers and trade mark applicants, since most words which fall to be considered before the highest legal tribunals do not fit into any of those three categories: they belong to three quite different categories, being words which may be: (i) adaptations of descriptive words; (ii) compounds made from descriptive words; or (iii) made-up words which direct the consumer towards the character or qualities of the goods for which the mark is to be used.

4.152 The words in the second three categories share the following characteristics: (i) they are lexical inventions, in the sense that they are not found in any dictionaries, and/or colloquial inventions, in the sense that they have a general meaning but not a specific one; (ii) they contain an element of description which does not of itself enable the goods or services on which they are used to be identified by anyone not already familiar with their use; and (iii) they have not usually been used by the applicant's competitors in a trade mark sense or in the course of advertising and marketing campaigns.

4.153 What general rules can we learn from the multitude of individual applications which are reflected in official actions and court decisions?

(a) Fusion of existing words

4.154 The fact that two known words are fused into a third, invented word, will not of itself make that third word registrable. It all depends on the words. WALKMAN was an example of an initially successful fusion of words: the conjunction of verb

---

[206] Council Directive 89/104, art 6(1); Council Regulation 40/94, art 12.

H. Descriptive marks

('walk') and noun ('man') is unusual and the words would be unlikely to follow each other in normal parlance. Two nouns in apposition may achieve the same registrable result: for example, DISCMAN for portable CD players. So too may the unnatural apposition of an adjective and preposition (ULTRAPLUS for plastic microwave ovenware) or an adjectival prefix and another adjective (as in BIO-MILD[207]).

Where the sequence of words is normal and those words, when taken together, both relate to the goods for which registration is sought, registration is a most unlikely outcome. For example, an application to register FOODSAVER for vacuum packaging machines failed: the words 'food' and 'saver', being merged into one, would form a functionally descriptive term. The fact that the graphic representation of the mark consisted of one fused word rather than two separate words would in any event be lost on radio audiences, who wouldn't be able to detect the difference.[208]

4.155

These principles do not apply where the first of two fused words is a 'concept' prefix like 'bio-', which refers to a subject matter which is 'biological' or oriented towards 'life'. Whether that word is attached to a noun or an adjective, it is likely to be regarded as descriptive or objectionable even where the allusion is not immediately apparent. Thus BIO-CLAIRE (French for 'BIO-CLEAR') was held unregistrable in the Benelux not only for water-purifying agents but even for additives to fish food which remove its pollutant effect.[209]

4.156

(b) Existing words in unused and unnatural formations

The exercise of turning an otherwise descriptive or non-distinctive noun into a verb does not automatically make it into a fancy term which would thus be entitled to registration, even though the resulting term is not found in the language in question. This is demonstrated by the OHIM Board of Appeal's rejection of the attempt to turn the noun 'enamel' into the verb ENAMELIZE and then register it as a trade mark for toothpaste.[210]

4.157

(c) Words that describe something that does not exist

The word mark SWEDISH FORMULA was registrable for soaps, cosmetics and shampoos, the OHIM Board of Appeal observing that there was no 'Swedish

4.158

---

[207] Issues relating to this fused word were referred to the ECJ in proceedings which appear to have become becalmed following the Advocate General's Opinion on 31 January 2002; see *Campina Melkunie BV v Benelux Merkenbureau*, Case C-265/00, 31 January 2002 (AG).
[208] *Tilia International's application*, Case R 57/1998-1 [1999] ETMR 191 (OHIM). One wonders how many people buy vacuum-packing machines in response to radio advertisements.
[209] *Bio-Claire International Ltd v Benelux Trade Marks Office* [1989] ETMR 251 (The Hague Court of Appeal).
[210] *Cosmedent Inc's application*, Case R 29/1998-3 [1998] ETMR 658.

formula' relating to the goods for which the applicant sought registration.²¹¹ The fact that the words might refer to some soap or shampoo formula which had not as yet been invented would not make a difference. In contrast the word mark POLY PADS was found to be unregistrable for saddle pads: although the words were not used together and were thus a colloquial invention, the OHIM Board of Appeal found that the word POLY was phonetically close to the highly obscure word 'poley', meaning a kind of saddle without a pommel. Accordingly the mark was descriptive of the product for which registration was sought.²¹²

(5) Why not register descriptive trade marks?

4.159 There is a great deal to say in favour of allowing the registration of most of the descriptive marks to which trade mark examiners and the courts take such regular and often violent exception. In particular, allowing such marks on to the register can make almost everyone happy.

4.160 First, *the trade mark applicant* gets his certificate without having to institute legal proceedings against the granting authority. This saves a lot of time and money, since the most active trade mark applicants may appear to the observer to have almost bottomless purses and endless patience. And if they get registration of a mark in two or more countries, it suddenly becomes part of their regional or global strategy and its registration in other countries becomes a desirable end in itself. Secondly, many of *the trade mark applicant's competitors* are fairly happy, because they have read the defences to trade mark infringement which all countries provide, under which the honest use of a word to describe their products will not infringe the trade mark anyway. Even if the increased facility for the registration of descriptive trade marks creates a greater likelihood of trade mark infringement, competitors are still happy because they know that the trade mark owner still has to shift the burden of proving that the descriptive use made of their marks is not honest.²¹³ Thirdly, *trade mark registries* will be happy, since a trade mark, once registered, produces a potentially eternal stream of renewal fees.

4.161 Will anyone not be happy? *Trade mark examiners*, possibly, since they will lose the unique and exquisite satisfaction of personally rejecting applications from giant enterprises like Procter & Gamble and Unilever and thus thwarting those great corporate plans (do people ever wonder what trade mark examiners tell their spouses or partners over dinner at the end of a long day in the office?). Some *competitors of the trade mark applicant* will also be unhappy, because legal advice or lack of financial resources will direct them to surrender or to settle claims which might well have been successfully defended. Finally *consumers* should be neutral to the

---

²¹¹ *Procter & Gamble Company's application*, Case R 85/1998-2 [1999] ETMR 559.
²¹² *Penny Makinson's application*, Case R 68/1998-3 [1999] ETMR 234.
²¹³ See eg *British Airways plc v Ryanair Ltd* [2001] ETMR 235 (HC).

registration of descriptive terms since, even though such terms are not registrable as trade marks, traders in every country use them and may even cultivate exclusive rights in them.[214]

Some economists may also be unhappy on the basis of a convoluted argument that, if competitors are prevented from making easy use of the best descriptive terms, they will have to search harder for suitable substitutes.[215] Such a search will be an expensive and inefficient allocation of corporate resources which may result in higher prices for consumers. This argument may make sense to economists in a market in which all competitors are selling identical products but has little else to commend it. For one thing, if all competitors are enabled to make a similar degree of easy use of the same best descriptive terms, consumers will find it more difficult to distinguish between competitors' products and will have to spend more time and effort in telling them apart. Secondly, establishing what constitutes the best terms for describing goods and services is nowadays an increasingly marketing- and advertising-led exercise. Thirdly, in our present era at any rate, in many areas of commerce including the sale of luxury goods, designer clothes, cars, drinks and non-staple foods, consumers discriminate between products on the basis of lifestyle expectations and not on the basis of the employment by competing businesses of descriptive terms. 4.162

I. Distinctiveness acquired through use

Readers will not have forgotten that inherently distinctive trade marks are registrable even in the absence of any evidence of distinctiveness which has already been acquired through their use. For those trade marks which are not so fortunate as to have been born distinctive, it is however necessary to prove that they have gained this elevated status. In the *Windsurfing* case[216] the ECJ gave some broad guidance as to when a trade mark can be said to have acquired distinctiveness as a result of the use which a trade mark applicant has made of it: 4.163

> —a trade mark acquires distinctive character following the use which has been made of it where the mark has come to identify the product in respect of which registration is applied for as originating from a particular undertaking and thus to distinguish that product from goods of other undertakings; [. . .]
> —in determining whether a trade mark has acquired distinctive character following the use

---

[214] See eg *Frank Reddaway & Co Ltd v George Banham & Co Ltd* [1896] AC 199 (HL), where the *prima facie* descriptive words 'camel hair belting', through constant use, had become sufficiently associated with the claimant for him to be able to stop competitors using it.
[215] Richard Posner and William M Landes, 'The Economics of Trademark Law' (1988) 78 TLR 267.
[216] *Windsurfing Chiemsee Produktions- und Vertriebs GmbH v Boots- und Segelzubehör Walter Huber and Franz Attenberger*, Joined Cases C-108 and 109/97 [1999] ETMR 585.

which has been made of it, the competent authority must make an overall assessment of the evidence that the mark has come to identify the product concerned as originating from a particular undertaking and thus to distinguish that product from goods of other undertakings;

— if the competent authority finds that a significant proportion of the relevant class of persons identify goods as originating from a particular undertaking because of the trade mark, it must hold the requirement for registering the mark to be satisfied;

—where the competent authority has particular difficulty in assessing the distinctive character of a mark in respect of which registration is applied for, Community law does not preclude it from having recourse, under the conditions laid down by its own national law, to an opinion poll as guidance for its judgment.

4.164 In other words: (i) it is not just *use* but *use as an identifier* which enables a trade mark to acquire distinctiveness; (ii) there must be *evidence* that the mark is used as an identifier; (iii) if a significant proportion of consumers use that mark to identify the applicant's goods, the application *must* be allowed; (iv) opinion polls may be relied on only if they constitute evidence of a mark's *distinctive character*.

4.165 These points are frequently misunderstood. For example, many people repeatedly fail to grasp the difference between evidence of use and evidence of distinctiveness acquired through use. Thus the words YOU'VE GOT MAIL are familiar to AOL Internet subscribers all over the world; the words pop up whenever they receive e-mail. But evidence of the ubiquity of the words YOU'VE GOT MAIL is not evidence that any particular goods or services can be said to be identified by them. Even AOL subscribers, on seeing them, assume that those words convey a message that e-mail has arrived and not that those words distinguish AOL's goods or services from anyone else's.[217]

4.166 There must be evidence not merely that people are familiar with the applicant's mark but that it is used as an identifier that its goods or services originate from a single undertaking. Thus it is easy to find evidence that men who employ electric shavers to remove unwanted facial hair are generally familiar with the appearance of the three-headed configuration of rotating blades on the Philips PHILISHAVE, but it is far less easy to construct evidence that those same men would assume that the three-head configuration was a trade mark that distinguished the product rather than being part of the product itself.[218] This is because any product shape can be regarded by consumers both as a design and as a trade mark; if it is regarded as a design, it need not be regarded as a design which is exclusive to a single maker.[219] Likewise, evidence that people have accessed the buy.com website in order to buy things is not evidence that the word mark BUY.COM has acquired a

---

[217] *America Online Inc's application*, Case R 209/2000-3 [2002] ETMR 59 (OHIM).
[218] See *Philips Electronics NV v Remington Consumer Products* [1998] ETMR 124 (HC); [1999] ETMR 816 (CA).
[219] *Henkel KGaA v OHIM*, Case T-30/00 [2002] ETMR 278 (CFI): bicoloured rectangular detergent tablet.

I. Distinctiveness acquired through use

distinctive quality as a trade mark rather than that those words are viewed as an Internet address.[220]

(1) Not all use is evidence of 'distinctiveness acquired through use'

4.167 Even where a sign has been used by a trade mark applicant with the intention of distinguishing goods, this use may not be evidence of acquired distinctiveness. This may be because the use relied on is use (i) with another trade mark, or (ii) as part of another trade mark or (iii) together with non-trade mark material.

4.168 The *Philips* case mentioned above is an example of the first of these situations: anyone seeing the word marks PHILIPS and PHILISHAVE as well as the distinctive Philips shield logo on the packaging of the shaver would be so convinced that the contents were made by Philips that it would be well-nigh impossible to establish that consumers relied upon the appearance of the shaver's head, either alone or in conjunction with other marks, as the means of distinguishing Philips products from those of competitors.

4.169 An example of the second case is illustrated by Nestlé's so-far unsuccessful attempt to register in the UK the word mark HAVE A BREAK as a trade mark for chocolate bars and other confectionery. The words were part of a famous slogan 'HAVE A BREAK . . . HAVE A KIT KAT' which had been widely used in marketing Kit Kat bars to generations of consumers. It was clear that the words were associated with Nestlé's product. However, since HAVE A BREAK had never been used without the words HAVE A KIT KAT, there was no evidence that the phrase had acquired distinctiveness in its own right.[221] While the logic of this reasoning is correct, on the facts it does no service to Nestlé and confers no benefit on that company's competitors: anyone else using those words would almost certainly face an action for passing off in respect of the misappropriated slogan.

4.170 An example of the third is the attempt to register as a CTM the words LAST MINUTE for Internet-related services. The applicant had ample evidence of use of the domain name lastminute.com, but that was not the same as the bare words LAST MINUTE.[222] It is possible for the words to have quite different meanings with or without the '.com' element: consider Amazon (river and rain-forest) with Amazon.com (online book and music sales service).

(2) How much proof will establish that distinctiveness has been acquired?

4.171 Evidence must show that the mark has been used and that its use has been as a

---

[220] *Buy.Com Inc's application*, Case R 638/2000-4 [2002] ETMR 540 (OHIM).
[221] *Société des Produits Nestlé SA v Mars UK Ltd*, 2 December 2002 [2003] FSR 684 (HC).
[222] *Last Minute Network Ltd's application*, Case R 1068/2000-2 [2002] ETMR 534 (OHIM).

trade mark[223] and not merely as some other form of reference to the goods or services in question. The evidence must normally relate solely to the period before the date of application to register the mark;[224] documentary evidence must be 'relevant, reliable and sufficient' and should relate to a specific time and place. Even if all these criteria are fulfilled, the application will still be rejected unless that evidence demonstrates not merely that the mark has been used but that it has acquired distinctiveness in the eyes of relevant consumers.[225] There is no point in submitting unused sheets of letterhead or key-ring tags bearing the mark in question, since they cannot establish acquired distinctiveness.

4.172 Although an applicant must prove that the mark has been used in the jurisdiction in which registration is sought,[226] he does not need to show that he was physically present in the jurisdiction at the time the mark was used. Thus an intellectual property law firm which advertised in Latvian publications and performed services on behalf of Latvian companies and patent agencies was held to have used its trade mark in Latvia even though it had no office there.[227]

4.173 It might be assumed that, the less inherently distinctive a sign is, the more persuading a granting authority will need before it concedes that the sign is distinctive. In some jurisdictions this may well be the case,[228] but in the EU the low level of distinctiveness necessary to achieve registration is all that need be proved and OHIM in particular does not appear to have made oppressive evidential demands upon applicants.

4.174 Evidence that one has successfully prevented competitors from using a sign in the past and that one has a policy of actively 'policing' unauthorized third-party use does not of itself demonstrate that the sign has acquired, or retained, a distinctive

---

[223] See eg *Labatt Brewing Co Ltd v Molson Canada* WTLR, 16 May 2003 (Federal Court Trial Division, Canada), where the applicant had used the *prima facie* non-distinctive terms OLAND EXPORT for fifteen years as a trade mark to distinguish its beers from those of its competitors, none of whom used the place name/surname OLAND for their beers.

[224] Council Directive 89/104, art 3(3) gives EU Member States the option of also taking into account evidence of distinctiveness acquired through use after the date of application or registration. This option, if exercised, will make it pointless to bring cancellation proceedings against trade marks which are distinctive at the time of the trial even if they were not previously distinctive. The UK's Trade Marks Act 1994, s 47(1), has exercised that option. The Benelux however has not; see *Campina Melkunie BV v Bureau Benelux des Marques* [2001] ETMR 392 (Benelux Court of Justice): BIOMILD.

[225] *Global Asset Management Ltd's application*, Case R 426/1999-2 [2001] ETMR 131 (OHIM).

[226] See eg *Boston Pizza International Inc v Boston Chicken Inc* WTLR, 11 April 2003, where the Canadian Federal Court of Appeal warned that distinctiveness acquired through use in the United States does not constitute evidence of acquired distinctiveness in Canada.

[227] *Tria Robit Agency v Jason* WTLR, 23 April 2003 (Supreme Court, Latvia).

[228] See eg Colombia where the descriptive and/or laudatory term SUPERIOR was accepted for registration for spirits on the basis that, in over forty years' use, it had in fact become a well-known mark: *Empresa Licorera de Santander's trade mark application*, 8 March 2002 (Colombian Trade Mark Office).

I. Distinctiveness acquired through use

character.²²⁹ In contrast, the fact that no satisfactory attempt has been made to prevent such use may be regarded as evidence that the sign is taken as being non-distinctive.²³⁰

(3) Whose use will count as evidence of distinctiveness acquired through use?

The trade mark applicant's use of his own sign will be of critical importance, but that is not to say that the use made of his sign by others will not also be of legal significance in establishing that the sign has acquired distinctiveness. It goes without saying that the use made by the applicant's licensees will count in his favour too. The New Zealand Court of Appeal has not ruled out the possibility that even adverse use by an unauthorized third party may be evidence of acquired distinctiveness: although this proposition may be 'difficult to accept', everything depends on the circumstances.²³¹ Presumably use in the form of importation and sale by a parallel trader would fit into this category. In European law there is nothing to prevent the unauthorized use of a sign by a competitor from accruing to the applicant's benefit. In fact logic dictates that, since the unauthorized use of the sign assumes that relevant consumers will recognize it and draw their own conclusions as to the merits of the contrasted goods or services, such use of the sign is quite strong evidence of factual distinctiveness.

4.175

(4) Acquired distinctiveness can overcome even absolute bars to registrability

Once acquired distinctiveness is proved, a trade mark ceases to be descriptive in the eyes of the consuming public for whom it has become distinctive. It also ceases to be a term which is customary in trade.²³² Nor is such a mark even deceptive. Thus, once armed with a new, secondary meaning, the trade mark MANPOWER could be validly registered in Austria for personnel services²³³ and the registration of RIGTIG JUICE ('Rigtig' being the Danish for 'real') could not be assailed even though that mark was used in respect of unreal juice: the mark had been in use so long that its literal meaning had been all but wiped out in respect of the trade mark owner's orange juice products.²³⁴

4.176

---

²²⁹ *Alcon Inc v OHIM, Dr Robert Winzer Pharma GmbH intervening*, Case T-237/01, 5 March 2003 (CFI).
²³⁰ *SA Bardinet v SCP Ego-Fruits (SCP Belat-Desprat intervening)* [2002] ETMR 1043 (Cour d'appel de Paris).
²³¹ *McCain Foods (Australia) Pty Ltd v ConAgra Inc*, 6 June 2002 (unreported).
²³² *Merz & Krell GmbH*, Case C-517/99 [2002] ETMR 231 (ECJ), para 37.
²³³ *Manpower ***** v Manpower Austria P***** GmbH, ***** [2002] ETMR 845 (Austrian Supreme Court).
²³⁴ *Rynkeby Foods A/S v Ministry of Foods, Agriculture and Fisheries* [2002] ETMR 136 (Danish High Court).

4.177 In the case of inherently distinctive marks which are the subject of CTM applications, we have seen that the mark must be absolutely registrable in each territory of the EU or the application will fail.[235] This is not so where an application is based on acquired distinctiveness: the mark in such an instance need only have acquired distinctiveness in 'at least a substantial part' of the EU territory.[236] The reason for this divergence of approach is clear: with absolute bars to registrability, the opposite of registrability is total unregistrability while, with acquired distinctiveness, the opposite of acquired distinctiveness is simply an absence of acquired distinctiveness. One hundred per cent acquired distinctiveness is so unusual a phenomenon that it would be unfairly burdensome to require proof at that level.[237]

4.178 The registration of inherently non-distinctive marks which have acquired a secondary distinctive meaning may not be possible in countries whose national laws are modelled on the pre-harmonization law of the UK. Thus in South Africa the Supreme Court of Appeal has held that the words PREMIER and PREMIER PACKAGE would remain unregistrable for banking services even if they became distinctive because they were reasonably required for use in banking.[238]

J. Relative grounds of unregistrability: a reminder

4.179 This chapter only addresses grounds upon which a trade mark must be refused registration because there is something inherently wrong with it. A trade mark application will also be refused if, though there is nothing wrong with the trade mark as such, its registration would result in a likelihood of confusion of the relevant consuming public. What this means in practice is discussed in detail in Chapter 10.

K. Conclusion

4.180 The impression this chapter *should* have given is that the criteria of registrability are fundamentally sound:

- they prevent the unfair monopolization of signs which either the public at large or a brand-owner's competitors need to use;
- they allow the monopolization of signs which no one other than their owners can legitimately lay claim to be able to use;

---

[235] *Ford Motor Company v OHIM*, Case T-91/99 [2000] ETMR 554 (CFI).
[236] *Ty Nant Spring Water Ltd's application*, Case R 5/1999-3 [1999] ETMR 974, 978 (OHIM).
[237] In *York trade mark* [1981] FSR 33 (HL) it was accepted that the word YORK was 100 per cent distinctive for trailers but, under the law then in force, the mark was still not registrable: it had to be distinctive *in law* as well as *in fact*.
[238] *First National Bank of Southern Africa Ltd v Barclays Bank plc* WTLR, 1 May 2003.

K. Conclusion

- they take into account the fact that words and signs do not retain a single permanent meaning.

Most of the cases reviewed in this chapter are atypical examples of trade mark applications. In all countries and regional jurisdictions the vast majority of trade mark applications are either allowed or rejected without a murmur: they are either clearly registrable or clearly unregistrable. This chapter has considered many trade marks which sit on the borderlines. That is why the battles to establish them on the register have been so keenly fought. As with most keenly fought battles where the outcome is uncertain, the outcome will sometimes depend on factors external to the legal process itself: the mood, temperament, philosophy, gender[239] and personal experiences of the adjudicators. **4.181**

The importance of this last factor cannot be minimized, because it is a problem which is peculiarly acute in the field of trade mark law. Courts can deal more objectively with issues as diverse as divorce, human rights, charterparties, commercial property transactions, medical negligence, software patent infringement and applications for asylum because, to the extent that judges encounter these issues at all outside the courts, they do so relatively infrequently. Yet every judge is a trade mark expert, even though he knows no law on the subject, by virtue of the fact that he is a consumer. Judges go shopping; they occasionally put the wrong shampoo in the supermarket trolley; they have their favourite cigars, golf equipment, cars and fashion accessories. It is difficult for a judge to suppress his daily-refreshed consumer reflexes when ruling on the registrability of a trade mark, particularly if the evidence before him is less persuasive than the power of his own personal impressions.[240] One senior British Law Lord not only conceded this point but sought to turn it into a virtue: **4.182**

> The judge's approach to the question [of confusion] should be the same as that of a jury. He, too, would be a potential buyer of the goods. He should, of course, be alert to the danger of allowing his own idiosyncratic knowledge or temperament to influence his decision, but the whole of his training in the practice of the law should have accustomed him to this, and this should provide the safety which in the case of a jury is provided by their number. That in issues of this kind judges are entitled to give effect to their own opinions as to the likelihood of deception or confusion and, in doing so, are not confined to the evidence of witnesses called at the trial is well established by decisions of this House itself.[241]

---

[239] Thus Ian Kilbey, ' "Baby-Dry": A Victory for the Ephemera of Advertising?' [2002] EIPR 493, 495, explains the *BABY-DRY* decision in terms of the judges all being men over the age at which they have to deal with incontinent babies.

[240] This is no mere assertion. The American Positivist school of jurimetrics has done much research on the correlation of judicial decisions with non-legal traits of members of the judiciary; see eg Glendon Schubert, *The Judicial Mind* (1965) and the school of thought which grew from this work.

[241] *GE trade mark* [1972] FSR 225, 235 per Lord Diplock.

4.183 The criteria of registrability are easy to understand and easy to apply. In relation to any given sign they enable a court or other tribunal to reach a decision on registrability which it intuitively prefers. Those same criteria allow this to be done without the need to torture either the wording of national trade mark legislation or the techniques of legal reasoning which permit that legislation to be interpreted so as to bring out its inner meaning. In general, the more complex and convoluted the reasoning applied by a court or tribunal in giving its decision on registrability, the more likely that reasoning is to be wrong.

4.184 Having considered the general principles attached to trade mark registration, we now examine some specific problem areas.

5

REGISTRABILITY OF SPECIFIC TYPES OF TRADE MARK

A. Introduction	
'They'll never copy this!'	
The moral of the story	5.01
B. Are there minimum and maximum criteria for registrability?	
(1) Simple marks	5.04
(2) Geometrical figures	5.06
(3) Complex marks	5.07
(a) 'Trade dress' in trading premises	5.08
(b) 'Trade dress' in the style of product designs	5.11
C. Identifiers which may not serve as trade marks	
(1) Barcodes	5.12
(2) Secret marks and hidden marks	5.15
D. Cultural emblems	
(1) Money	5.17
(2) Times and dates	5.19
(3) State emblems, official hallmarks and emblems of intergovernmental organizations	5.23
(4) Signs of the zodiac	5.24
E. Locators	
(1) Addresses and Internet addresses	5.25
(2) Telephone numbers	5.28
F. Issues relating to letters and numbers	
(1) Abbreviations and contractions	5.30
(2) Specific types of word mark	5.31
(a) Single letters	5.32
(b) Initials and acronyms	5.35
(c) Numbers	5.40
(d) Variations of type and font	5.41
G. Geographical marks	5.44
H. Trade dress and business formats	5.56
I. Names, titles and cultural icons	5.57
(1) Personal names are an emotive topic	5.58
(2) We may have to share our full names with trade mark owners	5.59
(3) We may have to share our surnames or forenames with trade mark owners	5.60

Chapter 5: Registrability of Specific Types of Trade Mark

	(4) We may find our path to fame and fortune blocked by an earlier person with the same name	5.62
	(5) Individuals and trade marks do not always reflect the same values	5.63
	(6) A person can register his name and then lose it to a third party	5.64
	(7) Dealing with name marks	5.65
	(8) Personal signatures	5.71
	(9) Titles of songs, books, films, etc	5.72
J.	Slogans	5.73
K.	Technology standards	5.78
L.	Product surfaces and shapes	
	(1) Designs applied to the outer surface of products	5.79
	(2) Product shapes	5.81
	(a) Product shapes cannot be registered if they result exclusively from the nature of the goods themselves	5.86
	(b) Product shapes cannot be registered if they consist exclusively of the shape of goods which is necessary to obtain a technical result	5.89
	(c) Product shapes cannot be registered if they exclusively give substantial value to the goods	5.94
	(d) Regular product shapes	5.95
	(e) Registration of a shape which marks the absence of a product	5.99
	(f) Bottles, packaging and containers	5.100
	(g) Features of products which have shape but are not shapes	5.105
	(h) Shapes incorporating variable text	5.106
	(i) Two-dimensional representations of three-dimensional products	5.107
	(3) Product shapes and 'limping' marks	5.109
M.	Non-traditional trade marks	
	(1) Olfactory marks	5.117
	(2) Colours	5.123
	(a) Single colours for goods and services	5.127
	(b) Single colours applied to only part of the goods	5.130
	(c) Colour combinations	5.131
	(d) Coloured versions of non-distinctive product shapes	5.132
	(3) Sound marks	5.134
	(4) Gestures and motions	5.140
	(5) Taste marks	5.143
	(6) Positional marks	5.144A
N.	Registration and the conduct of the applicant	5.145
O.	Building up a portfolio of registrations in order to cover unprotectable classes	5.146
P.	Conclusion	5.151

A. Introduction

'They'll never copy this!'

Magnus, the managing director of Acme Footwear, shook his head grimly. 'It's no good,' he groaned. 'Every time we come up with a new shoe, some damn fool

A. Introduction

competitor goes and steals it. You're supposed to be full of bright ideas, Higgins. What can we do?' Magnus turned to face Higgins, his mask of gloom reflected in the long faces of his product development team.

Higgins pushed his glasses up his forehead and scratched his hair with the back-end of his biro. 'Well, sir,' he began, a little haltingly. 'I think I've got a winning footwear product this time. It's called the EXCALIBUR. Would you like me to show you the proposal for it?'

'Get on with it, Higgins,' growled Magnus. 'I haven't got all day. Nor do the others here.' His head shook again, followed a microsecond later by those of his team.

'It's quite an unusual sports shoe design, sir,' said Higgins, turning over the pages of the flip-chart until he revealed the strikingly contoured, brightly coloured EXCALIBUR. 'But no one is going to steal it.'

Magnus winced at the sight of it. 'My goodness, Higgins,' he exclaimed. 'It's monstrous! It's disgusting! Who could have designed such a horrendous object?'

'The lawyers, sir. I went and asked the company's legal department what to do and they came up with this.' Higgins felt somehow comforted by the fact that it was the legal department and not the new product design group who had designed this fancy boot. They had been incredibly helpful when he sent them a memo asking for their aid. Could their sympathy be counted on, he wondered, if Magnus dismissed him on the spot for sheer incompetence?

'Are you a man or an imbecile, Higgins? Why on earth did you ask the lawyers to design the infernal thing?'

'You told me to, sir. You said I'd better make sure I spoke to the legal department before coming up with anything else for our competitors to rip off.' Only obeying orders had always been Higgins's personal philosophy for corporate success. It surely would not get him into trouble now.

'You fool. I wanted you to show the lawyers our next product and ask them how to protect it—not to design it themselves!' Magnus glowed incandescent with rage.

'Does that mean you don't want me to show you how it works, then, sir?' queried Higgins in a tone of respectful insolence which was guaranteed to annoy.

'Go on, then. Show us the worst! I don't suppose shoes designed by lawyers will turn out to be any worse than legal advice given by the design department.' Magnus shook his head again and resigned himself to Higgins's presentation. The team did likewise.

'The principle is simple,' began Higgins. He pointed at the illustrations of the proposed boot. 'We are going for maximum trade mark protection.'

'Well, I don't see what's so great about the word EXCALIBUR,' grumbled Magnus, who liked to think up the company's product names himself.

'The lawyers liked it, sir. They said it was easier to register as a trade mark than the last few sports shoes we brought out.'

'Which were?' glowered Magnus.

'SHOE-IN, FAST-FOOT, POWERBOOT, KICKIES . . . The lawyers said they thought they were a bit too descriptive and wouldn't be allowed to be registered.'

'But the sales department insisted on something that resonated with sports footwear,' Magnus reiterated. 'I mean. What's EXCALIBUR got to do with footwear? It's a blasted sword, isn't it? How can you sell shoes that sound like they've come out of Camelot? We need something more relevant, something like, er . . . like . . .' Magnus paused to await the inspiration that had already left him.

'Like NIKE? ADIDAS? REEBOK?' Higgins offered.

'Oh, all right then,' snapped Magnus, never the good loser. 'Get on with it.'

'EXCALIBUR is just the tip of the iceberg in terms of trade mark protection,' continued Higgins, warming to the task. 'Look at the shape of the sole: pretty, isn't it? We can register that as a trade mark. Not to mention that sweet little "sword and stone" logo.'

The product development team pretended to be furiously writing notes on their company pads while they watched Magnus's discomfiture. Higgins then resumed.

'But that's not all. Inside the heel we have installed an electronic sound unit. When you put the boots on, they play the theme from *Star Wars*. We can trade mark the tune. Then there's the colour-combination of mauve, gold and orange: no one else is using those colours so we can trade mark the colours. Best of all, we're impregnating the uppers and the lining with celebrity personal odour, reconstituted from the DNA of Princess Diana herself. We can register that too.' Higgins paused for applause. All that could be heard was the faint plop of Magnus falling from his chair on to the deep plush carpet of the boardroom. Higgins seized his chance.

'Right, men. Pick him up and put him out. Now, about the bootlaces, they are made from a particularly unusual material which feels quite distinctive to the touch. It goes without saying that we can register their look and feel as a trade mark . . .'

The moral of the story

5.01 The concept of the registrable trade mark has expanded widely beyond the 'traditional' notion of a word mark or logo. Accordingly the imagination of a new generation of legal and marketing enthusiasts such as our hero Higgins has been given over to conceiving ever-stranger gimmicks to which the law may at least in theory be able to extend a protective gauntlet.

5.02 As this chapter will later reveal, the level of trade mark protection obtainable from such non-traditional marks, even where they are registrable, may be disappointingly small: the scepticism of Magnus may not be so much the product of knee-jerk reaction as of prudent caution.

5.03 The general principles which govern absolute bars to registration have already been described, in Chapter 4. This chapter will look at specific kinds of trade mark subject matter and explain how the principles relating to absolute bars to registration in that chapter are applied, or could be applied, in specific instances. There is a further issue of registrability which is not however addressed in this chapter: the issues which arise when there is arguably nothing wrong with the trade mark but where a question arises as to the suitability of the applicant. This is the issue of 'bad faith' and it is discussed in Chapter 13.

B. Are there minimum and maximum criteria for registrability?

(1) Simple marks

5.04 In theory there is no reason why a trade mark should not be simple, so long as it has distinctive quality. A single black dot was successfully registered by the Dutch law firm NautaDutilh as a Benelux trade mark for legal services and, properly used on stationery and promotional materials, there is no doubt that it can serve this function well.

In *Corning's application* the Office for Harmonisation in the Internal Market (OHIM) examiner rejected an application to register a mark consisting of three ribs which were projecting from the circumference of an optical lens on the basis that it was excessively simple. The Board of Appeal disagreed, ruling that even excessive simplicity could not render a trade mark automatically non-distinctive: it was necessary to consider the consumer's reaction to it rather than the examiner's.[1] **5.05**

(2) Geometrical figures

An OHIM Board of Appeal has ruled that a mark consisting of no more than a line drawing of a 'simple, common and trivial' hexagon would be perceived by relevant consumers (of equipment for stables) as a simple hexagon with no other significance. Accordingly it could not serve as an 'indicator of origin or a source identifier'.[2] This decision seems somewhat ungenerous and may be viewed in sharp contrast with the Benelux law, which has tolerated the registration as a three-dimensional trade mark of a plain hexagonal shape for cheese.[3] **5.06**

(3) Complex marks

The length or complexity of a trade mark is not a measure of its inherent distinctiveness. Thus the fact that a single-word mark is thirty-four letters long might make it unusual, but both its content and the fact that other thirty-four-letter word marks might not be clearly distinguishable from it will both lean against its registrability.[4] **5.07**

(a) 'Trade dress' in trading premises

The registrability of a business format trade dress—a detailed description of the get-up and appearance of a shop, restaurant or other trade premises—has not yet conclusively been tested in European courts, though Planet Football's application to register its trade dress in the UK was not successful before the Registry or the Lord Chancellor's Appointed Person.[5] Even with such detailed descriptions it **5.08**

---

[1] *Corning Incorporated's application*, Case R 449/1999-2 [2001] ETMR 933.
[2] *De Boer Stalinrichtingen BV's application*, Case R 175/2000-4 [2001] ETMR 899, 904.
[3] *SA Kaasmakerij Passendale v Coopératives Réunies de l'Industrie du Lait Coberco* [2000] ETMR 840.
[4] *Telefon & Buch Verlags GmbH v OHIM*, Joined Cases T-357 and 358/99 [2001] ETMR 1004 (UNIVERSALKOMMUNIKATIONSVERZEICHNIS).
[5] *Jimmy Nicks Property Company Ltd's application* [1999] ETMR 445, 446: 'The trade mark for which the protection is sought is the interior of a building for use as a bar and/or restaurant, and/or

would be difficult for a competitor, on reading the graphic representation of a mark on the register, to know exactly what he was not allowed to do.

5.09 In the United States, the notion that trade dress in trading premises is protectable under trade mark law has developed further. The United States Supreme Court has recognized that 'it involves the total image of a product and may include features such as size, shape, color or color combinations, texture, graphics or even particular sales techniques'.[6] In the case in point, legal protection was extended to the Taco Cabana restaurant format:

> a festive eating atmosphere having interior dining and patio areas decorated with artifacts, bright colors, paintings and murals. The patio includes interior and exterior areas, with the interior patio capable of being sealed off from the outside patio by overhead garage doors. The stepped exterior of the building is a festive and vivid color scheme using top border paint and neon stripes. Bright awnings and umbrellas continue the theme.[7]

5.10 It is scarcely inconceivable that a graphic representation phrased in this manner would fulfil the criteria of registrability approved by the European Court of Justice (ECJ) that the representation of the mark be 'clear, precise, self-contained, easily accessible, intelligible, durable and objective'.[8]

(b) 'Trade dress' in the style of product designs

5.11 In Europe it appears that the overall 'style', 'fashion' or 'look' of a company's products is rarely likely to be registered as a trade mark. This is because the definition of an overall style or fashion is unlikely to be achieved with such clarity of expression that (i) it can be concisely graphically represented while (ii) at the same time being manifestly a representation of a single sign and not a broad concept. Even in the United States, where 'trade dress' doctrine provides for the protection of such amorphous concepts as trading premises (see para 5.09 above), the courts have been cautious in applying that protection.[9] In the *Wal-Mart* case[10] the Supreme Court narrowed trade dress doctrine by applying it to 'product packaging' but not 'product design'. The decor of the Taco Cabana restaurant was accordingly pro-

---

night-club, and/or entertainment space having an interior providing the appearance of the interior of a football/soccer stadium with a central area featuring a floor giving the appearance of a football/soccer pitch with goals at either end, an area bordering the central area representative of a spectator viewing area, an entrance into the central area provided by a tunnel with dugouts/coach seating on either side of the tunnel with sound effects of a football/soccer match with at least one servery in the interior having the appearance of a football/soccer ball.'

[6] *Two Pesos Inc v Taco Cabana* 505 US 763 (1992).
[7] *Two Pesos Inc v Taco Cabana* 932 F 2d 1113, 1117 (CA5 1991).
[8] *Sieckmann v Deutsches Patent- und Markenamt*, Case C-273/00 [2003] ETMR 466, paras 47–55.
[9] See Graeme Dinwoodie, 'Reconceptualizing the Inherent Distinctiveness of Product Design Trade Dress' (1997) 75 NCLR 471, 557.
[10] *Samara Brothers Inc v Wal-Mart Stores Inc* 120 SCt 1339 (2000).

C. Identifiers which may not serve as trade marks

tectable as 'product packaging', which consumers would tend to equate with a specific source. In contrast, the style or fashion of clothing described below was not protectable as 'product design' since consumers would not associate the design with a specific source.

> The protected trade dress will include most if not all of the following elements: seersucker fabric used exclusively; two or three identically shaped and symmetrically placed cloth appliqués (not screen printed) substantially similar to appliqués displaced on Samara clothing in vibrant colors integrated into the collar (which is typically large and white), collar line and/or pocket(s) (if any), single-piece, full-cut bodies; and the absence of three dimensional features, outlines and words. Essential to the 'Samara Look' is the method by which the design elements are combined on the garments. It is that amalgamation of the elements, . . . 'a distinctive combination of ingredients', which creates the uniform, protectable Samara look. . . . In particular, the placement of the appliqués, typically a row of two or three, along the collar or collar line of the garment and on any pockets is essential to the look.[11]

C. Identifiers which may not serve as trade marks

(1) Barcodes

5.12 Is a barcode registrable as a trade mark? In theory the answer should be 'yes'. A barcode is a sign, being a series of broad and narrow black lines which may be graphically represented. Further, its function is to enable a product to which it is attached to be distinguished from other products. If it could not do this, it would be useless as a barcode. Consumers know that barcodes are employed for a variety of purposes related to the identification of the product to which they are attached: to enable retail sales outlets to monitor the sale of stock and thus facilitate automatic reordering; to identify the wholesaler or importer through which goods passed on their way to the public; to identify batch numbers for quality-control purposes and also to mark the price. But no trade mark registry allows the registration of barcodes.

5.13 One reason why a barcode is arguably unregistrable is that consumers cannot read the data contained in them. This objection is itself dubious since the law does not demand that a trade mark has to be intelligible to the consumer without artificial aids such as barcode readers, any more than a trade mark has to be visible to people who don't wear glasses. Another reason, this time one which is fatal to a barcode's registration, is that each barcode is confusingly similar to each other barcode. On that basis, anyone seeking to identify a product or service on the strength of its barcode alone would almost certainly fail to do so. Thus a barcode as a trade mark would either fail to enable a consumer to identify a product or

---

[11] *Samara Bros Inc v Wal-Mart Stores Inc* 165 F 3d 120, 128–9 (2nd Cir 1998).

would be likely to mislead him into mistaking one product for another. Only if there were only one barcode would barcodes be registrable.

5.14 Apart from this a barcode will be unregistrable if it consists exclusively of signs which designate geographical origin, time of production or any of the other factors which fall within the classic list of data which may not be appropriated for exclusive use on account of their descriptive nature.[12] Despite this, the mere fact that a barcode is functional need not preclude it from registration as a trade mark in the unlikely event that it is also capable of serving a trade mark function and if consumers are trained to view it as such.

(2) Secret marks and hidden marks

5.15 Small and scarcely observable signs are often attached to goods so as to enable their manufacturer to identify them as being genuine or counterfeit. Since these markings cannot be detected by consumers or traders, they do not serve a trade mark function and should not therefore be registrable as trade marks.

5.16 Word marks which are only used as metatags may remain registrable despite the fact that the metatag is, under conditions of normal computer use, invisible to the consumer. If the consumer has to key the word into a search engine in order to locate and then gain access to the trade mark owner's website, that word is arguably being used as a trade mark even if this mode of trade mark use is somewhat unusual.

D. Cultural emblems

(1) Money

5.17 An OHIM Board of Appeal has expressed the view that words and signs in current use in signifying money will always be regarded by consumers as serving that function and cannot therefore serve as trade marks for any goods or services.[13] The same view has been expressed by the Polish Patent Office.[14] Presumably once a term or sign is no longer associated with currency (for example, terms such as 'guinea', 'groat', 'doubloon', 'louis'), or is associated with the currency of a country which most consumers will not recognize as being currency (for example, the kwacha in Zambia), this barrier to registration may no longer apply.

---

[12] See eg Council Directive 89/104, art 3(1)(c); Council Regulation 40/94, art 7(1)(c).
[13] *ABN Amro Holding NV's application*, Case R 190/1999-3 [2001] ETMR 90 (EURO word and symbol).
[14] *Grosz Sp Zoo's application*, 29 April 1998 (unreported) (Polish Patent Office, Board of Appeals).

D. Cultural emblems

5.18 In the Benelux a number of registrations have been granted for the trade mark 2.20371, which happens to be the official exchange rate of the Dutch guilder to the Euro.[15]

(2) Times and dates

5.19 In relation to date-sensitive products and services (for example, the variable vintage of wines), anything that appears to be a date is not distinctive and will not be registrable as a trade mark. Since consumers will look at it and say, 'Oh, look! That must be the date', they will not regard it as a trade mark at all.[16] If the nature of the date is such that it cannot be in any sense descriptive of the product in question (for example, 1437 in relation to mobile telephones), or if it is viewed as the date of foundation of a business depicted by the trade mark (for example, KRONENBOURG 1664 French lager), this barrier to registration will not apply.

5.20 Some dates have connotations which will make them unregistrable in some or possibly all goods and services sectors. For example, 1812 is unlikely to be registrable for musical products and services on account of the automatic association with Tchaikovsky's 1812 Overture. Dates such as 4 July (American Independence Day) and 14 July (Bastille Day in France) have a degree of national significance that will outweigh their ability to distinguish goods or services in the eye of the consumer and 9/11 (the American appellation for 11 September 2001) may remain unregistrable on account of its tragic connotations for some time to come.

5.21 Eras such as SIECLE 21 and XXIème Siècle (both French for 'twenty-first century') have been held to be not inherently unregistrable,[17] particularly when there is added subject matter (for example, TWENTY-FIRST CENTURY FOX).

5.22 The names of religious and pagan festivals are not automatically precluded from registration.[18] However, since words like 'Christmas', 'Ramadan' and 'Diwali' have such powerful primary meanings in their own right, the name of the festival will have to be incorporated with other terms or signs before the mark is regarded as being distinctive.

---

[15] I am grateful to Bas Kist (Shieldmark) for this and sundry other items of Benelux information in this chapter.

[16] *Allied Domecq plc's application* [1997] ETMR 253 (UK Trade Mark Registry): AD2000 unregistrable for alcoholic beverages.

[17] *Century 21 Real Estate Corporation's application*, Case R 135/1998-2 [1999] ETMR 781 (OHIM); *Casaubon and Vingt et Unième Siècle v 21st Century Film France* [1999] ETMR 787 (Cour d'appel de Paris).

[18] *Optos-Opus Sarl v SA Haribo Ricqlès Zan SA and others* [1999] ETMR 362 (Tribunal de Grande Instance de Paris) on HALLOWEEN.

(3) State emblems, official hallmarks and emblems of intergovernmental organizations

5.23 The unauthorized registration of state emblems such as national flags and armorial bearings, official signs and the emblems of intergovernmental organizations is prohibited under the Paris Convention[19] and therefore also under the national laws of that Convention's Member States. Countries may however determine for themselves whether this protection should be given even in the absence of evidence of confusion of the public.[20] It was accordingly open to a Dutch court to conclude that, in the absence of evidence of confusion or association, a trade mark which was validly registered for goods sold in a chain of drug stores did not infringe the rights enjoyed by the European Space Agency in a mark of similar appearance.[21]

(4) Signs of the zodiac

5.24 Despite their having been regarded as part of mankind's common culture for more than 2,000 years, signs of the zodiac have been regarded as freely registrable. Thus an application to register TÄHTIMERKKI KAURIS (Finnish for 'sign of the zodiac Capricorn') was allowed for teabags, notwithstanding an opposition based on a likelihood of confusion with an earlier mark HOROSCOPE for the same product.[22] Some signs of the zodiac are heavily used as trade marks, but CANCER as a freestanding mark remains available for most goods and services.

E. Locators

(1) Addresses and Internet addresses

5.25 Since a consumer, on seeing an address, will assume without further education that it is an address, he will not regard it as a trade mark. Applying this logic, which is referable both to terrestrial addresses and to domain names, an OHIM Board of Appeal rejected an application to register the word mark WWW.PRIMEBROKER.COM as a trade mark for software and services relating to the supply of business information.[23]

---

[19] Paris Convention, art 6*ter*.
[20] ibid, art 6*ter*(1)(c).
[21] *ESA (European Space Agency) v ETOS BV*, 1 October 2002 (unreported) (Haarlem District Court).
[22] *Aaro Forsman OY's application; opposition of Gilvaria OY* [2000] ETMR 142 (Supreme Administrative Court, Helsinki).
[23] *Nationsbanc Montgomery Securities LLC's application*, Case R 77/1999-2 [2000] ETMR 245.

E. Locators

Although the 'www' element is a clear indication that the words that follow it are a domain name, much the same result will pertain even in the absence of the 'www' although the reasoning may be different. An OHIM Board of Appeal refused registration of BUY.COM, not on the basis that it was an address but on the ground that it was inherently devoid of distinctive character. The Board did not say that *no* domain name could function as a trade mark, but more kindly stated that 'not *all* domain names are capable of performing the function of a trade mark'.[24] BUY.COM was however a non-starter: 'buy' described what people were expected to do on the applicant's website, while '.com' was a top-level generic term, signifying a domain name. The same fate befell INTERNET.COM which the Benelux Trade Mark Office regarded as consisting of the generic term 'Internet' and the non-distinctive term '.com'.[25] Domain names for which the Turkmenistan top-level domain abbreviation '.tm' is used may, however, possibly be registrable: would consumers, on seeing an address such as BUY.TM, view it initially as a trade mark first and only subsequently as a domain name?

5.26

Can a top-level generic term be registered? Logic would suggest that it cannot be regarded as ever being capable of distinguishing goods or services since: (i) it appears to be part of an address; (ii) it is by definition generic; and (iii) it is only the addition of the words which normally appear before it in the address string which give it any meaning in commerce. Nonetheless the Singapore Intellectual Property Office accepted an application by the Singapore Network Information Centre to register '.sg' as a trade mark for 'education, domain registration and internet connection services'. Following strong objections from ICANN this application was eventually abandoned.[26]

5.27

(2) Telephone numbers

Most telephone numbers—including those which are well known and heavily used by the consuming public in its dealings with a business—will be regarded as telephone numbers and not as trade marks. This applies not only to combinations of numbers alone but also to alphanumerical combinations such as 800-FLOWERS.[27] Where a telephone number is used as a trade mark and acquires distinctiveness through such use, it will eventually be capable of registration.[28] If a telephone number however acquires a secondary meaning (for example, as a song

5.28

---

[24] *Buy.Com Inc's application*, Case R 638/2000-4 [2002] ETMR 540, para 21 (emphasis added).
[25] *Mecklermedia Corporation v Benelux Trade Mark Office* [2001] ETMR 523 (Court of Appeal, The Hague).
[26] See Tan Tee Jim and Tan Wee Meng, 'Registration of ".sg" as a Trademark Abandoned' WTLR, 24 March 2003.
[27] *1-800 Flowers Inc v Phonenames Ltd* [2000] ETMR 369 (HC), affirmed by the Court of Appeal at [2002] FSR 191.
[28] *Pizza Pizza Ltd v Registrar of Trade-marks* (1989) 26 CPR (3d) 355 (Federal Court of Appeal, Canada).

title for the famous Glenn Miller melody PENNSYLVANIA 65000), it may not be regarded as a functioning telephone number by the relevant consuming public. If that be the case, there is no apparent bar to registration on the basis of lack of distinctive character. Where however the ownership of the telephone number lies in the hands of a telephone subscriber who is not connected with the trade mark proprietor, its registration may be contrary to public policy given the potential inconvenience which its exposure in the course of trade may inflict upon the subscriber.

5.29 Logically, while the word FLOWERS is clearly and correctly regarded as being generic for flowers, it cannot be concluded from that proposition that the telephone number 800-FLOWERS would also be so regarded. For while all florists use the word 'flowers', members of the public have an expectation that they do not all share the same telephone number and that, therefore, only one of them will be found by dialling 800-FLOWERS. Perhaps it is on this basis that in the United States the CAFC allowed the registration of 1-888-M-A-T-R-E-S-S (sic) for the service of selling mattresses. No one actually describes mattresses as '1-888-mattresses' when discussing them and, since there is no such thing as a '1-888 mat(t)ress', the term is not generic.[29] However, another United States court held the alphanumeric trade mark '1-800-PLUMBING' to be descriptive as 'immediately conveying the impression that a particular plumbing service is available by calling the telephone number'.[30] The court did not presumably consider whether its use of the phrase '*particular* plumbing service' actually suggested that the number was not descriptive but distinctive because it designated the source or origin of that service.

F. Issues relating to letters and numbers

(1) Abbreviations and contractions

5.30 Where an abbreviation is regarded as being either actually or potentially part of customary trade vocabulary, or might become so, the courts will not allow its registration. Thus BIOID, being a contraction of the words 'biometric identification', was not regarded as being distinctive of computer programs and services relating to biometric identification.[31]

(2) Specific types of word mark

5.31 Virtually any letter or combination of letters is potentially registrable as a trade

---

[29] *Re Dial-A-Mattress Operating Corp* 240 F 3d 1341 (Fed Cir 2001).
[30] *Cline v 1-888-Plumbing Group* 146 F Supp 2d 351, 362 (SDNY 2001).
[31] *BioID v OHIM*, Case T-91/01, 5 December 2002 (CFI).

F. Issues relating to letters and numbers

mark. Consider the following list: single letters (K for shoes), acronyms (WWF for the World Wide Fund for Nature charity, FIAT for Fabbrica Italiana Automobile Torino cars), nouns (APPLE for computers), adjectives (NEXT for clothing), verbs (WASH 'N' GO for shampoo), the definite article (THE for screws), pronouns (ELLE for magazines), adverbs (ALWAYS for sanitary products), slogans (DON'T LEAVE HOME WTHOUT IT for financial services), names (RENAULT for cars, YVES ST LAURENT for fashion items), geographical names (WATERFORD for glass) and specially coined words (PROZAC for happy pills). Words may be conjoined in forms which are found in normal use (COMPANYLINE) or not (BABY-DRY for babies' nappies; NETMEETING for computer software). Some specific problems relating to word marks are described below.

(a) Single letters

5.32 Although it is a somewhat brief and succinct indication of the origin of goods or services, even a single letter falls within the concept of a 'sign' and can be registered as a trade mark. Trade mark registries often display a degree of cautious resistance to registration. An application to register in Germany the letter K, for various goods including doors and windows, ironware, safes and letterboxes, was initially refused on the ground that, though K was a 'sign', it was devoid of distinctive character and had to be kept free for other traders to use. The Bundespatentgericht dismissed the applicant's appeal but he was finally successful before the Bundesgerichtshof. That court held that it should not be assumed that the threshold of distinctiveness should not be set too low: in other words, the existence of *any* distinctiveness, however small, meant that a mark was not devoid of distinctiveness.[32]

5.33 Where a single letter is portrayed as a figurative mark rather than as a word mark, its potential for registrability increases. This is because it is easier to visualize a figurative depiction of a letter serving to distinguish an undertaking's goods or services than to imagine how a simple and arguably unadorned letter might perform the same function. Even a fairly simple picture of a letter may be regarded as inherently distinctive. Thus the letter 'a' portrayed here (see Figure 5.1), initially rejected by the OHIM examiner as being devoid of distinctive character, was not regarded as such by the Board of Appeal which observed: 'although the design of the letter as such may not be unusual, . . ., it is the trade mark as a whole which must be considered . . .'. In this case the interrelation

Figure 5.1 Even a fairly simple picture of a letter may be regarded as inherently distinctive.

---

[32] *K trade mark* [2001] ETMR 1181.

of the black box and the assymetrical position of the letter added to its power to distinguish the goods and services (clothes and art exhibitions) for which registration was sought.[33]

5.34 The OHIM *Examination Guidelines* do not rule out the possibility that a single letter or digit, or two letters or digits, might possess distinctive character, but they suggest that this would only be the case in 'special circumstances'.[34]

(b) Initials and acronyms

5.35 Apart from having the capacity to spell a word, a combination of two or more letters may also symbolize a number or refer in short to a combination of two or more words. Abbreviations and acronyms are widely used in modern society and frequently become better known than the words they stand for. For this reason a trade mark applicant must expect any particularly short and snappy combination of letters to stand for something and thus have, in at least some sectors, a powerful secondary meaning. Even relatively cumbersome letters like WWF can have two or more separate and unrelated meanings; WWF has in fact been the subject of ferocious litigation unto the death.[35] Included in the price of success in getting a set of initials registered is the cost of policing and enforcing the integrity of letters which, since they may also stand for quite different things, can be difficult to police.

5.36 The fact that a set of letters has acquired a generic meaning within a particular sector will prevent its appropriation for sole use within that sector, even if the general public is quite unaware of it. Thus the letters DLC were wrongly registered as a Community trade mark (CTM) for razors and razor blades: since they stood for 'diamond-like carbon', a term in industrial use, they could not be captured by Gillette. Even though the vast majority of men who shaved using razor blades would not know what DLC stood for,

> scientists also form part of the general public. Male scientists shave, at least at times, and when they encounter DLC on a razor or on a razor blade, they know what it means.[36]

5.37 This comment should not be taken as a suggestion that the non-registrability of DLC is somehow there to benefit shavers. It is there to benefit Gillette's competitors, who can also use it.

---

[33] *Adolf Ahler AG's application*, Case R 91/1998-2, 28 May 1999 (unreported).
[34] *Examination Guidelines*, para 8.3: see *Fuji Photo Film Co Ltd's application*, Case R 4/1998-2 [1998] ETMR 343 (IX).
[35] *World Wide Fund for Nature and World Wildlife Fund Inc v World Wrestling Federation Entertainment Inc* [2002] ETMR 564 (CA).
[36] *Gillette Company's trade mark; application for a declaration of invalidity by Warner-Lambert & Company*, Case 000703579 [2002] ETMR 733, 745.

F. Issues relating to letters and numbers

5.38 The fact that a set of initials may stand for two different things will not enable it to achieve registrability if both those uses are taken as being generic in relation to the goods for which a mark is registered. Thus the letters BSS, meaning either 'buffered salt solution' or 'balanced salt solution', were wrongly registered as a CTM for sterile solutions for ophthalmic surgery.[37]

5.39 Even if a set of letters has not attained a high degree of recognition, the registry responsible for processing the application may have other ideas. Thus an application to register the letters TDdi as a trade mark for vehicles and spare parts was rejected by OHIM on the basis that the letters stood for 'turbo-diesel direct injection'.[38] The Board of Appeal was influenced by the fact that its *Acronyms, Initialisms & Abbreviations Dictionary* listed TD and DI as abbreviations for, respectively, 'turbo-diesel' and 'direct injection'. The combination of those two abbreviations was therefore held unregistrable. Even though there was no suggestion that the letter combination TDdi had in fact been used by anyone other than the applicant for registration, it was expected that it might be so used in the future.

(c) Numbers

5.40 An OHIM Board of Appeal refused registration of the numeral 7 for goods and services relating to sports cars and related goods and services. Although '7' was technically a 'sign', it was a sign which, the Board said, belonged to the public domain and was 'part of the store of signs available to all traders'. Without the addition of any 'unusual or fanciful feature' it could perform the basic function of a trade mark.[39]

(d) Variations of type and font

5.41 The use of an ornamental or fancy type font may result in an otherwise unregistrable sign becoming distinctive. However, the plainer the typography the less likely it is to be regarded as inherently distinctive. Thus the Court of First Instance (CFI) held a representation of the lower-case word 'electronica', for catalogues, trade fairs and trade conferences relating to electronic components, to be devoid of distinctive character: the fact that it was reproduced in the simple Helvetica font did nothing to make good the word's lack of distinctiveness.[40] The same result was reached by the same court when the word BioID (an abbreviation of 'biometric identification') was represented in the plain Arial font.[41]

---

[37] *Dr Robert Winzer Pharma GmbH's application to cancel a trade mark of Alcon Pharmaceuticals Ltd*, Case C000090134/1 [2000] ETMR 217, upheld on appeal in *Alcon Inc v OHIM, Dr Robert Winzer Pharma GmbH intervening*, Case T-237/01, 5 March 2003 (unreported) (CFI).
[38] *Ford Motor Company's application*, Case R 433/1999-1 [2000] ETMR 679.
[39] *Caterham Car Sales & Coachworks Ltd's application*, Case R 63/1999-3 [2000] ETMR 14, para 13.
[40] *Messe München GmbH v OHIM*, Case T-32/00 [2001] ETMR 135.
[41] *BioID v OHIM*, Case T-91/01 [2003] ETMR 766.

5.42 The substitution of the '@' sign for the letter 'a' will not make the word GLASS (ie GL@ss) distinctive of 'building materials including glass'.[42]

5.43 In the Benelux an entire font has been accepted for registration. The trade mark application featured a full print-out of the alphabet together with a description to the effect that the trade mark was the font itself.[43]

G. Geographical marks

5.44 This discussion omits reference to rights in protected geographical indications and protected designations of origin. These rights are discussed separately in Chapter 18.

5.45 Geographical terms and place names are capable of serving as trade marks; many have done so with great distinction (for example, YORK trailers, WATERFORD glass, PONTIAC, LINCOLN, GRANADA, TOLEDO cars, COLUMBIA films and sound recordings). European law, in common with that of many other jurisdictions, does however place a limitation upon their registrability. Directive 89/104 provides that there should be no registration of

> trade marks which consist exclusively of signs or indications which may serve, in trade, to designate . . . geographical origin . . . of the goods or of rendering of the service.[44]

5.46 The reason for this is obvious. Geographical terms are part of the common vocabulary of mankind: the imperative that traders be free to indicate where their goods come from is stronger than the desire of traders to appropriate them exclusively for their personal requirements. Indeed, this imperative is also protected through the availability as a defence to an infringement action of the honest use of a place name.[45]

5.47 This restriction quoted above does not speak specifically of place names; it speaks of signs or designations which 'designate geographical origin'. It therefore covers adjectival terms which are regional, such as NORDIC when used in respect of buildings for use as saunas.[46] The restriction also appears to cover words rather than figurative marks. Accordingly, while the word EUROPEAN is unregistrable for publications with European content, the representation of the words *THE EUROPEAN* (see Figure 5.2), featuring a bird flying across the letter O with a newspaper in its beak, was registrable.[47]

---

[42] *Pilkington plc's application* [2002] ETMR 206 (UK Trade Marks Registry).
[43] Wegener's trade mark, BX 665106.
[44] Council Directive 89/104, art 3(1)(c).
[45] Council Directive 89/104, art 6(1); Council Regulation 40/94, art 12.
[46] *Nordic Saunas Ltd's trade mark; application for revocation by Nordic Timber Council AB* [2002] ETMR 210 (UK Trade Mark Registry).
[47] *European Ltd v The Economist Newspaper Ltd* [1998] ETMR 307 (CA).

G. Geographical marks

Figure 5.2 *THE EUROPEAN*'s word-and-device mark is registrable.

It goes without saying that the scope of legal protection granted to such a mark, the most prominent feature of which is the word EUROPEAN, is very narrow. Accordingly that trade mark was not infringed by the publication by the defendant of a newspaper called *European Voice*. **5.48**

In Europe, where there is no possibility of a place name indicating geographical origin, it may safely be registered. A typical example would be the word mark NORTH POLE for bananas, because bananas do not grow in that region and have no natural connection with it.[48] Likewise, MARS bars have no apparent link with the red planet of the same name. Precisely the opposite approach appears to apply in the United States, which bars registration to names which are 'primarily geographically deceptively misdescriptive'.[49] On this basis, United States applications have been rejected for HOTEL MONACO for hotels which were not situated in the Principality of Monaco and had no connection with it,[50] as well as for CUBA L.A. for pre-recorded disks and cassette tapes which originated neither from Cuba nor from Los Angeles: the combination of two well-known place names did not lessen the geographical significance of either of them, notwithstanding the fact that no such place as 'Cuba L.A.' existed.[51] **5.49**

The ECJ has given careful thought to the meaning of the wording of the restriction upon the registrability of geographical marks[52] and has summarized the situation as follows: **5.50**

- it does not prohibit the registration of geographical names as trade marks *solely* where the names designate places which are, in the mind of the relevant class of persons, currently associated with the category of goods in question; it also applies to geographical names which are liable to be used in future . . . as an indication of the geographical origin of that category of goods;
- where there is currently no association in the mind of the relevant class of persons between the geographical name and the category of goods in question, the competent authority must assess whether it is reasonable to assume that such a

---

[48] *British Sugar plc v James Robertson & Sons Ltd* [1996] RPC 281, 306 (HC).
[49] Lanham Act, s 2(e)(3); 15 USC s 1052(e)(3).
[50] *Re Kimpton Hotel & Restaurant Group Inc* 55 USPQ 2d 1154 (TTAB 2000).
[51] *Re Narada Productions Inc* 57 USPQ 2d 1801 (TTAB 2001).
[52] *Windsurfing Chiemsee Produktions- und Vertriebs GmbH v Boots- und Segelzubehör Walter Huber and Franz Attenberger*, Joined Cases C-108 and 109/97 [1999] ETMR 585 (CHIEMSEE).

name is, in the mind of the relevant class of persons, capable of designating the geographical origin of that category of goods;
- in making that assessment, particular consideration should be given to the degree of familiarity amongst the relevant class of persons with the geographical name in question, with the characteristics of the place designated by that name, and with the category of goods concerned;
- it is not necessary for the goods to be manufactured in the geographical location in order for them to be associated with it.

5.51 Three further species of trade mark application have a geographical dimension which requires special consideration: the names of countries, the prefix EURO- and the word INTERNATIONAL.

5.52 Countries do not, as a matter of law, appear to own their own names.[53] For this reason country names are treated as being capable of being registered as trade marks and are subject to the same legal criteria as any other geographical sign for which registration is sought. Accordingly in the UK the word ICELAND has been registered for numerous goods and services which have no direct or obvious connection with that island; CANADA and GREENLAND, for example, are also found on the British register. There are however no single-word registrations of FRANCE and GERMANY.

5.53 In Europe at any rate EURO- is at best likely to be regarded as neutral and at worst likely to be ignored as being descriptive or non-distinctive: it all depends on what comes after it. Thus EUROLAMB for meat can only be descriptive or deceptive (depending on the origin and nature of the meat);[54] EUROCOOL is not inherently incapable of distinguishing the storage and transport of cold foods, though it may be descriptive of it;[55] EuroHealth only indirectly evokes 'financial affairs' and is registrable for them, but not for 'insurance affairs',[56] and so on. Even if EURO- is not used descriptively, it remains inherently non-distinctive and its marriage to a generic term will result in a sign which is incapable of distinguishing goods and thus unregistrable (for example, EUROCLIP for clips[57]). Until the mid-1990s an emblem of togetherness, peace and harmony, the prefix EURO- now appears to bear so many pejorative connotations (unpopular currency; mismanagement of regional affairs; allegations of corruption and cover-up) that there is much to be said for advising would-be trade mark owners to leave it alone—as most major brand-owners have done in previous decades.

---

[53] *Queen v Virtual Countries Inc*, WIPO D 2002-0754, 27 November 2002 (WIPO).
[54] *BOCM Pauls Ltd and Scottish Agricultural College's application* [1997] ETMR 420 (UK Trade Mark Registry).
[55] *Eurocool Logistik GmbH v OHIM*, Case T-34/00 [2003] ETMR 51 (CFI).
[56] *DKV Deutsche Krankenversicherung AG v OHIM* (EUROHEALTH), Case T-359/99 [2001] ECR II-1645; [2001] ETMR 919 (CFI).
[57] *IBP Industrial Products Ltd's application*, Case R 736/1999-2, 27 July 2001, OHIM OJ, 12/2002, p 2299, paras 10–12 (OHIM).

I. Names, titles and cultural icons

The word INTERNATIONAL is also overworked, if currently less redolent of pejorative meaning. As one OHIM Board of Appeal said: 5.54

> The word INTERNATIONAL is commonplace in business and simply indicates that an activity is pursued in many countries. Adjectives such as 'international', 'global', 'national' and 'European' may freely be used by any firm to indicate the geographical scale of its activities or aspirations, or to project an image reflecting the way in which it wishes to be perceived by consumers.[58]

With luck these will be the last words of this story.   5.55

H. Trade dress and business formats

There is nothing to exclude the trade dress of a business (for example, the format of a fast-food restaurant or dry-cleaning chain) from registration, so long as it satisfies the same criteria as any other trade marks, particularly that of graphic representation.[59] It is unlikely that, in Europe at any rate, all of the features of a shop's trade dress will be regarded as inherently distinctive since, until customers get used to its particular get-up and can recognize it for what it is, it will not be clear to the applicant or to the trade mark-granting authority precisely which elements of the get-up should be included within the trade mark application and which are to be regarded as part of the shop or service itself.   5.56

I. Names, titles and cultural icons

There is nothing in trade mark law to suggest that personal names should not be registrable as trade marks. Indeed, 'personal names' are mentioned explicitly among the examples of signs which may be registered as trade marks under TRIPs[60] and, in Europe, under Directive 89/104[61] and the CTM Regulation.[62]   5.57

---

[58] *International Paper Company's application*, Case R 868/200-2 [2003] ETMR 92, 95 (allowing INTERNATIONAL PAPER in respect only of paintbrushes, typewriters and other products having nothing to do with paper).

[59] This much is clear from the inconclusive decision in *Jimmy Nicks Property Company Ltd's application* [1999] ETMR 445, 446 (LCAP, Scotland) where the mark was graphically described as 'the interior of a building for use as a bar and/or restaurant, and/or night-club, and/or entertainment space having an interior providing the appearance of the interior of a football/soccer stadium with a central area featuring a floor giving the appearance of a football/soccer pitch with goals at either end, an area bordering the central area representative of a spectator viewing area, an entrance into the central area provided by a tunnel with dugouts/coach seating on either side of the tunnel with sound effects of a football/soccer match with at least one servery in the interior having the appearance of a football/soccer ball'.

[60] TRIPs Agreement, art 15.
[61] Council Directive 89/104, art 2.
[62] Council Regulation 40/94, art 4.

Chapter 5: Registrability of Specific Types of Trade Mark

(1) Personal names are an emotive topic

5.58 Despite the fact that personal names are, in principle, universally registrable as trade marks, the monopolization of names, and in particular surnames, is an emotive topic with a psychological as well as a legal agenda which is considered below.

(2) We may have to share our full names with trade mark owners

5.59 Real humans have been given names such as Harry Potter, James Bond, Henry Ford, Jack Daniels, Johnny Walker, Stuart Little and Donald Duck before—and perhaps surprisingly in some cases even after—those names were 'captured' by their respective trade mark owners. It is quite humiliating enough for a person to discover that his name has become an object of ridicule or amusement among his erstwhile friends and colleagues at work; it can be a further embarrassment to discover that his own potential for using his name has been diminished or whittled away entirely by virtue of its registration as a trade mark. However, unless the human who shares his name with a famous trade mark actually wants to pursue the same line of commerce, the existence of that trade mark will not unduly inconvenience him in the course of his trade.

(3) We may have to share our surnames or forenames with trade mark owners

5.60 If your name is Harry Potter or Stuart Little, you will be likely to endure a good deal of teasing for it; this is not so if your name is Mary Potter or Jason Little. But some surnames are registered as trade marks the evocative qualities of which can be an annoyance or embarrassment for everyone who shares them. ROTHSCHILD is a hallmark of financial services; MARS bars are a tasty and convenient substitute for a meal; PHILIPS makes washing machines. All Rothschilds are therefore expected to be rich; Marses must eat nothing but MARS bars while Philipses (and indeed Phillipses) have to endure tedious comments about their supposed connection to washing machines, and so on. Some names are so strongly associated with registered trade marks that the making of constant references to this association becomes a *leitmotif* in their bearers' lives: Daimler, Smirnoff, Nestlé, Hoover, Cadbury, Schweppes.

5.61 Some celebrity forenames have become so strongly associated with a single individual that the effect mentioned in the previous paragraph applies to them too. Examples include the forenames MADONNA, ELVIS and OSAMA.

(4) We may find our path to fame and fortune blocked by an earlier person with the same name

5.62 If you sing, your name is Elton John and you have ambitions to become a famous entertainer, you may be disappointed to discover that another singer of the same

I. Names, titles and cultural icons

name has already achieved notable repute. If the senior Mr John has registered his name as a trade mark for T-shirts, mugs, pillowcases and other celebrity memorabilia, your path to the exploitation of your stardom is blocked.[63] This is the case even if (i) you sing better than Mr John and (ii) your real name is Elton John, while the earlier Elton John has no greater claim to that name than that he adopted it in preference to the name Reginald Dwight.

(5) Individuals and trade marks do not always reflect the same values

Some name marks conjure up instantly recognizable values. GUCCI, for example, implies a particular strain of fashion; DISNEY suggests a wholesome, clean-cut American family lifestyle; FERRARI couples speed with glamour. No one is required to be fashionable, but anyone who goes off to meet an unknown Mr Gucci at the airport will not unreasonably personify him as possessing a Gucci-style persona. Likewise, one's reaction to an unwholesome individual with poor morals and unpleasant personal habits may be affected by the discovery that the person is surnamed DISNEY. This means that people whose names reflect values that they do not share have to bear the extra burden of disabusing the false expectations of others which they have done nothing to create.

5.63

(6) A person can register his name and then lose it to a third party

It happens from time to time that, when a person who registers his own name as a trade mark later assigns it to someone else, either he or a third party connected with him may wish to use it subsequently for professional or commercial purposes.[64] If a person assigns his trade marked name to another, he cannot be completely prevented from using his own name but the law greatly limits the scope of what he can do with it since the new trade mark owner can exercise the same rights against him as he can exercise against anyone else who uses the same mark without the new owner's consent.[65]

5.64

(7) Dealing with name marks

How does the law handle names? The question is answered in this chapter in

5.65

---

[63] See *Re Torres Valls*, 6 July 2001 [2002] ETMR N-53 (Spanish Supreme Court): Mr and Mrs Torres Vall were unable to register their surname TORRES VALL for sparkling wine since the TORRES mark was already registered for vermouth and wine.

[64] See eg Graeme Colquhoun, 'It's All in the Name . . .' (2003) 89 *LES News Exchange* 4, which outlines the loss by dress designer Elizabeth Emanuel of her own trade mark-registered name to downmarket fashion house Joe Bloggs.

[65] See eg *Centro Botanico Srl, Angelo Naj Oleari and Gruppo Cartorama SpA v Modafil di A Toniolo & C Sas*, [2003] ETMR 500 where the Tribunal of Milan (First Civil Division) refused to allow the use by another company of format 'CENTRO BOTANICO RANGES CREATED BY *Angelo Naj Oleari* CARTORAMA', where Naj Oleari had previously assigned his trade mark to another company.

general terms only. The problems raised by the names of dead and living celebrities are reviewed in greater depth in Chapter 15.

5.66 In general, national trade mark laws tend to regard common surnames (for example, O'SHEA, PATEL, LEE, BROWN, WONG, POPOVIC, SCHMIDT, PEDERSEN, MACDONALD depending on the jurisdiction) as being less inherently registrable than unusual ones (for example, WARHOL, NESTLE, PICASSO, RIMSKY-KORSAKOV). But should there be a uniform consequence, from the point of view of trade mark law, of a name being common or uncommon? After all, some areas of commerce are 'common' while others are 'uncommon'. Monopolization of names such as SMITH might inconvenience would-be competitors where the monopoly covers an area of economic activity in which market entry has few natural barriers, for example, in setting up a bar, a restaurant or a sweet shop. However, if the manufacture and sale of high-tech specialist electronic equipment for the aviation industry is monopolized by one SMITH, it is far less likely that many other Smiths would find themselves harshly excluded from being able to use their own name in that same market.

5.67 OHIM practice assumes that the fact that a surname is common does not of itself mean that it cannot be distinctive in respect of the goods or services for which an application is made.[66] A reference has however been made to the ECJ on the questions (i) whether common surnames should be considered non-distinctive in the absence of evidence of acquired distinctiveness and (ii) whether it was open to trade mark registries to allow registration on a 'first come, first served' basis or whether some more subtle basis should be developed.[67]

5.68 There is no uniformity in practice concerning the availability of surnames for registration as trade marks in Europe. In some Scandinavian jurisdictions, for example, an applicant is expected to obtain the consent of others who share that surname before the mark can be registered (in Finland this requirement goes wider than trade mark law, applying also to company names[68]). Where however the nature of the mark is such that the surname is effectively camouflaged by other material to the point that it would not be viewed as a surname, the mark's surnominal nature will be overlooked.[69]

---

[66] *Leroy Merlin Participations (SA) v K-2 Corp*, Case R 66/2001-4 [2003] ETMR 113 (OHIM): the name in this case was MERLIN for luggage.

[67] *Re Nichols plc*, 23 July 2003 (HC).

[68] See eg *Homer v Homer's Bar Maunlua OY and Homer's Bar Pihlajanmäki OY* [1998] ETMR 591, where the Supreme Court ruled that Mrs Eila Homer could prevent the registration of a company name including the word 'Homer's', notwithstanding that the name was: (i) commonly used outside Finland as a forename; (ii) associated with Homer Simpson; and (iii) used in the genitive case.

[69] *L'Oréal's application* [2000] ETMR 10 (the Finnish Administrative Court allowed the applicant's appeal against the refusal to allow the word-and-device mark PLENITUDE EXCELL A3: in that context the word 'Excell' would not be regarded as a surname).

I. Names, titles and cultural icons

Some common surnames are also adjectival, for example, Brown/Braun/Brun; White/Weiss/Blanc/Bianco; Green/Grun/Vert/Verdi. If this is the case the trade mark applicant may have to address issues of descriptiveness as well as surnominal frequency. Paradoxically, in such a case a trade mark's partially descriptive or allusive nature might actually enhance its registrability. Thus when Unilever sought to register MISTER LONG as a trade mark for ice creams and frozen confections, the application was refused on the basis that it would be viewed as a name and, since Long was an extremely common name, it lacked inherent distinctive character. However, once Unilever agreed to limit the specification of goods so as to include only elongated products, the word 'long' became descriptive rather than surnominal and the mark could proceed to grant.[70]

5.69

An OHIM Opposition Division has concluded that, where two trade marks share the same surname but feature different forenames, 'there is a conceptual similarity between both trade marks, although it is weak'; consumers will view the shared surname as a matter of coincidence rather than trade connection.[71]

5.70

(8) Personal signatures

A signature is the specific format in which a person signs his name. Like a personal name, a signature can be registered. Protection conferred by the registration of a signature will however be limited. If an applicant called John Smith produces a signature with a particular flourish, its registration *will* help him fend off competitors who have composed similar flourishes for their different names (Jack Smith, Joe Smith, John S. Mitt), but it will *not* help him to prevent the use of signatures of other John Smiths whose autographs are quite dissimilar unless he can satisfy a court that there is an overall similarity between them, taking into account their visual, aural and conceptual elements.[72]

5.71

(9) Titles of songs, books, films, etc

In principle there is no reason why the titles of songs, books and films should not be registered as trade marks. The famous song WALTZING MATILDA has been registered as a trade mark for a wide variety of goods and services in Australia. Where, however, the book title has a dominant secondary meaning, the German courts may take a different view. Thus where the book title *Winnetou* was registered as a trade mark for printed goods, film and production services and the production of books and magazines, the Bundesgerichtshof cancelled its

5.72

---

[70] *Unilever plc's application* [1999] ETMR 406 (LCAP).
[71] *Linda Jackson Pty Ltd's application; opposition of Jackson International Trading Company Kurt D Brühl Gesellschaft mbH & Co KG*, Case 520/2000 [2001] ETMR 376: LINDA JACKSON signature and DAVID JACKSON figurative mark insufficiently similar, even for the same goods.
[72] On the test of similarity of trade marks, see Chapter 10.

registrations, considering that the word WINNETOU had become so evocative of the idea of the noble Indian chief that it had lost its ability to distinguish goods or services and that it should be kept free for use by competitors.[73] If this decision is correct, publishers would be well advised to conjure up titles which are unlikely to be evocative and to avoid employing the name of a book's hero as the title.

J. Slogans

5.73 It is now accepted pretty well universally—though it was not always so—that slogans are registrable as trade marks. This does not mean that they are without their problems. First, it is often not apparent to consumers that a slogan, even if they associate it with a particular product or service, is supposed to distinguish those goods or services. Secondly, the best slogans from a marketing point of view are often those which are descriptive,[74] laudatory[75] or otherwise lacking in distinctive quality[76]—though even these slogans can gain distinctiveness through heavy use.[77]

5.74 There is no reason why a slogan which is quite unrelated to the goods or services for which registration is sought should not be initially registrable since its very lack of connection to them is an indication of distinctiveness.[78] Where that is not the case, one tribunal has concluded that

> the fact that the slogan could be regarded as a promotional text should be considered a positive property of a trade mark rather than a negative one, since it serves not only to identify the origin of the goods or services to which it relates but also performs a marketing function in that it draws attention to them.[79]

5.75 This somewhat upbeat appraisal of the marketing function of slogans would suggest that it may be easier for slogans to overcome the twin barriers of descriptiveness and lack of distinctive character through use than for some other types of

---

[73] *ZDF v Karl-May-Verlag*, 5 December 2002 (Bundesgerichtshof).

[74] *Fieldturf Inc's application*, Case R 462/2001-1, 15 May 2002 (unreported) (OHIM): LOOKS LIKE GRASS . . . FEELS LIKE GRASS . . . PLAYS LIKE GRASS not registrable for a synthetic grass surface.

[75] *Visa International Service Association's application*, Case R 46/1999-1 [2000] ETMR 263 (OHIM): THE WORLD'S BEST WAY TO PAY AND BE PAID not registrable for financial services; *Master Foods Ltd's application* [2001] ETMR 667 (Irish Patent Office): TOP BREEDERS RECOMMEND IT held not registrable for pet food.

[76] *'Partner With The Best' trade mark application* [1998] ETMR 679 (Bundespatentgericht): PARTNER WITH THE BEST.

[77] *Roux Laboratories Inc v Clairol Inc* 427 F 2d 823 (CCPA 1970) (HAIR COLOR SO NATURAL ONLY HER HAIRDRESSER KNOWS FOR SURE).

[78] *BECOME WHAT YOU ARE trade mark*, [2003] ETMR 879 (Republic of Turkey Appellate Court, Eleventh Tribunal).

[79] *Clinique Laboratories Inc's application*, Case R 73/1998-2 [1999] ETMR 750 (OHIM): BEAUTY ISN'T ABOUT LOOKING YOUNG BUT LOOKING GOOD.

K. Technology standards

trade mark (for example, product shapes and colours). A more cautious approach was however taken by the CFI to the slogan REAL PEOPLE, REAL SOLUTIONS for telemarketing services:

> . . . there is nothing about the term . . . that might, beyond its obvious promotional meaning, enable the relevant public to memorise the sign easily and instantly as a distinctive sign for the services designated. Even if the sign were used alone, . . ., the relevant public could not, in the absence of prior knowledge, perceive it other than in its promotional sense.[80]

5.76 Taking these two decisions together, there is little middle ground between (i) slogans which are so promotional that they cannot be perceived as anything other than slogans—which are desirable but not registrable—and (ii) slogans which convey no promotional information at all—which may be registrable but, from the applicant's point of view, may not be desirable. To this end the registrability of slogans upon evidence of acquired distinctiveness provides the practical solution: use the slogan (with or without other trade marks) in a trade mark manner, teach the public to respond to it as such and then secure its registration.

5.77 Some slogans themselves include a trade mark. For example, for many years in the UK the KIT KAT chocolate bar has been marketed under the slogan 'Have a break—have a KIT KAT'. Because this slogan was so heavily used, it became heavily ingrained in the nation's consciousness. Nestlé then applied unsuccessfully to register the first half of the slogan (HAVE A BREAK) as a trade mark. The words 'have a break' were well known to the relevant public, but they were not inherently distinctive of Nestlé's products. More to the point, their notoriety was earned through their use in the whole slogan 'Have a break—have a KIT KAT', but there was nothing to show that HAVE A BREAK, when not followed by HAVE A KIT KAT, had acquired its own independent distinctiveness through use.[81]

K. Technology standards

5.78 An OHIM Board of Appeal has refused an application to register the words BROADBAND CODE DIVISION MULTIPLE ACCESS as a trade mark for telecommunications goods and services. According to the examiner, the mark was a 'standard denomination of a technology in the field of communications' and was thus descriptive of goods and services which were compliant with that technical standard. The Board agreed. The fact that the applicant had devised the technology standard did not make it distinctive; nor did the Board accept the applicant's

---

[80] *Sykes Enterprises Inc v OHIM*, Case T-130/01 [2003] IP&T 213, para 29.
[81] *Société des Produits Nestlé SA v Mars UK Ltd* [2003] FSR 684 (HC). The Court of Appeal has now referred this issue to the ECJ; see *Société des Produits Nestlé SA v Mars UK Ltd* [2003] EWCA Civ 1072, 25 July 2003 (unreported) (CA).

assertion that the mark was tautologous since 'broadband' had the same meaning as 'code division multiple access' and that, therefore, the use of two descriptive terms where one would suffice made the mark less descriptive.[82]

L. Product surfaces and shapes

(1) Designs applied to the outer surface of products

5.79 In theory there is no reason why a design which is applied to the outer surface of goods should not be registrable as a trade mark: such a design has the physical characteristics of a registrable sign and has the potential to distinguish the goods or services of competing traders. In practice it may be difficult to persuade the registering authority that the pattern will be viewed by relevant consumers as a trade mark rather than as an ornamental or functional feature. In *Glaverbel's application* OHIM took the view that an abstract design as applied to the surface of glass products would cause consumers to view those products as being made of frosted glass since the design (see Figure 5.3) would not be apparent to the onlooker. This conclusion was accepted by the CFI[83] but is now under appeal to the ECJ.

5.80 Spotted and speckled patterns applied to the outer surface of a product can in theory distinguish it: for example, pink polka dots could distinguish the goods of one luggage manufacturer from those of his competitors. They cannot at present distinguish detergent tablets for the purposes of CTM registration, since the CFI has ruled that speckled tablets are (i) one of the most obvious solutions where various ingredients are to be combined in a detergent product and (ii) a commonplace feature of detergent solids.[84]

Figure 5.3 An abstract design as applied to the surface of glass products.

---

[82] *Interdigital Communications Corporation's application*, Case R 50/98-3 [1999] ETMR 758.
[83] *Glaverbel v OHIM*, Case T-36/01 [2003] ETMR 425. The application was however remitted on account of procedural defects.
[84] *Unilever plc v OHIM*, Case T-194/01, 5 March 2003 (unreported).

L. Product surfaces and shapes

(2) Product shapes[85]

So far, much of this chapter has focused on problems arising from the registration of word marks and two-dimensional visual marks. Three-dimensional product shapes may now also be protected as trade marks, either through the registration of the product shape itself or through the registration of a two-dimensional trade mark which could be infringed by its unauthorized reproduction in three-dimensional form.

5.81

There is no doubt that consumers are capable of recognizing the distinctive character of a product's shape, to the extent that they may even be confused as to the origin of two identically shaped products which bear different word trade marks.[86] The ECJ has stated in the most clear and unequivocal terms that the authorities that examine signs and grant trade marks are obliged to treat all signs equally and that there is no stricter test of registrability for product shapes than there is for any other category of sign.[87] It remains the case, however, that applications to register shapes are less likely to succeed than are applications to register most other types of sign[88] and that such marks, once granted, are probably more vulnerable to applications for cancellation.[89] There are three principal reasons for this: (i) the courts and granting authorities are cautious in conferring a potentially perpetual monopoly on the shape of a product where other forms of intellectual property protection such as patent, utility model or design law, confer protection of a shorter duration; (ii) it has proved difficult to establish that product shapes as viewed by consumers, particularly when used in conjunction with other more obvious trade marks, immediately strike the eye[90] as serving a trade mark function rather than just being a characteristic of the product; and (iii) it is unclear whether, even if consumers are clearly struck by the appearance of all or part of a product

5.82

---

[85] For a comprehensive review of OHIM practice on shape marks, see Arnaud Folliard-Monguiral and David Rogers, 'The Protection of Shapes by the Community Trade Mark' [2003] EIPR 169–79.

[86] On this basis the Court of Campobasso, Italy, awarded interim relief against a supplier of engine parts which slavishly imitated the shape of Honda's parts: *Honda Italia Industriale SpA v Kama Italia Import and Export Srl* WTLR, 12 May 2003.

[87] *Linde AG, Winward Industries Inc and Rado Uhren AG*, 24 October 2002, Joined Cases C-53/01 to C-55/01, [2003] ETMR 963.

[88] A survey of trade mark applications filed in Australia between January 1999 and June 2000, conducted by the Advisory Council of Intellectual Property, showed that, while 62% of all applications were accepted for registration, only 10% of shape, sound, scent and other unusual types of sign were accepted; see Colin Oberin, 'Registering Shape Trade Marks', *Intellectual Property Bulletin* (Allens Arthur Robinson), December 2002, pp 9–12.

[89] See eg *Mega Bloks Inc v Lego System A/S*, Case HG000095/ZO7 (Zurich Commercial Court): trade mark registration for LEGO block cancelled for loss of distinctiveness; *Philips Electronics NV v Remington Consumer Products* [1999] ETMR 816 (CA).

[90] See eg *Bongrain SA's trade mark application*, 21 March 2003 (unreported) (HC), in which the court held that the examiner was entitled to regard cheese in the form of a six-lobed flower as not possessing that striking character; accordingly evidence of acquired distinctiveness was required.

shape and associate it with the trade mark applicant, they would take that shape to be a trade mark rather than simply part of the design of the product in question. In this third context, the ECJ has been asked to rule whether consumer identification of the applicant's sign with the applicant, in the context of the existence of a *de facto* monopoly in the use of a sign consisting of a product shape (in this case a transparent collection chamber for bagless vacuum cleaners), can establish distinctiveness even if the sign has not previously been promoted as a trade mark.[91]

5.83 It is now plain that, since applications to register product shapes are not to be treated differently to other signs, other absolute bars to registration which apply to signs in general will apply to product shapes too.[92] Thus, even independently of other grounds upon which product shapes are specifically barred from registration,[93] a product shape which consists exclusively of

> signs or indications which may serve, in trade, to designate the kind, quality, quantity, intended purpose, value, geographical origin, or the time of production of the goods . . . , or other characteristics of the goods . . .[94]

will not be registrable unless it has first acquired distinctive character. Thinking in concrete terms, this point may be largely academic for two reasons. First, how many product shapes consisting *exclusively* of such indications even exist? We are presumably talking here of products which have no aesthetic or functional characteristics other than those listed. Secondly, how many of these products which are *exclusively* comprised of such indications is anyone ever likely to try to register as a trade mark?

5.84 The relative paucity of successful product shape applications creates uncertainty further down the line: since so few product shapes are validly registered, the number of trade mark infringement cases which involve them is very small indeed and it is difficult therefore to gauge the way in which courts will respond to issues which concern them. For example, a majority in the Australian Federal Court has allowed the registration of a 'millennium bug' insect shape.[95] This shape, while suggestive of insects in general, was not the shape of any specific insect. One of the judges observed:

> Theoretically it may be the case that the number of possible symmetrical arrangements [of insect features] is not infinite. Assuming that to be so, it is speculative . . . to draw conclusions about that number and whether the particular arrangement

---

[91] *Dyson Ltd v Registrar of Trade Marks*, 15 May 2003 (HC).
[92] *Linde AG, Winward Industries Inc and Rado Uhren AG*, 24 October 2002, Joined Cases C-53/01 to C-55/01, [2003] ETMR 963.
[93] Council Directive 89/104, art 3(1)(e); Council Regulation 40/94, art 7(1)(e).
[94] Council Directive 89/104, art 3(1)(c); Council Regulation 40/94, art 7(1)(c).
[95] *Kenman Kandy Australia Pty Ltd v Registrar of Trade Marks* [2002] FCAFC 273, discussed in Julia Baird, 'This Mark is So Attractive: It Should be Free for All to Use! An Australian Perspective on Functional Shape Marks' (2003) 52 IP Forum 26–37.

L. Product surfaces and shapes

has any significant impact upon the access of other traders to the use of insect like shapes as trade marks.

5.85 This displays the degree of uncertainty which is inherent in such marks. If a trader registers a three-dimensional shape of a clearly identifiable insect, such as a bee, it will be relatively easy to determine whether the shapes utilized by other traders resemble bees. The registration of the shape of a non-existent insect may however confer a greater degree of protection upon the trade mark owner in that consumers who are not as familiar with it (and whose memories are taken to reflect the human failing of imperfect recollection) will be likely to confuse it with a larger range of other insect shapes.

(a) Product shapes cannot be registered if they result exclusively from the nature of the goods themselves

5.86 Word marks and figurative marks which are descriptive cannot be registered. Accordingly neither the word COCONUT nor a picture of a coconut can be registered for coconuts. There is no ground of refusal of a trade mark for product shapes which directly corresponds to descriptiveness in respect of word and picture marks, but the fact that a shape mark's shape results from the product itself is an analogous ground for rejecting a trade mark application in Europe.[96]

5.87 What is not clear is whether the word 'nature' is to be taken literally. For example, coconuts have a shape which is derived from nature, but ice-cream desserts do not. While all ice-cream desserts may be recognizable as such by discerning consumers, there is no one shape which they may assume. Accordingly, it seems reasonable to suppose that the shape of an ice-cream dessert does not result from its 'nature',[97] although Plato's theory of forms[98] suggests the notional existence of an idealized ice-cream dessert of which the products in the shops are but pale earthly reflections. Yet some non-natural products are, on the whole, of more uniform a shape than ice-cream desserts: pencils, scissors, shoelaces, saucers, for example. Are the shapes of ice-cream desserts (see Figure 5.4) determined by their 'nature' or by their 'function'? Given that their function may determine their nature, this distinction may be meaningless.

---

[96] Council Directive 89/104, art 3(1)(e); Council Regulation 40/94, art 7(1)(e)(i).

[97] A reference of this question to the ECJ for a preliminary ruling in *Société des Produits Nestlé SA v Unilever plc*, [2003] ETMR 681 (HC) has subsequently been withdrawn. In *Procter & Gamble Company's application*, Case R 74/1998-3 [1999] ETMR 776; Case T-122/99 [2000] ETMR 580 the CFI considered that the shape of a soap bar did not result from the nature of the goods if other soap bars existed which did not have the same shape.

[98] Almost no one reads Plato today. More accessible is the short chapter on Plato in Jostein Gaarder, *Sophie's World* (1991).

Chapter 5: Registrability of Specific Types of Trade Mark

Figure 5.4 Are the shapes of these ice-cream desserts determined by their 'nature' or by their 'function'?

5.88 There was once a notion that a product cannot be a trade mark for itself[99] and that a trade mark should therefore be something added to the product. This axiom is not directly borne out by the notion of a trade mark consisting of 'any sign capable of being represented graphically, particularly . . . the shape of goods or of their packaging . . .' which is part of the leitmotif of TRIPs and European trade mark registration. It may be asked whether that axiom still represents an accurate picture of current trade mark law. In answer it may be suggested that, while the axiom still makes sense, it is probably an extreme expression of the operation of the law in Europe today. When a product is a trade mark for itself, consumers will often see the shape of that product as an indication of what the product is, rather than of who makes it. Even so, it seems harsh and probably unrealistic to pronounce that the shape of a product will *never* be an indicator of source: that outcome is not an impossibility although it will be quite rare and will demand a high level of proof of distinctive character.

(b) Product shapes cannot be registered if they consist exclusively of the shape of goods which is necessary to obtain a technical result

5.89 This principle is often referred to as that of 'functionality': a shape cannot be registered if it is functional. The term 'functional' is not used in European legislation but has been employed both by national courts and the ECJ. The general issue of 'functionality' occurs most frequently in respect of trade marks consisting of two- and three-dimensional product shapes, but in a slightly different context governs word marks and ordinary figurative marks too. Thus expressions like TEAR HERE TO OPEN or STIR BEFORE DRINKING may not be registered either because they are not trade marks at all or because they are incapable of distinguishing goods. For the same reason, images such as the picture of a court card in a pack of cards are not registrable.[100]

5.90 The bit of a product which performs its function cannot be registered as a trade mark in Europe since, even if people may think it looks good, it is not there to in-

---

[99] *Füllkörper trade mark application* [1997] ETMR 431 (Bundespatentgericht).
[100] *Société France Cartes v Naipes Heraclio Fournier SA*, Case R 766/2000-2 [2002] ETMR 1119 (OHIM).

L. Product surfaces and shapes

dicate a connection with a trade mark owner but to do a job of work.[101] Thus the teeth of a comb, the engine of a car or the Philips three-headed configuration of an electric shaver are regarded as having an exclusively functional role.[102]

5.91 Strictly speaking, virtually no product shape is exclusively determined by its function, even if that shape is itself determined by the shape or function of another article. Thus, while an electric plug may have to be a particular shape in order to fit into a socket, it could still fit the socket even if it were given a different shape, since the bits of the plug that do not fit the socket could have arbitrarily chosen dimensions. Likewise, as a majority of the judges in the Stockholm District Court concluded when it was their turn to consider the registrability of the Philips shaver, the functional advantages conferred upon the shaver by its shape could have been conferred by different versions of the same shape.[103] On this view, no product shape would ever be exclusively and necessarily determined by its technical function and the exclusion of functional shapes from registrability would never occur.[104] This view has however been decisively rejected by the ECJ on the basis that a shape does not perform a technical function any less simply because it could have looked different while still achieving the same technical end.[105]

5.92 Does the coexistence of other intellectual property rights in a product shape mean that the product is inherently functional? Not necessarily, it seems, since the conferring of a technical result is judged by trade mark law's own legal criteria. In Denmark a baby's high chair in which patent rights had expired but copyright still subsisted was held to be entitled to trade mark protection by virtue of its highly distinctive visual qualities.[106] Trade mark protection was accorded to the chair even though its shape and form was precisely that which gave it its value since, according to the court, the criterion of 'exclusively' could not be proven: the makers of the chair made other chairs which conferred the same technical advantage but without using the distinctive shape which the defendant had copied.

5.93 The foregoing comments apply only to the functionality of shapes. Other functional features, such as colours, are not explicitly excluded by the functionality provisions of European trade mark law but have nonetheless been excluded in some other jurisdictions. For example, in the United States the colour black was not registrable for boat motors because it fulfilled the function of making the

---

[101] Council Directive 89/104, art 3(1)(e); Council Regulation 40/94, art 7(1)(e)(ii).
[102] *Koninklijke Philips Electronics NV v Remington Consumer Products Ltd*, Case C-299/99 [2002] ETMR 81 (ECJ).
[103] *Ide Line Aktiebolag v Philips Electronics NV* [1997] ETMR 377.
[104] *Amp Inc v Utilux Pty Ltd* [1972] RPC 103 (HL).
[105] *Koninklijke Philips Electronics NV v Remington Consumer Products Ltd*, Case C-299/99 [2002] ETMR 955, para 84.
[106] *Stokke Fabrikker and another v Playmaster of Sweden AB (Ltd) and another* [1998] ETMR 395 (Ljungby District Court). This trade mark is currently the subject of litigation in the Netherlands.

motor appear smaller and was compatible with different coloured boats.[107] This result might be achieved in Germany through the doctrine of *Freihaltebedürfnis*, which might be invoked in order to keep the colour black free for use by other boat makers. There is also the likelihood that the colour black would be regarded as non-distinctive in that consumers would simply regard black as the colour of the motor and would not imagine that it was intended to serve as a trade mark. In such a case the non-registrability of an admittedly functional feature would depend on the chance finding of non-distinctiveness rather than the principle that its functionality should deprive it of registrability.

(c) Product shapes cannot be registered if they exclusively give substantial value to the goods

5.94 Instances of a trade mark for a shape exclusively giving substantial value to goods without also achieving a technical result are relatively rare events. Accordingly while 'substantial value' is sometimes raised in opposition or cancellation proceedings, it is generally the mute younger sister of the more eloquently pleaded argument of 'functionality'.

(d) Regular product shapes

5.95 While product shapes are registrable as trade marks, they may not be registered if: (i) the shape is viewed as inherently part of the product and not as a sign used in relation to it (since it will not be regarded as distinctive);[108] (ii) the shape is not visible to the consumer at the point at which he considers making his purchase;[109] or (iii) the shape is regarded as conferring some functional advantage upon it.

5.96 The registrability of Procter & Gamble's simple 'bone' shape for a bar of soap (see Figure 5.5) has proved the fulcrum upon which the legal issues of registrability and unregistrability are keenly balanced. The soap bar has a shape which is not used by competitors and which is not governed by the nature of soap itself.[110] On the other hand its shape is not apparent at the point of sale (on account of its wrapping), its concave feature

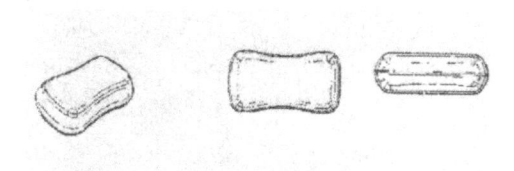

Figure 5.5 Procter & Gamble's simple 'bone' shape for a bar of soap.

---

[107] *Brunswick Corp v British Seagull Ltd*, 35 F 3d 1527, 1532 (CA Fed 1994).
[108] *Mag Instrument Inc v OHIM*, Case T-88/00 [2002] ETMR 665 (CFI): Maglite torch shapes regarded as being just part of the torch's design. This case is currently on appeal to the ECJ.
[109] *Procter & Gamble Company's application* [2000] ETMR 703 (Irish Patents Office).
[110] *Procter & Gamble Company v OHIM*, Case T-122/99 [2000] ETMR 580 (CFI).

L. Product surfaces and shapes

would not be instantly recognized as an indication of trade origin[111] and the 'bone' shape makes it easier for users to handle when the soap is wet.[112]

5.97 Trade mark registries have been relatively unsympathetic to applications of this nature. This may be seen both from the variety of grounds upon which they are rejected and from the tone of the rejections themselves. For example:

> the Coca-cola bottle, the Porsche Carrera, the Mini and the Rolls-Royce motor cars as products that can be identified by their shape alone are not helpful to the applicant's case ... [n]one of these products is sold in a wrapper ... and ... long after ... the product retains its original shape. The same does not hold for bars of soap sold in wrappers the shape of which is different to the shape of the bar of soap.[113]

5.98 But plain soap bars are not alone in facing difficulties in obtaining registration. Ornamental shapes have problems of their own. The fact that a product's shape is ornamental does not preclude it from being considered distinctive, whether the ornament covers the entire product[114] or is merely part of it.[115] If, however, the ornamental nature of the product is the function which it is intended to perform, its ornamental nature will not save it from unregistrability. This is what happened to a trade mark for the triangulated shape of chocolate shavings (see Figure 5.6): since they were intended to be sprinkled on to cakes in order to enhance their appearance, their ornament was their function and they had been improperly registered.[116]

Figure 5.6 A trade mark for the triangulated shape of chocolate shavings.

(e) Registration of a shape which marks the absence of a product

5.99 The Danish Dairy Board sought to invalidate a CTM for a doughnut-shaped cheese with a hole in the middle on the basis that, since other cheese products had holes in the middle, the mark lacked distinctive character. The OHIM Cancellation Division disagreed. In considering a mark's distinctive properties it is necessary to consider the mark as it appears on the goods themselves. In this instance, although the concept of the hole might be shared among many cheeses, each type of cheese will look different notwithstanding the presence of an identical

---

[111] *Procter & Gamble Company v OHIM*, Case T-63/01, 12 December 2002 (unreported) (CFI).
[112] *Procter & Gamble Company's application*, Case R 74/1998-3 [1999] ETMR 776 (OHIM).
[113] *Procter & Gamble Company's application* [2000] ETMR 703, 708–9 (Patents Office, Dublin).
[114] *Warman International Ltd's application*, Case R 82 /1999 [2000] ETMR 1159 (OHIM): shell-shaped ribbing on outer casing of pumps.
[115] *Valigeria Roncato SpA's application*, Case R 164/1998-1 [2000] ETMR 46 (OHIM): three-dimensional ornamental bulge on handbags.
[116] *Luijckx BV v ECC* [2000] ETMR 530 (Court of Appeal of 's Hertogenbosch, the Netherlands).

hole.[117] The Cancellation Division also added that the concept of the hole cannot itself be registered as a trade mark since it will always be part of a product, the shape of which also shows other features.

(f) Bottles, packaging and containers

5.100 Bottles, packaging and containers are now registrable subject matter. This does not mean that all bottles, packaging and containers can actually be registered. Only those which satisfy the same criteria of registrability as other types of trade marks will be registered.

5.101 An OHIM Board of Appeal refused an application to register 'the vacuum packing of an article of clothing in an envelope of plastic' for clothing because those words did not constitute a graphic representation of the applicant's trade mark. Said the Board:

> [I]t was considered essential that applicants present a clearly defined image of their mark . . . A mere description, not conveying the clear and precise appearance of the mark itself, cannot be considered to be a reproduction.[118]

5.102 Different vacuum-packed products look quite different from each other, it is true, and no doubt even a humble pairs of socks can be vacuum-packed in many stylistically different ways. However, the considerations that vacuum-packing (i) does not improve the quality of the socks and that (ii) it has not hitherto been considered by others as either a necessary or indeed a desirable procedure both lead to the conclusion that vacuum-packing as such is not inherently unregistrable. The need to delimit the concept of vacuum-packing by fixing its physical dimensions is reflected in the need which the Advocate General has advised the ECJ to recognize by delimiting the scope of colour trade marks.[119]

5.103 Although the dangers of 'limping trade marks' will be emphasized later in this chapter, the fact that a bottle is used in conjunction with other trade marks need not undermine its distinctive character. Possibly on account of the popularity of their contents, many bottles have indeed acquired a remarkably high degree of distinctiveness in their own right: examples include the curvaceous Coca-Cola bottle, the Yakult bottle[120] and the Dimple whisky bottle. One German court has observed that the widespread practice of employing peculiar bottle shapes reflects two assumptions: (i) that consumers do indeed pay attention to such shapes and (ii) that consumers' attention relates to the function of the bottle shape as an in-

---

[117] *Josef Rupp Gesellschaft mbH's Trade Mark; application for a declaration of invalidity by the Danish Dairy Board* [2002] ETMR 395.
[118] *Antoni and Alison's application*, Case R 4/97-2 [1998] ETMR 460, 463.
[119] *Libertel Groep BV v Benelux-Merkenbureau*, Case C-104/01 [2003] ETMR 508.
[120] On which see *Kabushiki Kaisha Yakult Honsha and others v Danone Nederland BV and others* [1998] ETMR 465 (District Court, The Hague).

L. Product surfaces and shapes

dication of origin.[121] This may be rather overstating the case, though. Consumers may view the bottle shape either as an indication of origin or as an attractive design (the latter being the case among those people who buy attractive bottles so that, once the contents are consumed, they can use them as candle-holders or lamp-stands).

5.104 No recognizable common standard has yet been set for the determination of the absolute quality of distinctiveness of a container shape. As with other types of mark there are three types of container: those which are entirely devoid of distinctive character, those which are inherently distinctive and those which hover between the two, *capable* of distinguishing goods but *incapable* of securing registration in the absence of evidence of actual distinctiveness acquired through use. The problem only lies in deciding which container fits into which category. OHIM has rejected two marks consisting of an accurate if 'marginally stylised' two-dimensional picture of a regular oil can (see Figure 5.7); the Board of Appeal described the graphic elements of the marks as 'utilitarian'.[122] A substantially less descriptive and more arbitrary bottle shape was rejected by the UK Trade Mark Registry (see Figure 5.8),[123] while a bottle of basic and unadorned simplicity was regarded in Portugal as being inherently distinctive (see Figure 5.9).[124]

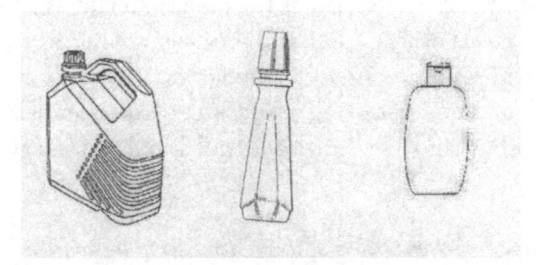

Figures 5.7–5.9 No recognizable common standard has yet been set for the determination of the absolute quality of distinctiveness of a container shape.

(g) Features of products which have shape but are not shapes

5.105 An application to register as a CTM a 'transparent bin forming part of a vacuum cleaner', without illustrating the shape of the bin, was refused. The applicant argued that the mark was not a word mark, a figurative mark or a three-dimensional mark but instead a 'feature' mark, referring to a quality of one of the features of the

---

[121] *Likoerflasche trade mark* [2002] ETMR 456 (Bundesgerichtshof).
[122] *British Petroleum Company plc's application*, Cases R 55/1998-2 and R 60/1998-2 [1999] ETMR 282, 286.
[123] *Fresh Breath Co Ltd's application* [2000] ETMR 644.
[124] *Jansen Pharmaceutica NV v Patent and Trade Marks Office* [2001] ETMR 663 (Civil Court of Lisbon).

product for which registration was sought.¹²⁵ As has been mentioned in the context of the registrability of packaging and containers, a similar conclusion was reached in an application to register as a CTM 'the vacuum packing of an article of clothing in an envelope of plastic'.¹²⁶ In each case the trade mark register would not give sufficient guidance to competitors as to what their own products were allowed to look like, even though many people would think that competitors would have little difficulty in understanding what it was that the respective applicants were trying to register.

(h) Shapes incorporating variable text

5.106 An applicant sought to register, for confectionery products, a mark consisting of 'a circular compressed tablet bearing a raised heart outline on both flat surfaces and containing within the heart outline on one side any one of several different words or phrases'. The application was refused on the basis that it appeared to presuppose knowledge on the part of traders of a confectionery product, marketed under the word trade mark LOVE HEARTS, which had been sold by the applicant for many years. Anyone who knew the product could instantly visualize it from the trade mark application, but those who were unfamiliar with it would not know what the mark consisted of and would therefore not know what it was they could not copy.¹²⁷ Matters such as the tablet's thickness and diameter, the positioning of the raised heart outline and the extent of the area available for additional text were not spelled out with sufficient clarity. However, the fact that the variable text content—consisting of succinctly expressed sentiments such as 'I love you', 'Lover boy' and 'Get lost'—was not stipulated as a ground for refusing registration.

(i) Two-dimensional representations of three-dimensional products

5.107 If an application to register a three-dimensional shape as a trade mark is likely to fail on the ground that the shape is functional or determined by the nature of the goods for which it is registered, the applicant may have better fortune if he applies to register a two-dimensional mark which is a non-literal representation of the shape of the product. This was formerly done by companies such as Cola-Cola in jurisdictions in which bottles and containers were not registrable. Even today on Coca-Cola cans on sale in the UK one sometimes sees a small-scale reproduction of the Coca-Cola bottle. This is not a gratuitous illustration which forms part of the can's artwork but a trade mark in the course of active service on behalf of its owner.

---

¹²⁵ *Notetry Limited's Application,* Case R 78/1998-1 [1999] ETMR 435 (OHIM): examiner's decision annulled on procedural grounds.
¹²⁶ *Antoni and Alison's application,* Case R 4/97-2 [1998] ETMR 460 (OHIM).
¹²⁷ *Swizzels Matlow Ltd's application* [2000] ETMR 58 (LCAP).

L. Product surfaces and shapes

5.108 Unlike a product shape, a graphic two-dimensional version of a three-dimensional product may be depicted in different ways. Accordingly, any sufficiently original depiction of that product will be regarded as inherently registrable.[128] In contrast, a fairly close depiction of the product which looks just like the product being sold under it may not however be registrable: customers looking at it would think it was just a picture of the product and not realize that it was supposed to be a trade mark at all.[129]

(3) Product shapes and 'limping' marks

5.109 The biggest problem raised by product shape trade marks is that of 'limping' trade marks, those which are used only in conjunction with other trade marks (generally word marks) which race ahead of the shape mark in terms of consumer recognition. In the High Court decision in the UK in the *Philips* shaver case, the judge had this to say:

> The . . . trade mark has never been used by Philips as the sole means of identification of trade source. It has never been trusted by Philips to do this job on its own, matter plainly relevant in considering acquired distinctiveness. It is at best a 'limping trade mark', needing the crutch of PHILISHAVE in use.[130]

5.110 The Court of Appeal preferred the word 'supporting' to 'limping',[131] although the Brussels Cour de Cassation has also described marks as 'limping' in the wider sense of any marks which are devoid of any distinctive character or are exclusively descriptive.[132]

5.111 There is a large difference between a supporting mark and a limping mark, since a limping mark supports nothing. The CFI has stated that this sort of sign might not even be recognized as a trade mark. In *Viking* it said:

> The applicant acknowledged that a product's commercial origin is ultimately identified on the basis of other distinguishing features, such as a word mark. This being so, consumers would not therefore see the juxtaposition of green and grey as a sign indicating that the goods came from the same undertaking but would see it merely as an aspect of the finish of the goods in question.[133]

---

[128] *Absperrpoller trade mark application* [1997] ETMR 176 (where the German Bundespatentgericht allowed the registration of a picture of a traffic bollard in respect of goods which included traffic bollards).
[129] *Car Wheel Rim trade mark application* [1998] ETMR 584 (Bundespatentgericht, Germany).
[130] *Philips Electronics NV v Remington Consumer Products* [1998] ETMR 124, 130 (Jacob J).
[131] *Philips Electronics NV v Remington Consumer Products* [1999] ETMR 816, 825 (Aldous LJ).
[132] *Lipton Ltd, Van Den Berg & Jurgens BV, Unilever Belgium and Unilever NV v Sara Lee/De NV and Douwe Egberts* [2002] ETMR 1073, 1077.
[133] *Viking-Umwelttechnik GmbH v OHIM*, Case T-316/00 [2003] ETMR 196, [2003] IP&T 25, para 6.

Chapter 5: Registrability of Specific Types of Trade Mark

5.112 BABY-DRY is an example of a supporting mark: in the accompanying illustration the words BABY-DRY appear on packages of PAMPERS disposable nappies, but in very much a subsidiary role (see Figure 5.10).

5.113 A trade mark owner who uses a subsidiary mark and does not want it to limp must avoid giving the impression that such a mark is used solely for the purpose of distinguishing its own products from one another, rather than distinguishing the owner's products from those of third parties. Some of the BABY-DRY packaging could be said to have created such an impression, although more recent marketing exercises are seeking to remove it.

Figure 5.10 An example of a supporting mark.

5.114 The use of a trade mark in a subsidiary role does not affect its inherent registrability: so long as a trade mark is able to distinguish its owner's goods or services from those of its competitors, it will be registrable even if it is actually used only to distinguish goods of the same manufacturer from one another. The question may still however be raised (as it was in *Philips*) as to whether such use is sufficient to resist a subsequent application to revoke a mark on the basis that it has not been used as a trade mark for the requisite period. This question is considered further in Chapter 13.

5.115 Not all countries tolerate the 'limping' mark. The practice in Iran, for example, is to allow the registrability of a three-dimensional mark only where a word mark or label is attached to it in the registration.[134] German practice is less extreme: it assumes that, since bottles (for example) are containers for their contents, the relevant consumers of those contents would view bottles primarily as containers unless it can be shown that they will also view them as having a descriptive function.[135] OHIM practice is to ask whether the consumer, seeing 'the bare shape of the applicant's packaging . . . would recognise it and associate it with a specific commercial source'.[136] Both the German and OHIM approaches leave open the possibility of registration but leave the burden with the applicant of proving the consumer's view.

5.116 From a marketing point of view, most modern product packaging or trade dress involves an often subtle mixture of origin indicators, with the result that few prod-

---

[134] *High Lights* (newsletter of the Law Offices of Dr Ali Laghaee & Associates Inc), vol 3, January 2003, p 1.
[135] *Likoerflasche trade mark* [2002] ETMR 456 (Bundesgerichtshof).
[136] *Cabot Safety Intermediate Corporation's application*, Case R 381/2000-1 [2001] ETMR 949 (OHIM).

ucts present the consumer with just a single trade mark. Does this mean that all actual or potentially registrable trade marks employed in the marketing of a single product or service are to some degree 'limping' in the sense that they are supported by one another? Probably not. Marketing practice invariably seeks to send the consumer a clear and unambiguous message and that is best done by a single word, logo, colour or other image. The lead trade mark catches the consumer's attention and satisfies him that he is making the purchase of his choice: the other trade marks are either part of the visual furniture of the packaging or trade dress or are being used in order to fend off the risk of revocation for non-use. A good example of this may be found in the case of a regular COCA-COLA can. Sometimes as many as four or five verbal or visual formulae which are depicted on the can will be identifiable as registered trade marks—but their trade mark function may not be realized by anyone who does not pick the can up and scrutinize it closely before purchase, a relatively abnormal pre-purchase consumer response for products of that nature.

M. Non-traditional trade marks

(1) Olfactory marks

5.117 A difficult and contentious issue raised by olfactory signs is that of whether they are even capable of graphic representation. An OHIM Board of Appeal[137] has considered that the words 'the smell of fresh cut grass' were an adequate graphic representation of that smell, a view which has subsequently been endorsed by another Board which found equally acceptable the verbal formula 'the scent of raspberries'.[138] In each case the Board considered that, since the smell was a well-known one with which anyone perusing the trade mark register would be familiar, further graphic representation would be unnecessary. A contrary—and authoritative—position was taken by the ECJ in *Sieckmann*.[139] Starting from a premiss shared by the OHIM Boards that 'a trade mark may consist of a sign which is not in itself capable of being perceived visually', for example, a smell, 'provided that . . . the representation is clear, precise, self-contained, easily accessible, intelligible, durable and objective', the Court concluded that neither the words 'balsamically fruity with a slight hint of cinnamon' nor the formula $C_6H_5-CH = CHCOOCH_3$ conformed to those criteria; the deposit of a sample in a container most certainly did not.

---

[137] *Vennootschap onder Firma Senta Aromatic Marketing's Application*, Case R 156/1998-2 [1999] ETMR 429.
[138] *Myles Ltd's application*, Case R 711/1999-3, [2003] ETMR 718 (OHIM).
[139] *Sieckmann v Deutsches Patent- und Markenamt*, Case C-273/00 [2003] ETMR 466.

5.118 For the avoidance of doubt it should be emphasized that, when the ECJ stated in *Sieckmann* that

> a trade mark may consist of a sign which is not in itself capable of being perceived visually, provided that . . . the representation is clear, precise, self-contained, easily accessible, intelligible, durable and objective[140]

it should not be thought that the same conditions do not equally apply in respect also of signs which *are* capable of being perceived visually, including colours, shapes, sounds, motions and gestures.

5.119 Smell marks, even if they are capable of being 'graphically represented', may never be usefully distinctive of the products to which they are applied. Their peculiar characteristics will pose fresh problems for the lawyer, consumer and market strategist alike. The OHIM Third Board of Appeal has stated that

> perception by the relevant trade circles is not the same with an olfactory mark as with a word mark. Even the novel forms of trade mark, such as colour marks, acoustic marks, taste marks or tactile marks, must have a functionally independent and autonomous character relative to the goods. Signs cannot be trade marks unless they spread out in space and can be perceived independently of the article of which they represent a property. This relationship between the goods and the trade mark should be stable and durable over time, so that the decision to purchase is always made regarding a trade mark which maintains the same state.[141]

5.120 If this statement is correct, it would appear that not only olfactory signs but also product shapes—particularly for products which lose their shape such as bars of soap—may not be regarded as registrable trade marks.

5.121 If anyone is in doubt as to whether real problems exist in employing olfactory signs as trade marks, let them consider the following situations in which tennis balls impregnated with the trade mark-protected smell of grass are on sale in a sports shop:

(i) the smell fills the entire shop, so customers cannot detect the tennis balls as being the source of the fresh grass smell;
(ii) the smell does not fill the entire shop, but does appear to emanate from the tennis-ball section: the consumer then depends on some visual or other cue (in other words a non-smell mark) in order to pick up one of a range of competing tennis balls which he thinks might be emitting the smell;
(iii) the smell is entirely obliterated by the smell of adjacent tennis balls, which have been impregnated by the odour of fried bacon. Could this be a form of unfair competition?
(iv) the balls are from last year's stock and the smell is no longer fresh: can the

---

[140] ibid, 476.
[141] *Myles Ltd's application*, Case R 711/1999-3 [2003] ETMR 718.

M. Non-traditional trade marks

trade mark owner object to their resale on the basis that the condition of the goods has changed? Or is it merely the condition of the trade mark which has changed?

(v) a supplier of seed for lawn tennis courts wishes to impregnate his seed bags with the allegedly descriptive smell of freshly cut grass. Would such an act infringe the olfactory mark as registered for tennis balls?

(vi) a competitor seeks to impregnate tennis balls with the scent of fresh pine. Would this be likely to cause confusion with the smell of fresh-cut grass?

5.122 In each of these situations it will be hard to capitalize on our current understanding as a means of determining how the law is likely to apply. In other situations our existing knowledge of the system will presumably be applicable by analogy. For example, the fact that many people may have an insufficiently delicate sense of smell to be able to identify fresh-cut grass as a trade mark for tennis balls is not a problem: there are many blind, partially sighted or illiterate consumers who cannot discern the word SCHWEPPES on the label of the tonic water bottle, but that word remains a trade mark nonetheless.

(2) Colours[142]

5.123 It was formerly accepted in Europe that a colour was capable of distinguishing the goods or services of one trader from those of another,[143] so long as its graphic representation consisted of a sample or illustration of the colour and not merely of a verbal description of it: the words 'orange'[144] and 'claimed colour green'[145] are not a graphic representation of any shade of the respective colours orange or green. However, the form in which a trade mark is graphically represented must be 'durable', but the deposit of a colour sample would be inadequate for that purpose if it were printed in ink which might fade.[146] The ECJ has now ruled that an applicant may designate a colour through the use of an internationally recognized colour code.[147]

---

[142] Charlotte Schulze, 'Registering Colour Trade Marks in the European Union' [2003] EIPR 55, 65, writes that 'The use of a variety of terms . . . ("abstract colour mark", "colour as such", "colour without contours", "colour *per se*" etc) both in the literature and in European case law clearly demonstrates the lack of a common concept for this type of mark'. This may be overstating the case in that the use of a variety of terms may indicate nothing more sinister than a richness of vocabulary with which to express our thoughts. My own choice of terminology is not intended to possess any deep conceptual significance.

[143] For a thorough discussion of issues raised by European colour marks, as well as problems resulting from other uncommon signs, see Stefano Sandri and Sergio Rizzo, *I Nuovi Marchi: forme, colori, odori, suoni e altro* (2002). See also the survey of legal writing, particularly from Germany, reviewed in Schulze (n 142 above) and Maria Cristina Caldarola, 'Questions Relating to Abstract Colour Trade Marks: Recent Developments in Germany' [2003] EIPR 248.

[144] *Orange Personal Communications Services Ltd's application* [1998] ETMR 337 (OHIM).

[145] *Aquatherm GmbH v Wavin SpA* [2002] EIPR N-33 (Court of Rovigo, Italy).

[146] ibid, para 32.

[147] ibid, para 68.

5.124 Colour marks suffer from hardships which are not faced by the more usual verbal and visual marks:

> While the public is used to seeing word or figurative marks as instantly identifying the commercial origin of the goods, the same is not necessarily true where the sign forms part of the look of the goods in respect of which registration of the sign is sought.[148]

5.125 Accordingly it is safer to rely upon the distinctiveness which a colour has acquired as a trade mark, because consumers have been taught to look for it and view it as a trade mark, than to file an application in the hope that the examiner will share one's sometimes optimistic view as to the distinctive quality of colours applied to goods. For the same reason the universal practice in the United States is to demand evidence that a colour has acquired secondary meaning as a trade mark before permitting it to be registered.[149] Although an OHIM Board of Appeal criticized an examiner for effectively reversing the burden of proof of distinctiveness in the case of an application to register a colour by challenging its distinctiveness simply *because* it was a colour,[150] the ECJ has since confirmed that a colour will almost never inherently be distinctive of the goods and services for which registration is sought:

> In the case of a colour *per se*, distinctiveness without any prior use is inconceivable save in exceptional circumstances, and particularly where the number of goods or services for which the mark is claimed is very restricted and the relevant market very specific.[151]

5.126 To satisfy the criterion of distinctiveness a colour should ideally be arbitrary and make no direct or indirect reference to the goods for which registration is sought. In one application to register a CTM, an application made by a manufacturer of chewing gum to register a particular shade of green was rejected by the Board of Appeal on the bases that (i) the colour would be needed by other makers of chewing gum whose flavour was the same colour (mint and, presumably, apple and lime) and that (ii) green also had ecological overtones.[152] Similar types of objections have been raised to colours by the CFI in cases involving three-dimensional

---

[148] *Viking-Umwelttechnik GmbH v OHIM*, Case T-316/00 [2003] ETMR 196, [2003] IP&T 25.
[149] *Qualitex Co v Jacobson Products Co* 514 US 159 (US Supreme Court 1995), discussed in Kevin M Jordan and Lynn M Jordan, '*Qualitex Co. v Jacobson Products Co.*, the Unanswered Question—Can Color Ever be Inherently Distinctive?' (1995) 85 TMR 371–98. Evidence of acquired distinctiveness in the United States will not however assist an application filed in Europe, even where the mark is registered in the United States and the *telle-quelle* rule is invoked; *Re Pink Fibreglass* [2002] EIPR N-39 (Court of Patent Appeals, Sweden).
[150] *National Car Rental Systems Inc's application*, Case R 194/2000-3, OHIM OJ 1/2003, 67 (application to register a dark green colour for car rental services in Class 39).
[151] *Libertel Groep BV v Benelux-Merkenbureau*, Case C-104/01, [2003] ETMR 807 (ECJ), para 66.
[152] *Wm Wrigley Jr Company's Application* [1999] ETMR 214 (OHIM).

M. Non-traditional trade marks

bicoloured detergent cubes.[153] The registration of colours as trade marks for services would appear to be less fraught with problems of this nature. This is because colours often allude to the nature or qualities of goods, but services—being devoid of colour—are rarely associated with specific colours and there is less need to leave colours available for other service suppliers to use.[154]

(a) Single colours for goods and services

5.127 Should a single colour be registrable in its own right or, in the absence of evidence of distinctiveness acquired through use, should it be necessary for it to be limited by some shape or other boundary which signifies that it is intended to be a trade mark and not just the mere colour of the product on which it appears? It was first thought by the Benelux Court[155] that any colour which is sufficiently arbitrary—in this case, turquoise for telecoms equipment—could serve as a trade mark. But, after that same court came to the contrary conclusion in *Libertel*,[156] the matter was referred to the ECJ for a ruling. In *Libertel* the Advocate General[157] advised the court to rule that a graphic representation of a trade mark was not in itself sufficient to merit registration: the application must be clear and precise as to the object of the mark; it should also be intelligible to competitors and consumers. For that reason, he submitted, a colour on its own without any form or shape should not be registered as a trade mark. The ECJ did not consider that colours had to be limited in terms of form or shape.[158]

5.128 Even if the Advocate General's Opinion in *Libertel* had been adopted with the result that colour registrations would be limited to specific shapes or forms, it is unclear whether that ruling would have been applicable on the facts considered by the Northern Ireland Court of Appeal where the trade mark before it, a particular shade of green which was registered in respect of petrol station services, had been illustrated in the trade mark application by the submission of a picture of a petrol station decorated in the applicant's green livery. The court ruled that the registration was not confined only to the dimensions of the specific design of the service station illustrated in the application, but would cover all petrol stations.[159] Since petrol stations are quite unalike in their shape, form and style (not least to comply with local planning restrictions or environmental and health regulations), it

---

[153] *Procter & Gamble Company v OHIM*, Case T-117/00 [2002] ETMR 174; *Henkel KGaA v OHIM*, Case T-30/00 [2002] ETMR 278.
[154] *KWS Saat AG v OHIM*, Case T-173/00 [2003] ETMR 288 (CFI).
[155] *Belgacom v Benelux Trade Mark Office* [2000] ETMR 286.
[156] See E Derclaye, 'ECJ to Decide "War of Colours" Between Belgian, Dutch Supreme Courts' [2001] 15 WIPR 11.
[157] *Libertel Groep BV v Benelux-Merkenbureau*, Case C-104/01 [2003] ETMR 508.
[158] *Libertel Groep BV v Benelux-Merkenbureau*, Case C-104/01, [2003] ETMR 807 (ECJ).
[159] *BP Amoco plc v John Kelly Ltd* [2001] ETMR 1021.

5.129 The cautious response of European law to the 'threat' of colour registrations may be contrasted unfavourably with the boldly decisive approach taken in Australia. On an application to register the arbitrary colour terracotta as a trade mark for non-metallic rigid irrigation pipe fittings, the Federal Court ruled the mark immediately registrable because it fulfilled what it viewed as the four key criteria of inherent registrability: (i) the colour was not descriptive; (ii) it was not functional; (iii) it was not the result of a normal manufacturing process; and (v) it was not used in an industry where colour was an important element of competition.[160] Even this approach is not a panacea for all arbitrary colour trade mark ailments. Although it provides a cure for lack of distinctive quality, it still leaves open the issue whether the relevant public would regard a colour as even being a trade mark. In practical terms, this is not a problem in Australia: either the trade mark is validly registered and used, in which case the public will soon learn to recognize its trade mark function, or the mark is not used in which case it is open to revocation. The fifth criterion enumerated above however has the potential to be highly limitative of the scope of the court's ruling: this is because, from the moment one competitor makes an issue of colour by registering one as a trade mark, it has surely become an important element of competition and would thus appear to preclude further colour registrations in that field of economic activity.

(b) Single colours applied to only part of the goods

5.130 The colour red as applied to the tips of fresh bananas has been registered as a trade mark in Australia.[161] Although the Australian registry has accepted that a single colour, as applied to goods, will have a low degree of capacity to distinguish goods, the applicant's mark appears to put itself forward as a strong case for registrability. Red is a strikingly unusual colour for yellow bananas; that colour is not needed by banana traders for any purpose and the technique of applying colours to the tips of bananas is itself novel.

(c) Colour combinations

5.131 Sometimes an applicant wants to register not a single colour but a combination of colours. In such an instance is it essential to indicate in the trade mark application not merely the colours but also their relative proportion to each other and the manner in which the applicant intends to use them? If this were not necessary, an applicant who registered silver and yellow in respect of vacuum cleaners might make yellow machines with silver trimmings or silver machines with yellow trim-

---

[160] *Philmac Pty Ltd v Registrar of Trade Marks* [2002] FCA 155.
[161] *Fada Pty Ltd (t/a Pacific Coast Eco-Bananas)'s application* WTLR, 19 May 2003.

M. Non-traditional trade marks

mings and, through a single registration, gain a monopoly to protect him against the use by competitors of either yellow or silver products.[162] The argument that an application should succeed even if the applicant has not determined the proportion of colours in relation to the specific products for which registration of the colour combination is sought has been accepted in principle by the German Bundesgerichtshof,[163] which observed that there were other grounds upon which such an application could be rejected, such as lack of distinctive character. Indeed, an application to register green and grey for gardening equipment has been firmly rejected by the CFI[164] on just these grounds: the fact that the application did not specify how the grey and green were to be used would result in consumers not noticing or recognizing that the 'sign' was an alleged trade mark.

(d) Coloured versions of non-distinctive product shapes

5.132 Subject to the comments made above concerning the registrability of colours, an otherwise unregistrable product shape will obtain a degree of trade mark protection if it is given one or more colours which can be registered in relation to that shape. In theory a trade mark can consist of the entire outer surface of a product to which it is applied. In practice, though, a consumer who looks at such a trade mark may not appreciate its trade mark quality. For example, if Perkins, a manufacturer of umbrellas, decides that all his umbrellas will have pink handles, his intention might well be to use the pinkness of a handle as a trade mark. Indeed, other umbrella makers may avoid use of that shade of pink altogether. If consumers say, 'Oh look, there's a Perkins umbrella; I know it's a Perkins umbrella because it has a pink handle', then the coloured product shape is clearly serving a trade mark function. If however consumers say 'Oh look, there's an umbrella with a pink handle', then Perkins and his team of marketers have a teaching job on their hands. Teaching the public to associate pink handles with Perkins' products is the real-world version of the oft-quoted phrase 'acquiring distinctiveness through use'. The importance of teaching the relevant consuming public cannot be overstated. In an application to cancel the registration of a trade mark consisting of a maroon-coloured inhaler, the hearing officer observed: 'there is nothing in the promotional material like an exhortation to "look for the one with the maroon tube" '.[165]

5.133 An example of the courts' lack of sympathy for coloured versions of non-distinctive product shapes may be found in the CFI's dismissal of an appeal against an

---

[162] *Notetry Ltd's application*, UK Trade Mark Registry transcript O/258/97, 29 December 1997 (unreported).
[163] *Yellow/Black* [1999] ETMR 677, *Yellow/Green* [2002] WRP 450.
[164] *Viking-Umwelttechnik GmbH v OHIM*, Case T-316/00 [2003] ETMR 196; [2003] IP&T 25.
[165] *Glaxo Group Ltd's trade mark; Riker Laboratories Inc's application for a declaration of invalidity* [2001] ETMR 96, para 42 (UK Trade Mark Registry).

OHIM Board of Appeal's refusal to register 'a square tablet with slightly rounded edges and corners, comprising two layers, the colours of which, white and pale green, are also claimed for registration' (in other words a bicoloured detergent tablet).[166] Correctly pointing out that consumers will view the detergent tablets as detergent tablets and not as trade marks for detergent tablets, the court added that the use of basic colours is commonplace for such products; that being so, distinctiveness of the entire mark cannot be established by pointing to the distinctiveness of, for example, the green part of the colour scheme alone.

(3) Sound marks

5.134   As with scent marks, sound marks provide problems relating both to whether they are capable of being 'graphically represented' and whether, if they can be, what the proper measure of their graphic representation should be. Where the sound mark consists of a tune, there is at least a choice as to the means by which that tune be identified. One may enter in the trade mark register: (i) a description of the tune's title (for example, 'Für Elise'); (ii) an account of the tune in sol-fa notation (E, D#, E, D#, E, D#, E, B, D, C, A); or (iii) a piece of music manuscript paper upon which the appropriate crochets, quavers and minims are recorded. As was pointed out by the Hague Court of Appeal,[167] none of these techniques actually records the sound made by the music. Following an appeal this case was referred to the ECJ for a preliminary ruling.[168] The Advocate General[169] has advised the ECJ to rule that registrable sound marks must be 'capable of being represented graphically in a clear, accurate, complete as such, easily accessible, comprehensive, durable and objective manner' and that the best way to achieve this was generally through the recording of the sound in a musical stave. This recommendation, if accepted, would allow for the registrability of tunes such as 'Für Elise'.

5.135   Some trade mark registries are reputedly content to accept sound recordings of, for example, tunes played by ice-cream chimes.[170] These recordings may admirably serve the function of being examinable by rival ice-cream vendors, but as the law stands they cannot be said to be 'graphically represented' in the sense that they are not written down and are not therefore strictly speaking 'graphic'. Sound recordings may well remain unregistrable in many jurisdictions until the margins of the law are adjusted in accordance with modern technology and common sense.

5.136   Sounds of a non-musical variety such as 'kukelekuuuuu',[171] dogs barking, ducks

---

[166] *Procter & Gamble Company v OHIM*, Case T-117/00 [2002] ETMR 174.
[167] *Shield Mark BV v Kist, trading as Memex* [2000] ETMR 147.
[168] *Shield Mark BV v Kist, trading as Memex* [2002] ETMR 2002 (Hoge Raad).
[169] *Shield Mark BV v Kist, trading as Memex*, Case C-283/01, [2003] ETMR 822 (AG).
[170] This is apparently the case in Sweden.
[171] 'Kukelekuuuuu' is the Dutch for 'cock-a-doodle-doo': the registrability of this sound was also considered in *Shield Mark BV v Kist, trading as Memex* (nn 167–9 above).

quacking, motor bikes roaring[172] or the squeak being made by the movement of a finger across the surface of a squeaky-clean plate, cannot be recorded in terms of musical notation at all. One might consider the approach adopted by OHIM to olfactory marks, allowing the registration of the smell of fresh-cut grass on the basis that everyone knows what that smell is like: but could that same approach be applied to sound marks? Probably not. Smells may vary in their intensity (one can contrast a faint smell with a strong one), but sounds are measured by four things—their duration, pitch, tone and volume. Words like 'the sound of church bells ringing', 'the sound of rain rattling on a metal roof' or 'the noise made by scraping a fingernail across the surface of a microphone' may well describe sounds with which we are familiar, but those words would be inadequate to enable the listener to identify an applicant's sound mark within the range of variables that his verbal parameters encompass. At the very least, therefore, verbal descriptions of even well-known sounds would need to be a lot more detailed and complex than verbal descriptions of well-known smells.

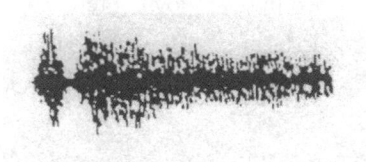

5.137

Non-musical sounds can be recorded, for example, by the use of a sonogram (see, for example, the sonogram image of the sound of a lion roaring,[173] depicted in Figure 5.11). It must however be questioned whether their registration and use as trade marks will necessarily enhance the reputation and integrity of the goods or services to which they would be applied, or indeed whether they will provide valuable weaponry in their proprietors' legal arsenal. This is because the scope of protection conferred upon non-musical sound marks is entirely unclear. Different breeds of dog give vent to different grades of bark: but would registration of the bark of, say, a mid-range dog such as a Golden Retriever provide a degree of monopoly protection which would prevent competitors from engaging the bark of a Rottweiler or a Chihuahua? There is also the issue of similarity of marks: would the master of a barking trade mark be able to resist the use by subsequent competitors of (i) the growl of a dog, (ii) a picture of a dog or (iii) the words BARKING DOG? It cannot be inferred from the existence of these problems that it would be improper to register such marks, but it is hoped that legislation would pave the way for the registrations of sounds of this nature in such a manner as to avoid those awkward issues being litigated on a case-by-case basis.

Figure 5.11 The sonogram image of the sound of a lion roaring.

---

[172] See *Honda Giken KKK and another v H-D Michigan Inc* 43 USPQ 2d 1526 (TTAB 1997), an opposition to Harley-Davidson's US application to register the 'roar' of its bikes as a trade mark. The application was eventually withdrawn.
[173] Metro-Goldwyn-Mayer Corp's trade mark US 73553567 ('The mark comprises a lion roaring').

5.138 OHIM has rejected an application to register the sound of a click, described as a 'click' in the application, since the word 'click' would not enable persons reading the application to recognize the sound itself.[174]

5.139 A sound mark must also be distinctive. A sign consisting of a short symphonic sound has been registered in Paraguay following testimony by the director of the Asunción Symphony Orchestra that the musical score was 'completely original and new' and that it was not similar to any other sounds. This approach would seem to miss the point: originality is a requirement of copyright law but not of trade mark law and a trade mark can only be considered to be distinctive in relation to the goods or services for which registration is sought.[175]

(4) Gestures and motions

5.140 Can a gesture be registered as a trade mark? The UK Trade Marks Registry has accepted for registration a mark, accompanied by a single photograph, which is described in the following terms:

> The mark is a gesture made by a person by tapping one side of his/her nose with an extended finger, normally the index finger of the hand on the side of the nose being tapped.[176]

5.141 The description and accompanying photograph are not without their difficulties. For example, the description of an action by means of a single still photograph is somewhat akin to the portrayal of a three-dimensional mark by means of a two-dimensional illustration: neither tells the full story. Nor can it easily be established as to what other gestures would constitute the 'similar' activities which define the outer scope of the protection which is accorded to granted trade marks. Neither the validity nor the scope of 'gesture' marks has yet been tested in the courts.

5.142 Several motion marks have been the subject of CTM applications. These include marks which give the appearance of motion, such as holograms, as well as of marks which require actual motion such as the 'revolving beaker with French fries' which rotates at between 500 and 700 revolutions per minute.[177]

---

[174] *Qlicksmart Pty Ltd's application*, Case R 1/1998-2 [1999] ETMR 190.
[175] *Dolby Laboratories Licensing Corporation's application*, 11 February 1999 (Paraguayan Trade Mark Office).
[176] UK Trade Mark No 2012603.
[177] CTM application 1222256. This and a selection of other unusual trade mark applications are reviewed in Stephen Völker, 'Registering New Forms with the CTM' (2002) 152 *Trademark World* 24–33.

(5) Taste marks

5.143 The Benelux Trade Mark Office has accepted applications to register trade marks in respect of the application of taste to goods.[178] The description of one such mark is 'The trade mark consists of the taste described applied to the goods (taste mark)', a description which appears to fall short of the rigorous standards for graphic representation required by the ECJ for olfactory and colour marks.

5.144 Taste marks raise other problems. For example, if the taste is applied to goods, it is not possible for such a trade mark to perform its essential function of guaranteeing the origin of the proprietor's goods or services unless it is actually sampled. Consumers may object to being expected to taste goods which have already been tasted and rejected by other consumers. Also, if the taste is inherently part of the goods themselves, for example, in the case of food and drink, it is difficult to regard the taste as also serving as a distinguishing badge in respect to those goods.

(6) Positional marks

5.144A The positioning of an otherwise unregistrable mark on or in relation to the goods for which registration is sought will not invest it with the quality of registrability. Thus in *Axion* the applicant sought to register, in respect of chocolate, cardboard packaging in the shape of a gold ingot.[179] On appeal to the Court of First Instance the applicant claimed that the packaging was inherently distinctive because it was to be displayed upside down. The court rejected this contention.

N. Registration and the conduct of the applicant

5.145 So far in this chapter, we have reviewed deficiencies in registrability which stem from the nature of the sign which an applicant seeks to register. The remainder of this chapter considers the human element: first we consider the legitimate and much-pursued ploy of obtaining protection for an actually or potentially unregistrable sign by erecting a portfolio of registrations around it. Then we consider the activities of applicants which are sufficiently unacceptable for the law not to allow any legal estate to be conferred in consequence of them.

---

[178] On this topic, see Bas Kist, 'Touch Me, Smell Me, Protect Me: Protecting Unconventional Trade Marks', conference paper, INTA 125th International Meeting, Amsterdam, May 2003. The example cited by Kist is trade mark BX 625 971, 'de smaak van drop' ('the taste of liquorice').

[179] *Axion SA and Christian Belce v Office for Harmonisation in the Internal Market*, Joined Cases T-324/01 and T-110/02, 30 April 2003 (unreported) (CFI).

O. Building up a portfolio of registrations in order to cover unprotectable classes

5.146 Trade mark registration is a game of strategy. With good planning, an applicant can secure trade mark protection even where it is not possible to apply directly for it. One way of doing this is by building up a web of registrations which are adjacent to the field in which registration is prohibited. Children will immediately identify this strategy as an adult version of 'joining up the dots'. How is this done?

5.147 Let us say that our target trade mark is the word mark LUSCIOUS LIPS, which we want to use for lipstick. The law is clear: descriptive marks cannot be registered and the phrase 'luscious lips' describes the desired end of all lipstick users. The first step is to file trade mark applications for LUSCIOUS LIPS in respect of products adjacent to lipstick, either in the sense of being applied to areas next to the lips or in the sense of being sold at sales counters next to those on which lipstick is displayed. We might therefore seek to register the word mark LUSCIOUS LIPS for face creams, moisturizers and powders, eye-liners and mascara—products for which those words are distinctive. If any competitor wants to call his lipstick LUSCIOUS LIPS, we can complain that he will confuse consumers who will associate his product with our 'family' of trade marks. To be on the safe side, we can also register the word mark LUSCIOUS LIFE for lipstick, since those words are not descriptive of lipstick's physical properties or metaphysical promise. Anyone else who even thinks of using LUSCIOUS LIPS for lipstick will hear the distant rustling of lawyers' writs. The final stage of this subtle procedure is to use the words LUSCIOUS LIPS as a trade mark for lipstick and argue, on account of the use you have made of that mark in relation to lipstick, that mark has acquired distinctive character. Even though the use you have made of the same mark on the adjacent goods does not actually count as use for the purpose of acquiring distinctive character for lipstick, it is almost impossible for the public to 'un-know' that mark in respect of those other products. Registration of LUSCIOUS LIPS is thus secured.

5.148 A simpler version of this procedure is reflected in the application made by Procter & Gamble to register as a CTM the word mark PERFECT BROW in respect of 'toilet soaps, toiletries, perfumery, essential oils, preparations for body and beauty care; preparations for the cleaning, care and beautification of the skin, hair lotions, cosmetics'. The examiner rejected the application in its totality, but the Board of Appeal addressed the reality of the situation: registration was barred in respect of only those products relating to brows. It had to be allowed in respect of all the other products. Once allowed in part, the application provided a hedge behind which the company's PERFECT BROW brand could be safely cultivated for perfect brow-related articles, free from any serious risk of trespass by other man-

P. Conclusion

ufacturers.[180] This policy does not just work for cosmetics manufacturers though: DaimlerChrysler have done exactly the same thing with their application to register CARCARD for a wide variety of goods and services, including the unregistrable 'target' area of information-carrying cards for use with motor vehicles. The CFI allowed registration for all the non-barred goods and services, adding:

> For the purposes of assessing a sign's descriptiveness in respect of a particular category of goods or service, whether the applicant for the trade mark in question is contemplating using or is actually using a particular marketing concept involving goods and services in other categories in addition to the goods and services within that category is immaterial. Whether or not there is a marketing concept is of no consequence to the right conferred by the Community trade mark. Furthermore, since a marketing concept is purely a matter of choice for the undertaking concerned, it may change after a sign has been registered as a Community trade mark and it cannot therefore have any bearing on the assessment of the sign's registrability.

In other words, OHIM is only concerned with the question of whether a sign is registrable as a trade mark. Whatever is done with the mark after registration takes place, for good or ill, is a matter of no concern.[181]   **5.149**

The strategy of building a hedge around an initially unregistrable mark which I have just described is employed in a slightly different form in which a trade mark owner, rather than obtaining a batch of registrations for the *same* mark in *different* classes, builds what is termed a 'family' of registrations for *different* marks in the *same* class. This technique is not used so much to obtain further registrations for the trade mark owner as to prevent unwanted registrations by third parties. It is described in more detail in Chapter 13.   **5.150**

P. Conclusion

This chapter shows how the basic principles of registration, outlined in the previous chapter, are put into effect in a large number of specific situations. Some of these situations strain our concept of normal commercial reality, for example, when applicants seek to register olfactory trade marks. Strain may also result from the ingenuity of the trade mark applicant in conjuring up situations in which fairly unpromising subject matter can be dressed up as a 'sign' for the sake of filing a trade mark application. On yet other occasions strain results from the efforts made by trade mark examiners (and the courts which handle appeals from them) to phrase in legal terms their absolute conviction that the trade mark before them should not be granted even though the words of their statute law, read literally, would appear to suggest otherwise.   **5.151**

---

[180] *Procter & Gamble Company's application*, Case R 110/1998-3 [2000] ETMR 174 (OHIM).
[181] *DaimlerChrysler AG v OHIM*, Case T-356/00 [2002] IP&T 815 (CFI).

5.152 The strain which is apparently inherent between the interests of trade mark applicants, their competitors, the public and the trade marks registry is not merely a by-product of how traders act in response to the law: it also flows from the way in which the trade mark system is constituted. For example, the 'graphic representation' requirement is unrelated to the key issue in trade mark law of whether a sign is capable of serving as a trade mark; but although it is more addressed to the formal requirements of a registration system, it makes an impact on the availability of legal protection. Some have argued therefore that it would make sense to allow other unequivocal ways of representing the sign, for example, by lodging with the granting office a sample of a shape. Another solution is to jettison the 'graphic representation' requirement entirely, replacing it with a doctrine of 'uncertainty'—that protection would only be withheld from a trade mark applicant or proprietor where his competitors were genuinely unable to deduce what the subject matter of legal protection was supposed to be. A third approach would be that of the United States, which is to live without a 'graphic representation' requirement and just get on with life.

6

TRADE MARKS AND GENERIC TERMS

A. Introduction	
Some thoughts on access to words	
The moral for 2003	6.01
What is meant by a 'generic term'?	6.03
B. 'Fencing in the commons': competing public and private claims upon words	6.07
(1) Commons and the polo test	6.11
(2) Words are not sheep	6.13
(3) Words multiply faster than trade marks	6.14
(4) Most uses of words registered as trade marks have no adverse legal consequence	6.15
(5) Mass abuse of trade marks: safety in numbers	6.16
(6) The public have higher interests than the preservation of the commons	6.18
(7) Are the interests of trade mark owners and consumers coterminous?	6.19
C. Legal issues relating to generic terms	
(1) What happens if a term is generic but not well known?	6.22
(2) Can you make someone else's trade mark a generic term?	6.23
(3) Unauthorized generic use of another's trade mark	6.24
(4) How can one prevent distinctive product names becoming generic?	6.27
(5) How can one prevent generic terms becoming trade marks?	6.30
(6) Can a mark be partially generic?	6.31
(7) Does the combination of two generic terms make a distinctive trade mark?	6.34
(8) Generic terms and the language factor	6.35
(9) Genericity depends on the nature of the goods as well as on the nature of the term	6.37
(10) Can a person's name become generic?	6.38
(11) Generic trade marks and the burden of proof	6.40
(12) Trade mark infringement is not excused by the addition of a generic term	6.44
D. Conclusion	6.45

A. Introduction

Some thoughts on access to words

1909
'Wealthy traders are habitually eager to enclose part of the great common of the

English language and to exclude the general public of the present day and of the future from access to the enclosure.'[1]

1984

'How is the Dictionary getting on?' said Winston, raising his voice to overcome the noise.

'Slowly,' said Syme. 'I'm on the adjectives. It's fascinating'.

He had brightened up immediately at the mention of Newspeak. He pushed his pannikin aside, took up his hunk of bread in one delicate hand and his cheese in the other, and leaned across the table so as to be able to speak without shouting.

'The Eleventh Edition is the definitive edition,' he said. 'We're getting the language into its final shape—the shape it's going to have when nobody speaks anything else. When we've finished with it, people like you will have to learn it all over again. You think, I dare say, that our chief job is inventing new words. But not a bit of it! We're destroying words—scores of them, hundreds of them, every day. We're cutting the language down to the bone. The Eleventh Edition won't contain a single word that will become obsolete before the year 2050'.

He bit hungrily into his bread and swallowed a couple of mouthfuls, then continued speaking, with a sort of pedant's passion. His thin dark face had become animated, his eyes had lost their mocking expression and grown almost dreamy.

'It's a beautiful thing, the destruction of words. Of course the great wastage is in the verbs and adjectives, but there are hundreds of nouns that can be got rid of as well. It isn't only the synonyms; there are also the antonyms. After all, what justification is there for a word which is simply the opposite of some other word? A word contains its opposite in itself. Take 'good', for instance. If you have a word like 'good', what need is there for a word like 'bad'? 'Ungood' will do just as well—better, because it's an exact opposite, which the other is not. Or again, if you want a stronger version of 'good', what sense is there in having a whole string of vague useless words like 'excellent' and 'splendid' and all the rest of them? 'Plusgood' covers the meaning, or 'doubleplusgood' if you want something stronger still. Of course we use those forms already. But in the final version of Newspeak there'll be nothing else. In the end the whole notion of goodness and badness will be covered by only six words—in reality, only one word. Don't you see the beauty of that, Winston? It was B.B.'s[2] idea originally, of course,' he added as an afterthought.

A sort of vapid eagerness flitted across Winston's face at the mention of Big Brother. Nevertheless Syme immediately detected a certain lack of enthusiasm.

'You haven't a real appreciation of Newspeak, Winston,' he said almost sadly. 'Even when you write it you're still thinking in Oldspeak. I've read some of those pieces that you write in *The Times* occasionally. They're good enough, but they're translations. In your heart you'd prefer to stick to Oldspeak, with all its vagueness and its useless shades of meaning. You don't grasp the beauty of the destruction of words. Do you know that Newspeak is the only language in the world whose vocabulary gets smaller every year?'

Winston did know that, of course. He smiled, sympathetically he hoped, not trusting himself to speak. Syme bit off another fragment of the dark-coloured bread, chewed it briefly, and went on:

---

[1] Sir Herbert Cozens-Hardy MR, *Joseph Crosfield & Son's application* ('PERFECTION') (1909) 26 RPC 837, 854.

[2] 'B.B.' = Big Brother.

A. Introduction

'Don't you see that the whole aim of Newspeak is to narrow the range of thought? In the end we shall make thoughtcrime literally impossible, because there will be no words in which to express it. Every concept that can ever be needed, will be expressed by exactly *one* word, with its meaning rigidly defined and all its subsidiary meanings rubbed out and forgotten. Already, in the Eleventh Edition, we're not far from that point. But the process will still be continuing long after you and I are dead. Every year fewer and fewer words, and the range of consciousness always a little smaller. Even now, of course, there's no reason or excuse for committing thoughtcrime. It's merely a question of self-discipline, reality-control. But in the end there won't be any need even for that. The Revolution will be complete when the language is perfect. Newspeak is Ingsoc and Ingsoc is Newspeak,' he added with a sort of mystical satisfaction. 'Has it ever occurred to you, Winston, that by the year 2050, at the very latest, not a single human being will be alive who could understand such a conversation as we are having now?'

'Except—'began Winston doubtfully, and he stopped.

It had been on the tip of his tongue to say 'Except the proles', but he checked himself, not feeling fully certain that this remark was not in some way unorthodox. Syme, however, had divined what he was about to say.

'The proles are not human beings,' he said carelessly. 'By 2050 earlier, probably— all real knowledge of Oldspeak will have disappeared. The whole literature of the past will have been destroyed. Chaucer, Shakespeare, Milton, Byron—they'll exist only in Newspeak versions, not merely changed into something different, but actually changed into something contradictory of what they used to be. Even the literature of the Party will change. Even the slogans will change. How could you have a slogan like 'freedom is slavery' when the concept of freedom has been abolished? The whole climate of thought will be different. In fact there will *be* no thought, as we understand it now. Orthodoxy means not thinking—not needing to think. Orthodoxy is unconsciousness'.[3]

The moral for 2003

6.01 The two extracts reproduced above reflect different aspects of the removal of words from the language. The first contemplates the placing of words under private control, while the second contemplates their complete elimination. A second's reflection is all that is needed to tell that the first is a far smaller threat to human expression than is the latter. Our intuition tells us that the former is a far more probable threat than the latter, but this chapter will argue that the languages we speak are under no threat whatsoever.

6.02 This chapter examines the two-way process by which words are 'taken' from the pool of common vocabulary when they are kidnapped and turned into trade marks, while other words, born in captivity within the private domain, are liberated by the public and turned from trade marks into generic terms.

---

[3] George Orwell, *1984*, ch 1.

What is meant by a 'generic term'?

6.03 'Generic term' does not have a precise legal meaning in international trade mark law or in European trade mark legislation.[4] For the purposes of this book, a 'generic term' is taken to be a term which indicates an article (i) without alluding to its source or origin and (ii) without specifying any particular qualities and characteristics which distinguish it from others of its kind. For example, the word 'scent' is a generic term which covers perfumes, aftershave lotions, eau-de-cologne and deodorants and the word 'apple' is generic in the sense that it does not inform the reader whether a particular fruit is green or red, sweet or sour. Generic terms also describe services, though it would seem that there are fewer serious consequences for trade mark registrations since they are not commonly the subject of litigation or registry hearings. Examples of generic terms relating to services might be 'dry-cleaning', 'drive-through', 'take-away', 'high-yield' and 'deferred interest'.

6.04 Where a word is a generic term, it may not be registered as a trade mark for the goods or service to which it directly applies.[5] It may however be registered for goods or services with which it has no connection. This is why APPLE may be registered as a trade mark for computers but not for apples and why SWORD may be registered for a razor blade but not for a sword. A small modification which is made to a generic term may be sufficient to deprive it of its status as a generic term without having the effect of making it distinctive and therefore registrable. Thus MÜSLI (or MUESLI), which is generic for a form of breakfast cereal, is no longer generic but still unregistrable as a trade mark if the suffix 'x' is added so as to create MÜSLIX.[6]

6.05 Since a word which is not originally generic may become generic at any stage in its life, it frequently happens that a coined word starts its life as a trade mark and later becomes a generic term. The rich and varied vocabulary of the English language is littered with such words: aspirin, linoleum, cornflakes and thermos are examples of words which have become generic in one or more English-speaking country. The phenomenon is not confined to English, though: frigidaire (France) and walkman (Austria) show that the French and German languages can be equally acquisitive.

6.06 Some trade marks have teetered on the brink of becoming generic terms because there is no convenient term for them in any language. Examples include HOOVER as a noun for vacuum cleaners and a verb indicating their function, FRISBEE for

---

[4] The term 'generic name' is used in the Lanham Act (see eg 15 USC, s 106(3)), but no statutory definition is provided for it.
[5] On the legal provisions relating to the registration of generic marks, see Chapter 4.
[6] *Kellogg Company v Pehuamar SA* WTLR, 22 May 2003 (Second Federal Court of Appeals for Buenos Aires, Argentina).

moulded plastic flying discs and YO-YO for the popular children's toy. Other trade marks stare into the same abyss because they have become synonymous with a particular product, even though there may exist perfectly good generic terms for them, because they have become cultural icons in their own right: for many people VALIUM, PROZAC, VIAGRA, FILOFAX and ROLLERBLADE may conjure up strong images of a lifestyle rather than a product.

B. 'Fencing in the commons': competing public and private claims upon words

A great debate[7] has taken place over the past century or so as to whether it is proper for trade mark law to permit an individual to 'fence in the commons' by facilitating the appropriation as private property of words which are the linguistic inheritance of us all. A common was a piece of land to which all people had access, for whatever purpose they so desired. Some might perhaps graze their sheep there; others might harvest hay; others still might utilize this asset by playing football on it. The main point is that the common provided a benefit to all. Once it became subject to private ownership and was fenced in, its role as a public resource ceased. **6.07**

Perhaps because (i) it has generally been enlisted in arguments against the protection of certain types of trade mark and (ii) it is a hypothetical domain with protean characteristics, the concept of the 'commons' has become emotive and threatens to obscure any serious objective consideration of the interplay between consumers, businesses and trade mark laws in real life. **6.08**

The concept of a linguistic commons[8] runs as follows: **6.09**

(i) language is an 'intellectual common', a resource to which all may contribute and from which all may freely draw, but which none may own;
(ii) despite the fact that language is an intellectual common which may be owned by none, the status of private property may be conferred upon those words which are made from it and which are termed 'intellectual goods' (for example, the words 'a', 'mars', 'day', 'help', 'you', 'work', 'rest' and 'play' are part of

---

[7] See Jennifer Davis, 'European Trade Mark Law and the Enclosure of the Commons' [2002] IPQ 342–67, and the sources to which she refers, for a good account of the nature and history of this debate. I am indebted to her for some cogent criticisms of my position on this issue. See also Spyros Maniatis, 'Trademark Rights: A Justification Based on Property' [2002] IPQ 123–71 for an Olympian overview of the topic and Jeremy Phillips, 'The Diminishing Domain' [1996] EIPR 429–31 on the recent growth of the private domain at the expense of public resources.

[8] This is only a simplification. There are many different constructs of the commons, characterized by different relations between the common owners and the intellectual content owned. See eg Peter Drahos, *A Philosophy of Intellectual Property* (1996), pp 57–8.

the common and thus incapable of ownership by no one, but the combination 'A MARS a day helps you work, rest and play' can be appropriated into private ownership);

(iii) there should be a justification for treating intellectual goods as property which explains it in terms of it conferring some sort of benefit to those who are excluded from its use. In the case of copyright, designs and patents there is a trade-off between the short-term exclusion and a subsequent eternal period in which those intellectual goods return to the common through their emergence as part of the 'public domain'. In the case of trade marks the justification may be framed in terms of consumers enjoying greater economic efficiency in the spread of market information upon which they exercise their choice, or in terms of their being less likely to be confused when exercising their choice;

(iv) to the extent that the content of the intellectual commons is appropriated into private ownership, there is a diminution of common resources. This diminution has an impact upon issues of economic efficiency in the allocation of resources as well as upon the cultural well-being of the community. For example, time and effort must be expended in searching for new free words and other signs to replace those which have been removed from the common pool.

6.10 'Commons' theories have been received with little criticism and one gets the impression that the notion of a 'common' has been accepted almost by default. But perhaps the time for a more critical evaluation has arrived. Rather than build a theoretical construct of 'intellectual commons' and then try to shoe-horn trade marks, patents, copyright, designs and other monopolistic laws into them, a greater challenge for the model-builders is to start with the law and the way the law influences actual behaviour, then to build the model which fits it.

(1) Commons and the polo test

6.11 So far as trade marks are concerned, any commons-based model will have to satisfy the polo test before it is entitled to be taken seriously. Consider the word 'polo': How many different meanings does it have? How many different traders simultaneously enjoy rights to use it (i) as exclusive owners, (ii) as users authorized by an owner of the word, (iii) as users who are not authorized by owners of the word but who are entitled to rely on provisions of the law which permit unauthorized use? How far do those rights and liberties affect other traders, members of the purchasing and non-purchasing publics? What are the economic and cultural effects of the answers to the foregoing questions?

6.12 The reality is that the physical analogy of the commons is unsustainable. Trade mark law poses no serious threat to the common linguistic or terminological inheritance of mankind at all, for at least the reasons outlined below.

B. Competing public and private claims upon words

(2) Words are not sheep

6.13 Sheep have characteristics which make them ideal for fencing in. Every sheep is, at any given time, either dead or alive, cloned or natural, male or female, inside the common or outside it. Despite its many virtues, the sheep is a creature of certainty and finitude.[9] This is not so for words. A word may bear many meanings at the same time, not just literally but in terms of metaphor. Words may be coined from nothing; they may fall out of use and then return to it; they are neither certain nor bound by precisely delimiting rules. They can exist simultaneously both inside the common and outside it. Not only can improper use change their meaning, but it can even change their capacity for ownership. Furthermore they are capable of co-existing with paraphrases, homonyms, homophones and a good deal more besides. To adopt so limitative a model for words as that of the common is to limit one's appreciation of their versatility.

(3) Words multiply faster than trade marks

6.14 New words enter the language at a far faster rate than trade marks are registered. This is not surprising, in that humans are faced with situations, emotions and technologies for which existing words provide only an imperfect means of expression. Neologisms, both in the form of single words and in the form of phrases, are constantly being coined; their acceptance is enhanced through their dissemination in the new media, particularly through the Internet, e-mail and text messaging. The total volume of words registered as trade marks creeps up far more slowly since: (i) they are limited by the range of goods and services for which registration is available and by the market for the supply of those goods and services; (ii) they cost money to acquire and maintain; and (iii) there are so many absolute and relative barriers to their being registered. In other words, the intellectual common is, for trade mark purposes, an effectively infinite resource, one which grows far more quickly than its stock of words which are attractive and useful for trade mark purposes can be depleted. It is also constantly topped up by the return of words from private control once those words cease to be able to serve as trade marks.

(4) Most uses of words registered as trade marks have no adverse legal consequence

6.15 The number of potentially infringing acts in respect of trade marks is small[10] and, even when a trade mark is registered, the range of legal defences to an action for trade mark infringement is very wide.[11] This is why we can use trade marks not

---

[9] This word has no apparent lexical validity, but only one of my many friends and colleagues who read this chapter challenged it—and even he knew what it was supposed to mean.
[10] See Chapter 7.
[11] See Chapter 8.

only in the course of conversation but even in the course of trade without having to look anxiously over our shoulders for signs that the Trade Mark Police are on our scent. That is also why we can allow the registration of BABY-DRY as a trade mark for babies' nappies, since the words 'baby' and 'dry' remain free for use even by competitors.[12]

(5) Mass abuse of trade marks: safety in numbers

6.16 In practical terms, a trade mark owner is defenceless—perhaps 'attackless' would be a better term—against a host of small-time abusers or misusers of his trade mark. If, for example, I have registered the trade mark HIPPOGRIFF for a particularly distinctive genre of carpet slippers and my product captures the imagination of the public, my current and future customers may find it more convenient to refer to that particular type of carpet slipper as a 'hippogriff', thus using it as a generic term. Most members of the public are indifferent to the legal status of this word. They have not studied trade mark law and have no conception of the difference between HIPPOGRIFF and hippogriff. They can, whatever my view of the subject, lift my trade mark from the private domain and place it firmly into ordinary speech.

6.17 If the consuming public chooses to use my trade mark as a generic term, there is not much I can do about it. Even if such use were to constitute an infringing use of the HIPPOGRIFF trade mark (which it does not[13]), the policy of suing one's actual or potential customers in such circumstances is at least questionable. It would also almost certainly cost far more to bring such actions than (i) to engage in a marketing and publicity drive in order to educate the public into using HIPPOGRIFF as a trade mark, not as a generic term or (ii) to coin another trade mark.

(6) The public have higher interests than the preservation of the commons

6.18 Even in the absence of a trade mark registration, the claimant manufacturer of 'camel hair belting', which is as descriptive or generic a way of indicating camel hair belting as one can think of, has been able to prevent a competitor using that term where the result of their use of it would confuse the public into believing that the competitor's product was connected with the claimant.[14] For as long as the protection of the public against confusion is recognized by the courts as holding a higher value than the protection of the public against the fencing off of the commons, decisions of this nature may be not only expected but justified.

---

[12] *Procter & Gamble Company v OHIM*, Case C-383/99 P [2002] ETMR 22 (ECJ).
[13] See Chapter 8, paras 8.83–8.84.
[14] *Frank Reddaway & Co Ltd v George Banham & Co Ltd* [1896] AC 199 (HL). Cf *McCain International Ltd v Country Fair Foods Ltd and another* [1981] RPC 69 (HC), where the court held that even a *de facto* monopoly on the use of the words OVEN CHIPS could not confer a protectable interest upon those generic words.

B. Competing public and private claims upon words

(7) Are the interests of trade mark owners and consumers coterminous?

6.19 It has been argued[15] that the neo-liberal foundation of current trade mark law, which sees a properly regulated trade mark regime as promoting competition, cannot always take into account the public interest, as distinct from the interests of trade mark owners. The reason why this is so, it is argued, is that the free-market argument of the neo-liberals is that, in a properly operating free market, the interests of trade mark proprietors and consumers would be coterminous. The neo-liberal view is criticized on the ground that, at least at the margins, there will always be the potential for a fundamental conflict between proprietors' interests and the public interest, a conflict which cannot be resolved by the current exceptions (as, it is maintained, the *Windsurfing Chiemsee* case[16] makes clear). This potential for conflict, together with the need to protect the public interest, is seen as a justification of the 'commons' argument and for the taking of a somewhat protectionist approach towards the preservation of the commons against the encroachment of the robber barons who would carve it up and carry it away with them.

6.20 The premiss that the interests of trade mark proprietors and consumers are coterminous is, to anyone who is not an economist and possibly to some people who are, a questionable one. The trade mark proprietor's immediate interest lies in reducing the consumer's choice and in the promotion of his own branded goods and services as against those of his competitors (if he has any: many trade mark proprietors are also patent owners); his interest also lies in maximizing profit and minimizing costs. The ownership of a trade mark in a market in which competitors exist is an expense in that the proprietor's brand values have to be advertised in order to persuade the consumer to vest him with the market power which he needs if he is to vanquish his competitors. In contrast the ownership of a trade mark in a market in which no competition exists or is possible is quite unnecessary and serves no purpose at all. If we now match up the interests of the consumer, we see that the same marketplace which favours one set of conditions for the trade mark owner will favour a very different one for the consumer. His interest is in being given a meaningful choice which he is capable of exercising in a meaningful manner. The premiss that the interests of proprietors and consumers are coterminous is thus thoroughly unappealing.

6.21 Is it then true to say that, if this premiss cannot be sustained, the only alternative is to take a public interest-oriented protectionist approach to the public's assets?

---

[15] Jennifer Davis, 'European Trade Mark Law and the Enclosure of the Commons' [2002] IPQ 342, 358.
[16] *Windsurfing Chiemsee Produktions- und Vertriebs GmbH v Boots- und Segelzubehör Walter Huber and Franz Attenberger*, Joined Cases C-108 and 109/97 [1999] ETMR 585 (ECJ).

This assumption is equally questionable. I have argued elsewhere in this book[17] that the function of trade mark law is to preserve a creative tension between the competing interests of all the players in the field. Whether this assertion is right or wrong, it calls for consideration of trade mark law on a wider basis than the bipolar model upon which the arguments in this section have so far been based. In terms of the protection of the consuming public, we should at least note that the consumer has the potential to make and break alliances with the trade mark owner, with his competitors, with non-competing businesses, with other consumers as individuals, with pressure groups and with government itself. It is submitted that, whether it is based on principles of paternalistic protectionism, heartless neo-liberalism or anything else in between, any trade mark system which enables many different and often conflicting interests to coexist in a generally profitable and beneficial manner should at least be taken seriously.

C. Legal issues relating to generic terms

(1) What happens if a term is generic but not well known?

6.22 Since trade marks of the 'aspirin' variety have become generic following their wide public use in a generic manner, it is tempting to assume that wide public acceptance of their generic nature is a precondition to their being deemed incapable of serving, or continuing to serve, as trade marks. This is not so. Terms which are unknown to the public at large, such as DLC[18] and BSS,[19] may still be generic even though their use is confined to narrow scientific or technical circles and a few specialist dictionaries and reference books.

(2) Can you make someone else's trade mark a generic term?

6.23 Since a trade mark may become generic when, having been used other than as a trade mark, it ceases to identify the trade mark proprietor's goods, it may be asked whether a third party can set out to make deliberate use of another's trade mark in a non-trade mark sense so as to render it generic. In theory third-party use of this nature can indeed result in the death of a trade mark's distinctive force, even if it is deliberate and malicious, since its effect has been to render a trade mark unserviceable as a trade mark. In practice, however, tribunals are reluctant to place great weight in revocation proceedings on evidence of genericity which consists of use by the applicant for revocation himself.[20]

---

[17] See Chapter 2, paras 2.53–2.58.
[18] An acronym for 'diamond-like carbon': *Gillette Company's trade mark; application for a declaration of invalidity by Warner-Lambert & Company*, Case 000703579 [2002] ETMR 733 (OHIM).
[19] An acronym for 'buffered salt solution' or 'buffered saline solution': *Alcon Inc v OHIM, Dr Robert Winzer Pharma GmbH intervening*, Case T-237/01, 5 March 2003 (unreported) (CFI).
[20] *Midland Wheel Supplies Ltd's application for revocation* [2000] ETMR 256 (UK Trade Mark

C. Legal issues relating to generic terms

(3) Unauthorized generic use of another's trade mark

6.24 The European model of trade mark infringement does not require EU Member States to protect trade mark owners against any activities of third parties other than for the purpose of distinguishing goods and services. Under the terms of the trade mark harmonization Directive[21] any Member State which wishes to provide separate and additional relief in respect of activities which damage the trade mark but do not involve its use for the purpose of distinguishing goods or services may however do so;[22] this presumably would entitle those countries to enact specific legislation relating to uses of a trade mark which render it generic.

6.25 What sort of genericity-producing activities would fall within the scope of this facility? Possibly where a newspaper feature or television programme on the disadvantages of using upright vacuum cleaners keeps referring to them as 'hoovers', with reference to their actual manufacture.[23]

6.26 In the United States it might be thought that the use of another's trade mark as a generic term would qualify as an act of 'dilution',[24] but it is difficult to see how such use—if not as part of a commercial activity—would fall within the scope of an actionable infringement.

(4) How can one prevent distinctive product names becoming generic?

6.27 It is easy to be wise with the benefit of hindsight. For example, when a French company registered the trade mark PIÑA COLADA[25] for alcoholic beverages other than beer in 1974, it could not have known how widespread the use and popularity of that trade mark would become.[26] If one does not start out with a well-thought-out policy for educating consumer and trade circles alike and for discouraging improper use, as well as a budget for promoting those aims, control of the trade mark can be quickly and irrevocably lost.

Registry): unsuccessful application to revoke MINILITE for car wheels. Further discussion of revocation is found in Chapter 13.

[21] Council Directive 89/104, art 5(5). The CTM Regulation does not contain an equivalent provision.

[22] *Robelco NV v Robeco NV*, Case C-23/01, [2003] ETMR 671(ECJ (Sixth Chamber)), para 36. The ECJ reference followed the incorporation of a company with a name which was very similar to another company's trade mark.

[23] For a similar incident involving shopping trolleys, see *SA Ateliers Réunis Caddie v Sarl Société Nouvelle de Presse et de Communication (SNPC)* [1999] ETMR 45 (Tribunal de Grande Instance de Paris), discussed in Chapter 8, paras 8.83–8.84.

[24] See 15 USC, s 1125.

[25] The mark means, literally, 'strained pineapple' in Spanish.

[26] *SA Bardinet v SCP Ego-Fruits (SCP Belat-Desprat intervening)* [2002] ETMR 1043 (Cour d'appel de Paris).

Chapter 6: Trade Marks and Generic Terms

6.28 Trade marks either become generic terms or, if they do not, are at least used by many people as if they are generic terms for one or more of the following reasons:

(i) the trade mark owner is the only maker of the product in the market, perhaps because of its patent or design protection (for example, LINOLEUM);

(ii) the public does not perceive any other convenient term for the goods or services for which they are used (for example, FRISBEE, VELCRO), perhaps in consequence of (i) above;

(iii) competitors want to cash in on the trade mark's popularity and high degree of public recall;

(iv) competitors make generic references to a trade mark (a good example, involving a geographical indication rather than a trade mark, occurred when a party applied for registration of the MILLENNIUM trade mark in France in respect of 'Champagne', treating that term as though it were generic);[27]

(v) the public is actually taught to use the trade mark as though it were a generic term ('Don't say brown [bread], say HOVIS');

(vi) the public makes the trade mark generic by taking it to its heart or treating it as a cultural icon (for example, when politicians are described as TEFLON Presidents because no blame ever sticks to them);

(vii) the word is treated as a generic term by compilers of dictionaries, word games and crossword puzzles in which the clue makes no reference to their protected legal status.[28]

6.29 Each of these actual or potential causes of genericity must be addressed on its own terms.[29] The best forms of treatment, taken singly or together as necessary, are as follows:

(i) when launching a product, first make sure the public has a convenient name for it which is not the trade mark even if it means coining a new word for it. Then teach that word to the trade press and to the public at large. Long and unmemorable paraphrases such as 'moulded flying plastic disk' encourage people to say 'frisbee';[30]

---

[27] *West v Nicolas Feuillatte SA and Yvon Mau SA*, 13 November 2002 (Cour d'appel de Reims).

[28] I am grateful to John Groom (Hallmark IP) for information concerning use of the UGLI trade mark for citrus fruit. UGLI is much used by crossword puzzle compilers since the English language contains few four letter words ending in 'i'.

[29] For a brief but helpful feature on taking steps to avoid genericity, see Juliana Viegas, 'Genericide: The Danger of Excessive Fame' (2003) 155 *Trademark World* 36–9.

[30] I am grateful to Jennifer Davis for the observation that, in the pharmaceutical industry, it may be desired to procure a pharmaceutical name for a product which is so long and complicated that practitioners will find it convenient to prescribe the product even once the patent has expired. In the pharmaceutical industry, however, the dangers of genericity are those which result from patent expiry rather than through loss of distinctiveness of the trade mark and some countries require the use of generic off-patent equivalents wherever possible. For further consideration of the role played by trade marks in the pharmaceutical sector, see Chapter 15.

C. Legal issues relating to generic terms

(ii) in advertising, marketing, packaging and even in one's own correspondence, try always to represent the trade mark as if it were a trade mark and not a product name, whether by printing it in capitals, by using an initial capital, by employing the ® symbol or by using distinctive typography and artwork;

(iii) do not engage in marketing exercises in which the trade mark is portrayed visually, in voice-overs or in dialogue as though it were a generic term;

(iv) be vigilant to monitor the activities not only of competitors but also the use to which the trade mark is put by authorized and unauthorized distributors, grey goods traders, resellers, repairers, websites[31] and so on;

(v) prepare and publicize where necessary any guidelines which you would like others to observe when using your trade mark, whether by means of a users' manual, a page on a website or any other appropriate means;

(vi) waste no time in applying to register a word as a trade mark, since an initially distinctive word can lose its distinctiveness before its proprietor gets round to registering it;[32] and

(vii) use the trade mark on products other than those for which the mark is likely to become a generic term (for example, the use of HOOVER on domestic electrical apparatus other than upright vacuum cleaners).

(5) How can one prevent generic terms becoming trade marks?

6.30 No generic term can be registered as a trade mark for its subject matter until it has acquired distinctiveness through use as a trade mark. It therefore follows that a trader who is aware that one of his competitors is using a generic term as though it were a trade mark should take steps to do so himself. If he and other competitors in the same field of commercial activity do not do this, then that term will eventually become synonymous with the trader who is using it as a trade mark and it may as well be registered as one.

(6) Can a mark be partially generic?

6.31 Trade marks distinguish goods while generic terms identify their nature. To say that a trade mark is partially generic appears at first sight as logically inconsistent as to say that a woman is partially pregnant. This is not however the case. Being distinctive and being generic are not mutually exclusive states. In the case of the woman who either is pregnant or is not pregnant, her status can be firmly and objectively established by reference to her own physical condition. In the case of a

---

[31] On which see *SA Bardinet v SCP Ego-Fruits (SCP Belat-Desprat intervening)* [2002] ETMR 1043 (Cour d'appel de Paris).

[32] See *Korean Florist Association v Kordes* WTLR, 14 March 2003 (Supreme Court, South Korea): RED SANDRA and KARDINAL roses were trade marks in Germany but, by the time the proprietor got round to applying to register these trade marks in South Korea, they were generally understood to be a variety of rose.

word, however, its status is determined by how people understand it. Some people, particularly in the field of trade mark practice but also in trading circles and indeed in the wider community, view the word VASELINE as a trade mark for a particular make of petroleum jelly; other people, whether because they have never encountered any other petroleum jelly or because they have never given any thought to the matter at all, assume that it is not VASELINE but Vaseline—a generic term for something they keep in a convenient jar in the bathroom cabinet.

6.32 The notion that a word can be simultaneously both a distinguishing mark and a generic term has been recognized in two cases. In the first,[33] a company registered the trade mark BOSTONGURKA in Sweden in 1979 for a specific type of chopped pickled cucumber. Twenty years later a competitor commenced the manufacture of its own chopped pickled cucumber which it too proposed to call 'Bostongurka' and commenced proceedings for the suspension of the BOSTONGURKA trade mark on the basis that it had become generic. The Stockholm District Court refused to suspend the trade mark. The Court agreed that the mark was being transformed into a generic term but ruled that, until that transformation was complete, the mark should remain on the register. At the date of the trial, while there was considerable evidence that the public regarded the word as a generic term, those who were most closely concerned with the product in trade circles still perceived BOSTONGURKA as a trade mark; opinion within trade circles was more important than that of shoppers or even shop assistants. This case has since been referred to the European Court of Justice (ECJ) for a preliminary ruling.[34]

6.33 In the second case[35] the issue was quite different. Here it was not a third-party user who went to court to free itself from the tyranny of a fading trade mark but the trade mark owner itself who went to court to stop an allegedly infringing use. The trade mark in question, SPORK, was registered for a utensil which was described as a 'combination of a spoon and a fork'. The defendant, who had used the word 'spork' in its price lists and in letters to its customers, denied infringement and claimed that it was not using the word 'spork' as a trade mark but as a term for a combination spoon and fork. The trial judge held that the mark had been infringed even though, as he found as a fact, it had become 'to some extent generic'. The Court of Appeal however allowed the defendant's appeal: if the mark had

---

[33] *Björnekulla Fruktindustrier Aktiebolag v Procordia Food Aktiebolag* [2002] ETMR 464 (Stockholm District Court).
[34] *Björnekulla Fruktindustrier Aktiebolag v Procordia Food Aktiebolag*, Case C-367/02 (on a reference from the Svea Hovrätt of 14 October 2002 on the following question: 'In cases where a product is handled at several stages before it reaches the consumer what is or are, under Article 12(2)(a) of the Trade Mark Directive, the relevant classes of persons for determining whether a trade mark has become the common name in the trade for a product in respect of which it is registered?').
[35] *D Green & Co (Stoke Newington) Ltd and Plastico Ltd v Regalzone Ltd* [2002] ETMR 241 (CA).

C. Legal issues relating to generic terms

become partially generic, the test of infringement was one of whether the recipients of the defendant's price lists and letters would have understood the word 'spork' to be a reference to the claimant's products (in which case the mark was infringed) or as a reference to a combination spoon and fork (in which the mark was not). In this case, on the facts, the use would not have been taken as an infringing use.[36]

(7) Does the combination of two generic terms make a distinctive trade mark?

6.34 This question has been considered by the ECJ in the COMPANYLINE case,[37] in which that court affirmed the basic principle for the assessment of all Community trade mark (CTM) applications: the distinctive character of a trade mark is assessed by taking the applicant's trade mark *as a whole*.[38] The words 'company' and 'line' may both be generic, but once they have been fused into COMPANYLINE it is the whole sign and not its constituent parts to which attention must be given. In this case, a global appreciation of these two generic terms did not make their fusion registrable: COMPANYLINE may no longer have been generic, but the fact that it was no longer generic did not mean that it had automatically become distinctive.

(8) Generic terms and the language factor

6.35 In most markets a term is not regarded as generic where it is not recognized by the relevant consumer as being generic. This means that foreign generic words can be successfully registered as trade marks in countries in which the foreign language is not understood.[39] A foreign term which is understood by the relevant public may however be regarded as generic.[40]

6.36 In the MATRAZEN case a German company argued that the registration in Spain of the German word for 'mattress' had adverse repercussions for the free movement of goods because the importation into Spain and subsequent sale of German mattresses bearing the word MATRAZEN could be impeded by the local registration of that generic term. The Court of First Instance disagreed, citing earlier ECJ jurisprudence to the effect that a national registration of a trade mark could not constitute an impediment to the free movement of goods, even though its exercise

---

[36] This approach is reminiscent of that taken by the ECJ in relation to non-infringing use in *Hölterhoff v Freiesleben* Case C-2/00 [2002] ETMR 917, discussed in Chapter 8, paras 8.45–8.46.
[37] *DKV Deutsche Krankenversicherung AG v OHIM,* Case C-104/00 P [2003] ETMR 241.
[38] ibid, para 21.
[39] *Matratzen v OHIM*, Case T-6/01 [2003] ETMR 392 (CFI): MATRAZEN, the German word for 'mattress', registrable for mattresses in Spain; *Tong Yang Confectionery Corporation's trade mark; application for cancellation by Lotte Confectionery Co Ltd* [2002] ETMR 219 (English term CHOCOPIE registrable for chocolate pies in Poland).
[40] *Lipton Ltd, Van Den Berg & Jurgens BV, Unilever Belgium and Unilever NV v Sara Lee/De NV and Douwe Egberts* [2002] ETMR 1073 (Cour de Cassation, Brussels): ICE TEA was found to be generic even though the words were English and the proper generic term was 'iced tea'.

may on an appropriate occasion be curbed.[41] The Court could have added that, since Spain did not apply different criteria to applications for national trade marks filed by Spanish and foreign applicants, the German company could itself have secured the registration of the generic term MATRAZEN if only the Spanish registrant hadn't had the idea first.[42]

(9) Genericity depends on the nature of the goods as well as on the nature of the term

6.37 The word 'horse' is generic for horses of the equine genus. It is not however a generic term for the genus into which 'clothes horse' or 'sea horse' falls. This example should remind readers that words are not generic in themselves: it is their use in relation to particular objects which makes them generic.[43] An OHIM Board of Appeal[44] applied this principle when an applicant sought to register the word mark K GLASS for, among other goods, 'glass in sheet form, ... not including glass fibre ...'. The application was refused on the basis that K GLASS was a term which was generic for fibre glass and for glass made from such fibre. The Board of Appeal set the examiner's decision aside. K GLASS might be generic for some types of glass, including glass fibre, but it was not generic for sheet glass; indeed, fibre glass was not even used in the production of sheet glass. The mark was therefore not barred from registration.

(10) Can a person's name become generic?

6.38 This issue was considered in a Dutch case[45] involving a trade mark consisting of the name of a fictional character, TARZAN. The defendant in this case, citing a dictionary definition '(often supposedly simple-minded) muscular man', maintained that TARZAN had become a generic term. The Court observed that the question to be considered was not whether TARZAN had become a generic term for a sort of person but whether it was generic for the goods in respect of which it was registered, in this case films and books. The defendant's argument was therefore misguided but the thought behind it was quite an interesting one.

6.39 Some names are certainly generic terms. In English, for example, Mae West was the name of an actress with a notable bust, but a mae west is an inflatable life-

---

[41] *Matratzen* (n 39 above), para 54, citing *Terrapin v Terranova*, Case 119/75 [1976] ECR 1039, para 5, *Dansk Supermarked*, Case 58/80 [1981] ECR 181, para 11.
[42] This idea was sparked off by reading *Deutsche Renault AG v Audi AG*, Case C-317/91 [1995] FSR 738.
[43] *Merz & Krell GmbH*, Case C-517/99 [2002] ETMR 231, para 27.
[44] *Pilkington plc's application*, Case R 81/1999-3 [2000] ETMR 1130.
[45] *Edgar Rice Burroughs Inc v Beukenoord BV and others* [2001] ETMR 1300 (Court of Appeal, Amsterdam).

C. Legal issues relating to generic terms

jacket. John Dory is the name of a fish, which is itself derived from the American term for a generic claimant in legal proceedings, John Doe;[46] a Jack Russell is a dog and Mickey Finn a laced drink. From the former British ruling classes we have acquired the linguistic legacy of the sandwich,[47] Earl Grey,[48] the cardigan[49] and Wellingtons.[50] Cockney rhyming slang has genericized the names Rosie Lee ('tea') and Jimmy Riddle ('piddle'). The Americans have an attenuated mumps virus called Jeryl Lynn.[51] Non-English speakers are not excluded from this process: Garibaldi, formerly a leader of the Italian *Risorgimento,* has become a biscuit baked with currants, the Marquis de Béchamel is cherished as the creator of béchamel sauce and the name of Bismarck, the redoubtable Iron Chancellor, has become a marinaded herring. All of this goes to show that the phenomenon of genericity is not confined to the sphere of trade mark law; it is a normal process in the development of language.

(11) Generic trade marks and the burden of proof

Once a trade mark is validly registered, it is presumed valid and remains valid until anyone can satisfy a court or trade mark-granting authority that it is valid no longer. Accordingly the trade mark owner does not have to prove that his trade mark does not consist of a generic term—it is for whoever assails its validity to bring proof to the contrary.[52] The courts, when faced with a valid registration certificate, do not decide that a trade mark has become generic on the basis of their own personal knowledge: they demand actual proof of genericity and mere unsubstantiated allegations do not suffice.[53] **6.40**

What sort of evidence of genericity do the courts prefer? Dictionaries have been used by trade mark-granting authorities in order to determine if a term is too generic to be allowed registration,[54] since the question under consideration is what a term actually means. But once a trade mark has been registered and the **6.41**

---

[46] Joining John Doe as a generic litigant is Richard Roe, a name which also has piscine connotations.
[47] Named after John Montagu, Fourth Earl of Sandwich.
[48] Named after the English Prime Minister (1764–1845).
[49] Named after the Seventh Earl of Cardigan.
[50] Named after the First Duke of Wellington.
[51] *Merck and Company's trade mark; SmithKline Beecham plc's application for a declaration of invalidity* [2000] ETMR 75 (HC). The virus was named after an unfortunate six-year-old girl, Jeryl Lynn Hilleman, who caught the virus in 1963.
[52] *TDC Forlag A/S v Medieforlaget Danmark A/S* [2003] ETMR 158 (Maritime and Commercial Court, Denmark): FAGBOG (Danish for 'reference book') held non-generic, having acquired distinctiveness through use before registration).
[53] *Pfizer Inc and Pfizer BV v Lestre Nederlandse Reformadviefbureau ENRA* [2001] ETMR 155 (District Court, Utrecht).
[54] See eg *Alcon Inc v OHIM, Dr Robert Winzer Pharma GmbH intervening,* Case T-237/01, 5 March 2003 (unreported) (CFI).

question arises as to whether it has become generic, dictionary definitions are not useful as evidence of trade use or of use in relevant consumer circles.[55]

6.42 In truth, dictionaries are not legal documents and reflect the gap which exists between the understanding of lawyers and that of lexicographers as to what trade marks and generic terms are. Writing in the United States in 1988 Landes and Posner observed:

> Courts may not be doing a very good job of determining when trademarks have become generic, at least if the dictionary can be considered an accurate inventory of words in general use by the relevant public (perhaps a big if). Of 35 illustrative examples in the McCarthy treatise of marks that courts have been held to be generic, 16 either do not appear at all in the most recent unabridged dictionary or, if they do appear, the meaning held to be generic is not included ... Of 17 illustrative examples of trademarks that courts have held not to be generic, seven nonetheless are listed in the dictionary with the rejected generic meaning.[56]

6.43 This does not mean that the courts have got it wrong, or that the dictionaries have erred. Courts and lexicographers can only determine the status of a word when confronted with reliable evidence of the manner in which it is used. Since the courts themselves have acknowledged that the same word can be both distinctive and generic,[57] it is scarcely surprising that judicial rulings and dictionary entries will reflect the ambiguity or lack of clarity which characterizes the way in which we use our words.

(12) Trade mark infringement is not excused by the addition of a generic term

6.44 In one French case the defendant, who was accused of infringing the IMAJE trade mark for printing ink and printing accessories by trading through the imaje-ink.com website, argued that the use of the claimant's trade mark was 'genericized' through the addition of the generic word 'ink' after the trade mark ('imaje-ink') and that visitors to the site would therefore view 'imaje-ink' as a reference to a type of ink sold by the defendant, not as a reference to its trade mark. The Cour d'appel de Paris rejected this curious submission.[58]

---

[55] *Du Pont de Nemours (EI) and Company v AMA VOF Antoon Michielsen Automobiles (trading as Protech Nederland Teflon Lakbescherming) and others* [2001] ETMR 777 (Appeal Court of 's-Hertegenbosch, the Netherlands); cf *Magna Ltd v Abdullah Ismail* [1998] IP Asia LR 176 (Register of Trade Marks, Karachi), where the fact that the word WIMPY was listed in the dictionary as a trade mark was taken as *prima facie* support for the fact that it was a trade mark and not a generic term. On the duty not to list a registered CTM in a dictionary as if it were a generic term, see Chapter 8.

[56] William Landes and Richard Posner, 'The Economics of Trademark Law' (1988) 78 TMR 267, 294.

[57] See paras 6.31–6.33 above.

[58] *Sarl Wolke Inks & Printers GmbH v SA Imaje* [2003] ETMR 849 (Cour d'appel de Paris).

D. Conclusion

In this chapter we have seen what constitutes a generic term and have reviewed the issues which arise where (i) an attempt is made to turn such a term into private property or (ii) to force private owners to relinquish their grip on terms which properly belong with the public. We have shown that, with care and good management, a registered trade mark can be shielded against the risk of becoming generic. We have also sought to show that the encroachment of trade mark rights upon language as used in trade or by the public at large does not in fact impose any serious threat to the 'commons'.   **6.45**

We now move to consider the concept of the infringing act.   **6.46**

PART C

LAWFUL AND UNLAWFUL USE OF TRADE MARKS

7
INFRINGING ACTS

A.	Introduction	
	Press Release	
	The moral of the Press Release	7.01
B.	**The scope of trade mark infringement**	
	(1) Infringement actions: the *raison d'être* for registering trade marks	7.03
	(2) What activities does the law regard as 'infringing' acts?	7.05
	(3) A taxonomy of infringing acts	7.10
C.	**Specific instances of infringing use**	
	(1) What sort of physical activities constitute 'use'?	7.16
	(2) Affixing a sign to goods or packaging	7.18
	(3) Offering to sell goods or to supply services	7.19
	(4) Import/export	7.21
	(5) Use on business papers and in advertisements	7.24
D.	**Further observations concerning infringing use**	
	(1) Motive and knowledge are largely irrelevant to the issue of infringement	7.26
	(2) Applying to register another's trade mark	7.28
	(3) Oral use	7.29
	(4) Domestic use for overseas purposes	7.30
	(5) Use on the Internet	7.31
	(6) 'Invisible' use	7.32
	(7) Is infringing use negated by a disclaimer?	7.35
E.	**The 'course of trade' requirement**	
	(1) Infringing use must be 'in the course of trade'	7.38
	(2) 'Course of trade' infringement: the issues	7.39
	(3) What does 'use in the course of trade' mean?	7.40
	(4) Is use 'in the course of trade' the same as 'trade mark use'?	7.43
	(5) 'Trade mark use' and the effect of disclaimers	7.46
	(6) *Arsenal v Reed*: the end of the line for 'trade mark use' in Europe	7.49
F.	**Infringement by the trade mark owner**	7.52
G.	**Secondary infringements and infringers**	
	(1) Secondary infringing acts: aiding, abetting, authorizing and procuring infringement	7.55
	(2) Vicarious liability	7.60
	(3) Joint tortfeasors	7.61
H.	**The United States perspective**	7.63
I.	**Conclusion**	7.65

Chapter 7: Infringing Acts

A. Introduction

Press Release

Summer Holidaymakers are Warned of the Dangers of Fake Products from Perfume and Spirits to Aircraft Parts[1]

The Anti-Counterfeiting Group has issued a warning to international travellers that not only their luggage but also the aircraft they travel on could contain dangerous fakes [. . .].

The Group's warning coincides with the publication of a new report by The Intellectual Property Institute (IPI) into The Social & Economic Effects of Counterfeiting. The report includes new information including the involvement of organised crime in counterfeiting and also the trade in counterfeit aircraft parts, which has led to many accidents globally. Aircraft fakes have been linked to no fewer than 174 US aircraft crashes or accidents between 1973 and 1996. Even the US President's Air Force One and Two are not immune to the counterfeiting problem: in 1997, the oxygen and fire extinguisher systems were found to be 'unapproved'.

The IPI's report concludes that such reported cases are the tip of the iceberg due to a reluctance by all sides of the industry to fully acknowledge the problem.

At the other end of the scale, the fakes that many people think are 'harmless'— such as perfume, tobacco, alcohol or clothing—are anything but. For example, in 1997, 22 people in Russia died after drinking fake vodka and similar fakes have since been seized by UK trading standards officers. In another case, a seizure of fake perfume by the RUC in Northern Ireland found that the contents included urine used as a stabiliser.

Trainers that maim growing feet, toys with parts that could choke young children, clothing with flammable fabrics are just a few of the ever-growing list of fakes that are flooding markets around the world.

But the harm caused by counterfeiting is not restricted to the immediate physical damage that they can cause. Each year, in the UK, 4,100 jobs and around £768 million are lost because of counterfeiting-wrecking industries whilst lower tax income and increased benefit costs drain funds away from vital public services. At the same time, buying fake goods funds criminals. There are proven links into criminal activity across the board, from burglary, drug dealing, prostitution and pornography right up to international organised crime and terrorism.

The National Criminal Intelligence Service (NCIS) reports that 26 per cent of organised crime groups are involved in product counterfeiting. According to John Anderson, Executive Secretary of the Anti-Counterfeiting Group:

> paramilitary organisations in Northern Ireland are known to be involved in sales of counterfeit products and the people behind the World Trade Centre bombing in the US funded their activities through sales of counterfeit t-shirts.

He added:

> We are very concerned that consumers should recognise the consequences of their purchasing decisions—especially when buying goods on their travels. It may seem a trivial matter to pick up a fake handbag or pair of jeans but these

---

[1] Anti-Counterfeiting Group Press Release, 6 July 2001.

are just the lowest level of an industry that is wholly criminal and that puts people's lives, health and livelihoods at risk for the sake of a quick and easy profit.

Dr Paul Leonard, Director of the IPI, said:

I think that the scale and nature of the counterfeit industry is not really understood by the public at large: there are severe social and economic consequences. I was particularly perturbed to see countries such as Poland and the Czech Republic featuring high on the list of sources of counterfeit goods in the EU. We are now looking to include such countries as part of the European Union and one has to wonder what the effect on legitimate business will be when the borders come down.

The moral of the Press Release

7.01 Although trade mark infringement comes in different shapes and sizes, the principle that the law should enable trade mark owners to deal firmly with infringement applies equally in all cases, regardless of the real or apparent severity of these infringements. In this context we must understand that our attitude towards infringement is not always consistent: people who buy fake ROLEX watches in the Far East and show them proudly to their friends for a good laugh are neither more nor less human than people who die in agony after being treated by fake pharmaceutical or medicinal products which bear a trusted trade mark. Not all infringements however involve the exact reproduction or counterfeiting of the trade marks of others: the damage caused by other types of infringement may be measured in terms of the confusion of consumers (when faced, for example, with a choice between HARVARD and JARVARD products) and also in terms of the weakening of consumer confidence in a brand (for example, where a mark with a reputation for excellence in a field of activity such as engineering, such as ROLLS-ROYCE, is 'kidnapped' for use on inferior goods or services in another field of commercial activity—razor blades, confectionery or nightclubs).

7.02 This chapter examines the legal bases upon which a trade mark may be considered to be infringed, not merely through counterfeiting (to which the introductory Press Release alludes) but through the many techniques which a trade mark owner's competitors have cultivated in order to obtain a benefit from the intellectual property of another.

B. The scope of trade mark infringement

(1) Infringement actions: the *raison d'être* for registering trade marks

7.03 A trader will see no reason for obtaining a registered trade mark if it cannot be used against competitors and others who seek to gain advantage through using it or whose activities are likely to damage it. Accordingly the value of the trade mark system depends on the extent to which the activities of others can be categorized by the trade mark owner as 'infringing acts' so that the full force of the legal system can be brought to bear against them.

7.04 From the standpoint of the trade mark owner, there are two types of activity that are regarded as reprehensible: infringing activities and objectionable activities. The former are unlawful and can be prevented by legal action, however trivial they may be; the latter are annoying but cannot be prevented, however much they may damage the integrity of the trade mark or the value of the brand it represents. This chapter will review the former; the latter will be discussed in Chapter 8. Unfair comparative advertising, in the context of its legitimate step-sister fair comparative advertising, is also discussed in Chapter 8.

(2) What activities does the law regard as 'infringing' acts?

7.05 The Agreement on Trade-Related Aspects of Intellectual Property Rights (TRIPs) takes a two-step approach towards trade mark infringement. It first prescribes that the following fundamental right should be conferred on trade mark proprietors:

> . . . the exclusive right to prevent all third parties not having the owner's consent from using in the course of trade identical or similar signs for goods or services which are identical or similar to those in respect of which the trademark is registered where such use would result in a likelihood of confusion.[2]

7.06 TRIPs then refers to the protection which all TRIPs Member States must accord[3] to well-known trade marks under the Paris Convention,[4] stipulating that the Paris Convention protection of well-known marks must be extended to cover (i) service marks as well as marks for goods[5] and (ii) 'goods or services which are not similar to those in respect of which a trademark is registered, provided that use of that trademark in relation to those goods or services would indicate a connection between those goods or services and the owner of the registered trademark and provided that the interests of the owner of the registered trademark are likely to be damaged by such use'.[6]

---

[2] TRIPs, art 16.
[3] ibid, art 2(1).
[4] The Paris Convention on the Protection of Industrial Property Rights, art 6*bis*, which provides, in its relevant part, that: '(1) The countries of the Union undertake, *ex officio* if their legislation so permits, or at the request of an interested party, . . . to prohibit the use, of a trademark which constitutes a reproduction, an imitation, or a translation, liable to create confusion, of a mark considered by the competent authority of the country of registration or use to be well known in that country as being already the mark of a person entitled to the benefits of this Convention and used for identical or similar goods. These provisions shall also apply when the essential part of the mark constitutes a reproduction of any such well-known mark or an imitation liable to create confusion therewith'.
[5] TRIPs, art 16(2).
[6] Paris Convention, art 6*bis*(3).

B. The scope of trade mark infringement

The EU's trade mark harmonization Directive contains a list of acts which the trade mark owner has the exclusive right to stop other people doing. According to the Directive: 7.07

> The registered trade mark shall confer on the proprietor exclusive rights therein. The proprietor shall be entitled to prevent all third parties not having his consent from using in the course of trade—
>
> (a) any sign which is identical with the trade mark in relation to goods or services which are identical with those for which the trade mark is registered;
> (b) any sign where, because of its identity with, or similarity to, the trade mark and the identity or similarity of the goods or services covered by the trade mark and the sign, there exists a likelihood of confusion on the part of the public, which includes the likelihood of association between the sign and the trade mark.[7]

The Directive also gives EU Member States the option[8] to provide that 7.08

> ... the proprietor shall be entitled to prevent all third parties not having his consent from using in the course of trade any sign which is identical with, or similar to, the trade mark in relation to goods or services which are not similar to those for which the trade mark is registered, where the latter has a reputation in the Member State and where use of that sign without due cause takes unfair advantage of, or is detrimental to, the distinctive character or the repute of the trade mark.

All three of the infringing acts described in the Directive are trade mark infringements under the Community Trade Mark (CTM) Regulation.[9] Figure 7.1 shows a schematic diagram of infringing acts. 7.09

(3) A taxonomy of infringing acts

Although some countries have closely followed the TRIPs rubric, others have passed infringement laws in their preferred style of legislative drafting. Nonetheless, the content of TRIPs is, broadly speaking, a matter of shared legal culture within the international community. Four distinct types of infringement can be extrapolated from the provisions of TRIPs, which are reflected in the two sets of European rules. To simplify the analysis of trade mark infringement which follows, this book will refer to them as 7.10

Type 1: Use of the identical trade mark on goods or services which are the same as those for which the trade mark is registered [example: I make and sell my own ROLEX watches, although Rolex owns the trade mark for watches].

Type 2: Use of (i) an identical mark for similar goods or services, or (ii) a similar mark for the same goods or services, or (iii) a similar mark for similar goods or services, where in each case there exists a likelihood of confusion

---

[7] Council Directive 89/104, art 5(1).
[8] ibid, art 5(2).
[9] Council Regulation 40/94, art 9(1).

Chapter 7: Infringing Acts

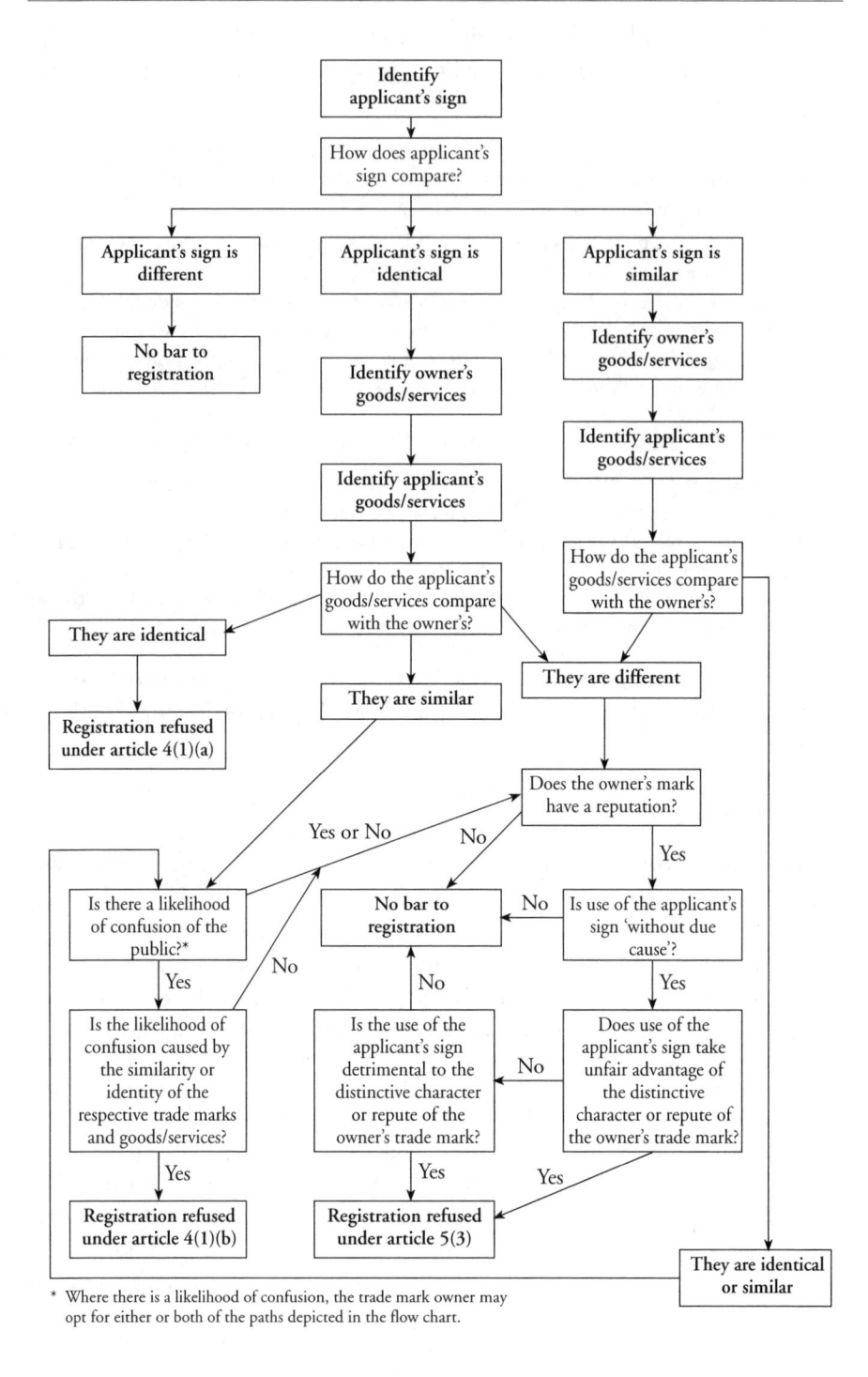

Figure 7.1 A schematic diagram of infringing acts under the Community Trade Mark Regulation, Council Regulation 40/94, art 5, taking into account the ECJ ruling in *Davidoff v Gofkid*.

B. *The scope of trade mark infringement*

on the part of the public [examples of each: (i) I call my non-alcoholic beer RIBENA; the trade mark RIBENA is already registered and used in respect of fruit juices; (ii) I call my perfume CHRISTINA DIOR; people buy it, thinking it to be a CHRISTIAN DIOR product; (iii) DENTINE is an existing trade mark for medicated chewing gum; I manufacture a medicated mouthwash under the trade mark DEN-KLEEN].

Type 3: Use of an identical or similar trade mark on goods or services which are quite different from those for which the trade mark is registered, where the user (i) obtains an unfair advantage from that trade mark or (ii) damages its reputation [examples of each: (i) when I promote a range of DOLBY hearing aids, people will assume that my hearing devices will have an advanced level of acoustic technology; (ii) I produce SONY jeans which are of poor quality and uncomfortable to wear, thereby making consumers reluctant to purchase other SONY products].

Type 4: Use of a well-known trade mark in respect of any goods or services to represent a connection between the user and the trade mark owner which damages the proprietor's interests [example: I open a retail pen shop called 'Mont Blanc'; the MONT BLANC trade mark is well known for pens but not for retail sales services. People visit the shop, do not like the range of low-quality mass-produced ball-point pens on offer and accordingly favour brands other than MONT BLANC in future].

Types 1, 2 and 3 were initially conceived as being mutually exclusive so that any alleged infringement which is of one type cannot at the same time be of another one. Nonetheless it is often necessary in legal proceedings to plead them together on the same facts. This is because it is sometimes unclear whether two trade marks, or indeed two sets of goods or services, are identical or similar: the court must decide on the facts whether Type 1, Type 2 or Type 3 is the appropriate ground upon which the trade mark proprietor may proceed against his adversary. Whether marks, goods and services are identical, confusingly similar, similar but not confusingly so, or indeed quite different, is considered at length in Chapter 10. The extent to which the European Court of Justice (ECJ) decision in *Davidoff v Gofkid* increases the potential for overlap between Type 2 and the Type 3 and 4 infringements is discussed in Chapter 11. **7.11**

In legal systems which are not based on the European model, such as the United States, there is more fluidity in categorizing infringement and, for example, causing confusion (a Type 2 infringing act) can be a factor in establishing dilution of a famous trade mark (a Type 3 and/or Type 4 infringing act).[10] Even within Europe, France does not appear to have wholly and consistently embraced the European model. In that jurisdiction, for example, the courts have continued to **7.12**

---

[10] *Nabisco, Inc et al v PF Brands Inc et al* (2d Cir 31 August 1999).

find a defendant liable for trade mark infringement where the parties' respective marks are different, but where the goods on which they are used are identical, without the need for the trade mark owner to prove that there is a likelihood of confusion.[11]

7.13 Types 3 and 4 are not mutually exclusive, since an activity which infringes Type 4 will generally be capable of infringing Type 3—but not vice versa. Most trade marks are well known because they are extensively used: Type 4 protects them because they are well known, while Type 3 protects them because their use has generated enough goodwill in their reputation to make it sufficiently attractive for another to use or abuse it.

7.14 Only in the case of Type 2 infringing acts is it necessary to consider the issue of confusion between the claimant's trade mark and the consequences of the defendant's activities. With Type 1 infringements, confusion is either considered irrelevant or is presumed and therefore need not be proved,[12] while with Type 3 and 4 infringement the damage which is addressed is damage caused by appropriating or assaulting a trade mark's reputation or distinctive character, not damage caused by befuddling the customer.[13]

7.15 The legal and commercial issues relating to the infringement of Type 3 and Type 4 marks are discussed further in Chapters 11 and 12.

C. Specific instances of infringing use

(1) What sort of physical activities constitute 'use'?

7.16 TRIPs does not go into detail as to what any given act of trade mark infringement physically entails. European legislation is however more forthcoming, providing a checklist of physical activities that are included within the scope of infringement.[14] Unauthorized use includes:

---

[11] See *Bouchard Pere & Fils v Pascal Bouchard*, 2 July 2002 (Cour de Cassation) (BOUCHARD PERE & FILS trade mark for wine infringed by PASCAL BOUCHARD); cf *AOM Minerve SA v INPI and another*, 15 December 2000 [2001] ETMR 1209 (Cour d'appel de Paris), in which, in the absence of evidence of a likelihood of confusion, POST'AIR could not be said to have infringed LA POSTE in respect of postal services.

[12] TRIPs Agreement, art 16(1).

[13] See the English High Court decision in *Pfizer Ltd and Pfizer Incorporated v Eurofood Link (United Kingdom) Ltd* [2000] ETMR 896, disposing of the contrary view taken in *BASF plc v CEP (UK) plc* [1996] ETMR 51 (HC) and *Baywatch Production Co Inc v The Home Video Channel* [1997] FSR 22 (HC). See also the pungent comment of Ray Black, '*Baywatch*: Sour Grapes or Justice' [1997] EIPR 39–42.

[14] Council Directive 89/104, art 5(3); Council Regulation 40/94, art 9(2).

C. Specific instances of infringing use

(a) affixing the sign to the goods or to their packaging;
(b) offering the goods, or putting them on the market or stocking them for these purposes under that sign, or offering or supplying services under that sign;
(c) importing or exporting the goods under the sign; and
(d) using the sign on business papers and in advertising.

Since this list is expressed to be non-exhaustive, the courts can add to it any activities which they consider to be a 'use'. Such a use will then constitute an infringement unless it falls explicitly within the scope of any of the statutory defences to infringement which the law provides. Let us now consider each of these specific uses in turn. 7.17

(2) Affixing a sign to goods or packaging

While the affixing of a sign to goods or packaging is an infringement, the mere printing or making of labels does not infringe the trade mark,[15] even though it may constitute an infringement of copyright in any artwork contained in the trade mark. In the UK and Ireland however, a person who puts a registered trade mark on to 'material intended to be used for labelling or packaging goods' is regarded as a party to any use of that material which infringes the trade mark, if he knew or had reason to believe that his application of the trade mark to the goods was not duly authorized by the proprietor or a licensee.[16] This should act as a natural deterrent to printers who are asked to print labels bearing well-known trade marks in suspicious circumstances, although the consequences of his being made a party to any subsequent infringing use are unclear. 7.18

(3) Offering to sell goods or to supply services

If I offer ROLEX watches for sale under a sign which reads 'These watches are fakes. They have no connection whatsoever with real ROLEX watches', am I still infringing the trade mark? After all, while the watches say 'ROLEX', I say 'NO-ROLEX'. The courts consider that such an offer constitutes an infringement of the trade mark even though the consumer is not confused or misled. This is correct. The sale of fake ROLEX watches under the ROLEX trade mark is a Type 1 infringement, which is actionable without the need to prove confusion.[17] 7.19

---

[15] *Beautimatic International Ltd v Mitchell International Pharmaceuticals Ltd and another* [1999] ETMR 912 (HC).
[16] Trade Marks Act 1994, s 10(5) (UK); Trade Marks Act 1996, s 14(5) (Ireland). This restriction is not found in Directive 89/104 but does not appear to be inconsistent with it.
[17] In *Arsenal Football Club plc v Matthew Reed* [2001] ETMR 860 the defendant sold merchandise under the legend 'the word . . . on the goods offered for sale are used solely to adorn the product and does not imply or indicate any affiliation or relationship with the manufacturers or distributors of any other product . . .', but did not even seek to rely upon this disclaimer in his defence to the trade mark infringement action.

7.20 If I offer LOREX watches under the same sign, can the sign stating 'These watches are fakes. They have no connection whatever with real ROLEX watches' absolve me of liability? This is a Type 2 infringement, where 'likelihood of confusion' must be proved. However, close scrutiny of the law does not provide an easy answer. TRIPs states that there should be infringement 'where such *use* would result in a likelihood of confusion'.[18] The EU's version of this[19] finds that there is infringement where, after comparing both (i) the respective trade marks and (ii) the goods or services for which they are used, there exists a likelihood of confusion on the part of the public. The TRIPs version therefore depends on the actual or probable facts of each case as it relates to the impact of the alleged infringing use upon the consumer, while the EU version focuses instead on the result of the twofold comparison. In practice this distinction may be of little consequence, since it is the similarity of the parties' respective marks and goods (the EU criterion) which establishes whether use of the allegedly infringing mark is likely to cause confusion (the TRIPs criterion).

(4) Import/export

7.21 Infringing goods remain infringing goods even if they are merely in transit between two other countries and are not destined to be put on sale in the country through which they are being transported.[20] This should be the case even if those goods do not infringe trade marks either in the country in which they originate or in their country of destination.

7.22 The fact that the importation has no market impact is not relevant to infringement through importation. Thus where a consignment of counterfeit WATERFORD glass, on its way from Bilbao in Spain to New York, entered the English port of Felixstowe without the defendant's knowledge so that it could be shifted from one ship to another, there had been infringement through importation.[21] Lack of market impact will however mean that, while a trade mark owner can obtain injunctive relief, delivery up or detention of goods, he will be unlikely to claim anything in excess of nominal damages: if goods are truly in transit, no damage has been done in the jurisdiction in which damages are sought.

7.23 In the UK it has been held that neither the act of printing labels bearing a UK-registered trade mark, nor the fixing of those labels on to packaging which was to be used on goods exported outside that jurisdiction, constitute an actionable in-

---

[18] Art 16(1).
[19] Council Directive 89/104, art 5(1); Council Regulation 40/94, art 9(1).
[20] *Salamander AG v Industria de Calcados Kissol Ltda, Too Vitl and Centra Anstalt* [1998] ETMR 94 (Supreme Court, Finland): goods en route from Brazil to Russia infringed registration in Finland; *Polo/Lauren Company LP v PT Dwidua Langgeng Pratama International Freight Forwarders*, Case C-383/98 [2000] ETMR 535 (ECJ): goods en route from Indonesia to Poland.
[21] *Waterford Wedgwood plc v David Nagli Ltd* [1998] FSR 92 (HC).

fringement of that trade mark.[22] This means that a third party who is the registered proprietor of the same mark in another country can lawfully outsource to a contractor in the UK the printing and affixation of labels for his products, which is good. It also means that the owner of the trade mark cannot nip in the bud a use of his trade mark which may lead to counterfeit goods bearing that trade mark entering markets in which their sale does infringe his rights, which is bad.

(5) Use on business papers and in advertisements

Perhaps the most extreme case of infringement under this heading occurred in a French case involving the trade mark EPSY, the name under which the claimant marketing company formerly traded.[23] The defendant, a competitor, published in *Marketing Magazine* an advertisement which included a brief *curriculum vitae* of one of its managers, who used to work for the claimant. This CV read:

7.24

> Jean Lagadec: ... After 12 years of experience in institutes of study (Motivation/Epsy/Synapse), he created Sylab ...

The Tribunal de Grande Instance held that this simple use of the name Epsy as a reference to where the defendant's manager acquired professional experience could not constitute a trade mark infringement. The Cour d'appel de Paris disagreed: it might be legitimate for Lagadec to use the name himself, but this was a use of the EPSY trade mark by the defendant for the purpose of advertising its own business and that use was an infringement under French law. This case may however reflect the continuing influence in France of the 'absolute right' theory of trade mark infringement,[24] since recent decisions of this nature cannot be found in other jurisdictions.

7.25

D. Further observations concerning infringing use

(1) Motive and knowledge are largely irrelevant to the issue of infringement

In civil infringement proceedings it is not normally necessary for the trade mark owner to prove that the defendant deliberately set out to infringe his trade mark. Nor is it necessary for the trade mark owner to prove that the defendant even had knowledge of his trade mark. Once a trade mark is registered, every other business in that jurisdiction is presumed to be familiar with it. The defendant's motive may

7.26

---

[22] *Beautimatic International Ltd v Mitchell International Pharmaceuticals Ltd and another* [1999] ETMR 912 (HC).
[23] *Sarl Sygroup and SA DCM v Société Sylab Ypsis and Jean Lagadec* [2001] ETMR 1275.
[24] See Isabel Davies (ed), *Sweet & Maxwell's European Trade Mark Litigation Handbook* (1998), para 6-37: 'no unauthorised party may use the trade mark of another in a commercial context without permission', an expression of sentiment which does not accord with the more detailed and specific content of Directive 89/104, art 5.

however be relevant to the extent to which he may exonerate himself from liability,[25] since Directive 89/104 and the CTM Regulation list a number of statutory defences based on honesty[26] and the range of court orders which a court is likely to bring to bear against a dishonest or deliberate defendant is wider than the range of remedies which it is likely to bring to bear against a blamelessly inadvertent one.

7.27 The defendant's motive and knowledge are significant issues in criminal proceedings and in proceedings for contempt of court, where a defendant who has already been found liable for infringement has acted in breach of, for example, a court order to discontinue his infringing acts or an order of delivery-up of infringing goods.[27]

(2) Applying to register another's trade mark

7.28 In some jurisdictions it is clear that the act of making an application to register another's trade mark will constitute an infringement of that trade mark,[28] presumably on the basis that it is an act done 'in the course of trade'. In some other countries it does not appear to have been established whether an infringing act has been committed at all.[29] Either way, a mark may be removed from the register in the event that it is found to have been registered in bad faith.[30]

(3) Oral use

7.29 It is not necessary for an act to be recorded in a permanent form such as print. Even an oral use of another's trade mark can be an infringing act. Thus using someone else's trade mark when announcing oneself as a trade representative,[31] or when answering the telephone,[32] can constitute an infringing act. Oral use is subject to the same criteria of infringement as any other type of use; accordingly an oral use of another's mark in a context which clearly does not lead customers to think that the defendant's goods originate with the claimant will not infringe that trade mark.[33]

---

[25] See eg *Aktiebolaget Volvo and another v Heritage (Leicester) Ltd* [2000] ETMR 940 (HC).
[26] See Chapter 8 (particularly paras 8.13–8.36).
[27] See Chapter 14 (particularly paras 14.33–14.35 and 14.39).
[28] ALVORADA *Trade Mark* [2003] ETMR 623 (Republic of Turkey Appellate Court Eleventh Tribunal). Infringement through making an application is also regularly asserted in French infringement proceedings.
[29] *Reality Group Ltd v Chance* [2002] FSR 13 (HC).
[30] For a detailed review of the law relating to bad faith in trade mark applications, see Chapter 13.
[31] *Premier Luggage and Bags Ltd v Premier Co (UK) Ltd and another* [2002] ETMR 787 (CA): the defendants' representatives called themselves 'Premier'.
[32] *Volvo Ltd v DS Larm Ltd and Dick Edvinsson* [2000] ETMR 299 (Swedish Supreme Court ruling against an unauthorized dealer in Volvo cars who answered the phone with the words 'Volvo service').
[33] *Hölterhoff v Freiesleben*, Case C-2/00 [2002] ETMR 917 (ECJ): use of trade mark for diamonds as a convenient reference to a specific style of diamond cut associated with the trade mark owner's diamonds.

D. Further observations concerning infringing use

(4) Domestic use for overseas purposes

7.30 The doing of an infringing act in the jurisdiction remains an infringement even if the ultimate market for the infringing product is another country.[34]

(5) Use on the Internet

7.31 The use of a trade mark on a website is capable of being an infringing use of that trade mark.[35] It has been accepted in the UK that the use of a trade mark on a website is not to be treated, at least in the absence of further evidence, as use of that trade mark in every jurisdiction to which the Internet extends.[36]

(6) 'Invisible' use

7.32 Need the use of a trade mark be visible to the consumer (i) at all, (ii) at the point of sale or (iii) at some other point in order to infringe that trade mark?

7.33 The use of another's trade mark as a metatag in order to draw an Internet user's attention to the existence of a website or banner which he is not actively seeking has been held to constitute an infringing use even though the Internet user may have no idea that the proprietor's trade mark, in machine-readable form, was employed for that purpose.[37]

7.34 The sale and distribution by the defendant of unauthorized copies of the claimant's pre-recorded video cassettes has been held to infringe the claimant's trade mark even though the trade mark in question was not visible at the point of sale: since it was encoded on to the video cassette tape itself, it could only be seen by viewers once they played the tape.[38]

(7) Is infringing use negated by a disclaimer?

7.35 Curiously there appears to be very little case law on the extent, if any, to which an alleged infringer can escape liability for infringement through attaching a disclaimer to his unauthorized use of another's trade mark. In one United States case[39] the defendant, who ran an Internet-based truck-locator service, used two of

---

[34] *Beautimatic International Ltd v Mitchell International Pharmaceuticals Ltd and another* [1999] ETMR 912 (HC).

[35] See Chapter 17, paras 17.51–17.63.

[36] *Euromarket Designs Incorporated v Peters and another* [2000] ETMR 1025 (HC); *1-800 Flowers Inc v Phonenames Ltd* [2002] FSR 191 (CA).

[37] See Chapter 17, paras 17.64–17.72.

[38] *Esquire Electronics v Executive Video* 1986 (2) 576 AD (South Africa). The Appellate Division of the Supreme Court overturned the trial court's ruling that the trade mark was used in relation to the film, but not in relation to the tape upon which it was magnetically recorded.

[39] *PACCAR Inc v TeleScan Technologies LLC*, No 00-2183, 5 February 2003 (US Court of Appeals for the Sixth Circuit).

the claimant's trade marks in the domain names of its websites as well as in metatags and as website 'wallpaper'. Visitors to those sites were confronted with a message:

> This web site provides a listing service for name brand products and has no affiliation with any manufacturer whose branded products are listed herein.

7.36 Dismissing the defendant's appeal, the appellate court affirmed the order of preliminary injunctive relief on the basis that the claimant had a strong likelihood of success at trial: the disclaimer—even if it did have the effect of escaping liability—arrived too late in that the defendant had already stolen surfers' initial interest by the use of the claimant's registered marks. The disclaimer defence is based on the premiss that 'initial confusion' may legitimately be caused to a consumer so long as that confusion is removed before the point at which the consumer makes a purchasing decision. European jurisprudence and case law do not however suggest that there is a basis for distinguishing between legitimate 'initial' confusion and illegitimate 'point of commitment' confusion.[40]

7.37 The use of the word 'imitation' or other similar added matter in front of another's trade mark (for example, IMITATION TISSOT for watches[41]) may also be intended to have the effect of a disclaimer of any connection between the user of that term and the trade mark proprietor and spare him liability for trade mark infringement. The use of a sign which contains a trade mark in this manner does not however appear to fall within the scope of any of the defences discussed in the following chapter.

E. The 'course of trade' requirement

(1) Infringing use must be 'in the course of trade'

7.38 The definitions in TRIPs, Directive 89/104 and the CTM Regulation of an infringing act all require that it be carried out 'in the course of trade'.[42] The meaning of this apparently bland and featureless phrase has sparked off some fierce controversy. Before we discuss that controversy further, let us seek to describe in general terms the issues which underlie it.

(2) 'Course of trade' infringement: the issues

7.39 There has been much debate on both sides of the Atlantic on the following issue:

---

[40] See eg *Sarl Le Book Editions v Sté EPC Edition Presse Communication and another* [1999] ETMR 554 (Tribunal de Grande Instance de Paris), discussed in Chapter 10, para 10.142.
[41] The 'Imitation X' phenomenon is discussed at length in Chapter 10, paras 10.18–10.20.
[42] See further paras 7.05–7.09 above.

E. The 'course of trade' requirement

Is there infringement whenever a person performs an act characterized as an infringing act with regard to another's trade mark, or must the use made of the trade mark also have to be its use *as* a trade mark. Andy Warhol's sequence of paintings of Campbell's soup cans is a case in point. The trade mark proprietor had registered the word CAMPBELL'S in relation to soup; Warhol had painted soup cans bearing the word CAMPBELL'S. In a narrow, literal sense he had used the registered mark (CAMPBELL'S) in respect of the goods for which it was registered (cans of soup) and could be regarded as an infringer. In a broader, metaphorical sense he was an artist creating art, not a food manufacturer creating food. Even the soup-consuming public recognized that Warhol's pictures were art and did not think of it as an invasion of Campbell's trade mark rights. But could the trade mark owner object that, while no direct and obvious loss of soup-can sales could be attributed to the popularity of the work of art, Warhol's trade in pictures reduced the ability of the CAMPBELL's trade mark to fulfil its trade mark function for soups? It could be argued, for example, that the CAMPBELL's trade mark underpinned and protected the brand values of sacred, family-oriented, warm, nourishing products while Warhol's use of the same trade mark would draw its family-oriented consumers to the antithetical values of violence, drug abuse, promiscuity and transvestism which characterized Warhol's alternative culture.

(3) What does 'use in the course of trade' mean?

7.40 The ECJ has observed that a use of a trade mark is 'use in the course of trade' where

> ... it takes place in the context of commercial activity with a view to economic advantage and not as a private matter.[43]

7.41 This is not a definition of 'use in the course of trade' but an observation concerning the circumstances in which such use generally occurs. In point of fact not all infringing use will be 'in the context of commercial activity with a view to economic advantage'. For example, if, without due cause, I perform acts which are detrimental to the repute of someone else's trade mark, the fact that such acts are not done with a view to my economic advantage would not make them any less infringing acts.

7.42 The ECJ has however made it clear that the words 'use in the course of trade' do mean a use which 'must affect or be liable to affect one of the functions of the mark' of the proprietor.[44] This requirement would appear to be a condition precedent to a finding that a trade mark has been infringed. It is plainly not a literal interpretation of the phrase 'in the course of trade' and it equally plainly requires the court, in infringement proceedings, to examine not merely the *characteristics* of

---

[43] *Arsenal Football Club plc v Matthew Reed*, Case C-206/01 [2003] ETMR 227 (ECJ), para 40.
[44] ibid, para 42.

the defendant's deeds but also their *consequences*. Since the trade mark right is a property right which serves the function of guaranteeing the origin of goods or services with which it is used,[45] an infringing use 'in the course of trade' is therefore any use which damages the capacity of that proprietary right to guarantee the origin of its proprietor's goods or services.

(4) Is use 'in the course of trade' the same as 'trade mark use'?

7.43 Until the dust started to settle on the ECJ ruling in *Arsenal v Reed*[46] it was argued with some force that, if an infringement only occurred where a prohibited act was performed 'in the course of trade', uses made of the proprietor's trade mark by the defendant which were not use 'as a trade mark' did not infringe. In this context, 'use as a trade mark' is a use which suggests that the origin of the defendant's goods or services is the same as that of the trade mark proprietor or that the two of them are somehow connected. For example, in the Andy Warhol example mentioned earlier,[47] putting a trade mark on a soup can would be a 'trade mark use' while painting it on to a canvas would not.

7.44 The same distinction between a 'trade mark' use and a 'non-trade mark' use may also be drawn in circumstances which are more obviously commercial and trade-based than in the Andy Warhol example. Such circumstances would include, for example, the use of another's trade mark which is not apparent at the point of sale or the point at which consumers might be expected to infer the existence of some link between the trade mark owner and the trade mark user. On this footing an Italian company printed albums into which children could stick portraits of famous footballers. Inside the albums the company printed the trade marks of the football teams for whom those footballers played. This use, which was not visible at the point of sale, was regarded as descriptive of the subject matter of the album and not therefore as being a use which fulfilled the functions of a trade mark.[48]

7.45 There is a further way in which the issue was analysed, by determining whether activities involving another's trade mark were even a species of 'use' at all. This approach can be seen from another case involving football stickers. The English Football Association (FA) put its trade mark, a 'three lions' crest, on to shirts which were subsequently worn by footballers who represented their country. A confectionery company, without first having sought the FA's permission, inserted in its products a series of collectable picture cards featuring photographs of footballers wearing shirts bearing that crest. The FA's use of the crest on the shirts was

---

[45] Council Directive 89/104, 10th recital; *Arsenal* (n 43 above), paras 32, 48.
[46] Discussed in greater detail in paras 7.49–7.51 below and in Chapter 8 (see paras 8.85–8.88).
[47] See further paras 7.10–7.15 above.
[48] *Milan AC SpA and Juventus FC SpA v Topps Italia Srl* [1999] ETMR 182 (Court of Milan). The reproduction of football club trade marks on separately sold stickers was however found to infringe.

E. The 'course of trade' requirement

a trade mark use, since it identified the FA as the source of those shirts, but the court held that the confectionery company's use of the crest was not a trade mark infringement. It could not be a 'use in the course of trade' because it was not even a 'use': that company sold confectionery, not shirts, and the crest was an incidental adornment of shirts which players happened to be wearing. Considering the examples of 'use' specified in article 5(3) of Directive 89/104,[49] the Court considered that it was unreal for the trade mark owner to suggest that its trade mark had been 'affixed' to the defendant's cards or that those cards had been put on the market under that mark.[50]

(5) 'Trade mark use' and the effect of disclaimers

7.46 If it were true to say that 'use in the course of trade' had to be a 'trade mark use', one way in which an unauthorized user could seek to escape liability for infringement would be for him to disclaim any notion that the trade mark has been used as a trade mark. Is it possible, by issuing a disclaimer, to remove the risk that one's use of another's trade mark will be seen as an infringing use? This approach is sometimes adopted by websites which offer 'replica goods' for sale. Fashiontime's website, for example, states:

> Fashiontime sells replica products for novelty purposes only. Anyone purchasing a watch from this site agrees to not pose the item as authentic and is for personal use only.[51]

7.47 This is only a general disclaimer and does not mention any trade marks by name. In contrast the Replicawatchworld website declares:

> Remember that we carry one of the largest selections of replica watches at the lowest prices. We will beat any price out there, guaranteed, so just ask. We carry replicas of Jacob & Co, Cartier, Breitling, Omega, Silverstein, and all others, along with an extensive selection of over 270 different replica Rolex models. Please contact us with any questions or requests.[52]

7.48 How has case law dealt with such disclaimers? In one Australian case a bootlegger sold CDs containing live recordings of the Rolling Stones rock group. Each disk carried a disclaimer stating that the recordings 'had not been authorised by the Rolling Stones group or by their record company'. The owner of the ROLLING STONES trade mark sued unsuccessfully for infringement: a majority of the judges considered that there was no infringement, since the words 'Rolling Stones' were used to indicate the name of the group, not as an indication of origin.[53] Where

---

[49] Implemented in the UK by the Trade Marks Act 1994, s 10(4).
[50] *Trebor Bassett Limited v The Football Association* [1997] FSR 211 (HC).
[51] www.fashiontime.net/commerce/Resources.htm#returns&warranty (verified 6 January 2003).
[52] www.replicawatchworld.com (verified 6 January 2003).
[53] *Musidor BV v Tansing (t/a Apple Music House)* (1994) ALR 593 (Federal Court of Australia, Full Court).

the connection between the proprietor's registered trade mark and the defendant's use of it is less blatant, liability for infringement can be avoided on similar facts even in the absence of a disclaimer, as can be seen from a Scottish case involving the pop group Wet Wet Wet.[54] This band failed to prevent the words protected by the registered trade mark WET WET WET being employed as part of the title of an unofficial book about that group. The obvious difference between the ROLLING STONES and WET WET WET cases is that, in the first, the bootleg CDs did in fact contain the work of the Rolling Stones, while the unauthorized book did not contain the *oeuvre* of Wet Wet Wet.

(6) *Arsenal v Reed*: the end of the line for 'trade mark use' in Europe

7.49 The question of whether use 'in the course of trade' is necessary may still remain live outside the EU, particularly where it relates to disclaimers and replica goods. However, the matter would now appear to be beyond debate in Europe itself. In the *cause célèbre* of *Arsenal v Reed* the acts complained of included the application of a trade mark-registered football team's name on an unlicensed scarf where, the defendant claimed, the use of the team's name was a use as a badge of loyalty, not a badge of origin and so consumers did not wrongly believe, basing their belief on the presence of the trade mark, that the goods originated from Arsenal Football Club. The court which referred this question observed that previous courts within the same jurisdiction were uncertain as to whether an infringing use had to be a use as a trade mark.[55]

7.50 The ECJ[56] has clearly indicated that there is not necessarily a dichotomy between 'trade mark use' (as characterized by use as a guarantee of origin) and 'non-trade mark use' (as characterized by use as a badge of loyalty): the same activity could be both, and indeed *would* be both, even if the same act was viewed as trade mark use by the trade mark owner and as non-trade mark use by the alleged infringer. Thus the use of another's trade mark as a badge of loyalty will constitute an infringing use,[57] as will any other use which damages the discharge of a trade mark's function of guaranteeing the origin of the trade mark owner's goods or services.

---

[54] *Bravado Merchandising Services Ltd v Mainstream Publishing (Edinburgh) Ltd* [1996] FSR 205 (Court of Session).

[55] See the contrasting views of Jacob J in *British Sugar plc v James Robertson & Sons Ltd* [1997] ETMR 118 (with which the Court of Appeal was in agreement in *Philips Electronics NV v Remington Consumer Products* [1999] ETMR 816) and *Philips Electronics NV v Remington Consumer Products* [1998] ETMR 124.

[56] *Arsenal Football Club plc v Matthew Reed*, Case C-206/01 [2003] ETMR 227, para 61.

[57] In *Arsenal Football Club plc v Matthew Reed* [2003] IP&T 75 the High Court refused to accept that, on the facts, an infringement had taken place. This decision was reversed by the Court of Appeal at [2003] ETMR 895. The Court of Milan, in *Gua Giù SNC v FC Internazionale Milano SpA* [2003] EIPR N-73, took a similar approach to the *Arsenal* trial court and granted a declaration of non-infringement to a party marketing INTER merchandise. It must be doubted whether this result could be achieved again in the light of the ECJ's *Arsenal* ruling.

F. Infringement by the trade mark owner

To conclude this discussion it is worth summarizing the position in the light of the Court of Appeal's ruling in *Arsenal v Reed*: **7.51**

(i) A trade mark is a property right which enables its holder to prevent uses that interfere with the specific function of a trade mark;

(ii) The specific function of a trade mark is to guarantee the origin of the goods or services for which it is registered;

(iii) A defendant's use that interferes with the essential function of a trade mark constitutes an infringement of that trade mark;

(iv) The unchecked use of the trade mark by a third party (except for a 'descriptive' use which is permitted by law) will impair the ability of the trade mark to communicate the fact that it is a guarantee of origin;

(v) Accordingly, therefore, all uses by third parties other than descriptive uses will be prohibited where both the signs and the goods are identical.

It is by no means certain that this conclusion reflects the position of the ECJ. For example, in *R v Johnstone*[58] (a decision of the House of Lords argued before judgment was given by the Court of Appeal in *Arsenal v Reed*, but not handed down until the following day) their Lordships agreed with the first three points listed above but thought that the effect of the ECJ's judgment was that only 'trade mark use', ie use which identifies the source of the defendant's goods, could interfere with the essential function of the trade mark and thus constitute infringement. Further, in the context of article 5(2) of Directive 89/104, the Advocate General in *Adidas v Fitnessworld*[59] has advised the ECJ that the use of another's trade mark as decoration or embellishment of the defendant's goods does not infringe where it is not a use which is perceived as distinguishing the origin of the defendant's goods. In doing so he distinguished *Arsenal v Reed*: **7.51A**

> That case concerned a claim for infringement under Article 5(1)(a), which provides for absolute protection in the case of identity between the mark and the sign and between the goods or services concerned and those for which the mark is registered. In that context the unauthorised use by a third party of the identical mark on identical goods was plainly trade mark use, notwithstanding that perception.[60]

F. Infringement by the trade mark owner

If infringement is so profitable, why don't trade mark owners 'infringe' their own trade marks? This question is not as stupid as it appears. Many trade mark owners, particularly those who make or market goods which are cheap to manufacture, are **7.52**

---

[58] *R v Johnstone* [2003] UKHL 28, 22 May 2003 (unreported), para 17.
[59] *Adidas-Salomon AG and Adidas Benelux BV v Fitnessworld Trading Ltd*, Case C-408/01, Opinion of 10 July 2003 (unreported) (ECJ), paras 52–62.
[60] ibid, para 62.

engaged in a constant battle against competitors who cannot be suppressed by normal judicial or market mechanisms. This is the case with pharmaceutical products, which may cost unimaginably large sums to discover and trial, but which are comprised of ingredients which may cost just a few pence. Once any patent protection for them has expired, they may legitimately be copied by generic pharmaceutical manufacturers. It is also the case for companies which develop exclusive scents, for which no patent protection is generally available, where 'smell-alike' products bearing different but often allusive brand names can erode or utterly destroy a promising market. Another example is found with designer watches: how many otherwise law-abiding people come back from the Far East proudly bearing fake ROLEX watches which they would not have had the nerve to steal if those watches had been genuine?

7.53 It is apparent that there is much money to be made from infringing trade marks. If so, the question should be asked why, for example, Rolex does not make its own genuine fake ROLEX watches. Presumably it would be able to employ higher standards of manufacture than its rip-off rivals; it would even be able to offer an international guarantee against breakage or malfunction (which none of its piratical competitors would be likely to match); more to the point, by achieving volume sales of its own 'fakes' it would be able to squeeze the pirates' profit margins and make real, unauthorized infringement less attractive. So great is the attraction and power of the ROLEX brand that even the sustained activities of infringers across the globe have failed to dim its lustre; it is therefore inconceivable that the supply of genuine fake ROLEX watches from the original source will damage the brand where the pirates themselves could not do so.

7.54 The idea of a company competing with itself is not novel. Some pharmaceutical companies manufacture both branded and generic versions of medicinal products, at premium and knockdown prices respectively.[61] Computer manufacturers have in the past 'cloned' their own branded products for the domestic end of their market.[62] And Nabisco have made house-branded WHEAT BISKS for sale by supermarkets in competition with their own WEETABIX.[63] So what is it that inhibits the notion of the trade mark owner making cheap fake versions of his own genuine products for sale to consumers who would not have bought the original non-fake version in the first place? So long as it remains possible to distinguish the genuine fake from (i) the real thing and (ii) third-party counterfeits, whether through packaging, materials, bar-coding, electronic tagging or any other technique, the quality and reputation of the genuine item, and therefore the reputation and value

---

[61] eg proprietary drug producer Merck has a specialized Merck Generics Group.
[62] Thus IBM-manufactured cut-price AMBRA clones for the UK market; see Jeremy Phillips, 'Unwanted Rivals' (1994) 40 *Managing Intellectual Property* 24–6.
[63] *United Biscuits (UK) Limited v Asda Stores Limited* [1997] RPC 513, 536 (HC).

of the trade mark which protects the brand, should not be jeopardized. On the other hand a trade mark owner may be reluctant to take a course of action which would highlight to consumers the fact that he could make a good quality product for a fraction of the price. This discovery might make consumers less willing to buy the real thing and the trade mark owner's monopoly profits would thereby be eroded, not to mention the trade mark's cachet of reputability.

G. Secondary infringements and infringers

(1) Secondary infringing acts: aiding, abetting, authorizing and procuring infringement

Neither TRIPs nor the major European trade mark laws directly address the extent to which acts which are preparatory to infringement as defined by law are themselves to be regarded as infringing acts. That does not mean that 'secondary' or 'preparatory' acts which lead to a statutorily defined infringement are not themselves civil legal wrongs under trade mark law, since many acts which are preparatory to another's infringing act are themselves explicitly listed in the pan-European legislation as primary infringements in their own right, for example, affixing the sign to the goods or to their packaging and stocking goods for infringing purposes.[64] **7.55**

Some countries take an even more inclusive approach, to the extent that even what might be regarded as 'secondary' infringers are themselves primarily liable for acts which are more remote from the primary infringement than those secondary acts listed in the Directive. Thus the Benelux Court of Justice has held that a general medical practitioner who gave a patient a prescription for '[trade mark] or similar generic product' was held both to have used and to have infringed the trade mark in question.[65] If this decision could still be achieved through the application of post-Directive 89/104 principles, it would place an extremely powerful tool in the hands of pharmaceutical trade mark owners. **7.56**

Although it is not common, some national laws make specific provision for secondary acts such as 'aiding and abetting' to be civilly actionable. In Turkey, for example, participating or assisting in, or abetting, infringing acts is itself an actionable infringement.[66] **7.57**

Outside the trade mark treaties and national or regional statute law, liability for secondary or preparatory acts may still be actionable under civil law. For example, **7.58**

---

[64] Council Directive 89/104, art 5(1); Council Regulation 40/94, art 9(1).
[65] *Nijs et al v Ciba-Geigy* Ing Cons 1984, 317.
[66] Decree-law on Trade Marks 556, art 61(e) (Turkey). Article 61(a)(c) of the same law additionally imposes severe penalties including imprisonment, fines and closure of the workplace.

the Austrian Civil Code[67] provides that a person who assists or encourages the committing of a civil wrong is himself liable for damages and Austrian jurisprudence is clear that the same provision will support an action for injunctive relief. Also noteworthy is the Civil Liability Act in Ireland, which provides that two or more people may be considered 'concurrent wrongdoers' even if the wrongdoing of one or more of them was only incidental to the damage incurred by the injured party. That Act goes further and renders each of them liable for the entire damage in respect of which they are concurrent wrongdoers.[68]

7.59 The common law may also offer support to the injured trade mark owner. For example, in the UK there is a little-used tort of civil conspiracy, which would render liable a person who shares a common design with others to commit a civil wrong (such as a trade mark infringement).[69]

(2) Vicarious liability

7.60 While many trade mark laws are silent on the issue, Austrian law specifically provides that an employer will be liable for the trade mark infringements carried on by his employees.[70]

(3) Joint tortfeasors

7.61 A further issue to consider is whether the party who performs the infringing act is the sole trade mark infringer or whether it is possible to join, as a joint wrongdoer or 'tortfeasor', another party such as the infringing party's parent company. Joint liability may be established by, for example, demonstrating that, while only one of the two parties committed the infringing act, the two parties shared a common design.

7.62 There may be particular advantages to joining another party. For example, (i) the parent company's assets may greatly exceed those of the actual infringer or (ii) it may be possible to bring proceedings in the jurisdiction in which the parent company is located. (Discussion of specific legal issues relating to joint tortfeasorship lies beyond the scope of this book.)

H. The United States perspective

7.63 Like Europe, the United States has also addressed these issues. The statutory provisions, in their relevant part, read as follows:

---

[67] General Civil Code, art 1302 (Austria).
[68] Civil Liability Act 1961, ss 11(1), 12(2) (Ireland).
[69] *Douglas, Zeta-Jones and another v Hello! Ltd and others*, 11 April 2003 (unreported) (HC).
[70] Trade Mark Law, art 54 (Austria).

H. The United States perspective

§32 (15 U.S.C. §1114). Remedies; infringement; innocent infringers

(1) Any person who shall, without the consent of the registrant—
(a) use in commerce any reproduction, counterfeit, copy, or colorable imitation of a registered mark in connection with the sale, offering for sale, distribution, or advertising of any goods or services on or in connection with which such use is likely to cause confusion, or to cause mistake, or to deceive; or
(b) reproduce, counterfeit, copy or colorably imitate a registered mark and apply such reproduction, counterfeit, copy or colorable imitation to labels, signs, prints, packages, wrappers, receptacles or advertisements intended to be used in commerce upon or in connection with the sale, offering for sale, distribution, or advertising of goods or services on or in connection with which such use is likely to cause confusion, or to cause mistake, or to deceive,

shall be liable in a civil action by the registrant for the remedies hereinafter provided . . .[71]

7.64 On reading these provisions one is instantly struck by how much more direct they are than their European equivalent and how much more formidably pro-trade mark owner is their mode of expression. To establish infringement one needs to show (i) a prohibited use (ii) which is without consent, (iii) which is in commerce and (iv) which is likely to confuse, mistake or deceive. Even though the United States law must, like European law, address the difficult issue of whether an alleged infringement is committed in the course of trade, the United States seems to have avoided the jurisprudential tangle over whether the infringing use is a 'trade mark use'[72] and it does not have to address arcane issues of 'likelihood of association'. There is no pussyfooting around 'without due cause' and 'distinctive character or repute'. Read over again the concept of trade mark infringement as encapsulated in TRIPs and ask yourself two questions: (i) which of the two great systems, the American or the European, better addresses the task of protecting registered trade marks? (ii) if you were taking liberties with the trade marks of others, under which of these two systems would you prefer to face an action for trade mark infringement?

---

[71] Lanham Act, s 32 (15 USC, s 1125).
[72] This is not to say that the same sort of factual problems do not arise in the US. In *Boston Professional Hockey Assoc, Inc v Dallas Cap & Emblem Mfg, Inc* 510 F 2d 1004 (5th Cir 1975) the defendant sold reproduction trade mark emblems that were unattached to any product. The court held in favour of the trade mark owner. This approach was rejected in *International Order of Job's Daughters v Lindeburg and Co* 633 F 2d 912; 208 USPQ 718 (9th Cir 1980), which held that the manufacture of jewellery in the form of the trade mark proprietor's insignia did not infringe the claimant's rights. In both cases the analysis appears refreshingly direct and fact-oriented when compared to European jurisprudence on the same issues.

Chapter 7: Infringing Acts

I. Conclusion

7.65 This chapter has sought to sketch out the scope of trade mark infringement and the nature of specific infringing acts, addressing the various different species of infringement and touching on some of the more interesting or sensitive issues which they raise. Type 3 and 4 infringements will be analysed in greater detail in Chapters 11 and 12. The boundaries of infringement will be reviewed in Chapter 8 and the legal mechanism for dealing with individual infringements will be discussed in Chapter 14.

7.66 From this chapter it can be seen that many, but by no means all, activities which trade mark owners find objectionable may be accommodated within the broad scope of the four definitions of trade mark infringement. Much time and effort has however been expended in debating issues relating to 'trade mark use' and 'non-trade mark use' and some of these debates are somewhat circular in appearance.

8

NON-INFRINGING ACTS

A. **Introduction**
  'I'm sure we can get away with it'
  The moral of the story — 8.01
B. **Taxonomy of non-infringing acts**
  (1) Why doesn't every unauthorized use of a trade mark infringe it? — 8.02
  (2) Non-infringing acts: the law — 8.08
    (a) Infringing use must be 'in the course of trade' — 8.11
C. **Acts for which specific defences are provided**
  (1) Fair use of descriptive terms — 8.13
    (a) Geographical origin of goods — 8.21
    (b) Intended purpose of goods — 8.22
    (c) Kind of service — 8.28
    (d) Quality of the goods — 8.29
    (e) Use of trade marks which are also the 'names' of goods — 8.30
  (2) The use of one's own name and address — 8.33
    (a) The use of corporate names — 8.34
    (b) The use of indicia of personal status — 8.36
  (3) Other activities that fall within the scope of 'infringement' but which are nonetheless permitted by law
    (a) Use of one's own registered trade mark — 8.37
    (b) Use of a trade mark which happens to be someone else's name — 8.43
    (c) Making use of the style of a trade mark but not the mark itself — 8.45
    (d) Local permitted use of a national trade mark — 8.47
    (e) Prior use — 8.50
    (f) Honest concurrent use — 8.51
D. **Acts which are permitted in principle, even without a statutory defence** — 8.52
  (1) Abuse of goods bearing trade marks — 8.53
  (2) Copying only the non-protected elements of the trade mark owner's product — 8.56
  (3) Incorporating only the weak part of another's mark into one's own trade mark — 8.57
  (4) Burying the trade mark in your own trade mark — 8.59
  (5) Freedom of speech — 8.60
    (a) Freedom of speech and derogatory reference to another's mark — 8.61
    (b) Trade marks and freedom of expression in the United States — 8.63
    (c) Do traders enjoy a 'freedom of commercial speech'? — 8.64
  (6) Parody, satire and irony — 8.66
    (a) Judicial responses — 8.67
    (b) The impact of comparative advertising — 8.70
    (c) The trade mark owner's revenge — 8.71

	(7) Hiding the infringing bits of an infringing use	8.72
	(8) Use in small advertisements	
	(a) 'Private small ads'	8.73
	(b) Marks too small to be discerned	8.75
	(9) Boycotts	8.76
	(10) Calling a product by its trade mark instead of by its product name	8.78
	(11) Half-infringing two separate marks	8.83
	(12) Using a trade mark as a badge of loyalty or allegiance	8.85
	(13) Calling one's dog Elvis	8.89
E.	**Limitation of actions**	8.90
F.	**Comparative advertising**	
	(1) Use of another's trade mark in the course of 'comparative advertising'	8.93
	(2) Comparative advertising and trade mark law	8.99
	(a) What does 'comparative advertising' have to do with trade mark law?	8.100
	(3) The Misleading and Comparative Advertising Directive	8.102
	(a) How does the Directive relate to trade mark law?	8.110
	(4) Voluntary codes of advertising practice	8.114
	(5) Treatment of 'comparative advertising' in the European Court of Justice	8.116
	(6) Treatment of 'comparative advertising' under national law in Europe	8.120
	(a) The UK statute	8.121
	(b) English case law	8.125
	(c) Other European case law	8.136
	(7) Comparative advertising in Europe: a tentative summary of key principles	8.141
	(a) How acceptable is the use of another's trade mark?	8.142
	(b) By what standard should the advertiser's behaviour be judged?	8.147
	(c) Who is the judge of 'honesty'?	8.150
	(d) Burden of proof	8.151
	(e) Dishonesty must be 'material'	8.153
	(f) Assessing the quantum of damage	8.156
	(g) Ordering an injunction	8.157
	(8) Comparative advertising: an exercise in principles and exceptions	8.158
	(9) Comparative advertising: some interesting problems to address	8.165
	(a) Does a third party's unauthorized use of a registered trade mark count as use for revocation purposes?	8.166
	(b) Does a third party's unauthorized use of an unregistered trade mark count as use for the purposes of distinctiveness acquired through use?	8.167
	(c) Infringement in comparative advertising where the mark used is not the same as the mark registered	8.168
	(d) How will comparative advertising involving 'new' types of trade mark be treated by the courts?	8.169
	(e) Endorsement transfer as comparative advertising	8.171
	(10) Comparative advertising in the United States	8.172
G.	**The effect of consent**	8.177
H.	**Conclusion**	8.179

A. Introduction

'I'm sure we can get away with it'

'Are you seriously going to make a James Bond film, Ernie?'

Ernie removed his spectacles, slowly polished them and returned them to their former position. Looking over their shiny metal rims he delivered his measured response. 'Of course I am, Betty. I've thought it all out. The film's going to be called *James Bond, Indiana Jones and Victoria's Davidson*. Not bad, eh? That should attract a little pre-launch excitement.' So long as your father's bank provides the production money, he thought.

'What sort of lunacy is that! How on earth do you reckon you can give a film a name like that and not end up in court,' snapped Betty. Having a talented boyfriend could be a liability at times, she mused. Do boyfriends ever grow up?

'Don't worry, there's no problem,' Ernie reassured her. She had heard that smug, slightly patronizing voice before. When he reversed her Ferrari into a fencepost after telling her there was enough room to back up.

'Of course there's a problem,' Betty expostulated. 'How are you going to be able to use the name James Bond? That's been trade marked. Everyone knows that.'

'No problem. It's not *the* James Bond, it's *another* James Bond. Look. Here's a photo of him. He's going to play himself,' explained Ernie.

'He doesn't look as though he's licensed to kill,' pondered Betty. 'How old is he?'

'Oh, he's quite old,' Ernie agreed. 'About fifty-seven, I think. Introducing James Bertram Algernon Bond. He's an accountant actually. But he always liked amateur dramatics. He did Professor Higgins in the local *My Fair Lady* last Christmas.'

'He doesn't look very sexy. And what about Indiana Jones? That's definitely a trade mark and I bet there's no one else around with such a dumb name.'

'Well, there's no problem using Indiana, because that's a place name and you can't stop people using place names. And there's no problem using Jones either, because that's a common surname. That's called the public domain, you know.' Once again Ernie oozed self-assurance.

But Betty was not so sure. 'But there are plenty of common surnames around and most of them don't go with Indiana. If you want to use a common surname, why don't you call him Indiana Singh?'

Ernie rolled his eyes. Another stupid question. 'Because it's not a musical.'

'And what about this Victoria's Davidson? What's that supposed to be about?'

'Well, you know there's a brand of lingerie called VICTORIA'S SECRET? And there's a bike called HARLEY DAVIDSON? I've gone and put them together. The film script is all about how James Bond and Indiana Jones team up to track down an international villain who rides around on a powerful motorbike in his underwear.' Ernie had all the answers.

'How did he get a powerful motorbike in his underwear?'

'Are you trying to be funny?'

'No,' bleated Betty, 'but I just don't understand. If VICTORIA'S SECRET and HARLEY DAVIDSON are trade marks, then isn't VICTORIA'S DAVIDSON a trade mark infringement too?'

'No problem, sweetings.' Ernie was really enjoying his moment of glory. 'VICTORIA'S SECRET is registered for knickers and HARLEY DAVIDSON is registered for motorbikes. I don't do knickers or bikes. I'm using the words for the title of a film.

There can't be any harm in that.'

'I suppose not,' murmured Betty. 'But what happens if anything does go wrong. What will you do then?'

'No problem.' Ernie smiled his most patient smile. 'I've got another film lined up.'

'What's that one?'

'*Bilbo Potter and the Towering Inferno.*'

The moral of the story

8.01 Not every annoying thing that someone other than a trade mark owner does to a trade mark actually infringes it. The dividing line between infringement and non-infringement can be a fine one. Sometimes liability will depend on the nature of the allegedly infringing act itself; sometimes it will also depend on the state of mind of the alleged infringer: did he know of the trade mark and did he act honestly with regard to it? This chapter will investigate some of the issues raised in escaping liability for trade mark infringement.

B. Taxonomy of non-infringing acts

(1) Why doesn't every unauthorized use of a trade mark infringe it?

8.02 The trade mark laws of all countries take great care to define the activities which constitute infringement of a valid trade mark. This care reflects the need for competitors of the trade mark owner to learn how they can safely trade and run their businesses without also running the risk of being sued by him. It is assumed, at least in the UK, that a businessman can run his business however he wants, unless there is some good legal reason why he should not do so.[1] Accordingly, if there is any doubt as to whether a trader has carried out an act which the law does not permit, or which the trade mark owner has not permitted, he will expect to receive the benefit of it.

8.03 The first type of non-infringing act considered here involves the unauthorized use of another's trade mark in a way which the law has failed to regulate at all. For example, in the musical *Evita* the eponymous heroine sings:

> I came from the people, they need to adore me
> So Christian Dior me from my head to my toes.
> I need to be dazzling, I want to be Rainbow High.
> They must have excitement, and so must I.[2]

8.04 There is no suggestion that this use of a famous trade mark as a verb is in any sense capable of serving as infringement of that mark. To give another example, the

---

[1] *Hodgkinson Corby Limited and another v Wards Mobility Services Limited* [1995] FSR 169, 174 per Jacob J.
[2] 'Rainbow High' (lyrics by Tim Rice).

B. Taxonomy of non-infringing acts

sports pages of most national newspapers carry photographs of athletes wearing sportswear with clearly visible logos: this too is not a use of the trade mark which requires the permission of the trade mark owner.

A second type of unauthorized use involves infringing acts which are specifically allowed. Sometimes this is because they are commercially trivial. For example, a holidaymaker brings back home with him a packet of cigarettes which was sold to him lawfully in Taiwan but the importation of which infringes the rights in a trade mark granted in his own land. Other types of unauthorized use are specifically allowed even though they may be economically highly significant and indeed quite commercially damaging to the trade mark owner: they may be permitted by the law because they are regarded as conferring some specific economic benefit, such as the importation of trade mark-protected products from a country in which they are marketed cheaply and their resale in another country where they fetch a higher price.[3]   **8.05**

A third type of non-infringing activity involves those acts which fall within the scope of statutory trade mark infringement and for which there is no statutory defence, but which do not infringe because someone has authorized them.[4]   **8.06**

This chapter will first consider the general principles of law which govern non-infringement and will then review all three types of non-infringing act.   **8.07**

(2) Non-infringing acts: the law

The concept of permitted but unauthorized[5] use of another's trade mark is well established. The Agreement on Trade-Related Aspects of Intellectual Property Law (TRIPs) itself permits Member States to provide limited exceptions to trade mark infringement such as   **8.08**

> fair use of descriptive terms, provided that such exceptions take account of the legitimate interests of the owner of the trademark and of third parties.[6]

Both Directive 89/104 and the Community Trade Mark (CTM) Regulation have explicitly provided for a number of limited exceptions to infringement. Under both the Directive[7] and the Regulation[8]   **8.09**

> The trade mark shall not entitle the proprietor to prohibit a third party from using, in the course of trade—

---

[3] See further Chapter 9.
[4] See further paras 8.177–8.178 below and Chapter 16.
[5] In this book 'permitted' means 'permitted by the law', while 'authorized' means 'authorized by the trade mark proprietor'.
[6] TRIPs, art 17.
[7] Council Directive 89/104, art 6(1).
[8] Council Regulation 40/94, art 12.

(a) his own name or address;
(b) indications concerning the kind, quality, quantity, intended purpose, value, geographical origin, the time of production of goods or of rendering of the service, or other characteristics of goods or services;
(c) the trade mark where it is necessary to indicate the intended purpose of a product or service, in particular as accessories or spare parts;

provided he uses them in accordance with honest practices in industrial or commercial matters'.

8.10 Figure 8.1 provides a diagrammatic account of trade mark defences and the scope of these defences is reviewed below in greater detail.

(a) Infringing use must be 'in the course of trade'

8.11 A trade mark is not infringed by an unauthorized use of it which is not 'in the course of trade'. The Court of First Instance (CFI) has ruled that the use of the euro symbol is not the use of a sign 'in the course of trade' even though it is used by traders and for the purpose of trade, since that symbol is used in front of numbers so as to indicate an amount of money. It is not used for the purpose of guaranteeing the origin of any goods or services.[9] The question whether there has been use 'in the course of trade' recurs later in this chapter and is discussed in some detail in the context of the use of a trade mark as a badge of loyalty by football fans.[10]

8.12 The use of another's trade mark as part of a name of a non-trading organization is not a use in the course of trade. On this basis the proprietor of the FORD trade mark in Brazil could not prevent the Association of Former Ford Dealers from using the word 'Ford' in its title.[11]

C. Acts for which specific defences are provided

(1) Fair use of descriptive terms

8.13 Unlike the law of copyright, trade mark law does not have a generally accepted defence of 'fair use' or 'fair dealing'. Instead, the law of most countries tends to list a number of specific categories of conduct which, if done fairly, do not constitute trade mark infringement. In contrast, the United States has developed, in addition to its own statutory defences,[12] a general principle of 'nominative fair use'.[13]

---

[9] *Travelex Global and Financial Services Ltd (formerly Thomas Cook Group Ltd) and Interpayment Services Ltd v Commission*, Case T-195/00, 10 April 2003 (CFI).
[10] See further paras 8.85–8.88 below.
[11] *Ford Motor Company v Association of Former Ford Distributors*, WTLR, 5 June 2003.
[12] See eg the defences listed in Lanham Act, s 43(c)(4), 15 USC, s 1125(c)(4).
[13] See *New Kids on the Block v New America Pub Inc* 971 F 2d 302 (9th Cir 1992): the proprietor of trade marks for the NEW KIDS series of toys failed to prevent two newspapers conducting phone-in surveys to find out which NEW KIDS products their readers liked best.

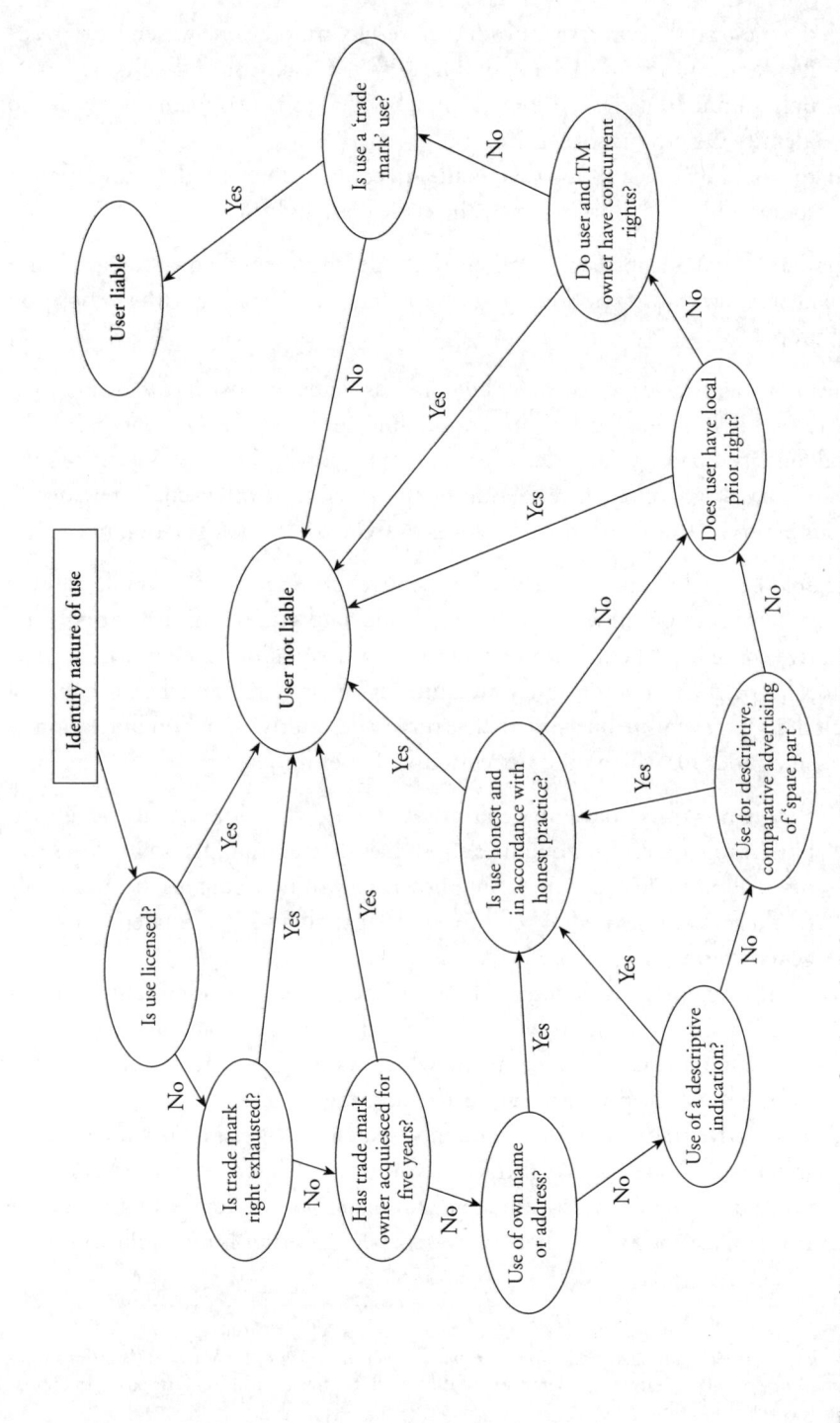

Figure 8.1 A diagrammatic account of trade mark defences (Council Directive 89/104, art 6(1); Council Regulation 40/94, art 12).

Under the nominative fair use doctrine an unauthorized use of another's trade mark will not infringe it where three conditions are fulfilled:

(i) the trade mark proprietor's product or service must be one which is not readily identifiable by the defendant if he does not make use of the trade mark;
(ii) only so much of the trade mark may be used as is reasonably necessary to identify the product or service; and
(iii) the user must do nothing that would, in conjunction with the mark, suggest sponsorship or endorsement by the trade mark holder.

8.14 This defence, which appears to embrace both descriptive and non-descriptive but nonetheless fair uses of another's trade mark, may be contrasted with the position in Europe.

8.15 The following paragraphs consider both 'fair use of descriptive terms', which article 17 of TRIPs mentions but does not define, and 'indications concerning the kind, quality, quantity, intended purpose, value, geographical origin, the time of production of goods or of rendering of the service, or other characteristics of goods or services' to which the two pieces of EU trade mark legislation refer.

8.16 It should be recalled that exclusively descriptive terms are not registrable as trade marks. That does not however mean that trade marks do not have a strongly descriptive content to them. On the contrary, many situations arise in which trade marks have a dual function. They are quite legitimately registered on account of their descriptive nature but nonetheless serve a descriptive function in relation to the same goods for which they are registered. For example

(i) a trade mark may have no descriptive content when it is actually registered but acquire descriptive qualities subsequently (for example, KIWI FRUIT was originally a trade mark for a fruit known as a Chinese gooseberry; eventually that term became used to refer to the fruit itself and it ultimately became a generic term);
(ii) a trade mark may have originally been a descriptive term but may have obtained a secondary, non-descriptive meaning (for example, Nestlé's TASTEE-FREEZ UK trade mark for ice cream, which was originally refused registration on account of its primary descriptive meaning[14]);
(iii) a figurative trade mark may contain verbal or visual elements which are descriptive, but it remains registrable because overall it serves a trade mark function rather than a descriptive one (for example, the representation of the words THE EUROPEAN in respect of newspapers covering Europe, illustrated in Chapter 5[15]);

---

[14] See *Tastee Freez International Ltd's application* [1960] RPC 255 (HC).
[15] For a further example, see *Tax Free trade mark application* [1998] ETMR 193 (Bundespatentgericht) in which a figurative representation of the words 'tax free for tourists Europe tax free shopping' was held registrable.

C. Acts for which specific defences are provided

(iv) car trade marks are, in the real world, used in a manner which is both distinctive and generic. Thus VOLVO distinguishes the cars made under that label from OLDSMOBILE, SKODA or SAAB. Yet automobile repairers describe themselves as being skilled in repairing a particular *genus* of car (we talk of 'Fords', 'BMWs' or 'Volkswagens') and owners continue to describe their cars by that *genus* long after they have been fitted with a multitude of parts which were not manufactured or supplied by the original maker.

8.17 The more efficiently trade mark registries handle trade mark applications, the fewer truly descriptive (rather than dual-function) marks will slip through the net. Even so, the fact that a trade mark can nonetheless be used by others as a descriptive term without offending the owner's legal rights shows that the position of competitors and of the general public remains well protected. The courts are however unlikely to allow the protection accorded by these provisions to be abused. In one English Court of Appeal decision, for example, a judge reflected that the function of the 'fair description' defence was

> to permit the characteristics of the defendant's goods or services, for example, in an advertisement, but not (whether alone or in conjunction with other words) to perform the dual function of indicating both the characteristics and the trade origin of the defendant's goods.[16]

8.18 In other words, the defendant can use another's mark as a descriptor, but not also as a trade mark. The judge continued:

> I do not believe that it can have been intended ... to allow the use of confusingly similar indications of the trade origin of the goods or services .... [T]o allow it would fundamentally subvert the policy which has hitherto underlain trade mark protection.

8.19 This opinion, subsequently reflected in the words of the European Court of Justice (ECJ),[17] currently represents a correct analysis of both the law and the commercial considerations which led to it. It is expected that this view will be reinforced by the ECJ in *Gerolsteiner*, in which the Advocate General recommended that the defendant's use of a geographical term as a trade mark was a factor that should be taken into account when considering the honesty of the defendant's conduct.[18]

8.20 Under the headings which follow, I have described how the defence of fair use of descriptive terms has been handled by the courts in various countries.

---

[16] *The European Ltd v The Economist Newspaper Ltd* [1998] ETMR 307, 316 per Millett LJ.
[17] *Windsurfing Chiemsee Produktions- und Vertriebs GmbH v Boots- und Segelzubehör Walter Huber and Franz Attenberger*, Joined Cases C-108 and 109/97 [1999] ETMR 585, para 28.
[18] *Gerolsteiner Brunnen GmbH & Co v Putsch GmbH*, Case C-100/02, 10 July 2003 (unreported) (ECJ Opinion of AG Stix-Hackl).

Chapter 8: Non-infringing Acts

(a) Geographical origin of goods

8.21 LAPHROAIG is a well-known trade mark in whisky-drinking circles. After the whisky was distilled at the Laphroaig Distillery in Scotland, some of it was sold under the LAPHROAIG trade mark for consumption by the public in its finished form, while the rest of it was sold, unbottled and untreated, for blending into other whisky products. The trade mark proprietor sold the untreated whisky on terms that it was not to be sold in bottles under the LAPHROAIG brand. The defendant, a bottling company, procured some of the untreated whisky and sold it under a label stating 'Islay single malt Scotch whisky from LAPHROAIG DISTILLERY'. The court concluded that the fact that the claimant had not put forward an arguable basis for disputing the 'place name' defence did not mean that it had failed to establish a *prima facie* case of trade mark infringement.[19]

(b) Intended purpose of goods

8.22 With one important exception this defence should rarely be capable of being successfully invoked. In most cases the consumer will be able to deduce the intended purpose of goods which he purchases from sources of information other than the trade mark of someone who has not manufactured those goods. Moreover, where it is through the use of another's trade mark that the intended purpose of goods is revealed to the consumer, it must be asked whether the trade mark itself performs a function which is descriptive or functional and which therefore suggests that the mark consists of a sign which should be left open for use by others. Where the party relying on this defence uses the allegedly infringed trade mark as all or part of his own trade mark, the defence will fail because it is difficult to characterize such use as being in accordance with honest commercial practices.[20]

8.23 The important exception is the use of another's trade mark in order to indicate product compatibility: this may be done, for example, by the use of statements such as 'this software has been written in order to reduce the frequency of crashes experienced by users of Microsoft Explorer in a Microsoft Windows environment' or 'this engine oil has been specifically designed in order to enhance the performance of BMW motors'. The use of another's trade mark is specifically condoned when it indicates that the product to which it is attached functions as a 'spare part' for the product with which that trade mark is associated, for example, 'these cartridges are compatible with all PARKER fountain pens'.

---

[19] *Allied Domecq Spirits & Wine Ltd v Murray McDavid Ltd* [1998] ETMR 61 (Court of Session, Scotland): interim relief was however recalled on the balance of convenience.

[20] *System 3R International AB v Erowa AG and Erowa Nordic AB* [2003] ETMR 916 (Stockholm District Court) (where 'combi' meant a product which had the function of combining with others and the claimant owned the COMBI CTM for chucks, the defendant called its own products EROWA Combi and EROWA CombiChuck).

C. Acts for which specific defences are provided

8.24 Even where compatibility with another's product is the unauthorized trade mark user's aim, he must be careful how he seeks to achieve it. Where a manufacturer of razor blades sought to indicate compatibility with Gillette's razor-blade holder he sold his blades in packages of much the same colour and decoration as Gillette's, bearing a formula along the lines of

> These razor blades fit the Sensor device of Gillette, and GILLETTE and SENSOR are registered trade marks of The Gillette Company

but not actually saying that his blades were not Gillette's. The Court of Appeal of The Hague preferred the following formula:

> These razor blades do not originate from The Gillette Company. It is however possible to use them in Gillette's Sensor holder.

8.25 This case was later remitted to a different Court of Appeal for consideration of a number of related issues, including those of (i) the significance of the argument that the razor blades were not a 'spare part' for the holder since the razor blade was the 'main product' which could function without the holder but not vice versa and (ii) Gillette's argument that none (or perhaps not more than one) of the many uses of their trade marks on the defendant's packages was actually 'necessary' in that the intended purpose of the razor blades could have been conveyed to consumers without using the trade marks.[21]

8.26 Another example of the fine line which divides an acceptable indication of one product's compatibility with another from a violation of another's right is shown in a Danish case[22] in which the defendant's website described its coffee filters both as 'MELITTA-style' and as being able to 'fit with MELITTA'. The first of those uses infringed; the latter was permitted.[23]

8.27 This defence has attracted the interest of some conspicuously undeserving defendants whose idea of 'necessity' has strained the courts' credulity. Thus the retention of the original manufacturer's registered trade mark on reconditioned batteries is not regarded as being necessary to indicate the intended purpose of those batteries.[24] Nor is it in any sense 'necessary' for a supplier of spare parts to appropriate an original equipment manufacturer's trade mark as part of a domain name in order to alert consumers to its own websites on which the trade mark proprietor's goods are sold.[25]

---

[21] *Hermans Groep BV v Gillette Nederland BV and The Gillette Company Inc* [2002] ETMR 150 (Supreme Court, The Hague).

[22] *Melitta SystemService and another v Coffilter International* (2003) 17 WIPR 6 (Supreme Court).

[23] The use of another's trade mark in indicating 'style' has been found permissible in a specific and far narrower context in *Hölterhoff v Freiesleben*, Case C-2/00 [2002] ETMR 917 (discussed at paras 8.45–8.46 below).

[24] *PAG Ltd v Hawke-Woods Ltd* [2002] ETMR 811 (HC).

[25] *Sarl Wolke Inks & Printers GmbH v SA Imaje* [2003] ETMR 849 (Cour d'appel de Paris).

(c) Kind of service

8.28 The owner of a Danish device mark consisting of a stylized form of the word TELE-MAEGLEREN ('tele-broker') for the analysis of telecommunications services sued the defendant company, a telecommunications routing agency, which named its client newsletter *Telemaegleren*. The court held that there was no infringement. Because the word TELE-MAEGLEREN was inherently descriptive of tele-broking, it was principally in the device and not in the word that the trade mark monopoly vested. The defendant's use of the word was indeed descriptive and there were no circumstances to lead the court to conclude that its use was unfair.[26]

(d) Quality of the goods

8.29 The French proprietor of two figurative trade marks for shampoo containing the words ULTRA DOUX ('ultra soft') sued a competitor who sold CLEANARGILE shampoo which added the words 'ultra doux' on the label. At first instance the court dismissed the infringement action, accepting that the defendant's use was descriptive.[27] On appeal however this decision was reversed: the words ULTRA DOUX were not the whole of the claimant's mark but they were by far the most prominent part of them and the defendant's launch of the 'ultra doux' descriptor occurred just at the point at which the trade mark proprietor was investing heavily in an advertising campaign for its product.[28] Presumably therefore the defendant's use was not in accord with honest commercial practice.

(e) Use of trade marks which are also the 'names' of goods

8.30 A body of case law has recently affirmed that it is not a trade mark infringement for a car dealer or repairer—even if he is not an official dealer—to employ the trade mark-protected name of the car in the description of his business. Thus the unauthorized use of slogans such as 'Volvos repaired here' or 'We specialize in BMWs' will be lawful.[29] However, it is not permitted to use the trade mark in such a way as to suggest falsely that one either is the trade mark owner (for example, by answering the phone with the word 'Volvo'[30]) or that one is an official dealer, distributor or in any other way connected with the trade mark owner.[31] The question has been posed, but not yet answered, as to whether such use of the trade marks of

---

[26] *Tele-Mægleren ApS v Netsource Danmark A/S* [2000] ETMR 523 (Maritime and Commercial Court, Denmark).
[27] *Laboratoire Garnier & Cie v Sté Copar* [1998] ETMR 114 (Tribunal de Grande Instance de Paris).
[28] *Laboratoire Garnier & Cie v Sté Copar* [2000] ETMR 1124 (Cour d'appel de Paris).
[29] *Bayerische Motorenwerke AG (BMW) and BMW Nederland BV v Deenik* [1999] ETMR 339 (ECJ).
[30] *Volvo Ltd v DS Larm Ltd and Dick Edvinsson* [2000] ETMR 299 (Sweden).
[31] *Aktiebolaget Volvo and another v Heritage (Leicester) Ltd* [2000] ETMR 940 (HC).

C. Acts for which specific defences are provided

the motor manufacturer is limited to word marks or whether it would include the use of figurative marks such as car logos.³²

8.31 The problem of trade mark-protected product names is not confined to cars. It also occurs in respect of other products which, being known by their trade mark, are not conveniently referred to by any other name. In one French case the defendant sought to justify his use of the trade mark-protected name by which the claimant's commercial databases were known, when selling information abstracted from those databases. This defence was bound to fail since, once the claimant showed that the abstracted data sold by the defendant infringed his copyright and database right, his use of the trade marks could not be regarded as being 'in accordance with honest practices in industrial or commercial matters'.³³

8.32 A similar result has been achieved in the United States where a Circuit Court of Appeal dismissed the notion that the sale of BEANIE BABIES toys from the bargain-beanies.com website constituted a dilution of that trade mark. Taking cognizance of the commercial reality of the marketplace, the Court said:

> You can't sell a branded product without using its brand name, that is, its trademark … That market [for second-hand toys as collectors' items] is unlikely to operate efficiently if sellers who specialize in serving it cannot use BEANIES to identify their business … [s]o that to forbid it to use Beanies in its business name and advertising (Web or otherwise) is like forbidding a used car dealer who specializes in selling Chevrolets to mention the name in his advertising.³⁴

(2) The use of one's own name and address

8.33 The honest use by a human being of his or her own genuine name cannot be prevented under trade mark law. This has been the case even before human rights law came into existence and is good news for anyone called Max Factor who is thinking of making or selling his own range of cosmetics. However, the use of one's name *as a trade mark* will not be tolerated by the law if another person owns a trade mark for the same name. This is because the public's interest in not being confused by the existence of two identical or nearly identical trade marks for the same product is given a higher legal value—and, in the hands of the trade mark owner, indubitably enjoys a higher commercial value—than the individual's right to use his own name. So Max Factor the Second can state on his products that he is their originator, but he cannot use the name MAX FACTOR as a trade mark.

---

[32] *Volkswagen AG and Audi AG v Garage X* [2003] ETMR 225 (Swiss Federal Court).
[33] *Société Reed Expositions France (Formerly Groupe Miller Freeman) v Société Tigest Sarl* [2003] ECDR 206 (Cour d'appel de Paris).
[34] *Ty Inc v Perryman*, 4 October 2002 (7th Cir Court of Appeals).

(a) The use of corporate names

8.34 What is the position regarding names other than human birth names? The situation is unclear. The question as to whether a company was entitled to make use of the 'own name' defence was raised in the UK in the complex *Scandecor* case, which was settled before the reference of this question to the ECJ could be made.[35] An English court has however ruled that, even if the defence is available to a company, it cannot rely on it when, having learned of the claimant's trade mark, it changes its name and style so as to resemble it more closely.[36] Nor can a human rely on an alleged nickname as a basis upon which to trade with another's trade mark.[37]

8.35 An English court has found that the use of the trade mark REED in the defendant's corporate name as part of a copyright notice on a website was an infringement of that trade mark.[38] This decision has been the subject of an appeal.

(b) The use of indicia of personal status

8.36 In the United States the former members of the BEACH BOYS pop group were not to be entitled, in the absence of an agreement to the contrary, to use for commercial purposes the trade mark of their old band.[39] However a former Playmate of the Year was permitted to use the trade mark-protected terms PLAYBOY, PLAYMATE and PLAYMATE OF THE YEAR 1981 on her personal website and also as a metatag.[40] The suggestion that the ex-Playmate could avoid use of Playboy's trade marks by describing herself as the 'nude model selected by Mr Hefner's magazine as its number one prototypical woman for the year 1981' was considered to be absurd.

(3) Other activities that fall within the scope of 'infringement' but which are nonetheless permitted by law

(a) Use of one's own registered trade mark

8.37 The law cannot be expected simultaneously to blow hot and cold. If it grants a person a trade mark monopoly, following a formal process of application and examination, it would be absurd to say in the same breath that the holder of that mark both owned the monopoly rights in that mark and was actually infringing someone else's mark. Where a later trade mark does indeed appear to overlap with

---

[35] *Scandecor Development AB v Scandecor Marketing AB and others* [2001] ETMR 800 (HL).
[36] *NAD Electronics Inc and another v NAD Computer Systems Ltd* [1997] FSR 380 (HC).
[37] *Biba Group Ltd v Biba Boutique* [1980] RPC 413 (HC), a passing-off case.
[38] *Reed Executive plc and Reed Solutions plc v Reed Business Information Limited, Reed Elsevier (UK) Limited and Totaljobs.Com Limited* [2003] RPC 207 (HC).
[39] *Brother Records Inc v Jardine*, 28 January 2003 (9th Cir): original Beach Boy prevented from performing as 'Beach Boys Family and Friends'.
[40] *Playboy Enterprises, Inc v Terri Welles* [2002] EIPR N-97 (9th Circuit Court of Appeals).

C. Acts for which specific defences are provided

an earlier one, the owner of the earlier mark may not assume that the use of the later mark is of necessity an infringement: logically it would seem necessary first to test the validity of the later mark by applying to have its registration cancelled or revoked. If the owner of the earlier mark succeeds in doing that, the user of the later trade mark, like a snail prised from its shell, is a succulent and vulnerable target.

8.38 Does the law specifically provide a trade mark owner with a defence when he seeks to use his own registered trade mark but is allegedly infringing another's mark? The two major pieces of European legislation make the same provision:

> The trade mark shall not entitle the proprietor to prohibit a third party from using, in the course of trade—
>
> ...
>
> (b) indications concerning the kind ... or other characteristics of goods or services; provided he uses them in accordance with honest practices in industrial or commercial matters.[41]

8.39 The defendant in our case is seeking to use, in the course of trade, *his own trade mark*—which must be regarded as an 'indication concerning the kind ... or other characteristics' of his goods or services—in order to distinguish his own goods or services. Further, the use of one's own trade mark to distinguish one's own goods or services is likely to be 'in accordance with honest practices in industrial and commercial matters'.

8.40 It can happen that the claimant in infringement proceedings actually holds the more recent of the two trade marks. This occurred in the *XTC* case[42] in which the claimant, who secured the 'XTC Ecstasy' trade mark in Austria for non-alcoholic drinks on 10 August, sued the defendant for selling XTC (eks)(ti:)(si:)' guarana drink. Although the defendant's own Austrian trade mark was granted on 9 September, a month after the claimant's, his mark stemmed from a Madrid Agreement international application which was entitled to the priority of an earlier Swiss registration dated 15 April. Accordingly, ruled the Austrian Supreme Court, the defendant could rely upon the use of his own mark in defence of the infringement action.

8.41 A party may not be able to rely on the fact that he is using his own trade mark if he is not using it in the manner in which it has been registered, unless any variation between the mark as registered and the mark as used is to a trivial or negligible extent. He certainly will not be able to rely on that defence if the mark actually used

---

[41] Council Directive 89/104, art 6(1); Council Regulation 40/94, art 12. (The UK Trade Marks Act 1994, s 11, which implements article 6 of the Directive, makes specific provision as follows: 'A registered trade mark is not infringed by the use of another registered trade mark in relation to goods or services for which the latter is registered ...'.)

[42] *XTC trade mark* [1998] ETMR 268.

lies somewhere between the mark which he has registered and a third party's famous mark.[43]

8.42 An interesting but ultimately doomed attempt was made in Hungary to excuse an otherwise infringing use of the trade mark MONTÁZS ('montage') where the claimant and the defendant were both publishers. The defendant published the *Heti Montázs* ('daily montage') advertising magazine, the title of which had been lawfully registered under the Press Act. According to the defendant it was the Press Act and not the Trade Marks Act which governed the legitimacy of the use of periodical titles and, since the defendant was using its own lawfully registered periodical title, it was immune from liability for trade mark infringement. The Supreme Court did not agree. Trade mark law and press law provided two separate and unrelated systems for protecting names and it was for the claimant to choose whichever avenue of relief it wanted.[44]

(b) Use of a trade mark which happens to be someone else's name

8.43 If I want to write a biography of a modern-day celebrity, for example, Madonna or Hugh Grant, I would almost certainly discover that the celebrity had been advised by his or her publicity agent to register that name as a trade mark. Among the things that celebrities register their names as trade marks for are many of the items which fall within Class 16 of the Nice Classification: posters, photographs, picture postcards, in fact pretty well everything made of paper and which enthusiastic devotees may wish to purchase. The question is therefore whether, by calling my book a title such as *The Life and Times of Madonna* or *A Brief Guide to the Philosophy of Hugh Grant*, will I be infringing their trade mark rights? The two celebrities might well resent the fact that I will be making a lot more money by selling even a mediocre book which bears their name on the cover than I could ever make from writing an excellent book on trade marks but which lacked so overt a reference to celebrity subject matter; they would even be right to allege that I was writing about them simply in order to cash in on the goodwill which vests in their names. But I would not be infringing their trade marks: my use of their names would be a descriptive use, relating to Madonna the person, not Madonna[45] the icon, to Hugh Grant the person and not Hugh Grant the merchantable commodity.[46]

---

[43] *Sanrio Co Ltd v Dong-A Pencil Co Ltd*, 27 November 2002 (Seoul High Court, South Korea): misappropriation of variant of the HELLO KITTY trade mark. This case is on appeal to the Supreme Court.

[44] MONTÁZS *trade mark* [2001] ETMR 275 (Supreme Court, Budapest).

[45] While on the subject of names, the following school playground riddle is too good to omit, even from a serious work of scholarship such as this. *Question*: 'George Bush has a short one; Arnold Schwarzenegger has a long one; Madonna doesn't have one; the Pope has one but doesn't use it. What is it?' *Answer*: 'A surname'.

[46] *Bravado Merchandising Services Ltd v Mainstream Publishing (Edinburgh) Ltd* [1996] FSR 205 (Scotland).

C. Acts for which specific defences are provided

8.44 Where the trade mark GLENN MILLER was registered in respect of concert services, the use by the defendant of the advertising slogan 'Bill Baker Remembering the Glenn Miller Army Air Force Band' was not considered to infringe it. The District Court of The Hague was not committed to the conclusion that the defendant's use even fell within the scope of infringement but, if it did, this use was an evocation of the memory of the original Glenn Miller orchestra and not an activity which the trade mark registration was capable of restraining.[47]

(c) Making use of the style of a trade mark but not the mark itself

8.45 Just as there is no copyright in a style, so too there is no protectable interest in the style of a trade mark. Accordingly, in one instance a proprietor registered trade marks consisting of (i) the words DEMOISELLE DE CHAMPAGNE and (ii) the shape and outer surface decoration of a champagne bottle which evoked a 'Belle epoque' image. The defendant did not infringe these two marks by appropriating for himself a similar 'Belle epoque' image when he named his champagne BELLE DE CHAMPAGNE and put it in a bottle which conveyed a similar ethos. He did however infringe the trade mark in the champagne bottle by making only non-distinctive changes to the proprietor's bottle decoration when he copied it.[48]

8.46 In the same way as the copying of a style is not an infringement of a trade mark, it is not an infringement to make an oral reference to a word trade mark where that trade mark is spoken of as the style of a product. Thus where a trader referred to the cutting of his diamonds in the 'spirit sun' and 'context cut' styles, he was not infringing the SPIRIT SUN and CONTEXT CUT trade mark registrations.[49] The use of those trade marks was intended to convey information about the particular characteristics of the appearance of those diamonds and would not have been taken by their purchaser as a representation that the diamonds were supplied or cut by the trade mark owner; according to the ECJ that was not a trade mark use.

(d) Local permitted use of a national trade mark

Under the European harmonization Directive **8.47**

> The trade mark shall not entitle the proprietor to prohibit a third party from using, in the course of trade, an earlier right which only applies in a particular locality if that right is recognised by the laws of the Member State in question and within the limits of the territory in which it is recognised.[50]

---

[47] *Glenn Miller Productions Inc and another v Stichting Bill Bakers Big Band Corporation* [1999] ETMR 247.
[48] *Vranken SA v Champagne H Germain et Fils SA* [1998] ETMR 390 (Cour d'appel de Paris).
[49] *Hölterhoff v Freiesleben*, Case C-2/00 [2002] ETMR 917.
[50] Council Directive 89/104, art 6(2); see also Council Regulation 40/94, art 8(4) which relates to grounds of opposition but not to granted trade marks. Article 6(2) applies as a defence to infringement of a CTM through the operation of Council Regulation 40/94, art 97(2).

8.48 This principle is similar to that which will be adopted when, on the enlargement of the European Union, the territorial protection conferred upon existing CTMs will be extended from fifteen countries to twenty-five: this extension will 'swamp' local registrations of trade marks which are adverse to the CTM but, in those countries in which the national mark is validly registered, its owner will be able to continue to use it.

8.49 How much local use will entitle the defendant to evade infringement? It is possible that a great deal of concentrated local use may assume more than purely local significance (for example, where a local business acquires national or even international renown[51]) and be capable of supporting an application for cancellation, but if it is too small it will be of no real significance at all and may be ignored. A Dutch court has suggested that local use must be 'intensive and continuous' if it is to be of any use to the party pleading it.[52]

(e) Prior use

8.50 The grant of a trade mark does not give the proprietor the right to prohibit any activity which commenced before the date of that trade mark's registration.[53] Thus registration of the trade mark RYTZ did not entitle that trade mark's proprietor to require a company, Rytz Industriebau, to cease use of that name under which it had been trading for more than twenty years.[54]

(f) Honest concurrent use

8.51 In the UK it is possible for two trade marks to be registered by competing traders for use in respect of the same goods. This happened when the American and Czech brewers of BUDWEISER beers were both held to have used that word in respect of the same product, 'beer, ale and porter'.[55] Each had an entitlement to the use of the mark; neither could exclude the other but both, presumably, can exclude any third party brave enough to try its luck in that jurisdiction with yet another BUDWEISER beer.

---

[51] eg Maxim's famous restaurant in Paris, which was held to have acquired transnational goodwill in *Maxim's Ltd v Dye* [1977] 1 WLR 1155. A less glamorous example is that of Harry Ramsden's original fish and chip shop, which was opened in Bradford in 1928. Ramsden's local shop was eventually patronized by customers.

[52] *?What If! Holdings Ltd v The What If Group BV* [2003] ETMR 481 (Hague District Court).

[53] Curiously, no provision to this effect exists in Directive 89/104, the CTM Regulation, the Paris Convention or TRIPs. Under UK law, the date of registration is taken to be the date on which the application for registration was made: Trade Marks Act 1994, ss 9(3), 43(3).

[54] *Rytz Cie SA v Rytz Industriebau AG* [2001] ETMR 363 (Federal Civil Court, Switzerland): no right to stop defendant registering rytz.ch domain name.

[55] Anheuser-Busch holds UK registration no 1125449, while Budejovicky Budvar holds UK registration no 1389680. See also *Anheuser-Busch Inc v Budejovicky Budvar NP* [2000] RPC 906.

D. Acts which are permitted in principle, even without a statutory defence

There are a range of activities that are permitted without the need for a specific defence, because they do not even fall within the scope of 'infringement'. These are discussed in the following paragraphs. **8.52**

(1) Abuse of goods bearing trade marks

The placement of products in a film may enhance those products' reputation and boost sales. Well-known examples of successful product placement include the use of Reese's Pieces to entice the much-loved alien in the children's classic *E.T.* and the succession of cars designated for James Bond over nearly half a century. Indeed, the concept of product placement has a poignant scene to itself in the perceptive comedy *The Truman Show*.[56] But the choice of product may by the same token also damage a product's reputation (for example, where a repugnant villain identifies his preference for a specific branded product), particularly where the trade mark is clearly depicted or the shape and nature of the product is clearly identifiable. If a film producer purchases products in which the trade mark right is exhausted there is nothing to stop him placing them in the hands of a particularly unpleasant or unsympathetic character. **8.53**

Many trade mark owners, particularly in the fashion industry, must silently grieve the purchase of their products by the wrong consumers. There have been anecdotal reports that sales by the Next chain of fashion shops dropped after the prime market of elegant young ladies became aware that their own mothers were buying the clothes which had been intended for the younger generation. Some abuses of a trade marked product are more subtle, since the eye of the consumer is not immediately drawn to them. For example, in the 1980s the Rolls Royce Motor Company made much of the fact that photographers were draping naked models over the bonnets of their vehicles for the purpose of taking pictures of an erotic nature. At the time, the company's trade mark department made many complaints concerning what was seen as a coarsening of the refined image which the trade mark was seeking to achieve.[57] **8.54**

Sometimes the trade mark abuse may give the trade mark a cachet of excitement which the trade mark owner, while not actually endorsing, does not actually disown. The MARS bar, for example, was not known for its erotic possibilities until the advent of 'Mars bar parties'.[58] The erotic potential of BARBIE and KEN children's dolls was **8.55**

---

[56] See further Kalle Lasn, *Culture Jam* (2000), p 107.
[57] Speech of Louis Gaze (Rolls Royce) at the first MARQUES conference, Vienna, 1986.
[58] 'Many parents were also very concerned about crude, explicit or "lewd" lessons on sex by adults

however utilized by one website operator, which used real Barbie and Ken dolls to demonstrate various positions.[59] In Europe in particular the laws relating to trade mark protection do not assist the owners of the ROLLS ROYCE, MARS, BARBIE and KEN trade marks where the acts complained of are done in relation to lawfully marketed and purchased products in respect of which the trade mark rights are exhausted. Article 5(2) of Directive 89/104, which provides relief against detriment to the repute of a trade mark,[60] will not avail the trade mark owner since the use of which he complains is use of the goods themselves rather than use of the mark. Some sort of defamation action, based on an alleged representation or implication that the trade mark owner has somehow endorsed or encouraged the sort of activities complained of, might possibly be argued but its prospects of success are a matter of speculation.

(2) Copying only the non-protected elements of the trade mark owner's product

8.56 Anything which is not covered by the protection of a trade mark, or which has been disclaimed in the application as falling outside the scope of its protection, can in theory be copied without running the risk of facing an action for trade mark infringement. However, a sufficiently angry trade mark owner may well sue even if there is little or no realistic likelihood of success, possibly alleging acts of unfair competition as an alternative ground of liability. In one Danish case the Supreme Court affirmed that, even where there is some similarity between the shape, size and colour scheme of the respective parties' products (in this case 100-gram chocolate blocks), trade mark protection cannot extend to features which are determined by their manufacture, such as the sealed flaps on a chocolate bar's wrapping which are actually the result of the use of a 'flow-pack' method of production.[61]

(3) Incorporating only the weak part of another's mark into one's own trade mark

8.57 Compound trade marks rarely contain elements which carry equally distinctive force. For example, NEW YORK KNICKS is registered as a trade mark in respect of a

---

"who should know better". Hence a national outcry in March 1994 after Leeds pupils of ten and eleven had "Mars Bar parties" explained to them in response to a question (using chocolate bars during oral sex) ... The lesson was by a nurse visiting from the Health Authority. One mother said: "When I heard about the lesson on affairs I was very upset, but my child was almost too embarrassed to talk to me about the lesson involving Mars bars."' (www.globalchange.com/books/rpl1.htm).

[59] See also the discussion of Barbie-like 'dungeon dolls' at paras 8.66–8.71 below.
[60] The ambit of this provision is discussed in depth in Chapter 11.
[61] *Alfred Ritter GmbH & Co KG and CK Chocolade A/S v Ion SA Cocoa & Chocolate Manufacturers* [1997] ETMR 103.

D. Acts which are permitted in principle

well-known NBA basketball team. This mark consists of three words: NEW (which is extremely common), YORK (which is far less common than NEW but nonetheless a frequently found surname and forms all or part of the name of at least three well-known cities) and KNICKS (which is relatively uncommon and highly distinctive). If I choose to call my basketball team the NEW JERSEY NETS, I have taken one-third of the words of NEW YORK KNICKS but no one would regard this as an infringement of the NEW YORK KNICKS trade mark since the only word held in common by the two team names, 'new', would be accounted to the fact that the names of the cities of New York and New Jersey share the word 'new'; the word 'new' in NEW YORK KNICKS would in any event be viewed together with 'York' as a geographical descriptor and not as a distinctive component in its own right. If however I adopted the team name NEW JERSEY KNICKS I would stand accused, at the very least, of a lack of imagination even if I were not regarded as a trade mark infringer.

This position has the support of case law. For example, in Denmark the use by Nike of the common word 'alpha' on its NIKE ALPHA PROJECT footwear was held not to infringe the ECCO ALPHA trade mark for the same goods.[62] Likewise in Latvia the use of the word mark BOLS INSIDE was not regarded as having infringed the well-known mark INTEL INSIDE.[63] 8.58

(4) Burying the trade mark in your own trade mark

Sometimes a trade mark—even a well-known or downright famous one—is buried so deeply in someone else's trade mark that no one would even imagine that they had anything to do with one another. This happened to Polo Ralph Lauren, whose POLO trade mark (registered for, among other things, perfumes and cosmetics) failed to mount an opposition to the registration of the mega-mark 10 ROYAL BERKSHIRE POLO CLUB for the same goods.[64] Although this was not an infringement case, it is submitted that the same principle would be applicable if it had been.[65] 8.59

(5) Freedom of speech

In modern European society the forces of free competition, in their attack on the sanctity of the trade mark monopoly, have now been joined by the forces of freedom of speech. Freedom of speech is a value which not only the Council of 8.60

---

[62] *Ecco Sko A/S v Nike Denmark ApS* [2001] ETMR 371 (City Court, Horsholm).
[63] *Intel Corporation v Distilleerijen Erven Lucas Bols BV* [2001] ETMR 1300 (Patent Office, Board of Appeal).
[64] *Royal Berkshire Polo Club's application* [2001] ETMR 826 (UK Trade Marks Registry).
[65] In one infringement case, *British Sugar plc v James Robertson & Sons Ltd* [1996] RPC 281, 294 the judge said *obiter*: 'No one but a crossword fanatic, for instance, would say that "treat" is present in "theatre atmosphere".'

Europe[66] but the European Union itself has come to accept and which is now enshrined in the domestic law of all EU Member States. This freedom supports the principle that we can speak ill of another's goods or services, even if this means making mention of his trade mark. Article 10 of the European Convention on Human Rights does contain derogations in favour of 'the protection of the reputations or rights of others ...', though whether this extends to protecting the reputation of CATTY-PUSS cat food against unflattering comments from the manufacturer of PUSSY-PURR cat food is a matter of debate. What then happens when those countries which protect freedom of speech are called upon to defend the right to make unauthorized use of another's trade mark, where that unauthorized use is in conflict with the interests or aims of the trade mark owner? Let us look at examples drawn from case law.

(a) Freedom of speech and derogatory reference to another's mark

8.61 In one French case the owner of the French registration of the trade marks DANONE objected to the use of its marks on the jeboycottedanone.net website in the context of attacks on the company's commercial and employment policy. The Tribunal de Grande Instance de Paris agreed that the right of freedom of speech protected the defendant's right to use the word DANONE, even though use of that word was protected by a trade mark registration; the right of freedom of speech did not however entitle the defendant to make use of that company's word-and-device marks.[67] However, the defendant's free speech argument was accepted on appeal.[68] It was also initially held, in an application for interim injunctive relief, that the right of free speech entitled Greenpeace to make use of the word mark ESSO, but not to portray it in the form E$$O.[69] However, in the consolidated appeal of the E$$O case[70] and a similar case in which Greenpeace had parodied a trade mark,[71] the Cour d'appel de Paris ruled that—whatever the position after a full trial—a constitutional entitlement to freedom of speech should not be inhibited by the exercise of third-party rights unless it was absolutely necessary to do so. In a case of this nature, freedom of speech should not be suppressed because, if the ESSO mark were found to be infringed, damages would always provide adequate compensation.

---

[66] European Convention on Human Rights, art 10: '1. Everyone has the right to freedom of expression ... 2. The exercise of these freedoms, since it carries with it duties and responsibilities, may be subject to ... restrictions ... in the interests of national security, territorial integrity or public safety, ... for the protection of the reputations or rights of others ...'.

[67] *Sté Gervais Danone v Société Le Riseau Voltaire, Société Gandhi, Valentin Lacambre* [2003] ETMR 321.

[68] *Sté Gervais Danone v Société Le Riseau Voltaire, Société Gandhi, Valentin Lacambre* WLTR, 14 July 2003.

[69] *Esso Société Anonyme Française SA v Association Greenpeace France and Société Internet.Fr* [2003] ETMR 441 (Tribunal de Grande Instance de Paris).

[70] *Association Greenpeace France v SA Société Esso* [2003] ETMR 867 (Cour d'appel de Paris).

[71] *SA Société des Participations du CEA v Greenpeace France et al* [2003] ETMR 870 (Cour d'appel de Paris), also discussed at paras 8.66–8.71 below in the context of a defence of parody.

D. Acts which are permitted in principle

In a case involving the use of trade marks as a means of identifying the source of infringing versions of commercial databases, the Cour d'appel de Paris has rather implied that article 10 of the European Convention on Human Rights, in granting a right of freedom of expression, should be regarded as addressing issues of opinion rather than the right to use another's trade mark for descriptive or identification purposes which is already specifically covered by trade mark law itself.[72]   8.62

(b) Trade marks and freedom of expression in the United States

In some European jurisdictions, in the still-evolving United Europe, trade mark law came first and the legal protection of freedom of expression came later. In the United States, in contrast, the First Amendment's constitutional protection of freedom of speech was well established before its potential for application in the realm of trade mark disputes was recognized. Since many trade mark disputes turn on whether a trade mark proprietor may suppress the use by the defendant of a word, logo or other image, opportunities for invoking freedom-of-speech arguments are widely available.[73] Recent case law has shown that the unauthorized registration of 'sucks' domain names, in which the word 'sucks' is appended as a suffix to a registered trade mark, will be protected as an exercise of the constitutional right of freedom of speech so long as that use is not commercial in nature.[74] This proviso means that the user is not seeking to make money from it himself, not that the use in question is not intended to have commercial consequences for the trade mark owner. Judging by the content of some 'sucks' sites, nothing short of the liquidation of the trade mark owner or some other major commercial disaster would satisfy the domain name registrant.   8.63

(c) Do traders enjoy a 'freedom of commercial speech'?

A completely different freedom-of-speech issue was raised in an Indian case in which the International Cricket Council sought to prevent the electronics company Philips engaging in 'ambush marketing'. Philips, a competitor of cricket's World Cup sponsor LG, promoted a competition which offered as prizes the prospect of free travel to South Africa and tickets for various cricket matches. The Council's action against Philips for 'ambush marketing' failed. The company had not actually made unauthorized use of any of the trade marks or copyright-protected material relating to the event and its use of the term 'World Cup' was in any event purely descriptive: more than that, Philips's promotion was constitutionally protected by freedom of commercial speech.[75]   8.64

---

[72] *Société Reed Expositions France (Formerly Groupe Miller Freeman) v Société Tigest Sarl* [2003] ECDR 206 (Cour d'appel de Paris).
[73] For a good review of the potential applicability of First Amendment arguments in the United States, see Arlen W Langvardt, 'Trademark Rights and First Amendment Wrongs: Protecting the Former Without Committing the Latter' (1998) 83 TMR 633.
[74] *Taubman Company v Mishkoff* 319 F 3d 770 (6th Cir 2003).
[75] *ICC (Development) International v Philips*, 31 January 2003 (High Court, Delhi).

Chapter 8: Non-infringing Acts

8.65 How far this approach is reflected in European practice is unclear. The Swedish Supreme Court has ruled that, where a party to litigation uses another's trade mark for an end which 'has a commercial purpose and ... at the same time regards purely commercial considerations as its object' will not benefit from its assertion of the right of freedom of expression.[76] A similar approach has been taken in France, where the use of the DIOR trade mark for the purpose of advertising a pirate videotape, 'Best of Dior', and the unauthorized webcast transmission of clips from a Dior fashion show could not be justified on the basis that the defendant had a right to transmit the news.[77]

(6) Parody, satire and irony

8.66 Because trade marks have the potential to convey powerfully evocative images, social commentators are drawn towards their use as a means of making an economic, environmental, political or social point. The use of the BARBIE trade mark in the song 'Barbie Girl'[78] is a case in point.[79] Another is the parody of the BLACK LABEL beer trade mark in the T-shirt slogan 'Black Labour—White Guilt' in South Africa.[80]

(a) Judicial responses

8.67 How do the courts handle complaints that a trade mark has been used in this manner? Although one of the best-known stereotypes in Europe is that of the humourless German, case law however suggests that the Germans appreciate as good a laugh as any of their European colleagues and that they also have a broader tolerance than most towards the parody of registered trade marks. In one case the then-current version of the Deutsche Telekom logo consisting of a letter 'T' and a set of dots was parodied by the defendants who produced postcards bearing the legend 'Toll! Alles Wird Teurer' ('Great! Everything is more expensive'), the word 'Teurer' ('more expensive') being represented in the style of Deutsche Telekom's mark. The subsequent infringement action was dismissed. The court held that there was no infringement but, even if there had been, the defendant's use was not actionable: it was not a trade mark use since it was an attempt to engage the

---

[76] *TV4 and TV Spartacus KB v Bröderna Lindströms Forlags AB*, noted in *Brandnews* 2/2003 (the OKEJ teen magazine obtained permission to publish copyright and trade mark-protected material but then also reproduced them in a calendar).

[77] *Christian Dior Couture v Fashion TV Paris and others* [2001] ETMR 126 (Tribunal de Grande Instance de Paris).

[78] *Mattel Inc v MCA Records Inc* 296 F 3d 894 (9th Cir 2000); cert denied 123 SupCt 993, discussed in Chapter 21.

[79] Many other examples are discussed and illustrated in Jeremy Phillips, 'Trademark Abuse' (1987) 8 *Trademark World* 24–31.

[80] *South African Breweries International (Finance) BV v Laugh It Off Promotions* WTLR, 28 May 2003 (HC): parody found to infringe trade mark.

D. Acts which are permitted in principle

claimant in a public debate about its pricing structure by poking fun at it.[81] The court reviewed earlier German decisions on trade mark disparagement and concluded that parody could serve as a defence not only where there existed no competitive relationship between the parties[82] but also where such a relationship existed and the possibility of an action for unfair competition might be raised. However, where there is no humour, there is no defence.[83]

8.68 The French approach to the 'sending up' of trade marks is inconsistent or, to be fair, consistent with the absence of the common-law doctrine of precedent. Where the proprietor of the TARZAN trade mark sued for infringement in respect of the defendant's use of TARZOON, LA HONTE DE LA JUNGLE ('Tarzoon, the disgrace of the jungle'), the court dismissed the action.[84] It did not do so on the basis of parody but on the ground that the length and composite nature of the defendant's sign left a very different impression from that of the single word TARZAN. This reasoning suggests that if the word TARZOON alone had been used, the claimant's action would have succeeded. In the French *Esso* case,[85] use of the trade mark ESSO in the satirical form E$$O was not permitted, since that use could damage the reputation of the claimant's trade mark. A defence of parody or satire was held to exist in an action for copyright infringement, but it did not avail the defendant in trade mark infringement proceedings.[86] *Esso* was not however followed in *CEA*,[87] where the same court refused to protect the trade mark owner against the use of a skull-and-crossbones version of its logo on the grounds (among others) that: (i) the parody was in relation to the trade mark owner's industrial nuclear activities and not in relation to the services in Class 38 for which it was registered; and that (ii) given the notoriety of Greenpeace, no one seeing the logo on its website would believe the trade mark owner had anything to do with the information sitting next to it on the same webpage.

8.69 A quite different form of 'sending up' of another's trade mark occurs where the trade mark owner's product is known and identified by its trade mark. This is the

---

[81] *'Alles Wird Teurer'* [1999] ETMR 49 (KG Berlin Court of Appeal).

[82] As in eg *BMW* GRUR 1986, 759, where the sale of joke BMW stickers adding the phrase 'Bumms Mal Wieder' ('Have sex again') was held not to infringe the BMW mark.

[83] Thus in *Disparagement of Trade Marks 1* GRUR 1994, 808 and *Disparagement of Trade Marks 2* GRUR 1995, 57 the use of the MARS and NIVEA trade marks on condom packets and stickers advertising them respectively was regarded as infringing use: there was no humour to redeem the situation and the infringing products could have been taken as advertisements for the claimants' goods.

[84] *Burroughs Inc and another v Picha, Valiza Films and others* [1978] EIPR European Digest, December, p iv (Tribunal de Grande Instance de Paris).

[85] Discussed at paras 8.60–8.65.

[86] *Esso Société Anonyme Française SA v Association Greenpeace France and Société Internet.Fr* [2003] ETMR 441 (Tribunal de Grande Instance de Paris).

[87] *SA Société des Participations du Commissariat à l'Energie Atomique v Greenpeace France et al*, 2 August 2002 (unreported) (Tribunal de Grande Instance de Paris), affirmed by the Cour d'appel de Paris at [2003] ETMR 870.

case with BARBIE, the trade mark which gives its name to (or takes its name from) the children's doll. In one case the manufacture and sale of dominatrix Barbie-like 'dungeon dolls' has been held not to infringe Mattel's United States trade marks,[88] not apparently on the basis of parody but on the more prosaic ground that the dominatrix did not constitute a use of the BARBIE trade mark.

(b) The impact of comparative advertising

8.70 When comparative advertising[89] becomes a more widespread phenomenon in continental Europe, the existence of a defence of parody, satire or irony will become far more important. Comparative advertising is now tolerated for the purpose of enabling consumers to become better informed about the goods or services they seek to purchase, but *how* one manufacturer informs another about the difference between his products and those of his competitors is open to argument. Will the fact that the use of another's mark is by way of parody be an extra factor in the advertiser's defence, as the German case law might suggest, or will it be an extra factor in the trade mark owner's armoury when he asserts that his trade mark has been denigrated and that any comparison made by the defendant is therefore an act of unfair advertising?

(c) The trade mark owner's revenge

8.71 Trade mark owners whose brands have been satirized or pilloried are not helpless to respond. Where the objectionable use comes from a competitor, it is open to them to retaliate in like kind by making fun of the parodist's trade mark in return, although many brand owners may consider this sort of conduct as beneath their corporate dignity. Perhaps the sweetest revenge was that extracted by DaimlerChrysler, owners of the MERCEDES trade mark which was the butt of the late Janis Joplin's song 'Mercedes Benz',[90] when they obtained the right to use that song in the company's own advertising campaign.

(7) Hiding the infringing bits of an infringing use

8.72 When Lindt successfully objected that a competitor's chocolate packaging infringed four of its trade marks, the competitor did not want to destroy the packaging so it overstuck the offending material with adhesive labels. Lindt considered

---

[88] Stuart Derrick, 'Barbie Ruling Rings Warning Bells', *Promotions & Incentives*, January 2003, p 23.
[89] Discussed at length later in this chapter (see paras 8.93–8.176).
[90] First recorded 10 January 1970. The lyrics of the first verse go 'Oh Lord, won't you buy me a Mercedes Benz? / My friends all drive Porsches, I must make amends. / Worked hard all my lifetime, no help from my friends, / So Lord, won't you buy me a Mercedes Benz?' This song was alluded to by the court in the *Barbie Girl* case (*Mattel Inc v MCA Records Inc* 296 F 3d 894 (9th Cir 2000); cert denied 123 Sup Ct 993), where the judge observed that no one hearing the song would assume that Joplin and Mercedes were in partnership.

D. Acts which are permitted in principle

this too to be an infringement, but the French Cour de Cassation disagreed.[91] At the point of sale of the defendant's chocolates the removable labels were protected by a cellophane wrapper and Lindt's marks could not therefore be used to promote their sale. Once they were sold, consumers could peel the labels off if they liked and read the previously 'invisible' advertisements, but that would not constitute an infringement of the trade marks.

(8) Use in small advertisements

(a) *'Private small ads'*

In a curious ruling which may not have survived the new European trade mark order, a publication carried a personal advertisement in its 'small ads' section. This advertisement read in its relevant part: 8.73

> For Sale: men's trousers, sizes 40–42, Hugo Boss. Suits, attractive prices, very good condition, new diff. colours. Phone ... Pref. evenings ...

The Tribunal de Grande Instance de Strasbourg ruled that this advertisement, having been placed under the 'Cleaning' section of the defendant's 'small ads' section, appeared to be a private advertisement and there was no evidence that it was placed within the framework of any economic activity. Accordingly the defendant could not be liable for publishing it.[92] It should be emphasized that, while the provisions of trade mark law in many countries which deal with criminal law or the seizure of goods at customs make special exceptions for 'private' rather than commercial infringing activities, it is not normally the case for the law of civil trade mark infringement to make explicit provision to except non-commercial infringing acts from liability: the European norm is simply to rely on the principle that infringing use be conducted 'in the course of trade'.[93] 8.74

(b) *Marks too small to be discerned*

Where an illustration of the defendant's packaging, which wrongly reproduced a number of the claimant's trade marks, was incorporated into an advertisement for its product, the claimant's action for trade mark infringement was dismissed by the French Cour de Cassation on the ground that the advertisement was, quite literally, a 'small ad'.[94] The scale of reproduction of the claimant's marks was so small on the illustration that consumers would be unable to discern them and there was therefore no unlawful reproduction of them. 8.75

---

[91] *SA Lindt & Sprüngli v Sté Chocometz* [1999] ETMR 315.
[92] *Sté Hugo Boss v Dernières Nouvelles d'Alsace and others* [1998] ETMR 197.
[93] Council Directive 89/104, art 5(1); Council Regulation 40/94, art 9(1).
[94] *SA Lindt & Sprüngli v Sté Chocometz* [1999] ETMR 315.

(9) Boycotts

8.76 Among the better known boycotts are those aimed at Nestlé products, in retaliation for what has been described as an unethical policy on the distribution of infant formula to mothers in Third World countries.[95] Typical of these is Baby Milk Action's breastfeeding.com website, which both lists and depicts numerous Nestlé products by reference to their trade marks and has even developed its own logo. Reports of decided cases do not reveal any action that Nestlé may have taken to enforce its trade mark rights against calls for a consumer boycott.

8.77 It is difficult to assess the long-term damage done to trade marks through consumer boycotts. The boycott of Barclays Bank because of its investment policy in apartheid-ridden South Africa led to that bank's eventual withdrawal from that country's financial market. Although that boycott is now a footnote in history and it is not suggested that Barclays' policy today is any better or worse than those of its competitors, anecdotal evidence suggests that some people still feel uncomfortable at the thought of using the banking services which they boycotted even three decades previously.

(10) Calling a product by its trade mark instead of by its product name

8.78 In an ideal world designed by trade mark owners for their own benefit, no trader or consumer would ever refer to a product solely by its trade mark. When asked what we drive, we would not say 'a BMW' but 'a motor car manufactured by the Bayerische Motorenwerke AG and put on to the market under the trade mark BMW'. Our children would not play MONOPOLY but 'a board game manufactured by John Waddington and sold under the name MONOPOLY', and so on. But humans are reluctant to be bound by so exacting a discipline and we use trade marks all the time as substitutes for nouns or verbs. Although this use may weaken the trade mark and ultimately kill it, when the trade mark has ceased exclusively to indicate a particular source of goods, its use does not constitute an infringement of the trade mark right in most civilized countries. France is a major exception here: an allegedly defamatory newspaper article which referred to shopping trolleys as CADDIES was regarded by the Tribunal de Grande Instance de Paris as an unlawful use which would bring about that mark's degeneration and granted an injunction accordingly.[96]

---

[95] The extent of this boycott is unclear, but an Internet search in November 2002 revealed that there were in excess of 2,500 web pages devoted to it.

[96] *SA Ateliers Réunis Caddie v Sarl Société Nouvelle de Presse et de Communication (SNPC)* [1999] ETMR 45. A claim of defamation on the same facts was dismissed on the basis of neat logic: if the defendant was using the word CADDIE generically, he could not have been using it to refer to the claimant's products.

D. Acts which are permitted in principle

8.79 Curiously, while some trade marks are killed by actual or apparently generic use (for example, THERMOS and ASPIRIN in the United States, WALKMAN[97] and TABASCO[98] in Austria, PIÑA COLADA in France[99]), others appear to be enhanced by it (for example, COKE universally). Much of the difference depends on whether this non-infringing use is tolerated by the trade mark owner. The trade mark owner is best advised to educate the general public either (i) not to use the trade mark except as a trade mark (for example, not to write 'valium' but 'VALIUM®') or (ii) to view the trade mark as applying to a wider range of goods than that for which it was originally associated (for example, by extending the use of CATERPILLAR from nearly generic earthmoving equipment to far from generic footwear and fashion goods).

8.80 The CTM Regulation provides that

> If the use of a Community trade mark in a dictionary, encyclopaedia or similar reference work gives the impression that it constitutes the generic name of the goods or services for which the trade mark is registered, the publisher of the work shall, at the request of the proprietor ... ensure that the reproduction of the trade mark at the latest in the next edition of the publication is accompanied by an indication that it is a registered trade mark.[100]

8.81 This provision, which is not found in any other trade mark law, is remarkable not only for (i) the relatively weak nature of the relief available to the trade mark owner[101] but also for (ii) its narrow scope of application and (iii) the limited nature of its potential for application to that Great Creator of generic use, the World Wide Web. Nonetheless its sentiment is to be applauded as a recognition of the frustration faced by trade mark owners when, often through no fault of their own, a privately owned word mark is adopted by mankind as a public resource.

8.82 On the subject of dictionaries, there is a division of legal opinion as to their worth as an index of whether a word is, or is becoming, generic. The Dutch[102] have taken the view that the inclusion of a trade mark in a dictionary is not its use 'in the course of trade' and that such use cannot in any event render a word—in this case

---

[97] *Sony Walkman Trade Mark* [2000] ETMR 890 (Austrian Supreme Court).
[98] *Tabasco Restaurant v Proprietor of the Tabasco Registered Trade Mark* [1998] ETMR 100 (Austrian Supreme Court).
[99] *SA Bardinet v SCP Ego-Fruits (SCP Belat-Desprat intervening)* [2002] ETMR 1043 (Cour d'appel de Paris).
[100] Regulation 40/94, art 10.
[101] P A C E Van der Kooij, *The Community Trade Mark Regulation: An Article by Article Guide*, para 2-067, expresses the opinion that failure to comply with this provision is actionable under article 14(2) of the Regulation. Even if it is actionable, it is difficult to imagine a court granting either substantial damages or a mandatory injunction.
[102] *Du Pont de Nemours (EI) and Company v AMA VOF Antoon Michielsen Automobiles (trading as Protech Nederland Teflon Lakbescherming) and others* [2001] ETMR 777 ('s-Hertogenbosch Appeal Court).

TEFLON[103]—generic. The First Cancellation Division of the Office for Harmonisation in the Internal Market (OHIM) has however found that dictionaries,[104] and also other reference books,[105] possess a rich seam of evidence as to how language is used. The two approaches are not necessarily in conflict: the Dutch have been asked to consider the legal status of trade marks which have been dragged into dictionaries, while the Cancellation Division has had to deal with dictionary words which have been dragged on to the trade marks register.

(11) Half-infringing two separate marks

8.83 Suppose I have a great affection for TOMMY HILFIGER fashion products and also for those of TED BAKER. When I launch my own business, can I brand them TOMMY BAKER and get away with it? Something like this actually happened in France, where the respective owners of the MEGA FORCE and SUPER POWER trade marks for computer games magazines both sued a competitor for calling its own magazine *Super Mega*. Since the elements 'borrowed' by the defendant were common prefixes which could not of themselves exercise a distinctive function, their aggregation in a competitor's magazine title did not infringe the trade mark of either of them singly; and if it could not infringe the trade marks as registered, it could not be said to half-infringe each of them when they were joined together.[106]

8.84 The conclusion that the fusion of two half-marks into a new hybrid mark will infringe neither of them is easy to accept on the facts of the *Super Mega* case, where both components of the fused mark lacked independent distinctive character, but how far this principle can be pushed is open to speculation. For example, where one of the family of 'EASY' marks (EASYJET, EASYCAR, EASYCINEMA, etc) is merged with a single word mark (for example, VIRGIN) into 'EASYVIRGIN' for airline services, it is quite likely that both original marks will have been infringed: 'EASY-' because of the strength of the family of marks to which EASYJET belongs and VIRGIN because the whole of this unusual and distinctive trade mark has been appropriated. A more difficult case is that of the merger of components of two trade marks where those components are more distinctive than SUPER and MEGA but less so than 'EASY-' and VIRGIN (for example, where CHRISTIAN DIOR and YVES ST LAURENT are fused into CHRISTIAN LAURENT).

---

[103] TEFLON is a trade mark for a product which deserves to be better known as polytetrafluoroethylene.
[104] See eg *Beiersdorf AG's trade mark; application for cancellation by L'Oreal*, Case C000835728/1 [2001] ETMR 187.
[105] See eg *Dr Robert Winzer Pharma GmbH's application to cancel a trade mark of Alcon Pharmaceuticals Ltd*, Case C000090134/1 [2000] ETMR 217.
[106] *Mega Press and Sumo Editions v Pressimage and Guidicelli* [2000] ETMR 403 (Cour d'appel de Paris).

D. Acts which are permitted in principle

(12) Using a trade mark as a badge of loyalty or allegiance

This question was considered by the ECJ in the hotly debated *Arsenal* case, following a reference from the English High Court. In brief, Arsenal, a famous football club, owned various trade marks including the word ARSENAL. Use of the ARSENAL trade mark was licensed to several manufacturers of football memorabilia, such as hats and scarves bearing the ARSENAL trade mark. Without Arsenal's permission one Reed, a street vendor, sold scarves and other goods which portrayed the word 'Arsenal'. The club sued for trade mark infringement and for passing off.   **8.85**

Before the High Court[107] Arsenal argued that there was a Type 1 infringement[108] ('same mark, same goods'). Reed not only denied infringement but counterclaimed for revocation of the ARSENAL mark on the basis that Arsenal had not used its own marks for a continuous period of five years.[109] To the surprise of many, the court was not prepared to find that there had been a trade mark infringement. As to passing off, the judge held that Arsenal had not proved that there had been any confusion as a result of Reed's use of its trade marks.[110] As to trade mark infringement the judge considered that the use of the mark both by the Arsenal club and by Reed might not even be a trade mark use: putting the word ARSENAL on to a football scarf was the use of the word as a 'badge of loyalty', not as a 'badge of origin'. Although this argument may appear to be strikingly out of sympathy with the aims of trade mark law, it is not without its logic. If the unauthorized use of a pop group's name on the cover of a book is not a 'trade mark' use, even if the group's name is registered for paper products in Class 16, because it shows that the book is a book *about* the pop group, not *originating from* the pop group,[111] could not a scarf bearing the word ARSENAL be a scarf *supporting* the Arsenal football team, not a scarf *originating from* the club?   **8.86**

The ECJ,[112] following the Advocate General's detailed analysis of current football business activity and not a little of its mythology,[113] rejected the notion that the unauthorized use of a trade mark had to be as a badge of loyalty *or* as a badge of origin: there was no reason why the same use could not be both. And so far as it was the use of another's trade mark as a badge of origin, it was an infringing use   **8.87**

---

[107] *Arsenal Football Club plc v Matthew Reed* [2001] ETMR 860 (Laddie J).
[108] See further Chapter 7, paras 7.10–7.15.
[109] On revocation for failure to use a registered trade mark for a continuous period of five years, see Chapter 13, paras 13.46ff.
[110] Although the passing-off decision was not appealed, the Court of Appeal, 21 May 2003 (unreported) expressed its doubt as to whether that conclusion was correct on the facts.
[111] *Bravado Merchandising Services Ltd v Mainstream Publishing (Edinburgh) Ltd* [1996] FSR 205 (Court of Session, Scotland): the *WET WET WET* case.
[112] *Arsenal Football Club plc v Matthew Reed*, Case C-206/01 [2003] ETMR 225.
[113] *Arsenal Football Club plc v Matthew Reed*, Case C-206/01 [2002] ETMR 975.

because it adversely affected the function of the ARSENAL trade mark as a guarantee of origin.

8.88 This was not the end of the story. The trial judge who referred the question nonetheless refused to find in favour of the football club as trade mark owner.[114] He concluded that, as Reed's use of Arsenal's trade marks was neither intended by him nor understood by the public as being a designation of origin, there could be no infringement because such use did not prejudice the essential function of the registered mark as a guarantee of the identity of origin of his goods or services. This decision was reversed on appeal.[115]

(13) Calling one's dog Elvis

8.89 The use of a trade mark as an appellation for a human being, however annoying it might be, cannot be prevented. If brand-abuse scourge Naomi Klein wishes to call her child Calvin, she can do so with impunity, notwithstanding the strength, legal nature and widespread reputation of the CALVIN KLEIN trade mark. Indeed the English High Court has expressed its position on celebrity names, whether registered as trade marks or not, in quite trenchant terms:

> Even if Elvis Presley was still alive, he would not be entitled to stop a fan from naming his son, his dog or goldfish, his car or his house Elvis or Elvis Presley simply by reason of the fact that it was the name given to him at birth by his parents. To stop the use of the whole or part of his name by another he would need to show that as a result of such use, the other person is invading some legally recognised right.[116]

E. Limitation of actions

8.90 All jurisdictions employ rules relating to the limitation of civil actions for trade mark infringement. These rules, which apply no less to actions to trade mark infringement than they apply to any other civil wrongs, are a matter of national civil law; they are generally found in special statutory provisions or in civil procedural codes.

8.91 A further set of rules on limitation apply specifically to trade marks granted within the Member States of the European Economic Area. These rules provide that, where the proprietor of the infringed trade mark has acquiesced, for a period of five successive years, in the use of a later trade mark which has been registered in that Member State while being aware of such use, he forfeits his entitlement to op-

---

[114] *Arsenal Football Club plc v Matthew Reed* [2003] IP&T 75.
[115] [2003] ETMR 895 (CA).
[116] *Elvis Presley Trade Marks* [1997] RPC 543, 547 (HC), per Laddie J.

F. Comparative advertising

pose the use of the later trade mark in respect of the goods or services for which the later trade mark has been used, unless registration of the later trade mark was applied for in bad faith.[117]

8.92 Limitation periods apply only in respect of actions brought by trade mark owners; they do not apply in respect of defences and counterclaims raised by the alleged infringer.

F. Comparative advertising

(1) Use of another's trade mark in the course of 'comparative advertising'

8.93 The most direct way to promote one's business at the expense of one's competitors is through comparative advertising. In a perfect market, all consumers will know all there is to know about the price, quality, availability and other characteristics of goods or services on offer to them and will make rational decisions based on that information. By informing consumers that its goods or services are superior to those of its competitors, a business improves the level of knowledge of consumers in the relevant market and makes it easier for them to choose the product which is most beneficial to them. But there is an important proviso: the improvement of consumers' knowledge can only be achieved for long as the advertising does not contain misinformation, which is always a risk if the education of consumers is entrusted to entities with vested interests.

8.94 So how does the use of another's trade mark contribute to the education of consumers? By relating information to the trade marks by which those goods or services are known (for example, 'POPPO is twice as nourishing as BIPPO and costs half the price'), the owner of the POPPO trade mark enhances his brand value and educates the public that products sold under his brand are better than those of an identifiable competitor. If the producer of BIPPO products is not driven out of business by this exercise, he will at least be forced to revise his pricing policy or his product formulation. This exercise, in theory, benefits the consumer and the owner of the trade mark for the more desirable of two or more competing products—but is it legal?

8.95 There are many ways in which comparative advertising can be done. Techniques include

(i) mentioning a competitor by name ('If you like Estée Lauder's products you'll love ours'[118]);

---

[117] Council Directive 89/104, art 9. A similar provision governs Community trade marks; see Council Regulation 40/94, art 53(1), (2).
[118] See *Diversified Marketing Inc v Estée Lauder Inc* 705 F Supp 128 (SDNY 1988).

(ii) mentioning the trade mark of a competing product (for example, in an advertisement for NOUVELLE toilet tissue: 'Softness guaranteed or we'll exchange it for ANDREX®'[119]);
(iii) not mentioning the name of the competitor or his trade mark but merely referring to 'the leading brand' in a field in which everyone knows what the leading brand is (for example, COCA-COLA is widely known to be the leading brand of soft drinks in many jurisdictions[120]) and
(iv) indicating which of one's products are compatible with those of a competitor by issuing a table in which the serial numbers of each party are listed.[121]

8.96 Comparison does not require that the person doing the advertising should make any claim that his goods or services are superior to those of his competitors. It accordingly includes circumstances in which an advertiser promotes his goods or services as a 'cheap and cheerful' alternative to the unquestionably superior goods or services of an upmarket competitor. Alternatively one may attract the consumer's attention by claiming: 'Our watches are still not as glamorous as ROLEX'.

8.97 In one sense comparison in advertising includes all generalizations made by advertisers in which no mention is made of specific competitors. For example, the statement

NIKE trainers out-run all others

conveys much the same message as

NIKE trainers out-run those of ADIDAS, PUMA, REEBOK etc.

8.98 In the first statement competitors are not mentioned by name but are merely generalized while, in the second statement, the words 'all others' which appear in the first statement have been expanded. Instinctively we regard the second statement as comparative advertising and the first as a mere boast, but in each case the relation between NIKE and all other brands remains one of adverse comparison, whether by implication (as in the first statement) or by express statement (as in the second).

(2) Comparative advertising and trade mark law

8.99 The Paris Convention, TRIPs and the classic pan-European trade mark laws do not even mention comparative advertising as a legal concept, from which we can infer that (i) an infringement action based on the use of another's use of a trade

---

[119] *Kimberley-Clark Limited v Fort Sterling Limited* [1997] FSR 877.
[120] See eg *Cola Test* (1987) GRUR 49, where the Bundesgerichtshof observed that, even in a comparison between three colas where no other colas were mentioned by name, people would assume that one of the other two was COCA-COLA. This would therefore constitute an indirect reference to a competitor's mark.
[121] As in *Toshiba Europe GmbH v Katun Germany GmbH*, Case C-112/99 [2002] ETMR 295.

F. Comparative advertising

mark in comparative advertising must be judged by the same legal criteria as any other type of trade mark infringement and that (ii) the defences already discussed earlier in this chapter will apply no more or less to comparative advertising than they would to any other form of unauthorized activity involving another's trade mark.

(a) What does 'comparative advertising' have to do with trade mark law?

8.100 In an era of acute brand consciousness, the easiest way to attract the attention of the public to one's goods or services is to 'brand' them with an attractive and memorable trade mark. It is also therefore easy to attract the attention of prospective customers or consumers by placing before them the familiar sound or appearance of a competitor's brand. Thus the hypothetical slogan

> Three times as many consumers prefer COKE to PEPSI

is a far more powerful message than

> Three times as many consumes prefer COKE to the carbonated cola beverage flavoured with vegetable extract and manufactured by or under licence from the Pepsi-Co Inc.

8.101 For this reason it can be appreciated both why it is that advertisers are often so eager to mention the trade marks of their competitors and why trade mark proprietors are so suspicious of all unauthorized uses to which their trade marks are put.

(3) The Misleading and Comparative Advertising Directive

8.102 Although the term 'comparative advertising' is missing from all the major provisions of international and European trade mark law, it does however appear in the Misleading and Comparative Advertising Directive.[122] That Directive defines 'advertising' extremely widely, as meaning

> the making of a representation in any form in connection with a trade, business, craft or profession in order to promote the supply of goods or services ....

8.103 The Directive then goes on to define 'comparative advertising' as

> any advertising which explicitly or by implication identifies a competitor or goods or services offered by a competitor.[123]

8.104 The definition of 'comparative advertising' requires that the advertiser identifies a *competitor* or the goods or services of a *competitor*. Accordingly practices such as using the legally protected word CHAMPAGNE in an advertisement for

---

[122] Council Directive 84/450 of 10 September 1984 concerning misleading and comparative advertising (as amended by Council Directive 97/55).
[123] ibid, art 2.

computers, or indeed mineral water, does not fall within its scope even though comparisons are made (such as 'Champagner bekommen, Sekt bezahlen: IBM Aptiva jetzt zum V-Preis'[124]) because sparkling wine is not sold in competition with computers.

8.105 The Misleading and Comparative Advertising Directive permits comparative advertising in article 3a if a number of conditions are met:

(a) it is not misleading …;
(b) it compares goods or services meeting the same needs or intended for the same purpose;
(c) it objectively compares one or more material, relevant, verifiable and representative features of those goods and services, which may include price;
(d) it does not create confusion in the market place between the advertiser and a competitor or between the advertiser's trade marks, trade names, other distinguishing marks, goods or services and those of a competitor;
(e) it does not discredit or denigrate the trade marks, trade names, other distinguishing marks, goods, services, activities or circumstances of a competitor;
(f) …[125]
(g) it does not take unfair advantage of the reputation of a trade mark, trade name or other distinguishing marks of a competitor or of the designation of origin of competing goods;
(h) it does not present goods or services as imitations or replicas of goods or services bearing a protected trade mark or trade name.

8.106 This list of criteria for a 'permitted' use of another's trade mark is very narrow and, for at least some trade mark lawyers, thoroughly difficult to apply. For example, by article 3a(b) the comparison must be of 'goods or services meeting the same needs or intended for the same purpose'. Since this phraseology is not found in Directive 89/104, it must be assumed that trade mark case law on the identity or similarity of goods or services will be of little relevance to its interpretation.

8.107 Whether it is assisted by trade mark case law or not, the comparison for the purposes of comparative advertising will definitely require some guidance. For example, does a SKODA meet the same needs as a LAMBORGHINI? Is it intended for the same purpose? Further difficulties are raised in applying article 3a(c), which requires that permitted comparisons be objective, relating to one or more material, relevant, verifiable and representative features. Does this exclude comparisons relating to preference in personal taste (for example, in double-blind sampling of COCA-COLA and PEPSI)? And how do you know whether people who prefer NUROFEN for their headaches actually get quicker relief than those who take other brands: perhaps they are more stoic and feel less pain in the first place. Finally, which features of a trade marked product are 'representative'? And who decides what they are?

---

[124] 'Get Champagne for the price of sparkling wine: IBM Aptiva now at a bargain price'; see *'Champagner Bekommen, Sekt Bezahlen'* [2002] ETMR 1091 (Bundesgerichtshof).
[125] This provision deals with 'products with designations of origin'.

F. Comparative advertising

8.108 A different sort of difficulty may arise from the non-congruence of the terminology of article 3a(d) with that of Directive 89/104 and the CTM Regulation. The former prohibits advertising which 'creates confusion' while the trade mark codes address situations in which 'there exists a likelihood of confusion', which includes 'the likelihood of association'.[126] The finer legal and practical consequences of these distinctions are not immediately apparent, but the concept of confusion for the purposes of comparative advertising is substantially narrower than for the purposes of trade mark application and infringement.

8.109 Other phrases within article 3a are more familiar to trade mark lawyers and may be expected to be interpreted in the same manner as Directive 89/104 and the CTM Regulation. Thus the concepts of denigration in article 3a(e) and unfair advantage in article 3a(g) may be understood in the light of interpretations of equivalent provisions of Directive 89/104 and the CTM Regulation.[127]

(a) How does the Directive relate to trade mark law?

8.110 Recitals 13 to 15 in the 1997 Preamble to the Misleading and Comparative Advertising Directive refer specifically to Directive 89/104. Recital 13 acknowledges that Directive 89/104 confers exclusive rights on trade mark owners. Recital 14 accepts that, for comparative advertising purposes, it may be essential for an advertiser to refer to another's trade mark. Recital 15 indicates that reference to another's trade mark should not infringe the trade mark right if it complies with the conditions laid down in the Misleading and Comparative Advertising Directive. From this it can be seen that it is very much the intention of the legislature to impose the leniencies of permitted comparative advertising over the stringencies of trade mark protection.

8.111 Was the passage of the amendments to the Misleading and Comparative Advertising Directive in 1997 intended to amend Council Directive 89/104? The view of at least one British judge[128] is that it did not, because it did not need to. Presumably the 1997 Directive merely gave guidance as to how the provisions of Directive 89/104 should be interpreted by the courts. Under the *Marleasing* principle,[129] the legislation passed by Member States to implement Directive 89/104 is to be read and interpreted in the light of the subsequent Misleading and Comparative Advertising Directive, so no further legislative adjustment is necessary. This conclusion fits in with the approach taken both in Finland[130] and in France, where comparative advertising involving trade marks has been legitimated by legislation outside the scope of national trade mark law.

---

[126] Council Directive 89/104, arts 4(1)(b), 5(1)(b); Council Regulation 40/94, arts 8(1)(b), 9(1)(b), discussed in depth in Chapter 10.
[127] For a full discussion of these concepts, see Chapter 12.
[128] *British Airways plc v Ryanair* [2001] ETMR 236, 245 per Jacob J.
[129] *Marleasing* Case 106/89 [1990] ECR I-4135.
[130] See the Law against Transactions Contrary to Good Business Practices.

8.112 Further evidence that the Misleading and Comparative Advertising Directive has no direct bearing on trade mark infringement may be gleaned from the fact that its thrust is principally regulatory. It requires Member States to establish mechanisms for preventing misleading advertisements reaching the public and for issuing 'stop orders' where such advertisements are promulgated,[131] but confers no private right upon trade mark owners (or any other individuals) to take action against misleading advertisements and grants no specific right to use another's trade mark for the purposes of comparison.

8.113 In one respect the Misleading and Comparative Advertising Directive may cause more problems than it seeks to solve. Although Recital 15 states that references to another's trade mark should not infringe the trade mark right if they comply with that Directive's conditions, it does not follow that references to another's trade mark which do not comply with the Directive will necessarily be regarded as trade mark infringements, particularly in the case of unauthorized uses of a trade mark which require proof of a likelihood of confusion before liability may be established.

(4) Voluntary codes of advertising practice

8.114 The Misleading and Unfair Advertising Directive does not preclude a degree of self-regulation on the part of industrial and commercial sectors which establish their own codes of advertising practice.[132] It is also regulated by the self-restraint imposed voluntarily through specific industry and trade groups (for example, the banking sector) and through the advertising profession itself. For example, in the UK the Committee of Advertising Practices has produced a Code of Practice which has this to say about the making of comparisons in advertising:

> *Comparisons with identified competitors and/or their products*
> 18.1 Comparative claims are permitted in the interests of vigorous competition and public information. They should neither mislead nor be likely to mislead.
> 18.2 They should compare products meeting the same needs or intended for the same purpose.
> 18.3 They should objectively compare one or more material, relevant, verifiable and representative features of those products, which may include price.
> 18.4 They should not create confusion between marketers and competitors or between marketers' products, trade marks, trade names or other distinguishing marks and those of competitors.
> 18.5 Certain EU agricultural products and foods are, because of their unique geographical area and method of production, given special protection by being registered as having a 'designation of origin'. Products with a designation of origin should be compared only with other products with the same designation.
> …

---

[131] Council Directive 84/450, art 4.
[132] ibid, art 5.

F. Comparative advertising

Denigration and unfair advantage

20.1   Although comparative claims are permitted, marketing communications that include comparisons with identifiable competitors and/or their products should not discredit or denigrate the products, trade marks, trade names, other distinguishing marks, activities or circumstances of competitors. Other marketing communications should not unfairly attack or discredit businesses or their products.

20.2   Marketers should not take undue advantage of the reputation of trade marks, trade names or other distinguishing marks of organisations or of the designation of origin of competing products.[133]

8.115   While none of this is 'rocket science', it does at least indicate that, in general terms and without specific reference to the level of sophistication or gullibility of consumers in different economic sectors, the advertising profession recognizes that there are some generally recognized standards. Breaches of voluntary codes such as this one are however generally devoid of legal sanctions. Moreover, at least one court has held that the standard by which comparative advertisements should be judged is that of the relevant consumer rather than the sector concerned.[134]

(5) Treatment of 'comparative advertising' in the European Court of Justice

8.116   The ECJ has had two opportunities to consider this issue, in *Toshiba v Katun*,[135] on a reference from the Landgericht Düsseldorf, and *Pippig v Hartlauer*,[136] on a reference from the Austrian Oberster Gerichtshof. The first of these cases involved the listing of competing equipment spare parts, part numbers and prices in a catalogue; the second was a more full-blooded comparison, where the defendant's advertisements featured the claimant's trade mark-protected logo as well as one of its shop fronts.

8.117   In *Toshiba v Katun* the Landgericht referred to the ECJ a complex sequence of questions relating to the meaning of articles 2(2a) and 3a(1)(c) of the Misleading and Comparative Advertising Directive, on which the Court made two rulings. First, the indication of product numbers by which an equipment manufacturer designates his spare parts could constitute comparative advertising which objectively compares one or more material, relevant, verifiable and representative features of goods. Secondly, the use of a competitor's distinguishing marks enables the advertiser to take unfair advantage of the reputation attached to those marks *only* if the effect of the reference to them is to create, in the minds of consumers, an association between the manufacturer and the competing supplier in that they associate the reputation of the manufacturer's products with the products of the competing supplier.

---

[133] Committee of Advertising Practice, *British Code of Advertising, Sales Promotion and Direct Marketing* (2003).
[134] *Barclays Bank plc v RBS Advanta* [1996] RPC 307; [1997] ETMR 199.
[135] *Toshiba Europe GmbH v Katun Germany GmbH*, Case C-112/99 [2002] ETMR 295.
[136] *Pippig Augenoptik GmbH & Co KG v Hartlauer Handelsgesellschaft mbH, Verlassenschaft Nach Dem Verstorbenen Franz Josef Hartlauer*, Case C-44/01, 8 April 2003 (unreported).

8.118 In making this ruling, the Court performed one of its favourite manoeuvres: it gave a ruling in which it explained the relevance of the Misleading and Comparative Advertising Directive in general terms but reminded the referring court that the question which lay at the heart of the matter, the standard of objective fairness or unfairness of the comparison, was an issue which remained to be decided on a case-by-case basis because it was ultimately a question of fact, not a question of law. The Court also made an important observation concerning the interplay between the two Directives: the leeway given under the Trade Marks Directive for the legitimate use of another's trade mark was broader than that given under the Advertising Directive for the making of comparative references. The Court concluded, having considered the purpose of the latter, that 'the conditions required of comparative advertising must be interpreted in the sense most favourable to it',[137] a sentiment which it repeated in *Pippig v Hartlauer*.[138]

8.119 The overall approach which the ECJ took in *Pippig v Hartlauer* was broadly similar, although it faced a more extensive range of issues to resolve,[139] and carried the law a long way beyond the earlier decision. The Court made the following rulings:

(i) the Misleading and Comparative Advertising Directive precluded the application of national laws which applied stricter standards for the regulation of comparative advertising than those laid down in the Directive (the right to impose stricter standards for the regulation of misleading advertising other than comparative advertising is however reserved under article 7 of the Directive);

(ii) while the advertiser is free to identify his competitor's brand name if he so chooses, the fact that he does not do so does not prevent a national court from concluding that its omission is capable of being misleading (this presumably occurs where consumers, on seeing the advertisement, will draw reasonable but incorrect inferences as to the identity of the unidentified competitor);

(iii) comparisons may be made between products which are purchased through different channels (in other words, price comparisons may be drawn between goods acquired through normal channels and those imported on the grey market);

(iv) the Directive does not preclude the practice of making a test purchase of a competitor's product before his own offer to sell that product has com-

---

[137] *Toshiba v Katun* (n 135 above), para 37.
[138] *Pippig v Hartlauer* (n 136 above), para 43.
[139] The facts, briefly stated, were that Pippig had three specialist opticians' shops which stocked premium products while Hartlauer sold mainly downmarket products and parallel-imported products. Hartlauer launched an advertising campaign with leaflets, radio and TV advertisements in which it showed, *inter alia*, a pair of spectacles purchased from Pippig, the Pippig logo and a shop front. The advertisements compared fifty-two of Pippig's prices adversely with its own, citing average savings and stating Pippig's profit margin. Some of the advertisements did not mention the fact that Pippig's and Hartlauer's spectacles had different lenses.

F. Comparative advertising

menced, so long as his resulting advertisement complies with the article 3a criteria listed earlier in this chapter (it is difficult to conceive how this innocuous activity could ever fall foul of any law, let alone a provision which is designed to permit and encourage competition);

(v) an otherwise fair comparison between the prices charged by the advertiser and his competitor does not become an unfair discrediting of the competitor only on account of the magnitude of the price differential or the number of unfavourable comparisons made (if this were otherwise, advertisers would be advised by their lawyers to make only minimal comparison of almost identically priced products); and

(vi) an otherwise fair comparison does not become unfair by virtue of the reproduction in an advertisement of the competitor's logo or a picture of its shop front in addition to its name (this is a relief: some businesses have well-known logos but, in the public's perception, obscure names).

(6) Treatment of 'comparative advertising' under national law in Europe

8.120 At present it appears that there has been little case law on comparative advertising in any European country outside the UK. For that reason the position under the law of that jurisdiction will be closely considered below. That is not to say that the laws of other jurisdictions are not worthy of consideration, but some countries appear to have actively discouraged comparative advertising. In France, for example, the law implementing the Misleading and Comparative Advertising Directive requires would-be comparative advertisers to make preliminary disclosure of their advertising copy to their competitor, who would thus be given the option to take pre-emptive legal action.[140] In other countries, for example, Germany, there has long existed a judicial culture of sternly protecting business reputations and of frowning upon the gratuitous citation of third-party trade marks for one's own benefit.[141]

(a) The UK statute

8.121 Before 30 October 1994 the use of another's trade mark in an advertisement which compared the advertiser's goods or services was a trade mark infringement, whether the comparison was true or false. This is now no longer the case. The use of another's trade mark will not now infringe it in the following circumstances laid out in section 10(6) of the Trade Marks Act 1994. Under this provision

---

[140] Loi no 2001-741 of 23 August 2001. The French have traditionally regarded comparative advertising as being contrary to their advertising culture; see eg *Volkswagen AG SA v Société Renault SA*, 23 September 1991 (Tribunal de Grande Instance de Paris), PIBD, 22 October 1991, p 576.

[141] For a view of the German and Spanish attitudes towards comparative advertising in general, see Eva M Dominguez Pérez, 'Review of Comparative Advertising: German Case Law in Light of the EC Directive' (2000) 1 IIC 20–51. See also Brunhilde Steckler and Frank Bachmann, 'Comparative Advertising in Germany with Regard to EC Law' [1997] EIPR 578–86.

> Nothing in the previous provisions of this section [ie the provisions which specify and define what normally does constitute trade mark infringement] shall be construed as preventing the use of a registered trade mark by any person for the purpose of identifying goods or services as those of the proprietor or a licensee.

8.122 If section 10(6) had stopped there, it would have permitted every imaginable type of trade mark-related comparison in advertising. The text however continues:

> But any such use otherwise than in accordance with honest practices in industrial and commercial matters shall be treated as infringing the registered trade mark if the use without due cause takes unfair advantage of, or is detrimental to, the distinctive character or repute of the trade mark.

8.123 Acute readers will notice that, though section 10(6) is full of words and phrases which are found in the main European trade mark legislation, the section as it stands is not found anywhere in either Council Directive 89/104 or Council Regulation 40/94. It is, for British trade mark lawyers, 'European' in the sense that it is not part of indigenous trade mark culture, but not 'European' in the sense that it directly implements any provision of European law. The first part of section 10(6) is what Sir Hugh Laddie has described as 'home grown', while the first part of its proviso is derived from the Paris Convention,[142] which in turn influenced the phraseology of Council Directive 89/104.[143]

8.124 In the following section the application of section 10(6) of the 1994 Act in various factual situations will be considered.

(b) English case law

8.125 *Barclays v Advanta*.[144] Advanta sent out 200,000 brochures advertising its ADVANTA Visa credit card. The brochure contained a tabular comparison of interest rates of various Visa credit cards, in which Barclays' leading BARCLAYCARD brand was made to appear an expensive and unattractive offer. Barclays sued for trade mark infringement under article 5(1) of Directive 89/104 (same mark, same services), alleging that Advanta's comparison was misleading and therefore dishonest. The comparison was allegedly misleading because it failed to draw the attention of consumers to the fact that the BARCLAYCARD Visa service (but not the ADVANTA card) offered various other benefits. Injunctive relief was sought. Advanta denied infringement, claiming that its use of the BARCLAYCARD trade mark was solely 'for the purpose of identifying goods or services as those of the proprietor' and that it was acting in accordance with 'honest practices in industrial or commercial matters'.[145]

---

[142] Paris Convention, art 10*bis*(2).
[143] See art 6(1).
[144] *Barclays Bank plc v RBS Advanta* [1996] RPC 307; [1997] ETMR 199 (HC).
[145] Trade Marks Act 1994, s 10(6).

F. Comparative advertising

The High Court refused to grant an injunction since Barclays had failed to establish an arguable case of trade mark infringement: it is for the claimant to satisfy the burden of proof that the defendant's use of his trade mark in an otherwise permitted comparison is not 'honest', but Barclays failed to establish on the facts that the 'members of a reasonable audience' would find the ADVANTA advertisements dishonest. Although advertisements for credit were regulated by law and there were voluntarily agreed nationwide Codes of Practice for credit advertisements, the standard of honesty by which the comparison had to be judged was that of the relevant public's own reasonable expectations, not by what credit companies thought the necessary level of public protection should be.

8.126

The Court stated that the primary objective of the proviso to section 10(6) of the Trade Marks Act 1994 was to allow comparative advertising, so long as it was 'honest'. The fact that the goods or services compared are not the same does not make the comparison dishonest: if it did, comparison would only be allowed between identical goods or services and the use of another's trade mark in comparative advertising would be virtually always prohibited. In this case the defendant's use of the claimant's trade mark was not shown to be dishonest.

8.127

Emaco and Electrolux v Dyson.[146] Two leading manufacturers of vacuum cleaners sold products under the ELECTROLUX and DYSON brands respectively. They engaged in advertising campaigns in which each made technical claims that, in independent tests, its product was superior to the other. In consequence of the respective advertising campaigns, each competitor sued the other for trade mark infringement and a peculiarly English tort, malicious falsehood (sometimes called 'slander of goods').[147] The Court dismissed both parties' claims for malicious falsehood but allowed each party's claim for trade mark infringement.

8.128

The Court first found that the tests upon which the comparisons were made were unfair, since the test results were obtained in each case under conditions of use which were not normal and which were designed to enhance the superiority of the advertiser's product over its competitor. In the Court's opinion, a reasonable member of the public would naturally assume that tests were conducted in respect of the normal mode of operation of the two products, which was not the case with the majority of results secured here. Both parties had therefore indulged in unfair comparative advertising.

8.129

Vodafone v Orange.[148] Vodafone, owner of the trade mark VODAFONE, sued rival mobile telephone service supplier Orange for trade mark infringement when its

8.130

---

[146] *Emaco Ltd and Aktienbolaget Electrolux v Dyson Appliances Ltd* [1999] ETMR 903 (HC).
[147] For a succinct account of malicious falsehood, see Peter Birks (ed), *English Private Law* (2000), vol I, paras 14.303–14.305.
[148] *Vodafone Group plc and another v Orange Personal Communications Services Ltd* [1997] FSR 34 (HC).

advertisements stated that 'Orange users save £20 every month' over subscribers to VODAFONE. The court disposed of this claim with vigour. Section 10(6) of the Trade Marks Act 1994 positively permitted comparative advertising, so long as the advertisement was not disqualified from its protection for lack of honesty. As the advertisement was not misleading and malice was not established, the claim for trade mark infringement therefore failed.

8.131 The reference to malice may seem a little surprising as malice is not normally a requirement of a successful action for trade mark infringement. Vodafone, like the parties in *Emaco and Electrolux v Dyson*, had also based its claim on malicious falsehood and the judge's reference to malice may therefore be taken as a reference to that ground of action.

8.132 In the course of his analysis of the law the judge also observed that with regard to trade marks

> ... there is no one meaning rule. If a comparison is significantly misleading on an objective basis to a substantial proportion of the reasonable audience, it is not an honest practice within the section.[149]

8.133 It is important to emphasize this point. A comparison made in the course of advertising may have more than one meaning, depending upon the understanding of its audience. For an action for trade mark infringement to succeed, it is only necessary for *one* of the meanings that the relevant consumer audience reasonably derives from it to be dishonest.

8.134 *British Airways v Ryanair*.[150] British Airways owned the trade mark BA for air travel services. Ryanair, a budget airline, advertised its prices in a most eye-catching fashion and compared them favourably with those of British Airways, who sued for trade mark infringement. British Airways' case was based on the fact that the comparisons were, it submitted, highly misleading. In the first place, the comparison did not inform the public that the conditions the airlines attached to their respective tickets were quite different. Secondly, British Airways flights were to airports in city centres or nearby while those of Ryanair were to airports many kilometres from the city. If taxi fares and other factors were taken into consideration, the cost of flying city-to-city with Ryanair would be nowhere near as cheap as the advertisements suggested.

8.135 The Court dismissed British Airways' action in stinging terms. The alleged deception, it concluded, was in informing the public that British Airways' fares were on average five times more expensive than those of Ryanair while in reality they were only three times more expensive. To the extent that Ryanair's advertisements

---

[149] ibid, 39.
[150] *British Airways plc v Ryanair Ltd* [2001] ETMR 235.

F. Comparative advertising

were misleading, they were not materially misleading since the point the advertisements were seeking to make, that flying with British Airways was very substantially more expensive than flying with Ryanair, remained the same.

(c) Other European case law

8.136 *Compare!*[151] The defendant, a distributor of fashion accessories, advertised high-quality fashion accessories at a reasonable price and invited consumers to compare his products with those offered in the catalogue of his competitor, whom he named by its trade mark. The Bundesgerichtshof confirmed that price comparisons were in principle acceptable under post-Directive 84/450 German law and that the use of the competitor's trade mark was legitimate in that the advertiser derived no benefit from any prestige that might be associated with it.

8.137 *Teknek Electronics v KSM.*[152] Teknek, a company that made tools for cleaning circuit boards, owned the TEKNEK trade mark. KSM, a company that distributed circuit board cleaning equipment made by Teknek and other manufacturers, began to sell its own equipment. It accordingly sent a newsletter and price list to about twenty of Teknek's distributors, advertising the benefits of its own products which were offered under the KSM trade mark. The price list compared TEKNEK products with those of KSM, listing the corresponding part numbers for each of them. Teknek obtained an *ex parte* interim injunction to stop KSM using its TEKNEK trade mark in the price comparison. KSM then applied unsuccessfully to have that injunction set aside.

8.138 KSM argued that there was not even a *prima facie* case of trade mark infringement to answer since the sole purpose of employing the TEKNEK trade mark was to enable a price comparison to be made between like products. The recipients of the newsletter and price list were Teknek's own distributors, who were fully aware that Teknek and KSM were competitors who did not sell each other's products. Accordingly there was no risk of confusion. Teknek maintained that, since KSM had no independent reputation as a manufacturer, recipients of the newsletter and price list would think that it was selling TEKNEK products under the KSM trade mark (as one Danish distributor of TEKNEK products had erroneously assumed).

8.139 The Court marginally varied the injunction but did not discharge it. The contention that the price list caused recipients to assume that TEKNEK products were being sold under the KSM trade mark constituted a 'triable issue' of infringement, which would be determined by evidence submitted at the full trial. In the meantime, the balance of convenience would be served by requiring KSM to make

---

[151] *Compare!* (1999) GRUR Int 453 (Bundesgerichtshof).
[152] *Teknek Electronics Ltd v KSM International Ltd* [1998] ETMR 522 (Court of Session: Lord Penrose).

comparisons without actually making reference to the TEKNEK trade mark. Since it was principally concerned with the position of the parties relative to each other pending the trial, the Court did not concern itself overmuch with the meaning of section 10(6), other than to observe, perhaps somewhat unhelpfully, that

> the taking of unfair advantage of the mark, or conduct detrimental to character of the mark, appears to refer to the conduct of the alleged infringer rather than to the origin of the goods.[153]

8.140 *Sabena v Ryanair*.[154] Ryanair attacked Sabena's high air fares with the straplines (i) 'Welcome Ryanair and its lowest fares. Goodbye Sabena and its outrageously expensive flights' and (ii) [on an advertisement featuring the Mannequin Pis statue] 'Pissed off with Sabena's high fares? Low fares have arrived in Belgium'. The advertisements contained no data relating to the respective airlines' pricing or services from which consumers could ascertain the truth of Ryanair's assertions. The Court held that the advertisements were misleading, offensive and damaging to Sabena's reputation.

(7) Comparative advertising in Europe: a tentative summary of key principles

8.141 The principles drawn from the cases discussed above may be tentatively summarized under the following headings.

(a) How acceptable is the use of another's trade mark?

8.142 The fact that the goods or services compared are not the same does not make the comparison dishonest: if it did, comparison would only be allowed between identical goods or services and the use of another's trade mark in comparative advertising would be virtually always prohibited (*Barclays Bank plc v RBS Advanta*).

8.143 Use of a trade mark for the purpose of insulting or denigrating its owner is not prohibited if the comparison made between the parties' goods or services is not dishonest, since denigration in accordance with honest practices is permissible (*British Airways v Ryanair*).

8.144 Use of a trade mark which does not enable the user to derive any benefit that might be attached to the prestige of that mark is legally acceptable (*Compare!*).

8.145 If the relevant consumer knows, or is likely to know, that the goods or services of the respective parties to the comparison are supplied on the basis of detailed contractual conditions which may vary considerably, the fact that the comparison makes no allusion to those conditions does not make the use of the trade mark owner's mark dishonest (*Barclays Bank plc v Advanta*; *British Airways v Ryanair*).

---

[153] ibid, 532.
[154] *Sabena v Ryanair*, 10 July 2001 (Brussels Commercial Court).

F. Comparative advertising

Even the omission of a competitor's trade mark from an advertisement may be misleading (*Pippig v Hartlauer*). **8.146**

(b) By what standard should the advertiser's behaviour be judged?

An advertisement which is otherwise fair does not become an unfair disparagement in view of the magnitude of the disparity of prices compared or the number of comparisons made (*Pippig v Hartlauer*). **8.147**

If an advertisement uses only relative terms such as 'outrageously expensive' or 'high' but provides no supporting data, it is not making a comparison which consumers can objectively judge (*Sabena*). **8.148**

Although advertisements in a specific trade sector may be regulated by law and there may be voluntarily agreed nationwide Codes of Practice for such advertisements, the standard of honesty by which the comparison must be judged is that of the relevant public's own reasonable expectations, not by what competing companies think the necessary level of public protection should be (*Barclays Bank plc v RBS Advanta*). **8.149**

(c) Who is the judge of 'honesty'?

The trade mark owner must establish objectively on the facts that the 'members of a reasonable audience' would find the comparison dishonest (*Barclays Bank plc v RBS Advanta*). **8.150**

(d) Burden of proof

It is for the trade mark owner to satisfy the burden of proof that the unauthorized use of his trade mark in an otherwise permitted comparison is not 'honest', not for the user to prove that his use is honest (*Barclays Bank plc v RBS Advanta*). **8.151**

Where the advertisement is objectively capable of bearing more than one meaning, the trade mark owner need prove that just one of those meanings is not 'honest' in order to succeed in his action (*Vodafone v Orange*). **8.152**

(e) Dishonesty must be 'material'

Where the substance of the comparison remains true, the fact that the data as represented in the advertisement is literally false will not render the advertisement dishonest (*British Airways v Ryanair*). **8.153**

Use of another's trade mark in making a price comparison is dishonest if it is 'materially' false, even where the sums involved are relatively small (*DSG v Comet Group plc*),[155] but not dishonest if it is not 'materially' false (*British Airways v Ryanair*). **8.154**

---

[155] *DSG Retail Ltd (t/a Currys) v Comet Group plc* [2002] FSR 899 (a malicious falsehood case).

8.155 The 'puffing' of one's own trade mark by making statements which appear to make the goods or services for which it is used seem more important than those of competitors, is not to be taken as an implicit denigration of the trade marks of competitors (*Jupiter v Johnson Fry*).[156]

(f) Assessing the quantum of damage

8.156 The whole point of comparative advertising, if it is to confer any benefit at all, is that it will increase the market share of the advertiser at the expense of the market share of the competitor whose trade mark he uses. This is so whether the comparison is honest or not. Accordingly, if the measure of damage inflicted by a dishonest comparison is the difference between an honestly inflicted loss and a dishonestly inflicted loss, the quantum of loss may be hard to compute and the courts will be reluctant to order an inquiry into damages (applying *Emaco and Electrolux v Dyson*).

(g) Ordering an injunction

8.157 Even if the nature of the comparison is honest, injunctive relief may be justified (at least on an interim basis) if there is an arguable likelihood of confusion, for example, where there is a genuine risk that recipients of the comparative advertisement will believe that the advertiser is selling the trade mark owner's products under his own trade mark (*Teknek v KSM*).

(8) Comparative advertising: an exercise in principles and exceptions

8.158 Anyone who is interested in how rules work might like to figure out the following propositions, which are based on the position which appears to pertain under UK law.

8.159 **Principle.** *It is permitted* to use signs and other intellectual creations employed by other enterprises without first obtaining authorization.[157]

8.160 **Exception to the principle.** *It is not permitted* to use a sign belonging to another enterprise where that sign is a registered trade mark and the unauthorized use of that sign is an act which falls within the scope of an infringing act.[158]

8.161 **Exception to the exception to the principle.** *It is permitted* to make an unauthorized use of another's trade mark in marketing which would otherwise infringe that trade mark, even though that trade mark is registered and the unauthorized

---

[156] *Jupiter Unit Trust Managers Ltd v Johnson Fry Asset Managers plc*, 19 April 2000 (HC) (an unreported malicious falsehood decision).
[157] *Hodgkinson Corby Ltd and another v Wards Mobility Services Ltd* [1995] FSR 169 (HC).
[158] Council Directive 89/104, art 5; Trade Marks Act 1994 (UK), s 10(1)–(3).

F. Comparative advertising

act falls within the scope of an infringing act, if it is a use of that mark for the purpose of referring to its proprietor's goods or services.[159]

Exception to the exception to the exception to the principle. *It is not permitted* to make an unauthorized use of another's trade mark in marketing, notwithstanding the fact that the use of that mark is for the purpose of referring to its proprietor's goods or services, if that reference takes unfair advantage of, or is detrimental to, the distinctive character or repute of the proprietor's trade mark.[160] **8.162**

Exception to the exception to the exception to the exception to the principle. *It is permitted* to make an unauthorized use of another's trade mark in marketing notwithstanding the fact that, while the use of that mark is for the purpose of referring to its proprietor's goods or services, it takes unfair advantage of, or is detrimental to, the distinctive character or repute of the proprietor's trade mark, so long as that use is not 'otherwise than in accordance with honest practices in industrial or commercial matters'.[161] **8.163**

Readers may draw from this curious edifice whatever conclusions they wish. **8.164**

(9) Comparative advertising: some interesting problems to address

It would be inappropriate to suggest that Europe has not yet got its thoughts together on the legal effects of using another's trade mark in comparative advertising, but it is fair to ask the following questions to which, it is submitted, there are no clear and firm answers: **8.165**

(a) Does a third party's unauthorized use of a registered trade mark count as use for revocation purposes?

If the proprietor of the BIPPO trade mark has not used his trade mark for a continuous period of five years, it can be attacked for non-use and revoked.[162] But what if, within that period, a competitor advertises 'POPPO has fewer calories per kilo than BIPPO and half the cholesterol'? Will POPPO's unauthorized use count in BIPPO's favour? It is possible that the Directive says yes ('revocation if ... it has not been put to genuine use',[163] but it doesn't say whose use) while the Regulation says no ('if ... the proprietor has not put the ... mark to genuine use'[164]). **8.166**

---

[159] Council Directive 89/104, art 6(1); Trade Marks Act 1994, ss 10(6), 11(2).
[160] Council Directive 89/104, art 5(5); Trade Marks Act 1994, proviso to s 10(6).
[161] Trade Marks Act 1994, proviso to s 10(6).
[162] See Chapter 13.
[163] Council Directive 89/104, art 12(1).
[164] Council Regulation 40/94, art 15(1).

(b) Does a third party's unauthorized use of an unregistered trade mark count as use for the purposes of distinctiveness acquired through use?

8.167 Let us suppose that the Easycredit Banking Corporation (EBC) has failed to obtain registration of the hypothetical EASYCREDIT trade mark because that word was not regarded as possessing distinctive character. EBC must then seek to persuade the granting authority that its mark has acquired distinctive character through use. Need such use be EBC's alone, or would the use of that mark by a competitor in a comparative advertisement such as 'SUPERLOAN offers half a percent off all EASYCREDIT interest rates' count as use for the purpose of enabling EBC to gain registration? Both the Directive[165] and the Regulation[166] suggest that even Superloan's adverse use would act to EBC's benefit, whether because that adverse use merely evidences EASYCREDIT's distinctive character or because it actually enhances it. Either way, logic dictates that Superloan's adverse use would suffice since what would be the point of Superloan comparing their rates with EASYCREDIT if the public *don't* recognize EASYCREDIT as a badge of EBC's credit services?

(c) Infringement in comparative advertising where the mark used is not the same as the mark registered

8.168 An advertiser may seek to reduce the threat of litigation by a trade mark proprietor by infiltrating into his advertisement a version of the compared mark which is not the same as that registered. By doing so he can (i) raise the burden of proof required by the trade mark owner by demanding that he establish a likelihood of confusion (for example, where MARKS & SPENCER is a retail chain's trade mark, by claiming 'our prices are 10% lower than SHARKS & SPENSIVE') and (ii) raise the question as to whether there has even been a 'trade mark use' at all (for example, where the registered trade mark is OBSESSION for perfume, 'Don't be obsessive about your choice of scent when you can enjoy a fragrance reminiscent of one of Calvin Klein's best-known products for a fraction of the price'). If the advertiser in each case is sure to make it plain that his goods or services are not those of the trade mark owner, the need to prove likelihood of confusion under trade mark law may prove an insurmountable burden, leaving trade mark proprietors to sue for unfair competition, passing off, malicious falsehood or such other remedies as may come to hand.

(d) How will comparative advertising involving 'new' types of trade mark be treated by the courts?

8.169 Most traditional comparative advertising involving trade marks does not require

---

[165] Council Directive 89/104, art 3(3).
[166] Council Regulation 40/94, art 7(3).

F. Comparative advertising

any great imagination on the part of the consuming public. BIPPO is compared with POPPO, EASYCREDIT with SUPERLOAN and no punches are pulled when it comes to mentioning trade marks by name. But what will happen in the era of new types of trade mark? Their very nature suggests that their potential for being subtly alluded to will be put to the test. Consider the following scenarios:

(i) Orange Telecommunications own a trade mark for the colour orange as well as for the word ORANGE. A competitor portrays a glamorous user of its own services squashing an orange beneath his or her foot.

(ii) The same competitor portrays a colour several shades darker than the shade of orange registered by Orange Telecommunications together with the text 'Some of our rivals have been feeling a bit off-colour recently. It's no wonder when you see how expensive their tariffs are'.

(iii) Nike's slogan JUST DO IT is perceived as a message which endorses participation in a healthy, relaxed sport and exercise-oriented lifestyle. A competitor seeks to communicate the ethos of achievement and success, rather than participative cool. In its advertisement it features a successful sports or other personality together with the slogan DON'T JUST DO IT.

8.170 It would be easy to say that the only 'true' comparative advertisements are those which provide factual data upon which the consumer can exercise his intellect and make a logical purchasing choice. But nowadays many trade marks, together with their competitors, are linked to aspirational or lifestyle brands. How does the consumer decide whether BENETTON is more fashionable than TOMMY HILFIGER? Style is a commodity as much as purchase price, quality or the nature of the fabric from which the respective products are made. In that sense, dressing up two cool persons in BENETTON clothes and featuring them walking nonchalantly past a couple of tramps wearing TOMMY HILFIGERS is just a way of saying 'our clothing is more responsive to the style demands of our market'. Or is it?

(e) Endorsement transfer as comparative advertising

8.171 Where a famous and influential personality has entered into an endorsement relationship with a high-profile brand, any lawyer who is awake to the danger that the personality in question may later be engaged to endorse a competitor's product will ensure that contractual provision is made to guard against it. If this is not done, consider the case where a celebrity who has previously endorsed coffee X appears on prime time television and announces with feigned sincerity: 'I used to drink other [unnamed] coffee but now I drink coffee Y I feel so much better. It tastes great and my doctor tells me it has less caffeine too'. The public will remember the celebrity's prior attachment to coffee X and will make the conceptual link between the rival products even if coffee Y's advertisement does not spell it out.

(10) Comparative advertising in the United States

8.172 In the United States the constitutional protection accorded to freedom of speech does not render trade mark proprietors helpless against their competitors. For although comparative advertising is permitted, section 43(a) of the Lanham Act[167] provides that:

> Any person who (B) in commercial advertising or promotion, misrepresents the nature, characteristics, qualities or geographical origin of his or her or another person's goods, or commercial activities, shall be liable in a civil action by any person who believes that he or she is likely to be damaged by such act.

8.173 What is 'commercial advertising or promotion' for these purposes?

> In order for representations to constitute 'commercial advertising or promotion' ... they must be (1) commercial speech; (2) by a defendant who is in commercial competition with plaintiff; (3) for the purpose of influencing consumers to buy defendant's goods or services. While the representations need not be made in a 'classic advertising campaign', but may consist instead of more informal types of 'promotion', the representations (4) must be disseminated sufficiently to the relevant purchasing public to constitute 'advertising' or 'promotion' within that industry.[168]

8.174 When applying this provision, no account is taken of mere statements of exaggerated opinion (for example, 'Better ingredients. Better Pizza'[169]). However, statements which have a clearly factual content to them and which are false will be clearly actionable. In one notable example, Clorox's television advertisement depicted its competitor's ZIPLOC SLIDE-LOC resealable storage bag side-by-side with a Clorox GLAD-LOCK bag, each bag being identified in the commercials by its trade mark. Each of the two bags contains an animated, talking goldfish in water. When the bags are turned upside-down, the SLIDE-LOC bag leaks rapidly while the GLAD-LOCK bag does not leak at all. The SLIDE-LOC goldfish, clearly distressed, says: 'My ZIPLOC Slider is dripping!'[170]

8.175 In addition to the provision cited above, the statutory regime which governs the wrongful dilution, tarnishment and blurring of another's trade mark applies equally to the use by an advertiser of another's trade mark in order to make a comparison. For example, the use of an altered version of the claimant's deer trade mark in a comparative advertisement has been the subject of interim injunctive relief as a possible violation of anti-dilution laws.[171] (This regime is discussed in Chapter 12.)

---

[167] 15 USC, s 1125(a)(1)(B).
[168] *Procter & Gamble Company and another v Randy L Haugen and others*, 23 August 2000 (US Court of Appeals 10th Cir), citing *Porous Media Corp v Pall Corp* 173 F 3d 1109, 1120–1 (8th Cir 1999).
[169] *Pizza Hut Inc v Papa John's International Inc* 27 F 3d 489 (5th Cir 2000).
[170] *Johnson (SC) & Son Inc v The Clorox Company* 241 F 3d 232 (2d Cir 2001).
[171] *Deere & Company v MTD Products Inc* 41 F 3d 39 (2d Cir 1994). The animated and altered version of claimant's deer was made to hop to a 'pinging noise'.

Where the use of another's trade mark in the course of comparison has the effect of confusing consumers, that use will be treated in the same way as any other non-comparative act which causes confusion between the trade marks of competitors.[172]

8.176

G. The effect of consent

There is a crucial range of activities that fall within the scope of 'infringement' and are not permitted by law, but which are permitted by the person exercising power over the trade mark—those done with consent. The best way to ensure that you are not infringing another's trade mark is to obtain a licence from its proprietor or other person who is empowered to grant a licence. Once a use has been licensed, the licensee who acts within the scope of that licence may not be sued for trade mark infringement, either by the trade mark owner or by a third party such as an exclusive licensee.[173]

8.177

Where a licensee exceeds the terms of his licence, he may be sued both for trade mark infringement and for breach of contract. This is therefore the fate that a licensee may expect to meet where, for example, he takes a licence to manufacture 100,000 branded baseball caps for the trade mark owner but actually makes 150,000 caps, delivering the promised 100,000 to the licensor and keeping the rest for himself to dispose of through unofficial channels. This practice, the manufacture of 'overruns', is common wherever manufacture of a trade marked product is outsourced and cannot conveniently be policed by the licensor. It is often difficult or impossible to detect, since the 50,000 overruns are identical to the 100,000 caps which the licensor ordered. Licensors should be aware that the manufacture of overruns is at least a possibility wherever an outsourcing licensee tenders an extremely competitive price for the supply of branded goods. (The licensing of trade marks is discussed further in Chapter 16.)

8.178

H. Conclusion

While the scope of infringing acts has been broadened in recent years, both on account of recent legislative developments in Europe and following the implementation of TRIPs on a near-global basis, the range of defences to an infringement action has expanded too.

8.179

---

[172] See eg *Norton Co v Newage Industries* 204 USPQ 382 (EDPA 1979); *Polyglycoat Corp v Environmental Chemicals Inc* 509 F Supp 36 (SDNY 1980).
[173] *Northern & Shell plc v Condé Nast and National Magazines Distributors Limited and another* [1995] RPC 117 (HC).

Chapter 8: Non-infringing Acts

8.180 This chapter has endeavoured to list the large number of activities which courts or statute law have deemed to be non-infringing. Taken in the short term, all of these activities cause annoyance to trade mark proprietors or their licensees. In the long term, however, the preponderant majority of these activities, when each is taken individually, is unlikely to impinge to any appreciable extent upon either the value or the validity of the non-infringed mark.

8.181 The most important defence to trade mark infringement, which affects the very right of the trade mark owner to place goods on the market in which his registration confers a monopoly, is considered separately in the next chapter.

9

EXHAUSTION OF TRADE MARK RIGHTS

A.	**Introduction**	
	Little Johnny goes shopping: the nightmare scenario	
	The nightmare scenario: could it happen here?	9.01
	(1) Implied contractual consent	9.03
	(2) Exhaustion of rights	9.07
	(3) Three different types of exhaustion	9.09
	(4) The morality of exhaustion	9.15
B.	**The legal basis of modern exhaustion law**	
	(1) International law and exhaustion	9.22
	(2) The European model: balancing competing interests	9.25
	(3) Can the exhaustion doctrine apply to trade marks for services?	9.29
C.	**The requirement of consent**	
	(1) What is the meaning of 'consent'?	9.36
	(2) Who has to prove whether consent has been given?	9.40
	(3) Is consent contagious?	9.50
D.	**Legitimate reasons for prohibiting further use of a trade mark**	
	(1) What is a 'legitimate reason'?	9.53
	(2) The condition of the goods is changed or impaired after they have been put on the market	9.56
	(3) The replacement of one medicinal product by another with different medical indications	9.60
	(4) The desire to maintain high retail prices in order to preserve the image of the trade marked goods as being luxury products	9.61
	(5) The desire to uphold the brand image associated with the trade mark	9.62
	(6) The need to preserve the integrity of fashion goods currently sold under the trade mark	9.64
E.	**Exhaustion and its relationship with other legal rights**	
	(1) Does exhaustion of trade mark rights automatically exhaust other rights too?	9.65
	(2) Exhaustion and unfair competition	9.68
	(3) Exhaustion and abuse of rights	9.70
	(a) Interference with legitimate trade	9.71
	(b) Abuse of rights and competition law	9.73
	(c) Abuse of human rights	9.74
F.	**Some interesting problems relating to exhaustion**	
	(1) Combinations of trade mark-protected products	9.75
	(2) Abusive use of products in which the trade mark right is exhausted	9.78
	(3) Resale of multipacks	9.79
	(4) Exhaustion and human rights	9.82

Chapter 9: Exhaustion of Trade Mark Rights

(5) Is tampering with a marketed product ever justified because it is 'necessary'?	9.83
(6) If I first market my products in a country which operates a global exhaustion policy, can I still rely on the exhaustion policy of other countries to keep out unwanted exports?	9.85
(7) Can I stop unwanted parallel imports by registering a slightly different trade mark in each country?	9.86
(8) If trading in parallel imports is so profitable, why don't trade mark owners do it too?	9.87
(9) What happens where the same trade mark is owned by different proprietors in different countries?	9.91
(10) Can consent be withdrawn?	9.93
(11) Is a possibility that exhaustion may not apply a ground of contractual illegality?	9.94
G. Conclusion	9.95

A. Introduction

Little Johnny goes shopping: the nightmare scenario

Little Johnny clutched his pocket money in his hand as he surveyed the tempting shelves. Today was pocket-money day. Brow furrowed, he scanned the counter, stacked high with packages of sweets and neat rows of chocolate bars. What would it be this week, he pondered, the SNICKERS or the MARS bar? Having survived a tough time on the streets and an even tougher time in the school playground, Johnny's decision was not long in coming. He needed strength and fortification. This week he would buy a MARS bar?

'A MARS please,' said Johnny, pointing to the object of his delight. He proffered the coins to Mr Patel. In his mind's eye he was already stripping the chocolate bar of its wrapper, sinking his well-brushed teeth into the decadent flesh, pressing the pliant caramel with his rasping, practised tongue. Mr Patel selected the uppermost MARS bar from the display and, weighing its pleasant bulk in his palm, held it out to his young, expectant customer.

'Not so fast! What do you think you're doing?'

Johnny and the honest merchant froze. It was a stern command; a voice spoke deep and hinted at untold authority. Its owner was wrapped in a long dark cape. Johnny wasn't sure if this man was a policeman, but he looked very official.

'I was buying a MARS bar, Mister. Honestly. I didn't do nothing wrong.' Johnny's parents had warned him how to handle a crisis. Be respectful and tell the truth.

'No, sonny, you didn't do anything wrong. But as for you . . . !' He toted an accusatory MARS bar at the unfortunate shopkeeper, who stood motionless with his hands raised above his head.

'But what have I done wrong?' queried the puzzled Patel.

'You've gone and been selling MARS bars again, that's what you've been doing wrong. You can't go around selling MARS bars, you know. It's against the law.'

'But I've been selling MARS bars for years. Everybody does. You can get them in all the shops. There's no law against selling MARS bar? Having survived a tough bars.' Patel's sense of moral outrage was strong, but it was not easy to argue with a man who was pointing a loaded MARS bar at his head. Anything might happen.

'You're not much of a lawyer, are you,' said the unwanted invader. 'Let me tell you this.' He paused to direct his portentous countenance to the miserable little Johnny,

A. Introduction

who had already begun to rue his confectionery preference. 'Mars, the company, owns MARS the trade mark. That means that only Mars the company can sell bars with MARS on them.'

Patel looked blankly at the man. His shop had entertained many strange customers over the years, but nothing like this.

'Let me explain again. I'll take it slowly this time,' said the man, suddenly sounding a little kinder. A patronizing sigh, a pause, an explanation. 'Do you know what MARS is?'

'Yes of course I do,' said Patel shortly, having decided that the man was trying to make a fool of him in front of a small but valued customer. 'It's a chocolate bar.'

'Aha! Got you there,' came the triumphant retort. 'No it isn't! Chocolate bar, he thinks it is, does he? It's not a chocolate bar,' he intoned, drawing out those words importantly. 'It's a . . . trade mark. And you've gone and infringed it, haven't you? The Mars company owns the MARS trade mark for chocolate bars and that means that they are the only company who can sell them as MARS bars. They've got an exclusive monopoly, you know.'

Now it was Patel's turn to furrow the brow. Monopoly was his cousin's favourite game and their families sometimes played it together on bank holidays. But what did MARS bars have to do with Advance to Mayfair and the street repairs in the Old Kent Road?

'But I bought them from the wholesaler so I could sell them again. In the shop. I don't want to eat them all myself,' he exclaimed. 'Or give them away.'

'You don't have to eat them all yourself,' announced the unwelcome inquisitor.

'What can I do with them then?'

'You can sell them.'

'But you just said I couldn't sell them. Only Mars the company can do that. That's what you just said.'

'No. You can sell the MARS bars. But what you can't do is sell them with the word MARS on them because that's the trade mark. Only Mars can do that.'

'You mean I have to take all the wrappers off?'

'Exactly.'

'But who will buy MARS bars without the wrappers on?'

'If you don't want to do that, you can always apply for a MARS bar sales licence.' The caped conversationalist thrust an official-looking piece of paper before him. 'Sign here!'

The nightmare scenario: could it happen here?

9.01 This nightmare scenario is pure fiction. Although it is true that trade mark law confers an absolute (if narrow)[1] monopoly upon the owner of a trade mark, allowing him alone to sell goods bearing that trade mark, that monopoly applies only until the first occasion that goods carrying his trade mark are sold. This happens when he sells the goods himself, as happens, for example, when Mars sells MARS bars to wholesalers. It also happens when goods bearing the trade mark are

---

[1] The monopoly is narrow in that (i) it does not generally extend beyond the goods or services for which it is registered and similar goods and services and in that (ii) the law lists numerous situations in which a third party's unlicensed use of the trade mark does not infringe it.

sold with his consent. This occurs when Tommy Hilfiger, who doesn't actually spend his days bottling aftershave and selling it, licenses Unilever to make and sell TOMMY HILFIGER products with his blessing.

9.02 The fact that goods bearing a trade mark have been legitimately sold does not mean that the trade mark owner is no longer entitled to trade mark protection. He may not however use his trade mark right to prevent the sale of those goods. The beneficial result of this is that people can buy and sell second-hand products on a day-to-day basis without risking a legal action for trade mark infringement. There are two legal mechanisms by which this beneficial result can be achieved. One is through the doctrine of 'implied contractual consent'. The other is through the doctrine of 'exhaustion of rights'. Both these doctrines will be discussed below. The main difference between them is that implied contractual consent is British,[2] obsolete[3] and operates well in only a few situations, while exhaustion is continental,[4] current[5] and works quite well in most situations.

(1) Implied contractual consent

9.03 The idea of implied contractual consent is straightforward. When a wholesaler buys from Mars a consignment of hundreds and thousands of MARS bars, Mars and the wholesaler clearly expect that members of the public will buy MARS bars from retail outlets such as shops, petrol stations and vending machines, rather than queue up at the factory gate to make their purchases. Indeed, Mars advertises its products directly to the public, most of whom will never enter into any contractual relationship with Mars at all. The wholesaler also clearly expects that it will sell its bars on to retailers. When, then, a wholesaler sells MARS bars to a retailer, Mars cannot then complain that this infringes the manufacturer's exclusive legal right to sell chocolate bars as MARS bars: it is the implicit fundament upon which the deal between them is struck.

9.04 The situation is somewhat different where the retailer seeks to sell MARS bars to humans (or 'ultimate consumers' as some lawyers prefer to call them). If the Mars company complains to the retailer that it is usurping the company's exclusive right

---

[2] 'Unless it can be shown . . . that there is some clear communication to the party to whom the article was sold, I apprehend that . . . he transfers with the goods necessarily the licence to use them wherever the purchaser pleases. When a man has purchased an article he expects to have control of it, and there must be some clear and explicit agreement to the contrary to justify the vendor in saying that he has not given the purchaser his licence to sell the article . . .' (*Betts v Wilmott* (1871) LR 6 Ch App 239, 245 per Lord Hatherley).

[3] The doctrine was implicitly superseded by the implementation in the European Economic Area of the exhaustion principle contained in article 7 of Directive 89/104.

[4] See eg Friedrich-Karl Beier, 'Territoriality of Trade Mark Law and International Trade' (1970) 1 IIC 48: German case law on exhaustion doctrine goes back to the nineteenth century.

[5] The doctrine of exhaustion is now expressly the norm in most countries and implicitly the norm in the others.

A. Introduction

to sell chocolates bearing the MARS trade mark, the retailer cannot argue that it was implicit in his contract with Mars that he would be allowed to do so, since he did not make a contract with Mars—his contract was made with the wholesaler instead. The retailer can say that there has been implied consent, but not that there has been implied *contractual* consent; under classical contract theory this does not avail the retailer since he cannot claim the implied benefit of a contract to which he was not a party.[6]

9.05 How does implied contract apply in the case of Little Johnny and Mr Patel? The contract of sale by Mars of MARS bars to a wholesaler includes an implicit agreement that the wholesaler can subsequently sell those bars to someone else. But when Mr Patel buys those MARS bars and seeks to sell them to Johnny, there is not actually a contract between him and Mars. Accordingly there is no contractually binding consent on the part of Mars to let Mr Patel sell Johnny his MARS bar.

9.06 Theoretically it would be possible to construct an implied contract between Mr Patel and Mars, to overcome this difficulty. We could say that Mars and Mr Patel are parties to a contract even though that company has not met Mr Patel and has had no direct dealings with him. Each party benefits the other: Mr Patel performs an action which is beneficial to Mars (ie selling MARS bars, which enables that company to retain its market share and thereby to make a profit by selling more products), in return for which Mars makes an implied promise which is beneficial to Mr Patel, which is not to sue him for trade mark infringement. In practice the implication of such a contract would probably be regarded as false and contrived.[7]

(2) Exhaustion of rights

9.07 The idea of 'exhaustion of rights' (or 'first sale' doctrine in the United States) is quite different from that of implied contractual consent. At its simplest it runs as follows. It is accepted that the owner of the MARS trade mark has the exclusive right to sell chocolate bars bearing the MARS trade mark and that this exclusive right will persist for as long as the MARS trade mark is registered. But trade marks don't exist in thin air: they only have an 'existence' if you put them on products, for example, on the wrapper of each MARS bar. In respect of each chocolate bar that comes off the conveyor belt in the Mars factory, Mars alone has the right to name that bar a MARS bar, to put the word MARS on the wrapper and sell it. However, once that MARS bar has been sold by Mars or with its consent (for example, if Mars had permitted another company to make and sell identically marked chocolate bars on its behalf), the ability of Mars or that other company to exercise its trade mark in respect of that

---

[6] This position has since been modified in the UK by the Contracts (Rights of Third Parties) Act 1999, which confers enforceable rights upon third parties unless those rights are explicitly excluded by the contract's parties.

[7] On such contracts, see G H Treitel, *Law of Contract* (1999), pp 540–1.

specific chocolate bar would be 'exhausted' and anyone who subsequently became its owner could sell it without the threat of legal action for infringing Mars's monopoly right to sell MARS bars.

9.08 Going back to the story of Little Johnny and Mr Patel, we now see how neatly the doctrine of exhaustion works. Mars has the legal monopoly to sell chocolate bars bearing the MARS trade mark. The MARS bar selected by Johnny was a confection in relation to which the trade mark right had been exhausted when Mars sold it to the wholesalers, who in turn sold it to Mr Patel. As a result of this, Mars cannot use its trade mark rights to prevent Mr Patel selling the MARS bar to Johnny.

(3) Three different types of exhaustion

9.09 Most countries have a national trade mark system,[8] which means that (i) the power of the trade mark monopoly extends only to the borders of the country which grants that monopoly and (ii) an act is only an infringement of that monopoly right if it is done within those borders or, if done outside them, has its effect within them.[9] Some countries, such as Switzerland, remain independent of others in the operation of their trade mark laws. Many other countries nowadays prefer to join with other countries in trading blocs, such as the European Economic Area (EEA) or the Andean Pact countries; this may have the consequence for their trade mark laws that an act done in one country within the bloc is regarded as an act done in all of them (for example, putting a MARS bar on sale in Athens has the same legal effect, within all EEA countries, as if that same MARS bar had been put on sale in Lisbon or Helsinki).

9.10 The way in which a country coexists with other countries can have a profound effect on the way it operates the doctrine of exhaustion. This can be seen from the fact that exhaustion comes in three basic sizes: national, regional and global (or international).

9.11 *National exhaustion* means that, if goods bearing a trade mark which is registered in the land of Strombolia are put on sale in Strombolia by the trade mark owner or with his consent, the trade mark owner cannot use his trade mark rights in order to prevent subsequent sales of those particular goods in Strombolia. But if the goods are put on sale in the neighbouring state of Vesuvia, the trade mark owner can sue anyone who imports them into Strombolia and subsequently sells them for trade mark infringement.

---

[8] A notable exception is the decision of Belgium, Luxembourg and the Netherlands to operate a common Benelux trade mark system.
[9] See *Bonnier Media Ltd v Greg Lloyd Smith and Kestrel Trading Corporation* [2002] ETMR 1050 (Court of Session (Scotland)).

A. Introduction

Regional exhaustion means that, if goods bearing a trade mark are put on sale in any country within a specific region by the trade mark owner or with his consent, the trade mark owner cannot stop subsequent sales of that product in his own country or in any other country in that region. But if the goods are put on sale in a country outside that region, the trade mark owner can sue anyone who imports them into that region and subsequently sells them for trade mark infringement. The EEA is one such region. Once goods are lawfully put on sale in any country within the EEA, they can happily circulate from country to country without ruffling anyone's trade mark rights. Another region, which exists in legal theory although not in terms of practice, is the hypothetical regional exhaustion which exists between China, Macau, Hong Kong and Taiwan.[10]

9.12

Global exhaustion means that, if goods bearing a trade mark are put on sale in a specific country by the trade mark owner or with his consent, the trade mark owner cannot stop subsequent sales of that product in that country or in any other country. The policy of global exhaustion is one which, with some limitations,[11] operates in the United States, in Canada and in Switzerland.

9.13

A person who exploits the exhaustion of trade mark rights in order to import goods from one country into another is often called a *parallel trader* or *parallel importer*, since the goods he sells or imports are sold in parallel with goods which are either non-imported or which have been imported from a source controlled by the trade mark owner. Goods sold by parallel traders are often referred to as *grey goods*, the origins of this metaphor being lost in the mists of time.[12] Accordingly parallel traders are also sometimes called *grey traders*.

9.14

(4) The morality of exhaustion

Is exhaustion of trade mark rights a good thing or a bad thing? The question cannot easily be answered in the abstract, since exhaustion of rights is no more good or bad than a fork, a hairbrush or a toothpick: it is the context of its use which gives it the quality of being good or bad. In the tale of Little Johnny which opened this chapter, exhaustion is clearly a good thing: it is the legal concept that enables Mr Patel to sell the MARS bar even though he is not the registered proprietor of the trade mark and it is the economic concept which enables downward pressure to be exerted on consumer prices.

9.15

---

[10] See Xiodong Yuan, 'Research on Trade Mark Parallel Imports in China' [2003] EIPR 224.
[11] Thus it may be possible to resist the importation of lawfully marketed foreign goods if the quality of those goods had been impaired or where differences between imported and indigenous products may damage the reputation of the trade mark. See *Colgate-Palmolive Ltd and another v Markwell Finance Ltd and another* [1988] RPC 283.
[12] Naomi Gross, 'Trade Mark Exhaustion: the UK Perspective' [2001] EIPR 224, 225 suggests that 'grey goods' was coined as a pejorative term for goods which were not as tainted as black market or counterfeit goods.

9.16 But can a different set of factual parameters lead the reader to the opposite response? Consider the following cases:

(i) The main constituent of toothpaste is chalk. Since chalk is cheap to quarry and bulky to transport, toothpaste manufacturers generally use local chalk when making their products. Chalk is not of a uniform quality; the chalk used in making toothpaste in Brazil is of inferior quality to that used for making the same product in England. The owners of the COLGATE trade mark make toothpaste both in Brazil and in England. A consignment of Brazilian COLGATE toothpaste is imported into England and sold there without the trade mark owner's consent. Satisfied customers of the English COLGATE product buy the imported Brazilian COLGATE and are disappointed with it. They may not want to buy COLGATE toothpaste again.[13]

(ii) Arthur buys a six-year-old second-hand FORD FOCUS car from a dealer in used cars. The vehicle's original brake pads, spark plugs, battery, tyres, gearbox and sundry other original components have been replaced by generic spare parts and the repair work was not done by Ford mechanics but by an untrained amateur. The car is unroadworthy and crashes, causing serious injury to other road users. The local newspaper quotes Arthur as saying: 'It just goes to show, you can't trust a FORD FOCUS'.

(iii) Nike, the lawful proprietor of the NIKE trade mark for footwear in most countries, outsources the manufacture of its running shoes to businesses in developing countries whose overheads are extremely low. These running shoes, which are then put on sale in the USA at prices which reflect the product's desirability, may not without Nike's permission be resold in other countries where even higher prices may be secured.

9.17 In the first case the COLGATE trade mark owner is not setting out to deceive the consumer by using the same trade mark for two different qualities of toothpaste: he is only bowing to the market reality which is that toothpaste must be made with local chalk if it is to be sold at a competitive price in the jurisdiction in which it is made. The trade mark owner has suffered damage to his mark's reputation and it is hard not to sympathize with him. Yet the importer and seller of the Brazilian toothpaste is also bowing to the market reality of arbitrage, acknowledging that profit is made when goods are bought where they are cheap and sold again when they are more expensive. With hindsight it is easy to see that the problem could have been avoided if the trade mark owner had established some clearly visible means of enabling English consumers to distinguish between different grades of toothpaste. However, there was no reason why he should have done so, since such humble domestic products as toothpaste are not normally so sensitive to regional price differentials.

---

[13] See *Colgate-Palmolive Ltd and another v Markwell Finance Ltd and another* [1988] RPC 283.

A. Introduction

In the second case the issue of exhaustion of rights is more disguised. It is the normal practice to describe cars by a pair of trade marks (the brand and the sub-brand, for example, FIAT PUNTO, RENAULT CLIO, NISSAN MICRA) even when reselling them when they are not in anything like their original condition. The brand and sub-brand are a form of shorthand for such terms as 'A vehicle originally manufactured by the FIAT company and sold as a FIAT PUNTO' and, in truth, whether through ignorance or indifference, there is no other convenient means of referring to such a vehicle other than by its trade mark. But in Arthur's case there is a damaging consequence which follows from an unauthorized and unstoppable sale of a car by someone who is not the owner of the trade mark.

9.18

In the third case we are forced to confront the emotive issue of exploitation of economically disadvantaged workers in the Third World. The law of trade marks is neutral to this issue. Nike's position under trade mark law is no different if it chooses to outsource its manufacture of running shoes to a factory in Germany, where overheads are high and labour is heavily protected by national and European law. The fact remains, however, that Nike is able to use its trade mark registrations in different countries in order to maintain price differentials. This practice is regarded by the EU as an abuse of monopoly (when done alone) or a distortion of competition (when done in concert with others[14]) if it occurs within or between Member States of that Union, but as a normal consequence of commercial life if it occurs as between a Member State and another country. This may be viewed as a pragmatic approach to the establishment of a European single market or as the adoption of double standards which depend on whether the price differentials occur within or outside 'Fortress Europe'.[15]

9.19

Exhaustion might be regarded as conferring a benefit both upon consumers and upon the market if goods in circulation are indeed genuine, were it not for the fact that trade mark owners may wish to exercise their entitlement to place the same trade mark on apparently identical goods of different quality which originate in different countries. It can be argued that, if it is the trade mark proprietor's own decision to market apparently identical goods which are actually of different quality, in different countries but bearing the same trade mark, it is for him to deal with the consequences of their subsequent circulation. By according a measure of extraterritorial protection to well-known marks, the law[16] acknowledges that those marks have an extraterritorial effect which is worthy of protection. Perhaps therefore, as a *quid pro quo*, trade mark proprietors should be prepared to accept

9.20

---

[14] See *Yves St Laurent Parfums SA v Javico International*, Case C-306/96 [1998] ECR I-1983 (ECJ), where an agreement to prevent the re-importation of branded goods into the EEA was held to infringe article 81 of the EC Treaty.
[15] This term was coined by the Americans to indicate a single market with metaphorically high walls around it so as to encourage intra-Europe trade while keeping non-European exports at bay.
[16] Paris Convention (discussed below), art 6*bis*.

the consequences if they put their well-known reputations at risk by confusingly using the same trade mark for products of different qualities. While it is perfectly legitimate to have different products to cater for differing local tastes, it may be questioned whether the use of the same trade mark is necessarily the best way of exploiting the market for products to fulfil those divergent tastes.

9.21 From this brief and somewhat trivialized analysis of complex and sensitive issues it should be apparent that the morality of exhaustion of trade mark rights is not a simple issue and that no one has a monopoly of justice when analysing it.

B. The legal basis of modern exhaustion law

(1) International law and exhaustion

9.22 Numerous international treaties specifically govern the operation of trade mark law. These treaties include: (i) the Paris Convention,[17] which requires countries to give legal protection to trade marks and to respect the rights of applicants from other Convention countries; (ii) the Madrid Agreement[18] and the Madrid Protocol,[19] which set up a system for obtaining protection in many countries by making just one application; and (iii) the Trademark Law Treaty of 1994, which attempts to sever the red tape attached to making trade mark applications. None of these treaties addresses the issue of exhaustion at all, leaving each country to decide for itself whether to provide for exhaustion of rights on a national, regional or global basis.

9.23 A further intellectual property law treaty, perhaps the most important of all such treaties today, is the Agreement on Trade-Related Aspects of Intellectual Property Rights of 1994. Popularly known as 'TRIPs', this treaty was part of a package of trade-related agreements which any country had to sign up to if it wanted to join the World Trade Organization (WTO) and trade with other nations on an equal, tariff-free and barrier-free footing. TRIPs requires all signatory countries to implement the internationally agreed minimum acceptable level of national trade mark protection[20] as well as the operative provisions of the Paris Convention relating to trade marks.[21] TRIPs even addresses an important if often overlooked aspect of trade mark-related trade law: the provision of special measures to enable customs authorities to detain imported goods at national borders until it can be

---

[17] Paris Convention for the Protection of Industrial Property (1883), as amended in 1979.
[18] Madrid Agreement Concerning the International Registration of Trade Marks (1891), as amended in 1979.
[19] Protocol relating to the Madrid Agreement Concerning the International Registration of Trade Marks 1989.
[20] TRIPs, s 2, arts 15–21.
[21] ibid, art 2.

B. The legal basis of modern exhaustion law

established whether they are genuine or fake.[22] But this bright modern treaty with such a promising name (for what could be more 'trade-related' than exhaustion of trade mark rights'?) has only this to say on the topic:

> ... nothing in this Agreement shall be used to address the issue of exhaustion of intellectual property rights.[23]

This is not because exhaustion was considered to be an unsuitable or irrelevant subject for consideration but because agreement could not be reached on a common position that was acceptable, or at any rate, unobjectionable, to all of the countries involved at TRIPs' negotiation phase.[24]

9.24

(2) The European model: balancing competing interests

In 1988 the Council of the European Communities proposed, in its harmonization Directive,[25] a set of laws which were to form the basis of domestic trade mark legislation in all of the then fifteen EU Member States. Some of its provisions were optional, but its treatment of exhaustion of rights was mandatory for all Member States.

9.25

The EU's preferred solution to the treatment of exhaustion of rights is found in article 7 of Directive 89/104:

9.26

> *Exhaustion of the rights conferred by a trade mark*
> 1. The trade mark shall not entitle the proprietor to prohibit its use in relation to goods which have been put on the market in the EEA under that trade mark by the proprietor or with his consent.
> 2. Paragraph 1 shall not apply where there exist legitimate reasons for the proprietor to oppose further commercialisation of the goods, especially where the condition of the goods is changed or impaired after they have been put on the market.

These rules have also been incorporated into the Community Trade Mark (CTM) Regulation[26] and it is expected that, by the end of 2004, they will govern a further ten entrants to the EU; equivalent legislation has also been implemented in Turkey. This makes the EU's legislative formula for the issue of exhaustion the most widely used legislative model in the world. Figure 9.1 shows a flowchart indicating the process of establishing whether a trade mark right has been exhausted within the EEA.

9.27

---

[22] ibid, s 4, arts 51–60.
[23] ibid, art 6.
[24] For a brief review of the negotiations leading to article 6 of TRIPs, see Daniel Gervais, *The TRIPs Agreement: Drafting History and Analysis* (1998), paras 2.39–2.41.
[25] First Council Directive 89/104 of 21 December 1988 to approximate the laws of the Member States relating to trade marks.
[26] Council Regulation of 20 December 1993 on the Community Trade Mark, art 13. For a brief discussion and some helpful antecedent references, see P Van der Kooij, *The Community Trade Mark Regulation: An Article by Article Guide* (2000), paras 2-077–2-081.

Chapter 9: Exhaustion of Trade Mark Rights

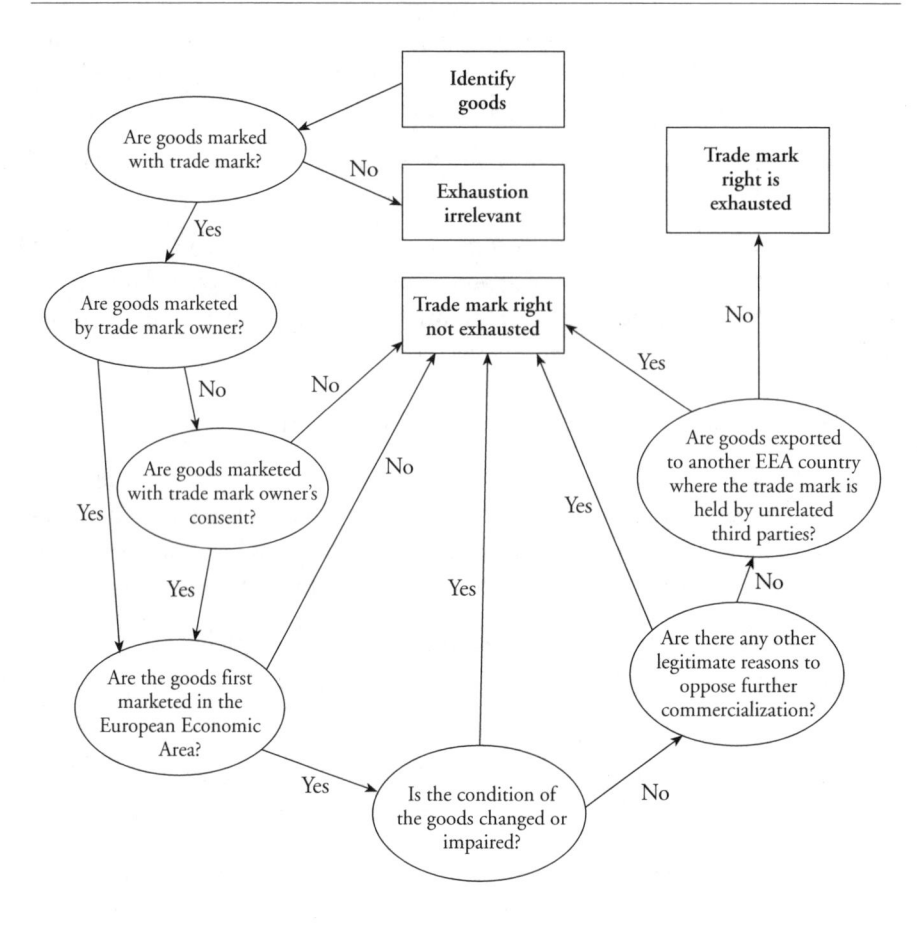

Figure 9.1 A flowchart indicating the process of establishing whether a trade mark right has been exhausted within the EEA (Council Directive 89/104, art 7; Council Regulation 40/94, art 13).

9.28 The chosen solution is only a partial solution in that it provides a general framework for resolving the question whether a trade mark right can be said to be exhausted in respect of any particular item, but it has left to the courts the resolution of a further set of questions. These questions are listed below and will be discussed individually.

(i) What is the meaning of 'consent' in article 7(1)? This question is far more complex than might be imagined. For example, do I consent to goods being put on the market in Europe if I put them on the market in Singapore but know that there is a good chance that they might be resold in the EU and do nothing about it? Is my consent to be measured by my words or deeds? And, once given, is my consent irrevocable?

(ii) Who has to prove whether there has been 'consent' to the putting of goods on to the market? This is a procedural issue with an obvious practical consequence: if all my goods bear a barcode containing details of their first marketing, but the same goods are later sold with the barcode having been defaced to make it unreadable, do I have to prove that those goods were put on the market without my consent or does the person selling them have to prove they were first marketed with my consent? Once the barcode has been eliminated, whoever has the burden of proof is likely to lose the case.

(iii) Is there such a concept as contagious consent? For example, if I have already agreed to the marketing of a batch of goods which are made for me by a particular factory, does that consent also cover batches of identical goods made for me in the same factory and being of the same quality, but for which I have not actually given my consent to marketing?

(iv) What is a 'legitimate reason' for the trade mark owner to prohibit further use of his trade mark? Does 'legitimate' bear its narrow meaning of 'permitted by law'—in which case there would be scarcely any situations in which a trade mark owner would have a legitimate reason for stopping subsequent trade in products he originally sold, or does it mean 'capable of being justified', in which case what sort of justification does he need?

(v) What constitutes a change of condition or an impairment of goods? Clearly, if a consignment of MARS bars has been left for a day under the burning sun, Mars would be most reluctant to think of someone buying them up for a nominal sum, refrigerating them until they regained their pristine firmness and then putting up a big sign saying 'MARS bars: Special Sale!' But this is an extreme case. Suppose that OBSESSION perfume was being sold in cardboard boxes which had become somewhat battered in transit. Could the trade mark owner resist further sales?

(vi) Does exhaustion of trade mark rights automatically imply exhaustion of other rights too? Directive 89/104 only governs trade marks, but goods sold under a trade mark may incorporate other intellectual property rights. For example, a logo will generally be comprised of artistic elements which attract copyright protection as well as trade mark protection. Does the fact that the trade mark owner's trade mark rights are exhausted mean that his copyright is equally exhausted? And can he still sue for passing off (an action available to the owner of a trade mark whether it is registered or not) or unfair competition?

(vii) Can the exhaustion doctrine apply to trade marks for services? The Directive specifies that exhaustion applies in respect of 'goods'. But trade marks may be registered for either goods or services. Does the Directive's silence as to services mean that the use of a trade mark in respect of services is (a) always exhausted, (b) never exhausted or (c) irrelevant to service marks?

(3) Can the exhaustion doctrine apply to trade marks for services?

9.29 If one looks literally at the words of the EU's Directive 89/104 and the CTM Regulation, it is plain that the defence to an action for trade mark infringement is only applicable where the owner of the trade mark has put his trade mark on to goods, because those provisions refer to the trade mark owner not being able to sue in respect of '*goods* which have been put on the market in the Community under that trade mark *by the proprietor or with his consent* [emphasis added]'. If the proprietor was the owner of a service mark, the defendant would not be able to point to any goods put on the market by the proprietor or with his consent.

9.30 There is however another question to ask: if the trade mark owner puts goods on to the market with his consent, do the Directive and the Regulation provide a defence where the defendant says that he is providing a service and not doing anything in relation to goods at all? For example, if I own the PEUGEOT trade mark both for motor cars and for the service of repairing them, and I then sell cars to which that PEUGEOT mark is affixed, can I use my trade mark rights in the car or in the repair service in order to stop a mechanic putting up a sign outside his workshop that reads 'Peugeots Repaired While You Wait'? Leaving aside the issues as to whether any other defences arise, does the defence of exhaustion apply?

9.31 The rider to the exhaustion principle[27] states that exhaustion of rights will not apply where 'there exist legitimate reasons for the proprietor to oppose further commercialisation of the goods, especially where the condition of the goods is changed or impaired after they have been put on the market'. From this one can argue that it can be inferred that, from the words 'to oppose further commercialisation of the goods', it is implicit that the defence of exhaustion is only intended to apply in respect of trade marks for goods. But the opposite can also be argued, that the words 'to oppose further commercialisation of the *goods*' are added because they specifically disapply the defence of exhaustion where the condition of the trade mark owner's original goods has been impaired but do not disapply it where the trade mark owner's mark is a service mark which has, for one reason or another, been applied to goods which are in circulation in the marketplace. This may happen, for example, where the Moneybank Corporation, which owns a trade mark MONEYBANK for banking and financial services but not for clothing, puts T-shirts on to the market bearing the legend 'MONEYBANK for all your banking needs'.

9.32 Going back to our Peugeot example, the ECJ has in fact considered whether the doctrine of exhaustion of rights was available to the supplier of services (in this case a motor mechanic and second-hand car salesman) who sought to use the leg-

---

[27] Council Directive 89/104, art 7; Council Regulation 40/94, art 12.

B. The legal basis of modern exhaustion law

ends 'Repairs and maintenance of BMWs' and 'Specialists in BMWs' and was sued by BMW for trade mark infringement. With regard to the advertising of second-hand cars the Court said:

> ... it is contrary to Article 7 of the directive for the proprietor of the BMW mark to prohibit the use of its mark by another person for the purpose of informing the public that he ... is a specialist in the sale of second-hand BMW cars, provided that the advertising concerns cars which have been put on the Community market under that mark by the proprietor or with its consent and that the way in which the mark is used in that advertising does not constitute a legitimate reason ... for the proprietor's opposition.[28]

The Court then addressed the question of advertising the maintenance of cars: **9.33**

> [T]he rule concerning exhaustion ... is not applicable to the advertisements relating to repair and maintenance ...
>
> Article 7 is intended to reconcile the interests of trade mark protection and those of free movement of goods ... by making the further commercialisation of a product bearing a trade mark possible ... Advertisements relating to car repair and maintenance do not affect further commercialisation of the goods ... .[29]

The advertisement of a BMW repair or maintenance service was however permitted by a separate provision of the Directive which provided that the use of another's trade marks would be permitted if that use were 'necessary to indicate the intended purpose of a product or service, ... provided he uses them in accordance with honest practices in industrial or commercial matters'.[30] Even though this latter provision clearly permits the use of a trade mark in advertising the repair of BMWs, the literal wording of article 7 is also wide enough to embrace it and it does so without the repair man having to prove that his use of the trade mark is 'necessary'. **9.34**

Not all other courts have taken the same view as the European Court of Justice (ECJ), particularly where the defendant is perceived as taking an unfair advantage through the use of the registered trade mark. In a Russian case[31] the owners of the KODAK trade mark for cameras took issue with the owners of a website, www.kodak.ru, which made available second-hand Kodak digital camera software and information concerning various Kodak products. The defendant argued that, since Kodak's trade mark rights in respect of products sold through the website were exhausted, it had no right to object to the legitimate use by the defendant of a domain name which accurately described the subject matter of his business. **9.35**

---

[28] *Bayerische Motowerke AG (BMW) and BMW Nederland BV v Deenik* [1999] ETMR 339, para 50.
[29] ibid, paras 56 and 57.
[30] ibid, para 58 quoting Council Directive 89/104, art 6(1).
[31] *Eastman Kodak Company Corporation v Grundul and the Russian Scientific and Research Institute for the Development of Public Networks* [2002] ETMR 776 (Federal Arbitration Court for Moscow).

The court concluded that Kodak's trade mark rights were not exhausted. Indeed, not only was the defendant infringing the KODAK trade mark by using it as part of the www.kodak.ru domain name as a means of selling Kodak products, but he also infringed the trade mark by putting a notice on the website stating that Kodak's trade mark rights were exhausted. By doing this, the Court concluded, the defendant was

> unfairly using on the internet the reputation inherent in the trade mark for the purpose of advertising his entrepreneurial activities.[32]

C. The requirement of consent

(1) What is the meaning of 'consent'?

9.36 This question is not as simple as it appears. It is beyond argument that, if I say to you 'I consent to you importing and reselling breakfast cereal under my KRUNCHABIX trade mark', I have given my explicit consent. But consider the following cases:

(i) I say: 'I consent to you importing and reselling breakfast cereal which I have placed on the market in the distant land of Beckistan under my KRUNCHABIX trade mark, but only if you agree to overstick the Beckistani label with an English translation of the ingredients'. This consent is explicit, but conditional—as is the case with most contractual licences.

(ii) I do not say anything but watch you import and resell KRUNCHABIX and do not do anything to stop you. Here there is no licence and no express consent, but by my actions I can be assumed to have assented to your actions—particularly if I continue to supply KRUNCHABIX for the Beckistan market. Even if I have not implicitly assented to your activities, it may be unfair for me to object later, after you have spent money, time and effort importing the cereal, setting up a distribution chain and advertising it.

(iii) I export KRUNCHABIX to Beckistan and tell the purchaser: 'you are welcome to do what you want with this product in Beckistan, but please don't send it back to the EEA'. This is a normal way of disposing of trade mark-bearing products which have become unpopular or unfashionable in the EEA. It is clear that I have not consented to the purchaser selling the cereal back into the EEA, but I haven't said this to anyone except him. Perhaps I just didn't want him to make a big profit by re-exporting the goods but didn't mind anyone else doing so.

---

[32] ibid, para 13.

C. The requirement of consent

(iv) As for (iii), but I tell the purchaser: 'you are welcome to do what you want with this product in Beckistan, but (a) please don't send it back to the EEA and (b) if you sell it rather than eat it all yourself, make it a term of your contract of sale that whoever buys it from you will not send it back to the EEA and will not let anyone to whom he sells it do the same'. Here my lack of consent to the reimportation of KRUNCHABIX is tangible.

9.37 Under the norms of European trade mark law which Directive 89/104 and the CTM Regulation impose, a trade mark owner's rights are exhausted in respect of specific goods once he puts those goods on to the market in the EEA himself or if he has either expressly or impliedly consented to those goods being marketed there.[33] The test of consent is objective ('are there grounds from which one can ascertain that the trade mark owner's unequivocal consent has been given?'), not subjective ('did the trade mark owner have it in his mind to give consent?'). Accordingly the formulation

> The distributor undertakes not to sell any Products outside the Territory and shall oblige his sub-distributors, sub-agents and/or retailers to refrain from such sales

which was employed by Zino Davidoff[34] is not objectively consonant with the trade mark owner's consent to reimportation, even if it does not explicitly require sub-distributors, sub-agents and retailers to impose similar terms on anyone who buys products from them.

9.38 It therefore appears reasonable to suppose that (i) there has been no such consent unless there is evidence that consent has been given and that (ii) equivocal consent (for example, the conditional assent which comes from a contractual licence as in case (i) above) is not unequivocal consent and will not therefore be sufficient. But is this second assumption correct? If I sell you KRUNCHABIX cereal and you do not pay me for it, it can be argued that I have not consented to any state of affairs in which I part with my product but do not get paid for it. Alternatively it can also be argued that I have indeed consented to its being put on the market and that, if you continue not to pay me, my quarrel is with you as my debtor and not with anyone who buys the cereal from you and tries to sell it to the general public. This question has not yet been addressed by the courts and its answer thus remains uncertain. In principle, however, it seems correct to assume that consent has been given and that the trade mark rights in the unpaid-for goods have been exhausted.

---

[33] *Zino Davidoff SA v A & G Imports Ltd; Levi Strauss & Co and Levi Strauss (UK) Ltd v Tesco Stores, Tesco plc and Costco Wholesale Ltd*, Joined Cases C-414/99, C-415/99 and C-416/00 [2002] ETMR 109, para 47 (ECJ).

[34] See *Zino Davidoff SA v A & G Imports Ltd* [1999] ETMR 700, 714.

9.39 One further question involving consent was considered in the *Primark* case: from what time does consent begin?[35] In this case Primark, who owned the PRIMARK and DENIM CO trade marks for jeans, sued Lollypop for trade mark infringement. Lollypop said they could not be infringers since they had obtained the jeans from Primark's own suppliers. The court was not disposed to accept that, if the suppliers had made the jeans to Primark's technical specifications and then sold them to Lollypop, the trade marks had been sewn on to those jeans with Primark's consent and the goods were not infringing products. In the judge's opinion, even if Primark gave its blessing to the manufacture of the jeans, it could not be said to have 'consented' to those jeans bearing its trade marks until it had adopted the jeans by taking delivery of them and satisfying themselves that the jeans were of the desired standard.

(2) Who has to prove whether consent has been given?

9.40 When little Johnny chose his MARS bar from Mr Patel's shop, he could not tell by looking at it whether it was put on the market with the blessing of Mars or not. Nor could Mr Patel. Even though machines can gather data from barcodes, their subtly encoded messages elude most humans. How much more so, when barcode information has been destroyed or defaced, or where there never was a barcode, will it be difficult or impossible to answer the question: 'Is this, or is this not, a consensual MARS bar?'

9.41 If an alleged fact cannot be proved, legal science offers one of two possible solutions. First, an alleged fact may be presumed unless the contrary can be established. Statutory presumptions are common in the field of intellectual property law—for example, trade marks and patents are presumed valid until they are proved to be invalid—but there is no statutory presumption that consent has not been given unless it can be proved that it has. Secondly, there is the normal principle of burden of proof, that if a person wants to rely on the truth of an alleged fact which he asserts, it is for him to prove it or it remains unproved.[36] Since in practice this means that whoever has to prove an unprovable fact loses the case, we can decide whether we favour trade mark owners or their adversaries by placing the burden of proof upon whichever of them we least prefer to win the case.

---

[35] *Primark Stores Ltd and Primark Holdings v Lollypop Clothing Ltd* [2001] ETMR 334 (HC).
[36] In *Zino Davidoff SA v A & G Imports Ltd* [1999] ETMR 700 (HC) Laddie J considered that implied consent to the re-importation into the EEA of goods placed on the market outside that area by the trade mark owner or with his consent should be presumed. This presumption has not withstood the ruling of the ECJ in *Zino Davidoff SA v A & G Imports Ltd; Levi Strauss & Co and Levi Strauss (UK) Ltd v Tesco Stores, Tesco plc and Costco Wholesale Ltd*, Joined Cases C-414/99, C-415/99 and C-416/00 [2002] ETMR 109.

C. The requirement of consent

9.42 The trade mark owner can legitimately argue that the burden of proof of showing that goods were marketed with the consent of the trade mark owner should be placed on the defendant: if the defendant wishes to rely on the proposition that the goods were placed on the market by the trade mark owner or with its consent, it is fair to require him to establish the facts upon which he seeks to rely. The trade mark owner may point out that a function of trade mark law is to protect the proprietor's investment of time, effort and money in establishing goodwill in his trade mark and in guarding the quality of products sold under that mark. Exhaustion of rights places a major limitation upon the trade mark owner's rights: it greatly weakens a monopoly which is already scarcely sufficient to enable the trade mark owner to police a vast and sophisticated market for counterfeit and infringing goods. Accordingly, to facilitate the trade mark owner's discharge of the important policing function, he should not additionally have to prove that mass-produced and highly mobile goods were *not* first placed on the market with his consent.

9.43 The person seeking to rely on the defence of exhaustion of rights can equally legitimately argue that the same burden of proof should be placed on the trade mark owner. After all, the trade mark owner can control the marking, identification and tagging of goods as well as the chain of distribution through which those goods reach the market. The subsequent dealer in those goods may have no idea of the chain of transactions which led to those goods reaching him and may not be in a position to compel businesses higher up the chain, with which he has had no personal dealings, to disclose information as to where those goods came from. Additionally, the cost and inconvenience of each dealer seeking to prove that the goods he sells were originally placed on the market with the consent of the trade mark owner would force up retail prices and greatly cut the profit margins upon which competition within the single European market (or indeed any other ostensibly free market) depends.

9.44 In practice the situation is complex, since a wholesaler which is an authorized dealer in a trade mark owner's products may buy those goods both directly from the manufacturer (where they are clearly placed on the market with the trade mark owner's consent) and also from other intermediaries. A retailer buying those products from the authorized wholesaler will assume that all products bought from that source are products in which the trade mark is exhausted. The situation becomes even more complex where the wholesaler buys products from a source which lies outside the EEA or where it is not possible to identify a 'paper trail' of documents or records which might indicate whether the products were first marketed with the consent of the trade mark owner.[37]

---

[37] See eg the facts of *Scapino BV and Ron Suwandi Sports BV v Basic Trademark SA* [2001] ETMR 294, in which the Amsterdam Court of Justice set aside an interim injunction on the basis that the defendants had established a 'sufficiently plausible' case that they were selling shoes first marketed with the trade mark owner's consent even though this could not be established on the evidence.

9.45 The situation in Europe is confused because neither piece of European trade mark legislation actually addresses it, thus leaving each EU Member State to do as it pleases. In Scotland, for instance, the Court of Session has reasoned that, since *prima facie* the only reason for interfering with a product's barcodes was to conceal the true origin of those goods, such interference could be viewed as evidence of invasion of the *prima facie* rights of the trade mark owner and interim injunctive relief should be given on that basis.[38] The ECJ has been asked to rule on this problem since, until there is a unified solution to it, parallel traders in imported goods will be advised to do so in those countries in which the trade mark owner must prove that those goods were not first marketed with his consent, while trade mark owners will be urged to sue in those countries in which it is for the subsequent trader to prove that no such consent existed. The Advocate General's opinion: (i) conceded that countries were free to adopt whichever rules of evidence they chose; (ii) stated that no rule of evidence should be acceptable if it was tantamount to a rule which deems the trade mark owner to have given its consent to the importation; and (iii) suggested that, to reflect a duty of co-operation on the part of the trade mark owner, the burden of proof should in some way be shared between the two parties.[39]

9.46 The Court affirmed that, in principle, there was nothing wrong in placing the burden of exhaustion upon the party seeking to rely upon it. But where a third party succeeds in establishing that

> there is a real risk of partitioning of national markets if he himself bears that burden of proof, particularly where the trade mark proprietor markets his products in the European Economic Area using an exclusive distribution system,[40]

then the burden of proof shifts on to the trade mark proprietor, who will then have to establish that his products were not initially placed in the EEA by him or with his consent. If, in this little game of evidential ping-pong, the proprietor can prove this, the burden of proof shifts once again to the third party to prove that, after the goods were first marketed outside the EEA without the proprietor's consent, they subsequently entered the EEA with that consent. If he cannot do this, the third party will be held liable for infringement whether consent was given or not.

9.47 This ruling invites two further questions. First, how on earth does the defendant set about proving that there is a real risk of partitioning of national markets if he, rather than the trade mark proprietor, has to bear the burden of proof that the goods were marketed in the EEA by the trade mark proprietor or with his consent?

---

[38] *Zino Davidoff SA v M & S Toiletries Ltd (No 2)* [2001] ETMR 112.
[39] *Van Doren + Q GmbH v Lifestyle + Sportswear Handelsgesellschaft mbG*, Case C-244/00 [2003] ETMR 561.
[40] *Van Doren + Q GmbH v Lifestyle + Sportswear Handelsgesellschaft mbG*, Case C-244/00 [2003] ETMR 922 (ECJ), para 42.

C. The requirement of consent

What sort of evidence is required in order to substantiate this risk? From whom may it be sought? Since 'real risk' presumably means more than 'theoretical risk', we are talking about a risk which *is* real and which is somehow caused by the placing of the burden of proof upon the defendant. Where there is no approved distribution system for goods of the type sold by the defendant and the goods are not conveniently coded or marked so that at least part of their passage into the EEA marketplace can be objectively verified, the defendant may have little upon which he can rely in support of the proposition that the goods were first marketed by the proprietor or with his consent. If there is an exclusive distribution system, it should be easier for him to point to a partitioning of the national markets since this is one of the benefits which a trade mark owner seeks to obtain from operating such a system. But the fact that an exclusive distribution system will have received the approval of the Commission will suggest that national courts will be unsympathetic to a third party's attempt to gatecrash it.

9.48 Secondly, is there a human rights issue to consider? The right to a fair trial is guaranteed under article 6 of the European Convention on Human Rights. It should therefore be considered whether it is fair for a defendant in trade mark proceedings to be required to prove a state of affairs—the proprietor's state of mind in relation to the marketing of products—which lies within the realm of the proprietor's control but not his own. Admittedly the standard to which proof must be made is not as high in civil actions as it is in criminal proceedings. Nonetheless, it will not suffice for the defendant to prove that he honestly believed the trade mark to be exhausted; nor will it avail him to show that he took all reasonable care to sell only approved stock. He must prove that the trade mark owner had put the goods on the internal market himself or that he had consented to them being put there.

9.49 The applicability of article 6 of the Convention has already been considered in the UK in the context of a criminal prosecution for trade mark infringement, where the defendant argued unsuccessfully that a statutory defence,[41] of being able to show that he believed on reasonable grounds that the use of the sign was not an infringement, was in breach of the Convention. The Court of Appeal maintained that this was a rule of evidence which, once the defendant showed reasonable grounds, shifted the burden of proof back to the prosecution to establish the defendant's guilt.[42] Such a device, the court considered, did not contravene article 6. The matter is not however beyond doubt and a ruling of the House of Lords is currently awaited.

---

[41] Trade Marks Act 1994, s 92(5).
[42] *R v Johnstone* [2003] ETMR 1.

(3) Is consent contagious?

9.50 If I consent to the sale of specific goods, for example, a batch of vodka which was bottled for sale under the SMIRNOFF trade mark, does my consent to products entering the market apply only to those specific bottles or does it also extend by implication to all other goods of the same specification, for example, any other bottles of SMIRNOFF vodka which were bottled on the same day? After all, 'goods which have been put on the market in the Community under that trade mark by the proprietor or with his consent' is an ambiguous phrase. It could mean 'those actual goods', meaning those bottles alone and no other bottles, or it could mean 'goods of that description', meaning any bottle of vodka which is in all essential physical details identical to those bottles and which, if it had been exchanged with any of the bottles marketed with the trade mark owner's actual consent, no one would have been any the wiser.

9.51 This issue has been considered by the ECJ in *Sebago*, in which the Court ruled that consent must be taken in its narrow sense, of being consent to the actual goods being marketed in the EEA.[43] In that case a hypermarket imported from El Salvador 2,561 pairs of shoes bearing the DOCKSIDES and SEBAGO trade marks. These shoes were perfectly genuine and, the hypermarket claimed, were similar to shoes which Sebago had already marketed in the EEA. The importation and sale of the El Salvadorean shoes, argued the hypermarket, should be permitted because it did not impair the function of the Sebago's trade marks, which was to indicate the origin and quality of its shoes. 'Such arguments', said Advocate General Jacobs, 'are extremely attractive' but they could not be accepted: their acceptance would effectively impose a rule of international exhaustion in place of the principle of regional exhaustion mandated by Community legislation.[44]

9.52 If, as appears to be the case, the ECJ's analysis in *Sebago* is correct, there can be no justification for national courts within the EU drawing the opposite conclusion.[45]

---

[43] *Sebago Inc and Ancienne Maison Dubois et Fils SA v GB-UNIC SA*, Case C-173/98 [1999] ETMR 681.
[44] *Sebago Inc and Ancienne Maison Dubois et Fils SA v GB-UNIC SA*, Case C-173/98 [1999] ETMR 467, 475–6.
[45] See for instance the September 2001 decision of the Spanish Supreme Court in *Bacardi y Compañía SA España v Dimexco SL and Destilerias de l'Urgell SA* [2003] ETMR 326, in which *Sebago* was not even cited.

D. Legitimate reasons for prohibiting further use of a trade mark

(1) What is a 'legitimate reason'?

Even if the trade mark owner has consented to the marketing of his goods, he can still oppose their further sale or distribution if there exists a 'legitimate reason' to oppose their further commercialization. In the case of little Johnny and the MARS bar (see the Introduction to this chapter), what might such a legitimate reason be?

9.53

It is clear that a 'legitimate reason' can mean a 'reason specifically provided for by law'. For example, if the MARS bars have been improperly stored or have come into contact with some noxious elements and are no longer fit for human consumption, it would be illegal for anyone to sell them. Likewise, if for any reason imported MARS bars contravened local ingredient-labelling regulations or their packaging infringed intellectual property rights which were owned locally by third parties, an entitlement to prevent their resale, even after they have been marketed with the trade mark owner's consent, would be 'legitimate' in the sense that it had been mandated by law.[46]

9.54

It is equally clear that the words 'legitimate reason' can be interpreted as going beyond a 'reason specifically provided for by law', in that the colloquial meaning of the word 'legitimate' embraces such notions as 'reasonable, sensible or valid'.[47] Let us look at some of these reasons.

9.55

(2) The condition of the goods is changed or impaired after they have been put on the market

This reason, which has been mentioned explicitly in the provisions of the Regulation and Directive cited above, has already proved to be a fertile source of litigation. In fact, one of the first decisions under national law was the German 'Dyed Jeans' case, in which that country's supreme appellate court expressed the opinion that the operations of bleaching, dyeing in garish colours and conversion into shorts could be regarded as a modification of LEVI's jeans which adversely affected the LEVI's brand to such an extent as to enable the defence of exhaustion to be disapplied.[48] For these purposes a change in the 'condition of the goods' includes a change in the form of packaging in which they are first put

9.56

---

[46] See eg *London Borough of Hackney v Cedar Trading Ltd* [1999] ETMR 801, where Coca-Cola cans imported from the Netherlands could not be sold lawfully in the UK because the ingredients were listed in Dutch.
[47] *Collins English Dictionary* (third edition, updated) (1994).
[48] *'Dyed Jeans'*, Bundesgerichtshof Case 1 ZR 210/93, [1997] ETMR 530.

on sale.⁴⁹ Similarly a South Korean court has held that the insertion of new non-Fuji film into a used disposable camera casing bearing the registered trade mark FUJIFILM constituted a sufficient change in the state of Fuji's disposable cameras to be actionable as a trade mark infringement.⁵⁰

9.57 Makers of luxury goods may be expected to object to anything done by a subsequent trader which spoils the appearance of their goods when they are subsequently marketed to consumers. Nonetheless even such goods may not be regarded as 'changed or impaired' if their label or packaging bears a barcode that has been obliterated or erased.⁵¹ An exception to this is the obliteration or erasure of information which legislation requires to be displayed on the product.⁵² In the case of functional goods the trade mark owner may still be able to persuade a court that there are sufficiently important quality control reasons for restricting sales of goods with deleted barcodes.⁵³ However, anyone who thinks he can with impunity open up the package of a French-marketed Sony PlayStation and add non-Sony adaptors and units for connecting PlayStations to British television sets will receive an unpleasant shock⁵⁴—and not in terms of voltage—unless he ensures that the consumers are not made to believe that the non-Sony components have been supplied by Sony.

9.58 Where the trade mark owner's goods are clearly damaged or impaired, the ultimate consumer will often find them repugnant and their sale will damage the trade mark's reputation. But what happens where it is only an intermediary, not the ultimate consumer, who sees the damage or impairment and the ultimate consumer is indifferent to it? This happened where a European entrepreneur obtained stocks of Microsoft software which was originally marketed in North America, removed the outer packaging (containing indications that the contents were not

---

⁴⁹ See eg *Elite Industries Ltd v Graziella Import Export Srl*, Case 1409/2002, WTLR, 17 June 2003, where the Criminal Division of the Romanian Supreme Court ruled that, in the absence of a 'legitimate reason' for repackaging the trade mark proprietor's coffee, any such repackaging would infringe its ELITE trade mark.

⁵⁰ *Fuji Film Co Ltd v Noh* WLTR, 21 July 2003.

⁵¹ See eg *Frits Loendersloot trading as F Loendersloot Internationale Expeditie v George Ballantine & Son Ltd and others*, Case C-349/95 [1998] ETMR 10 (ECJ); *Zino Davidoff SA v A & G Imports Ltd* [1999] ETMR 700 (HC), *Chanel SA Genève of Geneva and Chanel SA of Glaris v EPA AG* [1997] ETMR 352 (Swiss Federal Court, Lausanne). The United States courts take the opposite view; see *Davidoff & Cie SA and another v PLD International Corp* 263 F 3d 1297 (11 Cir 2001): obliteration of barcode information through use of white labels and etching tools held to constitute a change of condition in the goods that led to 'confusion' of the public; a stronger case for relief would appear to be *Montblanc-Simplo GmbH v Staples Inc* (unreported) (D Mass 3 May 2001): removal of serial numbers and PIX trade mark.

⁵² *Lancaster Group GmbH v Parfume Discount Sjaelland SpA*, Case UfR 2001.2105SH, 18 June 2001 (Maritime and Commercial Court, Denmark): product recall data required under EU Council Directive 76/768 deleted; cf *Zino Davidoff SA v A & G Imports Ltd* (n 51 above).

⁵³ *Reebok International Ltd v SA Cora and others* [1999] ETMR 649 (Court of Appeal, Brussels).

⁵⁴ *Sony Computer Entertainments Inc v Tesco Stores Ltd* [2000] ETMR 102 (HC).

D. Legitimate reasons for prohibiting further use of a trade mark

offered outside North America) and then sold the software in its inner brown cardboard casing to equipment manufacturers who subsequently sold pre-programmed computers in Europe. Exhaustion plainly could not apply because the software had not been put on the market within the EEA. The court however commented that, even if exhaustion were applicable, it would not assist the entrepreneur here because the depackaging of Microsoft's software would damage its reputation. Given the fact that the equipment manufacturers were probably quite neutral to the depackaging and the ultimate consumers would not have received it anyway, it may be asked whether this observation is correct.[55]

Changes to the condition of pharmaceutical products and their packaging are discussed in some detail in Chapter 15. **9.59**

(3) The replacement of one medicinal product by another with different medical indications

A trade mark owner who has a market authorization to sell a product with a specific medical formulation may at a later stage improve or reformulate his product. Can he then use his trade mark right in order to prevent the resale of 'old' products which were originally sold with the unimproved formulation? The ECJ[56] has given a very qualified 'yes' as the answer to this question: national law cannot legislate so as to provide for the trade mark owner to apply for a withdrawal of a market authorization which will automatically suspend a parallel trader's import licence; however, if a public health risk results from the coexistence of two differently formulated products in the same market, then restrictions upon the importation of the older version may be justified. **9.60**

(4) The desire to maintain high retail prices in order to preserve the image of the trade marked goods as being luxury products

It is unlikely that, argued in such overt and brazen terms, this plea would succeed in open court anywhere in Europe, since retail price maintenance is an axiomatic evil. But if one cannot legitimize retail price maintenance, one can at least obtain the European Commission's blessing for a selective distribution agreement which in reality will have much the same effect.[57] **9.61**

---

[55] *Microsoft Corporation v Computer Future Distribution Ltd* [1998] ETMR 597 (HC).
[56] *Ferring Arzneimittel GmbH v Eurim-Pharm Arzneimittel GmbH*, Case C-172/00 [2003] ETMR 115 (MINIRIN Spray revamped as MINIRIN Nasenspray).
[57] See eg the selective distribution network established by Givenchy (*Parfums Givenchy system of selective distribution* [1992] OJ L236/11), which was the subject of lively litigation in *BVBA Kruidvat v Commission of the European Communities*, Case T-87/92 [1997] ETMR 395.

(5) The desire to uphold the brand image associated with the trade mark

9.62 This argument, a toned down version of the high-prices argument discussed above, was used by Parfums Christian Dior, who objected to Evora buying up quantities of lawfully marketed scents such as EAU SAUVAGE, FAHRENHEIT and DUNE—normally sold in upmarket retail environments and duty free stores—and advertising them for sale in its downmarket Kruidvat retail chain.[58] The ECJ did not close the door entirely on this argument, but greatly narrowed its scope of application. The Court said that the trade mark owner may not oppose such use of his trade marks

> unless it is established that, having regard to the specific circumstances of the case, the use of those goods for that purpose seriously damages their reputation.[59]

9.63 The Court offered no examples. Perhaps under this ruling the exhaustion principle would apply where watches were sold without the bonus of point-of-sale service (where the use of such a watch would be unlikely seriously to damage the trade mark owner's reputation), but not where a retailer offered to supply a free packet of de-worming pills with every bar of SUCHARD chocolate.

(6) The need to preserve the integrity of fashion goods currently sold under the trade mark

9.64 As soon as this year's style comes into fashion, last year's is passé and no one who seriously pursues the ephemeral charms of fashion would be seen in last year's shape, length, texture or colour. So what happens to last year's unsold stock? Can the trade mark owner ensure that it does not come back to haunt the marketplace? This issue underpinned the landmark litigation in the *Silhouette* case,[60] in which the owner of the SILHOUETTE trade mark for sunglasses sold off a consignment of formerly fashionable stock to a Bulgarian dealer who was expected to dispose of these old frames within the states of Eastern Europe. In cases such as this it is precisely because the goods to which the mark is applied have *not* changed that the trade mark proprietor objects to their resale. No court has yet ruled, however, that one can sue resellers of old-fashioned goods for trade mark infringement. Nor have the courts yet had to contrast the position of durable goods, such as spectacle frames, with perishable goods such as chocolates, where 'sell by' issues may arise.

---

[58] *Parfums Christian Dior SA v Evora BV*, Case C-337/95 [1998] ETMR 26.
[59] ibid, 43.
[60] *Silhouette International Schmiedt GmbH & Co KG v Hartlauer Handelsgesellschaft mbH*, Case C-355/06 [1998] ETMR 539.

E. Exhaustion and its relationship with other legal rights

(1) Does exhaustion of trade mark rights automatically exhaust other rights too?

Goods sold by a trade mark owner or his licensee will almost certainly involve the commercial exploitation of intellectual property rights other than trade marks. For example, the product known as 'Viagra' was made by Pfizer in accordance with a patent for a substance for the treatment of male impotence; the unusual shape of the tablets was a creation which could attract protection in many countries under design law; then the labelling and artwork on the package and the printed instructions are also protected by copyright. The trade mark VIAGRA is thus only one item in the legal equation. If I buy a consignment of VIAGRA tablets in France and import them into Germany for resale there, Pfizer cannot object as trade mark owner to my doing so—but can Pfizer foil my plans by invoking any of the other legal rights? 9.65

In principle the answer is that exhaustion of rights does indeed apply both in respect of patents[61] and, in the case of copyright, even in a situation in which national law provides for exhaustion of trade marks but not copyright.[62] However, the fact that a trade mark right is exhausted does not entitle the parallel trader to take liberties with the trade mark owner's other intellectual property rights. For example, where he imports BURBERRY coats for sale, he cannot claim that he has a legal right, or indeed implied consent, to copy and use the trade mark owner's copyright-protected photographs for the purpose of advertising and selling those coats.[63] Not only are such photographs not part of the goods which have been put on to the market; the copyright in them may even be owned by third parties who have only licensed the trade mark proprietor to use them for limited purposes. 9.66

In practice the answer may not be so simple. The exhaustion of rights in goods is the exhaustion of rights *in rem* but national laws on fair trading, such as the tort of passing off, the law of unfair competition and market practices statutes in those countries which have them, can enable an injured party to bring an action *in personam* against the person who damages his business, irrespective of the fact that his trade mark rights may have been exhausted. Should it be possible for the law to 9.67

---

[61] See *Parke, Davis v Probel* [1968] ECR 55.
[62] See *Norwegian Government v Astra Norge AS* [2000] ECDR 20, an Advisory Opinion of the EFTA Court which invoked EU case law in concluding that national copyright law in the EEA may not have the effect of preventing parallel trade in pharmaceutical products on the facts before that court.
[63] *Burberrys Ltd v EMEC Co Ltd and Textjournal Co Ltd* [1998] IP Asia LR 129 (Seoul District Court, Korea), upheld on appeal to the Supreme Court; see *Kim, Choi & Lim Intellectual Property Law Newsletter*, January 2003, 7–8.

circumvent the principle of exhaustion of rights in circumstances such as this? Yes, on the assumption that exhaustion of rights is not an end in itself but merely an exception to the basic principle that a trade mark owner is entitled to enforce his rights in his property. To the extent that the laws which govern unfair competition and fair trading are focused more on the conduct of individuals than upon the broad sweep of legal principles, their flexibility is such that the courts can be expected not to apply them on facts which would unjustly preserve the trade mark owner's rights in his trade mark beyond the point at which his goods first reach the marketplace.

(2) Exhaustion and unfair competition

9.68 Where the doctrine of exhaustion applies, the trade mark owner's guns are spiked and he cannot sue for trade mark infringement, or for infringement of any other intellectual property right. But can he still sue the reseller of goods bought cheaply in one corner of the EU for expensive resale in the opposite corner by alleging that the resale is an act of unfair competition? The argument does not look promising: after all, how unfair is it for the allegedly unfair trader to buy goods cheaply and sell them more expensively elsewhere? Is that not what most traders normally do? Further, the trade mark owner has already had the opportunity to extract one profit from the sale of a product when he puts it on to the market. Why should he profit from the opportunities of others to make a profit of their own?

9.69 Unfair competition should not however be forgotten. It may be a weapon against parallel traders—particularly if it is wielded by someone other than the trade mark owner. For example, where, under a selective distribution agreement, an approved official distributor of trade marked goods invests heavily in the advertising and marketing of those goods, creating demand for the trade marked product, the training of staff to advise on them and so on, he may be effectively tilling the soil and sowing the seeds so that a parallel importer, buying in cut-price products and bearing few overheads, can come in and reap the profits which may swiftly overgrow the official distributor's business. That is unfair, in the sense that one business invests and another reaps the reward, and it is also competition, but is it 'unfair competition'? There appears to be no clear guidance on this point but, if it should transpire that the acts of the parallel trader do constitute an act of unfair competition, it is quite possible that a national distributor can sue even though the trade mark owner cannot.[64]

---

[64] This possibility appears to have been kept open by the Court of First Instance in *BVBA Kruidvat v Commission of the European Communities*, Case T-87/92 [1997] ETMR 395.

E. Exhaustion and its relationship with other legal rights

(3) Exhaustion and abuse of rights

9.70 The act of importation of lawfully marketed goods is simultaneously both fair (when viewed from the importer's angle and, if it results in cheap prices, from the customer's view too) and unfair (when viewed from the trade mark owner's and, where there is a selective distribution network, from the authorized distributors' view as well); the fact that the exercise of the trade mark monopoly may be portrayed as abusive does not however make it an 'abuse of rights'. The assertion of abuse of rights needs more legal substance if it is to succeed. In the following sections we consider some of the legal arguments by which assertions of abuse of a trade mark right have been buttressed.

(a) Interference with legitimate trade

9.71 If a trade mark owner uses his powerful legal monopoly solely in order to prevent a trader selling genuine articles bearing his trade mark, can it be argued that this use of trade mark law is a reprehensible 'abuse of rights' which the court should not even entertain? If trade mark law was created in order to clamp down on fakes and frauds, on counterfeiters and pirates, the argument runs that it has no business interfering in the business of traders in legitimate merchandise even if their sale of goods bearing a trade mark is a technical infringement of the trade mark right.

9.72 This argument was raised before the Brussels Tribunal de Commerce, which found it most attractive. The court thought that the use of legal action to stop the sale of lawfully manufactured shoes which had migrated to Belgium from El Salvador was 'nothing more than a scam, the nature of which is alien to the nature of a trade mark' because there were no legitimate motives for bringing such an action.[65] The opposite view was however taken by the Tribunal de Grande Instance de Paris, which considered that the bringing of an action to prevent the importation from the US of jeans for sale in France was not an act of unfair competition through abuse of rights.[66] This conclusion was supported by a ruling of the Appeals Court of The Hague that, in the absence of evidence that the trade mark owner is seeking to partition the market so as to maintain price differentials between Member States, an action for trade mark infringement may be brought in respect of the importation and sale of genuine goods.[67]

(b) Abuse of rights and competition law

9.73 In the context of European competition law, abuse of rights can also be argued in terms of whether a trade mark owner's use of his trade mark rights in order to

---

[65] *Sebago Inc and Ancienne Maison Dubois et Fils SA v GB-UNIC SA*, Case C-173/98 [1998] ETMR 187, 191.
[66] *Levi Strauss & Co and Levi Strauss Continental v Parkway Ltd* [2000] ETMR 977.
[67] *Parfums Christian Dior SA v Etos BV* [2000] ETMR 1057.

Chapter 9: Exhaustion of Trade Mark Rights

prevent the importation and sale of cheap but genuine products is an abuse of a dominant position under article 82 of the EC Treaty.[68] This argument will however be difficult to sustain for as long as the trade marked goods are part of a competitive market. Levi Strauss may have a complete dominance of the market for LEVI's jeans, but they are far from controlling the market for jeans in general. If the price of LEVI's jeans is higher than that of other brands and price-sensitive consumers will switch their allegiance, Levi Strauss can scarcely be said to be dominant in their market. Further, even if Levi Strauss was demonstrably in a dominant position within its market, it would still remain to be proved that an abuse of that position had occurred. The mere fact of dominance does not mean that any abuse of a dominant position has taken place: the abusive trade mark owner must have hindered competition by having recourse to activities other than those which are found in the course of normal competition.[69]

(c) Abuse of human rights

9.74 The possibility that the burden of proof in trade mark infringement cases may be in conflict with article 6 of the European Convention on Human Rights has already been mentioned above.[70] Other human rights arguments are that the enforcement of the trade mark owner's rights against genuine if infringing goods is contrary to the right to the defendant's right to his property[71] and also contrary to the defendant's right to exercise freedom of 'commercial speech'.[72] Both of these arguments were briskly rejected in *Levi Strauss v Tesco* when the referring court, having received its rulings on exhaustion from the ECJ, came to determine the merits of the action.[73]

F. Some interesting problems relating to exhaustion

(1) Combinations of trade mark-protected products

9.75 BACARDI and COKE are trade marks for popular drinks. Additionally, many people drink the two together as 'Bacardi and Coke' and ask for that combination by name when they order it in bars. Can an enterprising businessman buy quantities of both drinks, blend them himself and sell them as 'Bacardi and Coke', or is he courting potential disaster by simultaneously infringing two extremely valuable trade marks?

---

[68] On this hypothesis, see Thomas Heide, 'Trade Marks and Competition Law after *Davidoff*' [2003] EIPR 163–8.
[69] *Hoffmann-La Roche v Commission*, Case 88/76 [1979] ECR 461, para 91.
[70] See paras 9.40–9.49 above.
[71] European Convention on Human Rights, First Protocol, art 1.
[72] ibid, art 10.
[73] *Levi Strauss & Co and Levi Strauss (UK) Ltd v Tesco Stores Ltd and others* [2002] ETMR 1153, paras 38–44.

F. Some interesting problems relating to exhaustion

As has been stated, the principle of exhaustion does not generally apply 'where there exist legitimate reasons for the proprietor to oppose further commercialisation of the goods, especially where the condition of the goods is changed or impaired after they have been put on the market'.[74] In this case the condition of both sets of goods has changed, since the BACARDI rum has been diluted with COKE and the COKE carbonated beverage has been adulterated with BACARDI. But the mere fact that goods have changed or been impaired does not of necessity mean that they can't be resold: if that were the case, I could not use the registered trade mark by which my car is ubiquitously known when selling it second-hand with a few minor scratches and dents. In this case, apart from arguing that the right to enforce the BACARDI and COKE trade marks had been exhausted, the entrepreneur would also argue that he was using the words 'bacardi' and 'coke' descriptively, to indicate what sort of drink he was selling, rather than to indicate any trade connection with or authorization by the owners of the respective trade marks. Although this is a separate argument as to whether, on the assumption that the trade marks were not exhausted and could be enforced, the use was an infringing use, the two issues are not unconnected in a case where the trade mark-protected products have no other name by which they can easily be referred. By analogy, BMW is a trade mark and it is also a make of car in which the trade mark owner has the right to put it on the market. But even before the trade mark is exhausted, BMW is still the name of the car and the description of such a car as a BMW is not an infringement. If even before exhaustion one may call a BMW car a BMW, should one's entitlement to do so diminish after the car has been put on to the market and the trade mark right has been exhausted?

9.76

Despite this analysis, it is improbable that the courts would tolerate the use of the BACARDI and COKE trade marks in this manner, not least because of the damaging impact which it could have upon the individual value of each mark if the combined product were poorly received. The courts might also take account of the fact that a product which employed both the BACARDI and COKE trade marks was being concocted in circumstances in which neither of those trade mark owners had the opportunity to exercise any quality control, although it might be considered that quality control *after* the point at which the BACARDI and COKE products are put on the market should not be taken into account. In market terms, the entrepreneur's act would close the door upon the exploitation by the parties of opportunities for co-branding their own product and might reduce their opportunities to co-brand products with each other's competitors. If it were in a pro-competitive mood the European Commission might however take a more positive view, conjecturing the development of a new and readily

9.77

---

[74] See paras 9.25–9.28 above.

identifiable market for 'Bacardi and Coke' products in which all drinks' manufacturers, and not merely Bacardi and the Coca-Cola company, could compete.

(2) Abusive use of products in which the trade mark right is exhausted

9.78 This problem, which was mentioned in Chapter 8 in a slightly different context can be expressed simply enough: the owners of the trade marks for children's dolls BARBIE and KEN sold dolls which were used by a third party in order to illustrate various sexual positions on a magazine's website. Does this constitute an infringement of the trade mark and is exhaustion an issue here? Arguably the European version of the doctrine of exhaustion is not relevant because it only addresses acts of 'further commercialisation' of goods put on to the market, while the BARBIE and KEN activities complained of are not acts of further commercialization. However, the notion of 'further commercialisation' is neither defined nor explained: if people paid to gain access to the website, or if the use of BARBIE and KEN in this manner attracted extra advertising revenue, could their use be said to be akin to commercialization? There is a strong (but non-binding) analogy with copyright, where the commercialization of a work need not be limited to the making and selling of copies but would include public performances, broadcasts and cable transmissions.

(3) Resale of multipacks

9.79 At different times and in different cultures, packaged items have been known to have been sold individually. Cigarettes were often sold 'loose' in shops, while even today it is not uncommon for enterprising children to break open bags of confectionery and sell single sweets in the playground. This practice, which may or may not have the blessing of the trade mark owners concerned, would seem to have interesting repercussions for the doctrine of exhaustion of trade mark rights.

9.80 In a London supermarket last year (2002) I purchased a multipack of WALKERS ready salted crisps.[75] Each multipack contained six 25g packets of crisps. The outer packaging of the multipack bore no indication that Walkers intended to restrict the circulation within the EEA of goods lawfully marketed by them and bearing their trade mark, but the legend on the top of each of the 25g packets read 'MULTIPACK BAG NOT TO BE SOLD SEPARATELY'. On the reverse of the same packet a further legend read: 'THIS IS A PACK FROM A WALKERS CRISPS MULTIPACK AND MUST NOT BE SOLD SEPARATELY'. The question is: may I nonetheless buy multipacks and sell the small packages separately without infringing the WALKERS trade mark?

---

[75] The English term for what Americans call 'chips'.

F. Some interesting problems relating to exhaustion

It is not immediately apparent that the freshness, crispness or hygiene of the 25g package is reduced by virtue of its sale as a separate item. Indeed, the individual packets bear 'best before' data, as well as an address to which dissatisfied consumers can write. Complainants must however return not merely the packet and its contents but also the multipack wrapper. Since the multipack wrapper but not the inner bags carry barcodes, it is possible that Walkers must prohibit the separate sale of bags of crisps because the purchaser of a separate bag, having no access to the multipack wrapper, would be unable to return it to the manufacturers when seeking satisfaction. As against that, the requirement that the multipack wrapper be returned relates only to the consumer's entitlement to satisfaction in addition to his expressly preserved statutory rights, should the crisps prove to be of inadequate quality.

9.81

(4) Exhaustion and human rights

At least one court[76] has concluded that the exercise by a trade mark owner of his right to prevent the further commercialization of lawful goods in which the trade mark right was not exhausted does not constitute an infringement of the owner's right to own property, which included the right to sell that property.[77]

9.82

(5) Is tampering with a marketed product ever justified because it is 'necessary'?

This question has been answered by the ECJ in the context of the repackaging of pharmaceutical products and is discussed in greater detail in Chapter 16. If one were to filter out those elements of the Court's ruling which expressly address that sector, the Court's view would appear to be that making changes to a product lawfully first marketed in the EEA by the trade mark owner (or with his blessing) is

9.83

> ... objectively necessary ... if, without such [changes], effective access to the market concerned, or to a substantial part of that market, must be considered to be hindered as the result of strong resistance from a significant proportion of consumers ... .[78]

In the case of globally popular items such as MARS bars it is hard to imagine that any strong consumer resistance can only be overcome by making changes to the product. In the pharmaceutical sector, it is easy to see how patients may lack confidence in battered and well-travelled packets of medicine which are covered in

9.84

---

[76] *Levi Strauss & Co and Levi Strauss (UK) Ltd v Tesco Stores Ltd and others* [2002] ETMR 1153 (HC).

[77] See article 10 of the European Convention on Human Rights and article 1 of the First Protocol to that Convention. The right of property which that Convention protects may also be enjoyed by corporations.

[78] *Boehringer Ingelheim KG and Boehringer Ingelheim Pharma KG v Swingward Ltd*, Case C-143/00 [2002] ETMR 898; *Merck, Sharp & Dohme GmbH v Paranova Pharmazeutika Handels GmbH*, Case C-443/99 [2002] ETMR 923.

strange little stickers. Perhaps MARS bars and medicines lie at the two extremes, so far as market resistance is concerned, but it is submitted that most products will be polarized towards the MARS end of the spectrum rather than towards the medicinal end.

(6) If I first market my products in a country which operates a global exhaustion policy, can I still rely on the exhaustion policy of other countries to keep out unwanted exports?

9.85 If I place jeans on sale under the BIPPO trade mark in Switzerland, a country which operates a global exhaustion policy, I have placed my jeans on sale in a jurisdiction in which locally marketed BIPPO jeans must compete against jeans bearing the same trade mark and which are marketed in Greece by me or with my consent. Does this state of affairs restrict my ability to enforce my Greek trade mark so as to keep out BIPPO jeans which are first marketed by me in Switzerland? This question has not been formally resolved, although it was the subject of a somewhat opaque reference to the ECJ[79] which was subsequently withdrawn. One of the issues in that case was whether an EU Member State could withdraw the trade mark owner's entitlement to sue a parallel importer for infringement if the goods were first marketed in a country which, since it operated a global exhaustion policy itself, did not enable trade mark owners to do the same. On the face of it, there would appear to be nothing in either Directive 89/104 or the CTM Regulation to give direct support to such an argument.

(7) Can I stop unwanted parallel imports by registering a slightly different trade mark in each country?

9.86 Not if any of those countries are part of the EEA, even if the choice of slightly different trade marks in each country is motivated by purely honourable sentiments. For example, where a trade mark owner had registered, in respect of the same pharmaceutical product, the marks DALACIN in Denmark, Germany and Spain, DALACINE in France and DALACIN C elsewhere in Europe, the ECJ had to rule whether it would be possible for the proprietor to rely upon its Danish DALACIN registration when suing a parallel importer for marketing as DALACIN a quantity of imported genuine DALACINE and DALACIN C products from France and Greece. The Court ruled that, irrespective of the fact that the trade mark proprietor was not seeking to partition the market, since the different trade marks were the result of local trade mark registration problems and restrictive provisions imposed on

---

[79] *Calvin Klein Trademark Trust v Cowboyland A/S, Dansk Supermarked Administration A/S, HBN Marketing ApS, Progress (in the name of Peter Jensen) and Bilka Lavprisvarehus A/S*, Case C-4/98, referred to the ECJ by the Danish Maritime Commercial Court on 3 December 1997 but removed from the Register on 27 March 1999.

F. Some interesting problems relating to exhaustion

the trade mark owner, it could not invoke its local DALACIN registration in order to prevent the repackaging of the imported drugs where it was objectively necessary for the importer to do so. In this case, it may be presumed that the existence of one antibiotic product on the market under three different trade marks would do more harm than good, on the basis that consumers would impute the subtle variations between DALACIN, DALACIN C and DALACINE to different characteristics or strengths of closely related products.[80]

(8) If trading in parallel imports is so profitable, why don't trade mark owners do it too?

9.87 The use which a trade mark owner makes of its trade marks is driven by commercial considerations, the most important of which is the imperative to maximize the profitability of its assets and resources. Some trade mark owners make and sell products but do not wish to concern themselves with the mechanisms of distribution, transportation, storage, insurance, marketing and retail trade. Others prefer to retain a high degree of control over all aspects of the post-manufacture life of their products.

9.88 Competition authorities such as the European Commission like to view each separate phase of the exploitation of manufactured products as being subject to the beneficial influence of the marketplace. Thus, once a pack of BUDWEISER beer emerges from the production line, there is one competitive market for its distribution, another for its transportation, a third for the wholesaling of beer products and a fourth for retail sales. This way, the argument runs, market efficiencies will ensure that BUDWEISER will reach the consuming public at a potentially lower cost (if competitive savings are passed on to consumers) or at a greater profit (if they are not). The vertical integration of manufacturing and post-manufacturing activities may be suspected as having an inherently anti-competitive edge to it.[81] However, this competition-based prejudice against businesses taking a highly controlled and retentive policy towards their goods does not mean to say that the original manufacturer of goods cannot buy them back cheaply and resell them into markets in which they will fetch higher prices. What then stops them?

9.89 In many cases, trading in grey goods is an opportunistic exercise. For example, a retail outlet has ceased trading and its assets are being auctioned off to settle claims from creditors. Or an arbitrageur may hear that a particular consignment of a product is available for sale and can be diverted to a market in which it can more easily be disposed of (for example, denim products cannot be sold with facility in

---

[80] *Pharmacia & Upjohn SA v Paranova A/S*, Case C-379/97 [1999] ETMR 927.
[81] eg where it is an abuse of market power under the EC Treaty, art 82.

jurisdictions in which fashions keep changing, but their durable qualities ensure that they will always find purchasers in countries where considerations of fashion are less influential). Again, a quantity of branded food may be acquired at a discount when it is approaching the end of its shelf-life, then resold in a location in which sell-by dates are not a dominant factor in consumer choice. Or a quantity of cigarettes may be picked up as slightly spoiled stock following fire or flood damage. In all of these cases the profits made through purchase and sale may be considerable, yet they are one-off deals which depend on local knowledge and not on the development of regular and stable business relationships upon which most established businesses rely.

9.90 In other cases, the trade mark owner wants to cultivate the goodwill of those who normally distribute and sell his products, leaving him to concentrate on the design, the manufacture and the advertising of his products. This goodwill is not easily won by a trade mark owner who undercuts his distributors and retailers by establishing his own sales operation.

(9) What happens where the same trade mark is owned by different proprietors in different countries?

9.91 It can happen that a trade mark, let us call it POXO, is registered by different proprietors for shampoo in different EU countries: Fritz owns the German mark and Paolo the Italian. Both Fritz and Paolo put their POXO shampoo on to the market in their own countries. The principle of exhaustion of rights dictates that each POXO product can be sold and resold freely in its own country of origin as well as in countries such as Denmark, Belgium and Portugal where the mark has not been registered by anyone. But can Fritz's POXO products be imported into Italy for sale there?

9.92 The answer is 'no'. According to the ECJ, even if both trade marks were originally registered and owned by Paolo, who assigned the German mark to Fritz, the fact that the same mark was originally under the 'unitary control' of a single undertaking is of no avail once the possibility of exercising that unitary control is lost and neither POXO trade mark owner has any influence over the quality or manufacture of the products made by the other. This is the case both where the unitary control is lost through a voluntary assignment of one of the trade marks[82] and where it is lost through an act of state such as the appropriation of the trade mark in one jurisdiction in consequence of war.[83]

---

[82] *IHT Internationale Heiztechnik GmbH v Ideal Standard GmbH*, Case C-9/93 [1994] ECR I-2789, [1994] 3 CMLR 857, [1995] FSR 59.
[83] *CNL-Sucal NV v Hag GF AG* [1990] 3 CMLR 571 ('HAG II'), reversing the ECJ's earlier decision in *Van Zuylen Freres v HAG AG* [1974] ECR 731 ('HAG I').

F. Some interesting problems relating to exhaustion

(10) Can consent be withdrawn?

Can it be assumed that, once the trade mark owner puts goods on to the market or consents to their being put there, the legitimacy of those goods remains forever unassailable? Or can that legitimacy be retrospectively removed through the withdrawal of the trade mark owner's consent? This point was considered in an unusual case in which the importers of batches of clothing sent samples of each batch to a representative of Adidas, the trade mark owner, and asked it to verify whether or not they were genuine goods.[84] Adidas' representative, having confirmed that one batch was genuine, then changed its mind and informed the importer that the goods were counterfeit or, if genuine, had been imported from outside the EU and could not be resold within it. Adidas subsequently alleged trade mark infringement and sought summary judgment, while the importer maintained that the representative's approval constituted consent to resell the goods. The court gave judgment in Adidas' favour: the representative had acted speedily and retracted any consent that might have been given before any damage could have been done by selling the clothing.

9.93

(11) Is a possibility that exhaustion may not apply a ground of contractual illegality?

This question was touched upon in *Phytheron v Bourdon*,[85] in which Bourdon contracted to buy a quantity of a plant health product sold under the PREVICUR N trade mark. This product, made in Turkey, was subsequently lawfully imported into Germany from where it was to be delivered to France. Bourdon then refused to deliver the product, arguing that he could not do so without infringing the rights of the owner of the PREVICUR N trade mark in France. It appeared that the trade mark rights in France and Germany were owned by the same group of companies but that it was necessary to relabel the product for sale in France. On a preliminary reference from the Tribunal de Commerce, Pontoise, the ECJ ruled that, since the product had been lawfully imported into Germany and sold there, the trade mark rights in it were exhausted. It would appear from that ruling that Bourdon could not maintain that the contract was for an act which infringed French trade mark law and that it was therefore unlawful. If however, while the importation into Germany was lawful, the subsequent importation into France was not (for example, in a HAG-type situation in which the trade mark PREVICUR N was owned by unrelated companies who were using it in relation to the same goods), it is possible that different considerations would have applied.

9.94

---

[84] *Adidas-Saloman AG v Microhaven Ltd and others*, 24 March 2003 (unreported) (HC).
[85] *Phytheron International SA v Jean Bourdon SA*, Case C-352/95 [1997] ETMR 211 (ECJ).

G. Conclusion

9.95 Exhaustion doctrine is still relatively new for courts and trade mark owners, even in a number of legally sophisticated and economically mature jurisdictions. Accordingly we may expect to see a good deal more case law in the next decade as trade mark owners seek to close down the opportunities given to parallel traders to the greatest extent that the law provides, while grey-goods merchants strive to widen the hole which that doctrine has made in the trade mark monopoly.

9.96 There is no clear and unanswerable public interest in promoting the exhaustion of rights, since the public's interest is served both by the preservation of the integrity of goods bearing trade marks, which is perceived as being eroded by exhaustion doctrine, and by the price savings which exhaustion can bring. It is also difficult to judge this particular aspect of the operation of the trade mark system in the light of commercial and industrial experience, since trade mark law is a 'one size fits all' commodity: the same rules govern medicinal products, foods, clothes, cars and electrical goods—markets which behave quite differently to each other and in which the public interest may be found in quite different guises.

9.97 Given that a majority of countries both within and outside the EU favour global exhaustion, it is inconceivable that it will not ultimately win the day. At present there is no great momentum towards a change of policy within the EU,[86] but the main impetus towards reform is most likely to come from the WTO itself when global exhaustion is thrown in as a bargaining counter, a sop for those countries which will be asked to accept higher standards of domestic trade mark protection under the next TRIPs round and who will want to know what they will get in return for it.

---

[86] Following the communiqué of Commissioner Bolkestein of 18 May 2000 to the effect that the Commission did not propose to press for global exhaustion, although a majority of Member States favoured it, a Commission Report reviewing EU exhaustion policy was promised by the end of 2002. This Report does not appear to have materialized. Nor has there been any major public debate on the issue.

10

IDENTICAL AND SIMILAR MARKS, GOODS AND SERVICES

A. **Introduction**
   Real Madrid and the Real McCoy
   The moral of the story — 10.01
   (1) Why do we need to concern ourselves when different businesses use the same or similar trade marks? — 10.03
   (2) What does the law say about unauthorized use of the same or similar marks? — 10.06

B. **Identical and similar marks**
   (1) When are trade marks identical? — 10.10
      (a) Factors which suggest that the marks are identical — 10.13
      (b) Factors which suggest that trade marks are not identical — 10.14
      (c) The 'Imitation X' problem — 10.18
      (d) Sometimes it doesn't matter whether the mark is identical or merely similar — 10.21
   (2) When are trade marks similar? — 10.22
      (a) What is the legal yardstick by which trade marks are compared? — 10.23
      (b) Who is the judge of whether trade marks are similar? — 10.34
      (c) Similarity is patent, not latent — 10.36
   (3) Analysing similarity — 10.38
      (a) Visual similarity — 10.39
      (b) Aural similarity — 10.46
      (c) Conceptual similarity — 10.50
   (4) Aggregating the similarities of trade marks — 10.60
      (a) Marks which are visually and aurally similar, but not conceptually similar — 10.64
      (b) Marks which are visually similar, but aurally and conceptually dissimilar — 10.65
      (c) Marks which are visually and conceptually similar, but aurally dissimilar — 10.67
      (d) Marks which are aurally similar, but not visually or conceptually similar — 10.68
      (e) Marks which are conceptually similar, but not visually or aurally similar — 10.69
      (f) Marks which are aurally and conceptually similar, but visually dissimilar — 10.71
   (5) Comparison of simple marks — 10.73
   (6) When are trade marks different? — 10.75

C. **Identical and similar goods and services**
   (1) Comparison of goods and services — 10.76
   (2) When are goods identical? — 10.79
   (3) When are goods similar and when are they different? — 10.80
      (a) Products serving the same purpose — 10.85
      (b) Products sold in proximity to one another — 10.86
      (c) Products which are substitutable — 10.87
      (d) Products which are offered to the same public — 10.88
      (e) Products particularized in the trade mark specification — 10.89

(4) Can goods be 'conceptually' similar?		10.90
(5) Similarity of goods based on their apparently sharing a common source		10.93
(6) Similarity of goods: the problem of multiclass trade marks		10.97
(7) When are services identical?		10.98
(8) When are services similar and when are they different?		10.100
(9) When are goods similar to services?		10.101

D. **Likelihood of confusion**
  (1) When does similarity lead to confusion? The European approach — 10.103
    (a) A likelihood of confusion can be established where both trade marks have been used — 10.105
    (b) A likelihood of confusion can be established where one or even both trade marks have not actually been used — 10.108
    (c) The high degree of similarity between goods can enhance a likelihood of confusion but not create it — 10.111
    (d) Relevance of the inherent nature of the goods or services — 10.113
    (e) Relevance of outlets for the respective goods or services — 10.115
    (f) Relevance of non-distinctive or only weakly distinctive elements — 10.117
    (g) Relevance of jurisdictions in which the respective marks comfortably coexist without confusion — 10.121
    (h) Post-point of sale confusion must also be considered — 10.122
    (i) The more laboured is the task of establishing a link between the marks, the less likely it is to succeed — 10.124
  (2) Establishing confusion: the United States and Canada — 10.125
    (a) A 'market-oriented' approach — 10.129
    (b) Reverse confusion — 10.130
  (3) Is 'likelihood of confusion' a question of law or a question of fact? — 10.131
  (4) The yardstick of confusion: the reasonably well-informed consumer — 10.134
    (a) The consumer must be 'relevant' — 10.135
    (b) The consumer must be well informed — 10.138
    (c) The consumer must be averagely attentive and circumspect — 10.139
    (d) The consumer must be expected to suffer from imperfect recall — 10.140
  (5) What if the confusion is removed before the point of sale? — 10.142

E. **Likelihood of association**
  (1) Likelihood of confusion: does it include a 'likelihood of association'? — 10.143
  (2) What does 'likelihood of association' actually mean? — 10.150
  (3) How is a 'likelihood of association' established? — 10.152
  (4) If there is a likelihood of association, does a likelihood of confusion even need to be proved? — 10.154

F. **Conclusion** — 10.156

A. Introduction

Real Madrid and the Real McCoy

Maria picked the football scarf from the street vendor's stall and examined it critically. It was a lovely scarf, just the right size and colour; a perfect fashion accessory. Her boyfriend Juan was not so sure. The legend on the scarf read 'Real Madrid',[1] but Juan

---

[1] Real Madrid is the name of a famous Spanish football team.

A. Introduction

had not seen such a scarf either worn or displayed for sale at his favourite team's previous fixtures. 'Is this a real Real Madrid scarf?' he inquired.

'Of course it is,' insisted Carlos the street vendor, in a tone of injured innocence.

'But the Real Madrid scarves I've seen don't look like this one.'

'No. You don't understand,' explained Carlos patiently. Most of his customers didn't ask questions like this. 'This is a real scarf and it really comes from Madrid. That's why I had the words "Real Madrid" put on it.'

'Oh, right,' said Juan. Maria, meanwhile, had turned the scarf back-to-front and was trying to decipher a small label that had been stitched to one end of this. 'Does Tommy Hilfiger really make football scarves?'

'Ah, you didn't read the small print properly,' said Carlos. 'If you look closely, you'll see it isn't Tommy Hilfiger at all.'

'Are you sure?' queried Maria as she removed her shades, screwed up her pretty little face and peered more closely at the label. 'Oh, look, Juan, he's right. It isn't Tommy Hilfiger at all, it's Tammy Hilfiger. Isn't that extraordinary?'

'Not many people know about Tammy,' Carlos informed her. 'Very shy type, she is. But she makes a beautiful football scarf, doesn't she?'

'Don't people get confused, what with there being a Tommy Hilfiger and a Tammy Hilfiger?' queried Juan.

'Not people who really know about these things. You'd have to be quite ignorant to mistake Tammy for Tommy, wouldn't you? I mean, Tommy Hilfiger's quite common these days, a bit downmarket you might say—but Tammy caters for a more discriminating clientele.' Carlos beamed with pride. It wasn't often that he had the chance to use long words like 'discriminating.'

'Oh, look,' Maria piped up, 'there's something else on this label. It says "American Express." What's that got to do with Real Madrid scarves?'

'It's a reminder to my customers that they can pay by American Express if they want. It's a great convenience to be able to pay by plastic these days. You never know when you need your cash.'

The moral of the story

10.01 This story, if a little far-fetched, illustrates some of the realities of trade in trade mark-protected goods and services. Since the Real Madrid football club is the proprietor of the word mark REAL MADRID in respect of a range of football supporters' accessories such as scarves, that club would naturally wish to prevent the use of that mark on the same goods as those for which it had secured registration. This reflects the scenario of 'same mark, same goods'. 'Tammy Hilfiger' is subtly different from the TOMMY HILFIGER trade mark, which is also registered for clothing: this reflects 'similar mark, same goods'. The famous AMERICAN EXPRESS trade mark is registered for several types of goods and services, but not football scarves: this reflects 'same mark, different goods'.

10.02 This story depicts just three of the scenarios in which a trade mark owner is likely to want to take legal action against an unauthorized user of his trade mark. Where the case is one of 'same mark, same goods', the issue of infringement can be resolved easily, but in the other cases the trade mark owner's lawyer may have to consider numerous questions. These questions will puzzle any client who cannot understand why his lawyer is apparently reluctant to share his intuitive conclusion that infringement has taken place.

(1) Why do we need to concern ourselves when different businesses use the same or similar trade marks?

10.03 Even if it were not the law, it would be plain common sense to suppose that trade mark law would protect the owner of a trade mark against a competitor who (i) puts the same trade mark on his goods for which the trade mark owner has registered that trade mark, or (ii) who seeks to register the same mark for the same goods. The trade mark owner wants to protect his investment in developing his products and services so as to maintain their level of quality, not to mention his investment in advertising his branded goods and services. If he could not do so, his competitors could sell products under the same name. Without having to recoup the financial burden of investing in new products, in strategies for developing and strengthening the brand in the minds of consumers, and in advertisements, they would be able to sell the same products at considerably lower prices.

10.04 Consumers have an interest too. Many people who buy fake ROLEX watches either know a fake ROLEX when they see one or can guess that it is fake from the lowly and unglamorous circumstances of its sale. But those same people often have blind faith in the true and unsullied provenance of their medicines, their brake pads and other trade mark-bearing products to which they entrust their health and welfare. If we buy a medicine which turns out to be counterfeit, we can sue the shopkeeper for selling goods which are not of the appropriate quality; we can also report him to the relevant police or trading standards authority. But for the most part we trust the trade mark owner to police the integrity of his products for us by making sure that no counterfeit products even reach the shops. By protecting his trade marks against their unauthorized use by others, we enable him to perform this policing function at only the most marginal of cost to ourselves.

10.05 A further consumer interest exists, even if there is no risk through counterfeits, in being able to buy the product of one's choice. The link which trade mark owners establish with their customers is a powerful one; it provides the rock upon which most commercial investment is built. The trade mark owner provides a repeatable and predictable experience for the consumer, whether it be an experience of quality, image, value for money or anything else; the consumer in turn supplies a stream of continued business. That is why the integrity of trade marks is important; that it also why the relationship should not be abused, whether by interlopers or by the trade mark owners themselves.

A. Introduction

(2) What does the law say about unauthorized use of the same or similar marks?

10.06 It is generally accepted in both legal and consumer circles that the trade mark's owner should be able to prevent the unauthorized use of an identical trade mark in respect of identical goods or services under all circumstances. It is also generally accepted that, if there is a likelihood of confusion, the trade mark's owner should be able to prevent the unauthorized use of (i) a mark which is not identical but merely similar, in respect of identical goods or services, as well as (ii) a mark which is identical, in respect of goods or services which are not identical but merely similar. This position is reflected in the Agreement on Trade-Related Aspects of Intellectual Property Law (TRIPs), article 16(1) of which reads as follows:

> *Rights conferred*
> 1. The owner of a registered trademark shall have the exclusive right to prevent all third parties not having the owner's consent from using in the course of trade identical or similar signs for goods or services which are identical or similar to those in respect of which the trademark is registered where such use would result in a likelihood of confusion. In case of the use of an identical sign for identical goods or services, a likelihood of confusion shall be presumed. The rights described above shall not prejudice any existing prior rights, nor shall they affect the possibility of Members making rights available on the basis of use.

10.07 The owner of a trade mark can do this in one of two ways: by preventing anyone from using his mark, or by preventing anyone else applying to register a trade mark the use of which could be prevented. Article 16 of TRIPs only refers to the unauthorized use of another sign and does not specifically address attempts by others to register the same or a similar mark. However, the corresponding provisions in the domestic legislation of many countries (for example, those of the EU harmonization Directive[2] and the Community Trade Mark (CTM) Regulation[3]) effectively duplicate its terms by providing separately that competitors' marks which are identical or similar may be neither registered nor used. This is a simple way of reducing the likelihood of future infringements, as well as their attendant inconvenience and cost to legitimate trade mark users.

10.08 The rest of this chapter will deal with the legal criteria which establish

(i) whether trade marks are identical, similar or different;
(ii) whether goods and services are identical, similar or different;
(iii) whether a similarity between two trade marks is likely to cause confusion; and
(iv) whether there is a likelihood that two marks will be confusingly associated with one another.

---

[2] Council Directive 89/104, arts 4(1) and 5(1).
[3] Council Regulation 40/94, arts 8(1), 9(1)(a) and (b).

Chapter 10: Identical and Similar Marks, Goods and Services

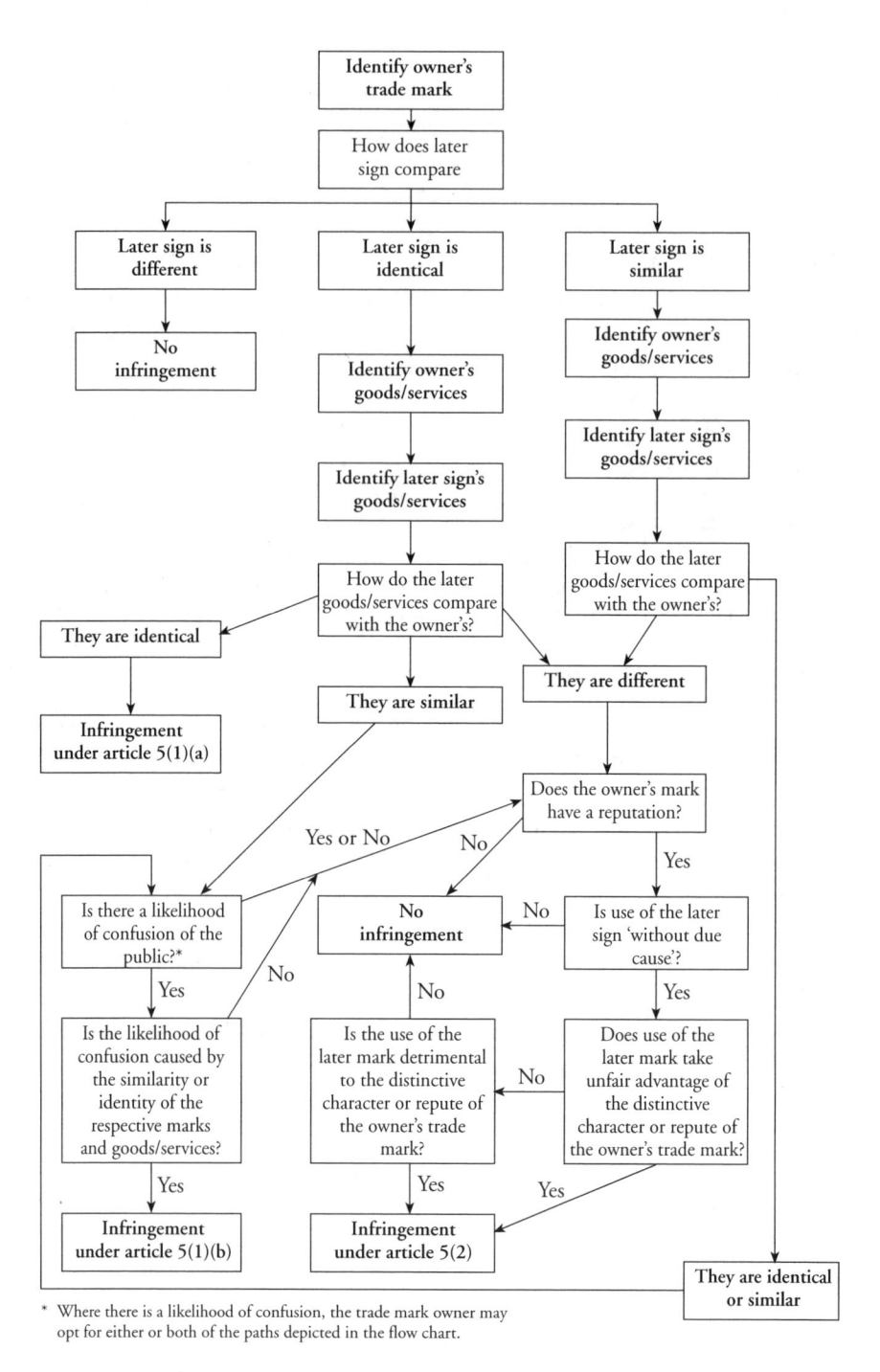

```
                    ┌──────────────────┐
                    │ Identify owner's │
                    │   trade mark     │
                    └────────┬─────────┘
                             ▼
                    ┌──────────────────┐
                    │  How does later  │
                    │   sign compare   │
                    └────────┬─────────┘
        ┌────────────────────┼────────────────────┐
        ▼                    ▼                    ▼
┌──────────────┐    ┌──────────────┐    ┌──────────────┐
│ Later sign is│    │ Later sign is│    │ Later sign is│
│  different   │    │   identical  │    │    similar   │
└──────┬───────┘    └──────┬───────┘    └──────┬───────┘
       ▼                   ▼                    ▼
┌──────────────┐   ┌──────────────────┐  ┌──────────────────┐
│      No      │   │ Identify owner's │  │ Identify owner's │
│ infringement │   │  goods/services  │  │  goods/services  │
└──────────────┘   └────────┬─────────┘  └────────┬─────────┘
                            ▼                     ▼
                   ┌──────────────────┐  ┌──────────────────┐
                   │ Identify later   │  │ Identify later   │
                   │ sign's goods/    │  │ sign's goods/    │
                   │    services      │  │    services      │
                   └────────┬─────────┘  └────────┬─────────┘
                            ▼                     ▼
                   ┌──────────────────┐  ┌──────────────────┐
                   │ How do the later │  │ How do the later │
                   │ goods/services   │  │ goods/services   │
                   │ compare with     │  │ compare with     │
                   │   the owner's?   │  │   the owner's?   │
                   └──────────────────┘  └──────────────────┘
```

Figure 10.1 Relative grounds for refusing an application (Council Directive 89/104, art 4), taking into account the ECJ ruling in *Davidoff v Gofkid*.

* Where there is a likelihood of confusion, the trade mark owner may opt for either or both of the paths depicted in the flow chart.

Key outcome boxes in the chart:
- They are identical → Infringement under article 5(1)(a)
- They are similar → (likelihood of confusion path)
- They are different → Does the owner's mark have a reputation?
- Is there a likelihood of confusion of the public?* → Yes → Is the likelihood of confusion caused by the similarity or identity of the respective marks and goods/services? → Yes → Infringement under article 5(1)(b)
- No infringement
- Is use of the later sign 'without due cause'? → Yes → Does use of the later mark take unfair advantage of the distinctive character or repute of the owner's trade mark? / Is the use of the later mark detrimental to the distinctive character or repute of the owner's trade mark? → Yes → Infringement under article 5(2)
- They are identical or similar

312

B. Identical and similar marks

Figure 10.1 is a schematic diagram of all of the grounds of refusal of registration which relate to the existence of another's trade mark. **10.09**

B. Identical and similar marks

(1) When are trade marks identical?

This question is not as easy as it appears. Consider the following scenario: a trade mark owner has registered the word ARTHUR as a trade mark for clothing. A competitor subsequently uses the trade mark ARTHUR ET FELICIE on similar clothing. Have they used the identical trade mark? The answer is both 'yes' and 'no'. In the sense that the word ARTHUR is used in its entirety by the owner of ARTHUR ET FELICIE, the use of ARTHUR ET FELICIE is the use of a mark which is identical to ARTHUR, the whole of ARTHUR's identity being subsumed within the words ARTHUR ET FELICIE. Yet ARTHUR ET FELICIE is three words, while ARTHUR is only one and it appears absurd to regard the two as being identical. The question whether the two marks were identical was referred by the Tribunal de Grande Instance de Paris[4] to the European Court of Justice (ECJ), which ruled that a mark is identical if **10.10**

> . . . it reproduces, without any modification or addition, all the elements constituting the trade mark or where, viewed as a whole, it contains differences so insignificant that they may go unnoticed by an average consumer.[5]

An example of an insignificant difference, drawn from another legal context, is that which existed between IBM's trade marks THINK PAD and THINKPAD.[6] **10.11**

Some courts have felt that the 'swamping' or swallowing up of the trade mark owner's trade mark into a larger mark is clearly the use of an 'identical' mark. For example, in the UK the use of the trade name 'William R Asprey' was the use of a trade mark which was identical to ASPREY.[7] Other tribunals have reached the opposite conclusion. The UK Trade Mark Registry, for example, concluded that the trade mark COMFORT AND JOY was not identical to JOY.[8] Where the word SLIM was part of a logo, albeit a prominent part, a Greek court **10.12**

---

[4] *SA Société LTJ Diffusion v Société SA Sadas Vertbaudet* [2001] ETMR 76.
[5] *SA Société LTJ Diffusion v SA Sadas*, Case C-291/00 of 20 March 2003 (unreported judgment), para 54, adopting a slightly tighter form of words than the Advocate General at [2002] ETMR 441, para A53.
[6] *International Business Machine Corp's application*, Case R 10/1998-2 [1998] ETMR 643, where IBM was able to base a CTM application for THINKPAD on the seniority of its Greek THINK PAD registration despite the fact that the Greek mark was written as two words while the CTM application was written as one.
[7] *Asprey & Garrard Ltd v WRA (Guns) Ltd and Asprey* [2002] ETMR 933 (CA).
[8] *Merri Mayers-Head's application; opposition of Jean Patou* [1997] ETMR 577.

concluded that the mark COOL AND SLIM was not only not identical but was not even similar.[9]

(a) Factors which suggest that the marks are identical

10.13 If the later sign contains material which is regarded as purely descriptive, it may be ignored in the course of comparison with the earlier mark. For example, if I have registered LOUIS VUITTON for luggage, my competitor cannot say that he has not used the same mark just because the label on his luggage bears the legend LOUIS VUITTON LUGGAGE.[10] Where the later sign contains its user's company name, that too has been disregarded by a Swedish Court when it considered the trade mark EROWA COMBICHUCK identical to the claimant's CTM COMBI.[11]

(b) Factors which suggest that trade marks are not identical

10.14 It is now widely accepted that a competitor who copies only part of the trade mark owner's registered mark has not used an identical mark, even though the part which was copied was the most prominent part of it. Thus the Cour d'appel de Paris has concluded that POST' AIR is not an identical mark to LA POSTE.[12]

10.15 Another criterion which will tilt the balance away from marks being identical and towards their being either merely similar or quite different is whether the material added by the later mark gives it a completely different meaning. This was recognized by the French Cour de Cassation, which conceded that the word mark FIRST was copied in its entirety in the mark FIRST LADY, but the association of 'First Lady' with the wife of the President of the United States completely changed the later mark's meaning.[13] Likewise the Cour d'appel de Paris perhaps surprisingly held that CHAMPION DU MONDE ('world champion') had a meaning which was quite different from that of the earlier mark CHAMPION.[14]

10.16 From these decisions it can be surmised that whether the different meaning is sufficient to dislodge the presumption of identity is not a precise science but remains a matter of subjective evaluation.

---

[9] *Slim International and Antineas Graikou v Delta Protypos Milk Industry* [2000] ETMR 409 (First Instance Court, Athens).
[10] This proposition appears from *AAH Pharmaceuticals Ltd v Vantagemax plc* [2003] ETMR 205 (HC), where the court considered that 'Vantage Rewards' for a customer award scheme was the same as the VANTAGE service mark for award schemes.
[11] *System 3R International AB v Erowa AG and Erowa Nordic AB* [2003] ETMR 916 (Stockholm District Court).
[12] *AOM Minerve SA v INPI and another* [2001] ETMR 1209.
[13] *Sarl Succès de Paris v SA Parfums Van Cleef et Arpels* [1999] ETMR 869. Cf *Vekaria v Kalatizadeh*, Case R 410/2001–1 [2003] ETMR 111, in which the OHIM Board of Appeal reckoned that the British public would associate both DIANA and PRINCESS DIANA with the same person.
[14] *Atlan v INPI and SA Promodès* [2001] ETMR 88.

B. Identical and similar marks

10.17 The subtraction of material from an earlier mark may not be an effective way of escaping a conclusion of similarity as the addition of fresh material. The Opposition Division of the Office for Harmonisation in the Internal Market (OHIM) thus considered STITCHES to be a similar mark to the earlier BROKEN STITCHES.[15]

(c) The 'Imitation X' problem

10.18 The Advocate General in ARTHUR ET FELICIE[16] considered a further aspect of identity: the difficulty of categorizing what he termed 'Imitation x' marks. In other words, if TISSOT is a trade mark for watches, would products sold under the sign IMITATION TISSOT be regarded as using the identical mark or not? If the word 'imitation' can be discounted as being descriptive, then at least one court would hold TISSOT and IMITATION TISSOT to be 'identical'.[17] This approach might well appeal to the Advocate General, who was alarmed at the prospect that, if (i) 'x' and 'Imitation x' could not be regarded as 'identical' and (ii) consumers were not confused into thinking that 'Imitation x' products were the real thing, a blatant abuse of the 'x' trade mark would go unremedied.[18]

10.19 Since, in the Advocate General's Opinion, the analysis of this issue was described as being 'neither necessary nor appropriate', it is unclear why he raised it at all. However, at the heart of his concern lay a deep question as to the fundamental role of articles 4(1)(a) and 5(1)(a) of the Directive in protecting trade mark owners. If those provisions are there in order to build a property-type fence around investment in a trade mark, they should apply to 'Imitation x' use which threatens that investment. If however they merely provide a convenient means for a trade mark owner to gain protection on the basis that confusion in the case of 'identical' marks is presumed (as article 16(1) of TRIPs states), it would be reasonable to suppose that the 'identical mark, identical goods or services' provisions should not be enlisted to aid the trade mark owner where (and if) the 'Imitation x' use can be proved not to result in confusion.

10.20 The ECJ's judgment in ARTHUR ET FELICIE does not discuss the 'Imitation x' problem and its ruling leaves that issue unclear. IMITATION TISSOT cannot be said to reproduce literally, 'without any modification or addition, all the elements constituting' the TISSOT trade mark. Nor, when viewed as a whole, does the addition of the

---

[15] *House of Stitches Pty Ltd's application; opposition of Bellini Warenvertriebsgesellschaft mbH*, Case B 16560 [1999] ETMR 994.
[16] *SA Société LTJ Diffusion v SA Sadas*, Case C-291/00 [2002] ETMR 441, para 48.
[17] *AAH Pharmaceuticals Ltd v Vantagemax plc* [2003] ETMR 205 (HC).
[18] This hypothesis assumed that, if 'x' and 'Imitation x' were used on the same product, the Directive would prohibit relief against 'unfair advantage' or 'detriment': the ECJ rejected this hypothesis in *Davidoff & Cie and Zino Davidoff SA v Gofkid Ltd*, Case C-292/00 [2003] ETMR 534, discussed in Chapter 11.

word IMITATION constitute a difference 'so insignificant that it may go unnoticed by an average consumer'. If the words could be separated, with IMITATION being regarded as an adjective describing the condition of the goods, not as a trade mark, while TISSOT is regarded as the whole of the trade mark, the problem would be solved.

(d) Sometimes it doesn't matter whether the mark is identical or merely similar

10.21 Since the law presumes that confusion exists between identical marks which are used for identical goods and services, it is obviously advantageous for a trade mark owner to be able to persuade a court or trade mark registry that his competitor's sign is 'identical' to his. If he can do so, he need not go through the often lengthy and expensive process of proving that there is a likelihood of confusion between his trade mark and that of his competitor. However, where the goods or services of his competitor are only similar to those for which he has registered his mark, he will have to prove that a likelihood of confusion exists irrespective of whether his trade mark and that of his competitor are identical or similar. In such a situation the court or tribunal will only consider whether the parties' respective marks are 'identical or similar' but does not need to trouble itself to determine which.

(2) When are trade marks similar?

10.22 Where trade marks are not identical, the fact that they are similar will enable the owner of the earlier mark to resist any use of a similar mark on identical or similar goods or services where confusion is likely to result. Accordingly it is necessary to pose the question as to when trade marks which are not identical are merely similar. This question cannot be asked until we have established the answer to two earlier questions: (i) what is the legal yardstick by which trade marks are compared? (ii) who is the judge of whether trade marks are similar?

(a) What is the legal yardstick by which trade marks are compared?

10.23 The ECJ was required to consider this question in *Sabèl v Puma*,[19] where it concluded that the comparison of trade marks should involve a

> global appreciation of the visual, aural or conceptual similarity of the marks in question, bearing in mind, in particular, their distinctive and dominant components.[20]

10.24 A global appreciation was necessary because

---

[19] *Sabèl BV v Puma AG, Rudolf Dassler Sport*, Case C-251/95 [1998] ETMR 1.
[20] ibid, para 23. To these criteria it may be necessary to add a further criterion of olfactory similarity, within the general context of sensory similarity; see *Adidas-Salomon AG and Adidas Benelux BV v Fitnessworld Trading Ltd*, Case C-408/01, Opinion of 10 July 2003 (unreported) (ECJ), para 43.

B. Identical and similar marks

The average consumer normally perceives a mark as a whole and does not proceed to analyse its various details.[21]

Although that Court was solemnly applying principles of EU law, it may be thought that this part of the ruling in that case represented something of a truism which is found in all trade mark systems: since trade marks generally consist of words which are read, spoken and understood, or of logos, containers or packaging which are seen and understood, there are no other useful ways of comparing marks other than by asking what they look like, what they sound like and what they mean. The rule does however require stating since it is not self-evident that each factor of a trade mark should be considered; nor is the degree of importance which should be given to each factor obvious. Without this clear statement it would be possible for a court to say, in the case of a primarily visual mark, that only its visual aspects should be considered when making a comparison between them. **10.25**

The *Sabèl v Puma* test emphasizes that one should, when comparing trade marks, bear in mind in particular their 'distinctive and dominant components'. What exactly does this verbal formula mean? It could mean, first, that one has to consider those features of each mark which distinguish it from all other marks which are unlike it; secondly, it could mean that one must consider those features which distinguish each of the two marks from the other. The first of these seems somewhat nonsensical since, when considering the similarity between two trade marks, their respective distinctive components would appear to be almost by definition irrelevant to their shared similarity: yet that is the more natural interpretation of the Court's words. The second approach therefore seems scarcely more sensible, for much the same reason: one would have expected a global appreciation of the similarity of two trade marks to bear in mind those areas of shared similarity rather than those features which serve to distinguish each from the other. In any event, since it is those features which trade marks have in common which cause consumers to confuse them, in principle we should ask not how far two marks differ from each other but how far their shared features will cause consumers to confuse them. **10.26**

In practice, we do indeed give weight to those areas of similarity between marks rather than focus on their differences. The French Cour de Cassation[22] has ruled that, when comparing marks—in this case OCEALINE and OCEALIA—one should focus on their similarities rather than their differences. A different approach was however adopted by the Spanish Supreme Court, when it upheld a decision that the trade marks REEBOK and REETRUCK were not graphically or aurally similar on account of the difference between the 'truc' and 'bo' elements which were contained within a shared outer casing of 'REE . . . K'.[23] **10.27**

---

[21] ibid.
[22] *Cuisine de la Mer Cuisimer SA v Maumenee, SA Meralim and Rambour* [2000] ETMR 880.
[23] REETRUCK trade mark application [2002] EIPR N-115.

Chapter 10: Identical and Similar Marks, Goods and Services

10.28 *Sabèl v Puma* remains only the beginning of the story of comparison of trade marks, for at least two reasons. First, its ruling does not explicitly take into account the registrability of simple or complex trade marks for 'new' subject matter such as smells and sounds.[24] Secondly, it does not advise overmuch on the relative significance of these three criteria. The failure to accord relative weight to them is not a problem where all three criteria (i) are fulfilled, in which case the two trade marks are bound to be similar (for example, PIGLET and PIGGIE); nor does it cause difficulties where none of the criteria are fulfilled, since the two marks cannot possibly be similar (for example, CAT and GRAPE). Difficulties arise where only one or two of the criteria are established, leaving grounds upon which it can be reasonably concluded both that the marks are similar and that they are not. This issue will be addressed later in the chapter.

10.29 The assessment of 'dominant' features in trade marks is little discussed in case law, but its importance is great. Where two trade marks share both similar and dissimilar features, they may be found to be similar where the shared feature is dominant but dissimilar where they are not. An elegant example of this may be found in the OHIM Board of Appeal decision[25] that the two figurative marks for clothing, depicted in Figure 10.2, were not similar. Unlike the Opposition Division, which considered that the word 'Arthur' was the dominant feature of each mark, the Board of Appeal considered that the marks were 'notably dissimilar' because the dominant feature of the mark on the right was the depiction of the friendly stylized aardvark.

Figure 10.2 The OHIM Board of Appeal considered these two figurative marks used on clothing to be 'notably dissimilar'.

10.30 This decision is easy to understand if one bears in mind that the relevant consumer of such clothes is taken to be the customer in the shop. Where retailers

---

[24] 'Sound' in this context means a sound which is not attached to a word mark by virtue of its pronunciation. The words COCA-COLA have a sound when they are pronounced and they thus have an aural element which is part of their identity. But it is not the sound which is registered: it is the words. Different speakers will sound them differently.

[25] *Marc Brown's Trade Mark Application; opposition of LTJ Diffusion* [2002] ETMR 653. Since clothes are rarely ordered orally but are usually chosen following inspection, comparison of the visual aspect of clothes marks is more important; cf beer, which is commonly asked for rather than chosen following inspection, where the oral element dominates: *Mystery Drinks GmbH v OHIM, Karlsberg Brauerei KG Weber Intervening*, Case T-99/01, 15 January 2003 (unreported) (CFI).

B. Identical and similar marks

order goods from wholesalers over the telephone, the goods of both parties would be called 'Arthur'. But people in the trade would be expected to know the difference between the two businesses, or at least not to remain confused between them for very long.

In the 'Arthur' case the OHIM First Board of Appeal stated: **10.31**

> It cannot be denied that trade marks are most often perceived visually, to the extent that they are usually graphic representations, using characters on their own or with drawings, with more or less colours and therefore the customer's attention is caught mainly by means of visual perception. Thus, even if the aural impact of a mark can obviously be of great importance in the identification of the product's origin, it can hardly be said that in the clothing sector customers use predominantly the name (*i.e.* the spelt word) to distinguish those products.[26]

One would imagine this to be true, which is why the contrary opinion of the Court of First Instance (CFI) in the FIFTIES case[27] is so disappointing. In that case the Court considered that the applicant's word mark FIFTIES would be confusingly similar to the earlier complex figurative mark (see Figure 10.3) on which the words 'Miss Fifties' could be read but could hardly be stated to be dominant. The CFI observed that, when considering the aural similarity of the marks—and it must be conceded that FIFTIES and 'Miss Fifties' are aurally similar—the visual content of the marks must be disregarded. But does that really entitle one to draw the conclusion that, on a global comparison, the marks are similar? It is a mistake to focus on aural similarity when addressing a complex word-and-device mark the verbal element of which is not dominant. The concern of the CFI as to there being a likelihood of confusion between MISS FIFTIES and FIFTIES would have been well founded if both were simply word marks. The effect of this decision is however to give the opponent a trade mark right which confers protection not only against use of the device as registered but also against the registration or use of the words FIFTIES and MISS FIFTIES—a very broad degree of protection for a complex trade mark in which the words 'Miss Fifties' played only a minor part. **10.32**

Figure 10.3 The complex FIFTIES figurative mark.

A different result was achieved by the First Instance Court of Athens, in a situation in which an attempt was made to assert that the words COOL AND SLIM were **10.33**

---

[26] *Marc Brown's Trade Mark Application; opposition of LTJ Diffusion* [2002] ETMR 653, 660.
[27] *Oberhauser v OHIM*, Case T-104/01 [2003] ETMR 739.

confusingly similar to the word-and-device mark SLIM. In this case, unlike the word FIFTIES, the word SLIM—the only common feature between the two marks—was specifically disregarded from the comparison on the basis that its use in COOL AND SLIM was predicated by the fact that it was descriptive of the product in question, diet ice cream.[28] As between the two parties the discounting of common descriptive material makes great sense, but one might ask whether the result could be justified if evidence were adduced that consumers were indeed confused.

(b) Who is the judge of whether trade marks are similar?

10.34 The standard by which the *similarity* of marks is measured would appear to be a matter of law which is considered by the court or tribunal which determines the issue. This issue should not be confused with two further questions: (i) whether two marks are *similar*; and (ii) whether two marks which are similar are *confusingly* similar (discussed below). These issues are matters of fact rather than law, which fall to be determined by reference to the 'relevant consumer'. The characteristics of this person are discussed below (see paras 10.134–10.141).

10.35 When considering the position of the reasonably well-informed consumer, one does so not merely in terms of his or her familiarity with the market in which the competing parties trade, but also by reference to the nature of that market. This being so, the relative importance of each of the factors which indicate similarity depends on the situation in which the products bearing the mark are encountered. Thus where it is customary for consumers to ask to be served with a specific product (for example, in a restaurant or bar), where they request others to procure the product for them (as in the case of non-prescription medicines for those who suffer mobility problems) or where purchase orders for products are habitually placed by telephone, a trade mark's aural element will be of correspondingly greater importance. In contrast, where the products are encountered in supermarkets or self-service food sales outlets, the aural element will be of diminished importance while the significance of visual elements will rise.

(c) Similarity is patent, not latent

10.36 The less it appears that two trade marks are similar, or the more effort and imagination is required in order to establish that similarity exists, the less likely any tribunal will be to conclude that they are indeed similar. When case law occasionally

---

[28] *Slim International and Antineas Graikou v Delta Protypos Milk Industry* [2000] ETMR 409 (First Instance Court, Athens). The opposite result was reached in *Budejovicky Budvar Narodni Podnik v Anheuser-Busch Inc* WTLR, 3 July 2003 (Examination Committee of the Romanian State Office for Inventions and Trade Marks), where AMERICAN BUD was held to be similar to BUD since the use of the word 'American' to denote the product's origin did not serve to differentiate it from the registered trade mark BUD.

B. Identical and similar marks

throws up exceptional decisions which run contrary to this proposition, they really stick out like sore thumbs and, unless they are decisions of a jurisdiction's highest court,[29] will generally be reversed on appeal.

If there is no similarity between an earlier registered trade mark and the applicant's trade mark in the form in which it appears in the application, the fact that it might be used in a manner which would be likely to confuse the relevant consumer should not be a relevant consideration. Thus the Supreme Court of Guatemala was right to affirm the decision to allow the registration of the sign 12939, which was challenged by the proprietor of the trade mark PEPSI.[30] On any straight comparison of 12939 and PEPSI there was palpably no similarity; the fact that the numeral 12939, when read in a mirror could be construed as a clumsy rendering of the word 'Pepsi' was an irrelevant consideration. If the applicant sought to use 12939 in its mirror image, it would not be using it in the form in which it was registered and would have no better right than any other infringer of the PEPSI trade mark.

10.37

(3) Analysing similarity

Now that *Sabèl v Puma* has identified the three criteria by which the similarity between two trade marks is established, we must examine the way in which the courts and trade mark registries go about their work in applying those criteria. Not surprisingly, since lawyers are lawyers, clients are fighting for a potentially everlasting legal monopoly and the stakes can be high, much thought has been given to what visual, aural and conceptual similarity mean as well as to the consequences of a trade mark being similar to another mark in only one or more, but not all, of the listed criteria.

10.38

(a) Visual similarity

Visual similarity is sometimes regarded as the king of the criteria of similarity. As the OHIM First Board of Appeal has said:

10.39

> It cannot be denied that trade marks are most often perceived visually, to the extent that they are usually graphic representations, using characters on their own or with drawings, with more or less colours and therefore the customer's attention is caught mainly by means of visual perception.[31]

The visual impact of trade marks also reflects their conceptual similarity. For example, while the trade mark POWER is contained in its entirety in the sign

10.40

---

[29] See eg the Spanish Supreme Court decision in *Comercial Iberica de Exclusivas Deportivas SA (Cidesport) v Nike International Ltd and American Nike SA* [2000] ETMR 189.
[30] *PepsiCo Inc v Productos Industriales, Comerciales y Agrícolas, Sociedad Anonima*, Case 128–97, 19 May 1998 (2001) 91 TMR 407.
[31] *Marc Brown's Trade Mark Application; opposition of LTJ Diffusion* [2002] ETMR 653.

POWERHOUSE, the two words have different meanings and it is impossible, when viewing the word POWERHOUSE, not to read the suffix -HOUSE.[32]

10.41 The visual element of trade marks has the advantage over the aural and conceptual elements in that it is so multifaceted: the visual element includes—in addition to any textual content—colour, shape, size and position, while the aural element—in addition to any melodic content—includes just pitch, tone and volume. The conceptual element does not exist in any physical dimension, but depends upon the cognitive ability of the consumer to extract a concept from either the appearance or sound of the mark. Another advantage of the visual and aural over the conceptual is that, with familiarity, the consumer's awareness of the first two is retained or enhanced by their constant repetition, whereas his awareness of the conceptual dimension weakens: this is because the sign develops a secondary meaning along the lines of 'this is a product made by X'. Thus many people now associate the word 'colt', originally both a horse and a surname, with guns.

10.42 What constitutes visual similarity is a difficult problem wherever a word mark is compared with a figurative mark which contains that word. This is because, where a word is registered as a trade mark and the applicant does not specify how he proposes to use that word, we can either say that *any* representation of the word in another's trade mark is visually similar to it, because they are comprised of the same letters, or that *only* a representation in exactly the same or a similar style or type font is visually similar. In other words, is MANGO visually similar to **Mango** since they contain the same letters, or is it actually dissimilar? The first approach appears to have been taken by the OHIM First Cancellation Division, which considered that the figurative mark SENSO DI DONNA (see Figure 10.4) was visually similar to the word mark SENSO.[33]

Figure 10.4 The SENSO DI DONNA figurative mark.

10.43 Where a mark is three-dimensional, one might have thought that visual similarity is the only one of the three *Sabèl v Puma* criteria which is capable of providing a meaningful comparison. A review of the cases discussed below (see paras 10.50–10.59) will show that this is not necessarily so. If the *Felix the Cat* case[34] is rightly decided, a three-dimensional salt cellar in the shape of a mouse may be regarded as 'similar' to a trade mark consisting of a three-dimensional representation of a cat on account of their cultural association, notwithstanding the fact that

---

[32] *Bata Ltd v Face Fashions CC* [2002] EIPR N-9 (Supreme Court of Appeal, South Africa).
[33] *Senso di Donna's trade mark; Kim Carl Meller's application for a declaration of invalidity*, Case C000616979/1 [2001] ETMR 38.
[34] *Sté Felix the Cat Productions Inc v Sté Polygram* [1999] ETMR 370.

B. Identical and similar marks

there is neither visual nor aural similarity. The Hague District Court did not however go beyond the purely visual when comparing a long, thin tube (for SMARTIES) with a short, wide one (for M & Ms).[35] If they had done, they would have found it difficult to avoid the conclusion that the concept of tubeness was common to them. It is submitted, for purely three-dimensional trade marks, that the Dutch approach is to be preferred. If this were not so, a salt cellar in the shape of a cat could be said to confer monopoly protection not only over cat-shapes but over any other creatures with which cats may be culturally associated: not just mice but dogs (dogs chase cats, just as cats chase mice), birds (Loony Tunes' SYLVESTER and TWEETY PIE) and owls (Edward Lear's 'The Owl and the Pussycat').

10.44 There is a special category of visual similarity called 'rather similar'. This was the term used by the OHIM Third Board of Appeal when ruling that the biscuit trade marks FOX'S and FUCHS looked 'rather similar',[36] in contrast with words like LANDAU, POTTER or HARMSEN which look 'very different'. The terms 'rather similar' and 'very different' do not exist in TRIPs or the CTM Regulation and it seems somehow disingenuous to suggest that words must be similar if they are not 'very different'.

10.45 There is an even more special category of visual similarity called 'not similar'. This category is exemplified by the decision of an OHIM Opposition Division[37] in which the two cockerel marks (see Figure 10.5), despite the immediately apparent striking similarity between them, were closely analysed and their differences listed at length. On a global assessment of the two marks, which is necessary because 'the average consumer normally perceives a mark as a whole and does not proceed to analyse its various details', how many people would have noticed the fact that 'there is a clear difference between the images of the feathers and the feet in each mark'? Fortunately there appear to be few cases in which this level of detail is dredged up in the decision-making process.

Figure 10.5 Are these two cockerel marks 'not similar'?

(b) Aural similarity

10.46 When considering the aural similarity of trade marks, trade mark lawyers find

---

[35] *Mars BV v Société des Produits Nestlé SA* [1999] ETMR 862.
[36] *Northern Foods Grocery Group Ltd's Application; opposition by Horace M Ostwald* [2002] ETMR 516, para 19.
[37] *Fromex SA's application; opposition of K H de Jong's Exporthandel BV*, Case B 43457 [1999] ETMR 989; cf the approach taken in *Cuisine de la Mer Cuisimer SA v Maumenee, SA Meralim and Rambour* [2000] ETMR 880, discussed above.

themselves sucked into the discipline of linguistics. Native English speakers take for granted the anomalies of English pronunciation which in turn amuse and frustrate those who must learn that language at school or thereafter. Why indeed should 'row' (to have a shouting match) and 'row' (to propel a boat) be pronounced differently, while 'ruff' and 'rough' or 'threw' and 'through' are homophones? But now, after seven years of CTM law, the English have had to learn how those who speak the EU's other ten languages pronounce English. Thus, when considering whether the English-language word mark FOX'S was similar to its German equivalent FUCHS in Germany, OHIM will take notice of the fact that Germans will treat FOX'S as a monosyllable, even though English biscuit-eaters would know that it was bisyllabic.[38]

10.47 If the relevant consuming public is, or should be, aware that a word comes from a foreign language, weight will be given to its foreign pronunciation. If however there is no reason to suspect that a word is foreign or that, even if it is suspected that it is foreign, the relevant consuming public would not know which language it belongs to, it will be assumed that those consumers will pronounce it as an indigenous word. Accordingly, wine drinkers who see a trade mark on a bottle of Champagne sparkling wine will be expected to have a go at pronouncing it in French, but there would be no reason to assume that the DRAMBUIE trade mark on a bottle of honey-flavoured whisky liqueur bearing an English-language label and hailing from Scotland should be pronounced as 'drom-bwee' rather than 'drambyooie'.

10.48 Following these principles, where Harvard College sought to protect its HARVARD mark for clothing against the registration of JARVARD for the same goods, there was nothing to suggest that JARVARD was a Spanish mark which would be pronounced by Spaniards as 'Harvard'; accordingly, it would be treated as though it would be pronounced 'Jarvard', not 'Harvard'.[39] Likewise, while the DAVINA and BABINA trade marks would be pronounced very differently in England, the 'V' of DAVINA would come out as a 'B' in Spanish, thus making the two marks almost aurally identical to Spanish speakers.[40]

10.49 An OHIM Opposition Division has opined that, 'in aural terms, vowels always have a more striking effect than consonants'.[41] It is not known whether this state-

---

[38] *Northern Foods Grocery Group Ltd's Application; opposition by Horace M Ostwald* [2002] ETMR 516.
[39] *Kundry SA's application; opposition by the President and Fellows of Harvard College* [1998] ETMR 178.
[40] *Brackenbrough's application; opposition of Säntis Management AG*, Case 1517/2000 [2001] ETMR 412.
[41] *Warsteiner Brauerei Gaus GmbH & Co KG's application; opposition of Brauerei Beck GmbH & Co*, Case 57/1998 [1999] ETMR 225, 230.

B. Identical and similar marks

ment has any basis in truth, but it does not appear to have been endorsed by the Board of Appeal.

(c) Conceptual similarity

The conceptual similarity of trade marks is established in at least three ways. **10.50**

(i) Conceptual similarity of subject matter. In *Sabèl v Puma* itself the issue in dispute related to shared subject matter: both parties' logos were representations of a 'springing wild cat'. Although the two logos were visually distinguishable, the idea behind them was not. In another cat case, *Al Gatto Nero v Le Chat Noir*,[42] a conceptual similarity was found to exist both in the visual images and in the words themselves ('gatto nero' and 'chat noir' being the Italian and French terms, respectively, for 'black cat'). **10.51**

There is no single satisfactory solution to the problem of language. Some nationalities (for example, the Scandinavian nations, the Germans and the Dutch) are known for their linguistic talents, while other nationalities are felt to demonstrate a degree of national pride (the French), insularity (the British) or peninsularity (the Spanish) which has made them peculiarly resistant to the acquisition of foreign tongues. This is reflected in their case law. The Cour d'appel de Paris, for example, has considered that there was no similarity between the French trade mark XXième SIECLE and 21ST CENTURY,[43] while the Court of Turin, Italy, was confident in its expectation that Italians would know that 'chat noir' was the French for 'gatto nero'. **10.52**

It is assumed that a word which conveys a concept and a visual image which conveys the same literal concept are conceptually similar. Accordingly the word 'cat' and a picture of a cat will be conceptually similar. It is not however clear whether there is any conceptual similarity between a word which conveys a concept and a visual image which conveys the same concept in a metaphorical manner. For example, Figure 10.6 is 'the Hershey kiss'.[44] It is difficult to conceive of this image being regarded by the chocolate-consuming public as conceptually similar to the word 'kiss'. **10.53**

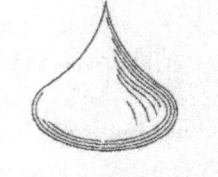

Figure 10.6 The Hershey kiss.

(ii) Conceptual similarity through the use by the incorporation of the same word into two figurative marks. Where a trade mark consists of words alone, any tribunal that is faced with the task of considering the concept which underlies that **10.54**

---

[42] *Al Gatto Nero Srl v Le Chat Noir* [1997] ETMR 371 (Court of Turin).
[43] *Casaubon and Vingt et Unième Siècle v 21st Century Film France* [1999] ETMR 787.
[44] *Hershey Foods Corporation v OHIM*, Case T-198/00, 5 June 2002 (CFI).

mark has nothing but words to work on; accordingly the meaning of the word(s) will inevitably define that underlying concept. This is not so in the case of genuinely figurative marks. It can be suggested that, proportionally as to the extent that the visual or artistic element of a mark rises above the mere selection of a particular typeface or the use of a plain geometric border, the probability increases that the courts will treat the concept as being derived from the mark's overall appearance. Accordingly, while the visually different trade marks EASY and EASY can clearly be said to be conceptually similar, the two 'easy' marks depicted here (see Figure 10.7) were correctly regarded by an OHIM Opposition Division as having no conceptual similarity whatsoever, the one conceptualizing a man holding a flag consisting of the letters 'e-a-s-y' and the other conceptualizing ease of spelling through the use of letter blocks.[45]

Figure 10.7 Two 'easy' marks which were correctly regarded by an OHIM Opposition Division as having no conceptual similarity.

10.55 **(iii) Conceptual similarity through cultural association.** The French Tribunal de Grande Instance considered that a conceptual similarity existed between FELIX THE CAT and FELIX LE SOURICEAU,[46] not because 'cat' and 'mouse' (*souriceau*) are conceptually similar but because of their fabled cultural association. The Cour d'appel de Paris has also indicated that a conceptual similarity existed between St John and St James, both being saints with Anglo-Saxon forenames.[47]

10.56 There is no conceptual similarity through shared meaninglessness. Although the fact that two marks may convey the same meaning may mean that they are conceptually similar, it does not follow, from the fact that both marks convey no meaning whatsoever, that if both concepts are meaningless they too are conceptually similar. So held an OHIM Board of Appeal, when comparing the pharmaceutical marks EVASIL and EXACYL.[48]

10.57 In one striking case an OHIM Board of Appeal concluded that the applicant's word mark ORANGEX was not similar to a word-and-device mark ORANGE X-PRESS:[49] it was conceded that both marks bore a conceptual reference to oranges, but this of itself was not enough to achieve conceptual similarity. Taking each

---

[45] *ABB Sadelmi SpA's application; opposition of the European Patents Organisation*, Case 3552/2002 of 28 November 2002 (unreported).
[46] *Sté Felix the Cat Productions Inc v Sté Polygram* [1999] ETMR 370.
[47] *Lyon v SA Rhums Martiniquais Saint-James* [1999] ETMR 188 (Cour d'appel de Paris).
[48] *Choay SA v Boehringer Ingelheim International GmbH*, Case R 273/1999–1 [2001] ETMR 693, para 17.
[49] *Orangex CA v Juan José Llombart Gavalda*, Case R 662/2001–1 [2003] ETMR 302.

B. Identical and similar marks

mark as a whole, the concept of ORANGEX did not clearly step beyond that of 'orange', while ORANGE X-PRESS embraced the concept of 'pressing' or 'express' in the sense of 'an extra quick process of orange-squeezing'. While it is correct that a single trade mark can contain more than a single concept, it is presumably necessary to ask whether the thing which most strikes the consumer about each of two compared trade marks is the same concept or the conceptual surplus. If a consumer thinks 'orange' and 'orange', he has fixed his attention on the similarity; if however he thinks 'orange' and 'press', then there is no conceptual similarity. If it had applied this test, bearing in mind that each of these marks was for orange juice extractors which themselves supplied the 'missing' element of '(ex)press' in the ORANGEX mark, the Board might have reached the opposite conclusion on the facts before it.

10.58 The majority of comparisons based on conceptual similarity relate to word marks, but the same principles apply where the conceptual comparison is to be made between purely figurative marks such as representations of the imprints of shoes.[50]

10.59 The fact that one mark is expressed in the singular while the other is expressed in the plural would not appear to constitute a conceptual difference between them.[51]

(4) Aggregating the similarities of trade marks

10.60 A simple arithmetical model for determining whether marks are similar would give a score of one to each of the three *Sabèl v Puma* criteria: visual, aural and conceptual similarity. Scores of 3–0 and 2–1 would ensure that two marks are regarded as similar, while 0–3 or 1–2 would exonerate the allegedly similar mark. Difficulties need not even arise where not all three criteria were applicable: for example, where the Latvian CARTIER trade mark was allegedly infringed by the word mark K ART J, the marks had no visual similarity, nor (the latter mark being meaningless) did they have any conceptual similarity, but normal Latvian rules of pronunciation ensured an aural similarity which gave Cartier victory by the slim but legally adequate margin of 1–0.[52] The only problem cases would be those where conceptual similarity was irrelevant (as where the two marks were both meaningless) and the remaining criteria fought out a 1–1 draw (for example, the homophonous but visually dissimilar KODAK and CAU D'ACQUE).

10.61 Although it would appear to have been accepted by the Cour d'appel de Paris in at least one case,[53] this simple arithmetical approach is not normally put into

---

[50] *Dr Martens International Trading GmbH's application; opposition of Lloyd Schuhfabrik Meyer & Co GmbH*, Case 165/2000 [2000] ETMR 1151.
[51] *Principles Retail Ltd's application; opposition of Manifattura Lane Gaetano Marzotto & Figli SpA*, Case 355/1999 [2000] ETMR 240 (PRINCIPLES and PRINCIPE).
[52] *Cartier International BV v Hammer Diamonds A/S* [2002] ETMR 1041.
[53] *Lyon v SA Rhums Martiniquais Saint-James* [1999] ETMR 188 (Cour d'appel de Paris).

practice. For one thing, it assumes that each of the three criteria of similarity is of equal weight, while one element of a trade mark may be far more dominant than the others.[54] For another thing, when an arithmetical aggregation is used, it may detract from the 'overall global impression' which might cause consumers to draw the confident conclusion that similarity existed notwithstanding differences which might be significant only in numerical terms. This being so, would it not be more efficient to dispense with the ritual of considering the three *Sabèl v Puma* features and simply to ask in the first place: 'is there an overall global similarity between these two trade marks?' We do not however take the direct route to our destination, for the following reasons: (i) the three-pronged analysis of visual, aural and conceptual similarity provides a useful checklist for ensuring that we do not overlook the main ways in which consumers equate trade marks with each other; (ii) once we have identified the ways in which trade marks may be said to resemble each other, we have also identified the ways in which consumers may be confused into believing one trade mark to be (or to be related to) another; (iii) the discipline of checking out the three cardinal criteria provides appellate courts with a framework within which to examine the thought-processes of a lower fact-finding tribunal; and (iv) the tripartite examination of similarity vests with the dignity of legal science a thought-process which is probably intuitive in the majority of instances. Law books do not readily suggest that trade mark examiners and courts first decide whether two trade marks are similar and then, having done so, they filter their intuitive decision back into the framework of what we are pleased to call legal reasoning. If this is indeed the case,[55] then we should at least be constrained to justify our highly subjective intuitive decisions by reference to the same shared and objective criteria.

10.62 In aggregating the three criteria, the mere fact that two marks are identical, both from a visual and from an aural view, is no guarantee that a court will even find them similar.[56] This is because the legal concept of visual identity applies where one mark is a complex mark, such as a figurative mark containing a dominant word, while the other mark consists of that word itself. It is ultimately the 'overall global impression' that counts.[57]

---

[54] Thus in *Alfa-Tel's application; opposition of Alcatel Altshom Compagnie Generale d'Electricité* [2001] ETMR 621, the Prague High Court refused to allow an appeal on the basis that the trade mark registry had failed to give equal weight to the three criteria.

[55] Which it may well be in some cases, eg the incredible and inexplicable conclusion of the Spanish Supreme Court in *Comercial Iberica de Exclusivas Deportivas SA (Cidesport) v Nike International Ltd and American Nike SA* [2000] ETMR 189 that two utterly different marks were confusingly similar.

[56] *Matratzen v OHIM*, Case T-6/01 [2003] ETMR 392 (CFI), paras 31, 32.

[57] *Sabèl v Puma*, Case C-251/95 [1998] ETMR 1; *Lloyd Schuhfabrik Meyer & Co GmbH v Klijsen Handel BV*, Case C-342/97 [1999] ETMR 10.

B. Identical and similar marks

The aggregation of criteria may lead to an element of 'double accounting' when calculating how similar two marks may be to one another. Thus a word-and-device mark JACK & DANNY'S ROCK CAFÉ was held to be confusingly similar to a quite different word-and-device mark HARD ROCK CAFÉ on the basis of the similarity of the words ROCK CAFÉ as well as the concept of a Rock Café.[58]

10.63

(a) Marks which are visually and aurally similar, but not conceptually similar

If two marks look similar and sound similar, they may be treated as similar even if they are conceptually quite unrelated to each other. For example, the Cour d'appel de Paris regarded ALOHA as being similar to OLA, their visual and aural similarity outweighing the fact that 'Ola' was the Spanish for 'hello' while 'Aloha' was the Hawaiian for 'love, happiness, welcome'.[59] The court expressed the view that the conceptual dissimilarity could be regarded because the average Frenchman would not understand Hawaiian, which rather suggests that had the words been similar but possessed of different meanings which Frenchmen would have understood, the marks might not have been regarded as similar. The OHIM Opposition Division has gone further and stated that, even where Englishmen would know the clear difference between FUNK and JUNK, the visual and aural criteria were sufficient to clinch a conclusion that the marks were similar.[60]

10.64

(b) Marks which are visually similar, but aurally and conceptually dissimilar

A typical situation in which visual similarity prevails over both aural and conceptual dissimilarity is that in which the overall appearance of the mark dominates it to the extent that its textual content is rendered of only secondary importance. The Court of Naples, Italy, recognized this in *Barilla v Danis* where the overall visual impact of the marks (see Figure 10.8) would clearly strike the public before the dissimilar textual element.[61]

10.65

Figure 10.8 Two marks where the overall appearance dominates to the extent that textual content is rendered of only secondary importance.

---

[58] *Neil King's application; opposition of Hard rock International plc and another* [2000] ETMR 22.
[59] *Société Corsetel v INPI and France Telecom* [2001] ETMR 930.
[60] *Seder's application; opposition of Funk*, Case 151/1999 [2000] ETMR 685. See also *Verify Interntional NV's application; opposition of Jörg Pohlmann*, Case 110/2000 [2000] ETMR 716, where the fact that English-speaking Germans would know the difference in meaning between ADSCORE and ADSTORE did not spare those marks from being deemed similar.
[61] *Barilla Alimentares SpA v Danis Srl and others* [1996] ETMR 43.

10.66 The same approach was adopted by the Spanish Supreme Court which, when ruling that the Nissan word-and-device mark was similar to that employed by Martini,[62] considered that the shared background of the trade marks would attract the public's attention more than the famous and highly distinctive word marks NISSAN and MARTINI which appeared in the foreground.

(c) Marks which are visually and conceptually similar, but aurally dissimilar

10.67 A pair of marks of this nature may be conceptualized since examples drawn from litigation have not been identified. A hypothetical example might consist of two device marks, each consisting of a picture of a happy-looking dog which is wagging its tail; the first dog is barking the word 'welcome' in English, while the second barks 'bienvenu' in French. Visually the two dogs look alike; perhaps they are even representations of the same breed. Conceptually the two marks express the same notion, that of a canine welcome. But 'welcome' sounds quite different from 'bienvenu'.

(d) Marks which are aurally similar, but not visually or conceptually similar

10.68 In one German decision the sign MOBILIX was held to be confusingly similar to OBELIX, both being used in the field of computers, notwithstanding their visual and conceptual dissimilarity.[63] It is however unusual for a finding of similarity to be reached on the basis of aural similarity alone. For example, in Ireland the CHANEL trade mark, phonetically similar but visually dissimilar to the word-and-device mark consisting of CHANELLE plus a sea horse, was not able to support an opposition based on similarity before the Irish Patents Office.[64] Similarly, where the two marks were visually dissimilar and had different meanings, the homophones EIRETEL and AIRTEL were not considered similar.[65] These cases however come with a caveat—CHANEL/LE involved pharmaceutical/veterinary products and EIRETEL/AIRTEL involved telecommunications and similar goods and services, in respect of which consumers are normally careful to study the goods or service on offer. A different result could be obtained in respect of 'bags of sweets', which shoppers ask for by name and with little attention to their strategic market options.

(e) Marks which are conceptually similar, but not visually or aurally similar

10.69 In the absence of any more tangible species of similarity, bare conceptual similarity is unlikely to be considered a sufficient basis upon which it can be concluded that two word marks are similar. Thus in one case no similarity was found to exist

---

[62] *Nissan Motor Iberica's application* [1999] ETMR 338.
[63] *Les Editions Albert René v Hauser* WTLR, 17 April 2003 (Landgericht, Munich).
[64] *Chanelle Pharmaceuticals Mfg Ltd v Chanel Ltd* [2003] ETMR 64.
[65] *Eiretel Ltd's application; opposition by Airtel Movil SA and another,* 10 June 2002 (unreported) (UK Trade Marks Registry).

B. Identical and similar marks

between the applicant's word mark DINOKIDS and the opponent's mark which consisted of an imaginative representation of a juvenile dinosaur together with the word DINO.[66] The fact that the concepts of 'young' and 'dinosaur' were common could not of itself lead to an overall assessment that the marks were similar. The same may also be true of figurative marks, where the conceptual similarity of shoe imprints was insufficient to enable the conclusion to be drawn that two shoe imprints of different appearance caused the respective marks to be regarded as similar.[67]

10.70 Sometimes the conceptual similarity can be divided into two segments. In one French case[68] the word marks LA FRESH WATER and EAU FRESH were conceptually similar but that similarity could be split between WATER/EAU, which had no visual or aural similarity, and the shared word FRESH which was only weakly distinctive and to some extent descriptive of the feeling derived from the use of the respective parties' products. In this instance the marks were held not to be confusingly similar.

(f) Marks which are aurally and conceptually similar, but visually dissimilar

10.71 This category, which does not in general appear to have been the subject of detailed legal analysis, would appear to be particularly applicable where word marks sound similar and convey a similar conceptual meaning but are written in different script.[69] In one OHIM case the Board of Appeal warned against the risk of assuming that, if words were phonetically similar, they were also of necessity conceptually similar. Thus even if the applicant's sign HOOLIGAN were phonetically similar to the opponent's mark OLLY GAN (though the contrary was found), it could not be assumed without proof that the words 'olly gan' shared with 'hooligan' the concept of an unruly and violent football supporter. The Board's warning is an apposite one[70] since, where words sound alike but look different, there is nothing to suggest that conceptual similarity should be measured by their sound rather than by their appearance. To put it another way, should the words RUFF and ROUGH be regarded as conceptually similar because they sound alike, or conceptually different because their appearance is quite different?

---

[66] *Herbalife International Inc's application; opposition of Haka Kunz GmbH*, Case B 52037 [1999] ETMR 882.
[67] *Dr Martens International Trading GmbH's application; opposition of Lloyd Schuhfabrik Meyer & Co GmbH*, Case 165/2000 [2000] ETMR 1151.
[68] *Lancôme Parfums et Beauté & Cie Snc v Jacques Bogart SA* (2003) 761 PIBD III-187 (Cour d'appel de Paris).
[69] A case in point, though any conceptual link between the marks is tenuous, is *Taam Teva (1988) Tivoli Ltd v Ambrosia Superb Ltd* WTLR, 15 May 2003 (Israeli Supreme Court), in which the word trade mark MEGA REPLEX, written in English lettering, infringed the claimant's MEGA-GLUFLEX trade mark which was written from right to left in Hebrew letters.
[70] *Dann and Backer v Société Provençale d'Achat et de Gestion (SPAG)*, Case R 1072/2000–2 [2003] ETMR 888 (OHIM Second Board of Appeal).

Chapter 10: Identical and Similar Marks, Goods and Services

10.72 The most important instance of conceptual and aural similarity but visual dissimilarity which is faced on a regular basis is that of the transliteration of trade marks. Many countries have populations which may not only speak different languages but even use different alphabets. Examples include Japan and China (which employ different alphabets for writing even the same language), Greece (where Greek and Latin alphabets are used side by side in commerce) and Israel (Hebrew, Arabic, Latin). How do these countries deal with marks which bear the same meaning and sound the same but look quite unlike and—in at least some circumstances—which are manifestly aimed at different groups of consumers or ultimate users? The normal approach is to regard the marks as being confusingly similar or at least to regard the transliteration of another's mark as an act of unfair competition.[71]

(5) Comparison of simple marks

10.73 Where trade marks are complex, their many features provide ample material for the exercise of comparison. But what happens in the case of simple trade marks? In theory the *Sabèl v Puma* approach applies equally to all trade marks, but what can one compare where both trade marks consist of, for example, fanciful portrayals of a single letter? Where the dominant element of each mark is the same letter, is one bound to conclude that the global overall assessment of the two marks is bound to result in their being found similar or, on the contrary, does the practice of disregarding weakly distinctive or non-distinctive elements[72] mean that, having disregarded the common letter, one focuses closely only on the differences? OHIM practice would appear to veer towards the second approach, with letters being regarded as dissimilar on account of a detailed analysis of their differences.[73] While this may be regrettable in theory, since one is supposed to focus on similarities when making the comparison,[74] it is probably the only practical way to handle the comparison of very weak trade marks such as portrayals of single letters.

10.74 When dealing with acronyms rather than single letters, the CFI has concluded that, for German consumers at any rate, ILS and ELS are both visually and aurally similar. They were verbally similar because 'the difference in a single letter does not prevent the marks being similar', even though a single letter is 33.3 per cent of the whole mark. They were aurally similar because 'the vowel phonemes "E" and

---

[71] In *Johnson & Johnson v Bandhaye Pezeshki Co* (Iran, noted in Raysan e-mail circular, 3 March 2003): VELBAND word mark in Latin/Farsi script.
[72] See eg *Askey Computer Corporation's application; opposition of Nokia Telecommunications OY* [2000] ETMR 214.
[73] *Loewe SA's application; opposition by Logoathletic Inc*, Case B 37889 [2000] ETMR 40; *Stillwater Designs and Audio Inc's application; opposition of Josefina Fernandez de la Fuenta Abellan*, Case B 7049 [2000] ETMR 35.
[74] *Cuisine de la Mer Cuisimer SA v Maumenee, SA Meralim and Rambour* [2000] ETMR 880.

"I" are pronounced similarly by Germans and the consonant phonemes "L" and "S" are pronounced the same'.[75] If this decision is correct, it will soon be difficult for organizations to use their acronyms without incurring the risk of infringing the registered trade marks of others.

(6) When are trade marks different?

10.75 If trade marks are not similar, they are different. Once a court concludes that trade marks are different, any complaint which is based on their identity or similarity will fail. Thus Unilever, having been unable to establish that a competitor's BENECOL trade mark was similar to its own BECEL, could not then establish a legal cause of action based on market survey evidence that confusion of the relevant consumers was likely.[76]

C. Identical and similar goods and services

(1) Comparison of goods and services

10.76 Having considered at length the question whether trade marks are identical, similar or downright different, it is now necessary to perform the same exercise in relation to (i) goods and (ii) services. It should be immediately apparent that, while the question is the same in each case, the comparison of goods and services requires a separate set of analytical tools: here we are not considering the cognitive ability to distinguish signs—a skill which can be taught to the illiterate, the uneducated, the mentally impaired and even to animals—but an ability to rationalize points of similarity or dissimilarity between goods or services which are actually at odds with the perceptional apparatus which enables us to discern differences in the appearance of trade marks.

10.77 By way of example, consider three apples. One is a Golden Delicious, one a Russet, one a Bramley. Golden Delicious has a smooth yellow-green complexion, the Russet a rough brown skin and the Bramley, in darker green with brownish patches, a slightly sticky surface. The apples also differ in size. Cut them in half and you can see at once that their flesh is differently textured; the smell and taste of each is also unique. No one who has sampled the three could ever confuse them, even in the dark. Yet they are the same 'goods': as a matter of definition they are all 'apples' and it is their appleness which distinguishes them from pears, plums, pomegranates or indeed any other fruit.

---

[75] *Institut Für Lernsysteme GmbH v OHIM*, Case T-388/00, 23 October 2002.
[76] *Unilever NV v Raisio Yhtyma OY and others* [1999] ETMR 847 (Appeal Court, The Hague).

10.78 There is another difference between the comparison of marks and the comparison of goods and services. The question of comparison of marks is a matter which uniquely troubles trade mark lawyers. However, what constitutes identical, similar or dissimilar goods or services is an issue which recurs elsewhere in the law (at least in Europe), both in competition law[77] and in data protection law.[78] In competition law the issue is posed differently: in order to establish whether an undertaking is dominant in its market, it is necessary to enquire as to what constitutes the 'market': do we say that bananas are similar to apples because they are both fruit, distributed by the same wholesalers and sold to the public by the same retailers, with the result that bananas and apples are part of the same market? Or do we stress that bananas and apples are not part of the same market: one is a hard fruit, the other soft; their storage requirements are different, as is their seasonality, so are they then not part of the same market at all? In data protection law the comparison of goods or services is phrased in terms comparable with those of trade mark law, but the object of data protection law is to protect the data subject against the abuse of information which he has provided to a data user, not to save a consumer from confusion or, more to the point, to save a business from the erosion of its goodwill.

(2) When are goods identical?

10.79 Some of the issues which affect a finding of identity between trade marks have corresponding roles to play in establishing identity between goods, but they have not yet been subjected to detailed legal scrutiny. These issues include, for example, the breadth of categorization by which goods are classed (for example, is a teapot 'identical' to a set of crockery which includes a teapot?) and the 'Imitation X' problem (is an imitation TISSOT watch identical to the genuine product?). There are also shades of difference which may cause the question to be asked as to whether goods are identical or merely similar. In one recent case the court found that free newspapers were not identical to newspapers for which payment was exacted,[79] notwithstanding the fact that there was no obvious physical difference between them. This decision suggests that the terminology employed in the specification of goods or services for which registration is obtained may be a crucial determinant of whether goods and services are identical or merely similar. The same cannot however be said where two parties' goods are registered within the same class under the Nice Classification scheme, since the range of goods or services covered by each class is very wide.[80]

---

[77] See *United Brands v Commission*, Case 27/76 [1978] ECR 207.
[78] Directive 2002/58 concerning the processing of personal data and the protection of privacy in the electronic communications sector, art 13(2).
[79] *Associated Newspapers Ltd and another v Express Newspapers* [2003] EWHC 1322 (Ch), 11 June 2003 (unreported) (Chancery Division).
[80] *Rhône Poulenc v Reckitt Benckiser* WTLR, 18 July 2003 (Colombian Trade Mark Office).

C. Identical and similar goods and services

(3) When are goods similar and when are they different?

10.80 This question has caused much difficulty within the EU, in the wake of the reference to the ECJ of a German trade mark application for the word mark CANNON.[81] The applicant wanted to register the trade mark for pre-recorded video cassettes, but an objection was raised that the almost identical CANON mark had already been registered for blank video cassettes. In an ideal world the Bundesgerichtshof would have asked for guidance as to how to tell whether pre-recorded and blank cassettes were similar goods. The issue was complicated, however, by the fact that the opponent's CANON mark was an extremely well-known trade mark. The question upon which the ECJ was asked to rule was whether, in determining whether the respective cassettes were similar goods for the purposes of establishing a likelihood of confusion, account could be taken of the fact that one party's goods was sold under a particularly distinctive trade mark. This question therefore fused together two issues which strict logic would be more than happy to separate: (i) whether the two sets of goods are similar; and (ii) whether, on account of their similarity as well as the additional similarity of the trade marks applied to them, a likelihood of confusion arises.

10.81 The ECJ is sometimes said to have ruled that goods are more similar if the trade mark applied to the earlier one of them is very well known but that they are less similar where the trade mark applied to the earlier goods is not well known. This is not what the ECJ said. The court actually said that

> ... the distinctive character of the earlier trade mark, and in particular its reputation, must be taken into account when determining whether the similarity between the goods or services covered by the two trade marks is sufficient to give rise to the likelihood of confusion.[82]

10.82 This does not mean that the distinctive character of the earlier mark makes the respective goods more similar, but that it makes it more likely to give rise to a likelihood of confusion where the goods' respective marks are also similar. Accordingly a lesser degree of similarity between the goods need be proved when seeking to establish a likelihood of confusion.

10.83 While the ECJ gave no explicit ruling on how to test goods for similarity,[83] it did establish a principle of proportionality: this principle also does not establish whether goods are similar, but it lays down that, the more similar the goods are, the lower is the degree of similarity of their respective trade marks which will

---

[81] CANNON trade mark application [1998] ETMR 77.
[82] *Canon Kabushiki Kaisha v Metro-Goldwyn-Mayer Inc*, Case C-39/97 [1999] ETMR 1, para 31.
[83] In paragraph 23 of the judgment the ECJ observed that one should look, *inter alia*, at the nature of the goods, their end users, their methods of use and whether they are in competition with each other or just complementary; but the ECJ took this question no further.

establish a likelihood of confusion whereas, the less similar the goods are, the greater will be the degree of similarity of marks which will be needed if the marks are to be regarded as likely to cause confusion.[84] This is not deeply profound jurisprudence; it is a bit like saying that, the lower the temperature in the oven, the longer it will take to bake a potato but that, the higher the temperature in the oven, the less time it will take for that potato to bake.

10.84 Case law within Europe has been, on the whole, robustly sensible in determining whether goods are similar are not. An OHIM Opposition Division has ruled that beer is similar to mineral water and fruit juice in Spain, where (i) the two products often serve the same purposes, (ii) they are sold side by side in the same shops and (iii) they are substitutable for one another.[85] The first and third grounds overlap closely with one another since, if products serve the same purpose, they are often likely to be substitutable too. There is a fourth consideration too, where (iv) the goods are offered to the same public.[86] Since these four grounds are the main means of determining similarity of goods and services, let us now consider them separately.

(a) Products serving the same purpose

10.85 Umbrellas and waterproof coats both serve the same purpose, that of keeping their user dry. They do so, however, in very different ways and most manufacturers of the one article do not extend their range of products so as to make the other. FIATs and Lamborghinis share one purpose (motorized propulsion) but not others (indicating wealth, status). 'Caps, boots, shoes and slippers' have been found similar to 'clothing' in that

> Caps, boots, shoes and slippers are meant for the head and feet respectively. Since clothing is meant for these parts as well as for other parts of the human body, they are of the same nature.[87]

(b) Products sold in proximity to one another

10.86 This ground of similarity has a long provenance in the UK where it has been extensively applied.[88] At a micro-level this approach is illogical but at a macro-level it possesses a high degree of functional utility. At the micro-level, the fact that two products are sold in proximity to one another does not make them objectively any more similar than if they were sold a long way apart. Umbrellas and waterproof

---

[84] ibid, para 17.
[85] *Cobra Beer Ltd's application; opposition of Alpabob AG* [2000] ETMR 638. The German Bundesgerichtshof has drawn the same conclusion regarding mineral water and alcohol-free drinks in *Queen's Club trade mark application* [1997] ETMR 345.
[86] *Humic SA's application; opposition of Sapec-Agro SA*, Case B911 [1999] ETMR 26.
[87] *Ducks Unlimited's application; opposition of Dr Rehfeld Handelsgesellschaft mbH*, Case 849/1999 [2000] ETMR 820, 823.
[88] See eg *Jellinek's application* (1946) 63 RPC 59.

C. Identical and similar goods and services

coats are manifestly different from one another; knives are never mistaken for spoons; toothbrushes bear no resemblance to toothpaste. Other odd couples for this purpose include rabbits and pheasants, hammers and nails, pencils and erasers. Yet while they are physically quite different, they are metaphysically united by a string of shopping concepts which weld them together in our mind in terms such as rain repellents, cutlery, toiletries, game, hardware and stationery. From the British, being a nation of shopkeepers,[89] there could scarcely have come a more apposite test of similarity of goods.

(c) Products which are substitutable

Umbrellas and waterproof coats may be functionally similar but they are not substitutable. You need a free hand and an absence of wind if you are going to be able to make use of an umbrella. FIATs and Lamborghinis are, for most purposes, substitutable in that, if you need to drive from A to B, either should be able to get you there. 10.87

(d) Products which are offered to the same public

It may be argued that, while the little FIAT and the mighty Lamborghini are technically both 'cars', they are not the same or even similar products since they are offered to quite different publics. Umbrellas and waterproof coats, however, are most certainly offered to those who have a need to stay dry. The District Court of Utrecht has held that pharmaceutical treatments for erectile dysfunctions and aphrodisiacs are 'similar products', at least for the purposes of granting interim relief.[90] The Bundesgerichtshof has held cashmere sweaters to be 'not dissimilar' to golf clubs where they are sold at golf tournaments.[91] 10.88

(e) Products particularized in the trade mark specification

Sometimes a trade mark application will describe the goods for which registration is sought in terms of 'all Xs and in particular X1 and X2'. Where this occurs, the fact that X1 and X2 are particularized does not support the argument that X3 or X4 are dissimilar to the goods for which the mark was registered. Thus in *Durferrit*[92] an applicant sought to register NU-TRIDE as a trade mark for 'chemicals, none consisting of or containing cyanide, all for use in the treatment of metals'. The opponent had previously registered TUFFTRIDE for 'inorganic salts, 10.89

---

[89] In my article 'Quality Control and the Napoleon Principle' (2001) 109 *Managing Intellectual Property* 42–4 I ascribed this term to Napoleon Bonaparte. I have since discovered that it was previously used by Adam Smith in *The Wealth of Nations* (1776): 'To found a great empire for the sole purpose of raising up a people of customers, may at first sight appear a project altogether unfit for a nation of shopkeepers; but extremely fit for a nation that is governed by shopkeepers'.
[90] *Pfizer Inc and Pfizer BV v Lestre Nederlandse Reformadviefbureau ENRA* [2001] ETMR 155.
[91] *Callaway Golf Company v Big Bertha Srl*/WTLR, 20 June 2003 (Bundesgerichtshof, Germany).
[92] *Durferrit GmbH v OHIM, Kolene Corporation Intervening*, Case T-224/01, 9 April 2003.

particularly cyanides and cyanates, for the treatment of metals by nitriding'. The CFI ruled that the particular mention of cyanides and cyanates from the opponent's mark and their specific exclusion from the applicant's mark, did not render the two sets of products dissimilar since 'chemicals . . . for the use in the treatment of metals' remained similar to 'inorganic salts . . . for the treatment of metals'.[93]

(4) Can goods be 'conceptually' similar?

10.90 The criteria by which the similarity of goods is compared are all at a relatively low level of abstraction. But would it be possible to identify similarity at a high level of abstraction? An attempt to do just this was rejected by the Cour d'appel de Paris,[94] where it was argued that 'caviar' was similar to 'tea and seasoning' on the bases, *inter alia*, that they came from the same geographical region, notably Iran. The court was unimpressed with this submission for a variety of factual reasons, but did not dismiss the principle which lay behind it. If people who purchase caviar, tea and seasoning would not normally associate those products with the place from which they actually came, this argument is unlikely ever to be successful.

10.91 A potentially stronger argument based on conceptual similarity of goods can be based on the classification system under the Nice Agreement: that goods should be regarded as similar on account of the fact that they share the same Nice classification. This argument might work in classes in which there is a relative homogeneity of products (for example, Class 15: musical instruments; Class 23: yarns and threads) but it would be unlikely to succeed in larger and more active classes such as Class 5 (pharmaceutical, veterinary and sanitary preparations, etc), Class 9 (practically anything that needs electricity, plus related products) or Class 16 (anything printed; stationery; office requisites). In one case before the OHIM Board of Appeal, two pharmaceutical products—one being a non-steroidal anti-inflammatory drug and the other being a treatment for prostate cancer, early puberty and endometritis—were ruled to be dissimilar when the only factor they had in common was their Class 5 categorization.[95]

10.92 Since goods and services must be compared on the basis of their factual similarity and not their conceptual similarity, it follows that no comparison should be made between the essential factual nature of the applicant's goods and the conceptual implication which an opponent's trade mark vests in his own quite different goods. Accordingly, where an application was made to register as a CTM the word mark VISA for 'access and crowd control identification bracelets manufactured

---

[93] ibid, paras 40–1.
[94] *SA Caviar Anzali v L'Institut National de La Propriété Industrielle, Sté Brugis (third party)* [2000] ETMR 513.
[95] *Laboratorios Menarini SA v Takeda Chemical Industries Ltd*, Case R 222/1999–2 [2001] ETMR 703.

C. Identical and similar goods and services

from synthetic plastic', the Opposition Division concluded that those bracelets were not similar to 'encoded cards, including magnetic cards'. There could be no similarity even though the former enable users of such bracelets to control admission to events, while the connotation of the word 'visa', used as a trade mark for the latter, is one of controlling admission.[96]

(5) Similarity of goods based on their apparently sharing a common source

10.93 The Court of Naples, Italy, considered that two computer programs named AL-BERT were similar products.[97] *Prima facie* this might seem a reasonable conclusion but, applying the four criteria discussed under the previous heading, it can be seen that we have a problem: (i) they were not, on any rationally identifiable criteria, products that served the same purpose: one was a software package which facilitated Internet use by Lotus software users, while the other managed a databank for works of art; (ii) they were not sold in proximity to one another (although they had been exhibited at the same trade fair, which was how they found out about each other); (iii) the products were manifestly not substitutable; and (iv) they were each offered to highly specific and entirely separate markets.

10.94 Commenting on such a scenario, the view of one English judge would appear to suggest quite forcefully that the conclusion of the Court of Naples was wrong:

> A piece of software which enables a computer to behave like a flight simulator is an entirely different product to software which, say, enables a computer to optically character read text or to design a chemical factory. In my view it is highly undesirable that a trader who is interested in one limited area of computer software should, by registration, obtain a statutory monopoly of infinite duration covering all types of software, including those that are far from his area of trading interest.[98]

10.95 The *Albert* decision can only be explained in one of the following three ways: (i) it is wrong; (ii) it is right but there exists some fifth factor which has not so far been identified; or (iii) computer programs are to be regarded as inherently similar, irrespective of their function and their target market.

10.96 The answer is that there is a fifth factor at work, as the court itself recognized: the apparent origin of the respective products. The two software packages were quite different in so many ways, but the relevant public of software users could have 'similarized' them by thinking that they came from the same manufacturer or software writer. Should this fifth factor be disallowed? We already factor whether the public considers that the goods share a common origin by virtue of the similarity of their

---

[96] *Precision Dynamics Corporation's application; opposition of Visa International Service Association*, Case 3479/2002, 29 November 2002 (unreported).
[97] *Data Professionals Srl v Mercantile Sistemi Srl* [1998] ETMR 670.
[98] *Mercury Communications Ltd v Mercury Interactive (UK) Ltd* [1995] FSR 850, 865 (HC), per Laddie J.

trade marks and to consider whether they share a common origin by virtue of their description as computer programs is effectively to count the same criterion, that of common origin, twice. Against that it can be argued that common origin is the issue which lies at the very crux of confusion. According to this view, confusion should be judged from the combination of similarity of marks *and* of goods; accordingly it should either be a relevant factor in establishing both similarity of goods *and* marks or as part of an independent question of whether there is confusion—a possibility which has now been ruled out by the 'global appreciation' approach.

(6) Similarity of goods: the problem of multiclass trade marks

10.97 A practical problem occurs where an applicant seeks to register a trade mark for a large number of goods and an opponent seeks to prevent him doing so, citing registration of the identical or similar mark in respect of a comparably large number of goods. When comparing goods, the question of similarity between goods potentially falls to be tested between each of the applicant's goods and each of the opponent's.[99] It is necessary to conduct these multiclass comparisons slowly and painstakingly if errors are to be avoided.

(7) When are services identical?

10.98 This issue is rarely raised. In *Avnet v Isoact*[100] the trade mark owner had registered AVNET for 'advertising and promotional services' in Class 35. The defendant ran an Internet service which offered customers a website through which they could publicize their products. The English High Court was asked whether the defendant's service was identical to that of the trade mark owner. On this point the judge said:

> Specifications for services should be scrutinised carefully and they should not be given a wide construction covering a vast range of activities. They should be confined to the substance, as it were, the core of the possible meanings attributable to the rather general phrase.[101]

10.99 The substance of the trade mark owner's 'advertising and promotional services' was in fact the sale of other people's goods through a printed catalogue. This being so, the parties' respective services were clearly not 'identical'. This decision reflects the position taken with regard to similarity of goods (discussed above): if purely conjectural, conceptual similarity will not be regarded as a sufficient basis for goods to be treated as similar, how much less so should a purely conjectural, conceptual identity be taken to be the true identity?

---

[99] A typical example of this can be found in *Zanella SNC's application; opposition by Zanella Confezioni SpA*, Case B 42053 [2000] ETMR 69.
[100] *Avnet Incorporated v Isoact Ltd* [1997] ETMR 562.
[101] ibid, 565.

C. Identical and similar goods and services

(8) When are services similar and when are they different?

10.100 There is no specific legal criterion by which the similarity of services must be measured. Nor is there any presumption that services either are, or are not, similar to one another and the onus of proving similarity lies with the party who asserts its existence. Some courts take a robust view of what constitutes similarity of services and are not easily persuaded by fanciful claims. Thus a Swedish court considered the services supplied by estate agents and travel agents to be quite different.[102] Likewise an English court had no difficulty in holding that the defendant's SMILECARE services did not infringe the claimant's SMILECARE trade mark, even though both related to dentists: one was for services provided *by* dentists to the public, while the other consisted of financial services provided *for* dentists.[103] Other courts appear to make the comparison from at a distance at which quite significant differences between services are glossed over. Thus a Danish court considered that estate agency services and home relocation services were similar since both related to change of accommodation and they were complementary to each other.[104]

(9) When are goods similar to services?

10.101 There is relatively little case law on whether goods are similar to services. The Tribunal de Grande Instance de Paris has ruled that printed materials (books, magazines, journals and newspapers) and radio stations are functionally 'similar' in so far as they both deliver information to the public.[105] The Cour d'appel de Paris has also found that the service of non-ferrous metal casting is similar to precious metals and jewellery.[106] In contrast, OHIM's Opposition Division has ruled that cigarettes are not similar to restaurants, even though cigarettes may be smoked in restaurants. According to the Division:

> In assessing the similarity, . . . all the relevant factors . . . should be taken into account. These factors include, *inter alia,* their nature, their end users and their method of use and whether they are in competition with each other or are complementary . . . Further factors include their origin and the pertinent distribution channels and sales outlets.[107]

---

[102] *Fritidsresor AB v Atlas Mediterraneo Sverige AB,* Brandnews 1/2003, p 1 (Helsingborg City Court, decision currently under appeal).
[103] *Harding v Smilecare Ltd* [2002] FSR 37 (HC).
[104] *Home A/S v Home From Home Relocation Services by Annemette Krogh Pedersen* [2003] ETMR 605 (Maritime and Commercial Court, Copenhagen).
[105] *SNC Prisma Presse v SA Europe 1 Telecompagnie* [1998] ETMR 515 ('ÇA M'INTERESSE' trade mark).
[106] *Haci Keles v Sté Megafonte and Evelyne Sitbon* [1997] ETMR 515.
[107] *Long John Silver's Inc's application; opposition of Swedish Match Sverige AB,* Case 458/2000 [2001] ETMR 120, para 20.

10.102 This statement, which is itself based on the ECJ's ruling in the *Canon* case,[108] is notable for three reasons. First, in its unedited form, it is apparent that it applies to comparisons between goods only and not to comparisons between goods and services. Secondly, the criterion of whether the compared items are 'in competition with each other or are complementary' is a difficult one to apply meaningfully on the facts: if I sell DELL computers and my competitor offers DELL computer services, how does the fact that those services are either complementary or competitive—or indeed both—affect the determination of whether they are similar? It is possible that 'complementary' in this instance includes synergistic products (for example, pancake flour is not similar to syrup, but confusion is highly possible in that both are ingredients of pancakes).[109] Although this reasoning does not make the two products any more similar to each other than they previously were, it tackles a very real threat of confusion which could damage the reputation in the earlier mark and block off the opportunity of its proprietor to expand his business into neighbouring commercial activities. Thirdly, it is not immediately and clearly apparent why the origin of goods and services, or indeed their pertinent distribution channels, should affect the issue of similarity: cigarettes may be supplied in restaurants and distributed within them, but so too may bottles of wine, toothpicks and bouquets of flowers. How much can we meaningfully learn from asking this question?

D. Likelihood of confusion

(1) When does similarity lead to confusion? The European approach

10.103 What is the relationship between similarity and confusion? Human beings who are unrelated often share the similar facial characteristics and mannerisms, yet people may not be confused between them. In the same way, unrelated products on the same shelf may have a certain similarity of appearance but still not confuse shoppers. Likewise where products which are not necessarily found next to each other in a retail setting bear similar trade marks, the trade mark on one may call to mind the trade mark of the other without inducing a mental state of confusion on the part of relevant consumers. On this basis, the applicant's trade mark AFTER SEX MINTS was regarded as calling into mind the opponent's AFTER EIGHT mint chocolate products but not as causing a likelihood of confusion.[110]

---

[108] *Canon Kabushiki Kaisha v Metro-Goldwyn-Mayer Inc*, Case C-39/97 [1999] ETMR 1.
[109] Relief was granted on this basis in *Aunt Jemima Mills Co v Rigney & Co*, 247 F 407 (2d Cir 1917), cert denied, 245 US 672 (1918).
[110] *Sweetmasters Ltd's application; opposition of Société des Produits Nestlé*, 25 February 2002 (UK Trade Mark Registry).

D. Likelihood of confusion

The ECJ[111] has identified two subsets of confusion: the direct and the indirect. Direct confusion occurs where two products or services are confused with each other. Indirect confusion occurs where it is not the products or services which are confused with each other but the owners of the trade mark or sign which each product or service uses. (Indirect confusion is discussed further in paras 10.143–10.149 below.)

10.104

(a) A likelihood of confusion can be established where both trade marks have been used

Once both marks are used as trade marks,[112] the question of likelihood of confusion becomes relatively simple to resolve, for three reasons. First, it is not proper for a court to guess how a registered-but-as-yet-unused trade mark may be used (this may be an important issue, since the size and positioning of a trade mark on a product for which it is registered may affect consumer perceptions) and a court need only

10.105

> assume the mark . . . is used in a normal and fair manner in relation to the goods for which it is registered and then . . . assess the likelihood of confusion and deception in relation to the way in which the defendant uses the mark, discounting external added matter or circumstances. The comparison is mark for mark.[113]

Secondly, evidence of coexistence without actual confusion is good evidence that there is no likelihood of confusion; thirdly, inferences can be drawn from the way in which trade marks are used as to how likely it is that confusing events will occur. For example, where the marks are not identical and one is used on extremely expensive goods while the other is used on much cheaper products, price alone may virtually guarantee that confusion is unlikely.[114] The fact that neither the trade mark proprietor nor his adversary have previously sought to object to the use of each other's marks is not of itself evidence of a lack of confusion.[115]

10.106

On a practical note, the fact that the alleged infringer has not yet commenced his use may prompt the trade mark proprietor to act quickly against him on the basis that evidence of actual confusion is sometimes hard to find and an argument of a likelihood of confusion based on hypothetical use may then appear more plausible.

10.107

---

[111] *Sabèl BV v Puma AG, Rudolf Dassler Sport*, Case C-251/95 [1998] ETMR 1, para 16.
[112] If the defendant's use is not use 'in the course of trade', then there cannot by definition be confusion; see *Travelex Global and Financial Services Ltd (formerly Thomas Cook Group Ltd) and Interpayment Services Ltd v Commission*, Case T-195/00, 10 April 2003 (CFI).
[113] *Natural Resources Inc v Origin Clothing Ltd* [1995] FSR 280, 284 per Jacob J.
[114] *GTR Group's application; opposition of Jean Patou* [1999] ETMR 164 (JOIS & JO and JOY perfumes).
[115] This point does not appear to have been considered in European jurisprudence but has been established in the United States; see *In re Majestic Distilling Co*, No 02–12243, 2 January 2003 (unreported) (Fed Cir).

(b) A likelihood of confusion can be established where one or even both trade marks have not actually been used

10.108 When the new European regime for trade marks came into existence, trade mark applications could be opposed not only by owners of earlier trade marks but also by users of earlier unregistered rights. Accordingly it seemed probable that the scenario in which an application for an unused mark was opposed by a right which was obtained through use would be a frequent occurrence. Experience of both national and CTMs has suggested however that this has not in fact been the case.[116]

10.109 It cannot be argued that, since the trade mark owner may never use his mark, it is not possible to prove a likelihood of confusion where his mark has not been used. As mentioned above in relation to the likelihood of confusion where both trade marks have been used (see para 10.105), in answer to this argument one British judge has said:

> In my judgment this point is misconceived. [The law] presupposes that the plaintiff's mark is in use or will come into use. It requires the court to assume the mark of the plaintiff is used in a normal and fair manner in relation to the goods for which it is registered and then to assess a likelihood of confusion in relation to the way the defendant uses its mark, discounting external added matter or circumstances. The comparison is mark for mark.[117]

10.110 This formula presumably applies, *mutatis mutandis,* even when neither party has used its mark. If it did not, the establishment of a likelihood of confusion during the five-year grace period before which a trade mark registrant must commence use of his mark would pose insoluble problems.

(c) The high degree of similarity between goods can enhance a likelihood of confusion but not create it

10.111 As was mentioned in the context of similarity of goods, the ECJ's *Canon* principle stated that the more similar goods or services are, the less similar a similar mark will need to be while still possessing the power to cause a likelihood of confusion.[118] There is however a point beyond which even this principle cannot be made to apply: the fact that both parties sold stationery could not make GRANDEE confusingly similar to LANDRE.[119]

10.112 In some non-European jurisdictions the converse argument is sometimes raised, that the fact that the parties' respective goods are so very different should lead to the conclusion that the public cannot be confused between them. So far as goods

---

[116] Gert Würtenburger, 'Risk of Confusion and Criteria to Determine the Same in European Community Trade Mark Law' [2002] EIPR 20, 29.
[117] *Origins Natural Resources Inc v Origin Clothing Ltd* [1995] FSR 280, 284 per Jacob J.
[118] *Canon Kabushiki Kaisha v Metro-Goldwyn-Mayer Inc*, Case C-39/97 [1999] ETMR 1.
[119] *Landré GmbH v International Paper Company*, Case R 39/2000–1 [2001] ETMR 794.

D. Likelihood of confusion

are concerned, this argument is superficially plausible: most people might confuse one watch with another but no one would confuse a watch with a cigar. But where the confusion relates to the guarantee of origin of goods, the fact that they bore the same trade mark could easily lead consumers to assume that ROLEX watches and ROLEX cigars shared a common source of one sort or another.[120]

(d) Relevance of the inherent nature of the goods or services

Consumers are more careful to distinguish some sorts of goods than others. Greater care is taken with regard to the names of competing medicines because, for example, the consequences of mistaking a laxative for a mouthwash can be startling. Likewise considerable attention may be given to the names of competing items like lipstick and nail varnish, where a mistake may result in a colour clash. Rather less intellectual effort is spent in discriminating between products where consumers are less sensitive to the outcome of their choice, for example, in the case of competing branded commodities such as apples, potatoes, milk or cheese. 10.113

The CFI has ruled that beer is not a commodity which, because of its inherent nature, is likely to be particularly carefully studied by consumers who would therefore be less likely to be confused between relatively similar MYSTERY and MIXERY trade marks: the argument that drivers would be particularly alert to the alcohol content accordingly failed.[121] 10.114

(e) Relevance of outlets for the respective goods or services

This criterion has already featured once in this chapter, as tending to suggest that goods are more likely to be considered 'similar' if they are sold in the same outlets or in the same areas of supermarkets. The same criterion is manifestly relevant to the question of likelihood of confusion, though its significance in this context is less clear. Do we say, as the Poles do, that people will be more likely to believe that similarly titled publications are related if they see them on display in newspaper kiosks and airport shops,[122] or should we say that consumers will be better able to tell them apart if they see them together than if they see only one and must rely on their imperfect memory? Both avenues of reasoning are available for use. 10.115

In an Australian action brought by the US sportswear company Nike International against the Spanish company Campomar, Nike held the NIKE registration for clothing, footwear and sportswear, while Campomar registered NIKE 10.116

---

[120] See *Montres Rolex SA v PT Permona*, Case 951/80 (Court of Appeal, Iran): ROLEX watches and ROLEX cigars held likely to confuse.
[121] *Mystery Drinks GmbH v OHIM, Karlsberg Brauerei KG Weber Intervening*, Case T-99/01, 15 January 2003 (unreported) (CFI).
[122] *Hola SA's trade mark; application for cancellation by G + J Gruner + Jahr Polska Sp Zoo & Co Spolka Komandytowa* [2002] ETMR 257 (HALO/HELLO).

for perfumes, soaps and essential oils. When Campomar launched a perfume called 'NIKE Sports Fragrance', Nike sued on various grounds and sought to expunge Campomar's registrations on the basis that they were likely to deceive or confuse consumers. Campomar's products were sold in the same outlets as other sports fragrances, including one marketed under the trade mark ADIDAS. Even if Campomar's conduct did not itself cause confusion, the fact that its product was sold next to the fragrance of one of Nike's great sports rivals would cause consumers to make the erroneous assumption that, if Adidas had indulged in brand extension, Nike had done so too.[123] These facts suggest that, when seeking to establish a likelihood of confusion, it is advisable to consider the inferences that can be drawn from the fact that the alleged infringer or unfair competitor shares outlets with the trade mark owner's competitors, rather than considering only the outlets shared by the two parties in dispute.

(f) Relevance of non-distinctive or only weakly distinctive elements

10.117 In seeking to determine whether the similarity between marks is likely to cause confusion, it might be thought that it is a sensible precaution first to excise from the equation those elements of the trade mark which are similar precisely because they refer to some external element to which both may claim entitlement to use. Is it not this approach which justified the decision of the ECJ to allow the registration of weakly distinctive marks such as BABY-DRY[124] for babies' nappies, knowing full well that competitors would also need to use words such as 'baby' and 'dry'? But that is not quite the approach which we do take. We do not refuse to take account of similar but descriptive elements: we do take them into account but only within the context of their overall significance within the marks which are being compared with each other. That is because their use in a later mark is not inherently blocked by the existence of an earlier mark, but will depend upon whether the immediate context of their use is liable to cause confusion.

10.118 In very many instances the fact that the shared element between two marks consists of descriptive or only weakly distinctive elements will mean that two similar marks will be allowed to coexist. For example, the Portuguese Court of Appeal considered that STREETBALL and SETBALL were not confusingly similar for clothing, footwear and headwear.[125] They both contained the word 'ball', which was well known to relevant Portuguese consumers and to which neither party could claim an exclusive entitlement. The Finnish Supreme Administrative Court took the same approach when determining that, once the weakly distinctive and commonly used prefix DYNA- had been disregarded,

---

[123] *Campomar Sociedad, Limitada v Nike International Ltd* [2000] HCA 12 (High Court of Australia).
[124] *Procter & Gamble Company v OHIM*, Case C-383/99 P [2002] ETMR 22 (BABY-DRY).
[125] *Adidas AG's application* [1996] ETMR 66.

D. Likelihood of confusion

there would be no risk of confusion between DYNANET and DYNALINK[126] and the Irish Patents Office used the same technique, disregarding the dominant prefix ORANG- when considering the likelihood of confusion between the word marks ORANGO and ORANGINA.[127]

10.119 What is true of prefixes would appear equally true of suffixes, according to the Danish Supreme Court which agreed that MEGASOL and PIKASOL were not similar trade marks for fish oil. Since so many trade marks in Class 5 ended in -SOL, that suffix could be disregarded, leaving MEGA- and PIKA- as plainly different indicia of their respective products.[128]

10.120 The approach to word marks would appear to apply equally to a comparison of figurative trade marks which contain words, OHIM's First Cancellation having found two word-and-device telecoms marks to be dissimilar once the common word DATA was ignored.[129] Even more spectacular was the decision of the same Division that two 'bank 24' marks (see Figure 10.9) were not confusingly similar.[130] Both marks represented twenty-four-hour banking 'in an almost descriptive manner' and it is likely that, short of an identical reproduction, most representations of similar features would not have been regarded as confusingly similar.

Figure 10.9 These two word-and-device marks were found to be not confusingly similar.

(g) Relevance of jurisdictions in which the respective marks comfortably coexist without confusion

10.121 The fact that two similar trade marks have coexisted without apparent difficulties in other jurisdictions is utterly irrelevant to the issue of whether their use together

---

[126] *Askey Computer Corporation's application; opposition of Nokia Telecommunications OY* [2000] ETMR 214.
[127] *Dairygold Co-operative Society Ltd's application; opposition of Austin Nichols & Co Inc* [2002] ETMR 1084. See also *Citicorp v Link Interchange Network Ltd* [2002] ETMR 1146 (HC), decided under the Trade Marks Act 1938, in which the weak prefix FX ('foreign exchange') was disregarded when comparing CITICORP FXLINK with the earlier mark LINK for foreign exchange services.
[128] *Lube A/S v Dansk Droge A/S* [2001] ETMR 343.
[129] *Deutsche Telekom AG's trade mark; Veiga's application for cancellation*, Case 000267724/1 [2000] ETMR 939. A similar approach was taken by the Austrian Supreme Court in *Deutsche Telekom AG, B***** v R***** AG, C***** Gesellschaft *** mbH* [2003] ETMR 170.
[130] *Din Bank A/S's trade mark; application for declaration of invalidity by Deutsche Bank Aktiengesellschaft*, Case 144C 001027374/1, 1 October 2001 (unreported) (OHIM Cancellation Division).

would lead to a likelihood of confusion in the country in which the question of confusing similarity has to be determined.[131] Local factors such as advertising, marketing and geographical distribution may provide good reasons why they have coexisted elsewhere.

(h) Post-point of sale confusion must also be considered

10.122 Neither Directive 89/104 nor the CTM Regulation stipulate the point of time at which the likelihood of confusion must be established. Clearly the fact that a consumer is confused *before* he makes a purchase is significant, but may significance also be attached to confusion which takes place *after* the purchase is made?[132]

10.123 *Prima facie* it may appear that post-purchase confusion is irrelevant, but careful reflection shows that this is not so. Consider the facts of an Irish case[133] in which similar biscuits were sold as MCVITIES COLLEGE CREAM and BOLANDS COTTAGE CREAM respectively. Since the two products were sold in quite different packaging and would not be mistaken on the supermarket shelves, the claims of trade mark infringement and passing off failed. However anyone who saw the unwrapped biscuits on a plate, who subsequently wished to purchase them but who lacked perfect recall, might have confused the two names when seeking to buy them on a future occasion. Much the same considerations may apply where the owner of, say, a camera which would not be confused with a competing brand at the point of sale, is confused as to which of two sets of accessories will be compatible with the one he owns. These two examples relate to circumstances in which a consumer, *after* having made one purchase, is confused *before* he makes a second one. In an action for passing off, the post-sale confusion of consumers has long been a sufficient basis upon which to sue[134] and it appears that the same approach has now been accepted by the Spanish Supreme Court in regard to trade marks.[135]

(i) The more laboured is the task of establishing a link between the marks, the less likely it is to succeed

10.124 In the *Stephanskreuz* case the question arose as to whether the word mark STEPHANSKREUZ ('Stephen's Cross') was liable to be confused with a label which contained a representation of a St Stephen's Crown, an image which appears on St Stephen's Cross. In dismissing the suggestion that there was any likelihood of confusion or association between them, the German

---

[131] *Icart SA's application; opposition of Beiersdorf AG*, Case B 1794 [2000] ETMR 180.
[132] This question has recently attracted attention in the United States too; see David Tichane, 'The Maturing Doctrine of Post-Sales Confusion' (1995) 85 TMR 399.
[133] *United Biscuits Ltd v Irish Biscuits Ltd* [1971] IR 16 (Irish High Court).
[134] *Reckitt & Colman v Borden* [1990] RPC 340 (HL): lemon juice containers differently presented at point of sale but looked similar once labels were removed.
[135] ACUPREL V AQUAPRED, 24 April 2002 (Spanish Supreme Court (Court III)).

D. Likelihood of confusion

Bundespatentgericht described the tortuous intellectual process which would have to be completed by any purchaser of wine who did in fact link them and observed that

> It would be stretching the concept of associative risk of confusion too far if it were to encompass every conceivable mental association, including a thought process which is not spontaneous.[136]

(2) Establishing confusion: the United States and Canada

The European checklist has been laboriously compiled by tracking themes which appear within the sprawling body of European case law. It is valuable to compare the issues which have troubled European tribunals with the checklist of thirteen factors (twelve substantive and one 'catch-all') for determining confusion adopted in the United States, which has been conveniently stated in a single Federal decision: **10.125**

(1) The similarity or dissimilarity of the marks in their entireties as to appearance, sound, connotation, and commercial impression.
(2) The similarity or dissimilarity and nature of the goods . . . described in an application or registration or in connection with which a prior mark is in use.
(3) The similarity or dissimilarity of established, likely-to-continue trade channels.
(4) The conditions under which and buyers to whom sales are made, *i.e.* impulse vs. careful, sophisticated purchasing.
(5) The fame of the prior mark . . .
(6) The number and nature of similar marks in use on similar goods.
(7) The nature and extent of any actual confusion.
(8) The length of time during and the conditions under which there has been concurrent use without evidence of actual confusion.
(9) The variety of goods on which a mark is or is not used . . .
(10) The market interface between the applicant and the owner of a prior mark . . .
(11) The extent to which the applicant has a right to exclude others from use of its mark on its goods.
(12) The extent of potential confusion . . .
(13) Any other established fact probative of the effect of use.[137]

---

[136] *Stephanskreuz Trade Mark Application* [1997] ETMR 182, 186.
[137] *In re EI du Pont de Nemours & Co* 476 F 2d 1357, 177 USPQ 563, 567 (CCPA 1973). This list of criteria is a good deal longer than the seven criteria laid down in *Polaroid Corp v Polarad Electronics Corp* 287 F 2d 492, 495 (2d Cir 1961) for the establishment of confusion between non-competing goods: (i) strength of the proprietor's mark; (ii) degree of similarity between marks; (iii) proximity of products; (iv) likelihood that the proprietor will 'bridge the gap' between the defendant's business and his own; (v) evidence of actual confusion; (vi) quality of the defendant's product; (vii) sophistication of the market.

10.126 This approach, which encapsulates the United States approach to determining confusion, is supplemented by case law that addresses the nature of the confusion itself. Thus 'initial interest' confusion, in which the consumer is briefly confused by a superficial similarity which is soon dispelled by further investigation, may be contrasted with the deeper, more persistent form of confusion which is traditionally associated with the behaviour of trade mark infringers. Where the trade mark owner and the alleged infringer are in non-competing businesses, initial interest confusion may be an insufficient basis upon which to succeed in a trade mark infringement action,[138] while a partial or complete overlap between the parties' respective businesses may result in even initial interest confusion being regarded as an infringement.[139]

10.127 Other countries have developed their own means of determining confusion, which may be founded on neither the European nor the United States models. In Canada, for example, when determining whether the applicant's mark CANNABIS CRUNCH would be confused with the opponent's CRISPY CRUNCH the Opposition Board[140] identified a five-point procedure for establishing confusion:

(i) how strong is the opponent's mark? [on the basis that, the stronger the mark, the greater the degree of protection to which it is entitled];
(ii) how long has the opponent's mark been used? [on the basis that, the longer the use, the greater the public recognition];
(iii) what is the nature of the respective parties' products; and
(iv) what is the nature of their respective businesses? [on the basis that, the greater the proximity in each case, the greater the likelihood of confusion]; and
(v) to what extent do the respective marks resemble each other?

10.128 In this case the opponents 'won' on the first four issues, but still lost because, by the fifth and crucial criterion, CANNABIS CRUNCH and CRISPY CRUNCH were not similar enough to confuse the relevant public.

(a) A 'market-oriented' approach

10.129 Unlike the European approach to establishing confusing similarity, which would appear to focus more on the juridical nature of the trade mark, the United States approach would appear to focus more on the role of the trade mark in the marketplace. One example of this is in the development of 'initial interest' confusion

---

[138] See eg *Checkpoint Systems Inc v Check Point Software Technologies Inc*, 104 F Supp 2d 427 (DNJ, 12 July 2000).
[139] See eg *Brookfield Communications Inc v West Coast Entertainment Corp* 174 F 3d 1056 (9th Cir. 22 April 1999).
[140] *Valliant-Saunders' application; opposition of Cadbury Trebor Allan*, Marketing Law, 26 May 2003.

D. Likelihood of confusion

itself, this being a concept which has not yet been generally recognized within Europe.[141] Another example may be found from a holding that the VENTURE trade mark for watches did not infringe the VENTURA mark for the same product, in which the trial court was strongly influenced by the fact that both VENTURE and VENTURA were used in a subsidiary manner: the public's perception of the two marks would be coloured by their non-prominent appearance as sub-brands of ESQ and SWATCH respectively.[142] However, while the manner of expression of the United States factors is markedly different from that of European law, it is doubtful whether any issue considered relevant to a finding of confusing similarity in Europe could be said to be excluded from consideration in the United States, or vice versa.

(b) Reverse confusion

United States case law has developed a concept of 'reverse confusion': the situation in which the public are not confused into believing that the defendant's goods are connected with the trade mark owner but where they are caused to believe that the trade mark owner's goods are in some way connected with the defendant. This scenario occurs where the trade mark owner has not used his trade mark at all, or has used it minimally, while the alleged infringer has used it widely.[143] European doctrine does not treat 'reverse confusion' as a concept separate from regular confusion since it is the fact of confusion, rather than the direction in which it travels, which determines liability. The fact that the confusion is 'reverse confusion' will however affect the availability of injunctive relief, the quantum of damages and the attractiveness of an account of profits.   10.130

(3) Is 'likelihood of confusion' a question of law or a question of fact?

The Swiss Federal Supreme Court has concluded that likelihood of confusion between trade marks is a question of fact, not a question of law.[144] Accordingly, as an appellate court it was entitled to conduct a full review of all the issues raised by the trial court; it did not need to admit or consider any fresh evidence and it could determine the issue of likelihood of confusion without having recourse to polls, surveys or other evidence.   10.131

---

[141] Cf *Playboy Enterprises Inc v Giannattasio* WTLR, 30 May 2003 (Court of Naples), discussed at Chapter 17, paras 17.09–17.10.

[142] *Swatch Group (US) Inc v Movado Corp* WTLR, 27 May 2003 (US District Court for the Southern District of New York).

[143] A good review of the doctrine is found in *Glow Industries Inc v Jennifer Lopez, Coty Inc & Does 1-20*, 252 F Supp 2d 962 (CD Cal 2002). In this case a small-scale cosmetics company selling GLOW products was 'swamped' by GLO BY J.LO. The infringement action was dismissed.

[144] *Denner AG v Rivella AG* [2001] ETMR 826 (RIVELLA and APIELLA soft drinks).

10.132 Within the EU and its individual Member States, the courts' appraisal of this question has been less extreme than that of the Swiss, but in the EU too there is a sentiment that, at least in part, the question of confusing similarity is a matter of law, not of fact. Consider this statement from *Lloyd v Klijsen*:

> The more similar the goods or services covered and the more distinctive the earlier mark, the greater will be the likelihood of confusion.[145]

10.133 This statement, with great respect to the ECJ, may be true in individual cases but in others it bears scant relation to reality. Let us leave aside for the moment the argument as to whether trade marks can be 'more' or 'less' distinctive, since the sole requirement of trade mark law is that a trade mark be 'distinctive', and concentrate on the real issue: does the fact that COCA-COLA is arguably the most distinctive trade mark on the planet mean that people will be more likely to confuse it with KOALA-COLA than if it had been a less distinctive trade mark? In truth and in logic a consumer is going to be confused by a third-party mark when seeking to identify a mark he knows less well and which is less distinctive. Go into a pharmacy where you find EUDERMIN bodycare products. You find EUCERIN products there too. Which one was it that you saw advertised? The reason for the likelihood of confusion was that neither brand is stamped into your consciousness. COCA-COLA is different. Can there be many people on the planet who could not distinguish it from its closest rivals, even if they do not drink it themselves?

(4) The yardstick of confusion: the reasonably well-informed consumer

10.134 In determining whether there is a likelihood of confusion, courts and trade mark registries must consider the effect of similarity of trade marks upon a hypothetical consumer who is 'reasonably well-informed and reasonably observant and circumspect'.[146] He will be: (i) the relevant consumer of the goods or services for which the trade marks are used (or to be used); (ii) well informed with regard to the products or services in question; and (iii) neither more nor less attentive than typical consumers of those products or services would be. This well-informed consumer is however (iv) not such a dedicated shopper that he always has both parties' products or services before him when he makes his choice between them (indeed, there may be no shops which stock both parties' products, particularly if they are 'in-house' brands). Let us examine these characteristics in turn.

---

[145] *Lloyd Schuhfabrik Meyer & Co GmbH v Klijsen Handel BV*, Case V-342/97 [1999] ETMR 10. This quote first appears as an apparent *non sequitur* in *Sabèl BV v Puma AG, Rudolf Dassler Sport*, Case C-251/95 [1998] ETMR 1, para 24.

[146] *Gut Springenheide GmbH, Tusky v Oberkreisdirektor des Kreises Steinfurt etc*, Case C-210/96 [1999] ETMR 425, cited in *Lloyd Schuhfabrik Meyer & Co GmbH v Klijsen Handel BV*, Case V-342/97 [1999] ETMR 690 and other ECJ trade mark decisions.

D. Likelihood of confusion

(a) The consumer must be 'relevant'

For many consumer products and services which are widely prevalent, the relevant consumer can be equated with the population at large: toothpaste, soft drinks, bank accounts and fast-food outlets are all within this category. The consumer needs to acquire little or no special background knowledge before he is equipped to make choices relating to such items. Other products are different, whether because of their small market appeal or their specialist nature. Thus the ordinary man in the street might be confused by the difference between MEMORY and MEMOREX, but sophisticated purchasers of computer equipment would not be.[147]

10.135

The ability of relevant consumers to discern subtle differences without being confused by them is nowhere more severely tested than when the relevant consumers are trade mark professionals themselves. This community is regularly confronted by firms with names such as MARKLAW, MARKFORCE, INTERMARK, INTERBRAND, MARKPRO, PROMARK, NOVAMARK, MARK-INVENTA, FIRSTMARK, ACEMARK, HIMARK, EUROMARK and MARKPLUS.

10.136

Where a party's trade mark is for pet food, the relevant consumer of that product is the purchaser of the pet food, not the pet itself,[148] although a German court has ruled that little girls of 4 years old and above are the 'relevant audience' for BETTY dolls[149] even though many little girls may not be in a position to make their own purchases.

10.137

(b) The consumer must be well informed

Where goods are expensive, the consumer will spend more time pondering over his purchase decision and will therefore be less likely to be confused into thinking that a LEGO-compatible toy building brick system is that of LEGO.[150] Where goods are cheap, or where decision-making is rushed, consumers are more likely to be confused.[151]

10.138

---

[147] *Memory (Ireland) Ltd v Telex Computers (Ireland) Ltd* [1978] EIPR European Digest (HC), December, v: '... likely customers of each company would be persons of education and intelligence, concerned to take a great deal of care in exercising their choice of purchases where such considerable sums of money were at stake.'

[148] *Lidl Stiftung & Co KG v Heinz Iberica, SA*, Case R 232/200–4 [2003] ETMR 312 (ORLANDO animal and human food). Cf the United States decision in *Recot Inc v M C Becton* 56 USPQ 2d 1859 (TTAB 2000), in which FIDO LAY dog treats were held confusingly similar to FRITO LAY snack foods.

[149] *Ohio Art Company and Bandai GmbH Toys and Entertainment v CreCon Spiel U Hobbyartikel GmbH* [2000] ETMR 756, 763 (Landgericht München I).

[150] *Lego and another v Distributor of B***** Building Blocks* [2001] ETMR 907.

[151] *Kimberley-Clark Ltd v Fort Sterling Ltd* [1997] FSR 877, 884 (CA) per Laddie J: 'A typical weekly family shop among the 25,000 different items ranged in a typical supermarket takes 40 minutes. Consumers tend to scan the shelves and make rapid purchase decisions. Consumers spend less than 10 seconds on average in front of packaged grocery shelves'.

Chapter 10: Identical and Similar Marks, Goods and Services

(c) The consumer must be averagely attentive and circumspect

10.139 The consumer will never mistake his favourite brand of cigarettes for another, whether through practised familiarity[152] or possibly through the ravages of addiction. Nor, in respect of any goods or services, will he confuse the stylized McDonald's yellow 'M' symbol with a pink heart-shaped 'M'.[153] He may however mistake his favourite beers and soft drinks, even if he is 'very experienced in respect of these goods'.[154]

(d) The consumer must be expected to suffer from imperfect recall

10.140 No national or regional trade mark law demands of consumers that they have a perfect memory. Sometimes shoppers will have only one of two similar products in front of them at the moment when the purchase decision is made and they will be considered likely to confuse the product before them with the competitor's product, the precise details of which they cannot recall.[155] Sometimes the confusion may result from the length of time which passes between occasions when consumers use products or services, for example, educational correspondence courses.[156]

10.141 The importance of imperfect recall cannot be overestimated. When considering whether the two letter marks depicted here (see Figure 10.10) were confusingly similar, the OHIM Opposition Division listed a number of typographical features which would probably make them quite distinctive in the view of a typographer, but which the averagely observant purchaser of photographic goods would be fairly certain to miss if he did not have the two marks in front of him at the same time. The two marks were therefore confusingly similar.[157]

Figure 10.10 Two confusingly similar marks.

---

[152] *British-American Tobacco (Holdings) Ltd's application; opposition of Fabriques de Tabac Réunis SA*, Case B598 [1999] ETMR 32 (HORIZON and ARISTON); *Lidl Stiftung & Co KG v The Savoy Hotel*, Case R 729/1999–2 [2001] ETMR 1284 (SAVOY and THE SAVOY).

[153] *Bertucci v McDonald's Corporation and others* [1999] ETMR 742 (Tribunal de Grande Instance de Paris).

[154] CAFFREY'S *application; opposition of CAFRE* [2002] Ent LR N-87 (Hungarian Supreme Court) Pfk IV 25.022/1999.

[155] *Northern Foods Grocery Group Ltd's Application; opposition by Horace M Ostwald* [2002] ETMR 516.

[156] *Institut Für Lernsysteme GmbH v OHIM*, Case T-388/00, 23 October 2002.

[157] *R Cable y Telecommunicationes Galicia SA's application; opposition of Ricoh Company Ltd*, Case 3475/2002, 28 November 2002 (unreported).

(5) What if the confusion is removed before the point of sale?

Once actual confusion between similar marks is proved, infringement results even if the confusion is later removed by the user of the later mark. Thus, where a trader took advantage of initial confusion in order to explain the difference between his product and that of his competitor and, in dispelling that confusion, to invite the consumer to purchase his product instead, damage to the trade mark owner remained even though confusion of the consumer had been 'remedied'. This technique, described by a French court[158] as 'doorstepping' or 'slipstreaming', was additionally an act of unfair competition.

10.142

E. Likelihood of association

(1) Likelihood of confusion: does it include a 'likelihood of association'?

The formulation of the rights conferred by a trade mark under article 16 of TRIPs[159] protects trade mark owners against a 'likelihood of confusion' but the two major planks of European trade mark protection, Directive 89/104 and the CTM Regulation, go further: they qualify the term 'likelihood of confusion' by adding the words 'which includes a likelihood of association'.[160] What do these words mean and what is their significance?

10.143

The terminology of 'likelihood of association' predates the mid-1990s movement towards common European law standards, owing its provenance to the pre-harmonization Benelux law.[161] That law employed a concept of 'resemblance of marks' rather than 'likelihood of confusion' as its criterion of infringement, there being a 'resemblance' between trade marks when their visual, aural or conceptual similarity is such as to establish an 'association' between them.[162] The term 'resemblance' was used in neither Directive 89/104 nor the CTM Regulation, but the words 'likelihood of association' were. Did this mean that the European provisions intended to establish the Benelux law as the pan-European standard?[163]

10.144

In *Wagamama* the English High Court, the first court to consider the additional words 'likelihood of association' in the post-harmonization period of European

10.145

---

[158] *Sarl Le Book Editions v Sté EPC Edition Presse Communication and another* [1999] ETMR 554 (Tribunal de Grande Instance de Paris).
[159] Article 16 is quoted in para 10.06 above.
[160] Council Directive 89/104, arts 4(1), 5(1); Council Regulation 40/94, arts 8(1), 9(1).
[161] Old Uniform Benelux Trade Mark Law, art 13A.
[162] *Jullien v Verschuere*, Case A 82/5, 20 May 1983, (1983) 4 Jur 36.
[163] This question provoked a lively debate: see eg Anselm Kamperman Sanders, 'The Return to *Wagamama*' [1996] EIPR 521; Peter Prescott, 'Think Before You Waga Finger' [1996] EIPR 317 and 'Has the Benelux Trade Mark Law Been Written Into the Directive?' [1997] EIPR 99.

trade mark history, concluded that they added nothing to the words 'likelihood of confusion'.[164] If, as the language of Directive 89/104 and the CTM Regulation suggested, 'likelihood of confusion' *included* a 'likelihood of association', the first category will as a matter of logic be broader than the second; any facts giving rise to a 'likelihood of association' must by their very nature already give rise to a 'likelihood of confusion'. Accordingly, the additional words were meaningless. The court could have added provocatively that, if the Directive and the Regulation bore the meaning for which the defendants argued, they would have employed the phrase 'likelihood of association, which includes a likelihood of confusion' rather than vice versa.

10.146 This view, which attracted a good deal of criticism, was however endorsed by the ECJ in *Sabèl v Puma*, which ruled:

> ... the mere association which the public might make between two trade marks as a result of their analogous semantic content is not itself a sufficient ground for concluding that there is a likelihood of confusion...[165]

10.147 This analysis would appear to have been completely misunderstood in a subsequent decision of the English Court of Appeal which, without discussion and for no apparent reason, has ruled that a successful claimant must prove that there is not only a likelihood of confusion *but also* a likelihood of association before he can succeed in a trade mark infringement action.[166]

10.148 Some scholars have persisted in advocating the virtues of the 'likelihood of association' approach over 'likelihood of confusion' and there is indeed much to say in its favour if you are a trade mark owner. Confusion can be difficult to prove (although there are cases in which evidence of confusion can be amassed even where as a matter of fact the defendant's trade mark is not similar to the claimant's[167]) and it will in general be easier to persuade a court or registry that there exists a 'likelihood of association', particularly where the earlier mark is unused, since some sort of association between trade marks or the goods or services on which they are used lies at the heart of every finding that there is a 'likelihood of confusion'. The notion of 'likelihood of association', being linked to the trade mark's real or conjectural reputation, is also more closely conceptually aligned to the protection accorded to trade marks against the use of the same or similar marks on completely different goods and services.[168]

---

[164] *Wagamama Ltd v City Centre Restaurants plc* [1996] ETMR 307 (HC).
[165] *Sabèl BV v Puma AG, Rudolf Dassler Sport*, Case C-251/95 [1998] ETMR 1, para 26.
[166] *Premier Luggage and Bags Ltd v Premier Co (UK) Ltd and another* [2002] ETMR 787.
[167] *Unilever NV v Raisio Yhtyma OY and others* [1999] ETMR 847 (Appeal Court, The Hague), discussed above.
[168] On such protection, see Chapter 11.

E. *Likelihood of association*

Against the desirability of adopting 'likelihood of association' as the normative test of interference by an undesirably similar mark, that test seems to work well for conventional trade marks but is untried in respect of trade marks consisting of single colours, colour combinations and product shapes, in respect of which a 'likelihood of association' may be too easily established, conferring an overwide degree of protection upon registered trade marks. Having said this, the concept of 'likelihood of association' in the sense in which Benelux lawyers understood it should not be discarded without first evaluating the lessons it can teach us.

10.149

(2) What does 'likelihood of association' actually mean?

'Likelihood of association' in its simplest form means that the public, because it associates the proprietor's trade mark with a later user's sign, is likely to think of products emanating from those enterprises as having come from connected businesses, or indeed from the same business. Thus consumers might imagine that RED BULL and BLACK BULL drinks come from the same producer.[169]

10.150

A question has been referred to the ECJ as to whether 'association' of a later mark with an earlier one also includes a situation in which the earlier trade mark is a word of average distinctiveness and the later mark is formed by adding to that earlier mark a well-known word or logo which already belonged to the applicant for the later mark.[170] It would be welcomed if the Court were to rule that whether there is an 'association' or not is a matter of fact for the national court to determine, not a matter of law for the ECJ to rule on.

10.151

(3) How is a 'likelihood of association' established?

The easiest way to prove that there exists a likelihood of association is to show that, on account of the actual or likely use of the two marks, relevant consumers will be led to believe that the goods of the respective competitors are associated—perhaps because they have some common source—or that one set of goods represent an extension of the product lines of the other. For example, Spanish consumers would be able to distinguish TED BAKER clothing from that of CLAUDIA BAKER, but they might view the former as a menswear brand related to the latter's women's clothing brand.[171]

10.152

The Utrecht District Court, when considering the likelihood of confusion between the trade marks YOU, YOURS and 4 YOU on the one hand and a device mark containing the words FASHION FOR YU on the other, doubted that the marks,

10.153

---

[169] *Scottish & Newcastle plc's application; opposition of Red Bull GmbH*, Case 863/2000 [2000] ETMR 1143.
[170] *Deutsche Telekom v Deutsche Krankenversicherung*, Case C-367/02 (reference to ECJ).
[171] *No Ordinary Designer Label Ltd v Comercial Fenicia de Exportación, SL* [2002] ETMR 527.

despite their similarity, would be confused by the public.[172] The court did however consider that there was a conceptual link, given that the second mark contained the word FASHION and the owner of the first mark employed the word 'mode' (being the Dutch for 'fashion'), thus establishing that there was not only a likelihood of association but a likelihood of confusion. The establishment of this conceptual link seems to go further than the law requires, since the connection made with 'mode' was not an association between the marks themselves but between the context in which they found themselves being used.

(4) If there is a likelihood of association, does a likelihood of confusion even need to be proved?

10.154 Adidas sued Marca Mode in the Netherlands for infringement of its famous three-stripe trade mark, which it alleged was being infringed by the unauthorized use of a two-stripe emblem. Marca Mode argued that there was no infringement since (i) it was not using the same mark as Adidas had registered and (ii) there was no actual or likely confusion between its own products and those of Adidas. If this was so, on an application of the *Sabèl v Puma* ruling, a 'likelihood of association' alone would not avail Adidas, who would have to establish a likelihood of confusion. A question was therefore referred to the ECJ[173] as to whether, in the case of a trade mark which was as particularly distinctive as that Adidas three-stripe emblem, it would be sufficient to prove in infringement proceedings that the likelihood of association was so great that a likelihood of confusion—even if it could not actually be proved—could not be excluded either. The ECJ answered this question in the negative: a likelihood of confusion must be proved since it cannot be presumed from a likelihood of association alone.[174]

10.155 This analysis does not greatly assist our understanding of the role 'likelihood of association'. The use of the word 'including' in the term 'likelihood of confusion, including a likelihood of association' suggests that association is a species of confusion. Yet if this is so, it gives an artificial and contrived meaning to the word 'association', which in ordinary language means something far wider than confusion. It is not possible to read both of the phrases with the word 'including' literally. The ECJ has stated that association serves to 'define the scope of confusion', but it is difficult to understand how it does so.

---

[172] *Hij Mannenmode BV v Nienhaus & Lotz GmbH* [1999] ETMR 730.
[173] *Marca Mode CV, Adidas AG and Adidas Benelux BV*, Case C-425/98 [2000] ETMR 723.
[174] In a decision on similar facts in Germany, the Bundesgerichtshof held that the court could not presume that consumers would *not* be confused on the basis that they had sensitized themselves to Adidas's three-stripe emblem to the point at which they would distinguish the defendant's two-stripe emblem; see *Three Stripes trade mark* [2002] ETMR 553.

F. Conclusion

10.156 The concepts of identity, similarity, confusion and association are surprisingly difficult to apply to the facts of individual cases. Bearing this in mind, the development of case law within Europe in the past decade has shown a remarkably healthy degree of consistency and common sense. The unifying effect of the rulings of the ECJ, together with an increased level of consistency in decisions of OHIM (particularly in some of the initially erratic Opposition Divisions) should encourage both trade mark owners and their competitors to believe that an era of stable and predictable application of the law is just round the corner, a position which it has occupied for a depressingly long time.

11

REPUTATION, UNFAIR ADVANTAGE AND DETRIMENT

A. **Introduction**	
A trade mark trasher confesses	
The moral of the story	11.01
(1) Background to the protection of trade marks which have a reputation	11.02
(a) Practical considerations	11.04
(b) The framework of the law	11.07
(c) Comparison of trade marks	11.12
(2) A note on concepts and terminology	11.14
(a) 'Dilution', 'blurring' and 'tarnishment'	11.15
(b) 'Distinctive character'	11.23
(c) 'Reputation' and 'repute'	11.25
(d) 'Unfair advantage'	11.29
B. **Reputation**	
(1) What is a 'reputation' and when does a trade mark have one?	11.30
(a) 'Reputation' in European law	11.33
(b) Reputation in relation to goods and services	11.36
(2) Does 'reputation' only mean that a trade mark be 'known'?	11.37
(3) 'Distinctive character' and 'repute'	11.40
(4) Does strong 'distinctive character' or 'repute' mean better protection?	11.44
(5) Proof of 'reputation' and other elements relating to protection of a mark's reputation	11.47
(a) The burden of proof	11.48
(b) Need for actual damage or merely that a probability of damage be proved?	11.50
(6) What is the difference between reputation and goodwill?	11.51
C. **Unfair advantage and detriment**	
(1) When is an unfair advantage or detrimental use 'without due cause'?	11.52
(2) What is an 'unfair advantage' relating to a trade mark's 'distinctive character'?	11.58
(3) What is an 'unfair advantage' relating to a trade mark's 'repute'? The *Dimple* case	11.60
(4) What is 'detrimental' to a trade mark's 'distinctive character'?	11.65
(5) What is 'detrimental' to a trade mark's repute?	11.73
(6) Is 'unfair advantage' or 'detriment' only an issue where there is also a likelihood of confusion?	11.82
(7) Is 'unfair advantage' or 'detriment' never an issue where the parties' respective goods or services are similar?	11.84
(8) Are there other forms of unfair advantage not covered by the *Dimple* principle?	11.94
D. **Conclusion**	11.95

Chapter 11: Reputation, Unfair Advantage and Detriment

A. Introduction

A trade mark trasher confesses

'It all started when I tried one of those GUBBO fruit-flavoured throat lozenges,' Jake said. 'I mean, I had a really sore throat and I bought these GUBBO things because of the adverts.'

'Go on,' said Detective Inspector Smith.

'You know those ads. The ones that say 'GUBBO brings relief in minutes. Money back if not satisfied.' Well, I took a couple of them. Apart from the fact they tasted horrid, they didn't do much for my throat either.'

'So what did you do then?' Smith prompted.

'I phoned up the Customer Care line and said the lozenges didn't work, so could I have my money back. They said no, so I said what about the "money back if not satisfied" bit? They said that meant money back if *they* weren't satisfied. But they were quite satisfied with my money so I couldn't have it back. That's when I started getting angry.'

'And then?'

'The first thing I did was to set up a website, www.dontsuckgubbo.com, to warn other suckers not to fall for Gubbo's dirty tricks. I organized some metatag links, so that anyone searching for 'GUBBO' or 'sore throat' would find my site.'

'What was on the website, Jake?'

'Lots of things. An article about my rage against Gubbo's lies. Obscene drawings of people swallowing GUBBO. Then there were the haikus.'

'Haikus?' There were no haikus to be found in the index to the police manual.

'My throat hurts like hell,

As raging sun beats parched earth.

GUBBO makes it worse.'

Smith recorded the incriminating haiku and shook his head. Sometimes villains committed acts for which there was just no rhyme or reason.

Jake continued. 'Then I decided to print some T-shirts with the slogan GUBBO KILLS on them.'

'But GUBBO surely doesn't kill, does it? That seems a bit extreme.' Smith checked himself. You weren't supposed to be judgmental when you were on the job.

'My throat was killing me,' explained Jake, 'because those GUBBOs didn't work. GUBBOs were killing my throat.' In case any further explanation were necessary he drew a finger across his throat.

'One moment. I'm just writing that down.'

'The next thing I did was to print some little cardboard boxes. They had BUGGO on the front in big letters. On the back they said 'Better than GUBBO.' Which they were.'

'What were, Jake? What did you put in the boxes?'

'Doggies' doings.'

Smith winced. Years in the police force had hardened him, but he was unprepared for anything quite as nasty as this. Was there no depravity to which trade mark trashers did not sink?

The moral of the story

11.01 In the long term there is just one way of establishing a good reputation and devel-

A. Introduction

oping goodwill in a brand name. That is by associating that name, in the mind of the consuming public, with goods or services that give them pleasure, or at least satisfaction. In contrast there are many ways of destroying that good reputation: by poking fun at it, by insulting it, by stealing it for use with inferior products or services, by confusing the public until they can't be sure whether the product they buy is the one they like or one they don't, and so on. The law provides various means whereby the trade mark owner can go to court in order to protect his trade mark against the activities of others, or to obtain compensation for the damage they have done to him. This chapter will look at the options available to the troubled trade mark owner whose mark has been used in a way that results in detriment to the mark or the derivation of an unfair advantage from its use.

(1) Background to the protection of trade marks which have a reputation

A registered trade mark is entitled to protection against the use or registration of an identical sign without the need for its proprietor to prove to the court that his registered mark possesses a reputation. The same applies to the protection to which a registered trade mark is entitled where it is likely to be confused with a sign used or intended to be registered by another. In all these cases a trade mark will gain the law's protection even if it has not yet been used. But there is an additional level of protection which is open to the owners of trade marks which have been used: that protection is the subject of this chapter. **11.02**

Once a trade mark owner has successfully invested in the development of a branded product or service, the goodwill derived from the brand serves as a valuable business asset. The brand both attracts and retains custom, providing a promise or reassurance of quality, good value for money or other desirable characteristics. Investment in trade mark registration is the best legal means of protecting the value of the goodwill in the brand but, as in other areas of business development, even investment in trade mark protection is subject to the law of diminishing returns, as the following section explains. **11.03**

(a) Practical considerations

Money spent in registering a trade mark for the goods and services for which it is used is money well spent, but the trade mark owner may wish to consider obtaining registration of his mark for use in relation to goods or services in which he has no interest. For example, registration of the JEAN-PAUL GAULTIER trade mark for a range of scents will protect the proprietor against counterfeit and confusingly similar products, but should time, money and effort be invested in registering the same trade mark for oven gloves, pencil sharpeners or ball-bearings? Such a course of action is not normally feasible. If the proprietor—as is most likely—does not use the JEAN-PAUL GAULTIER trade mark for oven gloves, pencil sharpeners or ball-bearings the registrations are open to challenge for non-use **11.04**

Chapter 11: Reputation, Unfair Advantage and Detriment

and may be revoked.¹ Once those registrations are revoked, they do not provide any protection at all.

11.05 Even if the portfolio of registrations for far-flung goods and services were not vulnerable to revocation, the expense of securing and maintaining this portfolio would be an unwelcome addition to the cost of looking after the JEAN-PAUL GAULTIER trade mark. Even trade mark owners must live within their means; the cost of monitoring and dealing with infringements and hostile third party registrations must come out of a corporate budget. The bigger the spend on registration, the less is left over for policing. As one commentator has said:

> The most famous marks are not used everywhere and cannot be registered and maintained in all the places and for all the categories in which infringements may arise. It is strange, but true, that most owners of famous marks are living beyond their means in the defence of their trade marks, in the sense that they must spend where they do not earn.²

11.06 For this reason it is vital for trade mark owners to obtain, in relation to their registration of trade marks for classes of goods and services which they *do* exploit commercially, the maximum degree of protection available in respect of goods and services to which they do *not* seek to extend the use of their trade marks. The framework for this protection is discussed in the following section.

(b) The framework of the law

11.07 In Chapter 7 we mentioned that the Agreement on Trade-Related Aspects of Intellectual Property Law (TRIPs)³ requires Member States to protect a registered trade mark against the use of that mark on

> goods or services which are *not similar* to those in respect of which a trademark is registered, provided that use of that trademark in relation to those goods or services would indicate *a connection between those goods or services and the owner of the registered trademark* and *provided that the interests of the owner of the registered trademark are likely to be damaged by such use* [emphasis added].⁴

11.08 The TRIPs provision mentioned above is reflected in the EU's trade mark approximation directive, Directive 89/104, article 5(2) of which gives EU Member States the option to provide that

> ... the proprietor shall be entitled to prevent all third parties not having his consent from using in the course of trade any sign which is identical with, or similar to, the trade mark in relation to goods or services which are *not similar* to those for which the trade mark is registered, *where the latter has a reputation* in the Member State *and*

---

¹ On revocation, see Chapter 13.
² Ronald J Lehrman, '"Reputation Without Use" and "Household Names"' (1986) 3 *Trademark World* 18, 27.
³ See TRIPs, art 16(3).
⁴ Paris Convention, art 6*bis*(3).

A. Introduction

where use of that sign without due cause takes unfair advantage of, or is detrimental to, the distinctive character or the repute of the trade mark [emphasis added].

Similar provision for such activities to be treated as infringements is made under the Community Trade Mark (CTM) Regulation.[5] Both Directive 89/104[6] and the Regulation[7] have corresponding provisions which enable a trade mark owner to prevent the registration of third-party applications under much the same circumstances.

11.09

The plain meaning of these provisions is that four species of wrongful act are identified:

11.10

(i) taking unfair advantage of the distinctive character of the earlier mark;
(ii) taking unfair advantage of the repute of the earlier mark;
(iii) inflicting detriment on the distinctive character of the earlier mark;
(iv) inflicting detriment on the repute of the earlier mark.[8]

In explaining the implications of these acts, this chapter will explore the nature of the protection enjoyed by a trade mark proprietor, both by virtue of its distinctive character and through the reputation which his trade mark has earned through use, where the unauthorized use of which he complains is a use in relation to goods or services which are entirely different to those for which he has registered his mark.

11.11

(c) Comparison of trade marks

For the purpose of comparing trade marks in order to ascertain whether they are identical, similar or dissimilar, the European Court of Justice (ECJ) has ruled that it is necessary to make a

11.12

> global appreciation of the visual, aural or conceptual similarity of the marks in question, bearing in mind, in particular, their distinctive and dominant components.[9]

It is assumed that the same 'global appreciation' approach to the comparison of trade marks is to be employed in the comparison of trade marks for the purpose of establishing their similarity or otherwise in the case of infringement through the taking of unfair advantage of or the infliction of detriment upon the trade mark of another.[10]

11.13

---

[5] Council Regulation 40/94, art 9(1)(c).
[6] Council Directive 89/104, art 4(4)(a).
[7] Council Regulation 40/94, art 8(5).
[8] *Hollywood SAS v Souza Cruz SA*, Case R 283/1999–3 [2002] ETMR 705.
[9] *Sabèl BV v Puma AG, Rudolf Dassler Sport*, Case C-251/95 [1998] ETMR 1, para 23, discussed in Chapter 10, paras 10.23–10.33.
[10] See Andrew Griffiths, 'The Impact of the Global Appreciation on the Boundaries of Trade Mark Protection' [2001] IPQ 326; *Premier Brands UK Ltd v Typhoon Europe Ltd* [2000] ETMR 1071 (HC).

(2) A note on concepts and terminology

11.14 Before considering the four types of wrongful act described under the previous heading and the law which relates to them, it is important to clarify some points relating to terminology and the conceptual devices which lawyers employ for the analysis of those acts. In particular, careful thought should be given to the use of the terms 'dilution', 'blurring' and 'tarnishment'. These words have already begun to enter the vocabulary of the Office for Harmonisation in the Internal Market (OHIM)[11] and some European national jurisdictions[12] as well as the writings of commentators.[13] Their meaning, which is not universally understood, is discussed in the next section. It is also necessary to understand what is meant by the 'distinctive character' of a trade mark, which is also discussed below (see paras 11.23–11.24).

(a) 'Dilution', 'blurring' and 'tarnishment'

11.15 Sometimes it is said that damage to a trade mark's 'distinctive character' is the result of 'blurring' in that its ability to distinguish the goods or services for which it was registered has been impaired by its coexistence with other marks. It is also sometimes said that damage to a trade mark's 'reputation' is the product of 'dilution' or 'tarnishment'. These metaphors, in the form in which they are generally used today, originate largely from the United States[14] and should be used only with the greatest caution in a context other than that of United States law. Two of the three concepts—'dilution' and 'tarnishment'—are found in the vocabulary of the United States legislation itself, in the context of the protection of famous marks. They are discussed further in Chapter 12.[15]

11.16 If care is not taken in defining one's terms or at least in placing them within a clearly recognizable legal context, what one means by 'dilution', in particular, may be misunderstood. There is also a danger that, as these terms become more widely interpreted by Federal and State courts in the United States, glosses and explanations of them which have a binding and statutory significance in the United States will be unthinkingly adopted into the legal analysis of those very many countries whose legislation does not contain those terms, with the danger of confused thinking, poor analysis and resulting legal uncertainty.

---

[11] See eg *Hollywood SAS v Souza Cruz SA*, Case R 283/1999-3 [2002] ETMR 705.

[12] See eg *Premier Brands UK Ltd v Typhoon Europe Ltd* [2000] ETMR 1071 (HC).

[13] eg Hazel Carty, 'Registered Trade Marks and Permissible Comparative Advertising' [2002] EIPR 294, 297–9 uses 'dilution' as a convenient shorthand term for relief against any use of the same or a similar mark for dissimilar goods or services.

[14] Although the word 'verwässert' ('watered down') was used in *Odol*, 25 *Juristische Wochenschrift* 502, XXV *Markenschutz und Wettbewerb* 265, as long ago as 1925 (Landsgericht, Elberfeld).

[15] See in particular para 12.13.

A. Introduction

Within the context of the protection accorded to famous trade marks, 'dilution' has been defined quite broadly under United States trade mark law since 1995 as

> the lessening of the capacity of a famous mark to identify and distinguish goods or services, regardless of the presence or absence of (1) competition between the owner of the famous mark and other parties, or (2) likelihood of confusion, mistake, or deception.[16]

11.17

This definition may be contrasted with the 'classic' explanation of dilution in American jurisprudence by Frank Schechter and his followers as an event which occurs when

> an awareness that a particular mark signifies a 'single thing coming from a single source' becomes instead an unmistaken, correct awareness that the mark signifies various things from various sources.[17]

11.18

The significance of that awareness is that it is the link which joins the trade mark to the consumer and thus vests that trade mark with 'selling power':

> The value of the modern trademark lies in its selling power . . . [T]his selling power depends . . . upon its own uniqueness and singularity . . . [and] such uniqueness or singularity is vitiated or impaired by its use upon . . . non-related goods.[18]

11.19

It is plain, from a consideration of Schechter's 1927 explanation of dilution together with the modern statutory version, that the former addresses what appears to be a sort of detriment to a truly distinctive trade mark's distinctive character, without regard to its fame, while the modern statutory version addresses the protection of famous marks.

11.20

Post-1995 United States Federal dilution may be effectively divided into two subsets: 'tarnishment' and 'blurring'. Tarnishment is broadly equivalent to acts which are detrimental to another's trade mark ('injury to business reputation'[19]), the protection of which under European law is discussed later in this chapter.[20]

11.21

---

[16] 'Dilution' was introduced into US Federal law via the Federal Trademark Dilution Act 1995; see now 15 USC, s 1127. A convenient review of earlier State dilution law can be found in Tony Martino, *Trademark Dilution* (1996).

[17] Beverly Pattishall, 'Dawning Acceptance of the Dilution Rationale for Trademark-Trade Identity Protection' (1984) 74 TMR 289, 300.

[18] Frank Schechter, 'The Rational Basis of Trademark Protection' (1927) 40 Harv LR 813, reprinted in (1970) 60 TMR 334, 345.

[19] *Moseley et al, dba Victor's Little Secret v V Secret Catalogue Inc* 537 US 418, 123 Sup Ct 1115 (2003).

[20] For an outstanding conceptual review of the role of tarnishment in United States law, see Robert Nelson, 'Unraveling the Trademark Rope: Tarnishment and its Proper Place in the Laws of Unfair Competition' (2002) 42 IDEA 133–79. Nelson argues that, logically, tarnishment cannot be a form of dilution in its classical sense because it is essentially a sort of implied likelihood of confusion, while dilution is not.

11.22 'Blurring' is a convenient shorthand term for 'the gradual whittling away or dispersion of the identity and hold upon the public mind of the mark or name by its use on non-competing goods'[21] or 'dilution of the distinctive quality of a trademark or trade name'.[22] The protection of trade marks against 'blurring' has been portrayed as an important role for trade mark law, particularly where the trade mark owes its distinctiveness and attractive force to the fact that it has been created especially for that purpose and it is not possible for other traders to stake a morally justifiable claim to be able to use it.[23]

11.22A In *Adidas v Fitnessworld*[24] the Advocate General observed that the concept of detriment to the distinctive character of a trade mark reflects what is generally referred to as dilution,[25] while the concept of detriment to the repute of a trade mark, often referred to as degradation or tarnishment of the mark describes the situation where the goods for which the infringing sign is used appeal to the public's senses in such a way that the trade mark's power of attraction is affected.[26] To this extent, at least, it appears that the ECJ is willing to employ the terminology of United States law.

(b) 'Distinctive character'

11.23 The term 'distinctive character' is found in the provisions of Directive 89/104 and the CTM Regulation which are cited above (see para 11.08). In the context of trade mark registration, the meaning of 'distinctive character' is discussed at length in Chapter 4. Can it be assumed that, in the context of protecting a trade mark which enjoys a reputation, the same meaning of 'distinctive character' applies?

11.24 The wording of neither Directive 89/104 nor the CTM Regulation suggests that the term 'distinctive character' should be treated differently in different contexts, but some commentators have wondered whether, in the case of a mark which is already known, protection of their reputation should depend upon that mark being *inherently* distinctive rather than distinctive only in result of the acquisition of distinctive character through use. This is a typically legalistic question which, while it may trouble trade mark theorists, is unlikely to occur to relevant consumers. One should be accordingly entitled to assume that *how* a trade mark came to acquire distinctive character is not an avenue of investigation which a court or trade

---

[21] Frank Schechter, 'The Rational Basis of Trademark Protection' (1927) 40 Harv LR 813, 827.
[22] *Moseley et al, dba Victor's Little Secret v V Secret Catalogue Inc* 537 US 418, 123 Sup Ct 1115 (2003).
[23] See Frank Schechter, 'Fog and Fiction in Trade-mark Protection' (1936) 36 Colum L Rev 60, 65.
[24] *Adidas-Salomon AG and Adidas Benelux BV v Fitnessworld Trading Ltd*, Case C-408/01, Opinion of 10 July 2003 (unreported) (ECJ).
[25] ibid, para 37.
[26] ibid, para 38.

A. Introduction

mark registry should ever need to pursue when deciding whether to protect that distinctive character.

(c) 'Reputation' and 'repute'

11.25 Article 5(2) of Directive 89/104 and article 9(1)(c) differentiate 'reputation' from 'repute' when they provide that

> ... the proprietor shall be entitled to prevent all third parties not having his consent from using in the course of trade any sign which is identical with, or similar to, the trade mark in relation to goods or services which are not similar to those for which the trade mark is registered, where the latter has a *reputation* in the Member State and where use of that sign without due cause takes unfair advantage of, or is detrimental to, the distinctive character or the *repute* of the trade mark [emphasis added].

11.26 This is confusing, since in colloquial English the words 'reputation' and 'repute' are often used as synonyms. On this terminological nicety, which is not found in other language versions of the same provisions,[27] an OHIM Board of Appeal had this to say:

> ... the fact that a trade mark has a reputation means that it is known by a significant part of the relevant public. On the other hand, a trade mark's reputation in the sense of recognition of the sign does not decide in advance the particular significance this reputation may have, in the sense of 'repute' or image, to which registration of the contested trade mark would be detrimental.[28]

11.27 In other words, the fact that consumers of chewing gum know of the existence of HOLLYWOOD chewing gum testifies to its *reputation*. The fact that they associate HOLLYWOOD chewing gum with a healthy lifestyle testifies to its *repute*.

11.28 It is noteworthy that the Board of Appeal, having explained the difference between 'reputation' and 'repute', then jettisoned the word 'repute' in favour of the non-statutory term 'image'.

(d) 'Unfair advantage'

11.29 The expression 'unfair advantage', which does not appear to have caused the courts any great difficulty to interpret, is considered below in the light of the German unfair competition ruling in *Dimple*.[29] The phrase 'unfair advantage' chimes in well with the French concept of 'parasitic trading', a term which is also drawn from that country's unfair competition law.[30]

---

[27] In the French version eg the word 'renomée' is used to render both 'reputation' and 'repute'.
[28] *Hollywood SAS v Souza Cruz SA*, Case R 283/1999-3 [2002] ETMR 705, para 61.
[29] See paras 11.60–11.64 below.
[30] *Yves Saint Laurent Parfums SA v Institut National des Appellations d'Origine* [1994] ECC 385 (use of miniature Champagne bottle and 'cork' stopper for YSL perfume held to be a form of 'parasitic trading' even though it would probably not damage the renown of the word Champagne).

Chapter 11: Reputation, Unfair Advantage and Detriment

B. Reputation

(1) What is a 'reputation' and when does a trade mark have one?

11.30 Although the word 'reputation' is constantly used by trade mark lawyers, brand managers, marketing consultants and even consumers, it is not found in TRIPs or in the Paris Convention on the Protection of Industrial Property. This omission is not surprising. Although the word 'reputation' is used in the trade mark legislation of many countries, including all those jurisdictions which have adopted the European model based on Directive 89/104, it is a word which takes on different meanings in accordance with its users. In relation to a trade mark, 'reputation' may mean the consequence of the fact that (i) consumers know that a trade mark is in use, (ii) competitors know that a trade mark is in use or (iii) consumers place a particular value on the trade mark in order to make or avoid making repeat purchases. Reputations may be made and lost, or even transferred from one commodity to another.

11.31 It is clear from this that a trade mark cannot acquire a reputation without being used in some way. This being so, those provisions of the law which protect a trade mark against unfair exploitation or detrimental activities on the part of competitors will not be able to come to assist a trade mark which, being unused, has no reputation.

11.32 The reputation of a trade mark may extend in different directions. It may be 'deep' in the sense that it penetrates a particular market to a very great extent (all gum-chewers will have heard of WRIGLEYS and all car-owners will know of FORD even if they have never driven one), or it may be 'wide' in the sense that it does not penetrate a specific market because it covers many separate markets (MARKS & SPENCER and DISNEY are extremely well known but are not tied to any particular product). The direction(s) in which a trade mark's reputation travels will affect the extent to which it can be protected against identical or similar trade marks. For example, while the WRIGLEYS trade mark is known for chewing gum, few people would connect it with the chewing gum manufacturer if they saw the same word in use on garden furniture, surgical appliances or knitting patterns. This is the basis on which trade marks like POLO can achieve extensive reputations in quite unrelated spheres of activity (motor vehicles, clothing and confectionery) in the hands of three unrelated proprietors. The reputation in MARKS & SPENCER would however be likely to extend beyond products sold by that chain of stores, to cover any goods or services which consumers would reasonably but incorrectly assume that chain dealt in.

(a) 'Reputation' in European law

11.33 The ECJ has considered the meaning of the term 'reputation' in *General Motors v Yplon*, a reference to the attempt of the owner of the trade mark CHEVY for motor

B. Reputation

vehicles to prevent its use on cleaning and polishing products. Since 'reputation' must be shown for the purpose of protecting a trade mark, the Court chose to explain 'reputation' by describing the protection which it conferred. Accordingly it ruled:

> ... in order to enjoy protection extending to non-similar products or services, a registered trade mark must be known by a significant part of the public concerned by *the products or services which it covers* [emphasis added].[31]

An unkind critic would observe that this is scarcely anything other than a statement of the blindingly obvious, but that comment would miss the significance of this ruling: it frees the concept of 'reputation' from the concepts of 'fame' or 'notoriety' with which it is so frequently confused. COCA-COLA has a reputation because it is famous, but many trade marks enjoy a very substantial reputation despite their manifest lack of fame. Trade marks such as VANDOREN (clarinet reeds), KNOCKANDO (malt whiskey) and EUTHYMOL (dentifrices) are not famous in the 'Coca-Cola' sense but, in the markets in which they are used, they are both known and well respected by what the ECJ calls the 'public concerned'. 11.34

The Court wisely did not reflect on how great a proportion of 'the public concerned' constitutes a 'significant' part. 'Significant' can mean 'big' or it can mean 'having some significance'; for legal purposes an absence of significance is also significant. The ECJ will not be easily drawn on this issue and will certainly not name a percentage of the relevant public as being the bright line beyond which significance is achieved.[32] 11.35

(b) Reputation in relation to goods and services

A trade mark's reputation does not exist in a vacuum: it attaches to goods or services on which it is used and cannot be expected as a matter of course to extend beyond them—though it may do so. Thus the reputation which the trade mark MERCEDES enjoyed in motor cars did not also encompass items of clothing.[33] Nor could the reputation of the word SEPHORA in relation to the retail sale of perfumes and cosmetics be said to cover the 'evaluation, creation, purchasing of beauty and perfumery stores'.[34] 11.36

---

[31] *General Motors Corporation v Yplon SA*, Case C-375/97 [1999] ETMR 950, para 31.
[32] In *Lloyd Schuhfabrik Meyer & Co GmbH v Klijsen Handel BV*, Case V-342/97 [1999] ETMR 690, para 24 the ECJ reflected this attitude in a slightly different context when, affirming its earlier ruling in *Windsurfing Chiemsee Produktions- und Vertriebs GmbH v Boots- und Segelzubehör Walter Huber and Franz Attenberger*, Joined Cases C-108 and 109/97 [1999] ETMR 585 it said: 'It is not possible to state in general terms, for example, by referring to given percentages relating to the degree of recognition attained by the mark within the relevant sector of the public, when a mark has a strong distinctive character'.
[33] *DaimlerChrysler AG v Alavi* [2001] ETMR 1069 (HC).
[34] *Inter Service Srl's application; opposition of Sephora SA*, Case 278/2000, 23 February 2003 (unreported) (OHIM Opposition Division).

(2) Does 'reputation' only mean that a trade mark be 'known'?

11.37 This book has quoted the English version of article 5(2) of Directive 89/104, which uses the word 'reputation'. English is however just one of the eleven official languages of the EU and the English text of Directives is of no greater authority than any of the others. Other versions of the Directive, including the French, German, Italian and Spanish—the four other 'official' languages of the CTM—protect marks which are 'known' or 'well known' rather than marks having a 'reputation'. What does this teach us about the meaning of the concept of 'reputation'?

11.38 This issue was considered by the ECJ, which described it as a 'nuance which does not entail any great contradiction'.[35] The word 'reputation', together with its foreign allies, suggests only that there is a 'knowledge threshold requirement' which a trade mark must meet before it is entitled to protection. The ECJ has wisely declined to fix that threshold, this being a job which falls within the province of national trial courts.

11.39 Another issue which remains open is whether 'reputation' is a bare knowledge requirement or whether 'reputation' must be *in relation to* something: for example, to goods or services, to quality or price, to geographical origin or some other factor. This issue may be devoid of almost any practical consequence, since it is hard to conceive of a situation in which a trade mark proprietor seeks to protect, against infringement or too-close-for-comfort registration, a trade mark which has 'reputation' in a vacuum. One such case may arise where a trade mark proprietor has registered the ZAPPO trade mark for, say, confectionery products; he does not then make or sell any such products but extensively promotes their forthcoming arrival with teaser advertisements ('ZAPPO is coming!'; 'ZAPPO will change your life'; 'ZAPPO—the ultimate cool' and so on). No member of the confectionery-eating classes even knows what ZAPPO is because the advertisements have coyly concealed the product. The entire nation is agog to discover what ZAPPO is. The proprietor then goes round to existing confectionery companies and offers to sell his ready-made brand to the highest bidder. Before he can do so, another company launches ZAPPOX cream for athlete's foot, instantly and perhaps irretrievably damaging ZAPPO's phantom reputation. However, even on these unusual facts it would appear that TRIPs, Directive 89/104 and the CTM Regulation formulations of protection relating to reputation (described at paras 11.02–11.03 above), would give ZAPPO's owner adequate protection.

---

[35] *General Motors Corporation v Yplon SA*, Case C-375/97 [1999] ETMR 950, para 22.

B. Reputation

(3) 'Distinctive character' and 'repute'

From the use of the separate terms 'distinctive character' and 'repute' in the European law provisions mentioned above, it is apparent that there are two separate types of damage which this head of infringement can inflict: (i) damage to a mark's distinctive character; and (ii) damage to its repute. While the term 'repute' has been described above as a trade mark's 'image',[36] 'distinctive character' lacks a single workable definition, so the question must be asked: what does that term mean?

11.40

We can say that the distinctive character of a trade mark is not considered in the abstract but only in relation to the goods or services for which its owner has registered it.[37] Thus CAMEL possesses a high degree of distinctive character for cigarettes but a low level of distinctive character for camels, dromedaries and their relevant parts and accessories.

11.41

What then is the relationship between 'distinctive character' and 'repute'? This point was considered in the English TY.PHOO/TYPHOON case, in which the judge observed:

11.42

> Depending on the width of meaning one gives to the word reputation, the differentness of a particular brand is either part of the repute of the mark or it is part of the distinctive character of the mark: either way it appears to me to be expressly within what is contemplated as being within the ambit of the intended protection of [the law]....[38]

On this analysis, the scope of protection accorded by the law to a trade mark's 'differentness' is a bit like the volume of an egg. The concepts of a mark's 'distinctive character' and its 'repute' are a bit like the egg yolk and the egg white in that, if the scope of one is bigger, then the scope of the other must be correspondingly smaller but it does not really matter (unless you are making meringue) since the scope of protection remains constant. This analogy does not however assist greatly in understanding the role played by the words 'distinctive character'.

11.43

(4) Does strong 'distinctive character' or 'repute' mean better protection?

According to the ECJ in *General Motors v Yplon*,[39] the stronger a mark's distinctive character and reputation, the easier it will be for its owner to establish detriment. This is a contentious position which at least one OHIM Board of Appeal

11.44

---

[36] See paras 11.25–11.28 above.
[37] *Ferrero oHG mbH v Annie Cornelia Beekenkamp*, Case R 214/2000–4, 4 December 2002 (unreported).
[38] *Premier Brands UK Ltd v Typhoon Europe Ltd* [2000] ETMR 1071 (HC).
[39] *General Motors Corp v Yplon SA*, Case C-375/97 [1999] ETMR 950 (ECJ), para 30; see also *Premier Brands UK Ltd v Typhoon Europe Ltd* (n 38 above).

has implicitly rejected when it suggested that, the more famous a trade mark is, the less likely people will be to mispronounce it in a manner which is phonetically similar to the trade mark of another.[40]

11.45 This discussion presupposes that the trade mark's distinctive character and repute repose within the field of commercial activity for which the trade mark is best known (as indeed is usually the case in infringement and opposition litigation). It sometimes happens, though, that a trade mark owner has a trade mark which is strongly distinctive and enjoys an extensive reputation in one field of activity but which is far less so in another. What happens in a case such as this?

11.46 This question was considered in an English case in which the owner of national and Community registrations for MERCEDES and MERCEDES-BENZ both for cars and for clothes brought infringement proceedings against the defendant, who sold Merc brand clothes from his Merc shop.[41] MERC(EDES) was extremely well known for cars, but its use on clothing was confined to 'T-shirt use', putting the trade mark on to clothes which were given away in order to advertise the claimant's cars. The court took the view, having first dismissed the claim relating to the clothing registration (ie similar mark, same goods), that the goodwill in the far better-known registration in respect of cars did not spill over into the market for clothing. The court did however leave open the possibility that it might.[42] The claim relating to infringement of the car registration was also rejected: it was not enough for the trade mark owner to consider the alleged infringer's use of his trade mark to be objectionable: he must also be able to point to some connection between his own use of a trade mark, with which the public was familiar, and any allegedly disparaging use which the defendant had made of it. If no mud from the allegedly disparaging use actually sticks to the trade mark, then that use is not to its detriment. A similar position was taken in the United States in the *VICTORIA'S SECRET* case,[43] where evidence that a colonel was offended by the defendant's use of a trade mark similar to that of the claimant was insufficient to support an action for dilution: it had also to be shown that the colonel thought less highly of the claimant's trade mark after the alleged dilution than he did before.

---

[40] *Ferrero oHG mbH v Jordi Tarrida Llopart*, Case R 186/2001–1 [2003] ETMR 188, para 20 (MON CHÉRI unlikely to be pronounced MONTXERI).

[41] *DaimlerChrysler AG v Alavi* [2001] ETMR 1069 (HC).

[42] 'There is no rule that T-shirt use of a mark primarily used in relation to some other kind of goods altogether, say computers, does not confer on the user a goodwill in relation to T-shirts. It is a question of fact in every case, but one should not blindly accept that this kind of advertising use necessarily gives rise to a protected goodwill in respect of the substrate which carries the advertisement' (ibid, para 20).

[43] *Moseley et al, dba Victor's Little Secret v V Secret Catalogue Inc* 537 US 418, 123 Sup Ct 1115 (2003).

B. Reputation

(5) Proof of 'reputation' and other elements relating to protection of a mark's reputation

Where a trade mark owner seeks to protect the integrity of the reputation of his trade mark, he must show that the trade mark possesses reputation—but proof of reputation, while a *necessary* condition of success, is by no means a *sufficient* condition.[44] The trade mark owner must also demonstrate successfully that, by means of its adverse registration or use of a trade mark, the other party is taking unfair advantage of his mark or is doing something which is detrimental to it. If the specifics of his case are not spelled out, he will fail in court, however great his reputation, since no court or tribunal will regard his case as being so self-evident that he does not have to argue it. If this were otherwise, any trade mark owner who proved reputation in his mark would be effectively entitled to blanket protection against the use of any similar mark for any goods or services whatsoever.[45] This remains the case even where 96.8 per cent of relevant consumers know the trade mark and over 90 per cent of them can correctly describe the product.[46]

11.47

(a) The burden of proof

Once the proprietor of an earlier trade mark is put to proof that an adverse application or use of another's mark takes unfair advantage of his trade mark or is detrimental to it, great care should be taken in determining the evidential standard which this proof must satisfy. If the level is too high, then proprietors will not be able to enjoy the benefit of the extended protection which is given to marks which have established a reputation; if however the level is too low, then the scope for the registration and use of trade marks by others will be unreasonably restricted.[47] How high should the civil burden of proof be in such cases?

11.48

In countries such as the UK and Ireland, the proprietor's case need only be made out on the 'balance of probabilities'. This being so, it is probably easier for the proprietor to oppose the registration of another's application on the ground of detriment than for him to establish detriment once the other party's mark is in actual use. If that use has not yet brought about any specific and identifiable damage to which the proprietor can point, the defendant in infringement proceedings will ask whether conjecture as to the likelihood of damage to the mark's reputation is

11.49

---

[44] In *Bravo Industry of Coffees SA (also trading as Bravo SA) v Fiat Auto SpA* [1997] ETMR 167 the Protodikeio (Athens) concluded that proof of reputation was a sufficient condition for success where the mark was 'invented for use upon a specific product' (such as COCA-COLA) but merely a necessary condition where it was not. It is however likely that this approach was intended only on an application for interim relief.
[45] *DUPLO/DUPLO*, Case R 802/1999–1, 5 June 2000 (unreported) (OHIM Board of Appeal).
[46] *Ferrero oHG mbH v Annie Cornelia Beekenkamp*, Case R 214/2000–4, 4 December 2002 (unreported).
[47] *Mitutoyo Corporation's application* [1999] ETMR 39 (Court of Patent Appeals, Sweden).

Chapter 11: Reputation, Unfair Advantage and Detriment

an adequate substitute for it. In the case where unfair advantage is alleged, the same considerations will apply where the unfair advantage is unrelated to the nature of the conduct leading to that advantage but, where the unfair advantage is based on identifiably wrongful conduct, it may be easier to establish a case where the trade mark owner can point to the damning nature of the defendant's activities.

(b) Need for actual damage or merely that a probability of damage be proved?

11.50   In European terms, the answer to this question depends on whether it is the *registration* or the *use* of another's sign to which the trade mark proprietor objects. In the case of registration, the trade mark owner need only demonstrate a 'simple probability'[48] that the sign would take unfair advantage of his earlier mark or be detrimental to it.[49] In the case of use, it appears that he must prove actual unfair advantage or detriment.[50]

(6) What is the difference between reputation and goodwill?

11.51   The existence of 'reputation' is the consequence of the fact that consumers know that a trade mark is being used somewhere in the world. In contrast 'goodwill' is the consequence that, because consumers in a particular jurisdiction know that a trade mark is used (in other words, that it has a reputation), they base their decision to purchase goods or services to which that trade mark is attached on the fact that they are attracted to those goods or services by virtue of the positive effect of that reputation. In this sense, goodwill would appear to be related to the concept of 'repute', the main difference being that a trade mark's 'repute' is its image in the eyes of consumers while the 'goodwill' is the economic consequence of the trade mark having that image.

C. Unfair advantage and detriment

(1) When is an unfair advantage or detrimental use 'without due cause'?

11.52   A use of another's trade mark which takes unfair advantage of it or inflicts detriment upon it must, if that use is to be an infringement of that trade mark, be 'without due cause'. What does this mean?

11.53   In the pre-harmonization *Lucas Bols* case the Benelux Court had to consider a very similar phrase, 'without justifiable reason'.[51] This phrase required consideration of

---

[48] *Hollywood SAS v Souza Cruz SA*, Case R 283/1999–3 [2002] ETMR 705, para 88.
[49] Council Directive 89/104, art 4(4)(a); Council Regulation 40/94, art 8(5).
[50] Council Directive 89/104, art 5(2); Council Regulation 40/94, art 9(1)(c).
[51] *Lucas Bols v Colgate-Palmolive* (1976) 7 IIC 420 (CLAERYN/KLAREIN).

C. Unfair advantage and detriment

what sort of reason was itself justifiable. The Court identified two situations in which use of another's mark was justifiable: first, where

> ... the user ... is under such a compulsion to use this very mark that he cannot honestly be asked to refrain from doing so regardless of the damage the owner of the mark would suffer from such use

and also where

> the user is entitled to the use of the mark in his own right and does not have to yield this right to that of the owner of the mark . . .[52]

11.54 This bifurcated approach which, the Benelux Court reminded us, ultimately depends on the trial judge's assessment of the specific facts of the case before him, has received the approval of the English High Court[53] subject to one qualification: that it is difficult to conceive of a situation in which an unauthorized user of a trade mark succeeds in taking unfair advantage of that trade mark other than 'without due cause' (though causing detriment to another's mark other than 'without due cause' is a scenario which it is altogether easier to imagine). Literally, the addition of the words 'without due cause' contemplates a situation where the defendant gains an advantage from the use of the mark which, were it not for the fact that he has a due cause for this use, would be unfair. Those words also give a court a degree of flexibility in a situation in which the allegedly infringing act confers some advantage or inflicts some detriment but where the justice of the case nonetheless leads the court to the conclusion that the defendant should not be liable.

11.55 An OHIM Board of Appeal, adopting the Benelux ruling in *Lucas Bols* on the meaning of 'due cause' as a general principle,[54] has held that the fact that an otherwise objectionable registration (and, by implication, infringing act) was subsequently allowed elsewhere in the EU does not constitute 'due cause' for what would otherwise be the infliction of a detriment or the securing of an unfair advantage.[55]

11.56 A Scottish court has ruled that the use of a trade mark, by an applicant for registration, does not become use 'without due cause' by virtue of the fact that the owner of another trade mark has commenced opposition proceedings against that application.[56]

---

[52] ibid, 425. A similar position was taken in *Hollywood SAS v Souza Cruz SA*, Case R 283/1999–3 [2002] ETMR 705.
[53] *Premier Brands UK Ltd v Typhoon Europe Ltd* [2000] ETMR 1071, 1098 (HC).
[54] *Hollywood SAS v Souza Cruz SA*, Case R 283/1999–3 [2002] ETMR 705, para 101.
[55] ibid, para 102.
[56] *Pebble Beach Company v Lombard Brands Ltd* [2003] ETMR 252 (Court of Session).

11.57 Where a toymaker launched construction toy puzzles made of interlocking wooden blocks, its choice of the trade mark INTEL-PLAY was considered by the High Court to infringe Intel Corp's INTEL trade mark, which was registered for merchandising products such as toys and computer products.[57] The fact that the defendant's toys were educational and that 'intel' was found at the beginning of words such as 'intelligent' and 'intellect' did not prevent the court concluding that the defendant had taken unfair advantage of the claimant's trade mark.

(2) What is an 'unfair advantage' relating to a trade mark's 'distinctive character'?

11.58 The OHIM Board of Appeal in *Hollywood*[58] identified four separate situations in which a trade mark was protected against the registration or use of the same or a similar mark on completely different goods or services than those for which it was registered.[59] The first of these was that of taking unfair advantage of a trade mark's distinctive character. Unlike the other three, which are discussed under the next three headings, the Board gave no example of this wrong. Although it should not be assumed that the failure to give an example was a consequence of there being no such thing as 'taking unfair advantage of a trade mark's distinctive character', it is extremely difficult to think of a factual situation in which such an event can occur. It may be for this reason that the Advocate General in *Adidas v Fitnessworld* was unable to draw a distinction between the two types of unfair advantage.[60] Possible instances of 'taking unfair advantage of a trade mark's distinctive character' might include the following scenarios:

(i) Where the trade mark has a *highly* distinctive character, by making gratuitous reference to it in one's advertising or promotional materials in order to attract the attention of consumers and then redirect it to one's own products without either damaging that mark or taking advantage of its repute. This could be done, for example, by running an advertisement in a motor enthusiasts' magazine consisting of a banner featuring in large print the message 'Free CHANEL No. 5 perfume for life!', followed by smaller print which reads 'We can't offer you anything as exciting as that, but use LUBE-O-SLICK engine oil and your car will feel just great'. The impact would not be as great if a message such as 'Free HONDA auto parts for life!' was used because the CHANEL trade mark, in relation to automobile products and services, has a greater degree of distinctive character than the HONDA trade mark and therefore stands out more.

---

[57] *Intel Corp v Sihra*, 24 January 2003 (unreported) (HC).
[58] *Hollywood SAS v Souza Cruz SA*, Case R 283/1999–3 [2002] ETMR 705.
[59] See paras 11.02–11.13 above.
[60] *Adidas-Salomon AG and Adidas Benelux BV v Fitnessworld Trading Ltd*, Case C-408/01, Opinion of 10 July 2003 (unreported) (ECJ), para 39.

C. Unfair advantage and detriment

(ii) Where the trade mark has a *low* degree of distinctive character in the eyes of the public despite possessing a substantial reputation, by using it in a generic sense in one's advertising. This could be achieved, for example, by using the trade mark HOOVER for the slogan: 'Do you suffer vacuum fatigue? Feeling all hoovered out? Try our new SUCKO vacuum cleaning system and freshen up your home'. Here the insinuation is that HOOVER is a tired-out, familiar old mark which is held out in contrast with the bright, fresh, exciting SUCKO product.

There may be some justification for the criticism that these examples are somewhat contrived and not entirely convincing. If, then, taking unfair advantage of another trade mark's distinctive character effectively does not happen, why would the Directive and the Regulation take the trouble to legislate that an act which takes unfair advantage of a trade mark's distinctive character is an infringement? One answer to this question is quite possibly that, in theoretical natural law terms, if (i) a trade mark's distinctive character is deserving of protection and if (ii) the taking of unfair advantage is a reprehensible act, then in principle the unfair advantage of a trade mark's distinctive character is an act which is inherently wrong and should fall within the scope of the trade mark right whether it can actually happen or not. But this answer is arguably as contrived as the scenarios suggested above. **11.59**

(3) What is an 'unfair advantage' relating to a trade mark's 'repute'? The *Dimple* case

Dimple, a German pre-harmonization decision under the German law of unfair competition, has greatly influenced trade mark thinking. In *Dimple* the Court explained the concept of 'unfair advantage' as follows: **11.60**

> . . . it constitutes an act of unfair competition to associate the quality of one's goods or services with that of prestigious competitive products for the purpose of exploiting the good reputation of a competitor's goods or services in order to enhance one's promotional efforts.[61]

This statement, subsequently endorsed by an English court,[62] and fortified by the Advocate General's Opinion in *Adidas v Fitnessworld*,[63] would seem to be a clear and incontrovertible statement of activities which fall within the category of acts conferring an 'unfair advantage'. **11.61**

In establishing that a trade mark applicant or alleged infringer has taken unfair advantage of his mark, the proprietor must go through a two-stage process. First he **11.62**

---

[61] *DIMPLE* (1985) 17 GRUR 529 (Bundesgerichtshof).
[62] *Premier Brands UK Ltd v Typhoon Europe Ltd* [2000] ETMR 1071, 1092 (HC).
[63] *Adidas-Salomon AG and Adidas Benelux BV v Fitnessworld Trading Ltd*, Case C-408/01, Opinion of 10 July 2003 (unreported) (ECJ), para 39.

must establish that the other party has obtained an advantage; next he must demonstrate that it is an advantage which is unfair. Not every appropriation of another's trade mark will confer any advantage. This may be because of the nature of the product for which the trade mark enjoys a reputation: trade marks such as AMPLEX (for products to mask the effects of halitosis) and ANUSOL (ointment to alleviate haemorrhoids) are unlikely to confer any benefits upon manufacturers of leisure wear, cosmetics or confectionery. The appropriation of another's trade mark may also bring no advantage on account of the nature of the product manufactured by the third party and the cultural distance between that product and the trade mark: thus the supplier of barbed-wire products may be expected to derive little obvious market benefit from the adoption of BARBIE as its trade mark.[64] The need to demonstrate that an advantage has been, or can be expected to be, secured from the use of another's mark should not be taken for granted.

11.63 That this is so may be seen from a Scottish case[65] in which the owner of a CTM registration of the words PEBBLE BEACH for goods and services in various classes, particularly those relating to the game of golf and golf resorts, sought interim injunctive relief against a Scottish company which sought to register as a trade mark and use the words PEBBLE BEACH for a Speyside malt whisky. The Court did not consider it self-evident that any association with golf or golf resorts should confer an advantage on a seller of whisky: if any connection between golf and whisky existed, it was 'tenuous and general'. Further, while accepting that the trade mark owner had a reputation in the registered mark, the court nonetheless formed the view that the owner did not even establish a *prima facie* case that any advantage had been gained by the defendant through the repute of the PEBBLE BEACH trade mark. The whisky label was not replete with golf-related illustrations and bore no material which might suggest any connection with the proprietor's golf resorts. If an advantage had been obtained, the court concluded, such advantage was *de minimis* and would not justify the award of injunctive relief.

11.64 The same case supports the proposition that not every advantage is an unfair advantage. The choice by the defendant of the words PEBBLE BEACH was supported by reasoning which was unrelated to the existence of the proprietor's trade mark: the reference to 'pebble' followed the use of the term 'pebble smooth' as a means of describing Speyside malt whisky and the word 'beach' alluded to the pebbles in Spey Bay forming the largest shingle bar in Scotland. Even if this reasoning had conferred an advantage on the whisky company, this advantage was not 'unfair'. Similar reasoning was employed in another pre-Directive German unfair compe-

---

[64] These points were recognized by the Bundesgerichtshof in *DIMPLE* (1985) 17 GRUR 529, when it considered that a reputation attached to whisky could be 'transferred' to men's cosmetics, but not to detergents.
[65] *Pebble Beach Company v Lombard Brands Ltd* [2003] ETMR 252 (Court of Session).

C. Unfair advantage and detriment

tition case in which the use of the word CAMEL by a travel agent who marketed Turkish holidays to travel agents was not regarded as the taking of an unfair advantage of the well-known CAMEL trade mark for cigarettes:[66] the exotic symbolism of the camel provided sufficient justification for his use.

(4) What is 'detrimental' to a trade mark's 'distinctive character'?

11.65 In a German pre-harmonization decision dating back to 1959, the Court explained the concept of 'detriment' as follows:

> [T]he owner of . . . a distinctive mark has a legitimate interest in continuing to maintain the position of exclusivity he acquired through large expenditures of time and money and that everything which could impair the originality and distinctive character of his distinctive mark, as well as the advertising effectiveness derived from its uniqueness, is to be avoided . . . Its basic purpose is not to prevent any form of confusion but to protect an acquired asset against impairment.[67]

11.66 This statement, which has since been endorsed by an English court[68] not only describes the nature of the detriment which the law seeks to avoid but emphasizes that, even before the harmonization process, it was necessary to contrast those types of infringement that *do* require evidence of confusion with those which *do not*.

11.67 Further consideration of the words 'detriment to distinctive character' was given in the *Mercedes* case[69] (discussed above), where Pumfrey J commented:

> I find the concept . . . somewhat fugitive. The presence of two similar marks where there was only one before seems to me to be detrimental to the distinctive character of the first. I am satisfied that this is not what the words are talking about.[70]

11.68 The learned judge then quoted a passage from Frederick Mostert's book, *Famous and Well-Known Marks*:

> Obviously, the more a trade mark is used on a wide variety of goods becoming saturated in the process, the less the particular mark will call to mind and focus the public's attention on the plaintiff's particular product. If, for example, the TIFFANY mark has become well-known in connection with jewellery, and it is used on a multiplicity of other goods such as chocolates, clothing, a motion picture house, and a restaurant, the likelihood that the TIFFANY mark will still exclusively call to mind the owner's jewellery products becomes increasingly diminished.[71]

---

[66] *Camel Tours* (1988) 19 IIC 695 (Bundesgerichtshof).
[67] *QUICK* (1959) GRUR 182 (Bundesgerichtshof).
[68] *Premier Brands UK Ltd v Typhoon Europe Ltd* [2000] ETMR 1071, 1092 (HC).
[69] *DaimlerChrysler AG v Alavi* [2001] ETMR 1069 (HC).
[70] ibid, 1104.
[71] Frederick Mostert, *Famous and Well-Known Marks* (1997), pp 58–9. The author is a former President of the INTA.

11.69 Whatever the judge was looking for, he did not find it in this approach, concerning which he commented:

> Read literally, this is simply a suggestion that once a mark acquires a reputation one can throw the specification of goods away. Any use of another mark will potentially have this effect if any member of the relevant public becomes aware of the second mark. Here, the point was not pressed, emphasis being placed on the element of detriment to the repute of the mark, and I prefer to come to no conclusion on it. It raises difficult conceptual problems.[72]

11.70 This seems a harsh criticism, since Mostert does not seek to assert that 'distinctive character' exists in a vacuum;[73] nor does he deny that its existence is determined by the specification of goods or services for which a trade mark is registered. In the abstract the word 'polo' may call to mind a variety of things: a Venetian explorer, cars, fashion garments, a style of collar which closely fits the neck, confectionery and ball games pursued respectively on horseback or in the water. That does not mean that, in relation to 'distinctive character', any of the extremely distinctive and well-known POLO trade marks has suffered some dreadful truncation of its vital force.

11.71 Since it is a trade mark's distinctive character which enables consumers to distinguish it from other signs, it is easy to conclude that *any* detriment to a mark's distinctive character *must* relate to the use of a sign which is identical or similar to it, thus eroding the distinctiveness of its character. Thus an OHIM Opposition Division has concluded that, where an application is made to register as a CTM a sign which is 'graphically similar' to an earlier registered trade mark, an improper use—and therefore prejudice the distinctive character of the earlier mark—could be assumed.[74]

11.72 An example of detriment to distinctive character which does *not* turn on the similarity of the parties' respective marks but on the different ethos of their respective products can be found in Intel's action to prevent the registration of the sign INTEL-PLAY for 'interlocking blocks being constructional toy puzzles'. According to the court, damage would be inflicted on the distinctive nature of the INTEL mark for high-quality, high-technology products where a similar mark was registered for such a markedly low technology product.[75] This decision itself raises

---

[72] *DaimlerChrysler AG v Alavi* [2001] ETMR 1069, 1105 (HC).

[73] The notion that 'distinctive character' exists as a commodity in its own right, divorced from the specifications of goods or services to which it is attached, does however appear to lie at the heart of Schechter's rationale for the protection of specifically created famous trade marks against dilution—this rationale does not appear to apply where the trade mark is highly distinctive for one category of goods but descriptive of others: see 'The Rational Basis of Trademark Protection' (1927) 40 Harv LR 813 (*Ringling Bros-Barnum & Bailey Combined Shows, Inc v Utah Division of Travel Development* 170 F 3d 449 (4th Cir 1999) understands Schechter in this way).

[74] *Campomar S.L's application; opposition of Nike International Ltd*, Case 102/1999 [2000] ETMR 50.

[75] *Intel Corp v Sihra*, 24 January 2003 (HC), para 24.

C. Unfair advantage and detriment

questions. Why, for example, did the court choose to consider this a case of detriment to distinctive character rather than detriment to the mark's reputation? And in what sense is there a detriment to the distinctive character of INTEL, there being no suggestion that the INTEL trade mark would function less effectively, in relation to the goods for which it was registered, if INTEL-PLAY was used for construction toys?

(5) What is 'detrimental' to a trade mark's repute?

11.73 If a trade mark's repute is its image, an event is clearly detrimental to that image if it reduces it in the eyes of relevant consumers. For example, Blade Brothers' SAFE-HANDS brand of razor blades may be positively and lucratively associated with safety until a number of prominent celebrities have well-publicized accidents with its products. Detriment to the repute of a trade mark is not synonymous with misconduct on the part of the third party seeking to use it. Thus in *NCDL*[76] the National Canine Defence League, a responsible registered charity, campaigned *against* dog abuse. However, its application to register a word-and-device mark which included the expression TOYS AREN'T US failed on the ground that the association of the opponent toy-seller's mark with dog abuse was detrimental to the repute of its TOYS "я" US word mark.

11.74 A useful seven-point checklist for establishing detriment to a trade mark's repute was drawn up by the hearing officer in a UK Trade Mark Registry case[77] brought by car-maker AUDI against a company manufacturing hearing aids for which it sought registration of the word AUDI-MED. The hearing officer considered the following factors:

(i) *Similarity of the respective marks*: AUDI hearing aids would be more easily associated with AUDI cars than would AUDI-MED hearing aids;
(ii) *Inherent distinctiveness of the earlier mark*: AUDI's distinctiveness was impaired by its similarity to the word 'audio';
(iii) *Extent of reputation enjoyed by the earlier mark*: in this case it was assumed to be high in relation to motor cars;
(iv) *Range of goods or services for which the earlier mark enjoyed its reputation*: the opponent's mark was essentially a 'one-product' mark;
(v) *Uniqueness of the mark in the marketplace*: Audi was the only proprietor in the UK of a trade mark consisting of the separate word AUDI (the question whether this uniqueness was affected by the existence of other marks on the register consisting of the separate word AUDIO was not raised);

---

[76] *National Canine Defence League's application; opposition of Geoffrey Inc*, Case O-213-03, 29 July 2003 (unreported) (Trade Mark Registry).
[77] *Audio Medical Devices Ltd's application; opposition of Audi AG* [1999] ETMR 1010.

(vi) *Are the parties' respective goods or services likely to be sold through the same outlets?* In this case cars and hearing aids are not sold through the same outlets;

(vii) *Would the earlier mark be any less distinctive after the advent of the later mark than it was before?* This proposition, which appears to impose a criterion of 'dilution' in the sense in which that term is defined under United States law, remains relevant to the issue of detriment since it invites quantification of the detriment in terms of dilution of the mark's primary quality—its distinctiveness. In this case, if there were any diminution of AUDI's distinctiveness it would be *de minimis*.

11.75 In listing this set of criteria the hearing officer did not actually pinpoint the specific relevance of each criterion to 'detriment to distinctive character' or 'detriment to a mark's repute', presumably leaving that question to be determined on the facts of each case.

11.76 Another approach to detriment to repute, which like the AUDI case also addresses the trade mechanism by which the reputation of an otherwise unimpeachable trade mark is sullied, may be found in an earlier German decision. In this case the proprietor of the MARS trade mark sued a defendant whose use of the same mark fell within an area of commerce in which the proprietor did not trade:

> If marks whose reputation was established ... only in connection with confectionery, in particular a candy-bar, and which marks have great advertising value for these goods, are used ... for labelling of contraceptive wrappers, then this circumstance alone suffices to impair the advertising power in regard to the original goods and, moreover, to ruin their positive image at least as far as part of the public is concerned ... for, by their very purpose, contraceptives evoke certain associations ... which significant portions of the addressed public would certainly rather do without when it comes to buying candy, and with which reputable candy manufacturers, in particular, rightfully do not wish to be identified because, as a rule, contraceptives do not appear to promote the sale or image of their products.
>
> Impairment ... and the disparagement of its good name cannot be ruled out on the basis that the gag item lacks any reference to the mark's owner, so that there is no way it could be associated with the latter. For, in the case at issue, the claimant's marks, nearly identical in word and appearance are used directly on the defendant's product in the manner of a trade mark, *i.e.* as an identifier ... [T]hey consequently also fulfil the mark's function as an indicator of product origin, *i.e.* they point to the claimant unless and until the consumer notices the inconspicuous, second reference to the origin of the defendant's company on the back of the package. Accordingly, association with the product 'contraceptives as promotional gifts' with the claimant's company appears quite conceivable in this case ...[78]

---

[78] *MARS* (1995) 26 IIC 282, I ZR 79/92. The High Court in *DaimlerChrysler AG v Alavi* [2001] ETMR 1069, 1104 commented that 'This passage is not particularly helpful on what is meant by disparagement when there is no confusion' but it is not clear why the court should have needed any greater help.

C. Unfair advantage and detriment

11.77 This case was one of trade mark infringement, where the nature of the infringing act itself helps to frame the concept of detriment within specific factual parameters. A rather different approach is however taken where the proceedings involve a trade mark proprietor opposing the grant of a trade mark which, if used, may damage his trade mark's ethos. This species of detriment came before an OHIM Board of Appeal in the HOLLYWOOD case,[79] in which the owner of the word mark HOLLYWOOD for chewing gum sought to prevent the applicant registering the same mark for cigarettes, tobacco products, lighters and matches. His argument was that the public associated his trade mark, in relation to chewing gum, with 'youth, health and dynamism', an association which would be destroyed as soon as the same word was attached to a product associated with addiction, health warnings, disease and death. The Opposition Division refused the opposition but the Board of Appeal allowed the chewing gum manufacturer's appeal in part. In its opinion, taking a careful, narrow class-by-class approach, the applicant's mark would be detrimental in respect of cigarettes and tobacco products but not for lighters or matches—products which even wholesome boy scouts presumably use when they can't find two sticks to rub together.

11.78 After finding that there was no similarity between chewing gum and cigarettes, the Board fastened on to the issue of detriment. Any detriment was for the opponent to prove and, since the applicant's cigarettes and other products were not on the market, the opponent's proof was likely to be confined to conjecture as to what the nature of the damage would be, rather than citing instances of actual damage. In this case the Board was content to accept the notion that cigarettes as a class of products possessed the negative traits which they were alleged to have in the proceedings before the Opposition Division.

11.79 How would the Board have acted if the defendant's HOLLYWOOD cigarettes were to be marketed on the basis of the same 'youth, health and dynamism' as the chewing gum manufacturer claimed for his own product? This may seem far-fetched, but anyone who recalls the cigarette advertisements of the 1960s will remember how powerful the 'youth, health and dynamism' message was to attract a new generation of young smokers. The Board's approach to this issue was to view the true values of cigarette brands to be those perceived by the public, not those intended by the trade mark owner:

> [I]n the commercial practice of promotional sponsorship, cigarette trade marks are often associated with the world of sport, vitality and *joie de vivre*. One need only think of the MARLBORO, FORTUNA, CAMEL, GAULOISES and MERIT trade marks. The fact that the proprietors of these trade marks have endeavoured to give them an image of sportsmanship, vitality, etc., does not mean that they have succeeded. In particular, this does not prove that . . . tobacco is not associated with a negative

---

[79] *Hollywood SAS v Souza Cruz SA*, Case R 283/1999–3 [2002] ETMR 705.

image which is precisely the opposite of that conveyed by the HOLLYWOOD trade mark. Instead, it illustrates the . . . need . . . to overcome a negative image and to reassure consumers.[80]

11.80 This statement is revealing. It suggests that the fact that cigarette smokers have to be assured that the brands they smoke convey an image of 'sportsmanship, vitality, etc' is indicative of the fact that such brands do not possess such characteristics and are not therefore associated with them. Accordingly, attempts to portray (for example) the HOLLYWOOD cigarette brand as being conducive to sporting activity would be no more productive than their portrayal in a negative sense, as being harmful to smokers. It also appears that detriment to the repute of a trade mark for chewing gum is viewed from the perspective of gum-chewers (who may not be presumed to possess a positive attitude towards smoking), not from the perspective of smokers (who for the most part have a positive attitude towards that practice).[81]

11.81 It is worth noting other cases in which tribunals have been required to consider whether the nature of the unauthorized user's or applicant's product was such as to require a ruling that the mark's registration or use would be detrimental to the reputation of an earlier trade mark. Thus Adidas' three-stripe mark,[82] Hilton International's HILTON word mark[83] and Visa's word mark[84] have been protected against unwanted registrations for alcoholic drinks, tents and condoms respectively, on the bases that those registrations would reflect the wrong ethos, vulgarize the mark or embarrass its owner. In contrast, an application to register EVEREADY for condoms was allowed[85] despite the objections of the proprietor of the earlier trade mark EVER READY for batteries: the hearing officer thought it unlikely that any normal and fair use of EVEREADY on condoms would damage the repute or distinctive character of the earlier mark. These cases demonstrate that the determination that a sign is detrimental to an earlier trade mark's repute is not a predictive science but depends upon the subjective evaluation of a basket of factors by a judge or hearing officer.

---

[80] ibid, para 96.
[81] Similarly, in *A/S Arovit Petfood's application; opposition of Chivas Brothers Ltd*, Case R 165/2002–1, 26 March 2003, para 60: detriment caused to the whisky trade mark CHIVAS REGAL by the animal food CHIVAS had to be viewed from the perspective of the whisky drinker.
[82] *Inlima SL's application; opposition of Adidas AG* [2000] ETMR 325 (UK Trade Mark Registry).
[83] *Hilton International Co and another v Raclet SA* [2001] ETMR 1113 (Tribunal de Grande Instance de Paris).
[84] *C A Sheimer (M) Sdn Bhd's application; opposition by Visa International Service Association* [1999] ETMR 519; [2000] ETMR 1170 (UK Trade Mark Registry).
[85] cf *Oasis Stores Ltd's application; opposition of Ever Ready plc* [1999] ETMR 531 (UK Trade Mark Registry).

C. Unfair advantage and detriment

(6) Is 'unfair advantage' or 'detriment' only an issue where there is also a likelihood of confusion?

This is currently a purely European question and it is premissed on the following syllogism: **11.82**

1. Trade marks are protected against unauthorized use on similar goods ONLY where their use on the latter is likely to cause confusion with the former;[86]
2. Trade marks are protected against unauthorized use on entirely different goods ONLY where their use on the latter take unfair advantage of, or cause detriment to, the distinctive character or repute of the former;[87]
3. Trade marks are entitled to greater protection against their unauthorized use on similar goods than against their unauthorized use on entirely different goods (a proposition which is apparently self-evident but which is not actually reflected in European trade mark law);
4. If, in the classical case of protection against the unauthorized use of trade marks on similar goods, it is necessary to prove a likelihood of confusion, how much more so is it necessary to do so when the unauthorized use is in respect of entirely different goods?

Although this syllogism was accepted in the UK in the *Baywatch* case,[88] it was however more greatly loved by free-market entrepreneurs and rogues than by jurisprudents. The ECJ in *Sabèl v Puma*[89] was quite matter-of-fact in commenting that no confusion was required in a 'different goods' situation; this view was accepted by the Advocate General in *General Motors v Yplon*, who nonetheless observed that some found the lack of a confusion requirement 'paradoxical'.[90] The *Baywatch* heresy was buried in VIAGRA/VIAGRENE,[91] later disinterred and then finally reburied in the TY.PHOO/TYPHOON case[92] by a judge who chose to summon the assistance of national case law from around Europe to buttress his already unassailable position. **11.83**

(7) Is 'unfair advantage' or 'detriment' never an issue where the parties' respective goods or services are similar?

As in the case of the previous discussion, this issue has also originated from a **11.84**

---

[86] Council Directive 89/104, arts 4(1)(b), 5(1)(b); Council Regulation 40/94, arts 8(1)(b), 9(1)(b).
[87] Council Directive 89/104, arts 4(3), 5(2); Council Regulation 40/94, arts 8(5), 9(1)(c).
[88] *Baywatch Production Co Inc v The Home Video Channel* [1997] FSR 22 (HC), following *BASF plc v CEP(UK) plc* [1996] ETMR 51 (HC).
[89] *Sabèl BV v Puma AG, Rudolf Dassler Sport*, Case C-251/95 [1998] ETMR 1, para 20.
[90] *General Motors Corporation v Yplon SA*, Case C-375/97, [1999] All ER 865, para 26.
[91] *Pfizer Ltd and Pfizer Incorporated v Eurofood Link (United Kingdom) Ltd* [2000] ETMR 896 (HC).
[92] *Premier Brands UK Ltd v Typhoon Europe Ltd* [2000] ETMR 1071 (HC).

peculiarly European context, in the ECJ decision in *Davidoff v Gofkid*. Davidoff's trade mark, registered for products in Classes 14 (items made of precious metals) and 34 (tobacco products), consisted of a fanciful depiction of the word DAVIDOFF; Gofkid subsequently registered in Germany its own trade mark, DURFFEE, for more or less the same goods in the same classes, the word DURFFEE being depicted in similar typography to DAVIDOFF. Davidoff objected to Gofkid's use of the DURFFEE mark, not so much on the basis that its discerning customers would be confused between the two trade marks but on the basis that Gofkid had sought to latch on to the reputation of the DAVIDOFF mark and that its emulation by DURFFEE damaged it in that DURFFEE products would be regarded as being cheap, lower-quality products.

11.85 If Gofkid's products had been different (for example, car tyres or powdered eggs), Davidoff could have commenced proceedings based on the German implementation of article 5(2) of Directive 89/104, alleging the equation of 'earlier mark with reputation + similar mark without authorization + different goods + detriment to earlier mark + no excuse = infringement'. But since both Davidoff and Gofkid made and sold the same products, Davidoff's route had to be the article 5(1) equation of 'similar marks + same goods + likelihood of confusion = infringement'. What Davidoff wanted was something between the two: 'earlier mark with reputation + similar mark without authorization + same goods + detriment to earlier mark + no excuse = infringement'—but the Directive offered no apparent route to court for such a complaint.

11.86 Before continuing Davidoff's saga, we should pause for a moment and ask whether there is a lacuna in trade mark protection. Is no protection against 'unfair advantage' or 'undue detriment' given to a trade mark which has been used and has gained a reputation, against a later sign which is the same or similar and which is being used for the same or similar goods or services as those for which the earlier trade mark was registered? If, in articles 4(1)(b) and 5(1)(b) of the Directive, the words 'likelihood of confusion . . . , *which includes* a likelihood of association'[93] had read 'likelihood of confusion *or* a likelihood of association', there would have been no lacuna since it would be precisely that likelihood of association between the two marks that the 'unfair advantage' or 'detriment' would manifest itself. If there were no such association on the part of the relevant consumer, there could be neither an unfair advantage gained nor a detriment inflicted. But we—unlike the ECJ—are obliged to take the words of the Directive as we find them. In any event, that court has already rejected the possibility of reading into those words any meaning other than a narrow one.[94]

---

[93] The meaning of this phrase is discussed in depth in Chapter 10, paras 10.143–10.155.
[94] See *Sabèl BV v Puma AG, Rudolf Dassler Sport*, Case C-251/95 [1998] ETMR 1.

C. Unfair advantage and detriment

11.87 Assuming DAVIDOFF and DURFFEE to be similar marks, for similar goods, and assuming that there was no 'likelihood of confusion' between them, should we be concerned that an alleged 'unfair advantage' derived by Gofkid or 'detriment' inflicted by that company should not be an actionable wrong? It is not easy to conjure up any set of facts in which: (i) two marks are registered for the same or similar goods or services; (ii) the two marks were similar; (iii) there is no likelihood at all of any confusion; and (iv) none of the statutory defences to an action for trade mark infringement applies but nonetheless (v) the later mark, without due cause, takes advantage of the earlier mark or is detrimental to it.[95] Can it therefore be that the lacuna is a problem in theoretical but not in practical terms? Since this question will not answer itself and there is no present likelihood of a court having to answer it, we must live with it until we can deduce an answer for ourselves.

11.88 Davidoff's legal proceedings against use of the Durffee trade mark were initially unsuccessful since neither the trial court nor the appeal court considered their respective marks to be similar. On a further appeal the Bundesgerichtshof thought that the marks *were* similar and concluded that it was therefore necessary for a further finding to be made as to whether they were confusingly so. The Bundesgerichtshof then referred to the ECJ two questions relating to the apparent anomaly that detriment to the reputation of a trade mark, through the unauthorized use of a similar mark, could be stopped where the unauthorized use was on quite dissimilar goods but not where it was on the same or similar goods. This anomaly was seen as resulting in a lacuna in the protection which the law accorded to used trade marks.

11.89 The first question which the Bundesgerichtshof referred to the ECJ was:

> (1) Are the provisions of . . . Article 5(2) . . . to be interpreted (and where appropriate applied) as also entitling the Member States to provide more extensive protection for well-known marks in cases where the later mark is used or to be used for goods or services identical with or similar to those in respect of which the earlier mark is registered?

11.90 In the event that the ECJ should answer 'no', the Bundesgerichtshof added a supplementary question:

> (2) Are the grounds mentioned in Article . . . 5(2) of the Trade Mark Directive . . . exhaustive in regulating when it is permissible for provisions protecting well-known marks to be retained under national law, or may those articles be supplemented by national rules protecting well-known marks against later signs which are used or to be used in respect of identical or similar goods or services?

11.91 In the event, the second question remained unanswered, the ECJ ruling that the Member States were entitled to provide specific protection under registered trade

---

[95] The point made by Advocate General Jacobs in *Davidoff & Cie and Zino Davidoff SA v Gofkid Ltd*, Case C-292/00 [2002] ETMR 1219, [2003] FSR 50.

Chapter 11: Reputation, Unfair Advantage and Detriment

mark law for well-known registered trade marks in cases where a later mark or sign, which is identical with or similar to the registered mark, is intended to be used or is used for goods or services identical with or similar to those covered by the registered mark.[96] In this ruling the ECJ gave no specific guidance as to what constituted 'specific protection'.

11.92 The Court's answer is a surprising and, for some, an unexpected one.[97] In reaching its decision the ECJ adopted the unusual path of refusing to follow the Opinion of the Advocate General[98] who considered that (i) there was nothing in the Directive's recitals or in the plain meaning of its provisions to suggest that the Directive contemplated a wider degree of protection than that which it expressly provided and that (ii) there was no apparent need to confer a wider degree of protection than that specified by the Directive itself since adequate protection was already conferred through its 'similar goods and services' provisions. Another difficulty raised in this case was the employment of the phrase 'well-known marks', both by the referring court and in the ECJ's response. It does not appear to have been expressly intended that this ruling applies in respect of 'well-known marks' but not in respect of marks which, while possessing reputation, are not well-known but, if that is not the case, is this case teaching us, contrary to the ECJ's earlier reasoning,[99] that the provisions relating to the meaning of 'reputation' refer in fact to well-known marks and not merely to marks which have crossed the 'knowledge threshold' discussed above.

11.93 It was not at the time of writing known how many EU Member States would be seeking to amend their national trade mark law in the light of the ECJ's ruling in *Davidoff v Gofkid* in order to provide further protection against the taking of unfair advantage or the infliction of detriment against applicants or users in the same or similar fields of commerce. Since Portugal supported Davidoff's case we may suppose that it will be among the first to do so; the UK, which opposed it, may well be the last. In the Opinion of Advocate General Jacobs in *Adidas v Fitnessworld*[100] article 5(2) of Council Directive 89/104 is not correctly implemented unless the proprietor of a trade mark with a reputation is entitled to oppose the use of the mark in relation to similar goods or services as well as those which are identical or similar to those for which the trade mark is registered. The Court's response to this Opinion is eagerly awaited.

---

[96] *Davidoff & Cie and Zino Davidoff SA v Gofkid Ltd*, Case C-292/00 [2003] ETMR 534.
[97] See eg Hedwig Schmidt, '"Likelihood of Confusion" in European Trademarks: Where Are We Now?' [2002] EIPR 463, 465.
[98] *Davidoff & Cie and Zino Davidoff SA v Gofkid Ltd*, Case C-292/00 [2002] ETMR 1219, [2003] FSR 50.
[99] *General Motors Corporation v Yplon SA*, Case C-375/97 [1999] ETMR 950, paras 22–5.
[100] *Adidas-Salomon AG and Adidas Benelux BV v Fitnessworld Trading Ltd*, Case C-408/01, Opinion of 10 July 2003 (unreported) (ECJ), para 34.

(8) Are there other forms of unfair advantage not covered by the *Dimple* principle?

To recap, *Dimple*[101] regarded as an unfair advantage any act which associated 'the quality of one's goods or services with that of prestigious competitive products for the purpose of exploiting the good reputation of a competitor's goods or services in order to enhance one's promotional efforts'.[102] While all acts which fall within this definition may be regarded as conferring an unfair advantage, there is nothing to suggest that this is an all-embracing definition. Without addressing definitional issues, case law has supported the contention that other types of unfair advantage exist. One such example involved the gratuitous use of the HUGO BOSS word-and-device trade marks by a tour operator, so as to attract the attention of would-be customers for its trips to the Hugo Boss factory in Germany. This use was held in France to constitute a trade mark infringement[103] even though the advertiser did not in any meaningful sense associate its services with the quality of Hugo Boss products.

11.94

D. Conclusion

In this chapter we have seen how a trade mark's reputation, and the goodwill in that reputation, are protected both against hostile trade mark applications and against unauthorized third-party use in areas of commerce which are far distant from its own. We have also examined the 'lacuna' issue, the ruling in *Davidoff v Gofkid* and the Advocate General's Opinion in *Adidas v Fitnessworld*.

11.95

This is an unsettled area of law, which cannot be comprehended on its own. In order to obtain a fuller picture of the situation, it is necessary to consider also the protection given to well-known and famous marks, which is discussed in the next chapter.

11.96

---

[101] *DIMPLE* (1985) 17 GRUR 529, discussed in paras 11.60–11.64 above.
[102] Cited in *Premier Brands UK Ltd v Typhoon Europe Ltd* [2000] ETMR 1071, 1092 (HC).
[103] *Sté Hugo Boss v Dernierès Nouvelles d'Alsace and others* [1998] ETMR 197 (Tribunal de Grande Instance de Strasbourg).

12

WELL-KNOWN MARKS, FAMOUS MARKS AND DILUTION

Author's note. This chapter follows the previous chapter, 'Reputation, Unfair Advantage and Detriment', which addresses the degree of protection which is given to trade marks which have a reputation. The protection described in that chapter applies also to trade marks which are well known or famous. I have assumed that anyone who is reading this chapter will have read the previous chapter first. Perhaps perversely, almost every one of the expert readers who were invited to pass comment on this chapter did so without having read the previous one. Unless you are visiting this chapter for the purpose of reading a specific feature which is listed in the Table of Contents, it is recommended that you read the previous chapter first.

A. **Introduction**
   D is for doggerel
   The moral of the poem   12.01
   (1) Practical and legal background
       (a) Practical considerations   12.04
       (b) The international framework for the protection of well-known trade marks   12.05
   (2) The definition of 'famous' and 'well-known' trade marks   12.09
       (a) Blurring the difference between 'well-known' and 'famous' marks   12.11
       (b) 'Famous' trade marks: the United States definition   12.12
       (c) The problem of intense but limited fame   12.17
   (3) Are 'well-known' marks more famous than 'famous' marks?   12.24

B. **Europe**
   (1) The position under European law   12.25
   (2) How does Europe manage with so little legal provision for famous trade marks?   12.31
   (3) Further European national perspectives on well-known marks which may be famous   12.33
   (4) Well-known marks in a complex single market   12.37
   (5) What happens when a trade mark becomes famous?   12.40
   (6) The duration of fame   12.42
   (7) Relief against wrongful registration of a famous mark   12.44
   (8) Relief against infringement of a famous mark   12.45
   (9) The position of the consumer   12.47

C. **Famous mark protection in the United States**
   (1) The 'anti-dilution' approach   12.49
   (2) Dilution and the burden of proof   12.53
   (3) Interim injunctive relief against dilution   12.54

(4) The doctrine of progressive encroachment	12.56
(5) Multiparty dilution of a famous mark	12.58
(6) The 1999 WIPO recommendations	12.60
(7) United States, ECJ and WIPO guidelines for 'famous marks' contrasted	12.67
D. Conclusion	12.69

A. Introduction

D is for doggerel

A is ARMANI, for clothes-conscious geezers;
B is BACARDI, the drink for young breezers.

C is for COKE, with bubbles of passion;
D is for DIOR, an icon of fashion.

E is for ESSO, to power your car;
F is for FIAT, to drive you afar.

G is for GILLETTE, the popular blade;
H is for HILTON, where many have stayed.

I is for INTEL, the chip that's inside;
J is JUVENTUS, for football with pride.

K is for KODAK, for camera and lens;
L is for LANCÔME, to make chicks of hens.

M is for MARS bars, as tasty as toffee;
N is for NESCAFÉ soluble coffee.

O is OBSESSION, the subtlest of scents;
P is for POLO's smart clothing for gents.

Q is for Q-TIPS, to clean ears without trouble;
R is for REMINGTON, to shave off your stubble.

S is for SMIRNOFF, for pleasurable sipping;
T is for TEFLON, to keep omelettes slipping.

U is for UMBRO, for players who win;
V is for VOLVO, to drive safely in.

W is for WATERFORD's crystal cut glass;
X is for XEROX, to make copies fast.

Y is for YAHOO! which keeps you online;
Z is for ZANTAC, to make tummies fine.

Each mark's a pearl of celebrated fame,
With lustrous repute it shouts its name.
But all face risk from unscrupulous foes
Whose fake wares wretched shoppers chose.

A. Introduction

> To make marks famous we've worked so hard,
> But let us heed the words of the Bard:
> Who steals my purse steals only trash—
> While stealing good names earns the cash.[1]
>
> *The moral of the poem*

The two previous chapters have looked at (i) the protection given to trade marks against a likelihood of confusion and (ii) the protection given to trade marks on account of their reputation. The first of these types of protection was conferred irrespective of whether the infringed mark had been used at all, while the second depended upon the existence of reputation but not on its magnitude of scale. Some trade marks are used but little known, while others are well known. However, each of the trade marks mentioned in the doggerel above is so well known that it could be said to be a household word. **12.01**

Household word-type trade marks face the risk that they may become generic (see Chapter 6). They also face—since they have proved their popularity and profitability—a far greater threat of misappropriation by 'unscrupulous foes' than is faced by unused or little-known trade marks (dealing with unscrupulous foes is covered in great detail in the section dealing with bad faith in Chapter 13[2]). **12.02**

But does the fame of some trade marks entitle them to an extra degree of protection against predatory trade practices? And, perhaps more importantly, should it? These issues lie at the heart of this chapter. **12.03**

(1) Practical and legal background

(a) Practical considerations

As has been mentioned in the previous chapter,[3] where a trade mark possesses a degree of reputation the theoretical possibility of registering a trade mark for all goods and services, not just those for which a trade mark proprietor wishes to use the trade mark, is not a practical reality. This is even more the case with well-known or famous marks, since the spread of fame may cause the trade mark proprietor to take expensive action to protect his trade mark not only for goods and services in which he has no interest but even in countries in which he does not trade. It is thus imperative for the owner of a well-known or famous trade mark to maximize the degree of protection accorded by the law without his having to embark upon an expensive and impractical international filing programme. The **12.04**

---

[1] cf William Shakespeare, *Othello,* Act III, Scene III: 'Who steals my purse steals trash; 'tis something, nothing; 'Twas mine, 'tis his, and has been slave to thousands. But he that filches from me my good name robs me of that which not enriches him and makes me poor indeed'.

[2] See also para 12.44 below and Frederick Mostert, *Famous and Well-Known Marks* (1997), pp 33–49.

[3] See Chapter 11, paras 11.60–11.64.

framework of legal protection for such trade marks is laid out in the following section.

(b) The international framework for the protection of well-known trade marks

12.05　The Paris Convention contains special provision for well-known marks in article 6*bis*:

> (1) The countries of the Union undertake . . . to refuse or to cancel the registration, and to prohibit the use, of a trademark which constitutes a reproduction, an imitation, or a translation, liable to create confusion, of a mark considered by the competent authority of the country of registration or use to be well known in that country as being already the mark of a person entitled to the benefits of this Convention and used for identical or similar goods. These provisions shall also apply when the essential part of the mark constitutes a reproduction of any such well-known mark or an imitation liable to create confusion therewith.

12.06　In French the expression 'well-known marks' comes out as 'marques notoires', which then sometimes find their way back into English under the somewhat disreputable soubriquet of 'notorious marks'.

12.07　Article 16 of the Agreement on Trade-Related Aspects of Intellectual Property Rights (TRIPs) embellishes the level of Paris Convention protection by adding:

> 2. Article 6*bis* of the Paris Convention (1967) shall apply, *mutatis mutandis*, to services. In determining whether a trademark is well known, Members shall take account of the knowledge of the trademark in the relevant sector of the public, including knowledge in the Member concerned which has been obtained as a result of the promotion of the trademark.
> 3. Article 6*bis* of the Paris Convention (1967) shall apply, *mutatis mutandis*, to goods or services which are not similar to those in respect of which a trademark is registered, provided that use of that trademark in relation to those goods or services would indicate a connection between those goods or services and the owner of the registered trademark and provided that the interests of the owner of the registered trademark are likely to be damaged by such use.

12.08　Acute readers will have noticed that the word 'famous' is not mentioned in either the Paris Convention or the TRIPs provision. Nor is there any mention of the need to protect consumers against the misappropriation or wrongful use of well-known marks. 'Famous' marks and their relationship to 'well-known' marks will be considered later in this chapter,[4] as will the position of the consumer.[5]

---

[4] See paras 12.09–12.24 below.
[5] See paras 12.47–12.48 below.

A. Introduction

(2) The definition of 'famous' and 'well-known' trade marks

12.09 Although 'famous mark' is not a term employed in the Paris Convention, in TRIPs, in Directive 89/104 or in the Community Trade Mark (CTM) Regulation, it is a term which is used in the trade mark legislation of the United States (discussed at length later in this chapter). It is also a term which recurs in discussions relating to the extent of protection which the law should accord to trade marks which are merely known, well known or truly famous. In this section we will therefore consider some of the definitional problems which arise when it is necessary to determine whether a trade mark is 'famous' or 'well known'. This exercise is a frustrating one: we all know some famous trade marks and can identify them when we see them, but what is it that makes them well known or famous in law?[6]

12.10 The exercise of finding a definition is an important one, not solely because it is necessary if we are to protect well-known or famous marks but also because it is necessary if we are to refuse to protect, as well-known or famous marks, those marks which are *not* well known or famous. If we were only concerned with protecting ultra-famous trade marks such as COCA-COLA, we might be tempted to argue that it is self-evident that COCA-COLA is famous and that, instead of having to define in law what constitutes 'famous' and then apply the law to the facts, the courts and trade mark granting authorities should simply take judicial notice of the fact COCA-COLA is famous.[7] But we have to have an objective standard which will enable a judge to explain to an owner who thinks *his* trade mark is famous: 'I'm sorry but, however famous your trade mark is to you (in fact), it isn't famous to me (in law)'.

(a) Blurring the difference between 'well-known' and 'famous' marks

12.11 The terminology of famous and well-known marks is unhelpfully imprecise. Article 6*bis* of the Paris Convention sought to protect 'well-known' marks against the use by others of those marks on *identical or similar* goods. In contrast, the original dilution doctrine propounded by Frank Schechter sought to protect trade marks against the use by others of those marks on *non-related* goods.[8] It would have been convenient at this point to use the term 'well known' to refer to the protection of a used trade mark against its direct competitors and to employ the term 'famous' to refer to the protection of a used trade mark against non-competing businesses. This opportunity has now been lost for good, since the protection of

---

[6] Many different jurisdictions now have guidelines as to whether a mark is 'famous' or 'well known'; see eg those countries discussed by Frederick Mostert, *Famous and Well-Known Marks* (1997), ch 1.

[7] See Julian Gyngell and Allan Poulter, *A User's Guide to Trade Marks and Passing Off* (1998), para 1.11: '[I]n the majority of cases the notoriety of the mark may almost be a matter for judicial notice'.

[8] See Chapter 11, paras 11.14–11.29 and the sources cited there.

well-known marks under the Paris Convention has now been extended to use in relation to goods and services which are unrelated,[9] while statutory dilution doctrine now protects famous trade marks regardless of whether they are used by competing businesses.[10]

(b) 'Famous' trade marks: the United States definition

12.12 Some trade marks are so well known that their fame transcends the bounds of normal trade mark law. Marks in this category are not limited to those listed in our piece of doggerel. But what defines 'fame' for legal purposes? The answer given in the United States is probably the most apposite, since that jurisdiction has the greatest quantity of experience in seeking to define a famous mark for legal purposes and there is no doubt that its experience has been at least partially formative in the position taken by the World Intellectual Property Organization (WIPO) on that issue.[11]

12.13 The United States Federal legislation considers a trade mark's fame to be a compound issue, fame being comprised of one or more of a number of criteria:

> In determining whether a mark is distinctive and *famous*, a court may consider factors such as, but not limited to—
> (A) the degree of inherent or acquired distinctiveness of the mark;
> (B) the duration and extent of use of the mark in connection with the goods or services with which the mark is used;
> (C) the duration and extent of advertising and publicity of the mark;
> (D) the geographical extent of the trading area in which the mark is used;
> (E) the channels of trade for the goods or services with which the mark is used;
> (F) the degree of recognition of the mark in the trading areas and channels of trade used by the mark's owner and the person against whom the injunction is sought;
> (G) the nature and extent of use of the same or similar marks by third parties;
> . . .[12]

12.14 Even without going to the jurisprudence in order to see how these terms are interpreted, we can appreciate that their relevance to the issue of fame is clear and should demand no further explanation. It should also be apparent that these measuring rods by which a mark's fame are measured are also of equal applicability to the questions (i) whether a trade mark is 'well known' for Paris Convention purposes and (ii) whether a trade mark has 'reputation' for European national and CTM purposes. The Lanham Act should not be criticized for employing the same

---

[9] TRIPs Agreement, art 16(3).
[10] 15 USC, s 1127.
[11] See Chapter 12, paras 12.60–12.68.
[12] Lanham Act, s 43 (15 USC, s 1125). This analysis does not discuss the protection of famous marks under the laws of individual States within the United States.

A. Introduction

criteria for measuring both distinctiveness and fame, since a famous trade mark which lacks distinctiveness is *ex hypothesi* serving as a generic term.[13]

Looking at the US criteria which we have listed, their potential applicability to the facts of individual cases is clear. A trade mark which is specially created for its impact, such as KODAK, will be better able to attract swift fame than a mark such as PIZZA EXPRESS, which has to be learned by the public if it is to be regarded as more than a description of a fast-food outlet selling pizzas, while the scale and extent of publicity given to even an initially mundane trade mark can impel it towards fame more swiftly than a highly distinctive but unpublicized trade mark. Since the duration and extent of a trade mark's use will increase the likelihood of its fame developing and being sustained, it is not surprising that a British court held that an exceptional trade mark such as VIAGRA became a household name within a matter of months of its launch.[14] A heavily advertised trade mark will initially gain notoriety more swiftly than a word-of-mouth brand, though BODY SHOP achieved the remarkable feat of becoming famous by stealth.[15] A product promoted under a trade mark in New York and California will almost inevitably experience fame before products which are launched and marketed in the open spaces of Wyoming or Nebraska. Trade marks attached to products which are co-promoted along with international high-profile trade marks such as those found on KELLOGG's or MCDONALD's products will obtain an extra boost to their visibility, and so on.

12.15

This is what the law says and it is difficult to come up with any other tests that might have any value in court.[16] One could, for example, say that a trade mark has become famous when, on its mention in a book or film, there is no need to explain the reference to it—but this rule of thumb works well only with word marks. It has no obvious field of application in relation to product shapes and other marks which are difficult to separate out from the product for which they are used. In addition, its inclusion may be a sign that it has become a generic term rather than a famous trade mark.

12.16

(c) The problem of intense but limited fame

Fame is not an eternal and constant thing. It may be limited in many ways. A few examples will elucidate the point.

12.17

---

[13] The European Court of Justice (ECJ) has arguably also moved towards 'merging' the notions of distinctiveness and reputation, by employing the factors relating to acquired distinctiveness in *Windsurfing Chiemsee Produktions- und Vertriebs GmbH v Boots- und Segelzubehör Walter Huber and Franz Attenberger*, Joined Cases C-108 and 109/97 [1999] ETMR 585 as part of the test of reputation in *Lloyd Schuhfabrik Meyer & Co GmbH v Klijsen Handel BV*, Case V-342/97 [1999] ETMR 690.

[14] *Pfizer Ltd and Pfizer Incorporated v Eurofood Link (United Kingdom) Ltd* [2000] ETMR 896.

[15] Naomi Klein, *No Logo* (2000), p 20.

[16] The 1999 Paris Union and WIPO recommendations, discussed in para 12.16 below, enlist much the same criteria as those of the United States law.

Chapter 12: Well-known Marks, Famous Marks and Dilution

12.18 **(i) Fame may be limited in time.** The heroes of today are the forgotten men and women of the future. Any reader who has experienced the pleasures of tourism will be familiar with the Ozymandias syndrome:[17] on visiting many public places one encounters statues and monuments to people whose names were once mentioned throughout their country in terms of fear or admiration. We no longer have any idea who most of these people are. They have passed from fame to a condition of prominent and highly exposed obscurity. As the speed of our lives accelerates and the number of famous people increases accordingly, the amount of attention which we can accord to them decreases accordingly. This is what Warhol meant when he said: 'In the future, everybody will be world famous for 15 minutes'.[18] The fame of trade marks is also sometimes purely temporary. Record labels (REGAL ZONOPHONE), cars (STUDEBAKER, SUNBEAM, PANHARD, SIMCA, HISPANO-SUIZA and airlines (TWA, PAN-AM, BOAC) are among the categories of goods for which trade marks which were once familiar now exercise their influence chiefly within the jurisdiction of the land of Nostalgia.

12.19 **(ii) Fame may be limited in space.** Another joy of travel is the discovery that shops in different countries stock brands of goods of which one has never heard of at home but which seem to be advertised and sold everywhere when one is on holiday.[19] Sometimes the fame of goods in one country but not in another is a consequence of those goods having a market in one country but not another: for example, the repute attached to even prominent trade marks attached to skiing products may not spread greatly to countries in which few people ski.

12.20 **(iii) Fame may be limited in cultural terms.** An Englishman who is forced to listen to a conversation between two Americans on the subject of the performance of baseball stars will soon discover the cultural relativity of fame. He will be consoled by the fact that an American will feel much the same if he finds himself listening to a discussion between two Englishmen on the performance of prominent proponents of the game of cricket.

12.21 **(iv) Fame may be limited in social terms.** Auntie Maisie's home-baked apple pie may be famous among her nieces, nephews, cousins and other clan members—but, to those of us who are not members of her family, her fame is something of a secret, if not an irrelevance.

---

[17] 'I met a traveller from an antique land / Who said:—Two vast and trunkless legs of stone / Stand in the desert. Near them on the sand, / Half sunk, a shatter'd visage lies, whose frown / And wrinkled lip and sneer of cold command / Which yet survive, stamp'd on these lifeless things, / The hand that mock'd them and the heart that fed. / And on the pedestal these words appear: / 'My name is Ozymandias, king of kings: / Look on my works, ye mighty, and despair!' / Nothing beside remains: round the decay / Of that colossal wreck, boundless and bare, / The lone and level sands stretch far away.' (P. B. Shelley, 'Ozymandias' (1818)).

[18] *Andy Warhol* (exhibition catalogue, 1968).

[19] I am indebted to Michael Edenborough for the example of DODO lager on Réunion.

B. Europe

12.22 (v) **Fame may be limited in professional or industrial terms.** Where specialist goods or services are provided within a niche market, their name may be famous to those within that niche but not outside it. To people working within the field of trade mark law, words like 'WIPO' and 'INTA' probably achieve 100 per cent recognition. Yet they mean nothing to most laymen.

12.23 The point behind these truisms will already have been realized by the acute reader: if fame is neither constant nor absolute, how does the law cope with its inconsistency and its relative nature? Does the fact that a court has ruled that a trade mark was well known or famous in 1995 mean that it should be required to do the same in 2005? In what circumstances should the law come to the aid of a partially famous mark because it is famous at least in part—and when should it withhold that aid on account of that mark's partial obscurity? How does one cope with geographically local fame where the proposed use of a trade mark by a third party falls both within and without the area of that fame, or with fame in a niche area when the proposed third party use lies outside that niche?[20] These are difficult issues to address in principle, given the tendency of trade mark owners to demand a level of protection which exceeds that necessary for the protection of their immediate trade interests and the tendency of many parties to encroach upon the reputation of established trade marks to at least the greatest possible legal extent.

(3) Are 'well-known' marks more famous than 'famous' marks?

12.24 In normal speech, to be famous is more than to be well known. But considering the application of the European standard of the well-known mark against the United States standard of the famous mark, it may be wondered whether the threshold of protection of famous marks in the United States is potentially lower than the threshold for the protection of well-known marks in Europe. It is too early to judge but, once the same mark becomes the subject of protective litigation on both sides of the Atlantic, the answer to this question may become apparent.

B. Europe

(1) The position under European law

12.25 How do the two major pieces of European trade mark law implement article 6*bis*

---

[20] Inconsistencies in seeking to resolve these issues in the United States have been considered in context by Dyann Kostello, 'Grappling with the Limits of Fame Under the FTDA: Do Marks Famous Only in a Niche Market or Limited Geographical Area Qualify for Protection?' (2001) 91 TMR 1133–49.

of the Paris Convention and its TRIPs add-on? Although the final recital to the Preamble of Directive 89/104 confirms that the Directive's provisions are 'entirely consistent' with the Paris Convention, its English text contains scarcely a mention of the words 'well known' in relation to trade marks.[21] The registration of another's 'well-known' mark is a ground upon which a trade mark application can be refused, or registration invalidated,[22] but the rights conferred against infringers are egalitarian in their nature and treat all used trade marks in a similar manner, protecting them by virtue of their reputation[23] even if they are not well known.

12.26 The approach taken by the CTM Regulation corresponds to that adopted by Directive 89/104. The registration of another's 'well-known' mark is a ground of refusal of a trade mark application,[24] or registration invalidated.[25] Once again, the rights conferred against infringers treat all used trade marks in a similar manner, regardless of whether they are well known.[26]

12.27 This relatively straightforward analysis has been thrown into some small uncertainty by the ECJ in *Davidoff v Gofkid*[27] when it chose, in the English version of its decision, to refer to the protection granted under Directive 89/104[28] to trade marks which have 'a reputation in the Member State' as being the protection of 'well-known marks'. Does this mean that 'marks with a reputation' and 'well-known marks' are now synonymous? The ECJ itself in *General Motors v Yplon*[29] noted that the marks 'having a reputation' in the English were 'well-known' marks in the French, German, Italian and Spanish versions of Directive 89/104 and considered this no more than a 'nuance which does not entail any great contradiction'.[30] Regardless of the terminology employed, a trade mark must be known to a particular extent before it is entitled to receive the protection accorded to such a mark. This extent is reached where the mark is known by a significant part of the public concerned with the goods sold under that trade mark.

---

[21] Paris Convention, art 6*bis*(1).
[22] Council Regulation 89/104, art 4(2)(d).
[23] Council Regulation 89/104, art 5(2), on which see Chapter 11. The Trade Marks Act 1994, s 56, gives foreign 'well-known' marks only the level of protection required by the Paris Convention, that is to say, protection against use on identical or similar goods which is likely to cause confusion.
[24] Council Regulation 40/94, art 8(2)(c).
[25] ibid, art 52.
[26] ibid, art 9(1)(c). In contrast, the South African anti-dilution provisions are drafted in virtually the same terms as the protection which Council Regulation 40/94 accords to any mark with a reputation, but appears to limit its applicability to well-known marks alone; see *South African Breweries International (Finance) BV v Laugh It Off Promotions* WTLR, 28 May 2003.
[27] *Davidoff & Cie and Zino Davidoff SA v Gofkid Ltd*, Case C-292/00 [2002] ETMR 1219, [2003] FSR 50 (Advocate General's Opinion); [2003] ETMR 534 (ECJ), discussed in Chapter 11, paras 11.84–11.93.
[28] Council Directive 89/104, arts 4(4)(a) and 5(2).
[29] *General Motors Corp v Yplon SA*, Case C-375/97 [1999] ETMR 950; see also Chapter 11, paras 11.30–11.51.
[30] ibid, para 22.

B. Europe

12.28 One final point should be mentioned. Directive 89/104 states that, for the purpose of refusing a national trade mark application or invalidating a subsequent grant, the words 'well known' mean

> well known in a Member State, in the sense in which the words 'well-known' are used in Article 6*bis* of the Paris Convention.[31]

12.29 In theory this qualification, which is not found in those provisions in Directive 89/104 that refer to marks being (in English) marks with a reputation and (in French, German, Italian and Spanish) well-known marks, suggests that it is somehow for the Paris Union rather than the ECJ to determine what 'well known' means for article 6*bis* purposes. In practice, the Paris Union countries have so far failed to come up with a consensus or understanding as to what 'well known' means, though they may one day do so.[32]

12.30 Not all European jurisdictions however take their lead from the Directive. Monaco, for example, provides that article 6*bis* of the Paris Convention is directly applicable in that principality.[33]

(2) How does Europe manage with so little legal provision for famous trade marks?

12.31 It has been noted by commentators that European trade mark law makes very little specific provision for the protection of famous trade marks as a separate category of subject matter of legal protection.[34] Surprisingly little damage would appear to be done to famous marks through the paucity of European national and Community legislation relating to them, at least if reported decisions of the courts and trade mark registries are a reliable indicator.

12.32 Where an opposition is based on a truly famous mark, the examining authority appears to intuit the imperative need to act firmly in order to guard against even small threats of erosion of its status. For example, one Opposition Division of the Office for Harmonisation in the Internal Market (OHIM) has taken the view that the reputation of the protected word OLYMPIC is so high that any use of that word, for any class of goods or services at all, would constitute both the taking of an unfair advantage and the infliction of undue detriment.[35]

---

[31] Council Directive 89/104, art 4(2)(d).
[32] See paras 12.60–12.68 below.
[33] Sovereign decree No 5687 of 29 October 1975.
[34] See eg Pier Luigi Ronaglia, 'Should We Use Guns and Missiles to Protect Famous Trademarks in Europe?' (1998) 88 TMR 551.
[35] *Belmont Olympic SA's application; opposition of the Comité International Olympique* [2000] ETMR 919 (rejecting an application to register a word-and-device mark FAMILY CLUB BELMONT OLYMPIC for transport, storage and business administration services).

(3) Further European national perspectives on well-known marks which may be famous

12.33 The Czech Industrial Property Office has observed, in relation to the trade mark DURACELL,[36] that a trade mark's being well known has certain consequences. One is that a wrongful applicant to register it stands to benefit from the well-known mark's distinctive character, regardless of the classes of goods or services for which it is registered. The fact that this is so might suggest a mark which is famous in the sense that it would be recognized by relevant consumers for all classes of goods and services for which trade marks may be registered, rather than one which is merely well known within the parameters of its particular market.

12.34 The Lisbon Court of Appeals was invited to consider the 'advertising function' of a trade mark as the key to its fame or repute. The appellant, arguing for the cancellation of a competitor's trade mark, maintained that a function of the trade mark is to advertise or proclaim the characteristics of its goods or services to the public. That function should not accordingly be impaired by it having to coexist, on the register or in the marketplace, with another mark. If impairment of this advertising function occurred, then the trade mark's inherent global property would be damaged or devalued.[37] The more famous the trade mark, the greater the likelihood that even remote and unconnected use of an identical or similar sign by others would damage that inherent advertising function. The appellant's appeal failed, possibly because its argument was made the wrong way round: it can be argued that, if a trade mark is famous, damage to its advertising function should be remedied—but it cannot be argued that, because there is damage to a trade mark's advertising function, the trade mark is famous. It is notable that earlier successful Portuguese actions to protect famous trade marks were founded on allegations of unfair competition or fraud rather than upon assertion of damage to their advertising function.[38]

12.35 The French courts have taken a fairly strict line towards the protection which might be termed the penumbra of famous marks—variations of marks which evoke them rather than repeat them letter for letter. Thus the Cour de Cassation has refused to conclude that the trade mark OLYMPRIX (French for 'OLYMPRICE'), used by its proprietor when advertising its annual 'low price' marketing campaign, infringed the famous trade marks OLYMPIQUE and JEUX OLYMPIQUES.[39] Since the Court did not go into detail in its reasoning, we do not know if it

---

[36] DURACELL trade mark [1999] ETMR 583.
[37] Indústria e Comércio de Cosméticos Natura AS's application [2001] ETMR 783 (Portugal).
[38] See MARLBORO–SCOTCH WHISKY, Industrial Property Bulletin, 10/1981, p 1980 (Civil Court 3, Lisbon); also the decision of the Lisbon Court of Appeal of 3 July 1990 (registration of COKE refused for cleaning, hygienic and perfume products).
[39] Groupement d'Achat des Centres Leclerc v Comité National Olympique et Sportif Français and others [2001] ETMR 367.

rejected the contention that OLYMPRIX was 'a trademark which constitutes a reproduction [or] an imitation' under article 6*bis* of the Paris Convention against which OLYMPIQUE required protection. The Court did however state that, while the relevant provision of French law[40] protected famous marks, it did not expressly prohibit their evocation in a similar form. This decision may be contrasted with the English decision that VIAGRENE constituted an infringement of VIAGRA even though the legislative provision which protected it conferred that protection on the basis of 'reputation' alone, without the need to argue that VIAGRA was either 'well known' or 'famous'.[41]

What can be learned from these three single instances? Until the ECJ lays down guidance on the subject or comity between members of the judiciary at the highest levels of national law establishes judicial consensus, (i) protection of trade marks which are well known or famous will vary from country to country and (ii) the scope of protection under national law will be defined by considerations derived from diverse national legal traditions rather than from a common stock of shared jurisprudence. A touch of quaint local charm is always welcome, while the suppression of national legal and cultural tendencies is rarely so. However, one wonders how much benefit is obtained by trade mark owners, their competitors and consumers when the protection which is available to well-known and famous marks is not so much a coat of armour as a patchwork quilt.

12.36

(4) Well-known marks in a complex single market

The notion of a mark being well known began as a nationally applicable concept. It was therefore necessary to ask whether a mark was well known only in the country in which protection was sought. The phenomenon of single markets such as that of the European Union raises an interesting issue: what if a mark is well known in one country within the single market but unknown within another?

12.37

European trade mark law has tangentially addressed this issue through the ruling of the ECJ that the CHEVY trade mark must be taken to have a reputation throughout the Benelux countries, which operate a single trade mark registration system, if it can be shown that 'it is known by a significant part of the public concerned in a substantial part of the territory'—even if that 'substantial part' is just one part of one of the three countries within the Benelux zone.[42] The countries of the Andean Pact[43] addressed the same issue more directly when they determined that, for the purposes of recognition of a famous mark, the recognition of a mark's famous status in any one of those five countries should be treated as sufficient to support a

12.38

---

[40] Intellectual Property Code (France), art L713-5.
[41] *Pfizer Ltd and Pfizer Incorporated v Eurofood Link (United Kingdom) Ltd* [2000] ETMR 896.
[42] *General Motors Corporation v Yplon SA*, Case C-375/97 [1999] ETMR 950, para 31.
[43] Bolivia, Colombia, Ecuador, Peru, Venezuela.

finding that it is famous in the others, even in the absence of evidence to that effect.[44]

12.39 This solution is commendably efficient in terms of dispute resolution: it protects all countries in the same economic zone against the problems caused by multiple ownership of trade marks at a time when their economies are coming closer together and it also confers a wider degree of protection on famous marks than that to which they would be entitled under national law. It may also be seen as unduly restrictive of the freedom of traders to select and use trade marks to which, within the context of their own national markets, there may be no legal objection. In commercial and economic terms, however, the limitation placed upon traders in terms of using the trade mark of their choice is more of a theoretical hardship than a real one because the pool from which new trade marks are chosen is, in practice, inexhaustible. The question may also be raised as to why an applicant should seek to register in one country a trade mark which is famous in a neighbouring one if not for the purpose of taking advantage of its fame.

(5) What happens when a trade mark becomes famous?

12.40 Where a trade mark starts off as a regular trade mark and becomes famous at some stage after it has been registered, what is the status of acts of third parties which began before the mark became famous and continued thereafter? The answer is clear. In Europe it seems that the date upon which the alleged wrongdoer commenced its use is the operative date for liability purposes. Thus where a manufacturer of MAC Cat and MAC Dog food traded in those products in Germany from 1983, it was necessary to consider whether MCDONALD'S portfolio of trade marks commencing with MC- or MAC- had sufficient reputation in 1983 to protect it against its adversary.[45] Likewise, *Elle* magazine is very famous in many countries, but the proprietors of the ELLE trade mark could not prove that it was famous in Poland in 1984 and therefore failed to prevent registration of the same mark for cosmetics.[46] A similar approach is taken in the United States.[47]

12.41 But do other considerations apply once those trade marks attain superstar status as famous marks? In principle a prior *bona fide* continuous user of a name or trade mark can carry on using his trade mark, regardless of what happens in the marketplace after that use commences. Trade mark owners have tried hard, and may

---

[44] Decision 344 of the Andean Community, art 83(d).
[45] *McDonald's Corporation and McDonald's Deutschland Inc v Rahmer* [2000] ETMR 91 (Bundesgerichtshof).
[46] *J B Cosmetics SP ZOO Kamienczyk N/Bugiem's trade mark* [2000] ETMR 722 (Polish Patent Office).
[47] *AM General Corp v DaimlerChrysler Corp*, No 02-1816 (7th Cir 18 November 2002).

perhaps have failed,[48] to uproot earlier users of identical or similar trade marks[49] and it would take a grave shift in public and legal opinion before the law moved any closer to protecting them against earlier users than it already does.

(6) The duration of fame

We have seen that a trade mark may acquire fame extremely quickly.[50] But how long does that fame last? More to the point, from a practical lawyer's perspective, does fame have to be proved afresh each time a trade mark owner goes to court to protect his famous mark? Logically, if the fame of a trade mark must be established before a judicial tribunal or trade mark registry on the first occasion that the owner seeks protection, he must do so also on subsequent occasions since it is a mark's fame at the time it is threatened which determines the nature of the legal response to that threat. This position was taken by the Peruvian Trade Mark Office when Mars, having successfully established the fame of the MARS trade mark in 1994, sought to cancel a similar mark granted in 1999. The Supreme Court disagreed, taking the view that fame, once established, should be presumed from the fact that products bearing the famous mark remained continuously on the market.[51] Likewise, the fact that a trade mark has been held in an earlier decision not to be famous may be regarded as a matter of *res judicata* when the fame of that mark is asserted in subsequent proceedings.[52]

12.42

From a practical point of view this decision can be justified, since it spares trade mark proprietors the inconvenience of preparing evidence of what, in the vast majority of cases, will be obvious to both the judge and to the defendant. On the other hand, famous marks *do* lose their fame[53] and the case of a trade mark which is on its way to losing its fame while keeping its reputation is not an easy one to resolve. An analogous position which presents itself for comparison is that of the distinctive mark which is on its way to losing its distinctive character, but this analogy is weak: a mark can be simultaneously both distinctive (to a small number of experts) and

12.43

---

[48] Instances of success on the part of trade mark owners in driving away earlier users through legal threats, unlike failures, are not publicized.
[49] See eg *McDonald's Corporation v McDonald's Corporation Limited & Vincent Chang* [1997] FSR 760, *Société des Produits Nestlé SA v Pro Fiducia Treuhand AG* [2002] ETMR 351.
[50] *Pfizer Ltd and Pfizer Incorporated v Eurofood Link (United Kingdom) Ltd* [2000] ETMR 896 (HC).
[51] *Mars v Miski* (2003) 4 WIPR 13 (Supreme Court, Peru).
[52] *Enterprise Rent-a-Car Co v Advantage Rent-a-Car Inc* WTLR, 18 July 2003 (CAFC).
[53] See eg the trade marks mentioned at paras 12.17–12.24 above. See also *Quality Bakers*, 27 April 2000 (The Hague Court of Appeal), where the formerly famous CORN KING trade mark for bread was cancelled for non-use after it was shown that only 221 loaves of CORN KING bread had been sold in the previous five years. The court held that 'well-known mark' protection under article 6*bis* of the Paris Convention was intended to apply to trade marks which had lapsed for non-use.

non-distinctive (to the consuming public[54]) but it is hard to see how a mark can be both famous and non-famous.

(7) Relief against wrongful registration of a famous mark

12.44 As we have seen above, article 6*bis* of the Paris Convention requires that trade marks which fall within the scope of its protection should not be registered by any person who is not entitled to its benefit. Where such a person wrongfully registers another's trade mark, the cancellation of that registration is the most appropriate relief. Where the mark is sufficiently well known that it is difficult for the wrongful registrant to plead convincingly that he did not know of its existence, or where he certainly should have discovered its existence before he registered the mark, the owner of the well-known mark will generally be able to plead that the registration contrary to article 6*bis* was made in bad faith.[55] The advantage of being able to claim that the registration was sought in bad faith is that there is no limitation period beyond which an application for relief is time-barred.[56] Thus in a Dutch case the owner of the well-known trade mark MARIE CLAIRE for the fashion magazine *Marie Claire* was able, by successfully alleging bad faith, to obtain the cancellation of a hostile MARIE CLAIRE Benelux registration for socks, stockings and underwear a good decade after its original registration in 1992.[57]

(8) Relief against infringement of a famous mark

12.45 When the proprietor of a famous trade mark sues for infringement, injunctive relief is usually the most important consideration. This is because not only the trade mark's ability to serve as a designator of origin or quality but also its inherent value or 'advertising function' (to use the Portuguese term[58]) is in danger of persistent long-term erosion if the threat to that trade mark is not immediately nipped in the bud. Owners of trade marks are generally vigilant to police their marks and swift to act when danger threatens. Accordingly, a review of the cases shows that actions for interim injunctive relief are the commonest, followed by actions for final injunctive relief. Damages awards are relatively infrequent because the defendant is rarely allowed enough time to inflict damage. For the same reason, where a third party seeks to register an identical or dangerously close trade mark, oppositions are far more common than actions for cancellation.

---

[54] See *Björnekulla Fruktindustrier Aktiebolag v Procordia Food Aktiebolag* [2002] ETMR 464 (Sweden, referred to the ECJ).
[55] On registrations made in bad faith, see Chapter 13.
[56] Paris Convention, art 6*bis* (3).
[57] *Marie Claire Album SA v Ipko-Amcor BV*, Case 00/2268 (District Court, The Hague).
[58] See *Indústria e Comércio de Cosméticos Natura AS's application* [2001] ETMR 783 (Lisbon Court of Appeals).

C. Famous mark protection in the United States

The Monaco Court of First Instance, in a case involving the improper registration of VIAGRA for telematic services and computer software, has indicated that injunctive relief and non-compensatory damages is all that the proprietor of even a famous mark can expect, unless it can show evidence of actual damage.[59] **12.46**

(9) The position of the consumer

When considering the problems relating to trade marks which are liable to mislead or confuse the public, much has been made of the specific interests and capabilities of the consumer. This is because the consumer who is confused is the consumer who buys the wrong product. If he buys the wrong product, he is annoyed with his purchase and the shop he buys it from is annoyed when the consumer returns it (assuming that the consumer hasn't already consumed it). It follows from this that the likelihood that a consumer will be confused between a trade mark and an allegedly infringing sign is determined by the courts' looking at the alleged confusion through the eyes of those consumers who would typically be confused. **12.47**

In contrast, where legal issues address the protection of well-known marks, the position of the consumer is given far less prominence. That is not to say that there is no role for the consumer, though. A trade mark's reputation, as well as its repute,[60] can only be found to exist and then be quantified by reference to consumers of the goods or services for which it is registered. Legal mechanisms for the protection of well-known or famous marks do however appear to depend far less upon the typical consumer's response, relying instead upon other criteria such as the extent to which the trade mark owner has successfully invested in establishing a distinctive and possibly unique image. Another factor which is considered in relation to well-known and famous marks but which is unrelated to the consumer's perception of the parties' respective marks is the extent to which the use of the later mark constitutes an unfair appropriation of the labour and efforts of the owner of the earlier one. **12.48**

C. Famous mark protection in the United States

(1) The 'anti-dilution' approach

The provisions of Federal[61] United States law are more sophisticated and focused **12.49**

---

[59] *Pfizer Inc v Monaco Télématique en Abrégé MC TEL* [2001] ETMR 169 (the 'non-compensatory' damages were fixed at FFr 50,000, about €7,600 or $8,000: not a fortune but not token either).
[60] See Chapter 11, paras 11.25–11.28.
[61] In addition to Federal anti-dilution law, anti-dilution statutes exist in many States including California, Florida, Georgia, Illinois, Massachusetts, New York and Pennsylvania: for an account of the working of these State laws, see Tony Martino, *Trademark Dilution* (1996). A list of States and anti-dilution protection currently offered by them may be accessed from the INTA website (www.inta.org).

than those of their European counterparts. In their relevant part they read (with added emphasis) as follows:[62]

> *False designations of origin; false description or representation*
> (c) (1) The owner of a *famous* mark shall be entitled, subject to the principles of equity and upon such terms as the court deems reasonable, to an injunction against another person's commercial use in commerce of a mark or trade name, if such use begins after the mark has become *famous* and causes *dilution* of the distinctive quality of the mark, and to obtain such other relief as is provided in this subsection . . .
> (2) In an action brought under this subsection, the owner of the *famous* mark shall be entitled only to injunctive relief as set forth in section 34 unless the person against whom the injunction is sought wilfully intended to trade on the owner's reputation or to cause *dilution* of the famous mark. If such wilful intent is proven, the owner of the famous mark shall also be entitled to the remedies set forth in sections 35(a) and 36, subject to the discretion of the court and the principles of equity . . .

12.50 Dilution is defined in section 45 of the Lanham Act (15 USC, s 1127), as follows:

> [T]he lessening of the capacity of a famous mark to identify and distinguish goods or services, regardless of the presence or absence of (1) competition between the owner of the famous mark and other parties, or (2) likelihood of confusion, mistake, or deception.

12.51 How does 'dilution' relate to other concepts with which we have sought to evaluate the scope of the protection of known, well-known and famous marks? An OHIM Board of Appeal has observed that dilution is a narrower concept than detriment since, while evidence of dilution is evidence of detriment, the opposite proposition is not true.[63] Dilution may also be contrasted with unfair advantage, since dilution is of necessity measured from the point of view of the senior right owner while unfair advantage is measured from the position of the contentious applicant or allegedly infringing user.[64]

12.52 It is unclear whether a trade mark must be merely famous, or both famous and distinctive. This is because, while the protection of a trade mark against dilution in section 43(c)(1) is initially expressed as being accorded to a trade mark which is famous, that same provision later lays down guidance 'in determining whether a mark is distinctive and famous'.[65] In *Nabisco v P F Brands Inc*[66] a Second Circuit court ruled emphatically that protection against dilution was only available to

---

[62] Lanham Act, s 43 (15 USC, s 1125).
[63] *Hollywood SAS v Souza Cruz SA*, Case R 283/1999-3 [2002] ETMR 705.
[64] *Pfizer Ltd and Pfizer Incorporated v Eurofood Link (United Kingdom) Ltd* [2000] ETMR 896, [2000] IP&T 280, para 37.
[65] This guidance is discussed in paras 12.67–12.68 below.
[66] *Nabisco v P F Brands Inc* 191 F 3d 208, 227–8 (2d Cir 1999): goldfish-shaped cracker held to be famous and inherently distinctive. The Court said: 'A mark can be famous without being at all distinctive, as in the cases of AMERICAN AIRLINES, AMERICAN TOBACCO COMPANY, BRITISH AIRWAYS . . . [A] famous mark that has acquired secondary meaning is not distinctive as that term is used in the federal anti-dilution statute, and is . . . not entitled to protection'.

C. Famous mark protection in the United States

trade marks which were both famous and inherently distinctive, while in the *Times Mirror* case a Third Circuit court has equally emphatically ruled that there is no separate requirement to find that a trade mark is both famous *and* distinctive.[67]

(2) Dilution and the burden of proof

The position under Federal United States law is that, in the context of an action for 'dilution',[68] the trade mark owner must prove more than a likelihood of damage. Where the owner of the well-known VICTORIA'S SECRET trade mark for lingerie objected to the sale of 'unwholesome, tawdry merchandise' from a retail store in Elizabethtown, Kentucky, named 'Victor's Little Secret', that court held that the trade mark owner could not succeed except on proof of actual damage.[69] This appears to be similar to the position in Europe where, under Directive 89/104 and the CTM Regulation,[70] an infringing act is one which actually takes advantage of, or is detrimental to, the distinctive character or repute of a trade mark (though how this is proved will remain a matter of national law).[71] 12.53

(3) Interim injunctive relief against dilution

If *VICTORIA'S SECRET* is correct, an interesting problem relates to the means by which a trade mark owner may persuade a court to grant an injunction *before* the alleged dilution takes place. From the trade mark owner's point of view, it is always better to prevent damage occurring than to wait until it has occurred and then try to stop it. But, according to *VICTORIA'S SECRET*, an action for dilution cannot succeed unless actual dilution occurs. Where the allegedly diluting trade mark is the same as the trade mark owner's (for example, KODAK for cameras, KODAK for toothpicks), the fact that the two marks are the same is regarded as circumstantial evidence of dilution, so a court would not find it hard to accept, even before KODAK toothpicks reach the shops, that their sale would dilute the KODAK trade mark for cameras. But where KODAK sells cameras and a trader plans to sell KO DA KAI judo mats, there is no circumstantial evidence of dilution and Kodak will have to adduce evidence at the trial. 12.54

In such a situation, before KO DA KAI judo mats are launched and there is plainly no dilution, would it be sufficient for Kodak to seek an interim injunction by proving the existence of its own KODAK trade mark and arguing that there exists a 12.55

---

[67] *Times Mirror Magazine Inc v Las Vegas Sports News LLC* 212 F 3d 157, 167 (3d Cir 2000): THE SPORTING NEWS newspaper title held to be famous, though not inherently distinctive.

[68] Discussed in the next chapter; see especially Chapter 12, paras 12.49–12.55ff.

[69] *Moseley et al, dba Victor's Little Secret v V Secret Catalogue Inc* 537 US 418, 123 Sup Ct 1115 (2003).

[70] Council Directive 89/104, art 5(2); Council Regulation 40/94, art 9(1)(c).

[71] *General Motors Corp v Yplon SA*, Case C-375/97 [1999] ETMR 120, para 43.

likelihood of dilution? Since evidence of a likelihood of dilution would not be sufficient basis upon which to succeed at a full trial, it is improbable that such evidence would be a sufficient basis for securing interim relief either. Another suggestion is that the trade mark owner submit two sets of consumer survey evidence: one to support the notion that the claimant's trade mark is a famous mark within the meaning of the Lanham Act, the other to support the contention that, *if* a product or service bearing the defendant's intended trade mark were to be launched, they would regard the claimant's trade mark as having lost some of its distinctive quality and that they would thereby think less of products or services bearing the claimant's trade mark. Irrespective of whether a court would be prepared to accept hypothetical survey evidence at all, the 'two survey' approach does seem an expensive, cumbersome and inconvenient route to interim relief.

(4) The doctrine of progressive encroachment

12.56 Under United States case law[72] it has been established that a trade mark owner may pursue a *de minimis* infringer on the basis that even a trivial infringement may serve to dilute the distinctive character of his trade mark. If however he chooses not to sue but decides to tolerate *de minimis* encroachments upon the distinctive character of his famous mark, he may do so without running the risk that, when he later seeks to enforce his claim against an alleged diluting use, he will be prevented from doing so by legal doctrines such as laches (delay), acquiescence or estoppel.

12.57 This doctrine has no exact equivalent in Europe, where minor encroachments upon the rights of a trade mark owner in his well-known trade mark are actionable but where issues such as laches, acquiescence and estoppel would fall to be determined by national law in the jurisdiction in which they were raised.

(5) Multiparty dilution of a famous mark

12.58 Let us consider the position of MON CHÉRI liqueur-filled cherry pralines in Europe, in respect of which the proprietor's attempts to prevent some arguably distant dilutionary trade mark applications were reviewed in the previous chapter. MON CHÉRI products are currently famous, which is more than can be said for MONTXERI liqueurs[73] or BONCÈRI cherry tomatoes which hover around the fringes of the consumer's consciousness but stay just out of reach of opposition or infringement proceedings.[74] We could add MONT CHERRY for a chocolate dessert

---

[72] *SunAmerica Corp v Sun Life Assurance Co of Canada*, 77 F 3d 1325, 1345 (11th Cir 1996). See also J Thomas McCarthy, *McCarthy on Trademarks and Unfair Competition* (1997), para 31.19.
[73] *Ferrero oHG mbH v Jordi Tarrida Llopart*, Case R 186/2001-1 [2003] ETMR 188.
[74] *Ferrero oHG mbH v Annie Cornelia Beekenkamp*, Case R 214/2002-4, 4 December 2002 (unreported).

C. Famous mark protection in the United States

mounted by a cherry, MUNCHERIE for a cherry encrusted with liqueur-saturated crystallized sugar, LONG CHÉRI for a cool cherry/praline flavoured alcopop. Very soon MON CHÉRI would start to look like another tired and faded piece of me-too marketing in a field crowded with similar-sounding cherry references. But what can be done about it?

12.59 Where a trade mark giant is attacked by pygmies, no one trader can be held legally responsible for anyone's activities but his own. Assuming that the dilutionary assailants are not acting in concert, there would not even be a possibility of an action for conspiracy against them; nor would the situation appear to be one in which an action for unfair competition would lie. Moreover, while the attack of the first pygmy might be fended off by interim injunctive relief if he was foolish enough to bring his own sign sufficiently close to the trade mark proprietor's as to attract liability, once he is joined by many others out there with their sound-alike brands it is well-nigh impossible for the trade mark giant to establish and sustain a commercially viable claim to protect his reputation.

(6) The 1999 WIPO recommendations

12.60 A set of recommendations[75] concerning the protection of well-known marks was agreed in 1999 by the Assembly of the Paris Union and the WIPO General Assembly (the two Assemblies being drawn from largely the same countries). The recommendations propose a number of guidelines for the protection of famous marks, any of which may be used by Paris Convention Member States. They appear to be aimed at enhancing the law of those countries which do not adequately protect well-known marks rather than seeking to amend the existing laws of those jurisdictions which do.

12.61 At present these recommendations are not enforceable propositions of law. Despite this, both the degree of consensus which they reflect and their intellectual origin as propositions based on national law suggest that they may be accorded at least some persuasive value in jurisdictions which require the protection of well-known trade marks and where no better or more legally influential guidance exists.

12.62 Article 2 of the recommendations consists of guidance in determining whether a mark is 'well-known' in a Member State. Competent authorities must take account of 'any factors from which it may be inferred that the mark is well known'. These include:

---

[75] WIPO, *Joint Recommendation Concerning Provisions on the Protection of Well-Known Marks* (2000).

(i) the degree of knowledge or recognition of the mark in the relevant sector of the public;
(ii) the duration, extent and geographical area of any use of the mark;
(iii) the duration, extent and geographical area of any promotion of the mark, including advertising or publicity and the presentation, at fairs or exhibitions, of the goods and/or services to which the mark applies;
(iv) the duration and geographical area of any registrations, and/or any applications for registration, of the mark, to the extent that they reflect use or recognition of the mark;
(v) the record of successful enforcement of rights in the mark, in particular, the extent to which the mark was recognized as well known by competent authorities;
(vi) the value associated with the mark.

12.63 These criteria are not without their difficulties, which may be why article 2 adds that they 'are not preconditions' and that some—and or even none—may be relevant in any given instance: every determination should depend on its own circumstances. One wonders how many marks become well known nowadays on the basis of use in 'fairs and exhibitions', platforms which were manifestly more important in trade terms in the nineteenth century than they are today.[76] Likewise, the reference to trade mark applications, 'to the extent that they reflect use or recognition of the mark', is curious. Is this a reference to *telle-quelle* applications[77] or an allusion to applications where the trade mark is claiming distinctiveness acquired through use?

12.64 Of equal significance is the list of factors which, article 2(3) states, should *not* be required as criteria of being well known:

(i) that the mark has been used in, or that the mark has been registered or that an application for registration of the mark has been filed in or in respect of, the Member State;
(ii) that the mark is well known in, or that the mark has been registered or that an application for registration of the mark has been filed in or in respect of, any jurisdiction other than the Member State;
(iii) that the mark is well known by the public at large in the Member State.

12.65 The first and second of these non-criteria enable a trade mark to become famous on the basis that it has, through strategic product placements, been mentioned on American sitcoms which are then repeated frequently in target countries, regardless of whether any registration strategy has yet matured in that jurisdiction or any

---

[76] The fairs and exhibitions to which this provision applies are those which fall within the terms of the Convention on International Exhibitions (Paris, 22 November 1928), as revised.

[77] Discussed in Chapter 4.

D. Conclusion

other. The third reflects the possibility of a court finding that MCDONALD'S was not regarded as well known in South Africa since only the wealthy white minority, and not the black 'public at large' would be familiar with it.[78]

Once a mark is deemed well known, article 3 requires that Member States protect it against 'conflicting marks, business identifiers[79] and domain names, at least with effect from the time when the mark has become well known in the Member State'. Articles 4 (dealing with conflicting marks) and 5 (dealing with business identifiers) specify the nature of the protection conferred, listing both American-style 'impairment and dilution' and European-style 'unfair advantage'.

(7) United States, ECJ and WIPO guidelines for 'famous marks' contrasted

If we place article 2 of the WIPO recommendations, section 43 of the Lanham Act and the ECJ's comments in *General Motors v Yplon*[80] in juxtaposition, we can group together several of the indicia of fame (in the case of Lanham and the United States) and reputation (in the case of Europe). This juxtaposition is best portrayed in diagrammatic format (see Table 12.1).

Let us leave aside the ECJ criteria and focus on the WIPO and Lanham Act lists, since it is those which focus fully on a mark's true celebrity rather than on it being merely known. Even (i) taking into account the possible consequences of those two sets of respective criteria being interpreted in different ways and (ii) allowing for the fact that each has one criterion for which there is no counterpart, it is apparent that they are both flexible and thus reassuringly imprecise in their potential application to the facts of any specific situation. It is difficult, if not impossible, to think of any relatively well-known trade mark in the world today which, within its jurisdiction, would be bound to satisfy the 'famous mark' criteria of the United States but fail that of the WIPO recommendations, or vice versa.

D. Conclusion

In this chapter we have reviewed the concepts of the well-known and famous marks. We have examined international, European and United States law for approaches to them and we have found that, in general, they are well protected by law even though the means of achieving protection is sometimes unclear in its path or uncertain in its objectives.

---

[78] See the discussion in *McDonalds Corporation v Joburgers Drive-Inn Restaurant (Pty) Ltd and Anor & McDonalds Corporation v Dax Prop CC and Anor* [1996] (4) All SA 4.
[79] Defined in article 1 as 'any sign used to identify a business of a natural person, a legal person, an organization or an association'.
[80] *General Motors Corp v Yplon SA*, Case C-375/97 [1999] ETMR 950 (ECJ).

Chapter 12: Well-known Marks, Famous Marks and Dilution

12.70 In the following chapter we visit the 'killing fields', in which applications for trade mark registration are thwarted and even granted registrations may be dispatched.

Table 12.1 Juxtaposition of the indicia of fame: article 2 of the WIPO recommendations, section 43 of the Lanham Act and the ECJ's comments in *General Motors v Yplon*.

	WIPO Joint memorandum	United States	European Union
Knowledge or recognition by the public	*Article 2(1)(b)(1)* The degree of knowledge or recognition of the mark in the relevant sector of the public.	*Section 43(c)(1)(F)* The degree of recognition of the mark in the trading areas and channels of trade used by the mark's owner and the person against whom the injunction is sought.	*General Motors, para 23* Knowledge of the mark by a significant part of the public concerned for the products or services which it covers.
Duration and extent of any use of the mark	*Article 2(1)(b)(2)* The duration, extent and geographical area of any use of the mark.	*Section 43(c)(1)(B)* The duration and extent of use of the mark in connection with the goods or services with which the mark is used.	*General Motors, para 27* The intensity, geographical extent and duration of the use.
Geographical extent of fame	*Article 2(1)(b)(5)* The record of successful enforcement of rights in the mark, in particular, the extent to which the mark was recognized as well known by competent authorities.	*Section 43(c)(1)(D)* The geographical extent of the trading area in which the mark is used.	*General motors, para 28* Reputation must exist in a 'substantial part' of the territory.
	Explanatory Note 2.8 Explains that successful enforcement and recognition of a mark as being well known in, for example, *neighbouring countries* may serve as an indicator as to whether a mark is well known in a particular state.	Fame that is limited to a geographical niche area may[1] or may not[2] be sufficient.	

---

[1] See *Avery Dennison Corp v Sumpton* 189 F 3d 368, 51 USPQ 2d 1801 (9 Cir 1999) which says that fame in a localized trading area may be sufficient where the plaintiff's trading area includes that trading area of the defendant.

[2] The legislative history of section 43(c) states that 'the geographical fame of the [plaintiff's] mark must extend throughout a substantial portion of the US' (House Report 104-374 (30 November 1995), 1996 US CCAN 1029, 1034). This was cited in *Syndicate Sales Inc v Hampshire Paper Corp* 192 F 3d 633, 52 USPQ 2d 1035 (7th Cir 1999) where the Court held that fame in a geographical niche market is insufficient. See also *Times Mirror Magazines Inc v Las Vegas Sporting News LLC* 212 F 3d 157, 54 USPQ 2d 1577 (3d Cir 2000). See, further, J Thomas McCarthy, *McCarthy on Trademarks and Unfair Competition* (1996), §24:92.

D. Conclusion

Table 12.1 *continued*

	WIPO Joint memorandum	United States *Article 2(2)(d)*	European Union
	A Member State may determine that a mark is well known even if it is not well known or known in *that* state, in which case, according to *Article 2(3)(b)*, it may require that the mark be well known in one or more *other* jurisdictions.		
Advertising and promotion of the mark	*Article 2(1)(b)(3)* The duration, extent and geographical area of any promotion of the mark, including advertising or publicity and the presentation, at fairs or exhibitions, of the goods and/or services to which the trade mark applies.	*Section 43(c)(1)(C)* The duration and extent of advertising and publicity of the mark.	*General Motors, para 27* The size of the investment in promoting the mark.
Registration of the mark	*Article 2(1)(b)(4)* The duration and geographical area of any registrations, and/ or any applications for registration of the mark, to the extent that they reflect use or recognition of the mark.	*Section 43(c)(1)(H)* Whether the mark was registered under the Act of 3 March 1881, or the Act of 20 February 1905, or on the principal register.	No equivalent in the EU although no mark can form the basis of an infringement action under article 5(2) unless it is registered in the Member State in question or, in the case of a Community trade mark, on the Community trade mark register.
Successful enforcement of the mark	*Article 2(1)(b)(5)* The record of successful enforcement of rights in the mark, in particular, the extent to which the mark was recognized as well known by competent authorities.	No US Equivalent	No European Equivalent
The value associated with the mark	*Article 2(1)(b)(6)* The value associated with the mark.	No US Equivalent	No European Equivalent

Table 12.1 *continued*

	WIPO Joint memorandum	United States *Article 2(2)(d)*	European Union
Recognition of the mark in specific trade sectors	*Article 2(1)(b)(1)* The degree of knowledge or recognition of the mark in the *relevant sector* of the public. **Together with** *Article 2(2)(a)* Which states that relevant sectors of the public shall include, but shall not necessarily be limited to: (i) actual and/or potential consumers of the type of goods and/or services to which the mark applies; (ii) persons involved in channels of distribution of the type of goods and/or services to which the mark applied; (iii) business circles dealing with the type of goods and/or services to which the mark applies **and** *Article 2(2)(b)* Where a mark is determined to be *well known* in at least *one* relevant sector of the public in a Member State, the mark *shall* be considered by the Member State to be a well-known mark **and** *Article 2(2)(c)* Where a mark is determined to be *known* in at least *one* relevant sector of the public in a Member State, the mark *may* be considered by the Member State to be a well-known mark.	*Section 43(c)(1)(E)* The channels of trade for the goods or services with which the mark is used. *Times Mirror Magazines Inc v Las Vegas Sports News, LLC* and *Syndicate Sales Inc v Hampshire Paper Corp* Fame in a niche market composed only of purchasers or users of the type of goods or services the claimant provides is sufficient, but dilution protection will only be provided if the junior user markets his goods or services in the same niche market.	*General Motors, para 24* Reputation may be acquired in the eyes of the public at large or a more specialized public, such as traders in a specific sector.
Use by third parties	No Equivalent in the joint recommendations	*Section 43(c)(1)(G)* The nature and extent of use of the same or similar marks by third parties	**No European Equivalent**

D. Conclusion

Table 12.1 *continued*

	WIPO Joint memorandum	United States *Article 2(2)(d)*	European Union
Strength of the mark	No equivalent in the joint recommendations	Section 43(c)(1)(A) The degree of inherent or acquired distinctiveness of the mark.	No European Equivalent although this factor is relevant to the substantive issue[3]

---

[3] While strength of the mark is not relevant to the assessment of whether a mark has a reputation in the EU, strong marks are afforded greater protection under both article 5(2) and 5(1)(b). In *General Motors v Yplon* (para 30), the ECJ stated that 'the stronger the earlier mark's distinctive character and reputation the easier it will be to accept that detriment has been caused to it.' The OHIM Board of Appeal in *Hollywood SAS v Souza Cruz SA* (para 115) has added that unfair advantage is also more likely if the mark has a strong distinctive character and reputation. Similarly, in *Cannon KK v Metro-Goldwyn-Mayer Inc* (para 18), the ECJ confirmed that confusion is more likely to occur where earlier marks have 'a highly distinctive character, either per se or because of the reputation they possess on the market.'

13

THE KILLING FIELDS: OPPOSITION, CANCELLATION AND REVOCATION

A.	**Introduction**	
	A knock at the door	
	The moral of the story	13.01
	(1) Structure of the chapter	13.02
	(2) Opposition proceedings	13.03
	(3) Cancellation proceedings	13.07
	(4) Grounds of opposition and cancellation	13.09
	(5) Revocation proceedings and grounds of revocation	13.11
	(6) *Locus standi* to oppose, cancel or revoke a trade mark	13.13
B.	**Opposition**	
	(1) Opposition and 'invisible' attacks	13.16
	(2) Intention of the applicant	13.18
	(3) Opposition based on families of marks	13.19
	(a) Opposition based on large families	13.20
	(b) Opposition based on single-parent families	13.22
	(c) Ignoring the family: the OHIM approach	13.23
	(d) Families of device marks	13.25
	(4) Use of the opponent's mark must be significant	13.26
	(5) The opponent's mark must be geographically relevant	13.32
	(6) Prior proceedings and contractual arrangements	13.33
C.	**Cancellation**	
	(1) Cancellation on absolute grounds	13.35
	(2) Cancellation based on prior third-party use	13.39
	(3) Cancellation on relative grounds	13.40
	(4) 'Central attack' and the Madrid Agreement	13.42
D.	**Revocation**	13.46
	(1) Non-use in relation to different classes of goods and services	13.50
	(2) What is 'genuine use' of a trade mark?	13.51
	(3) Proper reasons for non-use	13.59
	(4) The mark must be used in the form in which the mark is registered	13.61
	(5) Evidence of use	13.63
	(6) Trade marks remain valid until they are revoked	13.64
	(7) A trade mark may be re-registered after revocation	13.65
	(8) Revocation of part of a registration	13.67
E.	**Suspension of trade mark applications and of hostilities in general**	13.70

Chapter 13: The Killing Fields: Opposition, Cancellation and Revocation

F.	Trade mark systems and 'bad faith'	13.72
	(1) 'Bad faith' in EU law	13.75
	(2) 'Bad faith' in European domestic trade mark law	13.82
	(3) Persuasive grounds of 'bad faith'	13.85
	(a) Unauthorized filing by the trade mark owner's agent or representative	13.86
	(b) Misuse of rights	13.90
	(c) Abuse of 'direct relations'	13.92
	(d) Use of the registered mark in a manner other than as registered	13.95
	(e) Registration of a later mark with actual knowledge of the earlier mark	13.96
	(f) Registration of another party's famous mark	13.98
	(g) Failure to behave in a prudent commercial manner	13.99
	(h) *Bona fide* belief in one's entitlement to file a trade mark application does not mean that the application is not made in bad faith	13.101
	(i) The certain knowledge that one's application will be successfully opposed	13.102
	(4) Things which do not positively suggest that there is 'bad faith'	13.103
	(a) Using the trade mark monopoly in order to extend an expired patent monopoly	13.104
	(b) Registration of the name of deceased celebrities	13.105
	(c) Timing of the application	13.106
	(d) Amendment of the application	13.107
	(e) Lack of veracity in the application	13.108
	(f) Mere similarity between the registered trade mark and the earlier mark	13.109
	(g) Translation of the earlier trade mark into another language	13.110
	(h) Proximity of the registered trade mark to an international non-proprietary name	13.111
	(5) Things which do suggest that there is no 'bad faith'	13.112
	(a) Length of time the applicant uses the mark openly before filing the application	13.113
	(b) Plausibility of the applicant's explanation as to how he chose the trade mark	13.114
	(c) The offer of a coexistence agreement	13.116
	(d) The concept of the 'previous prior user'	13.117
	(6) 'Bad faith' and the nature of the earlier trade mark	13.118
	(a) Does the earlier trade mark need to have been used?	13.119
	(b) Where does the earlier trade mark need to have been used?	13.120
	(c) Does the earlier trade mark need to have a reputation?	13.121
	(d) Does the use of the earlier mark need to be continuous?	13.122
	(e) Does the earlier mark have to be identical or similar to the challenged mark?	13.123
	(7) 'Bad faith' and intent to use	13.124
	(8) Overwide registration as 'bad faith'	13.130
	(9) 'Bad faith' and procedural issues	13.143
	(a) When need the registering office raise the issue of bad faith?	13.144
	(b) Which tribunal deals with bad-faith claims?	13.145
	(c) The burden of proof of bad faith: rebutting the presumption of good faith	13.147
	(d) *Locus standi* to plead bad faith	13.148
G.	Conclusion	13.149

A. Introduction

A knock at the door

Business was definitely bad, mused Marmaduke as he scanned the horizon for distant orders. The rag trade was definitely sluggish—or at least his little corner of it was. There was no doubt about it: people were still wearing clothes, but not those lovingly

A. Introduction

designed and stitched together by his eponymous outfit Marmaduke Modes. Pausing for a moment to reshuffle the pile of unpaid bills on his desk, Marmaduke returned to the gentle privacy of his thoughts and to his precious dream of making the big time with his fashion house.

Suddenly there was a sharp, businesslike knock at the door. Leaping up, Marmaduke swiftly scooped up a fistful of invoices, threats and final demands and tucked them artfully out of sight in the fridge, straightened his tie, patted his hair down and threw back his shoulders with an air of confidence and swung open the door. This must surely be a customer, he thought. But he was wrong. Two men stood before him. One was tall and gruff, the other short and greasy.

'Are you Mr Modes?' queried the short, greasy one.

'No, my name's Marmaduke Sparrow. It's my business that's called Marmaduke Modes. You know, Marmaduke Sparrow trading as Marmaduke Modes and all that stuff.'

'Oh, I see, Mr Modes,' continued Short and Greasy. 'Well, can you let us in, please? We're from the Ministry and we've come to inspect your trade marks.'

'I didn't know they needed inspecting,' responded Marmaduke, a little surprised. 'I thought that once you got them they just lasted forever and that was that.' The sudden thought struck Marmaduke that perhaps the Ministry was considering placing a large order with him for uniforms for the inspectorate.

'Been reading fairytales, son?' This was the tall gruff one. 'Can't be too careful with trade marks, you know. We caught someone hoarding them last week, we did. And do you know what we did to him?' He arched his brows, looked deeply into Marmaduke's eyes and waited for his host to blink first, which he did.

'No, what did you do to him?' Marmaduke was becoming alarmed. Prospects of a Ministry contract faded.

'Tell him, son,' said Tall and Gruff.

'We had him . . . expunged. That's what we did. Right out there in the street. In front of all the neighbours. We expunged him, we did.' Short and Greasy spoke with an obvious warmth for his employment duties.

'Well, what's that got to do with me?' gulped Marmaduke, wondering what it felt like to be expunged.

'We have reason to suspect that you are harbouring an unused mark, Mr Modes.' Short and Greasy paused for effect, then continued: 'It goes by the name of MARMADUKE FASHIONS. Do you remember MARMADUKE FASHIONS?'

'Can't say I do,' responded Marmaduke, tramlines of perplexity traversing his brow. 'Oh, wait . . . yes, I think I did register one of those. Must have been a few years ago now.'

'It was nine years ago, Mr Modes.' It was Tall and Gruff's turn again. 'Nine years is a long stretch for not using a mark. I'm afraid we are going to have to report this one.'

'What . . . what will happen to me?' Marmaduke's nether lip quivered. This could mean the end of his business dreams.

Tall and Gruff shrugged his shoulders in a gesture of indifference. 'It's not up to me to decide, mate. But the Ministry may decide to have you revoked.'

Marmaduke was despondent. But he still had one last trade mark hope. It was only a few short months ago that he had filed an application to register his trading name MARMADUKE MODES as a trade mark for fashion garments and accessories. Surely that would be all right?

'Oh, and another thing,' said Short and Greasy. 'Don't think for a minute that we don't know all about your MARMADUKE MODES application. We know all about that one. Nice little mark, isn't it? You wouldn't want anything to . . . to happen to it, would you?'

'What would you like, good sir? I can offer you a smashing new suit. One each, if you like,' pleaded Marmaduke. 'But please, please don't harm my MARMADUKE MODES application.'

'I'm sorry, Mr Modes,' said T and G, sounding almost sympathetic, 'but we don't accept gifts when we're on duty. Just office fees. And it's bad news about your application. Too close to SQUIRREL MODES. We had to put it down.'

Marmaduke shed a tear. The game was up.

The moral of the story

13.01 In the real world there is no Ministry to visit businesses and protect the purity of the trade mark register by rooting out unworthy marks and applications. Keeping the registry clean is the function of traders themselves. They do this (i) through seeking to remove 'dead wood' in the form of old, unused marks which perform no commercial function and merely inconvenience later businesses and (ii) by opposing attempts to register as trade marks those signs which have no right to be on the register. This chapter is dedicated to the techniques involved in killing live marks and applications and in removing dead and dying marks from the commercial battlefield.

(1) Structure of the chapter

13.02 In this chapter we will first introduce the concepts of opposition, cancellation and revocation. Then we will look more closely at the functional characteristics of each of these weapons, which have the potential to wield great destructive force against the registration of a trade mark.

(2) Opposition proceedings

13.03 Opposition is a procedure which enables a third party to prevent a trade mark applicant getting his mark registered. For Community trade marks (CTMs) the opposition procedure may only be invoked by proprietors of earlier marks or signs where the ground of opposition is based on what would be a *relative* ground of refusal of the application.[1] Where the ground upon which registration is objected to is an *absolute* ground for refusal of registration, the would-be opponent must content himself by writing a letter to the Office for Harmonisation in the Internal Market (OHIM) in which he expresses his observations as to registrability since there is no formal procedure for opposition in such a case.[2]

---

[1] Council Regulation 40/94, art 42.
[2] Council Regulation 40/94, art 41; see also *Durferrit GmbH v OHIM, Kolene Corporation Intervening*, Case T-224/01, 9 April 2003, paras 73–4.

A. Introduction

If I own a registered trade mark or even merely use a sign as though it were a trade mark, most countries provide a mechanism by which I can oppose another person's application to register a trade mark which I consider to be (i) identical or (ii) confusingly similar, or which either (iii) seeks to take unfair advantage of the distinctive character or repute of my mark or (iv) is detrimental to it. By the effective use of this mechanism I can stifle a competitor's branding aspirations or at least weaken them by depriving him of the strong legal protection accorded to trade marks.

13.04

A good example of the effective use of opposition proceedings is the policy which has been pursued in many countries by McDonald's. The word mark MCDONALD'S is derived from a surname which is common in all countries where Scotsmen and their descendants are found; its prefix Mc- is even more common. MCDONALD'S is therefore far more vulnerable to the threat of registrations of similar marks than, for example, an invented name like HÄAGEN-DAZS. McDonald's has accordingly sought to oppose all potentially conflicting applications for trade marks for fast-food restaurants commencing with the prefix Mc-. Once other traders become aware that any application to register a Mc- mark for anything to do with high-street food outlets is likely to be met by opposition proceedings which are potentially expensive, time-consuming and stress-inducing, even when the opposition fails, those other traders soon learn how to file applications for trade marks that do not begin with Mc-.

13.05

Proceedings based on relative grounds of opposition are very much like trade mark infringement proceedings in that the grounds upon which an application may be rejected are those upon which an infringing act may be prevented. The fact that an application is successfully opposed does not however lead to the automatic conclusion that the opponent as owner of an earlier mark will be able to secure injunctive relief against the applicant for use of the rejected mark. That is because opposition proceedings are concerned with the ability of an applicant to acquire proprietary rights in the mark for which he sought registration, while injunctive relief is concerned with the opponent's ability to protect his proprietary rights.[3]

13.06

(3) Cancellation proceedings

Proceedings for cancellation (sometimes also termed invalidity or nullity) provide a means by which a trade mark which should not have been registered may be removed from the register. Accordingly where opposition proceedings fail, or if an interested party is asleep to the danger of a competitor's application until it is too late, cancellation proceedings can be launched so as to have the unwanted mark expunged from the register. It is in principle more difficult to eliminate another

13.07

---

[3] For a case in point, see *Wellcome Foundation Co Ltd v Dairy Farm Management Co Ltd* [1998] IP Asia LR 40 (Thailand).

person's trade mark by cancelling it than to oppose it when it is still only at the application stage, since a granted trade mark is presumed valid until the contrary is proved.

13.08 It is unusual for anyone to seek cancellation of someone else's trade mark solely on the ground that he does not like it and thinks it shouldn't remain on the register. So what is the motivation which underlies an application to cancel another's trade mark? Cancellation is generally sought when the applicant for cancellation considers that his freedom to market his own goods or services in the manner he chooses has been unfairly restricted through the grant of trade mark rights to the proprietor in a sign which he too feels that he is entitled to use. The invalidity of a trade mark is often raised as a counterclaim in trade mark infringement proceedings in which the defendant considers that he is being sued for infringing a trade mark which should not have been granted in the first place.

(4) Grounds of opposition and cancellation

13.09 There are two types of ground of opposition and cancellation. One is based on the inherent unregistrability of the disputed sign (an 'absolute' ground). The other is founded on the likelihood that the disputed sign will be confused with, or otherwise interfere with, an earlier trade mark or other intellectual property right belonging to the opponent or applicant for cancellation (a 'relative' ground).[4] The absolute grounds correspond to the grounds of non-registrability which are discussed in detail in Chapters 4 and 5. The relative grounds correspond to the grounds upon which marks may be confused with each other (reviewed in Chapter 10) or upon which a use of another's trade mark is adjudged to be detrimental to another's earlier mark or to be taking unfair advantage of its reputation, discussed in Chapters 11 and 12.

13.10 In addition to the grounds mentioned above, a trade mark application may be opposed or, if a trade mark is granted, it may be cancelled on the basis that the application to register it was made in bad faith. This ground is discussed in great detail later in this chapter (see paras 13.72–13.148).

(5) Revocation proceedings and grounds of revocation

13.11 Even where a trade mark has been validly registered, it may still be removed from the register, normally on that ground that it has not been used for a continuous period of time. TRIPs stipulates that a trade mark registration may be revoked after three years' non-use,

---

[4] Not all trade mark systems allow for oppositions based on absolute grounds; see Council Regulation 40/94, art 42(1), which limits CTM oppositions to relative grounds alone.

A. Introduction

unless valid reasons based on the existence of obstacles to such use are shown by the trademark owner. Circumstances arising independently of the will of the owner of the trademark which constitute an obstacle to the use of the trademark, such as import restrictions on or other government requirements for goods or services protected by the trademark shall be recognised as valid reasons for non-use.[5]

In both the EU[6] and the United States[7] the period of non-use which is tolerated before revocation may be sought is a generous five years. Unlike the United States, the EU has imposed upon trade mark owners a requirement which is stricter than that of TRIPs in that such use has to be 'genuine'. **13.12**

(6) *Locus standi* to oppose, cancel or revoke a trade mark

The public at large has a shared interest in keeping generic, descriptive and confusing trade marks off the register. Accordingly it is sometimes the case in trade mark systems that any person can seek to oppose, cancel or revoke a trade mark which offends against one or more of the absolute or relative grounds of non-registrability. But this is not always so. Some jurisdictions have more restrictive rules as to who may attack an incumbent trade mark. In one Dutch case, for example, the party seeking the revocation of a Benelux trade mark was held to be only allowed to do so in respect of the registration of that mark in those classes of goods for which the trade mark proprietor and the applicant for revocation were direct competitors.[8] In a French case the applicant for revocation had to satisfy the requirement of being an 'interested party'[9] by demonstrating that it wished to use a mark which would infringe the registered mark unless revocation were ordered.[10] **13.13**

The CTM Regulation has its own set of rules for determining who may apply to OHIM, and in what circumstances, for revocation or a declaration of invalidity. Essentially, (i) anyone may seek revocation,[11] (ii) anyone may seek cancellation on absolute grounds,[12] (iii) only certain specified holders or users of an earlier mark may oppose[13] an application or seek cancellation[14] on relative grounds concerning the earlier mark and (iv) only the owners of other intellectual property rights may seek cancellation on relative grounds concerning those rights.[15] **13.14**

---

[5] TRIPs Agreement, art 19(1).
[6] Council Directive 89/104, art 12(1); Council Regulation 40/94, art 15(1).
[7] 15 USC, s 1058.
[8] *Hij Mannenmode BV v Nienhaus & Lotz GmbH* [1999] ETMR 730 (District Court, Utrecht).
[9] French Intellectual Property Code, art L714–5.
[10] *SA Jean Lempereur v SA Jifi-Madison* [1999] ETMR 1005 (Cour d'appel de Paris).
[11] Council Regulation 40/94, arts 50, 55(1)(a).
[12] ibid, arts 51, 55(1)(a).
[13] ibid, art 42(1).
[14] ibid, arts 52(1), 55(1)(b).
[15] ibid, arts 52(2), 55(1)(b).

13.15 Where CTM and national rules on *locus standi* are not in harmony, the strange and undesirable result may transpire that, where a trade mark owner holds overlapping national and CTMs, a competitor may have *locus standi* to seek revocation or cancellation of one but not the other.

B. Opposition

(1) Opposition and 'invisible' attacks

13.16 Both cancellation and revocation proceedings are relatively easy to anticipate or predict. Revocation is generally a consequence of a mark remaining unused, a circumstance of which the trade mark proprietor is—or should be—only too painfully aware. Cancellation too is often the consequence of an application having been made in bad faith or of an applicant having sought to appropriate a sign which his competitors believe they too should be able to use.

13.17 A feature which sets opposition proceedings apart from revocation and cancellation is the fact that opposition to a trade mark application can spring from a source which was unknown to the applicant and could not even be identified by him at the date when he filed his application. This is because oppositions are based on prior third-party rights which may not be trade marks at all (for example, copyright or design right); they may be based on the use of an unregistered sign which cannot be searched and identified; they may be based on a prior and as yet unpublished application to register a mark and, worst of all, the opposition may be based on the prior filing of a trade mark application in any of the countries which belong to the Paris Union.[16] All of this applies to oppositions based not only on a mark which is the same as the applicant's but on oppositions based on a trade mark which is different but may be confused or associated with his trade mark.

(2) Intention of the applicant

13.18 Where the applicant for registration has deliberately stolen another's trade mark and seeks to register it, the application is made in bad faith[17] and will be rejected. This does not mean that the opponent is required to prove in all cases that the trade mark applicant intended to cause deception or confusion. The grounds of opposition apply even when the trade mark applicant is morally blameless[18]—

---

[16] The Paris Union countries include the preponderant majority of trade mark-granting jurisdictions in the world and all of the commercially significant ones. For an example of a Colombian application to register VIASAT CORPORATIVO being successfully opposed on the basis of an unpublished Australian application which was filed a month before, see *Viasat Inc v Sociedad Telefónica SA* WTLR, 3 April 2003 (Colombia Trade Mark Office).

[17] See paras 13.72–13.148 below.

[18] *Montex Holdings Ltd v Controller* [2000] ETMR 658 (High Court, Ireland): application to reg-

B. Opposition

which is just as well if one considers how difficult it can be to prove the applicant's state of mind when the application is filed.

(3) Opposition based on families of marks

13.19 One of the most interesting techniques for preventing competitors' marks taking root in the trade mark register is that of developing a 'family' of registered marks. The *paterfamilias* of the family is the trade mark owner and his children are his trade marks. Each child is distinguishable from the others, but the family resemblance is strong—so strong, in fact, that the *paterfamilias* can and will feel obliged to deny the paternity of any putative third-party 'sibling'. The way in which a 'family' based opposition may be launched is discussed in the following sections.

(a) Opposition based on large families

13.20 Family-based opposition is most effective where the opponent's family is a large one. An excellent example may be found in the case of Ronald McDonald's fast-food family of trade marks. Starting with MCDONALD's itself, the family grew to include not only BIG MAC but (among others) the following:

MCBACON	MCCAFE	MCCHEESE
MCCHICKEN	MCCRISPY	MCCROISSANT
MCDONUT	MCDOUBLE	MCEXPRESS
MCFEAST	MCFLURRY	MCMENU
MCMUFFIN	MCNUGGETS	MCPIZZA
MCRIB	MCSINGLE	MCTRIPLE

13.21 Any other applicant for a fast-food trade mark will soon be alerted to the existence of this large and flourishing family. What's more, since the McDonald's Corporation is not beyond the age of child-bearing, *lebensraum* must be found on the trade mark register for future offspring (MCTOMATO, MCGHERKIN, MCNOODLE, MCSPINACH and MCWIENER had still not made it on to the trade mark register at the time of writing).

(b) Opposition based on single-parent families

13.22 Opposition proceedings encourage large families since they are more effective when the power of a number of clearly related trade marks is brought to bear against the applicant's mark. Small families simply do not have the same power. In an early OHIM Opposition, the brewers of BECK beers sought to resist the registration of the word mark ISENBECK for beer and claimed, among other things, that since they had also obtained the HAAKEBECK trade mark for beer, the public would assume that any beer with 'BECK' in its name must be part of their beer family. The

---

ister DIESEL for jeans successfully opposed despite *bona fides* of applicant. (Decision under pre-harmonization Trade Marks Act 1963.)

Opposition Division dismissed this claim on the evidence since Beck did not show whether, or to what extent, the HAAKEBECK mark was used.[19]

(c) Ignoring the family: the OHIM approach

13.23 A quite different approach towards family-based oppositions was employed by an OHIM Opposition Division in the *LIFESOURCE* case.[20] The applicant sought to register LIFESOURCE as a word mark for goods in Classes 5, 30 and 32 including vitamin and mineral supplements, dietetic products and pharmaceutical substances. Novartis opposed, citing its prior registrations of DIETSOURCE, ISOSOURCE, FIBERSOURCE, CITRISOURCE, SANDOSOURCE and RESOURCE for dietetic and medicinal substances in Class 5. Surely this family of six could see off the challenge of an interloper bearing the -SOURCE surname?

13.24 The Opposition Division was not impressed by the opponent's display of kinsmanship. First, it held, family resemblance may be apparent to the opponent but its impact upon the relevant public cannot be presumed and must therefore be proved: it is in any event just one of the circumstances of the case which must be considered when asking whether LIFESOURCE was likely to be confused with any of the six family members. Novartis offered no evidence that its opposing marks not only enjoyed individual reputations but also shared a 'family' reputation. If such proof had been available, Novartis could have based its opposition on 'indirect confusion'[21]—confusion which included a likelihood of association between LIFESOURCE and the Novartis family. On the facts, held the Opposition Division, LIFESOURCE was not confusingly similar to any of Novartis' marks.[22]

Figure 13.1 Some of the TORRES family of marks.

---

[19] *Warsteiner Brauerei Gaus GmbH & Co KG's application; opposition of Brauerei Beck GmbH & Co*, Case 57/1998 [1999] ETMR 225.

[20] *Lifesource International Inc's application; opposition of Novartis Nutrition AG*, Case 2844/2000 [2001] ETMR 1227.

[21] ibid, para 25. The term 'indirect confusion' is not used in Council Regulation 40/94 but was borrowed by the Opposition Division from *Sabèl BV v Puma AG, Rudolf Dassler Sport*, Case C-251/95 [1998] ETMR 1 (ECJ), para 16. In that case the term meant confusion not between the goods but between their makers.

[22] In *Infamous Nut Co Ltd's trade marks* [2003] RPC 126 (LCAP) the principle was applied of comparing the applicant's mark with each of the opponent's individual marks individually and not as a 'family'.

B. *Opposition*

(d) Families of device marks

Just as an opposition may be based upon a family of word marks, it may also be made on the basis of a likelihood of confusion with a family of figurative marks. Success will however be more difficult to achieve where the opponent's family of figurative marks has little familial similarity and the main shared feature is a word which is not the same as that used in the applicant's mark. That is why the TORRES family of marks (in Figure 13.1) failed to stop the registration of TORREMAR (see Figure 13.2[23]). As in *LIFESOURCE*, where there was no evidence of consumer perception of family kinship it was for the court to determine the outcome of the opposition on the basis of the opponent's 'best bet', which in this case was held to be the word mark TORRES and not any of the figurative marks.

Figure 13.2 The Torres family of marks failed to stop the registration of TORREMAR.

13.25

(4) Use of the opponent's mark must be significant

If a trade mark application is going to be stopped in its tracks, the degree of use which the opponent claims to have made of his own identical or similar mark should be of sufficient stature to achieve the desired end. It would be remarkable if, for example, I could stop an applicant registering SQUIDGE for fruit juices throughout the territory of the EU on the ground that I had set up a stall in my front garden and sold a drink which I informally called SQUIDGE to passers-by in Golders Green.

13.26

Under the CTM Regulation, when an opposition is lodged on the ground that the opponent holds an identical or similar earlier trade mark, the CTM applicant is entitled to attack his attacker and ask for evidence of genuine use of the opponent's mark during the previous five years. This challenge often seems to catch CTM opponents off-guard. For example, when FIAT opposed Volkswagen's application to register LUPO as a trade mark for motor vehicles, citing its earlier Italian registration of LUPO, Volkswagen demanded proof of use of the earlier mark. All FIAT could manage was one price list, two newspaper advertisements and two invoices, none of which related to vehicle sales during the five-year period, as well as some evidence of use of the LUPETTO trade mark. The Opposition Division had no difficulty in rejecting the opposition on this basis.[24] In circumstances such as this,

13.27

---

[23] *TORREMAR trade mark* [2003] RPC 89 (LCAP).
[24] *Volkswagen AG's application; opposition of FIAT Veicoli Industriali SpA (Iveco SpA)*, Case 1269/1999 [2000] ETMR 320.

the opponent will not only be unable to prevent an application being granted but will also be drawing public attention to the fact that one or more of his trade marks has apparently remained unused for at least five years.

13.28 Not only must evidence of the opponent's use of its own mark relate to the five-year period prior to the application date of the opposed mark, but it must also show where the use took place and what was the extent of that use.[25] Such items as a photograph of the opponent's premises, stickers reading PAYLESS RENT A CAR a picture of a car with the words PAYLESS RENT A CAR or a keyring fob bearing the same legend do not count as sufficient evidence for such purposes.[26]

13.29 So far as CTMs are concerned, use must be of more than 'purely local significance' if it is to be invoked in CTM opposition proceedings.[27] For these purposes the use of an unregistered mark in the UK is of more than 'mere local significance'.[28]

13.30 Where a CTM applicant challenges an opponent's claim which is based on an earlier trade mark, the opponent must prove that he has made 'genuine use' of his own mark during the five years preceding the date of publication of the application. For this purpose

> ... genuine use implies real use of the mark on the market concerned for the purpose of identifying the goods or services. Genuine use is therefore to be regarded as excluding minimal or insufficient use when determining that a mark is being put to real, effective use on a particular market. In that regard, even if it is the owner's intention to make real use of his trade mark, if the trade mark is not objectively present on the market in a manner that is effective, consistent over time and stable in terms of the configuration of the sign, so that it cannot be perceived by consumers as an indication of the origin of the goods or services in question, there is no genuine use of the trade mark.[29]

13.31 It follows from this that genuine use of a trade mark excludes artificial use for the purpose of maintaining the mark on the register; the mark must not only be present in a substantial part of the territory where it is protected but it must be present in a capacity in which it exercises its essential function of identifying the commercial origin of the goods or services, thus enabling a consumer who

---

[25] On which see *Marco-Chemie Eugen Martin KG Chemische Fabrik v Aldemar AG*, Case R 644/2000–4, OHIM OJ 2/2003, 375 (OHIM Board of Appeal).

[26] *Payless Car Rental System Inc's application; opposition of Canary Islands Car SA*, Case 198/2000 [2000] ETMR 1136 (OHIM Opposition Division).

[27] Council Regulation 40/94, art 8(4).

[28] *McCann-Erickson Advertising Ltd's application; opposition of Momentum Integrated Communications Ltd*, Case 2149/2000 [2001] ETMR 540 (OHIM): UK use of MOMENTUM for advertising and other services prevented registration of a CTM for the same mark.

[29] *Kabushiki Kaisha Fernandes v OHIM*, Case T-39/01, 12 December 2002 (CFI), para 36.

B. Opposition

acquires them to repeat the experience, if it proves to be positive, or to avoid it, if it proves to be negative, on the occasion of a subsequent purchase.[30]

(5) The opponent's mark must be geographically relevant

Where an application was made to register the word-and-device mark MOSKOVSKAYA as a CTM for vodka, an opposition was lodged which was based on the earlier registration in Latvia of the same trade mark. Latvia was not, at the time of the application, an EU Member State and the opponent failed to furnish evidence that MOSKOVSKAYA was a well-known foreign mark in any of the EU Member States. The opposition was thus inevitably bound to fail, notwithstanding a ruling of the Latvian Supreme Court that the opponent was exclusively entitled to use that word for vodka.[31]

13.32

(6) Prior proceedings and contractual arrangements

It sometimes happens that the subject matter of opposition proceedings has already been adjudicated by another court or tribunal in the same jurisdiction. Where that happens, it is necessary to consider whether the opposition has to be fought out afresh or whether the result of the earlier decision will effectively determine the outcome of the later one too. For example, after a trade mark consisting of a two-dimensional representation of the Philips three-headed shaver configuration had been ruled invalid by a UK court, Philips applied to register a trade mark which was a very similar modification of the invalidated mark. Remington opposed on the ground that since the grounds upon which the original trade mark had been invalidated were grounds that applied equally to the second application, the merits of the second application had been effectively dealt with and, as a matter of *res judicata*, the application must be rejected. The court dismissed both of these arguments. *Res judicata* applied only if the facts of an earlier case were identical (ie if Philips had sought to register a sign which was exactly the same as the mark which had just been declared invalid). This was not however the case where the subsequent trade mark application was for a modified form of the original mark.[32]

13.33

Sometimes the outcome of an opposition may be determined by previous contractual dealings between the trade mark applicant and his opponent. For example, where the applicant to register COMPAIR as a trade mark in Germany entered into a coexistence agreement with another party who also used the COMPAIR mark but for different goods, under the terms of which each party agreed that there was

13.34

---

[30] *Rewe-Zentral v OHIM*, Case T-79/00 [2002] ETMR 1109, para 26 (CFI).
[31] *Vzao Sojuzplodimport's application; opposition of Latvijas Balzams*, Case 62/1999 [2000] ETMR 618 (OHIM Opposition Division).
[32] *Philips Electronics NV v Remington Consumer Products Ltd (No 2)* [1999] ETMR 835 (HC).

no likelihood of confusion between their respective products, the German registrant could not subsequently argue that there was a likelihood of confusion in Germany between his own registration there and the other party's subsequent CTM application.[33]

C. Cancellation

(1) Cancellation on absolute grounds

13.35 When considering whether a trade mark registration should be cancelled on absolute grounds, for example, that the trade mark is generic,[34] non-distinctive,[35] or deceptive,[36] the same principles which govern the mark's suitability for registration will apply. Accordingly, where a registered trade mark is challenged for lack of distinctive character, the challenged trade mark's distinctiveness must be examined taking the registered mark as a whole[37] and not through a process of salami-slicing,[38] in the same manner as it would have been examined prior to registration.

13.36 An applicant for cancellation, when challenging a mark's validity on the basis that it is no longer distinctive, cannot rely on evidence of his own infringing use of the registered mark.[39]

13.37 Issues of *locus standi* may limit the manner in which an application for cancellation on absolute grounds falls to be considered. Thus in French infringement proceedings a defendant raised the non-distinctive quality of the claimant's trade mark, citing the fact that twenty-three versions of the same or an almost identical mark were used or registered for the same services by other traders. The court

---

[33] *CompAir Ltd v Naber + Co KG*, Case R 590/1999–2, OHIM OJ 2/2003, 341 (OHIM Board of Appeal).
[34] *Rugby Football Union and Nike European Operations Netherlands BV v Cotton Traders Ltd* [2002] 861 (HC): white rose emblem a 'descriptive or generic' emblem for English rugby team.
[35] See eg *Beiersdorf AG's trade mark; application for cancellation by L'Oréal*, Case C000835728/1 [2001] ETMR 187 (OHIM): POUDRE LIBRE NATURELLE incapable of serving as a trade mark for stopping facial skin from shining.
[36] See eg *Kaysersberg SA and another v Scott Paper and others* [1997] ETMR 188 (Corte di Cassazione, Italy), where the COTONELLE trade mark was declared invalid insofar as it was registered for items which were not made of cotton. See also the reported order that Swedish food manufacturer Wasa abandon its twenty-seven-year use of MORAKNAECKE for crackerbread on the ground that the product was no longer manufactured in the town of Mora (http://news.bbc.co.uk/1/hi/business/2989935.stm).
[37] *Deutscher Teeverband eV's application for cancellation* (TEEKAMPAGNE) [2000] ETMR 546 (OHIM Cancellation Division).
[38] On 'salami-slicing', see Chapter 4, paras 4.98–4.103.
[39] *Farside Clothing Ltd et al v Caricline Ventures Ltd* 2002 FCA 466, 12 November 2002 (Federal Court of Appeal, Canada): infringer of the PHARSYDE mark failed in his attack on that mark's distinctiveness which was caused by his own use of FARSYDE.

C. Cancellation

however concluded that the defendant could cite the effect only of those other marks in which he had a proprietary interest.[40]

The role of the OHIM Cancellation Division has been stated in terms which summarize the approach taken in proceedings before it on an appeal from an OHIM examiner: **13.38**

> When examining an application . . . the examiner enjoys a certain degree of discretion. . . . [C]ancellation proceedings provide a means of rectification of clear mistakes, they do not provide means of execution of the same scope of discretion with a different result, *ie* they do not provide the possibility of having a decision replaced by another, different one within the same scope of discretion.[41]

(2) Cancellation based on prior third-party use

Just as opposition proceedings based on the opponent's prior use could have been brought against a trade mark during its application phase, so too can cancellation proceedings be brought which are based on the applicant for cancellation's prior use. In such circumstances the use in question must be genuine and it must be use in the course of trade. Where Volkswagen secured the registration of the CTM IFM International Fleet Management, a Belgian company called International Fleet Management sought to cancel the registration. Evidence of use included invoices sent by that company to its parent company, Interleasing. The OHIM Cancellation Division held that correspondence between a parent company and a subsidiary did not constitute evidence of use 'in the course of trade' in principle and, since no evidence was submitted that Belgian law regarded it as such, the application for cancellation had to fail.[42] **13.39**

(3) Cancellation on relative grounds

Can a trade mark registration be cancelled on relative grounds where the party seeking cancellation relies on use of his own earlier mark or name by others rather than his own use? In theory he should be able to do so, certainly where the use has his permission (as in the case of use by licensees) and also where the use is lawful but unauthorized (for example, in the case of use by third parties in comparative advertisements). Case law does not however support this position. In a case where an applicant sought cancellation of a Benelux registered trade mark on the basis that he had a prior entitlement to that mark which was based on use within the **13.40**

---

[40] *Sté Recife v Sté Recife* [2001] ETMR 182 (Cour d'appel de Paris): RECIFE mark not invalidated by other uses of RECIF and RECIFE.
[41] *Cahill May Roberts Ltd's application for a declaration of invalidity; Medicine Shoppe International's trade mark*, Case C000172734/1 [2000] ETMR 794.
[42] *Volkswagen Leasing GmbH's trade mark; International Fleet Management NV's application for cancellation*, Case C000525824/1 [2001] ETMR 1170.

Benelux, the court ruled that the use upon which the applicant for cancellation seeks to found his prior entitlement must either be by the applicant for cancellation himself or by others with his consent. The unlicensed use of his mark by third parties such as travel agents was insufficient for this purpose.[43] The Polish Supreme Court has also held that where, following an act of privatization, a state-owned enterprise was divided up into several different enterprises and its trade mark was assigned to another company in the private sector, it was not open to other privatized segments of the former state enterprise to challenge the validity of the mark on the basis of their own pre-privatization use of it.[44]

13.41 An application for cancellation on relative grounds is not without its hazards. In the confusingly difficult *Scandecor* case each of the two Scandecor parties was successful in persuading the court that, by reason of the use made by each of them of the SCANDECOR trade mark, the trade mark registered in the name of the other was no longer distinctive. Accordingly both parties' trade marks were cancelled.[45]

(4) 'Central attack' and the Madrid Agreement

13.42 The Madrid Agreement[46] is the earlier of the two international filing systems for trade marks. Although it has been superseded by the Madrid Protocol its continuing importance should not be overlooked because it remains in use and its provisions govern the legal relationship between countries which have acceded to the Agreement but not the Protocol.

13.43 Briefly stated, a trade mark proprietor who is a national of a Madrid Agreement country and who has secured the registration of his trade mark in his own country may use that registration as a springboard for registering the same trade mark in some or all of the other Madrid Agreement countries by lodging an international application with the International Trademark Bureau of the World Intellectual Property Organization (WIPO) in Geneva. This application is then forwarded to national trade mark offices. If an application, once forwarded, is not refused by a national office, the trade mark registration is automatically granted twelve months later.

13.44 The national trade marks which derive from a Madrid Agreement application become independent national registrations five years after the date the international

---

[43] *Le Lido SA v Nationale Stichting tot Exploitatie van Casinospelen in Nederland and another* [1997] ETMR 537 (Court of Cassation, the Netherlands): French owner of LE LIDO for a Parisian nightclub could not rely on use by travel agents so as to cancel Benelux registration of LIDO for entertainment services.
[44] *Spolka Akcyjna PPCH's trade mark* [2001] ETMR 770: CALYPSO ice-cream trade mark unimpeachable.
[45] *Scandecor Development AB v Scandecor Marketing AB* [1999] FSR 26 (CA).
[46] Madrid Agreement Concerning the International Registration of Marks 1891 (as amended on 14 April 1979).

D. Revocation

application is filed.[47] But if, within that period, the applicant's original home registration is attacked and subsequently lost, in whole or in part, then the protection obtained under the Madrid Agreement in all the other countries is lost.[48] An assault upon the applicant's original domestic registration in order to eliminate protection in the countries designated in the international registration is usually referred to as 'central attack'.

It does not appear that, on a day-to-day basis, the risk of central attack has posed a major practical problem for trade mark owners within Madrid Agreement countries. Notwithstanding this, the proposition that a trade mark registration must be lost in countries B, C and D because that registration has lost its validity in country A is illogical; the need to accept 'central attack' proved to be a deterrent factor which discouraged many countries from acceding to the Agreement. It is notable that the Madrid Protocol contains no corresponding provision. **13.45**

D. Revocation

Both of the major European codes of trade mark law provide that a trade mark may be revoked following non-use for a continuous period of five years.[49] Immediately after there has been five years' continuous non-use, an application for revocation may be made.[50] If the trade mark owner suddenly gets wind of the threat to his unused mark and starts using it, that use will not avail him unless he started using his mark more than three months before the applicant for revocation commenced his action. **13.46**

Revocation under the European codes may also be sought where, **13.47**

> in consequence of acts or inactivity of the proprietor, it has become the common name in the trade for a product or service in respect of which it is registered[51]

and also where

> in consequence of the use made of it by the proprietor of the trade mark or with his consent in respect of the goods or services for which it is registered, it is liable to mislead the public, particularly as to the nature, quality or geographical origin of those goods or services.[52]

---

[47] Madrid Agreement, art 6(2).
[48] ibid, art 6(3).
[49] Council Directive 89/104, art 12(1); Council Regulation 40/94, art 50(1)(a).
[50] *Philosophy Inc v Ferretti Studio Srl* [2003] ETMR 97, [2003] RPC 287 (CA): no requirement to wait three months before filing for revocation.
[51] Council Directive 89/104, art 12(2)(a); Council Regulation 40/94, art 50(1)(b).
[52] Council Directive 89/104, art 12(2)(b); Council Regulation 40/94, art 50(1)(c).

13.48 Where a trade mark has become a common name in the trade, the correct procedure for removing the mark from the register is by means of revocation proceedings. If a declaration of invalidity is sought, the court or tribunal seised of the application will consider whether the sign was correctly registered in the first place rather than whether it is still valid. To give a striking example, the Venezuelan trade mark registry ruled that the word mark CORN FLAKES was generic but valid: it was generic in 2003, when the ruling was made, but valid in 1988 when it was first registered.[53]

13.49 In practice almost all revocation proceedings are based on non-use.

(1) Non-use in relation to different classes of goods and services

13.50 The owners of the VISA trade mark for credit-card services had also registered the VISA mark in Class 16 of the register for 'newspapers, magazines and publishing services'. When Jibena, a publisher, later registered VISA POUR LE MUSCLE, VISA POUR LE BEAUTE and VISA POUR LE BODY BUILDING as trade marks, the credit-card company sued for trade mark infringement. Jibena successfully counterclaimed for revocation of the VISA registration for publications: although that trade mark had been heavily used for credit cards, it had not been used in respect of publications.[54]

(2) What is 'genuine use' of a trade mark?

13.51 Under the English language versions of Directive 89/104 and the CTM Regulation a trade mark risks revocation if it has not been put to 'genuine use' for a period of five years. Other versions of these laws do not employ the same vocabulary. As the Court of First Instance (CFI) has observed:

> 36. . . . The German (*'ernsthafte Benutzung*'), French (*'usage sérieux*'), Italian (*'seriamente utilizzata*') and Portuguese (*'utilizaçao séria*') versions state the requirement of serious use. The English version ('genuine use') has the same meaning. On the other hand, the Spanish version uses the expression actual use (*uso efectivo*), which also corresponds to the wording of the ninth recital in the preamble to Regulation 40/94 in the German, English, Spanish, French and Italian versions. Lastly, the Dutch version (*'normaal gebruik*') places a slightly different emphasis, namely requiring normal use.
> 37. Accordingly, contrary to the applicant's claim, it is not possible to contrast genuine use with real use. It is by contrast necessary to define genuine use by taking account of the different language versions . . . on the one hand, and of the ninth recital in the preamble to that regulation, on the other.[55]

---

[53] *Maizoro SA de CV v Kellogg Company* WTLR, 6 May 2003.
[54] *Visa International (US) v Editions Jibena* [1998] ETMR 580 (Cour de Cassation, France).
[55] *Goulbourn v OHIM, Redcats SA intervening*, Case T-174/01, 12 March 2003, para 37.

D. Revocation

That recital reads: **13.52**

> Whereas there is no justification for protecting Community trade marks or, as against them, any trade mark which has been registered before them, except where the trade marks are actually used.

Taking into account the use of the notion of *actual* use in the ninth recital and the employment of the terms *genuine, serious* and *normal* use, it is submitted that our first consideration should be whether a trade mark has been *actually* used since, logically, actual use is a condition precedent for the existence of any specific variety of use. If there has been no actual use, that is to say no use at all, there is no justification for allowing that mark to remain usefully on the register or for entitling its proprietor to block a subsequent application for registration made by another. If there has been actual use, our next step is to consider whether it is *genuine, serious* or *normal*. If the trade mark is used in the ordinary course of commerce, the question of genuine, serious or normal use is unlikely to be challenged. If however there is something abnormal or pathological about its use, we must look behind the superficial evidence and use and consider its significance. For example, is the use evidenced only by transactions between related companies? Is use deliberately kept unpublicized or hidden from normal channels of commercial information? Is use confined to the printing of the trade mark on receipts, certificates of warranty or other post-contractual stationery? Is use only made in conjunction with other, far more visible and better-known trade marks in circumstances in which consumers would not recognize the use as being a trade mark use? The answers to these questions need not result in the automatic conclusion that there has been no genuine, serious or normal use of a trade mark but they will at least call for some plausible explanation from the trade mark proprietor as to why the use of his trade mark has been confined within such atypical parameters of commercial practice. **13.53**

The degree of use which a trade mark owner need prove if he is to withstand a challenge based on non-use of his mark has been considered by the European Court of Justice (ECJ),[56] on a reference from the Netherlands. The case arose from a situation in which the owner of the Benelux trade mark MINIMAX for fire extinguishers, having lost the right to sell new extinguishers, continued using the mark when selling components and extinguishing substances for customers' existing devices. The applicant for revocation argued that, if the trade mark owner was no longer selling new products under the MINIMAX trade mark, it was no longer making a 'genuine use' of that trade mark. The ECJ ruled as follows: **13.54**

> [T]here is genuine use of a trade mark where the mark is used in accordance with its essential function, which is to guarantee the identity of the origin of the goods or services for which it is registered, in order to create or preserve an outlet for those

---

[56] *Ansul BV v Ajax Brandbeveiliging BV*, Case C-40/01, 11 March 2003 (unreported).

goods or services; genuine use does not include token use for the sole purpose of preserving the rights conferred by the mark.[57]

13.55 The Court did not stop there but helpfully mentioned four specific points which a tribunal should address when asking whether a trade mark has been genuinely used:

> When assessing whether use of the trade mark is genuine, regard must be had to all the facts and circumstances relevant to establishing whether the commercial exploitation of the mark is real, particularly (i) whether such use is viewed as warranted in the economic sector concerned to maintain or create a share in the market for the goods or services protected by the mark, (ii) the nature of those goods or services, (iii) the characteristics of the market and (iv) the scale and frequency of use of the mark [Roman numerals added].[58]

13.56 Finally the ECJ addressed the issue in the case which generated the reference to it in the first place:

> The fact that a mark is not used for goods newly available on the market but for goods that were sold in the past does not mean that its use is not genuine, if the proprietor makes actual use of the same mark for component parts that are integral to the make-up or structure of such goods, or for goods or services directly connected with the goods previously sold and intended to meet the needs of customers of those goods.[59]

13.57 It is significant that the ECJ did not require, as a condition of the use being genuine, that it also be 'continuous', as the Advocate General had proposed.[60] Even intermittent or occasional use may therefore be sufficient to protect a registered trade mark against an application for revocation so long as the ECJ's 'genuine use' criteria are satisfied. The ECJ has still to resolve a question referred to it[61] as to whether, even if use is 'genuine', it is still on so small a scale that it is effectively *de minimis* and should therefore be ignored. The ECJ should also be asked whether use in the form of test-marketing constitutes 'genuine use'. While national courts have held that it does, they have done so in the context of different statutory provisions.[62] Moreover, use of a trade mark in a situation such as test-marketing, where there is no opportunity for a consumer to make a repeat purchase, may be

---

[57] ibid, para 43.
[58] ibid.
[59] ibid.
[60] *Ansul BV v Ajax Brandbeveiliging BV: C-40/01* (Advocate General's Opinion, 2 July 2002), para 68.
[61] *Laboratories Goemar SA's trade marks; application for revocation by La Mer Technology Inc* [2002] ETMR 382 (HC); see also *Re Laboratories Goemar SA* [2003] EWHC 1382 (Ch), 20 June 2003 (unreported) (HC).
[62] See eg *Gerber Products Co v Gerber Foods International Ltd* [2002] ETMR 882 (HC), affirmed by the Court of Appeal 12 December 2002 (unreported), a decision on the pre-Directive Trade Marks Act 1938, and a Canadian decision, *ConAgra Foods Inc v Fetherstonhaugh & Co* WTLR, 2 April 2003 (Federal Court of Canada) (KID CUISINE).

D. Revocation

regarded as falling outside the essential function of a trade mark. Against that, a use of a trade mark which is conditional in the sense that it will be used again if the consuming public respond well to it is not excluded from being regarded as a genuine use.

Outside the EU, different standards of acceptable use prevail. Thus in Indonesia the sale of just 150 cigarettes by a Sumatran company under its DAVIDOFF registered trade mark was regarded as sufficient use in the normal course of trade to stave off a revocation claim.[63]   13.58

(3) Proper reasons for non-use

Where the trade mark owner has a proper reason for not having used his trade mark, it will not be revoked. But what constitutes a proper reason for non-use? The TRIPs rubric of   13.59

> circumstances arising independently of the will of the owner of the trademark which constitute an obstacle to the use of the trademark, such as import restrictions on or other government requirements for goods or services protected by the trademark[64]

suggest that events which lie outside the will, or at least the control, of the trade mark proprietor will be excused. Such events include the fact that the proposed use is not lawful until certain legal requirements which lie outside the control of the trade mark owner have been fulfilled.[65] They may also include the trade mark owner's failure to establish a satisfactory means of manufacturing the products to which the goods were intended to be applied, despite the fact that he had invested time and money in product development.[66] The fact that the marketing and packaging of a projected new product were not completed because the trade mark owner kept redesigning the product's overall appearance was not however regarded as a proper reason for non-use.[67]

The burden of proving that the reasons for the non-use of a trade mark are genuine falls on the trade mark owner.[68]   13.60

---

[63] *Reemtsma Cigarettenfabriken GmbH v NV Sumatra Tobacco Trading Company* WTLR, 22 April 2003. Reemtsma, as licensee of the 'real' Davidoff, is believed to have appealed against this decision.
[64] TRIPs, art 19(1).
[65] HENNAFLOR *trade mark* [2001] ETMR 132 (High Court, Prague): licensee not permitted to use the licensed mark until the Registry had recorded the licence. On account of internal registry problems, this was not done before revocation proceedings had been instituted.
[66] *Nestlé UK Ltd v Zeta Espacial SA* [2000] ETMR 226 (HC): the product concerned was lollipops having a centre filled with gasified particles.
[67] *Glen Catrine Bonded Warehouse Ltd's application for revocation* [1996] ETMR 56 (UK Trade Mark Registry).
[68] *Philosophy Inc v Ferretti Studio Srl* [2003] ETMR 97 (CA).

(4) The mark must be used in the form in which the mark is registered

13.61 If a trade mark proprietor is to be safe from a revocation action, it is not enough for him to have made genuine use of the mark: he must have made use of it in a form which does not differ significantly[69] from the form of the mark as registered. Thus, where the trade mark as registered consisted of a rectangular label featuring the words 'Fino Bandera' as well as 'Fino Bandera— Rainera Pérez Maria-Salúcar de Barrameda' and the Spanish national colours, the proprietor could not argue that the use of this most elaborate mark was achieved through use of the word 'Bandera'.[70] Likewise, use of the word ELLE in upper case letters was not regarded as use of a registered figurative trade mark depicted here (see Figure 13.3).[71] In contrast, the trade mark SECOND SKIN avoided revocation when it was represented as 2ND SKIN[72] because the difference between the two representations was insignificant.

Figure 13.3 Use of the word ELLE in upper case letters was not regarded as use of a registered figurative trade mark depicted here.

13.62 The advent of m-commerce and the increased use of mobile phones in the marketing of goods and services may result in the use of some trade marks in a somewhat condensed and approximate form since, at the time of writing, most mobile phones' display facilities are not capable of rendering stylized trade marks with the degree of subtlety, or indeed in the colour(s), of the reproduction of the mark as found on the trade mark register. Until technology improves to the point at which any discrepancy between the mark as registered and the mark as it appears on-screen is removed, trade mark owners should ensure that the version which phone users see is as close to the registered version of the trade mark as possible.

(5) Evidence of use

13.63 Proof of use in revocation proceedings is similar to that in opposition proceedings in which the opponent is called upon to demonstrate that he has used his own trade mark within the previous five years before he may use that mark in support of his challenge against a later application.[73] A trade mark owner may not rely upon evidence which does not demonstrate the fact that his trade mark has been

---

[69] See eg Council Directive 89/104, art 10(2); Council Regulation 40/94, art 15(2).
[70] *Re Bandera* [1999] ETMR 337 (Spanish Supreme Court).
[71] *Safeway Stores plc v Hachette Filipacchi Presse* [1997] ETMR 552 (HC).
[72] SECOND SKIN *trade mark* [2002] ETMR 326 (UK Trade Mark Registry).
[73] See paras 13.26–13.31 above.

D. Revocation

used in the course of trade. Thus it is insufficient to place before a court evidence such as advertising material which features the proprietor's trade mark unless there is also evidence that the advertising material has been distributed or used: advertisements which bear no date, and invoices to show that advertising material has been purchased, are insufficient.[74]

(6) Trade marks remain valid until they are revoked

The proprietor of the word mark JOY in France for goods and services in all classes of the trade mark register sued a publisher for launching a German-language youth magazine called *Joy* and for reproducing the word 'joy' on 500 T-shirts bearing the slogan 'Joy One Year'. The publisher counterclaimed for revocation for non-use of the JOY trade mark in Classes 16 (printed products) and 25 (clothes). The court had no difficulty in establishing that the proprietor had failed to use JOY in those classes and revoked the registrations. However, until those registrations were revoked they were valid and, therefore, had been infringed. The proprietor was therefore awarded infringement damages.[75] It has been held in the UK that, unless the pleadings of the applicant for revocation specify that an earlier date is sought, revocation will take effect with effect from the date of the court's order.[76]

13.64

(7) A trade mark may be re-registered after revocation

The TRI-OMINOS trade mark was originally registered in the Benelux for toys and games in 1981. Three years later that registration was revoked for non-use, so in 1988 the previous owner registered it again. The Benelux Court of Justice ruled that the second registration was governed by exactly the same rules as any other registration. It could not derive priority based on the earlier revoked mark; nor was it tainted with bad faith on the ground that the earlier registration was unused. Accordingly the later registration was valid.[77]

13.65

Even where revocation is no more than a possibility, there is apparently no inherent bar to a trade mark proprietor filing a second application to register a mark which he already owns, even if it is for the same goods or services as the earlier one.[78] In such a situation the trade mark registry may nonetheless consider that, in the circumstances of the application, it has been made in bad faith.

13.66

---

[74] *Manpower Inc v Manpower Temporar Personal GmbH*, 16 April 2003 (Supreme Court, Hungary).
[75] *Jean Patou SA v Sté Zag Zeitschriftn Verlag AG and another* [1999] ETMR 157 (Cour d'appel de Paris).
[76] *Omega SA v Omega Engineering Ltd* [2003] EWHC, 3 June 2003.
[77] *Erich Perner Kunststoffwerke v Pressman Toy Corporation* [1997] ETMR 159 (Benelux Court of Justice).
[78] See the Privy Council decision of *Unilever plc and another v Cussons (New Zealand) Pty Ltd* [1998] RPC 369, on an appeal from the New Zealand Court of Appeal, citing *Natural Resources Inc v Origin Clothing Ltd* [1995] FSR 280 (HC).

(8) Revocation of part of a registration

13.67 It is possible to revoke only part of a registration. For example, if a trade mark is registered for a specification of goods that contains products both X and Y, but the mark is used only for X, registration for Y may be cancelled without adversely affecting the power of the trade mark to continue to protect the proprietor's use of X. What happens is that the court or granting authority puts a pencil line through the words in the registration certificate that should not be there. Thus where the MINERVA trade mark was registered for a specification of goods that listed 'paper and paper articles; printed matter; stationery' but the mark was not used for 'printed matter', registration for 'printed matter other than stationery' was revoked without adversely affecting the power of the trade mark to continue to protect the proprietor's use of MINERVA on the other specified products.[79]

13.68 If the registration is for a broad category of goods, such as 'cosmetics', but the registration is descriptive or non-distinctive for some of the goods in that category, it is OHIM and British practice to cancel the whole registration rather than try to guess what goods or services the proprietor should be entitled to retain.[80] As the Cancellation Division wisely commented:

> The Office itself cannot draft a proper list of goods and services for the holder of the mark... [W]e... do not have sufficient insight into the sector of trade at issue, and specifically not into the holder's expertise and capacity. Secondly, and more importantly, the setting up of a list on the Office's own motion would possibly force something on the holder which he commercially does not wish to be entitled to, and indirectly forced to make use of in order not to face difficulties under the user requirement. Further, any initiative of the Office in this respect would, in all likelihood, result in irritation on the part of competitors.[81]

13.69 If the registration is for a category of goods or services which is not so broad as to be incapable of repair, the courts may restrict its scope through the judicious addition of limitative words. For example, in one case the court considered that the registration of the FREESTYLE trade mark for (among other things) 'Arrangement and booking of travel, tours and cruises; escorting travellers and arranging the escorting of travellers; providing tourist office services; all included in Class 39' should be limited through the inclusion in its specification of the words 'for holidays'.[82] Likewise the registration of ESB for 'beers' was whittled down to 'bitter beers' after a court considered that the word 'beers' was broad enough to include

---

[79] *Pomaco Ltd's trade mark; application for revocation by Reed Consumer Books Ltd* [2001] ETMR 1013 (HC).
[80] *Beiersdorf AG's trade mark; application for cancellation by L'Oréal*, Case C000835728/1 [2001] ETMR 187: registration of POUDRE LIBRE NATURELLE for 'cosmetics' declared invalid in its entirety because it was not distinctive for face powders.
[81] ibid, para 19.
[82] *Thomson Holidays v Norwegian Cruise* [2003] IP&T 299 (CA).

lagers, which were actually a different product[83] and, where the DECON mark was registered for 'cleansing and decontaminating substances and preparations', the court amended the registration by adding the limitative words 'all for non-domestic use'.[84]

E. Suspension of trade mark applications and of hostilities in general

In some jurisdictions it is possible to apply for the suspension of a trade mark application until such time as an issue relating to the legal status of the trade mark has been judicially determined in separate proceedings. Where it exists, the power to suspend an application is exercised sparingly. For example, where the trade mark applicant seeks to register a sign which is not the same as a sign he is using and for which he is being sued for trade mark infringement, suspension will not be ordered.[85] 13.70

It may also be possible for the trade mark applicant to seek a stay of opposition proceedings, pending the outcome of other litigation involving the same or even a highly similar trade mark.[86] 13.71

F. Trade mark systems and 'bad faith'

Although the applicant's sign may be registrable as a trade mark, an application to register it may still be refused, or its registration cancelled, if the applicant was not the right person to seek to register it. This is the case where one person tries to register a mark which rightfully belongs to someone else. Such an application is said to be made in 'bad faith'. As a proportion of all applications, those which are truly filed in bad faith are only a tiny minority. In some jurisdictions,[87] 'bad faith' is routinely alleged along with any other objection to registration that an opponent can think of. In other countries little reliance appears to be placed on that doctrine at all.[88] 13.72

---

[83] *West (t/a Eastenders) v Fuller Smith and Turner plc* [2002] FSR 822, [2003] ETMR 376 (HC), affirmed on appeal 31 January 2003 (unreported) (CA).
[84] ibid.
[85] *S-P's trade mark application; application by K S to suspend the trade mark registration proceedings* [1999] ETMR 335 (Board of Appeals, Polish Patent Office).
[86] *Philips Electronics NV v Remington Consumer Products Ltd (No 2)* [1999] ETMR 835 (HC).
[87] The UK appears to be a case in point.
[88] See eg *Eli Lilly & Co v Salenab Nigeria Ltd* (FHC/LCS/534/99) WTLR, 1 April 2003 (Federal High Court, Nigeria): Salenab, a former distributor of Eli Lilly products, secured registration of eight pharmaceutical trade marks consisting of the name LILLY in combination with other trade marks owned by Lilly. The Federal Court ordered their deletion from the register on the ground that all eight were identical or confusingly similar to Lilly's. In most other jurisdictions the case would have been determined on the basis of an absence of good faith.

13.73 Although the requirement of good faith in making trade mark applications is not new, it is only in recent years that the courts in many countries have been called upon to explain and clarify what constitutes 'bad faith' and to contemplate its consequences. The recent increase in interest in 'bad faith' in Europe has been manifested by a sudden increase in the number of 'bad-faith' cases. This is because the CTM now requires applications originating from either inside or outside the EU to be measured by the same criteria of bad faith, regardless of the norms of national law in the applicants' countries of origin. Additionally, the use of the same term in Directive 89/104 demands that a similar measure of meaning be given to it in a group of countries whose national and regional[89] trade mark jurisdictions span a historically broad range of legal cultures.

13.74 The manner in which the EU's national courts and trade mark registries wrestle with bad faith-related problems is of more than academic interest since fixing standards for bad faith touches upon at least four practical points:

(i) if the standard of good faith required by trade mark applicants is uniformly too low, a trade mark which is derived from a single business may easily be legitimately registered by different applicants in different countries;
(ii) if the standard of good faith is too high, unnecessary barriers may hinder the efficient functioning of the trade mark registration process;
(iii) if different countries employ different standards, then whoever is able to establish an earlier priority date for a trade mark in the jurisdiction in which he first applies will be able to benefit from that early priority date when opposing subsequent applications by third parties; and
(iv) if there is a dichotomy between the standards employed by national or regional trade mark registries on the one hand and the standards employed by the OHIM on the other, there may be substantial implications for the degree of attractiveness or utility of the pan-European registration system.

(1) 'Bad faith' in EU law

13.75 Under Directive 89/104 Member States have the option to provide that

> a trade mark shall not be registered or, if registered, shall be liable to be declared invalid where and to the extent that the application for registration of the trade mark was made by the applicant in bad faith.[90]

13.76 Moreover

> a trade mark shall not be registered or, if registered, shall be liable to be declared invalid where, and to the extent that the trade mark is liable to be confused with a

---

[89] Belgium, the Netherlands and Luxembourg share a common regional 'Benelux' trade mark law, while leaving issues such as infringement to be dealt with under national law.
[90] Council Directive 89/104, art 3(2)(d).

mark which was in use abroad on the filing date of the application and which is still in use there, provided that at the date of the application the applicant was acting in bad faith.[91]

Where a trade mark is registered in bad faith, its fate is that it will not enjoy everlasting peace and security. Even in a situation in which the owner of an earlier trade mark might otherwise be unable to assail a later mark because he has acquiesced in its use for a period of five years, his acquiescence will not count against him where the later mark was registered in bad faith.[92] **13.77**

The CTM Regulation contains similar, though by no means identical, provisions. Thus a CTM must be declared invalid where the applicant was acting in bad faith when he filed the application;[93] the five-year period of acquiescence which would otherwise forfeit one's right to challenge a later CTM registration or sue for infringement does not apply where the later CTM was registered in bad faith;[94] the right of the holder of a prior right in a particular locality to resist the exploitation of a CTM in that locality, which might also be lost through five years' acquiescence, is also preserved where the CTM was applied for in bad faith.[95] The main difference between the Directive and the Regulation is that, under the former, bad faith is an absolute ground for refusing an application while, under the latter, it is merely a ground of cancellation.[96] **13.78**

Neither the Directive nor the Regulation specifies what bad faith means. However, the Regulation expressly provides[97] that an application may be opposed on the ground that it was made by an agent or representative of the trade mark owner, in his own name and without the proprietor's consent. This ground of opposition is not specifically described as being 'bad faith' although there is little doubt that the acts embraced within it would be regarded as such. **13.79**

The fact that 'bad faith' has been considered in a number of cases involving CTMs means that a body of coherent doctrine is building up. In contrast, doctrine on 'bad faith' under the Directive is inevitably going to be, at least initially, **13.80**

---

[91] ibid, art 4(4)(g).
[92] '... it is important, for reasons of legal certainty and without inequitably prejudicing the interests of a proprietor of an earlier trade mark, to provide that the latter may no longer request a declaration of invalidity nor may he oppose the use of a trade mark subsequent to his own of which he has knowingly tolerated the use for a substantial length of time, unless the application for the subsequent trade mark was made in bad faith'. The bad-faith provision in the 11th recital to Directive 89/104, which is based on article 6*bis*(3) of the Paris Convention, is canonized in article 9(1) of the Directive.
[93] Council Regulation 40/94, art 51(1)(b).
[94] ibid, art 53(1), 53(2).
[95] ibid, art 107(2).
[96] This is also the approach taken in Germany (see Markengesetz, art 50(1)(4)) and in Portugal (Industrial Property Code, art 214(6)).
[97] Council Regulation 40/94, art 8(3).

Chapter 13: The Killing Fields: Opposition, Cancellation and Revocation

less coherent since it is derived from a variety of different tribunals in different countries. The position of OHIM is that

> ... the concept of bad faith in the Regulation is narrow, implying or involving, but not limited to, actual or constructive fraud, or a design to mislead or deceive another, or any other sinister motive. It is to be understood as including a dishonest intention.[98]

13.81 How does this approach compare with that taken by domestic tribunals within Europe?

(2) 'Bad faith' in European domestic trade mark law

13.82 All fifteen EU Member States, together with the three EFTA states[99] with which the EU forms the European Economic Area, have implemented the normative provisions of the Directive within their domestic trade mark law. By the time the next group of ten countries joins the EU on 1 May 2004,[100] its members will also have implemented the Directive, as will some countries whose accession to the EU may still be some time away.[101] This means that the substantial majority of European jurisdictions have now been required to engage with the concept of 'bad faith' in registry procedures or in their case law.

13.83 Some countries have employed the concept of 'good faith' as well as that of 'bad faith'. For example, in the UK,

> [t]he application shall state that the trade mark is being used, by the applicant or with his consent, in relation to those goods or services, or that he has a *bona fide* intention that it should be so used.[102]

13.84 Since the opposite of a *bona fide* intention is 'bad faith', that concept inevitably falls to be considered in that context too. In focusing on the issue of 'bad faith', this chapter will draw principally on the issue of bad faith as it affects the immediate circumstances of the trade mark application.

(3) Persuasive grounds of 'bad faith'

13.85 Under this heading we list the grounds of alleged bad faith on the part of a trade mark applicant which have resulted in the cancellation of a registration.

---

[98] *Decon Laboratories Ltd v Fred Baker Scientific Ltd and Veltek Associates Ltd* [2001] ETMR 486, para 32 (referring to *Trillium Digital Systems Inc's trade mark; Harte-Hanks Data Technologies' application for a declaration of invalidity*, Case C000053447/1 [2000] ETMR 1054).
[99] Iceland, Norway and Liechtenstein.
[100] Cyprus, Czech Republic, Estonia, Hungary, Latvia, Lithuania, Malta, Poland, Slovenia and Slovakia.
[101] The largest and most economically significant of these countries is Turkey.
[102] Trade Marks Act 1994, s 32(3). This provision has no analogue within either the Directive or the CTM Regulation.

F. Trade mark systems and 'bad faith'

(a) Unauthorized filing by the trade mark owner's agent or representative

This ground of bad faith, which is derived from article 6*septies* of the Paris Convention, is not controversial, although its precise measure of application is unclear. A good example of its potentially restricted field of operation may be found in a Polish case in which a local company, which imported products from the Canadian trade mark owner, decided to register in Poland a trade mark, DURAL DURA KOTE, which was a composite of trade marks used by the Canadian company in Poland but never registered there. The Polish Patent Office considered that the Polish company was not, in a strict legal sense, an agent or representative of the Canadian business but concluded that the application had nonetheless been filed in bad faith.[103] Spanish jurisprudence has confirmed that the bad faith of an agent or representative of the proprietor is not 'laundered' when applications made in bad faith are transferred to the agent's successor in title.[104]

13.86

It appears to be generally understood in Italy that the unauthorized filing of a trade mark by the trade mark proprietor's agent or representative is the 'bad faith' to which Directive 89/104 refers.[105] This opinion links 'bad faith' under modern European trade mark law with the corresponding provision of the Paris Convention. It has also been suggested that the implementing provision of Italian law[106] would cover a situation in which a distributor of the trade mark owner's goods lodges an unauthorized application as well as one in which, through the existence of some other relationship with a third party, the trade mark owner's path to filing his own trade mark is blocked.

13.87

In one surprising case an application filed in Italy by an agent of the party who claimed ownership of a trade mark was not challenged for bad faith where the agent filed an application to register the trade mark just three days before the agency agreement was even entered into. The court considered that the agent could not be in breach of any obligations under an agency contract into which it had not yet entered.[107]

13.88

Where an unauthorized trade mark application has been filed by the trade mark proprietor's director, resulting in the grant of that application, a UK court has ordered the assignment of that mark to the proprietor, thus allowing it to retain the benefit of the improper filing.[108]

13.89

---

[103] *Tajer Firma Handlowa Sciwiarski Tadeusz's Trade Mark; Multibond Inc's Application for Cancellation* [2002] ETMR 491 (Board of Appeal, Polish Patent Office).
[104] *Orient Watch Co Ltd v Rita HB* [2002] EIPR N-94 (Supreme Court, Spain).
[105] See Davies (ed), *Sweet & Maxwell's European Trade Mark Litigation Handbook* (1998), paras 10–12.
[106] Trade Marks Law (Italy), art 22(2).
[107] *Videogruppo SpA v Agenzia GP Srl* [2002] ETMR 1003 (Court of Appeal, Turin).
[108] *Ball v The Eden Project Ltd and another* [2001] ETMR 966 (HC).

(b) Misuse of rights

13.90 In Germany a trade mark is registered in 'bad faith' where the registration is the consequence of a misuse of rights or where it is otherwise unfair. Although the origins of this position antedate the implementation of Directive 89/104, it is still the currently held position. Under German doctrine, misuse of rights includes 'blocking'—the practice of registering a trade mark which the applicant does not intend to exploit itself in order that another business should find its path to the marketplace blocked.[109] Where this happens, not only will the trade mark be annulled for bad faith but the wrongful registrant may itself be sued for unfair competition.[110] 'Bad faith' also includes the 'unfair disturbance of a protectable acquired status' where an earlier trader has an interest in a sign which falls short of being a registered trade mark.

13.91 A curious variant of 'blocking' theory may be found in one British case in which the applicant sought to register the trade mark DEMON ALE for beer on the somewhat illogical basis that, since this word was an anagram of 'lemonade', DEMON ALE would be rendered unregistrable in respect of alcopops. Although the LCAP (Lord Chancellor's Appointed Person) considered that the case based on bad faith had not been properly made out, the application was nonetheless successfully opposed.[111]

(c) Abuse of 'direct relations'

13.92 The Uniform Benelux Trade Mark Law provides that

> ... no right to a mark shall be acquired by ... (6) filing effected in bad faith, including, inter alia ... (b) filing effected by a person who, as a result of direct relations with a third party, knows that during the preceding three years the said party has, in good faith and in the normal manner, used a like mark for similar goods or services outside the Benelux territory, unless the said third party has given his consent or such knowledge was obtained only after the person effecting the filing had started to use the mark within the Benelux territory.[112]

13.93 This provision is neither required nor directly considered by the Directive, although it bears some similarity to the optional provision of its article 4(4)(g). On a reference to the Benelux Court of Justice it was held that 'direct relations', within the meaning of the Benelux Court, included even relations with a representative

---

[109] eg: (i) *EQUI 2000* (GRUR 2000, 1032, 1034) where the EQUI trade mark was registered in order to prevent a legitimate registration being made for EQUI 2000; and (ii) *CLASSE E* (GRUR 2001, 242, 244) in which the mark CLASSE E was filed in order to prevent the filing of E-CLASS. This concept has been recognized in the UK, but at a rather lower level; see OXYFRESH *Trade Mark* (UK Trade Mark Registry, 25 March 1999), where 'blocking' was inferred after the applicant wrote to the 'real' Oxyfresh and offered to sell it the trade mark for US$19,250.

[110] *NeutralRed trade mark* [1998] ETMR 277 (OLG Karlsruhe).

[111] *Demon Ale trade mark* [2000] RPC 345 (UK Trade Marks Registry).

[112] Uniform Benelux Trade Mark Law, art 4(6).

F. Trade mark systems and 'bad faith'

of the trade mark owner.[113] Accordingly a trade mark was registered in bad faith in the Benelux if the applicant knew, as a result of discussions with the trade mark owner's parent company, that the mark in question was currently in use for similar goods outside the Benelux.

Even in the absence of a specific provision such as that found in Benelux law, a 'direct relations' rule may be applied as a normal application of 'bad-faith' principles. Thus where a former UK distributor of an Australian company's BE NATURAL product, having been prevented from registering that trade mark in the UK, registered it as a CTM, the Cancellation Division had no difficulty in expunging its registration.[114]   13.94

(d) Use of the registered mark in a manner other than as registered

In the BETTY'S KITCHEN CORONATION STREET case the UK Trade Mark Registry concluded that the fact that the registrant placed the two sets of words, BETTY'S KITCHEN and CORONATION STREET, far apart and in different styles, was evidence that the mark was not intended to be used in the manner of its registration. Since 'Coronation Street' by itself was the name of a British soap opera of well-nigh iconic cultural status, the registration of those words alone would not have been achievable by the applicant; the addition of 'Betty's Kitchen' enabled the mark to gain registration but in its subsequent use the separation of the two sets of words gave the impression of a link with the soap opera. Accordingly the hearing officer held that the mark had been applied for in bad faith.[115]   13.95

(e) Registration of a later mark with actual knowledge of the earlier mark

It is generally agreed that, where the later applicant has actual knowledge of an earlier trade mark, that knowledge plays some part in determining bad faith. Different jurisdictions however give different weight to it. In Sweden, for example, it is regarded as a necessary condition without which the later registration cannot be regarded as having been made in bad faith.[116] Knowledge of an earlier mark   13.96

---

[113] *Intergro v Interbuy* [2003] ETMR 152.
[114] *Multiple Marketing Ltd's trade mark; Surene Pty's application for cancellation*, Case C000479899/1 [2001] ETMR 131 (OHIM).
[115] BETTY'S KITCHEN CORONATION STREET *trade mark* [2001] RPC 825.
[116] *Travaux préparatoires* to the Swedish Trade Marks Law, SOU 1958: 10, pp 288 and 289. See also FÄRGTEMA COLOR TREND (RÅ 1984 2:37) where the Administrative Appeal Court held that the fact that the applicant was very likely to have knowledge of the use by an American company of the trade mark COLORBLEND was an insufficient basis upon which to establish that its application had been made in bad faith, and BUDGET BILUTHYRNING AB (Svea Court of Appeal, 27 November 1981), a case under the Swedish Business Names Act, in which a Swedish company was allowed to register its name because the opponent could not prove that that company knew of any of its registration of the word BUDGET in thirty-eight different jurisdictions.

is also essential if bad faith is to be proved in Norway.[117] In Estonia the GULF trade mark was held to have been registered in bad faith where a member of the applicant company's board had lived in the Netherlands, where the opponent had extensively used its trade mark; the Board of Appeal ruled that the board member should have been aware of the GULF mark and its notoriety in the Benelux countries.[118]

13.97 Although knowledge must in principle be proved, it may be taken to exist in Sweden where the applicant is a former employee of the party alleging bad faith[119] or where the applicant and the party objecting to registration conducted their business from the same address and had both used the disputed mark.[120] In Turkey (see further para 13.98 below) actual knowledge is not required and Sweden is itself considering introducing the requirement that the later applicant 'knew or ought to have known' of the earlier application[121] (the standard which the British courts appear to adopt).[122]

(f) Registration of another party's famous mark

13.98 Even where a finding of 'bad faith' requires a technical legal requirement of knowledge on the part of the applicant, this requirement is presumed in the case of an unauthorized filing of a famous mark. On that basis the owners of the CAMPARI trade mark were able to prevent the registration in Turkey of a word mark which included that mark.[123] The applicant's good faith is measured at the date of filing of the application. Accordingly Microsoft was unable in the UK to invalidate the registrations WINDOWPRO, WINDOWBASE and WINDOWSHEET for software products in Class 9: application for registration of those marks was made in 1991, some years before Microsoft's WINDOWS became a household word and a year or so earlier than Microsoft had been able to persuade the USPTO that the word was distinctive of its own products rather than being merely generic.[124]

---

[117] See Davies (ed), *Sweet & Maxwell's European Trade Mark Litigation Handbook* (1998), paras 11–14.

[118] *Gulf International Lubricants Ltd v Gulf Oil Estonia AS* WTLR, 4 July 2003 (Patent and Trade Mark Office, Board of Appeal, Estonia).

[119] This is also the case in the UK; see *Mickey Dees (Nightclub) Trade Mark* [1998] RPC 359 (Trade Mark Registry).

[120] HAMMARBY MARINCENTER trade mark (RÅ 1988 no 296) (Administrative Appeal Court, Sweden).

[121] SOU 2001: 26, p 438.

[122] *Etat Française v Bernard Matthews plc* [2002] ETMR 1098 (HC), reported sub nom *LABEL ROUGE trade mark* [2003] FSR 13.

[123] *Davide Campari Milano SpA v Özal/Finkol Giyim Sanayi ve Ticaret Ltd Şti* [2002] ETMR 856 (Istanbul Court of First Instance).

[124] *Software Products International Inc's trade marks; applications by Microsoft Corporation for declarations of invalidity*, transcript O/256/97 of 30 December 1997 (unreported) (UK Trade Mark Registry). See also *J B Cosmetics' trade mark* [2000] ETMR 722 (Board of Appeals, Polish Patent Office) where the owner of the trade mark ELLE for the well-known magazine could not show that

F. Trade mark systems and 'bad faith'

(g) Failure to behave in a prudent commercial manner

In the Turkish *Alvorada* case the applicant obtained registration in Turkey of the ALVORADA trade mark for teas.[125] This trade mark had already been registered by a competitor in fifteen other countries. The Republic of Turkey Appellate Court observed that, under article 21(2) of the Commercial Code, businesses were required to behave in a prudent manner which placed them under the obligation of familiarizing themselves with their competitors' trade marks. Even if the applicant had registered the ALVORADA trade mark in complete and genuine ignorance of the third party's mark, its failure to acquaint itself with competitors' brands constituted an act of bad faith which was sufficient to vitiate its trade mark registration. A similar result was obtained in Poland, where it has been held that even a negligent filing of another's trade mark may constitute bad faith.[126]

13.99

Although a failure to behave in a prudent manner is not an explicit legal requirement in the UK, it was considered in the *Gromax* case where the judge stated:

13.100

> I shall not attempt to define bad faith . . . Plainly it includes dishonesty and, as I would hold, includes also some dealings which fall short of the standards of acceptable commercial behaviour observed by reasonable and experienced men in the particular area being examined. Parliament has wisely not attempted to explain in detail what is or is not bad faith in this context; how far a dealing must so fall short in order to amount to bad faith is a matter best left to be adjudged not by some paraphrase by the Courts (which leads to the danger of the Courts then construing not the Act but the paraphrase) but by reference to the words of the Act and upon a regard to all material surrounding circumstances.[127]

(h) Bona fide *belief in one's entitlement to file a trade mark application does not mean that the application is not made in bad faith*

Under UK law at any rate, the concept of 'bad faith' is generally measured subjectively, but not exclusively so.[128] Accordingly an applicant who honestly and genuinely deludes himself that he is entitled to file a trade mark application will not be assisted by his subjective honesty; nor can he insist that any allegation has to be

13.101

---

a 1984 registration of the same word in Communist Poland as a trade mark for cosmetics was made in bad faith: in that year *Elle* magazine was not available in Poland and the proprietor could not be said to have acted in bad faith in trying to register its mark.

[125] ALVORADA trade mark [2003] ETMR 623 (Republic of Turkey Appellate Court, Eleventh Tribunal).

[126] CORVINA trade mark, 18 December 2001 (unreported) (Polish Patent Office). See also the US decision in *Medinol Ltd v NeuroVasx Inc* WTLR, 12 June 2003 (TTAB), in which an applicant's oversight was treated as 'fraudulent' because it 'should have known' of facts concerning its own use which it stated in support of its application.

[127] *Gromax Plasticulture Ltd v Don & Low Nonwovens Ltd* [1999] RPC 367, 379 (HC), per Lindsay J.

[128] ibid, per Lindsay J: 'I shall not attempt to define bad faith . . . Plainly it includes dishonesty'.

established both objectively and subjectively (in other words, where proof must be brought both that the applicant fell short of honest standards and that he knew his conduct had fallen short of them[129]). Thus in an application for summary judgment[130] the claimant, a representative member of an unincorporated association sought a declaration of invalidity of the defendant's LONG POINT trade mark. The unincorporated association had previously organized furniture exhibitions under the name 'Long Point' and the defendant registered its mark after it had been expelled from the association. The defendant maintained, among other things, that it did not apply in bad faith since it held a *bona fide* belief that it was entitled to that name. Lawrence Collins J gave summary judgment for the claimant without considering the point in depth and without establishing the defendant's state of mind. A wider degree of bad faith than merely that encapsulated within subjective dishonesty was also preferred by Pumfrey J in *Decon v Fred Baker*. Commenting on the subjective approach adopted by the court in *Gromax* he said:

> This approach would mean that the validity of the registration could depend upon the advice received by the proprietor, since the scope of the specification of goods is normally, if not always, a matter upon which the proprietor would be advised by his professional advisers, if the proprietor genuinely informs the professional advisors [sic] as to the scope of his use and his intended use and is advised by them to take an unjustifiably wide specification of goods his conduct could not be criticised. On the other hand a proprietor who was advised that his specification of goods was too wide and decided to chance his arm might be open to criticism . . . This may be thought to be anomalous when one is considering the intended and actual use of the mark and a suitable specification of goods. In my judgment, the validity of registrations should not, in this context, depend upon subjective considerations. In my judgment, the underlying objection might well be thought to be far closer to the idea that the proprietor should lose his registration to the extent to which a reasonable person in his position would know that the specification of goods as applied for was too wide. However, it is not necessary to express a concluded view on this point and I do not do so.[131]

(i) The certain knowledge that one's application will be successfully opposed

13.102 In a UK application to register the word VISA for contraceptives, the LCAP expressed the opinion that the fact that the VISA trade mark was so well known that it was not possible to find that any of the goods for which the applicant sought registration would be free from objection was itself sufficient to justify a finding of bad faith.[132]

---

[129] DAAWAT *trade mark* [2003] RPC 187.
[130] *Artistic Upholstery Ltd v Art Forma (Furniture Ltd)* [2000] FSR 311.
[131] *Decon Laboratories Ltd v Fred Baker Scientific Ltd and another* [2001] ETMR 486, 502.
[132] *C A Sheimer (M) Sdn Bhd's application* [2000] RPC 484 (LCAP).

F. Trade mark systems and 'bad faith'

(4) Things which do not positively suggest that there is 'bad faith'

13.103 In contrast with the previous list, the cases reviewed under this heading are those in which a court or tribunal, without specifically ruling out the possibility that the grounds alleged could never constitute bad faith, did not positively affirm that those grounds actually did constitute bad faith.

(a) Using the trade mark monopoly in order to extend an expired patent monopoly

13.104 Is a trade mark application made in bad faith if the intention of the applicant is to obtain, through the registration of a product shape as a trade mark, an effective extension of a patent monopoly? This suggestion was made in a recent UK case, Nestlé v Unilever,[133] where it was vigorously rejected. Said the court:

> I need say little about this allegation—it was based on a suggestion that somehow a patent monopoly was being extended. That is miles from bad faith. An allegation of bad faith should only be made when dishonesty or something approaching it (such as conduct falling short of acceptable commercial behaviour) can properly be alleged with full particulars. It is a serious allegation, not one to be thrown in the pot along with other, more conventional points . . . Not surprisingly it failed in this case.

(b) Registration of the name of deceased celebrities

13.105 In the JANE AUSTEN case the applicant sought to register the word mark JANE AUSTEN for toiletries, Jane Austen being the name of a celebrated novelist. The Jane Austen Memorial Trust, which owned the Jane Austen House and ran the Jane Austen Museum, opposed the application on various grounds, including bad faith. The UK Trade Mark Registry hearing officer commented that, since there was no public policy argument against the registration of the name of a deceased historical figure as a trade mark, it may be presumed that an application to do so, even without the consent or tacit acceptance of related persons or bodies, would not of itself be regarded as an application made in bad faith.[134]

(c) Timing of the application

13.106 La Chemise Lacoste opposed an application to register, as a trade mark in various classes, a device consisting of a representation of a reptile over the word 'Kaimann' in stylized writing enclosed within two ovals. Bad faith was among the numerous grounds of opposition, the opponent maintaining that the fact that the applicant delayed for a substantial period of time after seeking registration of the mark in Germany before seeking to register the same mark in the UK was suggestive of bad faith. The hearing officer dismissed the opposition on all grounds, observing that

---

[133] Société des Produits Nestlé SA v Unilever plc, 18 December 2002 (unreported) (HC), para 7.
[134] JANE AUSTEN application, 12 July 1999 (unreported) (UK Trade Marks Registry).

there was nothing in the evidence that went any way towards establishing that Kaimann's application was anything other than *bona fide*.[135]

(d) Amendment of the application

13.107 In the UK the High Court has held, on an appeal from the Trade Mark Registry, that an applicant's attempt to amend his application to register the word mark CAREMIX for goods in Class 11 rather than Class 7 did not constitute evidence of bad faith on his part.[136]

(e) Lack of veracity in the application

13.108 In the *VISA* application,[137] the LCAP said that lack of veracity in connection with a trade mark application did not necessarily constitute bad faith. This is presumably because the making of false statements by the applicant could be the result of negligence or inadvertence as well as *mala fides*.

(f) Mere similarity between the registered trade mark and the earlier mark

13.109 OHIM's Cancellation Division has concluded that the similarity between the mark allegedly registered in bad faith (AROMATONIC) and the earlier mark (AROME TONIQUE) is an insufficient basis upon which to draw a conclusion that the junior mark was registered in bad faith, even where the later registrant knew of the existence of the earlier mark.[138]

(g) Translation of the earlier trade mark into another language

13.110 In the *DEMON ALE* case,[139] discussed above, the opponent who alleged bad faith on the part of the trade mark applicant was the proprietor of the earlier registered trade mark BIERE DU DEMON (French for 'Demon's beer'). This was not considered to be decisive as to the issue of bad faith.

(h) Proximity of the registered trade mark to an international non-proprietary name

13.111 The fact that a pharmaceutical trade mark, OMEPRAZOK, was registered for a word which was almost identical to an international non-proprietary product name, OMEPRAZOL, did not appear to be, in Germany at least, a ground upon which the applicant's bad faith was argued.[140]

---

[135] *Wilhelm Kaimann's application*, 19 May 1999 (unreported) (UK Trade Mark Registry).
[136] *Altecnic Ltd v Reliance Water Controls Ltd* [2001] RPC 13.
[137] *C A Sheimer (M) Sdn Bhd's application; opposition by Visa International Service Association* [2000] RPC 484 (LCAP).
[138] *Lancôme Parfums et Beauté & Cie's trade mark; application for revocation by Laboratoires Décléor* [2001] ETMR 981 (OHIM).
[139] *Demon Ale trade mark* [2000] RPC 345.
[140] OMEPRAZOK *trade mark* [2003] ETMR 662 (Bundesgerichtshof).

F. Trade mark systems and 'bad faith'

(5) Things which do suggest that there is no 'bad faith'

The issues listed below contribute to the debate in that, by basing submissions upon them, the applicant should be able to protect his application from the allegation of bad faith.

13.112

(a) Length of time the applicant uses the mark openly before filing the application

In the UK SKYLIFT case[141] the applicant applied in 1996 for registration of a trade mark which it had been using, without any previous suggestion that this was an infringing use of another's trade mark, since 1989. The hearing officer doubted that an applicant who had been openly using a trade mark for seven years before applying to register it could be said to have acted in bad faith in filing the application.

13.113

(b) Plausibility of the applicant's explanation as to how he chose the trade mark

A UK application to register WACKERS for various toys in Class 28 was opposed by a US company, which claimed that the applicant had copied the idea of the mark from its goods when they were being exhibited at a trade fair in the United States. The applicant denied appropriating the mark and filed a statutory declaration to the effect that it was looking for a trade mark that would fit with 'Wacky Warehouse', the name used for a children's play area in public houses owned by a client of the applicant. The hearing officer dismissed the opposition. Since the opponent had offered no evidence to support its allegation that the trade mark had been copied from its own products, while the applicant had offered an explanation as to how it had come by the name WACKERS, an allegation of bad faith could not be sustained.[142]

13.114

In another case a Polish registration of the word-and-device mark GAPPOL for clothes was challenged by the American clothing company the Gap, which maintained that GAPPOL was a Polish version of its famous GAP trade mark. The application failed, the Polish Patent Office noting that the trade mark proprietor had chosen the name GAPPOL as a derivation from a dog's name, Gappa.[143] Whether this argument would have succeeded if the two marks had not been held to be similar is a matter of conjecture.

13.115

(c) The offer of a coexistence agreement

According to the OHIM Cancellation Division, the fact that a trade mark proprietor proposes a coexistence agreement, in respect of another trade mark owner

13.116

---

[141] SKYLIFT *trade mark*, 19 July 2000 (unreported) (UK Trade Mark Registry).
[142] *Wackers application*, 27 November 1998 (unreported) (UK Trade Mark Registry).
[143] *Porczynska Marzena Gappol Przedsiebiorstwo Prywatne's trade mark; The Gap Inc's application for cancellation* [2001] ETMR 1056.

whose earlier trade mark is different, is positive evidence that its registration was not made in bad faith.[144] This is because, by first approaching the proprietor of the earlier trade mark, a subsequent applicant puts the earlier proprietor on notice of his intended course of conduct.

(d) The concept of the 'previous prior user'

13.117 Under the Benelux trade marks law an applicant is regarded as having acted in bad faith if, with knowledge that another trader is already applying the same sign to his goods or services, he subsequently applies to register that sign for the same goods or services.[145] However, this is not the case where the applicant's own use of the same unregistered sign antedates the use of the other party. In effect, if the opponent is a prior user, the applicant is himself the 'previous prior user' and is regarded as acting in good faith because the function of his application is to rectify his omission to apply on an earlier occasion. The future of this doctrine is however uncertain. Where Unilever first used a Mexican taco shape for an ice cream product and a competitor, Artic, later adopted the same, Unilever's subsequent trade mark application for that product shape was held by the Court of Appeal in The Hague to be in bad faith on the basis that, while Unilever knew of Artic's prior use, Arctic did not know that Unilever would later apply for registration of that shape as a trade mark and—having ascertained that Unilever had not applied to register that shape—need not assume that it would eventually do so.[146] This issue has been referred for a preliminary ruling to the Benelux Court of Justice.[147]

(6) 'Bad faith' and the nature of the earlier trade mark

13.118 The success of applications to prevent or cancel a registration on the basis of bad faith is not merely a matter of the ill health of the applicant's trade mark. Sometimes it is necessary to consider additionally the function and qualities of the trade mark of the person who alleges bad faith. Such instances are reviewed below.

(a) Does the earlier trade mark need to have been used?

13.119 The *travaux préparatoires* of the Swedish Trade Marks Law require that there must have been actual use of the earlier trade mark: mere preparations to use a trade mark would not constitute a ground upon which the party claiming bad faith would be able to succeed.[148] This view is at odds with the position taken by the OHIM First Cancellation Division, which is that bad faith is proved where it is

---

[144] *Lancôme Parfums et Beauté & Cie's trade mark; application for revocation by Laboratoires Décléor* [2001] ETMR 981.
[145] Benelux Trade Marks Act, s 6(4)(a).
[146] *Unilever v Arctic*, Case C01/036, HR 24 January 2003.
[147] See note by Tjeerd Overdijk, 'Ice Cold Bad Faith?' in the Steinhauser Hoogenraad newsletter 2/2003, p 3.
[148] Prop 1960: 167, p 106; SOU 1958: 10, p 288.

F. Trade mark systems and 'bad faith'

shown that a subsequent applicant has merely attended meetings at which the intention of another business to use a trade mark has been communicated to him.[149] It is submitted that the position taken by the Cancellation Division is to be preferred since they provide a greater disincentive to dishonesty.

(b) Where does the earlier trade mark need to have been used?

13.120 The optional provision of article 4(4)(g) of the Directive refers to the situation in which the earlier mark was used 'abroad' at the date of the later application and was still being used (presumably at the time cancellation proceedings were instituted). It is in this sense that Italy has implemented article 4(4)(g);[150] the earlier mark must however be well known in commercial circles. In contrast with this Sweden has regarded use both under its own regime and outside it as a sufficient basis upon which to lodge a bad-faith claim against the later registered trade mark. Accordingly an application to register GOLDEN LIGHTS for cigarettes and tobacco in Sweden was bound to fail once the applicant acknowledged that it knew of the KENT GOLDEN LIGHTS trade mark in the United States.[151]

(c) Does the earlier trade mark need to have a reputation?

13.121 The Swedish *travaux préparatoires* consider that the extent, if any, to which the earlier trade mark need have acquired a reputation is not an issue which is material to the finding of bad faith. Although the point does not appear to have been considered elsewhere, the Swedish view is not considered controversial.

(d) Does the use of the earlier mark need to be continuous?

13.122 Anything which leads to a suggestion that an earlier trade mark has been abandoned will make it extremely difficult for an attack on a subsequent registration to succeed. Accordingly, if there is a cessation in the use of the earlier mark, it may be necessary to consider how a reasonable trader would have viewed that non-use.[152]

(e) Does the earlier mark have to be identical or similar to the challenged mark?

13.123 Sweden is considering introducing the requirement that only the user of an identical or confusingly similar trade mark be able to launch a bad-faith challenge on a later mark.[153] From this it may be inferred that the only grounds of bad faith recognized in Sweden are those which relate to the appropriation of an earlier trade mark.

---

[149] *Interkrenn Maschinen Vertriebs GmbH's Trade Mark; Application for Declaration of Invalidity by Horst Detmers* [2002] ETMR 27.
[150] Trade Marks Law (Italy), art 22(2).
[151] *GOLDEN LIGHTS* (RÅ 1984 Ab 122).
[152] See Swedish *travaux préparatoires*, SOU 1958: 10, p 288.
[153] SOU 2001: 26, p 186.

(7) 'Bad faith' and intent to use

13.124   TRIPs gives its Member States the option of making the registrability of a trade mark depend on use. However,

> actual use of a trademark shall not be a condition for filing an application for registration.[154]

13.125   The United States[155] and the UK[156] require applicants to state their *bona fide* intention to use a mark for which application is made, although foreign applicants are not obliged to have used a mark prior to registration.[157] However both OHIM[158] and national courts[159] have explicitly stated that, in respect of CTMs, there is no 'intention to use' requirement. An applicant can apply for a trade mark whether he intends to use it or not and, once he gets his registration, he has five years in which to use it. If he makes genuine use of the mark within that period, the mark's validity may not be challenged in revocation proceedings based on five years' continuous non-use. If no such use is made, then the registration is vulnerable to attack. It follows from this that the fact that there is no 'intention to use' a CTM cannot constitute 'bad faith', even though a CTM may have been registered in respect of more goods or services than the applicant intended to use it for.

13.126   Under national law the situation may be different. For example, Italian law prior to implementation of the Directive took the view that registering a trade mark in order to sell it to another party was an act of bad faith in that the registrant sought to obtain what he did not himself intend to use.[160] But it appears to be the view that compliance with the Directive does not require this position to be maintained.

13.127   UK case law has discussed the notion of 'intention to use' as a ground of bad faith more fully than other jurisdictions. In *South Cone v Bessant*[161] an opposition to an application to register the trade mark REEF was lodged on the grounds, *inter alia*, that the application was made in bad faith and that there was no *bona fide* intention to use it as a trade mark. The use in question was a pop group's use of REEF on

---

[154] TRIPs, art 15(3). This provision adds that an application may not be refused on the sole ground that no use has taken place within three years of the date of application.
[155] 15 USC, s 1051(b)(1).
[156] Trade Marks Act 1994, s 32(3); Form TM3.
[157] 15 USC, s 1126(e).
[158] *Trillium Digital Systems Inc's trade mark; Harte-Hanks Data Technologies' application for a declaration of invalidity*, Case C000053447/1 [2000] ETMR 1054; *Senso di Donna trade mark* [2001] ETMR 5.
[159] *Decon Laboratories Ltd v Fred Baker Scientific Ltd and another* [2001] ETMR 486 (Pumfrey J).
[160] See the decision of the Court of Milan, 10 March 1980, Giur Ann Dir Ind 80, 271, in which an application to register the words BEVETE COCA COLA ('drink Coca Cola') was held null and void.
[161] *South Cone Incorporated v Bessant and others (trading as Reef)* [2002] RPC 387 (Pumfrey J). An appeal against this decision was allowed on other grounds sub nom REEF *trade mark* [2003] RPC 101.

F. Trade mark systems and 'bad faith'

promotional items of clothing. The judge, referring to the relevant provision of the UK Trade Marks Act 1994, said:

> Subsection 3(6) of the Act provides that a trade mark shall not be registered if or to the extent that the application is made in bad faith. This provision is found in the ... Directive ... and in the ... Regulation. The only basis on which this ground is advanced is that the applicants do not have any *bona fide* intention to use the trade mark *as a trade mark,* relying on section 32(3).[162]

13.128 After citing that provision, which provides that the applicant must state that the mark is being, or will be, used or that he has a *bona fide* intention that it be so used, he added:

> This is a 'home-grown' provision, and has no parallel in the ... Directive. It states a requirement for the contents of the application. I have expressed the view elsewhere that lack of a *bona fide* intention to use a mark on the date of application does not provide a ground of revocation of a Community trade mark under the Regulation (see *Decon v Fred Baker* [2001] ETMR 486).
>
> ... I would be very reluctant to import into that 1994 Act a concept which does not appear in the Directive or the Regulation and which did not represent the law under the 1938 Act.

13.129 From these statements it is clear that, in the judge's view, lack of intention to use is emphatically not a subset of 'bad faith' even though it may be one of a number of factors which the court will wish to take into account when reaching its decision.

(8) Overwide registration as 'bad faith'

13.130 Although OHIM does not generally interfere with overwide specifications, the UK Trade Marks Registry will routinely raise the issue of bad faith wherever an applicant makes a claim to register the mark for 'All goods' or 'All services' within a Class, for 'All machines' in Class 7 and for 'Electric, electrical and/or electronic apparatus, devices, equipment and instruments' in Class 9, as well as 'Personal and social services rendered by others to meet the needs of individuals' in Class 45.[163] The rationale for this interference is that, since those Classes are so wide and encompass so many different types of goods and services, the protection given by an overwide registration may be greatly wider than that actually needed by the applicant. The notion that a trade mark has been registered in 'bad faith' if it has been registered in respect of a wider range of goods or services than those for which the applicant actually sought to use it is a subject which has been discussed in two important UK decisions, *Decon v Fred Baker* and *Wyeth v Knoll,* both of which are reviewed below.[164]

---

[162] ibid, para 7.
[163] UK Patent Office Practice Amendment Notice PAN 8/02 of 19 June 2002.
[164] On this subject see also David Wilkinson's excellent review of overbroad specifications in the four stages of a trade mark's life, as well as his analysis of the problems either raised or solved by the OHIM *Trillium* case in 'Broad Trade Mark Specifications' [2002] ETMR 227–31.

13.131 In *Decon v Fred Baker*[165] Decon sued for infringement of their UK and Community marks for DECON which, Fred Baker maintained, had been registered in bad faith since there was no intention to use that mark, either at the date of application or thereafter, for any goods except 'goods intended for non-domestic use'.

13.132 Since 'bad faith' under both the CTM Regulation and UK national legislation fell to be considered, the judge had this to say on the interplay between UK and Community law:

> 29. The Community trade mark is less than five years old and may not therefore be revoked either in whole or in part for non-use. The defendants seek to obtain the same result by alleging that the mark is liable to revocation under Article 51(1) of the Regulation on the ground that the applicant was acting in bad faith when he filed the application for the trade mark. What is said is that the applicant had no bona fide intention to use the mark in respect of any of the goods covered by the specification of goods other than goods intended for non-domestic use either at the time when the mark was registered or at any time thereafter. So it is alleged that to the extent to which the specification of goods extends beyond that which I have held the English mark should be restricted to then the mark should be revoked to that extent.
>
> 30. Although concerned with bad faith, Article 51(3) [of the CTM Regulation] allows for revocation in respect of some only of the goods or services in respect to which the mark is registered, so suggesting that the proprietor may exhibit bad faith in respect of some only of the goods comprised within the specification of goods. In my view, there are two considerations to take into account. The first and, I believe, most important is that the legislature has seen fit to accord the proprietor five years during which he is not obliged to demonstrate use of the mark at all. At the same time, it is open to the proprietor to enter into other transactions in respect of the mark even if he does not himself intend to use it. For example, he may license the mark for use upon other goods falling within the specification and the use by the licensee will be deemed to be the proprietor's use; see Article 15(3). These considerations have led the First Cancellation Division of . . . OHIM . . . to hold in *Trillium TM*[166] that the objection of bad faith is available only in very limited circumstances. After pointing out that in the United Kingdom an application for a trade mark under section 32(3) of the 1994 Act is required to be accompanied by a statement that the mark is being used by the applicant or with his consent in relation to the goods or services in relation to which it is sought to be registered or that he has a bona fide intention that it should be so used, the Division says that on the contrary under the Regulation (but not under the Directive, which is silent on the point) there is no requirement for such a statement. The Division says that in general, and as a matter of principle, it is entirely left to the applicant to file a list of goods and services as long as he sees fit i.e. a list exceeding his actual scope of business activity, and try later to expand his activities in order to be able to show genuine use CTM or face revocation under Article 51(a) CTMR and other sanctions, respectively.[167]

---

[165] *Decon Laboratories Ltd v Fred Baker Scientific Ltd and Veltek Associates Ltd* [2001] ETMR 486 (Pumfrey J).

[166] [2000] ETMR 1054.

[167] *Decon Laboratories Ltd v Fred Baker Scientific Ltd and Veltek Associates Ltd* [2001] ETMR 486, 502 (Pumfrey J).

F. Trade mark systems and 'bad faith'

13.133 Up to this point the judge could accept the Cancellation Division's position, but he was troubled by its subsequent postulate:

> They point out that there may be cases where an applicant files a list of goods and services which does not have the slightest connection with his actual economic activity and in such cases it might be worth considering Article 51(1)(b) of the CTMR. I have some difficulty with this approach. What does not have the slightest connection with his actual economic activity mean? This was another case of a registration of a mark in relation to computer software. It cannot be seriously contended that games software is related to telecommunications switching software, which was the applicant's only field of economic activity. I cannot believe that the Division was saying that if the specification of goods had read Games software, telecommunications switching software, software for controlling automotive production lines it would have been revoked as to the first and last parts of the specification, but not if it just read computer software. I regret to say that I find the suggested distinction unworkable. Either Article 51(1)(b) is available where there is no bona fide intention to use the mark (whether by licensing or otherwise) during the first five years, or it is not.[168]

13.134 It may have been the Cancellation Division's intention to suggest that the complete lack of connection between an applicant's field of business and the goods or services specified in his application, while not actually proof of bad faith, was one of a number of evidential factors which would lead one to conclude that the application was made in bad faith. But that is not how the learned judge viewed its position.

13.135 The judge then addressed an issue of policy—the establishment of consistency between the UK Trade Mark Registry and the OHIM and the repercussions for overwide registrations.

> 34. In my judgment, it would be desirable for there to be consistency between the UK and OHIM on this topic. Whilst the First Cancellation Division is only a tribunal of first instance (and may not be a judicial tribunal) its views represent the practice of OHIM . . . If I ignore the reference to constructive fraud in the *Trillium* case, and concentrate on the essential element of dishonesty, it seems to me that this construction of the Regulation is a tenable one, and is supported by the fact that there is no express requirement to have an intention to use the mark at the outset. In considering questions under the Regulation, I am part of the same legal system as OHIM, and this construction is, I think, a construction to which I should adhere in the interests of consistency . . .
> 35. If this view is right, it is improbable (but not impossible) that a decision as to the width of a specification of goods would lack good faith.[169]

13.136 A similar result was obtained through a quite different route in *Wyeth v Knoll*.[170]

---

[168] ibid, 498.
[169] ibid, 504.
[170] *Wyeth (formerly American Home Products Corporation) v Knoll Aktiengesellschaft*, reported as *Knoll AG's trade mark* [2003] RPC 175 (HC).

A challenge to a mark's validity was made on the basis that, while the application was made for all pharmaceutical products, the applicant never intended to use it for any products other than obesity treatments. Neuberger J's treatment of the issues involved is thorough, instructive and firmly based on the view of bad faith taken by the court in the *Gromax* case.[171]

13.137 On the overall merits of the application the judge made his own position clear:

> I have considerable difficulty in accepting that the defendant could be said to have been guilty of bad faith in expressing an intention to use the mark in issue for pharmaceutical preparations and substances and dietetic substances adapted for medical use. After all, the defendant had a firm and developed intention to use the mark for pharmaceutical preparations and substances for the treatment of obesity, and contemplated that it might use it in connection with other pharmaceutical products.[172]

13.138 But it still remained to address the issues. The first of these was to consider why the defendant's list of products for which registration was sought came to be so wide. Was the selection of goods itself an act of bad faith? The judge thought not:

> Although the role of the Classes [of the Nice Agreement] can be overstated, it is nonetheless not without significance that the defendant made its application by repeating the first part of Class 5 of that Schedule, the remainder being plasters, materials for dressings; material for stopping teeth, dental wax; disinfectants; preparation for destroying vermin; fungicides, herbicides. The defendant made its application by reference to the terms set out in a Class identified in the Order, and, presumably consciously, only applied for registration in respect of some of the goods in that Class. That is scarcely redolent of greed, let alone bad faith.[173]

13.139 Even if the defendant had been greedy, was its failure to draft the trade mark application more tightly a sign of bad faith. Again, the answer was no:

> I think it is a little difficult to describe the defendant as wanting in good faith simply because it failed to draft its application more critically or with greater precision.[174]

13.140 Having already concluded that the defendant had a 'firm and developed intention to use the mark for pharmaceutical preparations and substances for the treatment of obesity' and 'contemplated that it might use it in connection with other pharmaceutical products', the judge added that *bona fides* might be found even in a conditional intention to use:

> Given that there is no doubt that the defendant had a firm and developed intention to use the mark in connection with obesity products, I think it is of real assistance to its case that it had a contemplation, or, to put it another way, a provisional or con-

---

[171] *Gromax Plasticulture Limited v Don & Low Nonwovens Limited* [1999] RPC 367.
[172] *Wyeth (formerly American Home Products Corporation) v Knoll Aktiengesellschaft*, reported as *Knoll AG's trade mark* [2003] RPC 175, para 21 (HC).
[173] ibid, para 22.
[174] ibid, para 23.

ditional intention, of using it in relation to other pharmaceutical products . . . [W]hether a contemplated use, or a possible or conditional intention to use, can suffice must depend upon the circumstances.[175]

13.141 The judge then took another approach, contrasting an intention to use the mark in respect of specific products (which was problematic on account of the breadth of products claimed) and intention to use the same mark as a corporate logo:

> Thus, if the defendant in the present case could show a firm and settled intention to use a mark as its corporate logo, and it is a pharmaceutical company, I would have thought it hard to argue against the proposition that it would be entitled to register that mark in relation to pharmaceutical preparations and substances generally . . . Section 3(6) of the 1994 Act . . . involves alleging not merely that the applicant has framed its claim too widely, but that it was guilty of bad faith. The precise meaning of bad faith may vary depending on its linguistic context and purpose, but it must, I think, always involve a degree of dishonesty, or at least something approaching dishonesty. To say that one intends to use a mark in connection with pharmaceutical substances, when one intends to use the mark in connection with a specific category of pharmaceutical substances, does not appear to me, as a matter of ordinary language or concept, to amount to want of good faith . . .[176]

13.142 The *Decon* and *Wyeth* cases thus demonstrate quite different ways in which the issue of bad faith in making applications with arguably overwide specifications can be addressed.

(9) 'Bad faith' and procedural issues

13.143 Having reviewed the substantive issues relating to bad faith, it is worth taking note of some of the procedural issues which relate to the manner in which challenges to a trade mark applicant's *bona fides* are processed.

(a) When need the registering office raise the issue of bad faith?

13.144 Trade mark applications in Europe, as well as granted trade marks, are open to two types of challenge: those on absolute grounds (ie that there is an inherent defect in the sign which the applicant seeks to register) and those on relative grounds (ie that there is nothing inherently wrong with the sign but it conflicts with other signs or with the legal interests of third parties). Although the bad faith of the applicant is listed along with the other absolute grounds of refusal of registration under article 3 of the Directive, its logical home is alongside the relative grounds of refusal listed in article 4 since bad faith, like the other relative grounds, addresses the relationship between an applicant's trade mark and the rights of third parties. Probably for this reason Sweden already treats bad faith as a relative ground, which the Patent and Registration Office will only consider where it is

---

[175] ibid, para 24.
[176] ibid, para 27.

raised by the owner of the earlier trade mark.[177] This reform will bring Sweden into line with the *de facto* practice of most other trade mark systems since, whatever the juridical status of applications made in bad faith, it is difficult for national and regional trade mark registries to act as bad-faith police.

(b) Which tribunal deals with bad-faith claims?

13.145 In the case of CTMs, the issue of bad faith is, of necessity, dealt with by OHIM's Cancellation Divisions. Neither the Cancellation Divisions nor the OHIM Boards of Appeal to which appeals are made are strictly speaking courts, so the cancellation procedure in the case of allegations of bad faith is effectively an administrative office procedure. CTM Courts do not have jurisdiction to hear original cancellation claims, although they can hear counterclaims both for revocation and for a declaration of invalidity.[178]

13.146 In the case of national trade marks, the situation naturally differs from country to country. It is quite normal for an application for a declaration of invalidity to be made before a court. Spain does not currently provide an administrative means of cancelling bad-faith trade marks, although its Patent and Trade Mark Office will submit to the opinion of the courts on this issue.[179] In Sweden, where the position is the same, an amendment is currently being contemplated which would provide an office procedure whereby bad-faith cancellations can be processed or, where appropriate, transferred to a court.[180]

(c) The burden of proof of bad faith: rebutting the presumption of good faith

13.147 British courts, addressing the issue of establishing bad faith, have held that good faith was to be presumed in a trade mark application unless there was evidence to the contrary which was sufficient to rebut that presumption.[181] This is also the position in Sweden.

(d) Locus standi *to plead bad faith*

13.148 In the UK, in Germany and in Sweden there is no specific *locus standi* requirement: any person may therefore challenge the lack of *bona fides* of a trade mark. However in Sweden the courts will only cancel the registration of a trade mark where its continued registration would be detrimental to the person who objects to it.

---

[177] Swedish Trade Mark Act, s 14(4).
[178] CTMR, arts 92(d), 96.
[179] See Davies (ed), *Sweet & Maxwell's European Trade Mark Litigation Handbook* (1998), paras 13–34.
[180] SOU 2001: 26, pp 448, 449, 451 and 452.
[181] *FSS Trade Mark* [2001] RPC 40 (HC); DAAWAT *trade mark* [2003] RPC 187 (LCAP).

G. Conclusion

This chapter has reviewed the challenges which can kill a trade mark both before and after it reaches the relatively safe harbour of registration. The laws of opposition, cancellation and revocation are rather less homogeneous than those of, for example, registration or infringement since they are often coloured by local procedural requirements. The application of those laws to the facts is also more discretionary than in the case of registration or infringement. This is because challenges to the trade mark monopoly must strike a balance between (i) the need to protect investment in brands and (ii) the need to keep undeserving trade marks off the register where (iii) the interests of third parties are articulated with sufficient clarity.

13.149

On the subject of 'bad faith', while that concept is firmly embedded in European trade mark law and jurisprudence, there is a substantial degree of variation in the establishment of the principles by which a trade mark applicant's conduct may be described as being in 'bad faith'. In this respect 'bad faith', like the treatment of public policy issues and damages for the deliberate infringement of intellectual property rights,[182] reflects the consideration that national laws within Europe at any rate, are more likely to differ on morally sensitive issues than on those which are morally neutral.

13.150

There is also a wide degree of latitude in determining how principles of law relating to 'bad faith' should be applied on the facts of individual cases. Notwithstanding this, it appears that there is a gradual drift towards a common approach. This drift will take time unless it can be accelerated by firm rulings from the ECJ.

13.151

---

[182] See Nigel Swycher and Mark Parsons, 'IPR Damages: A Pan-European Perspective', *Global Counsel*, September 2002, pp 35–40.

14

TRADE MARKS IN COURT

A. **Introduction**
   In pursuit of justice
   The moral of the story — 14.01
   (1) Legal machinery for enforcement — 14.02
   (2) Scope of this chapter — 14.04

B. **Preliminary issues in trade mark litigation**
   (1) Proof that a trade mark exists — 14.06
      (a) Proof that rights held under a trade mark exist — 14.07
      (b) From when do trade mark rights exist? — 14.08
   (2) Choice of jurisdiction — 14.09
   (3) Courts' powers — 14.16
   (4) Community trade mark courts — 14.18
   (5) Burden of proof in infringement cases — 14.20
   (6) Auditing and disclosure of information — 14.23
   (7) Judicial comments on trade marks — 14.26
   (8) Publication of the court's decision — 14.27

C. **Injunctive relief**
   (1) Final injunctions — 14.29
      (a) When will an injunction be ordered? — 14.32
      (b) The form of the injunction — 14.33
      (c) The geographical scope of the injunction — 14.35A
      (d) Proportionality of the injunction — 14.36
      (e) Post-expiry injunctions — 14.38
      (f) Against whom may an injunction be granted? — 14.39
      (g) What happens if an injunction is disobeyed? — 14.40
      (h) The effect of delay and acquiescence on injunctive relief — 14.42
      (i) When an injunction will not be granted — 14.43
      (j) Injunctions where the infringing act has already stopped — 14.46
      (k) No trade mark injunction will be awarded as ancillary relief for patent infringement — 14.47
      (l) Does loss of registration entail termination of the injunction? — 14.48
   (2) Interim injunctions: general principles — 14.49
      (a) *Ex parte* and *inter partes* injunctions — 14.53
      (b) The two preconditions for success in interim applications — 14.56
      (c) Evidence of the claimant's right — 14.58
      (d) An urgent need for relief — 14.59
      (e) The balance of convenience — 14.63
      (f) Interim relief will not be available where damage to the trade mark is small and not permanent — 14.65
      (g) Interim relief before the trade mark is registered — 14.66

Chapter 14: Trade Marks in Court

(h) Interim relief may be available even before a trade mark is used		14.67
(i) Interim relief will not be ordered if it is unfair on the defendant		14.68
(j) The effect of the conduct of the parties on the application for relief		14.70
(k) What happens after interim relief is granted?		14.72

D. Pecuniary relief
- (1) Damages — 14.76
  - (a) Damages where licences are granted — 14.80
  - (b) Damages where licences are not granted — 14.84
  - (c) Inquiries into damages — 14.88
  - (d) Inquiries in the case of comparative advertisements — 14.89
  - (e) Moral damages — 14.90
- (2) Account of profits — 14.92

E. Dealing with infringing goods
- (1) Seizure of the defendant's goods — 14.95
- (2) Delivery up and destruction — 14.98

F. Liability for making groundless threats — 14.101
- (1) Unjustified threats under international law — 14.105
- (2) Threats actions in the UK — 14.108
- (3) What is a threat? — 14.113
- (4) Threats in other circumstances — 14.115

G. Declaration of non-infringement — 14.116

H. Competition law
- (1) Claim of unlawful agreement or concerted practice — 14.118
- (2) Claim of abuse of a dominant position — 14.120

I. Conclusion — 14.123

A. Introduction

In pursuit of justice

'Do you know what I want to do to that disgusting person, that ... that *insect*?' Maude screamed, 'I want to have him *hanged*, that's what I want.'

From deep within a well-worn leather armchair in his shabby office, Cyril shook his head sadly in a futile gesture of sympathy. 'I'm afraid we can't do that.' This was one client interview that was not going to pass smoothly. One of the worst side-effects of an economic downturn was that opportunities to pick and choose one's clients were few and far between.

'Why not? That brute infringed my trade mark, didn't he?' Maude's lower lip quivered. She was not a happy trade mark proprietor.

'Yes, he did,' Cyril concurred. 'But capital punishment is not usually ordered against trade mark infringers.' And never by the civil courts, he quietly reminded himself.

'Why not? It's a dreadful thing to do. I don't think there's any punishment that's too severe for them, those ... those *parasites*.' Maude clenched her little fists in rage, then returned her hands to her lap. Motionless for a moment as if engaged in deep and sudden thought, she suddenly sprang to life again. 'So what can I do to him? Can we pull his fingernails out?'

A. Introduction

'No, not that either.'

'Prison?'

'Not for committing a *civil* wrong, I'm afraid.' The difference between civil and criminal meant little to Maude, who had long believed that the court system was established for the purpose of exacting retribution on wrongdoers.

'So what happens, then? Nothing, I suppose! No wonder the world's in such a bad way at the moment when these infringers can just walk out of court scot-free.'

'No, not at all,' Cyril reassured her. 'There's plenty the courts can do.'

'Such as?' Maude's whole body, in Cyril's mind's eye, had curved into the shape of an accusatory question mark, her coal-black eyes blazing with fresh anger. What was worse, she wondered? Trade mark infringers who did things when they shouldn't, or courts that did absolutely nothing even when they should?

'We can seek an injunction,' Cyril suggested hopefully.

'A what?' Maude was a successful fashion designer and her label was much sought-after (particularly, on this occasion, by an unscrupulous former colleague who had just become a somewhat unlawful competitor). But she had not hitherto been well versed in the law. The word 'injunction' sounded to her like a cross between an engine and a junction. Perhaps it was something to do with the railway service?

'An injunction,' Cyril repeated. 'It's a court order that tells the defendant he must stop infringing your trade mark.'

'That's pretty stupid, isn't it?' Maude retorted.

'Why?' Now it was Cyril's turn to ask the questions.

'Stands to reason, doesn't it?' The blinding light of clear reason cast no shadow across Maude's radiantly open countenance. She continued: 'If you've got a trade mark, then no one else is allowed to use it.'

Cyril nodded hesitantly.

'So if a court gives one of these injunction things, all it's doing is telling the man he can't do what he's not allowed to do anyway. That's right, isn't it?'

Another hesitant nod.

'So if he's not allowed to use my trade mark *before* the court gives him an injunction and he's not allowed to use my trade mark *after* the court gives him an injunction, he's not being stopped from doing anything he was allowed to do in the first place, is he?'

A final nod.

'So there's not much point in me suing him in the first place.' Maude was flushed with triumph and the warm realization that she had finally learned to think like a lawyer, or at least like Cyril whose forensic skills seemed to her to match his dreadful dress sense. And then a further thought troubled her newly gained tranquillity: one of the worst side-effects of an economic downturn was that one couldn't be more fussy about one's choice of law firm.

The moral of the story

14.01 Maude's expectations, though couched in extreme terms, mirror the more modest expectations of trade mark owners throughout the world that their trade marks, once registered, will be protected. These expectations are often crushed when they discover, like Maude, that trade marks do not enforce themselves and that substantive trade mark law appears to provide as many defences to infringement as there are ways of infringing and that trade mark enforcement is impeded

Chapter 14: Trade Marks in Court

by impartial procedural rules which exist to ensure fair play. Finally, like a clockwork duck in the hands of a small child, trade mark enforcement machinery does not keep working unless it is rewound at each step of the way; if it is overwound, it simply ceases to function.

(1) Legal machinery for enforcement

14.02 While trade mark law exists for the purpose of granting and enforcing trade marks, the judicial system of each country exists for the purpose of administering and distributing justice through the fair application of all its laws.

14.03 There is no point in trying to enforce a trade mark against an infringer unless a legal machinery for enforcement is in place and fully functioning. The Agreement on Trade-Related Intellectual Property Rights (TRIPs) has recognized this by imposing on its Member States the following requirements:

(i) to ensure that national enforcement procedures 'permit effective action against any act of infringement . . . , including expeditious remedies to prevent infringement and remedies which constitute a deterrent to further infringements';[1]

(ii) to have enforcement procedures which are 'fair and equitable', 'not . . . unnecessarily complicated or costly' and must not 'entail unreasonable timelimits or unwarranted delays';[2]

(iii) to provide for a judicial review of administrative procedures and of initial judicial decisions (except for acquittals in criminal proceedings);[3]

(iv) to provide relief in the form of final injunctions,[4] interim injunctions,[5] damages[6] and 'other remedies' (destruction of infringing goods or their removal from commerce[7]), on the basis that the simple removal of a trade mark from infringing goods should only in exceptional circumstances permit the release of those goods into channels of commerce;

(v) to grant judicial authorities the right to order an infringer to disclose the identity of producers or distributors of infringing goods.[8]

(2) Scope of this chapter

14.04 This chapter will review the powers granted to the courts to deal with infringers

---

[1] TRIPs, art 41(1).
[2] ibid, art 41(2).
[3] ibid, art 41(4).
[4] ibid, art 44.
[5] ibid, art 50.
[6] ibid, art 45.
[7] ibid, art 46.
[8] ibid, art 47.

B. Preliminary issues in trade mark litigation

and will contrast the manner in which these powers are wielded in different countries. It will also look at some of the means by which alleged infringers can counterattack and either head off an action for infringement completely or at least seize the initiative from the trade mark proprietor who seeks to protect his proprietary rights.

There are four important topics which this chapter will not address. The first is that of costs. Although the manner in which costs are awarded may have a powerful impact on the decisions (i) to embark upon litigation, (ii) to contest an action and (iii) to settle a dispute once the parties have locked horns, it is too big a subject, with too great a degree of divergence between national practices, to admit of a proportionately concise and helpful discussion within this volume. For the same reason this chapter does not discuss the applicability of criminal law to trade mark infringement. The third topic omitted from this chapter is the availability of modes of alternative dispute resolution (ADR) such as arbitration and mediation. This topic is one in which generalized guidance in a book of this scale could never reflect the wealth of practical experience upon which ADR is built. The fourth topic is the recognition of orders made by foreign courts, a subject which is of relevance to trade mark law[9] but which extends far beyond its borders. **14.05**

B. Preliminary issues in trade mark litigation

(1) Proof that a trade mark exists

Before the court of any country can rule on an allegation of trade mark infringement, it must first establish that the claimant has a trade mark right. The existence of a valid registration certificate, indicating: (i) the identity of the trade mark itself; (ii) the goods or services for which it is registered; (iii) the date of the registration; and (iv) the identity of the trade mark proprietor, is best for these purposes. Sometimes it happens that the claimant cannot show such a right, as, for example, where the certificate is held in the name of a previous proprietor from whom the claimant has taken an assignment or a licence, or where the claimant has changed its corporate name and this is not yet reflected in its trade mark registrations. In such a case, most national courts will accept any reliable evidence to substantiate the claimant's entitlement. **14.06**

(a) Proof that rights held under a trade mark exist

In the UK the fact that a claimant cannot substantiate his entitlement to the trade **14.07**

---

[9] See eg *UNIC Centre Sarl v Harrow Crown Court and others* [2000] ETMR 595, [2000] IP&T 205 (HC), *Prudential Assurance Co Ltd v Prudential Insurance Company of America* [2002] ETMR 1013, [2003] FSR 97 (HC); 13 March 2003 (CA).

mark through registration of his interest may affect his ability to claim damages or an account of profits in infringement proceedings;[10] this factor will not however affect his ability to secure interim injunctive relief.

(b) From when do trade mark rights exist?

14.08 Directive 89/104 does not specify the point from which a trade mark right exists, leaving it to each Member State to determine that point for itself. In the UK[11] and Ireland,[12] for example, rights in trade marks which have been granted take effect retrospectively to the date upon which the application was first made. The retrospective nature of those rights does not however mean that they can be asserted in respect of any right derived from the use of a sign which a third party makes before the trade mark proprietor's application date and which continues beyond that date.[13]

(2) Choice of jurisdiction

14.09 Before a trade mark owner goes to court to sue an infringer, he must identify the appropriate court in which to sue him. As a starting point, each country's trade mark law may not be invoked for the sole purpose of seeking to enforce or protect trade marks granted in other countries.[14] Although the trade mark owner may have no choice as to the court in which he brings proceedings,[15] he may be in a position to choose the jurisdiction in which he commences his action. This can happen, for example, when alleged infringement is taking place in several different countries. Although an infringer will be sued in a forum determined by the trade mark proprietor, he may be in a position to preselect the jurisdiction in which he defends an infringement action if, before the proprietor launches proceedings, the infringer seeks a declaration in the country of his choice that he is not infringing that trade mark. A claimant may wish to commence proceedings in a specific country in order to obtain interim relief or to seek disclosure of evidence from the defendant, but then seek permanent relief in another court. A claimant may also be able choose one jurisdiction for obtaining an order and then attempt to enforce it in a second.[16]

---

[10] Trade Marks Act 1994, s 25(4).
[11] ibid, ss 9(3), 40(3).
[12] Trade Marks Act 1996, ss 13(3), 45(3).
[13] *Inter Lotto (UK) Ltd v Camelot Group plc* [2003] 3 All ER 191 (HC): right based on HOT-PICKS trade mark for lottery services could not be used against pre-application and subsequent use of HOT PICK sign for same services.
[14] See eg *Nogueras v City of Barcelona*, WTLR, 9 June 2003 (US Court of Appeals, 4th Cir): US Lanham Act cannot protect alleged rights to Spanish trade marks.
[15] eg when suing in France, where proceedings must be brought in the *situs* in which the defendant is located; see *Odyssée Interactive v L'Ile des Médias*, 2 December 2002 (Tribunal de Grande Instance de Grenoble).
[16] This is precisely what happened in *Italian Leather SpA v WECO Polstermöbel GmbH & Co,*

B. Preliminary issues in trade mark litigation

Within the EU the determination of jurisdictional issues is governed by the Brussels Convention of 1968, which has been incorporated into EU law by the Brussels Regulation of 2001.[17] These provisions make just one specific reference to trade marks, when they provide that any dispute concerning the registration or validity of a trade mark or other registered industrial property right must be determined in the courts of the country which grants that right.[18] **14.10**

The United States has its own criteria for determining jurisdiction both at Federal and at State level, which is important when it is remembered that the United States operates parallel Federal and State trade mark systems. Some States have cultivated extensive 'long arm' jurisdictional rules which enable them to hear claims against remote defendants who might not have appreciated that their business dealings could lead to an action before a United States court. The United States courts have also affirmed that conduct is actionable under the Lanham Act as a 'use in commerce' where the defendant advertises his trade mark in that jurisdiction, even if the services he renders lie elsewhere.[19] **14.11**

Although it is desirable that all disputes concerning the same parties and involving the same trade mark should be heard together by the same court, there may be circumstances in which this is not possible and where different national jurisdictions must rule on different facets of the same dispute. Thus even where trade mark infringement proceedings are pending in Germany, a passing-off claim made within the context of the same dispute will need to be heard in England since the common-law doctrine of passing off is not part of German law.[20] **14.12**

Where the alleged infringement involves the operation of a website which is hosted outside the trade mark owner's own country, the emergent pattern appears to be that jurisdiction will be accepted if the website is intended to be accessed in the country in which the trade mark is registered and the damage done by the infringement is accordingly inflicted there, but not otherwise. Thus the Tribunal of Rome has declined jurisdiction where the Italian owner of the CARPOINT trade mark sought to sue Microsoft over its use of the carpoint.msn.com website for selling cars in the United States,[21] while the Scottish Court of Session accepted jurisdiction where the local proprietor of the 'business a.m.' word-and-device **14.13**

Case C-80/00 [2003] ETMR 130 (ECJ) where an Italian claimant, unable to obtain relief in Germany, secured a favourable order in Italy and then tried unsuccessfully to enforce it in the court which first refused it.

[17] Council Regulation 44/2001 on jurisdiction and the recognition and enforcement of judgments in civil and commercial matters (Denmark remains a member of the Brussels Convention but has opted out of the Brussels Regulation).
[18] Council Regulation 44/2001, art 22(4).
[19] *International Bancorp LLC and others v Société des Bains et Mer du Cercle des Etrangers à Monaco*, Case No 02–1364, 3 December 2002 (EDVa 2002).
[20] *Mecklermedia Corporation and another v DC Congress GmbH* [1997] ETMR 265 (HC).
[21] *Carpoint SpA v Microsoft Corporation* [2000] ETMR 802 (Tribunale de Roma).

mark for newspapers sought to sue defendants based in Greece and Mauritius for operating businessam.com, a website aimed at Scottish users.[22]

14.14 The Community Trade Mark (CTM) Regulation contains a number of rules relating to jurisdictional issues relating to the trade marks granted by Office for Harmonisation in the Internal Market (OHIM). For example, where actions are brought which involve the same parties and the same cause of actions in two or more countries, but one involves the infringement of a CTM and the other the infringement of a national mark, any court other than that first seised of the action is required to decline jurisdiction, whether on its own motion or where its jurisdiction is contested.[23] Directive 89/104 contains no equivalent provisions.

14.15 The operation of the rules which govern the choice of jurisdiction is a discipline in its own right.[24] Its coverage lies outside the scope of this work, which will confine itself to reminding readers that the factors involved in the choice of a jurisdiction in which to sue or be sued are many: they include the subject matter of the litigation (for example, a national court cannot invalidate a trade mark right granted by another country's trade mark registry), the expense of litigation, timing, requirements relating to security for costs and damages in respect of foreign parties, the value of that jurisdiction as a market, the nature of the judicial relief sought, the risk of appeal and the likelihood of success in court.

(3) Courts' powers

14.16 The courts have a broad range of weapons at their disposal: damages, injunctions, delivery up or destruction of infringing goods are available in almost all jurisdictions, while some countries[25] also provide for the advertisement of the decision in the national or local press as a means of alerting the relevant consuming public to the infringing nature of a particular trade mark use. The removal of an offending trade mark may also be ordered where it does not affect the condition of the goods to which it has been applied.[26]

---

[22] *Bonnier Media Ltd v Greg Lloyd Smith and Kestrel Trading Corp* [2002] ETMR 1050 (Court of Session).
[23] Council Regulation 40/94, art 105(1). See also art 105(2), (3) and (4) and a rare case on these provisions: *Prudential Assurance Co Ltd v Prudential Insurance Company of America* [2002] ETMR 1013, [2003] FSR 97 (HC); 13 March 2003 (CA), in which it was held that a decision of a French court on the dissimilarity of PRUMERICA to the opponent's PRU and PRUDENTIAL marks did not bind an English court which was seised of infringement proceedings involving, *inter alia*, the same marks.
[24] See eg James Fawcett and Paul Torremans, *Intellectual Property and Private International Law* (1998) for a comprehensive overview of the topic. See also Annette Kur, 'International Hague Convention on Jurisdiction and Foreign Judgments: A Way Forward for IP' [2002] EIPR 175–83 on the competing merits of jurisdiction in the country of registration or the country of the defendant's domicile.
[25] Countries which provide for the publication of legal decisions include Belgium, France and Italy.
[26] *Boehringer Ingelheim Pharma KG v Eurim-Pharm Arzneimittel GmbH* [2003] ETMR 491 (Bundesgerichtshof).

14.17 The courts generally confine their orders to their own territories.[27] Some national courts in Europe have either made extraterritorial orders in order to prevent infringing actions taking place even abroad[28] or have indicated their readiness to do so in an appropriate case.[29] In the United States, Federal statutes—including the Lanham Act, which covers trade marks—presumptively lack extraterritorial reach.[30] The long arm of United States law may however stretch even into Europe in exceptional circumstances such as where (i) the defendant (an Italian citizen conducting business in Italy) was a United States resident of forty years' standing, (ii) the foreign infringing activity had a substantial impact on United States commerce and (iii) the proposed injunction would not conflict with foreign law.[31]

(4) Community trade mark courts

14.18 Since the CTM is a pan-EU right, each EU Member State has been asked to nominate both first- and second-instance 'Community trade mark courts' from its own national courts for the purpose of hearing and disposing of certain issues involving CTMs.[32] These issues include infringement proceedings and the determination of counterclaims for cancellation or revocation of the claimant's CTMs, but not actions brought by a claimant in order to revoke or cancel another's CTM.[33]

14.19 Where the CTM Regulation is silent, national CTM courts must apply their own national law.[34] This principle explicitly applies with regard to legal sanctions[35] and to 'provisional and protective measures'[36] such as interim injunctions and orders relating to the search of a suspected infringer's premises or the seizure of infringing articles or evidence relating to them.

---

[27] See eg *SpeechWorks Ltd v SpeechWorks International Incorporated* [2000] ETMR 982 where the Court of Session considered the implications of extending an order from Scotland to England.

[28] *Consorzio per la Promozione dello Speck v Christanell, Handle Tyrol and Lidl Italia Srl* [1998] ETMR 537 (Tribunale di Bolzano): injunctive relief ordered against defendants in Austria and Germany as well as Italy. See also *John Walker & Sons Ltd and another v Henry Ost and Company Ltd and another* [1970] FSR 63 (HC).

[29] In *Re Sacher* [2000] ETMR 185 the Austrian Supreme Court indicated its preparedness to grant interim injunctive relief in all Paris Convention Member States, so long as it had before it (i) evidence of allegedly infringing activities and (ii) evidence as to the law of each of those countries.

[30] *Alcar Group v Corporate Performance Systems Ltd* 109 F Supp 2d 948 (ND Ill 2000): US law does not apply to unauthorized post-licence sale of products in Germany. The court said (at 952): 'If [the claimant] has a trademark case, it is under British, German or other EC Law'.

[31] *AV by Versace Inc v Gianni Versace SpA* 126 F Supp 2d 328 (SDNY 2001).

[32] A current list of CTM courts can be found on the OHIM website at http://oami.eu.int/pdf/aspects/Co026-ann.pdf.

[33] Council Regulation 40/94, art 92.

[34] ibid, art 97(2).

[35] ibid, art 98.

[36] ibid, art 99.

(5) Burden of proof in infringement cases

14.20 It is the responsibility of the claimant to satisfy the burden of proof that there has been an infringement of his trade mark. This burden is met, *prima facie,* by the claimant proving (i) that the trade mark exists,[37] (ii) that he has an entitlement to it and (iii) that the defendant is doing some act which may be described as falling within the scope of an infringing act as defined by his national or regional trade mark regime. Once this is done, the burden shifts to the defendant to show that he has a defence. Perhaps he is not infringing or, even if he is technically infringing, he is nonetheless not liable: for example, he may show that the trade mark is invalid or revocable, that his actions do not constitute infringing acts because the law provides a specific defence, that he has acted with the consent or acquiescence of the claimant or that the trade mark rights have been exhausted. If the defendant cannot do that, the court will enter judgment for the claimant.

14.21 The burden of proof in cases in which the defendant pleads exhaustion of the trade mark proprietor's right is discussed in Chapter 9.

14.22 When a claimant succeeds in proving that infringement has taken place, his obligation to prove his case does not end at that point. In some countries the successful claimant is required to show he has suffered actual pecuniary or non-pecuniary loss before damages are granted,[38] while in others he is entitled to receive damages on a 'willing licensee' basis even if he can prove no actual loss at all.[39] Further, where infringing products are found in the defendant's possession, only those products which are shown to have infringed the claimant's rights can be regarded as infringing products: the rest must be regarded as non-infringing until proof of their unlawful provenance can be demonstrated.[40]

(6) Auditing and disclosure of information

14.23 Sometimes the trade mark owner is as much concerned to obtain information as it is to stop infringing acts or seek recompense for the damage done by them. For example, it may be important for the trade mark owner to discover the name of the defendant's supplier of infringing products, or to ascertain the identity of those to whom the defendant has supplied them. The trade mark owner may also want to know how much stock an infringer holds. One Dutch court has acceded

---

[37] It is normal for a granted trade mark to be presumed valid: see eg ibid, art 95; Trade Marks Act 1994 (UK), s 72.
[38] *Barilla Alimentares SpA v Danis Srl and others*, 20 March 2002 [2003] ETMR N-4 (Court of Naples); *Morgan Crucible Company plc v AB Svejseteknik ApS* [2001] EIPR N-78 (Maritime and Commercial Court, Denmark).
[39] *Reed Executive plc and Reed Solutions plc v Reed Business Information Ltd, Reed Elsevier (UK) Ltd and Totaljobs.Com Ltd (No 2)* [2003] Info TLR 60 (HC).
[40] *Chloé Société Anonyme v Føtex A/S* [1997] ETMR 131 (Maritime and Commercial Court, Denmark).

B. Preliminary issues in trade mark litigation

to a claimant's request that information concerning stocks, suppliers and customers be audited by the infringer's accountants, in preference to the claimant having to rely on the infringer's word alone,[41] but it is not known whether the courts in other European jurisdictions would go so far in seeking to verify the information sought by the claimant.

14.24 It is not only by bringing an action against an infringer that a trade mark owner can obtain information concerning the circulation of infringing goods. In a Dutch case involving the importation of medicinal products into the EEA where those products were differently formulated for use in non-EEA countries, the trade mark owner successfully brought proceedings which were not directed against the infringers at all but against a transport company which had innocently shipped the goods from a non-EEA supplier to a German company; that company was ordered to disclose the source from which it acquired the infringing products.[42] In the UK it is common practice, where infringement proceedings have been commenced, to seek disclosure of information from parties other than the actual infringer through a *Norwich Pharmacal* order.[43]

14.25 In an appropriate case the trade mark owner can force the customs authorities to disclose information. Under EU law it is possible for trade mark owners to secure a temporary suspension of the transit of any goods which enter the EU for long enough to enable them to find out if those goods are counterfeit or not.[44] The European Court of Justice (ECJ)[45] has ruled that this Regulation overrides any provisions of national law which seek to protect the confidential nature of the identity of the parties who send or receive such goods. Accordingly, once goods that have been seized by customs have been found to infringe a trade mark, the customs authorities can be compelled to disclose information which will enable the trade mark owner to proceed against importers and distributors.

(7) Judicial comments on trade marks

14.26 Although a court, in dismissing the trade mark owner's action, will occasionally pass comment on the validity of his trade mark,[46] there is no well-established

---

[41] *Braun Aktiengesellschaft v Elbeka Electro BV* [1998] ETMR 259 (County Court, Breda).
[42] *Boehringer Ingelheim Pharma KG v GTO Expeditie BV and others*, 19 February 2003 (Court of The Hague).
[43] Now known as an order against a party who is not a party, this procedure is usually referred to by the name of the case in which it was established, *Norwich Pharmacal Co v Commissioners for Customs and Excise* [1974] AC 133 (HL).
[44] Council Regulation 3295/94 laying down measures to prohibit the release for free circulation, export, re-export or entry for a suspensive procedure of counterfeit and pirated goods.
[45] *Adidas AG's reference*, Case C-223/98 [1999] ETMR 960 (ECJ).
[46] See eg *French Connection Ltd v Sutton* [2000] ETMR 341, where an English High Court judge passed comment on the unsuitability for registration as the trade mark of the claimant's word mark FCUK.

practice as to what the court may do to it. Where the defendant does not counter-claim for invalidity of the trade mark registration, the courts appear to leave it on the register even if they believe that it is not validly registered.[47]

(8) Publication of the court's decision

14.27 In many countries (but not in the UK) the courts routinely order, at the request of the successful trade mark owner, the publication of the court decision in one or more newspapers and also on the defendant's website.[48] This relief is not often discussed by the courts but its rationale is well summarized in the following dictum of the Brussels Commercial Court:

> [T]he plaintiff demands the publication of the judgment in four daily or weekly newspapers of its choice. The defendant ... accepts that publication of the judgment in the context of a trade mark infringement offers the trade mark holder the possibility of informing bona fide buyers and potential clientele that it really was acting against trade mark infringements.
>
> The publication of the judgments in some way compensates for the deterioration of the attractive power and the convincing character of the plaintiff's three-stripe trade mark. In this way the public is warned against infringing activities.[49]

14.28 Publication of the court's decision may also go some way towards mitigating the damage which results from the defendant's wrongful act.

C. Injunctive relief

(1) Final injunctions

14.29 A final injunction in trade mark infringement proceedings is an order that requires the infringer to refrain from performing any further infringing acts. Sometimes the injunction will be coupled with other relief, such as damages in respect of infringing acts which have already been performed.

14.30 An injunction may take immediate effect or may be delayed until a later date, for example, the date by which it is feasible to cease the infringing act or the date by which infringing products which still remain in the defendant's shops will have been sold. In one French case a successful English claimant obtained injunctive relief against use of its CONQUEROR trade mark for paper products, but the French defendant was given a whole year in which to cease infringing activity in

---

[47] See eg *Ty Nant Spring Water Ltd v Lemon & Co Srl* [1999] ETMR 969, where the Court of Naples dismissed Ty Nant's infringement action on the ground that its cobalt blue colour mark was not distinctive but did not annul the registration.
[48] *Hugo Boss* (4 Ob 174/02w) WTLR, 6 May 2003 (Austrian Supreme Court).
[49] *Adidas AG v NV Famco* [1998] ETMR 616, 624–5 (Brussels Commercial Court).

C. Injunctive relief

the light of the length of time and magnitude of the scale of the infringer's activities.[50]

When an injunction is granted against an infringer, does that mean that he may not use the proprietor's trade mark at all, or that he may carry on using the infringed trade mark but only in a manner which was non-infringing before the injunction was granted? This issue was discussed in a Swedish case in which an unlicensed VOLVO maintenance, repair and recovery service was ordered to stop various activities which clearly infringed the trade mark. The Appeal Court was of the opinion that the injunction should be varied so as to entitle the defendant to make such use of the VOLVO trade mark as was permitted in the 'Volvo Corporate Identity Programme Manual'. The Supreme Court disagreed. Reinstating the order of the Stockholm City Court, it left the terms of the injunction unlimited: the unauthorized but legally permitted use of a trade mark under Directive 89/104, it reasoned, presupposed that such use had to be made in accordance with honest business practices, which was manifestly not the case where the defendant was an infringer.[51] This decision may be criticized on the basis that, while the absence of honest business practices relates to the past, injunctive relief is addressed to the conduct of the infringer in the future. What legal or commercial policy objective is being served by prohibiting an infringer from performing an activity which the law permits? **14.31**

(a) When will an injunction be ordered?

The principal justification of an injunction against trade mark infringement is that it forces the infringer to stop doing, both at the time of the infringement and in the future, something which interferes with the intangible property rights and commercial expectations of the trade mark owner and of any other person entitled to use those rights. This justification remains valid even though damages might provide adequate compensation for the trade mark owner (for example, where the owner of the POWER PIZZA trade mark for takeaway pizzerias does not sell pizzas himself but operates through a national web of non-exclusive licensees, if the infringer sets up his own unauthorized POWER PIZZA in a town where no licensee has yet been appointed). *A fortiori* the injunction also provides protection for the trade mark owner against types of harm for which the award of monetary damages would not provide adequate compensation, for example, where the infringement has resulted in a loss of consumer confidence or brand credibility, or where the trade mark has been 'debased'.[52] **14.32**

---

[50] *SA Papeterie Hamelin v Wiggins Teape Ltd* [2000] ETMR 1047 (Cour d'appel de Paris).
[51] *Volvo Ltd v D S Larm Ltd and Dick Edvinsson* [2000] ETMR 299 (Supreme Court, Sweden).
[52] *Ferrari SpA v Power Horse and others* [1997] ETMR 84 (Court of Milan, Italy).

(b) The form of the injunction

14.33 How wide should be the form in which the order contained in the injunction is expressed? For example, Knorr owns the trade mark POT NOODLE for food products containing noodles. If I choose to sell food products which are emphatically intended to be eaten by humans and not dogs, I might wish to call it NOT POODLE. Knorr would be advised to seek an injunction, which would order me to desist. Should I be ordered 'not to use the trade mark NOT POODLE' or should I be required 'not to use the trade mark NOT POODLE or any other trade mark which is confusingly similar to POT NOODLE'? Since the court only found NOT POODLE to be an infringing mark, I don't know how it would react to, for example, a dispute involving the rebranding of my food products as PONTOODLE. If the injunction were issued in the first format, Knorr would have to go to court again to prove infringement; in the second, Knorr could have me committed for contempt of court.

14.34 This issue was raised in a UK patent case[53] in which the trial judge questioned the wisdom of granting an injunction in the form of a general order to the defendant not to infringe the patent. Translating the judge's reasoning from patents to trade marks, it runs as follows: if a defendant is found to have infringed a trade mark by making his own mark insufficiently different from that of the claimant, the form of words of the injunction should reflect that by ordering him only not to do those acts that have been found by the court to constitute infringement. This will leave him free to try again to find a trade mark which is not too close to that of the claimant, free from the fear that he will be in breach of the injunction and thus in contempt of court if his next attempt to escape infringement is equally unsuccessful. Further, where an injuncted defendant is obliged to distance his trade mark further from that of the claimant's than he might otherwise have done if he had not already been enjoined, there is an element of reduction in competition. If he does not have this freedom, then he is disadvantaged *vis-à-vis* other third parties who can risk infringing the trade mark without the threat of contempt of court proceedings. Although the Court of Appeal disapproved of this approach,[54] preferring the traditional form of order, it may be attractive where the infringed trade mark right has been conferred upon a product shape which competitors find it difficult to avoid completely.

14.35 The notion of the 'tailored injunction' as a means of enabling businesses with similar names to function on the Internet, where risks of confusion or 'interference' between non-competing concerns are high, has already been countenanced in the

---

[53] *Coflexip SA v Stolt Comex Seaway MS Ltd* [1999] FSR 473 (HC), followed in the trade mark infringement action of *Beautimatic International Ltd v Mitchell International Pharmaceuticals Ltd and another* [1999] ETMR 912 (HC).

[54] *Coflexip SA v Stolt Comex Seaway MS Ltd* [2001] RPC 182.

C. Injunctive relief

United States. In such instances an injunction will not absolutely prohibit the use of a claimant's name but will indicate with some degree of precision the manner or circumstances in which the defendant may use it.[55]

(c) The geographical scope of the injunction

An injunction should not have the effect of conferring upon the trade mark owner a wider degree of protection than that within which his interests require to be protected. Thus in the *American Eagle* case a United States court overturned the trial court's nationwide injunction where the trade mark proprietor had only used his trade mark within certain territories within the United States.[56]

14.35A

(d) Proportionality of the injunction

Where the scale of damage inflicted on a trade mark owner through an infringement is likely to be small, it is open to a court to refuse to grant injunctive relief. Where the damage caused by the infringement is not purely economic but relates to the repute of the claimant's mark, the fact that economic loss is proportionally trivial will not outweigh the need to continue to protect the trade mark's image against even small encroachments. Thus in a passing-off case brought by the Scotch Whisky Association against the intended sale of Isle of Man 'white whiskey' (redistilled blended Scotch whisky), the defendants could not escape an injunction by maintaining that the level of trade in white whiskey was so small that injunctive relief would be disproportionate. The Court's words are worthy of note:

14.36

> The real risk of damage . . . is the commencement of an insidious process of erosion of the integrity of the reputation or 'aura' of true whisky which the defendant rightly accepted that it has in the minds of potential consumers . . . Once the integrity of the undoubted concept of whisky made in the traditional manner is allowed to be breached it seems to me that . . . it is difficult to see where the line is to be drawn, and the true whisky producers . . . will see the increasingly damaged reputation of whisky by products less and less like true whisky being called 'whisky'.[57]

In rejecting the argument that an injunction would provide relief which was disproportionate to the damage done by the defendant, the court was effectively prohibiting the sale of 'white whiskey' for fear of the encouraging or permissive consequences which those sales might have for the making of further sales of different products by traders who were not party to these proceedings.

14.37

---

[55] See the cases discussed in Anandashankar Mazumdar, 'Courts are Beginning to Grasp the Idea that Similar Marks can Coexist on the Internet' [2003] ECLR 293–4.
[56] *Emergency One v American Fire Eagle Engine Company* WTLR, 24 July 2003 (4 Cir 2003).
[57] *Scotch Whisky Association v Glen Kella* [1997] ETMR 470, 492 (HC).

(e) Post-expiry injunctions

14.38 Even where a trade mark lapses through non-renewal of the registration, injunctive relief may be granted to the trade mark proprietor who, through continued use of the expired mark, continues to enjoy a degree of protectable goodwill in it.[58] In such a case the fact that the trade mark has lapsed or is invalid does not disqualify its owner from seeking injunctive relief on principles of unfair competition or passing off. In contrast, where a trade mark is revoked for non-use, further use by the defendant will not be restrained even if he has been ordered to pay damages for his infringing acts prior to the revocation.[59]

(f) Against whom may an injunction be granted?

14.39 An injunction may be awarded against almost any infringer, whether he be the prime mover of the infringement or a distant, indirect or secondary infringer such as the proprietor of a newspaper which carries advertisements in which an infringement of another's trade mark appears.[60] An exception to this principle is that an Internet service provider (ISP) who takes reasonable steps to abate an infringement, once that infringement is drawn to its attention, will not be liable in trade mark infringement proceedings and no injunctive order will be made against an ISP in such circumstances.[61]

(g) What happens if an injunction is disobeyed?

14.40 Any act of disobedience of an injunction, like disobedience to any court order, is generally treated as a serious legal matter. In some countries the injunctive order contains daily fines for non-compliance. In the UK the defendant who defies an injunction is in 'contempt of court'.[62] He can be sent to prison for up to two years,[63] be made to pay a fine and can have his assets sequestered.

---

[58] *Azienda Agragia Perda Rubia v Cantina Sociale Ogliastria* [2001] ETMR 1114 (Tribunal di Lanusei, Italy).

[59] *Jean Patou SA v Sté Zag Zeitschriftn Verlag AG and another* [1999] ETMR 157 (Cour d'appel de Paris).

[60] *Ferrari SpA v Power Horse and others* [1997] ETMR 84 (Court of Milan, Italy); *Sté Hugo Boss v Dernierès Nouvelles d'Alsace and others* [1998] ETMR 197 (Tribunal de Grande Instance de Strasbourg, France).

[61] See *Sté Gervais Danone v Société Le Riseau Voltaire, Société Gandhi, Valentin Lacambre* [2003] ETMR 321 (Tribunal de Grande Instance de Paris). In *Esso Société Anonyme Française SA v Association Greenpeace France and Société Internet.Fr* [2003] ETMR 441 the Tribunal de Grande Instance de Paris concluded that an ISP was not in fact exonerated from injunctive relief but did not actually make an order against it. Where it has been implemented, article 12 of the E-Commerce Directive (Directive 2000/31 on certain legal aspects of information society services, in particular electronic commerce, in the Internal Market) exempts an ISP from liability, but only where it is a 'mere conduit'.

[62] See paras 14.33–14.35 above.

[63] Small, innocent breaches of an injunction need not necessarily lead the trade mark infringer into prison for contempt of court; see *British Telecommunications plc v Nextcall Telecom plc* [2000] ETMR 943 (HC).

C. Injunctive relief

An injunction will only bind parties to the case. Thus, where an order was made against the World Wrestling Federation whereby it was required to stop various infringing acts and to take steps to cause its licensees to cease infringing the World Wide Fund for Nature's WWF trade mark, a licensee of the Federation was able to secure a declaration that its continued sale of video games within which was encoded the WWF trade mark was neither a breach of the injunction nor a contempt of court.[64]

14.41

(h) The effect of delay and acquiescence on injunctive relief

Where a final injunction is sought, neither the fact that the infringer has infringed for a long time nor the fact that the trade mark owner has taken a long time to respond to the infringement are necessarily fatal to an application for permanent relief. Thus the Danish Supreme Court, reversing the decision of the Maritime and Commercial Court, held that the owner of the GRAMMY trade mark for awards made by the National Academy of Recording Arts & Sciences, was entitled to an injunction against the defendants' use of the mark DANSK GRAMMY even though the infringing DANSK GRAMMY awards were made each year from 1989 and the trade mark owner did not object before 1997.[65]

14.42

(i) When an injunction will not be granted

Injunctive relief is usually granted at the discretion of the court, which will weigh up all the factors which are relevant to the case before making an order. Relevant considerations may include the conduct of the successful claimant and the infringing defendant both before and after the infringement, whether the defendant is still trading at the time the order is made, the extent to which the claimant actually suffers damage through the infringing acts, and so on. Procedural issues will also be taken into account, such as whether the trade mark owner has raised issues before the court so late that the infringer is unable to respond to them.[66] Neither of the two considerations, (i) that the damage done through the infringing acts is conveniently quantifiable or (ii) that the claimant has licensed other users of the trade mark, gives the defendant the right to opt to pay damages rather than face an injunction.

14.43

An injunction is most unlikely to be granted where the court considers that there is neither actual evidence of damage nor a likelihood of confusion or damage to the trade mark owner through the alleged infringement.[67]

14.44

---

[64] *World Wide Fund for Nature and World Wildlife Fund Inc v World Wrestling Federation Entertainment Inc and another*, 27 March 2003 (CA).
[65] *National Academy of Recording Arts & Sciences Inc v International Federation of Phonographic Industry Danmark* [2001] ETMR 219 (Supreme Court, Denmark).
[66] *?What If! Holdings Ltd v The What If Group BV* [2003] ETMR 481 (District Court, The Hague), para 5.
[67] *French Connection Ltd v Sutton* [2000] ETMR 341 (HC): application for interim relief: no evidence of confusion of FCUK trade mark and fcuk.com domain name.

14.45 Where the trade mark proprietor was a foreign entity which did not exploit the trade mark itself but merely licensed its use by others, the Austrian Supreme Court upheld a decision to grant an injunction to restrain the infringing acts on the basis that they constituted acts of unfair competition, leaving open the question whether the claimant could have succeeded on the ground of trade mark infringement.[68]

(j) Injunctions where the infringing act has already stopped

14.46 An injunction may not be granted where the court considers that the infringing act has ceased and there is no likelihood of it ever being repeated[69] (this may be the case where the defendant has already accepted that it was in the wrong and has since modified its marketing or advertising activities accordingly). Where however the court can be persuaded that, notwithstanding the cessation of infringement, further infringing acts may result, the cessation of infringement is no bar to final injunctive relief.[70]

(k) No trade mark injunction will be awarded as ancillary relief for patent infringement

14.47 Sometimes it is not the claimant's trade mark that the claimant seeks to stop the defendant using, but the defendant's own trade mark. This happened in a UK patent infringement[71] case in which the successful claimant asked the court to order the defendant not to use its own VORTEX trade mark for a period of six months in relation to bagless upright vacuum cleaners. The basis of the argument was that the defendant, through its patent infringement, had been able to build up goodwill in the reputation of its VORTEX trade mark, to the detriment of the claimant. If the defendant were allowed to continue use of its VORTEX trade mark, having developed its goodwill on the strength of its use on infringing machines, it would have derived a secondary advantage from its patent infringement. The court refused this unusual application. In the first place, it could not be said that the benefit gained through the use of its trade mark was a foreseeable consequence which flowed from its wrongful use of the claimant's patent. Secondly, the order would be unfair to the defendant in that it would also prohibit the use of VORTEX in relation to innocent and non-infringing sales of products as well as on the sale of infringing machines. The court did not however say that an injunction to prohibit the use of a patent infringer's trade mark could *never* be granted.

---

[68] *The Football Association Ltd, GB v Distributors of Football Strips* [1997] ETMR 229 (Supreme Court, Austria).
[69] *United Biscuits (UK) Limited v Asda Stores Limited* [1997] RPC 513 (HC); cf *Iliad SA v Cédric A*, 7 January 2003 (Tribunal de Grande Instance de Paris), where an injunction was granted fifteen months after the infringement had ceased.
[70] *Sony Computer Entertainment Inc v Lee* WTLR, 8 April 2003 (High Court of Kuala Lumpur, Malaysia): infringing PLAYSTATION CD-ROMS had already been seized; such goods are easy to procure, easy to sell and highly profitable to trade in.
[71] *Dyson Appliances Ltd v Hoover Ltd (No 2)* [2001] RPC 544 (HC).

C. Injunctive relief

(1) Does loss of registration entail termination of the injunction?

14.48 Does an injunction continue in force even if the claimant's trade mark has expired or been cancelled or revoked? This issue does not appear to have been judicially considered and it is not as straightforward as it appears. This is because the claimant may have based his action on claims other than trade mark infringement, such as passing off or unfair competition, and the terms in which the court's order is made may be directed specifically towards the actions of which the claimant complained rather than towards the nature of the right or rights which have been infringed. In principle, however, courts grant injunctive relief in order to protect the right of the proprietor to exercise the essential functions of his trade mark. Once a trade mark ceases to be of effect, it is difficult to justify its continued protection even where the defendant's conduct has been unlawful or dishonest.

(2) Interim injunctions:[72] general principles

14.49 Sometimes the cost of litigation is likely to be unacceptably high to an alleged infringer or a substantial delay is likely to occur between an interim hearing and the full trial of the issue of infringement. In such instances the defendant may find it commercially unattractive to persist in denying liability for infringement: an action may go no further than the stage at which an interim injunction is granted and may never reach full trial at all. Accordingly an understanding of the mechanism by which the courts will grant interim injunctive relief is vital for any business with product or service names which may come into conflict with its competitors.

14.50 Hearings on interim relief are generally very tightly focused on determining the merits of granting or refusing an interim remedy. They therefore concentrate on the period between the interim hearing and the full trial. Such hearings are not intended to provide an opportunity for the defendant to air any defence which is based on past events, such as whether the trade mark owner was previously in breach of the local Trade Practices Act or other unfair competition law.[73] Nor are interim proceedings the appropriate time for a defendant to raise the defence that the claimant's trade mark has become a generic term.[74] In the UK and some other common-law jurisdictions, however, the principle that 'he who comes to equity

---

[72] The term 'interim relief' is employed in this book, although the word 'interlocutory' is still widely used. TRIPs and the CTM employ the vocabulary of 'provisional measures' (see eg TRIPs, art 50, Council Regulation 40/94, art 99).

[73] *Christien t/a Rose's Lace Boutique and another v BVBA Parcles* [2000] ETMR 1 (Brussels Court of Appeal).

[74] *Nichols (N N) plc v Mehran Bottles (Private) Ltd* (2001) 91 TMR 477 (Sindh High Court, Pakistan): the claimant, proprietor of the VIMTO mark, secured interim relief to stop the use of PAKOLA VIMTO.

must come with clean hands'[75] may require the court to consider the ethical nature of the past conduct of the respective parties.

14.51 In some jurisdictions the court may refuse to grant an interim injunction since it is not strictly merited on the facts of the trade mark applicant's claim, but will nonetheless seek to bring on the full trial earlier than might otherwise be the case. This is what happened in one Irish case[76] in which the owner of the trade mark SOLPADEINE for a pain-killer sought interim relief against the use of SOLFEN for a similar product. Since after five months' aggressive marketing by the defendant, the claimant had not actually been able to identify anyone who had actually been confused between the two products, the court reckoned that the likelihood of confusion between them was not high enough to warrant interim relief;[77] yet there was clearly a triable issue. Accordingly a speedy trial was ordered.

14.52 The fact that an injunction is not expressed as being of a temporary nature does not mean that the courts may not, in granting an injunction, fix a further hearing, following which further relief against infringement would be considered.[78]

(a) Ex parte and inter partes injunctions

14.53 Ideally a court will prefer to hear both sides of the argument before deciding whether to grant an interim injunction. An application for interim relief made by the trade mark owner and opposed by the defendant—a so-called *inter partes* application—is however not always possible. Sometimes, upon receipt of a letter from the trade mark owner's lawyers before a legal action is commenced, the defendant simply disappears, only to reappear when he feels it safe to do so; sometimes it is not the defendant who disappears but the allegedly infringing goods; on other occasions it is neither the defendant nor the goods that disappear, but only the documentary or other evidence which links them to manufacturers, suppliers, distributors or customers. In such circumstances the trade mark owner does not really want to trumpet his claims in advance—he wants to get his court order beforehand and then surprise the defendant with it. An application which the trade mark owner makes for interim relief, without the presence of the defendant, is called an *ex parte* application.

14.54 In the UK various forms of *ex parte*[79] relief are available, including search orders

---

[75] See I C F Spry, *The Principles of Equitable Remedies* (2001), pp 246–8, 494–500.
[76] *SmithKline Beecham plc and others v Antigen Pharmaceuticals Ltd* [1999] ETMR 512 (High Court, Ireland).
[77] A similar conclusion was reached in *Beecham Group plc v Munro Wholesale Medical Supplies Ltd* [2001] ETMR 318 (Court of Session, Scotland), where the sophistication of the market for pharmaceutical products was a factor in reducing the likelihood of confusion.
[78] *Zino Davidoff SA v M & S Toiletries Ltd* [2000] ETMR 622 (Court of Session, Scotland).
[79] In England and Wales the term '*ex parte*' has been officially replaced by 'order without notice' and *inter partes* by 'on notice'. The old Latin terms however show a remarkable degree of persistence.

C. Injunctive relief

which enable the trade mark owner to gain access to evidence and prevent its destruction,[80] as well as those which stop the defendant spiriting his assets out of the country before a hearing can be arranged.[81] In Germany too the Civil Procedural Code provides for *ex parte* relief in sufficiently urgent cases where irreparable harm would otherwise occur.[82]

Although Dutch law does not provide for *ex parte* injunctions, it protects the trade mark owner's needs in other ways, for example, through attachment orders which can be made against an alleged infringer even before infringement proceedings are initiated.[83] In contrast, Belgian law provides for the *saisie-description*, an efficient *ex parte* tool that enables the trade mark owner to obtain measures of discovery and seizure against alleged infringements: the suspected infringer receives no advance notice of the visit by a court-appointed expert who is empowered to take samples of allegedly infringing products, to analyse them and to draft a report that will subsequently serve as evidence in proceedings on the merits.[84] The French *saisie contrefaçon*[85] and Italian *descrizione giudiziaria*[86] procedures may be used to even greater effect since they allow seizure of the entire allegedly infringing inventory. 14.55

(b) The two preconditions for success in interim applications

The Italian courts require, as a precondition of interim relief, the fulfilment of two threshold criteria: the trade mark owner must prove *fumus boni juris* (the existence of the right which he seeks to enforce) and he must show that there is *periculum in mora* (urgency in the need for the court to grant relief).[87] In theory the absence of either criterion is fatal, however strongly evidenced the other one may be. In practice, the Italian courts have been prepared to accept, in lieu of proof of the existence of the right, a presumption that it exists which is based on the difficulty which a claimant may face when seeking to bring an action in a very short time-frame.[88] 14.56

---

[80] Formerly known as *Anton Piller* orders, after one of the early cases in which they were employed.
[81] CPR, r 25(1)(f) and (g), on which see David Kitchin and others, *Kerly's Law of Trade Marks and Trade Names* (2001), paras 18-206–18-207.
[82] Isabel Davies (ed), *Sweet & Maxwell's European Trade Mark Litigation Handbook* (1998), para 7–102.
[83] ibid, para 4–95.
[84] Ruben Peeters, 'Search and Seizure', Bird & Bird website, 31 July 2002.
[85] Intellectual Property Code, art L716–7.
[86] Isabel Davies (ed), *Sweet & Maxwell's European Trade Mark Litigation Handbook* (1998), para 10–78.
[87] The criterion of urgency has been adopted by the ECJ: see its ruling in *Hermès International v FHT Marketing Choice BV*, Case C-53/96 [1998] ETMR 425, para 34.
[88] *Levi Spa v Iniziative Srl* [2003] ETMR N-3 (Court of Monza).

14.57 Although there may be some difference in emphasis, the twofold Italian approach can be seen in other European jurisdictions too, as the following paragraphs will show.

(c) Evidence of the claimant's right

14.58 The claimant must demonstrate that he is entitled to sue for trade mark infringement. In the absence of a valid trade mark certificate (which may be difficult to obtain at short notice on account of the complexities of a company's internal organizational structure or something as simple as national holidays) or a certified copy of it, an affidavit or statement of truth on the part of the claimant will generally suffice.

(d) An urgent need for relief

14.59 The trade mark owner must first establish that there is at least a plausible allegation of trade mark infringement because, without an allegation that the trade mark has been infringed, there is no ground for the court's intervention at all. Then he must show that the need for relief is urgent in that he cannot wait for a decision until the date of a trial which may not be concluded until several months, or in some cases even years, in the future. An allegation of infringement will usually be supported by evidence showing that the claimant's trade mark and the sign used by the defendant are identical or similar and by explaining how the defendant's use of that sign fits within one or more of the infringing acts stipulated by national law. At this early stage in the litigation the court may be influenced by evidence of even a single episode of actual confusion,[89] even if that evidence might not of itself be sufficient basis for the award of a final injunction. A court may also be influenced by factors such as the fact that damages might not be an adequate remedy if injunctive relief is not granted, or by the fact that any losses caused to the alleged defendant would be adequately compensated by the trade mark owner giving a cross-undertaking in damages.

14.60 Since there must be an element of urgency in the trade mark proprietor's request for interim relief, it follows that any delay in bringing an action may prejudice his chances of obtaining protection prior to the trial. In one French case[90] the trade mark owner was unable to deny that it knew of the allegedly infringing acts ten months prior to its application for interim relief: that delay in seeking the court's interim assistance was fatal. In the Dutch *kort geding* procedure a complaint is no longer regarded as urgent when six months has elapsed since the trade mark owner

---

[89] Thus in *Teknek Electronics Ltd v KSM International Ltd* [1998] ETMR 522 (Court of Session, Scotland), the court was influenced by a single instance of confusion which might, at the full trial, have not been regarded as being of real substance.

[90] *Skis Rossignol SA and another v SA Head Tyroli Sports & HTM Sport SpA* [1999] ETMR 450 (Tribunal de Grande Instance de Grenoble).

C. Injunctive relief

became aware of the infringing act.[91] In Germany, depending on the court, a claim will cease to be regarded as urgent between one and three months after the trade mark proprietor has become aware of the allegedly infringing act.[92]

The fact that the parties' respective products are competing in a field in which technological change is swift will also influence a court's decision to provide temporary protection for a trade mark. This factor swayed the Court of Naples[93] when it ordered one company to stop selling bicoloured detergent tablets—a technological innovation in their time—similar to those for which another company had secured trade mark registrations. As the court said, even a finding of liability on the merits would not avail the trade mark owner if he had to submit to the temporary use of his mark by the defendant

14.61

> ... because, at the time of the decision on the merits, further technological developments or different marketing choices could render commercially useless the right recognised only after a delay.[94]

The urgency demanded by the courts is not always matched by the nature of their interim relief. Thus in one case a publisher obtained a preliminary injunction against the use of its FORMAT trade mark in the defendant's format.at domain name but the defendant was given two weeks within which to comply with it.[95]

14.62

(e) The balance of convenience

Once the claimant has established his entitlement to the trade mark and the existence of an urgent need for relief, the court must decide whether it is right to grant the interim relief asked for. This is because the defendant may have an even more urgent need for there not to be relief. For example, if the allegedly infringing goods have a short shelf-life but the trial of the full action is unlikely to take place for six months, the effect of ordering the defendant not to sell them until the trial of the action could be commercially disastrous. Likewise, if the claimant has not yet used his trade mark but the defendant has invested heavily in advertising and manufacturing a product bearing an allegedly infringing mark, or where the defendant has been able to establish a market for infringing products,[96] the defendant's reasons for there not being an interim injunction may be more powerful than the proprietor's reasons for wanting one. In the UK and Ireland the courts

14.63

---

[91] Isabel Davies (ed), *Sweet & Maxwell's European Trade Mark Litigation Handbook* (1998), para 4–91.
[92] ibid, para 7–99.
[93] *Benckiser NV and Benckiser Italia SpA v Henkel SpA and others* [1999] ETMR 614 (Court of Naples).
[94] ibid, 647.
[95] *Format Gesellschaft mbH and another v Wirtschafts-Trend Zeitschriftenverlags Ges mbH* [2002] ETMR 472 (Austrian Supreme Court).
[96] *Beecham Group plc v Munro Wholesale Medical Supplies Ltd* [2001] ETMR 318 (Court of Session, Scotland).

consider a powerful cocktail of criteria which relate to the 'balance of convenience'—would the inconvenience to the defendant if the injunction *were* granted outweigh the convenience to the claimant, and would the convenience to the defendant if the injunction *were not* granted outweigh the inconvenience to the claimant.[97]

14.64 Once it is accepted that it is necessary to achieve some sort of balance of convenience between the conflicting interests of trade mark owner and alleged infringer, an interim order can become a sophisticated and complex tool for preserving the *status quo ante* in part or in whole. The potential versatility of interim orders can be seen from the approach taken by the Court of Appeal of Jamaica in an action brought by the internationally famous McDonald's against a local prior trader of the same name,[98] where the interests of each trader as well as the need to protect the consuming public had to be carefully weighed before a balance of convenience could be identified.

(f) Interim relief will not be available where damage to the trade mark is small and not permanent

14.65 In one Scottish case involving the sale of whisky which allegedly infringed the LAPHROAIG trade mark the Court of Session, having already granted interim relief on an *ex parte* application, retracted that relief once it discovered that the alleged infringement was of finite extent and on a very small scale: the trade mark proprietor's goodwill in its trade mark would be scarcely damaged if the allegedly infringing goods were sold and that damage was not regarded as being irreparable.[99]

(g) Interim relief before the trade mark is registered

14.66 In some jurisdictions, notably Greece,[100] Italy[101] and the Netherlands[102] (but not the UK), the courts are willing to grant injunctive relief against trade mark infringement in order to protect an application even before the trade mark has been granted. Where a country provides this facility for its national trade marks, it is obliged to provide the same level of protection for CTMs.[103]

---

[97] *American Cyanamid v Ethicon* [1975] AC 396 (HL), applied in *Symonds Cider & English Wine Co Ltd v Showerings (Ireland) Ltd* [1997] ETMR 238 (High Court, Ireland).
[98] *McDonald's Corporation v McDonald's Corporation Limited & Vincent Chang* [1997] FSR 760 (Court of Appeal, Jamaica).
[99] *Allied Domecq Spirits & Wine Ltd v Murray McDavid Ltd* [1998] ETMR 61 (Court of Session, Scotland).
[100] See *Slim International and Antineas Graikou v Delta Protypos Milk Industry* [2000] ETMR 409 (First Instance Court, Athens).
[101] Trade Mark Act, art 61.
[102] *Rowling v Uitgeverji Byblos*, 3 April 2003 (unreported) (District Court of Amsterdam).
[103] Council Regulation 40/94, art 99.

C. Injunctive relief

(h) Interim relief may be available even before a trade mark is used

14.67 In a Scottish case[104] the owner of the DISCOVERY CHANNEL trade mark for radio and cable transmission services sought an interim injunction to halt the impending broadcast of the 'Discovery 102' local radio station in Dundee, 'The City of Discovery'. The trade mark owner had no imminent plans to use its trade mark for radio services, though it planned to do so eventually. Overturning the trial judge's refusal of relief on the basis that the trade mark owner had done nothing to establish its use in relation to radio, an appellate court held that the fact that the trade mark owner had not yet commenced use of its trade mark for radio services was not of itself a ground for withholding interim relief, since the defendant had also not yet launched its station.

(i) Interim relief will not be ordered if it is unfair on the defendant

14.68 Since interim injunctions provide temporary relief until the full trial can take place, the courts in most countries are fairly sensitive to the need to establish a reasonable balance between the interests of the conflicting parties until that event occurs. This means not inflicting on either party a degree of harm which cannot be easily righted at a later stage, or which is disproportionate to the allegations raised in each case. Accordingly a Scottish court refused to grant interim injunctive relief to the owner of the PEBBLE BEACH trade mark for golf resorts and sundry spin-off merchandise products, where the defendant was selling PEBBLE BEACH whisky.[105] The defendant's highly important Christmas marketing campaign was already underway: it was too late for him to change his product's name and, if he missed that year's seasonal opportunity, his main chance of profit for the year would be lost.

14.69 The trade mark proprietor may be required to give an undertaking to pay the defendant damages to compensate him for any loss suffered as a result of interim relief being granted if it is concluded, at the trial of the substantive issue of infringement, that the defendant was not an infringer after all.[106] Likewise, a defendant against whom an interim injunction is not granted may be required to undertake to compensate the trade mark proprietor in respect of any use of the trade mark which, in the absence of an injunction, he should be obliged to pay; it may also be possible for him to make a payment into court on account of any damages which may be awarded against him. The courts will take account of the ability of

---

[104] *Discovery Communications Inc v Discovery FM Ltd* [2000] ETMR 516 (Court of Session, Scotland).
[105] *Pebble Beach Company v Lombard Brands Ltd* [2003] ETMR 250 (Court of Session, Scotland).
[106] These damages can be substantial: in *Lube A/S v Dansk Droge A/S* [2001] ETMR 343 (Supreme Court, Denmark) damages payable by the trade mark owner totalled some 600,000 kr (around £54,000 or €80,000).

both parties to make any necessary undertakings or payments of this nature when determining whether to grant interim relief.[107]

(j) The effect of the conduct of the parties on the application for relief

14.70 Since injunctive relief is generally granted as a matter of discretion, the court will be concerned not only with the balance of convenience but also with such matters as the conduct of the parties. These include, for example, the fact that one (or both) of the litigants has acted in bad faith.

14.71 Sometimes a claimant may be prevented from obtaining interim relief because, through his conduct, he has given the impression that he was not going to object to the allegedly infringing act. In one case a defendant unsuccessfully sought to persuade a Scottish court that, since the defendant had launched his own allegedly infringing business in the trade mark owner's hotel without having faced any objection from the hotel's management, the trade mark owner had acquiesced in the alleged infringement and was barred from seeking relief.[108]

(k) What happens after interim relief is granted?

14.72 Even in the relatively recent past, the grant of interim relief would more often than not be not just the first salvo in the battle of the parties but also the final and decisive shot. This was because, if a defendant was held back from using the disputed trade mark even for a few months, his inability to promote goods or services using that mark within the marketplace would be a major impediment to profitable trade. No business wants to have capital, workforce and marketing know-how tied up in a project which it cannot press on with until the future outcome of an uncertain event (the full trial) is known. In such circumstances, options such as (i) choosing another trade mark for one's own goods or services or (ii) infringing someone else's trade mark—depending on the integrity and ambition of the defendant—became commercially more desirable. Once an interim injunction was granted, the trade mark owner whose prime objective was to stop new infringements rather than to gain recompense for old ones would frequently not pursue the action further by seeking to have the interim order made permanent. The dilatory action or indeed inaction of the claimant was particularly annoying to the defendant who believed in the legitimacy of his activity and wished to see the case through to the end.

---

[107] *SpeechWorks Ltd v SpeechWorks International Incorporated* [2000] ETMR 982 (Court of Session, Scotland). For a general review of these issues, see *American Cyanamid v Ethicon* [1975] AC 396 (HL).

[108] *Gleneagles Hotels Limited v Quillco 100 Limited and Toni Antioniou*, 1 April 2003 (Outer House, Court of Session, Scotland): GLENEAGLES FILM STUDIOS development launched in the famous GLENEAGLES Hotel.

D. Pecuniary relief

14.73 TRIPs has changed this scenario to a considerable extent. By article 50(6)[109]

> ... provisional measures ... shall, upon request by the defendant, be revoked or otherwise cease to have effect, if proceedings leading to a decision on the merits of the case are not initiated within a reasonable period, to be determined by the judicial authority ordering the measures where a Member's law so permits or, in the absence of such a determination, not to exceed 20 working days or 31 calendar days, whichever is the longer.

14.74 This now means that the boot is on the other foot. Once the trade mark owner secures *inter partes* interim relief, he has to take active steps to pursue a decision following a full trial, if he does not want the injuncted defendant to ask for the interim order to be revoked or suspended.[110] A defendant can accordingly seek to stretch the trade mark owner's resources by pressing him to go to trial, the cost and inconvenience of which can be substantial—particularly where the trade mark owner is seeking to protect many trade marks against many defendants but the defendant is only infringing the one trade mark of the claimant. If the defendant does not request the revocation or suspension of the interim order, it will not automatically cease to have effect at the end of the period stipulated by article 50(6).[111]

14.75 Once the application and scope of article 50 was raised, the prospect of a major revision of the injunction-granting practices of national courts throughout Europe appeared likely, but this has not yet occurred. This may be because the cost of testing and interpreting this provision inevitably falls on the litigants, who may have better things to do with their material resources than pay for the further development of legal doctrine.

D. Pecuniary relief

(1) Damages

14.76 In all jurisdictions it is possible for the owner of the infringed trade mark to obtain an award of damages from the infringer. Damages are usually awarded only after a trial of the merits, but in the Benelux countries some courts have ordered an apparently infringing defendant to pay the trade mark owner an advance of damages or ill-gotten gains pending a full hearing on the issue of liability.[112]

---

[109] The ECJ has jurisdiction, in a field of Community intellectual property law upon which the EU has legislated, to apply and interpret this provision on a reference from a national court regarding provisional measures; see *Parfums Christian Dior SA v Tuk Consultancy BV*, Case C-300/98 [2001] ETMR 277 (ECJ).

[110] *Hermès International v FHT Marketing Choice BV*, Case C-53/96 [1998] ETMR 425 (ECJ), para 34.

[111] *Schieving-Nijstad VOF and others v Groeneweld*, Case C-89/99 [2002] ETMR 34 (ECJ), paras 56–61.

[112] Isabel Davies (ed), *Sweet & Maxwell's European Trade Mark Litigation Handbook* (1998), para 4.52.

14.77 The way in which damages are calculated appears to differ substantially from country to country. In some jurisdictions (for example, the UK, Denmark and Germany) an award of damages—if compensation cannot be agreed by the parties—is based on actual evidence of loss, often supplemented by arithmetical computations; in France, however, the successful claimant will expect to receive automatic damages even where actual loss cannot be proved, as well as damages for the expense and inconvenience of having to go to court in the first place.[113] In countries such as Spain and Portugal it appears to this author, writing as a relative outsider, that the sum awarded is based on the judge's subjective evaluation of the scale of the damage.

14.78 The main basis upon which damages are awarded in civil litigation is that of compensation: there may however be other grounds on which damages are awarded, for example, to punish the infringer for his wrongful acts or to deter him (and, through him, perhaps others) from doing them again. These grounds are however more the province of criminal law than civil litigation.[114]

14.79 Where damages are awarded on a compensatory basis, the trade mark owner should receive an amount of money which restores him to the position he would have been in, had his trade mark not been infringed in the first place. This exercise in compensation is likely to be addressed in different ways, depending on whether the trade mark owner habitually grants licences to use his trade mark—in which case there is at least some objective evidence as to what the proprietor charges for the use of his trade mark and therefore a clue as to what he may be considered to have lost through the infringer's failure to take a licence—or whether the trade mark owner does not license use by others. Both of these types of compensatory damages are considered below.

(a) Damages where licences are granted

14.80 If the trade mark owner exploits his trade mark by licensing the merchandising rights in it to others, he should not forget to tell the court what sort of loss he has suffered. Thus in one Italian case a trade mark owner was refused damages because, although his mark had been infringed, he had not pleaded that he had suffered any loss, whether through loss of royalties from his licensees or in any other way.[115]

---

[113] Civil Procedural Code, art 700.
[114] In the UK the Law Commission's Report No 247, *Aggravated, Exemplary and Restitutionary Damages* (1997) recommended the introduction of 'punitive' damages for infringement of intellectual property rights. This proposal has not yet been acted upon.
[115] *Centro Botanico Srl, Angelo Naj Oleari and Gruppo Cartorama SpA v Modafil di A Toniolo & C Sas* [2003] ETMR 500 (Tribunal of Milan).

D. Pecuniary relief

Assuming that the trade mark owner claims the loss of licence royalty income, how much is a licence worth? The 'going rate' for a trade mark licence is, at least in the UK, the starting point for the calculation of infringement damages against an unlicensed infringer. Does that mean that such an infringer, having been refused a licence, can infringe at will and will have to pay no more than he would have done if he had been a legitimate licensee? If, as the courts have repeatedly stated, damages for trade mark infringement are compensatory, this may well be the case unless there is also some other basis upon which damages for trade mark infringement can be awarded. **14.81**

The Danish courts have considered damages in the context of the problem which occurred where a trade mark proprietor was a regular licensor with a highly selective and expensive licensing policy (which militated towards damages being assessed at a high level), while the defendant's infringement—the reproduction of the WWF panda logo in a newspaper's title page—was the result of negligence, of relatively short duration and unlikely to affect the licensor's sales (which would suggest a low level). In the event the court sided with the defendant: the infringement was relatively inconspicuous and there was nothing to indicate to the court either that the claimant had suffered, or that the defendant had benefited, from the infringement.[116] Accordingly, with the claimant demanding damages of 500,000 kroner (around £45,000 or €67,000) and the defendant offering one-fifth of that, the court awarded damages of 100,000 kroner (around £9,000 or €13,200). **14.82**

Whether licences are granted or not, the availability of unlicensed and therefore infringing products in the marketplace may have the effect of depressing prices. If the proprietor is a licensor, depressed prices will mean lower royalties from his legitimate licensees; if the proprietor is not a licensor but sells his products himself, depressed prices mean lower profits. Although this issue does not appear to have been explicitly raised in any recent European trade mark case, loss incurred through price depression has been recognized as a head of damages in at least one patent case.[117] **14.83**

(b) Damages where licences are not granted

Where the injured trade mark owner does not normally issue licences, there is often no indication as to how either he or the market in which he trades values the trade mark and, therefore, no indication as to how much value one places on the damage done by infringement. In England the starting point for the assessment of the quantum of damages is to seek to establish how much the infringer would have paid the trade mark owner on a 'user' basis, on the fictitious assumption that the **14.84**

---

[116] *WWF Danmark and WWF-World Wide Fund for Nature v Den Blå Avis A/S* [1999] ETMR 300 (Maritime and Commercial Court, Denmark).
[117] *Gerber Garment Technology Ltd v Lectra Systems Ltd* [1997] RPC 443 (CA).

trade mark owner was a willing licensor and that the infringer was a willing licensee.[118] The fact that the English courts take this as their starting point indicates how fond they are of the notion that the damage inflicted by an infringer has a notional price which is fixed by how much the proprietor would be prepared to accept for the violation of his trade mark. Some trade mark owners—particularly those who neither outsource their manufacturing nor license their trade marks under any terms—find this distasteful: it is a bit like assessing damages in favour of an angler, from whom a magnificent trout has been stolen, on the basis of how much his thief would have paid him if he had bought it. It should be emphasized, though, that the willing licensor/licensee presumption is only a starting point. In theory it does not restrict the ability of the courts to award a larger (or indeed smaller) sum based on evidence or on its own estimate as to how badly the goodwill in a trade mark has been damaged by the infringement.[119]

14.85 Danish practice is to assess damages as a percentage of the infringer's turnover from the infringement. In one recent case where a parallel importer of a pharmaceutical product repackaged genuine products but 'co-branded' them by adding its own name and logo to that of the trade mark owner, damages were assessed at 5 per cent of the defendant's infringement-based turnover.[120]

14.86 The German practice has been to recognize two different bases for making an award of damages where the reasonable royalty principle, described above, does not apply. The first is to seek to estimate the scale of the trade mark owner's lost turnover and, from that, to calculate his lost profits—an approach which is particularly suitable where the prime role of the trade mark relates to its use in the sale of products.[121] The second is to seek to estimate the scale of the infringer's profits, so long as those profits can be shown to arise wholly from the infringing act and not to any other commercial activity on the infringer's behalf.[122]

14.87 The French approach towards the calculation of damages where there is no licence norm is quite different. Recent jurisprudence reveals that damages may be substantial, if not large, even where the trade marks themselves are not in any sense household words. Thus in one 2001 case, where the infringing act consisted of listing a set of infringing databases of exhibitors' details by the names of the exhibitions to which those databases related, the amount of damages for trade mark infringement ranged from the same amount as that awarded for infringement of

---

[118] *Reed Executive plc and Reed Solutions plc v Reed Business Information Limited, Reed Elsevier (UK) Limited and Totaljobs.Com Limited (No 2)* [2003] InfoTLR 60 (unreported) (HC).
[119] In practice, however, according to one eminent English barrister, it probably does restrict the court's ability.
[120] *AstraZeneca AB v Orifarm A/S*, 4 January 2002 [2002] EIPR N-92 (Supreme Court, Denmark).
[121] *Iris v Urus* GRUR 1966, I 457 (Bundesgerichtshof).
[122] *Vita Sulfa* GRUR 1961, I 354 (Bundesgerichtshof).

D. Pecuniary relief

database right to one-fifth of that sum: two of the companies within the claimant's group were awarded damages of 20,000FF (around £2,000 or €3,000), the third receiving ten times that amount.[123]

The Portuguese courts have considered that the mere fact that the unauthorized use of another's trade mark has continued for four years is itself evidence of damage. On this basis at least one court has ordered the infringer to pay equitable damages in the absence of evidence of the exact quantum of damages.[124]

14.87A

(c) Inquiries into damages

Sometimes the successful claimant may have no idea as to the scale or nature of the damage flowing from the infringement. In such cases jurisdictions such as the UK and Ireland offer him the opportunity to seek an inquiry into damages, this inquiry being conducted in accordance with the specific instructions of the court. Where the court awards an inquiry into damages for trade mark infringement, it will indicate whether or not the basis of the damages award is that of a hypothetical licence, while also taking into account the extent to which the defendant benefited from the infringement—a issue which seems superficially more appropriate to an order of an account of profits than an inquiry into damages.[125]

14.88

(d) Inquiries in the case of comparative advertisements

Where the infringing act is the use of another's mark for the purpose of comparative advertising which the court has considered to be unfair, the basis for the computation of damages is unclear. In one English case the judge observed that the whole point of comparative advertising, if it is to confer any benefit on the advertiser at all, is that it will increase his market share at the expense of the market share of the competitor whose trade mark he uses. This is so whether the comparison is honest or not. Accordingly, if the measure of damage inflicted by a dishonest comparison is the difference between an honestly inflicted loss and a dishonestly inflicted loss, the quantum of loss may be hard to compute and the courts will be reluctant to order an inquiry into damages.[126]

14.89

(e) Moral damages

It is generally understood that the proprietor's right in his trade mark is a property right and that, since the trade mark is a piece of property in commerce, compensation for damage inflicted upon it is to be assessed on the basis of the proprietor's

14.90

---

[123] *Société Reed Expositions France (Formerly Groupe Miller Freeman) v Société Tigest Sarl* [2003] ECDR 206 (Cour d'appel de Paris).
[124] *Les Editions Albert René Sarl v Madaleno* WTLR, 23 July 2003 (Court of Golegã).
[125] *Reed Executive plc and Reed Solutions plc v Reed Business Information Limited, Reed Elsevier (UK) Limited and Totaljobs.Com Limited (No 2)* [2003] InfoTLR 60 (HC).
[126] *Emaco Ltd and Aktienbolaget Electrolux v Dyson Appliances Ltd* [1999] ETMR 903 (HC).

economic loss. Much the same applies to damages for infringement of patent rights. With regard to copyright, however, the law of all Berne Convention Members is supposed to recognize the existence of two types of right—the economic right and the moral right—and to compensate the injured author, where appropriate for injury to both rights.[127] What is the difference between the economic right and the moral right? The economic right, which may be sold or licensed to others, is the right to reproduce, distribute or perform a protected work, while the moral right is a personal, inalienable right to be acknowledged as a work's author, to object to distortions and mutilations of that work and, in some countries, also the rights to determine when a work is finished and to withdraw it from publication if the author considers publication prejudicial to his reputation.

14.91 Where a trade mark is a logo, a design or other work which is also protected by copyright, it is possible that its creator—who may be the trade mark owner but is more likely to be a creative third party—will be able to recover compensation for damage to his moral rights. This sort of damage to moral rights does not appear to be the same as the use of the term 'moral damages' in some countries to refer to damage relating to the diminution of the goodwill in the infringed mark rather than calculable damage relating to lost sales or lost profits.[128]

(2) Account of profits

14.92 Sometimes an infringer's use of a trade mark has resulted in profit to the infringer but has not actually caused any serious damage to the trade mark proprietor. This may happen where the infringement involves the importation and sale of genuine 'grey goods' which were first marketed outside the European Economic Area, in circumstances where the trade mark proprietor has not been left with any unsold stock in his own hands. It may also happen where the defendant has made and sold good quality infringing products of his own but has not affected the trade mark owner's sales. In such a situation the trade mark owner may opt to receive an account of the profits earned by the defendant rather than an inquiry into damages.

14.93 The basis upon which an account of profits is ordered will vary from country to country. In Germany, for example, the account of profits is seen as a means of compensating the claimant for the loss of his own profits[129] and as an appropriate sanction against infringing behaviour against vulnerable intellectual property rights[130] rather than as merely a manner of transferring one person's profits to another.

---

[127] Berne Convention for the Protection of Literary and Artistic Works, art 6*bis*.
[128] *Louis Vuitton Distribuição v Caliente Comércio de Modas* WTLR, 30 May 2003 (Superior Court of Justice, Brazil): $4,000 'moral damages' awarded for damage to the value of the LOUIS VUITTON trade mark.
[129] *Objective loss calculation*, I ZR 16/93, 2 February 1995 (Bundesgerichtshof).
[130] *Treatment of overheads in profit calculations* [2002] ECDR 289 (Bundesgerichtshof).

E. Dealing with infringing goods

An account of profits should not be confused with an inquiry into damages. An account of profits is an order, available in the UK and in some other countries, that further evidence be produced and information gathered for the purpose of calculating a monetary award which is appropriate to the true loss which the claimant has suffered in consequence of the infringement. **14.94**

E. Dealing with infringing goods

(1) Seizure of the defendant's goods

In most countries the seizure of infringing goods by the appropriate authorities may be ordered. Seizure may be employed not just as a final remedy but even, in interim proceedings, as an adjunct to an injunction.[131] **14.95**

What happens to goods once they are seized? This issue has been addressed by TRIPs in the following manner: **14.96**

> In order to create an effective deterrent to infringement, the judicial authorities shall have the authority to order that goods that they have found to be infringing be, without compensation of any sort, disposed of outside the channels of commerce in such a manner as to avoid any harm caused to the right holder, or, unless, this would be contrary to existing constitutional requirements, destroyed. . . . In considering such requests, the need for proportionality between the seriousness of the infringement and the remedies ordered as well as the interests of third parties shall be taken into account. In regard to counterfeit trademark goods, the simple removal of the trademark unlawfully affixed shall not be sufficient, other than in exceptional cases, to permit release of the goods into the channel of commerce.[132]

The British-based charity International Aid Trust has sought to dispose of seized counterfeit goods by arranging for any attached trade marks to be removed by convicted prisoners and for the trade mark-free goods to be sent to recipients in developing countries who would certainly not be in a position to purchase the genuine product. **14.97**

(2) Delivery up and destruction

Delivery up is an order by which infringing products find their way into the trade mark proprietor's hands. Sometimes delivery up is ordered for the purpose of the destruction of infringing goods by the trade mark owner. Destruction, as its name suggests, is an order that the infringing goods be destroyed. Destruction is popular with trade mark owners because it provides photo-opportunities involving **14.98**

---

[131] *Benckiser NV and Benckiser Italia SpA v Henkel SpA and others* [1999] ETMR 614 (Court of Naples, Italy).
[132] TRIPs, art 46 ('Other remedies').

steam-rollers or other appropriate industrial machinery reducing quantities of counterfeit or otherwise infringing products to a squashed or mangled pulp. Unlike damages and injunctive relief, destruction may be ordered by the competent customs authorities of EU Member States,[133] even if no civil trial has taken place on the issue of infringement.[134]

14.99 The German Bundesgerichtshof has ruled that, where the infringing act consisted of the use of a trade mark on what turned out to be the unnecessary repackaging of a genuine parallel-imported pharmaceutical product, it was appropriate to order the destruction of the packaging alone. Although compliance with this order might be most annoyingly inconvenient for the defendant, the court ruled that that did not offend the principle of proportionality.[135]

14.100 Not all delivery up is for the purpose of destruction. Where, for example, the trade mark owner seeks delivery up of genuine goods in which the local trade mark right has not been exhausted, the trade mark owner has at least the opportunity of selling the goods himself. This effectively provides the trade mark owner with a second income stream from putting the infringing goods on the market. In such circumstances a delivery up order may be made subject to the payment to the defendant by the trade mark owner of a proportion of the purchase price of the goods.[136]

F. Liability for making groundless threats

14.101 No normal person goes about his business in the hope of being sued. The cost and inconvenience of successfully defending an action, not to mention the commercial uncertainty to which pending litigation subjects a business, are factors which make most businesses risk-averse. Accordingly it is a natural response for a business, when threatened with trade mark infringement litigation, to seek to avoid even making a successful defence of its position if a profitable low-risk alternative position can be adopted. The risk-averse nature of traders has however been recognized by trade mark owners in the past as a means by which they can unfairly extend *de facto* the monopoly which they enjoy *de jure*.

---

[133] Council Regulation 3295/94 laying down measures concerning the entry into the Community and the export and re-export from the Community of goods infringing certain intellectual property rights, art 8(1).
[134] See eg *Adidas-Salomon AG's application*, Case 2000:119 (unreported) (Finnish Supreme Court).
[135] *Boehringer Ingelheim Pharma KG v Eurim-Pharm Arzneimittel GmbH* [2003] ETMR 491 (Bundesgerichtshof).
[136] eg in *Braun Aktiengesellschaft v Elbeka Electro BV* [1998] ETMR 259 the Breda County Court (the Netherlands) awarded delivery up but ordered the successful claimant to pay the infringer 50% of the purchase price of the infringing goods.

F. Liability for making groundless threats

Consider the following situation: Bingo and Bongo are two traders who sell electronic tortoise-warmers. Bingo, having registered the word mark BINGO for his tortoise-warmers and then having advertised them heavily, is enraged to discover that retail sales of Bongo products have remained constant. Bingo then writes to retailers who sell both Bingo's and Bongo's products together, advising them that the sale of Bongo products infringes the BINGO trade mark and threatening to sue them for dealing in infringing goods. He also writes to wholesalers and distributors of Bongo products, telling them the same thing. The recipients of these letters do not want to be sued and think to themselves: 'since the profit earned by dealing with BINGO products is the same as that earned by dealing with Bongo's, we lose nothing if we stop dealing in Bongo's. Why then should we go to court to defend our right to sell Bongo's?' Bongo loses sales outlets and, after reducing his manufacturing output to match falling demand, cannot achieve the necessary economies of scale and is soon producing far fewer tortoise-warmers than Bingo is, but at a higher price. Members of the price-sensitive public abandon Bongo's products and flock to buy those of Bingo. By adopting this underhand and unethical strategy, Bingo can wipe Bongo out of the market for tortoise-warmers even though the sale of Bongo products does not infringe the BINGO trade mark. 14.102

Trade mark law in the UK[137] and Ireland[138] provides that the making of groundless threats of this nature is itself an actionable civil wrong. The trade mark laws of most other jurisdictions do not contain similar provisions, although the making of such threats may constitute an act of unfair competition or an abuse of rights under ordinary principles of civil law.[139] 14.103

Although it is not a threat in itself, the use of the ® registered trade mark symbol in relation to a trade mark which has not been registered is generally treated as being unlawful. The use of that symbol is a representation that the user has the legal authority to sue an unauthorized user for trade mark infringement. Since the use of one's own trade mark registration may constitute a defence to an action for infringement, the ® symbol is sometimes used by infringers who seek to avoid a threat of litigation rather than as a threat itself.[140] 14.104

(1) Unjustified threats under international law

The Paris Convention, TRIPs, the Directive 89/104 and the CTM Regulation have in common the fact that they make no express provision for the circumstance 14.105

---

[137] Trade Marks Act 1994, s 21, discussed at paras 14.113–14.115 below.
[138] Trade Marks Act 1996, s 24.
[139] See eg Council of Europe, *Abuse of Rights and Equivalent Concepts: the Principle and its Present-Day Applications* (Proceedings of the 19th Colloquy on European Law 1989, Luxembourg 1990); French Civil Code, arts 552, 1382.
[140] See eg *Red Bull Sweden AB v Energi Trading I Skara Handelsbolag and Energi Trading I Skara AB (in bankruptcy)* [2002] ETMR 758 (Swedish Market Court).

in which a trade mark owner, without legal justification, threatens to commence infringement proceedings against an alleged infringer. But two of those international codes are not quite silent on the subject. Under the Paris Convention

> false allegations in the course of trade of such a nature as to discredit the establishment, the goods, or the industrial or commercial activities, of a competitor[141]

are prohibited as acts of unfair competition and an unjustified threat to sue a third party for trade mark infringement *may* in certain circumstances be encompassed within that narrow provision.

14.106 TRIPs does not address the threats issue directly either, but it provides as follows:

> The judicial authorities shall have the authority to order a party at whose request measures were taken and who has abused enforcement procedures to provide to a party wrongfully enjoined or restrained adequate compensation for the injury suffered because of such abuse.[142]

14.107 This provision at least appears to require the compensation of an unjustly threatened party who, for example, has been at the wrong end of a groundless threat to the point that interim injunctive relief has been ordered against him. But neither the Paris Convention nor TRIPs go as far as the laws of the UK or Ireland, both of which specifically provide that groundless threats to sue for trade mark infringement are themselves actionable torts which lay their perpetrators open to an action for damages or other relief.

(2) Threats actions in the UK

14.108 The threats action in the UK does *not* apply where proceedings for an alleged trade mark infringement relate to the following acts: applying a trade mark to goods or their packaging, the importation of goods to which a trade mark has been applied or the supply of services.[143] This means that the trade mark proprietor can still with impunity threaten infringement proceedings against the primary infringer who actually makes the infringing goods. Given that most manufactured goods sold in the UK are no longer made in that jurisdiction, opportunities to threaten that primary infringer are probably of decreasing frequency.

14.109 Where a groundless threat is made, the court may award damages, injunctive relief against the continuance of the threat and a declaration that the threat is unjustifiable.[144]

---

[141] Paris Convention on the Protection of Industrial Property, art 10*bis*(3).
[142] TRIPs, art 48(1).
[143] Trade Marks Act 1994, s 21(1).
[144] ibid, s 21(2).

F. Liability for making groundless threats

It may be thought that a threats action arises only where a groundless threat is made by the trade mark owner to the alleged infringer. This is not necessarily so. Not merely the trade mark proprietor but 'a person'[145]—who need not be the trade mark proprietor and will often be his solicitor—will be liable for making a threat and 'any person aggrieved',[146] whether the alleged infringer or not, may bring a threats action. Thus in our example of Bingo and Bongo above, where Bingo (or his solicitor) makes a threat against a retailer or distributor of Bongo's products, Bongo too may be a 'person aggrieved' even though no threat has been made against him. Anyone making a threat against a small business with slender resources should thus consider whether he will face threats proceedings brought by a bigger and better-resourced business which is adversely affected by that threat. **14.110**

A threat may be actionable even if it is made outside the UK, if the words constitute a threat when received by the recipient within the UK.[147] A groundless threat to sue another for infringing a CTM is also actionable, both in the UK[148] and in Ireland.[149] **14.111**

The only statutory defence which is open where a threats action is brought is for the defendant (who has made the threat) to show that the acts in respect of which it threatened proceedings do, or would, infringe the trade mark. **14.112**

(3) What is a threat?

The test of whether a statement is a threat is an objective one. Some forms of words are so clearly threats that it would be difficult to persuade a court that they were made with innocent intent. Statements such as 'Our client is the registered proprietor of the BINGO trade mark for tortoise-warmers. If you do not desist from selling Bongo tortoise-warmers within the next seven days in infringement of our client's trade mark, we have been instructed to issue proceedings against you for trade mark infringement' are no mere harmless jest. On the other hand expressions such as 'We note that you are selling Bongo tortoise-warmers. We think you should be selling BINGO products instead. In this connection we are prepared to make you an offer you can't refuse' are altogether more subtle and may, on their surface, be considered as genial commercial initiatives rather than as a veiled threat of possibly extrajudicial action. The courts therefore take the view that it is not the words alone which constitute a threat, but the circumstances in which **14.113**

---

[145] ibid, s 21(1).
[146] ibid.
[147] *Prince plc v Prince Sports Group Ltd* [1998] FSR 21 (HC).
[148] Trade Marks Act 1994, s 52; CTM Regulations 1996, reg 4.
[149] Trade Marks Act 1996, s 57(4).

they are communicated and the manner in which they are likely to be received which determines whether there is a threat.[150]

14.114 Even a letter written by a solicitor who refuses to confirm that his client will *not* bring infringement proceedings in the UK, in a situation in which infringement proceedings had been brought on the same facts in Ireland, may be capable of being construed as a groundless threat for the purposes of interim proceedings.[151]

(4) Threats in other circumstances

14.115 It does not appear that the making of unjustified threats *against* a trade mark proprietor, for example, by threatening to initiate cancellation or revocation proceedings, is an actionable wrong even in those jurisdictions which provide for relief against groundless threats made *by* a trade mark proprietor.

G. Declaration of non-infringement

14.116 It is always gratifying for a defendant to be vindicated by a court's decision that he has not in fact infringed the trade mark proprietor's rights. But it is generally better for his nervous system, as well as for his financial standing, if he doesn't have to defend himself in court in the first place. Accordingly, where it is an available option, a person who seeks to use a trade mark which, he believes, does not infringe another's trade mark right may institute proceedings for a declaration of non-infringement. By such a declaration the court rules that, if the defendant makes a specific use of a sign in the course of trade, that use will not infringe the rights of a specific trade mark owner named in the proceedings.

14.117 Although the declaration of non-infringement is a common feature of patent law, it appears to be of limited availability in trade mark law. Italian law recognizes this valuable form of relief, which has been invoked for the purpose of showing that, since a proprietor's rights in the NATIVA trade mark for soaps, cosmetics, perfumes and other products had lapsed in part for non-use in respect of cosmetics, third-party use of NATIVA DI CUPRA for the same products would not infringe the earlier right.[152]

---

[150] See *Brain v Ingledew Brown Bennington & Garret* [1996] FSR 341 (CA), esp at 349.
[151] *L'Oréal (UK) Ltd and another v Johnson & Johnson and another* [2000] ETMR 691 (HC).
[152] *Farmaceutici Dott. Ciccarelli v Aboca di Mercati Valentino Sas* [2003] EIPR N-72 (Court of Milan).

H. Competition law

(1) Claim of unlawful agreement of concerted practice

14.118 Article 81 (formerly article 85) of the EC Treaty[153] prohibits any agreement or concerted practice between undertakings which may affect trade between Member States and which has as its object the prevention or distortion of competition within the Common Market. The ECJ has held that this provision applies to agreements and concerted practices involving trade marks.[154] From the standpoint of a defendant in trade mark infringement proceedings, it is therefore worth considering whether what looks for all the world like a regular trade mark infringement action can be dressed up in terms which make it appear to be a distortion of competition within the Common Market. If this approach is successful, the defendant may undermine the trade mark proprietor's action completely.

14.119 A submission based on article 81 was raised by two importers of pharmaceutical products whom Glaxo, Wellcome, SmithKline Beecham, Boehringer Ingelheim and Eli Lilly sued for trade mark infringement. The importers maintained that the actions brought against them by the five trade mark owners—who between them enjoyed a large share of the pharmaceutical products market—constituted a concerted practice. Following a preliminary hearing the importers were allowed to amend their defences to the trade mark infringement action so as to plead a breach of article 81 on the basis that there was an arguable basis upon which to argue that defence.[155]

(2) Claim of abuse of a dominant position

14.120 Article 82 (formerly article 86) of the EC Treaty states that any abuse by one or more undertakings of a dominant position within the Common Market or any part of it shall be prohibited as being incompatible with the Common Market so far as it may affect trade between Member States.[156] The exercise of a trade mark right by its proprietor is unlikely by itself to constitute an abuse of a dominant position since the trade mark right does not stand as a substantial barrier to trade: a competitor can, at least in theory, supply the same goods or services to the same consuming public under a different trade mark. Before article 82 applies to the exploitation of a trade mark, as the ECJ has said:

---

[153] See also the UK's Competition Act 1998, s 2, which applies in respect of agreements that distort competition within that jurisdiction.
[154] *Sirena Srl v Eda Srl*, Case 40/70 [1971] ECR 69 (ECJ), criticized in Guy Tritton, *Intellectual Property in Europe* (2002), paras 7-123–7-124.
[155] *Glaxo Group and others v Dowelhurst Ltd and others* [2000] ETMR 118 (HC). This defence does not however appear to have been argued at trial; see *Glaxo Group and others v Dowelhurst Ltd and others*, 6 February 2003 (unreported) (HC).
[156] The Competition Act 1998, s 18, contains an equivalent provision dealing with abuse of a dominant position within the UK.

> ... the trade mark owner should have the power to prevent the maintenance of effective competition in a considerable part of the market in question, taking into account, in particular, the possible existence and the position of products or distributors who market similar or substitute products.[157]

14.121 Where this is the case, the dominant position enjoyed by the trade mark owner may be derived from economies of scale, pre-eminence in the market which has been established by a patent, or indeed a number of other factors that are not directly related to the wielding of trade mark rights. Accordingly, little attention has focused on the role played by trade marks in establishing and preserving a dominant and anti-competitive position.

14.122 An unsuccessful attempt was made to invoke the 'abuse of dominant position' argument in a UK case in which Claritas, a leading supplier of 'lifestyle' information sought to restrain the posting by the Post Office of some seven million direct mail questionnaires.[158] The Post Office had set up a subsidiary company, Postal Preference Service (PPS), which was intended to compete with Claritas in the gathering and supply of lifestyle information. The direct mail questionnaires which were to be sent out on behalf of PPS, unlike those of Claritas, were to bear the Post Office's prestigious Royal Mail logo. Claritas sought interim injunctive relief on the basis that the Post Office's refusal to license its own use of the Royal Mail logo while using that logo on PPS' mailshots was an abuse of its dominant position in the UK. The court disagreed: a refusal to license an intellectual property right could be an abuse of rights if it effectively excluded a competitor from entering a market, but this was not the case here. Claritas was already well established, with a market share of between 40 and 50 per cent; further, the market dominated by the Post Office (ie the market for posting letters and packages) and the market in which the alleged abuse occurred (ie the market for the gathering and supply of lifestyle information) were quite different.

I. Conclusion

14.123 This chapter has sought to describe the scope of judicial relief granted by the courts. It should be apparent that, with the exception of the court's powers to award compensatory damages against defendants who make themselves into involuntary licensees, the courts have an adequate array of tools in their judicial toolbox for the job they have to do. It is however important to emphasize that the result in each case which comes before the courts depends upon its own facts: there is no guarantee that trade mark owners, like Maude in the story which introduced this chapter, will be able to obtain all or any of the remedies mentioned in it.

---

[157] *Sirena Srl v Eda Srl*, Case 40/70 [1971] ECR 69 (ECJ), para 16.
[158] *Claritas (UK) Ltd v Post Office and Postal Preference Service Ltd* [2001] ETMR 679 (HC).

PART D

TRADE MARKS IN INDUSTRY AND COMMERCE

15

TRANSACTIONS INVOLVING TRADE MARKS

A.	**Introduction**	
	The trade mark tango	
	It takes two to tango	15.01
B.	**The nature of trade mark transactions**	
	(1) Trade marks as property	15.02
	(2) Types of transaction	15.05
	(a) Assignments	15.06
	(b) Licences	15.09
C.	**Basic legal provisions governing transactions**	
	(1) Assignment and licensing of trade marks under national and international law	15.14
	(2) Assignment with or without goodwill	15.18
	(3) Registration of transactions	15.25
D.	**Classification of trade mark licences**	15.26
	(1) Exclusive licences	15.27
	(2) Sole licences	15.29
	(3) Non-exclusive licences	15.30
	(4) Compulsory licences	15.31
	(5) Sublicences	15.34
E.	**The consequences of being a licensee**	15.35
	(1) Licensees' liability for trade mark infringement	15.37
	(2) Licensee estoppel	15.38
	(3) No-challenge obligations	15.41
F.	**Internal transactions and external transactions**	15.42
G.	**Some examples of trade mark transactions**	15.47
	(1) Securitizations	15.48
	(2) Franchising	15.50
	(3) Character merchandising	15.57
	(4) Sponsorship	15.60
	(5) Endorsement	15.63
	(6) Co-branding	15.66
	(7) Outsourcing	15.69
H.	**Important issues in trade mark licences**	15.71
	(1) Geography	15.72
	(2) Commencement	15.75

	(3) Duration	15.76
	(4) Premature and mature termination	15.77
	(5) Subject matter	15.79
	(6) Royalties and other payments	15.81
	(7) Change of control	15.83
	(8) Quality control	15.86
I.	Litigation of trade mark transactions	15.88
J.	The valuation of trade marks	15.93
K.	Conclusion	15.98

A. Introduction

The trade mark tango

Legal anthropology, the study of the ritual behaviour and tribal rites of lawyers, is the key to any functional analysis of the legal system. Through his academic connections the author of this book, though not a legal anthropologist himself, has been able to procure the results of some fascinating research in this little-recognized field of human conduct. These research results focus on the behavioural patterns of the transactional intellectual property lawyer, a hitherto little-known species which scholars now recognize as forming two distinctive subspecies: (i) the in-house lawyer and (ii) the private practitioner. Their behavioural patterns are in many instances quite similar, for example, with regard to rituals such as 'meetings', 'telephone calls' and establishing superiority over a lower form of life known as 'secretaries'. There are however some striking differences, the principal one being that the private practitioner must court the in-house lawyer, whom he will pursue relentlessly until the relationship is consummated by a ritual called 'giving instructions to act'. It appears however that these relationships are frequently neither permanent nor exclusive.

A little-known fact concerning the lives of transactional intellectual property lawyers, culled from months of patient monitoring by legal anthropologists, is that they don't actually spend their lives doing deals. Indeed, research teams have, through months of patient observation, obtained video clips of these delightful creatures at leisure. Since transactional intellectual property lawyers are rarely seen outside their offices during the hours of daylight, most of the footage of their nocturnal activities has been recorded with the use of infrared lenses. Although the clarity of the images could be better, we have been privileged to observe a thrilling insight into what transaction intellectual property lawyers do when they are not, for example, engaged in trade mark assignments or licences.

We should state at the outset that, as befits these dedicated creatures, even their leisure activities mirror the professional pursuits in which they engage during the twenty or so billable hours of each working day. Preferred pursuits include fishing (for clients), boxing (documents in files) and, quite surprisingly, dancing—a pursuit in which the in-house lawyer gains much practice but sometimes little proficiency. Most popular among this year's dance fads is the Trade Mark Tango, or TMT. According to the leading legal anthropologists in the field, the TMT goes something like this:

A. Introduction

1. Select your partner

One of the partners in the Trade Mark Tango belongs to a business which owns a trade mark; the other represents a business that wants to use that trade mark. When doing the TMT, remember that it takes two to tango. Make sure your partner has the assets you need if the two of you are to co-operate. If he doesn't own the trade mark you're interested in, he can't license it to you.

2. Don't start until the music begins

It should be plain to you and your partner that you should both begin to tango at the same time, so make sure you agree upon a convenient commencement date for your shared activities (see also point 9 below, 'What happens when the music stops?').

3. Face the music together

The more successfully you and your partner dance to the tune of the TMT, the more you will attract the attention of other dancers who want to save themselves the trouble of working out their own dance routines by copying yours (sometimes called 'infringers'). The best of these infringers ('counterfeiters') copy your dance routine so well that spectators who watch the TMT are convinced that they are watching you. This state of affairs should never be allowed to develop. You and your partner must face the music together and deal firmly with these infringers at all times. If you are lucky, the adjudicators at the dance (or 'the judiciary', for short) will make them stop doing your dance and will even give you all their money.

4. Careful where you throw your partner

The TMT is a colourful dance, often with lots of boldly improvised steps. This is because the tune to which the tango is danced (sometimes called 'prevailing market conditions') may suddenly change at a moment's notice. If the tune, the tempo or even the rhythm suddenly change, you and your partner should have some shared understanding as to what you both propose to do, or you may find that you have thrown your partner into the arms of another dancer.

5. Give your partner proper support

There are occasions when one or other of the partners attempting the TMT will be caught on the hop, wrong-footed by a sudden twist in the dance. When this happens, you may be well within your rights to let your partner crash to the floor in an undignified heap—particularly if his troubles are of his own making. But do you really want this to happen? If other prospective partners see how little you help your current partner if he gets into trouble, they may not want to tango with you later. It may be better to bend over backwards (a difficult step to execute at the best of times) to assist a struggling partner, especially if he doesn't stumble often.

6. Mind where you put your feet

In the trade mark tango, you can only stand on territory that has been licensed by your partner. Put your feet down anywhere else and you are outside the terms of your licence. This can mean that you are in breach of contract to your partner, who may be able to stop the dance without waiting for the music to finish (in dancing parlance this is called a 'terminating event') or you may find that you are treading on the tails of other dancers (sometimes called 'trade mark infringement').

7. If you can't see where you're going

When one partner advances, the other is in retreat. If you are tangoing together, this means that you have to be able to rely on the judgment of your partner. If you trust him not to steer you into a brick wall or over a parapet, that's your business, but you may just want to take some warranties from him before the dancing starts.

8. Changing partners in mid-dance

It may happen that you or your partner will be dancing happily away and then suddenly one or the other of you will simply cease to exist. This happens when one of you 'merges' with another dancer or is 'acquired' by one. Your dance rules should provide in advance as to whether the surviving partner has to carry on dancing with a new partner whom he did not seek to dance with initially, or whether he can retire from the TMT, put his feet up and have a few refreshing lagers.

9. What happens when the music stops?

That's up to you. Your partner may go off in search of fresh dancing partners if you didn't take the precaution of securing an option on a second dance before you started the first one. But one thing is certain—if you try to carry on dancing when the music has stopped, your partner may regard this as an unpardonable liberty and may not want to try a trade mark tango with you ever again.

It takes two to tango

15.01 The moral of this story should be simple. In any trade mark transaction it takes two to tango. Each party must co-operate with the other in a spirit of openness and with each nurturing expectations which, if not actually shared with the other party, are clearly understood by him. This chapter examines the legal framework within which trade mark transactions are carried out and also considers some of the types of transaction in which trade mark owners and their representatives are regularly engaged.

B. The nature of trade mark transactions

(1) Trade marks as property

15.02 It is generally accepted in national trade mark law that registered trade marks, applications for registered trade marks and, in common-law jurisdictions,[1] even unregistered trade marks are forms of 'property'.[2] Like land, cars and lawnmowers they can be bought and sold, leased and hired. The property rights of trade mark owners in Europe cannot be restricted unless those restrictions correspond to Community objectives to which they are not disproportionate.[3] In those cases where the owner is a human being and not a company or other legal person, trade marks pass to the beneficiaries of the owner's will or, if the owner makes no will, they obey the normal rules for the devolution of title upon intestacy. If trade marks are valuable they can be mortgaged or used as security for loans.

---

[1] *Sprints Ltd v Comptroller of Customs (Mauritius) and another* [2000] IP&T 735, 737 (PC, Mauritius): 'At common law, the right of property in a distinctive mark is acquired by a trader merely by using it on or in connection with his goods, irrespective of the length of such user and without proof of recognition by the public as a mark distinctive of the user's goods'.

[2] The same cannot necessarily be said of matter which may incorporate a trade mark, such as a domain name; see Sheldon Burshtein, 'A Domain Name is Not Intellectual Property' (2002) 11 *World E-Commerce & IP Report* 9–11.

[3] *R v Secretary of State for Health, ex p British American Tobacco (Investments) Ltd and Imperial*

B. The nature of trade mark transactions

For those who are interested, there are different philosophical bases for the notion of the trade mark as 'property'.[4] Although this book does not discuss the issues involved, they are recommended holiday reading for serious trade mark students and practitioners who wish to understand the function of trade marks within a wider jurisprudential context than is provided by the intellectual straitjacket of the Paris Convention, the Agreement on Trade-Related Aspects of Intellectual Property Rights (TRIPs) and the two Madrids.[5]

15.03

The proposition that the law treats trade marks as property is one which has a staggeringly important consequence: it enables businesses to perform transactions involving trade marks. This does not just mean that a man can sell a trade mark and walk away with a pocketful of money. It also means that two or more people can use the same trade mark at the same time, either for the same goods and services[6] or for different ones.[7] The proposition that one can trade in trade marks has legitimated activities which we all take for granted in our daily lives: franchising, merchandising, sponsorship and endorsement. The legal basis for these activities and others will be discussed in this chapter, together with some of the main principles which underpin the trade mark owner's ability to maximize the benefit of his trade mark by allowing its use by others.

15.04

(2) Types of transaction

There are two legally significant acts which one can perform with a trade mark. One can transfer it to another person (lawyers usually call this an assignment); or one can license other people to use it. Each of these types of transaction is discussed in greater detail below.

15.05

(a) Assignments

The assignment of a trade mark is a transfer of ownership in it from its proprietor (the assignor) to another party (the assignee). Once a trade mark owner has assigned a trade mark, he has no further interest in the rights which he has assigned. The granting office which issued the trade mark must be informed of the assignment so that there is an official and publicly accessible record of the change of ownership and so that renewal fees are sent to the right owner.

15.06

Tobacco Ltd, supported by Japan Tobacco Inc and JT International SA, Case C-491/01 [2003] ETMR 547 (ECJ): property rights of owners of tobacco trade marks not unduly restricted by limitation as to parts of the cigarette box on which their trade marks might be displayed.

[4] For two recent treatments of the subject, see J W Harris, *Property & Justice* (1996) and Spyros Maniatis, 'Trademark Rights: A Justification Based on Property' [2002] IPQ 123 (together with the many sources cited therein).

[5] On which see Chapter 3.

[6] See eg the practice of business format franchising discussed at paras 15.50–15.56 below.

[7] See eg the practice of character merchandising discussed at paras 15.57–15.59 below.

15.07 Sometimes the trade mark owner contracts to assign his trade mark to an assignee but the legal formalities of assignment are not completed.[8] In such a circumstance the courts will treat the assignee as having an 'equitable' or 'beneficial' interest in the trade mark: the assignor is regarded as if he owns the trade mark but holds it in trust for the benefit of the assignee who can call upon him not only to enforce the trade mark against third parties but also to complete the formalities of assignment.

15.08 The vast majority of transfers of ownership are the result of a consensually agreed contract between traders, often in the context of the sale of the business to which the trade marks belong. Some trade marks are transferred as part of the estate of a dead proprietor or as part of the assets of a company which has gone into liquidation. Other trade marks may be transferred *de facto* when the company which owns them is itself sold to a third party who takes a controlling interest it.[9]

(b) Licences[10]

15.09 A licence of a trade mark is a permission granted by its proprietor (the licensor) to another party (the licensee). Once a trade mark owner has licensed a trade mark, he remains its owner, although an exclusive licensee[11] may, for all intents and purposes, grant rights to another licensee. Most trade mark licences are granted under contract and, where this is the case, the terms of the contract will dictate what the licensee is allowed to do. In some countries the granting office which issued the trade mark must be informed of the licence so that there is an official and publicly accessible record of the permitted use.[12]

15.10 In an ideal world, all trade mark licences would be recorded in writing so that there could be no doubt as to their terms. It is however the case that many trade mark licences are oral; their terms may be expressed between the parties or may simply have evolved through understandings or patterns of conduct between a trade mark owner and a third party. It is for the party who relies on the terms of a trade mark licence to prove its existence.

15.11 Some licences are not granted as the result of a consensual contract. A licence may be implied by the court even if the licensor does not appreciate that he has licensed his trade mark. A licence may also be effectively imposed on parties through the rules of equitable estoppel, where a trade mark owner has not actually licensed the use of his trade mark but has given a third party the clear impression that, if the

---

[8] eg in the UK an assignment must be in writing and signed by the assignor: Trade Marks Act 1994, s 25(3).
[9] Council Regulation 40/94, art 17(2).
[10] On trade mark licensing in general, see Neil J Wilkof, *Trade Mark Licensing* (2004).
[11] Explained at paras 15.27–15.28 below.
[12] See eg the Trade Marks Act 1994, s 25(4) (UK) and the Trade Marks Act 1996, s 29(4) (Ireland).

latter uses that trade mark, the owner will not sue him for trade mark infringement.

Depending on the context, a trade mark proprietor may be disinclined to grant a licence, preferring instead to covenant not to assert his rights: such a covenant is typically framed in terms of permitting a third party to continue its current manner of use of the trade mark but not to develop that use any further; alternatively the proprietor may permit that third party to use the trade mark only for a finite period of time in order to deplete existing inventories of branded goods or materials. **15.12**

In the United States and Canada[13] a trade mark licensee may, by virtue of the fact that he has taken a licence to use the trade mark, be estopped from denying its validity.[14] **15.13**

C. Basic legal provisions governing transactions

(1) Assignment and licensing of trade marks under national and international law

Since no legal formalities are required under international law for the assignment or licensing of trade marks, most such transactions are treated as regular contracts which are governed by the law of the country of the transaction (or by any other law agreed by them). TRIPs fortifies the role of national law in this regard: **15.14**

> Members may determine conditions on the licensing and assignment of trademarks, it being understood that the compulsory licensing of trademarks shall not be permitted . . .[15]

Directive 89/104 does not address the assignment of trade marks at all, leaving it to each EU Member State to determine the parameters of trade mark assignment for itself. The Directive does however say this about licences: **15.15**

> 1. A trade mark may be licensed for some or all of the goods or services for which it is registered and for the whole or part of the Member State concerned. A licence may be exclusive or non-exclusive.
> 2. The proprietor of a trade mark may invoke the rights conferred by that trade mark against a licensee who contravenes any provision in his licensing contract with regard to its duration, the form covered by the registration in which the trade mark

---

[13] *Anne of Green Gables Licensing Authority and Heirs of L M Montgomery v Avonlea Traditions*, 10 March 2000 (OSCJ).
[14] *Seven-Up Bottling Co v Seven-Up Co*, 561 F 2d 1275, 1279 (8th Cir 1977); *Pacific Supply Co-op v Farmers Union Cent Exch, Inc*, 318 F 2d 894, 908–9 (9th Cir 1963).
[15] TRIPs, art 21. On compulsory licences; see further the discussion at para 15.30 below.

may be used, the scope of the goods or services for which the licence is granted, the territory in which the trade mark may be affixed, or the quality of the goods manufactured or of the services provided by the licensee.[16]

15.16 A trade mark can be licensed for all of the goods and services for which it is registered or for just one or more of them. Thus if I own the FIFI registered trade mark for dog food, canine accessories, dog-obedience training services and dog-storage services for holidaying pet-owners, I can license to four different people my right to use the FIFI trade mark in each of these classes. It equally appears from these provisions that a trade mark may be assigned for all or any of the goods and services for which it is registered. Thus if I own the FIFI trade mark for dog food, canine accessories, dog-obedience training services and dog-storage services for holidaying pet-owners, I can assign to four different people my right to the FIFI trade mark in each of these classes (I can also make each a licensee).

15.17 The Community Trade Mark (CTM) Regulation echoes the provisions found in Directive 89/104, adding that a licensee may bring infringement proceedings if he has the CTM proprietor's consent and that an exclusive licensee may bring infringement proceedings where the proprietor has declined to do so himself.[17] That Regulation also addresses assignments. It stipulates that a CTM may be transferred only in its entirety and for the whole area of the Community[18] (although it may be licensed on a territory-by-territory basis[19]) and that the transfer of an undertaking will normally include the transfer of its CTMs too.[20] Assignments of CTMs which are not the result of a court judgment must be made in writing and signed by both parties if they are not to be void.[21] Where a CTM is registered in the name of an agent or representative of its proprietor but without his authorization, the proprietor is entitled to demand that it be assigned to him.[22]

(2) Assignment with or without goodwill

15.18 It was formerly believed by many people that, since the trade mark forged so powerful a link between the identity of its proprietor and the goods or services he provided, the use of that trade mark by any person other than the trade mark's owner would deceive the public.[23] According to this opinion the trade mark could only be transferred as part of the proprietor's business with which it was associated. A

---

[16] Council Directive 89/104, art 8.
[17] Council Regulation 40/94, art 22.
[18] ibid, art 16(1).
[19] ibid, art 22.
[20] ibid, art 17(2).
[21] ibid, art 17(3).
[22] ibid, art 18.
[23] On the changing public perception of the role of trade marks, see the speech of Lord Nicholls in *Scandecor Development AB v Scandecor Marketing AB and others* [2001] ETMR 800, [2001] IP&T 676 (HL).

C. Basic legal provisions governing transactions

separate objection to the sale of a trade mark 'in gross' (in other words, without the business to which it is attached) was based on economic rather than moral grounds:

> The answer relates to the economic function of trademarks in providing useful information, which would be more costly to obtain elsewhere about a good's attributes.[24]

15.19 Where a trade mark is used first for the goods of company A and later for the goods of company B, it is quite simply a waste of economic resources for consumers to have to find this out. For whatever reason, the United States has been a firm proponent of the principle that a trade mark should only be assigned together with its associated goodwill.[25]

15.20 Many people however disagreed with the perception that the use of a trade mark by someone other than its original owner was deceptive. In their opinion it might have been justified in the nineteenth and early twentieth centuries, when most companies made their own products and there was little licensing or outsourcing. In post-World War II conditions, however, as manufacture of products by undertakings other than the trade mark owner began to become the norm, it had become apparent to many that both industry and the public at large gradually were increasingly accustomed to seeing producers, products and trade marks as being less quintessentially bound in with each other.

15.21 In international terms, the assignment of trade marks separately from the business to which they were attached was first addressed by the Paris Convention, which sanctioned the transfer of a trade mark both with and without its accompanying business:

> (1) When, in accordance with the law of a country of the Union, the assignment of a mark is valid only if it takes place at the same time as the transfer of the business or goodwill to which the mark belongs, it shall suffice for the recognition of such validity that the portion of the business or goodwill located in that country be transferred to the assignee, together with the exclusive right to manufacture in the said country, or to sell therein, the goods bearing the mark assigned.
> (2) The foregoing provision does not impose upon the countries of the Union any obligation to regard as valid the assignment of any mark the use of which by the assignee would, in fact, be of such a nature as to mislead the public, particularly as regards the origin, nature, or essential qualities, of the goods to which the mark is applied.[26]

---

[24] William M Landes and Richard Posner, 'The Economics of Trademark Law' (1988) 78 TMR 267, 283. This notion is also used to support the argument that the owners of unpopular trade marks should not be allowed to change them: Louis Tompos, 'Badwill' [2003] Harv Law Rev 1845.
[25] See eg *Marshak v Green* 746 F 2d 927, 929 (2d Cir 1984).
[26] Paris Convention on the Protection of Industrial Property, art 6*quater*.

15.22 It is now widely accepted that a trade mark should be an object of property in its own right. In purely physical terms it remains true that a trade mark may only be registered and used in respect of goods and services. Even so, the trade mark is no longer treated as the handmaiden of the business to which those goods or services relate. Accordingly in many jurisdictions (including all of the Member States of the EU) a trade mark may now be assigned either together with the business in which it was used, or separately from it. This shift is reflected in TRIPs, which states:

> Members may determine conditions on the licensing and assignment of trademarks, it being understood that . . . the owner of a registered trademark shall have the right to assign the trademark with or without the transfer of the business to which the trademark belongs.[27]

15.23 Echoing this, the CTM Regulation states:

> A Community trade mark may be transferred, separately from any transfer of the undertaking in respect of some or all of the goods or services for which it is registered.[28]

15.24 These are welcome developments. A trade mark may be the most valuable asset a business possesses and, indeed, the proprietor's only business may be principally that of licensing its trade marks. In addition it is difficult to maintain that any deceit is practised on the public by the practice of assigning a trade mark from one business to another and, in the improbable event that the public is likely to be misled by such a transaction, at least one trade mark system takes steps to prevent the assignment taking full effect.[29]

(3) Registration of transactions

15.25 Although international laws on trade marks do not require the assignment or licence of a trade mark to be recorded with the relevant trade mark registry, it is standard practice for national law to provide for such transactions to be notified to the granting office so that information on the register can be kept up-to-date. A well-maintained trade mark register provides the public with relatively reliable information as to who owns a trade mark and who is entitled to use it. A failure to record an assignment, licence or security interest in a trade mark may result in the limitation of the rightholder's entitlement to obtain damages in infringement proceedings[30] and may render the rights of the assignee or licensee ineffective against the rights of a subsequent registered assignee or licensee.[31]

---

[27] TRIPs, art 21.
[28] Council Regulation 40/94, art 17(1).
[29] See ibid, art 17(4) in respect of the transfer of CTMs. This is an option for which the Paris Convention, art 6*quater* (discussed later) provides. Directive 89/104 provides for revocation of a trade mark on the same ground; see art 12(2)(d).
[30] See eg Trade Marks Act 1994, s 25(4) (UK). See also a patents case, *LG Electronics Inc v NCR Financial Solutions Group Ltd* [2003] FSR 428, in which it was held that, following a failure to register a transaction, the right of subsequent assignees to obtain damages would also be lost.
[31] See eg Trade Marks Act 1994, s 25(3) (UK).

D. Classification of trade mark licences

There are different types of trade mark licence. The main categories of licence are listed in the following sections. **15.26**

(1) Exclusive licences

An exclusive licence permits a single licensee to use the trade mark to the exclusion of all other parties, including the trade mark owner himself. Since the right granted to the exclusive licensee is so extensive, it is generally the case that an exclusive licence will cost more than any other sort. A hypothetical example of a typical exclusive licence would be the rights granted by the Australian brewer of COBBER beer who seeks to establish a foothold in the geographically distant European market by granting a local European concern, OzBeers Imports Ltd, the exclusive right to make, distribute and sell COBBER ales. **15.27**

In some jurisdictions an exclusive licensee may be able to bring infringement proceedings in his own name,[32] or where he has called upon the proprietor to sue for infringement but the proprietor has declined to do so.[33] **15.28**

(2) Sole licences

While the term 'exclusive licence' is used as a term of art in intellectual property law, the term 'sole' licence is not. For this reason it is not uncommon to find a licence to grant 'the sole and exclusive right' to an intellectual property right. Such usage should be avoided, because the term 'sole licence' is more properly used in contrast to an exclusive licence and permits a single licensee, in addition to the trade mark proprietor, to use the trade mark. Such a licence may have a commercial effect which is similar to an exclusive licence where, for example, the licensor reserves to himself the right to use his trade mark but does not do so at all or if conditions attached to the licence are fulfilled by the licensee. For example, a licensor may reserve to himself the right to make and sell dog food under the FIFI registered trade mark if the licensee fails to meet monthly manufacture and sale targets for three consecutive months. **15.29**

(3) Non-exclusive licences

A non-exclusive licence permits any number of licensees to use the trade mark on the footing that what they are permitted to do may also be permitted to others. A typical example might be a franchise for a takeaway bacon fry-up business format **15.30**

---

[32] This is the case eg in the UK (Trade Marks Act 1994, s 31(1)) and in Ireland (Trade Marks Act 1996, s 35(2)). Such proceedings may not however be brought against the proprietor.
[33] This is the case eg in France; see the Intellectual Property Code, art L 716–5.

granted by PIGG-WHIZZ to entrepreneurs who wish to run PIGG-WHIZZ outlets in towns and cities across the country. In some jurisdictions a non-exclusive licensee may be able to bring infringement proceedings in his own name where he has the permission of the trade mark proprietor to do so,[34] or where he has called upon the proprietor to sue for infringement but the proprietor has declined to do so.[35]

(4) Compulsory licences

15.31 A compulsory licence is a non-consensual licence which is granted against the will of the trade mark proprietor. There is no provision in the Paris Convention or in any other piece of international legislation for the granting of compulsory licences, even though compulsory licences may be granted, in appropriate circumstances, for patents,[36] utility models[37] and designs.[38] Indeed, TRIPs specifies that compulsory licensing of trade marks is *not* permitted.[39] This does not however mean that the compulsory licensing of trade marks is a dead issue. The scope of registrability for trade marks is potentially very wide; so is the scope of protection of both patents and designs. Accordingly, where trade mark protection is secured for a product shape which is also the subject of patent, utility model or design protection, or for a design feature which is also protected under design law, a compulsory licence to make the product shape or design feature will automatically involve making use of the corresponding trade mark.

15.32 In the United States the compulsory licensing of trade marks has been something of a live issue. In one instance[40] the Federal Trade Commission (FTC) proposed the creation of five completely new companies and sought to require three major cereal manufacturers (Kellogg, General Mills and General Food) to license their trade marks. In another case,[41] following a finding by the FTC that the REALEMON trade mark enjoyed market dominance in the market for lemon juice, the court agreed that the grant of a compulsory licence of the REALEMON trade mark was a form of relief which it could impose.

---

[34] This is the case eg with CTMs; see Council Regulation 40/94, art 22(3).
[35] This is the case eg in the UK (Trade Marks Act 1994, s 30(2)) and Ireland (Trade Marks Act 1996, s 34(2)).
[36] Paris Convention, art 5A(2); TRIPs, art 31.
[37] ibid, art 5A(5).
[38] From the fact that the Paris Convention, art 5B prohibits forfeiture of a design right but is silent as to compulsory licences, it may be possible to infer that compulsory licensing of designs is permitted (as it is in the UK; see the Registered Designs Act 1949, s 10 and the Copyright, Designs and Patents Act 1988, s 240 (compulsory licence for Crown use)).
[39] TRIPs, art 21.
[40] *FTC v Cereal Companies*, noted in Sol Goldstein, 'A Study of Compulsory Licensing' (1977) *Les Nouvelles* 122–5. See also Carlos M Correa, 'Intellectual Property Rights and the Use of Compulsory Licenses: Options for Developing Countries' (www.southcentre.org/publications/complicence/toc.htm).
[41] *Borden Inc v Federal Trade Commission* 674 F 2d 498 (6th Cir 1982).

E. The consequences of being a licensee

Where national law provides for the compulsory licence of an intellectual property right, it also provides that compensation be payable to the owner of that right.[42] It is not known whether, in the case of the compulsory licence of a patent- or design-protected product shape, the assessment of the compensation would have to be made on the basis that unauthorized use had also been made of the corresponding trade mark. **15.33**

(5) Sublicences

As the term suggests, a sublicence is a licence which is granted to a licensee by another licensee. Since the Paris Convention, TRIPs, Directive 89/104 and the CTM Regulation are all silent as to sublicences, the extent to which a sublicence may be granted depends upon the terms of national law, which may be split between trade mark legislation, specific commercial codes and general principles of contract law. In the UK a licensee may sublicense a trade mark only where his own licence provides for him to do so.[43] **15.34**

E. The consequences of being a licensee

The first and most obvious consequence of being a licensee is that one can perform acts which an unlicensed trader cannot. The licensee is however something of an 'invisible' user of the proprietor's trade mark in that, for the purposes of (i) identifying the owner of goodwill,[44] (ii) establishing whether the proprietor has failed to use the licensed mark during the previous five years[45] and (iii) determining whether a trade mark applicant has applied to register a trade mark in good faith,[46] use by a licensee is treated as though it were use by the proprietor and not by himself. **15.35**

There are further consequences of being a licensee, some of which are summarized below. **15.36**

(1) Licensees' liability for trade mark infringement

It is clear from the text of Directive 89/104 that, where a licensee is in breach of the terms of a licensing contract, the trade mark proprietor may sue him for trade **15.37**

---

[42] See eg Patents Act 1977, ss 57, 57A (UK).
[43] Trade Marks Act 1994, s 28(4).
[44] Thus where a franchisee of a fast-food business format owns a site from which he trades under another's trade mark, he may enjoy goodwill in trade generated by the site but not in goodwill generated by the use of the licensed trade mark: this division of goodwill is not normally provided for in trade mark licences.
[45] See eg Chapter 13, paras 13.26–13.31 and 13.50.
[46] See Chapter 13, paras 13.72–13.148.

mark infringement[47] as well as for breach of contract. The importance of this provision is often overlooked. Trade mark infringement is a civil delict or tort which can have quite different parameters of liability from breach of contract. In the UK, for example, a trade mark infringement and a breach of contract—even where they are the same act—may have different limitation periods within which proceedings must be started, different rules on the mitigation of avoidable loss, on causation and remoteness of damage and indeed on the assessment of the quantum of damages. Moreover, depending on the terms of the trade mark licence, contractual limitations of liability may be imposed as well as other provisions applicable to a claim for breach of contract which would not necessarily be applicable to the corresponding claim based on trade mark infringement.

(2) Licensee estoppel

15.38 In the United States there is a doctrine known as 'licensee estoppel' which dictates that, once a person has consented to the terms of an agreement under which he appears to have accepted that he requires a licence to use a trade mark, he cannot during the currency of that licence challenge the validity of that trade mark.[48]

15.39 The basis for licensee estoppel is the sentiment that it is inconsistent for a licensee both to acknowledge the legitimacy of a trade mark's registration by taking a licence to use it and then to deny the validity of that registration. This basis is determined by considerations of equity rather than by the exigencies of trade: if I want to use your DIAL-O-MATIC trade mark for automatic telephone dialling systems, even if I am convinced that it is descriptive and should never have been registered, the transactional cost of obtaining a licence may be small, my use may commence almost immediately and the number of other uses of the same mark may be limited. If however I wish to stand by my principles and have the mark expunged from the register, it may take me years of expensive litigation to obtain cancellation of the registration and, once the registration is eliminated, my other competitors will be able to enjoy the fruits of my labour and use DIAL-O-MATIC too. In such circumstances there is little to encourage a trader to stick to his principles.

15.40 It is not clear whether and, if so, to what extent, licensee estoppel is part of the trade mark law of countries other than the United States[49] and there are grounds upon which that doctrine may be criticized: (i) it seems wrong in principle that,

---

[47] Council Directive 89/104, art 8(2).
[48] See *Professional Golfers Association v Bankers L & C Co* 514 F 2d 665, 671 (5th Cir 1975).
[49] Neil Wilkof, *Trade Mark Licensing* (1994) argues that the doctrine applies in the UK. See also Aidan Robertson, 'Is the Licensee Estoppel Rule Still Good Law? Was It Ever?' [1991] EIPR 373 (although this article deals with the issue under patent law, no compelling logic suggests that what is true for patent licensing is not also true for trade mark licensing).

F. Internal transactions and external transactions

where a right has been improperly granted by a public authority, the owner of that right should be able to protect it against a challenge by permitting the use of its subject matter to others who may not then challenge it; (ii) the licensee may be disadvantaged by taking a licence if, after he has done so, third parties can negotiate better licence terms by threatening cancellation proceedings; and (iii) any doctrine which has the effect of prolonging the existence of a private intellectual property right which should not have been granted or which, having been properly granted, should be annulled, also has the effect of restricting competition.

(3) No-challenge obligations

One step beyond the principle of licensee estoppel is the inclusion in trade mark licences of express no-challenge clauses, which either seek to prohibit the licensee from challenging the validity of the licensor's trade mark or stipulate that any challenge to the validity of that mark is taken as notice of termination of the licence. In principle, no-challenge clauses are enforceable so long as they do not produce an anti-competitive effect. However, where the effect of a no-challenge clause was to prevent a licensee challenging a trade mark of the licensor which had not been used for more than five years, such a clause has been held to be void under European competition law.[50] In the United States too the right of a licensee to challenge the validity of a certification mark, despite the existence of a no-challenge clause, has been upheld where there is a countervailing public interest in permitting the challenge.[51] **15.41**

F. Internal transactions and external transactions

Some trade mark transactions are strictly 'internal': they affect only the trade mark owner and do not in any way affect the way a trade mark functions as a guarantee of the origin of goods or services for which it is registered. For example, the Acme Balaclava Company (ABC) has registered the ACME trade mark for Balaclava helmets in many countries. ABC's accountants advise it to make itself more tax-efficient. Accordingly ABC restructures itself into a group of related companies: Acme International is incorporated as the management base through which its subsidiaries Acme Europe, Acme Asia-Pacific and Acme America function. The ACME trade mark is assigned to Acme Holdings, an offshore company based in the Netherlands Antilles. Acme Holdings then licenses the use of its ACME trade mark and other valuable intellectual properties to each of its subsidiaries. It is quite possible that, even in the cut-throat market for the sale of Balaclava helmets in the face **15.42**

---

[50] *British American Tobacco Cigaretten-Fabriken GmbH v Commission*, Case C-35/83 [1985] ECR 363 (ECJ).
[51] *Idaho Potato Commission v M&M Produce Farm and Sales* (2d Cir 2003).

of global warming, not even ABC's keenest competitors would even notice this complex transaction.

15.43 Other trade mark transactions are highly visible. For example, Elvin B. Kelvin, a wannabe tycoon and the owner of the BISON-BURGER fast-food burger bar, Hickety Ridge, Tennessippi, is determined to fulfil the American dream and become a leading player in the international burger market, ahead of market leaders MCDONALD'S and BURGER KING. Through an imaginative licensing programme Kelvin secures franchisees for the BISON-BURGER format in the United States, Canada, Europe and beyond. Then he teams up with the producers of the cult film THE MATRIX RELOADED and is thus able to launch its new fleet of burger products, led by the double-decker flagship the BISON MATRIXBURGER RELOADED. This burger is then endorsed by major celebrities including Nicole Kidman, Eminem, Venus Williams and Luciano Pavarotti, all of whose trade mark-protected names are linked with the BISON MATRIXBURGER product range. The public is instantly captivated and sales of bison meat hit record proportions. Transactions such as these are highly visible because visibility is what they are meant to achieve. They are thus 'external' rather than internal in their impact.

15.44 The law does not draw any distinctions between internal and external transactions. More attention is given to external transactions, by investors,[52] by the public at large and by the legal profession, but in reality it is often the invisible internal transactions that provide the rock-solid foundation upon which a brand-based business is able to thrive.

15.45 The ACME example cited above was a transaction motivated by tax advice. The principles that underlie such transactions are simple: if the licensing of a trade mark generates royalty income, then the tax on that income for which the trade mark owner is liable should be paid in the jurisdiction in which the rate of taxation is at its lowest. Expenses incurred in the promotion of the trade mark and of goods and services for which it is registered should be incurred where they have the greatest capacity to offset tax liability. Advice on the realization of these two principles is complex and lies beyond the scope of this book.[53]

15.46 Other commercial imperatives may call for the structuring of an 'intra-group' licensing agreement: these include complex securitization arrangements whereby financiers take security over some but not all of the group's assets. There may be reason to place the group's trade mark portfolio within a separate company which

---

[52] See Suzanna Hawkes, *Licensing Intellectual Property: Share Price Movements and Analysts' Perceptions* (2003) on the correspondence between share movements and the publication of financial statements concerning trade mark licensing and other intellectual property rights.

[53] For extensive specialist coverage of this topic, see Nigel Eastaway, Richard Gallafent and Victor Dauppe, *Intellectual Property Law and Taxation* (2003).

G. Some examples of trade mark transactions

may or may not form part of the security package and then to put into place licensing arrangements which permit the group's operating companies to use those trade marks.

G. Some examples of trade mark transactions

The binary mode of trade mark transactions is simple: every transaction may be characterized only as an assignment or a licence. However, within this severely limiting framework there has developed a panoply of techniques for exploiting trade mark rights in different sectors and for a wide range of purposes. Some of the better known techniques are summarized below. 15.47

(1) Securitizations

In many jurisdictions today, trade marks can be mortgaged or used as security for loans.[54] This practice is not widespread,[55] nor is it likely to become so, for as long as capital is relatively easy to borrow and companies can employ as security assets which are less vital to the continuance of their business than their trade marks.[56] 15.48

Some forms of securitization for loans are more complex. An example is a sale and leaseback arrangement, whereby the trade mark owner actually parts with title to his trade mark in return for an exclusive right to use it. Such a transaction may contain provisions which enable the assignor or another company in the same group to exercise an option to repurchase the trade mark at a later stage. 15.49

(2) Franchising[57]

One of the most successful ways of developing a business, whether as a trade mark licensor or as a licensee, is through the mechanism of a business format franchise. Well-known franchising exercises which have benefited franchisors and franchisees alike over recent decades include 7-ELEVEN, AMTRAK, DOMINOS PIZZA, DUNKIN' DONUTS, DYNO-ROD, KFC, KWIK COPY, MANGO, MCDONALD'S, WIMPY and WSI INTERNET. 15.50

---

[54] See eg Council Regulation 40/94, art 19(1).
[55] Jay Eisbruck, 'Credit Analysis of Patent and Trademark Royalty Securitisation: Rating Agency Perspective', in Joff Wild (ed), *Building and Enforcing Intellectual Property Value: An International Guide for the Boardroom 2003* (2003), describes two securitizations. The first related to the BILL BLASS trade mark, the second to CANDIE's branded footwear and licensed product lines. In each case the securitization depended upon the trade mark owner's ability to prove a long history of royalty generation at a rate sufficient to cover the debt.
[56] See Jeremy Phillips, 'Intellectual Property as Security for Debt Finance: A Time to Advance' [1997] EIPR 276–7.
[57] On franchising in general, see John Adams and K V Pritchard Jones, *Franchising* (1997) and Martin Mendelsohn and Robin Bynoe (eds), *Franchising* (1995).

15.51 It is plain to see that a trade mark licence is central to the relationship between a franchisor and his franchisees. The franchised business format is built around a brand identity which is, generally speaking, meant to be applied uniformly throughout the entire franchise. For this reason, trade mark licences within the context of franchising tend to be more prescriptive than most other species of trade mark licence: the franchisor dictates the terms and the franchisees have little scope for individual variation of the franchise norm. Thus, while it is common for trade mark licences to contain terms in which the licensor requires the licensee to maintain a particular quality of production or service supply, a franchise trade mark licence will legislate for quality control in great and specific detail.

15.52 The franchise technique is simple: I create a business which has a clearly identifiable format; I make sure that the bits which are visible and can be copied are protected by registered trade marks and other intellectual property rights such as copyright and design right; I make sure that the bits which are not visible are carefully described in a know-how manual. Once I have done this, I put the business into operation and see if it succeeds. If it does, I can then find licensees (or franchisees) to whom I can license both the visible and the invisible bits. If the business proposition is attractive enough, my prospective franchisees will be willing to pay me royalties on the use of my intellectual property rights and a proportion of their turnover. More than that, they will even be willing to pay their own start-up costs in securing business premises and in converting them to my franchise format.

15.53 From the franchisor's point of view, the licensing of franchises is far less capital-intensive than the establishment of a centrally owned chain of shops. Franchisors can thus derive income from the spread of their franchisees' operations without incurring large debts and heavy interest repayments. Franchisees also benefit, since regional or national advertising of many different franchised outlets with the same trade mark-protected name is far more cost-effective than the painful and often unsuccessful experience of trying to establish a new business on the strength of local advertising alone. It is also far easier to borrow money for the acquisition of a well-tried and tested franchise than to raise capital for more speculative activities. Trade mark franchising involves collective supply arrangements whereby franchisees enjoy the benefit of volume discounts as a result of sourcing from a common supplier. There may well be other benefits to franchisees such as the ability to use centralized information technology systems and the gaining of access to the franchisor's business expertise and commercial relationships with other businesses and institutions.

15.54 Franchising disputes most certainly arise but, in Europe at any rate, they rarely reach the level at which they are published in law reports.[58] This is because most

---

[58] An exception is the somewhat tangential decision in *Benincasa v Dentalkit Srl*, Case C-296/95

G. Some examples of trade mark transactions

franchise contracts provide for the resolution of disputes through arbitration, mediation or other non-judicial processes. The use of alternative systems of dispute resolution (ADR) enables trade mark licensors to resolve a dispute with a single licensee without all the other licensees getting to hear about it and asking themselves whether they too ought to have a grievance. The discreet veil in which ADR enwraps franchise disputes may also serve the useful function (from the franchisor's point of view) of shielding prospective franchisees from publicity which might otherwise discourage them from seeking a franchise licence.

Within the EU it was at one time thought that business franchising was potentially anti-competitive because of its potential to impose contractual limits on the extent to which franchisees could compete with one another. For example, competition law would apply where a franchisor could impose limits to the extent to which the holder of a PRONUPTIA franchise in one area might seek or receive business from an area in which another PRONUPTIA franchisee was trading.[59] This led to the introduction of a Regulation[60] which indicated the form which franchise schemes could take without being regarded as contravening the competition laws of the EC Treaty, particularly article 85 (now article 81) which rendered void those agreements which had the effect of distorting or preventing competition within all or a substantial part of the EU. Once it was appreciated that franchising schemes do not so much hamper competition as encourage it by enabling different franchise groups to compete effectively against each other, the need for a special Regulation for franchising was doubted and the Regulation was allowed to expire.[61]

15.55

The only provision of European competition law which now addresses trade mark licences for business format franchises is a general provision, Regulation 2790/99,[62] which gives the go-ahead to a broad range of vertical agreements between, for example, franchisors and franchisees which are generally pro-competitive in their effect.

15.56

(3) Character merchandising[63]

Whether a character is real (JENNIFER LOPEZ, RUUD VAN NISTELROY), fictional but

15.57

[1997] ETMR 447 in which the ECJ ruled that a franchisee was not a 'consumer' within the meaning of the Brussels Convention on jurisdiction and the enforcement of judgments in civil and commercial matters.

[59] See *Pronuptia de Paris GmbH v Pronuptia de Paris Irmgard Schillgalis*, Case C-161/84 [1986] ECR 353.

[60] Commission Regulation 4087/88 on the application of article 85(3) of the Treaty to franchise agreements.

[61] Regulation 4087/88 expired on 1 December 1999.

[62] Commission Regulation 2790/99 on the application of article 81(3) of the Treaty to categories of vertical agreements and concerted practices.

[63] On this topic see eg John Adams, *Character Merchandising* (1996); Shelley Lane, 'The

with human characteristics (PRINCESS LEIA, SPOCK) or entirely fictional (YOGI BEAR, MINNIE MOUSE), his or her popularity may reach a level at which members of the consuming public wish to associate themselves with that character. Manifestations of this phenomenon include wearing shirts with footballers' names on the back, snuggling into a duvet decorated with images of 101 DALMATIONS and the purchase of poster-size portraits to adorn one's walls. The registration of a trade mark for the purpose of 'trafficking' in it, making no goods but merely licensing its use by others willing to pay for the privilege, is the most secure basis for the practice known as 'character merchandising'.

15.58 In the UK trafficking in trade marks was once so strongly frowned upon that it was a ground upon which a trade mark application could be refused or a registration cancelled.[64] The law has since moved on and the perceived threat that all available and suitable trade marks would be registered by speculators, who would then hold the commercial world to ransom by licensing them to the highest bidders, does not however seem to have materialized.

15.59 In terms of trade mark law, character merchandising is no different from any other species of trade mark licence. In practical terms, however, it is characterized by the need to deal with numerous issues. The following points in particular should be noted:

(i) Since the 'shelf-life' of a merchandised character may be fleeting (for example, a football star may be sold from one team to another; British readers may also recall the nation's temporary obsession with such now-obscure characters as Mr Blobby and Eddie the Eagle), the licence terms should reflect the commercial realities which that shelf-life imposes;

(ii) Typical merchandised goods are particularly vulnerable to counterfeiting. Accordingly provision should be made where possible for adequate policing and reporting of likely infringements, particularly at events at which merchandised performers may be appearing;

(iii) Quality-control provisions should be imposed and rigorously implemented. A child's affection for LUKE SKYWALKER products will be severely damaged if merchandised produce bearing his name and likeness disintegrates and causes him pain. There may also be product-liability issues where licensed goods are defective and cause harm.

Problems of Personality Merchandising in English Law: The King, the Princess and the Penguins' (1999) *Yearbook of Media and Copyright Law* 28; and Simon Smith, *Image, Persona and the Law* (2001).

[64] *HOLLY HOBBIE trade mark* [1984] FSR 199; [1984] RPC 329 (HL).

G. Some examples of trade mark transactions

(4) Sponsorship[65]

In its pure form, sponsorship is a form of trade mark licence in which it is the trade mark owner himself who pays money or confers some other form of benefit upon the licensee in return for the promotion of his name by the licensee. This sort of trade mark licence can make the trade mark proprietor appear to be a great patron of the arts ('This play is brought to you by FIZZ-UP Sparkling Lemonade'), or it may seek to convey a market image of a licensor who is heavily involved at the top level of its field of commerce ('The SMUGGO Match-Play Championship. Sponsored by SMUGGO, international golf's most popular golfing equipment'). Sometimes the word 'sponsorship' is used in marketing circles as a euphemism for any form of paid-for advertising, without any connotation of trade mark licensing.[66]

15.60

The trade mark owner, as sponsor, should take pains to ensure that it will derive the benefits from the sponsorship. He should ensure that the licensee has the most current version of the trade mark and that, if plans are made to restyle the trade mark during the currency of the sponsorship deal, the sponsored licensee is kept well informed. It is also prudent to seek to guard against any damage which may be suffered as a result of the choice by the licensee of a new sponsor who may be a competitor of the first one. Thus if an event first sponsored by FIZZ-UP Sparkling Lemonade is, in later years, sponsored by its arch rival FIZZOLA Bubble Juice, consumers may feel that the change of sponsor is caused not so much by commercial considerations such as the amount of money offered in exchange for the publicity but by the fact that FIZZOLA has been generally considered a more popular product than FIZZ-UP.

15.61

Depending on the particular circumstances, the trade mark proprietor may play no more active a role in the sponsorship than simply to lend the sponsored licensee the use of his name and brand, the licensee taking upon himself all the responsibility for planning, promoting and conducting the sponsored activities. In such cases the proprietor may find that his lack of control places him at commercial and legal risk. If the sponsored activities are poorly conceived and executed, or if they cause harm to members of an audience or to participants in an event (for example, a yacht race in which competitors are drowned or injured), the resulting publicity would reflect poorly on the sponsor's image. To reduce these risks the sponsor should ensure that he secures rights of approval over those areas within the sponsored activity from which, if things go wrong, brand or trade mark damage can be foreseen. He should also retain the right to approve the manner in which the licensed trade marks are

15.62

---

[65] On sponsorship, see Hayley Stallard (ed) *Bagehot on Sponsorship, Endorsement and Merchandising* (1998).
[66] See eg the about.com e-shopping website, where advertisers can pay to provide 'sponsored links of the day'.

used. The sponsor should also seek contractual assurances that a suitable level of skill will be displayed in planning and carrying out the sponsored activities and that, where necessary, indemnities and insurance cover are taken out.

15.62A The party which believes itself to be the beneficiary of a sponsorship contract should take care to ensure that there is indeed a contract in place and that the parties have not merely been involved in precontractual negotiations.[67]

(5) Endorsement[68]

15.63 Endorsement is a form of trade mark licence in which the trade mark owner—typically a well-known individual but sometimes an organization—receives payment from the licensee in return for the right to use the endorser's name or likeness in relation to the endorsement of the qualities of the licensee's products or services. This form of licence is heavily used in the sports sectors, where depending on your point of view, (i) it is increasingly difficult to persuade the consuming public to purchase any sports equipment which has not been endorsed by a current or past personality who has excelled in that line of sport or (ii) it is increasingly difficult for the public to purchase any sports equipment which has not had its cost inflated through the routine and often meaningless association of the product with the name of someone who may never even have used it.

15.64 In the field of sports endorsement, there is the unwritten assumption that endorsement is only meaningful if it comes from a notable achiever in the relevant field of sport. Accordingly one might expect to see a tennis racket endorsed by Pete Sampras, Venus Williams or Boris Becker but not (say) by Nelson Mandela, Mick Jagger or Alfred Brendel. In other fields of commercial activity, endorsement is often commercially more effective where the endorsement comes from a user-friendly personality with whom consumers can identify rather than with a true expert. Thus 'wine of the month'-type offers may be more profitably endorsed by respectable media personalities (if this is not a contradiction in terms) and not by intimidatingly professional wine buffs who can identify, from a single inhalation of the vintage, the side of the grape upon which the sun shone.

15.65 In the case of most product or service endorsements the good name and integrity of the endorsing personality is vital. Provision should therefore be made where there is any risk that continued association with a personality's tarnished image will damage the licensee. For example, after Ben Johnson was stripped of his Seoul 1988 Olympic gold medal for steroid abuse, several of the companies whose prod-

---

[67] *Jordan Grand Prix Ltd v Vodafone Group plc* [2003] EWHC 1965 (Comm), 4 August 2003 (unreported) (Commercial Court).
[68] On product endorsement, see Hayley Stallard (ed) *Bagehot on Sponsorship, Endorsement and Merchandising* (1998).

G. Some examples of trade mark transactions

ucts had received his endorsements hastened to terminate them.[69] Termination can only bring an end to further damage; it cannot however assist the licensee who has paid for advertisements in magazines which remain in circulation for weeks and sometimes months after the termination takes place.

(6) Co-branding[70]

In the terminology of transactions,[71] co-branding is any venture in which the owners of two or more brands will lend their intellectual property to a vehicle for their joint exploitation. Sometimes co-branding is the result of a carefully negotiated contract which seeks both to promote and to protect the synergy of two well-matched brands. For example, in the traditional washing machine/detergent co-branding tie-in in the 1950s and early 1960s, co-branding might take the form of mutual endorsements and advertisements with the format 'We recommend SCRUBBO for use in WASHWHITE washing machines' in return for 'For best results with SCRUBBO, why not buy the new WASHWHITE twin-tub?' **15.66**

Nowadays some of the most informal and off-the-peg trade mark licences take the form of co-branding. An example is the Business Wire Internet news service: any partner can co-brand and run its own brand name or trade mark in front of the name BUSINESS WIRE, specifying its own parameters for the provision by Business Wire of tailored news delivered to visitors to the co-branding partner's website. The advantages of this arrangement are obvious: Business Wire gets extra publicity for its brand and acquires further opportunities to attract paid-for advertising to its portals, while the co-branding partner obtains a free dedicated Internet news service. **15.67**

From a legal point of view, the main problem of co-branding is that, just as the buoyancy of one brand may assist the other, any problem faced by one brand may have the potential to run the other down. For example, if a much-loved fictional character such as MICKEY MOUSE were tied into a co-branding promotion with MCDONALD's fast-food outlets, offering MCMOUSE portions for small children and other attractions, any negative publicity received by MCDONALD's, such as allegations regarding nutritional issues or relating to its environmental impact and employment practices, could have an adverse impact on the profile and commercial value of MICKEY MOUSE too. Likewise, a tie-in between MCDONALD's and the fictional characters in a new film could have an adverse impact on MCDONALD's if the film became an instant box-office flop. For this reason any serious co-branding contract may need to address the need for early termination of the licence and its foreseeable financial consequences. **15.68**

---

[69] It is not known whether Mr Johnson received any endorsement offers from steroid manufacturers.
[70] On which see Tom Blackett and Bob Boad, *Co-Branding: The Science of Alliance* (1999).
[71] Cf the use of the same term in the context of the repackaging of goods; see Chapter 16, paras 16.26–16.28.

(7) Outsourcing

15.69 It is nowadays a frequent occurrence for a business to outsource one or more of its functions to another business which operates as an independent service provider. Examples of outsourcing include the delivery of manufactured products and raw materials as well as the off-site processing of commercial or financial data by computer agencies.

15.70 Sometimes the service provider to whom a business function is outsourced will assume a 'front line' role in which he has direct contact with the trade mark proprietor's customers, for example, where a call centre is engaged to process incoming messages, or where telesales teams are recruited to promote products. Let us take the hypothetical case of CHEAPCASH, an Internet banking company which decides to enter the motor insurance market by contracting with SAFERISK, an independent motor insurance company which administers the Internet banking company's business under the CHEAPCASH name. Motorists do not realize that they are dealing with SAFERISK and not CHEAPCASH because SAFERISK, when dealing with the public on CHEAPCASH's behalf, only uses the CHEAPCASH trade mark and thus creates the impression that it is not a separate entity at all. In such situations a trade mark licence should be firmly emplaced, giving SAFERISK the flexibility to run its business in a profitable manner while yet imposing upon the company sufficient constraints to make the outsourced business 'seamless' with that of CHEAPCASH—particularly by making SAFERISK's operations reflect the ethos and the quality standards which the banking portal's customers have come to expect from any business bearing the CHEAPCASH name.

H. Important issues in trade mark licences

15.71 Under this heading are mentioned a selection of some of the more important issues which are sometimes found missing from trade mark licences, particularly (but not exclusively) those entered without the benefit of professional legal advice. This list is not intended to be exhaustive; it is purely illustrative. There are lengthy and detailed analyses[72] of techniques and problems arising from trade mark licensing, including issues such as the impact of competition law,[73] the insolvency of either party, choice of law to govern the terms of the licence and choice of forum in which any dispute is to be heard.[74] None of those issues are covered here.

---

[72] See eg Neil J Wilkof, *Trade Mark Licensing* (2004).
[73] On which see also Guy Tritton, *Intellectual Property in Europe* (2002).
[74] On which see James Fawcett and Paul Torremans, *Intellectual Property and Private International Law* (1998).

H. Important issues in trade mark licences

(1) Geography

A trade mark licence should stipulate the jurisdiction(s) to which it applies. Where a licensor holds trade mark registrations for numerous countries, the licensee may erroneously assume that the licence covers all of them and make his calculations accordingly. Given the issues which are raised by exhaustion of rights,[75] the licensee should consider whether he needs a licence to do anything relating to the trade marks in country A if he proposes later to sell them in country B (or vice versa). For example, does a licence to sell goods in one country include a right to import goods first into another country or to repackage them there? **15.72**

Some places named in licences are not countries. 'Europe' and 'America' are two notable examples. 'Great Britain' is England, Scotland and Wales, but excludes Northern Ireland (a province of the island of Ireland but not part of the Republic of Ireland). Other terms which, without precise definition, may lead to misunderstanding include (in alphabetical order) 'Continental Europe', 'Cyprus', 'Macedonia', 'Russia', 'Scandinavia' and 'Yugoslavia'. **15.73**

The widespread commercialization of businesses through the use of the Internet has complicated the issue of territorial scope still further. Since most Internet websites are accessible throughout the electronic world, trade mark licences for Internet use may need to be tailored to reflect the parties' intentions and the nature of the risks which international cyberexploitation of a trade mark may bring. **15.74**

(2) Commencement

A trade mark licence will frequently be expressed as lasting for x years. But when is the licence intended to start? From the date the agreement is signed, from the date the licensee is first in a position to take advantage of it or from any other date? **15.75**

(3) Duration

The considerations are the same as above, but lie at the other end of the contract. Since a trade mark is potentially renewable for all eternity, a trade mark licence can be drafted which has that effect. This may be of advantage to either or both parties to the licence but it is rarely what they contemplate. **15.76**

(4) Premature and mature termination

Both parties should ask themselves what they think should happen when the licence ends. The end of a licence may be a long-expected event. Even so, the end of the contract may still come as a surprise to its parties, who may not have considered **15.77**

---

[75] See Chapter 9.

what happens to licensed products which are made before the expiry of the licence but are not distributed or sold when the expiry date kicks in. The licensee may be left with thousands of cute little CURLIE CUDDLES white bunnies that he is anxious to sell, while the licensor (if he is earnestly seeking a new licensee for his CURLIE CUDDLES range of products) will not want that prospective new licensee to see hordes of cute little white bunnies piled high in retailers' 'special reductions' bins.

15.78 The end of the licence may, in contrast, be triggered by some sudden event such as a serious and material breach of one of its terms by one of the parties. In such a case, the parties should consider what their position is and how best it may be protected. A clause along the lines of 'in the event of any breach of the terms of this licence by the licensee, the licence shall be terminated with immediate effect' might look as though it is for the benefit of the trade mark owner as licensor, but it will come to the assistance of a licensee who is unhappy with the terms of the licence and who only needs to breach a term of it in order to terminate it.[76]

(5) Subject matter

15.79 A trade mark licence should stipulate the trade mark or marks—or indeed the trade mark applications—to which the licence applies. Failure to do so can be the cause of misunderstanding. For example, if I take a licence to use 'the CURLIE CUDDLES trade mark', I may not know that the trade mark owner actually has two trade mark registrations, one for the word mark CURLIE CUDDLES and one for a figurative mark consisting of the words CURLIE CUDDLES in a particular format and garlanded with little rabbit images. One of them may be a UK mark, the other a CTM. The contract should specify which mark or marks it includes, giving the registration number or some other means of clearly identifying it.

15.80 Depending on the context, it may be worth including provisions which address the addition of new trade marks to the licence where the trade mark licensor continues to create entirely new brands or to evolve variations upon brands which are already in existence.

(6) Royalties and other payments

15.81 Although some people may have expressed the view that the business community is mercenary, profit-obsessed and thoroughly money-oriented, there is little evidence of this in some trade mark licences, where monetary matters are mentioned in fleeting, almost embarrassed and certainly inadequate terms. An annual royalty

---

[76] Cf *Alghussein Establishment v Eton College* [1991] 1 All ER 267 (HL) which held that a party cannot avoid its contractual obligations by virtue of its own breach.

H. Important issues in trade mark licences

may be expressed in terms of 'five per cent per annum',[77] a bald phrase in great need of elucidation. Five per cent of what? Paid when? And with what degree of frequency? In which currency? To whom? By what means? Who pays transaction charges? How is the five per cent to be verified? And at whose expense? And indeed, why five per cent at all?[78]

15.82 Where the trade mark is part of a package of intellectual property rights, thought should be given to the benefits which may be obtained in the allocation of royalties between them. For example, if a licence includes a weak trade mark (or a not-yet granted trade mark which is under opposition), a strong design right, some industrial know-how and continuing consultancy services, it may be worth shifting payments from the trade mark element of the licence to the other elements which are more likely to endure (it can be difficult to extract royalties for a trade mark licence if that trade mark has been subsequently invalidated).

(7) Change of control

15.83 If I license the use of my trade mark to a friendly licensee, I should remember that he may later fall into enemy hands. If this gives me cause for concern (as it may particularly do if the trade mark licence is tied to the licence of my own proprietary know-how and sensitive trade information), I should take steps to ensure that, if my licensee experiences a change of control which effectively puts him into the enemy camp, I should be able to terminate the licence.

15.84 Change of control may also occur where a business restructures or subdivides. In such circumstances it is imperative for the restructured business to address the issues of trade mark ownership and control. If this issue is not explicitly addressed, two or more separate companies may simply assume that they are entitled to continue to use the same trade mark for the same goods, with the result that the trade mark is liable to be revoked: if the same trade mark has become an indicator of the goods of two or more independent businesses, it may have ceased to be distinctive of the goods of either of them or may even be deceptive.[79]

15.85 The protection of a trade mark licensor against a licensee's change of control has been the subject of litigation in two recent cases which illustrate the lengths that parties will go to when seeking to escape the effects of change of control provisions. In the first, Rothmans International—a member of the Rothmans group of

---

[77] A regrettable consequence of the decline in the teaching of Latin at school is the increasing inability to distinguish between payments due 'per annum' and those stipulated to be 'per anum'.

[78] Alexander Poltorak and Paul Lerner, *Essentials of Intellectual Property* (2002), p 91, give the astounding piece of advice: 'If you haven't a clue what royalty rate to request, start with a demand for 5%, and you won't be far wrong'. But why? If 5% isn't far wrong, presumably 6% or 7% also aren't far wrong—and you might get more.

[79] See *Scandecor Development AB v Scandecor Marketing AB and others* [1999] FSR 26 (CA).

companies—was the licensee of the MARLBORO cigarette trade mark in the UK. The Rothmans group of companies, including Rothmans International, fell under the control of rival tobacco company BAT. Philip Morris, having imposed a 'change of control' clause in the licence, sought and obtained a declaration that there had been a change of control. BAT sought to persuade the court that, since the immediate ownership of Rothmans International remained unchanged, the fact that the whole group had come under its ownership did not mean that there had been a change of control of Rothmans International. The court, whose decision was upheld on appeal, disagreed.[80] In the second case, a similar result was reached when the licensee of the MINITRAN trade mark for an angina drug merged on a minority basis with another company which had 'effective control' over it. The court considered that the words 'effective control' meant much the same as 'control' on the basis that control which is not effective is not control and that even the fact that the licensee's parent company could in theory gang up with other shareholders to defeat the new controlling interest did not change the fact that there had been a change of control.[81]

(8) Quality control

15.86   In the UK and in jurisdictions influenced by its pre-1994 laws, quality control was an essential element of a trade mark licence. To the extent that the trade mark proprietor carefully regulated and policed the use of his trade mark by a licensee, the licensee's use was truly capable of being regarded as use by the proprietor himself; where more than one licensee or manufacturer produced or sold goods under the licence, the consumer was not confused into believing that the same trade mark was used by competing traders for different qualities of goods. Even where there was no legal imperative to impose quality controls upon a licensee, there remained a commercial imperative: the value of the goodwill in the trade mark would diminish if its owner allowed shoddy products to be sold under it.

15.87   The current British view appears to be that, since there is now no legal requirement on the part of a licensor to establish performance targets and monitor the product quality of his licensees' goods in Europe, whether a trade mark proprietor imposes quality controls upon his licensees is purely a matter of how he perceives his own self-interest.[82] In practice most trade mark owners see important commercial purposes being served by quality-control requirements and do generally include them in their licence agreements.

---

[80] *Philip Morris Products Inc and another v Rothmans International Enterprises Ltd and another* [2001] ETMR 1250 (CA).
[81] *Sanofi-Synthélabo SpA v 3M Healthcare Ltd and another* [2003] ETMR 586 (HC).
[82] *Scandecor Development AB v Scandecor Marketing AB and others* [2001] ETMR 800, [2001] IP&T 676 (HL).

I. Litigation of trade mark transactions

Most trade mark transactions fortunately do not get litigated. Those that do are most often the agreements in which the greatest degree of ambiguity is left to be resolved by post-contractual construction. Accordingly since there is some basis upon which both parties can assert the rectitude of their claim, a ruling by a third party, often a court, is required. **15.88**

There are several explanations as to why trade mark contracts are often left ambiguous or incomplete. The parties may have not addressed important issues at all; they may have addressed them but not realized that the form in which their resolution was expressed was inadequate; or they may have avoided them completely for fear that, if they pressed for agreement where none might be forthcoming, no contract would ever be concluded. However, even the careful and diligent pursuit of agreement is no guarantee that the interpretation of a contract will not fall to be adjudicated in court. This point is illustrated by two cases, one involving a contract which was formally negotiated with the aid of professional advisers, the other of which, the result of relatively informal communications between senior executives of the two parties, had yet to be accepted as having any binding effect. The contrast is appealing because there are several similarities between the two cases. In each of these cases the trade marks involved were internationally known; on each occasion there was an agreement to anticipate future disputes and to avoid litigation by carving out territories and roles for both parties; in each the European party thought there was a binding contract and the United States party thought there wasn't. **15.89**

The first of these cases was the battle between the World Wide Fund for Nature and the World Wrestling Federation for control of the WWF trade mark.[83] In that case the court rejected the contention that an agreement which sought to limit one party's right to use the WWF mark was void as a distortion of competition within the EU or as an unlawful restraint of trade under the common law. The fact that the agreement was freely negotiated by properly advised parties who knew their respective interests and who were aware of the consequences of their actions made it difficult for either party to allege at a later stage that the agreement was unreasonable. **15.90**

In the second case, the respective parties were fighting for the right to register and use the PRUDENTIAL trade mark and other similar trade marks for insurance services.[84] The substantive issues arising from this case are still to be resolved, but it **15.91**

---

[83] *World Wide Fund for Nature and World Wildlife Fund Inc v World Wrestling Federation Entertainment Inc* [2002] ETMR 564, [2003] IP&T 98 (CA). See also Ilanah Simon, 'Pandering to Their Whims? WWF: The Second Round' [2002] Ent LR 161.
[84] *Prudential Assurance Co Ltd v Prudential Insurance Company of America* [2002] ETMR 1013, [2003] FSR 97 (HC); [2003] ETMR 873 (CA).

turns on the issue of whether correspondence between senior representatives of the respective parties over a period of time could be regarded as a contractual determination of those parties' rights.

15.92 A final commonsense point on the issue of litigation is that, however good a trade mark transaction is, there is always a risk of it getting to court if the parties who enter into it later forget about it. This happened in *Pitman v Nominet*,[85] where a company split into two separate entities, each of which was entitled to use the name PITMAN for specific purposes only. If this perfectly good agreement between them had been observed instead of being left in a drawer, then their subsequent tussle for control of Internet domain names could have been avoided.

J. The valuation of trade marks[86]

15.93 Almost every assignment and licence involving a trade mark presupposes that the trade mark has some sort of value to its parties, whether that value is commercial or purely sentimental. But how does one place a value on a trade mark?

15.94 Since the mid-1980s a great deal of activity has taken place in the field of trade mark valuation. The placing of a value on a trade mark has been done for many reasons: to ascertain a fair price for a sale between businesses at arm's length or an objective price for transfer pricing purposes where the businesses are related; to plump up a company's paper worth in its annual accounts;[87] to ward off unwanted takeover bids which undervalue the target company's assets; to enable banks to know how much money they can advance on the security of a trade mark and even to give a trade mark owner an idea of the relative merits of building up an in-house brand or buying in a brand owned by a third party.

15.95 Several different methodologies have been proposed for the calculation of the value of a brand or trade mark.[88] In short, they are:

(i) Excess operating profits: which profits generated by the trade mark proprietor are earned over and above the profits of similar businesses which lack the trade mark? This approach, which depends upon excess profits being identifiable, is

---

[85] *Pitman Training Limited and another v Nominet UK and another* [1997] FSR 797 (HC). See also Jeremy Phillips, 'Two Lessons in Name Management' (1997) 72 *Managing Intellectual Property* 24–6.

[86] On this topic see eg John Sykes and Kelvin King, *Valuation and Exploitation of Intellectual Property and Intangible Assets* (2003) and Raymond Perrier (ed), *Brand Valuation* (1997).

[87] For the purpose of including acquired brands on corporate balance sheets, the UK Accounting Standards Board has brought out two accounting standards, FRS10 and FRS11.

[88] For a brief summary of methodologies, see Caroline Woodward, 'Valuation of Intellectual Property', in Joff Wild (ed), *Building and Enforcing Intellectual Property Value: An International Guide for the Boardroom 2003* (2003).

J. The valuation of trade marks

difficult because similar businesses will generally have their own trade marks too.

(ii) Premium pricing: what is the value of the fact that consumers will pay more for the trade mark proprietor's branded product than for the unbranded or differently branded products of a competitor? This approach is unsuitable where the brand to be valued is not a premium brand.

(iii) Cost savings: how much does the trade mark proprietor expect to save through owning the trade mark? Such savings can be made if the use of an existing brand saves the trade mark proprietor the expense of developing a new brand.

(iv) Royalty savings: how much does the trade mark proprietor expect to save by using his own trade mark rather than through paying royalties to use the trade mark of a third party?

(v) Market value: how much would similar trade marks fetch when they are sold on the open market? This approach is based on a comparison of factors such as the ratio between the price paid and the value of sales derived from the acquired asset.

(vi) Replacement cost: if the trade mark owner were to lose his trade mark, how much would the trade mark owner need to pay for a trade mark with sufficient market power to replace it?

15.96 These methodologies may be used alone or in conjunction with each other so as to achieve a 'cocktail' of values. None of them appears to be based on a watertight scientific technique since the subjectivities of human impression can never be eliminated from the valuation process; yet most of them have some merit and even relatively weak guides which are consistently applied will give a better idea as to the value of marks than fairly good guides which are inconsistently applied. For that reason if no other there is often therefore some advantage in seeking valuations from those who have been around the longest and have done plenty of them.

15.97 A cynic would observe that, in commercial terms, it is probable that the majority of trade marks are probably of little or no commercial value at all: if one were to substitute, on the products and services for which they are used, another quite different trade mark, most proprietor's sales figures would probably show little or no appreciable move in any direction. Proof of this is the fact that most trade marks—and in particular the little mom 'n' pop street-corner trade marks—are never infringed. Could this same fact be construed as proof of the effective deterrent value of the trade mark and its accompanying ® sign? Probably not. There is plenty of trade mark infringement afoot, but the infringers tend to concentrate on the best-defended and best-resourced trade marks, for it is in the infringement of such marks that the biggest profits are made. Why bother infringing most of the ordinary, unexciting trade marks that hover at the fringes of our consumer awareness, when untold riches beckon through the unlawful emulation of magical incantations such as CARTIER, CHANEL, NIKE and ROLEX?

K. Conclusion

15.98 This chapter has sought to show that the law provides a framework within which trade mark owners and those who contract with them can exploit the inherent value and the money-making potential of trade marks. The legal cupboard is not quite bare—it has just two ingredients in assignments and licences—but from those two ingredients a prudent trade mark proprietor and a willing contractual partner can bake a remarkable selection of cakes.

15.99 This chapter has also sought to demonstrate the existence of some obstacles to successful contractual exploitation of trade mark rights which despite, or perhaps because of, their size are frequently missed in the course of business. However, even the most prudent of planning and the most distinguished of draftsmanship is no guarantee that a trade mark transaction will evade the scrutiny of the courts.

16

TRADE MARKS IN SPECIFIC SECTORS

A. **Introduction**	
Darwin's finches and the origin of species	
B. **Pharmaceutical marks**	16.01
(1) The naming of pharmaceutical products	16.02
(2) Uniformity of pharmaceutical trade marks	16.06
(3) Parallel importation: the special position of pharmaceutical products	16.08
(a) Repackaging, relabelling and overstickering	16.11
(b) What constitutes 'repackaging'?	16.12
(c) What is the function of 'prior notice' in repackaging cases?	16.13
(d) Is there a doctrine of 'necessity'?	16.16
(e) Can an importer rebrand the imported products with the trade mark of the country of importation?	16.24
(f) Adding a trade mark, logo or features of package design to the imported goods	16.26
(g) Can the importer repackage and relabel branded goods as generic goods?	16.29
(4) Pharmaceutical trade marks and withdrawal of market authorizations	16.30
(5) Confusion between pharmaceutical trade marks	
(a) An exercise in risk analysis	16.31
(b) Special considerations relating to the pharmaceutical products market	16.35
C. **Retail sales service marks**	16.37
(1) The position under international law	16.39
(2) Retail services in the United States and in Europe	16.41
(3) Problems arising from the interrelation of trade marks for products and service marks for retail sales	16.46
(4) Retail sales, e-tail sales and modern technologies	16.49
D. **Celebrity trade marks**	16.50
(1) Live celebrities	16.53
(2) Dead celebrities	16.57
(a) Dead celebrity names: private ownership and public policy	16.58
(b) Protection of dead and live celebrity names against non-identical signs	16.59
(c) Vehicles for the protection of dead celebrities' names	16.61
(3) Celebrities' signatures	16.63
(4) Collective celebrities	16.64
(5) Fictional celebrities	16.65
(6) Events as celebrities	16.71
E. **Conclusion**	16.73

A. Introduction

Darwin's finches and the origin of species

According to tradition, when Charles Darwin landed in the Galápagos Islands in 1835, he gathered samples of thirteen species of finch.[1] These finches formed a closely knit genealogical group, although they enjoyed widely different lifestyles. Deducing from these observations that the differences between the thirteen species of finch were somehow derived from their divergent lifestyles, Darwin and his colleagues theorized that the format of the basic finch had evolved in response to the immediate environment in which it lived.

There is a close analogy between the behaviour of Darwin's finches in the Galápagos and that of trade mark practice in different sectors. Our trade mark laws are of the 'one size fits all' variety, but the way in which trade marks are conceived, registered and used can differ substantially as between commercial and industrial sectors. In this chapter we look at the way trade mark law and practice have developed in the diverse and unrelated fields of pharmaceutical products, the retail sales sector and in the protection of celebrity names and concepts.

B. Pharmaceutical marks[2]

16.01 No one has died of a trade mark, but many people have died through taking the wrong medicaments—too frequently as a result of confusing one medicine with another. The 'life and death' factor of avoiding confusion in giving names to medicines and pharmaceutical preparations is therefore accorded a high priority in the development of pharmaceutical trade mark law and practice. It should not however be thought that this is the only area in which 'life and death factors' are important. For many people with food allergies, confusion between proprietary confectionery products can also be fatal, as can the confusion of automobile or aeroplane spare parts. But the primacy of the safety factor has shaped the development of trade mark law and practice far less in those fields of commerce. Together with the safety factor, the potential for the truly international exploitation of pharmaceutical products and the massive imbalance between research and development costs on the one hand and manufacturing costs on the other are features which combine to give the pharmaceutical trade mark sector its own very clearly defined characteristics within trade mark practice.

---

[1] See Stephen Jay Gould, 'Darwin at Sea—and the Virtues of Port', in *The Flamingo's Smile* (1985), which brings down both the popular traditional account of the discovery of evolution and the true, somewhat less romantic version.

[2] For a general overview of legal problem areas within the pharmaceutical sector, see Shelley Lane with Jeremy Phillips, *Trade Mark Legislation and the Pharmaceutical Industry* (1999). For a stirring, if melodramatic account of the role of the sector, see Derek Rossitter, 'Life and Death, Comfort and Pain, Hope and Despair' (1987) 6 *Trademark World* 28–33. A valuable overview of branding and marketing aspects can be found in Tom Blackett and Rebecca Robins (eds), *Brand Medicine: The Role of Branding in the Pharmaceutical Industry* (2001).

B. Pharmaceutical marks

(1) The naming of pharmaceutical products

Pharmaceutical products can be divided into two groups: 'over the counter' (OTC) and 'prescription only' preparations. OTC products can be purchased by ordinary consumers in supermarkets and in specialist retail outlets. Prescription-only products cannot be purchased by the consumer on demand: they must be prescribed by a qualified medical practitioner and dispensed, together with instructions for their use, by a qualified pharmacist. There is some overlap between the two categories, since medical practitioners may prescribe OTC products and consumers who are aware of the trade mark of prescription-only products may ask for them by name (for example, PROZAC for fluoxetine, ZANTAC for ranitidine). Nonetheless, the commercial function of the trade mark in each market is quite different. **16.02**

Since OTC products are available on request and without prescription, it is possible for manufacturers to market them directly to consumers through regular advertising. Accordingly many such products have easily memorized and user-friendly trade marks. Examples of well-known OTC products include most oral-hygiene products, analgesics, contraceptives, laxatives, as well as treatments for indigestion, baldness and athlete's foot. Popular brands in these fields include NUROFEN (ibuprofen painkiller), NIZORAL (anti-dandruff shampoo) and AVEENO (colloidal oat bath meal for eczema). **16.03**

In contrast, prescription-only products are marketed by their manufacturers to the physicians who prescribe them. Accordingly their trade marks are usually chosen in order to make them sound non-memorable, very serious and pseudo-scientific. OTC products may have cheerful, snappy and allusive names like KWELLS (promethazine for travel-sickness) and OPTREX (eye bath with boric acid and witch hazel), but prescription-only products may have to live with stern, serious-sounding trade marks like VOLTAROL (anti-inflammatory diclofenac). There are exceptions, such as the attractively named prescription-only YASMIN contraceptive pill. **16.04**

In truth, prescription products have three names: (i) their trade mark; (ii) the descriptive term which defines the chemical structure of their active ingredients; and (iii) their International Non-Proprietary Names (INNs),[3] which are designed to be an easy means of referring to the generic version of the product. An INN may not be registered as a trade mark for a product to which it refers, since it is effectively a generic term, but that does not prevent pharmaceutical trade mark applicants choosing names which allude to the INN (such as AMOXIL for amoxycillin) or even trying to secure registration for a trade mark which is as close as it can be **16.05**

---

[3] For a good introduction to INNs, see Agathe Wehrli, 'Pharmaceuticals: Trademarks Versus Generic Names' (1986) 4 *Trademark World* 31.

to the forbidden INN. The value of INNs is also eroded by the fact that trade marks which are virtually identical to them may be registered for other pharmaceutical products which do not contain the same active ingredients. Accordingly the word OMEPRAZOK was registrable for 'pharmaceutical, veterinary and sanitary preparations; dietetic substances adapted for medical use, food for babies; plasters, materials for dressings' in Germany since it did not contain the active ingredients of the INN for a treatment for ulcers, Omeprazol.[4]

(2) Uniformity of pharmaceutical trade marks

16.06 In any single market, be it just one country or a compound single market made up of a large number of Member States, it is desirable for any pharmaceutical product to be designated by the same, uniform trade mark wherever it is sold. The uniformity of a product's trade mark saves the inconvenience and embarrassment which may occur where a consumer asks for, or a physician seeks to prescribe, a product by reference to one name when it is known locally by another. Under EU law it was until recently believed by many that a certificate of marketing authorization[5] would not be granted for a new medicinal product unless the applicant could show that he had secured registration of a single trade mark by which that product was to be known throughout the territory of the EU. This view has very properly been rejected by the Court of First Instance (CFI): where proper reasons exist for having different names in different jurisdictions and there is no serious health risk, the public interest in making medicaments available under different trade marks to people who need it outweighs the inconvenience of it not being available at all.[6]

16.07 One mark per pharmaceutical product is not just a preference in terms of health and safety: it is also an issue in European competition law, where the use of different trade marks for the same medicine in different countries looks suspiciously like an attempt to partition the single market into lots of little Member State-sized units in order to limit supplies and keep prices high. But even competition law recognizes that in theory there may be *bona fide* reasons for a drug company to use a separate trade mark for each national market. For example, the mark under which the product was originally launched may not be available in some countries because it, or a mark close enough to be confused with it, has already been registered by someone else.[7]

---

[4] OMEPRAZOK *Trade Mark* [2003] ETMR 662 (Bundesgerichtshof). Omeprazol(e) is better known when sold under the trade mark LOSEC.

[5] A certificate of marketing authorization (CMA) must be received from the European Agency for the Evaluation of Medicinal Products (EMEA) or a national certification authority before a medicinal product can be sold within the EU or its Member States.

[6] *Dr Karl Thomae GmbH, supported by the European Federation of Pharmaceutical Industries and Associations (EFPIA) v Commission of the European Communities, supported by the Council of the European Union,* Case T-123/00, 10 December 2002 (unreported) (CFI (Fifth Chamber)).

[7] *Pharmacia & Upjohn SA v Paranova A/S,* Case C-379/97 [1999] ETMR 937 (ECJ).

B. Pharmaceutical marks

(3) Parallel importation: the special position of pharmaceutical products

16.08 When Spain and Portugal became members of the EU, pharmaceutical products were not subject to patent protection. The terms under which their accession was negotiated included transitional provisions which enabled those nations to control the price at which pharmaceutical and medicinal products could be sold.[8] Accordingly entrepreneurs in those countries ordered large quantities of products, which could be procured very cheaply and then exported to countries such as Denmark, Sweden and the UK, where the unrestricted pricing policies in those markets enabled parallel importers of such products to resell them at a handsome profit. Although pharmaceutical companies could not refuse to supply their products to Spain or Portugal, since this was contrary to European law, they did everything in their power to make it difficult for the dealers in parallel-imported products to benefit from this state of affairs.

16.09 In the debate between original product manufacturers and parallel importers, which has taken place both in court and outside it, both sides claim to have justice on their side. The original product manufacturers maintained both that (i) their legitimate expectation of profit had been sabotaged by letting Spain and Portugal impose artificially low prices with which their legitimate distributors must compete throughout Europe and that (ii) when parallel traders repackaged and relabelled their goods, damage was done to the goodwill in their most treasured assets, their trade marks. The parallel importers argued that (i) what they were doing was in keeping with not just the law of trade marks but also the principles of free-market economics and that (ii) they were benefiting the ill and the needy by making expensive products available at a far lower price, also reducing the cost to the taxpayer of medicines purchased by the state.

16.10 Justice is a child of promiscuous times. She has smiled on both warring parties. So too, taking their cue from Justice, have the courts, as the sections below will indicate.

(a) Repackaging, relabelling and overstickering

16.11 Even before the introduction of Directive 89/104 and the Community Trade Mark (CTM) Regulation, the European Court of Justice (ECJ) had ruled that the repackaging of parallel-imported pharmaceutical products and the application to the new packages of the original manufacturer's trade mark would not infringe that trade mark where there was a need to repackage those products—for example, to conform with national packaging or labelling laws—and where the repackaging operation did not adversely affect the quality of those pharmaceutical

---

[8] On the background to this see eg *Merck & Co Inc v Primecrown Ltd*, Joined Cases C-267/95 and 268/95 [1997] FSR 237 (ECJ).

goods.⁹ These principles were affirmed and clarified in the first cases on Directive 89/104 to reach the Court, in its consolidated decision in *Bristol-Myers Squibb v Paranova*.¹⁰ In that ruling the Court laid down that a trade mark owner could not oppose the subsequent marketing of a repackaged product where the following cumulative conditions were fulfilled:

(i) enforcement of the trade mark right would have the effect of contributing towards the artificial partitioning of the market as between EU Member States (for example, where the trade mark owner deliberately employs different packaging in each country, thus forcing the importer to repackage whenever the product is to be imported from one country to another);

(ii) the repackaging must not harm the original condition of the product (including the instructions for use);

(iii) the new packaging must clearly state both the details of the original manufacturer and the repackager and the origin of any additional articles that originated from third parties other than the original manufacturer;

(iv) the presentation of the repackaged product must not be such as to damage the reputation of the trade mark or its owner by being of poor quality, defective or untidy; and

(v) the parallel importer must notify the trade mark owner before he imports the goods and, if requested, supply him with a sample.

(b) What constitutes 'repackaging'?

16.12 The Advocate General of the ECJ has advised the Court that even the sticking together of two five-packs of INSUMAN insulin marketed in France so as to form a 'ten-pack' for the German market is sufficiently an act of 'repackaging' for the resulting product not to be counted as a genuine 'ten-pack'.¹¹

(c) What is the function of 'prior notice' in repackaging cases?

16.13 The five requirements in *Bristol-Myers Squibb v Paranova* conclude with that of notice: if you want to repackage pharmaceutical products, you must let the trade mark owner know first and be prepared to give him a sample. The requirement is based on commonsense. If the trade mark proprietor has an objection to the

---

⁹ See *Hoffmann-La Roche v Centrafarm*, Case 102/77 [1978] ECR 1139 (ECJ); *Centrafarm v American Home Products Corp* [1978] ECR 1823 (ECJ).

¹⁰ *Bristol-Myers Squibb v Paranova A/S; CH Boehringer Sohn and others v Paranova A/S; Bayer Aktiengesellschaft and another v Paranova A/S*, Joined Cases C-427/93, C-429/93 and C-436/93 [1996] ETMR 1 (ECJ).

¹¹ *Aventis Pharma Deutschland GmbH v Kohlpharma GmbH and another* [2003] ETMR 143 (ECJ): this case is governed by Council Regulation 2309/93 laying down Community procedures for the authorization and supervision of medicinal products for human and veterinary use and establishing a European Agency for the Evaluation of Medicinal Products, not the regular trade mark laws.

B. Pharmaceutical marks

repackaging, it is better and cheaper for him to raise it and for the matter to be disposed of before the repackaged goods go on sale rather than afterwards, since by doing so the cost and inconvenience of recalling and destroying either the pharmaceutical products or their packaging may thus be avoided. The ECJ has subsequently explained its position on the issue with greater clarity:

> [A] parallel importer must . . . in order to be entitled to repackage trade marked pharmaceutical products, fulfil the requirement of prior notice. If the parallel importer does not satisfy that requirement, the trade mark proprietor may oppose the marketing of the repackaged pharmaceutical product. It is incumbent on the parallel importer himself to give notice to the trade mark proprietor of the intended repackaging. In the event of dispute, it is for the national court to assess, in the light of all the relevant circumstances, whether the proprietor had a reasonable time to react to the intended repackaging.[12]

16.14 In a subsequent British case, the High Court cited this decision and held that

> . . . it can be an actionable wrong to fail to give advance notice to the proprietor that you will not be infringing his rights.[13]

16.15 This may well be the case, but it is difficult to pinpoint any provision in Directive 89/104, the CTM Regulation or indeed the Trade Marks Act 1994 which adds, to the list of other infringing acts, the failure to notify the trade mark owner of the repackaging of what might well be a non-infringing product.

(d) Is there a doctrine of 'necessity'?[14]

16.16 A difficult question addressed in European trade mark law is whether repackaging or relabelling is only allowed where there is an objective necessity for it. For example, where a country requires that medicines sold within its borders must be labelled with instructions or ingredient lists in that country's language, it can be understood that a trader would be prevented from taking advantage of the exhaustion of trade mark rights if it could only sell quantities of that product in the country in which it bought it. Likewise, where one country requires that a particular product be sold in packages of ten and its neighbour requires that the product be sold in packages of twelve, repackaging is necessary if that product is to be resold in that neighbouring state. But are repackaging and relabelling permitted only where it is objectively necessary? And, if so, does 'necessity' mean exclusively legal necessity or does it include economic necessity?

---

[12] *Boehringer Ingelheim KG and Boehringer Ingelheim Pharma KG v Swingward Ltd*, Case C-143/00 [2002] ETMR 898 (ECJ), para 68.
[13] *Glaxo Group and others v Dowelhurst Ltd and others*, 6 February 2003 (HC), para 38.
[14] On this topic, see eg Dominic Dryden and Susie Middlemiss, 'Parallel Importation of Repackaged Goods: Is "Necessity" Really Necessary?' [2003] JBL 82–9; Naomi Gross and Lucy Harrold, 'Fighting for Pharmaceutical Profits' [2002] EIPR 497–503; and Stephen Whybrow and Lucy Kilshaw, 'Repackaging Ruled Out' (2003) 155 *Trademark World* 17–18.

16.17 The ECJ in *Bristol-Myers Squibb v Paranova* considered that repackaging was only justifiable if it was necessary.[15] This view was then strongly supported by national case law. Thus in Denmark, in respect of a product which Danish law did not require to be labelled exclusively in Danish, all the importer needed to do was to place a Danish-language sticker containing relevant information on the original box: the repackaging was unnecessary and therefore constituted an infringement of the trade mark.[16] The same rule applies where the contents of the imported product are in the same quantity as that required by the country of importation: relabelling is permitted, to the extent that it is required, while repackaging is unnecessary and is therefore prohibited.[17]

16.18 While the doctrine of necessity was becoming firmly established in national law, it was noted that the provisions of Directive 89/104 and the CTM Regulation did not contain any reference to that concept. Was it therefore a mirage, a piece of jurisprudential ectoplasm which had no genuine legal substance? Or was it part of official European jurisprudence all along, part of the implicit spirit of the new European law even if, like lovers' sighs, the doctrine of necessity was too well felt to require articulation in the law? The answer came in *Boehringer Ingelheim Pharma KG v Swingward* when the Court ruled that

> replacement packaging of pharmaceutical products is objectively necessary within the meaning of the Court's case law if, without such repackaging, effective access to the market concerned, or to a substantial part of that market, must be considered to be hindered as the result of strong resistance from a substantial proportion of consumers to relabelled pharmaceutical products.[18]

16.19 This ruling, which *prima facie* comes out in support of legal, economic and cultural necessity being grounds upon which repackaging can be carried out, is phrased in terms which actually limit the scope of the doctrine of necessity.

16.20 In the first place one must ask whether, without repackaging, there is no effective access to the market in the country of importation. Does 'without repackaging' mean also 'without advertising and marketing of the unrepackaged product?' If it can be shown that access to the market is the result of a failure of the parallel importer to promote the product in an appropriately appealing manner, then it is not the absence of repackaging but the absence of initiative and effort which bars effective access to the market.

---

[15] *Bristol-Myers Squibb v Paranova A/S; CH Boehringer Sohn and others v Paranova A/S; Bayer Aktiengesellschaft and another v Paranova A/S*, Joined Cases C-427/93, C-429/93 & C-436/93 [1996] ETMR 1, para 56.

[16] *Løvens Kemiske Fabrik Produktionsaktielskab v Paranova A/S* [2001] ETMR 302 (Østre Landrets Domme, Denmark): DAIVONEX imported from Spain.

[17] *Løvens Kemiske Fabrik Produktionsaktielskab v Orifarm A/S*, Case 214/2001 WTLR, 20 March 2003 (Supreme Court, Denmark).

[18] *Boehringer Ingelheim KG and Boehringer Ingelheim Pharma KG v Swingward Ltd*, Case C-143/00 [2002] ETMR 898 (ECJ), para 54.

B. Pharmaceutical marks

Secondly, what does 'strong resistance' mean? 'Strong resistance' is presumably more powerful than 'weak resistance', which the parallel importer could be expected to overcome without having to resort to repackaging; and both 'strong resistance' and 'weak resistance' are more powerful than 'mere inertia'. Presumably the burden of proving that there is strong resistance will lie with the party seeking to rely upon it—the parallel importer—in which case it will be interesting to see how this burden of proof will be discharged. **16.21**

Thirdly, who are the consumers? So far as OTC preparations are concerned, the consumer is presumably the Swede with a sore throat or the Dane with a dreadful hangover. But with regard to prescription-only products, are we talking about the common folk of Northern Europe or about their skilled medically qualified practitioners, who may be expected to offer less resistance to unrepackaged or unrelabelled products? **16.22**

It would be a brave man indeed who could say, hand on heart, that none of these questions will find their way to Luxembourg. **16.23**

(e) Can an importer rebrand the imported products with the trade mark of the country of importation?

It has already been established that a trade mark proprietor may have a lawful reason for maintaining different brand names for the same pharmaceutical product in different EEA countries,[19] so long as he is not seeking to partition the single market by doing so. Does this therefore mean that the proprietor of multiple trade marks for the same product may not object where a parallel importer of pharmaceutical products removes the brand name from the country of purchase and replaces it with the trade mark of the country of importation? In a Swedish case the trade mark owner made a product which was sold as LIMOVAN in Spain but as IMOVANE in Sweden.[20] An importer imported LIMOVAN into Sweden where he repackaged and resold it as IMOVANE. The trade mark proprietor's action for infringement was successful. There was no evidence that the trade mark proprietor was seeking to partition the Internal Market and no reason why the importer should not have sold the product as LIMOVAN: the fact that greater commercial advantage could be secured by changing the trade mark was not a reason why the importer should be allowed to rebrand the goods, since there was no 'objective necessity' for it to do so. Indeed, the change of brand was an attempt on the part of the importer to gain a free ride on the goodwill generated by the trade mark owner through advertising and marketing its product under the name IMOVANE. **16.24**

---

[19] *Pharmacia & Upjohn SA v Paranova A/S*, Case C-379/97 [1999] ETMR 937 (ECJ), cited at para 16.07 above.
[20] *Aventis Pharma Aktiebolag v Paranova Läkemedel Aktiebolag* [2001] ETMR 652 (City Court, Stockholm).

A similar result was achieved in Denmark, where the rebranding of Portuguese GUTALAX laxatives as LAXOBERAL was held to infringe the trade mark proprietor's rights for the same reason.[21]

16.25 Where a rebranding exercise of this nature takes place, the courts will take into account the impact of the likely change of trade mark when determining whether to grant interim relief. Thus in one case an importer of paroxetine bought it in France, where it was branded DEROXAT and dispatched it to Scotland for relabelling as SEROXAT, the trade mark under which it was to be sold in Sweden. The trade mark owner sought interim injunctive relief, which was refused. The court observed that the repackaged paroxetine bore a label stating, in Swedish, that the tablets inside the box were marked DEROXAT but that the box had been relabelled as SEROXAT; under those circumstances not only was there no real scope for confusion but it was difficult to see what damage the trade mark owner would suffer to its trade mark right. Accordingly this was not an appropriate case for interim relief.[22]

(f) Adding a trade mark, logo or features of package design to the imported goods

16.26 The courts are willing to allow the importer and reseller of pharmaceutical products to buy and sell goods in which the trade mark proprietor's rights have been exhausted, since that is precisely what exhaustion policy demands.[23] But the courts are equally reluctant to allow importers to use this facility as a springboard from which they can launch the marketing of their own brands. Accordingly, while a parallel trader is obliged to print details of its identity on any repackaging,[24] the Danish Supreme Court has ruled that it is not open to a parallel trader to add its own logo or other markings to repackaged goods,[25] a practice which is sometimes described as 'co-branding'.[26]

16.27 The question whether a trade mark owner can object to the use of his mark on packaging which the parallel importer has equipped with 'stripes and/or other graphic elements that make up a part of the design of the packaging' has been referred for an advisory ruling to the EFTA Court.[27]

---

[21] *Boehringer Ingelheim Danmark A/S and others v Orifarm A/S* [2002] ETMR 223 (Court of Odense).

[22] *Beecham Group plc v Munro Wholesale Medical Supplies Ltd* [2001] ETMR 318 (Outer House, Court of Session, Scotland).

[23] For the basic provisions of EEA exhaustion policy, see Council Directive 89/104, art 7; Council Regulation 40/94, art 13. For a detailed discussion see Chapter 9.

[24] See *Bristol-Myers Squibb v Paranova A/S etc*, Joined Cases C-427/93, C-429/93 and C-436/93 [1996] ETMR 1 (ECJ).

[25] *Løvens Kemiske Fabrik Produktionsaktielskab v Orifarm A/S*, Case 214/2001 WTLR, 20 March 2003 (Supreme Court, Denmark).

[26] See eg *Glaxo Group and others v Dowelhurst Ltd and others* [2003] EWHC 110 (Ch) [2003] 2 CMLR 248, para 23.

[27] *Paranova AS v Merck & Co Inc*, Case C-3/02, request for advisory opinion, 17 December 2002.

B. Pharmaceutical marks

Where the EMEA has granted the trade mark proprietor a certificate of marketing authorization which enables him to sell a medicinal product under his own trade mark throughout Europe, additional labelling requirements may still be imposed in respect of individual countries in which that product is sold. To that end, the European Commission adopted the concept of the 'blue box', a portion of the certified product's labelling which is given over to the publication of information of purely national interest—so long as that information is approved by the EMEA. Information inserted in the blue box may relate, for example, to the details of a local distributor of the medicinal product. The CFI has ruled that there is no reason to bar the inclusion in the 'blue box' of the local distributor's trade mark or logo since its inclusion will not cause confusion as to the origin of the approved medicinal product but will, on the contrary, provide information which may be of assistance to consumers.[28]

16.28

(g) Can the importer repackage and relabel branded goods as generic goods?

Many countries have now introduced medicinal prescription rules which require physicians to prescribe generic products in preference to more expensive branded products, or which permit pharmacists to substitute generic products for branded ones unless the prescribing physician insists on the issue of the branded version. In such circumstances it may be advantageous for the parallel importer, having purchased proprietary medicines very cheaply in one country, to import them into another and then by removing the original trade mark genericize them in order to enhance the prospect of a swift sale. The Danish Supreme Court has ruled that this practice is also unacceptable and constitutes an infringement of the trade mark[29] although it is difficult to understand the principle of trade mark law under which this should be so.[30]

16.29

(4) Pharmaceutical trade marks and withdrawal of market authorizations

Where a proprietary pharmaceutical company has a marketing authorization[31] which entitles it to sell an approved product under a particular trade mark in the EU, may it shrug off the competition of parallel traders by (i) changing the formulation of its product, (ii) surrendering its authorization, thus invalidating a parallel trader's import licence, then (iii) objecting to the importation of products

16.30

---

[28] *A Menarini—Industrie Farmaceutiche Riunite SRL (European Federation of Pharmaceutical Industries and Associations, intervening) v Commission*, Case T-179/00 [2002] ETMR 1131 (ECJ).

[29] *Løvens Kemiske Fabrik Produktionsaktielskab v Orifarm A/S*, Case 214/2001 WTLR, 20 March 2003 (Supreme Court, Denmark).

[30] Laddie J in *Glaxo Group and others v Dowelhurst Ltd and others* [2003] 2 CMLR 248, para 22, considered that 'debranding' a product could not be a trade mark infringement: 'If the mark is completely removed from all parts of the product and its packaging, the importer is no longer using it and there cannot be infringement which is a wrong which is dependent upon use of the mark'.

[31] On which see paras 16.06–16.08 and 16.26–16.28 above.

in which the trade mark right is exhausted but which are no longer covered by a valid marketing authorization (CMA)? This question arose before the ECJ after Ferring changed the formulation of its MINIRIN spray antidiuretic product. The new product was to be sold as MINIRIN Nasenspray. Ferring surrendered its German authorization for MINIRIN spray and then objected to Eurim-Pharm importing the old version. The availability of the two products side by side, it argued, would confuse the public. The ECJ[32] ruled that any provision of national law which enabled a trade mark owner to secure the automatic invalidation of a parallel import licence by surrendering its own authorization was precluded by EU competition law.[33] The Court qualified this ruling by stating that, if the coexistence of differently formulated products with the same trade mark caused a risk to public health, importation of the old version of the product might be justified.

(5) Confusion between pharmaceutical trade marks

(a) An exercise in risk analysis

16.31 Some courts have considered that, where prescription-only products have similar names, the likelihood of confusion is lower than it would be for other types of goods. This is because, if those products are prescribed by a qualified medical practitioner and are then dispensed by a qualified pharmacist, people who have had the benefit of professional training and expertise in the medical field will be unlikely to confuse products with which they deal regularly in the discharge of their professional duties.[34] Other tribunals have considered that the great danger of a consumer taking the wrong product demands that a greater distance be placed between pharmaceutical trade marks before it is considered that there is no likelihood of confusion.[35] One court has even ordered the cancellation of the ANDAK pharmaceutical trade mark on account of the risk of its being confused with ZANTAC even though the owner of ANDAK had not yet decided what pharmaceutical product(s) to use it on.[36]

16.32 A Board of Appeal of the Office for Harmonisation in the Internal Market (OHIM) has taken the view that these two opposing views are both valid and are therefore capable of cancelling each other out:

---

[32] *Ferring Arzneimittel GmbH v Eurim-Pharm Arzneimittel GmbH*, Case C-172/00 [2003] ETMR 115 (ECJ), followed in *Paranova Oy*, Case C-113/01, 8 May 2003 (ECJ).

[33] Such an activity would be a quantitative restriction on imports under article 28 EC of the Treaty.

[34] *Pfizer Inc and Pfizer A/S v Durascan Medical Products A/S* [1997] ETMR 85, 96 (Danish Supreme Court): VIBRAMYCIN not likely to be confused with VIBRADOX, both being antibiotics.

[35] See eg *Pliva D D Zagreb's application* [2000] ETMR 594 (Board of Appeals, Polish Patent Office): RECTOCIN so close to RASTOCIN as to constitute a danger to health, even though there was little danger of suitably qualified persons mistaking them.

[36] *Glaxo Group Ltd v Knoll Aktiengesellschaft* [1999] ETMR 358 (Maritime and Commercial Court, Denmark).

B. Pharmaceutical marks

In some Member States the view is taken that a likelihood of confusion should be accepted more readily in the case of medicines on account of the serious consequences that can ensue if the patient takes the wrong product. In other countries the view is taken that pharmaceutical trade marks will not be confused so easily because the consumer has the assistance of qualified professionals and is particularly attentive to differences... because of the importance of taking the right product.

In the Board's view, the conflicting considerations... are likely to cancel each other out in many cases, with the result that no special criteria need be applied to trade marks for pharmaceutical products...[37]

16.33 This view would be commendable if we were to be concerned only with the likelihood of confusion before or at the point when the consumer acquires the medicine. No respectable physician or pharmacist would ever confuse the hypothetical PONGOCYL eye ointment and PONCOGYL as a treatment for the removal of ear wax. But we must also consider why we ask whether the consumer is likely to be confused. Is it just because we want to protect brands or also because we want to protect consumers? If the latter, then we must ask not just whether PONGOCYL and PONCOGYL are confusingly similar to the qualified professional but also what will be running through the consumer's mind six months after he goes to his medicine cabinet and sees his PONGOCYL next to his wife's PONCOGYL. If we start to consider the consequences of post-transaction confusion, we cannot realistically maintain that the professional expertise of physicians and pharmacists militates towards a reduced risk of confusion.

16.34 Where the respective trade marks relate to products which are available over the counter and not on prescription, the supposed protection provided by the professional expertise of physicians and pharmacists will not exist anyway. It is thus disappointing that, in a case where the applicant sought to register ACAMOL for a painkiller and the opponent based its opposition on the earlier German trade mark AGAROL for laxatives, an OHIM Board of Appeal appeared to assume that the only time at which a consumer might confuse the respective products was at the point of sale.[38] The Board thus rejected the policy argument that there should be extra protection against confusion for pharmaceuticals on the ground that the consequences of taking a laxative instead of a painkiller (or vice versa) were not particularly serious. One wonders if any member of the Board of Appeal would take the same view if informed that he was about to undergo delicate surgery at the hands of a surgeon who had just taken a laxative instead of a painkiller.

---

[37] *Choay SA v Boehringer Ingelheim International GmbH*, Case R 273/1999–1 [2001] ETMR 693, paras 19–20 (OHIM): EXACYL prescription-only drug for haemorrhagic disorders unlikely to be confused with EVASIL treatment for premenstrual disorders.

[38] *Gödecke AG v Teva Pharmaceutical Industries Limited*, 15 May 2000 (2001) 32 IIC 326 (OHIM First Board of Appeal).

(b) Special considerations relating to the pharmaceutical products market

16.35 Unlike many markets for consumer goods, the pharmaceutical products market is a market in which the competing parties tend to have a high degree of familiarity with each other's products. This is because very many state-of-the-art products are covered by patent protection and, in the case of those products which are not patented, the identity or similarity of products can be ascertained by reference to their pharmaceutical names and to the approval processes to which medicines must submit in order to obtain authorization certificates before they can be sold.

16.36 Although most players in the pharmaceutical market have financial resources which make it possible for them to litigate extensively against one another, it is notable that, while trade mark oppositions as between original product manufacturers are extremely common, actions for cancellation are far less common and actual infringement proceedings brought by one proprietary pharmaceutical company against another are relatively rare.

C. Retail sales service marks

16.37 The registration of trade marks for the service of the retail sale of goods was long regarded in Europe as anathema. The main objection was that, by registering the name of a shop as a service mark, the service mark proprietor could control and ultimately stifle the choice of trade marks on the part of manufacturers of goods. To give a simple example, if I registered the name TRIXIE as a trade mark for my department store, I could reasonably expect to be able to object to and ultimately control the use of TRIXIE as a trade mark by the makers of clothing, furniture, bedding, kitchenware, toys, electrical equipment and most other categories of goods sold in department stores. This control would be based on the hypothesis that anyone buying TRIXIE duvets from a TRIXIE shop could reasonably suppose that the same enterprise was responsible for them both. There were two other token objections to the registration of trade marks for retail services, neither of which required serious rebuttal: (i) that there was no specific provision for them in the various classes listed in the Nice Classification scheme and (ii) that the sale of other people's goods was not really a service at all since it did not affect the nature of the goods sold but merely transferred the ownership of goods on display in shops from their owner to the customer.

16.38 Against the view that retail service marks should not be registered, the arguments in favour looked much stronger. The differences between trade marks and service marks, and between service marks for the retail supply of goods and service marks for other services, are deep and meaningful in the minds of judges, trade mark examiners and legal practitioners—but those differences are meaningless to the vast

C. Retail sales service marks

majority of consumers. The man in the street does not view a trade mark on goods as being qualitatively different to the name of a shop; it is not uncommon today for shoppers to be as loyal to shops as they are to the brands of goods they purchase. Indeed, with the growth of 'in-house' and 'own product' branding, the distinction between trade marks for goods and service marks for retail sales has become blurred in the eyes of many.

(1) The position under international law

16.39 So should retail sales services be entitled to trade mark registration? The international conventions shed some light on this question. The Paris Convention requires that Paris Union states protect service marks but does not demand that they be registrable as trade marks.[39] Although that Convention requires that the nature of the *goods* for which a trade mark registration must not form an obstacle to its registration,[40] it also says nothing about obstacles to the registration of *services*. The Agreement on Trade-Related Aspects of Intellectual Property Law (TRIPs) is however explicit:

> The nature of the goods or services to which a trademark is to be applied shall in no case form an obstacle to registration of a trademark.[41]

16.40 This would suggest that, unless it can be shown that the provision of retail sales is not a service at all, there is no apparent justification for preventing the registration of service marks for retail services.

(2) Retail services in the United States and in Europe

16.41 In the United States the Lanham Act makes no distinction between the registration of service marks for retail sales services and any other species of service mark. The failure to make such a distinction has not apparently caused any problems in the United States. In that most fertile of jurisdictions for the cultivation of brand-based opportunities, the non-controversial registration of service marks for retail sales has produced most of the world's best-known retail service marks: WALMART, NIKETOWN and TOYS "Я" US, to name but a few.

16.42 In Europe, however, while neither Directive 89/104 nor the CTM Regulation actually barred retail service marks from registration, it was long accepted that they should not be registered. This understanding was enshrined in the OHIM President's Communication of 7 October 1999[42] and even the British, the so-called 'nation of shopkeepers', for once did not object. The Japanese, much of

---

[39] Paris Convention on the Protection of Industrial Property, arts 1(2), 6*sexies*.
[40] ibid, art 7.
[41] TRIPs, art 15(4).
[42] This Communication was itself based upon the Joint Statements of the Minutes of the Council Meeting made when the CTM Regulation was adopted in 1993.

whose commercial law has been influenced by German jurisprudence, also refused to permit the registration of retail service marks.[43]

16.43 The face of European retail trade was changed by an OHIM Board of Appeal decision, *Giacomelli*, in which the applicant sought to register a figurative mark containing the word GIACOMELLI for Class 35 services of

> Bringing together, for the benefit of others, a variety of goods . . . to enable consumers to view and buy the products; organisation of exhibitions in halls and showrooms for commercial or advertising purposes.[44]

16.44 The Board's view was that, so long as an application did not seek to register the mark for the service of selling *all* goods but restricted itself to specific identifiable categories of goods, there was no reason in law or principle why it should not be able to do so. Noting that, by and large, the goodwill of a retail business is built upon the service it provides, the Board added that even the fact that a retail store operated on a self-service basis should not lessen its prospects of gaining trade mark registration as a retail service.[45]

16.45 The willingness of OHIM and some other national registries to allow the registration of trade marks for retail services has not been reflected by the practice in Germany, where an apparent reluctance to allow such registrations has resulted in the reference to the ECJ of a request for a preliminary ruling on the question 'is retailing of goods a service within the meaning of article 2 of the Directive'.[46] The German view is based on the assumption that since, in the EC Treaty itself, services are defined as being 'normally provided for remuneration',[47] any service which may be the subject of a trade mark registration must involve the provision of some service for which remuneration is provided, for example, by reference to 'gathering together various goods of different origin into an assortment, and offering them for sale in an homogeneous environment'.[48] While the outcome of this reference is eagerly sought, it need only be added that it seems wrong in principle that the interpretation of the meaning of words in the highly focused text of Directive 89/104 should be made to depend upon a definition in the EC Treaty which was not drafted with the registrability of trade marks in mind.

---

[43] This remains the position even today; see *Esprit International v Commissioner of the Japanese Patent Office* Heisei (gyo-ke) 105, 31 January 2001 and John Tessensohn and Shusaku Yamamoto, 'Japan Denies Trade Mark Registration for Retail Services' [2003] EIPR 381–3.
[44] *Giacomelli Sport SpA's application*, Case R 46/1998–2 [2000] ETMR 277 (OHIM).
[45] ibid, para 20.
[46] *Praktiker Bau- und HeimwerkemÄrkte AG*, reference by the Bundespatentgericht to the European Court of Justice, 15 October 2002.
[47] EC Treaty, art 50.
[48] See INTA submission in the *Praktiker* reference in support of the applicant's position, 20 March 2003 (www.inta.org/downloads/brief_praktiker.pdf).

C. Retail sales service marks

(3) Problems arising from the interrelation of trade marks for products and service marks for retail sales

If we may assume that service mark registration is available for retail sales, how do we resolve any problems that arise where a retailer, by virtue of his retail service registration, can control and dominate the choice (or use) of brand names for goods? In other words if I have registered the word mark SATURN as a retail service mark for a shop that specializes in selling hi-fi equipment, can I bar the registration by a third party of SATURN for such equipment? This problem exists in its mirror image too: if I manufacture SATURN hi-fi equipment, can I stop a retailer of such equipment calling his shop Saturn or registering that word as a trade mark?

16.46

In practice, the issue of potential confusion between the same or similar trade marks for goods and for equivalent retail services is capable of being resolved through the application of domestic laws of unfair competition and passing off. That this may be the case does not however mean that a consideration of trade mark law should not be undertaken since there is a matter of principle at stake. If the manufacture of SATURN hi-fis and the sale of hi-fis under the SATURN trade mark are 'similar' commercial activities and there is a likelihood of confusion between them, both Directive 89/104[49] and the CTM Regulation[50] will protect the earlier registrant against the activities of his later competitor. But, if this is so, it may appear that, by registering a trade mark only for goods, one may also be obtaining automatic protection for retail services.

16.47

A robust approach to this issue has been taken in Australia, where a majority of the Federal Court of Appeal held that the Woolworths retail chain could register the service mark WOOLWORTHS METRO, notwithstanding that many of the goods it sold, but did not make, contained the word METRO within their own trade marks.[51] According to the majority, since WOOLWORTHS was a famous mark, no one would associate METRO products with WOOLWORTHS METRO retail services. The dissenting judge considered that confusion might arise if consumers shortened WOOLWORTHS METRO to METRO alone. It is submitted that the majority's view is better: the decision to refuse registration should not be based on a contingency such as how consumers, rather than businesses, might come to use their trade marks.

16.48

(4) Retail sales, e-tail sales and modern technologies

It is logical to conclude that, to the extent that a service mark may be registered for

16.49

---

[49] Council Directive 89/104, arts 4(1)(b), 5(1)(b).
[50] Council Regulation 40/94, arts 8(1)(b), 9(1)(b).
[51] *Woolworths' trade mark application* [1999] FCA 1020 (Australian Federal Court of Appeal).

retail sales, it should be equally registrable where the service of providing retail sales is furnished by means other than that of the conventional shop. For example, where retail sales are effected both through high street stores and Internet websites, it would be anomalous if the sale of products through one medium was a 'service' for trade mark registration purposes but the sale of products through the other was not. This principle seems to have been accepted in Germany, where one division of the Bundespatentgericht has taken the view that the same rules that govern the registration of marks for conventional retail services also govern, for example, 'the sale and auction of goods through call centres' and that, accordingly such services must also specify the goods which were to be sold through those call centres.[52]

D. Celebrity trade marks

16.50 The definitions in TRIPs, Directive 89/104 and the CTM Regulation[53] all include 'personal names' in the non-exclusive list of things that constitute registrable signs. These definitions do not distinguish between the names of people who are celebrities and the names of those people are not. In truth, celebrity is a relative term and the law is wise to draw no clear divisions between personal names. If it did seek to draw distinctions between them, it might wish to recognize the special position of at least some of the following groupings:

(i) *universal celebrities*: some people are so well known that their names may be mentioned in practically any circles without the need to explain who they are, for example, United States President George Bush, Microsoft's Bill Gates and the popular entertainer Michael Jackson. On account of the dominance of American culture in the world's media, the preponderant majority of names in this category are American.

(ii) *regional or local celebrities*: for example, the singer JOHNNY HALLIDAY in France.

(iii) *celebrities within a narrow field of activity*: the name of Eric Bristow is synonymous with the game of darts,[54] in which he has been five times world champion and four times North American champion—but the vast majority of people who do not follow the game of darts have never heard of him.

(iv) *potential and former celebrities*: some people's moment of fame is yet to come (for example, child prodigies who may become the next generation of con-

---

[52] SMARTWEB trade mark application [2003] ETMR 272 (Bundespatentgericht): SMARTWEB not registrable for call centre sales services relating to unspecified goods, whether or not those services related to the Internet.
[53] See Chapter 4, especially paras 4.04–4.06.
[54] www.cyberdarts.com/pros/EricBristowBio.html.

D. Celebrity trade marks

cert violinists and pianists), while the fame of others is sadly and often irretrievably lost (many members of this class are sports and television personalities of previous generations). Sometimes one celebrity will eclipse the fame of another with the same name (George Bush today means the United States President; George Bush twelve years ago meant his father).

(v) *vicarious celebrities*: although the children or other relations of celebrities may have no claim to celebrity in their own right, their proximity to 'real' celebrities may enable them to enjoy vicarious celebrity status. An example of this was President Jimmy Carter's brother Billy.

(vi) *the real and assumed names of celebrities*: when, like a butterfly emerging from its chrysalis, Elton John sloughed off his pervious identity as Reg Dwight, he left behind him a name which could be a potentially useful commercial asset, as did the privacy-loving Greta Garbo (formerly Greta Louisa Gustafsson). Some celebrities are known only by their adopted name or pseudonym because we don't know their real identity: Jack the Ripper is a case in point.

(vii) *dead celebrities*: this category includes such diverse celebrities as Joan of Arc, Kemal Ataturk, St Thomas Aquinas, Maria Callas, Florence Nightingale, Yuri Gagarin, Attila the Hun and the Marquis de Sade.

(viii) *live celebrities*: for example, Celine Dion, Kofi Annan, Anna Kournikova, Michael Shumacher and the Pope.

(ix) *fictional celebrities*: this class contains some of the best-loved celebrity names, such as James Bond, Winnie-the-Pooh, Sherlock Holmes, Tintin, Bart Simpson, Paddington Bear, Mickey Mouse and Harry Potter.

(x) *celebrities from folklore*: this clubbable group includes such personalities as the Abominable Snowman, the Yeti, Bigfoot and Father Christmas.

(xi) *collective celebrities*: this category relates to people who may or may not enjoy fame as individuals but whose collaboration with others provides a separate and potentially enduring basis for their celebrity, for example, The Seven Samurai, The Magnificent Seven and The Beatles. Following the popularization of kung fu by the late Bruce Lee, the Shaolin monks from China's Henan Province found it necessary to protect and to control the exploitation of their identity through the registration of SHAOLIN as a trade mark.[55]

These groupings are not exclusive and a celebrity name may be classed within more than one of them. Although they have no inherent legal status, they are a convenient means for reviewing recent case law on celebrity trade marks. Some of them are accordingly discussed further below. **16.51**

---

[55] The SHAOLIN trade mark has now been registered for many classes of goods and services in the name of Henan Shaolin Temple Industrial Development Ltd; see *INTA Bulletin*, 15 November 2002, p 6.

16.52 While this chapter deals principally with names, celebrities may also seek to protect through trade mark registration a number of other features with which they may be famously associated. These features include their faces (or parts of faces, such as Mick Jagger's lips) or overall appearance, their voices[56] and items which are associated with them (for example, Charlie Chaplin's cane and boots or Groucho Marx's moustache). In general, though, it is names that tend to be the most enduring subject matter: unlike faces and other physical features, they do not normally change with time;[57] nor do they vary (in the case of actors, for example) in accordance with the celebrity's role.

(1) Live celebrities

16.53 A celebrity has no greater entitlement to register his name as a trade mark than does any other individual. In Europe the same criteria of distinctive character and graphical representation, both at Community level and under national law, apply to the registration of a celebrity's name as apply to any other sign. A court in the UK has emphasized that, since English law recognizes no right of personality, not even a celebrity can be said to own his own name while still alive and the fact that a name is both famous and unique does not mean that it automatically possesses distinctive character in relation to goods or services.[58]

16.54 In many jurisdictions all individuals—and not merely celebrities—enjoy a right of privacy.[59] Although rights in trade marks are clearly not intended to perform the function of buttressing the individual's right of privacy, it is plain that they may be invoked for that purpose, for example, so as to prevent the unauthorized use of a personal name by a third party who is publishing material of a private nature where the use of that name appears to serve as an endorsement of that material's contents. In the UK it has also been recognized that a right to the privacy of a celebrity wedding may be 'sold' to the highest bidder;[60] but this too is not strictly within the scope of registered trade mark law.

16.55 As in the case of any other trade mark application, a celebrity's name will not be registered if it is confusingly similar to an earlier trade mark which has been registered for the same or similar services. On this basis French inline blade star Taïg Khris could not register his unusual forename TAÏG for perfumes and cosmetics,

---

[56] The misappropriation of Bette Midler's voice singing the song 'Do You Want to Dance?' by the Ford Motor Company was held to be a violation of her right of publicity under Californian state law; see *Bette Midler v Ford Motor Co*, 849 F 2d 460 (9th Cir 1988).

[57] Cf Prince Roger Nelson, later known as Prince and subsequently as The Artist Formerly Known as Prince (being identified only by a logo).

[58] ELVISLY YOURS *trade mark* [1999] RPC 567 (CA).

[59] This right is enshrined eg in the Universal Declaration of Human Rights, art 12, and in the European Convention on Human Rights, art 8.

[60] *Douglas and others v Hello! Ltd* [2001] QB 967 (CA).

D. Celebrity trade marks

since another company had already registered TAIGA for the same products.[61] If however he had sought to register his full name TAÏG KHRIS, the application would have been quite likely to succeed.

16.56 It is the practice of the granting authorities in many jurisdictions to allow the registration of the name of a live celebrity only upon receipt of evidence that the application does not conflict with any rights which that celebrity may hold. Thus, for example, an application to register the word mark LUCIANO PAVAROTTI in Greece for perfumes and toiletries could not proceed until the tenor provided a declaration that the application was not in conflict with his own right of personality.[62]

(2) Dead celebrities[63]

16.57 Some dead celebrities are so much a part of a nation's cultural heritage that many people regard them as a national asset.[64] Wolfgang Amadeus Mozart has certainly acquired that status in Austria, where local traders appear to derive greater financial benefit and stability from the use of his name and likeness than he was able to enjoy in his lifetime through the composition of music; these traders jostle cheek-by-jowl with others who have succeeded in registering MOZART (or indeed AMADEUS) for certain classes of goods or services. The novelist Jane Austen has achieved much the same status in England, where an application to register JANE AUSTEN for toiletries was refused on the basis that members of the public, seeing the words 'Jane Austen' on those goods, would view them as indicating Jane Austen memorabilia rather than an indication of trade origin.[65] The Registry observed in this case that there appeared to be an inverse relationship between a dead celebrity's fame and the ability of his or her name to function as a trade mark: the more famous the name, the less likely the public would be to regard it, in the absence of evidence of distinctiveness acquired through use, as an indication of origin.

---

[61] *Khris, Taïg v INPI, ex p Loius Vuitton Malletier* [2001] ETMR 194 (Cour d'appel de Paris).

[62] *Guaber Srl v Greece* [1999] ETMR 879 (Athens Administrative First Instance Court).

[63] On some of the issues relating to rights in dead celebrities, see Jeremy Phillips, 'Life After Death' [1998] EIPR 201.

[64] This issue has been thoughtfully explored within the context of United States law by Nicholas J Jollymore, 'Expiration of the Right of Publicity: When Symbolic Names and Images Pass Into the Public Domain' (1994) 84 TMR 125. A wider review of the policy considerations is found in Rosemary J Coombe, 'Objects of Property and Subjects of Politics: Intellectual Property Laws and Democratic Dialogue' (1991) 69 Texas L Rev 1853.

[65] *Corsair Toiletries Ltd's application; opposition by Jane Austen Memorial Trust* [1999] ETMR 1038 (UK Trade Mark Registry). A similar result was achieved in *Executrices of the Estate of Diana Princess of Wales' application* [2001] ETMR 254 (UK Trade Mark Registry), where DIANA PRINCESS OF WALES was held unregistrable in the absence of evidence of acquired distinctiveness.

(a) Dead celebrity names: private ownership and public policy

16.58 In Poland[66] the registration of the name of a distinguished king, JAN III SOBIESKI, as a trade mark for cigarettes was refused on the basis that it was 'contrary to principles of social coexistence' by violating the respect due to a great national leader. The Supreme Court remitted the application for re-examination, stating that 'principles of social coexistence' were not immutable and that they had to be considered in the light of each individual case. Since the names of other notable Poles, including the composer and pianist Frederick Chopin, had been registered without apparently causing damage to the fabric of Polish society, there was no objection to the disputed application.

(b) Protection of dead and live celebrity names against non-identical signs

16.59 In the case of regular, non-celebrity trade marks, protection against the adverse use of similar trade marks is valuable because it enables consumers to make purchasing choices without the risk of being confused. Thus a customer who wishes to buy a MONTBLANC pen is entitled to make a choice which does not mislead him into believing that a BLANCMANGE pen would fit his requirement.

16.60 Where a celebrity name is registered as a trade mark, the same degree of protection is accorded to the trade mark owner by law. In practice, however, the level of protection for celebrity names may be narrower than for other kinds of mark. This is because the relevant consumer is familiar with the conceptual meaning of the name as a whole and, if he is drawn to purchase products bearing the name, he will in general notice variations such as non-equivalent spellings. On that basis, he is less likely, as a matter of fact, to be confused. Thus, for example, a customer who sees the word mark PQASSO on teaching materials may call in mind the fact that the word is similar to the PICASSO trade mark but would be quite unlikely to link it with the artist Pablo Picasso in his guise as a posthumous trading entity.[67] Likewise, although the two marks are similar, a consumer who sees the PICARO trade mark on motor vehicles will be unlikely to view it as being connected to Picasso.[68] As an OHIM Board of Appeal said in this case,

> [A]ny phonetic and/or visual similarity between the two signs is overcome by the conceptual impact of the name PICASSO ...
>
> As a matter of fact the inherent distinctive character of the sign PICASSO is so high that any perceptible difference may be apt to exclude any likelihood of confusion on the side of the consumers concerned.[69]

---

[66] *JAN III SOBIESKI trade mark* [1999] ETMR 874 (Supreme Court, Poland).

[67] *Farley's application; opposition by the joint ownership on the monopoly of the intellectual property attached to the work of Pablo Picasso* [2002] ETMR 336 (UK Trade Mark Registry).

[68] *DaimlerChrysler Aktiengesellschaft's application; opposition of Succession Picasso*, Decision 2/2001 [2002] ETMR 346 (OHIM Opposition Division), upheld on appeal in *Succession Picasso v DaimlerChrysler Aktiengesellschaft*, R 0247/2001–3 [2002] ETMR 953 (OHIM Board of Appeal).

[69] *Succession Picasso v DaimlerChrysler Aktiengesellschaft*, R 0247/2001–3 [2002] ETMR 953, paras 19, 20 (OHIM).

D. Celebrity trade marks

(c) Vehicles for the protection of dead celebrities' names

16.61 In the absence of a trade mark registration, which may be difficult to secure on account of widespread use by third parties, the names of long-dead kings and heroes are public property. It is increasingly the case however that the names of modern deceased celebrities are protected by trade marks and other intellectual property rights. This happens where a trust or other body is established (whether during the celebrity's life or thereafter) for the exploitation of the celebrity's name and likeness or the preservation of the celebrity's reputation. In such circumstances there is often an acute tension between the trust's desire to control the manner of exploitation of the celebrity's image and the public's desire to claim what it regards as its own. After all, since it is usually the support of the public that makes a celebrity into a celebrity, the public may feel that it has already paid for the privilege of exploiting the celebrity's name or likeness.

16.62 Case law has demonstrated that the establishment of a trust or similar body to administer and exploit personality rights may not always be able to protect deceased personalities against trade mark registrations. This is because the body in question cannot have a better right to object to trade mark applications than did the original celebrity. Thus when the Hebrew University of Jerusalem, to whom the late Albert Einstein had bequeathed the use of his name and likeness, opposed an application to register as a CTM the word Café EinStein for foods and beverages, an OHIM Opposition Division found that, despite Einstein's immense fame as a scientist, neither his name nor his likeness were 'signs used in the course of trade' upon which the opposition could be founded.[70] A completely different outcome relating to the same personality was achieved in Japan, where an application to cancel the stylized mark EINSTEIN for clothes succeeded on the violation of norms of public order and morality.[71]

(3) Celebrities' signatures

16.63 The signature of a celebrity, like any other signature, is registrable as a trade mark. An argument that copyright exists in a celebrity's signature and that the owner of the copyright has the right to prevent a third party registering the celebrity's name as a trade mark was not accepted in the UK: even if copyright subsists in a signature (which is by no means certain), a signature is a figurative sign and the rights in it vest primarily in its appearance, not its content.[72]

---

[70] *Einstein Stadtcafé Verwaltungs- und Betriebsgesellschaft mbH's application; opposition of the Hebrew University of Jerusalem*, Case 506/2000 [2000] ETMR 952 (OHIM).
[71] *Re Einstein* [2001] EIPR N-136 (Trade Mark Opposition Board, Japan); John Tessensohn and Shusaku Yamamoto, 'Piratical Japanese Trade Mark Registrations Invalidated on Public Order and Morality Grounds' [2003] EIPR 203.
[72] *Anne Frank Stichting's trade marks* [1998] ETMR 687 (UK Trade Mark Registry).

(4) Collective celebrities

16.64 A former member of a pop group can perform under his own name, which he may register as a trade mark. Where that group's name has been registered as a trade mark, he may not however perform under that name without the trade mark owner's authorization.[73]

(5) Fictional celebrities

16.65 Some of the best-loved trade marks of our time have been fictional celebrities: TARZAN, JAMES BOND, LUKE SKYWALKER, LARA CROFT. Even WIMPY and JEEP were originally coined as names for fictional characters in *Popeye* stories.[74]

16.66 In contrast with the relatively narrow protection accorded to the names of real people, whether dead or alive, against the registration or use of non-identical names,[75] the protection enjoyed by fictional celebrities would appear to be somewhat wider. Thus the proprietor of the HARRY POTTER trade mark was able to persuade a Dutch court both that the little wizard's name was visually and phonetically similar to the girl's name 'Tanja Grotter'[76] and that HARRY POTTER would suffer the indignity of dilution at Ms Grotter's hands.

16.67 Fictional celebrities, like their real-life counterparts, may fade with time. Long John Silver was a colourful and (to children) quite scary character in Robert Louis Stevenson's *Treasure Island*. Indeed, in some parts of the world the book may even still be read. Yet when an application was made to register LONG JOHN SILVER'S as a CTM for foods, confections and restaurant franchises, the OHIM Opposition Division made no reference to the mark's distinguished literary provenance.[77] Indeed, the only claim to fame was made by the proprietor of an earlier trade mark, JOHN SILVER, which was registered in Sweden for cigarettes and which, the opponent pleaded, was a famous mark under article 6*bis* of the Paris Convention.

16.68 While the unauthorized use of a pop group's name as part of the title of a book is regarded as a descriptive use of a trade mark and not as a use in the course of trade,

---

[73] Cf *Manton and others v Van Day and others* [2001] ETMR 1114 (HC) where an application for interim injunctive relief against an allegedly unauthorized use of the BUCK'S FIZZ trade mark failed following more than five years' acquiescence. See also *Brother Records Inc v Jardine* CV 99–3829 HLH, 28 January 2003 (9th Cir 2003), in which the BEACH BOYS trade mark was not automatically available for use by former band members.

[74] Jeremy Phillips, 'Elzie Segar, Intellectual Property Creator Extraordinary' [1986] EIPR 373.

[75] See paras 16.59–16.60 above.

[76] *Rowling v Uitgeverji Byblos* [2003] ECDR 245.

[77] *Long John Silver's Inc's application; opposition of Swedish Match Sverige AB*, Case 458/2000 [2001] ETMR 120 (OHIM).

D. Celebrity trade marks

the same need not be said of fictional names.[78] Thus the use of the name Tarzan in the defendant's copyright-infringing video cassette title *Tarzan van den Apen*[79] was held to have infringed the trade mark TARZAN. The trade mark proprietor itself used the TARZAN trade mark in the titles of various books and films, to indicate products which contained stories of Tarzan, his girlfriend Jane and a community of monkeys; the defendant's use of the word 'Tarzan' fulfilled exactly the same function.[80]

A more difficult issue arising from the TARZAN case is that of whether a fictional character can attain 'generic' status. The court rejected the defendant's submission that 'Tarzan' had become generic for an '(often supposedly simple-minded) muscular man', notwithstanding a dictionary definition brought in support of its position. However, in the German WINNETOU case[81] it was held that Winnetou, a character in a book by Karl May in which copyright expired, could not be registered as a trade mark since it had become evocative of the epitome of a noble Indian chief and thus needed to be kept free for use by competitors. **16.69**

Where fictional characters stem from the same television programme or book and are associated with it, it will not be possible for a third party to register the name of any of those characters as a trade mark without creating the suggestion that the use of that trade mark is in some way connected with the book itself. Thus registration of the characters ZUKINIS IN BIKINIS would falsely suggest a link to the Australian television programme Bananas in Pyjamas in which the Zukinis featured.[82] **16.70**

(6) Events as celebrities

Strictly speaking an event cannot be regarded as a celebrity, since it is not a person. Events can however be promoted and exploited through the use of merchandise in much the same manner as the names and likenesses of celebrities. Further, the identity of an individual and of an event may coalesce. For example, where merchandised produce is sold to mark the coronation of a monarch, a royal wedding, a Papal visit or a farewell concert performance by an ageing rock icon, it may be unclear whether it is the event, the personality or the combination of them both which drives the sale of commemorative goods. **16.71**

---

[78] *Bravado Merchandising Services Ltd v Mainstream Publishing (Edinburgh) Ltd* [1996] FSR 205 (Court of Session, Scotland): use of WET WET WET trade mark not infringed by book title *A Sweet Little Mystery—Wet Wet Wet—The Inside Story*.
[79] Dutch for 'Tarzan of the Apes'.
[80] *Edgar Rice Burroughs Inc v Beukenoord BV and others* [2001] ETMR 1300 (Court of Appeal, Amsterdam).
[81] *ZDF v Karl-May-Verlag*, 5 December 2002 (Bundesgerichtshof).
[82] See Baker & McKenzie Australian Trade Mark Update, February 2003, p 3.

16.72 There is little civil case law on the status of events within Europe. An Indian court has sensibly noted that there is no right of publicity in the International Cricket World Cup since it is an event and not a person.[83]

E. Conclusion

16.73 The various segments of this chapter, dealing with the pharmaceutical sector, the retail sales sector and celebrities' rights in their own names, do not only illustrate that trade mark law is capable of serving three quite disparate sectors of the economy. They also illustrate the manner in which trade mark law is able to adapt itself to the needs and requirements of each sector.

16.74 The selection of these three sectors of commerce was based not only on their economic or cultural importance but also on the availability of interesting case law to illustrate the manner in which trade mark law adapts to a particular sector. If other sectors had been analysed, such as fashion products and accessories, fast-moving consumer foods, industrial chemicals, travel and leisure services or office equipment, the same facility for adaptation would still be discernible.

---

[83] *ICC (Development) International v Philips*, 31 January 2003 (High Court, Delhi).

17

TRADE MARKS ON THE INTERNET

A.	**Introduction**	
	A safe haven for cybersquatters	
	The moral of the story	17.01
B.	**Use of another's trade mark as a domain name**	17.02
	(1) What sort of infringing act is it to add a '.TLD' to another's trade mark?	17.05
	(2) The defence of use of a trade mark as a descriptive term	17.08
	(3) Is the use of the trade mark in the domain name a use 'in the course of trade'?	17.09
	(4) Use of a trade mark in a post-domain path	17.11
	(5) Factors which tilt the odds in favour of the trade mark owner	17.15
	(6) Factors which tilt the odds against the trade mark owner	17.20
	(7) Liability for allocation of infringing domain names	17.25
	(8) Trade mark-friendly domains	17.26
	(9) The United States approach	17.27
	(10) Resolution of domain name disputes under ICANN and similar rules	17.32
	(a) The complainant's 'trade mark' need not be registered	17.36
	(b) 'Sucks' and other critical or hostile domain names	17.37
	(c) Registration of 'near misses'	17.39
	(d) Appropriation of a 'famous mark' is presumed to be evidence of bad faith	17.42
	(e) Proving bad faith where a trade mark is also an ordinary word	17.45
	(f) Other circumstantial evidence of bad faith	17.47
	(g) Reverse domain-name hijacking	17.48
	(h) Evidence of confusion	17.49
C.	**Use of another's trade mark on a web page**	17.51
	(1) In which country is the use of another's trade mark on a website a 'use in the course of trade'?	17.52
	(2) Use of another's trade mark in order to sell the goods of the trade mark owner	17.53
	(3) Unauthorized use of advertisements	17.54
	(a) Genuine advertisements	17.55
	(b) Subvertisements	17.57
	(4) Use of another's trade mark as part of a copyright notice	17.63
D.	**Use of another's trade mark as a metatag**	17.64
	(1) Permissible uses of another's trade mark as a metatag	17.67
	(2) Impermissible uses of another's trade mark as a metatag	17.69
E.	**Use of another's trade mark as the name of an Internet service provider**	17.73
F.	**Conclusion**	17.74

Chapter 17: Trade Marks on the Internet

A. Introduction

A safe haven for cybersquatters[1]

Trade mark owners have occupied themselves for much of the past few years chasing cybersquatters. Like elephants trying to swat gnats, they expend an amount of time and effort which is disproportionate to the benefits attained and often hit themselves harder than they hit their intended foe. All sorts of relief against cybersquatters has been tried: civil and criminal litigation, arbitration and mediation, ignoring them, buying them out—but, as with gnats, so too with cybersquatters, the relief is only temporary and they soon come back again in even greater numbers. Worse still, each time they return they have learnt a few more tricks to use against the unfortunate trade mark proprietor: they are exercising their right of fair comment, they have a constitutionally protected freedom of expression, their name just so happens to be Mr Pepsicola, your trade mark is a generic term in their country, they aren't competing with you but are using the site for their own perfectly inoffensive activity, and so on.

The situation has been made worse by the decision to create and operate a new set of generic top-level domains (gTLDs).[2] This may possibly be inspired by the misbelief that the reason why everyone wants to register domain names with eBay or PlayStation is that there are just not enough names to go round. Accordingly let's have .biz, .info, .name and so on, to give the punters more choice. But this approach will not distract the cybersquatters: they want a domain name with COKE, NIKE or whatever and the growth of new gTLDs isn't going to change that fact. The provision of more gTLDs just makes trade marks appear in the eyes of the cybersquatters as a larger and more vulnerable target.

Having said all this, we should actually recognize that those people who routinely abuse and defile trade marks *off* the Internet, without attracting anything other than the admiration of their friends and the opprobrium of their enemies, must be given the opportunity to do the same *on* the Internet, under carefully controlled conditions in which any possible damage to trade mark owners is strictly limited. But how can this be done?

The solution to the problem is simple. Let us provide a new set of gTLDs—let us call them the 'safe haven' gTLDs—specifically for the benefit of all the cybersquatters, cybersuckers, nerds, geeks, pervs, twerps (or whatever) whose misplaced or unwanted attention so embarrasses trade mark owners. These new gTLDs would be as follows:

.not For websites having absolutely nothing to do with the trade mark owner (for example, chanelno5.not indicates a website for smellalike perfumes which are guaranteed not to have been manufactured by CHANEL. Also, for film buffs there is also waynesworld.not);

.haha As the name suggests, for websites poking fun at the trade mark or its owner (for example, benetton.haha, for photographs of the sort of people unfortunate enough to end up in BENETTON's shock advertisements actually wearing BENETTON clothes);

.love For those of us who can't control our feelings (for example, princessdiana.love, bigmac.love, vwbeetle.love: need one say more?);

---

[1] Based on the author's Opinion published in *Trademark World*, April 2003, p 66.

[2] In November 2000 seven new gTLDs were proposed: .biz, .info, .name, .pro, .aero, .coop and .museum. These came into operation during 2001–2.

B. Use of another's trade mark as a domain name

.hate As above, *mutatis mutandis*.

.pirate For serious counterfeits and unauthorized replica models of trade mark protected products (for example, rolex.pirate for fake ROLEX watches made by shifty entrepreneurs, or bmwbrakepad.pirate—a godsend for any dealer who has occasionally been tricked into buying the legitimate product).

.outlaw For unauthorized imports, repackaged or reconditioned versions of the real thing (thus levis.outlaw for the sale of legitimate LEVI'S products in Europe at United States prices, or viagra.outlaw for supplies of the genuine article which passed their use-by date while heading through the Gobi desert on a caravan towards their eventual resale in Amsterdam).

No trade mark owner would be entitled to challenge the sanctity of any of these 'safe haven' names or even to confer any degree of legitimacy on it. Only pirates, outlaws and other undesirables would be able to assert a higher degree of entitlement. Arbitration would be according to the rules of the International Committee for Accessing New Technologies (ICANT). For all of these gTLDs there would be not a 'sunrise' period but a 'sunset' period. At the end of this period any cybersquatters' sites which remain with .com, .net and .org gTLDs would be automatically 'shunted' to the nearest available safe-haven gTLD.

These sites will of course be rigorously policed by trade mark owners. This is fine and proper, since it is the trade mark owner who suffers when freedom of speech is exercised in a manner which is irresponsible. So long as everyone knows what .not, .pirate and the rest actually mean, no ordinary consumer or Internet user is likely to be duped into what they are for. Who knows, we might even see a decrease in time, effort and money spent in chasing cybersquatters.

The moral of the story

17.01 The Internet is a sector of activity in which trade mark owners and trade mark users have suddenly found themselves in conflict. The Internet was not designed for the convenience of trade mark owners. Nor was trade mark law specifically directed towards the circumstances in which trade marks are used on the Internet. The story seeks to illustrate the sort of problems faced by trade mark owners when they are faced with unconventional foes but have only conventional weapons with which to deal with them. This chapter looks at several Internet-related problems in which some fundamental assumptions of trade mark law and practice have been challenged.

B. Use of another's trade mark as a domain name

17.02 In this context we address problems which are mainly met by word marks since they are, at the present state of Internet technology, the only trade marks which are capable of being used, in the form in which they are registered, as part of a domain name. But this does not mean that proprietors of other marks do not also face problems. For example, where a trade mark is a logo, a colour, a product shape or even a sound, a domain name which incorporates a verbal description of it may be seen as a potential act of infringement.

17.03 Trade mark law in Europe, unlike that of the United States,[3] makes no special provision for the use of another's trade mark as part of a domain name, leaving it to the courts to apply general principles of trade mark law to the specific circumstances of the Internet. It has been argued that this legally conservative approach is correct[4] and that the general principles which govern trade mark infringement should be adequate to rise to the challenge of dealing with uses of a trade mark in any context which interfere with the essential function of the trade mark. The case law reviewed below would suggest that this conservative approach has so far been justified.

17.04 When considering the issues discussed under this heading, readers may wish to consider asking whether the result would have been different if the domain name complained of, in suitably transfigured format, had appeared as the title of a book, an advertising brochure or in some other paper-based format. Although it is quicker and cheaper for a cybersquatter to set up a website under the name 'esso-sucks.com' than to publish a book or pamphlet called *Esso Sucks*, and although the Internet enables far more potential readers to access it, the condition for legal action in each case is the same: the owner of a trade mark objects to the use of his trade mark as part of a product which identifies him as an object of criticism. The same applies where the object of the exercise is not to apply political or economic pressure but to gain commercial advantage. For example, if I propose to sell second-hand and reconditioned FORD motor cars, is there any difference in legal terms between me setting up a cheapfordsforall.com website and printing a price list headed 'Cheap Fords for All?'. If the Aristotelian ideal of treating like cases in a like manner is an objective of our legal system, we should ask whether our application of trade mark law to the recent threats of cybersquatting and domain name abuse is consistent with the approach which we would have taken to similar threats posed by more familiar technologies.

(1) What sort of infringing act is it to add a '.TLD' to another's trade mark?

17.05 The format which is common to every domain name is that it consists of one or more word, each of which is followed by a dot, which in turn is followed by a top-level domain (TLD). For example, in the name sidney.sausages.com, 'sidney' is a third-level domain, 'sausages' is a second-level domain and '.com' is the TLD. Where a trade mark is registered for clothing and a competitor appropriates that very trade mark as the name of its website as a gateway for the sale of clothing by adding a TLD, the trade mark proprietor must consider his options. If his trade mark is registered for commercial activities in the same line of business as the defendant, he will have to proceed on the basis of a Type 1 infringement ('same

---

[3] Discussed at paras 17.27–17.31 below.
[4] Spyros Maniatis, 'Trade Mark Law and Domain Names: Back to Basics?' [2002] EIPR 397.

B. Use of another's trade mark as a domain name

mark, same goods or services'):[5] the TLD would not be viewed as part of the trade mark but as part of an address.[6] In this context it does not matter whether the defendant uses the zara.it website as a gateway for the sale of ZARA clothes or for the sale of the products of its competitors.[7] If however the defendant's website and activities relate to goods or premises which are quite different from those of the trade mark owner, a Type 3 or Type 4 infringement action ('same or similar mark, entirely different goods or services') should be considered.[8]

17.06 If a TLD or other matter is added to the claimant's trade mark, the defendant's domain name will infringe the claimant's registered trade mark if it is regarded as being similar to it, in which case a Type 2 infringement claim must be considered ('similar mark, similar goods or services, plus likelihood of confusion').[9] In this context the PETA case in the United States has shown how wide the concept of confusion may be stretched in order to find an undeserving defendant liable for trade mark infringement.[10]

17.07 Where a domain name which incorporates another's registered trade mark has not been used, at least one court has ruled that an unused domain cannot be regarded as goods or services which are 'similar' to those for which the trade mark was registered.[11] If an unused domain name does not constitute 'similar' goods or services, does it then constitute 'dissimilar' goods or services? One British court has indicated its preparedness to treat it as such, though some doubt was expressed as to whether the retention of an unused domain name was a use 'in the course of trade'.[12]

(2) The defence of use of a trade mark as a descriptive term

17.08 Can the defendant justify its use of the trade mark in the domain name by maintaining that the use is descriptive, in the same way in which the use of a metatag for a purely descriptive purpose is justified?[13] After all, if you keep bees, should not the use of the word 'beehive' be available to you for use in your domain name even

---

[5] On Type 1 infringement, see Chapter 7 (particularly paras 7.10–7.15).
[6] *Buy.Com Inc's application*, Case R 638/2000–4 [2002] ETMR 540 (OHIM).
[7] See eg *Inditex SA v Compagna Mercantile SRL* [2002] ETMR 9 (Tribunal of Turin): ZARA trade mark infringed by use of zara.it website.
[8] On Type 3 and 4 infringements, see Chapter 7 (particularly paras 7.10–7.15).
[9] On Type 2 infringement, see Chapter 7 (particularly paras 7.10–7.15).
[10] In *People for the Ethical Treatment of Animals v Doughney* 263 F 3d 359, 60 USPQ 2d 1209 (4th Cir 2001), the defendant's registration of www.peta.org and its subsequent use in an alleged parody promotion of the activities of 'People Eating Tasty Animals' was held to infringe the claimant's trade mark.
[11] *Zewillis v Baan Nordic A/S*, Case B-3553–97, 26 November 1999 (Østre Landsret, Denmark).
[12] *British Telecommunications plc and others v One in a Million Ltd and others* [1999] ETMR 61, 92–3 (CA).
[13] See *Monster Board BV v VNU Business Publications BV* [2002] ETMR 1 (Court of Appeal, The Hague), discussed below.

if the word is also the trade mark of an extremely well-known department store?[14] The answer is no, where the trade mark is an arbitrary or coined term which has no use in the language of the jurisdiction other than as a trade mark. Thus while one may argue that the use of the APPLE trade mark in a domain name indicates something to do with apples, one cannot argue (as the defendant did in *Rolex v Fogtmann*[15]) that the use of ROLEX in the rolex.dk domain indicates something to do with Rolexes as a genre rather than with the business activities of the Rolex company. Distinguishing the ECJ decision in *BMW v Deenik* which permitted the use of the BMW trade mark in advertisements for the repair or servicing of BMWs, the court observed that the use of another's trade mark in a domain name is more than a mere description of a business: it is the use of that mark as a 'shop façade' through which to attract business.[16] The *Rolex v Fogtmann* court also dismissed the notion that the defendant could justify use of the ROLEX trade mark because he was dealing with second-hand watches in which the trade mark rights were exhausted.[17]

(3) Is the use of the trade mark in the domain name a use 'in the course of trade'?

17.09 Since businesses use the Internet for commercial purposes it would be simple to conclude that any use of a trade mark as part of the domain name of a business website is a use 'in the course of trade'[18] and therefore a trade mark infringement. This assumption however requires the qualification that use, in any given country, depends upon the circumstances of the case: what was the intention of the website owner and what would an Internet user assume on seeing the website?[19] Thus the use of the name 'Crate and Barrel' by an Irish store-owner in the domain name crateandbarrel.ie was not regarded as a use of the CRATE AND BARREL trade mark which the claimant, a United States business, had registered in the UK. Since there was no evidence that the defendant traded, or indeed sought to trade, in the UK, the accessibility of its website to British shoppers could not lead the

---

[14] *Magazijn 'De Bijenkorf' BV v Accelerated Information BV* [2002] ETMR 676 (WIPO): the respondent rather spoilt this argument by using the website not for bee-keeping but for pornography.
[15] *Montres Rolex SA v Fogtmann* [2001] ETMR 424 (Maritime and Commercial Court, Denmark).
[16] *Bayerische Motorenwerke AG (BMW) and BMW Nederland BV v Deenik*, Case C-63/97 [1999] ETMR 339 (ECJ).
[17] A similar argument was rejected by the Moscow Arbitration Court in *Eastman Kodak Company Corp v Grundul and the Russian Scientific and Research Institute for the Development of Public Networks* [2002] ETMR 776. Cf *Bravilor Bonamat BV v Boumann Hotelbenodigdhenden BV*, 10 August 2000 (2002) 92 TMR 273 (District Court, Amsterdam), where the court held that since the claimant's rights in BRAVILOR coffee machines had been exhausted and since the claimant already owned the bravilor.com domain name there was no absolute necessity for it to have the bravilor.nl domain name as well.
[18] Council Directive 89/104, art 5(1); Council Regulation 40/94, art 9(1).
[19] *Euromarket Designs Incorporated v Peters and another* [2000] ETMR 1025 (HC).

B. Use of another's trade mark as a domain name

court to conclude that there had been a use of CRATE AND BARREL in the course of trade in the UK.

An Italian court has stated that a domain name is a 'distinctive sign used as a means of commercial communication' and that, therefore, the use of a domain name is an activity which is governed by Italian trade marks law.[20] The same court has laid down some principles for comparing registered trade marks with domain names in order to ascertain whether the use of the domain name is likely to cause confusion: (i) since domain names can only consist of numbers and letters, figurative elements of the trade mark should be disregarded when making a comparison; (ii) the fact that a domain name has a top-level code is not in itself sufficient ground for establishing that there is no confusion; (iii) 'initial interest' confusion[21] where an Internet user alights upon the defendant's site, realizes that it is not the site he was looking for and then goes elsewhere, is sufficient confusion for the purposes of trade mark infringement since it can cause an undue advantage to the domain name owner or prejudice the interests of the trade mark owner. 17.10

(4) Use of a trade mark in a post-domain path

When we think of an Internet domain name, our thoughts tend to focus on the name's 'pure' form, the form in which we can most easily remember it (for example, www.inta.org for the International Trademark Association), but each web page has its own address and in many cases that address contains a good deal of information to the right of the TLD. For example, at www.inta.org/press/pr2003_06.shtml we find news of the establishment of an INTA special committee to review the law on famous trade marks in the light of the VICTORIA'S SECRET case. We have seen how the use of another's trade mark in the main part of the domain name may infringe the rights in that trade mark, but would the inclusion of the same mark in the stream of information which follows the TLD (or 'post-domain path') also infringe that trade mark? 17.11

This question was considered in a United States case in which the claimant company's LAP TRAVELER trade mark was included by an Internet-based sales company, a2z Mobile Office Solutions, in the address www.a2zsolutions.com/desks/floor/laptraveler/dkfl-1t.htm, this being the page on its website from which it sold LAP TRAVELER portable computer stands. One of the former co-owners of the claimant company then produced a new portable computer stand, THE MOBILE DESK The claimant ceased doing business with a2z and asked it to remove references to LAP TRAVELER from its website. A2z did not do so, but sold THE 17.12

---

[20] *Playboy Enterprises Inc v Giannattasio* WTLR, 30 May 2003 (Court of Naples).
[21] See Chapter 10, paras 10.125–10.130.

MOBILE DESK products from the original LAP TRAVELER web page. The claimant's action for trade mark infringement failed. In the opinion of the court the presence of the LAP TRAVELER in the web page's post-domain path was unlikely to cause any confusion because, in that location, it was not going to be regarded as suggesting an indication of source: the post-domain path is merely an indicator as to how the website's data is organized with the host computer's files.[22]

17.13 It is unclear whether a court would take the same view when applying the European standard of confusion. Since both parties were using the same trade mark (LAP TRAVELER) to indicate the same goods (portable computer stands), the court would have to consider whether the defendant's use was 'in the course of trade' and, as such, whether such use interfered with the ability of the claimant's trade mark to perform its essential function as a guarantor of the origin of the goods. At the very least, the use of laptraveler within the post-domain path could have the effect of weakening or even genericizing the distinctive character of that trade mark by designating laptraveler as the part of the domain from which THE MOBILE DESK products were sold.

17.14 Can a reference to a trade mark as part of a post-domain path really have any effect on the trade mark's function as a guarantor of origin if no one actually pays any attention to the post-domain path? It could be argued that most people navigate their way by following a link from the main website and so will never enter the post-domain path into the address bar (eg rather than entering www.oup.co.uk/aliceinwonderland, most people would first go to www.oup.co.uk and follow successive links for children's books, Lewis Carroll and *Alice in Wonderland*). Other people may not use the address bar at all but find their way to what they want through search engines, with the result that their attention will never be drawn to the post-level domain name unless they happen to glance upwards. Against this, it should be remembered that the defendant's use of LAP TRAVELER was in a commercial context: if purchasers of THE MOBILE DESK products over the Internet were to print paper copies of their orders, sales notes, delivery notes or acknowledgments of payments from www.a2zsolutions.com/desks/ floor/laptraveler/dkfl-1t.htm, they would generate permanent commercial records relating to THE MOBILE DESK products but which bore the word laptraveler.

(5) Factors which tilt the odds in favour of the trade mark owner

17.15 The trade mark is strengthened by being also the proprietor's company name. The trade mark owner's claim against the domain name user will be stronger where (i) the trade mark is also the owner's company name and (ii) the two parties are competitors, since any use of the domain name will more powerfully suggest a

---

[22] *Interactive Products Corp v a2z Mobile Office Solutions Inc* 326 F 3d 687 (6th Cir 2003).

B. Use of another's trade mark as a domain name

connection with the trade mark owner. Thus where a company, Format, was also the proprietor of the FORMAT trade mark, the Austrian Supreme Court had no difficulty in ordering interim relief against a competitor in the publishing industry who registered the format.at domain name.[23] The same principle works the other way round, where the claimant owns a trade mark and a closely related domain name and seeks to stop a competitor turning that trade mark into a company name.[24]

The domain name registrant has no obvious reason for selecting the name. If a party registers a domain name to which he has no obvious entitlement and which he is unlikely to be able to use at all without attracting legal action, it will be difficult for him to persuade a court that he is entitled to keep and use it to the detriment of the trade mark owner. In other words, if your name is John Travolta, you have at least some excuse for seeking to incorporate john.travolta into your domain name, but if your name is John Smith, the choice of 'travolta' may seem a trifle surprising. In the UK, irrespective of whether the registration of a domain name is an actionable trade mark infringement, such registration may constitute an 'instrument of fraud' which may be restrained or remedied through an action for passing off.[25] The 'instrument of fraud' argument should be even stronger where the choice of that name relates not only to a well-known business but where the domain name registrant has registered the name hours after a significant event such as the announcement of a merger[26] or the launch of a new product.[27]   17.16

The defendant practises the serial registration of trade marks as domain names. Where a trade mark owner can show that there is a pattern of behaviour on the part of the defendant which involves the serial registration of domain names including the trade marks of other traders, the domain name registrant will find it more difficult to maintain his entitlement to such a domain name.[28]   17.17

---

[23] *Format Gesellschaft mbH and another v Wirtschafts-Trend Zeitschriftenverlags Ges mbH* [2002] ETMR 472 (Supreme Court, Austria).
[24] See *Advernet SL v Ozucom SL* [1999] ETMR 1037 (First Instance Court, Bilbao), in which the proprietor of the OZÚ trade mark and ozu.es domain name obtained injunctive relief and damages against an ex-employee who registered Ozucom as a company name and ozu.com as its corresponding domain name.
[25] *British Telecommunications plc and others v One in a Million Ltd and others* [1999] ETMR 61 (HC, CA).
[26] See *Perfetti SpA, Van Melle NV and Van Melle Nederland BV v MIC* [2002] ETMR 52 (WIPO), where the respondent registered the domain names perfetti-vanmelle.com and perfettivanmelle.com just two days after the merger of the owners of the PERFETTI and VAN MELLE trade marks.
[27] *Format Gesellschaft mbH and another v Wirtschafts-Trend Zeitschriftenverlags Ges mbH* [2002] ETMR 472 (Supreme Court, Austria): defendant's domain name registered three hours and 55 minutes after claimant's product launch.
[28] *British Telecommunications plc and others v One in a Million Ltd and others* (n 25 above), where the defendant company had registered a string of domain names incorporating the names of well-known shops and enterprises.

17.18 **The defendant uses the contested site for the sale of products not supplied by the trade mark owner.** A domain name registrant is entitled to use, as part of a domain name, a trade mark by which a product is known if he is using that website for the purpose of selling that product, so long as that use is not a dishonest use or a use which causes confusion.[29] Where however he registers a domain name such as davidoffshop.com for the purpose of selling goods only a small fraction of which are connected to the DAVIDOFF trade mark, the National Arbitration Forum has held the use of that domain name to be in bad faith.[30] In this context there does not appear to be any distinction between the domain name registrant who sells goods which are primarily sourced from the trade mark owner and one who sells goods which are derived from parallel trade or second-hand sources.

17.19 **The registration of the domain name appears to be for the purpose of blocking the trade mark owner's own registration.** In a situation in which the domain name registrant appears to have registered a domain name in order to prevent a trade mark owner gaining it for himself, the circumstances may point to his having committed an act of unfair competition.[31]

(6) Factors which tilt the odds against the trade mark owner

17.20 **The weakly distinctive or non-distinctive nature of the trade mark.** In an Austrian case the claimant, proprietor of the JUSLINE trade mark for the provision of legal services and other goods and services, commenced proceedings against the defendant, a company which registered the jusline.com domain name and offered to sell or lease it to the claimant, alleging that this was a form of blackmail.[32] The Supreme Court dismissed the claimant's appeal on the basis that JUSLINE was not a 'freely invented word' and that it had been registered as a trade mark without proof of its having acquired distinctiveness through use. Since the average Internet user would regard the word 'jusline' as a combination of 'jus' (the Latin for 'law') and 'line' (being a connection to the Internet), the word would not be viewed as a trade mark.

17.21 A similar issue was addressed where FREEBIES, a United States trade mark since 1977 for periodicals carrying information on free mail-order offerings, had been allowed to lapse and was subsequently re-registered. During the period in which the trade mark had lapsed, a registrant obtained the freebie.com domain name and used it for a computer system for tracking retail transactions. Overturning the

---

[29] *Ty Inc v Perryman,* 4 October 2002 (7th Cir Court of Appeals).
[30] *Davidoff & Cie SA v Muriel* WTLR, 4 April 2003 (NAF, majority decision); see also *Philip Morris Inc v Tsypkin* WTLR, 7 May 2003 (WIPO), where discount-marlboro-cigarettes.com was used for the sale of the products of Philip Morris's competitors.
[31] See eg *Format Gesellschaft mbH and another v Wirtschafts-Trend Zeitschriftenverlags Ges mbH* [2002] ETMR 472; *Magnetics v Diskcopy,* CF 751/00 (Tel Aviv District Court 2001).
[32] *Jusline GmbH v O****** [1999] ETMR 173 (Supreme Court, Austria).

B. Use of another's trade mark as a domain name

National Arbitration Forum's decision that the domain name should be returned to the trade mark owner, a Virginia court[33] considered that the trade mark FREEBIES had lost whatever distinctiveness it had and could be regarded as generic. Accordingly FREEBIES was not entitled to receive the special protection of trade marks under the Lanham Act.[34]

The existence of an obvious reason for selecting the name. Nestlé, as proprietors of the MAGGI trade mark, were right to be vigilant as to the unauthorized use of that trade mark as part of a third-party domain name—but Romeo Maggi had a good and obvious reason to register his surname in the domain name maggi.com.[35] Trade marks which are invented words will generally be better protected against cybersquatters than trade marks which already exist as words, surnames or place names. 17.22

The remoteness of the defendant's commercial interests from those of the trade mark owner. Where the registrant, a business called Zaras but which traded as Zara, had registered the zara.gr domain name for the purpose of marketing its industrial coffee grinding machines, a Greek court considered that there was little likelihood that there would be any confusion on the part of customers seeking to purchase fashion products bearing the claimant's ZARA trade mark.[36] 17.23

The existence of appropriate added matter. The more words are added to the trade mark when formulating a domain name, the less likely it is that members of the public will be confused into believing that that website bearing the domain name originates from the trade mark owner. Thus the DANONE trade mark was not infringed by the defendant's use of jeboycottedanone.net ('je boycotte' being the French for 'I boycott'[37]) since the unauthorized use of the DANONE trade mark in the context of the added subject matter diluted its ability to communicate the suggestion that the website was connected with the trade mark owner. This conclusion would obviously not apply if the added subject matter was neutral (for example, 'danonedairyproducts.net') or positively suggested a connection (for example, 'enjoydanoneeveryday.net'). 17.24

---

[33] *Retail Services Inc v Freebies Publishing* 247 F Supp 2d 822 (EDVa 2003).
[34] See further paras 17.27–17.31 below.
[35] *Société des Produits Nestlé SA v Pro Fiducia Treuhand AG* [2002] ETMR 351 (WIPO).
[36] *Re Zaras* [2003] ECC 34 (Monomeles Protodikeio Athinon, Athens). Given that the parties' respective trade marks were dissimilar, it is presumed that the court's consideration of the issue of confusion was attributable to the fact that the claim was made partly for trade mark infringement and partly for unfair competition.
[37] *Sté Gervais Danone v Société Le Riseau Voltaire, Société Gandhi, Valentin Lacambre* [2003] ETMR 321 (Tribunal de Grande Instance de Paris).

(7) Liability for allocation of infringing domain names

17.25 Does a domain name allocation agency incur any liability for allowing an applicant to register as a domain name a name which wrongfully incorporates the trade mark of another? In dismissing an action brought against a domain name authority by a political party which owned an unregistered trade mark, the Austrian Supreme Court considered that it was simply not feasible for the authority to monitor the legitimacy of every domain name applicant's claim to be able to use the name of its choice.[38] This decision is surely right, given the impossibility of determining, for example, which of a number of legitimate users of the word 'polo' should be entitled to the exclusive use of that word as part of a domain name.[39]

(8) Trade mark-friendly domains

17.26 Recognizing that more can be done to respect the integrity of trade marks even when they are used on the medium of the Internet, the French Association for Cooperation in Internet Naming (AFNIC) has introduced a new second-level domain '.tm.fr'. Use of the .tm.fr domain is available only to proprietors of trade marks registered in France.[40] Presumably French consumers who visit websites ending with .tm.fr will feel secure that they are dealing with the genuine trade mark proprietor. It may however be asked whether, by promoting the interests of French trade mark owners, this policy discriminates unfairly against, for example, French or foreign proprietors of Community trade marks (CTMs) whose registrations also cover the territory of France.

(9) The United States approach

17.27 The United States, as the cradle of the Internet, was relatively swift to adopt a comprehensive legislative solution for cybersquatting by third parties. Under its purpose-built legislation[41]

> (d)(1)(A) A person shall be liable in a civil action by the owner of a mark, including a personal name which is protected as a mark under this section, if, without regard to the goods or services of the parties, that person—
>
>> (i) has a bad faith intent to profit from that mark, including a personal name which is protected as a mark under this section; and
>> (ii) registers, traffics in, or uses a domain name that—

---

[38] *FPOE v Nic.at* [2003] ETMR 25: the claim was brought under the relevant provisions of the Austrian Civil Code, not domestic trade mark law.

[39] On the 'Polo question', see Chapter 6.

[40] See Karina Dimidjian and Claire Lazard, 'New ".tm.fr" Domain Names for Mark Owners' WTLR, 17 April 2003.

[41] Passed as the Anticybersquatting Consumer Protection Act 1999, this legislation was incorporated into the Lanham Act as section 43(d) (15 USC, s 1025(d)).

B. Use of another's trade mark as a domain name

(I) in the case of a mark that is distinctive at the time of registration of the domain name, is identical or confusingly similar to that mark;

(II) in the case of a famous mark that is famous at the time of registration of the domain name, is identical or confusingly similar to or dilutive of that mark; or

(III) is a trademark, word, or name protected by reason of section 706 of title 18, United States Code, or section 220506 of title 36, United States Code.

(B)(i) In determining whether a person has a bad faith intent described under subparagraph (A), a court may consider factors such as, but not limited to—

(I) the trademark or other intellectual property rights of the person, if any, in the domain name;

(II) the extent to which the domain name consists of the legal name of the person or a name that is otherwise commonly used to identify that person;

(III) the person's prior use, if any, of the domain name in connection with the bona fide offering of any goods or services;

(IV) the person's bona fide noncommercial or fair use of the mark in a site accessible under the domain name;

(V) the person's intent to divert consumers from the mark owner's online location to a site accessible under the domain name that could harm the goodwill represented by the mark, either for commercial gain or with the intent to tarnish or disparage the mark, by creating a likelihood of confusion as to the source, sponsorship, affiliation, or endorsement of the site;

(VI) the person's offer to transfer, sell, or otherwise assign the domain name to the mark owner or any third party for financial gain without having used, or having an intent to use, the domain name in the bona fide offering of any goods or services, or the person's prior conduct indicating a pattern of such conduct;

(VII) the person's provision of material and misleading false contact information when applying for the registration of the domain name, the person's intentional failure to maintain accurate contact information, or the person's prior conduct indicating a pattern of such conduct;

(VIII) the person's registration or acquisition of multiple domain names which the person knows are identical or confusingly similar to marks of others that are distinctive at the time of registration of such domain names, or dilutive of famous marks of others that are famous at the time of registration of such domain names, without regard to the goods or services of the parties; and

(IX) the extent to which the mark incorporated in the person's domain name registration is or is not distinctive and famous . . .

(ii) Bad faith intent . . . shall not be found in any case in which the court determines that the person believed and had reasonable grounds to believe that the use of the domain name was a fair use or otherwise lawful.

(C) In any civil action involving the registration, trafficking, or use of a domain name under this paragraph, a court may order the forfeiture or cancellation of the domain name or the transfer of the domain name to the owner of the mark.

(D) A person shall be liable for using a domain name under subparagraph (A) only if that person is the domain name registrant or that registrant's authorized licensee.

(E) As used in this paragraph, the term traffics in refers to transactions that include, but are not limited to, sales, purchases, loans, pledges, licenses, exchanges of currency, and any other transfer for consideration or receipt in exchange for consideration.

Chapter 17: Trade Marks on the Internet

(2)(A) The owner of a mark may file an *in rem* civil action against a domain name . . . if—

    (i) the domain name violates any right of the owner of a mark registered in the Patent and Trademark Office, or protected under subsection (a) or (c); and
    (ii) the court finds that the owner—

        (I) is not able to obtain *in personam* jurisdiction over a person who would have been a defendant in a civil action under paragraph (1); or
        (II) through due diligence was not able to find a person who would have been a defendant in a civil action under paragraph (1) by—

            (aa) sending a notice of the alleged violation and intent to proceed under this paragraph to the registrant of the domain name . . . ; and
            (bb) publishing notice of the action as the court may direct promptly after filing the action.

(B) . . .
(C) In an *in rem* action under this paragraph, a domain name shall be deemed to have its situs in the judicial district in which—

    (i) the domain name registrar, registry, or other domain name authority that registered or assigned the domain name is located; or
    (ii) documents sufficient to establish control and authority regarding the disposition of the registration and use of the domain name are deposited with the court.

(D)(i) The remedies in an *in rem* action under this paragraph shall be limited to a court order for the forfeiture or cancellation of the domain name or the transfer of the domain name to the owner of the mark. Upon receipt of written notification of a filed, stamped copy of a complaint filed by the owner of a mark in a United States district court under this paragraph, the domain name registrar, domain name registry, or other domain name authority shall—

    (I) expeditiously deposit with the court documents sufficient to establish the court's control and authority regarding the disposition of the registration and use of the domain name to the court; and
    (II) not transfer, suspend, or otherwise modify the domain name during the pendency of the action, except upon order of the court.

(ii) The domain name registrar or registry or other domain name authority shall not be liable for injunctive or monetary relief under this paragraph except in the case of bad faith or reckless disregard, which includes a willful failure to comply with any such court order.

(3) The civil action established under paragraph (1) and the *in rem* action established under paragraph (2), and any remedy available under either such action, shall be in addition to any other civil action or remedy otherwise applicable.

(4) The *in rem* jurisdiction established under paragraph (2) shall be in addition to any other jurisdiction that otherwise exists, whether *in rem* or *in personam*.

17.28 It appears from the content of these provisions that they are intended to provide a body of law which addresses the wrongful use of another's trade mark in a domain name through the operation of a sealed-in subset of trade mark laws which is self-sufficient and highly focused on its subject matter. Thus the 'bad faith' requirement which a trade mark owner must prove is specifically a 'bad faith intent to profit' requirement with its own list of criteria. Admittedly this list is non-exclusive and thus

B. Use of another's trade mark as a domain name

offers the opportunity for litigants to cite 'bad faith' doctrine from mainstream trade mark precedents, but the detailed and highly focused nature of bad-faith criteria leave little scope for such activity.

17.29 The issue of liability is interesting. Only the person who registers the domain name and his authorized licensee may be liable for registering another's trade mark with a bad-faith intent to profit. Thus Internet service providers (ISPs), operators of search engines and Internet users who visit sites bearing the offending trade mark are absolved of any liability. The 'sale' of another's trade mark to the highest bidder for use as a metatag or as a trigger for the release of a pop-up banner do not incur liability under this provision.[42]

17.30 The provisions reproduced above address all the major issues raised by trade mark owners, in particular by enabling them to bring an *in rem* action in order to secure a troublesome domain name where *in personam* proceedings cannot be employed in order to obtain satisfaction. Since is not necessary to exhaust *in personam* proceedings before seeking *in rem* relief, trade mark owners can commence proceedings against the domain which is the object of their wrath without wasting valuable time and incurring both research and litigation expense in hunting the domain's instigator.[43] Another advantage of *in rem* proceedings is that it may deprive or, at worst, restrict the right of the owner of the disputed domain name to wrest jurisdiction from the United States courts through *in personam* litigation in a foreign court.[44]

17.31 In terms of removing uncertainty and of demonstrating the thrust of legislative intent, the US law addressed the problems of cybersquatting relatively early in the cybersquatting era. In contrast trade mark owners in Europe were required to deal with these issues on a problem-by-problem, country-by-country basis; and in European jurisdictions many of the problems addressed by statute in the United States remain unresolved. It has however been argued[45] that the United States law has gone too far and that, in applying the rigours of dilution doctrine to domain names, the law has a tendency to prevent the use of 'non-competing, non-identical

---

[42] Cf *Estée Lauder Cosmetics and others v Fragrance Counter Inc and Excite Inc* [2000] ETMR 843 (where the Hamburg District Court held such activity to be both a trade mark infringement and an act of unfair competition). An action brought in the US, *Estée Lauder Inc v Fragrance Counter* 1999 US Dist LEXIS 14825 (SDNY 1999), was eventually settled when iBeauty, the successor in title of the Fragrance Company, voluntarily agreed to refrain from using the Estée Lauder trade marks as Internet keywords.

[43] *Caesar's World Inc v Caesar's Palace.com and others* 112 F Supp 2d 502 (EDVa 2000).

[44] *GlobalSantaFe Group v Globalsantafe.com* WTLR, 15 April 2003: the Eastern Court for the District of Virginia ordered *in rem* relief notwithstanding a subsequent order of the District Court of Seoul, Korea.

[45] Matthew D Caudill, 'Beyond the Cheese: Discerning What Causes Dilution Under 15 USC s.1125(c): A Recommendation to Whittle Away the Liberal Application of Trademark Dilution to Internet Domain Names' (2002) xiii Fordham Int Prop, Media and Ent Law Jl 231.

marks that have a speculative possibility of diluting a famous mark' and that the application of dilution doctrine to domain names should therefore be suspended.[46]

(10) Resolution of domain name disputes under ICANN and similar rules

17.32 Litigation is an expensive pastime and the problems faced by trade mark owners in seeking to preserve the integrity of their trade marks against a multitude of small-time fraudsters, cybersquatters and those with personal grievances are well chronicled.[47] To address these problems by providing a cheap and swift means of removing bad-faith domain name registrations or of transferring them to injured trade mark owners, the ICANN[48] Uniform Domain-Name Dispute Resolution Policy (UDRP) and Rules were implemented.

17.33 The ICANN Policy governs the practice of domain name registrars when a registered domain name is disputed, while the Rules determine the substantive criteria and the procedures employed by the mediators who operate dispute-resolution service providers. The ICANN rules only address disputes involving universal top-level domains (TLDs) like .com, .net, .org, .biz and .info and they only apply where the name in dispute is a second-level domain. Accordingly a dispute relating to a domain such as www.kodack.com would fall to be determined by ICANN rules, but not one relating to www.kodack.cameras.com. Domain name registries which allocate national TLDs generally employ dispute-resolution policies and rules which are very similar to those of ICANN.

17.34 In short, under the UDRP a complainant may trigger a mandatory administrative proceeding before a dispute-resolution panel by alleging that: (i) a registrant has registered a domain name which is identical or confusingly similar to his own trade mark or service mark; (ii) that the registrant has 'no rights or legitimate interests' in respect of the domain name; and (iii) that the registrant's domain name has been registered and is being used in bad faith.[49] For these purposes 'bad faith' is defined as: (i) the registration or acquisition of the domain name for the primary purpose of selling or leasing it to the trade mark owner; (ii) registration for the purpose of blocking the trade mark owner's own registration; (iii) registration for the purpose of disrupting a competitor's business; or (iv) an attempt to attract Internet users to the registrant's site by creating a likelihood of confusion between that site and the trade mark owner's trade mark.[50]

---

[46] See also *Sporty's Farm LLC v Sportsman's Market, Inc* 202 F 3d 489 (2d Cir 2000); cert denied 147 LEd 2d 984 (Sup Ct 2000): 'it is clear that the new law was adopted to provide courts with a preferable alternative to stretching federal dilution law when dealing with cybersquatting cases'.
[47] See eg the cases and incidents cited in the Anti-Counterfeiting Group newsletter.
[48] Internet Corporation for Assigned Names and Numbers.
[49] UDRP, para 4(a).
[50] ibid, para 4(b).

B. Use of another's trade mark as a domain name

The mediation of domain name claims is a vast subject in its own right and will not be addressed in detail in this book. What this chapter seeks to do is to summarize briefly the extent to which the ICANN system can provide relief for trade mark proprietors against cybersquatters and to examine the overall impact of this system. In doing so, the following points ((a)–(h)) may be asserted. **17.35**

(a) The complainant's 'trade mark' need not be registered

The registrant in one complaint registered the names of numerous well-known authors and then approached novelist Jeanette Winterson, offering to transfer to her three websites which incorporated her name in exchange for 3 per cent of her gross book sales for 1999. The WIPO panellist considered that the name in which the novelist wrote was an unregistered trade mark and that paragraph 4(a) of the UDRP did not require that the owner of a 'trade mark or service mark' had to register it before the offending websites could be transferred to her.[51] A similar conclusion was reached where the complainant's name was not only not a trade mark but, as an organ of the Dutch state, could not even be registered as a trade mark, but where protection of that name was nonetheless provided.[52] **17.36**

(b) 'Sucks' and other critical or hostile domain names

The registration of a domain name for the purpose of focusing criticism upon the activities or products of a trade mark owner is regarded as a perfectly legitimate thing to do. However, that domain name should not be such as to mislead Internet users into thinking that they have reached the trade mark owner's website when they have reached the site which is hostile to it. Thus a site criticizing the attitude of the Leonard Cheshire Foundation towards disabled people was legitimate, but it could not be called leonard-cheshire.com since the use of that name would confuse the public.[53] A website with a name like ihateleonardcheshire.com would be easier to defend. **17.37**

In the United States in particular, the expression 'sucks' has been used extensively by disgruntled consumers and by (usually former) employees of large companies as a means of publicizing private grievances or airing serious environmental or economic issues regarding them. Some panellists have concluded that trade mark owners should not have to tolerate the existence of 'sucks' sites, which are often not understood by foreigners and which can damage the reputation of their trade **17.38**

---

[51] *Winterson v Hogarth*, Decision 200–0235 [2000] ETMR 783 (WIPO).
[52] *Netherlands v Goldnames Inc*, Decision 2001–0520 [2001] ETMR 1062 (WIPO): 'The States General' protectable even though it was not a trade mark but the name of the bicameral parliament of the Kingdom of the Netherlands.
[53] *Leonard Cheshire Foundation v Darke*, Decision 2000–0131 [2001] ETMR 991 (WIPO). A split decision of a WIPO Panel in *Legal & General Group plc v Image Plus* (2003) 157 *Trademark World* 17 took the opposite view, concluding that the registrant's legitimate right to run a complaints site justified its use of the legal-and-general.com domain name.

marks.⁵⁴ Other panellists have taken a more robust view of them and consider that the use of such sites is part and parcel of the respect for freedom of expression which one should expect to find in any free and open society.

(c) Registration of 'near misses'

17.39 Not everyone is a competent speller; nor is everyone a competent typist. Those who spell well but type inaccurately, or vice versa, often find themselves misspelling the search words—including trade marks—through which they seek to navigate the Internet. Well-known trade marks which are frequently misspelled include GUINNESS (often GUINESS), PROCTER (not PROCTOR) AND GAMBLE, the whisky mark LAPHROAIG and the vodka mark STOLICHNAYA. Whoever registers domain names incorporating 'near miss' spellings is thus likely to secure many extra accidental visits from which he can benefit, whether by 'mouse-trapping' surfers and subjecting them to a barrage of inescapable advertisements or by luring them into pornographic or other sites which it was not their intention to visit.

17.40 In one complaint the deliberate misspelling of a bank's name, lakaixa.com for LA CAIXA, was regarded as a sufficient ground for ordering the transfer of the domain name. Said the panellist:

> Although converting 'c's into 'k's is a way of expressing feelings similar to those expressed by the word sucks in English, this practice is part of a countercultural Latin jargon and is unlikely to be understood by most internet users throughout the world.

17.41 In other words, most people wouldn't know that lakaixa.com was an act of biting political-economic satire: that name would thus function as a near-miss which it was not legitimate for the registrant to retain.⁵⁵

(d) Appropriation of a 'famous mark' is presumed to be evidence of bad faith

17.42 Where a domain registrant obtained the scaniabilar.com domain name, the Swedish motor vehicle manufacturer Scania complained, maintaining that it owned the SCANIA trade mark in Sweden and the United States for motor vehicles and that the registrant's use of scaniabilar.com (Swedish for 'Scania cars') would lead Internet users to assume that that website was Scania's official website. The WIPO panellist concluded that the fame of the SCANIA trade mark was so great that the registrant could not reasonably maintain he was unaware of it.⁵⁶

---

⁵⁴ See eg *Diageo plc v John Zuccarini and Cupcake Patrol*, Decision 2000–0996 [2001] ETMR 466 (WIPO).
⁵⁵ *Caixa d'Estalvis y Pensions de Barcelona v Namezero.com*, Decision 2001–0360 [2001] ETMR 1239 (WIPO).
⁵⁶ *Scania CV AB v Leif Westlye*, Decision 2000–0169 [2000] ETMR 767 (WIPO).

B. *Use of another's trade mark as a domain name*

17.43 A spurious explanation as to how the registrant came to select a domain name is unlikely to be persuasive with a WIPO panellist. Thus when Christian Dior objected to the registration of the babydior.com and babydior.net domain names, the registrant's explanation that 'babydior' alluded to a purple dinosaur which the registrant had created in order to use for educational purposes did not prevent the panellist holding that the trade marks DIOR, CHRISTIAN DIOR and BABY DIOR were clearly well-known trade marks under Article 6*bis* of the Paris Convention and should be protected against a bad-faith registration such as this.[57]

17.44 Not all panellists are prepared to presume bad faith on facts such as these. For example, where the well-known Italian football club Sampdoria objected to the adverse registration of sampdoria.com, the panellist agreed that the domain name's main component was identical to the complainant's SAMPDORIA trade mark and that the registrant had no legitimate interest in using it (since 'Sampdoria' was not a place name but a contraction of two former football club names, Sampierdarenese Doria and Andrea Doria, no one had a better claim to use the word than the club itself). However, the club had neither established that SAMPDORIA was a famous mark nor submitted evidence that the domain name was registered and used in bad faith. The complaint thus failed.[58]

(e) *Proving bad faith where a trade mark is also an ordinary word*

17.45 Invented words like XEROX, NESQUIK and SCANIA are easier to protect against cybersquatting since it is usually hard for a domain name registrant to justify his interest in the use of that word. The same cannot be said for even well-known trade marks like APPLE, since fruit traders have as much reason to wish to register apple.com as do computer manufacturers.

17.46 A panellist refused to return the avengers.com domain name to the company which owned the copyright in the cult television series *The Avengers* (for which, surprisingly, no trade mark had been registered). The registrant maintained that it proposed to use avengers.com for the marketing of 'recreational submarine leisure tours'. The complainant's mark was not so famous, nor the evidence of bad faith so compelling, as to require the panellist to find that there had been bad faith on the registrant's part. If the complainant's mark had not been an ordinary word with a meaning other than that which indicated the television series, the complaint would have stood a greater opportunity of succeeding.[59]

---

[57] *Christian Dior Couture SA v Liage International Inc*, Decision 2000–0098 [2000] ETMR 773 (WIPO).
[58] *Unione Calcio Sampdoria SpA v Titan Hancocks*, Decision 2000–0523 [2000] ETMR 1017 (WIPO).
[59] *Canal+ Image UK Ltd v VanityMail Services Inc*, Decision FA0006000094946 [2001] ETMR 418 (WIPO).

(f) Other circumstantial evidence of bad faith

17.47 Where a domain name registration for rtlgroup.com was made shortly after intense press speculation that two companies intended to merge under the name RTL Group, the speed at which the registration was effected, the fact that it was put up for sale just twelve days after it was registered and the fact that the registrant's name was 'This Domain is for Sale' were all circumstances which caused the three-man WIPO panel to find that the domain had been registered in bad faith.[60]

(g) Reverse domain-name hijacking

17.48 ICANN policy protects innocent and *bona fide* registrants of domain names against acts of bullying ('reverse domain-name hijacking') which are designed to shake their domain names free from them. Thus where the owners of the MAGGI trade mark for soups sought to pressurize the registrant into relinquishing control of the maggi.com domain name, the panellist was heavily critical of the trade mark owner's lack of candour in bringing its complaint when it knew of the registrant's interest. The registrant did not compete in the market for soup and had no intention of selling the site to the MAGGI trade mark owner: it was a company owned by one Romeo Maggi, who sought to use the site for the benefit of the Maggi family.[61]

(h) Evidence of confusion

17.49 The Netherlands State Information Office was generally known in that country by its postal address 'Postbus 51'. Where a registrant appropriated that name for his postbus51.com domain name, he resisted an application for its transfer by arguing that no Internet user would confuse his own postbus51.com website with the complainant's official website postbus51.nl. The panellists disagreed. Even though .com was commonly used for commercial sites, it could not be assumed that an Internet user would automatically assume that postbus51.com was a commercial site and not connected with the State Information Office.[62]

17.50 It has been considered that the use of disclaimers on a website, even if they may be effective to prevent an Internet user believing wrongly that he has visited a trade mark owner's site, is not necessarily determinative of the complainant's application for transfer of a website. Such disclaimers operate only after the deception or confusion has kicked in and it is possible that, so far as the trade mark owner's reputation in his trade mark is concerned, the damage through the disputed domain name registration has already been done.[63]

---

[60] *CLT-UFA Société Anonyme v This Domain is for Sale and Sean Gajadhar*, Decision 2000–0801 [2001] ETMR 446 (WIPO).
[61] *Société des Produits Nestlé SA v Pro Fiducia Treuhand AG* [2002] 351 (WIPO).
[62] *Netherlands v Humlum*, Decision 2002–0248 [2002] ETMR 1213 (WIPO).
[63] *Leonard Cheshire Foundation v Darke*, Decision 2000–0131 [2001] ETMR 991 (WIPO).

C. Use of another's trade mark on a web page

The appropriation of another's trade mark as part of one's domain name is the most visible and high-profile form of Internet-related trade mark infringement, but there are other ways too. In the following paragraphs we will review some of the other means by which third parties, whether through deliberate or inadvertent action, infringe a trade mark owner's rights or reduce the cachet of his registered trade mark.[64] **17.51**

(1) In which country is the use of another's trade mark on a website a 'use in the course of trade'?

When a trade mark appears on a commercial web page which is accessible to Internet users throughout the world, has there been a 'use in the course of trade' in every country from which it is accessible? This point has been considered in the UK where it was concluded that use, in any given country, depends upon the circumstances of the case: what was the intention of the website owner and what would an Internet user assume on seeing the website?[65] From this it follows that, if I use the PANGOLIN trade mark for polymer piping by displaying it on my website when marketing polymer piping to British builders, the fact that surfers from St Vincent and the Grenadines can visit my website does not therefore constitute use in that exotic jurisdiction. **17.52**

(2) Use of another's trade mark in order to sell the goods of the trade mark owner

In principle, if I want to sell bottles of CHANEL perfume I can do so in any way I choose. This includes offering those bottles for sale on the Internet by featuring them on my web page, even if I identify them by their trade marks. This freedom is however limited by the normal rules on the infringement of trade marks. Accordingly any business conduct which is not permissible when it is done offline remains equally impermissible when carried on through the medium of the Internet. If I may not decant CHANEL eau de toilet into perfume bottles and sell it as CHANEL perfume, the fact that I do this through my web page does not make such an activity any more lawful than it was before.[66] **17.53**

---

[64] For a recent review of this topic, see David Bainbridge, 'Infringement of Trademarks on Web Pages' (2003) 19 CL&SR 124–30.
[65] *1-800 Flowers Inc v Phonenames Ltd* [2000] ETMR 369, [2000] IP&T 325 (HC); [2002] FSR 191, [2001] IP&T 810 (CA).
[66] *Sté Chanel v SA Citycom* [2000] ETMR 1068 (Tribunal de Grande Instance de Paris).

(3) Unauthorized use of advertisements

17.54 Because of its unique degree of accessibility, the Internet is a perfect medium for the dissemination of advertising material. Two problems in particular need to be addressed here: the unauthorized transmission of genuine advertisements and the dissemination of apparently unauthorized or spoof advertising material. Neither of these problems is unique to the Internet, but each will be discussed in this chapter because it is within the context of the Internet that these practices seem to be most prevalent.

(a) Genuine advertisements

17.55 A strange phenomenon in Internet circles, particularly it seems in regard to peer-to-peer network services such as Kazaa and Grokster,[67] is the placement of advertisements for well-known products and services on the Internet by third parties without the consent of those who appear to be the advertisers. Although the advertisements may have been posted on to websites in error, it is also possible that they are placed there in order to create the impression that they are paid-for advertising which has been placed by major brand-owners. This false impression may suggest to Internet users that a site carrying such advertising must be 'legitimate' and can lead other advertisers to consider placing their own paid-for advertising in the same media.

17.56 From the point of view of European trade mark law the position would appear simple: running an advertisement which features a trade mark is a Type 1 ('same mark, same goods or services') infringement.[68] The main problem is how the courts would deal with it. Although many trade mark owners would seek actively to disassociate themselves from the suggestion that they would advertise on, for example, portals leading to the supply of pornography, real damage may be hard to prove and, in at least some cases, it is possible that the trade mark owner has derived some unsolicited benefit through positive consumer responses to the unrequested advertisements. This is one of those areas in respect of which harmonization of European law and practice is far from complete.

(b) Subvertisements

17.57 Into this category fall the following:

(i) spoof advertisements which are created in order to criticize, denigrate or make fun of a well-known branded product or service;

---

[67] See Yinka Adegoke, 'Top Brands Start to Pull Ads from P2P Networks' *New Media Age*, 24 April 2003, 1.
[68] On the categorization of trade mark infringements, see Chapter 7.

C. Use of another's trade mark on a web page

(ii) genuine advertisements which are circulated on the Internet only, possibly because they do not fulfil the legal or advisory criteria that would entitle them to be displayed on television or in the printed media in all of the countries for which they are intended;
(iii) copies of genuine advertisements, usually billboard posters, which have been doctored so as to convey a message other than that intended by the trade mark owner;[69] and
(iv) advertisements the provenance of which is unknown and which, if challenged, the trade mark owner disowns but which promote an image or ethos which some prospective purchasers may find appealing.

Many of these advertisements exploit themes of sex or violence;[70] they are generally spread by viral marketing, through Internet users who send each other links to materials which they find appealing and which are posted on certain websites.[71] The same material is often posted on 'blogs'.[72] The propensity for viral marketing to spread the word and thereby to promote products and services is quite remarkable.[73] Because they are addressed to the consuming public in a somewhat unorthodox manner and may have no actual or admitted connection with the trade mark owner, this chapter refers to them as subvertisements or underground advertisements.

17.58

In terms of trade mark infringement, these underground advertisements do pose a number of problems the most obvious of which is that it can be hard to pinpoint their source. At the bottom end of the scale, anyone with a digital camera can record an advertisement and post it on a convenient host site. At the other end of the scale, well-resourced teams deploy actors and equipment in such a way as to create subvertisements which are indistinguishable in quality—if not content—from genuine advertisements. Unless the creators of these advertisements announce their identity, there may be no obvious culprit for a trade mark owner to sue. And even where the advertisement's creator or producer is identified by name, there still remains the task of tracking the jurisdiction in which he operates. If the advertisement causes damage or embarrassment in a jurisdiction in which the

17.59

---

[69] See eg the advertisements for VW Commando, Land Rover, Vauxhall Tigra and Audi on subvertise.org/theme.php?theme=CAR.
[70] A controversial example is a pair of purported advertisements for Puma products which employ explicitly sexual imagery: see www.memefirst.com/images/blah/blah1.jpg and blah2.jpg respectively. Puma disavowed the images, warned the operators of the memefirst and adrant websites that it was 'reserving its legal steps' (felixsalmon.com) and sent a cease-and-desist letter to Gawker (www.gawker.com).
[71] A selection of such advertisements may be found on www.punchbaby.com/clip_ads.htm.
[72] A 'blog' (short for 'weblog') is an Internet web page that records the regular comments or postings of the individual who controls it. Examples include The Trademark Blog from the Law Offices of Martin Schwimmer (trademark.blog.us/blog/) and the ipkat.com IP blog.
[73] See eg the case histories cited by The Viral Factory on its website http://www.theviralfactory.com/.

17.60 Since the advertisement's progenitors are unlikely to face legal action, the trade mark owner may contemplate suing the ISP who hosts the offending website. Where the ISP is a 'mere conduit', who did not initiate the advertisement, select its recipients or select or modify its contents, EU Member States are obliged to ensure that the ISP bears no liability for hosting it.[74] In the United States the issue appears less clear. Both in the case of the party who creates and posts the advertisement and in the case of the ISP it will be necessary to prove that the defendant's use of the proprietor's trade mark is a commercial use, whether the basis of his legal action is for a regular trade mark infringement[75] or for dilution.[76]

17.61 In terms of substantive liability for the content of the advertisement, if the advertisement has been composed and disseminated by the trade mark owner (if he admits to it) or with his approval, there will be no infringement and, if the advertisement is a spoof or a meme,[77] there will be a classic Type 1 'same mark, same goods or services' infringement action.[78] However, the extent to which defences based on freedom of expression will be allowed to prevail is quite uncertain.[79] There is also a difficult issue of determining the extent, if any, to which some of these advertisements damage the value of the trade mark since, within particular market niches, they may well enhance the trade mark's image. For example, the marketing of a trade mark-protected brand through a film clip which employs explicit sexual imagery or dialogue may be considered repugnant by the public at large while yet establishing credibility with a generation of young Internet users.[80] In other cases the nature of the advertisement suggests that the potential for damage to the trade mark is substantial within all segments of society. An example of this is the spoof 'Nokia kitty' advertisement in which, within the context of an apparent advertisement for a NOKIA video phone, a cat is portrayed as being spun round a room by a fast-rotating ceiling fan before being smashed against a wall.[81]

---

[74] Directive 2000/31 (the E-commerce Directive), art 12.
[75] Lanham Act, s 43(a)(1).
[76] ibid, s 43(c)(1).
[77] 'Meme', defined as 'a unit of information which moves from brain to brain to brain' (Kalle Lasn, *Culture Jam* (2000), p 123), is a term sometimes used to denote an original advertisement which has been metamorphosed so as to convey quite the opposite message from that which the advertiser intended.
[78] See Chapter 7, paras 7.10–7.15.
[79] On freedom of speech defences, see Chapter 8, paras 8.60–8.65.
[80] See eg 'Indecent Proposal', a spoof MASTERCARD advertisement directed by Scott Quigley and available on www.yjd40.dial.pipex.com/mastercard.html.
[81] 'Nokia kitty' advertisement: www.ad-rag.com/103616.php.

D. Use of another's trade mark as a metatag

The issue which ultimately falls to be determined is the extent to which trade mark owners are to be allowed to control the uses in advertising to which their trade marks are put by others, bearing in mind the fact that once a spoof advertisement or meme is accessible through the Internet, it is practically impossible for the trade mark owner to eradicate it and that, unlike traditional forms of electronic advertising on the television or radio, spoofs and memes may persist forever. It is hoped that the debate over the control of trade marks on the Internet is one in which all interested parties will have their say and that the issues involved will not be left to be resolved, on a case-by-case basis, by courts which may be ill advised as to the commercial, technological and political undercurrents of the storm-swept sea upon which trade mark rights are tossed. **17.62**

(4) Use of another's trade mark as part of a copyright notice

In the UK it has been held that the inclusion of the word 'Reed' in the copyright strapline 'Copyright Reed Business Information 1999', on a website publicizing employment opportunities, infringed the claimant's REED word trade mark for employment agency services.[82] **17.63**

D. Use of another's trade mark as a metatag

A metatag[83] is a word which is written on a web page in an electronic language such as HTML. When attached to a web page, the metatag is not normally visible to Internet users but its invisible presence is detected by Internet search engines which have been instructed to search for it. If a word which is selected to serve as a metatag is a registered trade mark, it follows that anyone using a search engine such as Alta Vista or Google will be given a list of answers to his search inquiry ('hits') which will include pages which bear some reference to that metatag. A search for some words, for example, 'polo', will throw up references both to trade marks and to other, non-trade mark meanings of the word such as the games played on horseback or in the water, a fashion for the neck of certain garments and the surname of a famous explorer. Where however a trade mark is an invented word, it is reasonable to suppose that all 'hits' identified by a search engine would be in at least some manner related to that trade mark. **17.64**

If a business has a dull and unimaginative name, for example, the Northern Urban and District Glazing and Window Frame Company, many Internet users will lose patience looking for it via a conventional search: nor is there an easy and obvious **17.65**

---

[82] *Reed Executive plc and Reed Solutions plc v Reed Business Information Ltd, Reed Elsevier (UK) Ltd and Totaljobs.Com Ltd* [2003] RPC 207, [2003] IP&T 220 (HC).

[83] For a good review of metatag issues, see Askan Deutsch, 'Concealed Infringement and Web Pages: Metatags and US Trademark Law' (2000) 7–8 IIC 845.

way of searching for it if you can't remember the name. It is however possible to secure a large number of visitors to the company's web pages by using as metatags such popular and easy-to-spell words as 'nike' and 'sex'.

17.66 The unauthorized use of another business's trade mark as a metatag or magnet to draw Internet users to one's own website has been the subject of extensive, not to mention expensive, litigation in Europe, the United States and elsewhere. This litigation has now broadly clarified our understanding of the circumstances in which unauthorized metatagging is permitted, although each new shift in the technology produces unforeseen opportunities for both trade mark owners and their competitors to exploit their own strengths and each other's weaknesses. In the following sections I hope to summarize some of the most significant recent cases and to offer some general guidance on the implications of metatag use for trade mark owners.

(1) Permissible uses of another's trade mark as a metatag

17.67 **Use of the trade mark as an ordinary part of speech.** The trade mark INTERMEDI-AIR (the Dutch term for 'intermediary') was registered for magazines and online services relating to the advertisement of employment vacancies. Its use as a metatag by another company was prohibited by the trial judge but permitted on appeal.[84] The use was regarded as a fair descriptive use of the term for 'intermediary'; that word did not appear in the defendant's advertisements and it was not used as a trade mark in the contexts in which it did appear.[85]

17.68 **Use for free speech purposes.** The Tribunal de Grande Instance de Paris concluded, in proceedings for interim injunctive relief, that where the trade mark ESSO was used as a metatag for the purpose of drawing the intention of Internet browsers to a Greenpeace web page which criticized Esso's environmental policies, such use could not even constitute an arguable infringement at the trial.[86]

(2) Impermissible uses of another's trade mark as a metatag

17.69 **The use of the trade mark as a metatag by a direct competitor of the trade mark proprietor.** Where two businesses provided computer software for the road haulage industry and one of them owned the ROADRUNNER trade mark, the use of the word 'roadrunner' as a metatag so as to attract web-users to the defendant's

---

[84] *Monster Board BV v VNU Business Publications BV* [2002] ETMR 1 (Court of Appeal, The Hague).

[85] Whether this reasoning is still justified in the light of the ECJ decision in *Arsenal Football Club plc v Matthew Reed*, Case C-206/01 [2003] ETMR 227 (ECJ); [2003] IP&T 43 (ECJ) is open to doubt.

[86] *Esso Société Anonyme Française SA v Association Greenpeace France and Société Internet.Fr* [2003] ETMR 441.

D. Use of another's trade mark as a metatag

website was held to be an infringement of the ROADRUNNER trade mark.[87] In France, even in the absence of a registered trade mark, the mere unauthorized use of a third party's registered company name or business name by a competitor, which directs Internet users to a competitor's website, is an actionable civil wrong for which damages may be awarded.[88]

The 'sale' of key words by search engine operators. The owners of the Excite search engine 'sold' the right to use third parties' trade marks as key words. By this means, web-users who typed in those trade marks as Internet search terms would be led to the advertising materials and websites of those businesses who had 'bought' those rights as well as to the websites of the trade mark owners. The Hamburg District Court held that this constituted both trade mark infringement and an act of unfair competition.[89] There are however other forms of commercial exploitation of trade marks by search-engine operators the legality of which has not yet been established. For example, may a search-engine operator charge a lawful user of another's trade mark (such as a repairer of BMW cars or a retail supplier of NOKIA phones) for the right to have search hits for its own website displayed before hits for the trade mark owner himself? Google has recently been reported as having acceded to eBay's request that Google ban advertisers from bidding for the right to use eBay's trade marks as key words, irrespective of whether those advertisers had the right to use those marks.[90] In principle there appears to be no reason why every profitable third-party commercial activity which relates to the lawful use of another's trade mark should itself be regarded as an infringement of that trade mark, but it would be unwise to predict the position that will be taken by the courts in an area as sensitive to political and commercial considerations as that of the Internet. 17.70

Use where the defendant is aware of confusion even before the metatag is used. Even when there is no suggestion of trade mark infringement, there may be a history of confusion between two traders with identical or similar names and that confusion may be exacerbated where technological convergence brings the two traders' interests closer together. This is exactly what happened where an employment agency and a publisher of magazines, both featuring the word Reed in their names, sought to use the Internet. Members of the public occasionally confused the two Reeds or thought them to be connected, but no real harm was done until 17.71

---

[87] *Roadtech Computer Systems Ltd v Mandata (Management and Data Services) Ltd* [2000] ETMR 970 (HC).
[88] *Sté Fabrication et d'Outillage de la Brie (SFOB) v Sté Notter GmbH*, 13 March 2002 (Cour d'appel de Paris).
[89] *Estée Lauder Cosmetics and others v Fragrance Counter Inc and Excite Inc* [2000] ETMR 843 (Hamburg District Court).
[90] See Stefanie Olsen, 'Trademarks May Stymie Online Searches', www.news.zdnet.co.uk/business/legal/0,39020651,39115824,00.htm, 20 August 2003.

both took to cyberspace. The employment agency (which owned the REED trade mark for employment agency services) sought to promote job vacancies and recruitment opportunities via its website while the publisher sought to exploit the long-standing publication of employment advertisements in its paper products by making them accessible online. The fact that, even before the era of the Internet, the publisher was aware of the risk of confusion counted against it in its claim that its use of the word 'Reed' on its website, on banners and in metatags was an honest commercial practice.[91]

17.72 **Overuse of the metatag.** The owner of the pharmaceutical trade mark PYCNOGENOL sued the operator of the healthierlife.com website, through which various pharmaceutical products including those of the trade mark owner's competitors were sold. The use which the defendant made of the PYCNOGENOL trade mark through its metatags was so extensive, a US Court of Appeals ruled, that it created the impression that the trade mark proprietor had some sort of relationship with him, possibly as a sponsor.[92]

E. Use of another's trade mark as the name of an Internet service provider

17.73 An company which owned the AVNET trade mark for advertising services 'included in Class 35' sued the defendant for trade mark infringement when it used the name Avnet (a contraction of the words 'Aviation Network') as the name of an ISP which offered Internet users the opportunity to acquire websites through which they could advertise their own businesses. The court held that the use of Avnet as the name of an ISP did not add up to the provision of advertising and promotional services. The court added that, even if the defendant's use of that name did constitute use of the mark for such services, it was not used for the provision of such services as were comprehended by advertising included in Class 35.[93]

F. Conclusion

17.74 This chapter has briefly reviewed many of the problems faced by trade mark owners which have been raised by the development of the Internet, together with a range of options which they may wish to pursue.

---

[91] *Reed Executive plc and Reed Solutions plc v Reed Business Information Ltd, Reed Elsevier (UK) Ltd and Totaljobs.Com Ltd* [2003] RPC 207, [2003] IP&T 220 (HC).
[92] *Horphag Research Ltd v Pellegrini (t/a Healthdiscovery.com)* 328 F 3d 1108 (9th Cir 2003).
[93] *Avnet Incorporated v Isoact Ltd* [1997] ETMR 562 (HC). Class 35 includes such services as the rental and leasing of billboards, screens, hoardings and other displays.

F. Conclusion

At the time of writing, the Internet—despite its unquestioned status as the single most important technological and cultural influence on most aspects of trade and commerce in our lifetimes—is still a relatively new phenomenon and one which almost certainly has not even come close to maturity. This phenomenon poses a problem for lawyers: do we seek to legislate for the Internet as it grows, as the Americans have done, or do we endeavour to apply old laws to new situations, as the British and other European nations have preferred to do? The American approach offers security to trade mark owners, comfort to investors and predictability to Internet users and third parties. The European approach offers uncertainty but fosters a spirit of empiricism in which Europe's common law jurisdictions are experienced as well as a degree of doctrinal flexibility which preserves the fabric of the *corpus juris* as a living juridical organism which is capable of accommodating change.

17.75

18

GEOGRAPHICAL INDICATIONS AND OTHER FORMS OF PROTECTION

A.	Introduction	
	Auntie Marjorie's Problem Page	
	The proof of the pudding	18.01
B.	The protection of geographical indications	
	(1) Geographical indications	18.04
	(2) Designations of origin under international law	18.08
	(a) The basic level of protection	18.15
	(b) Additional protection for wines and spirits	18.16
	(c) Further international negotiation	18.20
C.	GIs in the European Union	18.21
	(1) Foods and agricultural products	18.22
	(a) The application process	18.28
	(b) GIs from non-EU countries	18.29
	(c) Scope of protection and enforcement	18.30
	(d) The position of conflicting trade marks and trade mark applications	18.34
	(e) Can the geographical area of a protected name be changed?	18.35
	(2) Protection of alcoholic beverages	18.36
D.	GIs under national law in Europe	18.38
E.	The interface between GI protection and trade mark protection	18.41
	(1) The ECJ's perspective	18.42
	(2) The perspective of the national courts	18.46
F.	Case law of the European Court of Justice	
	(1) PDOs and parallel protection under national law	18.47
	(2) The free movement of goods	18.49
G.	Future plans for GIs	18.52
H.	Company name registrations	18.54
I.	Protection of titles	18.55
J.	Certification marks, guarantee marks and collective marks	18.56
K.	Conclusion	18.60

Chapter 18: Geographical Indications and other Forms of Protection

A. Introduction

Auntie Marjorie's Problem Page

Dear Auntie Marjorie,
I've invited some lawyer friends for dinner and I really don't know what to make for them. To make matters worse they are trade mark lawyers, who are well known to be the most discerning and gastronomically discriminating of legal practitioners. I'm starting to panic—please help!
Yours desperately,
Hungry of Hampstead

Dear Hungry,
Lawyers are indeed hard to satisfy and you are quite right to fear trade mark lawyers, who are known to be the most demanding in this regard. But never fear! Follow my easy instructions below for an easy summer dinner party and you'll cook a meal that will impress even the most intellectual property-savvy solicitors.
Good luck!
Auntie Marjorie

Aperitifs
As your guests arrive, serve a variety of the following:
Avellana de Reus (hazelnuts)
Amêndoa Douro (almond)
Kelifoto fistiki Phtiotidas (pistachios)
Olives noires de Nyons (olives)
Konservolia Piliou Volou (olives)

Asparagus Soup
500g Asparago verde di Altedo
3 Scalogno di Romagna
1 large Patata Kato Nevrokopiou
2 cloves of Ail rose de Lautrec
2 pints boiling Gemminger Mineralquelle
2 tablespoons of Toscano olive oil
25g Beurre Charentes-Poitou
Squeeze of Limone Costa d'Amalfi juice
Seasoning
Crème fraîche fluide d'Alsace to serve

1. Prepare the spears of Asparago verde di Altedo by cutting off and discarding the woody ends, cutting off and retaining one tip for each person in order to form a garnish. Cut the remaining asparagus into 1cm chunks.
2. Peel and dice the Scalogno di Romagna. Sauté in the Toscano olive oil without browning.
3. Peel and dice the potato and the cloves of Ail rose de Lautrec. Add to the Scalogno di Romagna together with the Beurre Charentes-Poitou and a dash of Limone Costa d'Amalfi juice. Sauté for 3 minutes without browning.
4. Add the boiling Gemminger Mineralquelle and the reserved asparagus tips. Cook for three or four minutes and then remove the tips and reserve for a garnish.
5. Add the remaining asparagus chunks and cook until boiling then lower the heat and simmer until the potato and asparagus are soft – about an hour.
6. Blend until smooth. Season to taste.
7. Serve immediately, garnished with a swirl of Crème fraîche fluide d'Alsace and an asparagus tip in each bowl.

A. Introduction

Salmon *au Bébé-Sec*

1 1–1.5kg Clare Island Salmon
1 Limone di Sorrento
20ml of Katlenburger Burgbergquelle
20ml Aceto balsamico tradizionale di Modena
Huile d'Olive de la Vallée des Baux-de-Provence for brushing

1. Pre-heat the oven to Gas Mark 2/150°C. Place enough tin-foil to cover a 1–1.5kg Clare Island salmon on a large baking tray.
2. Oil the foil generously with the huile d'Olive de la Vallée des Baux-de-Provence.
3. Place the salmon on top of the oiled foil. Season it inside and out.
4. Thinly slice half a limone di Sorrento into 3 or 4 slices and place on top of the Clare Island salmon.
5. Sprinkle 20ml of Katlenburger Burgbergquelle and 20ml of Aceto balsamico tradizionale di Modena on top of the salmon. Then wrap the foil around the salmon, completely enclosing it. Work quickly to prevent the liquids from spilling out. If necessary, enclose in a further piece of foil.
6. Place the salmon in the pre-heated oven. Cook for 15 minutes per 500g and an additional 10 minutes thereafter.
7. Remove from the oven and leave at room temperature for 20 minutes. Remove the skin. Serve garnished with slices of the other half of the limone di Sorento and the *Sauce du secret victorien*.

Sauce *du secret victorien*

2 egg yolks
75g Beurre d'Ardenne
1 tablespoon of citrinos do Algarve juice
2 tablespoons of Rilchinger Armandus Quelle

1. Heat 1 tablespoon of the juice of a citrinos do Algarve and 2 tablespoons of Rilchinger Armandus Quelle in a bowl over simmering Rilchinger Armandus Quelle.
2. Add two egg yolks and whisk until the mixture thickens.
3. Whisk in 75g of softened butter – I prefer Beurre d'Ardenne, but if you really can't get hold of that you could use Beurre rose de la marque nationale Grand-Duché de Luxembourg and season.
4. Serve with the *Salmon au Bébé-Sec*.

Steamed Jersey Royal Potatoes

1. Scrape clean 4 Jersey Royal Potatoes per person.
2. Steam for 20 to 30 minutes until soft.
3. Serve tossed in Beurre Charentes-Poitou.

Carrot salad

500g Lammefjordsgulerod
1 Arancia rossa di Sicilia
1 Limone di Sorrento
1 teaspoon Meli Elatis Menalou Vanilia

1. Peel and grate the Lammefjordsgulerod into a salad bowl.
2. Make a dressing by whisking together the juice of the Arancia rossa di Sicilia and the Limone di Sorrento and the Meli Elatis Menalou Vanilia.
3. Pour over the Lammefjordsgulerod. Mix and serve.

Chapter 18: Geographical Indications and other Forms of Protection

Green salad

2 Raw Spreewälder Gurken
4 Pomodoro S. Marzano dell'Agro Sarnese-Nocerino
½ Radicchio variegato di Castelfranco
½ Mâche nantaise
1 Pimentón de Murcia
5 tablespoons Olympia olive oil
3 tablespoons Aceto balsamico tradizionale di Reggio Emilia

1. Remove the leaves from the Radicchio variegato di Castelfranco and Mâche nantaise, wash thoroughly and tear into a large salad bowl.
2. Wash and slice the Spreewälder Gurken. Add to the salad bowl.
3. Wash, deseed and slice the Pimentón de Murcia. Add to the salad bowl.
4. Wash the Pomodoro S. Marzano dell'Agro Sarnese-Nocerino. Cut into eighths and add to the salad bowl.
5. In a screw-top jar make a dressing by shaking together 5 tablespoons of Olympia olive oil and 3 tablespoons of Aceto balsamico tradizionale di Reggio Emilia.
6. Pour over the salad.
7. Toss the salad and serve.

Fruit salad

4 Xera Syka Kymis (figs)
2 Arancia rossa di Sicilia (oranges)
1 Melon du Haut Poitou (melon)
150g Kerasia Tragana Rodochoriou (cherries)
50g Kumquat Kerkyras (kumquats)
150g Mirabelles de Lorraine (grapes)
300ml Cornish Clotted Cream

1. Wash the Xera Syka Kymis, Kerasia Tragana Rodochoriou, Mirabelles de Lorraine and Kumquat Kerkyras.
2. Remove the Mirabelles de Lorraine from their stalk. Remove the pips from the Kerasia Tragana Rodochoriou and place both fruits in a large serving dish.
3. Peel and segment the Arancia rossa di Sicilia. Add to the serving dish.
4. Peel and deseed the Melon du Haut Poitou and cut into bite-size chunks. Add to the serving dish.
5. Cut the Xera Syka Kymis into quarters and then cut the quarters in half. Add to the serving dish.
6. Cut the Kumquat Kerkyras into halves. Add to the serving dish.
7. Gently toss the fruits so that they are evenly distributed throughout the salad. Cover and chill.
8. Serve with Cornish Clotted Cream.

Cheeseboard

Fromage de Herve	Danablu	Altenburger Ziegenkäse
Xynomyzithra Kritis	Quesucos de Liébana	Bleu d'Auvergne
Imokilly Regato	Gorgonzola	Noord-Hollandse Gouda
Tiroler Alpkäse	Svecia	Single Gloucester
Queijo de Castelo Branco	Muscat du Ventoux	

Petits Fours

Lübecker Marzipan   Turrón de Alicante

B. The protection of geographical indications

To Drink

Wine list	Other beverages
Riesling Hochgewächs	Herefordshire cider
Est! Est!! Est!!! di Montefiascone	Bayerisches Bier
Hessische Bergstraße	Bad Hersfelder
Colli del Trasimeno	Naturquelle
	Graf Meinhard Quelle
	Giessen

The proof of the pudding

By far the most important of the legal regimes included in this chapter is that which protects geographical indications (GIs), for which a framework of international and national protection exists and which is currently the subject of a good deal of debate. The other topics included in this chapter are mentioned in outline only. The recipes described above draw almost exclusively upon GIs which are not generic or descriptive terms but which are protected appellations under the law of the EU. 18.01

GIs generally describe foods and drinks which are made to a uniformly high standard, thereby attracting premium prices; they also reflect the cultural variety of an era from which the homogenized pan-European palate had not yet emerged, when food was hand-crafted rather than manufactured and packaged for mass production and mass consumption in distant lands. Accordingly these indications are not only loved by connoisseurs and gourmands; they are also vigorously protected by those producers who alone are permitted to use them. 18.02

This chapter discusses GIs in addition to an assortment of rights in words or names which are protected by statutory legal schemes but which are not registered trade marks. The coverage given to some of them in this chapter is brief and introductory; they are included in this book so that they should not escape from the trade mark expert's peripheral vision, rather than for the purpose of satisfying any deep-seated curiosity as to their function and practical value. 18.03

B. The protection of geographical indications

(1) Geographical indications

GIs confer rights that resemble trade marks in that (i) they are applied to goods and (ii) they serve to distinguish them from other goods. In other ways, however, they behave quite differently from trade marks. Take the GI Gorgonzola for cheese, for example. The fact that this term is a GI enables those who use it to seek protection against competitors who make cheeses with similar characteristics but which originate from regions which lie outside the town in the Po Valley in which Gorgonzola is produced. The term may also act as a bar to those who seek to register the same 18.04

Chapter 18: Geographical Indications and other Forms of Protection

term or a variant of it as a trade mark. However, the word Gorgonzola is not a 'property' in the sense in which trade marks are 'property' because, in relation to the cheese for which it is a protected term, it cannot be bought, sold or licensed. Special rules govern the use of the word Gorgonzola even by those cheese makers who live within the requisite geographical catchment area and, once a term has been accepted as a GI, its specification may be effectively fossilized if provision is not made for its revision in the light of new food technologies or market conditions. This is because, while trade marks can be used on improved and reformulated versions of well-known products without confusing or disappointing the relevant consuming public, GIs are designed to be used on products which enjoy the sanction of tradition.

18.05 Table 18.1 sets out the major differences between trade marks and GIs.

18.06 There is a major geo-commercial difference between GIs and trade marks too. An almost overwhelming majority of the world's most significant trade marks hail from the United States or are controlled by United States corporations. In contrast, it is this author's purely subjective impression that it is quite probable that the majority of the world's most significant GIs at present are still of European origin. That may be either a cause or a consequence of the European Commission's activity in promoting the protection of GIs as well as an explanation as to why the intervention of the European Court of Justice (ECJ) has been sought on so many occasions in recent years; it may also explain why the Commission has been receiving such a steady stream of notifications of new GIs from EU Member States over the past few years.

18.07 In the EU context, GIs are divided into two species: protected designations of origin (PDOs) and protected geographical indications (PGIs). PDOs and PGIs are discussed below along with the ECJ decisions in which they have been considered. GI is however the term by which both PDOs and PGIs are described in the Agreement on Trade-Related Aspects of Intellectual Property Law (TRIPs).[1]

(2) Designations of origin under international law

18.08 Before considering the position under the law of the EU, the international framework within which it functions should first be understood.

18.09 The Paris Convention affirms that the protection of industrial property has as its objects (among other things) 'indications of source or appellations of origin'[2] but makes no specific reference to their mode of protection, leaving that protection to the provision of suitable legal remedies for unfair competition.[3] Building upon

---

[1] TRIPs, s 3.
[2] Paris Convention, art 1(2).
[3] ibid, art 10*ter*.

B. The protection of geographical indications

Table 18.1 The major differences between trade marks and GIs.

	Trade marks (CTM and national European)	Geographical indications (Regulation 2081/92)
Subject matter	All goods and services falling within Classes 1 to 45 of he Nice Classification (ie almost everything)	Agricultural products and food-stuffs
Eligibility for registration	Must be a 'sign' which is graphically represented and can distinguish goods/services of different undertakings	Must fulfil definition of a PDO or PGI (art 2) and possess a specification that defines a set of designated characteristics (art 4)
Duration	Ten years, indefinitely renewable for further ten-year periods	No limit specified
Applicant	The proprietor of a sign	The 'Group', being any association of producers/processors of the protected product (art 5)
Assignment	Possible	Impossible, since GI is not a property right
Licensing	Possible	Impossible for the product designated, though the Group may register a GI as a trade mark for goods other than those protected by the GI and can license it
Non-distinctive and descriptive terms	Unregistrable, though they may become registrable if they acquire distinctiveness through use	Unregistrable
Can generic terms be registered?	No, though they may become registrable if they acquire distinctiveness through use	No (art 13(1))
Can mark/GI become generic?	Yes	No (art 13(3))
Protection against unfair competition?	Only within scope of Directive 89/104, art 5(2) and corresponding provisions	Yes, within the terms of art 13, especially art 13(1)(d)
Scope of geographical protection	Pan-European (CTM), regional (Benelux) or national	Pan-European
Opposition/ revocation/ cancellation	All available; some jurisdictions have rules on *locus standi*	Member States may object to the Commission (art 7)
Use requirements	No use needed before application; five years in which to use before registration may be challenged for non-use	It is implicit that the PDO or PGI must be in use before it qualifies for proection (see art 2)
Action to enforce rights	Trade mark infringement action before national or CTM court	Duty on Member States to protect GIs but no mechanism for protection stipulated

this, the Lisbon Agreement of 1958[4] provided for the establishment of a dedicated system for the deposit of 'appellations of origin' with an International Bureau operated by the World Intellectual Property Organization (WIPO). Under the Lisbon Agreement, each signatory state is required to protect the appellations of origin registered by the other states. An 'appellation of origin' for this purpose is

> ... the geographical name of a country, region, or locality, which serves to designate a product originating therein, the quality and characteristics of which are due exclusively or essentially to the geographical environment, including natural and human factors.[5]

18.10 This definition protects geographical names alone, thus appearing to exclude terms which indicate a product's origin but which are not place names (for example, Speck ham[6]).

18.11 By 15 April 2003 the Lisbon Agreement had secured just twenty participating states, the most economically significant being France, Italy and Mexico.

18.12 TRIPs took the protection of GIs a stage further by tying it to a package of commitments which countries had to accept as a condition of the World Trade Organization (WTO). TRIPs contains three articles which deal with GIs. Article 22 defines them for TRIPs purposes as:

> ... indications which identify a good as originating in the territory of a Member, or a region or locality in that territory, where a given quality, reputation or other characteristic of the good is essentially attributable to its geographical origin.[7]

18.13 This definition goes further than that of the Lisbon Agreement by including indications which are not actually place names.

18.14 How does the TRIPs definition of a GI work in practice? If, say, curried pigeons from Perpignon are produced in a particular and distinctive manner which relates to the raw materials, climate or indigenous know-how and talent of people from the region of Perpignon, then Perpignon may be regarded as a GI for curried pigeons that originate from Perpignon. If however curried pigeons taste much the same wherever they come from, the fact that a regular supply of curried pigeons comes from Perpignon does not of itself enable the place name Perpignon to be used as a GI.

---

[4] Lisbon Agreement for the Protection of Appellations of Origin and their International Registration 1958, as amended in 1979.
[5] ibid, art 2.
[6] On the protection of which see *Consorzio per la Promozione dello Speck v Christanell, Handle Tyrol and Lidl Italia Srl* [1998] ETMR 537 (Tribunale di Bolzano).
[7] TRIPs, art 22(1).

B. The protection of geographical indications

(a) The basic level of protection

In respect of GIs covered by TRIPs, each TRIPs Member is obliged to provide the legal means for interested parties to prevent (i) the use of a GI on goods where that use misleadingly suggests that the goods to which it is attached come from somewhere other than their true place of origin[8] as well as (ii) any act of unfair competition.[9] In other words, I may not affix the word Perpignon on curried pigeons which originate from, say, Pisa. TRIPs does not specify what is to happen if I were to affix the word Pernipong to curried pigeons, since that is not a use of the GI itself, the use of a confusingly similar term would most probably constitute an act of unfair competition or passing off under the domestic law of each Member.

18.15

(b) Additional protection for wines and spirits

As with cheeses and cured meats, the names of wines and spirits can evoke generic or descriptive connotations. Some cheese designations, such as cheddar, have ceased to serve as GIs and are now truly generic terms.[10] Once a product name becomes generic, attempts to turn back the tide and reinstate them as GIs are fiercely resisted: the Commission's efforts to redesignate Feta cheese as having a purely Greek geographical connotation have so far met with little enthusiasm from the Danish dairy industry which produces a substantial proportion of the world's Feta and has used that term for more than half a century.[11]

18.16

The producers of wines and spirits have to address the same threats and the use of terms such as 'Spanish champagne', 'Elderflower champagne', 'South African sherry' and 'Welsh whisky' has provoked legal action. The wine and spirits lobby has however presumably demonstrated that it is more powerful than the cheese and meat lobbies since TRIPs requires Members to give extra protection to wines and spirits. Interested parties must be given the legal means

18.17

> . . . to prevent use of a geographical indication identifying wines . . . or spirits not originating in the place indicated by the geographical indication in question, even where the true origin of the goods is indicated or the geographical indication is used in translation or accompanied by expressions such as 'kind', 'type', 'style', 'imitation' or the like.

This requirement addresses for GIs an issue which remains unclear under trade mark law: the legality of 'imitation x' product descriptors.[12] While 'Imitation

18.18

---

[8] ibid, art 22(2)(a).
[9] ibid, art 22(2)(b).
[10] The issues of genericity concerning GIs closely parallel those of trade mark law; see in particular Chapter 6.
[11] See eg *Denmark, Germany and France v The Commission*, Joined Cases C-289, 293 and 299/96 [1999] ETMR 478 (ECJ). On 14 October 2002 Feta was again designated as an exclusively Greek cheese. The Danes have indicated their willingness to challenge this designation again.
[12] 'Imitation X' issues are discussed in Chapter 10, paras 10.18–10.20.

ROLEX' may be either identical to ROLEX (in which case a likelihood of confusion need not be proved) or merely similar to it (in which case a likelihood of confusion must be established), 'Imitation Burgundy' will infringe the Burgundy GI so long as it misleads the public or constitutes an act of unfair competition.

18.19 Although this requirement applies to the impermissible use of a protected GI on wines or spirits, but not on other products, the use of a GI on products other than wines or spirits may still be proscribed by law. For example, if I were to use the term Champagne on a bottle of bubble bath, those who control the use of that term would be able to draw upon trade mark rights, passing off or unfair competition rules[13] in order to prevent me doing so.

(c) Further international negotiation

18.20 In the case of wines (but not spirits) which are eligible for GI protection, provision is made for negotiations to be undertaken in the Council of TRIPs for the establishment of a multilateral system of notification and registration of GIs.[14] Provision is then made for the parameters within which those negotiations are to take place and for the operation of national systems for the protection of GIs and trade marks in the meantime.[15]

C. GIs in the European Union

18.21 The position adopted by the EU is that, once a sign is identified as a GI by the authorities in the country in which it originated, it should be entitled to protection as a GI throughout the EU. The system established for the protection of GIs thus required Member States to determine which GIs protected under national law should attract full pan-Union protection and then to register them accordingly with the European Commission. The purely national protection of other appellations was then to be phased out following the passage of a term of five years.[16]

(1) Foods and agricultural products

18.22 Under Regulation 2081/92[17] each Member State must provide for the legal pro-

---

[13] See TRIPs, art 22(2)(b), which states that all GIs (and not just those for wines and spirits) should enjoy the benefit of protection against an act of unfair competition within the meaning of art 10*bis* of the Paris Convention.

[14] TRIPs, art 23(4).

[15] ibid, art 24.

[16] See *Commission of the European Communities v French Republic*, Case C-6/02, 6 March 2003 (ECJ).

[17] Council Regulation 2081/92 on the protection of geographical indications and designations of origin for agricultural products and foodstuffs. Implementing regulations for Regulation 2081/92 are found in Commission Regulation 2037/93.

C. GIs in the European Union

tection of GIs for agricultural products and foodstuffs, including beers and mineral waters (separate legislation exists for the protection of the names of wines and spirits[18]). Regulation 2081/92 protects PDOs and PGIs.[19] Although the definition of PDOs and PGIs states that both forms of protection must be for the name of a region, place or (exceptionally) country which is used to describe a food or agricultural product which originates from that named place, 'certain traditional geographical or non-geographical names' may also be considered as designations of origin, thus enabling terms such as Speck to be protected in respect of ham.[20]

In addition to Regulation 2081/92, Regulation 2082/92[21] protects GIs for principally processed foods such as chocolate, pastas, prepared dishes, prepared sauces, soups, stocks, ice creams and sorbets. These items may be accorded a Certificate of Specific Character (CSC, often called TSGs, for Traditional Speciality Guaranteed) on the basis of their traditional nature rather than their physical origin. An example of a CSC is the term Traditional Farmfresh Turkey, which is promoted under the GOLDEN PROMISE brand by members of the Traditional Farmfresh Turkey Association.[22] Manufacturers of PDOs, PGIs and TSGs are all entitled to bear the respective official logo which attests to their status. TSGs, which may be registered and protected in the same manner as PDOs and PGIs, will not be mentioned further in this chapter. 18.23

What, then, is the difference between a PDO and a PGI? 18.24

(i) a PDO protects a food or product which essentially or exclusively owes its quality or characteristics to a 'particular geographical environment with its inherent natural and human factors', where the production, processing *and* preparation of the food or product must take place in the defined geographical area.
(ii) a PGI protects a food or product which possesses 'a specific quality, reputation or other characteristics attributable to that geographical origin', where the production *or* processing *or* preparation of the food or product must take place in the defined geographical area.

From these definitions, which relate solely to criteria of location and manufacture, it appears that there is little legal difference between a PDO and a PGI. The 18.25

---

[18] See paras 18.36–18.37 below.
[19] Regulation 2081/92, art 2(2). A current list of PDOs and PGIs (but not the details of their manufacture or preparation) can be found at www.europa.eu.int/comm/agriculture/qual/en/1bbab_en.htm.
[20] Regulation 2081/92, art 2(3).
[21] Regulation 2082/92 on certificates of specific character for agricultural products and foodstuffs.
[22] Ministry of Agriculture, Food and Fisheries Press Release (168/00), 18 May 2000.

Chapter 18: Geographical Indications and other Forms of Protection

requirements for establishing the existence of a PGI are less onerous than those of a PDO, which means that all PDOs are also PGIs (but not vice versa). Quality is not an issue and a product which is designated a PDO may be of better or worse quality than a PGI without affecting its legal status. Since the Regulation does not differentiate between the nature of the protection to which PDOs and PGIs are entitled, it may be asked why a distinction between them needs to be maintained.

18.26 In the case of both PDOs and PGIs, the description of the products for which GI protection is accorded is somewhat reminiscent of a patent specification. The product specification of the PDO for the Parmigiano Reggiano cheese is as follows:

> Semi-fat hard cheese obtained from cooked and slowly matured paste. It is made with cow's milk from animals whose feeding mainly consists of forage from the area of origin. The milk used is raw and cannot undergo any thermal treatments. The use of additives is strictly forbidden.
>
> The milk from the evening milking and that from the morning milking is delivered to the dairy within two hours from the end of each milking. Milk can be cooled immediately after milking and kept at a temperature not below 18 °C. The milking time of each one of the two milkings allowed daily must be limited within 4 hours of time.
>
> The evening milk is partly skimmed by removing the cream naturally risen to the surface in open-top stainless steel basins. The morning milk, immediately after arriving at the dairy, is mixed with the partly skimmed milk from the previous evening. It may also be partially skimmed by removing the naturally risen cream.
>
> A maximum of 15% of the morning milk may be kept for processing on the following day. In this case, the milk must be kept in the dairy in suitable refrigerated containers, equipped with special agitators and at a minimum temperature of 10°C, and poured into the resting basins in the evening of the same day.
>
> Starter whey is then added to the milk. This is a natural starter culture of lactic ferments obtained from the spontaneous acidification of the whey remaining after the previous day's cheese processing.
>
> The milk curdling takes place inside copper vats shaped like truncated cones with the exclusive use of calf rennet. After curdling, the curd is broken up into grains and cooked. These curd grains are then left to settle to the bottom of the vat in order to form a compact mass. The cheese mass is subsequently placed into special moulds for the moulding process.
>
> After a few days, cheeses are salted in a bath of salt solution. Maturation must last at least 12 months starting from the cheese moulding. In summer, the temperature of maturation rooms must not be lower than 16°C.
>
> Parmigiano-Reggiano cheese has the following features:
> cylinder shape with slightly convex to straight sides, upper and lower faces slightly chamfered;
> dimensions: diameter of upper and lower faces from 35 to 45 cm; side height from 20 to 26 cm;
> minimum wheel weight: 30 kg;
> external appearance: natural gold-coloured rind;
> paste colour: from pale straw-yellow to straw-yellow;
> typical aroma and taste of the mass: fragrant, delicate, tasty yet not sharp;

C. GIs in the European Union

paste texture: fine granules, breaks in brittles;
rind thickness: approximately 6 mm;
fat content: minimum 32% of dry matter

For anything that is not specified herein, the procedure sanctioned by local, fair and consistent usages shall be applied. Any changes shall be subject to the favourable outcome of experiments and studies assessed by the Consorzio del Parmigiano-Reggiano, which, if positive, may lead to an amendment of the Production Regulations.

Production region: territory of the provinces of Parma, Reggio Emilia, Modena and Mantua on the right bank of the River Po and Bologna on the left bank of the River Reno.

It can be seen from this specification that the designation Parmigiano Reggiano represents a complex combination of features: ingredients, milking instructions, ranges of temperature, method of production, method of maturation, data pertinent to shape, size, smell, taste, consistency and general appearance as well as geographical origin. The specification also leaves open the possibility of undergoing change in time. 18.27

(a) The application process

The mechanism of protection is simple. Each EU Member State, through whichever authority it so appoints, must notify the Commission of a proposed PDO or PGI. The notification will contain a description of the food or product for which protection is sought, together with a detailed technical specification as to its means of production. An application for protection must therefore be made directly to the relevant national authority. In most circumstances, applications must be made by an association of producers or processors of the same product each of whom may be in competition with the others but who believe that they and their fellow producers alone are entitled to use the GI concerned. Once the authority approves the application it will forward it to the Commission, which has six months in which to examine and verify it. The main responsibility for the Commission is that of guarding against the protection of generic terms, which are expressly excluded from being able to obtain GI status.[23] 18.28

(b) GIs from non-EU countries

Where a non-EU country provides reciprocal protection for EU-originating GIs, it may be able to obtain protection for its own GIs under Regulation 2081/92[24] and Regulation 2082/91.[25] The Commission's website does not however list the GIs which are protected in the EU but which do not originate from that economic zone. 18.29

---

[23] Regulation 2081/92, art 3.
[24] ibid, art 12.
[25] Regulation 2082/91, art 16.

(c) Scope of protection and enforcement

18.30 Once a name is registered as a PDO or as a PGI in the EU it is protected against five things:

(i) direct or indirect use of the same name for products not within its registration if those products are comparable with such products or that use seeks to exploit the GI's reputation (for example, the PARMA ham GI would give protection against the use of PARMA for other pig products such as pork; it would also give protection against PARMA mustard for consumption with PARMA ham). This protection corresponds to that given to trade marks under article 5(1)(a) and (b) of Directive 89/104.

(ii) misuse, imitation or evocation of the GI, even if the true origin of goods bearing such a sign is indicated (for example, the GI Newcastle brown ale could expect protection against 'Newsparkle brown ale, brewed in Sunderland');

(iii) the reproduction of the protected name translated or accompanied by expressions such as 'style', 'type', 'method', 'as produced in', 'imitation'[26] and so on;

(iv) any other false or misleading indication or packaging or advertising as to the product's origin which may convey a false impression;

(v) any other practice liable to mislead the public as to the origin of the product (for example, sticking French flags and fleur-de-lis emblems all over a Danish tribute Brie-style cheese).[27]

18.31 An EU Member State may enforce rights in a GI even where a product which allegedly infringes those rights has been made purely for export to another EU Member State and will be neither sold nor consumed in its country of manufacture. On that basis Italy was entitled to bring proceedings against the producer of a 'parmesan' grated cheese which did not satisfy the requirements for being sold under the PDO Parmigiano Reggiano and which was destined for France.[28]

18.32 Since Regulation 2081/92[29] is not directly actionable against 'economic operators' (the ECJ's favoured term for people who produce, grate (or slice) then package products contrary to the specification of a PDO[30]), it is left to each EU Member State to produce its own enforcement mechanism. In some countries a breach of Regulation 2081/92 is directly actionable on the part of the group that

---

[26] On which see paras 18.16–18.19 above.
[27] Regulation 2081/92, art 13(1).
[28] *Dante Bigi* [2003] ETMR 707 (ECJ).
[29] The direct actionability of infractions of the EU Regulations providing for the registration of GIs has not been tested before the ECJ, but it would appear that they would also be incapable of supporting direct legal action for the same reason as Regulation 2081/92.
[30] *Consorzio del Prosciutto di Parma and Salumificio S Rita*, Case C-108/01, 20 May 2003 (ECJ); *Ravil Sarl v Bellon Import Sarl and Biraghi SpA*, Case C-469/00, 20 May 2003 (ECJ).

C. GIs in the European Union

applied for protection in the first place. In the United Kingdom enforcement is believed to be left in the hands of local trading standards authorities, although it may be possible for a trade group or indeed for an individual trader to bring an action for passing off on an appropriately promising set of facts.[31]

Whether a GI has been infringed is a matter for determination by the national court. The ECJ[32] has held that the fact that different national courts may come to contradictory conclusions as to whether there has been an infringement does not constitute a threat to the free movement of goods within the Community.

18.33

(d) The position of conflicting trade marks and trade mark applications

Once a PDO or PGI is registered, Member States may not allow the registration as a trade mark of any sign which would, if used, infringe the rights to which those GIs are entitled.[33] In theory a conflicting trade mark which was registered in good faith before the date upon which the application for PDO or PGI protection was sought may continue.[34] In 1999 however a French court ordered the revocation of the BAIN DE CHAMPAGNE ('Champagne bath') trade mark for perfume, which was registered in 1923, on the basis that this registration was taking undue advantage through the use of the famous name Champagne.[35]

18.34

(e) Can the geographical area of a protected name be changed?

The German authorities adopted regulations to designate Altenburger Ziegenkäse as a designated appellation for cheeses made in a number of districts which included Altenburg and Wurzen. After the Commission accepted Altenburger Ziegenkäse as a PDO, the two companies which produced that cheese in the Altenburg region complained that the designation was too wide since it included areas of Saxony, in particular Wurzen, which lay outside Altenburg and that the specification of the PDO should be restricted accordingly. In its ruling the ECJ explained that the correct method of challenging the specification of a PDO is through an action brought against the relevant national authority under national

18.35

---

[31] But passing off may be difficult or impossible to establish on the facts; see *Consorzio del Prosciutto di Parma v Marks & Spencer plc* [1991] RPC 351 (CA).

[32] *Consorzio per la Tutela Formaggio Gorgonzola v Käserei Champignon Hofmeister GmbH & Co KG and Eduard Bracharz GmbH*, Case C-87/97 [1999] ETMR 454 (ECJ): Cambozola may therefore constitute an infringement of the Gorgonzola PDO in some countries but not others, depending on what consumer response the name Cambozola evokes. See also *Gorgonzola/Cambozola* [1999] ETMR 135 (Upper County Court, Frankfurt am Main), in which the court held Cambozola to be neither an imitation nor an adaptation of Gorgonzola.

[33] Regulation 2081/92, art 14(1).

[34] ibid, art 14(2).

[35] *Comité Interprofessionel du Vin de Champagne v SA Parfums Caron* (1999) 685 PIBD, III-442 (Tribunal de Grande Instance de Paris). The name BAIN DE CHAMPAGNE was allegedly chosen for a wealthy gentleman who enjoyed bathing in that commodity.

law.³⁶ Only once that avenue of relief is exhausted, and only once the complainants could prove that it was impossible for them to bring proceedings against allegedly unfairly competing manufacturers of Altenburger Ziegenkäse cheese under national law, could proceedings be brought against the Commission.

(2) Protection of alcoholic beverages

18.36 Within the EU the names of wines and grape musts are protected by Regulation 2392/89;³⁷ the names of sparkling and aerated wines are protected by Regulation 2333/92.³⁸ Like Regulation 2081/92 on the protection of agricultural products and foodstuffs, these Regulations have centralized registration mechanisms which are activated within individual Member States and they confer a similar standard of protection upon the names which are covered by such registration.

18.37 Regulation 2392/89 and Regulation 2333/92 do not accord automatic and absolute protection to the names of wines which are protected under them against any form of unauthorized use in respect of other wine products. Thus in one case the name protected under Regulation 2333/92 was that of a wine made from Riesling grapes, Riesling Hochgewächs; the claimant, an organization which was responsible for protecting wine names in Germany, subsequently challenged the defendant's right to use the registered trade mark KESSLER HOCHGEWÄCHS, which had been made from Chardonnay grapes for over sixty years. According to the ECJ, there is no infringement of the protected wine name unless the claimant can prove before the relevant national court that (i) the use of name which includes part of the designation of a protected wine is likely to be confused with the protected name and that (ii) the use of the disputed name is likely to mislead consumers and thereby affect their economic behaviour.³⁹

---

³⁶ *Molkerei Groddbraunshain GmbH and Bene Nahrungsmittel GmbH v Commission*, Case C-447/98 P [2002] ETMR 605 (ECJ). See also *Carl Kühne GmbH and Co KG Rich Hengstenberg GmbH and another v Jütro Konservenfabrik GmbH & Co KG*, Case C-269/99 [2003] ETMR 36 (ECJ), in which the Court refused to invalidate the PGI Spreewälder Gurken at the instance of a defendant to an action brought in Germany.
³⁷ Regulation 2392/89 laying down general rules for the description and presentation of wines and grape musts, as amended by Regulation 2603/95.
³⁸ Regulation 2333/92 laying down general rules for the description and presentation of sparkling wines and aerated sparkling wines [1992] OJ L231/9.
³⁹ *Verbraucherschutzverein EV v Sektkellerei GC Kessler GmbH und Co*, Case C-303/97 [1999] ETMR 269 (ECJ).

D. GIs under national law in Europe

While each EU Member State is also a Member of TRIPs, which requires that GIs be protected, the provisions of TRIPs do not specify the mechanism whereby that protection is attained. There is no doubt that the operation within EU Member States of Regulation 2081/92 and corresponding Regulations for alcoholic beverages provides a measure of protection which the WTO would regard as acceptable in terms of fulfilling TRIPs obligations, but it is open to the courts to provide further protection if they so desire (such extra protection being subject to EU rules on the free movement of goods[40]). Thus, for example, in the United Kingdom the law of passing off has in the past protected the use of the words Champagne[41] and Sherry.[42] More recently, protection has been given to the word Swiss in relation to Swiss chocolate, even though (i) there is no single product specification for Swiss chocolate and (ii) not all chocolate manufactured by Swiss *chocolatiers* is manufactured in Switzerland.[43] In the same manner German unfair competition law has protected the use of the protected designation Champagne against use in advertisements for cheap computers.[44]

18.38

The fact that a designation has GI status under Regulation 2081/92 or one of the other Regulations which protect geographical appellations does not mean that its status is inviolate under national law. Apart from the fact that parties affected by designations made under them may challenge them under national law,[45] EU Member States may also enact legislation which prohibits the use of GIs if they are potentially misleading by virtue of the fact that no link remains between the characteristics of a product and its geographical provenance. Thus, according to the ECJ, under German law it was possible to protect consumers against any confusion that might arise from the fact that WARSTEINER beer was produced forty kilometres down the road from Warstein in neighbouring Paderborn.[46]

18.39

---

[40] See *Guimont, Jean-Pierre*, Case C-448/989 [2001] ETMR 145 (ECJ), discussed below.
[41] See eg *Taittinger SA v Allbev Ltd* [1994] 4 All ER 75 (CA), *Bulmer (HP) Ltd v J Bollinger SA (No 3)* [1978] RPC 79 (CA).
[42] See *Consejo Regulador de las Denominaciones Jerez-Xeres-Sherry y Manzanilla de Sanlucar de Barrameda v Mathew Clark & Sons Ltd* [1992] FSR 525 (HC); *Vine Products Ltd v Mackenzie & Co Ltd (No 3)* [1967] FSR 402 (HC).
[43] *Chocosuisse, Kraft Jacobs Suchard (Schweiz) AG and Chocoladefabriken Lindt & Sprüngli (Schweiz) AB v Cadbury Ltd* [1999] ETMR 1020 (CA).
[44] *'Champagner Bekommen, Sekt Bezahlen'* [2002] ETMR 1091 (Bundesgerichtshof).
[45] *Molkerei Groddbraunshain GmbH and Bene Nahrungsmittel GmbH v Commission*, Case C-447/98 P [2002] ETMR 605 (ECJ).
[46] *Schutzverband Gegen Unwesen in der Wirtschaft eV v Warsteiner Brauerei Haus Bramer GmbH & Co KG*, Case C-312/98 [2003] ETMR 76 (ECJ). The Bundesgerichtshof ultimately concluded that the interests of consumers in getting their WARSTEINER beer from Paderborn prevailed over the need to prevent the false labelling of the beer's physical origin; see *Schutzverband Gegen Unwesen in der Wirtschaft eV v Warsteiner Brauerei Haus Bramer GmbH & Co KG* [2002] EIPR N-110.

18.40 The protection of PDOs and PGIs within the single market of the EU runs coextensively with the protection under national law of appellations from third-party countries outside the EU which are protected under bilateral treaties.[47] To the extent that these treaties are not incompatible with existing provisions of EU law they remain enforceable: their applicability and interpretation is a matter for the relevant national courts to determine.[48] The volume of case law on the legal status and enforcement of these treaties has recently grown apace for the reason that the former Czechoslovakia had entered into a number of such arrangements for the purpose of protecting the appellation Budweis, from which is derived the contentious short form 'Bud'.[49]

E. The interface between GI protection and trade mark protection

18.41 The GI regime in Europe presupposes the existence of parallel forms of protection, GI protection for the name of the product itself and trade mark protection for the individual source from which that product arose. There is nothing contradictory in this: only one wine may be termed Champagne but it may be supplied under a variety of trade marks indicating its origin such as BOLLINGER, MOËT ET CHANDON, VEUVE CLICQUOT or KRUG. Indeed, in the case of wines specific provision is made for the coexistence of GIs and trade marks.[50]

(1) The ECJ's perspective

18.42 In the *Hochgewächs* case[51] the organization policing the use of wine names sought to prohibit the use of the trade mark KESSLER HOCHGEWÄCHS on the ground that it was allegedly infringing the protected wine designation Riesling Hochgewächs. On a reference for a preliminary ruling the German Bundesgerichtshof asked the ECJ a question of vital interest to trade mark owners:

> [If the use of a national trade mark falls within the scope of protection conferred on wine names by Regulation 2333/92], may the industrial property right which the owner of the brand has acquired by reason of the traditional undisturbed use of his

---

[47] Bilateral treaties between EU Member States would appear now to be subordinate to the current regime for PDOs and PGIs; see *Ravil Sarl v Bellon Import Sarl and Biraghi SpA*, Case C-469/00, 20 May 2003 (ECJ).
[48] See *Budejovicky Budvar NP v Rudolf Ammersin GmbH*, Case C-216/01 (Advocate General's Opinion, 22 May 2003).
[49] On the 'Bud' treaty issues, see *Budejovicky Budvar Narodni Podnik v Anheuser-Busch Inc* [2002] ETMR 1182, Anheuser-Busch Inc v Budejovicky Budvar Narodni Podnik [2001] ETMR 74.
[50] Regulation 2333/92, art 13(2).
[51] *Verbraucherschutzverein EV v Sektkellerei G C Kessler GmbH und Co*, Case C-303/97 [1999] ETMR 269 (ECJ), discussed at paras 18.36–18.37 above.

E. The interface between GI protection and trade mark protection

description in Germany, as a higher-ranking interest deserving protection, preclude the application [of the prohibition under Regulation 2333/92]?

18.43 The Court considered that, in the light of its answer to an earlier question, it would be 'devoid of purpose' for it to answer this question too. It is however implicit, from that Court's approach to the issue of conflict between a pan-EU GI and a national trade mark, that the determining factor is that of the protection of the consumer. In establishing whether use of the national brand fell within the scope of activities prohibited by Regulation 2333/92,

> ... it is for the national court to assess whether an appellation, brand name or advertising statement may be misleading... In this case it is for the national court to assess in the light of circumstances whether, bearing in mind the consumers to whom it is addressed, a brand name or its component parts are liable to be confused with all or part of the description of certain wines. In that respect... the national court must also take into account the presumed expectations of the average consumer...[52]

18.44 This rather suggests that, if consumers identify the defendant's wine label with the defendant's product and not with the protected GI, the courts must give effect to that degree of identification: if they did otherwise, protection of the GI against the trade mark would not protect consumers against confusion but would actually cause confusion—at least in the short term until consumers would be 're-educated' as to the meaning of the sign. If the use of the wine trade mark was however liable to confuse the relevant public, then the GI should be protected against such confusing use. This issue is much the same as that faced in registered trade mark law, where a sign which is originally descriptive gradually acquires a secondary meaning in the eyes of the relevant consuming public: once this is done, the courts are obliged to respect the fact that the term has effectively changed its meaning within the sector in which products bearing it are consumed.[53]

18.45 A similar approach was taken by the same Court where the dispute focused not on a well-established earlier trade mark but on a subsequent trade mark application. A trade mark applicant sought to register, as a word mark for wines, the sign LES CADETS D'AQUITAINE, which it proposed to use on wines from Bergerac, a region within Aquitaine. The French trade mark registry, whose decision was upheld by the Cour d'appel, refused the registration on the ground that LES CADETS D'AQUITAINE contained the controlled word Aquitaine but was not a description for which the relevant laws on wine appellations had made provision. The Cour de Cassation referred the case to the ECJ for a preliminary ruling. That Court ruled that Regulation 2392/89 did not prohibit the use of the word Aquitaine *per se*. Even though LES CADETS D'AQUITAINE contained the protected geographical reference Aquitaine and was intended for use on wines, its registration as a trade

---

[52] ibid, para 36.
[53] On acquired distinctiveness in trade mark law, see Chapter 4, paras 4.163–4.178.

mark should only be prohibited if there was a real risk that its use would confuse consumers and alter their economic behaviour.[54]

(2) The perspective of the national courts

18.46 An Italian court has held that, in principle, there is no reason why a trade mark should not combine a GI. Each has its own function: the GI reassures consumers that, through a connection with its place of origin, a product is of a particular quality. The trade mark does not specifically address the issue of quality but informs consumers as to that product's origin. Accordingly the use of the GI Pilsener together with the defendant's trade mark TUBORG was not in principle unlawful.[55] The same court added that where, in trade mark infringement proceedings, the only element of the claimant's trade mark which the defendant used was the GI which was incorporated within it, it was the law relating to the protection of GIs and not trade mark law which governed the dispute between them. In this case, therefore, the trade mark PILSEN URQUELL could not be infringed by the use of the brand name TUBORG PILSENER.

F. Case law of the European Court of Justice

(1) PDOs and parallel protection under national law

18.47 Once a PDO is registered, a Member State may not adopt provisions of its own national law which have the effect of altering the protection which it sought for that PDO. Accordingly, after the French government had requested the PDO protection of Époisses de Bougogne for cheese, it could not then broaden that protection under national law so that it covered Époisses alone.[56]

18.48 Where a food product is protected as a PDO, its protection—subject to the vagaries of the national courts—extends throughout Europe. But where a food product is given a narrow specification under the national law of one EU Member State alone while the same product is manufactured and sold under a broader specification in the rest of the Union, the ECJ has ruled that the narrow specification operates as a restriction on the free movement of goods. That was the fate of French Decree 88-1206, which prohibited the use of the designation Emmenthal on rindless cheeses. The ECJ was impressed by the fact that the World Health Organization and the UN Food and Agriculture Organization's *codex alimentar-*

---

[54] *Borie Manoux Sarl v Directeur de l'Institut de la Propriété Industrielle*, Case C-81/01 [2003] ETMR 367 (ECJ).
[55] Pilsen Urquell v Industrie Poretti SpA [1998] ETMR 168 (Supreme Court of Cassation, Italy).
[56] *Chiciak, Fromagèrie Chiciak and Fol*, Joined Cases C-129 and 130/97 [1998] ETMR 550 (ECJ).

F. Case law of the European Court of Justice

ius defined Emmenthal as a cheese which might be given that name even in the absence of a rind.[57]

(2) The free movement of goods

The ECJ has considered issues involving PDOs and the free movement of goods on several occasions. This is not surprising since the specifications of PDOs and PGIs sometimes extend not only to the production of the protected product but also to activities which may take place a long way down the chain of commerce, such as the slicing and packaging of ham, the grating and packaging of cheese or the bottling of wines. To the extent that such specifications are valid and enforceable, they interfere with the development of competitive markets for the performance of activities which lie downstream of the initial production process. **18.49**

In the first ECJ case on PDOs to address the issue of free movement of goods,[58] Belgium brought an action against Spain for a declaration that the limitation of the term Rioja to wine bottled in the Rioja region was a quantitative restriction upon the bulk export of goods, since it was not possible to sell as Rioja any wine which had been pumped into tankers and then driven to Belgium for bottling and sale there. The ECJ did not consider this to be a quantitative restriction on exports: the wine could be sold and rebottled—but it couldn't be resold as Rioja. In the Court's view the bottling was an important operation which, if not carried out in accordance with strict requirements, might impair the wine's quality. The bulk transportation of wine might have a similar consequence. On this basis the restriction of the use of the term Rioja to wine bottled locally was justifiable. **18.50**

A similar issue arose in two cases which were decided on the same day, *Ravil*[59] and *Parma*.[60] In each case the specification for the product covered by the PDO had to receive its final preparation in its area of production (in *Ravil* this was the grating and packaging of Grana Panado cheese; in *Parma* this was the slicing and packaging of Parma ham). In each case it was argued that, by requiring these final steps to be done in their region of production, the PDO had the effect of a quantitative restriction upon the export of such products. However, restrictions such as these were justifiable under article 30 of the EC Treaty for the sake of the protection of the intellectual property rights which those products enjoyed. **18.51**

---

[57] *Guimont, Jean-Pierre*, Case C-448/989 [2001] ETMR 145 (ECJ).
[58] *Belgium (Kingdom of) v Spain (Kingdom of)*, Case C-388/95 [2000] ETMR 999 (ECJ).
[59] *Ravil Sarl v Bellon Import Sarl and Biraghi SpA*, Case C-469/00, 20 May 2003 (ECJ).
[60] *Consorzio del Prosciutto di Parma and Salumificio S Rita*, Case C-108/01, 20 May 2003 (ECJ).

G. Future plans for GIs

18.52 From 10 to 11 June 2003 the WTO and the WIPO jointly hosted a meeting of producers of regional food and drink products from twenty-four countries, the first such meeting to have taken place. The fruit of this meeting was the formation of the Organization for an International Geographical Indications Network (ORIGIN), a cross-border lobby group for greater protection of consumers against misleading use of GIs. At present the EU countries (which are rich in actual and potential GI-protectable products) and the developing countries (which see GI protection as a relatively investment-free means of protecting terms such as Darjeeling tea and Basmati rice) are united in their enthusiasm for (i) providing more protection for GIs and (ii) extending the range of products for which GI protection is available. Against them are ranged a small but powerful and articulate group of mainly former colonial countries which have traded extensively using the appellations which earlier colonists brought over with them: this group of countries includes the United States, Australia and most of Latin America. The first role of ORIGIN will presumably be to put further pressure on these recalcitrant nations in the hope that further GI protection will be achieved.[61]

18.53 In Europe the current set of reform plans are less radical, being more in the nature of fine-tuning of the current system so as to enhance its performance rather than proposals for root-and-branch change. The European Parliament has adopted the European Commission's proposal to update Council Regulation 2081/92 by (i) extending the range of products covered so as to include mustard pastes, pastas, wool, osier and tobacco products, (ii) providing for the cancellation of registration where the registrant waives protection or where the denotation no longer meets the selection criteria and (iv) precluding applicants from seeking to register PDOs and PGIs that refer to a country neighbouring an EU Member State, unless the neighbouring state is a joint applicant.

H. Company name registrations

18.54 Contrary to the belief of many non-lawyers, both in the United Kingdom and elsewhere the registration of a company name confers none of the powers of a registered trade mark. Where a company name is registered, the principal benefit which registration confers is that no other company may subsequently be registered with an identical or nearly identical name. It is only through trading under a company name or through registering it as a trade mark that any enforceable

---

[61] See Stephanie Bodoni, 'Producers Worldwide Team Up to Protect Food Names', *MIP Week*, 15 June 2003.

right may be obtained against third parties. Where a company name is used, the protection which the company enjoys by virtue of its use is neither greater nor smaller than the protection granted to a trading name which is not also the registered name of a company.

I. Protection of titles

In Germany special protection is accorded to the titles of books, plays, films and similar works.[62] This protection would appear to enable the owner of a title to prevent third-party registration of the title as a trade mark and, since protection of titles was accorded under the Unfair Competition Law even before the enactment of the present trade mark statute, it may be supposed that protection against other forms of unfair competition is also provided.[63] In Denmark the existence of an earlier film title may provide the ground upon which a subsequent trade mark application may be refused.[64]

18.55

J. Certification marks, guarantee marks and collective marks

A certification mark is a mark which indicates that goods or services for which it is used have qualities or characteristics which are certified by its proprietor.[65] A collective mark, otherwise known as an 'association mark',[66] is similar to a certification mark except that it is owned by an association and its use is limited to members of that association.[67] A guarantee mark is a mark which guarantees 'the common characteristics of undertakings, production methods, geographical signs and the quality of those undertakings'.[68]

18.56

This book deals with certification, guarantee and collective marks in only the barest outline since, taking a panoramic sweep across the peaks and troughs of European and international trade mark law, they are few in number and cast almost no shadow.[69]

18.57

---

[62] Trade Marks Act, ss 5, 15 (Germany).
[63] *FTOS* [1999] ETMR 338 (Bundesgerichtshof).
[64] *VN Legetøj A/S v Patentankenævnet* [2001] ETMR 529 (Maritime and Commercial Court).
[65] See eg Trade Marks Act 1994, s 50(1) (UK); Trade Marks Act 1996, s 55(1) (Ireland).
[66] Paris Convention, art 7 *bis*.
[67] See eg Trade Marks Act 1994, s 49(1) (UK), Trade Marks Act 1996 s 54(1) (Ireland).
[68] Definition adapted from www.bogazicipatent.com.tr.
[69] For a thorough and scholarly analysis of certification marks, see Jeffrey Belson's excellent book, *Certification Marks* (2002); see also Jeffrey Belson, 'Certification Marks, Guarantees and Trust' [2002] EIPR 340.

18.58 Subject to the making of small but necessary amendments so as to cater for their specific characteristics, certification, guarantee and collective marks will in general obey much the same rules of registration, opposition, cancellation, renewal and infringement as regular trade marks. Directive 89/104 does not require EU Member States to provide for the registration of certification marks, guarantee marks or collective marks. However, where a Member State elects to do so, article 15 provides as follows:

> *Special provisions in respect of collective marks, guarantee marks and certification marks*
>
> 1. Without prejudice to Article 4 [relative grounds for refusal of a trade mark application], Member States whose laws authorise the registration of collective marks or of guarantee or certification marks may provide that such marks shall not be registered, or shall be revoked or declared invalid, on grounds additional to those specified in Articles 3 [absolute grounds for refusal] and 12 [revocation for non-use] where the function of those marks so requires.
>
> 2. By way of derogation from Article 3(1)(c) [marks exclusively consisting of geographical descriptors absolutely barred from registration], Member States may provide that signs or indications which may serve, in trade, to designate the geographical origin of the goods or services may constitute collective, guarantee or certification marks. Such a mark does not entitle the proprietor to prohibit a third party from using in the course of trade such signs or indications, provided he uses them in accordance with honest practices in industrial or commercial matters; in particular, such a mark may not be invoked against a third party who is entitled to use a geographical name.

18.59 Because there are so relatively few of these marks, cases in which they are litigated are extremely uncommon. However, in one important recent case a Swedish court has ruled that the protection accorded by the registration of a collective mark may overlap with that accorded to PGIs under Regulation 2081/92.[70] Accordingly the organization which was responsible for the protection of the PGI Champagne for sparkling wines was able to sue a local vendor of Champagne spectacle frames for infringement of its collective mark. The sale of such frames was, the court held, a taking of an undue advantage of the claimant's repute without due cause.

K. Conclusion

18.60 No one whose business or professional activities depend on a good working knowledge of trade mark law can ignore the impact of GIs, any more than the creators of culinary masterpieces which opened this chapter can ignore them. Apart from giving an assurance of quality to consumers, GIs provide protection in respect of words whose geographical nature may make them descriptive or even

---

[70] *Institut National des Appellations d'Origine v Handelshuset OPEX AB*, Case 99–004 WTLR, 7 April 2003 (Court of Patent Appeals, Sweden).

K. Conclusion

generic. They also block the registration of signs which traders may wish to convert into trade marks. As the developing countries flex their numerical muscles in future rounds of TRIPs and other international trade-based conventions, we may expect to see a substantial increase in the number of classes of products attracting GI protection. Indeed, it may well be that GIs from developing countries will establish themselves as valuable intellectual properties, designating ranges of goods on the shelves of the developed world, with a good deal more commercial success than regular branded goods from those same countries.

In contrast, certification marks and collective marks, despite their potential importance, look set to retain no more than a marginal role in the commercial exploitation and protection of goodwill. This may be because they provide an option for protection which few business interests seriously consider or because they are perceived as being less flexible to exploit and transfer. **18.61**

PART E

ISSUES FOR TRADE MARK OWNERS

19

CHOOSING A TRADE MARK

A.	**Introduction**	
	The Invention of Love	
	The moral of the story	19.01
B.	**Legal considerations**	19.03
	(1) Do not choose a trade mark which is too reminiscent of a better-known one	19.04
	(2) Do not use anything as a trade mark if it actually belongs to someone else	19.05
	(3) Do not choose a trade mark that is manifestly descriptive or highly allusive unless you have the budget to cultivate it	19.06
	(4) Avoid a trade mark which your competitors are likely to regard as deceptive	19.07
	(5) Refrain from using sensitive words and parts of words	19.09
C.	**Cultural considerations**	19.10
	(1) Sectoral or tribal considerations	19.11
	(2) Linguistic considerations	19.12
	(3) Political correctness	19.14
	(4) Brand values and taboos	19.17
D.	**Business considerations**	19.19
	(1) Do the trade marks owned by or licensed to a business cover its activities?	19.21
	(2) Is the cost of maintaining the trade mark portfolio justified?	19.22
	(3) Is it worth hanging on to a trade mark if one can take a licence to use someone else's?	19.23
E.	**Psychological considerations**	19.24
F.	**Conclusion**	19.25

A. Introduction

The Invention of Love

In 1997 Tom Stoppard published a play called *The Invention of Love*. This play focuses on the life of the poet and classicist A E Housman and his relationship with various celebrities of his age including John Ruskin, Oscar Wilde, Walter Pater and Benjamin Jowett. It was not widely known that, after leaving Oxford without a degree, Housman spent some time working as a trade mark examiner in the UK Patent Office. The following dialogue between Housman and his friend Jackson, a patent examiner, is drawn from the play:

Jackson: Every age thinks it's the modern age, but this one really is. Electricity is going to change everything. Everything! We had an electric corset sent in today.
Housman: One that lights up?
Jackson. I've never thought of it before, but in a way the Patent Office is the gatekeeper to the new age.
Housman: An Examiner of Electrical Specifications may be, but it's not the same with us toiling down in Trade Marks. I had sore throat lozenges today, an application to register a wonderfully woebegone giraffe—raised rather a subtle point in Trade Marks regulation, actually: it seems that there is already a giraffe at large, wearing twelve styles of celluloid collar, but, and here's the nub, a *happy* giraffe, in fact a preening self-satisfied giraffe. The question arises—is the registered giraffe Platonic?,[1] are all God's giraffes *in esse et in posse*[2] to be rendered unto the Houndsditch Novelty Collar Company?[3]

The moral of the story

19.01 In the late nineteenth century the choice of trade mark was often predicated by considerations of a physical nature. The giraffe, being a creature with a characteristically long neck, was thus the natural branding choice both for the manufacturers of collars and of throat lozenges. In case the public would not make the immediate connection between the trade mark and the nature of the goods, the giraffe for throat lozenges was portrayed as suffering the hardships of a sore throat, while the giraffe registered for collars—which gave their users an air of stiff-necked self-importance—was 'preeningly self-satisfied'.

19.02 Since the era of Housman the exercise of uniting a trade mark with a product or service has gradually become far more allusive than the conventions of nineteenth-century branding allowed. In 2003 the only representation of a giraffe on the register which Housman helped run is registered for restaurants and wine bars,[4] where giraffes are neither found nor served. There are also many trade marks today which it would be difficult to imagine succeeding commercially in the late nineteenth century: FCUK, POISON and (in lands over which Queen Victoria reigned) VICTORIA'S SECRET, for example. This chapter will look at the exercise of choosing a trade mark from a variety of perspectives.

B. Legal considerations

19.03 Trade mark practitioners usually have about as much direct input into the choice of a client's trade mark as they have in the choice of the names of a client's children.

---

[1] This is a reference to Plato's Theory of Forms. Housman is asking whether all giraffes are individual entities or whether they are merely a pale reflection of an ideal giraffe, from which all giraffes take their form and character.
[2] Latin for 'in existence and in potential'.
[3] *The Invention of Love* (1997), p 55.
[4] UK trade mark no 2181388.

B. Legal considerations

This is regrettable because experienced trade mark practitioners can save their clients a lot of time, expense and embarrassment. Typical of the legal guidance which businesses fail to obtain are the following key axioms.

(1) Do not choose a trade mark which is too reminiscent of a better-known one

19.04 Once a brand is successful, it inevitably attracts 'me-too' followers, whether in the same field of commercial activity or not. A good example of this is the large number of businesses that now use the "Я" US suffix, actively or subconsciously taking their lead from the imaginative TOYS "я" US brand. If another business is using a brand, 'me-too' businesses will find that one or more of the following consequences will occur: (i) they will be sued for infringing the trade mark rights of the earlier business; (ii) even if they are not sued, they will find that the strong link between their own brand and the prominent earlier one makes it more difficult for them to extend their brand's image into other areas than if they had selected a more distinctive brand.

(2) Do not use anything as a trade mark if it actually belongs to someone else

19.05 Where a business chooses artwork as a logo, it is easy to forget that someone else probably owns the copyright in it and may not want to see his work appropriated as another person's trade mark.[5] This happens even where a logo is created specifically for a business but where arrangements are not made to assign the copyright in the logo to the trade mark applicant.[6]

(3) Do not choose a trade mark that is manifestly descriptive or highly allusive unless you have the budget to cultivate it

19.06 Thus FROOT LOOPS is ultimately capable of attaining distinctiveness as a fruit-flavoured, loop-shaped breakfast cereal if it is sufficiently heavily used in connection with that product that the public learn to recognize that FROOT LOOPS indicate Kelloggs to be their source, but when Kelloggs attain their goal it will be at the cost of a great deal of legal and marketing effort.[7]

(4) Avoid a trade mark which your competitors are likely to regard as deceptive

19.07 In one sense many highly successful trade marks are literally deceptive, but that

---

[5] *AUVI Trade Mark* [1995] FSR 288 (High Court, Singapore).
[6] *Hutchison Personal Communications Limited v Hook Advertising Limited and others* [1996] FSR 549 (HC).
[7] Cf *FROOT LOOPS Trade Mark* [1998] RPC 240 (Lord Chancellor's Appointed Person).

does not cause problems for registrability. FAIRY liquid is neither made by nor extracted from fairies. CROSS pens are not particularly irritable. There is no bull's blood in Hungarian BULL'S BLOOD wine and CHURCH shoes have no religious affiliation.

19.08 However, marks which deceive or mislead may not be registrable.[8] Even if a mark does not actually mislead, you will be likely to waste valuable money-making time in court if your major competitor thinks it does. Was Nestlé's attack on Kenco's application to register KENCO—THE REAL COFFEE EXPERTS not a reasonably foreseeable consequence of Kenco's having chosen so provocative a mark?[9]

(5) Refrain from using sensitive words and parts of words

19.09 Even apparently innocent words like BIO, ORGANIC and CHOCOLATE can be loaded with legal significance where legislation governs the terms under which they may be used on labels for foodstuffs, whether as part of a trade mark or not.[10]

C. Cultural considerations

19.10 The suitability of a trade mark is not merely achieved by keeping the lawyers happy. There are other considerations of a more subtle variety. For example, a trade mark which appeals to one segment of society may, by its very appeal, simultaneously alienate another segment of society. The trade mark FCUK is a case in point: so far as fashion-conscious youngsters and their parents are concerned, action and reaction may well be equal and opposite. Other trade marks may lose appeal because of their linguistic or other semantic qualities, while others again may be deemed politically incorrect. In all of these situations the function of a trade mark in distinguishing goods or services is not impaired, but its ability to attract favourable responses from consumers may be impaired.

(1) Sectoral or tribal considerations

19.11 The word mark CRUSADER has been registered for goods and services in numerous classes. The notion of a crusader is very positive in some quarters (for example, the fictional character Batman is lauded as 'The Caped Crusader'). But there are some ethnic groups for whom the word mark CRUSADER has uncomfortable or pejorative connotations. Is it worth choosing a trade mark which

---

[8] See Chapter 4, paras 4.50–4.52.
[9] *Kraft Jacobs Suchard Limited's Application; Opposition by Nestlé UK Limited* [2001] ETMR 54 (UK Trade Mark Registry).
[10] See Chapter 4, paras 4.41–4.49.

C. Cultural considerations

may convey such connotations? (A more recent instance of tribalism may be found in the profound distaste which some Manchester City football supporters have for the owners of the well-known brands which sponsor neighbouring Manchester United.)

(2) Linguistic considerations

Linguistic considerations should also be considered. Was the Whirlpool Corporation right to market its washing machine products in Spain under the WHIRLPOOL trade mark, when the word 'whirlpool' had no obvious Spanish pronunciation? And should cars have been marketed in England under the trade mark SEAT, which carries more credibility in Spain where a seat is not something you sit on? **19.12**

There is no one obviously right answer to the 'Whirlpool question' since, with good marketing, the problems faced by a consumer in pronouncing a trade mark (i) at all or (ii) correctly can enhance a trade mark's memorability and thus enrich its ability to retain the loyal custom of its consumers. Thus, in the alcoholic beverages sector, much has been made of the apparent difficulty of pronouncing trade marks such as LAPHROAIG and, in the 1960s, COCKBURN port was promoted by publicizing the information, apparently known only by connoisseurs of good port, that the correct pronunciation of that word was not 'cock-burn' but 'co-burn'. **19.13**

(3) Political correctness

Political correctness must also be recognized as a significant cultural force within the marketing process. In the United Kingdom the Robertson gollywog was a powerful icon for generations of children who had no idea that it had any conceptual link with black people, let alone any pejorative connotation through the word 'wog'. However, as a victim of attacks based on the alleged perception of the mark as an emblem of racial stigmatization, the gollywog trade mark was marginalized and ultimately axed. In the United States six trade mark registrations of the WASHINGTON REDSKINS basketball team were cancelled after activists objected that the word 'Redskin' was a disparaging term for Native Americans[11] and the same fate awaits even allegedly humorous trade marks such as ONLY A BREAST IN THE MOUTH IS BETTER THAN A LEG IN THE HAND which, though registered for a self-service restaurant, was taken to have disparaged women.[12] **19.14**

Political correctness does not apparently come to the assistance of religious organizations, possibly as a *quid pro quo* for the failure of many religious organizations **19.15**

---

[11] *Harjo v Pro Football Inc*, 50 USPQ 2d 1705 (TTAB 1999).
[12] *Bromberg v Carmel Self Service Inc* 198 USPQ 176 (TTAB 1978).

to support the notion of political correctness. Thus the Unification Church, often referred to (disparagingly) as 'the Moonies', failed to persuade a court that the trade mark MOONIES, registered for a novelty doll which dropped its pants, was a disparagement of its movement.[13]

19.16 It is also probable that political correctness is not a problem when a term which is used as a trade mark disparages a majority rather than a minority of the population. Thus terms like GRINGO[14] and POM[15] are found on the United Kingdom register and do not appear to have caused any noticeable offence.

(4) Brand values and taboos

19.17 Trade marks owners inevitably seek to capture the brand values which are most popular with consumers: foods must be nourishing, healthy or fun; clothing must be stylish, functional or sexy; cars must be fast, safe or technologically advanced, and so on. As a result, quite distinctive trade marks often reflect so closely the values of their closest competitors that, despite their apparent distinctiveness, the consuming public views products bearing those marks as being effectively substitutes for one another. In the past it was common to aim the content of the trade mark itself towards the value which its owner endorsed (for example, HIS MASTER'S VOICE for apparatus for the faithful recording and reproduction of sounds, PRUDENTIAL for insurance policies taken out on the basis of prudence, DURACELL and EVER READY to support the virtue of reliability in batteries and READER'S DIGEST to exemplify potted literacy for the partially educated). This function is now generally performed through marketing rather than through the choice of trade mark.

19.18 A current technique for attracting the attention of consumers, thus separating one's products from the crowded centre of the marketplace, is to reflect or endorse values which shock the consumer and which may even lead him to confront matters which, in not merely marketing terms but also in social terms are considered taboo. This approach has been adopted successfully by companies such as French Connection through its choice of the FCUK trade mark and by Diesel and Benetton, which chose neutral trade marks but promoted them through shock marketing. In recent years, Benetton's exploitation of the generally neglected values of 'death, illness, suffering, piety'[16] has attracted not just increased sales but also moral opprobrium and occasionally the threat of legal action. The commercial

---

[13] *Re In Over Our Heads Inc* 16 USPQ 2d 1653 (TTAB 1990).
[14] Term used by Latin Americans to denote a person from an English-speaking country: registered for, among other things, clothing, luggage and accessories.
[15] Term used by Australians to denote the English, usually in the phrases 'whingeing Pom' or 'Pommie bastards': registered for various types of clothing.
[16] Henning Hartwig, 'United Against Taboo' (2003) 157 *Trademark World* 36, 37.

exploitation of commodities of human suffering such as HIV and prisoners awaiting execution on death row may be in good taste or bad, depending on one's personal perspective; they may prove lucrative or not, but such activity is ultimately likely to remain protected as an exercise of the right of freedom of speech.

D. Business considerations

19.19 Most books on choosing a brand stress how important it is to select a brand which enables a product or service to stand out from its competitors.[17] This advice chimes well with trade mark law, which permits the registration only of those signs which have distinctive character. However, this piece of branding advice is not always appropriate. There is no single branding and trade mark strategy. Each company seeking to build its business will have its own immediate, medium-term and long-term aims, its peculiar financial, geographical and cultural characteristics, its own view of the market in which it competes. Not all companies have significant funds or credit facilities; not all companies are happy to gamble away the security of a low-risk, low-profit enterprise. Most importantly, not all businesses want their products to stand out from the opposition: many aim specifically to brand their goods or services in such a way as to encapsulate and reflect the same norms and values of their competitors. A trade mark for such a company need only (i) fulfil the minimum criterion of distinctiveness, (ii) be not too descriptive to register and (iii) be not too similar to be able to use.

19.20 Probably the most important piece of generalized advice which addresses the business dimension of trade marks is this: make sure that your trade marks fit your business plan. The suitability of a portfolio of trade mark registrations can be ascertained by running through the checklist below.

(1) Do the trade marks owned by or licensed to a business cover its activities?

19.21 Neither trade mark registration nor the protection which they confer will expand automatically when a business does. As new products and services are developed, they may bring the business into markets for which its existing trade mark registrations offer no legal protection. Fortunately a registered trade mark confers protection against the use of the same or a similar trade mark in areas of business which are similar to those for which it is registered. If the trade mark is well enough established it may even provide some protection against its use in quite

---

[17] Typical of this approach is that taken by John Murphy in *Brand Strategy* (1990), especially chs 1–4, and by Tom Blackett and Graham Denton, 'Developing New Brands', in John Murphy (ed), *Branding: A Key Marketing Tool* (1987).

different business activities too.[18] Bearing this in mind, some growth in the provision of core areas of a business' products and services may be protected by existing trade mark registrations—but it should not be assumed that this is so.

(2) Is the cost of maintaining the trade mark portfolio justified?

19.22 Trade marks have to be registered, audited, monitored, renewed and, occasionally, litigated. Could some or all of the cost of these activities be better spent on other and possibly more profitable items or activities? The diversion of resources from registered trade marks to other activities need not denude a business of its legal protection, bearing in mind the availability of at least a basic level of protection for unregistered names and get-up through passing off or unfair competition law and the reduction of trade mark-related spend may be justified. Some trade marks are retained for years after the products or services for which they were used have become marginal to the interests of their owners. Other trade marks, particularly if they are somewhat descriptive, do seem to be rather 'accident-prone' and are the subject of frequent inadvertent encroachment on the part of other traders. Is it worth persevering with them, or would a complete change generate long-term advantages and savings?

(3) Is it worth hanging on to a trade mark if one can take a licence to use someone else's?

19.23 If a business wishes to develop in the field of fast food, hotel services or any other area in which the franchising of business formats is commonplace, it is worth considering the pros and cons of taking a licence to use an established trade mark (HOLIDAY INN, PRONTOPRINT, KFC for example) rather than seeking to develop one's own, initially local goodwill at one's own expense and effort.

E. Psychological considerations

19.24 The psychology of branding and of choosing trade marks is such an important subject that it has an entire chapter to itself.[19]

F. Conclusion

19.25 The choice of a trade mark has important legal, cultural and commercial

---

[18] See Chapters 11 and 12.
[19] See Chapter 20.

F. Conclusion

repercussions. Accordingly the consideration of those repercussions should be on the agenda of a business before a mark is chosen. If not, it is common for the same considerations to be reviewed as part of a damage limitation exercise after a product or service has been launched.

20

THE PSYCHOLOGY OF TRADE MARKS

A.	**Introduction**	
	'Filboid Studge, the Story of a Mouse That Helped' *by 'Saki' (H H Munro)*	
	What does the psychology of branding have to do with trade mark law?	20.01
B.	**The trade mark as an icon of brand loyalty**	
	(1) The trade mark as the measure of difference between goods or services	20.03
	(2) What is brand loyalty?	20.06
	(3) The cultivation of brand loyalty	20.07
	(4) Are there impermissible limits to brand loyalty?	20.10
C.	**Branding strategy in action**	
	(1) Promising more: the psychology of brand extension	20.13
	(2) When the brand is captured by the consumer	20.17
	(3) Damage to brands	20.20
	(4) Negative branding	20.24
D.	**Some aspects of brand psychology**	
	(1) The psychology of infringement	20.26
	(2) The psychology of comparative advertising	20.29
E.	**Conclusion**	20.32

A. Introduction

'Filboid Studge, the Story of a Mouse That Helped' *by 'Saki' (H H Munro)*

'I want to marry your daughter,' said Mark Spayley with faltering eagerness. 'I am only an artist with an income of two hundred a year, and she is the daughter of an enormously wealthy man, so I suppose you will think my offer a piece of presumption.'

Duncan Dullamy, the great company inflator, showed no outward sign of displeasure. As a matter of fact, he was secretly relieved at the prospect of finding even a two-hundred-a-year husband for his daughter Leonore. A crisis was rapidly rushing upon him, from which he knew he would emerge with neither money nor credit; all his recent ventures had fallen flat, and flattest of all had gone the wonderful new breakfast food, Pipenta, on the advertisement of which he had sunk such huge sums. It could scarcely be called a drug in the market; people bought drugs, but no one bought Pipenta.

Chapter 20: The Psychology of Trade Marks

'Would you marry Leonore if she were a poor man's daughter?' asked the man of phantom wealth.

'Yes,' said Mark, wisely avoiding the error of over-protestation. And to his astonishment Leonore's father not only gave his consent, but suggested a fairly early date for the wedding.

'I wish I could show my gratitude in some way,' said Mark with genuine emotion. 'I'm afraid it's rather like the mouse proposing to help the lion.'

'Get people to buy that beastly muck,' said Dullamy, nodding savagely at a poster of the despised Pipenta, 'and you'll have done more than any of my agents have been able to accomplish.'

'It wants a better name,' said Mark reflectively, 'and something distinctive in the poster line. Anyway, I'll have a shot at it.'

Three weeks later the world was advised of the coming of a new breakfast food, heralded under the resounding name of 'Filboid Studge'. Spayley put forth no pictures of massive babies springing up with fungus-like rapidity under its forcing influence, or of representatives of the leading nations of the world scrambling with fatuous eagerness for its possession. One huge sombre poster depicted the Damned in Hell suffering a new torment from their inability to get at the Filboid Studge which elegant young fiends held in transparent bowls just beyond their reach. The scene was rendered even more gruesome by a subtle suggestion of the features of leading men and women of the day in the portrayal of the Lost Souls; prominent individuals of both political parties, Society hostesses, well-known dramatic authors and novelists, and distinguished aeroplanists were dimly recognizable in that doomed throng; noted lights of the musical comedy stage flickered wanly in the shades of the Inferno, smiling still from force of habit, but with the fearsome smiling rage of baffled effort. The poster bore no fulsome allusions to the merits of the new breakfast food, but a single grim statement ran in bold letters along its base: 'They cannot buy it now.'

Spayley had grasped the fact that people will do things from a sense of duty which they would never attempt as a pleasure. There are thousands of respectable middle-class men who, if you found them unexpectedly in a Turkish bath, would explain in all sincerity that a doctor had ordered them to take Turkish baths; if you told them in return that you went there because you liked it, they would stare in pained wonder at the frivolity of your motive. In the same way, whenever a massacre of Armenians is reported from Asia Minor, every one assumes that it has been carried out 'under orders' from somewhere or another; no one seems to think that there are people who might *like* to kill their neighbours now and then.

And so it was with the new breakfast food. No one would have eaten Filboid Studge as a pleasure, but the grim austerity of its advertisement drove housewives in shoals to the grocers' shops to clamour for an immediate supply. In small kitchens solemn pigtailed daughters helped depressed mothers to perform the primitive ritual of its preparation. On the breakfast-tables of cheerless parlours it was partaken of in silence. Once the womenfolk discovered that it was thoroughly unpalatable, their zeal in forcing it on their households knew no bounds. 'You haven't eaten your Filboid Studge!' would be screamed at the appetiteless clerk as he hurried wearily from the breakfast-table, and his evening meal would be prefaced by a warmed-up mess which would be explained as 'your Filboid Studge that you didn't eat this morning.' Those strange fanatics who ostentatiously mortify themselves, inwardly and outwardly, with health biscuits and health garments, battened aggressively on the new food. Earnest spectacled young men devoured it on the steps of the National Liberal Club. A bishop who did not believe in a future state preached against the poster, and a peer's daughter died from eating too much of the compound. A further advertisement was obtained when an infantry regiment mutinied and shot its officers rather than eat the nauseous mess; fortunately, Lord Birrell of Blatherstone, who was *War Minister* at the moment, saved the situation by his happy epigram, that 'Discipline to be effective must be optional.'

Filboid Studge had become a household word, but Dullamy wisely realized that it was not necessarily the last word in breakfast dietary; its supremacy would be challenged as soon as some yet more unpalatable food should be put on the market. There might even be a reaction in favour of something tasty and appetizing, and the Puritan austerity of the moment might be banished from domestic cookery. At an opportune moment, therefore, he sold out his interests in the article which had brought him in colossal wealth at a critical juncture, and placed his financial reputation beyond the reach of cavil. As for Leonore, who was now an heiress on a far greater scale than ever before, he naturally found her something a vast deal higher in the husband market than a two-hundred-a-year poster designer. Mark Spayley, the brainmouse who had helped the financial lion with such untoward effect, was left to curse the day he produced the wonder-working poster.

'After all,' said Clovis, meeting him shortly afterwards at his club, 'you have this doubtful consolation, that 'tis not in mortals to countermand success.'

What does the psychology of branding have to do with trade mark law?

20.01 This story, published before the First World War, demonstrates: (i) the capacity of a brand to influence decision-making on the part of the consumer; (ii) the necessity of choosing the brand which is appropriate for the relevant market; (iii) the power which a brand unleashes when attached to the right marketing strategy; as well as (iv) the importance of establishing one's rights to creative work through the conclusion of written contracts between co-operating parties. We see the same story today, though perhaps too closely to appreciate it. TOMMY HILFIGER, for example, is a brand which has demonstrated its capacity to influence consumer choice; the marketing strategy for it was brilliantly conceived. But would the same strategy have worked if it had been executed in relation to the hypothetical brand name ELMER WIMP?

20.02 The selection of a name is merely one of several psychological dimensions to the development of brands based on the firm platform of trade mark protection. The previous chapter looked at issues arising from the need to choose a trade mark; this chapter examines some of those other psychological considerations.

B. The trade mark as an icon of brand loyalty

(1) The trade mark as the measure of difference between goods or services

20.03 Where a number of businesses compete against each other in the same market, classical trade mark theory has tended to run along the following logic:

(i) each business within the market provides goods or services for consumers at a specific and identifiable level of quality and at a price which reflects the cost of production together with a reasonable mark-up for profit;
(ii) as a result of each competing business producing that identifiable standard of goods or services at its own unique price, consumers recognize that those goods or services are not of uniform quality or of uniform price; and
(iii) the trade mark attached to those goods or services is the means (a) by which the consumer identifies their competing sources and (b) by which the consumer is enabled to make repeat purchases of goods and services which satisfy him and/or to avoid making repeat purchases of goods and services which displease him.

20.04 Increasingly in modern commerce the first premiss in this three-stage reasoning is coming under assault. This is because such considerations as (i) the need to comply with health and safety requirements, (ii) the need to comply with product labelling requirements, (iii) the convergence of the properties of both goods and services in the light of perceived consumer preferences, (iv) the demands of fashion and (v) the use of common outsourced suppliers gravitate towards the gradual homogenization of both the quality and the price of products. This trend has been expressed most succinctly by the head of one of Europe's leading design houses:

> Look at financial services, petrol retailing, airlines and the chemical industry, just to take some broad industrial and commercial areas at random. In all of these activities there is very little or no real difference between the products and services of the leading players in terms of price, quality and service. Being as good as the best of the competition is now sufficient only to enable an organisation to stay in the race.
>
> In these situations emotional factors, being liked, admired or respected more than the competition, help the organisation to win. And that is why so many organisations now invest so heavily in what is increasingly being called corporate branding.[1]

20.05 This is a sophisticated and eloquent way of telling us that the only real and meaningful difference between goods and services in those fields of commerce is not the quality of competing goods and services and it is not the price—it is the trade mark itself. Where that is the case, corporate resources are increasingly directed at making the public love its brand and in using its trade mark rights (and, where appropriate, other intellectual property rights) as a means of removing or reducing 'interference' with the signs and icons through which it establishes brand loyalty.

(2) What is brand loyalty?

20.06 Like love between human beings, brand loyalty is a phenomenon which it is eas-

---

[1] Wolff Olins, *The New Guide to Identity: How to Create and Sustain Change through Managing Identity* (1995), p 30.

B. The trademark as an icon of brand loyalty

ier to experience than to explain rationally. This book is not the place to explain it. Suffice it to say that a brand may exercise particular power over its consumers; the trade mark is the legal anchor which protects the brand from drifting away from its owner's control. Attack the trade mark and you weaken the brand. That is why, although competition law is not concerned with protecting brand values, trade mark law is. And that is why there is a powerful and continuing tension between those forces which seek to promote comparative advertising and those forces which wish to minimize or indeed suppress it.

(3) The cultivation of brand loyalty

Once a consumer identifies his satisfaction with a product or service with the brand by which it is known, a strong bond of loyalty may be established. This loyalty is particularly pronounced where a product has distinctive characteristics (for example, a favourite brand of drink, confectionery or perfume) which cannot be easily replicated by that product's competitors. Examples of products with distinctive qualities that attract intense loyalty are GAULOISES cigarettes, JACK DANIEL's whiskey and CHANEL NO 5 perfume. The same loyalty is noticeable even where the goods of competitors are entirely substitutable for each other and it is only the trade mark itself which conveys values that the consumer finds attractive, as in the case of casual shirts which may be indistinguishable from each other if it were not for the POLO, LACOSTE or equivalent logo. Where, as in the case of POLO and LACOSTE, the brand exudes a 'lifestyle' message, a consumer's adherence to that lifestyle strengthens that brand loyalty even further. 20.07

Some forms of loyalty do not depend upon the quality of the product branded or upon the power of the brand's ethos. Football clubs, for example, have enjoyed the loyalty of their supporters on account of a variety of factors: locality, family and social ties and peer-group approval have all shaped the attachment of the supporters to a team irrespective of (i) the quality of football played or (ii) the style of football practised. Clubs such as Real Madrid, Barcelona and Manchester United have however reached out beyond the level of a purely parochial relationship with their supporters. They have turned themselves into truly international brands, offering their supporter-consumers a range of goods (many of which are quite unrelated to football) using trade marks in order to exploit this loyalty to the full. 20.08

The trade mark monopoly cannot prevent the copying of products or services themselves, but it can provide some degree of protection for the relationship between brand owner and consumer by preventing the use or registration of trade marks designed to weaken the brand's appeal or distinctive characteristics. The trade mark can also protect brand loyalty when the original source of that loyalty no longer produces the goods on which the brand is based. For example, loyalty to KENTUCKY FRIED CHICKEN did not expire with the death in 1980 of Colonel 20.09

Harlan Sanders; nor did BEN 'N' JERRYS aficionados abandon their ice cream of choice once the product was acquired by Unilever.

(4) Are there impermissible limits to brand loyalty?

20.10 As between a trade mark owner and his consumer, the relationship can be as close or as distant as the respective parties wish and prevailing market conditions dictate. But the European Commission is vigilant in ensuring that the same techniques as those employed in branding are not employed by EU Member States for impermissible purposes. This vigilance is necessary if the EU's competition policy—of which trade mark and geographical appellation protection forms a major part—is to be respected.

20.11 Accordingly, it is possible, both in principle and in practice, to use a place name as a trade mark (for example, CHIEMSEE for sportswear[2]). It is also possible to employ a place name as a designation which relates to the particular qualities or characteristics of goods originating from that place (for example, CHAMPAGNE for a type of wine manufactured in the Champagne region of France by the *methode Champagnoise*). It is not however possible to use a place name as a means of attracting custom which is based solely on the fact that goods originate from that place, irrespective of the fact that goods of equivalent quality and price may also be available on the market: that would make the consumer's market choice depend upon economically irrational factors such as the nationality or location of origin of the goods, which would favour more populous geographical regions and retard the free movement of goods. Thus, for example, it was impermissible under article 28 of the EC Treaty to reserve the sign 'Markenqualität aus deutschen Landen' ('quality label for produce made in Germany') for quality produce made in Germany.[3] Nor could the French continue to reserve for French products such terms as 'Salaisons d'Auvergne' ('Salted meats from the Auvergne'), 'Savoie', 'Normandie' and 'Lorraine' (these being regions of France) unless those terms were used as geographical appellations for products with specifically designated characteristics.[4]

20.12 Nationalism can be evoked in more subtle ways than through the use of labels. The use of the colours of the national flag in the colour-coding of both trade marks and the livery of goods and services can achieve this end. American goods which are branded in red, white and blue (colours used heavily in conjunction with TOMMY HILFIGER and PEPSI COLA products, for example) can effortlessly sug-

---

[2] *Windsurfing Chiemsee Produktions- und Vertriebs GmbH v Boots- und Segelzubehör Walter Huber and Franz Attenberger*, Joined Cases C-108 and 109/97 [1999] ETMR 585 (ECJ).
[3] *Commission of the European Communities v Federal Republic of Germany*, Case C-325/00 [2003] ETMR 417 (ECJ).
[4] *Commission v French Republic*, Case C-6/02, 6 March 2003 (ECJ).

gest a connection to all-American values. There is also a down side to this: when a country is unpopular (for example, products originating in the United States were the subject of localized boycotts in some Middle East communities which were heavily out of sympathy with its decision to invade Iraq in 2003), the nationalistic colour-coding policy can result in the loss of custom from even those consumers who cannot recognize the unfamiliar lettering of the brand but recognize its colour scheme. Curiously the association of a nationalistic colour with leading brands does not appear to have impaired their path towards market globalization. This may indicate either that such colour schemes have a positive impact even abroad, or that the vast majority of consumers are indifferent to the colour scheme's significance.

C. Branding strategy in action

(1) Promising more: the psychology of brand extension

20.13 Where a trade mark owner has established a particular relationship with his consuming public, he may want to build upon this relationship if he can identify the positive attributes of his brand and then transfer them to other products or services which those same consumers may wish to buy or use. For example, that sector of the public which enjoys visiting STARBUCKS coffee shops can be persuaded to purchase bags of STARBUCKS coffee for use at home, as well as STARBUCKS hardware (mugs, cafetières and so on). The ambience of Starbucks products and the expectation of pleasure transfers well from one area to another which is related to it. A version of brand extension along similar lines with which most of us are familiar is the legend: 'If you liked the book, you'll love the film' (or, more likely nowadays, if you liked the film you'll love the tie-ins'[5]).

20.14 Occasionally an exercise in brand extension will succeed even where there is no connection at all between the users or purchasers of the original branded product and purchasers of products to which the brand is extended. Where this happens, it is not so much the consumers' expectations of fulfilment as the brand owner's own ethos which is the subject of the successful brand extension. The CATERPILLAR brand was first used for earth-moving equipment and the purchasers of such equipment were not the prime market for the fashionable clothing and footwear to which the brand was extended—but the ethos of rugged good looks and durability did transfer. Other examples include the extension of HARLEY DAVIDSON from motorcycles to cosmetics and deodorants, where the ethos of cool hedonism transferred to a whole generation of non-bikers, as well as the launch of

---

[5] The film *The Matrix Reloaded* generated tie-ins which included DVD, CD, VHS versions, computer games, posters, fetus hats and a virtual Nebuchadnezzar assembly kit.

affinity credit-card schemes and telecom services by football clubs, charities and other non-banking organizations.

20.15 A useful exercise in brand extension is to take some well-known brands which possess a particular ethos and conjecture as to which products or services would most closely fit in with that ethos. The VOLVO vehicle brand, for example, conveys (among other things) an image of safety. This could enable the VOLVO brand to succeed when used on products such as locks, safes, mountain climbing equipment and parachutes, as well as security services. The BODY SHOP brand conveys the notion of possessing both an ecological and an economic conscience: it could be extended from cosmetics and body maintenance accessories to foods, clothes, alternative medicinal treatments and the like.

20.16 Where neither the consumers' expectations nor the brand's ethos are transferred, the result is likely to fail. An example of this was the extension of the CADBURY's brand from chocolate to powdered instant mashed potatoes. It is not difficult to think of other examples: they can be ridiculous. For example, FERRARI from cars to hot-water bottles, PIZZA HUT from pizza restaurants to pension funds, TAMPAX from female sanitary products to men's fashions, SAMSONITE from luggage to ice cream and INTEL from semiconductor chips to cigarettes.

(2) When the brand is captured by the consumer

20.17 Ownership of a trade mark enables a brand owner to control many facets of his brand's development and thereby keep the initiative when dealing with competitors and other traders. By creating and promulgating a brand ethos, the trade mark owner attracts and stimulates custom and seeks to ensure, through his ownership of the mark, that the benefit of the goodwill and reputation in the brand will be within his power. Yet control of the trade mark may be lost to consumers. The 'revolt' by loyal COCA-COLA drinkers over the proposed change to that product's formula is a case in point which is chronicled later on in this book.[6]

20.18 A more serious threat to the trade mark proprietor's control of his brand comes where his most loyal and faithful customers seek not so much to preserve the brand's heritage against unwanted change, which is what happened in the COCA-COLA case, but where they actively seize and subvert the brand for their own purposes and re-establish its ethos in the minds of the general public as something quite different from what the trade mark owner intended. This has happened when relatively neutral products have been associated with violence. A case in point is the hijacking of DOCTOR MARTEN boots by various groups:

---

[6] See Chapter 21, paras 21.25–21.29.

C. Branding strategy in action

You don't need to be a skinhead to indulge in some tough bovver boy style. Toughen up your image with tight turned up jeans and jackets in faded or bleached denim (skinheads were the originators of splashing Domestos on denim), bomber jackets, braces and a pair of 16 hole Dr Marten boots. This look was once only associated with right-wing fascists but since it's been adopted by gay men and its roots in 60s Ska and Mod culture have been revived, you won't be labelled a hooligan.[7]

There are three things a brand owner can do where this occurs: (i) he can seek to dissociate himself from the politics or culture of the group(s) which have taken over his brand, (ii) he can seek actively to build on this unsolicited image and its concomitant goodwill or (iii) he can ignore the problem and hope it goes away. The first course of action is likely to alienate existing loyal customers and may thus be seen as an act of betrayal, while not necessarily guaranteeing that any new and more brand-acceptable loyalists will replace them. The second approach will please existing loyalists but may discourage the wider purchasing public from making purchases and experiencing the quality of the product. The third approach, particularly where fashions change rapidly, where memories are short or where an age-based target market is replaced by fresh consumers who move into the same age group, may well be the best in the long term. 20.19

(3) Damage to brands

A brand can become damaged or destroyed and, when this occurs, the value of related trade marks will decrease or may disappear entirely.[8] In the 1980s, for example, a popular product was sold in the United Kingdom under the trade mark SLIMMERS AYDS. When the pandemic Acquired Immune Deficiency Syndrome became referred to as 'Aids', this being a condition which led to sufferers contracting diseases which wasted their bodies, use of the term SLIMMERS AYDS became an embarrassment to shoppers. 20.20

There is no general legal power vested in a trade mark proprietor which entitles him to object to the public picking on his trade mark as a name for an ailment. This being so, what steps can the trade mark owner take to avoid or minimize damage? Probably the best thing one can do in the case of a widespread and persistent ailment is to change the trade name at the earliest possible opportunity, reckoning that the news value of the change will itself generate a good deal of gratuitous publicity. In the case of ailments which are likely to be little known beyond a small circle of doctors, scientists, patients and their families, it may not be worth doing anything. 20.21

---

[7] See www.widemedia.com/fashionuk/news/2000/07/07news0000560.html.
[8] For a lively account of the concept of 'badwill' in a damaged brand and its relation to goodwill, see Louis Tompos, 'Badwill' (2003) 116 Harv Law Rev 1845–67.

Chapter 20: The Psychology of Trade Marks

20.22 Some damage to a brand is self-inflicted, for example, in 1990 where benzene was accidentally introduced into some bottles of PERRIER mineral water, resulting in the loss of an estimated 140 million bottles of water and causing long-term loss of confidence in the PERRIER brand. Other damage may be inflicted by third parties, such as the tampering with TYLENOL painkillers at retail outlets.[9] Other damage still may result from unforeseen accidents such as the Exxon Valdez oil spill off Alaska in 1989. Even such routine events as the manner in which a corporation lays off its staff can have a localized impact on the power of that company's brand.[10]

20.23 The common factor in instances such as these is that the image of the brand among consumers in general and the public at large is badly shaken. It is remarkable that so few major brands should have been damaged in this way during a period in which staple commodities such as eggs (carrying salmonella), beef (carrying Creutzfeldt-Jakob Disease), tuna (mercury) and farmed salmon (carrying a whole cocktail of noxious elements) have seen their own generic reputations suffer severely. Perhaps the relative buoyancy of brands is a consequence of the care which trade mark owners take in cultivating them.

(4) Negative branding

20.24 Between the nineteenth century and the 1960s, trade marks tended to be bright, cheerful, things which portrayed a wholesome image to the consuming public. From the 1960s onwards the cultural revolution which so affected personal and social *mores* made its mark on branding policy too. While much effort was directed prior to the 1960s towards the securing of trade marks such as SUNLIGHT and PERFECTION, we have seen in the past two generations a trend towards the registration of trade marks such as POISON for perfume and FCUK for clothing. Examples of dubious taste in less-well known marks registered in the United Kingdom include DEATH (cigarettes) and SNOTBLASTER (essential oils). We have yet to see marks such as CARRION for meat products, but the concept is now no longer unthinkably shocking.

20.25 The choice of trade marks with negative imagery reflects the mood of a consumer market which, though not often non-conformist, often wishes to be perceived as such. An interesting issue which the use of these marks poses is whether the relationship between trade mark owner and consumer can be sustained as the consumer progresses from rebellion and through various stages of non-conformity

---

[9] Such damage need not be permanent: the commendably vigorous response of TYLENOL to the threat of tampering resulted in the restoration of brand loyalty and indeed in its increase.

[10] A survey of 1,200 recently laid-off workers conducted by Vault Inc in 2001 revealed that 54% of those laid off said they would not recommend the company's products or services to others on the basis of the way their lay-off was handled: see www.accountingnet.com/x31751.xml.

until he reaches the stages of 'individuality' (a positive label for 'non-conformity' which is usually reserved for those who have more purchasing power) and ultimately to conformity. Since trade marks are so image-oriented, it is probably best to have a whole set of product ranges, each with its own separate trade mark-protected ethos, through which the young consumer may pass on his journey towards middle age and beyond. A branding policy which takes account of consumer image shifts over time will therefore accommodate the affluent youngster who is ready to replace his ready-to-shock style for something a little smoother.

D. Some aspects of brand psychology

(1) The psychology of infringement

The risk that a trade mark will be infringed is the *raison d'être* for trade mark registration as well as the outcome for which trade mark proprietors have the least desire. Although the vast majority of trade mark rights are never infringed at all and a good number of actual infringements are probably never spotted, the whole of the registration system is ultimately directed to what is a relatively infrequent outcome, the infringement trial. **20.26**

Where an infringement is detected or suspected by the trade mark owner, infringement litigation is just one of a number of possible outcomes. Among the other options available to the trade mark owner are the following: (i) do nothing; (ii) sell the trade mark to someone else who is prepared to do something; (iii) turn the alleged infringer into a licensee; (iv) seek to resolve any differences of position through mediation; or (v) commit oneself to a non-judicial but legally binding determination by an arbitrator. The choice of outcome will depend on a cocktail of factors: the cost of taking action, the cost of inaction, the availability of time and resources, the likelihood of success or failure, the extent to which the trade mark owner is prepared to take risks, his desire to deter other prospective infringers and so on. **20.27**

Viewed from the point of view of the infringer, infringement is not just a state of affairs in which a trader uses a sign which falls within the scope of protection which the law confers upon a registered trade mark: it is often the product of a complex set of thought processes. Bear in mind the following reflections: **20.28**

(i) Infringement of a trade mark may be seen as a strong endorsement of the brand's worth. To put it another way, if a trade mark isn't worth infringing, perhaps it isn't worth having. Colloquially it is said that 'imitation is the sincerest form of flattery'. That imitation certainly gives the trade mark owner a sense of whether his goods are setting the agenda for others to follow or whether he is engaged in pursuit of ascendancy in the eyes of the consuming public.

(ii) At the point at which counterfeit goods are brought to the market, the 'leverage' of the infringed brand is exposed, giving consumers and competitors alike a notion of the difference between what it can cost to make the product and what the legitimate market is prepared to pay for it. Thus both actual counterfeiting and the threat of it may act as a regulator of the trade mark owner's pricing policy. Brand owners find this frustrating because, as they correctly point out, they incur the cost of research, testing, developing and marketing not only their commercially successful products but also their commercially unsuccessful ones, while counterfeiters cherry-pick only the commercially successful products and incur none of the brand owners' overheads.

(iii) In the case of counterfeiting, each infringer depends, for his advantage, upon the trade mark owner enforcing the trade mark monopoly against all other infringers except himself. If a trade mark-protected product is not policed in this manner, an infringer finds that his profit margins are eroded by the sale of infringing products by other infringers and that the credibility of the infringed brand suffers from widespread copying. When the point is reached at which the credibility of the brand suffers, the goodwill in the infringed brand will diminish and, in proportion to this diminution, his opportunity to sustain profit margins also shrinks.

(2) The psychology of comparative advertising

20.29 Comparative advertising is a mechanism for enabling the champion of one product or service to get a market advantage over a competitor. There is no limit to the scale of advantage which may be obtained. In a perfect market, assuming a fully informed body of consumers and the same degree of availability of all competing products at the same price, we should imagine that a successful exercise in comparative advertising will drive out of business the competitor whose goods or services have been adversely compared. As such, comparative advertising achieves the survival of the fittest: it has been called 'perhaps the crudest form of commercial Darwinism'.[11]

20.30 Since the trade mark is generally the means by which a product or service is known, competition theory justifies the use of a competitor's trade mark as the most efficient means of informing the consumer of the deficiencies or inadequacies of the goods or services which he might otherwise buy. The consumer may however have a stable relationship with the owner of that trade mark, based on considerations which run counter to the elimination of weak traders through the exercise of consumer choice. These considerations exasperate economists but not lawyers (particularly trade mark lawyers).

---

[11] Sonya Willimsky, 'Comparative Advertising: an Overview' [1996] EIPR 649.

E. Conclusion

So why do people buy inferior products? There are many reasons. For example, if there is less demand for them, they may be more speedily or cheaply available. The consumer may own shares in the company making the inferior goods and thus wish to support it. The product might not be the best, but at least it fits the same space on the cupboard shelf as did its predecessor. The consumer may want to make a statement as to his character by not being perceived as a 'me-too' purchaser of all the leading lines in the shops, and so on. The consumer may also experience the phenomenon of brand loyalty (discussed in the next chapter). **20.31**

E. Conclusion

Brand loyalty and brand strategy have a psychological dimension which it is important to recognize. This is because the relationship between the brand owner and consumer is a form of property which, within certain specific parameters, depends upon the trade mark for its protection. By paying sufficient attention to that psychological dimension, it should be possible to maximize the advantage which a valid trade mark confers. **20.32**

21

TRADE MARKS, IMAGES, ICONS AND SOCIAL RESPONSIBILITY

A.	Introduction	
	'Kiss me here, touch there'	
	The moral of the story	21.01
B.	*No Logo*: the thesis	21.03
C.	No excuse: formulating a response	21.15
D.	No chance: brand power and goodwill	21.24
E.	No change: why the public's best weapons may never be adequately utilized	21.29
F.	No fear: why the consumer apocalypse may never happen	21.38
G.	No Armageddon: the threat of trade mark litigation	21.40
H.	Conclusion	21.44

A. Introduction

'Kiss me here, touch there'[1]

'If you're not on the team of a company large enough to control a significant part of the playing field, and can't afford your very own team of lawyers, you don't get to play.'

That is the lesson, it would seem, of Mattel's [trademark] suit against the Danish pop band Aqua and its label MCA. Mattel charged that the band's hit song 'Barbie Girl'—which contains lyrics like 'Kiss me here, touch there, hanky panky'—wrongfully sexualizes its wholesome blonde. Mattel went to court in September 1997 charging Aqua with trademark infringement and unfair competition. The toy manufacturer asked for damages and for the album to be removed from stores and destroyed. Aqua won the dispute . . .

Although the music itself is pure cotton candy, the Aqua case is worth considering . . . It also highlighted the uncomfortable tension between the expansive logic of branding—the corporate desire for full cultural integration—and the petty logic of

---

[1] Extracted from Naomi Klein, *No Logo* (2000), pp 180–1.

Chapter 21: Trade Marks, Images, Icons and Social Responsibility

these legal crusades. Who if not Barbie is as much cultural symbol as product? Barbie, after all, is the archetypal space invader, a cultural imperialist in pink. She is the one who paints entire towns fuchsia to celebrate 'Barbie Month'. She is the Zen mistress who for the past four decades has insisted on being everything to young girls—doctor, bimbo, teenager, career girl, Unicef ambassador . . .

The people at Mattel weren't interested in talking about Barbie the cultural icon when they launched the Aqua suit, however. 'This is a business issue, not a freedom of speech issue', a Mattel spokesman told *Billboard*. 'This is a $2 billion company, and we don't want it messed around with, and situations like this gradually lead to brand erosion' . . .

But while this fight against erosion seems reasonable in the context of brands competing with each other, it's a different matter when looked at from the lens of aggressive lifestyle branding—and from that perspective, a re-examination of the public's right to respond to these 'private' images seems urgently required. Mattel, for instance, has reaped huge profits by encouraging young girls to build elaborate dream lives round their doll, but it still wants that relationship to be a monologue. The toy company, which boasts of having 'as many as 100 different [trademark] investigations going on at any time throughout the world', is almost comically aggressive in protecting this formula. Among other feats, its lawyers have shut down a riot girl zine called *Hey, There, Barbie Girl!* And successfully blocked the distribution of Todd Haynes's documentary *Superstar: The Karen Carpenter Story*, a re-enactment of the life of the anorexic pop star using Barbies as puppets (legal pressure also came from Carpenter's family).

It seems fitting that Aqua member Sten Rasted says he got the idea for the song 'Barbie Girl' after visiting 'an art-museum exhibition for kids on Barbie'. In an effort to have its star doll inaugurated as a cultural artefact, Mattel has in recent years been mounting travelling exhibits of old Barbies which claim to tell the history of America through 'America's favourite doll'. Some of these shows are put on by Mattel, others by private collectors working closely with the company, a relationship that ensures that unpleasant chapters in Barbie's history—the feminist backlash against the doll, say, or Barbie the cigarette model—are mysteriously absent. There is no question that Barbie, like a handful of other classic brands, is an icon and artefact in addition to being a children's toy. But Mattel . . . wants to be treated as an important pop-culture artefact at the same time as it seeks to maintain complete proprietary control over its historical and cultural legacy. It's a process that ultimately gags cultural criticism, using copyright and trademark laws as effective tools to silence all unwanted opposition.

The moral of the story

21.01 This trade mark infringement action, from which Mattel unsuccessfully appealed,[2] reflects the desire of the trade mark owner to 'have his cake and eat it': to

---

[2] *Mattel Inc v MCA Records Inc* 296 F 3d 894 (9th Cir 2000); cert denied 123 Sup Ct 993. The court ruled that the use of 'Barbie Girl' as the title and subject of a pop song neither infringed nor diluted the BARBIE trade mark. The US Supreme Court subsequently denied Mattel a petition for writ of *certiorari*. In the light of the subsequent Supreme Court decision in *Moseley et al, dba Victor's Little Secret v V Secret Catalogue Inc* 537 US 418, 123 Sup Ct 1115 (2003) that a trade mark owner must prove actual damage rather than a likelihood of damage in dilution proceedings, Mattel's legal position now appears even weaker than before.

establish a commercially viable brand which assumes the status of a cultural icon and then, through the use of legal rules which were originally designed in order to protect it against competitors, to preserve the integrity of the brand against parody, satire, criticism and any other unwanted 'noise' which interferes with the message which the brand owner seeks to transmit to the consumer. But criticism of Mattel's conduct should not be confused with criticism of the law itself: the same rules which enable the Mattels of this world to assert the power of the BARBIE trade mark are the rules which civil-rights icon Rosa Parks successfully invoked against the producers of a rap song, 'Rosa Parks', whose invocation of her name was held to have no artistic relevance to that song.[3]

21.02 In this chapter we examine the situation which arises when a trade mark transcends the status of a brand[4] and becomes a cultural icon with a forceful and influential personality of its own. This examination is conducted chiefly through the eyes of one of modern branding's most serious and influential critics.

B. *No Logo*: the thesis

21.03 In her book *No Logo* (2000) Naomi Klein raises a passionately argued case against the owners of some of the largest internationally established brands. It should not be thought that, since Klein is a journalist rather than a lawyer, her case does not require to be answered or that it can be brushed aside.[5] Even if every assertion she has made were provably false (which is not the case), the care with which she has assembled her case and provided sources for her allegations would entitle her to receive a fairly reasoned response from the trade mark community and not a trite dismissal. The charges which Klein makes against modern 'big business' practices in general and the activities of the major brand owners in particular occupy some hundreds of pages and will not be replicated in this chapter. Klein's thesis is based on the following propositions.

21.04 1. Companies have redirected their attention from the manufacture of products to the creation of brand ethos. Instead of making and selling goods, they increasingly create and market images. Unlike the manufacture of goods, which ties up capital in plant, labour and production costs, the creation of images is an intellectual activity which requires relatively little capital investment[6] but a correspondingly

---

[3] *Parks v LaFace Records* No 99–2495, 12 May 2003 (6th Cir 2003): the court considered that the repetition of the words 'move to the back of the bus' in the song's chorus did not allude to civil-rights issues but to the pop group OutKast being of higher quality than its competitors.

[4] For a description of the concept of a 'brand', see Chapter 1.

[5] For a perfect example of a patronizing *in hominem* brush-off which seeks to ridicule Klein while patently failing to address her case, see 'Why Naomi Klein Needs to Grow Up', *The Economist*, 9 November 2002, p 86.

[6] *No Logo*, ch 1 ('New Branded World').

heavy spend in advertising.[7] In relation to this proposition it must be conceded that trade mark law facilitates this practice since it enables trade mark owners to protect and develop their brands without the need for them to be the physical source and origin of their goods.[8]

21.05 2. When an image which is associated with a brand expands in popularity and power, it intrudes into the cultural life of those societies to which it is exposed and by which it is adopted. This intrusion may be achieved by conventional advertising and also by the sponsorship of events and institutions and by the association of the brand with activities which fall outside the apparent context of the brand itself.[9] Depending on one's standpoint the injection of private brand-injected funding into public and cultural events may be viewed as an act of social responsibility,[10] as a necessary evil where other sources of funding have failed to materialize or as an act of economic colonialism.

21.06 3. This intrusion makes itself felt not only in the regular advertising and media but also in the invasion of private space and communal space (for example, in the school curriculum and school premises). At this point the image conveyed by the brand is not something outside the consumer, to which individuals or groups of consumers aspire, but becomes a 'social experience' or a 'lived reality'.[11]

21.07 4. As tax revenues collected from the major brand-owning companies continue to fall as a proportion of public income, the role played by brand-owners in subsidizing and effectively subverting public events for their advantage increases. The brand-owners are thus able to adopt the mantle of public benefactors when what they are actually doing is creating further platforms for the integration of their brand into consumer consciousness.[12]

21.08 5. As global brands continue to gain power, the economies of scale which their owners can achieve, together with the outsourcing of manufacture to some of the world's most impoverished and therefore cheapest labour zones, have the effect of killing smaller competition, thus (i) homogenizing town-centre shopping areas and (ii) if not actually eliminating genuine consumer choice, narrowing it down

---

[7] The vital significance of advertising is reflected in the German motto 'Wer nicht wirbt, stirbt' ('The one who does not advertise . . . dies').
[8] Under 15 USC, s 1125(a)(1)(A) trade mark owners are protected against confusion with regard to matters as far from goods' physical origin as 'affiliation, connection, association . . . sponsorship or approval'. In the EU *Canon Kabushiki Kaisha v Metro-Goldwyn-Mayer Inc*, Case C-39/97 [1999] ETMR 1 establishes that trade mark owners are protected against acts which induce the belief that the goods come from 'economically linked undertakings', regardless of those goods' origin.
[9] ibid.
[10] Marcel Knobil, '"No Logo" Brand Fails to Deliver', 13 *British Brands*, Spring 2001, p 1.
[11] *No Logo*, ch 2 ('The Brand Expands').
[12] ibid.

B. *No Logo: the thesis*

to choice between large-scale competitors only.[13] The process of killing off smaller competition is a collusive one in that it requires the continued support of consumers, who may not realize the consequences of their actions.

6. Since the big brands have ceased to serve solely a trade mark function but have become cultural icons in their own right, the public have a genuine expectation that they too can make use of them. The brand-owning corporations do not allow this to happen, wielding intellectual property rights such as copyright and trade marks in order to prevent even trivial uses being made of their brand image[14] as well as the use of their brand by fanzines.

21.09

7. The advertising-bearing media such as the press and the television industry are increasingly dependent on the income which they earn from a smaller number of large, powerful brand-owners. This in turn enables the brand-owners to manipulate these media and discourage or prevent their carrying news items and features which may be adverse to the interests of the brand-owners or the images portrayed by their brands, thus creating

21.10

> a picture of corporate space as a fascist state where we all salute the logo and have little opportunity for criticism because our newspapers, television stations, Internet servers, streets and retail spaces are all controlled by multinational corporate interests.[15]

Another contemporary critic of big-brandism, Kalle Lasn visualizes an even bleaker outcome. In strikingly emotive language he describes the absorption by the state itself of the corporate fascism to which Klein refers:

21.11

> *America is no longer a country. It's a multitrillion-dollar brand.* America™ is essentially no different than McDonalds, Marlboro or General Motors. It's an image sold not only to the citizens of the U.S.A. but to consumers worldwide. The American brand is associated with catchwords such as democracy, opportunity and freedom. But like cigarettes that are sold as symbols of vitality and youthful rebellion, the American reality is very different from its brand image. America™ has been subverted by corporate agendas. Its elected officials bow before corporate power as a condition of their survival in office. A collective sense of powerlessness and disillusionment has set in. A deeply felt sense of betrayal is brewing.[16]

8. Ultimately consumers will resent the absence of free cultural space and, motivated by their sense of betrayal by the brands for which they have not voted but

21.12

---

[13] *No Logo*, ch 6 ('Brand Bombing'). For a further powerfully expressed account of this phenomenon, see Susan George, 'Corporate Globalisation' in Bircham and Charlton, *Anti Capitalism: A Guide to the Movement* (2001), pp 11–24.

[14] *No Logo*, ch 8 ('Corporate Censorship'), esp the examples cited at pp 176–80.

[15] ibid, p 187. This statement is inaccurately described as Klein's thesis in 'Pro Logo: The Case for Brands', *The Economist*, 8 September 2001, p 9.

[16] *Culture Jam* (2000), Introduction, p xii.

have purchased into power, they will rise up against their oppressors. Lasn cites a familiar case in point:

> In the 1998 film *The Truman Show* a corporation adopts Truman Burbank at birth, then carefully scripts a whirl of product placement and impression management into his life, which is televised live, twenty-four hours a day. The only time Truman upsets that managed order, when he catches a glimpse of the real world behind his scripted life, is when he does something spontaneous. Slowly he comes to realize that only a chain of spontaneous acts will lead to salvation. The culture jammer is seized by a similar sense of urgency to do something, anything, to escape the consumerist script.[17]

21.13   But Truman Burbank was just an enlightened individual and *The Truman Show* had a happy ending. Reality, in Klein's eyes, has employed a different team of scriptwriters:

> As more people discover the brand-name secrets of the global logo web, their outrage will fuel the next big political movement, a vast wave of opposition targeting transnational corporations, particularly those with very high name-brand recognition.[18]

21.14   Again, Lasn writes in militant terms:

> We will strike by unswooshing America™, by organising resistance against the power trust that owns and manages that brand. Like Marlboro and Nike, America™ has splashed its logo everywhere.[19]

C. No excuse: formulating a response

21.15   The accusations of brand abuse are serious and they hurt all conscientious brand owners. This is because the building of a successful brand is, at least in its initial stages, almost entirely dependent upon giving the consumer sufficient satisfaction to enable the brand owner and the consumer to strike up and then maintain a relationship. Yet these criticisms state clearly that this relationship is one which is good for the brand owner and bad for the consumer, bad for the economy, bad for the environment and bad for the principle of choice.

21.16   One way to address these criticisms is to say that the consumer is a voluntary party to the alleged abuses: if that's what the consumer wants, then that's what the consumer gets since that is the natural order of things. Just as psychologists are familiar with the phenomenon that humans often form deeply loving bonds with partners who abuse their faith, their trust and their bodies, we too can claim familiarity with—if not deep understanding of—the consumer who forms the

---

[17] ibid, p 107.
[18] *No Logo*, p xviii.
[19] *Culture Jam*, p xvi.

C. No excuse: formulating a response

equivalent of a deeply loving bond with a brand which ultimately damages him. But this is not a response. In human terms, legislation adopts a paternalistic role and intervenes to protect the abused partner, at least in fields such as medicine, health and safety and product liability. This is scarcely the case for alleged brand abuse.

How, then, should the socially aware, objectively honest trade mark proprietor or lawyer approach the task of responding to these points? **21.17**

First, we should recognize that Klein's case has not been built upon the misfeasance of all brand owners in respect of all brands. The issues which she raises are addressed to a number of globalized brands which, though of enormous power, are only a small fraction of all brands. The vast majority of brand owners are not indicted by Klein's accusations. Brand owners are not accused where their brands are (i) not actually globalized or in the process of becoming so, (ii) non-aspirational and not in danger of becoming cultural icons, and which (iii) do not seek (arguably cynically, if legally) to exploit the environment or social and economic conditions and, in so doing so, to create a disjunction between the brand owner's public and private personas. We should also recognize that it is not brands themselves that Klein criticizes, but what their owners are doing with them.[20] Once it is understood that the target of Klein's criticism is the behaviour of a relatively small number of brand-mighty corporate potentates, it can be seen that it is no response to Klein's case to say 'Most brand owners don't behave that way'. Perhaps, however, we should acknowledge that many businesses which are not brand-bullies are influenced by the corporate ethos, the charisma and the enormous potential for profit which those global enterprises exude. **21.18**

We cannot pretend that powerful corporations do not seek to maximize their power in the marketplace and elsewhere, in order to maximize the profitability of their commercial activities. That is not in itself a wrong: it is the reason why they function in an open economy and it is also the reason why our pension funds buy shares in them. But while we welcome maximization of market power, we may not welcome the abuse of a company's power within its chosen markets if its activities are inherently anti-competitive (for example, dividing markets, limiting supplies, imposing retail price maintenance) since those activities will tend to weaken or destroy the degree of consumer choice which keeps open markets efficient. **21.19**

The smaller and more highly focused a company is, the greater is the likelihood that it will be able to set and then fulfil its corporate aims. Most big brand-owners in the 1950s and 1960s were large multilayered structures which encompassed most or all of the key component functions of design, manufacture, **21.20**

---

[20] Tim Ambler, *Are Brands Good for Britain?* (British Brands Group Inaugural Lecture 2000), p 3.

storage, distribution, marketing and sales. By the 1990s these companies had either metamorphosed into, or been replaced by, small lean enterprises which, having outsourced their manufacturing and other labour-intensive functions, were built around brand concepts. This should not be surprising: a relatively compact group of executives within the same small company can more easily share the same aims and aspirations than can the directors, marketers, shop-floor labourers and accountants who often work in separate locations and whose aspirations are frequently a matter of mutual indifference. In short, a small and highly focused company can be expected to use its power, for good or ill, more efficiently than a large and cumbersome one.

21.21 The law is not unprepared for the possibility that businesses will seek to exercise their financial and legal power in a way which is harmful to existing economic and social values. Accordingly the law often provides, in areas such as pay, labour relations and health and safety at work, for minimum standards which must be obeyed by all, however inconvenient this may be to business interests. Legal recognition of the potential dangers of market abuse may take the form of laws against monopolies, cartels and the abuse of dominant market power. Legislation to achieve such ends has been introduced in most countries and has formed the backbone of the EU's economic policy for the past forty years.[21]

21.22 The laws which require businesses to be socially and economically responsible may impinge little upon the activities of many of the new generation of brand-owners. Brand-owning companies may, for example, be legally based in jurisdictions in which tax liability is minimized or eliminated; the manufacture of their products may be outsourced to jurisdictions in which the protection of labour is token and unenforceable. They trade in countries whose laws prevent the abuse of trade mark rights, but those laws do not address the power of the brand. This is because the trade mark is a purely legal concept (a monopoly over the use of a sign in relation to goods and services), operating in a purely commercial context (a market). The brand, however, is a 'cross-over' concept: it is an image or message which is embodied in icons which are protected by trade marks, while being embedded in cultural as well as commercial contexts. It can therefore be assumed that checks on the abuse of trade mark monopolies will not be brought to bear on abuses of the power exerted by the owner of a brand image.

---

[21] For an excellent account of the principles through which EU seeks to rein in intellectual property rights in cases of actual or apprehended abuse, see Inge Govaere, *The Use and Abuse of Intellectual Property Rights in EC Law* (1996); see also Guy Tritton, *Intellectual Property in Europe* (2002). It has been suggested however that EU policy towards IP rights has become increasingly tolerant of them; see Jeremy Phillips, 'Pariah, Piranha or Partner: The New View of Intellectual Property in Europe' [1998] IPQ 107–12.

D. No chance: brand power and goodwill

Klein recognizes that the power of the brand can be turned against a brand-owner, through the use of adverse publicity. This is the case whether the brand-owner has abused its power or not. Thus the impact upon the McDonald's Corporation of its ultimately technically successful defamation action against the 'McDonald's Two' was almost certainly far more negative than it must have originally calculated when it launched legal proceedings to protect its famous brands against some serious but initially underpublicized allegations concerning rain-forest depletion, health and cruelty to animals and employees.[22] Means of leveraging this counter-power against brand-owners can be expensive or of limited availability if they are confined to the use of the traditional advertising and marketing media, but the power of informal communication through e-mail circulars, use of the Internet and through viral anti-marketing cannot be underestimated. 21.23

D. No chance: brand power and goodwill

The fact that a brand's power can be turned against the brand-owner enables us to identify an important distinction between businesses which are brand-based and those which are not. A business which has no public profile can far more easily escape public attention, and is thus far more difficult to call to account, than a company whose very brands are deeply etched in the consciousness of all. That is why calls to boycott companies such as Nestlé, Shell or Nike resonate within our minds far more than calls to boycott lesser-known rivals or, for example, companies which make generic products for a variety of companies or who supply own-brand products for supermarkets, whose behaviour towards employees or the environment may be more reprehensible. But calling a brand-based company to task for real or alleged misdeeds is always going to be a hard task for those who seek to do it. What makes this task so hard? 21.24

The answer in this case is 'goodwill'. Popular brands possess what one British court has called 'the attractive force that brings in custom'.[23] When people see the word NIKE or the swoosh, they do not see a piece of information to which their feelings are neutral. They have been trained to respond positively to NIKE and swoosh alike by powerful advertising, peer-group influence and lifestyle aspirations which, it should not be forgotten, may be backed up by pleasant and positive experiences such as visits to Nike Town retail outlets and the purchase of stylish and desirable high-quality products. It is possible to call Nike to account, pulling it towards the issues arising from its trading practices as one might pull a bull by the ring on the end of its nose. But anyone who does so must first overcome that groundswell of consumer goodwill which, it should also not be forgotten, 21.25

---

[22] See *No Logo*, pp 387–95 and sources cited therein.
[23] *Inland Revenue Commissioners v Muller & Co's Margarine Ltd* [1901] AC 217.

Nike did not inherit or find in the street but sweated to establish with its consuming public.

21.26 The same can be said about brands in other areas of commercial activity. Even forty years of research, lobbying, litigation and legal restrictions aimed against the tobacco industry have not killed the power of its major cigarette brands (although the fact that the products concerned are addictive probably plays an important part in the persistence of brand power in that market). Other brands have so far survived allegations of insider dealing,[24] political[25] and tax[26] improprieties, poor standards of manufacture[27] and low levels of customer satisfaction with services[28] (but not, it seems, allegations of Satanism[29]).

21.27 How does one then counter the powerfully positive effect of goodwill? There is no one simple answer to this. In recent years companies probably more often damage or destroy their brand power themselves than see it destroyed by others. Different types of brand are particularly vulnerable to different threats, depending on their image. For example, VOLVO, being synonymous with safety, would be open to threat if its safety-image were undermined. Likewise the wholesome image of BODY SHOP would be sullied if it were shown to be polluting the environment and exploiting indigenous inhabitants of developing countries. But attacks on a brand's integrity cannot always be shoe-horned conveniently into those zones of vulnerability.

21.28 An alternative approach is to vest the power of the brand in the consumers themselves.[30] Although this may sound far-fetched, there is one well-known occasion in which a consumer revolt forced a company's hand: that was in May 1985 when the Coca-Cola Company mounted its attempted relaunch of a new, improved and differently formulated cola beverage under the treasured COCA-COLA trade mark. The relaunch was not an irrational decision: it was built upon

---

[24] eg MARTHA STEWART: 'Martha's Fall From Grace', www.guardian.co.uk/Print/0,3858,4445370,00.html.

[25] See eg FORMULA ONE's alleged purchase of influence through a £1 million donation to the Labour Party in the UK: www.news.bbc.co.uk/1/hi/uk_politics/931708.stm.

[26] eg ERBITUX, after ImClone Systems' founder Sam Waksal was ordered to repay nearly $4.3m in fines and back taxes; see Erin Mcclam, 'ImClone's Founder Gets Seven Years in Prison', 10 June 2003, www.wallstreetbaloney.com.

[27] A notable example is SKODA, which came through decades of bad car jokes (*Question*: 'Why does a SKODA have a heated rear window?' *Answer*: 'To warm your hands when you're pushing it') but is now a respected marque within the VOLKSWAGEN family.

[28] eg the jibe that Italian airline ALITALIA was the acronym for 'Aircraft Landing In Tokyo. All Luggage In Amsterdam'.

[29] The decline and fall of the Procter & Gamble 'moon and stars' logo is chronicled on http://www.ship-of-fools.com/Myths/02Myth.html and *Procter & Gamble: The House That Ivory Built* (1988), p 7.

[30] It has been asserted, with some justification, that consumers already have more power over big-brand companies than over others; see 'Pro Logo: The Case for Brands', *The Economist*, 8 September 2001, p 9; 'Who's Wearing the Trousers?', *The Economist*, 8 September 2001, pp 27–9.

solid laboratory work and consumer research. It was the consumers' reaction which was arguably irrational, but it won the day. Within a short time of the relaunch Coca-Cola had received more than 400,000 phone calls and over 200,000 letters and postcards from angry consumers. Consumer action groups were formed and, in the face of such intense and hostile lobbying, the brand owner retreated.[31] Would anything have been achieved if 600,000 consumers had taken the same trouble in lobbying a recalcitrant brand owner on behalf of a more politically or economically sensitive issue? The answer is unknown, though it may be realistic to concede that (i) consumers who have been so stirred into action against a company may be reluctant to patronize it and that (ii) a business which faces the opposition of consumers may prefer to write off the possible benefits of obtaining their custom and spare itself the embarrassment of conceding that it is in the wrong.

E. No change: why the public's best weapons may never be adequately utilized

Ultimately, as Klein herself recognizes, the two most successful weapons against brand abuse are consumer knowledge and consumer rage. An informed and discriminating consumer will not allow himself to be 'dumbed down' by aspirational advertising messages and will look behind the products and services on offer. The consumer, once in possession of information which he finds disturbing, may then not merely exercise his consumer choice by avoiding a brand which displeases him but may also challenge that brand and take active steps to put the situation right. Where that happens, the brand owner will be faced with a choice of its own: whether to spend its resources on fighting the challenge or on accepting the criticism and rectifying it.   **21.29**

There is little likelihood that these two consumer weapons will be effectively brought to bear in the short term. There are at least six reasons for this.   **21.30**

First, the allocation of information in the marketplace is asymmetric. Although the concept of the perfect market assumes that the consumer has full knowledge of all the characteristics of the products in the relevant market, the brand-owner generally has far more knowledge of the consumer than the consumer has about the competitors with whom he shares the marketplace. Brand owners accurately target, stimulate and motivate prospective purchasers on the basis of sales research, data capture, psychological profiling and a host of other techniques. Those purchasers in contrast base their purchasing upon not only fact-based criteria such as price and satisfaction with past purchases but also upon factors such as what   **21.31**

---

[31] Donald Keough, 'The Importance of Brand Power', in Paul Stobart (ed), *Brand Power* (1994), pp 26–8.

they think their friends or classmates would say: is their acquisition cool or is it sad? The bigger the brand's bandwagon, the more likely it is that the cool/sad issue will dominate rational choice.

21.32 Secondly it is far from the case that most consumers of high-profile branded products actually want to know what lies behind the brand. Most women who love their pet dogs and treat them with the utmost kindness simply do not want to know whether the cosmetic products they wear have been tested on live puppies in laboratories. Nor do most youngsters who buy trainers want to know of the economic and social circumstances of children their own age who manufacture them in far-off lands. Nor indeed do most men want to know the environmental cost of obtaining the fuel which propels the car of their dreams (or, if they are less affluent, the car of their realities). This is not to say that they should not be told these unwanted truths, but that the response of consumers to these truths is likely to vary as to the strength of various thoughts and feelings which consumers have at any given time. To give one trivial example, a consumer of mass-produced, arguably unhealthy, choice-destroying and environmentally disastrous fast-food products will be more sympathetic to the thesis in *No Logo* when he has just eaten them and is no longer hungry than he would be if he hadn't eaten for ten hours and had just been seduced by the wafting smell of a sizzling burger.

21.33 Thirdly, consumers do not behave in a rational manner. There is no evidence to suggest that, even when armed with all the information they could ever need about the manufacturing, marketing and environmental stances taken by brand owners, consumers *en masse* make the right decisions—assuming (i) that we even know what rational consumer behaviour actually is and (ii) that, at any point at which a choice is about to be made, there is only one consumer response which is rational. Some consumers, when told of the outsourcing policies of trainer manufacturers, feel ashamed and resolve to change their purchasing habits. More, however, experience momentary embarrassment and then forget about them. Others, again, are genuinely indifferent: they are only interested in their trainers. Still others will feel angry and resentful that their choice of trainer has been questioned. Another group will consider it right and proper to keep on purchasing those outsourced products, citing the need to provide and stimulate even poorly paid employment in areas in which rural destitution has led to migration of the young unemployed to free ports and industrial zones. All of these responses can be understood and all of them can either be described as rational or at any rate rationalized—but all these responses, however varied, have all been triggered by the same event, the unsolicited communication of unwanted consumer information. Is there a rightful hierarchy of human responses to this information? Probably not.

21.34 Fourthly, there is no community of interest between consumers. A consumer who rages against one particular actual or perceived injustice may be immune to even

E. No change: why the public's best weapons may never be adequately utilized

feelings of gentle indignation with regard to another one. This is probably why more people campaign against vivisection conducted against domestic pets than against the factory-like conditions of battery hens. Fewer still stand up for the rights of farmed fish and no one at all protests against the exploitation of whole colonies of bees for their life-sustaining honey. Since there is no community of interest, individual consumers may unite with others from time to time to bring their grievances to bear but, being few and scattered in respect of each issue, they may struggle to make their complaint felt. It is no accident that those protests which have made the greatest impact, such as the disruptions of world economic summits and 'Reclaim the Streets' activities, have involved coalitions of disparate groups of protesters rather than a specific single-interest pressure group.[32]

Fifthly, it is easier to identify what people are protesting *against* than to establish what it is that they are protesting *for*. In *No Logo* Klein stresses both the need and the ability of consumers to reassert their own values in the face of the brand values which they are being asked or compelled to adopt. But while the value of the brand is constant and clearly identifiable, the values of individual consumers are not. For example, among those who protest against Nestlé's existing programmes for the distribution and marketing of infant formula in developing countries, there are those on one side who would happily settle for little gentle modification of Nestlé's programme so as to make the relative merits of breast-feeding and bottle-feeding better understood, while there are those on the other side who would be reluctant to settle for anything less than the dismemberment of Nestlé and the payment of reparation. The community of consumers is united against Nestlé but not necessarily united in favour of a single outcome. **21.35**

Sixthly it is probable that, in an era which more than any other has witnessed the breakdown of traditional norms of family and community life, pitting individual against individual and generation against generation, the lifestyle brand almost certainly conveys a large degree of identity upon people who cannot identify anywhere else because they have neither a family nor a community to which they belong. For such people, a challenge to the influence of an aspirational brand in their lives is a challenge to their very being. And not all brand values are negative—even if they may sometimes seem that way to the critical or discerning analyst. Coca-Cola's overt and explicit attempts to ally itself with the qualities of 'freedom, democracy, equality and a new beginning' begat the 'I'd Like to Buy the World a Coke' advertising campaign in 1971.[33] This campaign may have been synthetic, a corny manipulation of ideals and sentiments for the sake of increased sales, but **21.36**

---

[32] *No Logo*, pp 311–22 and the sources cited therein.
[33] See Donald Keough, 'The Importance of Brand Power' in Paul Stobart (ed), *Brand Power* (1994), pp 18–23. Keough was formerly President and Chief Operating Officer of the Coca-Cola Company.

Chapter 21: Trade Marks, Images, Icons and Social Responsibility

the values it represented were real enough. Back in the 1970s one commentator observed:

> What's great about this country is that America started the tradition where the richest consumers buy essentially the same things as the poorest. You can be watching TV and see Coca-Cola, and you can know that the President drinks Coke, Liz Taylor drinks Coke, and just think, you can drink Coke too. A Coke is a Coke and no amount of money can get you a better Coke than the one the bum on the corner is drinking. All Cokes are the same and all Cokes are good. Liz Taylor knows it, the President knows it, the bum knows it and you know it.[34]

21.37 This view reflects the egalitarian flavour of Coca-Cola, a brand value which is probably as true today as it was in the 1970s.

F. No fear: why the consumer apocalypse may never happen

21.38 Klein's predicted scenario assumes that the brand owners ('brand bullies', as they are sometimes described) will persist in their habits and that nothing short of a furious political movement, taking to the streets and venting their fury, will change the present situation. It is difficult to know if Klein views this consumer apocalypse as a 'best-case' scenario because it will result in the abatement of the abuses she describes, or a 'worst-case' one on account of the anarchy and *anomie* which appear to be all the new order has to offer.

21.39 Without taking anything away from Klein's account of the magnitude of the problem, the view from other crystal balls may be that the consumer apocalypse is unlikely to happen. Such a perspective may be cultivated after considering the following:

(i) Klein and her colleagues have themselves done a great deal to prevent their prophecies from being fulfilled by writing in such incisive and emotive terms about the issues and by attracting so much attention to them. Lack of consumer awareness has already been mentioned above as a significant contributor to the persistence of brand abuse. There is no doubt, however, that in the past two years the level of consumer awareness has taken a sharply upward turn. This is not solely through the sale of copies of *No Logo*. The Internet has proven to be an ideal medium both for the making available of vital facts and for their discussion. Moreover the judicious use of trade marks and brand names as metatags, sanctioned by the courts,[35] not to mention the reluctant

---

[34] Andy Warhol, *The Philosophy of Andy Warhol (from A to B and Back Again)* (1975), cited in Donald Keough, 'The Importance of Brand Power', in Paul Stobart (ed), *Brand Power* (1994), p 31.
[35] See eg *Sté Gervais Danone v Société Le Riseau Voltaire, Société Gandhi, Valentin Lacambre* [2003] ETMR 321; *Association Greenpeace France v SA Société Esso* [2003] ETMR 441 (Cour d'appel de Paris).

F. No fear: why the consumer apocalypse may never happen

concession by ICANN arbitrators that websites critical of brands can indeed be registered in good faith,[36] has given those who seek discussion the chance of finding it.

(ii) Within the developed world and beyond it, there has grown in the past two years a climate of increasing scepticism with regard to the acceptance of conventional wisdom. Thus issues as diverse as the safety and desirability of genetically modified crops, human and animal cloning, the treatment of asylum seekers, the combating of both government and private-enterprise terrorism and the availability of patented treatments of the HIV pandemic have seen an unprecedented increase in debate at consumer levels well below those at which decision-makers traditionally flourish. As a result of this increased debate, sometimes supplemented by spontaneous outbreaks of carefully orchestrated vandalism, governments modify their positions and supermarkets take products off their shelves.

(iii) The brand bullies, encouraged by their shareholders, will always steer for the areas of highest profit or best return on their investment. When there is no advantage to be gained from opening more MCDONALD's because consumers want fewer of them, McDonald's will focus on some other project such as its healthy lifestyle PRET A MANGER outlets. When the fashion moves from coffee to some other beverage, STARBUCKS will shift its focus too. Consumers have some say in this process and more of them now need little encouragement to participate in it.

(iv) Klein's case is sharp because, as is the entitlement of any issue-based campaigner, she has selected the instances and allegations which best suit her cause. This is not to say that she has entirely neglected the charitable activities and social or environmental benefaction of large and brand-owning companies. However, the 'doing-good' role of large corporations—which she concedes on a number of occasions—is not the main object of her thesis (except in the case of BODY SHOP, where 'doing good' is portrayed as part of the exercise of consumer manipulation). Klein has speculated as to whether these benefactions are an adequate substitute for the tax contributions which many of these companies are not paying, but that too is outside the main thrust of her thesis. The point, however, is this: companies do buy extra goodwill through their charitable activities[37] and the power of these actions is not lost on those who benefit. It is unlikely that the time will be ripe for a grand consumer revolution when, across the board, there is a fund of gratitude felt by institutions as well as individuals towards even badly behaving companies.

---

[36] See eg the discussion in *Leonard Cheshire Foundation v Darke*, Decision 2000–0131 [2001] ETMR 991.

[37] Marcel Knobil gives some examples of large-scale corporate benefaction in his brief piece, '"No

Chapter 21: Trade Marks, Images, Icons and Social Responsibility

G. No Armageddon: the threat of trade mark litigation

21.40 At this point we should return to the theme which prefaced this chapter: the ability of trade mark owners to create brands which evolve into cultural icons that are rendered invulnerable by trade mark law to the sort of dialogue which the public demands: the dialogue of criticism through parody, satire and other means which, in the eyes of the brand owner, damage the commercial or cultural value of that icon.

21.41 A review of the lengthy list of non-infringing acts listed in Chapter 8 should give the public at large some greater confidence in the ability of trade mark law to provide a responsible balance between the interest of the brand owner in preserving his property and the interest of the consuming public in using that property. From that chapter it can be seen that the trade mark owner is well protected against (i) unfair competitive uses of his mark and (ii) acts of market vandalism and opportunism by competitors in other markets, but scarcely protected against the consuming public itself.

21.42 The main point of Klein's citation of the 'Barbie Girl' saga was not in fact to show that users of cultural icons had no rights but to demonstrate that only those who were both brave enough to defy the brand owner and rich enough to be able to afford the litigation could risk attempting to exercise those rights. This is certainly the case where the unauthorized use of the brand as cultural icon is overt, large-scale and lucrative for the user. But it is not the case where the unauthorized user is small and poorly funded and the cost of pursuing him is disproportionate to the benefit involved. For as long as Mattel remains a profit-seeking enterprise, every instance of litigation in which it engages—from actions against recording companies like MCA to actions against mom-and-pop stores that decorate birthday cakes with Barbie effigies—remains a commercial decision. If Mattel recognizes (or can be made to recognize) that greater financial good and commercial stability can be achieved by not suing than by suing, that company too will follow that path.

21.43 Earlier in this chapter we spoke of the need to educate the consumer better and to raise his level of consciousness of what lies behind the brand. Education of the brand owner is also necessary. This is apparent if one considers the following points:

(i) The need to protect a business's investment in a brand against all forms of erosion—whether through dilution, blurring, tarnishment or any other legal

---

Logo" Brand Fails to Deliver', 13 *British Brands*, Spring 2001, p 1 and the anonymous author of 'Who's Wearing the Trousers?', *The Economist*, 8 September 2001, p 29 points out that brands such as CADBURY and HERSHEY were actually built upon the philanthropic activities of their owners.

G. No Armageddon: the threat of trade mark litigation

concept—is a legitimate need and corporate lawyers educate their clients to respond to threats of erosion wherever they appear. However, some brand owners are apparently encouraged to consider litigation as an automatic first response to any unauthorized use of their brands, while others are not. The unauthorized use of a brand can be a compliment as well as an insult; it can strengthen the power and the recognition of the brand as well as diminish or dilute it. When kids draw brand icons on a graffiti-covered wall, they do more damage to the wall than to the street-cred of the brand. As a first step, therefore, brand owners should be taught that litigation need not be the first step but the last course of action, after all else fails.[38]

(ii) Brand owners need to understand that not every consumer is one of their consumers and that the spread of power-brands can build up fear, resentment and anger in those who are not a brand-owner's customers. Part of consumer choice is the facility of members of the public to avoid constant confrontation by brands for which they have no affinity.

(iii) Brand owners have to realize that trade mark laws have built-in mechanisms which require them to face criticism, even if that criticism explicitly mentions the trade marks upon which the brand is based. This book has already discussed the valuable and underused technique of comparative advertising.[39] In a market where all players behave in a manner which is equally reprehensible, comparative advertising is of little value; but where players are divided into good guys and bad guys, whether in terms of product quality, pricing, environmental impact or anything else, the good guys should be encouraged at least to understand and appreciate the relative safety of the measures they can take. Individuals can also criticize brand owners, safe in the knowledge that fair and responsible criticism will always be protected by freedom of speech. Brand owners should be encouraged to respect this right and not to seek to suppress criticism on the pretext that they are protecting trade marks when they are not under threat.

(iv) Brand owners must accept that the inconsistencies which they identify in the positions of their critics are a natural and inevitable consequence of a certain 'cubism'—a simultaneous viewing of the same phenomenon from different sides. Consumers want choice, but many of them also enjoy giving exclusive custom to the brands of their choice; consumers want cheap, well-made goods which Third World outsourcing with policed quality-control can bring, but they also want the employment opportunities which non-outsourced manufacture can bring. Brand owners want to feel that they 'own'

---

[38] In the UK and Ireland 'threats' proceedings may be brought against a trade mark owner who makes what turns out to be a baseless threat to pursue infringement proceedings against an innocent party; in other countries such threats may be actionable as acts of unfair competition; see Chapter 14, paras 14.101–14.115.
[39] Chapter 8.

their consumers, while consumers like to feel they 'own' their adopted brands. The same inconsistencies appear in the laws which regulate brand-owners' businesses, where intellectual property rights grant powerful monopolies which competition laws then break down again. There is no single 'right' or 'wrong' position: what we have is a perpetually shifting state of creative interaction and conflict between the interests of brand-owners, their competitors and their consumers. The law is not a one-way street in which all legal policy issues travel in a single direction: there is two-way traffic and the law must be ready and able to facilitate travel in both directions.

H. Conclusion

21.44 Naomi Klein's anxieties concerning the power and influence of major brands are not misplaced, but the abuses which she addresses are not confined to brand owners: they are found within large corporations of many descriptions. The rectification of those abuses is not the exclusive province of the trade mark and brand-protection community. Klein has argued that trade mark law is a tool in the hands of brand owners which facilitates the manipulation of consumers. However, trade mark law is a two-edged sword. While it helps to protect brand manipulators by granting them a powerful exclusive right, that same body of law provides for a wide range of defences to infringement in the interests of freedom of speech, competition and honest use.

BIBLIOGRAPHY

A.	Introduction	669
B.	Legal reference works, law books and monographs	669
C.	Non-law books and monographs	672
D.	Legal articles and conference papers	673
E.	Non-legal articles	678
F.	Materials drawn from the Internet	679

A. Introduction

This bibliography contains references to works which have been cited in footnotes. It also contains details of works which, if not explicitly cited, have nonetheless influenced me and have formed part of the intellectual roughage upon which my diet of trade mark reading over the past few years has been based.

B. Legal reference works, law books and monographs

Adams, John, *Character Merchandising*, 2nd edn (London: Butterworths, 1996)
—— and K V Pritchard Jones, *Franchising*, 4th edn (London: Butterworths, 1997)
Advertising Standards Authority, *British Code of Advertising, Sales Promotion and Direct Marketing*, 11th edn (London, 2003)
Arden, Thomas P, *Protection of Nontraditional Marks* (New York: INTA, 2000)
Belson, Jeffrey, *Certification Marks* (London: Sweet & Maxwell, 2002)
Birks, Peter (ed), *English Private Law* (Oxford: Oxford University Press, 2000)
Bynoe, Robin: see Mendelsohn, Martin
Coombe, Rosemary J, *The Cultural Life of Intellectual Properties: Authorship, Appropriation and the Law* (Durham, NC: Duke University Press, 1998)
Council of Europe, *Abuse of Rights and Equivalent Concepts: The Principle and its Present-Day Applications* (Proceedings of the 19th Colloquy on European Law 1989) (Luxembourg, 1990).

Craig, Paul and Gráinne De Búrca, *EU Law: Text, Cases and Materials*, 3rd edn (Oxford: Oxford University Press, 2002), ch 6.

Dauppe, Victor: see Eastaway, Nigel

Davies, Isabel M (ed), *Sweet & Maxwell's European Trade Mark Litigation Handbook* (London: Sweet & Maxwell, 1998)

Davies, Margaret and Ngaire Naffine, *Are Persons Property?* (Aldershot: Ashgate/Dartmouth, 2001)

Dawson, Norma and Alison Firth (eds), *Trade Marks Retrospective* (Perspectives in Intellectual Property, vol 7) (London: Sweet & Maxwell, 2000)

De Búrca, Gráinne: see Craig, Paul

Drahos, Peter, *A Philosophy of Intellectual Property* (Aldershot: Dartmouth Publishing Co, 1996)

Dreyfuss, Rochelle, Diane L Zimmerman and Harry First (eds), *Expanding the Boundaries of Intellectual Property: Innovation Policy for the Knowledge Society* (Oxford: Oxford University Press, 2001)

Eastaway, Nigel, Richard Gallafent and Victor Dauppe, *Intellectual Property Law and Taxation*, 6th edn (London: Sweet & Maxwell, 2003)

Edward, David, *Trade Marks, Descriptions of Origin and the Internal Market: What Lies Behind the Silhouette?* (London: IPI, 2001), republished as 'Trade Marks, Descriptions of Origin and the Internal Market' [2001] IPQ 135–45

Fawcett, James and Paul Torremans, *Intellectual Property and Private International Law* (Oxford: Oxford University Press, 1998)

First, Harry: see Dreyfuss, Rochelle

Firth, Alison, *Trade Marks: The New Law* (London: Jordans, 1995)

—— see also Dawson, Norma and Phillips, Jeremy

Gallafent, Richard: see Eastaway, Nigel

Gervais, Daniel, *The TRIPs Agreement: Drafting History and Analysis* (London: Sweet & Maxwell, 1998)

Gilson, Jerome, Anne Gilson Lalonde and Karin Green, *Trade Mark Protection and Practice* (New York: Matthew Bender, looseleaf)

Govaere, Inge, *The Use and Abuse of Intellectual Property Rights in EC Law* (London: Sweet & Maxwell, 1996)

Gyngell, Julian and Allan Poulter, *A User's Guide to Trade Marks and Passing Off*, 2nd edn (London: Butterworths, 1998)

Isaac, Belinda, *Brand Protection Matters* (London: Sweet & Maxwell, 2000)

King, Kelvin: see Sykes, John

Kitchen, David, David Llewelyn, James Mellor, Richard Meade and Thomas Moody-Stuart, *Kerly's Law of Trade Marks and Trade Names*, 13th edn (London: Sweet & Maxwell, 2001)

Lane, Shelley, 'The Problems of Personality Merchandising in English Law: The King, the Princess and the Penguins' *Yearbook of Media and Copyright Law* (Oxford: Oxford University Press, 1999), 28–66

B. Legal reference works, law books, and monographs

—— with Jeremy Phillips, *Trade Mark Legislation and the Pharmaceutical Industry* (London: Office of Health Economics, 1999)

Law Commission Report No 247, *Aggravated, Exemplary and Restitutionary Damages* (London: HMSO, 1997)

Lontai, Endre, *Unification of Law in the Field of International Intellectual Property* (Budapest: Akadémiai Kiadó, 1994)

Martino, Tony, *Trademark Dilution* (Oxford: Clarendon Press, 1996)

McCarthy, J Thomas, *McCarthy on Trademarks and Unfair Competition*, 4th edn (New York: Clark Boardman Callaghan, 1997)

Mendelsohn, Martin and Robin Bynoe (eds), *Franchising* (London: Sweet & Maxwell, 1995)

Michael, Amanda, *A Practical Guide to Trade Mark Law* (London: Sweet & Maxwell, 2002)

Morcom, Christopher, Ashley Roughton and James Graham, *The Modern Law of Trade Marks* (London: Butterworths, 1999)

Mostert, Frederick W, *Famous and Well-Known Marks* (London: Butterworths, 1997)

Naffine, Ngaire: see Davies, Margaret

Oliver, Peter, *Free Movement of Goods in the European Community* (London: Sweet & Maxwell, 1996)

Phillips, Jeremy: see Lane, Shelley

—— and Alison Firth, *Introduction to Intellectual Property Law*, 4th edn (London: Butterworths, 2002)

Poltorak, Alexander and Paul Lerner, *Essentials of Intellectual Property* (New York: John Wiley, 2002)

Poulter, Allan: see Gyngell, Julian

Prime, Terence, *European Intellectual Property Law* (Aldershot: Ashgate/Dartmouth, 2000)

Pritchard Jones, K V: see Adams, John

Richards, William: see Tatham, David

Rizzo, Sergio: see Sandri, Stefano

Rothnie, Warwick A, *Parallel Imports* (London: Sweet & Maxwell, 1993)

Sandri, Stefano and Rizzo, Sergio, *I Nuovi Marchi: Forme, Colori, Odori, Suoni e Altro* (IPSOA, 2002).

Schechter, Frank, *The Historical Foundation of Trade-mark Law* (New York: Columbia University Legal Studies, 1925)

Simon, Ilanah, 'Trade Marks' in *European Union Law Reporter* (London: CCH, 2003)

Smith, Simon, *Image, Persona and the Law* (London: Sweet & Maxwell, 2001)

Spry, I C F, *The Principles of Equitable Remedies*, 6th edn (Sydney: LBC Information Services, Sydney, 2001)

Stallard, Hayley (ed), *Bagehot on Sponsorship, Endorsement and Merchandising*, 2nd edn (London: Sweet & Maxwell, 1998)

Sykes, John and Kelvin King, *Valuation and Exploitation of Intellectual Property and Intangible Rights* (Welwyn Garden City: emis, 2003)

Tatham, David and William Richards, *ECTA Guide to European Union Trade Mark Legislation* (London: Sweet & Maxwell, 1998)

Torremans, Paul: see Fawcett, James

Treitel, G H, *Law of Contract*, 10th edn (London: Sweet & Maxwell, 1999)

Tritton, Guy, *Intellectual Property in Europe*, 2nd edn (London: Sweet & Maxwell, 2002)

Van der Kooij, P A C E, *The Community Trade Mark Regulation: An Article by Article Guide* (London: Sweet & Maxwell, 2000)

Wadlow, Christopher, *The Law of Passing Off*, 2nd edn (London: Sweet & Maxwell, 1994)

Wilkof, Neil J, *Trade Mark Licensing*, 2nd edn (London: Sweet & Maxwell, 2004)

WIPO, *Joint Recommendation Concerning Provisions on the Protection of Well-Known Marks* (Geneva, 2000)

Zimmerman, Diane L: see Dreyfuss, Rochelle

C. Non-law books and monographs

Ambler, Tim, *Are Brands Good for Britain?* (British Brands Group Inaugural Lecture 2000)

Anon, *Brands: An International Review* (London: Mercury Books, 1990)

—— *Naming* (London: Interbrand, undated)

—— *Procter & Gamble: The House That Ivory Built* (Lincolnwood, Ill, NTC Business Books, 1988)

—— *Riding for the Brand* (American Express, 1985)

Bircham, Emma and John Charlton, *Anti Capitalism: A Guide to the Movement* (London: Bookmarks Publications, 2001)

Blackett, Tom and Bob Boad, *Co-Branding: The Science of Alliance* (Basingstoke: Macmillan Business, 1999)

—— and Rebecca Robins (eds), *Brand Medicine: The Role of Branding in the Pharmaceutical Industry* (Basingstoke: Palgrave, 2001)

Boad, Bob: see Blackett, Tom

Charlton, John: see Bircham, Emma

Clifton, Rita and Esther Maughan (eds), *The Future of Brands* (Basingstoke: Macmillan Business, 2000)

Eisbruck, Jay, 'Credit Analysis of Patent and Trademark Royalty Securitisation: Rating Agency Perspective', in Joff Wild (ed), *Building and Enforcing Intellectual Property Value: An International Guide for the Boardroom 2003* (London: Globe White Page, 2003)

Fletcher, Alan, *The Art of Looking Sideways* (London: Phaedon, 2001)

Gaarder, Jorstein, *Sophie's World* (first published by H Aschehoug & Co, Oslo, 1991) (London: Phoenix House, 1996)
Gould, Stephen Jay, *The Flamingo's Smile* (Penguin, Harmondsworth 1985)
Harris, J W, *Property & Justice* (Oxford: Oxford University Press, 1996)
Hawkes, Suzanna, *Licensing Intellectual Property: Share Price Movements and Analysts' Perceptions* (Bembridge: Palladian Law Publishing, 2003)
Javed, Naseem, *Naming for Power* (New York: Linkbridge Publishing, 1993)
Klein, Naomi, *No Logo* (London: Flamingo, 2000)
Kochan, Nicholas (ed), *The World's Greatest Brands* (Basingstoke: Macmillan Business, 1996)
Lasn, Kalle, *Culture Jam* (New York: Quill, 2000)
Murphy, John, *Brand Strategy* (Cambridge: Director Books, 1990)
—— (ed), *Branding: A Key Marketing Tool* (Basingstoke: Macmillan, 1987)
Perrier, Raymond (ed), *Brand Valuation*, 3rd edn (London: Premier Books, 1997)
Phillips, Jeremy, *Charles Dickens and 'The Poor Man's Tale of a Patent'* (Oxford: ESC, 1984)
Pinker, Steven, *Words and Rules: The Ingredients of Language* (London: Phoenix, 1999)
Robins, Rebecca: see Blackett, Tom
Schubert, Glendon, *The Judicial Mind* (New York: Free Press, 1965)
Southgate, Paul, *Total Branding by Design* (London: Kogan Page, 1994)
Stobart, Paul (ed), *Brand Power* (London: Macmillan, 1994)
Stoppard, Tom, *The Invention of Love* (London: Faber and Faber, 1997)
Wild, Joff (ed), *Building and Enforcing Intellectual Property Value: An International Guide for the Boardroom 2003* (London: Globe White Page, 2003)
—— *Maximising the Value of Intellectual Property* (London: Euromoney Publications, 1997)
Wolff Olins, *The New Guide to Identity: How to Create and Sustain Change through Managing Identity* (London: Design Council, 1995)
Woodward, Caroline, 'Valuation of Intellectual Property', in Joff Wild (ed), *Building and Enforcing Intellectual Property Value: An International Guide for the Boardroom 2003* (London: Globe White Page, 2003)

D. Legal articles and conference papers

Bainbridge, David, 'Infringement of Trademarks on Web Pages' (2003) Vol 19(2) CL&SR 124–30.
Baird, Julia, 'This Mark is So Attractive: It Should be Free for All to Use! An Australian Perspective on Functional Shape Marks' (2003) 52 IP Forum 26–37

Baird, Stephen R, 'Moral Intervention in the Trademark Arena: Banning the Registration of Scandalous and Immoral Trademarks' (1993) 83 TMR 661–800

Bastian, Eva-Marina, 'Comparative Advertising in Germany: Present System and Implementation of EC Directive' (2000) 2 IIC 151–61

Beier, Friedrich-Karl, 'Territoriality of Trade Mark Law and International Trade' (1970) 1 IIC 48–72

Belson, Jeffrey, 'Certification Marks, Guarantees and Trust' [2002] EIPR 340–52

Black, Ray, 'Baywatch: Sour Grapes or Justice' [1997] EIPR 39–42

Blakeney, Michael, 'The Impact of the TRIPs Agreement in the Asia Pacific Region' [1996] EIPR 544–54

Buffon, Charles E, 'United States: Owners Prevail over Altered and Decoded Goods' (2002) 144 *Trademark World* 23–7

Burshtein, Sheldon, 'A Domain Name is Not Intellectual Property' (2002) 11/02 *World E-Commerce & IP Report* 9–11

Caldarola, Maria Cristina, 'Questions Relating to Abstract Colour Trade Marks: Recent Developments in Germany' [2003] EIPR 248–55

Carty, Hazel, 'Registered Trade Marks and Permissible Comparative Advertising' [2002] EIPR 294–300

Caudill, Matthew D, 'Beyond the Cheese: Discerning What Causes Dilution Under 15 USC s 1125(c)—A Recommendation to Whittle Away the Liberal Application of Trademark Dilution to Internet Domain Names' (2002) xiii Fordham Int Prop, Media and Ent Law Jl 231–67

Chaudri, Abida, 'Graphically Speaking: Registering Smell, Colour and Sound Marks in the UK and Europe' (2003) 157 *Trademark World* 26–9

Cohen, Felix, 'Transcendental Nonsense and the Functional Approach' (1935) 35 Colum L Rev 809–49

Colquhoun, Graeme, 'It's All in the Name . . .' (2003) 89 *LES News Exchange* 4

Coombe, Rosemary J, 'Objects of Property and Subjects of Politics: Intellectual Property Laws and Democratic Dialogue' (1991) 69 Texas L Rev 1853

Davis, Jennifer, 'European Trade Mark Law and the Enclosure of the Commons' [2002] IPQ 342–67

—— 'To Protect or Serve? European Trade Mark Law and the Decline of the Public Interest' [2003] EIPR 180–7

Davis Jr, Theodore H, 'Registration of Scandalous, Immoral and Disparaging Matter Under Section 2(a) of the Lanham Act: Can One Man's Vulgarity be Another's Registered Trademark?' (1993) 83 TMR 801–62

Deutsch, Askan, 'Concealed Infringement and Web Pages: Metatags and US Trademark Law' (2000) 7–8 IIC 845–85

Dinwoodie, Graeme, 'Reconceptualizing the Inherent Distinctiveness of Product Design Trade Dress' (1997) 75 NCLR 471

D. Legal articles and conference papers

Dominguez Pérez, Eva M, 'Review of Comparative Advertising: German Case Law in Light of the EC Directive' (2000) 1 IIC 20–51

Dryden, Dominic and Susie Middlemiss, 'Parallel Importation of Repackaged Goods: Is "Necessity" Really Necessary?' [2003] JBL 82–9

Dyrberg, Peter and Mikael Skylv, 'Does Trade Mark Infringement Require that the Infringing Use be Trade Mark Use and, if so, What is Trade Mark Use?' [2003] EIPR 229–33

Folliard-Monguiral, Arnaud and David Rogers, 'The Protection of Shapes by the Community Trade Mark' [2003] EIPR 169–79

Gigliotti, Lisa M, 'Beyond Name and Likeness: Should California's Expansion of the Right of Publicity Protect Non-Human Identity?' (1993) 83 TMR 64–76

Gold, Tibor Z, 'Community Trade Marks in Transition' (2003) 126 MIP 55–9

Goldstein, Sol, 'A Study of Compulsory Licensing' (1977) *Les Nouvelles* 122–5

Griffiths, Andrew, 'Modernising Trade Mark Law and Promoting Economic Efficiency: An Evaluation of the BABY-DRY Judgment and its Aftermath' [2003] IPQ 1–37

—— 'The Impact of the Global Appreciation on the Boundaries of Trade Mark Protection' [2001] IPQ 326–60

Gross, Naomi, 'Trade Mark Exhaustion: The Final Chapter?' [2002] EIPR 92–6

—— 'Trade Mark Exhaustion: The UK Perspective' [2001] EIPR 224–37

—— and Lucy Harrold, 'Fighting for Pharmaceutical Profits' [2002] EIPR 497–503

Harrold, Lucy: see Gross, Naomi

Hartwig, Henning, 'United Against Taboo' (2003) 157 *Trademark World* 36–41

Heide, Thomas, 'Trade Marks and Competition Law after *Davidoff*' [2003] EIPR 163–8

Jollymore, Nicholas J, 'Expiration of the Right of Publicity: When Symbolic Names and Images Pass Into the Public Domain' (1994) 84 TMR 125–54

Jordan, Kevin M and Lynn M Jordan, '*Qualitex Co v Jacobson Products Co*: The Unanswered Question—Can Color Ever be Inherently Distinctive?' (1995) 85 TMR 371–98

Kamperman Sanders, Anselm, 'The Return to *Wagamama*' [1996] EIPR 521–5

—— and Spyros Maniatis, 'A Consumer Trade Mark: Protection Based on Origin and Quality' [1993] EIPR 406–15

Keeling, David, 'About Kinetic Watches, Easy Banking and Nappies That Keep a Baby Dry: A Review of Recent European Case Law on Absolute Grounds for Refusing to Register Trade Marks' [2003] IPQ 131–62

Kilbey, Ian '"Baby-Dry": A Victory for the Ephemera of Advertising?' [2002] EIPR 493–7

Kilshaw, Lucy: see Whybrow, Stephen

Kist, Bas, 'Touch Me, Smell Me, Protect Me: Protecting Unconventional Trade

Marks' (conference paper, INTA 125th International Meeting, Amsterdam, May 2003)

Klein, Sheldon and Leo Loughlin, 'Trademarks by Popular Demand?' (2002) 151 *Trademark World* 20–2

Korah, Valentine, 'Dividing the Common Market Through Industrial Property Rights' (1972) 35 MLR 634–43

Kostello, Dyann, 'Grappling With the Limits of Fame Under the FTDA: Do Marks Famous Only in a Niche Market or Limited Geographical Area Qualify for Protection?' (2001) 91 TMR 1133–49

Kur, Annette, 'Identical Marks Belonging to Different Owners in Different Countries: How Can They Co-exist in Cyberspace?' (2000) JWIP 307–19

—— '*Glaxo et al v Dowelhurst*: Time for the ECJ to Change its Attitude Towards Repackaging?' [2000] IPQ 301–7

—— 'International Hague Convention on Jurisdiction and Foreign Judgments: A Way Forward for IP' [2002] EIPR 175–83

Langvardt, Arlen W, 'Trademark Rights and First Amendment Wrongs: Protecting the Former Without Committing the Latter' (1998) 83 TMR 633–60

Lehrman, Ronald, '"Reputation Without Use" and "Household Names"' (1986) 3 *Trademark World* 18–27

Maniatis, Spyros, 'Trade Mark Law and Domain Names: Back to Basics?' [2002] EIPR 397–408

—— 'Trademark Rights: A Justification Based on Property' [2002] IPQ 123–71

—— see also Kamperman Sanders, Anselm

Mazumdar, Anandashankar, 'Courts are Beginning to Grasp the Idea that Similar Marks can Coexist on the Internet' [2003] ECLR 293–4

McGee, A and G Scanlan, 'Phantom Intellectual Property Rights' [2000] IPQ 264–85

Middlemiss, Susie and Jeremy Phillips, 'Bad Faith in European Trade Mark Law and Practice' [2003] EIPR 397–405

—— see also Dryden, Dominic

Mostert, Frederick, 'Authenticity: The Timeless Quest' (2003) 156 *Trademark World* 22–4

Nelson, Robert, 'Unraveling the Trademark Rope: Tarnishment and its Proper Place in the Laws of Unfair Competition' (2002) 42 IDEA 133–79

Oberin, Colin, 'Registering Shape Trade Marks', *Intellectual Property Bulletin* (Allens Arthur Robinson), December 2002, pp 9–12

Osborne, Dawn, 'Metatags and the *Reed* Case: A Few Discordant Notes' (2002) 7 *Communications Law* 5, 155–8

Parsons, Mark: see Swycher, Nigel

Pattishall, Beverly, 'Dawning Acceptance of the Dilution Rationale for Trademark-Trade Identity Protection' (1984) 74 TMR 289–310

D. Legal articles and conference papers

Pfeiffer, Tim, 'Descriptive Trade Marks: The Impact of the *Baby-Dry* Case Considered' [2002] EIPR 373–80

Phillips, Jeremy, 'Intellectual Property as Security for Debt Finance: A Time to Advance' [1997] EIPR 276–7

—— 'Interlocutory Injunctions and Intellectual Property: A Review of *American Cyanamid v Ethicon* in the Light of *Series 5 Software*' [1997] JBL 486–92

—— 'Life After Death' [1998] EIPR 201–3

—— 'Pariah, Piranha or Partner: The New View of Intellectual Property in Europe' [1998] IPQ 107–12

—— 'Quality Control and the Napoleon Principle' (2001) 109 *Managing Intellectual Property* 42–4

—— 'The Diminishing Domain' [1996] EIPR 429–30

—— 'Two Lessons in Name Management' (1997) 72 *Managing Intellectual Property* 24–6

—— see also Middlemiss, Susie

Prescott, Peter, 'Has the Benelux Trade Mark Law Been Written Into the Directive?' [1997] EIPR 99–102

—— 'Think Before You Waga Finger' [1996] EIPR 317–21

Richardson, Megan, 'Copyright in Trade Marks? On Understanding Trade Mark Dilution' [2000] IPQ 66–83

Robertson, Aidan, 'Is the Licensee Estoppel Rule Still Good Law? Was It Ever?' [1991] EIPR 373–9

Rogers, David: see Folliard-Monguiral, Arnaud

Ronaglia, Pier Luigi, 'Should We Use Guns and Missiles to Protect Famous Trademarks in Europe?' (1998) 88 TMR 551–63

Schechter, Frank, 'Fog and Fiction in Trade-mark Protection' (1936) 36 Columbia L Rev 60

—— 'The Rational Basis of Trademark Protection' (1927) 40 Harv LR 813, reprinted in (1970) 60 TMR 334

Schmidt, Hedvig, '"Likelihood of Confusion" in European Trademarks: Where are We Now?' [2002] EIPR 463–5

Schulze, Charlotte, 'Registering Colour Trade Marks in the European Union' [2003] EIPR 55–67

Simon, Ilanah, 'Pandering to Their Whims? WWF: The Second Round' [2002] Ent LR 161–4

—— 'What's Cooking at the CFI? More Guidance on Descriptive and Non-distinctive Trade Marks' [2003] EIPR 322

Skylv, Mikael: see Dyrberg, Peter

Steckler, Brunhilde and Frank Bachmann, 'Comparative Advertising in Germany with Regard to EC Law' [1997] EIPR 578–86

Swann, Jerre B, 'Dilution Redefined for the Year 2002' (2002) 92 TMR 585–625

Swycher, Nigel and Mark Parsons, 'IPR Damages: A Pan-European Perspective', *Global Counsel*, September 2002, pp 35–40

Tatham, David, 'WIPO Resolution on Well-known Marks: A Small Step or a Giant Leap?' [2000] IPQ 127–37

Tessensohn, John and Shusaku Yamamoto, 'Japan Denies Trade Mark Registration for Retail Services' [2003] EIPR 381–3

—— and —— 'Piratical Japanese Trade Mark Registrations Invalidated on Public Order and Morality Grounds' [2003] EIPR 203–6

Tichane, David M, 'The Maturing Doctrine of Post-Sales Confusion' (1995) 85 TMR 399–423

Tompos, Louis, 'Badwill' (2003) 116 Harv Law Rev 1845–67

Viegas, Juliana, 'Genericide: The Danger of Excessive Fame' (2003) 155 *Trademark World* 36–9

Völker, Stephen, 'Registering New Forms with the CTM' (2002) 152 *Trademark World* 24–33

Wehrli, Agathe, 'Pharmaceuticals: Trademarks Versus Generic Names' (1986) 4 *Trademark World* 31–3

Whybrow, Stephen and Lucy Kilshaw, 'Repackaging Ruled Out' (2003) *Trademark World* 17–18

Wilkinson, David, 'Broad Trade Mark Specifications' [2002] ETMR 227–31

Willimsky, Sonya, 'Comparative Advertising: An Overview' [1996] EIPR 649–53

Würtenburger, Gert, 'Enforcement of Community Trade Mark Rights' [2002] IPQ 402–17

—— 'Risk of Confusion and Criteria to Determine the Same in European Community Trade Mark Law' [2002] EIPR 20–9

Xiodong Yuan, 'Research on Trade Mark Parallel Imports in China' [2003] EIPR 224–8

Yamamoto, Shusaku: see Tessensohn, John

E. Non-legal articles

Adegoke, Yinka, 'Top Brands Start to Pull Ads from P2P Networks', *New Media Age*, 24 April 2003, 1

Anon, 'Pro Logo: The Case for Brands', *The Economist*, 8 September 2001, p 9

—— 'Who's Wearing the Trousers?', *The Economist*, 8 September 2001, pp 27–9

Derrick, Stuart, 'Barbie Ruling Rings Warning Bells', *Promotions & Incentives*, January 2003, p 23

Friedland, Julian, 'Ideation and Appropriation: Wittgenstein on Intellectual Property' (2001) 12 *Law and Critique* 185–99

Knobil, Marcel, '"No Logo" Brand Fails to Deliver', 13 *British Brands*, Spring 2001, p 1

Landes, William M and Richard Posner, 'The Economics of Trademark Law' (1988) 78 TMR 267–306

Martin, Brian, 'Against Intellectual Property' (1995) 21 *Philosophy and Social Action* 7–22

Phillips, Jeremy, 'A Safe Haven for Cybersquatters' (2003) 156 *Trademark World* 66

—— 'An Empire Made of Bricks: A Brief Appraisal of LEGO' [1987] EIPR 363–6

—— 'Do National Brands have a Future in the European Market?' [1991] EIPR 191–4

—— 'Elzie Segar, Intellectual Property Creator Extraordinary' [1986] EIPR 373–6

—— 'Fakin' It' [1999] EIPR 275–8

—— 'Trademark Abuse' (1987) 8 *Trademark World* 24–31

—— 'Unwanted Rivals' (1994) 40 *Managing Intellectual Property* 24–6

Posner, Richard: see Landes, William M

Rossitter, Derek, 'Life and Death, Comfort and Pain, Hope and Despair' (1987) 6 *Trademark World* 28–33

F. Materials drawn from the Internet

Anon, 'Layoff Practices Linked to Brand Damage, Andersen Survey Shows', www.accountingnet.com/x31751.xml

Bodoni, Stephanie, 'Producers Worldwide Team Up to Protect Food Names', *MIP Week*, 15 June 2003

Correa, Carlos M, 'Intellectual Property Rights and the Use of Compulsory Licenses: Options for Developing Countries (working paper prepared with the assistance of members of the Centre for Advanced Studies, University of Buenos Aires, Argentina, www.southcentre.org/publications/complicence/toc.htm)

Dimidjian, Karina and Claire Lazard, 'New ".tm.fr" Domain Names for Mark Owners' WTLR, 17 April 2003

Liss, David, 'The Brands We Love to Hate', The Brand Channel, 20 March 2003, www.brandchannel.com/features_effects.asp?id+150

Mamudi, Sam, 'Lawmakers Vote to End Diversion', *MIP Week*, 1 June 2003

Mcclam, Erin, 'ImClone's Founder Gets Seven Years in Prison', 10 June 2003, www.wallstreetbaloney.com

Olsen, Stefanie, 'Trademarks May Stymie Online Searches', 20 August 2003, news.zdnet.co.uk/business/legal/0,39020651,39115824,00.htm

Peeters, Ruben, 'Search and Seizure', 31 July 2002, Bird & Bird website (www.twobirds.com/newsAndPublications)

Tan Tee, Jim and Tan Wee Meng, 'Registration of ".sg" as a Trademark Abandoned' WTLR, 24 March 2003

GLOSSARY

absolute grounds the reasons connected to a mark's inherent nature (as opposed to the use of a similar mark by another undertaking) for which the mark may be refused registration, or for which, if it is registered, it is liable to be invalidated. For example, a mark will be refused registration if it describes the goods for which it is to be used.

ambush marketing advertising by an undertaking at an event sponsored by one of its rivals.

assignment the complete transfer of a property right from one person or entity to another person or entity.

blurring use of a trade mark by a third party that causes the mark to become less distinctive.

brand the image that an undertaking attempts to create for its products or services.

British Brands Group (BBG) (www.britishbrandsgroup.org.uk) an association of British brand owners that promotes brands and the benefits they bring in the UK.

cancellation the removal from the trade mark register of a trade mark on the ground that it should not have been registered in the first place.

certification mark a mark which indicates that the goods or services bearing it have been approved with respect to one or more of their characteristics by the proprietor of the certification mark.

claimant the term used in England and Wales (as well as in this book) to indicate the party that commences legal proceedings. In the United States and in most other English-speaking countries the claimant is known as the plaintiff.

co-branding (i) any venture in which the owners of two or more brands will lend their intellectual property to a vehicle for their joint exploitation; (ii) the placing by a parallel trader of his own trade mark alongside the trade mark of the original manufacturer on repackaged products in which the original manufacturer's trade mark right may have been exhausted.

collective mark a mark held by an association of undertakings that is used to distinguish the goods or services of the members of that undertaking from the goods or services of other undertakings.

Community trade mark (CTM) a unitary trade mark, created by Council Regulation 40/94 of 20 December 1993 on the Community trade mark. The CTM has the same legal effect in all the Member States of the European Union by virtue of a single trade mark registration.

comparative advertising advertising by an undertaking that directly or indirectly makes reference to a competitor's products.

copyright the right of an author to prevent his literary, artistic or other protected creation from being copied.

counterclaim an argument that the claimant has in some way broken the law, raised by the defendant in response to the claimant's allegation that the defendant has broken the law.

Court of First Instance the lower court of the European Court of Justice, which hears appeals from the Office of Harmonisation in the Internal Market as well as appeals from the European Commission on competition issues.

cyberpiracy see **cybersquatting**.

cybersquatting the registration of another undertaking's trade mark as a domain name in bad faith.

deceptive mark a mark that gives a false message that is likely to be believed by consumers about some characteristic of the mark-owner's goods or services. For example, using the mark HAND MADE BY JANE would be deceptive for goods that are mass-produced in a factory in Hong Kong but using the mark NORTH POLE for bananas would *not* be deceptive because nobody believes that bananas are grown in the North Pole.

de minimis a matter is *de minimis* if it so insignificant that it is ignored by the law. From the Latin motto *de minimis non curat lex* (the law does not concern itself with small things).

delivery up the surrender of infringing materials by the infringer, usually to the rightowner or a person designated by the rightowner.

descriptive mark a mark that consists of indications of the kind, quality, quantity, intended purpose, value, geographical origin or other characteristics of the goods or services for which it is used, for example, SOFT for cushions.

descrizione giudiziaria Italian court procedure for obtaining pre-trial disclosure of information and seizure of allegedly infringing products.

design the appearance of a product or any part of it.

dilution use of a trade mark by a third party that damages the mark's ability to function as a trade mark, either by blurring or by tarnishment.

Glossary

the Directive First Directive 89/104 of 21 December 1988 to approximate the laws of the Member States relating to trade marks. This Directive harmonizes the trade mark laws of the Member States of the European Union.

distinctive mark a mark that enables consumers to recognise that the goods on which it is used comes from a specific (although possibly anonymous) undertaking and to tell those goods apart from the goods of other undertakings. This can be by virtue of the intrinsic nature of the mark itself (in which case the mark is inherently distinctive) or because consumers have been educated to recognize that the mark refers to a specific undertaking (in which case the mark has acquired distinctiveness).

domain name the alphanumeric mask that represents the numeric IP address of a computer on which a website is located. For example, the domain name of Oxford University Press is www.oup.co.uk.

endorsement the grant of a licence to use the name of a person who is either a celebrity or is well known in a specific sector as a means of indicating his approval of endorsed goods or services by.

estoppel a situation where, because of his previous actions or inaction, a person is precluded from relying on a point that he would otherwise be able to argue.

European Community Trademark Association (ECTA) (www.ecta.org) an association of European Union trade mark lawyers.

European Court of Justice (http://curia.eu.int) the judicial branch of the European Union. The European Court of Justice (ECJ) sits in Luxembourg. It hears appeals from the Court of First Instance (CFI) and responds to questions on issues of law referred to it under the preliminary reference procedure by the courts of the Member States of the European Union.

ex parte an action that takes place with only one party in attendance, either because the second party is absent (this is now termed 'without notice' in England and Wales) or because there is no second party—for example, when a trade mark is refused registration under the absolute grounds because the matter is heard before the trade mark registry and no other party is involved.

exclusive licence a licence giving the licensor the sole right to use the property in question.

exhaustion a state of affairs in which a trade mark owner is no longer able to enforce his trade mark rights with regard to specific goods after the goods bearing that trade mark have been put on the market with his consent.

expunging removing.

famous mark a mark that is well known by the population *as a whole* in a specific territory.

Glossary

figurative mark a mark consisting of a pictorial representation, such as a logo or a design, with or without a word mark or of a word mark on its own in fancy lettering.

generic (i) a term that describes the type of goods for which it is used and that is incapable of functioning as a trade mark for those goods (for example, BOOK is generic for bound sheets of printed paper); (ii) generic drugs are drugs with the same chemical composition as drugs that were previously protected under a patent. Generics are sold under a proprietary mark, rather than under the original trade mark used for the drugs during the duration of patent protection.

geographical indication the name of a product (usually coinciding with a geographical place-name) that is reserved for undertakings producing that product in a specific location because the quality or nature of the product is dependent on geographical factors or skills that are only present in the place from which the product originates.

goodwill this is generally defined as 'the attractive force which brings in custom'. In other words, it is the thing that causes consumers to purchase (or make repeat purchases) of a particular product. Goodwill cannot exist in the abstract. It must inhere in something. For example, a consumer may see the name of a product, know that he has had good experiences with products by that name in the past and choose to buy the product for that reason, in which case the manufacturer of the product has goodwill in the name of the product.

grey goods genuine goods that have been parallel imported into a jurisdiction from another jurisdiction without the trade mark owner's consent.

house mark the mark used by a retailer on the goods that are made especially for that retailer. For example, the former house mark of MARKS AND SPENCER was ST MICHAEL. House marks are sometimes known as an 'own brands'. The concept of the house mark (also sometimes called an umbrella mark) has been extended to cover the use of a primary trade mark under which a range of products are sold, for example, FORD is the house brand for a name of cars with names such as KA, FOCUS and FIESTA.

infringement use of a trade mark by a third party that encroaches on the trade mark owner's exclusive rights in the trade mark.

injunction a court order that prevents a person or undertaking from doing a certain act or acts.

interim relief a temporary award given at an early stage of proceedings before a full trial has taken place.

international registration registration under the Madrid Agreement or the Madrid Protocol (see below).

International Trademark Association (INTA) (www.inta.org) a US-based but internationally focused association of trade mark owners that plays an active lobbying role and publishes a range of texts, including the *Trademark Reporter* journal.

invalidity the cancellation of a trade mark that has been registered even though it does not satisfy the requirements for the registration as a trade mark.

kort geding a court procedure in the Netherlands by which a trade mark owner can seek urgent temporary relief against infringement.

Lanham Act the United States trade mark legislation, also known as Title 15 of the United States Code.

licence a contractual right to make use of another's property.

locus standi the entitlement of a specific person or entity to argue a case before a court.

Madrid Agreement The Madrid Agreement on the International Registration of Marks, a treaty allowing the owner of a registered trade mark to make a single centralized application for the grant of national trade mark rights in the countries that he designates, as long as those countries are parties to the Madrid Agreement.

Madrid Protocol The Protocol Relating to the Madrid Agreement Concerning the International Registration of Marks. Like the Madrid Agreement, the Protocol sets up a scheme for centralized applications for national trade mark rights although there are numerous differences between the two schemes.

mark with a reputation a mark that is known by a specific proportion of the population and as a result is protected against use by third parties on dissimilar goods. The exact percentage necessary varies in accordance with the facts of the case in question.

MARQUES (www.marques.org) the Association of European Trade Mark Owners.

misrepresentation an express or implied statement that deceives consumers. This statement does not have to be put into words by the misrepresentor. For example, if trader A is known for the distinctive shape of his bottles and trader B starts using bottles of the same shape for his soft-drinks, causing consumers to think that trader B's soft drinks are made by trader A, trader B has made a misrepresentation by using that shape of bottle.

Nice Agreement the treaty setting out the details of the various classes into which goods can be divided, particularly for the purposes of registration of trade marks. For example, Class 4 covers 'Industrial oils and greases; lubricants; dust absorbing, wetting and binding compositions; fuels (including motor spirit) and illuminants;

candles, wick.' The Nice Classifications are often used and accepted even in countries that are not party to the Nice Agreement.

non-exclusive licence a licence that gives the licensee the right to use the property in question, but allows the licensor to grant further licences to use the same property to other undertakings.

Office for Harmonisation in the Internal Market (OHIM) (www.oami.eu.int) the European Union institution that administers the Community trade mark (see above), as well as the Community design regime.

opposition proceedings brought by a third party who maintains that the mark that a trade mark applicant has applied for is unregistrable.

parallel importation the process of importing genuine goods from a jurisdiction where they have been put on the market with the trade mark proprietor's consent into another jurisdiction where the trade mark proprietor has not consented to their being marketed.

Paris Convention the Paris Convention for the Protection of Industrial Property Rights, which established the Paris Union for the Protection of Industrial Property Rights. The Paris Convention sets out the minimum intellectual property rights that must be recognized by the members of the Paris Union and regulates the recognition by members of the Paris Union of intellectual property rights belonging to non-nationals.

patent the legal protection granted to inventions.

passing off a form of unfair competition law found in common-law countries and which involves an undertaking misrepresenting his goods as the goods of another undertaking.

permitted use a use of another's trade mark which is permitted by law, regardless of whether it has been authorized by the trade mark owner.

provisional measures temporary measures (such as the awarding of an interim injunction) taken in expectation of a full trial.

the Regulation Council Regulation 40/94 of 20 December 1993 on the Community trade mark. This regulation creates the Community trade mark (see above).

relative grounds reasons for which a mark can be refused registration, or invalidated if it is registered, based on a conflict with an earlier trade mark.

relief the award of damages, an injunction and/or costs or any other award made against the unsuccessful party for the benefit of the successful party in a court action.

Glossary

remedy a synonym for 'relief' (see above).

revocation the removal from a trade mark register of a trade mark which was originally validly registered but which, usually on account of non-use, has ceased to be so.

saisie contrefaçon French court procedure for obtaining pre-trial disclosure of information and seizure of allegedly infringing products.

saisie-description Belgian court procedure for obtaining pre-trial disclosure of information and seizure of allegedly infringing products.

salami-slicing analysing an element of a trade mark in isolation, without considering how that element interacts with all of the other elements of the trade mark.

service mark a trade mark registered in respect of the provision of services.

sign any carrier/communicator of information. The term is often used in European trade mark law to describe a would-be trade mark that is unregistrable or a trade mark that has not been registered.

sponsorship financial support granted to cultural, sporting or educational events or institutions by businesses, often in return for an obligation to display the name, logo and/or trade mark of the sponsoring business.

tarnishment use of a trade mark by a third party that causes negative associations to adhere to the earlier trade mark. Generally this will involve use of the mark in an unwholesome or unsavoury context, or on goods that are unwholesome, unsavoury or poor quality.

third party a person or entity other than the proprietor of the trade mark.

trade mark a sign capable of distinguishing the goods of one undertaking from the goods of another undertaking.

trade mark portfolio all of the trade marks owned by a company.

TRIPs the Agreement on Trade-Related Aspects of Intellectual Property Rights, appended to the World Trade Organization Agreement. TRIPs details the minimum intellectual property protection that all members of the World Trade Organization must provide.

unauthorized use use of another's trade mark for which the user obtained no authorization. Such use may be an infringement but need not, as where the use is not one which falls within the definition of an infringing act.

unfair competition actions taken during the course of trade that are considered, through the eyes of the law, to unacceptably impinge on the rights of another trader. The threshold of what is considered 'unfair' varies greatly between various countries. For example, Germany has a general prohibition on all competitive acts which are *contra bonos mores* while passing-off law in the UK only provides relief when a misrepresentation has taken place.

United Kingdom Patent Office (www.patent.gov.uk) the United Kingdom government entity that is responsible for granting and registering patents, designs and trade marks in the United Kingdom, as well as for maintaining the patent, design and trade mark register.

United States Patent and Trademark Office (USPTO) (www.uspto.gov) the United States government entity that is responsible for granting and registering patents and federal trade marks in the United States, as well as for maintaining the patent and trade mark register.

well-known mark a mark that has a wider degree of recognition than the majority of marks generally in use. For a mark to be famous it generally has to be recognized by the population as a whole, while a well-known mark usually only need be recognized by its target market.

word-and-device mark a trade mark consisting of both a word and a logo, picture or design.

World Intellectual Property Organization (WIPO) (www.wipo.int) an international organization that is part of the United Nations and is responsible for the harmonization of national intellectual property legislation and procedures, the exchange of intellectual property information, the resolution of certain intellectual property disputes and various other functions connected to the development and administration of intellectual property laws worldwide.

INDEX OF WORD MARKS

Note: Case names are in *italics*

4 YOU	10.153	AMPLEX	11.62
7	5.40	AMTRAK	15.50
7-ELEVEN	15.50	*ANDAK*	16.31
10 ROYAL BERKSHIRE POLO CLUB	8.59	ANDREX	2.41, 8.95
101 DALMATIONS	15.57	ANUSOL	11.62
1-800-PLUMBING	5.29	ANZAC	4.17
1-888-M-A-T-R-E-S-S	5.29	*APOTEKET*	4.54
800-FLOWERS	5.28, 5.29	APPLE	1.02, 1.03, 1.06, 4.150, 5.31, 6.04, 17.08, 17.45
21ST CENTURY	10.52		
ABSOLUT	4.60	AQUASCUTUM	4.114
ACAMOL	16.34	*AROMATONIC*	13.109
ACEMARK	10.137	*AROME TONIQUE*	13.109
ACME	15.42, 15.45	ARSENAL	2.30, 2.33, 2.38, 7.43, 7.49, 7.51, 8.84, 8.85, 8.86
ACME AMERICA	15.42		
ACME ASIA-EUROPE	15.42		
ACME EUROPE	15.42	ARTHUR	1.03, 10.10
ACME HOLDINGS	15.42	*ARTHUR*	10.29, 10.30, 10.31
ADIDAS	2.27, 4.116, 7.51, 8.97, 9.93, 10.117, 11.81	ARTHUR ET FELICIE	1.03
		ARTHUR ET FELICIE	10.10, 10.18, 10.20
ADIDAS	10.154, 11.22A, 11.58, 11.61, 11.93, 11.95	ASPIRIN	6.05, 8.79
		ASPREY	10.12
ADVANTA	8.125, 8.126	AUDI	11.74, 11.76
ADVANTA	8.142, 8.145, 8.149, 8.150, 8.151, 8.153, 8.154	AUDI-MED	11.74
		AVEENO	16.03
		AVENGERS	17.46
AFTER EIGHT	10.103	AVNET	10.98, 17.73
AFTER SEX MINTS	10.103	*AXION*	5.144A
AGAROL	16.34		
AIRTEL	10.68	BABINA	10.48
AL GATTO NERO	10.51	*BABY DIOR*	17.43
ALBERT	10.93, 10.96	BABYDIOR.NET	17.43
ALOHA	10.64	BABY-DRY	4.76, 4.78, 4.98, 4.100, 4.104, 4.111, 4.136, 4.149, 10.117
ALTENBURGER ZIEGENKASE	18.35		
ALVORADA	13.99	BABY-DRY	1.36, 4.99, 4.100, 4.133, 4.147, 4.148, 4.149, 5.31, 5.112, 5.113, 6.15
ALWAYS	5.31		
AMAZON.COM	4.170		
AMBROSIA	4.42		
AMERICAN EXPRESS	1.09	BACARDI	9.75, 9.76, 9.77
AMOXIL	16.05	BACARDI BREEZER	1.17

Index of Word Marks

BAIN DE CHAMPAGNE	18.34	BMW	17.08
BALSAMICALLY FRUITY		BOAC	12.18
WITH A SLIGHT HINT		BODY SHOP	12.15, 20.15, 21.27,
OF CINNAMON	5.117		21.39
BANANA	4.68, 4.69	BOEHRINGER INGELHEIM	14.119
BANANAS IN PYJAMAS	16.70	BOEING	2.41
BANDERA	13.61	BOLANDS COTTAGE	
BANK 24	10.120	CREAM	10.123
BARBIE	8.55, 8.66, 8.69, 9.78,	BOLLINGER	18.41
	21.01, 21.42	BOLS INSIDE	8.58
BARCELONA	20.08	BOSTONGURKA	6.32
BARCLAYCARD	8.125	BOVRIL	4.116
BARCLAYS BANK	8.77	BRAVO	4.83
BARCLAYS BANK	8.142, 8.145, 8.149,	BRITISH AIRWAYS	8.134, 8.135, 8.143,
	8.150, 8.151, 8.153,		8.145, 8.153
	8.154	BROADBAND CODE	
BARILLA	10.65	DOUBLE DIVISION	
BAYWATCH	11.83	MULTIPLE ACCESS	5.78
BE NATURAL	13.94	BROKEN STITCHES	10.17
BEACH BOYS	8.36	BRUSCHETTA	4.59
BEANIE BABIES	8.32	BSS	5.38, 6.22
BEAUTY ISN'T ABOUT		BUD	18.40
LOOKING YOUNG		BUDWEIS	18.40
BUT LOOKING GOOD	4.111	BUDWEISER	8.51, 9.88
BECHAMEL	6.39	BULLS' BLOOD	19.07
BECKS	13.22	BURBERRY	2.40, 9.66
BELLE DE CHAMPAGNE	8.45	BURGER KING	15.43
BEN 'N' JERRYS	20.09	BUSINESS WIRE	15.67
BENECOL	10.76	BUY.COM	4.166, 5.26
BENNETTON	2.40, 8.170, 19.18	BUY.TM	5.26
BEQUEMLICKEIT	4.132		
BETON-APOTEKET	4.54	CADBURY	5.60, 20.16
BETTER INGREDIENTS,		CADDIES	8.78
BETTER PIZZA	8.174	CAFE EINSTEIN	16.62
BETTY	10.136	CALVIN KLEIN	8.89, 8.168
BETTY'S KITCHEN	13.95	CAMEL	11.41, 11.79
BIERE DU DEMON	13.110	CAMEL	11.64
BIG MAC	1.06	CAMPBELL'S	7.39
BILLCLINTON	4.35	CANADA	5.52
BIO	4.45, 19.09	CANCER	5.24
BIO-CLAIRE	4.156	CANNABIS CRUNCH	10.127, 10.128
BIO-CLEAR	4.156	CANNON	10.80
BioID	4.62, 5.30, 5.41	CANON	10.80, 10.102, 10.111
BIO-MILD	4.155	CARCARD	5.148
BIRD'S EYE	4.42	CARDIGAN	6.39
BISMARCK	6.39	CAREMIX	13.107
BLACK BULL	10.150	CARPOINT	14.13
BLACK LABEL	8.66	CARRION	20.24
BLANCMANGE	16.59	CARTIER	10.60, 15.97
BLOOD PRESSURE WATCH	4.123, 4.144	CARTIER FRANCE	4.47
BLOODSTREAM	4.123	CATERPILLAR	8.79, 20.14
BMW	4.26, 8.16, 8.23, 8.30,	CHAMPAGNE	1.06, 6.28, 8.104,
	8.78, 9.32, 9.34, 9.76,		10.47, 18.17, 18.19,
	17.70		18.41, 18.59, 20.11

Index of Word Marks

CHAMPION	10.15	CRUSADER	19.11
CHAMPION DU MONDE	10.15	CUBA L.A.	5.49
CHANEL	15.97, 17.53		
CHANEL	10.68	DAIMLER	5.60
CHANEL NO.5	11.58, 20.07	DALACIN	9.86
CHANELLE	10.69	DALACIN C	9.86
CHEMFINDER	4.118, 4.119, 4.120, 4.122	DALACINE	9.86
		DANIS	10.65
CHEVY	1.02	DANONE	8.61, 17.24
CHEVY	11.33	DANSK GRAMMY	14.42
CHIEMSEE	20.11	DAS PRINZIP DER BEQUEMLICHKEIT	4.113, 4.132
CHIVAS REGAL	1.23		
CHOCOLATE	19.09	DAVIDOFF	11.84, 11.85, 11.86, 11.87, 11.88, 11.93, 11.95, 12.27, 13.58, 17.18
CHRISTIAN DIOR	7.10, 8.03, 8.84, 17.43		
CHRISTIAN LAURENT	8.84		
CHRISTINA DIOR	7.10		
CHURCH SHOES	19.07	DAVINA	10.48
CINE ACTION	4.111	DEATH	4.143, 20.24
CITRISOURCE	13.23	DECON	13.69, 13.130, 13.131, 13.142
CITY OF DISCOVERY	14.67		
CLAUDIA BAKER	10.152	DELL	10.102
CLEANARGILE	8.29	DEMOISELLE DE CHAMPAGNE	8.45
COBBER	15.27		
COCA COLA	1.16, 1.17, 1.18, 1.19, 2.04, 5.116, 8.95, 8.107, 11.34, 12.10, 20.17, 20.18, 21.24, 21.28, 21.36, 21.37	DEMON ALE	13.91, 13.110
		DE-NIC	4.48
		DENIM CO	9.39
		DEN-KLEEN	7.10
		DENTINE	7.10
COCA-COLA	10.133	DEROXAT	16.25
COCKBURN	19.13	DIAL-O-MATIC	15.39
COCONUT	5.86	DIESEL	19.18
COKE	1.01, 1.02, 8.79, 8.100, 9.75, 9.76, 9.77	DIET COKE	1.17, 1.19
		DIETSOURCE	13.23
COLGATE	2.25, 9.16, 9.17	DIMPLE	11.29, 11.94
COLIBRI	4.116	DINERS CLUBCARD	2.41
COLUMBIA	5.45	DINO	10.69
COMBI	10.13	DINOKIDS	10.69
COMFORT AND JOY	10.12	DIOR	8.65
COMFORT PLUS	4.139	DIOR	17.40
COMPAIR	13.34	DISCMAN	4.154
COMPANYLINE	5.31, 6.34	DISCOVERY 102	14.67
COMPANYLINE	6.34	DISCOVERY CHANNEL	14.67
COMPARE!	8.136, 8.144	DISNEY	5.63
COMPLETE	4.84	DISNEY WORLD	1.06
CONQUEROR	14.30	DLC	5.36, 5.37, 6.22
CONTEXT CUT	8.46	DOCKSIDES	9.51
COOL AND SLIM	10.12	DOCTOR MARTEN	20.18
COOL AND SLIM	10.33	DOLBY	7.10
CORNFLAKES	6.05	DOMINOS PIZZA	15.50
CORN FLAKES	13.48	DONALD DUCK	1.06
CORONATION STREET	13.95	DON'T LEAVE HOME WITHOUT IT	5.31
CRATE AND BARREL	17.09		
CRISPY CRUNCH	10.127, 10.128	DOUBLEMINT	4.117, 4.130, 4.139
CROSS	1.09, 4.150, 19.07	DRAINS "я" US	1.20

Index of Word Marks

DRAMBUIE	10.47	EURO-HEALTH	5.53
DRIZABONE	4.114	EURO-LAMB	4.49, 5.53
DRY-BABY	4.148	EUROMARK	10.136
DUNE	9.62	EUROPABANK	4.42
DUNKIN' DONUTS	15.50	EUROPEAN	5.47, 5.48, 8.16
DURACELL	19.17	EUROPEAN VOICE	5.48
DURACELL	12.33	EUTHYMOL	11.34
DURAL DURA KOTE	13.86	EVASIL	10.56
DURFFEE	11.84, 11.87, 11.88	EVER READY	11.81, 19.17
DYED JEANS	9.56	EVERREADY	11.81
DYNALINK	10.118	EXACYL	10.56
DYNANET	10.118	EXTRA SPECIAL BITTER	4.64
DYNO-ROD	15.50	EXTRA STRONG BITTER	4.64
DYSON	8.128, 8.156	EXXON	4.01
DYSON	8.131		
		FAHRENHEIT	9.62
EARL GREY	6.39	FAIRY LIQUID	19.07
EASYBANK	4.117, 4.138	*FASHION FOR Y U*	10.153
EASYCAR	8.84	FCUK	4.37, 19.02, 19.10,
EASYCINEMA	8.84		19.18, 20.24
EASYCREDIT	8.167, 8.169	*FELIX LE SOURICEAU*	10.56
EASYJET	8.84	*FELIX THE CAT*	10.42, 10.56
EASYVIRGIN	8.84	FERRARI	5.63, 20.16
EAU FRESH	10.70	FIAT	2.24, 5.31, 10.85,
EAU SAUVAGE	9.62		10.88, 13.26
ECCO ALPHA	8.58	FIAT PUNTO	9.18
ECO	4.45	*FIBERSOURCE*	13.23
EIRETEL	10.68	FIDEL CASTRO	4.35
ELECTROLUX	8.128	FIFTIES	10.32, 10.33
ELECTROLUX	8.131, 8.157	FILOFAX	6.06
ELLE	5.31	FINNAIR	1.09
ELLE	12.40, 13.61	*FINO BANDERA*	13.61
ELLOS	4.134	FINO BANDERA –	
ELS	10.74	RAINERA PEREZ	
ELTON JOHN	5.62	MARIA- SALUCAR	
ELVIS	5.61, 8.89	DE BARRAMEDA	13.61
EMACO	8.131, 8.156	FIRST	10.15
EMMENTHAL	18.48	FIRST LADY	10.15
ENAMELIZE	4.157	FIRSTMARK	10.136
EPOISSES DE BOUGOGNE	18.47	FLOWERS	5.29
EPSY	7.24, 7.25	FLU-SHIELD	4.138
ERGOPANEL	4.71	FOODSAVER	4.155
EROWA COMBICHUCK	10.13	FOR YOU	4.137
ESB	13.69	FORD	8.12, 8.16, 11.32,
ESQ	10.129		17.04
ESSO	8.61, 8.68	FORD FOCUS	1.19, 1.24, 9.16
ESSO	17.68	FORD JAGUAR	1.19
ESTEE LAUDER	8.95	FORD MUSTANG	1.24
E.T.	8.53	FORD THUNDERBIRD	1.24
EUCERIN	10.133	*FORMAT*	14.62, 17.15
EUDERMIN	10.133	FORMATIL	4.115
EURO-	5.57, 5.51, 5.53	FORTUNA	11.79
EUROCLIP	5.53	FOX'S	10.44, 10.46
EURO-COOL	5.53	FRANCE	5.52

692

Index of Word Marks

FREEBIES	17.21	HARD ROCK CAFE	10.63
FREESTYLE	13.69	HARLEY DAVIDSON	20.14
FRIGIDAIRE	6.05	HARMSEN	10.44
FRISBEE	1.01, 6.06, 6.28	HARRODS	1.23
FROOT LOOPS	19.06	*HARRY POTTER*	16.66
FUCHS	10.44, 10.46	*HARTLAUER*	8.146
FUJIFILM	9.56	HARVARD	7.01, 10.48
FUNK	10.64	HAVE A BREAK	4.169, 5.77
		HAVE A KIT KAT	4.169
GAP	13.115	HEINEKEN	1.14, 2.27
GAPPOL	13.115	HERMES	2.40
GARDOL	4.114	HERSHEY KISS	10.53
GARIBALDI	6.39	*HETI MONTAZS*	8.42
GAULOISES	11.79, 20.07	HEWLETT-PACKARD	2.41
GENERAL FOOD	15.32	HILTON	11.81
GENERAL MILLS	15.32	HIMARK	10.136
GENERAL MOTORS	11.83, 12.27, 12.67	HIS MASTER'S VOICE	19.17
GENESCAN	4.69, 4.149	HISPANO-SUIZA	12.18
GEO	4.105	HOLIDAY INN	19.23
GERMANY	5.52	HOLLYWOOD	11.27, 11.79, 11.80
GERMANY: A THOUSAND-YEAR OLD ENEMY OF POLAND	4.56	*HOLLYWOOD*	11.58, 11.77, 11.79
		HONDA	11.58
GEROLSTEINER	8.19	HOOLIGAN	10.71
GIACOMELLI	16.43	HOOVER	1.01, 5.60, 6.06, 6.29, 11.58
GILLETTE	8.24		
GIROFORM	4.63	HOROSCOPE	5.24
GLAD-LOCK	8.169	HOTEL MONACO	5.49
GL@SS	5.42	HOVIS	6.28
GLAXO	14.119	HUGO BOSS	8.73, 11.94
GLENN MILLER	8.44	HYUNDAI	2.24
GOD MORGON APELSIN JUICE MED FRUKTKOTT	4.106	ICELAND	5.52
		IDEAL	4.82, 4.86
GOLDEN LIGHTS	13.120	IFM INTERNATIONAL FLEET MANAGEMENT	13.39
GOLDEN PROMISE	18.23		
GORGONZOLA	1.06, 18.04	*ILS*	10.74
GRAMMY	14.42	IMAJE	6.44
GRANA PANADO	18.51	*IMOVANE*	16.24
GRANADA	5.45	*INSUMAN*	16.12
GRANDEE	10.111	*INTEL*	20.16
GREENLAND	5.52	*INTEL*	11.57, 11.72
GRINGO	19.16	INTEL INSIDE	8.58
GROKSTER	17.55	*INTEL-PLAY*	11.57, 11.72
GROMAX	13.100, 13.136	INTERBRAND	10.136
GUCCI	5.63	INTERMARK	10.136
GUINNESS	17.39	*INTERMEDIAIR*	17.67
GULF	13.96	INTERNATIONAL	5.51, 5.54
GUTALAX	16.24	INTERNATIONAL FLEET MANAGEMENT	13.39
HAAGEN-DAZS	2.40, 4.01, 13.05	INTERNET.COM	5.26
HAAKEBECK	13.22	INTERPOL	4.17
HAG	9.94	ISENBECK	13.22
HALLOWEEN	4.39	*ISOSOURCE*	13.23

Index of Word Marks

JACK & DANNY'S ROCK CAFE	10.63	KWIK COPY	15.50
JACK DANIEL'S	20.07	LA CAIXA	17.40, 17.41
JAGUAR	1.19	*LA CHEMISE LACOSTE*	13.106
JAMES BOND	8.53, 16.65	*LA FRESH WATER*	10.70
JAN III SOBIESKI	16.58	LA HONTE DE LA JUNGLE	8.68
JANE AUSTEN	13.105, 16.57	LA PIZZA DE ST-TROPEZ	4.38
JARVARD	7.01, 10.48	*LA POSTE*	10.14
JEAN-PAUL GAULTIER	11.04, 11.05	LABEL	4.149
JEEP	16.65	LACOSTE	20.07
JENNIFER LOPEZ	15.57	LAMBORGHINI	8.107, 10.85, 10.889
JERYL LYNN	6.39	LANDAU	10.44
JEUX OLYMPIQUES	12.35	*LANDRE*	10.111
JOHANNES PAUL II	4.35	*LAP TRAVELER*	17.12, 17.13, 17.14
JOHN SILVER	16.67	LAPHROAIG	8.21, 17.39, 19.13
JOHNSON FRY	8.155	*LAPHROAIG*	14.65
JOY	2.41, 10.12	LARA CROFT	16.65
JOY	13.64	LAST MINUTE	4.170
JOY ONE YEAR	13.64	*LAXOBERAL*	16.24
JUNK	10.65	*LE CHAT NOIR*	10.51
JUPITER	8.156	LEGO	4.116, 10.138
JUSLINE	17.20	LEONARD-CHESHIRE.COM	17.37
JUST DO IT	8.170	*LES CADETS D'AQUITAINE*	18.45
		LEVI STRAUSS	9.73, 9.74
K	5.31, 5.32	LEVI'S	9.56, 9.73, 9.74
K GLASS	6.37	*LIBERTEL*	5.127, 5.128
KART	10.60	*LIFESOURCE*	13.23, 13.24, 13.25
KAZAA	17.55	*LIMOVAN*	16.24
KELLOGG'S	2.44, 12.15, 15.32	LINCOLN	5.45
KEN	8.55, 9.78	LINDT	8.72
KENCO – THE REAL COFFEE EXPERTS	19.08	*LINDE*	4.124
		LINGUAPHONE	4.114
KENT GOLDEN LIGHTS	13.120	LINOLEUM	6.05, 6.28
KENTUCKY FRIED CHICKEN	20.09	LITE	4.62, 4.130
		LONG CHERI	12.58
KESSLER HOCHGEWACHS	18.37, 18.42	*LONG JOHN SILVER*	16.67
KEYMAIL	4.115	*LONG POINT*	13.101
KFC	15.50, 19.23	*LORRAINE*	20.11
KIKU	4.144	LOUIS VUITTON	10.13
KITCHENS "я" US	1.20	LOVE HEARTS	5.106
KIT KAT	5.77	*LUCAS BOLS*	11.53, 11.55
KIT PRO	4.100	*LUCIANO PAVAROTTI*	16.56
KIT SUPER PRO	4.100	LUKE SKYWALKER	15.59, 16.65
KIWI	4.42, 4.43	LUPETTO	13.26
KIWI FRUIT	8.16	LUPO	13.26
KNOCKANDO	11.34		
KODAK	4.01, 4.116, 9.35, 10.60, 12.15, 12.54, 12.55	MAC CAT FOOD	12.40
		MAC DOG FOOD	12.40
		MADONNA	5.61
KRONENBOURG 1664	5.19	MAE WEST	6.39
KRUG	18.41	MAG	2.50
KSM	8.137, 8.139, 8.158	*MAGGI*	17.22, 17.48
KUKELEKUUUUU	5.136	MAIL	4.124
KWELLS	16.04	MANCHESTER UNITED	20.08

694

Index of Word Marks

M&Ms	10.43	MCTRIPLE	13.20
MANGO	10.42, 15.50	MCVITIES COLLEGE	
MANPOWER	4.176	CREAM	10.123
MARCA MODE	10.155	MEGA FORCE	8.83
MARIE CLAIRE	12.44	*MEGA-*	10.119
MARIGOLD	4.131	*MEGASOL*	10.119
MARKENQUALITAT		MELITTA	8.26
AUS DEUTSCHEN		MEMOREX	10.135
LANDEN	20.11	MEMORY	10.135
MARKFORCE	10.136	MERC	1.02
MARK-INVENTA	10.136	MERCEDES	8.71, 11.36
MARKLAW	10.136	*MERCEDES*	11.46
MARKPLUS	10.136	MERIT	11.79
MARKPRO	10.136	METRO	16.48
MARKS & SPENCER	8.168, 11.32	MICKEY FINN	6.39
MARLBORO	11.79	MICKEY MOUSE	1.06, 2.27, 15.68
MARLBORO	15.85	MILLENNIUM	6.28
MARS	5.49, 5.60, 6.09, 8.55,	*MINERVA*	13.67
	9.01, 9.03, 9.04,	*MINIMAX*	13.54
	9.05, 9.06, 9.07, 9.08,	*MINIRIN*	16.30
	9.09, 9.15, 9.28,	*MINITRAN*	15.85
	9.40, 9.53, 9.54, 9.84	MINNIE MOUSE	15.57
MARS	12.42	*MISS FIFTIES*	10.32
MARTINI	10.66	MISTER LONG	5.69
MATRATZEN	4.144, 6.36	*MIXERY*	10.114
MATRAZEN	6.36	MOBILE DESK	17.12, 17.13,
MATRIX RELOADED	15.43		17.14
MAX FACTOR	8.33	*MOBILIX*	10.68
MAXIMA	4.85	MOET ET CHANDON	18.41
MCBACON	13.20	*MOONIES*	19.15
MCCAFE	13.20	*MOSKOVSKAYA*	13.32
MCCHEESE	13.20	MON CHERI	12.58
MCCHICKEN	13.20	MONEYBANK	9.31
MCCRISPY	13.20	MONOPOLY	8.78
MCCROISSANT	13.20	MONT BLANC	7.10
MCDONALDS	1.06, 1.21, 10.139,	MONT CHERRY	12.58
	12.15, 12.40,	MONTAZS	8.42
	13.05, 13.20, 13.21,	MONTBLANC	16.59
	14.64, 15.43, 15.50,	MONTCHERI	12.58
	15.68, 21.39	MONTXERI	12.58
MCDONALD'S	12.65	MOTHERCARE	4.139
MCDONUT	13.20	MOZART	16.57
MCDOUBLE	13.20	MUESLI	6.04
MCEXPRESS	13.20	MULTI 2'N 1	4.111
MCFEAST	13.20	MUNCHERIE	12.58
MCFLURRY	13.20	MUSLI	6.04
MCL PARFUMS DE PARIS	4.46, 4.47	MUSLIX	6.04
MCMENU	13.20	*MYSTERY*	10.114
MCMOUSE	15.68		
MCMUFFIN	13.20	NABISCO	12.52
MCNUGGETS	13.20	*NATIVA*	14.117
MCPIZZA	13.20	*NATIVA DI CUPRA*	14.117
MCRIB	13.20	*NCDL*	11.73
MCSINGLE	13.20	NESQUIK	17.45

Index of Word Marks

NESTLE	2.41, 5.60, 5.66, 8.76, 21.24	ORANGE MAID	4.141
		ORANGE X-PRESS	10.57
NESTLE	13.104	ORANGEX	1.03
NETMEETING	4.117, 4.133, 5.31	*ORANGEX*	10.57
NEURONE	4.70	ORANGEXPRESS	1.03
NEW BORN BABY	4.113, 4.122, 4.133, 4.136	*ORANGEXPRESS*	10.58
		ORANGINA	10.119
NEW BORN BABY	4.136	ORANGO	10.119
NEW JERSEY NETS	8.57	ORGANIC	19.09
NEW YORK KNICKS	8.57	ORGANIC ESSENTIALS	4.143
NEWCASTLE BROWN ALE	18.30		
NEWSPARKLE BROWN ALE	18.30	PAMPERS	4.149, 5.112
NEXT	5.31, 8.54	PAN-AM	12.18
NIKE	2.27, 2.40, 8.97, 8.98, 8.169, 9.16, 9.19, 15.97, 21.24, 21.25	PANGOLIN	17.52
		PANHARD	12.18
		PARFUMS CHRISTIAN DIOR	9.62
NIKE	10.116	PARKER	8.23
NIKE ALPHA PROJECT	8.58	*PARMA*	18.51
NIKE SPORTS FRAGRANCE	10.116	PARMA HAM	18.30
NIKETOWN	16.41, 21.25	PARMIGIANO REGGIANO	18.26, 18.27
NISSAN	10.67	PARTNER WITH THE BEST	4.53
NISSAN MICRO	9.18	PAYLESS RENT	13.28
NIZORAL	16.03	PAYLESS RENT A CAR	13.28
NOGENOL	17.72	*PEBBLE BEACH*	11.63, 11.64, 14.68
NOKIA	17.61, 17.70	PENGUIN	1.02, 2.56
NORDIC	5.47	PENNSYLVANIA 65000	5.28
NORMANDIE	20.11	PEPSI	4.26, 4.150, 8.100, 8.107
NORTH POLE	5.49		
NOUVELLE	8.95	*PEPSI*	10.37
NOVAMARK	10.136	PEPSI COLA	1.17, 1.19, 20.12
NUROFEN	8.107, 16.03	PERFECT BROW	5.148
NU-TRIDE	10.89	PERFECTION	20.24
		PERFECTIONISTS	4.83
OBELIX	10.68	PERRIER	20.22
OBERON	4.65	*PETA*	17.06
OBSESSION	8.168, 9.28	PETIT BEBE	4.136
OCEALIA	10.27	PEUGEOT	9.30
OCEALINE	10.27	*PEUGEOT*	9.32
OLDSMOBILE	8.16	PHILIPS	4.168, 5.60
OLLYGAN	10.71	PHILISHAVE	4.166, 4.168, 5.110
OLYMPIC	12.32		
OLYMPIQUE	12.35	PICASSO	5.66, 16.60
OLYMPRIX	12.35	*PIKA-*	10.119
OMEPRAZOK	16.05	*PIKASOL*	10.119
OMEPRAZOK	13.111	*PILSEN URQUELL*	18.46
OMEPRAZOL	13.111	PINA COLADA	6.27, 8.79
ONLY A BREAST IN THE MOUTH IS BETTER THAN A LEG IN THE HAND	19.14	*PIPPIG*	8.146
		PITMAN	15.92
		PIZZA EXPRESS	12.15
		PIZZA HUT	20.18
OPTREX	16.03	PLANET FOOTBALL	5.08
ORANG-	10.118	PLAYBOY	8.36
ORANGE	1.02, 4.141, 8.169	PLAYMATE	8.36
ORANGE	8.131, 8.152		

696

Index of Word Marks

PLAYMATE OF THE YEAR 1981	8.36	REED	8.35, 17.71
POISON	4.143, 19.02, 20.24	REED	17.63, 17.71
POLAROID	4.150	REEF	13.127
POLICE	4.17	REESE'S PIECES	8.53
POLO	2.56, 6.11, 8.59, 11.32, 11.70, 17.64, 20.07	REETRUCK	10.27
		REGAL ZONOPHONE	12.18
		RENAULT	5.31
POLYPADS	4.158	RENAULT CLIO	9.18
POM	19.16	REPLICAWATCHWORLD	7.47
PONTIAC	5.45	*RESOURCE*	13.23
PORK – THE OTHER WHITE MEAT	3.50	RIBENA	7.10
		RIESLING HOCHGEWACHS	18.37
PORSCHE	2.24	*RIGTIG JUICE*	4.176
POST'AIR	10.14	*RIOJA*	18.50
POSTBUS 51	17.49	ROADRUNNER	17.69
POSTBUS51.COM	17.49	ROCK CAFE	10.63
POT NOODLE	14.33	ROLEX	1.09, 2.40, 4.01, 4.116, 7.01, 7.10, 7.19, 7.20, 7.52, 7.53, 8.96, 10.04, 10.112, 15.97, 18.18
POTTER	10.44		
POWERHOUSE	10.40		
PQASSO	16.60		
PREMIER	4.178	ROLEX	17.08
PREMIER PACKAGE	4.178	ROLLERBLADE	6.06
PRET A MANGER	21.39	ROLLING STONES	7.48
PREVICUR	9.94	ROLLS ROYCE	2.40, 7.01, 8.54, 8.55
PREVICUR N	9.94	*ROSA PARKS*	21.01
PRIMARK	9.39	ROSIE LEE	6.39
PRINCESS LEIA	15.57	ROTHSCHILD	5.60
PROCTOR AND GAMBLE	17.39	ROYAL MAIL	14.122
PROMARK	10.136	*RTLGROUP.COM*	17.47
PRONTOPRINT	19.23	*RYANAIR*	8.134, 8.135, 8.140, 8.143, 8.145, 8.153, 8.154
PRONUPTIA	15.55		
PROZAC	5.31, 6.06, 16.02		
PRUDENTIAL	19.17	RYTZ	8.50
PRUDENTIAL	15.91		
PUFFIN	2.56	SAAB	8.16
PUMA	8.97	*SABEL*	10.23, 10.26, 10.28, 10.38, 10.43, 10.51, 10.6, 10.73, 10.146, 10.154, 11.83
PUMA	10.23, 10.26, 10.28, 10.38, 10.43, 10.51, 10.60, 10.61, 10.73, 10.146, 10.154, 11.82		
		SABENA	8.140, 8.148
PYCNOGENOL	17.72	*SAFE-HANDS*	11.73
		SAINT-PETERSBOURG	4.47
QUALITEX	1.36	*SALAISONS D'AUVERGNE*	20.11
		SAMARA LOOK	5.11
RATZ "Я" US	1.20	*SAMPDORIA*	17.44
RAVIL	18.51	SAMSONITE	20.16
READER'S DIGEST	19.17	*SANDOSOURCE*	13.23
REAL MADRID	10.01, 20.08	SATURN	16.46, 16.47
REAL PEOPLE, REAL SOLUTIONS	5.75	*SAVOIE*	20.11
		SCANDECOR	8.34, 13.41
REALEMON	15.32	SCANIA	17.42
RED BULL	10.150	SCHWEPPES	5.60, 5.122
REEBOX	10.27	SEAT	19.12
REEBOX	8.97	*SEBAGO*	9.51, 9.52

Index of Word Marks

SENSO DI DONNA	10.42	*TAIG*	16.55
SENSOR	8.24	*TAIG KHRIS*	16.55
SEPHORA	11.36	*TAIGA*	16.55
SEROXAT	16.25	TAMPAX	4.116, 20.16
SETBALL	10.118	*TANJA GROTTER*	16.66
SEX PATCH	4.36	TARZAN	6.38, 8.68, 16.65
SHAOLIN	16.50	*TARZAN*	16.68, 16.69
SHELL	21.24	TARZOON	8.68
SIECLE 21	5.20	TASTEE-FREEZ	8.16
SILHOUETTE	1.36, 9.64	TAX FREE	4.69
SIMCA	12.18	TD<small>DI</small>	5.39
SKODA	8.16, 8.107	TECHNOCITE	4.111
SKYLIFT	13.113	TED BAKER	8.83
SLIDE-LOC	8.169	*TED BAKER*	10.152
SLIMMERS AYDS	20.20	TEFLON	6.28
SMARTIES	10.43	*TEKNEK*	8.13, 8.138, 8.158
SMARTWEB	4.144	TELE-MAEGLEREN	8.28
SMILECARE	10.100	TESCO	1.23
SMIRNOFF	4.47, 5.60, 9.50	THANK YOU	4.106
SMITHKLINE BEECHAM	14.119	THE	4.86, 5.31
SNOTBLASTER	20.24	THERMOS	6.05, 8.79
SOCIAL AND POLITICAL		THINK PAD	10.11
MONTHLY: A		THINKPAD	10.11
EUROPEAN MORAL		*TIMES MIRROR*	12.42
TRIBUNAL	4.56	TINY PENIS	4.37
SOLFEN	14.51	TISSOT	10.79
SOLPADEINE	14.51	*TISSOT*	10.18, 10.20
SONY	7.10	TOLEDO	5.45
SPIRIT SUN	8.46	TOLL! ALLES WIRD	
SPOCK	15.57	TEURER	8.67
SPORK	6.33	TOMMY BAKER	8.83
STARBUCKS	20.13, 21.39	TOMMY HILFIGER	2.27, 8.83, 8.170, 9.01,
STEPHANSKREUZ	10.124		10.01, 20.01, 20.12
STITCHES	10.17	*TORREMAR*	13.25
STOLICHNAYA	17.39	*TORRES*	13.25
STREETBALL	10.118	TOYS AREN'T US	11.73
STUDEBAKER	12.18	TOYS "Я" US	1.20, 1.21, 11.73,
SUCHARD	9.63		16.41, 19.04
SUN MAID	4.42, 4.44	TRANSLATIONS	4.70
SUNBEAM	12.18	TREAT	4.127
SUNLIGHT	20.24	*TRILLIUM*	13.132
SUNNY DELIGHT	4.141	*TRI-OMINOS*	13.65
SUPER MEGA	8.83, 8.84	TRIVIAL PURSUIT	4.143
SUPER POWER	8.83	*TRIXIE*	16.37
SUPERLOAN	8.167, 8.169	TUBORG	18.46
SUPREME	4.84	*TUBORG PILSENER*	18.46
SWATCH	10.129	*TUFFTRIDE*	10.89
SWEDISH FORMULA	4.158	TURBO	4.141
SWORD	6.04	TWA	12.18
SYLVESTER	10.43	TWEETY PIE	10.43
		TWENTY-FIRST	
TABASCO	8.79	CENTURY FOX	5.22
TACO CABANA	5.09, 5.11	TYLENOL	20.22
TAHTIMERKKI KAURIS	5.24	*TY.PHOO*	11.42, 11.83

Index of Word Marks

TYPHOON	11.42, 11.83	WECOVER	4.22
		WEETABIX	7.54
ULTRA DOUX	8.29	WELLCOME	14.119
ULTRAPLUS	4.78, 4.87, 4.100, 4.103, 4.154	WELLINGTONS	6.39
		WET WET WET	7.48
UNILEVER	13.104	WHEAT BISKS	7.54
VALIUM	6.06, 8.79	WHIRLPOOL	19.12
VANDOREN	11.34	WIMPY	15.50, 16.65
VASELINE	6.31	*WINDOWBASE*	13.98
VELCRO	4.150, 6.28	*WINDOWPRO*	13.98
VENTURA	10.129	*WINDOWS*	13.98
VENTURE	10.129	*WINDOWSHEET*	13.98
VESTORWORLD	4.117	*WINDSURFING*	
VEUVE CLICQUOT	18.41	*CHIEMSEE*	4.78, 4.163, 6.19
VIAGRA	3.49, 4.01, 6.06, 9.65, 12.15	WINNETOU	5.72, 16.69
		WOOLWORTHS	16.48
VIAGRA	11.83, 12.35, 12.46	WOOLWORTHS METRO	16.48
VIAGRENE	11.83, 12.35	WORLD CUP	8.64
VICTORIA'S SECRET	1.29, 4.39, 19.02	*WRIGLEY*	4.141
VICTORIA'S SECRET	11.46, 12.53, 12.54, 17.11	WRIGLEYS	11.32
		WSI INTERNET	15.50
VICTOR'S LITTLE SECRET	12.53	WWF	5.31, 5.35
VIKING	5.111	*WWF*	14.41, 15.90
VIRGIN	8.84	WWW.PRIMEBROKER.COM	5.25
VISA	2.56, 10.92	*WYETH*	13.130, 13.142
VISA	13.50, 13.102, 13.108		
VISA POUR LE BEAUTE	13.50	XEROX	4.01, 4.116, 17.45
VISA POUR LE BODY BUILDING	13.50	XTC	8.40
VISA POUR LE MUSCLE	13.50	XTC ECSTASY	8.40
VISION DIRECT	4.121	XTC (EKS)(TI:)(SI:)	8.40
VISION DIRECT	4.121	XTRA	4.84
VITALITE	4.115	XXI<small>EME</small> SIECLE	5.21, 10.52
VODAFONE	8.130, 8.131, 8.152		
VOLKSWAGEN	8.16, 13.39	YASMIN	16.04
VOLTAROL	16.04	YES	4.83
VOLVO	8.16, 8.30, 20.15, 21.27	YOGI BEAR	15.57
		YORK	5.45
VOLVO	14.31	YOU	4.137
VORTEX	14.47	*YOU*	10.153
		YOURS	4.137
WACKERS	13.114	*YOURS*	10.153
WACKY WAREHOUSE	13.114	YOU'VE GOT MAIL	4.31, 4.165
WAGAMAMA	10.145	YO-YO	6.06
WALKERS	9.80	YVES ST LAURENT	5.31, 8.84
WALKMAN	1.02, 4.154, 6.05, 8.79		
W<small>AL</small>-M<small>ART</small>	5.11, 16.41	ZANTAC	2.10, 2.25, 4.116, 16.02
WALTZING MATILDA	5.72	*ZANTAC*	16.31
WARHOL	5.66	ZARA	17.05
WARSTEINER	18.39	*ZARA*	17.23
WASH 'N' GO	5.31	*ZINO DAVIDOFF*	9.37
WASHINGTON REDSKINS	19.14	ZIPLOC SLIDE LOC	8.174
WATERFORD	5.45, 7.22	ZUKINIS IN BIKINIS	16.70
W<small>EB</small>R<small>ECORD</small>	4.115		

INDEX

abbreviations 5.30
absolute grounds
  acquired distinctiveness 4.176–4.178
  bad faith 13.144
  cancellation 13.09, 13.14, 13.35–13.38
  opposition to registration 13.03, 13.09
  registrability 4.16–4.23, 4.32, 5.03
  revocation 13.14
  shapes 5.83
abuse of brands 21.15–21.23, 21.29, 21.38–21.39, 21.44
abuse of rights
  Belgium 9.72
  brands 21.15–21.23, 21.29, 21.38–21.39, 21.44
  dominant position, abuse of a 9.73
  EC law, 9.73–9.74
  European Convention on Human Rights 9.74
  exhaustion of rights 9.70–9.74
  fair trials 9.74
  France 9.72
  freedom of speech 9.74
  generic marks and terms 6.16–6.17
  legitimate trade, interference with 9.71–9.72
  mass 6.16–6.17
  monopolies 9.19, 9.70–9.71
  Netherlands 9.72
  non-infringing acts 8.53–8.55
  property rights 9.74
  selective distribution networks 9.70
  Trade Mark Directive 8.55
  unfair competition 9.72–9.73
  websites 8.55
abuse of trade marks 6.16–6.17
academic experts, writings of 3.18
account of profits 14.92–14.94
  damages, inquiries into 14.92, 14.94
  Germany 14.93
  grey goods 14.92
  parallel imports 14.92
acquired distinctiveness 4.80, 4.163–4.178
  absolute bars to registrability 4.176–4.178
  applicant's use 4.175
  Austria 4.176
  Community Trade Mark Regulations 4.177
  customary trade use 4.176
  EC law 4.173, 4.175
  evidence 4.167–4.170
    documentary 4.171
    identifiers, use as 4.164–4.166
    use of 4.165
  identifiers, use as 4.164–4.166
  jurisdiction, use in the 4.172
  Latvia 4.172
  licensees, use by 4.175
  New Zealand 4.175
  opinion polls 4.164
  proof, level of 4.171–4.174
  secondary distinctiveness 4.178
  South Africa 4.178
  third parties, use by unauthorized 4.175
acquiescence 12.56–12.57, 13.77–13.78, 14.42
acronyms 5.35–5.39, 10.73
adjectival surnames 5.69
administrative bodies, decisions of 1.32
ADR (alternative dispute resolution) 14.05, 15.54
addresses 5.25–5.27
administration of registration systems 3.02, 3.04
advantage *see* **unfair advantage and detriment**
adverse publicity 21.23
advertising *see also* **comparative advertising**
  brand 21.04–21.06, 21.10
  car maintenance 9.32–9.34
  franchising 15.53
  France 8.72, 8.74–8.75
  infringement 7.24–7.25
  Internet 17.73
  mere puffs 2.48
  morality 2.48
  No Logo thesis 21.04–21.06, 21.10
  non-infringing acts 8.72–8.75
  notice-based systems 3.37
  pharmaceutical marks 16.03
  private adverts 8.73–8.74
  revocation 13.63
  small adverts, use of marks in 8.73–8.75
  sponsorship 15.60
  spoof 17.57, 17.62
  subvertisements 17.57–17.61
  websites 17.55–17.57, 17.62
  well known and famous marks 12.34–12.35, 12.45

Index

affiliation *see* loyalty or allegiance, badges of
affixing signs to goods or packaging 7.18
African Industrial Property Organization,
    Banjui Agreement on 3.09
Agreement on Trade-Related Aspects of
    Intellectual Property Law *see* TRIPs
agricultural products 18.22–18.35
aiding, abetting, authorizing and procuring
    infringement 7.55–7.59
alcoholic beverages 18.16–18.20, 18.22,
    18.36–18.37, 18.41–18.44
allegiance *see* loyalty or allegiance, badges of
allusive marks 4.114–4.115, 4.133–4.135,
    4.141, 19.06
alphanumeric numbers 5.29
alternative dispute resolution 14.05, 15.54
ambiguous terms 4.139
ambush marketing 8.64
amorial bearings 4.08
Andean Pact 3.09, 12.38
annulment *see* cancellation
appellations of origin *see* geographical
    indications
applications
    amendment of 3.42, 13.107
    bad faith 13.106–13.108, 13.113–13.115
    examination of 3.33–3.39
    fax, by 3.40
    national applications, conversion into 3.48
    publication of 3.40
    revocation 13.14
    systems for processing 2.17
arbitrary embellishments 4.111–4.113
aspirational brands 8.170–8.171
assignment 15.06–15.08, 15.16
    bad faith 13.88
    beneficial interest in 15.07
    Community Trade Mark Regulation 15.17,
        15.23
    contracts 15.08, 15.14
    damages 15.25
    deceit 15.24
    enforcement 15.07
    formalities 15.07, 15.14
    goodwill 15.18–15.24
    international laws 15.14–15.17
    meaning 15.06
    names 5.64
    national laws 15.14–15.17
    Paris Convention 15.21
    record of 15.06
    registration 15.25
    Trade Mark Directive 15.15
    TRIPs 15.14, 15.22

United States 15.19
valuation 15.93
association, likelihood of 10.143–10.155
    Benelux 10.143, 10.148
    Community Trade Mark Regulation
        10.143–10.145
    confusion, likelihood of 10.143–10.149,
        10.154–10.155
    distinctiveness 10.151, 10.154
    EC law 10.144–10.146, 10.151,
        10.154–10.155
    establishing 10.152–10.153
    meaning 10.150–10.151
    Netherlands 10.153, 10.154
    proof of 10.154–10.155
    resemblance of marks 10.144
    similarity and 10.143–10.145
    Trade Mark Directive 10.143–10.145
association marks 18.56
auditing of information 14.23–14.25
aural marks *see* sound marks
Australia
    celebrities 16.70
    colours 5.129, 5.130
    confusion 10.116
    infringement 7.48
    retail sales service marks 16.48
    shapes 5.84
    titles 5.72
Austria
    acquired distinctiveness 4.176
    celebrities 16.57
    damages for secondary infringement 7.58
    domain names 17.20, 17.25
    infringement 7.58, 7.60
    injunctions, final 14.45
    non-infringing acts 8.40
    vicarious liability 7.60

bad faith 13.72–13.148, 13.150
    absolute grounds 13.144
    abuse of direct relations 13.92–13.94
    acquiescence 13.77–13.78
    agency 13.87
    amendment of applications 13.107
    assignment 13.88
    Benelux 13.92–13.94, 13.117
    blocking 13.90–13.91
    bona fide entitlement to file application 13.101
    burden of proof 13.147
    cancellation 13.10, 13.16, 13.85,
        13.145–13.146, 13.148
    celebrities, registration of name of deceased
        13.105

Index

bad faith (*cont.*):
  coexistence agreement, offer of a 13.116
  commercial manner, failure to behave in a prudent 13.99–13.100
  Community Trade Mark Regulations 13.73, 13.78–13.80, 13.94, 13.125, 13.131–13.135
  continuous use 13.122
  domain names 17.18-17.19, 17.28–17.29, 17.32, 17.42–17.47
  duration of open use before filing applications 13.113
  earlier trade mark
    continuous use 13.122
    identical or similar 13.123
    nature of the 13.118–13.123
    reputation of 13.121
    use of 13.119
  EC law 13.73–13.82, 13.132, 13.151
  Estonia 13.96
  Europe 13.82–13.83, 13.150
  evidence of, circumstantial 17.47
  explanation, plausibility of applicant's 13.114–13.115
  Germany 13.90, 13.148
  good faith 13.83
    rebutting the presumption of 13.147
  grounds of
    absolute 13.144
    persuasive 13.85–13.102
    relative 13.144
  identical marks 13.123
  injunctions, interim 14.70
  intent to use 13.124–13.128
  Italy 13.87–13.88, 13.120, 13.126
  knowledge
    earlier marks of, registration with 13.96–13.97
    opposition, of 13.102
    well known marks, registration of third party's 13.98
  misuse of rights 13.90–13.91
  Netherlands 13.96, 13.117
  Norway 13.96
  OHIM 13.80, 13.109, 13.116, 13.119, 13.125, 13.130–13.135, 13.145
  opposition 13.10, 13.18, 13.79, 13.102
  overwide registration 13.130–13.142
  Paris Convention 13.86
  patent monopolies, extending 13.104
  Poland 13.86, 13.99, 13.115
  previous prior user 13.117
  procedural issues 13.143–13.148
  proof of 13.101, 17.45–17.46
  proximity to international non-proprietary names 13.111
  registration, in 13.72–13.148, 12.44
  relative grounds 13.144
  reputation 13.121
  revocation 13.65–13.66, 13.145
  similarity 13.109, 13.123
  Spain 13.86, 13.146
  standing 13.148
  Sweden 13.96–13.97, 13.119–13.121, 13.123, 13.144, 13.146–13.148
  time for raising the issue of 13.144
  timing of the application 13.106
  Trade Mark Directive 13.73–13.82, 13.90, 13.120, 13.126
  translation into another language 13.110
  tribunals dealing with 13.145–13.146
  TRIPs 13.124
  Turkey 13.97, 13.98–13.99
  United States 13.120, 13.125
  use in a manner other than registered 13.95
  veracity on the application, lack of 13.108
  well known and famous marks 12.44, 13.98, 17.42–17.44
Bangui Agreement on an African Industrial Property Organization 3.09
Banjul Protocol on Marks 3.09
barcodes, registration of 5.12–5.14
Belgium
  abuse of rights 9.72
  distinctiveness 4.22
  geographical indications 18.50
  injunctions, interim 14.55
  publication of the court's decision 14.27
  registrability 4.22
  shapes 5.110
beneficial interests 15.07
beneficiaries of trade marks
  comparative advertising 2.06
  consumers 2.10
  counterfeiters 2.07
  dishonest traders 2.06
  fees for administering the trade mark system 2.08
  goodwill 2.05–2.06
  infringers 2.07
  legal profession 2.09
  purchasers 2.10
  state 2.08
  trade mark owners 2.05
  traders, dishonest and honest 2.06
Benelux *see also* **Belgium, Netherlands**
  association, likelihood of 10.144, 10.149
  bad faith 13.92–13.94, 13.117

Benelux *(cont.)*:
   Benelux Treaty on the Uniform Trade Mark Law 3.09
   colours 5.127
   damages 14.76
   fonts 5.43
   infringement 7.56
   money 5.18
   revocation 13.54, 13.65
   taste marks 5.143
   unfair advantage and detriment 11.53–11.55
   well known and famous marks 12.38, 12.44
Berne Convention 14.90
blogs 17.58
blurring 11.14–11.22A
book titles 5.72
bottles 5.100–5.104, 5.107, 5.115
boycotts 8.76–8.77, 21.24
brand abuse 21.15–21.23, 21.29, 21.38–21.39, 21.44
brand loyalty 20.03–20.12
   capture by the consumer 20.19
   cultivation of 20.07–20.09
   distinctiveness 20.07, 20.09
   EC law 20.10–20.11
   ethos of the brand 20.08
   free movement of goods 20.11
   geographical appellations 20.11
   icons 20.03–20.12
   lifestyle 20.07
   limits to 20.10–12.12
   measure of difference between goods and services, as 20.03–20.05
   meaning of 20.06
   monopolies 20.09
   nationalism 20.12
   place names 20.11
   psychology of trade marks 20.03–20.12
   substitutability 20.07
   unfair competition 20.10
   United States 20.12
brands *see also* **brand loyalty**
   abuse of 21.15–21.23, 21.29, 21.38–21.39, 21.44
   adverse publicity 21.23
   advertising 21.04–21.06, 21.10
   aspirational brands 8.169–8.170
   big business practices 21.03
   boycotts 21.24
   bullies 21.38–21.39
   capture by customers 20.17–20.23
   charitable activities of owners 21.39
   choosing trade marks 19.01–19.02, 19.04, 19.19
   co-branding 15.66–15.68
   collusion 21.08
   competition, killing off 21.08
   consumers
      abuse, as voluntary parties to 21.16
      apocalypse 21.38–21.39
      challenges, by 21.29–21.32
      community of interests, no 21.34
      knowledge 21.29–21.33, 21.39, 21.43
      rationality 21.33
      scepticism 21.39
      values, reasserting 21.35
   contracts 15.66, 15.68
   corporate aims 20.20
   corporate fascism 21.11
   criticism of 21.40, 21.43
   culture
      icons, as 21.09, 21.18, 21.22, 21.40, 21.42
      intrusion into the 21.05–21.06
   damage to 20.20–20.21
   dumbing down 21.29
   EC law 9.62–9.63
   economic values, harming 21.21
   economies of scale 21.09
   ethos 20.14–20.18, 21.04
   exhaustion of rights 9.62–9.63
   extension of 1.21, 20.13–20.16
   function of 1.18
   function of trade marks 1.15–1.17
   globalization 21.08, 21.18
   goodwill 11.01, 11.03, 21.24–21.28
   health and safety 20.21
   house marks 1.24
   image of 21.04–21.07
      upholding 9.62–9.63
   Internet, consumer awareness and 21.39
   investments, protection of 21.43
   labour exploitation 21.08, 21.32–21.33
   labour standards, need for minimum 20.21–20.22
   licences 15.67
   lifestyle 8.169–8.170, 21.36
   litigation, threat of 21.40–21.43
   market abuse 21.21
   marketplace 21.31
   maximization of market power 21.18–21.19
   McDonald's defamation case 21.23
   media manipulation 21.10
   negative branding 20.24–20.25
   No Logo thesis 21.03–21.22, 21.29, 21.35, 21.38–21.39, 21.42, 21.44
   non-conformity 20.25
   outsourcing 21.08
   power of 21.24–21.28

Index

brands (*cont.*):
  primary 1.24
  public benefactors, owners as 21.07
  psychology of 20.03–20.32
  reputation 11.01, 11.03
  retail sales service marks 16.46
  secondary trade marks 1.17
  social values, harming 21.21
  sponsorship 21.05
  strategy, psychology of brand 20.13–20.25
  sub-brands 1.19, 1.24, 9.16, 9.18
  synonym with trade mark, as 1.14
  tax
    jurisdictions, location in low 21.22
    revenues 21.07
  trade marks and 1.14–1.21
  unfair competition 21.21
  United States as a brand 21.11, 21.14
  values 19.17–19.18, 21.25–21.37
Brazil 8.12
Brussels Convention 1968 14.10
Brussels Regulation 2001 14.10
burden of proof
  bad faith 13.147
  comparative advertising 8.151–8.152, 8.168
  consent 9.41–9.49
  damages 14.22
  dilution of famous marks 12.53
  exhaustion of rights 9.41–9.49, 14.20–14.21
  generic marks and terms 6.40–6.43
  infringement 14.20–14.22
  non-use 13.60
  parallel imports 16.21
  preliminary issues 14.20–14.22
  reputation 11.48–11.50
  revocation 13.60
  similarity 10.100
  unfair advantage and detriment 11.48–11.50
business formats 5.56, 5.98
business names 1.13
business papers, use of marks on 7.24–7.25
business reputation *see* reputation

Canada 10.127–10.128, 15.13
cancellation 3.46
  absolute grounds 13.09, 13.14, 13.35–13.38
  bad faith 13.10, 13.16, 13.85, 13.145–13.146, 13.148
  Benelux 13.40
  central attack 13.42–13.45
  Community Trade Mark Regulation 13.14, 13.39
  confusion 13.09
  counterclaims 13.08
  dictionaries 8.82
  distinctiveness 13.35–13.37, 13.41
  France 13.37
  genuine prior use 13.39
  grounds of 13.09–13.10, 13.35–13.38, 13.40–13.41
  Madrid Agreement and Protocol, central attack and 13.42–13.45
  motive for 13.08
  OHIM 13.38, 13.39
  pharmaceutical marks 16.36
  Poland 13.40
  prior use
    own 13.40–13.41
    third parties, by 13.39, 13.40
  proceedings 13.07–13.08, 13.35–13.45, 13.149
  relative grounds 13.09, 13.14, 13.40–13.41
  shapes 5.82
  standing 13.13–13.15, 13.37
  threats 14.115
  unfair advantage or detriment 13.09
  well known and famous marks 12.44
  WIPO 13.43
capture of brands by consumers 20.17–20.23
cars
  descriptive marks, fair use of 8.16, 8.30
  dealers and distributors 8.30
  exhaustion of rights 9.16, 9.18, 9.32–9.34
  maintenance of, advertising the 9.32–9.34
  sub-brands of 9.16, 9.18
Cartagena Agreement (Andean Pact) 3.09
case law 1.28–1.37
  administrative bodies, decisions of 1.32
  Court of First Instance 3.13
  EFTA Court 3.14
  European Court of Justice 1.32, 1.36, 3.13
  examples, as 1.33
  hierarchy of nations 1.28–1.31
  hypotheses, as working 1.35
  landmark decisions 1.36–1.37
  national courts, decisions of 3.15
  OHIM 1.32
  precedent, cases as 1.32–1.33
  trade mark examiners, decisions of 1.32–1.33
  TRIPs 1.31
  United States 1.29, 1.36
  well-known marks 1.31
celebrities 16.50–16.72
  Australia 16.70
  Austria 16.57
  bad faith 13.105
  collective 16.50, 16.64
  commemorative goods 16.71

Index

celebrities (*cont.*):
  Community Trade Mark Regulation 3.51,
    16.50, 16.62, 16.67
  comparative advertising 8.171
  confusion 16.55, 16.59
  copyright 16.63, 16.68–16.69
  dead 13.105, 16.50, 16.57–16.62
  descriptive terms 16.68
  distinctiveness 16.53
  endorsement 8.171, 15.63–15.65
  Europe 16.53
  events, as 16.71–16.72
  features 16.52
  fictional 16.50, 16.65–16.70
  folklore 16.50
  former 16.50
  generic terms, fictional characters and 16.69
  Germany 16.69
  graphical representation 16.53
  Greece 16.56
  live 16.50, 16.53–16.56, 16.59–16.60
  local 16.50
  names 5.61, 8.43
    assumed 16.50
    confusing similarity 16.55
    dead celebrities 13.105, 16.58–16.62
    fictional celebrities 16.65–16.70
    live 16.59–16.60
    non-infringing acts 8.89
    personal 16.50, 16.54
    registration 13.105, 15.60
  narrow filed of activity, within a 16.50
  Netherlands 16.66
  Paris Convention 16.67
  personal names 16.50, 16.54
  personality rights 16.53, 16.56, 16.62
  Poland 16.58
  potential 16.50
  privacy 16.54
  public policy 16.58
  regional 16.50
  registration 13.105, 16.52–16.53, 16.60
  signatures 16.63
  Sweden 16.67
  Trade Mark Directives 16.50
  TRIPs 16.50
  universal 16.50
  vicarious 16.50
certificates of marketing authorization 16.06,
  16.28, 16.35
certification marks 15.41, 18.56, 18.58, 18.61
character merchandising 15.57–15.59
charitable activities 21.39
choice of jurisdiction 14.09–14.15

  Brussels Convention 1968 14.10
  Brussels Regulation 2001 14.10
  causes of action, same 14.14
  Community Trade Mark Regulation 14.14
  Italy 14.13
  OHIM 14.14
  passing off 14.12
  pending proceedings 14.12
  preliminary issues 14.09–14.15
  same parties 14.14
  Scotland 14.13
  Trade Mark Directive 14.14
  United States 14.11
  websites 14.13
choosing trade marks 19.01–19.25
  allusive marks 19.06
  better-known trade marks, avoiding marks too
    reminiscent of 19.04
  branding 19.01–19.02, 19.04, 19.19
  business considerations 19.19–19.23
  copyright 19.05
  cost of maintaining portfolio 19.22
  coverage 19.21
  cultural considerations 19.10–19.18
  deceptive marks 19.07–19.08
  descriptive marks 19.06
  distinctiveness 19.19
  franchising 19.23
  infringement 19.04
  licensing, advantages of 19.23
  logos 19.05
  legal considerations 19.03–19.09
  sensitive words and parts of words, avoidance
    of 19.09
classification of trade marks 3.28–3.32, 10.91,
  16.37
cliches 4.107
co-branding 15.66–15.68
codes of practice, voluntary 8.114, 8.117, 8.127,
  8.149
coexistence agreements, offers of 13.116
collective marks 18.56, 18.61
  celebrities 16.50, 16.64
  EC law 18.59
  registrability 18.58–18.59
  Sweden 5.79
  Trade Mark Directive 18.58
colloquial inventions 4.152
colours 5.123–5.133
  Australia 5.129, 5.130
  Benelux 5.127
  combinations of 5.131
  Community Trade Mark Regulation 5.126
  comparative advertising 8.169

Index

colours (*cont.*):
   competitors' use of 5.129
   distinctiveness 4.103, 4.108, 5.93, 5.127, 5.129, 5.131–5.133
   EC law 4.108, 5.123, 5.126–5.129, 5.131, 5.133
   functionality 5.93
   Germany 5.131
   graphic representation 5.123
   Northern Ireland 5.128
   OHIM 5.125, 5.133
   part of goods, single colours applied to only 5.130
   registrability 5.123–5.125
   shapes 5.93, 5.132–5.133
   single colours 5.127–5.129
   United States 5.125
combinations of letters 5.31, 5.35, 5.39
commemorative goods 16.71
Community Trade Mark Regulation 3.09 *see also* OHIM
   acquired distinctiveness 4.177
   annulment by national courts 3.51
   assignment 15.17, 15.23
   association, likelihood of 10.144–10.145
   bad faith 13.73, 13.78–13.80, 13.94, 13.125, 13.131–13.135
   cancellation 13.14, 13.39
   celebrities 16.50, 16.62, 16.67
   colours 5.126
   comparative advertising 8.109, 8.166–8.167
   confusion 10.122
   consent, exhaustion of rights and 9.37
   course of trade requirement 7.26
   Court of First Instance 3.48
   courts 3.47, 14.18–14.19
   descriptive terms 4.145
   dilution of famous marks 12.53
   distinctiveness 4.100, 11.23–11.24
   domain names 17.26
   enforcement 14.18–14.19
   European Court of Justice 3.48
   exhaustion of rights 9.27, 9.29–9.30, 9.37, 9.56, 9.85
   generic marks and terms 4.58–4.59, 6.34, 8.80–8.82
   genuine use 13.51–13.58
   gestures and motions 5.142
   graphical representations 4.24
   immoral and illegal marks 4.35
   infringement 7.09, 7.26, 7.38
   jurisdiction, choice of 14.14
   licensing 15.17, 15.34
   member states' trade marks 3.47–351
   names 5.57
   national application, conversion into 3.48
   national laws 3.47, 14.19
   national procedural rules 3.48
   non-infringing acts 8.09, 8.48, 8.80–8.81
   opposition 13.03, 13.27–13.30
   overlapping registrations 3.49–3.50
   parallel imports 16.11, 16.15, 16.18
   publicly reserved terms 4.57
   registrability 4.13, 4.52, 4.57
   retail sales service marks 16.42, 16.47
   reputation 11.09, 11.23–11.24, 11.39
   revocation 13.14, 13.51–13.58
   same mark under CTM and national law, registration of 3.49–3.50
   seniority to national marks 3.48
   shapes 5.105
   standing 13.14–13.15
   surfaces 5.80
   tellequelle principle 4.13
   threats 14.105
   unfair advantage and detriment 11.59, 11.63
   well known and famous marks 12.09, 12.14, 12.26
companies
   corporate aims 20.20
   corporate designations, registrability of 4.53
   corporate fascism 21.11
   domain names 17.15–17.17
   names 1.13, 8.34–8.35, 18.54
   registrations 18.54
compatibility, indications of product 8.23–8.26
comparative advertising 8.93–8.176, 21.43
   beneficiaries of trade marks 2.06
   burden of proof 8.151–8.152, 8.168
   celebrities, endorsement transfer and 8.171
   codes, voluntary 8.114–8.115, 8.126, 8.149
   colours 8.169
   Community Trade Mark Regulation 8.109, 8.166–8.167
   confusion 8.108, 8.113, 8.157, 8.168, 8.176
   damages 8.156, 14.89
   definition 8.102–8.104
   denigration 8.143, 8.155
   dishonesty 8.125–8.127, 8.130, 8.133, 8.144–8.145, 8.150–8.156
   disparagement 8.147
   distinctiveness 8.162–8.163, 8.167
   EC law 8.116–8.119
   endorsement transfer 8.171
   Europe 8.121–8.156, 8.164
   exaggerated statements of opinion 8.174
   Finland 8.111
   France 8.111, 8.120

Index

comparative advertising (*cont.*):
  freedom of speech 8.172–8.174
  generalizations 8.96–8.97
  Germany 8.120–8.137
  injunctions 8.158
  lifestyle or aspirational brands 8.169–8.170
  logos, reproduction of 8.119
  malice 8.129–8.130
  Misleading and Comparative Advertising Directive 8.102–8.114, 8.117–8.120, 8.166–8.167
  new types of trade marks 8.169–8.170
  omissions 8.146
  Paris Convention 8.99
  parodies, satire and irony 8.69
  permitted use 8.105–8.106
  prices 8.120, 8.137–8.139, 8.147–8.148, 8.154
  principles and exceptions 8.158–8.164
  psychology of 20.29–30.31
  puffing 8.155
  registered, mark used not same as 8.168
  revocation 8.166
  spare parts 8.117–8.118
  standard of behaviour 8.147–8.149
  techniques of 8.97
  test purchases 8.119
  third parties' mark in the course of, use of 8.93–8.98, 8.142–8.146, 8.166–8.167
  Trade Mark Directive 8.106, 8.108–8.111, 8.118, 8.124, 8.126
  Trade Marks Act 1994 (UK) 8.111–8.136
  TRIPs 8.99
  United States 8.172–8.176
comparison of goods and services 10.76–10.78, 11.12–11.13
competition *see* unfair competition
complex marks
  business formats 5.08
  distinctiveness 5.07
  EC law 5.10, 5.11
  get up of shops 5.08, 5.56
  registrability 5.07–5.11
  trade dress in trading premises 5.08–5.10
  trade dress in the style of product designs 5.11
compulsory licences 15.31–15.32
computers 4.30 *see also* Internet
conceptions 1.01–1.08
concerted practices 14.118–14.119
conflicts of interest 2.54, 2.58
confusion 2.14–2.15, 10.103–10.142
  association, likelihood of 10.143–10.149
  Australia 10.116
  barcodes 5.13

  both trade marks, use of 10.105–10.107
  Canada 10.127–10.128
  cancellation 13.09
  celebrities 16.55, 16.59
  Community Trade Mark Regulation 10.122
  comparative advertising 8.108, 8.113, 8.157, 8.168, 8.176
  consumers
    attentive and circumspect, averagely 10.139
    reasonably well-informed 10.134–10.141
    recall, suffering from imperfect 10.140–10.141
    relevant 10.135–10.137
  Denmark 10.119
  direct 10.104
  domain names 17.06, 17.10, 17.12–17.13, 17.24, 17.34, 17.49–17.50
  EC law 10.103–10.124, 10.129, 10.132–10.133
  emblems 5.23
  exhaustion of rights 9.20
  Finland 10.118
  France 10.142
  generic marks and terms 6.18
  geographical indications 18.18
  Germany 10.122, 10.137
  high degree of similarity 10.111–10.112
  hypothetical use 10.107
  identical marks 10.05, 10.20
  indirect 10.104
  inferences 10.106
  infringement 7.12, 7.14, 7.20, 7.36
  inherent nature of the goods and services 10.113–10.114
  initial interest 10.126, 10.129
  injunctions 14.44, 14.51
  Ireland 10.118, 10.123
  jurisdictions in which marks co-exist without 10.121
  loyalty or allegiance, badges of 8.86
  market-oriented approach 10.129
  metatags 17.71
  names 16.55
  non-distinctive or weakly distinctive elements, relevance of 10.117–10.120
  not been used, one or both marks have 10.108–10.110
  OHIM 10.120, 10.141
  opposition 10.108, 13.09, 13.18, 13.24–13.25, 13.34
  outlets for respective goods or services 10.115–10.116
  parallel imports 16.25
  passing off 10.123

Index

confusion *(cont.)*:
  pharmaceutical marks 16.01, 16.31–16.36
  Portugal 10.118
  post-point of sale 10.123–10.124
  proof of 10.154–10.155
  questions of law and questions of fact 10.131–10.133
  reasonably well-informed consumers 10.134–10.141
  recall, consumers suffering from imperfect 10.140–10.141
  registrability 4.182
  removal from point of sale 10.142
  reputation 11.02, 11.04
  retail sales service marks 16.47–16.48
  reverse 10.130
  similarity 7.20, 10.27, 10.31–10.33, 10.80–10.82, 10.96, 10.102
  Switzerland 10.130–10.131
  Trade Mark Directive 10.122
  unfair competition 10.142
  unfair advantage and detriment 11.66, 11.82–11.88
  United States 7.12, 7.36, 8.177, 10.125–10.126, 10.129–10.130
  well known and famous marks 9.20, 12.47
connotations 5.20
consent, exhaustion of rights and 9.28, 9.36–9.52
  burden of proof 9.41–9.49
  Community Trade Mark Regulation 9.37
  contagious 9.28, 9.50–9.52
  distribution 9.37, 9.43, 9.47
  EC law 9.45–9.47, 9.50–9.52, 9.93
  European Convention on Human Rights 9.48–9.49
  European Economic Area 9.46–9.47, 9.51
  evidence 9.45–9.48
  fair trials 9.48–9.49
  imports 9.36, 9.93
  licences 9.36
  meaning of 9.36–9.39
  monopolies 9.42
  parallel imports 9.45
  presumptions 9.41
  proof of 9.40–9.47
  resales 9.93
  Scotland 9.45
  Trade Mark Directive 9.37
  wholesalers 9.44
  withdrawal of 9.93
conspiracy 7.59, 12.59
consumers
  apocalypse 21.39–21.39
  attentive and circumspect 10.139
  average 4.90–4.91, 10.139
  beneficiaries of trade marks 2.10
  brands 21.29–21.34, 21.39, 21.43
    abuse of, as voluntary parties to 21.16
  capture of brands by the 20.17–20.23
  challenges by 21.29–21.32
  community of interests, no 21.34
  confusion 10.134–10.141
  coterminous interests of trade mark owners and 6.19–6.21
  distinctiveness 4.90–4.91
  freedom of speech 2.56
  generic marks and terms 6.19–6.21
  Internet, awareness of the 21.39
  knowledge 10.134–10.141, 21.29–21.33, 21.39, 21.43
  position of 2.13–2.15
  protection
  rationality 21.33
  recall, suffering from imperfect 10.140–10.141
  relevant 2.15, 10.135–10.137
  satisfaction with quality of 2.35
  scepticism 21.39
  shapes, recognition of 5.109
  values of, reasserting the 21.35
contagious confusion 9.28, 9.50–9.52
contempt of court 7.27, 14.34, 14.40
containers 5.100–5.105, 5.107, 5.112–5.113, 5.115
contractions 5.30
contracts 15.89–15.91
  assignment 15.08, 15.14
  co-branding 15.66, 15.68
  exhaustion of rights 9.94
  franchising 15.54–15.55
  illegality 9.94
  implied contractual consent doctrine 9.02–9.06
  licensing 15.09, 15.14, 15.37, 15.77–15.78
  opposition 13.34
  sponsorship 15.62–15.62A
conventions *see* **treaties and regional agreements**
copyright
  Berne Convention 14.90
  celebrities 16.63, 16.68–16.69
  choosing trade marks 19.05
  damages 14.90–14.91
  exhaustion of rights 9.66
  fictional celebrities 16.68–16.69
  functionality 5.92
  notices 17.63
  originality 5.139
  parodies, satire and irony 8.68

copyright (*cont.*):
  registrability 4.50–4.52
  shapes 5.92
  signatures 16.63
  websites 17.63
costs 14.05
counterfeiting
  beneficiaries of trade marks 2.07
  character merchandising 15.59
  developing countries 2.10
  pharmaceuticals 2.10
country names 5.52
course of trade requirement
  Community Trade Mark Regulation 7.38
  domain names 17.09–17.10, 17.13
  EC law 7.38, 7.40–7.42, 7.45, 7.49–7.51
  infringement 7.38–7.51
  meaning 7.40–7.52
  non-infringing acts 8.11
  Trade Mark Directive 7.38, 7.45
  trade mark use and 7.43–7.45
  TRIPs 7.38
  websites 17.52
Court of First Instance 3.13, 3.48
criminal proceedings 7.27
critical domain names 17.37–17.38
cultural considerations *see also* **cultural emblems**
  brands
    icons 21.09, 21.18, 21.22, 21.42
    intrusion into culture of 21.05–21.06
    values, of 19.17–19.18, 21.40, 21.42
  choosing trade marks and 19.10–19.18
  cultural relativism 4.83
  distinctiveness 19.17
  emblems 5.17–5.24
  icons 5.57–5.72, 21.09, 21.18, 21.22, 21.40, 21.42
  intrusion of brands into culture 21.05–21.06
  laudatory terms 4.83
  linguistic considerations 19.12–19.13
  No Logo thesis 21.09, 21.18, 21.22, 21.42
  political correctness 19.14–19.16
  registrability 5.17–5.24, 5.57–5.72
  religious organizations 19.15
  sectoral or tribal considerations 19.11
  similarity 10.55–10.59
  taboos 19.17–19.18
  well known and famous marks 12.20
cultural emblems
  dates 5.19–5.22
  hallmarks 5.23
  intergovernmental organizations 5.23
  money 5.17
  state emblems 5.23
  times 5.19–5.22
  zodiac signs 5.24
currency 5.17–5.18, 8.11
customary trade terms
  abbreviations 5.30
  acquired distinctiveness 4.176
  descriptive terms 4.60
  EC law 4.61, 4.64–4.65
  laudatory terms 4.81
  letters 5.30
  registrability 4.58–4.66, 4.75
customs 14.25
cybersquatters 17.04, 17.22, 17.27–17.31, 17.35, 17.45
Czech Republic 12.33
Czechoslovakia, former 18.40

damages 14.76–14.91
  account of profits 14.92, 14.94
  assessment of 8.156, 14.77, 14.84–14.89
  assignment 15.25
  Austria 7.58
  Benelux 14.76
  burden of proof 14.22
  comparative advertising 8.156, 14.89
  compensatory 14.78–14.79
  copyright 14.90–14.91
  Denmark 14.82, 14.85
  economic rights 14.90
  France 14.77, 14.87
  Germany 14.86
  infringement 7.58
  injunctions 14.32, 14.43, 14.59, 14.69
  inquiries into 14.88–14.89, 14.92, 14.94
  Italy 14.80
  licences 14.79–14.87A, 15.25, 15.33
  loss of profits 14.86
  moral rights 14.90–14.91
  parallel imports 14.85
  Portugal 14.77, 14.87A
  revocation 13.64
  royalties 14.80–14.83, 14.86
  Spain 14.77
  threats 14.107, 14.109
  well known and famous marks 12.46
data protection 10.78
dates as cultural emblems 5.19–5.22
deceased persons
  bad faith 13.105
  celebrities 16.50, 16.57–16.62
    names of 16.58–16.62
    registration of names of 13.105
  names 16.58–16.62

Index

deceit 15.24
deceptive marks
  choosing trade marks 19.07–19.08
  denials of deception 4.48
  EC law 4.41, 4.45
  geographical indications 4.46
  immoral and illegal marks 4.33
  legitimate trade marks, deceptiveness of 4.42
  opposition 13.18
  registrability 4.41–4.49, 4.56
  Trade Mark Directive 4.41
  United States 4.44
decisions, publication of 14.27
declarations of non-infringement 14.116–14.117
defamation 8.55
definition of a trade mark 1.09
delivery up and destruction 14.98–14.100
denigration
  comparative advertising 8.102–8.104
Denmark
  confusion 10.119
  damages 14.82, 14.85
  functionality 5.92
  injunctions, final 14.42
  non-infringing acts 8.56, 8.58
  parallel imports 16.71, 16.24, 16.26, 16.29
  registrability 4.51
  shapes 5.92, 5.99
  titles 18.55
depository systems 3.36, 3.38
design
  adding features of 16.26–16.28
  licensing 15.31, 15.33
  parallel imports 16.26–16.28
  pharmaceutical marks 16.26–16.28
  registrability 4.50, 4.52
  surfaces 5.79–5.80
  trade dress 5.11
descriptive terms 4.60, 4.128–4.162
  allowing registration of, reasons for 4.159–4.162
  allusiveness 4.133–4.135, 4.141
  ambiguous terms 4.139
  applicants,
    advantages of registration for 4.160
    disadvantages of registration for 4.161
  available for use, need to keep word or mark 4.69–4.70
  car trade marks 8,16, 8.30
  celebrities 16.68
  certificates 4.160
  choosing trade marks 19.06
  colloquial inventions 4.152
  Community Trade Mark Regulation 4.145
  compatibility, indications of product 8.23–8.26
  competitors, advantages of registration for 4.160
  customary trade terms 4.60
  dealers and distributors 8.30
  describing something that does not exist, words 4.158
  dilution 8.32
  distinctiveness and 4.21–4.22, 4.70, 4.104
    competitors, non-use by 4.123
    inability to guess a product's nature 4.119
    invented descriptive marks and 4.150
    low threshold of 4.146–4.149
    registrability 4.21–4.22, 4.70
  domain names 17.08
  EC law
    exclusively descriptive marks 4.128, 4.134
    fair use 8.15, 8.19
    immaterial descriptiveness 4.143–4.145
    registrability 4.21
  examiners 4.161
  exclusively 4.128–4.142
  fair use of 8.13, 8.15–8.17, 8.19, 8.21–8.32
  figurative marks 8.16
  France 8.31
  function, descriptiveness of the 4.138
  fusion of existing words 4.154–4.156
  geographical indications 8.19, 8.21
  Germany 4.144
  gestures and motions 5.140–5.141
  immaterial descriptiveness 4.143–4.145
  infringement 4.160
  intended purpose of goods 8.22–8.27
  invented 4.150–4.158
  Ireland 4.138–4.139, 4.144
  lexical inventions 4.152
  low threshold of inherent distinctiveness 4.146–4.149
  market, descriptiveness of 4.136–4.137
  multilingual countries, in 4.140
  names 5.69
    goods of, use of marks which are also 8.30–8.32
  necessity 8.27
  Netherlands 4.137
  nominative use of fair use doctrine 8.13
  non-infringing acts 8.08
  OHIM 4.143, 4.157
  pharmaceutical marks 16.05
  quality 8.29
  registrability 4.21–4.22, 4.50, 4.52, 4.60, 4.68–4.70, 4.128–4.162

descriptive terms (*cont.*):
  registration 8.16–8.17
  registries, advantages of registration for 4.160
  services, kinds of 8.28
  shapes 5.86
  South Korea 4.135
  spare parts 8.23–8.26
  substitutes 4.162
  suggestive allusions 4.141
  times and dates 5.19
  TRIPs 8.15
  United States 8.13, 8.32
  unused and unnatural formations, existing words in 4.157
  user, descriptiveness of the ultimate 4.136–4.137
destruction and delivery up 14.98–14.100
detriment *see* **unfair advantage and detriment**
developing countries
  examinations of applications 3.38
  labour exploitation 9.16, 9.18, 21.32–21.33
  pharmaceuticals, fake 2.10
  seized goods of, use in 14.97
  WIPO 3.38
device marks 13.25
dictionaries
  cancellation 8.82
  Community Trade Mark Regulation 8.80–9.82
  generic marks and terms 6.41–6.43, 8.80–8.82
  Netherlands 8.81
  non-infringing acts 8.80–8.82
  OHIM 8.82
dilution of famous marks
  acquiescence 12.56–12.57
  blurring 11.21–11.22
  burden of proof 12.53
  Community Trade Mark Regulation 12.53
  conspiracy 12.59
  definition 12.50
  descriptive marks, fair use of 8.32
  distinctiveness 11.22A, 12.52, 12.55–12.56
  domain names 17.31
  encroachment, doctrine of progressive 12.56–12.57
  estoppel 12.56–12.57
  generic marks and terms 6.26
  infringement 7.12
  injunctions, interim 12.54–12.55, 12.59
  laches 12.56–12.57
  likelihood of 12.54–12.55
  meaning 11.18
  multiparty 12.58–12.59
  OHIM 12.51
  reputation 11.14–11.22A
  statutory 12.11
  survey evidence 12.55
  tarnishment 11.21
  Trade Mark Directive 12.53
  trivial infringement 12.56
  unfair advantage and detriment 12.51
  unfair competition 12.59
  United States 6.26, 7.12, 11.15–11.21, 12.49–12.59
directives *see* **Trade Mark Directive**
disclaimers 3.43, 7.35–7.36, 7.46–7.49, 17.50
disclosure 14.24–14.25
discovery 14.55
disparagement 8.148
distinctiveness 4.07, 4.88–4.127 *see also* **acquired distinctiveness, confusion**
  abbreviations 5.30
  allusiveness 4.114–4.115
  arbitrary embellishments 4.111–4.113
  association, likelihood of 10.151, 10.154
  available for use, need to keep word or mark 4.70, 4.75–4.76
  average consumer, in the eyes of the relatively 4.90–4.91
  banality 4.111–4.113
  Belgium 4.22
  brand loyalty 20.07, 20.09
  cancellation 13.35–13.37, 13.41
  celebrities 16.53
  choosing trade marks 19.19
  clichés 4.107
  colours 4.103, 4.108, 5.125–5.127, 5.129, 5.131–5.133
  common use as monopolies, signs in 4.105–4.109
  Community Trade Mark Regulation 4.100, 11.23–11.24
  comparative advertising 8.162–8.163, 8.167
  competitors
    non-use of term by 4.123
    use of term by 4.124
  complex marks 5.07
  containers 5.103–5.104
  cultural considerations, 19.17
  descriptive marks 4.21–4.22, 4.70, 4.104
    competitors non-use of term 4.123
    inability to guess a product's nature 4.119
    inventive 4.150
    low threshold of distinctiveness 4.146–4.149
    registrability 4.21–4.22, 4.70
  dilution of famous marks 11.22A, 12.52, 12.55–12.56
  diminishing 4.96
  domain names 5.26, 17.20–17.21

Index

distinctiveness (*cont.*):
  EC law 4.75–4.76, 4.92–4.93, 4.98–4.99
    allusiveness 4.115
    colours 4.108
    commonplace, signs that are 4.108–4.109
    level of distinctiveness 4.125
    originality and 4.113
    registrability 4.75–4.76
  figurative elements, strengthening by addition of 4.105
  figurative marks 5.33
  France 4.104, 4.111
  generic marks and terms 6.27–6.30, 7.34, 6.43
  goods and services, consideration in relation to 4.97
  grammatical errors 4.116–4.117
  graphical representations 4.25
  inability to guess a product's nature 4.119
  laudatory terms 4.84
  letters 5.30, 5.32–5.33
  level of, same 4.125–4.127
  lexical invention 4.116–4.117
  limping trade marks 5.110
  memorable nature, enhanced by a mark's 4.110
  monopolies 4.105–4.109
  names 5.67, 5.69
  negative 4.104
  OHIM 4.118–4.122
  olfactory marks 5.119
  originality, lack of 4.111–4.113
  partial 4.95
  perversity 4.116–4.117
  positional marks 5.144A
  presumption of 4.94
  quantification, arithmetic 4.92–4.93
  reputation 11.15, 11.20, 11.22–11.24, 11.40–11.46
  shapes 5.82–5.83, 5.92–5.93, 5.95, 5.98–5.99, 5.103–5.104, 5.110
  similarity 10.25, 10.80–10.82
  simple marks 5.04
  single letters 5.32–5.33
  sound marks 5.139
  technology standards 5.78
  telephone numbers 5.28
  territory, existence throughout the 4.95–4.96
  times and dates 5.19
  trade dress 5.56
  Trade Mark Directive 11.23–11.24
  TRIPs 4.88
  type, variations of 5.41
  unfair advantage and detriment 11.58–11.59, 11.65–11.75, 11.81
  United States 4.114, 12.14
  well-known and famous marks, dilution of 12.14, 12.43, 12.52, 12.55–12.56, 12.63
  whole, considered in relation to the mark as a 4.98–4.104

distribution
  abuse of rights 9.70
  cars 8.30
  consent, exhaustion of rights and 9.37, 9.43, 9.47
  descriptive marks, fair use of 8.30
  EC law 9.61
  exclusive 9.47
  exhaustion of rights 9.61, 9.69
  selective 9.61, 9.69, 9.70

domain names
  added matter, existence of appropriate 17.24
  allocation of infringing 17.25
  Austria 17.20, 17.25
  bad faith 17.18, 17.28–17.29, 17.32, 17.42–17.44
    circumstantial evidence of 17.47
    proof of 17.45–17.46
  blocking owner's own registration 17.19
  Community Trade Mark Regulation 17.26
  company name, strengthened by being also the proprietor's 17.15–17.17
  confusion 17.06, 17.10, 17.12–17.13, 17.24, 17.34, 17.49–17.50
  course of trade requirement 17.09–17.10, 17.13
  critical names 17.37–17.38
  cybersquatters 17.04, 17.22, 17.27–17.31, 17.35, 17.45
  descriptive term, defence of use of trade mark as 17.08
  dilution of famous marks 17.31
  disclaimers 17.50
  dispute resolution 17.32–17.50
  distinctiveness 5.26
    weak or non-distinctiveness 17.20–17.21
  Europe 17.03
  exhaustion of rights 9.35
  France 17.26
  fraud 17.16
  friendly names, trade mark 17.26
  generic terms 5.26–5.27
  Greece 17.23
  hostile names 17.37–17.38
  ICANN Uniform Domain Name Dispute Resolution Policy 17.32–17.50, 21.39
  infringement 17.05–17.06, 17.09, 17.25
  Internet service providers 17.29
  Italy 17.10
  metatags 17.08, 17.29

Index

domain names (*cont.*):
  near misses, registration of 17.39–17.41
  Netherlands 17.49
  non-use 17.07
  obvious reason for selection of 17.22
  OHIM 5.25–5.26
  Paris Convention 17.43
  passing off 17.16
  post-domain path, use of a trade mark in a 17.11–17.14
  registrability 5.25–5.27
  registration 17.34
    blocking owner's own 17.19
    ICANN 17.36
    near misses, of 17.39–17.41
    serial 17.17
  remoteness of commercial interests 17.23
  reverse name hijacking 17.48
  sale of products, use of site for 17.18
  selection of
    no obvious reason for 17.16
    obvious reason for 17.22, 17.43
  second level 17.25
  serial registration 17.17
  similarity 17.07
  Singapore 5.27
  'sucks' names 8.63, 17.37–17.38
  Sweden 17.42
  top level 5.26–5.27, 17.05–17.07, 17.11, 17.33
  third parties' trade marks as 17.02–17.50
  transfer of 17.32, 17.36, 17.40, 17.49
  United States 17.06, 17.12, 17.21, 17.27–17.31, 17.38
  well known and famous marks 17.31, 17.42–17.44
dominant position, abuse of 9.73, 10.78, 14.120–14.122
double accounting 10.63
due cause, unfair advantage and detriment without 11.52–11.57
dumbing down 21.29

EC law *see also* **Community Trade Mark Regulation, Trade Mark Directive**
  abuse of a dominant position 9.73
  acquired distinctiveness 4.173, 4.175
  association, likelihood of 10.144–10.146, 10.150, 10.154–10.155
  bad faith 13.73–13.82, 13.132, 13.151
  brands
    image of, upholding the 9.62–9.63
    loyalty to 20.10–20.11
  collective marks 18.59

  colours 5.123, 5.126–5.129, 5.131, 5.133
  commonplace, signs that are 4.108–4.109
  comparative advertising 8.102–8.114, 8.116–8.120, 8.166–8.167
  complex marks 5.10, 5.11
  confusion 10.103–10.124, 10.129, 10.132–10.133
  consent, exhaustion of rights and 9.45–9.47, 9.50–9.52, 9.93
  Court of First Instance 3.13, 3.48
  customary trade terms 4.61, 4.64–4.65
  deceptive marks 4.41, 4.45
  descriptive terms 4.128, 4.134, 4.143–14.145
    fair use of 8.15, 8.19
    registrability 4.21
  disclosure 14.25
  distinctiveness 4.75–4.76, 4.92–4.93, 4.98–4.99
    allusiveness 4.115
    colours 4.108
    commonplace, signs that are 4.108–4.109
    level of distinctiveness 4.125
    originality and 4.113
    registrability 4.75–4.76
  distribution 9.61
  European Court of Justice 1.32, 1.36, 2.29, 3.09, 3.13, 3.48
  exhaustion of rights 9.25–9.28, 9.91–9.92, 9.94, 9.97
    consent and 9.45–9.47, 9.50–9.52, 9.93
    legitimate reasons for prohibiting further use 9.61–9.63
    parallel imports 9.88
    tampering with marketed products 9.83
    third countries, exhaustion policy of 9.85
    unfair competition and 9.68, 9.88
  franchising 15.55–15.56
  free movement of goods 18.30–18.33, 18.49–18.51, 20.11
  freedom of speech 8.60
  functionality 5.89–5.93
  geographical indications 18.06, 18.16, 18.21–18.53
  graphical representations 4.24–4.25
  identical marks 10.10, 10.18–10.20, 10.78
  immoral and illegal marks 4.32, 4.34–4.36
  infringement 7.16, 7.20
    course of trade requirement 7.38, 7.40–7.42, 7.45, 7.49–7.51
    United States and 7.63–7.64
  laudatory terms 4.87
  limping trade marks 5.111
  loyalty or allegiance, badges of 2.38, 8.85–8.88
  non-infringing acts 8.11

Index

EC law (cont.):
  non-use 13.12
  olfactory marks 5.117–5.118
  origin of goods and services 2.29
  originality and 4.113
  parallel imports 9.88, 16.11–16.23, 16.28
  packaging 5.102
  pharmaceutical marks 16.06, 16.08, 16.30
  place names, registration of 5.45, 5.49–5.50, 5.53
  positional marks 5.144A
  property, trade marks as 15.02
  quality 2.36–2.37
  registrability 4.05–4.06, 4.21, 4.55, 4.75–4.76
  reputation 11.08–11.09, 11.12, 11.22A, 11.33–11.40, 11.44–11.46
  retail sales service marks 16.42–16.45
  revocation 13.12, 13.51–13.58
  selective distribution agreements 9.61
  shapes 4.21, 5.82, 5.88–5.93, 5.102, 5.111
  similarity 10.23–10.28, 10.32, 10.80–10.83, 10.102
  sound marks 5.134
  tampering with marketed products 9.83
  third countries, exhaustion policy of 9.85
  trade dress 5.10–5.11
  type, variations of 5.41
  unfair competition 3.73, 9.68, 9.88, 10.78, 14.118–14.119, 20.10
  unfair advantage and detriment 11.55, 11.82–11.93
  United States
    course of trade requirement 7.63–7.64
    infringement 7.63–7.64
    well known and famous marks 12.67–12.68
  well known and famous marks 12.27–12.39, 12.67–12.68
economic loss 14.36
economic rights 14.90
economies of scale 21.08
EEA see European Economic Area
EFTA Court 3.14
embellishments 4.111–4.113
emblems
  confusion 5.23
  cultural 5.17–5.24
  intergovernmental organisations of 5.23
  Paris Convention 4.08
  registrability 4.08, 5.17–5.24
  state 5.23
encoding 7.34
encroachment, doctrine of progressive 12.56–12.57
endorsement 15.43, 15.63–15.65
  celebrities 8.172, 15.63–15.65
  comparative advertising 8.171
  infringement 20.28
  licences 15.63–15.65
  sports 15.63–15.64
  transfer 8.171
enforcement 14.01–14.05, 15.88–15.92
  alternative dispute resolution 14.05
  assignment 15.07
  Community Trade Mark Regulation courts 14.18–14.19
  costs 14.05
  courts
    decisions, publication of 14.27
    powers 14.16–14.17
  dealing with infringing goods 14.95–14.100
  declarations of non-infringement 14.116–14.117
  delivery up and destruction 14.98–14.100
  extraterritoriality 14.17
  functions of the trade mark system 2.17
  geographical indications 18.30–18.33
  judicial comments 14.26
  legal machinery 14.02–14.03
  preliminary issues 14.06–14.28
  protected designations of origin 18.30–18.33
  protected geographical indications 18.30–18.33
  publication of the court's decision 14.27–14.28
  seizure 14.25, 14.95–14.97
  threats
    brand owners, by 21.40–21.43
    liability for making groundless 14.101–14.115
  treaties and regional agreements 3.07
  TRIPs 14.03
  United States, extraterritoriality and 14.17
Estonia 13.96
estoppel 12.56–12.57, 15.09, 15.17, 15.27–15.29
euro symbol 8.11
Europe see also EC law, Particular countries (eg France)
  bad faith 13.82–13.83, 13.150
  celebrities 16.53
  comparative advertising 8.120–8.156, 8.164
  domain names 17.03
  Internet 17.75
  jurisdiction 1.25
  revocation 13.46–13.47
  well known and famous marks 12.25–12.48
European Convention on Human Rights
  abuse of rights 9.74
  consent, exhaustion of rights and 9.48–9.49

Index

European Convention on Human Rights (*cont.*):
    exhaustion of rights 9.48–9.49, 9.82
    fair trials 9.48–9.49, 9.74
    freedom of speech 8.60, 8.62
    property rights 9.74, 9.82
    registrability 4.56
European Court of Justice 1.32, 1.36, 2.29, 3.09, 3.13, 3.48
European Economic Area
    consent, exhaustion of rights and 9.46–9.47, 9.51
    exhaustion of rights 9.12, 9.83
    limitation of actions 8.91
European Union *see* EC law
events as celebrities 16.71, 16.72
evidence 14.06–14.08 *see also* burden of proof
    acquired distinctiveness 4.167–4.171
    bad faith 17.47
    consent, exhaustion of rights and 9.45–9.48
    dilution of famous marks 12.55
    documentary 4.171
    domain names 17.47
    injunctions, interim 14.58, 14.59
    survey 12.55
    time for existence of trade marks 14.08
    Trade Mark Directive 14.08
    revocation 13.63
    use, of 13.63
ex parte injunctions 14.53–14.55
examination of applications 3.33–3.39
    applicants and examiners, relationship with 3.39
    decisions 1.32–1.33
    depository systems 3.38
    descriptive terms 4.161
    developing countries 3.38
    discretion 3.34
    notice based systems 3.38
    presumption of registrability 3.34
    purity of the register 3.34
    TRIPs 3.38
exclusive rights 7.07, 9.03–9.04, 9.07
exhaustion of rights 9.01, 9.07–9.97 *see also* consent, exhaustion of rights and, legitimate reasons for prohibiting further use, exhaustion and
    abuse of rights 9.70–9.74
    abusive use of products where trade mark exhausted 9.78
    automatic exhaustion of other rights 9.65–9.67
    burden of proof 14.20–14.21
    cars
        maintenance of, advertising the 9.32–9.34
        sub-brands of 9.16, 9.18
    change of condition 9.28
    combination of trade mark-protected products 9.75–9.77
    commercialization, further 9.78, 9.82
    Community Trade Mark Regulation 9.27, 9.29–9.30, 9.85
    confusion 9.20
    contractual illegality 9.94
    copyright 9.66
    domain names 9.35
    EC law 9.25–9.28, 9.91–9.92, 9.94, 9.97
        parallel imports 9.88
        tampering with marketed products 9.83
        third countries, exhaustion policy of 9.85
        unfair competition and 9.68, 9.88
    European Economic Area 9.12, 9.83
    exclusive rights 9.07
    exploitation of workers 9.16, 9.19
    exports 9.85
    extraterritoriality 9.20
    global 2.12, 9.13–9.14, 9.85, 9.97
    goodwill 9.90
    identical goods 9.20
    impairment of goods 9.28, 9.31
    imports 9.11–9.12, 9.14, 9.17, 9.94
    international law 9.22–9.24, 9.51
    legal basis of 9.22–9.35
    legal rights and, relationship with other 9.65–9.74
    licensing 9.66, 15.72
    Madrid Agreement and Protocol 9.22
    monopolies 9.01, 9.07–9.09, 9.19
    morality of 9.15–9.21
    multipacks, resales of 9.79–9.81
    national 9.11
    origin of goods and services 2.25
    outsourcing 9.16, 9.19
    parallel imports 9.14, 9.66, 9.95
        competition 9.88
        EC law 9.88
        goodwill 9.90
        grey goods 9.14, 9.89
        profitability of 9.87–9.90
        registration of slightly different marks in each country 9.86
        third countries, exhaustion policy of 9.85
        unfair competition and 9.69
        unwanted, stopping 9.86
    Paris Convention 9.22–9.23
    passing off 9.67
    patents 9.65–9.66
    pharmaceuticals 9.84
    prices 9.16–9.17, 9.19
    property rights 9.82

Index

exhaustion of rights (*cont.*):
　public interest 9.95
　quality 9.16–9.17, 9.20, 9.77
　regional 9.12, 9.51
　resales 9.68, 9.79–9.81
　Russia 9.35
　same trade mark owned by different proprietors in different countries 9.91–9.92
　selective distribution agreements 9.69
　service marks 9.28–9.35
　tampering with marketed products due to necessity 9.83–9.84
　third countries, exhaustion policy of 9.85
　trading blocks 9.09
　Trade Mark Directive 9.25–9.30, 9.85
　Trademark Law Treaty 1994 9.22
　TRIPs 9.23–9.24, 9.97
　types of 9.09–9.14
　unfair competition 9.67–9.69
　well known marks 9.20
experts, writings of learned 3.18
expression *see* freedom of speech

fair trials 9.48–9.49, 9.74
fair use of descriptive terms
　car trade marks 8.16, 8.30
　compatibility, indications of product 8.23–8.26
　dealers and distributors, car 8.30
　dilution 8.32
　EC law 8.15, 8.19
　figurative trade marks 8.16
　France 8.31
　geographical origin of goods 8.19, 8.21
　intended purpose of goods 8.22–8.27
　names of goods, use of marks which are also 8.30–8.32
　necessity 8.27
　nominative fair use doctrine in 8.13
　quality of the goods 8.29
　registration 8.16–8.17
　services, kinds of 8.28
　spare parts 8.23–8.26
　TRIPs 8.15
　United States 8.13, 8.32
families of marks 13.19–13.25
famous marks *see* well known and famous marks
famous persons *see* celebrities
fashion goods
　lifestyle statements 2.40
　preserving the integrity of 9.64
　resale of 9.64
feature marks 5.89
features of celebrities 16.52

fees 2.08
festivals 5.22
fictional characters 16.50, 16.65–16.70
figurative marks
　descriptive marks, fair use of 8.16
　distinctiveness 4.105, 5.33
　letters 5.33
　opposition 13.25
　similarity 10.42, 10.54, 10.58, 10.62, 10.69
film titles 5.72, 18.55
final injunctions 14.29–14.48
　acquiescence 14.42
　Austria 14.45
　breach of 14.40–14.41
　confusion 14.44
　contempt of court 14.34, 14.40
　damages 14.32, 14.43
　delay 14.30, 14.42
　Denmark 14.42
　economic loss 14.36
　form of the injunction 14.33–14.35
　France 14.30
　geographical scope of 14.35A
　goodwill 14.38
　Internet 14.35, 14.39
　loss of registration, effect of 14.48
　passing off 14.36, 14.38, 14.48
　patent infringement, ancillary relief for 14.47
　persons against whom granted 14.39
　post-expiry 14.38
　proportionality 14.36–14.37
　revocation 14.38
　Sweden 14.31
　tailored 14.35
　time for ordering 14.32
　Trade Mark Directive 14.31
　unfair competition 14.38, 14.45, 14.48
　United States 14.35–14.35A
　well known and famous marks 12.45
Finland 8.111, 10.118
first sale doctrine *see* exhaustion of rights
fitness for human consumption 9.54
flags 4.08, 5.23
folklore 16.50
fonts 5.41–5.43
food
　exhaustion of rights 9.54
　fitness for human consumption 9.54
　geographical indications 18.22–18.35, 18.48–18.49
　ingredients of 2.04
　safety 2.04
　well known and famous trade marks 2.04
former celebrities 16.50

Index

France
- abuse of rights 9.72
- advertising 8.72, 8.74–8.75
- cancellation 13.37
- comparative advertising 8.111, 8.120
- confusion 10.142
- damages 14.77, 14.87
- descriptive marks, fair use of 8.31
- distinctiveness 4.104, 4.111
- domain names 17.26
- freedom of speech 8.61–8.62, 8.65
- geographical indications 18.34, 18.45, 18.47–18.48
- identical marks 10.10, 10.15
- immoral and illegal marks 4.38–4.39
- injunctions, final 14.30
- infringement 7.24–7.25
- injunctions, interim 14.55, 14.60
- metatags 17.68, 17.69
- non-infringing acts 8.72, 8.74, 8.78, 8.83
- parodies, satire and irony 8.68
- Paris Convention 12.35
- revocation 13.13, 13.64
- similarity 10.26, 10.52, 10.55, 10.61, 10.64, 10.70, 10.91, 10.102
- unfair advantage and detriment 11.29, 11.94
- well known and famous marks 12.02, 12.35

franchising 15.50–15.56
- advertising 15.53
- alternative dispute resolution 15.54
- choosing trade marks 19.23
- competition law 15.55–15.56
- contracts 15.54–15.55
- EC law 15.55–15.56
- licences 15.30, 15.51–15.54
- royalties 15.52

fraud 17.16

free movement of goods 18.30–18.33, 18.49–18.51, 20.11

freedom of speech
- abuse of rights 9.74
- ambush marketing 8.64
- comparative advertising 8.172–8.174
- derogatory references to another's mark 8.61
- EC law 8.60
- European Convention on Human Rights 8.60, 8.62
- France 8.61–8.62, 8.65
- India, ambush marketing in 8.64
- metatags 17.68
- non-infringing acts 8.60–8.65
- parodies 8.61
- registrability 4.56
- sucks domain names 8.63

- Sweden 8.65
- United States 8.63, 8.172–8.174
- websites 17.61

functionality 5.89–5.93, 5.98, 5.106

functions of the trade mark system 2.02–2.04, 2.16–2.58
- applications, systems for processing 2.17
- competing businesses 2.56
- conflicting interests 2.54, 2.58
- consumers 2.56
- creative tension, equilibrium of 2.54–2.55
- distinguishing goods 1.17
- enforcement 2.17
- identity of the origin of goods and services, guaranteeing the 2.30–2.33
- lifestyle statements, enabling consumers to make 2.39–2.41
- model-building 2.17–2.22
- morality of trade mark law 2.17–2.22
- non-competing businesses 2.56
- origin of goods and services, physical 2.24–2.29
- pathology of trade marks 2.42–2.43
- quality of goods and services, guaranteeing 2.34–2.37
- real 2.53–2.54
- support or affiliation, serving as a 2.38

generic marks and terms 6.01–6.46
- abuse of trade marks, mass 6.16–6.17
- become, trade marks which 6.05
- burden of proof 6.40–6.43
- celebrities 16.69
- combination of two generic marks 6.34
- commons
  - fencing in the 6.07–6.21, 6.45
  - linguistic, concept of a 6.09–6.10
  - polo test 6.11–6.12
- Community Trade Mark Regulation 4.58–4.59, 6.34, 8.80–8.82
- competition 6.19–6.20
- confusion 6.18
- consumers and trade marks owners, coterminous interests of 6.19–6.21
- dictionaries 6.41–6.43, 8.80–8.82
- dilution 6.26
- distinctiveness 6.27–6.30, 6.34, 6.43
- distinguishing marks 6.32
- domain names 5.26–5.27
- EC law 4.61–4.64, 6.24, 6.36
- 'fencing in the commons' 6.07–6.21, 6.45
- fictional characters 16.69
- foreign language 6.35–6.36
- France 6.44

generic marks and terms (*cont.*):
   free market 6.19
   free movement of goods 6.36
   geographical indications 18.28
   household words 12.02
   infringement 6.15–6.17, 6.26, 6.33, 6.44, 7.52, 7.54
   injunctions, interim 14.50
   language
      changes in 4.65
      foreign 6.35–6.36
      multiplication of words in the 6.14
      removal of words from the 6.01–6.02
   letters 5.36–5.37
   meaning of 6.03–6.06
   modifications to 6.04
   names 6.38–6.39
   nature of the goods, depending on the 6.37
   Netherlands 6.38, 8.82
   non-infringing acts 8.78–8.82
   OHIM 6.37, 8.82
   parallel imports 16.29
   partially 6.31–6.33
   pharmaceutical marks 16.29
   polo test, commons and the 6.11–6.12
   prevention
      distinctive names becoming, of 6.27–6.29
      generic terms becoming trade marks, of 6.30
   private property, words as 6.09, 6.45
   protectionism 6.21
   public and private claims on words, competing 6.07–6.21
   public interest 6.19, 6.21
   registrability 4.56–4.66
   registration 6.04, 6.30, 6.40
   repackaging and relabelling 16.29
   revocation 13.48
   services 6.03–6.04
   Sweden 6.32
   telephone numbers 5.29
   third parties' trade mark generic, making 6.23
   Trade Mark Directive 4.58–4.59, 6.24
   unauthorized generic use 6.24–6.26
   United States, dilution in 6.26
   well known, generic but not 6.22
genuine use
   cancellation 13.39
   Community Trade Mark Regulation 13.51–13.58
   opposition 13.27, 13.30–13.31
   proper reasons for 13.59–13.60
   revocation 13.51–13.61
   TRIPs 13.59
geographical indications 18.01–18.53
   agricultural products 18.22–18.35
   alcoholic beverages 18.16–18.20, 18.22, 18.36–18.37, 18.41–18.44
   application process 18.28
   basic level of protection 18.15
   Belgium 18.50
   brand loyalty 20.11
   Certificates of Specific Character 18.23
   change of geographical area 18.35
   conflicting trade marks and trade mark applications 18.34
   confusion 18.18
   Czechoslovakia, former 18.40
   deceptive marks 4.46
   descriptive marks, fair use of 8.19, 8.21
   EC law 18.06, 18.16, 18.21–18.53
   enforcement 18.30–18.33
   foods 18.22–18.35, 18.48–18.49
   France 18.34, 18.45, 18.47–18.48
   free movement of goods 18.49–18.51
   future plans for 18.52–18.53
   generic terms 18.28
   Germany 18.37, 18.38–18.39
   injunctions, final 14.35A
   interface between trade mark law and 18.41–18.46
   international law 18.08–18.20
   international negotiation, further 18.20
   Italy 18.31
   Lisbon Agreement 1958 18.09, 18.11, 18.13
   national courts 18.33, 18.46
   national laws 18.38–18.40
   non-EU countries, from 18.29
   Organization for an International Geographical Indications Network (ORIGIN) 18.52
   Paris Convention 18.09
   passing off 18.32, 18.38
   protected designations of origin (PDOs) 18.07, 18.22
      application process 18.28
      bilateral treaties, protection under 18.40
      change of geographical area 18.35
      conflicting trade marks and trade mark applications 18.34
      enforcement and protection, scope of 18.30–18.33
      free movement of goods 18.49–18.51
      parallel protection under national law 18.47–18.48
      protected geographical indications 18.24–18.26
   protected geographical indications (PGOs) 18.07, 18.22
      application process 18.28

geographical indications (*cont.*):
  protected geographical indications (PGOs) (*cont.*):
    bilateral treaties, protection under 18.40
    change of geographical area 18.35
    conflicting trade marks and trade mark applications 18.34
    enforcement and protection, scope of 18.30–18.33
    protected designations of origin 18.24–18.26
    registrability 5.44–5.55
    quantitative restrictions 18.50–18.51
    scope of protection and enforcement 18.30–18.33
    Switzerland 18.38
    TRIPs 18.07, 18.12, 18.14–18.17, 18.20, 18.38, 18.60
    unfair competition 18.09, 18.18, 18.38
    United States 18.06
    wines and spirits, additional protection of 18.16–18.20, 18.22, 18.36–18.37, 18.41–18.44
    WIPO 18.09, 18.52
    World Trade Organization 18.12, 18.52
geographical terms *see* **geographical indications**, **place names**
geometrical figures 5.06
Germany
  account of profits 14.93
  bad faith 13.90, 13.148
  celebrities 16.69
  colours 5.131
  comparative advertising 8.120, 8.136
  confusion 10.124, 10.137
  damages 14.86
  delivery up and destruction 14.99
  descriptive terms 4.144
  exhaustion of rights 9.56
  geographical indications 18.37, 18.38–18.39
  injunctions, interim 14.54, 14.60
  laudatory terms 4.83
  letters 5.32
  limping trade marks 5.115
  metatags 17.70
  opposition 13.34
  Paris Convention 4.12
  parodies, satire and irony 8.68
  registrability 4.12, 4.51, 4.53, 4.67–4.80
  retail sales service marks 16.45, 16.49
  shapes 5.93, 5.103, 5.115
  similarity 10.46, 10.69, 10.89
  tellequelle principle 4.12
  titles 5.72, 18.55
  unfair advantage and detriment 11.29, 11.60–11.66
  unfair competition 11.29
  well known and famous marks 12.40
gestures and motions 5.140–5.142
  Community Trade Mark Regulation 5.142
  descriptions 5.140–5.141
  photographs of 5.140–5.141
  registrability 5.140–5.142
get up of shops 5.08
globalization 21.08, 21.18
good faith
  bad faith 13.83
  presumption of, rebutting the 13.147
goodwill
  assignment 15.18–15.24
  beneficiaries of trade marks 2.05–2.06
  brands 11.01, 11.03, 21.24–21.28
  capture by consumers 21.28
  effects of 21.26–21.27
  exhaustion of rights 9.90
  infringement 20.28
  injunctions, final 14.38
  licensing 15.35, 15.86
  parallel imports 9.90, 16.09, 16.24
  reputation 11.01, 11.03, 11.51
  retail sales service marks 16.44
grammatical errors 4.116–4.117
graphical representations
  celebrities 16.53
  colours 5.123
  Community Trade Mark Regulation 4.24
  computers, 4.30
  distinctiveness, 4.25
  EC law 4.24–4.25
  olfactory marks 5.117, 5.119
  register, function of the 4.24–4.30
  registrability 4.24–4.30, 5.152
  signs 4.26
  similarity 10.27
  smells 4.26–4.27
  sounds 4.26–4.27, 5.134–5.135
  taste marks 5.143
  Trade Mark Directive 4.24
  TRIPs 4.24–4.26
Greece
  celebrities 16.56
  domain names 17.23
  identical marks 10.12
  injunctions, interim 14.66
  similarity 10.33
grey goods 9.14, 9.89, 14.92
guarantee marks 18.56, 18.58
Guatemala 10.37

Index

hallmarks 5.23
health and safety 20.21
hidden and secret marks 5.15–5.16
hijacking, reverse domain name 17.48
history, trade marks and 1.38–1.39
honest and dishonest practices
   beneficiaries of trade mark system and 2.06
   comparative advertising 8.125–8.127, 8.130, 8.133, 8.144–8.145, 8.150–8.156
   concurrent use 8.51
   non-infringing acts 8.51
   place names, use of 5.46
hostile domain names 17.37–17.38
hosting 17.60
house marks 1.22–1.24
human rights *see* European Convention on Human Rights, freedom of speech
humour *see* parodies, satire and irony
Hungary 8.42
hybrid marks, fusion of 8.83–8.84

ICANN Uniform Domain Name Dispute Resolution Policy 17.32–17.50, 21.39
icons
   cultural, brands as 21.09, 21.18, 21.22, 21.40, 21.40
   psychology of brands 20.03–20.12
   registrability of cultural 5.57–5.72
identical marks 1.03, 10.03–10.74
   bad faith 13.123
   comparison of goods and services 10.76–10.78
   confusion 10.06, 10.21
   data protection 10.78
   dominant position 10.79
   EC law 10.10, 10.18–10.20
   exhaustion of rights 9.20
   factors suggesting marks are identical 10.13
   factors suggesting marks are not identical 10.14–10.17
   France 10.10, 10.15
   goods and services 10.01, 10.98–10.99
   Greece 10.12
   imitation x problem 10.18–10.20
   infringement 10.01–10.02
   integrity of trade marks, importance of 10.03–10.04
   names 8.33
   OHIM 10.17
   part of mark, copying 10.14
   services 10.97–10.98
   similar marks and 7.10, 10.79
   subtraction of material from earlier marks 10.17
   Sweden 10.13
   TRIPs 10.06–10.07
   unauthorized use of 10.06–10.09
   well known and famous marks 12.11
   when goods are identical 10.79
   when marks are identical 10.10–10.21
identifiers 5.12–5.16
identity
   functions of the trade mark system 2.30–2.33
   goods, of 2.30–2.33
   origin of goods and services 2.28, 2.30–2.33
   physical origin of, actual 2.35
   practices, of
   services, of 2.30–3.33
illegality 9.94 *see also* immoral and illegal marks
image
   exhaustion of rights 9.62–9.63
   No Logo thesis 21.04–21.05, 21.07
   upholding the brand 9.62–9.63
imitation
   identical marks 10.18–10.20
   infringement 7.37
   word, use of 7.37
   x problem 10.18–10.20
immoral and illegal marks
   Community Trade Mark 4.35
   deceptive marks 4.33
   EC law 4.32, 4.34–4.36
   France 4.38–4.39
   Ireland 4.36
   obscenity 4.40
   OHIM 4.36–4.37
   Poland 4.32
   public policy 4.32, 4.34–4.35, 4.38–4.40
   registrability 4.32–4.40, 4.56
   sexual content, marks with 4.35–4.36
   Trade Mark Directive 4.32
impairment of goods 9.28, 9.31, 9.56–9.59
implied contractual consent doctrine 9.02–9.06
imports *see* parallel imports
India, ambush marketing in 8.64
infringement 7.01–7.66 *see also* non-infringing acts
   advertisements, use in 7.24–7.25
   affixing signs to goods or packaging 7.18
   aiding, abetting, authorizing and procuring 7.55–7.59
   applications to register 7.28
   Australia 7.48
   Austria 7.58, 7.60
   bad faith 7.28
   beneficiaries of trade marks, infringers as 2.07
   Benelux 7.56
   burden of proof 14.20–14.22
   business papers, use on 7.24–7.25

infringement (*cont.*):
  choices of outcome 20.27
  choosing trade marks 19.04
  civil proceedings, motive and knowledge in 7.26
  Community Trade Mark Regulation 7.09, 7.26, 7.38
  confusion 7.12, 7.14, 7.20, 7.36
  conspiracy, civil 7.59
  contempt of court 7.27
  counterfeiting 2.07, 15.59
  course of trade requirement 7.38–7.51
    Community Trade Mark Regulation 7.38
    EC law 7.38, 7.40–7.42, 7.45, 7.49–7.51
    meaning 7.40–7.42
    trade mark use, whether same as 7.43–7.45
  criminal proceedings, motive and knowledge in 7.27
  damages 7.58
  declarations of non-infringement 14.116–14.117
  descriptive terms 4.160
  different goods and services, use on 7.10
  dilution of well known marks 7.12
  disclaimers 7.35–7.37
    trade mark use and 7.46–7.49
  disclosure 14.24–14.25
  domain names 17.05–17.06, 17.09, 17.25
  domestic use for overseas purposes 7.30
  EC law 7.16, 7.20
    course of trade requirement 7.38, 7.40–7.42, 7.45, 7.49–7.51
    United States and 7.63–7.64
  endorsement of the brand, as 20.28
  exclusive rights 7.07
  exports 7.21–7.23
  fakes 7.52–7.54
  France 7.24–7.25
  generic marks 7.52, 7.54
  goodwill 20.28
  harm done by 7.01, 7.10
  identical marks 7.10, 10.01–10.02
  imitation, use of word 7.37
  imports 7.21–7.23
  innocent 2.11
  intention 2.11
  Internet, use on the 7.31, 7.33, 7.35–7.36
  invisible use 7.32–7.34
  Ireland, concurrent wrongdoers in 7.58
  joint wrongdoers 7.58, 7.61–7.62
  knowledge 7.26–7.27
  labelling 7.18, 7.23
  licensing 15.28, 15.30, 15.37
  loyalty, badges of, 7.49–7.51
  metatags 7.33
  motive 7.26–7.27
  offering to sell goods or to supply services 7.19–7.20
  oral use 7.29
  overseas purposes, domestic use for 7.30
  owner, by trade mark 7.52–7.54
  packaging 7.18, 7.23
  Paris Convention 7.06
  patents 14.47
  pharmaceuticals 7.52, 7.54, 7.56, 16.36
  physical activities constituting use 7.16–7.17
  preparatory acts 7.55, 7.58
  psychology of 20.26–20.28
  registration
    reasons for 7.03–7.04
    third parties' trade mark of, application for 7.28
  reputation, damage to 7.10
  scope of 7.03–7.15
  secondary infringement and infringers 7.55–7.62
  signs to goods of packaging, affixing 7.18
  similar goods and services 7.10, 7.20
  specific instances of 7.16–7.25
  taxonomy of infringing acts 7.10–7.15
  Trade Mark Directive 7.07–7.09, 7.26, 7.38, 7.45, 7.56
  trade mark use 7.31–7.51, 7.66
  TRIPs 7.05–7.06, 7.10, 7.16, 7.20, 7.38, 7.55, 7.64
  trivial 12.56
  Turkey, secondary infringement in 7.57
  types of 7.10–7.15, 7.65
  United States 7.12, 7.63–7.64
    confusion 7.36
    disclaimers, Internet and 7.35–7.36
    EC law and 7.63–7.64
    trade mark use 7.64
  valuation 15.97
  vicarious liability 7.60
  video cassettes, marks encoded on 7.34
  websites, use on 7.31
  well known and famous marks 7.06, 7.10, 7.12–7.13, 12.45–12.46
ingredients of food and drink 2.04
inherent distinctiveness
initials and acronyms 5.35–5.39, 10.73
injunctions *see also* **final injunctions, interim injunctions**
  comparative advertising 8.157
  opposition 13.06
  seizure 14.95
  threats 14.109

insurance 15.91
integrity of trade marks, importance of
    10.03–10.04
interim injunctions 14.49–14.75
    bad faith 14.70
    balance of convenience 14.63–14.64
    Belgium 14.55
    conduct of the parties 14.70–14.71
    confusion 14.51
    damages 14.59, 14.69
    delay 14.60
    dilution of famous marks 12.54–12.55, 12.59
    discovery 14.55
    ex parte 14.53–14.55
    evidence 14.58, 14.59
    fairness 14.68–14.69
    France 14.55, 14.60
    generic terms 14.50
    Germany 14.54, 14.60
    Greece 14.66
    Ireland 14.51, 14.63
    Italy 14.55–14.57, 14.61, 14.66
    Netherlands 14.55, 14.60, 14.66
    preconditions for success 14.56–14.62
    registration, before 14.66
    Scotland 14.65, 14.67, 14.68, 14.71
    search orders 14.54
    seizure 14.55
    TRIPs 14.73
    unfair competition 14.50
    urgent cases 14.56, 14.59–14.62
    well known and famous marks 12.45,
        12.54–12.55, 12.59
intergovernmental organizations, emblems of
    5.23
international law *see also* **particular treaties,**
    agreements and conventions (eg
    TRIPs)
    assignment 15.14–15.17
    exhaustion of rights 9.22–9.24, 9.51
    geographical indications 18.08–18.20
    licensing 15.14–15.17
    registrability 4.08–4.15
    threats 14.105–14.107
    well known and famous marks 12.05–12.08
International Non-Proprietary Names 16.05
Internet 17.01 *see also* **domain names, metatags**
    addresses, registrability of 5.25–5.27
    advertising 17.73
    brands 21.39
    consumer awareness of the 21.39
    disclaimers 7.35–7.36
    Europe 17.75
    infringement 7.31, 7.33, 7.35–7.36

injunctions, final 14.25, 14.39
jurisdiction 15.74
licensing 15.74
search engines 5.16, 17.64, 17.70
secret and hidden marks 5.16
service providers 14.39, 17.29, 17.60, 17.73
United States 7.35–7.36, 17.75
intestacy 15.02
invalidity *see* **cancellation of registration**
investments
    brands, in 21.43
    reputation 11.03–11.04
invisible use of marks 7.32–7.34
Iran, shapes and 5.115
Ireland
    concurrent wrongdoers, in 7.58
    confusion 10.118, 10.124
    descriptive terms 4.138–4.139, 4.144
    immoral and illegal marks 4.36
    infringement 7.58
    injunctions, interim 14.51, 14.63
    retrospectivity 14.08
    threats 14.103, 14.111, 14.114
    unfair advantage and detriment 11.49
irony *see* **parodies, satire and irony**
Italy
    bad faith 13.87–13.88, 13.120, 13.126
    damages 14.80
    declarations of non-infringement 14.117
    domain names 17.10
    geographical indications 18.31
    injunctions, interim 14.55–14.57, 14.61,
        14.66
    jurisdiction, choice of 14.13
    similarity 10.52, 10.65, 10.94–10.95

joint wrongdoers 7.58, 7.61–7.62
judicial comments 14.26
jurisdiction 1.25–1.27 *see also* **choice of**
    jurisdiction
    acquired distinctiveness 4.172
    comparative approach 1.25
    Europe 1.25
    Internet 15.74
    licensing 15.72–15.74
    national registration 3.22
    natural variation factor 1.26

Klein, Naomi see No Logo **thesis**

labelling
    generic goods 16.29
    infringement 7.18, 7.23
    overstickering 16.11

Index

labelling (*cont.*):
  packaging 7.18, 7.23
  parallel imports 16.11–16.29
  relabelling 16.11–16.29
labour
  exploitation 9.16, 9.18, 21.08, 21.32–21.33
  standards, need for minimum 21.21–21.22
laches 12.56–12.57
landmark decisions 1.36–1.37
language
  bad faith 13.110
  culture 19.12–19.13
  descriptive terms 4.140
  multilingual countries 4.140
  reputation 11.37
  similarity 10.47–10.49, 10.52, 10.72
  Trade Mark Directive 11.37
  translations 13.110
  transliteration 10.72
Latvia
  acquired distinctiveness 4.172
  non-infringing acts 8.58
  opposition 13.32
laudatory terms
  available, terms to be kept 4.81
  cultural relativism 4.83
  customary trade marks 4.81
  distinctiveness 4.84
  EC law 4.87
  Germany 4.83
  OHIM 4.84–4.86
  registrability 4.81–4.87
legitimate reasons for prohibiting further use, exhaustion and 9.28, 9.31, 9.53–9.64
  brand image, upholding the 9.62–9.63
  combination of trade mark-protected products 9.76
  Community Trade Mark Regulation 9.56
  condition of goods 9.56–9.59
  EC law
    brand image, upholding the 9.62–9.63
    selective distribution agreements and 9.61
  fashion goods, preserving the integrity of 9.64
  fitness for human consumption 9.54
  Germany 9.56
  impairment of goods 9.56–9.59
  luxury goods 9.57, 9.61–9.63
  meaning of 9.53–9.55
  medicinal products by another with different indications, replacement of 9.60
  obliteration and erasure of information 9.57
  packaging 9.58
  parallel trade 9.60
  prices for luxury goods, maintaining 9.61

  reputation 9.58
  resale of fashion goods 9.64
  retail price maintenance 9.61
  selective distribution agreements 9.61
  South Korea 9.56
  Trade Mark Directive 9.56
legitimate trade, interference with a 9.71–9.72
letters
  abbreviations 5.30
  acronyms 5.35–5.39, 10.73
  combinations of 5.31, 5.35, 5.39
  distinctiveness 5.30, 5.32–5.33
  figurative marks 5.33
  generic terms 5.36–5.37
  Germany 5.32
  initials and acronyms 5.35–5.39, 10.73
  OHIM 5.34, 5.39
  recognition, degree of 5.39
  registrability 5.30–5.39
  simple marks 10.73
  single 5.32–5.34
lexical inventions 4.116–4.117, 4.152
licensing 15.09–15.13, 15.16, 15.71–15.87
  acquired distinctiveness 4.175
  breach 15.78
  Canada 15.13
  certification marks 15.41
  change of control 15.83–15.85
  character merchandising 15.58–15.59
  choosing trade marks 19.23
  classification of 15.26–15.41
  co-branding 15.67
  commencement 15.75
  Community Trade Mark Regulation 15.17, 15.34
  compulsory licences 15.31–15.33
  consent, exhaustion of rights and 9.36
  consequences of being a licensee 15.35–15.41
  contracts 15.09, 15.14, 15.37, 15.77–15.78
  damages 14.79–14.87A, 15.25, 15.33
  designs 15.31, 15.33
  duration 15.76
  endorsements 15.63–15.65
  estoppel 15.11, 15.13, 15.38–15.41
  exceeding the terms of 8.178
  exclusive licences 15.09, 15.17, 15.27–15.29
  exhaustion of rights 9.36, 9.66, 15.72
  external transactions 15.43
  formalities 15.14
  franchising 15.30, 15.51–15.54
  geography 15.72–15.74
  goodwill 15.35, 15.86
  infringement 15.28, 15.30, 15.37
  internal transactions 15.42

Index

licensing (*cont.*):
  international laws 15.14–15.17
  Internet 15.74
  intra-group 15.46
  jurisdiction 15.72–15.74
  limitation periods 15.37
  national laws 15.14–15.17
  no challenge obligations 15.41
  non-exclusive licences 15.30
  non-infringing acts 8.177–8.178
  non-use 15.35
  origin of goods and services 2.26
  overruns 8.178
  Paris Convention 15.31, 15.34
  patents 15.33
  quality control 15.86–15.87
  record of 15.09–15.10
  registration 15.25
  restructuring 15.84
  royalties 15.45, 15.81–15.82
  sole 15.29
  sponsorship 15.60–15.62
  sub-licences 15.34
  subject matter 15.79–15.80
  termination 15.77–15.78, 15.83
  Trade Mark Directive 15.14, 15.17, 15.34, 15.37
  TRIPs 15.14, 15.31, 15.34
  unfair competition 14.122
  United States 15.13
    certification marks 15.41
    compulsory licensing in 15.32
    estoppel 15.38–15.40
  utility models 15.31
  valuation 15.93
lifestyle statements
  brands 20.07, 21.36
  comparative advertising 8.169–8.170
  fashion trade marks 2.40
  functions of the trade mark system 2.39–2.41
likelihood of association *see* association, likelihood of
limitation of actions 8.90–8.92, 15.37
limping trade marks 5.103, 5.109–5.116
Lisbon Agreement 1958 18.09, 18.11, 18.13
local celebrities 16.50
locators 5.25–5.29
locus standi see standing
logos
  adding 16.26–16.28
  choosing trade marks 19.05
  comparative advertising 8.119
  parallel imports 16.26–16.28
  pharmaceutical marks 16.26–16.28

loyalty or allegiance, badges of 8.11 *see also* brand loyalty
  confusion 8.86
  EC law 8.85–8.88
  functions of the trade mark system 2.38
  infringement 7.49–7.51
  non-infringing acts 8.11, 8.85–8.88
  origin, badge of 2.33, 8.87–8.88
  passing off 8.86
luxury goods 9.57, 9.61–9.63

Madrid Agreement and Protocol on the International Registration of Marks 3.06
  cancellation 13.42–13.45
  exhaustion of rights 9.22
  international registration 3.25
  WIPO 3.25
memes 17.62
mere conduits 17.60
mere puffs 2.48
metatags
  competitors, use by 17.69
  confusion 17.71
  domain names 17.08, 17.29
  France 17.68, 17.69
  freedom of speech 17.68
  Germany 17.70
  impermissible uses of trade marks 17.69–17.72
  infringement 7.33
  names 8.36
  overuse of 17.72
  permissible uses of trade marks as 17.67–17.68
  search engines 17.64, 17.70
  secret marks and hidden marks 5.16
  speech, ordinary part of 17.67
  third parties' trade marks as 17.64–17.72
  websites 17.64
media manipulation 21.10
medicines *see* pharmaceuticals
misuse of rights 13.90–13.91
mobile commerce 13.62
Monaco 12.30, 12.46
money
  Benelux 5.18
  cultural emblems, as 5.17
  euro symbol 8.11
  OHIM 5.17
  Poland 5.17
  registrability 5.17–5.18
monopolies
  abuse of rights 9.19, 9.70–9.71
  bad faith 13.105
  brand loyalty 20.09
  consent, exhaustion of rights and 9.42

725

monopolies (*cont.*):
  disclaimers 3.43
  distinctiveness 4.105–4.109
  exhaustion of rights 9.01, 9.07–9.09, 9.19
  names 5.66
  non-infringing acts 8.37
  patent, extension of 13.104
  shapes 5.82
moral rights 14.90–14.91
morality *see also* **immoral and illegal marks**
  advertising, mere puffs and 2.48
  copying 2.46–2.47, 2.49–2.50
  exhaustion of rights 9.15–9.21
  functions of the trade mark system 2.17–2.22
  intention 2.51
  lying 2.45, 2.48, 2.50
  neutral acts unlawful, making 2.50
  registration contrary to
motions and gestures 5.140–5.142
motor vehicles *see* **cars**
multipacks 9.79–9.81

names *see also* **domain names, place names**
  adjectival surnames 5.69
  assignment 5.64
  assumed names 16.50
  bad faith 13.105
  business names 1.13
  celebrities 5.61, 8.43
    assumed names 16.50
    bad faith 13.105
    confusion 16.55
    dead 16.58–16.62
    fictional celebrities 16.65–16.70
    live 16.59–16.60
    non-infringing acts 8.89
    registration of names of 13.105
  Community Trade Mark Regulations 5.57
  companies, registration of 18.54
  confusion 16.55
  corporate 8.34–8.35
  dead celebrities 16.58–16.62
  dealing with name marks 5.65–5.70
  descriptiveness 5.69
  distinctiveness 5.67, 5.69
  EC law 5.67
  emotive topic, as 5.58
  fictional celebrities 16.65–16.70
  identical marks 8.33
  metatags 8.36
  monopolies 5.66
  nicknames 8.34
  non-infringing acts 8.33–8.36, 8.89,
    8.43–8.44, 8.89

  OHIM 5.67, 5.70
  personal 5.57–5.71, 8.33–8.36, 16.50, 16.54
  pharmaceutical marks 16.02–16.05
  registrability 5.57–5.72
  registration 13.105, 15.60, 18.54
  same name, persons with the 5.62
  sharing with trade mark owners 5.59–5.61
  signatures, personal 5.71
  status, use of indicia of personal 8.36
  third parties, losing names to 5.64
  Trade Mark Directive 5.57
  TRIPs 5.57
  United States 8.36
  values 5.63
  websites 8.35–8.37
national courts
  annulment by 3.51
  Community Trade Mark Regulation 3.51
  decisions of 3.15
  geographical indications 18.33, 18.46
nationalism 20.12
natural variation factor 1.26
negative branding 20.24–20.25
Netherlands
  abuse of rights 9.72
  association, likelihood of 10.153, 10.154
  auditing 14.23
  bad faith 13.96, 13.117
  celebrities 16.66
  descriptive terms 4.137
  dictionaries 8.82
  disclosure 14.24
  domain names 17.49
  generic marks and terms 6.38, 8.82
  injunctions, interim 14.55, 14.60, 14.66
  non-infringing acts 8.49
  revocation 13.13
  similarity 10.88
  simple marks 5.04
  well known and famous marks 12.44
New Zealand 4.175
Nice Classification 3.30–3.32, 10.91, 16.37
nicknames 8.34
no challenge obligations 15.41
***No Logo* thesis** 21.03–21.18
  adverse publicity 21.23
  advertising 21.04–21.06, 21.10
  brand abuse 21.15–21.23, 21.29,
    21.38–21.39, 21.44
  brand bullies 21.39–21.40
  brand ethos 21.04
  competition, killing off 21.08
  consumer apocalypse 21.38–21.39
  corporate aims 20.20

Index

No Logo thesis *(cont.):*
  corporate fascism 21.11
  culture
    icons, brands as 21.09, 21.18, 21.22, 21.42
    intrusion of brands into 21.05–21.06
  economic values, harming 21.21
  economies of scale 21.08
  exploitation of labour 21.08
  globalization 21.18
  health and safety 20.21
  image 21.04–21.07
  labour standards, need for minimum 21.21–21.22
  market abuse 21.21
  maximization of market power 21.18–21.19
  media manipulation 21.10
  outsourcing 21.08
  public benefactors, brand owners as 21.07
  social values, harming 21.21
  tax jurisdictions, location in low 21.22
  unfair competition 21.21
  values, reasserting consumer 21.35
non-conformity 20.25
non-infringing acts 8.01–8.181 *see also* comparative advertising, fair use of descriptive terms
  abuse of goods bearing trade marks 8.53–8.55
  advertisements
    France 8.72, 8.74–8.75
    private 8.73–8.74
    small, use in 8.73–8.75
  Austria 8.40
  boycotts 8.76–8.77
  Brazil 8.12
  burying the trade mark in own trade mark 8.59
  calling a product by its trade mark instead of its product name 8.78–8.82
  celebrity names 8.89
  Community Trade Mark Regulation 8.09
    generic use 8.80–8.81
    local permitted use of a national trade mark 8.48
  consent, effect of 8.177–8.178
  course of trade, infringing use in the 8.11
  defamation 8.55
  defences provided, acts for which specific 8.13–8.51
  Denmark 8.56, 8.58
  descriptive terms 8.08
  dictionaries 8.80–8.82
  EC law 8.11
  economic benefit, conferring 8.05
  euro symbol 8.11
  France 8.72, 8.74, 8.78, 8.83
  freedom of speech 8.60–8.65
  generic use 8.78–8.82
  half-infringing two separate marks 8.83–8.84
  hiding the infringing parts of an infringing use 8.72
  honest concurrent use 8.51
  Hungary 8.42
  hybrid marks, fusion of two marks in 8.83–8.84
  Latvia 8.58
  licences 8.177–8.178
  limitation of actions 8.90–8.92
  local permitted use of national trade mark 8.47–8.49
  loyalty, badges of 8.11, 8.85–8.88
  monopolies 8.37
  name and addresses
    celebrities 8.89
    third parties, of 8.43–8.44, 8.89
    use of one's own 8.33–8.36
  national trade mark, local permitted use of 8.47–8.49
  Netherlands 8.49
  non-protected elements, copying the 8.56
  non-trading organizations 8.12
  oral references to styles 8.46
  owners, use by trade mark 8.37–8.42
  parodies, satire and irony 8.66–8.71
  permitted by law, infringing activities 8.37–8.51
  principle, infringing activities permitted in 8.52–8.89
  prior use 8.50
  priority 8.40
  product placement 8.53
  secondary infringement 8.06
  style of mark, using the 8.45–8.46
  taxonomy of 8.02–8.12
  titles of periodicals in Hungary 8.42
  Trade Mark Directive 8.09
    abuse of goods bearing trade marks 8.55
    local permitted use of a national trade mark 8.47
    unfair advantage or detriment 8.55
  TRIPs 8.08
  trivial use 8.04, 8.41
  unauthorized use 8.01–8.12
  unfair advantage and detriment 8.55
  unfair competition 8.56
  weak part of another's trade mark, incorporating 8.57–8.58
  websites 8.55
  well known and famous trade marks 8.03–8.04, 8.41, 8.59

non-use
  burden of proof 13.60
  distinctiveness 4.123
  domain names 17.07
  EC law 13.12
  licensing 15.35
  genuine 13.12
  revocation 13.11–13.12, 13.16, 13.49–13.50, 13.60
  United States 13.12
Northern Ireland 5.125, 5.133
Norway 13.96
Norwich Pharmacal **orders** 14.24
notice-based systems 3.19, 3.37–3.38
notorious marks *see* **well-known and famous marks**
nullification *see* **cancellation of registration**
numbers
  OHIM 5.40
  public domain, part of the 5.40
  registrability 5.40
  telephone 5.28–5.29

obliteration and erasure of information 9.57
obscenity 4.40
Office of Harmonisation in the Internal Market *see* **OHIM**
OHIM 3.51
  bad faith 13.80, 13.109, 13.116, 13.125, 13.130–13.135, 13.145
  cancellation 13.38, 13.39
  case law 1.32
  confusion 10.120, 10.140
  containers 5.104
  descriptive terms 4.144, 4.157
  dictionaries 8.82
  dilution of famous marks 12.51
  distinctiveness 4.118–4.122
  domain names 5.25–5.26
  geometrical figures 5.06
  identical marks 10.17
  immoral and illegal marks 4.36–4.37
  jurisdiction, choice of 14.14
  laudatory terms 4.84–4.86
  letters 5.34, 5.39
  money 5.17
  names 5.67, 5.70
  numbers 5.40
  olfactory marks 5.117–5.119
  opposition 13.03, 13.22
  packaging 5.105, 5.115
  pharmaceutical marks 16.32, 16.34
  reputation 11.14, 11.26–11.28, 11.44
  retail sales service marks 16.42–16.44
  revocation 13.68
  similarity 10.29, 10.31, 10.39, 10.45, 10.49, 10.56–10.57, 10.64, 10.71, 10.84, 10.91–10.92, 10.101
  simple marks 5.05, 10.73
  sound marks 5.138
  surfaces 5.79
  technology standards 5.78
  unfair advantage and detriment 11.55, 11.58, 11.71, 11.77–11.80
  well known and famous marks 12.32, 12.51
olfactory marks 5.117–5.122
  distinctiveness 5.119
  EC law 5.117–5.118
  graphical representation 5.117, 5.119
  OHIM 5.117–5.119
  registrability 5.117–5.122, 5.151
opinion polls 4.164
opposition to registration 3.41, 13.16–13.34
  absolute grounds of 13.03, 13.09
  bad faith 13.10, 13.18, 13.79, 13.102
  Community Trade Mark Regulations 13.03, 13.27–13.30
  confusion 10.108, 13.09, 13.18, 13.24–13.25, 13.34
  contractual arrangements 13.34
  deception 13.18
  device marks 13.25
  families of marks, based on 13.19–13.25
    device marks of 13.25
    figurative marks 13.24
    ignoring 13.23–13.24
    large 13.20–13.21
    OHIM 13.22–13.24
    single parent 13.22
  figurative marks 13.25
  genuine use 13.27, 13.30–13.31
  geographical relevance 13.32
  Germany 13.34
  grounds of 13.03, 13.09–13.10, 13.18–13.25
  injunctions 13.06
  intention of the applicant 13.18
  invisible attacks 13.16–13.17
  knowledge of 13.102
  Latvia 13.32
  OHIM 13.03, 13.22
  pharmaceutical marks 16.36
  prior proceedings 13.33
  proceedings 13.03–13.06, 13.16–13.34, 13.149
  relative grounds of 13.03, 13.06, 13.09
  res judicata 13.33
  significant use of the opponent's mark 13.26–13.31

Index

opposition to registration (*cont.*):
  standing 13.13–13.15
  stay of proceedings 13.71
  third party rights 13.17
  unfair advantage and detriment 13.09
  well known and famous marks 12.45
oral use of marks 7.29
Organization for an International Geographical Indications Network (ORIGIN) 18.52
origin of goods and services
  actual physical, identification of 2.24–2.29
  badge of 2.24, 2.27, 2.33
  competition 2.31
  European Court of Justice 2.29
  exhaustion of rights 2.25
  functions of the trade mark system 2.24.2.29
  identification 2.28, 2.30–2.33
  licensing 2.26
  loyalty, badge of 2.33, 8.87–8.88
  outsourcing 2.26
  quality 2.25, 2.35
  shapes 5.116
originality 4.111–4.113, 5.139
origins, marks of *see* geographical indications, origin of goods and services
ornamental shapes 5.98
outsourcing 15.69–15.70, 21.08
overseas purposes, domestic use of marks for 7.30
overstickering 16.11
own names 5.57–5.71, 8.33–8.36, 16.50, 16.54

packaging
  affixing signs to 7.18, 7.24–7.25
  containers 5.100–5.105, 5.107, 5.112–5.113, 5.115
  EC law 5.102
  exhaustion of rights 9.58
  generic goods 16.29
  infringement 7.18, 7.23–7.25
  labelling 7.18, 7.23
  OHIM 5.101, 5.115
  parallel imports 16.11–16.29
  positional marks 5.144A
  repackaging 16.11–16.29
  shapes 5.100–5.105, 5.107, 5.112–5.113, 5.115–5.116
pagan festivals 5.22
Paraguay, sound marks and 5.139
parallel imports
  account of profits 14.92
  adding trade marks, logos or features of design 16.26–16.28
  burden of proof 16.21
  certificates of marketing authorization 16.28
  Community Trade Mark 16.11, 16.15, 16.18
  confusion 16.25
  consent, exhaustion of rights and 9.45
  damages 14.85
  delivery up and destruction 14.99
  Denmark 16.17, 16.24, 16.26, 16.29
  design features, adding 16.26–16.28
  EC law 9.88, 16.11–16.23, 16.28
  exhaustion of rights 9.14, 9.66, 9.95
    competition 9.88
    consent 9.45
    EC law 9.88
    goodwill 9.90
    grey goods 9.14, 9.89
    legitimate reasons for prohibiting further use 9.60
    profitability of 9.87–9.90
    registration of slightly different marks in each country 9.86
    third countries, exhaustion policy of 9.85
    unfair competition and 9.69
    unwanted, stopping 9.86
  generic goods, repackaging and relabelling as 16.29
  goodwill 9.90, 16.09, 16.24
  grey goods 9.14, 9.89, 14.92
  logos 16.26–16.28
  necessity, doctrine of 16.16–16.23
  overstickering 16.11
  pharmaceutical marks 16.08–16.30
  Portugal 16.08
  profitability of 9.87–9.90
  rebranding with trade mark of country of importation 16.24–16.25
  registration of slightly different marks in each country 9.86
  relabelling 16.11–16.29
  repackaging 16.11–16.29
    conditions for 16.11
    necessity, doctrine of 16.16–16.23
    prior notice 16.13–16.15
    what constitutes 16.12
  Spain 16.08
  springboard doctrine 16.26
  Sweden 16.24–16.25
  third countries, exhaustion policy of 9.85
  Trade Mark Directive 16.11, 16.15, 16.18
  unfair competition 9.88
  unwanted, stopping 9.86
Paris Convention on the Protection of Industrial Property 3.06
  assignment 15.21

Paris Convention on the Protection of Industrial Property (*cont.*):
  bad faith 13.86
  celebrities 16.67
  comparative advertising 8.99
  domain names 17.43
  exhaustion of rights 9.22–9.23
  France 12.35
  geographical indications 18.09
  infringement 7.06
  licensing 15.31, 15.34
  registrability 4.08–4.14
  retail sales service marks 16.39
  threats 14.105, 14.107
  well known and famous marks 12.05, 12.07, 12.09, 12.11, 12.14, 12.25
    France 12.35
    Monaco 12.30
    WIPO recommendations 12.60
    wrongful registration 12.44
parodies, satire and irony
  comparative advertising 8.70
  copyright 8.68
  France 8.68
  freedom of speech 8.61
  Germany 8.67
  non-infringing acts 8.66–8.71
  United States 8.69
passing off
  confusion 10.123
  domain names 17.16
  exhaustion of rights 9.67
  geographical indications 18.32, 18.38
  injunctions, final 14.36, 14.38, 14.48
  jurisdiction, choice of 14.12
  loyalty or allegiance, badges of 8.86
  retail sales service marks 16.47
patents
  bad faith 13.104
  exhaustion of rights 9.65–9.66
  infringement 14.47
  injunctions, final 14.47
  licensing 15.33
  monopolies, extension of 13.104
  pharmaceutical marks 16.08, 16.35
pathology of trade marks 2.42–2.43
PDO *see* **protected designations of origin (PDOs)**
personality rights 16.53, 16.56, 16.62
Peru 12.42
PGI *see* **protected geographical indications (PGOs)**
pharmaceutical marks 16.01–16.36
  advertising 16.03

  authorization, withdrawal of market 16.30
  cancellation 16.36
  certificates of marketing authorization 16.06, 16.28, 16.35
  competition law 16.07
  confusion 16.01, 16.31–16.36
  counterfeiting 2.10
  descriptive terms 16.05
  design, adding features to 16.26–16.28
  developing countries 2.10
  EC law 16.06, 16.08, 16.30
  exhaustion of rights 9.60, 9.84
  generic goods, repackaging and relabelling branded goods as 16.29
  indications, replacement with product with different 9.60
  infringement 7.52, 7.54, 7.56, 16.36
  International Non-Proprietary Names (INNS) 16.05
  marketing 16.03
  naming 16.02–16.05
  necessity, doctrine of 16.16–16.23
  logos, adding 16.26–16.28
  OHIM 16.32, 16.34
  opposition 16.36
  over the counter 16.02–16.03, 16.22
  overstickering 16.11
  parallel imports 16.08–16.30
  patents 16.08, 16.35
  Portugal 16.08
  prescription only 16.02, 16.04, 16.31, 16.34
  prior notice of repackaging 16.13–16.15
  rebranding 16.24–16.25
  relabelling 16.11, 16.29
  repackaging 16.11–16.15, 16.29
  risk analysis 16.31–16.34
  safety 16.01, 16.07
  Spain 16.08
  uniformity of 16.06–16.07
  withdrawal of market authorization 16.30
photographs, gestures and motions in 5.140–5.141
physical activities constituting use 7.16–7.17
place names *see also* **geographical indications**
  brand loyalty 20.11
  country names 5.52
  EC law 5.45, 5.49–5.50, 5.53
  honest use of 5.46
  opposition 13.32
  regional terms 5.47
  registration of 5.45, 5.47, 5.49–5.50, 5.52–5.53
  Trade Mark Directive 5.45
  United States 5.49

Index

Poland
  bad faith 13.86, 13.99, 13.115
  cancellation 13.40
  celebrities 16.58
  immoral and illegal marks 4.32
  money 5.17
  registrability 4.56
  well known and famous marks 12.40
political correctness 19.14–19.16
portfolio of registrations
  adjacent registrations 5.146
  Community Trade Mark Regulation 5.148
  confusion 5.147
  cost of maintaining 19.22
  descriptive marks 5.147–5.148
  distinctiveness 5.147
  EC law 5.148
  families of trade marks 5.147, 5.150
  OHIM 5.149
  unprotectable classes, to protect 5.145–5.150
Portugal
  confusion 10.118
  damages 14.77, 14.87A
  parallel imports 16.08
  pharmaceutical marks 16.08
  shapes 5.104
  unfair advantage and detriment 11.93
  well known and famous marks 12.34
positional marks 5.144A
practice statements 3.16–3.17
precedent 1.32–1.33
preliminary issues 14.06–14.28
  auditing and disclosure of information 14.23–14.25
  burden of proof 14.20–14.22
  choice of jurisdiction 14.09–14.15
  enforcement 14.06–14.28
  proof 14.06–14.14.08
  judicial comments 14.26
  publication of the court's decision 14.27–14.28
preparatory acts of infringement 7.55, 7.58
prices
  comparative advertising 8.120, 8.137–8.139, 8.147–8.148, 8.154
  exhaustion of rights 9.16–9.17, 9.19, 9.61
  luxury goods 9.61
  retail price maintenance 9.61
prior use
  bad faith 13.117
  cancellation 13.39–13.40
  genuine 13.39
  non-infringing acts 8.50
  own 13.40–13.41
  previous prior user 13.117

  third parties 13.39, 13.40
product placement 8.53, 12.65
profits, account of 14.92–14.94
privacy of celebrities 16.54
processional experts, writings of 3.18
proof *see* burden of proof
property
  EC law 15.02
  European Convention on Human Rights 9.74
  exhaustion of rights 9.82
  generic marks and terms 6.09, 6.45
  intestacy 15.02
  private, words as 6.09, 6.45
  rights 9.74, 9.82
  trade marks, as 15.02–15.04
proportionality 10.83, 14.36–14.37, 14.99
protected designations of origin (PDOs) 18.07, 18.22
  application process 18.28
  bilateral treaties, protection under 18.40
  change of geographical area 18.35
  conflicting trade marks and trade mark applications 18.34
  enforcement and protection, scope of 18.30–18.33
  free movement of goods 18.49–18.51
  parallel protection under national law 18.47–18.48
  protected geographical indications 18.24–18.26
protected geographical indications (PGOs) 18.07, 18.22
  application process 18.28
  bilateral treaties, protection under 18.40
  change of geographical area 18.35
  conflicting trade marks and trade mark applications 18.34
  enforcement and protection, scope of 18.30–18.33
  protected designations of origin 18.24–18.26
protectionism 6.21
psychology of trade marks 20.01–20.32
  brand loyalty, as icons of 20.03–20.12
  branding strategy 20.13–20.25
  comparative advertising 20.29–20.31
  infringement 20.26–20.28
public benefactors, owners as 21.07
public domain, part of the 5.40
public figures *see* celebrities
public policy
  celebrities 15.58
  generic marks and terms 6.19, 6.21
  immoral and illegal marks 4.32, 4.34–4.35, 4.38–4.40

public policy (*cont.*):
  registrability 4.32–4.49
  registration contrary to 4.32, 4.34–4.35, 4.38–4.40
  telephone numbers 5.28
publication of decisions 14.27
publicity, adverse 21.23
publicly reserved terms 4.53–4.57
puffing 2.48, 8.155

quality of goods and services
  character merchandising 15.59
  consumer satisfaction 2.35
  descriptive marks, fair use of 8.29
  EC law 2.36–2.37
  exhaustion of rights 9.16–9.17, 9.20, 9.77
  functions of the trade mark system, guaranteeing 2.17, 2.34–2.37
  origin 2.25, 2.35
  producers, definition of 2.37
  United States 2.34
  well known and famous marks 9.20
quantification, arithmetic 4.92, 4.93
quantitative restrictions 18.50–18.51

regional agreements *see* **treaties and regional agreements**
regional celebrities 16.50
regional exhaustion of rights 9.12, 9.51
regional registration 3.23–3.24
regional terms 5.47
registrability 4.01–4.184 *see also* **distinctiveness**
  abbreviations 5.30
  absolute bars to registration 4.16–4.23, 4.32, 5.03
  acronyms 5.35–5.39, 10.73
  addresses 5.25–5.27
  amorial bearings 4.08
  automatic 4.01
  available for use, need to keep word or mark 4.67–4.80
    distinctiveness 4.70, 4.75–4.76
    EC law and 4.72–4.80
    scope of protection of granted applications 4.69–4.71
  barcodes 5.12–5.14
  Belgium 4.22
  business formats 5.56
  celebrities 16.52–16.53, 16.60
    names of dead 13.105, 15.60
  certification marks 18.58
  collective marks 18.58–18.59
  colours 5.123–5.133
  Community Trade Mark Regulation 4.52
  publicly reserved terms 4.57
  tellequelle principle 4.13
  company names 18.54
  complex marks 5.07–5.11
  conduct of the applicant 5.145
  confusion 4.182
  contractions 5.30
  copyright, infringement of 4.50–4.52
  corporate designations 4.53
  criteria for 4.02–4.184
    minimum and maximum 5.04–5.11
  cultural emblems 5.17–5.24
  cultural icons 5.57–5.72
  customary trade terms 4.58–4.66, 4.75
  deceptive marks 4.41–4.49, 4.56
  Denmark 4.51
  descriptive marks 4.60, 4.128–4.162
    available for use, need to keep word or mark 4.69–4.70
    distinctiveness and 4.21–4.22, 4.70
  design rights, infringement of 4.50, 4.52
  domain names 5.25–5.27, 17.17, 17.19, 17.34, 17.36, 17.39–17.41
  EC law 4.05–4.06, 4.21, 4.55
    descriptive marks 4.21
    distinctiveness 4.75–4.76
    shapes 4.21
  emblems
    cultural 5.17–5.24
    intergovernmental organisations, of 5.23
    Paris Convention 4.08
  European Court of Human Rights 4.56
  flags 4.08, 5.23
  font, variations of 5.41–5.43
  freedom of expression 4.56
  generic terms 4.58–4.66, 6.04, 6.30, 6.40
  geographical marks 5.44–5.55
  geometrical figures 5.06
  Germany 4.12, 4.51
    available for use, keeping words or signs 4.67–4.80
    publicly reserved terms 4.53
  gestures and motions 5.140–5.142
  graphical representation 4.24–4.30, 5.152
  grounds of unregistrability as independent of each other 4.20–4.23
  guarantee marks 18.58
  identifiers not serving as trade marks 5.12–5.16
  immoral and illegal marks 4.32–4.40, 4.56
  initials 5.35–5.39
  international law, registration under 4.08–4.15
  Internet addresses 5.25–5.27
  laudatory terms 4.81–4.87
  letters, issues relating to 5.30–5.39

Index

registrability (*cont.*):
  locators 5.25–5.29
  money 5.17–5.18
  names 5.57–5.72
    companies 18.54
    dead celebrities 13.105, 15.60
  non-traditional trade marks 5.117–5.144A
  numbers, issues relating to 5.40
  numerals 5.40
  official hallmarks 5.23
  olfactory marks 5.117–5.122, 5.151
  Paris Convention 4.08–4.14
    armorial bearings 4.08
    emblems 4.08
    flags 4.08, 5.23
    tellequelle principle 4.10–4.13
  place names 5.45–5.47, 5.49–5.50, 5.52–5.53
  Poland 4.56
  policy grounds, not registrable on 4.32–4.49
  portfolio of registrations to protect
    unprotectable classes 5.145–5.150
  positional marks 5.144A
  presumption of 3.34
  public interest 4.17
  publicly reserved terms 4.53–4.57
  refusal of registration
    Paris Convention 4.08–4.09
    relative grounds of 4.179
  rejection of, grounds for 4.20–4.23
  relative bars to registration 4.16, 4.179
  secret marks and hidden marks 5.15–5.16
  shapes 4.21, 5.81–5.116, 5.120
  signatures, personal 5.71
  signs 4.01, 4.06–4.08
    not regarded as trade marks 4.31
    other traders may want to use, that
      4.50–4.87
  simple marks 5.04–5.05
  single letters 5.32–5.34
  slogans 5.73–5.77
  sounds 5.134–5.139
  state emblems 5.23
  subject matter, protectable 4.04
  surfaces of shapes 5.79–5.80
  Sweden 18.59
  taste 5.143–5.144
  technology standards 5.78
  telephone numbers 5.28–5.29
  tellequelle principle 4.10–4.13
  terminology 4.07
  times and dates 5.19–5.22
  titles 5.57–5.72
  trade dress 5.56
  Trade Mark Directive 4.05, 4.19, 4.52
  TRIPs 4.04, 4.06
  Turkey 4.12
  type, variations of 5.41–5.43
  types of trade marks, specific 5.1–5.152
  uncertainty, doctrine of 5.152
  well known and famous marks 12.44, 13.98
  words
    invented 4.01
    specific types of mark 5.31–5.43
  World Trade Organization 4.04
  zodiac signs 5.24
registration *see also* **cancellation of registration, opposition to registration, registrability, revocation of registration**
  administration 3.02, 3.04
  applications
    amendment of 3.42
    examination of 3.33–3.39
    fax, by 3.40
    publication of 3.40
  assignment 15.25
  bad faith 12.44, 13.72–13.148
  certification of trade marks 3.44
  classification 3.28–3.32
  delay 3.02
  depository systems 3.36, 3.38
  descriptive marks, fair use of 8.16–8.17
  disclaimer of monopolies 3.43
  examination of applications 3.33–3.39
  grant of trade marks 3.44–3.45
  infringement 7.03–7.04, 7.28
  injunctions before, interim 14.66
  international registration 3.25
  licensing 15.25
  Madrid Agreement and Protocol 3.25
  main features of 3.26–3.46
  national registration 3.21–3.22
    jurisdiction and 3.22
    Nice Classification 3.32
  Nice Classification 3.30–3.32
  notice-based systems 3.19, 3.37–3.38
  overlapping 3.49–3.50
  post-grant challenge 3.46
  publication of applications 3.40
  purity of the register 3.34
  reasons for 7.03–7.04
  regional registration 3.23–3.24
  register
    classes, division into 3.29–3.32
    contents of 3.26, 3.28
    existence of a 3.26
    functions of 3.27, 4.24–4.30
    purity of the 3.34
    re-checking 3.28

Index

registration (*cont.*):
  reputation 11.14, 11.26–11.28, 11.44
  retail sales service marks 16.37–16.39
  systems 3.02–3.04, 3.19–3.46
  theory 3.20
  transactions in trade marks 15.25
  validity, presumption of 3.45
relative grounds for refusal of registration
  cancellation 13.09, 13.14, 13.40–13.41
  opposition 13.03, 13.06, 13.09
  registrability 4.16, 4.179
  revocation 13.14
religion 5.22, 19.15
reputation 11.01–11.51, 12.01
  bad faith 13.121
  blurring 11.14–11.22A
  brand names, goodwill in 11.01, 11.03
  burden of proof 11.48–11.50
  Community Trade Mark Regulation 11.09, 11.23–11.24, 11.39
  comparison of trade marks 11.12–11.13
  concepts 11.14–11.36
  confusion 11.02, 11.04
  deep 11.32
  dilution 11.14–11.22A
    blurring 11.21–11.22
    definition 11.18
    distinctiveness 11.22A
    tarnishment 11.21
    United States 11.15–11.21
  distinctiveness 11.15, 11.20, 11.22–11.24, 11.40–11.46
    protection, better 11.44–11.46
    Community Trade Mark Regulation 11.23–11.24
    dilution 11.22A
    repute and 11.40–11.43
    Trade Mark Directive 11.23–11.24
  EC law 11.08–11.09, 11.12, 11.22A, 11.33–11.40, 11.44–11.46
  exhaustion of rights 9.58
  global appreciation 11.13
  goods, in relation to 11.36
  goodwill
    brand names 11.01, 11.03
    difference between reputation and 11.51
  infringement 7.10
  investment 11.03–11.04
  known, need for trade marks to be 11.37–11.39
  languages 11.37
  meaning 11.30–11.39
  OHIM 11.14, 11.26–11.28, 11.44
  proof of 11.47–11.50
  registration 11.02, 11.04–11.10
  repute and
    distinctive character and 11.40–11.43
    protection, better 11.44–11.46
    reputation and 11.25–11.28
  services, in relation to 11.36
  tarnishment 11.14–11.22A
  terminology 11.14–11.36
  Trade Mark Directive 11.09, 11.23–11.25, 11.30, 11.37–11.39
  TRIPs 11.07–11.08, 11.39
  unfair advantage or detriment 11.01, 11.11, 11.13, 11.29, 11.48
    repute and 11.60–11.64, 11.73–11.81
  United States 11.46
    blurring 11.21
    dilution 11.15–11.21
    famous marks 11.15, 11.17
    tarnishment 11.15–11.21
  use, need for 11.31
  well know and famous marks 11.44, 12.04, 12.14, 12.27, 12.35, 12.38, 12.43, 12.48, 12.67
    dilution 11.15, 11.17
    tarnishment 11.15
    United States 11.15–11.19
  wide 11.32
res judicata 13.33
resales
  consent 9.93
  exhaustion of rights 9.64, 9.68, 9.79–9.81, 9.93
  fashion products 9.64
  multipacks 9.79–9.89
retail price maintenance 9.61
retail sales service marks 16.37–16.49
  Australia 16.48
  brand names 16.46
  Community Trade Mark Regulations 16.42, 16.47
  confusion 16.47–16.48
  EC law 16.42–16.45
  Germany 16.45, 16.49
  goodwill 16.44
  Nice Classification 16.37
  OHIM 16.42–16.44
  Paris Convention 16.39
  passing off 16.47
  registration 16.37–16.49
  products and, interrelationship between trade marks for 16.46–16.48
  Trade Mark Directive 16.42, 16.45, 16.47
  TRIPs 16.39
  unfair competition 16.47

retail sales service marks (*cont.*):
  United States 16.41
  websites 16.49
retailers house marks 1.22–1.23
retrospectivity 14.08
reverse domain name hijacking 17.48
revocation of registration
  absolute grounds 13.14
  advertising, evidence of use and 13.63
  applications for Community trade marks 13.14
  bad faith 13.65–13.66, 13.145
  Benelux 13.54, 13.65
  burden of proof 13.60
  Community Trade Mark Regulation 13.14, 13.51–13.58
  comparative advertising 8.166
  continuous use 13.46
  damages 13.64
  EC law
    genuine use and 13.51–13.58
    non-use and 13.12
  Europe 13.46–13.47
  evidence of use 13.63
  form in which registered, use in the 13.61–13.62
  France 13.13, 13.64
  generic marks 13.48
  genuine use 13.51–13.58, 13.61
    proper reasons for 13.59–13.60
    TRIPs 13.59
  grounds 13.14
  injunctions, final 14.38
  mobile commerce 13.62
  Netherlands 13.13
  non-use, for 13.11–13.12, 13.16, 13.49–13.50
    burden of proof 13.60
    EC law 13.12
    genuine 13.12
    TRIPs 13.59
    United States 13.12
  OHIM 13.68
  part of registration, revocation of 13.67–13.69
  proceedings 13.11–13.12, 13.46–13.69, 13.149
  re-registration after 13.65–13.66
  relative grounds 13.14
  standing 13.13–13.15
  threats 14.105
  Trade Mark Directive 13.51
  TRIPs 13.11–13.12, 13.59
  United States, non-use and 13.12
  validity of marks until 13.64
royalties
  damages 14.80–14.83, 14.86

  franchising 15.52
  licensing 15.45, 15.81–15.82
Russia 9.35

sale and leaseback 15.49
satire *see* parodies, satire and irony
Scotland
  consent, exhaustion of rights and 9.45
  injunctions, interim 14.65, 14.67, 14.68, 14.71
  jurisdiction, choice of 14.13
  unfair advantage and detriment 11.55
search engines 5.16, 17.64, 17.70
search orders 14.54
secondary infringement and infringers 7.55–7.62, 8.06
secondary marks 1.17
secondary meaning, acquisition of 5.28
secret marks and hidden marks 5.15–5.16
sectoral considerations 19.11
securitizations 15.48–15.49
seizure 14.95–14.97
  developing countries, use of goods seized in 14.97
  disclosure 14.24
  enforcement 14.25, 14.95–14.97
  injunctions 14.55, 14.95
  TRIPs 14.96
selective distribution 9.69, 9.70
sensitive words 19.09
services
  complementary 10.102
  definition 1.09
  descriptive marks, fair use of 8.29
  exhaustion of rights 9.28–9.35
  generic marks and terms 6.03–6.04
  identical marks 10.01, 10.98–10.99
  misappropriation of trade marks 2.10
  origin of 2.24–2.33
  reputation 11.36
  retail sales service marks 16.37–16.49
sexual content, marks with a 4.35–4.36
shapes
  absence of a product, marking the 5.99
  absolute bars to registration 5.83
  Australia 5.84
  Belgium 5.110
  bottles 5.100–5.104, 5.107, 5.115
  cancellation 5.82
  co-existence of other intellectual property rights 5.92
  colours 5.93, 5.132–5.133
  Community Trade Mark Regulation 5.105
  consumer recognition 5.109

shapes (*cont.*):
  containers 5.100–5.105, 5.107, 5.112–5.113, 5.115
  copyright 5.92
  Denmark 5.92, 5.99
  descriptive marks 5.86
  distinctiveness 5.82, 5.83, 5.92–5.93, 5.95, 5.98–5.99
    colours 5.93
    containers 5.103–5.104
    limping trade marks 5.110
  EC law 5.82, 5.88, 5.89–5.93
    functionality 5.89–5.93
    limping trade marks 5.111
    packaging 5.102
    registrability 4.21
  feature marks 5.105
  figurative marks 5.89
  functionality 5.89–5.95, 5.98
    colours 5.93
    copyright 5.92
    Denmark 5.92
    three-dimensional marks 5.106
  Germany 5.93, 5.103, 5.115
  indicator of source, as 5.88
  Iran 5.115
  limping trade marks 5.103, 5.109–5.116
    consumer recognition 5.109
    EC law 5.111
    Germany 5.115
    Iran 5.115
    supporting trade marks 5.110–5.112
  marketing 5.116
  monopolies 5.82
  nature of the goods themselves, resulting from 5.86–5.88
  OHIM 5.101, 5.104, 5.115
  origin indicators 5.116
  ornamental shapes 5.98
  packaging 5.100–5.105, 5.107, 5.112–5.113, 5.115–5.116
  Portugal 5.104
  registrability 4.21, 5.81–5.116, 5.120
  regular product 5.95–5.98
  shapes, features of products which have shape but are not 5.105
  technical result, consisting exclusively of shape of goods necessary for 5.89–5.93
  three-dimensional 5.81, 5.85, 5.89, 5.107, 5.115
  trade dress 5.116
  TRIPs 5.88
  two-dimensional 5.81, 5.89, 5.104, 5.107
  United States 5.93

value to the goods, giving substantial 5.94
variable text, incorporating 5.106
word marks 5.89
signatures 5.71, 16.63
signs 1.12, 1.15
  affixing 7.18, 7.24–7.25
  commonplace 4.108–4.109
  distinctiveness 4.105–4.109
  graphical representations 4.26
  monopolies 4.105–4.109
  registrability 4.01, 4.06–4.08
    not regarded as trade marks 4.31
    other traders may want to use, that 4.50–4.87
  zodiac 5.24
similar goods and services 10.01, 10.76–10.78, 10.80–10.97, 10.100–10.102
  abstraction, level of 10.91
  association, likelihood of 10.143–10.155
  bad faith 13.109, 13.122
  burden of proof 10.100
  complementary services 10.102
  conceptual similarity 10.90–10.92
  confusion 7.20, 10.80–10.82, 10.96, 10.102
  distinctiveness 10.80–10.82
  domain names 17.07
  EC law 10.80–10.83, 10.102
  France 10.90, 10.101
  Germany 10.88
  high degree of similarity 10.111–10.112
  identical marks 7.10, 10.79
  infringement 7.10, 7.20
  Italy 10.93–10.95
  multiclass trade marks 10.97
  Netherlands 10.88
  Nice Classification 10.91
  OHIM 10.84, 10.91–10.92, 10.101
  proportionality 10.83
  proximity to one another, products sold in 10.86
  same public, products offered to the 10.88
  same purposes, products serving the same 10.85
  source, sharing a common 10.93–10.96
  specification, products particularized in the, 10.89
  substitutability 10.87, 10.93
  Sweden 10.100
  unfair advantage and detriment 11.84–11.93
  well known and famous marks 10.80, 12.11
similar marks
  aggregating similarities 10.60–10.72
  analysing 10.38–10.58
  association, likelihood of 10.143–10.155

similar marks (*cont.*):
  aural similarity 10.23, 10.27, 10.32, 10.41, 10.43, 10.46–10.50, 10.61–10.74
  bad faith 13.109, 13.123
  conceptual similarity 10.23, 10.40–10.41, 10.51–10.62, 10.65–10.72
    cultural association, through 10.55–10.59
    incorporation of same worked into two figurative words 10.55
    subject matter, of 10.52–10.54
  confusion 10.27, 10.32–10.34
  cultural association, through 10.56–10.60
  distinctiveness 10.26
  domain names 17.07
  dominant components 10.26, 10.29, 10.61–10.62
  double accounting 10.63
  EC law 10.23–10.28, 10.32
  familiarity with the market 10.35
  figurative marks 10.42, 10.54, 10.58, 10.62, 10.69
  France 10.27, 10.52, 10.55, 10.61, 10.64, 10.70
  Germany 10.45, 10.68
  global appreciation 10.24, 10.26, 10.61–10.62
  graphical similarity 10.27
  Greece 10.33
  Guatemala 10.37
  high degree of similarity 10.111–10.112
  incorporation of the same word into two figurative marks 10.54
  Italy 10.52, 10.65
  language 10.47–10.49, 10.52, 10.72
  legal yardstick 10.23–10.33
  meaningless, shared 10.56
  'not similar' 10.45
  OHIM 10.29, 10.31, 10.39, 10.45. 10.49, 10.56–10.57, 10.64, 10.71
  patent or latent similarity 10.36–10.37
  'rather similar' 10.44
  simple marks 10.73–10.74
  sound marks 5.137
  Spain 10.27, 10.66
  standard of similarity 10.34–10.35
  surveys 10.75
  three-dimensional marks 10.43
  transliteration 10.72
  visual similarity 10.23, 10.39–10.45, 10.51, 10.53–10.54, 10.61–10.72
  when marks are 10.22–10.74
simple marks
  acronyms 10.73
  aural similarity 10.74
  distinctiveness 5.04
  letters 10.74
  Netherlands 5.04
  OHIM 5.05, 10.73
  registrability 5.04–5.05
  similarity 10.73–10.74
  verbal similarity 10.74
Singapore 5.27
slogans, registration of 5.73–5.77
smells *see* **olfactory marks**
song titles 5.72
sound marks 5.134–5.139
  distinctiveness 5.139
  EC law 5.134
  graphical representation 4.26–4.27, 5.134–5.135
  non-musical sounds 5.136–5.137
  OHIM 5.138
  originality 5.139
  Paraguay 5.139
  registrability 5.134–5.139
  similarity 5.137, 10.23, 10.27, 10.32, 10.41, 10.43, 10.46–10.50, 10.61–10.74
  sonograms 5.137
  tunes 5.134
  verbal descriptions 5.136
sources of trade mark law 3.05–3.18
  case law 3.13–3.15
  legislation 3.11–3.12
  practice statements 3.16–3.17
  trade mark registries, rulings of regional and national 3.16–3.17
  treaties and regional agreements 3.06–3.10
  writings of academic and processional experts, learned 3.18
South Africa 4.178
South Korea 4.135, 9.56
Spain
  bad faith 13.86, 13.146
  damages 14.77
  parallel imports 16.08
  pharmaceutical marks 16.08
  similarity 10.27, 10.66
spare parts defence 8.23–8.26, 8.116–8.118
speech *see* **freedom of speech**
sponsorship 15.60–15.62A
  advertising 15.60
  approval rights 15.62
  brand image 21.05
  contracts 15.62–15.62A
  licences 15.60–15.62
sports endorsements 15.63–15.64
springboard doctrine 16.26

Index

standing
  bad faith 13.148
  cancellation 13.13–13.15, 13.37
  Community Trade Mark Regulation
    13.14–13.15
  opposition 13.13–13.15
  revocation 13.13–13.15
state
  beneficiaries of trade marks 2.08
  emblems 5.23
style of the mark, using the 8.45–8.46
sub-brands 1.19, 1.24, 9.16, 9.18
substitutability 4.162, 10.87, 10.93, 20.07
subtraction of material 10.17
subvertisements 17.57–17.61
'sucks' websites 8.63, 17.37–17.38
suggestive allusions 4.141
support *see* loyalty or allegiance, badges of 8.11, 8.85–8.88
surfaces 5.79–5.80
surnames, registration of 5.60, 5.63–5.69
survey evidence 10.75, 12.55
suspension 13.70–13.71
Sweden
  bad faith 13.96–13.97, 13.119–13.121,
    13.123, 13.144, 13.146–13.148
  celebrities 16.67
  collective marks 18.59
  domain names 17.42
  freedom of speech 8.65
  generic marks and terms 6.32
  identical marks 10.13
  injunctions, final 14.31
  parallel imports 16.25–16.25
  registrability 18.59
  similarity 10.100
Switzerland 10.131–10.132, 18.38
symbol, use of the registered trade mark 14.104

taboos 19.17–19.18
tampering 9.83–9.84
tarnishment 11.14–11.22A
taste marks 5.143–5.144
tax 15.45, 21.07, 21.22
taxonomy
  infringing acts 7.10–7.15
  non-infringing acts 8.02–8.12
technology standards 5.78
telephone numbers, registration of 5.28–5.29
***tellequelle* principle** 4.10–4.13
test purchases 8.119
threats 14.101–14.115
  brands 21.40–21.43
  cancellation 14.115

  Community Trade Mark Regulation 14.105
  damages 14.107, 14.109
  enforcement 14.101–14.115
  groundless, liability for making 14.101–14.115
  injunctions 14.109
  international law 14.105–14.107
  Ireland 14.103, 14.111, 14.114
  meaning 14.113–14.114
  Paris Convention 14.105, 14.107
  registered trade mark symbol, use of 14.104
  revocation 14.115
  Trade Mark Directive 14.105
  TRIPs 14.105–14.107
  unfair competition 14.105
three-dimensional marks 5.81, 5.85, 5.89, 5.107, 5.115, 10.43
times and dates
  connotations of 5.20
  cultural emblems, as 5.19–5.22
  descriptive marks 5.19
  distinctiveness 5.19
  national significance of 5.20
  registrability 5.19–5.22
  religious and pagan festivals 5.22
time limits 8.90–8.92, 15.37
titles
  Australia 5.72
  books 5.72
  Denmark 18.55
  films 5.72, 18.55
  Germany 5.72, 18.55
  Hungary 8.42
  non-infringing acts 8.42
  periodicals 8.42
  protection of 18.55
  registrability 5.57–5.72
  songs 5.72
  unfair competition 18.55
trade dress 5.08–5.10, 5.56, 5.116
Trade Mark Directive
  abuse of goods bearing trade marks 8.55
  assignment 15.15
  association, likelihood of 10.143–10.145
  bad faith 13.73–13.82, 13.90, 13.120, 13.126
  celebrities 16.50
  certification marks 18.58
  collective marks 18.58
  comparative advertising 8.106, 8.108–8.111, 8.118, 8.123, 8.125
  confusion 10.122
  consent, exhaustion of rights and 9.37
  course of trade requirement 7.38, 7.45
  deceptive marks 4.41
  detriment 8.55

Index

Trade Mark Directive (*cont.*):
  distinctiveness 11.23–11.24
  exhaustion of rights 9.25–9.30, 9.85
    consent 9.37
    legitimate reasons for prohibiting further use 9.56
  generic marks and terms 4.58–4.59, 6.24
  graphical representation 4.24
  guarantee marks 18.58
  immoral and illegal marks 4.32
  infringement 7.07–7.09, 7.26, 7.38, 7.45, 7.56
  injunctions, final 14.31
  jurisdiction, choice of 14.14
  languages 11.37
  licensing 15.14, 15.17, 15.34, 15.37
  names 5.45, 5.57
  non-infringing acts 8.09, 8.47, 8.55
  parallel imports 16.11, 16.15, 16.18
  place names 5.45
  registrability 4.05, 4.19, 4.52
  reputation 11.09, 11.23–11.25, 11.30, 11.37–11.39
  retail sales service marks 16.42, 16.45, 16.47
  retrospectivity 14.08
  revocation 13.51
  secondary infringement 7.56
  unfair advantage and detriment 11.59
  well known and famous marks 12.25–12.30
trade mark transactions 15.02–15.25 *see also* **assignments, licensing**
  character merchandising 15.57–15.59
  co-branding 15.66–15.68
  contracts 15.89–15.91
  endorsements 15.43, 15.63–15.65
  examples of 15.47–15.70
  franchising 15.43, 15.50–15.56
  insurance 15.91
  internal and external 15.42–15.46
  litigation of 15.88–15.92
  outsourcing 15.69–15.70
  property, trade marks as 15.02–15.04
  registration of 15.25
  securitization 15.48–15.49
  sponsorship 15.60–15.62A
  tax 15.45
  types of 15.05–15.13
  valuation of trade marks 15.93–15.97
Trademark Law Treaty 3.06, 9.22
trade names 1.13
Trade-Related Aspects of Intellectual Property Law Agreement *see* **TRIPs**
translations 13.110
transliteration 10.73
treaties and regional agreements
  Andean Pact 3.09
  Bangui Agreement on an African Industrial Property Organization 3.09
  Banjul Protocol on Marks 3.09
  Benelux Treaty on the Uniform Trade Mark Law 3.09
  bilateral 3.08
  Cartagena Agreement 3.09
  Community Trade Mark 3.09
  enforcement 3.07
  European Court of Justice 3.10
  Harmonization Directive 3.10
  international multilateral conventions 3.06–3.07
  regional treaties 3.09
tribal considerations 19.11
TRIPs 3.06
  assignment 15.14, 15.22
  bad faith 13.124
  case law 1.31
  celebrities 16.50
  comparative advertising 8.99
  course of trade requirement 7.38
  descriptive marks, fair use of 8.15
  dispute settlement 3.07
  distinctiveness 4.88
  enforcement 14.03
  examination of applications 3.38
  exhaustion of rights 9.23–9.24, 9.97
  genuine use 13.59
  geographical indications 18.07, 18.12, 18.14–18.17, 18.20, 18.38, 18.60
  graphical representation 4.24–4.26
  identical marks 10.06–10.07
  infringement 7.05–7.06, 7.10, 7.16, 7.20, 7.38, 7.55, 7.57, 7.64
  injunctions, interim 14.73
  licensing 15.14, 15.31, 15.34
  names 5.57
  non-infringing acts 8.08
  non-use 13.59
  registrability 4.04, 4.06
  reputation 11.07–11.08, 11.39
  retail sales service marks 16.39
  revocation 13.11–13.12, 13.59
  seizure 14.96
  shapes 5.88
  threats 14.105–14.107
  well known and famous marks 12.07, 12.09
tunes 5.134
Turkey
  bad faith 13.97, 13.98–13.99
  registrability 4.12
  secondary infringement 7.57

Index

two-dimensional shapes 5.81, 5.89, 5.104, 5.107

uncertainty, doctrine of 5.152
unfair advantage and detriment 11.01,
    11.52–11.94
  Benelux 11.53–11.55
  burden of proof 11.48–11.50
  cancellation 13.09
  checklist 11.74
  Community Trade Mark Regulation 11.59,
    11.63
  confusion 11.66, 11.82–11.88
  damage, need for actual or probability of 11.50
  dilution of famous marks 12.51
  distinctiveness 11.58–11.59, 11.65–11.75,
    11.81
  due cause, without 11.52–11.57
  EC law 11.55, 11.82–11.93
  France 11.29, 11.94
  Germany 11.29, 11.60–11.66
  Ireland 11.49
  non-infringing acts 8.55
  OHIM 11.55, 11.58, 11.71, 11.77–11.80
  opposition 13.09
  Portugal 11.93
  proof of 11.78
  reputation 11.01, 11.11, 11.13, 11.29, 11.48
    repute and 11.60–11.64, 11.73–11.81
  retail sales service marks 16.47
  Scotland 11.55
  similar goods and services 11.84–11.93
  Trade Mark Directive 8.55, 11.59
  unfair competition 11.29
  well known and famous marks 11.68, 11.70,
    11.92, 12.32, 12.51
unfair competition
  abuse of rights 9.72–9.73
  barriers to trade 14.120
  brands
    loyalty 20.10
    No Logo thesis 21.08, 21.21
  concerted practices 14.118–14.119
  confusion 10.142
  dilution of famous marks 12.59
  dominant position 9.73, 10.78,
    14.120–14.122
  EC law 9.68, 9.73, 9.88, 14.118–14.122,
    15.90, 20.10
  exhaustion of rights 9.67–9.69
  franchising 15.55–15.56
  generic marks and terms 6.19–6.20
  geographical indications 18.09, 18.18, 18.38
  Germany 11.29
  identical marks 10.76–10.78

  injunctions 14.38, 14.45, 14.48, 14.50
  licensing 14.122
  litigation 15.90
  No Logo thesis 21.08, 21.21
  non-infringing acts 8.56
  origin of goods and services 2.31
  parallel imports 9.69, 9.88
  pharmaceutical marks 16.07
  threats 14.105
  titles 18.55
  unfair advantage and detriment 11.29
  United States 15.90
  well known and famous marks, dilution of
    12.59
United States
  assignment 15.19
  bad faith 13.120, 13.125
  blurring 11.21
  brand
    as a 21.11–230.12, 21.14
    loyalty 20.12
  case law 1.29, 1.36
  certification marks 15.41
  colours 5.125
  comparative advertising 8.172–8.176
  complex marks 5.09
  compulsory licensing 15.32
  confusion 7.12, 7.36, 8.176, 10.125–10.126,
    10.129–10.130
  deceptive marks 4.44
  descriptive marks, fair use of 8.13, 8.32
  dilution of well-known marks 6.26, 7.12, 8.32,
    11.15–11.21, 12.49–12.59
  disclaimers 7.35–7.36
  distinctiveness 4.114, 12.14
  domain names 17.06, 17.12, 17.21,
    17.27–17.31, 17.38
  EC law and 7.63–7.64, 12.67–12.68
  enforcement 14.17
  estoppel 15.38–15.40
  extraterritoriality 14.17
  freedom of speech 8.63, 8.174
  generic marks and terms 6.26
  geographical indications 18.06
  infringement 7.12, 7.35–7.36, 7.60, 7.63–7.64
  injunctions, final 14.35–14.35A
  Internet 7.35–7.36, 17.75
  jurisdiction, choice of 14.11
  landmark decisions 1.36
  licensing 15.13, 15.32, 15.38–15.41
  names 5.63, 8.36
  nationalism 20.12
  non-use 13.12
  parodies, satire and irony 8.69

Index

United States (*cont.*):
   place names, registration of 5.149
   quality 2.34
   reputation 11.15–11.21, 11.31–11.32, 11.46
   retail sales service marks 16.41
   revocation 13.12
   shapes 5.93
   telephone numbers 5.28
   trade dress 5.09
   trade mark use and 7.64
   sucks websites 17.38
   unfair competition 15.90
   websites 17.60
   well known marks 12.40
     dilution 7.12, 11.15–11.21, 12.49–12.59
     distinctiveness 12.14
     EC law and 12.67–12.68
     European standard of well known marks and 12.24m 12.67–12.68
     famous marks 11.15–11.19, 12.09, 12.13–12.16, 12.24, 12.49–12.68
     WIPO recommendations 12.67–12.68
   WIPO recommendations 12.67–12.68
unregistered trade marks 1.11
use *see also* **course of trade requirement, fair use of descriptive terms, non-use, prior use**
   availability for 4.69–4.70, 4.75–4.76
   common 4.105–4.109
   continuous 13.46, 13.122
   customary trade 4.176
   evidence 13.63
   genuine 13.27, 13.30–13.31, 13.39, 13.51–13.58, 17.51–17.58
   honest 5.46, 8.51
   hypothetical 10.107
   infringing 17.67–17.72
   intent to use 13.124–13.128
   invisible 7.32–7.34
   oral 7.29
   other than registered, in manner 13.95
   overseas purposes, domestic for 7.30
   overuse 17.72
   owners, by 7.30, 8.37–8.42
   permitted 8.105–8.106
   physical activities, constituting 7.16–7.17
   significant 13.26–13.31
   trade mark, as 7.31–7.51, 7.66
   trivial 8.04, 8.41
utility models 15.31

valuation of trade marks 15.93–15.97
   assignment 15.93
   brands 21.25–21.37
   infringement 15.97

   licences 15.93
   methodologies 15.95–15.96
   shapes 5.94
vicarious liability 7.60, 16.50
victims of trade mark law 2.11–2.12
video cassettes, marks encoded on 7.34
viral marketing 17.58
visual perceptibility *see* **graphical representation**
visual similarity 10.23, 10.39–10.45, 10.51, 10.53–10.54, 10.61–10.72

websites *see also* **domain names**
   abuse of goods bearing trade marks 8.55
   advertisements
     genuine 17.55–17.57
     spoof 17.57, 17.62
     unauthorized use of 17.54–17.62
   blogs 17.58
   copyright notice, use of third parties' trade mark as 17.63
   course of trade requirement 17.52
   freedom of expression 17.61
   hosting 17.60
   infringement 7.31
   Internet service providers 17.60
   jurisdiction, choice of 14.13
   memes 17.62
   mere conduits 17.60
   metatags 17.64
   names 8.35–8.37
   non-infringing acts 8.55
   retail sales service marks 16.49
   sale of goods of trade mark owner 17.53
   subvertisements 17.57–17.61
   'sucks' 8.63, 17.37–17.38
   third parties' trade marks on 17.51–17.63
   United States 17.38, 17.60
   viral marketing 17.58
well known and famous marks *see also* **dilution of famous marks**
   adverse publicity 21.23
   advertising 12.34–12.35, 12.45
   Andean Pact 12.38
   bad faith 12.44, 13.98, 17.42–17.44
   Benelux 12.38, 12.44
   burying own trade mark in 8.59
   cancellation 12.44
   case law 1.31
   Community Trade Mark Regulation 12.09, 12.14, 12.26
   confusion 9.20, 12.47
   consumer, position of the 12.47–12.48
   criteria 12.13, 12.15, 12.62–12.68
   cultural terms, fame limited in 12.20

well known and famous marks (*cont.*):
  Czech Republic 12.33
  damages 12.46
  definition of well known and famous marks
      12.09–12.23
    Trade Mark Directive, in 12.28
    United States and 12.13–12.16
  difference between well known and famous
      marks 12.11
  distinctiveness 12.14, 12.43, 12.63
  domain names 17.31, 17.42–17.44
  duration and extent of use 12.15
  duration of fame 12.42–12.43
  EC law 12.27–12.39, 12.67–12.68
  European well-known marks 12.25–12.48
    single market, in a 12.37–12.39
    US standard of famous marks and 12.24
    WIPO recommendations 12.67–12.68
  exhaustion of rights 9.20
  extraterritoriality 9.20
  food safety 2.04
  France 12.02, 12.35
  generic marks and terms 6.22
  Germany 12.40
  identical goods 12.11
  industrial terms, fame limited in 12.22–12.23
  infringement 7.06, 7.10, 7.12–7.13,
      12.45–12.46
  injunctions 12.45–12.46
  intense but limited fame 12.17–12.21
  international framework of protection of
      12.05–12.08
  knowledge of registration of third party 13.98
  Monaco 12.30, 12.46
  Netherlands 12.44
  non-infringing acts 8.03–8.04, 8.41, 8.59
  OHIM 12.32
  opposition 12.45
  Paris Convention 12.05, 12.07, 12.09, 12.11,
      12.14, 12.25
    France 12.35
    Monaco 12.30
    WIPO recommendations 12.60
    wrongful registration, relief against
      12.44
  Peru 12.42
  Poland 12.40
  Portugal 12.34
  product placements 12.65
  professional terms, fame limited in
      12.22–12.23
  proof of 12.42
  quality 9.20
  registration
    bad faith 12.44, 13.98
    relief against wrongful 12.44
  reputation 11.15–11.19, 11.44, 12.04, 12.14,
      12.27, 12.35, 12.38, 12.43, 12.48,
      12.67
  similarity 10.80, 12.11
  social terms, fame limited in 12.21
  space, limited in 12.19
  specialist goods or services 12.22
  tarnishment 11.15
  third parties 12.40
  time, limited in 12.18
  Trade Mark Directive 12.25–12.30
  TRIPs 12.07, 12.09
  ultra famous marks 12.10
  unfair advantage and detriment 11.68, 11.70,
      11.92, 12.32
  United States 12.40
    distinctiveness 12.14
    EC law and 12.67–12.68
    European standard of well known marks and
      12.24, 12.67–12.68
    famous marks 11.15–11.19, 12.09,
      12.13–12.16, 12.24, 12.49–12.68
    WIPO recommendations 12.67–12.68
  WIPO recommendations 12.60–12.68
wholesalers 9.44
wines and spirits 18.16–18.20, 18.22,
    18.36–18.37, 18.41–18.44
WIPO
  cancellation 13.43
  developing countries 3.38
  geographical indications 18.09, 18.52
  Madrid Agreement and Protocol 3.25
  Paris Convention 12.30
  United States 12.67–12.68
  well known and famous marks 12.60–12.68
World Intellectual Property Organization *see*
    WIPO
World Trade Organization 4.04, 18.12, 18.52
writings of academic and processional experts,
    learned 3.18

zodiac signs 5.24